Sourcebook on Rhetoric

Key Concepts in Contemporary Rhetorical Studies

James Jasinski

Sage Publications
International Educational and Professional Publisher
Thousand Oaks ▪ London ▪ New Delhi

To my parents for their many years of love and support

For information:

Sage Publications, Inc.
2455 Teller Road
Thousand Oaks, California 91320
E-mail: order@sagepub.com

Sage Publications Ltd.
6 Bonhill Street
London EC2A 4PU
United Kingdom

Sage Publications India Pvt. Ltd.
M-32 Market
Greater Kailash I
New Delhi 110 048 India

Printed in the United States of America

Library of Congress Cataloging-in-Publication Data

Jasinski, James.
Sourcebook on rhetoric : key concepts in contemporary rhetorical studies / by James Jasinski.
p. cm. — (Rhetoric and society)
Includes bibliographical references and index.
ISBN 0-7619-0504-9
1. Rhetoric—Dictionaries. I. Title. II. Rhetoric & society (Thousand Oaks, Calif.)
PN172 .J37 2001
808'.003—dc21 2001001625

04 05 06 10 9 8 7 6 5 4 3 2

Acquiring Editor: Margaret H. Seawell
Editorial Assistant: Alicia Carter
Production Editor: Claudia A. Hoffman
Editorial Assistant: Cindy Bear
Copy Editor: D. J. Peck
Typesetter: Marion Warren
Cover Designer: Jane M. Quaney

Contents

Glossary Of Concepts

Foreword

Herbert W. Simons

It is my pleasure to introduce this very odd but extremely useful reference work. Arranged as one might arrange a dictionary or an encyclopedia, it is rather a highly textured introduction to contemporary rhetorical theory, one that sacrifices comprehensiveness for depth over the limited array of key concepts that it covers. Missing from the Glossary of Concepts, for example, is the term *example,* yet the book is exemplary in the many examples it provides to illustrate included concepts. Moreover, the book's index provides the equivalent of a second and more detailed glossary of terms, pointing readers to the many terminological contexts in which the indexed terms are relevant.

These linkages, also highlighted in the text itself, permit efficient travel across the terrain that is rhetoric. Readers will, of course, choose their own itineraries, exploring connections that Jasinski could not possibly have anticipated. Those readers who were reared in the literary/compositional/English department tradition of rhetorical studies, for example, might begin with words such as **narrative** that already are familiar to them, but then, having become convinced that their tradition says not enough about rhetoric as an adaptive art, might venture to the oral/oratorical/communication studies side of the street for an introduction to **rhetorical situation.** The venturesome rhetorician in a communication studies department might likewise move from the familiar (e.g., **debate, apologia**) to the unfamiliar, finding in Bloom's (1973) poetics of influence precisely the metaphor needed to analyze the oratory of Malcolm X. A decided virtue of this book is its broad range of pivotal terms—reason enough for students in English or communication studies to purchase it or make liberal use of it at their reference libraries.

It is instructive to apply Jasinski's concepts to the book itself. The first concept discussed in the preface is *conversation,* but its use—such as Burke's (1957) in the *Philosophy of Literary Form*—is metaphorical. Jasinski purports to record the conversation that is contemporary rhetorical studies, but he also is one of the conversationalists, making clear in his introduction that he is sympathetic to efforts to rein in "rhetoric," restricting it to the civic arena or at least keeping public discourse as its focus.

Yet in spite of good intellectual conversation, Jasinski's introduction to rhetoric's nature and scope is fair to the globalists, those who would have us look for rhetoric—or at least rhetorical dimensions—in virtually all human acts and artifacts. Jasinski also *accents* what he knows best, which is American public address, past and present. This is at once a limitation of the book but also a strength; it gives depth to the book, albeit at a sacrifice to range.

But who among us can do justice to a globalized view of the range of rhetoric? And that indeed is a reason why Jasinski favors a more restricted view.

Jasinski notes in the preface that this book began as an eight-page mimeo handout. Years later, it was made ready for Sage Publications' Rhetoric & Society series, consisting of books of about 200 pages each. But as Jasinski set to work on his key concepts, he found that he had much too much to say about them. Fortunately, as the size of the entries grew, Jasinski grew with them, becoming in the process of fashioning this singular book a singular adept teacher of contemporary rhetorical theory.

Beginning students of rhetoric might take issue with this last claim. They might find, for example, that the introduction to rhetoric is too difficult, the many meanings explored are excessive, and the introduction's "conversation" is disturbingly inconclusive. But this is a highly commendable introductory essay, one that should be better appreciated as other terms in the book are scrutinized, digested, and made a part of readers' inner conversations. Not all of the terms in the book will require scrutiny; that depends on the chosen itinerary. But many entries will repay repeated readings.

References and Additional Reading

Bloom, H. (1973). *The anxiety of influence.* New York: Oxford University Press.

Burke, K. (1957). *The philosophy of literary form* (rev. ed.). New York: Vintage.

Preface

In a well-known passage from *The Philosophy of Literary Form,* Kenneth Burke described human existence as an "unending conversation." Burke (1957) wrote,

> Imagine that you enter a parlor. You come late. When you arrive, others have long preceded you, and they are engaged in a heated discussion, a discussion too heated for them to pause and tell you exactly what it is about. In fact, the discussion had already begun long before any of them got there, so that no one present is qualified to retrace for you all the steps that had gone before. You listen for a while, until you decide that you have caught the tenor of the argument; then you put in your oar. Someone answers; you answer him [sic]; another comes to your defense; another aligns himself against you, to either the embarrassment or gratification of your opponent, depending upon the quality of your ally's assistance. However, the discussion is interminable. The hour grows late, [and] you must depart. And you do depart, with the discussion still vigorously in progress. (pp. 94-96)

I have composed this book on the assumption that academic disciplines, as a slice of human existence, partake of our unending conversation. To put the point more directly, I have approached the discipline of rhetorical studies as a conversation. This book strives to describe the conversation that is the contemporary discipline of rhetorical studies. Like any conversation, rhetorical studies features multiple voices, idioms, and perspectives, and this book tries to incorporate the various voices, idioms, and perspectives that constitute contemporary rhetorical studies. As Burke suggested in his discussion of the unending conversation, no one is ever qualified to provide a complete account of the conversation of human life. The same is true for the conversation that is rhetorical studies. No one is qualified to provide an exhaustive definitive account of its shape and contours. But this book tries to provide its readers with an introduction to most of the major issues, themes, and arguments that engage the attention of rhetorical scholars at the beginning of the 21st century.

After the introductory essay that reviews the vexing question of how to define the term *rhetoric,* the book consists of a series of alphabetically organized entries, beginning with the Bakhtinian concept of **accent** and ending with the emerging concept of the **vernacular.** Each entry tries to define its central concept, provide practical illustrations of the concept when that is appropriate, discuss some of the key scholarship that has addressed the concept, and identify some of the more important studies by rhetorical scholars that have engaged the concept in some way. A number of concepts do not receive extended treatment in a separate entry but are discussed in the course of treating a broader concept. If a concept in which readers are interested does not have a specific entry devoted to it, they should check the index at the back of the book to see whether it is listed there and discussed as part of a different entry. For example, there is not an entry for Burke's concept of *bridging device* or Stephen Toulmin's sense of *warrant,* but each concept is discussed briefly as part of a broader topic (e.g., **transcendence, argument**). Terms in boldface in the text indicate that there are specific entries for those terms or forms of those terms. Secondary terms listed in the index are italicized in the text on their first mention in an entry.

The book attempts to do something more than provide a detached or objective account of the conversation that is rhetorical studies.[1] In many of the entries, I have tried to enact or purposefully "stage" conversational episodes by bringing voices or idioms that have not yet noticed or engaged each other into some contact. For example, in the entry for **feminine style,** I have tried to suggest some possible points of contact between this idea and work being done on seemingly disparate concepts such as **judgment, prudence,** and **social knowledge.** The aim of these moments in the book is heuristic—an effort to suggest new paths that our disciplinary conversation might wish to pursue and an attempt to sketch out possible lines of critical and conceptual inquiry. At these moments, to return to Burke's metaphor, I have put in my "oar" and tried to contribute to, rather than simply describe, the conversation of rhetorical studies.

Conversations, and books about conversations, are collaborative communal accomplishments. That certainly is the case with this book. Numerous individuals have contributed to its development. Dilip Gaonkar was an early, and constant, supporter of the project. Bob Ivie, Kathryn Olson, Mike Osborn, and Herb Simons read the initial proposal and an early draft and made many wonderful suggestions for improving the book. Steve Browne, Melissa Deem, Bonnie Dow, Peter Ehrenhaus, Tom Farrell, Mike Greco, Bob Hariman, Forbes Hill, Mike Leff, John Lucaites, A. Susan Owen, Mark Pollock, Ed Schiappa, John Sloop, Barbara Warnick, and Wade Williams answered questions, provided resources, and/or read and commented on specific entries. Dan Emory, Andrew Gooding, Steve Klien, and Beth Manolescu provided important bibliographic assistance. Heidi Van Middlesworth, Alicia Carter, and Margaret Seawell provided expert editorial guidance. My wife, Jody Dyer Jasinski, created the artwork and provided constant encouragement and support during the lengthy process of research and writing.

Finally, this project began as an eight page mimeo handout I prepared in 1988 for my Introduction to Rhetorical Theory and Criticism course at Southern Illinois University. Since then, I have used portions of the book as handouts and/or reading packets in various classes. Through the years, my students have provided valuable feedback and been a continual source of inspiration. I especially want to thank my students at the University of Puget Sound who read and responded to major sections of the book over the past 3 years. This book tries to do what its eight-page mimeo ancestor first set out to do—introduce students to, and get them excited about, the discipline of contemporary rhetorical studies.

Note

1. I leave aside, for the time being, the important question of whether it is possible to produce an impartial detached account of anything.

Reference

Burke, K. (1957). *The philosophy of literary form* (rev. ed.). New York: Vintage.

Acknowledgments

Excerpts from Woody Allen's "My Speech to the Graduates" reprinted by permission. © 1979, Woody Allen. All rights reserved.

Excerpts from William Bennett reprinted by permission. William J. Bennett served as director of the Office of National Drug Control Policy under President George Bush. He currently is co-director of Empower America and co-chairman of the Partnership for a Drug-Free America.

Excerpt from Robert Bridges, *Poetical Works,* © 1936 Oxford University Press. Reprinted by permission.

Calvin and Hobbes © 1991 Watterson. Reprinted by permission of Universal Press Syndicate. All rights reserved.

Excerpt from Mona Charen reprinted by permission of Mona Charen and Creators Syndicate Inc.

Excerpts from © Dilbert reprinted by permission of UFS.

Excerpt from Terry Goodkind, *Stone of Tears,* © 1995, Terry Goodkind. Used by permission of the author, Tor Books, and the author's agent, Scovil Chichak Galen Literary Agent, Inc.

Excerpt from James N. Gregory reprinted by permission of the Seattle Times Company © 1998.

Excerpt from George Kennan, "Sources of Soviet Conduct," reprinted by permission of *Foreign Affairs.* © 1987 by the Council on Foreign Relations Inc.

Excerpt from C. S. Lewis, *Surprised by Joy,* © C. S. Lewis Pte. Ltd. 1955 and renewed 1984 by Arthur Owen Barfield, reprinted by permission of Harcourt Inc.

Excerpts from Barry Lopez, "Apologia," reprinted by permission of Sterling Lord Literistic Inc. © 1998 by Barry Lopez.

Excerpt from Charles Madigan © 1993 Chicago Tribune Company. All rights reserved. Used with permission.

Excerpt from Michael Moore, *Downsize This!* © 1996 by Michael Moore. Reprinted by permission of Crown Publishers, a division of Random House Inc.

Excerpt from P. J. O'Rourke, "Taking Drugs—Seriously," *Rolling Stone,* November 30, 1989, by Straight Arrow Publishers Inc. Reprinted by permission. All rights reserved.

Excerpt from the *Seattle Post-Intelligencer* © 1998 reprinted with permission of the *Seattle Post-Intelligencer.*

Excerpt from the *St. Louis Post-Dispatch* reprinted with permission.

Excerpts from Jacob Sullum, "Capital Punishment—Yes," reprinted with permission from the June 1990 issue of *Reason* Magazine. © 2000 by the Reason Foundation, 3415 S. Sepulveda Blvd., Suite 400, Los Angeles, CA 90034.

Excerpt from George Will, © 1998, The Washington Post Writers Group. Reprinted with permission.

Excerpt from Herman Wouk, *The Caine Mutiny,* reprinted by permission of Random House Inc.

Introduction: On Defining Rhetoric as an Object of Intellectual Inquiry

This book is designed to introduce readers to the intellectual world, as well as the academic sub-discipline, of rhetorical studies.[1] Before proceeding into an examination of the terminology, or the lexicon, of contemporary rhetorical studies, it is appropriate to reflect on the definitional ambiguities of the term rhetoric itself. Rhetoric has, and seemingly always has had, multiple meanings. Variations on the meaning of rhetoric often reflect different attitudes toward language and linguistic representation and, even more particularly, the use of language for persuasive purposes. One common sense of the term, constituting a tradition of thought stretching from the Greek philosopher Plato to our contemporary world, links rhetoric with artifice, the artificial, mere appearances, or the simply decorative. For Plato, rhetoric was a pseudo-art and, like poetry, an ignoble public practice. Numerous contemporary expressions such as the phrase "mere rhetoric" and the customary opposition of someone's "rhetoric" to his or her actions or deeds continue the Platonic denigration of rhetoric. The Platonic tradition's negative or pejorative sense of rhetoric is intertwined with a marked ambivalence toward language. Ambivalence toward language—the feeling that it is both beneficial and dangerous, a tool for building human community and a device for tearing it apart, a medium for representing knowledge (or, in more common parlance, "stating the facts") and a vehicle for distorting or deceiving—was a key element in the thought of most of the major early modern philosophers such as Descartes, Locke, and Kant (Bender & Wellbery, 1990).[2] The concept of rhetoric, or what it might possibly mean, is entangled in this persistent ambivalence toward language.

Whereas Plato, and the many thinkers who followed in his path, was inclined toward a negative view of language, a considerable number of other thinkers over the years have leaned in the opposite direction. A more positive understanding of rhetoric emerged within the writings of those individuals who stressed the beneficial capacity of language, speech, and discourse. Isocrates, one of the early Greek thinkers in the sophistic tradition, believed that language, and especially persuasive oratory or rhetoric, was a force for civilization and human advancement. In a famous speech titled "Antidosis," Isocrates maintained,

> The art of discourse . . . is the source of most of our blessings. . . . Because there has been implanted in us the power to persuade each other and to make clear to each other whatever we desire, not only have we escaped the life of wild beasts, but we have come together and founded cities and made laws and invented arts; and, generally speaking, there is no institution devised by man [sic] which the power of speech has not helped us to establish.[3]

Isocrates' celebration of language and rhetoric developed into a tradition of thought that extended from Aristotle and the Greek Sophists, through Cicero and Quintilian, into the humanist movement of the European Renaissance (Seigel, 1968), and continues today in the works of numerous theorists and critics whose ideas are discussed more fully throughout the remainder of this book.

Although sketching the antagonistic traditions of thought about language and rhetoric helps to reconstruct the intellectual context in which rhetorical thinking has occurred, it does not provide an adequate understanding of the substance of rhetorical thinking. For more than two millennia, philosophers, teachers, scholars, and citizen advocates have discussed the concept of rhetoric and formulated definitions of it. Looking back on this multivoiced **tradition** of thought, Ehninger (1968) wrote,

> The continuing dialogue on the question, What is rhetoric? except as an academic exercise, is largely profitless. If there is no one generic rhetoric which, like a Platonic idea, is lurking in the shadows awaiting him [sic] who shall have the acuteness to discern it, the search for a defining quality can only end in error or frustration. (p. 140)

Ehninger's observation guides the discussion that follows. The aim is not to uncover an absolute or final definition of rhetoric. Rather, the discussion tries to outline *some* of the key issues involved in the activity of trying to define rhetoric. Reflection on these issues should provide readers with an introduction to the conversation that is contemporary rhetorical studies.

Bryant (1973) identified both a problem and a place to begin this undertaking. He wrote, "Over the centuries, one great trouble with the term *rhetoric* has been that it is used loosely for the art, the artifact, and a quality of discourse; and often the reference of the designation is quite unclear" (p. 3). Other disciplines such as literary studies have evolved "a full complement of useful differentiating terms for artist, art, and output"—poet, poetics, and poetry. But "with rhetoric, we are in something of a mess" (p. 3; see also Gaonkar, 1993). Rhetorical studies lack the differentiating terms found in literary studies for the artifact or the product and the theory or the art; the term *rhetoric* is used to refer to both a particular type of *practice*[4] and a *theory* that tries to guide and/or explain that practice. Burke (1950) recovered the terms *rhetorica utens* (meaning rhetoric as practice) and *rhetorica docens* (meaning rhetoric as theory) to help alleviate the ambiguity. Unlike many of his terminological innovations, the utens-docens distinction has not been widely employed by rhetorical scholars in the more than 50 years since Burke published *A Rhetoric of Motives.* Contemporary theorists and critics continue to use "rhetoric" to refer to certain discursive practices as well as to certain forms of theory or modes of theorizing.[5] But what specific types of discursive practice are rhetorical? What constitutes a theory or art of rhetoric? These questions need to be considered more carefully.

Rhetorica Utens: Rhetoric as Discursive Practice

There are a number of strategies we might employ to define rhetoric as a practice or language performance (Gaonkar, 1990a). One

	Normal (Literal)	**Literary/Rhetorical** (Figurative)
Function	problem solving/ coordinate action	world disclosing
Evaluative standard	validity conditions (e.g., logical consistency)	success (not subject to consistency standard)
Principal discursive technique	argument	style

Figure I.1. Habermas on Forms of Communication

common approach to the definitional task has been an effort to identify the most basic or elemental forms of human communication so as to then specify one form as "rhetoric." For some contemporary thinkers, there are *two* essential forms of practice. The exact nature of each form is open to dispute, but to a significant degree, the various "two-form" characterizations are indebted to the common distinction between *literal* and *figurative* language use. What is the basis for this distinction? Definitions of what constitutes literal and figurative language use have varied over time. A relatively common contemporary definition holds that language is used literally when the established rules for practice, or grammar, are followed; language is used figuratively when the established rules are ignored or disregarded. What has been the trajectory of the literal-figurative distinction?

We can detect its presence in the recent work of the German philosopher and social theorist Jürgen Habermas. Habermas (1987) sought to distinguish between normal or everyday communication[6] and a second form that is literary and/or rhetorical. Based on this twofold distinction, Habermas's writing provides the matrix depicted in Figure I.1. For Habermas, rhetoric as practice can be defined through association and opposition. Rhetoric is associated with the figurative and literary use of language, and both are then opposed to normal or literal language use. Habermas acknowledged that these two forms are not mutually exclusive. As one of Habermas's principal explicators, Thomas McCarthy, noted, "We are dealing here with a continuum" (McCarthy, 1987, p. xiii). But McCarthy also pointed out that Habermas "insists on distinguishing those contexts in which the poetic function predominates, and thus structurally determines discourse, from those in which it plays a subordinate role" (p. xiii). We can distinguish the two types of practice by noting the dominant function. Literary/rhetorical discourse functions as a force of innovation and novelty; it reveals or "discloses" what previously had been concealed, and it identifies new possibilities of thought and action. It does so largely by way of the resources of linguistic style (e.g., *metaphor*) and is evaluated on the degree to which the world-disclosing function has been actualized (e.g., has the discourse produced any effects, and has it been successful in revealing new possibilities to people?). Normal or everyday discourse functions to solve practical problems such as questions of public policy and to organize or coordinate human interaction. It is evaluated not on the grounds of success but rather according to the degree to which it measures up to certain enduring standards that Habermas described as validity conditions.[7] And the principal discursive vehicle of everyday communicative practice is reason giving or **argument.**

Habermas's (1987) argument was directed against a trend in contemporary philosophy and literary theory to conflate or collapse the distinctions between the two dominant forms of discourse. Confusing literary/rhetorical and normal everyday discourse creates problems, Habermas argued, because each mode or form conforms to different standards for evaluation. We understand and judge normal communication by the degree to which speakers and writers redeem or support validity claims. We expect people to speak the truth and to be truthful about their intentions, and we use these standards to evaluate what people say to us. If a politician distorts the facts, misrepresents his or her intentions, or employs ambiguous language, then we use the inherent validity conditions of normal communication as a basis for a negative judgment. These normal standards do not apply to literary/rhetorical practices; we do not judge a novel or poem in the same way as we judge normal communication. Habermas's concern was that if we collapse this distinction, or if we blur everyday and literary/rhetorical discourse, then we will lose the standards of normal communication and all communication will be judged on the literary/rhetorical standard of success; truth, appropriateness, truthfulness, and intelligibility will not matter so long as the practice—the novel, the poem, or (perhaps more dangerously) the political speech—produces results.

The American philosopher Richard Rorty, at times an intellectual opponent of Habermas, nevertheless developed a similar two-part scheme of discursive types. Loosely extending Thomas Kuhn's distinction between normal science and revolutionary science,[8] Rorty (1979, 1989) argued that there are two basic situations: stable situations (in which people generally agree on the ends they want to achieve and disagree only on the means) and unstable situations (in which everything, ends as well as means, is up for grabs). During stable periods, people tend to use literal language and fashion arguments to solve practical problems. During periods of instability, normal or stable communication does little good. Rorty suggested that normal argument is of minor value when it comes to ends; people cannot argue about ends, only means. In these unstable situations, people begin to use words in new ways, create new languages largely through the device of metaphor, and (in Habermas's terms) create or "disclose" new worlds or new ends that eventually create a different but stable situation. Once the new paradigm is in place, practices become stabilized and new routines are established. In terms of politics, the shift from feudalism to state-based nationalism, or the shift from a monarchical system to a republic, embodies the stable-unstable contrast described by Rorty. For a period of time (that may last for generations), talk is unfamiliar; people do not argue with each other so much as try out or experiment with new words and languages. Once new ends are in place (and people begin to see the world in terms of nation-states rather than in terms of feudal lords), a stable form of language practice develops to sustain the new order.

Rorty and Habermas developed roughly parallel descriptions of two dominant modes of discourse. The biggest difference between them is that Rorty tended to find the discourse of unstable periods more interesting, whereas Habermas believed that normal or stable communication is more central to the basic task of coordinating human action. Rorty saw considerable value in unleashing abnormal, unfamiliar, metaphorical language; he suggested that all of the great conceptual advances emerge when people break the rules. Habermas (1987) claimed to appreciate the value of world-disclosing discourse. But he nevertheless maintained that the "rhetorical elements" that tend to surface in everyday discourse—the abnormal and unfamiliar practices that Rorty praised—need to be "tamed" (p. 209).

Rhetorical scholar Richard Lanham also employed a central antithetical contrast in his work on the history of rhetorical theory. But in Lanham's (1976) case, the contrast was not simply an opposition between two types of discourse; it was a struggle between two views of human nature (see also Fish, 1989, pp. 478-485). By moving from types of discourse to views of human nature, Lanham reconceptualized the struggle in anthropological terms.[9] On one side is *homo seriosus,* defender of the real, the rational, the familiar, the ordinary, and the everyday. On the other side is *homo rhetoricus,* proponent of a world of appearances, artifice, novelty, playfulness, and the unexpected.

Habermas, Rorty, and Lanham described and enacted a long-standing, deep-seated conceptual tension or opposition that has helped to shape the possibilities of rhetoric.[10] The key question is *how* this struggle has shaped our understanding of rhetoric as a form of practice. At the risk of oversimplification, this long-standing struggle cultivated two ways of defining rhetorical practice. One definition emerged largely in American departments of speech early in the 20th century.[11] The other definition, largely European in ancestry, reflects the continued influence of Peter Ramus's reworking of the classical tradition of rhetoric during the 16th century.

Many of the exponents of rhetorical studies in the newly created departments of speech during the early 20th century would recognize Habermas's contrast between normal everyday discourse and literary/aesthetic discourse. But they would have rejected one key element in his formulation. Scholars such as Hudson (1923; see also Wichelns, 1925/1962) frequently employed the practical/aesthetic antithesis as a way of clarifying the nature of rhetorical practice. But these scholars, unlike Habermas, did not contrast rhetoric with ordinary language practices; they did the opposite. Hudson, Wichelns, and other early advocates of rhetorical studies maintained that rhetorical practice can be understood as something different from literature, poetry, and other aesthetic forms of discursive practice. In a famous passage, Hudson (1923) wrote,

> The writer in pure literature has his [sic] eye on his subject; his subject has filled his mind and engaged his interest, and he must tell about it; his task is expression; his form and style are organic with his subject. The writer of rhetorical discourse has his eye upon the audience and occasion; his task is persuasion; his form and style are organic with the occasion. (p. 177)

The founders of the contemporary rhetorical tradition in speech argued that rhetorical practice is concerned with the real world, whereas aesthetic and literary practices focus on an imaginary world.[12] Rhetorical practices consequently are bound to the moment in time and space when they were produced in a way that aesthetic or literary texts are not. Aesthetic or literary texts embody a universal appeal, whereas rhetorical works focus on particular moments in the lives of political communities. *Hamlet* has spoken to audiences across the centuries, whereas a speech by a 19th-century abolitionist or women's suffrage advocate spoke to the problems, concerns, and needs of a particular, historically specific community. In 1965, Edwin Black encapsulated the initial mainstream speech communication definition of rhetoric as practice when he wrote, "Rhetorical discourses are those discourses, spoken or written, which aim to influence men [sic]" (Black, 1965/1978, p. 15).

Whereas American rhetoricians have focused on the literal, the practical, and the pragmatic, the European understanding of rhetorical practice emphasizes the figurative, the aesthetic, and the formal (e.g., Dubois et al., 1981). This is the sense of rhetoric that Habermas had in mind when he linked rhetoric and literary discourse. The range of rhetoric began to be narrowed during the 16th century, thanks in large part to the works of Peter Ramus (Conley, 1990; Kennedy, 1980). For Ramus, rhetoric was primarily the study of **style.** Consistent with this Ramistic tradition, the literary scholar Paul de Man defined rhetoric as "the study of tropes and figures" and specifically denied any connection to persuasion (de Man, 1979, p. 6).[13] But de Man's Ramistic narrowing of rhetoric is part of a larger strategy that both redefines and, paradoxically, enlarges the scope of rhetorical practice. For de Man, virtually all language practice, but especially the form of practice that purports to be merely descriptive or literal, is at some level ultimately figurative; various rhetorical tropes and figures saturate discourse and allow it to create the illusion of truth. Discussing Nietzsche's insights, de Man wrote, "The trope is not a derived, marginal, or aberrant form of language but the linguistic paradigm par excellence. The figurative structure is not one linguistic mode among others, but it characterizes language as such" (p. 105). Whereas de Man followed the European trend and narrowed rhetoric to the realm of tropes and figures, he went on, following Nietzsche, to locate a figurative element in virtually all language practice. Rhetoric, as a form of "intralinguistic" discursive practice, is everywhere (p. 8). De Man's understanding of rhetorical practice as the play of tropes and figures, or as "the figural dimension in language," is representative of a significant trend in contemporary scholarship (Gaonkar, 1987, p. 484).[14]

The opposition between the literal and the figurative, or the ordinary and the aesthetic, helped to generate two competing definitions of rhetorical practice. We have de Man's "intralinguistic" sense of rhetoric as the incessant play of tropes and figures in language practice, and we have an extralinguistic sense of rhetoric as a particular strand of literal ordinary language practice that is practical, pragmatic, and persuasive in its orientation. Both definitions have large followings, and both have apparent limitations. For a large number of contemporary rhetorical scholars, the focus on explicit practical persuasion begun during the early part of the 20th century is too narrow and limited. As early as the 1950s, scholars such as Donald Bryant began to broaden the range of ordinary language practices that constitute the realm of rhetorical practice (Bryant, 1953; see also the entry for **exposition**). The range of practices that fall within the orbit of rhetoric has continued to expand, thanks in part to the influence of thinkers such as de Man and Jacques Derrida (e.g., Derrida, 1977) who began to question the adequacy of categories such as "the ordinary" and "the literal." The rhetorical, or the figurative aspect of language, was everywhere. This expansion of rhetoric has led, in turn, to the feeling among some rhetorical scholars that the domain of rhetorical practice has become too broad and expansive. The tendency to think about language practice by way of dichotomies and oppositions has given way to alternative strategies for defining the nature of rhetorical practice. Nevertheless, the dichotomies literal-figurative, rhetoric-aesthetic, persuasion-trope, and argument-style still inhabit contemporary thought about language and human communication and, hence, continue to exert some influence on how rhetorical practice is conceptualized.

One alternative to the binary definitional strategy is to exploit the apparent human fascination with three-part schemes (e.g., the Christian trinity, the Hegelian dialectic). Some thinkers over the years have identified three basic forms of language practice. There is some evidence of this approach during the classical period, for example, in discussions that distinguished between rhetoric, poetic or **narrative**, and dialectic or philosophical discourse.[15] The contemporary literary and legal scholar James Boyd White relied on this classical trivium (White, 1984) when he equated philosophical discourse with the pursuit of truth, aesthetic discourse with the pursuit of beauty, and rhetorical discourse with the pursuit of justice (with justice being, for White, the essential ingredient in human community). Something close to this trivium can be detected in some of Habermas's (1984, pp. 235-242) thinking about human communication. Starting with his assumption that there are three basic "orientations" that an individual can have to the world (objective, subjective, and intersubjective), it is possible to uncover the three basic forms lurking in the wings. Traditional philosophical discourse, and its modern cousin scientific discourse, has an objective orientation to the world; the world is an object to be known, described, and controlled. Aesthetic discourse (e.g., poems, novels) and art in general (e.g., painting, music) has a subjective orientation to the world; the objective of these practices is not description and mastery but rather self-expression. Finally, rhetorical discourse (for Habermas, this form of practice is restricted to legal and moral discourse) has an intersubjective orientation to the world; the objective of this form of practice is neither knowledge and truth nor self-expression and beauty but rather interaction with a world consisting of fellow creatures. Rhetorical, intersubjectively oriented practices create, maintain, modify, and overturn the communal world(s) that humans share in common (even if individuals differ with respect to their ability to shape that communal world).[16]

One virtue of a three-part scheme is that rhetorical practice usually is positioned in the middle. As such, it inevitably will contain elements from the discursive forms that reside on either side; rhetorical practice will raise issues of truth (the proper concern of philosophical and, more and more today, scientific discourse) and contain elements of formal beauty and self-expression (the focus of aesthetic practice). But these elements are not dominant in rhetorical discourse. Conceived as a middle ground between the traditional philosophical quest for truth and the aesthetic pursuit of beauty and self-expression, rhetorical discourse constitutes and reconstitutes intersubjective communities; it promotes intersubjective **identification** by overcoming the divisions that plague humanity. But positioning rhetoric as a discursive middle ground also has limitations. As any advocate who has tried to defend a middle ground can attest, middle positions are notoriously unstable. Conceived as a middle ground, rhetorical practice is susceptible to Plato's critique. There is no real *substance* to rhetoric; it is simply a collection of discursive tricks. Another problem with this type of three-part scheme is that real-world discursive practices frequently violate the functions assigned to the different categories. Sociologists of science argue that scientific discourse does not simply transmit objective knowledge; it also establishes and maintains a community of scientists. In at least some cases, scientific discourse exhibits traces of rhetorical activity.[17] When pushed with concrete examples such as those uncovered by sociologists of science, the three forms begin to collapse into each other. The question remains: Is it possible to identify distinct forms of human communication and, in so doing, identify a specific form that can be considered "rhetoric"?[18]

The inability to establish clear and immutable distinctions between different forms of language practice has led large numbers of scholars to abandon any efforts to locate or identify essential forms of communication. This approach, an outgrowth of the expansion of rhetoric discussed earlier, sometimes is referred to as the *undifferentiated textuality* thesis. Adherents of the thesis maintain that all linguistic and discursive practices—scientific reports, poems, newspaper articles, political speeches, philosophical treatises, legal contracts, corporate "advertorials," radical manifestos, advice columns, and so on—are essentially the same. They can have multiple functions, appear in different contexts, be produced by one person or prepared by a committee, and be written in any of a number of idioms or combinations of idioms. But despite these apparent differences, all of these discursive practices result in a "text." They consist of words, the words combine into sentences, and the sentences combine into paragraphs; the words, sentences, and paragraphs cohere into structures and configurations that reveal various types of patterns. The words, sentences, paragraphs, and patterns enter into relationships with each other; they can, among other possible relationships, support, qualify, contest, subvert, and/or ignore each other. And out of this mix of words, sentences, paragraphs, idioms, patterns, and interrelationships comes something ephemeral but sometimes enduring, something intangible but nevertheless real, something inherently particular but capable of subsequent rearticulation in different contexts. This something is discursive *force.*

When people use language, they do not simply employ it as a passive tool for depicting or representing the world. Nor does language serve only as a device that allows people to externalize their internal thoughts. These restrictive views of linguistic **representation** have been largely discarded in contemporary scholarship. More and more scholars are embracing a *constructivist* or *constitutive* understanding of language practice. Put simply, when people use language, they are participating in the ongoing (re)construction of the world.[19] Fish (1989) noted how, in many disciplines,

> there is evidence of . . . the realization . . . that the givens of any field of activity—including the facts it commands, the procedures it trusts in, and the values it expresses and extends—are socially and politically constructed, are fashioned by man [sic] rather than delivered by God or nature. (p. 485)

Fish continued this line of argument a few pages later when he commented on the Searle-Derrida "debate" about "ordinary" language. In this context, Fish observed,

> The "obvious" cannot be opposed to the "staged," as Searle assumes, because it is simply the achievement of a staging that has been particularly successful. One does not escape the rhetorical by fleeing to the protected area of basic communication and common sense because common sense in whatever form it happens to take is always a rhetorical—partial, partisan, interested—construction. (pp. 491-492)

Along similar lines, Bash (1995) described how the social constructionist position

> stipulates that what we commonly accept as real, the familiar world within which and in relation to which we plan our activities and act them out—both in their day-to-day detail and in the broader strategies in terms of which we conduct our lives—this reality, in effect, is an artifact of the way in which we have elaborated our particular culture and this given shape to our society. (p. 26)[20]

The constructivist position does not entail the idea that language can magically conjure up material objects from thin air. Rather, language and discursive practice mediates, or links, people and their surrounding world. As Shotter (1993b) observed, "We 'see' just as much 'through' our words as through our eyes" (p. 14).[21] But this linking process never is passive or neutral. Whereas language and discourse make the world understandable and accessible, they always present the world in particular ways. Fish (1989) noted,

> Whatever reports a particular language (natural or artificial) offers us will be the report on the world as it is seen from within some particular situation; there is no other aperspectival way to see and no language other than situation-dependent language—an interested, rhetorical language—in which to report. (p. 488)[22]

Language and discourse do not create natural disasters, nor do they simply neutrally report these events; rather, language and discourse shape or construct how we will understand events such as earthquakes and tornadoes (consider that, at various times, these events would have been understood as acts of God, the result of fate, or the consequence of the scientific laws of physics).

But how does language construct reality? Our language practices have constructive power because discourse exudes perspective, it exudes influence, and it exudes force.[23] Discursive force is manifest through grammar and syntax, tropes and figures, structural patterns of **arrangement** or disposition, vocabulary and word choice, explicit **argument**, and other forms of discursive strategy. This force can be experienced by the text's producers, by an immediate audience, by subsequent readers distant in time and space, by interested bystanders, by opponents in a social controversy, or by individuals who never have directly encountered the text in their entire lives (e.g., the North American Indians who experienced the force of texts produced by European colonizers for hundreds of years). According to the undifferentiated textuality thesis, all texts exert a force, but not in the same degree or magnitude. Paraphrasing Derrida, Fish (1989) remarked, "This does not mean . . . that all rhetorical constructions are equal, just that they are equally rhetorical" (p. 492). Texts may differ in their degrees of force, but they all are essentially the same.

How do the undifferentiated textuality thesis and the social constructionist position influence the effort to define rhetoric as a practice? Some scholars in contemporary rhetorical studies embrace both ideas. The basic argument can be represented in a traditional first figure syllogism (A → B, B → C, A → C):

Social reality is the product of discursive force.
Discursive force is best understood as rhetorical practice.
Social reality is constructed through rhetorical practice.

The combination of the undifferentiated textuality thesis and social constructionism is the universalization of rhetoric; all discursive practice can be considered "rhetorical."[24] But notice the shift in the last sentence from "rhetoric" (a substantive noun) to "rhetorical" (an adjective). When scholars talk about the universalization of rhetoric (e.g., Gaonkar, 1993), we need to understand that what has been universalized is a particular *quality* or *function* of discourse, not a specific type or form of discourse. There is some ambiguity between form and function in the definitions of rhetorical practice introduced by the founders of the speech field. The function of persuasion invariably was a part of their definitions, but it was subordinated by formal considerations. Scholars from Hudson and Wichelns to Black hoped to identify an object of inquiry—rhetoric—that was on the same plane as, yet different from, the widely recognized object of literary studies. Over time, and thanks to a variety of intellectual trends (some of which have been noted here), the form-function relationship has been reversed. Universal rhetoric is functional. Scholars who subscribe to this definition of rhetorical practice study the force, or the power, of language; they study the "rhetoricity" or "rhetoricality" of any and every type of discursive practice. Through this form-function reversal and universalizing impulse, rhetorical studies emerges as the preeminent intellectual discipline.[25]

The impulse to universalize rhetoric has been resisted in at least two ways. First, a number of scholars accept the shift from form to function as the most appropriate way of defining rhetorical practice. But they then try to narrow the expansive equation of discursive force and rhetorical function that exists in a globalized conception of rhetorical practice. In the speech/communication studies field, the emphasis tends to be on the traditional idea of persuasion. Rhetoric is understood as the persuasive *dimension* of discursive and symbolic practice (Brummett, 1994; Bryant, 1973; Medhurst & Benson, 1984; Weaver, 1971).[26] Bryant (1953) took tentative steps in this direction when he wrote, "I am almost forced to the position that whatever we do or say or write, or even think, in explanation of anything, or in support, or in extenuation, or in despite of anything, evinces rhetorical symptoms" (p. 401). Frye (1957) also was moving in this direction around the same time when he observed that "all structures in words are partly rhetorical. . . . the notion of a scientific or philosophical verbal structure free of rhetorical elements is an illusion" (p. 350). LaCapra (1985) continued this trend when he asserted, "Rhetoric is a dimension of all language use rather than a separable set of uses or a realm of discourse" (p. 17). Commenting on the state of rhetorical studies during the late 1980s, Leff (1987) noted "the shift . . . from a kind of discourse to a dimension in discourse, from an emphasis on certain products to an emphasis on a certain kind of activity" (p. 3). If rhetoric is the persuasive dimension in discursive practice, then it becomes possible to identify practices that are more or less rhetorical (based on the degree to which the persuasive dimension stands out) while still examining the persuasive dimension, or the rhetoric, of a wide variety of practices (e.g., the rhetoric of newsmagazines, the rhetoric of popular song lyrics, the rhetoric of advertising, the rhetoric of science, the rhetoric of judicial opinion, the rhetoric of film). The dimensionalizing of rhetoric has proven to be an extremely attractive definitional option,[27] but it is not without limitations. LaRue (1995) suggested that the root meaning of rhetoric as persuasion, even when persuasion is transformed into a function or dimension of discourse, "is not enough to ground a common discipline, since speech and writing can persuade in many different ways and at many different levels of conscious and unconscious operation" (p. 3).[28] So, although the dimensional definition might unify a number of scholars, LaRue questioned whether it is sufficient to organize and integrate their intellectual labor.

Other scholars in the field of rhetorical studies agree that foundational distinctions between types or forms of practice are untenable, but these scholars still want to restrict the scope of what is meant by rhetoric as practice. The motivation behind these efforts to delimit rhetoric as practice varies. Garver's (1994) reconstruction of Aristotle's (1954) *Rhetoric* as a guide to civic practice was motivated by ethical concerns. Garver recognized the potential for rhetorical practice to evolve into a "universal" or "professional" art where the external end—instrumental success or persuasion—becomes dominant at the expense of the internal end of moral excellence (pp. 45-51). But this universalizing impulse can be resisted, Garver argued, by recovering Aristotle's vision of a "restricted" or "civic" form of rhetorical practice. For Garver, a restricted or civic understanding of rhetorical practice allows for the essentially ethical reconciliation between the competing ends of practice—excellence and instrumental success. When rhetorical practice is universalized, as it is in the idea of undifferentiated textuality, victory or success emerges as the only end of practice and the ethical relationship between advocate and audience is lost. Garver explained, "When accomplishing the external end becomes the only value, then rhetoric needs additional moral restraints distinct from the activity of argument itself" to protect the community and prevent cultural decline (p. 48). But a restricted or civic rhetoric

> is [a form of practice] in which more than the external goal is at stake. The audience is not an enemy, and the civic rhetorician must construct a civic relation between himself [sic] and the audience. . . . Civic rhetoric aims at an identity between the speaker making arguments and the audience receiving them. (pp. 46-47)

Restricting the scope of rhetorical practice to civic or political discourse provides a set of artistic and ethical standards by which it can be evaluated.

Some other scholars in the rhetorical studies community move in a somewhat similar direction. In a number of essays, Leff has tried to resist the globalization of rhetoric (e.g., Leff, 1987, 1997b). His primary motivation is pedagogical and focused on disciplinary development. Leff (1997b) acknowledged, "It is now generally agreed that rhetoric is not a property of certain kinds of texts but a process that inheres in all discursive practices and that influences social consciousness at every level of its manifestation" (p. 131). He then conceded, "Theoretically, I find it difficult to dispute the status of rhetoric as a global process. I do not know of any abstract principle that would distinguish some discourses as rhetorical and others as non-rhetorical" (p. 132). But Leff then tried to argue that there are practical and pragmatic reasons for a more restrained approach to defining rhetorical practice. He wrote, "The view that all discourse is rhetorical expresses a theoretical truism that has limited practical value for the critic. Global conceptions of rhetoric cannot adequately account for the differing kinds of rhetoric that appear and develop in the social world" (p. 132). Leff encouraged rhetorical critics to concentrate their attention on public or civic discourse for practical reasons. Critics, like effective advocates and practitioners, must "master a genre" of practice (p. 132). And the genre of public or civic discourse provides rhetorical scholars with a genre that not only is sanctioned by the ancient tradition of rhetoric but also is of tremendous social and historical significance.

For different reasons, Garver and Leff have favored a rather traditional definition of rhetoric as public or civic discursive practice. But what is meant by rhetoric as a public or civic practice? These terms, like the term *rhetoric* itself, are slippery. To define rhetoric as a public or civic practice typically means that rhetorical practices, which are capable of assuming different discursive forms (e.g., speeches, essays, pamphlets), address issues of public concern or interest.[29] Which deodorant a person uses, or which brand of dishwashing detergent a person buys, is not commonly considered a public issue. Consumer choices like these, and a range of additional choices that all of us make on a regular basis, occur outside of what we collectively constitute as the public realm. Messages aimed at influencing consumer decisions might involve persuasion but, given Garver's and Leff's restricted definition of rhetorical practice, would not be considered rhetorical. But we need to acknowledge that the shape of the public realm can be altered discursively so that choices not thought to be of public consequence become public issues. A person might prefer to use an aerosol spray deodorant. Advocates on behalf of scientific or environmental groups might release information about the possible harmful effects of aerosol spray emissions on the environment. Now the person's consumer choice begins to take on public significance because the atmosphere is something that people hold in common. The advocates are creating a public issue by, in part, altering the shape of the **public sphere.** Once the choice has been politicized or moved into the public sphere, messages that once were thought to be commercial and nonrhetorical now take on rhetorical significance.[30]

As the preceding example tried to illustrate, the publicness or civic quality of an issue can change. Practices once thought to be outside the public realm (e.g., treatment of a spouse) can be brought into the public realm, and practices once thought to be integral to the public realm (e.g., religion) can be displaced (although, in this case, the controversy in the United States continues). Employing the concept of public or civic as a way of locating and defining rhetorical practice cannot be exact. As the boundaries shift, certain practices and issues move into and out of the public realm, and consequently, the attribution of the label "rhetorical" to the discourse that addresses these practices and issues can change as well. This definitional strategy allows for a degree of substantive stability as well as change over time.

The discussion in this section has described some of the more prominent ways in which scholars have defined rhetoric as a form of discursive or language practice. These definitions include (a) rhetoric as practical persuasive discourse; (b) rhetoric as the use of tropes and figures; (c) rhetoric as a type of *middle ground* practice concerned with justice and/or creating and maintaining a community (intersubjectivity); (d) rhetoric as attitude, perspective, and/or discursive force (universalized rhetoric); (e) rhetoric as the persuasive *dimension* of discursive and symbolic practice; and (f) rhetoric as public or civic discourse.[31] These definitions of rhetorical practice are not necessarily mutually exclusive,[32] and there are some affinities among the various definitions. But important tensions—rhetoric as form versus rhetoric as function, product versus process—persist. Appreciating similarities and differences, even when those differences are subtle, is important when trying to understand how the term *rhetoric* is being used by specific scholars or critics. All of the definitions have attractive features, and all appear to have certain limitations. During various historical periods, the identity of rhetoric as a cultural practice was unproblematic. That clearly is not the case today. It is uncertain whether rhetoric as practice will achieve a coherent identity any time in the near future. In the meantime, rhetoricians, as well as other scholars who have appropriated the term *rhetoric,* must struggle with its ambiguous meanings.

Rhetorica Docens: Rhetoric as Theory

At the outset, it was noted that rhetoric means both a type of discursive practice and the activity of thinking about or theorizing that practice. The utens-docens distinction seems to assume that there are clear differences between the activity of producing a practical text (e.g., a public speech advocating a prochoice position on the abortion controversy)/the result of that activity (the speech text) and the activity of thinking about practice that leads to the production of a theoretical text (e.g., a lecture in a classroom about what is going on in the discourse of the abortion controversy)/the theoretical text (an essay in a scholarly journal). For scholars such as Habermas and Leff, this assumption is obvious and correct; practical activity/practical texts and theoretical activity/theoretical texts are different types of things and should not be conflated. But the proponents of the undifferentiated textuality position would challenge the obviousness of this assumption. Scholars adhering to this position maintain that there are no essential differences between these activities and the texts that result from them. All discursive practice, whatever its **genre** or purpose, results in a text whose force can be analyzed. But the analysis of the force of one text (an essay endorsing a policy position) simply leads to the production of another text (a piece of criticism) and another text (proposing a theory of policy discourse) that are not fundamentally different from each other. It is, therefore, quite reasonable to talk about something like the rhetoric of rhetoric (Cahn, 1993; Gaonkar, 1993). The texts that make up the tradition of rhetorical thinking are not fundamentally different from the texts that constitute the traditions of rhetorical practice. Although there might not be an absolute distinction between practical activity and theoretical activity, scholars have, as a matter of convenience, differentiated these activities and their resulting texts. We can talk about the meaning of rhetoric as a form of theory, or as something different from the meaning of rhetoric as a form of practice, while still acknowledging the textuality, or the rhetoricity, of theoretical discourse.[33]

So, what does it mean to talk about rhetoric as a way of thinking about practice or as a form of theory? Nearly 50 years ago, Bryant (1953) surveyed the field of rhetorical studies so as to map its important features. Bryant discussed four specific aspects of rhetorical theory that remain extremely useful as a way of sorting out the domain, or the meaning, of rhetorical theory (cf. Natanson, 1955).

We can label Bryant's first aspect "instrumental" or "productive." This sense of rhetorical theory often goes by the term *art.* What is an instrumental theory or an art of rhetoric? The most common manifestation of this form of rhetorical thinking is as a prescriptive handbook (for an exception, see Kaufer & Butler, 1996). Many of the earliest books on the subject of rhetoric took this form. They provided advice to speakers (and eventually writers) on how to proceed in certain situations (how to proceed with a friendly audience, a hostile audience, etc.). Most college textbooks for public speaking courses and self-help books on how to become a more effective public speaker continue this tradition of thinking. To offer advice, the earliest prescriptive handbooks typically engaged in some elementary forms of analysis. The handbooks of classical antiquity dissected rhetorical practice so as to identify the elements of the art (see the entry for **canon of rhetoric**), describe the usual parts of a speech and note their common functions (see the entry for **arrangement**), provide typologies of persuasive strategies or the **modes of proof** and **stylistic** tactics, and describe the common types or **genres** of rhetorical practice (Ehninger, 1968).

Contemporary commentators on the classical tradition of rhetorical theory have raised an important question. Discussing Aristotle's (1954) *Rhetoric*, Beiner (1983) wrote,

> What is not so clear is whether he understood [rhetoric] as the necessarily imperfect medium within which political life is conducted or whether he also saw it as a positive expression of the mediated quality of social life. . . . But what remains open to question is whether his *Rhetoric* was merely a handbook for the instrumental employment of this medium or whether it pointed toward an affirmation of the medium itself. (p. 96)

The interpretive issues that Beiner introduced are important because they raise the question of rhetoric's status—as practice and as theory—in Aristotle's thought. If Aristotle's *Rhetoric* was simply a handbook, on par with a contemporary public speaking textbook, then the theoretical possibilities of rhetoric are quite limited. But if Aristotle understood the practice of rhetoric, and the process of theorizing about that practice, in more positive terms, then the possibilities for both practice and theorizing are expanded.

A related issue raised by some of the first writers on rhetoric is whether or not the art of rhetoric could be reduced to rules and put down on paper. One tradition of thought believed that rhetorical art could be condensed into precepts or rules that can be followed (often discussed as the "technical" or "prescriptive" tradition). A different tradition of thought, best represented by the Roman statesmen and rhetorician Cicero in his mature writing, held that the art of rhetoric existed only in actual practice or performance.[34] Prescriptive handbooks were rejected as an inadequate embodiment of the art. If the art was embodied in practice, then the only way of learning the art—of becoming a master practitioner—was to study exemplary performances so as to replicate the artfulness of those performances in subsequent practice. Students of rhetoric in this tradition did not learn rules. Rather, they engaged in a complex process of *imitation* to internalize the artfulness of acknowledged masterpieces. As students internalized the art, they would be able to produce effective, or eloquent, rhetorical discourse (see the entry for **invention**).

The second aspect in Bryant's map of rhetorical studies is an extension on this early interest in studying actual practice. We can label this dimension "critical" or "interpretive." The thrust of this aspect has changed over time. In classical rhetorical education, interpretation and discourse production were interconnected (Leff, 1997a); reading rhetorical practice facilitated the production of discourse. In contemporary rhetorical studies, interpretation and criticism often are regarded as independent activities that lack an immanent connection to the production of rhetorical discourse (Gaonkar, 1993). The separation of criticism and interpretation from discourse production in rhetorical studies parallels a similar development in the area of literary studies. Learning to become an expert discerning reader, given that reading is at the heart of interpretation and criticism, has become as important as learning to become an expert practitioner or advocate. The critical or interpretive aspect of rhetorical theory focuses on the way in which rhetoricians read the texts produced through rhetorical practice (see the entry for **criticism**).

Discussion of this aspect of theory in the contemporary tradition of rhetorical studies typically focuses on the idea of critical *method*. Over the past few decades, numerous methods for reading rhetorical texts have been proposed, illustrated, attacked, defended, modified, and abandoned.[35] Some critical methods specify in great detail what readers should do as they encounter and read a text, whereas other methods provide only a rough framework or a general perspective that can be employed by critics or readers. Some contemporary rhetorical scholars maintain that the idea of method, imported from the realm of science where the ideal of "scientific method" is seen as a way of guaranteeing the production of knowledge, is an inappropriate model for the activity of rhetorical criticism and interpretation. The end of this activity, they often claim, is not the production of knowledge (the aim of scientific experimentation) but rather the achievement of understanding. Understanding someone is not the same thing as gaining knowledge about someone. An individual might know various facts about another person, but does that mean that the individual understands who the other person is? So, a number of contemporary rhetorical scholars urge students and colleagues to, rather than blindly following a single method, encounter rhetorical practices and texts directly, engaging in a process that sometimes is called **close reading** or close textual analysis. Through this activity, readers try to discover what is going on in a text in its own terms.

Other scholars, within the tradition of rhetorical studies and in adjacent traditions of thinking, respond by maintaining that it is impossible to encounter a text strictly on its own terms. Reading, we are told, never is a neutral activity; just as facts do not "speak for themselves," the words in a speech, a novel, a poem, or an essay never speak directly to the readers. When we read any text, we always are relying on something, not necessarily any specific critical or interpretive method but rather certain conceptual screens that allow the words of the speech, essay, or poem to mean something for us. As different readers encounter the words on this page, different conceptual screens—some unique to specific individuals and others shared by people because of where they grew up, where they went to school, what their parents taught them, and many other factors—are activated. The words on the page do not literally change; they remain the same (at least physically), but they are not read in precisely the same way. The conceptual screen that allows one group of people to understand an inside joke is not available to others who, in most cases, do not understand the joke. Reading, then, involves more than paying careful attention to the words, sentences, patterns, and images in the text; it also involves paying attention to the conceptual screens that make reading possible.[36]

The fact, according to this line of interpretive theory, that reading never is neutral, or that the words produced by a speaker or printed on a page always are filtered by conceptual screens, has been disputed by other critics. Critics who object to this line of thought argue that the "reading never is neutral" position entails interpretive anarchy because ultimately each individual will have a unique conceptual screen that filters every message he or she encounters. Given an infinite number of conceptual screens, the possibility of people agreeing on an interpretation of a text is almost nonexistent. No agreement among readers on interpretation *is* interpretive anarchy (e.g., Hirsch, 1967). Fish (1980) responded to this line of argument in his book, *Is There a Text in This Class?* According to Fish, scholars who worry about interpretive anarchy are effectively making a mountain out of a molehill. How so? Because those scholars assume a world of isolated individuals, all of whom possess their own unique conceptual screens. Fish would not deny people a degree of uniqueness, but he emphasized the existence of "interpretive communities" and "interpretive conventions" that make interpretive anarchy impossible. Fish wrote that communication occurs within situations, and

> to be in a situation is already to be in possession of (or to be possessed by) a structure of assumptions, of practices understood to be relevant in relation to purposes and goals

> that are already in place; and it is within the assumption of these purposes and goals that any utterance is *immediately* heard. (p. 318)

Fish insisted that the process of interpretation always is constrained by a specific situation, an institutional structure, and cultural norms. In Fish's view, people cannot create outlandish interpretations *unless* they are willing to violate situational, institutional, and cultural structures and norms. Given the sanctions that follow from such willful violations, they do not occur very often. Fish concluded that the fact that readers read texts differently, or the fact that meanings are not "in" the text, is not something that scholars and theorists need to worry about.

There are other important issues related to the critical and interpretive aspect of rhetorical thinking. For example, a question of concern to some rhetorical scholars is whether or not there is a distinctly *rhetorical* form of interpretation, a way of reading that distinguishes the rhetorical critic's interpretive habits and conventions.[37] Consider a text such as the Declaration of Independence. Students might be asked to read this text in a history class, a political science class, an English class focusing on American political literature, or a class in early American public address taught by a rhetorical scholar. In what ways might the readings of this document produced in these four classes differ? Would the historian encourage his or her class to read the document in ways that are significantly different from how the political scientist, the literary specialist, and the rhetorician read the text? Or, imagine that a group of, say, five rhetoricians read the Declaration of Independence, with each approaching the text from a different critical method discussed in a contemporary textbook on rhetorical criticism. Would these five readings be linked in some way? Would someone be able to read these different analyses and conclude that they all were written by rhetorical critics? These all are important **metacritical** questions to which there are no simple answers. But these are some of the questions that continue to shape the second aspect of rhetorical theory.

Following Bryant, we can label the third aspect of rhetorical theory "social." Numerous issues constitute this domain of rhetorical thinking. First, thinking about rhetorical practice involves thinking about where that practice takes place. Thinking about where rhetorical practices occur leads in different directions. One line of thought focuses on the idea of the "rhetorical situation" (Bitzer, 1968; see also the entry for **situation, rhetorical**) and its constituent elements—*exigences, constraints/resources,* and **audiences.** Related to the idea of rhetorical situations is the concept of **genre.** As situations continue to recur over time and space, the responses they elicit typically share certain characteristics. Genre scholars explore this social aspect of rhetorical practice. Another line of thought investigates the relationship between rhetorical practice and various social and political institutions. Studies of presidential rhetoric, corporate advocacy, legal or **forensic discourse,** journalism, and the rhetoric of inquiry, among other lines of research, focus (at least in part) on the relationship between discursive practices and their institutional setting (Campbell & Jamieson, 1990; Hart, 1987). A fourth avenue of social inquiry involves reflection on the relationship between rhetorical practice and the *public* and **public sphere.**[38] Rhetorical scholars, along with colleagues in other disciplines, are interested in the nature of the contemporary public sphere and on the essentially recursive or interactive relationship between rhetorical practice and the public realm. Other scholars direct their attention to the idea of the public. Is there such a thing? Has there ever been a public in the United States? What does it mean to address "the public"? How do people behave differently when they act as members of the public rather than as private individuals? How do issues of race, ethnicity, gender, class, and religion influence a person's ability to become part of the public? Can we appeal to people in terms of their class or ethnic backgrounds at the same time as we appeal to them as members of the public?

Another important trend in social rhetorical theory is inquiry into the **effects of rhetorical practice.** During the early decades of the rebirth of rhetorical studies in the United States, the idea of discursive effect typically was limited to the action or actions taken by an immediate audience (Black, 1965/1978). When studying campaign discourse, the principal effect we would be interested in is the election outcome. How did people vote? Did the discourse of either candidate have a substantial impact on the outcome of the race? Some earlier scholars extended this approach and tried to measure, in some quantifiable way, the effects of messages on the audience. Effects inquiry along these lines rarely is found in the contemporary tradition of rhetorical studies. Thanks, in part, to the *constructivist* intellectual movement discussed earlier, scholars in rhetorical studies and other disciplines have begun to investigate the way in which language—in all its practical manifestations—helps to construct or constitute social reality. Over the past decade, rhetoricians have begun to explore the **constitutive** capacity of rhetorical practice.[39] In exploring this capacity, scholars have moved well beyond the ways in which words can influence how people vote. Scholars now ask questions such as the following. How does rhetorical practice shape our understanding of the past (e.g., the "meaning" of the war in Vietnam) and of what might be possible in the present (e.g., whether we can intervene in Bosnia given the legacy of Vietnam)? How does rhetorical practice construct our understanding of racial or ethnic categories? How does rhetorical practice shape and reshape the values and fundamental concepts or **ideographs** (e.g., liberty, equality, justice) that make community possible?

Finally, Bryant labeled the fourth aspect of rhetorical theory "philosophical." In the contemporary tradition of rhetorical studies, philosophical reflection on the nature of rhetoric can be traced to essays such as Natanson's (1955) "The Limits of Rhetoric." After suggesting the need for such reflection, Natanson wrote, "The question naturally arises, What, after all, is the subject matter of the philosophy of rhetoric? . . . What problems constitute the subject matter of the philosophy of rhetoric, and how may such a philosophy be articulated?" (p. 137). We cannot answer these questions unless we have a working definition of philosophy. Natanson provided the following: "Philosophy [is] the critique of presuppositions." Philosophical inquiry, he continued, has a *synthetic* component that "seeks to comprehend the nature of reality" and an *analytic* component that "attempts to bring to clarity the meaning of terms [or concepts] which are basic and crucial to the conceptual structure of all special disciplines" (p. 138). He maintained that both components of philosophy come together in "the systematic and persistent exploration of elements and themes which are taken for granted [both in] commonsense reality and in the special disciplines" (p. 138).

Natanson's sense of philosophy's mission is very traditional. This traditional view considers philosophy to be the ultimate form of intellectual inquiry; all the various forms of human practice and the other intellectual disciplines submit to its scrutiny. Natanson (1955) proposed the following as a partial list of topics in rhetorical studies that might benefit from careful philosophical scrutiny:

> the relationship between language and what language denotes; the relationship between mind and what the mind is aware of; the relationship between knowledge and what knowledge is "of"; the relationship between consciousness and its various contents . . ., the relationship of speaker and listener, the persuader and the one persuaded, [the] judger and the thing judged. (p. 138)

In suggesting these topics, Natanson anticipated some of the issues that would capture the attention of rhetorical scholars starting during the 1960s—the question of rhetoric's **epistemic** status, the nature of language and the process of linguistic **representation,** and the process of inducing **judgment** by way of **argument** and artistic **modes of proof.** The type of self-scrutiny that Natanson labeled "philosophy" has become a fixture in contemporary rhetorical studies (e.g., Cherwitz, 1990).

Natanson's traditionalism depicts philosophy lording over other modes of thinking. Philosophy reveals and/or helps to clarify the *foundations* of all knowledge, all values, and all human practices. But what if there are no foundations to be revealed or clarified? What if there is nothing firm or permanent supporting our beliefs, values, and modes of action? People have been posing these seemingly heretical questions for as long as philosophers have been engaged in the task of establishing foundations. A world without firm foundations guaranteed by *philosophy* is a world of incessant talk, abundant discourse, and *undifferentiated textuality.* For some scholars, these *are* the conditions of our world (despite the fact that many people cling to the illusions of stable foundations), and these conditions reveal ours to be a decidedly rhetorical (in a specific sense of the term) world. And what of "theory" in such a thoroughly rhetorical world? Theoretical labor does not end, but the status of theory and its objectives change. Natanson's idea of "critique" remains, but it is radicalized. Instead of the critique of presuppositions, theory becomes the critique of certain lingering metaphysical desires—the desire for foundations, the desire for stability, the desire for *absolute presence,*[40] and the desire for a fixed center around which coherence can be established. In short, theory becomes conceptual and discursive *deconstruction.*[41]

As is often the case, there is a potential (if unstable) middle ground between a Natansonian foundationalist approach to a philosophy of rhetoric and the decidedly anti-foundationalist ideas of *universalized rhetoric, radical contingency,* and undifferentiated textuality.[42] Some scholars suggest that although there *may* be absolute foundations in some spheres of human existence (e.g., an "objective" sphere) and for some types of practice (e.g., science), the world where rhetoric is practiced (at least traditionally) is fundamentally **contingent.** To live together, people must make decisions. And these decisions are contingent. No decisions are absolutely determined; alternative possibilities always are present. And to make matters worse, people normally do not have all the time in the world to reach decisions. Philosophical controversies can, and often do, go on for centuries; practical problems that require decisions and collective action usually need some closure.[43]

What type of philosophy of rhetoric emerges from this middle ground position? The middle ground between foundationalism and anti-foundationalism explores the link between rhetoric and *practical philosophy.* As Toulmin (1988) noted, the neglected tradition of practical philosophy stresses four sets of topics—the oral, the particular, the local, and the timely—that are pillars of classical rhetorical thinking. Theoretical reflection on these, and other closely related, topics (e.g., **prudence/phronesis, decorum, local stability**) has been an important feature of contemporary rhetorical studies.

The discussion of the fourth aspect of rhetorical theory has tried to describe three broad ways of proceeding: the foundationalist stance, the anti-foundationalist counterstance, and a middle ground between the two. We can conclude this overview of the philosophical aspect of rhetorical theory by considering a simple question: What have rhetoricians been doing in the realm of the philosophy of rhetoric? What theoretical questions and issues have been on the agenda of contemporary rhetorical scholars? Over the past few decades, rhetoricians have taken up a number of important issues including rhetoric's **epistemic** status (What is "knowledge," and does rhetorical practice create or constitute knowledge? Is all knowledge the product of rhetorical practice or only certain spheres or types of knowledge?), questions regarding human reason and rationality (Is reason monolithic, or are there different forms of reasoning? What is the relationship between the human propensity to tell stories, or the idea of **narrativity,** and the various forms of reasoning?), the relationship between gender and theory (Has rhetorical theory proceeded in a patriarchal manner? What alternative modes of theorizing, such as **invitational rhetoric,** might be possible?), the experience of time and temporality (Is time a "natural" phenomenon experienced the same way by all people, or is the experience of time predicated on, or conditioned by, discursive practice? What are the basic modes of temporal experience? How are these modes represented by language?), problems arising from language and linguisticality (How does language work? Is there a foundational function of language? Is language primarily a mechanism for **representing** things clearly? How central is the realm of **figurative** language, especially *metaphor,* to human thinking and rhetorical practice?), and the nature of human character and **subjectivity** (What is the individual "person"? Are we all unique, autonomous, self-directing creatures, or are we essentially conditioned "subjects" of various regimes of discourse? How do we negotiate the various subject positions, or roles, that we find ourselves in? What capacity, if any, do individuals possess to constitute themselves discursively or to engage in the process of "self-fashioning"? What relationship exists between who we were last year or last week, who we are today, and who we might be tomorrow? What role do our rhetorical choices and performances play in maintaining and/or subverting the relationship among our past, present, and future selves?). As some readers will recognize, many of these issues and questions have had a central place in a number of intellectual traditions for quite a long time. Rhetoricians, and the tradition of rhetorical thought, are participants in an ongoing and, to reinvoke the image borrowed from Burke, unending conversation about language, discourse, and what it means to be human.

This introduction has tried to outline some of the key features and important implications of how the term *rhetoric* is used in the contemporary tradition of rhetorical studies. It cannot replace, and is not meant to replace, a careful examination of, and perhaps the eventual entry into, that tradition of thought. The glossary of concepts that follows is intended to render that tradition more accessible, useful, and inviting.

Notes

1. The focus of this book is on the tradition of rhetorical studies as it has been revived and developed in American departments of speech communication and/or communication studies. But rhetoric has become an interdisciplinary object of concern. Eagleton (1983) noted rhetoric's increasing centrality when he wrote, "Rhetoric, or discourse theory, shares with formalism, structuralism, and semiotics an interest in the formal devices of language, but like reception theory is also concerned with how these devices are actually effective at the point of 'consumption'; its preoccupation with discourse as a form of power and desire can learn much from deconstruction and psychoanalytic theory, and its belief that discourse can be a humanly transformative affair shares a good deal with liberal humanism" (p. 206). The interdisciplinary nature of rhetorical studies is reflected in this introductory essay and many of the entries that follow.

2. Gustafson (1992) described the historical tendency to view language as "an instrument . . . which could, on the one hand, help preserve order and liberty, but also an instrument which could, on the other hand, become a source of tyranny and corruption" (p. 12). Rahe's (1994) history of republican thought also touches frequently on this topic. Rahe wrote that speech, or logos, usually was understood as "a double-edged sword" (Vol. 1, p. 41). As Gustafson (1992) noted, the ancient Greeks had a term for something that could be both a "cure" and a "poison"—*pharmakon.* Language and rhetoric frequently are described with imagery that leads back to the Greek idea of the pharmakon.

3. For more information on Isocrates' attitude toward language and speech, see Jaeger (1939, pp. 46-70). On Isocrates' potential relevance today, see Schiappa (1995).

4. As will be discussed in more detail later, reflection on rhetoric as practice has developed its own internal dichotomy between *form* and *function* or between *product* and *process.*

5. Commenting on the state of rhetorical scholarship during the 1950s, Natanson (1955) remarked, "The fundamental difficulty, it seems to me, that has confused the discussion is a failure on the part of the analyst to distinguish between the theory of rhetoric and the practice of rhetoric" (p. 133). But simply distinguishing theory and practice might not be sufficient. Discussing a variation on the practice-theory ambiguity, Culler (1978) described the "paradoxical definition" of rhetoric as both "the ability to produce an event" and "a code to be obeyed." That is, "rhetoric is repeatedly defined either as persuasion or as an inventory of conventional tropes" (p. 608). Culler maintained that it is either a persuasive event or a description of structures. But Culler's assessment of this definitional ambiguity moved in a much more radical direction than that of scholars such as Bryant and Natanson, who merely lamented its existence. For Culler, "the relationship between trope [structure or theory] and persuasion [event or practice] is always problematic and discontinuous. On the one hand, description of structures never suffices to account for an event; and, on the other hand, though one can describe the structures and figures of a discourse, one can never be certain what sort of events these discourses may have produced. The relationship between structure and event is incalculable, which is why rhetoric is fated, as the name of this incalculable textuality, to be simultaneously and alternatively a discourse of structure and event" (p. 608). Culler read the practice-theory ambiguity as more than a lexical accident. It identifies an aporia, a paradox, or a tension at the very core of the tradition of rhetorical studies. He suggested that there is no way of stabilizing the event-structure or practice-theory relationship. Hence, rhetorical studies is an inherently unstable discipline, or to paraphrase Plato, rhetoric has no substance. The questions about rhetoric's stability and substance have proven exceedingly difficult to escape (Gaonkar, 1990b).

6. Habermas (1984) argued that the realm of normal communication can be further segmented into spheres of practice such as science, politics, and law and that it is perfected in a specific type of practice that Habermas labeled "discourse."

7. Habermas (1987) identified "logical consistency" as a key evaluative standard in his discussion of Derrida (p. 188). In other work, Habermas (1979, 1984) provided a more detailed account of the claims inherent in all normal or serious (nonfigurative) communicative practice. Those claims are truth, rightness, sincerity, and comprehensibility.

8. *Normal science* refers to those practices that are present during periods of paradigmatic stability (e.g., the nature of scientific practice during the period of Newtonian physics). *Revolutionary science* refers to those practices that emerge during periods of paradigmatic instability and shift (e.g., the nature of scientific practice during the period when there was a shift from a Newtonian view of the universe to an Einsteinian one).

9. Lanham's (1976) anthropological dichotomy might be compared and contrasted with Blumenberg's (1987) similar project.

10. As Fish (1989) remarked, "The history of Western thought could be written as the history of this quarrel" (p. 484).

11. Johnson (1991) and Kinneavy (1990) described the shifting contours of rhetoric as a practice in American higher education.

12. The distinction that the early exponents of rhetorical studies had in mind was something like this. Charles Dickens frequently wrote about London in his novels. Even though his account of London in his fictional works was based on the real London, the novels depicted an imaginary London. Dickens' novels were realistic *fiction*, not accounts of actual reality. On the other hand, in speeches on practical social questions, Dickens inevitably had to deal first and foremost with the real London, not the London of his imagination. As we will see later in this introductory essay, the distinction between "real" and "imaginary" might not be as clear as earlier generations of American rhetorical scholars believed.

13. De Man (1979) credited the philosopher Nietzsche with this innovation. Most scholars of the history of rhetorical theory question this attribution. Nietzsche did call attention to the epistemic significance of tropes and figures, a topic that de Man developed at length. For analyses of de Man's discussion of rhetoric, see Kastely (1997) and Vickers (1988).

14. For a different sense of rhetoric that relies heavily on the tropological possibilities of language, see Grassi (1980).

15. See Frye (1957, p. 243) and Hauser (1991, pp. 15-22). A variation on this trivium can be found in Trimpi's (1983) discussion of formal, cognitive, and judicative modes of discourse.

16. The relationship between rhetoric and intersubjectivity was developed at length by Wells (1996).

17. This issue is treated more fully in the entry for **inquiry, rhetoric of.**

18. Linguist Roman Jakobson outlined one of the more elaborate models of human communication. Jakobson's (1960) model of communication identified six parts: *addresser* (e.g., speaker, writer, source, encoder), *addressee* (e.g., reader, **audience**), *context, contact, code,* and *message.* In any instance of communication, one of these six elements will be emphasized; hence, a particular function, and a particular form, will be instantiated. Jakobson was not interested in specifying the nature of rhetorical discourse. His primary concern was in identifying the essence of "poetic" expression. But his discussion of the *conative* function, which is designed to provoke a specific reaction in the addressee, resembles the instrumentalist equation of rhetoric with overt persuasion.

19. Leff (1998) suggested that much of the recent scholarship in rhetorical studies is united in the basic idea that discursive practice is a constitutive or generative medium.

20. For additional insight into social constructionism, see Shotter (1993a, 1993b) and volumes in the Sage Publications series, *Inquiries in Social Constructionism*, edited by Kenneth Gergen and John Shotter.

21. Or, as Burke (1966) observed, "Much that we take as observations about 'reality' may be but the spinning out of possibilities implicit in our particular choice of terms" (p. 46).

22. A similar point was made by Weaver (1971). See the discussion in the entry for **sermonic, language as.**

23. Fish (1989) wrote, "Force is simply a (pejorative) name for the thrust or assertion of some point of view" (p. 521). Force is, then, a general term that encapsulates related concepts such as Weaver's (1971) sense of language as sermonic and Burke's (1950) belief that language always conveys an attitude.

24. This claim should not be seen as implying that all discursive practice is *only* rhetoric. Every instance of discursive practice can be rhetorical while also falling into other categories such as "poem," "scientific report," or "solicitation letter."

25. Bender and Wellbery (1990) wrote that our age is that of "a generalized rhetoric that penetrates to the deepest levels of human experience. . . . Rhetoric is no longer the title of a doctrine and a practice, nor a form of cultural memory; it becomes instead something like the condition of our existence" (p. 25). On the relationship between rhetoric and experience, see also McGee (1982).

26. The addition of the term *symbolic* here signals an interest in visual as well as verbal or linguistic persuasion.

27. But a tension between rhetoric as a thing or product and rhetoric as a dimension or function persists. See Chatman (1990, p. 193) and Leff (1987).

28. LaRue (1995) indirectly echoed Gaonkar's (1993) observation that because there is no clear institutional structure that unifies persuasive discourse or public advocacy, as there is for "literary" discourse, it is difficult to craft a definition that might organize a discipline.

29. Dewey's (1927) discussion of "public acts" has had a significant impact on American rhetorical scholars. Dewey wrote, "We take . . . our point of departure from the objective fact that human acts have consequences upon others, that some of these consequences are perceived, and that their perception leads to subsequent effort to control action so as to secure some consequences and avoid others. Following this clew [sic], we are led to remark that the consequences are of two kinds, those which affect the persons directly engaged in a transaction and those which affect others beyond those immediately concerned. In this distinction, we find the germ of the distinction between the private and the public. . . . When the consequences of an action are confined, or are thought to be confined, mainly to the persons directly engaged in it, the transaction is a private one. . . . Yet if [for example] it is found that the consequences of conversation extend beyond the two directly concerned, that they affect the welfare of many others, the act requires a public capacity, whether the conversation be carried on by a king and his minister or by Cataline and a fellow conspirator or by merchants planning to monopolize a market" (pp. 12-13).

30. A deodorant manufacturer might produce messages that, in addition to their primary objective of commercial persuasion, try to position the manufacturer and the product as environmentally friendly. The message would then be a *hybrid* in that it raises both public and nonpublic claims.

31. This list is not exhaustive. For a more elaborate account of nine "senses" of rhetoric, see Benson (1978).

32. In some cases, a theorist will subscribe to somewhat different definitions. Weaver (1971), for example, at one moment supported the globalized rhetoric position ("Rhetoric is cognate with language" [p. 176]) but then tempered this universal definition by discussing rhetoric in dimensional terms ("Any utterance is capable of rhetorical function or aspect. If one looks widely enough, one can discover its rhetorical dimension" [p. 177]).

33. Mailloux (1991) suggested that we simply treat "theory as practice about practice" (p. 241).

34. On this distinction, see Conley (1990) and Sloane (1997).

35. The careers of most of these methods can be traced in textbooks such as Brock, Scott, and Chesebro (1990) and Foss (1996).

36. On the idea of "conceptual screens," see Burke's (1966) discussion of *terministic screens.*

37. See Gaonkar's (1993) discussion of what he termed the *rhetorical signature* or the habits that identify a critic as someone from the tradition of contemporary rhetorical studies.

38. Theoretical reflection on, and critical studies of, the public and public sphere have been of considerable importance to the strategy of defining rhetorical practice as public or civic discourse.

39. Some scholars (e.g., Leff, 1992) have found hints of the constitutive perspective in the writings of some of the earliest thinkers on rhetoric. So, in a sense, the constitutive "turn" in rhetorical studies also is a "return" to a neglected part of its tradition.

40. The discussion here is gesturing toward Jacques Derrida's concept of *presence.* Readers are invited to take up the potentially interesting conceptual issue of the relationship between Derrida's sense of presence and that developed by Perelman and Olbrechts-Tyteca (1969) discussed in the entry for **presence.**

41. Anything close to a thorough discussion of the topic of deconstruction is beyond the scope of this introductory essay. Short discussions of the topic can be

found in any number of glossaries or dictionaries of literary or cultural studies terms. More elaborate introductions can be found in Agger (1998) and Sarup (1989).

42. Fish (1989) wrote, "Anti-foundationalism is a thesis about how foundations emerge, and in contradistinction to the assumptions that foundations do not emerge but simply are anchoring the universe and thought from a point above history and culture, it says that foundations are local and temporal phenomena and are always vulnerable to challenges from other localities and other times" (pp. 29-30).

43. As most contemporary rhetorical theorists will argue, situational decision making and closure does not mean that practical questions do not resurface. Rhetorical discourse is, from the perspective of the local situation, finalizable. But from a broad historical perspective, it is commonly unfinalizable.

References and Additional Reading

Agger, B. (1998). *Critical social theories: An introduction.* Boulder, CO: Westview.

Aristotle. (1954). *Rhetoric* (W. R. Roberts, Trans.). New York: Modern Library.

Bash, H. H. (1995). *Social problems and social movements: An exploration into the sociological construction of alternative realities.* Atlantic Highlands, NJ: Humanities Press.

Beiner, R. (1983). *Political judgment.* Chicago: University of Chicago Press.

Bender, J., & Wellbery, D. E. (1990). Rhetoricality: On the modernist return of rhetoric. In J. Bender & D. E. Wellbery (Eds.), *The ends of rhetoric: History, theory, practice.* Stanford, CA: Stanford University Press.

Benson, T. W. (1978). The senses of rhetoric: A topical system for critics. *Central States Speech Journal, 29,* 237-250.

Bitzer, L. (1968). The rhetorical situation. *Philosophy and Rhetoric, 1,* 1-14.

Black, E. (1978). *Rhetorical criticism: A study in method.* Madison: University of Wisconsin Press. (Original work published 1965)

Blumenberg, H. (1987). An anthropological approach to the contemporary significance of rhetoric (R. M. Wallace, Trans.). In K. Baynes, J. Bohman, & T. McCarthy (Eds.), *After philosophy: End or transformation?* Cambridge, MA: MIT Press.

Brock, B. L., Scott, R. L., & Chesebro, J. W. (Eds.). (1990). *Methods of rhetorical criticism: A twentieth-century perspective* (3rd ed.). Detroit, MI: Wayne State University Press.

Brummett, B. (1994). *Rhetoric in popular culture.* New York: St. Martin's.

Bryant, D. C. (1953). Rhetoric: Its functions and its scope. *Quarterly Journal of Speech, 39,* 401-424.

Bryant, D. C. (1973). *Rhetorical dimensions in criticism.* Baton Rouge: Louisiana State University Press.

Burke, K. (1950). *A rhetoric of motives.* New York: Prentice Hall.

Burke, K. (1966). *Language as symbolic action: Essays on life, literature, and method.* Berkeley: University of California Press.

Cahn, M. (1993). The rhetoric of rhetoric: Six tropes of disciplinary self-constitution. In R. H. Roberts & J. M. Good (Eds.), *The recovery of rhetoric: Persuasive discourse and disciplinarity in the human sciences.* Charlottesville: University of Virginia Press.

Campbell, K. K., & Jamieson, K. H. (1990). *Deeds done in words: Presidential rhetoric and the genres of governance.* Chicago: University of Chicago Press.

Chatman, S. (1990). *Coming to terms: The rhetoric of narrative in fiction and film.* Ithaca, NY: Cornell University Press.

Cherwitz, R. A. (Ed.). (1990). *Rhetoric and philosophy.* Hillsdale, NJ: Lawrence Erlbaum.

Conley, T. M. (1990). *Rhetoric in the European tradition.* New York: Longman.

Culler, J. (1978). On trope and persuasion. *New Literary History, 9,* 607-618.

de Man, P. (1979). *Allegories of reading: Figural language in Rousseau, Nietzsche, Rilke, and Proust.* New Haven, CT: Yale University Press.

Derrida, J. (1977). Signature event context. *Glyph, 1,* 172-197. (Johns Hopkins Textual Studies)

Dewey, J. (1927). *The public and its problems.* New York: Henry Holt.

Dubois, J., Edeline, F., Klinkenberg, J.-M., Minguet, P., Pire, F., & Trinon, H. (1981). *A general rhetoric* (P. B. Burrell & E. M. Slotkin, Trans.). Baltimore, MD: Johns Hopkins University Press.

Eagleton, T. (1983). *Literary theory: An introduction.* Minneapolis: University of Minnesota Press.

Ehninger, D. (1968). On systems of rhetoric. *Philosophy and Rhetoric, 1,* 131-144.

Fish, S. (1980). *Is there a text in this class? The authority of interpretive communities.* Cambridge, MA: Harvard University Press.

Fish, S. (1989). *Doing what comes naturally: Change, rhetoric, and the practice of theory in literary and legal studies.* Durham, NC: Duke University Press.

Foss, S. K. (1996). *Rhetorical criticism: Exploration and practice* (2nd ed.). Prospect Heights, IL: Waveland.

Frye, N. (1957). *Anatomy of criticism: Four essays.* Princeton, NJ: Princeton University Press.

Gaonkar, D. P. (1987). Deconstruction and rhetorical analysis: The case of Paul de Man. *Quarterly Journal of Speech, 73,* 482-498.

Gaonkar, D. P. (1990a). Object and method in rhetorical criticism: From Wichelns to Leff and McGee. *Western Journal of Speech Communication, 54,* 290-316.

Gaonkar, D. P. (1990b). Rhetoric and its double: Reflections on the rhetorical turn in the human sciences. In

H. W. Simons (Ed.), *The rhetorical turn: Invention and persuasion in the conduct of inquiry.* Chicago: University of Chicago Press.

Gaonkar, D. P. (1993). The idea of rhetoric in the rhetoric of science. *Southern Communication Journal,* 258-295.

Garver, E. (1994). *Aristotle's RHETORIC: An art of character.* Chicago: University of Chicago Press.

Grassi, E. (1980). *Rhetoric as philosophy: The humanist tradition.* University Park: Pennsylvania State University Press.

Gustafson, T. (1992). *Representative words: Politics, literature, and the American language, 1776-1865.* Cambridge, UK: Cambridge University Press.

Habermas, J. (1979). *Communication and the evolution of society* (T. McCarthy, Trans.). Boston: Beacon.

Habermas, J. (1984). *The theory of communicative action: Reason and the rationalization of society* (Vol. 1, T. McCarthy, Trans.). Boston: Beacon.

Habermas, J. (1987). *The philosophical discourse of modernity* (F. Lawrence, Trans.). Cambridge, MA: MIT Press.

Hart, R. P. (1987). *The sound of leadership: Presidential communication in the modern age.* Chicago: University of Chicago Press.

Hauser, G. A. (1991). *Introduction to rhetorical theory.* Prospect Heights, IL: Waveland.

Hirsch, E. D., Jr. (1967). *Validity in interpretation.* New Haven, CT: Yale University Press.

Hudson, H. H. (1923). The field of rhetoric. *Quarterly Journal of Speech Education, 9,* 167-180.

Jaeger, W. (1939). *Paideia: The ideals of Greek culture* (G. Highet, Trans.). New York: Oxford University Press.

Jakobson, R. (1960). Closing statement: Linguistics and poetics. In T. A. Sebeok (Ed.), *Style in language.* Cambridge, MA: MIT Press.

Johnson, N. (1991). *Nineteenth-century rhetoric in North America.* Carbondale: Southern Illinois University Press.

Kastely, J. L. (1997). *Rethinking the rhetorical tradition: From Plato to postmodernism.* New Haven, CT: Yale University Press.

Kaufer, D. S., & Butler, B. S. (1996). *Rhetoric and the arts of design.* Mahwah, NJ: Lawrence Erlbaum.

Kennedy, G. A. (1980). *Classical rhetoric and its Christian and secular tradition from ancient to modern times.* Chapel Hill: University of North Carolina Press.

Kinneavy, J. L. (1990). Contemporary rhetoric. In W. B. Horner (Ed.), *The present state of scholarship in historical and contemporary rhetoric* (rev. ed.). Columbia: University of Missouri Press.

LaCapra, D. (1985). *History and criticism.* Ithaca, NY: Cornell University Press.

Lanham, R. (1976). *The motives of eloquence.* New Haven, CT: Yale University Press.

LaRue, L. H. (1995). *Constitutional law as fiction: Narrative in the rhetoric of authority.* University Park: Pennsylvania State University Press.

Leff, M. (1987). The habitation of rhetoric. In J. W. Wenzel (Ed.), *Argument and critical practices: Proceedings of the Fifth SCA/AFA Conference on Argumentation.* Annandale, VA: Speech Communication Association.

Leff, M. (1992). Things made by words: Reflections on textual criticism. *Quarterly Journal of Speech, 78,* 223-231.

Leff, M. (1997a). The idea of rhetoric as interpretive practice: A humanist's response to Gaonkar. In A. G. Gross & W. M. Keith (Eds.), *Rhetorical hermeneutics: Invention and interpretation in the age of science.* Albany: State University of New York Press.

Leff, M. C. (1997b). Lincoln among the nineteenth-century orators. In T. W. Benson (Ed.), *Rhetoric and political culture in nineteenth-century America.* East Lansing: Michigan State University Press.

Leff, M. (1998). Cicero's *Pro Murena* and the strong defense of rhetoric. *Rhetoric and Public Affairs, 1,* 61-88.

Leff, M. C., & Procario, M. C. (1985). Rhetorical theory in speech communication. In T. W. Benson (Ed.), *Speech communication in the twentieth century.* Carbondale: Southern Illinois University Press.

Mailloux, S. (1991). Rhetorical hermeneutics revisited. *Text and Performance Quarterly, 11,* 233-248.

McCarthy, T. (1987). Introduction. In J. Habermas, *The philosophical discourse of modernity* (F. Lawrence, Trans.). Cambridge, MA: MIT Press.

McGee, M. C. (1982). A materialist's conception of rhetoric. In R. E. McKerrow (Ed.), *Explorations in rhetoric: Studies in honor of Douglas Ehninger.* Glenview, IL: Scott, Foresman.

Medhurst, M. J., & Benson, T. W. (1984). Rhetorical studies in a media age. In M. J. Medhurst & T. W. Benson (Eds.), *Rhetorical dimensions in media: A critical casebook* (rev. ed.). Dubuque, IA: Kendall/Hunt.

Natanson, M. (1955). The limits of rhetoric. *Quarterly Journal of Speech, 41,* 133-139.

Perelman, C., & Olbrechts-Tyteca, L. (1969). *The new rhetoric* (J. Wilkinson & P. Weaver, Trans.). Notre Dame, IN: University of Notre Dame Press.

Rahe, P. A. (1994). *Republics ancient and modern* (3 vols.). Chapel Hill: University of North Carolina Press.

Rorty, R. (1979). *Philosophy and the mirror of nature.* Princeton, NJ: Princeton University Press.

Rorty, R. (1989). *Contingency, irony, and solidarity.* Cambridge, UK: Cambridge University Press.

Sarup, M. (1989). *An introductory guide to post-structuralism and postmodernism.* Athens: University of Georgia Press.

Schiappa, E. (1995). Isocrates' *philosophia* and contemporary pragmatism. In S. Mailloux (Ed.), *Rhetoric, sophistry, pragmatism.* Cambridge, UK: Cambridge University Press.

Seigel, J. (1968). *Rhetoric and philosophy in Renaissance humanism: The union of eloquence and wisdom, Petrarch to Valla.* Princeton, NJ: Princeton University Press.

Shotter, J. (1993a). *Conversational realities: Constructing life through language.* Newbury Park, CA: Sage.

Shotter, J. (1993b). *Cultural politics of everyday life: Social constructionism, rhetoric, and knowing of the third kind.* Toronto: University of Toronto Press.

Sloane, T. O. (1997). *On the contrary: The protocol of traditional rhetoric.* Washington, DC: Catholic University of America Press.

Toulmin, S. (1988). The recovery of practical philosophy. *The American Scholar, 57,* 337-352.

Trimpi, W. (1983). *Muses of one mind: The literary analysis of experience and its continuity.* Princeton, NJ: Princeton University Press.

Vickers, B. (1988). *In defense of rhetoric.* Oxford, UK: Clarendon.

Weaver, R. (1971). Language is sermonic. In R. L. Johannesen (Ed.), *Contemporary theories of rhetoric: Selected readings.* New York: Harper & Row.

Wells, S. (1996). *Sweet reason: Rhetoric and the discourses of modernity.* Chicago: University of Chicago Press.

White, J. B. (1984). *When words lose their meaning: Constitutions and reconstitutions of language, character, and community.* Chicago: University of Chicago Press.

Wichelns, H. A. (1962). The literary criticism of oratory. In A. M. Drummond (Ed.), *Studies in rhetoric and public speaking in honor of James Albert Winans.* New York: Russell and Russell. (Original work published 1925)

Winterowd, W. R. (1990). *The rhetoric of the "other" literature.* Carbondale: Southern Illinois University Press.

Glossary of Concepts

ACCENT

We typically use the word **accent** to describe the regional variations in spoken language (e.g., in the United States, we speak of a "southern accent" or a "Brooklyn accent") or as a way of indicating stress patterns in pronunciation (e.g., accent marks). A more general sense of the term, accent as a distinctive manner of spoken or written expression, is being recovered in various spheres of criticism, thanks largely to the influence of the Russian literary theorist Mikhail Bakhtin and the Russian linguist V. N. Voloshinov. Bakhtin's writings on the nature of prose discourse are beginning to have an impact on the tradition of rhetorical studies.[1] Bakhtin's sense of accent or related terms such as *inflection* points to the way in which nuances of meaning can be achieved discursively. It is common to speak about how "**tone** of voice" can convey different meanings (e.g., how the meaning of an expression changes if said "sarcastically"). For Bakhtin (1981), all language use involves inflections and accentuations because of the very nature of language itself as a public and social phenomenon. He wrote,

> The word in language is [always] half someone else's. It becomes "one's own" only when the speaker populates it with his own intention, his own accent, when he appropriates the word, adapting it to his own semantic and expressive intention. Prior to this moment of appropriation, the word does not exist in a neutral and impersonal language (it is not, after all, out of the dictionary that the speaker gets his words!), but rather it exists in other people's mouths, in other people's contexts, serving other people's intentions; it is from there that one must take the word and make it one's own. . . . Language is not a neutral medium that passes freely and easily into the private property of the speaker's intentions; it is populated—overpopulated—with the intentions of others. Expropriating it, forcing it to submit to one's own intentions and accents, is a difficult and complicated process. (pp. 293-294)[2]

We make words "our own" in different ways.[3] One way in which we accomplish this task is through forms of accentuation and inflection. But the accents or inflections that people give to words are not the result of purely individual choice. Bakhtin observed that particular forms of discourse, or **genres,** have their own "accentual system"; that is, they exhibit certain regularized patterns for making words mean certain things (e.g., the word *property* has one type of accent or emphasis when used in the genre of political philosophy and another when used in real estate transactions).

Voloshinov (1986) also stressed the importance of accent or *intonation* in discursive practice. Words—or, in Voloshinov's terminology, signs—have no real meaning apart from their situated use where individuals rely on "evaluative accents" (p. 80) or "expressive intonations" (p. 103) to give words meaning and to provide discourse with its thematic substance.[4] Voloshinov emphasized the *multiaccentuality* of signs or words that results from social struggle. Although his focus was on *class* struggle, the insights can be extended to various forms of ideological, generational, religious, and racial/gender struggles that make language a force in life. He wrote,

> Thus, various different classes [or groups] will use one and the same language. As a result, differently oriented accents intersect in every ideological sign [or word]. Sign becomes an arena of class struggle. . . . It is thanks to this intersecting of accents that a sign maintains its vitality and dynamism and the capacity for further development. (p. 23)

This point is reaffirmed later in Voloshinov's book where he wrote, "It is precisely a word's multiaccentuality that makes it a living thing" (p. 81). Voloshinov observed that dominant groups within a society strive to contain the possibilities of multiaccentuality. These dominant groups attempt to give words a single meaning (rendering them "uniaccentual" [p. 23]), a meaning that serves their interests and helps to perpetuate their social position. Like Bakhtin, Voloshinov observed that the growth of uniaccentual words is a danger that must be resisted.

Bakhtin and Voloshinov anticipated Burke's (1950) emphasis on "tonality" as a crucial persuasive force (p. 98). But the concepts of accent, intonation, tonality, and inflection often are hard to grasp outside the context of situated discursive practice. Let us consider a piece of discourse, the Second Amendment of the Constitution. It reads, "A well-regulated militia, being necessary to the security of a free state, the right of the people to keep and bear arms, shall not be infringed." How might different advocates or rhetorical agents give it particular inflections or accents? When members of the National Rifle Association (NRA) repeat these words or gesture toward them, they tend to emphasize, highlight, or accent the last part of the amendment that prohibits infringement on a person's right to own a gun (of any type whatsoever). Supporters of gun control, as well as a number of judges over the years, tend to highlight or accentuate the first part of the amendment that apparently links the right to service in a militia. Consider a third group of advocates. In their 1966 party platform and program, representatives of the Black Panthers wrote,

> We believe we can end police brutality in our black community by organizing black self-defense groups that are dedicated to defending our black community from racist police oppression and brutality. The Second Amendment to the Constitution of the United States gives a right to bear arms. We therefore believe that all black people should arm themselves for self-defense.

At one level, the Black Panthers were accentuating the amendment along the same lines as does the NRA in that they emphasized the right to bear arms. But should we conclude from this similarity that the accentual processes of the NRA and the Black Panthers are identical? Despite the NRA's efforts to recruit black members over the past few years, it seems safe to conclude that there is a wide ideological gulf between the NRA and the Black Panthers. That gulf, according to theorists such as Bakhtin and Voloshinov, can be detected by a careful reconstruction of the accents of the discourse. The Black Panthers' gesture to the Second Amendment was confrontative, aggressive, and rather threatening (especially to a white audience in 1966). Although the NRA certainly is an aggressive and confrontational organization, its use or appropriation of the Second Amendment does not convey the radical fury—the "in-your-face motherf****r" feeling—of the Black Panthers. This brief analysis only scratches the surface of how the Second

Amendment is accented in different ways, and for different reasons, by different advocates.[5]

For Bakhtin and Voloshinov, all discursive practice and every resulting **text** is a product of language appropriation. In creating messages, rhetorical actors do not conjure their words out of thin air; rather, they borrow words and expressions from the various languages or *idioms* with which they are familiar. Sometimes this borrowing process is explicit (e.g., quotations from other sources), but frequently it is more indirect or unacknowledged. **Inventional** creativity is the result of the process of accentuation or how advocates and rhetorical actors make words work in different ways. Consider a second example of accentuation. In a speech delivered before the National Convention of Colored Citizens in 1843, Henry Highland Garnet urged slaves to engage in physical resistance to the institution of slavery. As part of his appeal, Garnet borrowed "an old and true saying that 'if hereditary bondsmen would be free, they must themselves strike the first blow.' " This saying is a paraphrase derived from the British poet George Byron's *Childe Harold's Pilgrimage* (Byron, 1818/1991), which reads,

> Hereditary bondsmen! Know ye not
>
> Who would be free themselves must strike the blow?
>
> By their right arms the conquest must be wrought?

In appropriating Byron's words, Garnet gave them a new accent. How? In this case, the process was rather simple; Garnet abandoned Byron's use of the **rhetorical question** form and phrased the observation as a direct assertion. What was tentative and indirect in Byron was, through a rather simple form of reaccentuation, rendered straightforward and direct by Garnet.

Here is an example of some rather common ways in which the printed word is accented. A Students for a Democratic Society (SDS) anti-war pamphlet from 1969 stated,

> And young people all over the country go to prisons that are called schools, are trained for jobs that don't exist or serve no one's real interest but the boss's, and, to top it all, get told that Vietnam is the place to defend their "freedom."

First, the concept of "school" is reaccented by way of a comparison (a weak form of *metaphor*) with "prisons." But also notice how the *ultimate term* or **ideograph** "freedom" is reaccented through its placement in quotation marks. Most basic grammar books recognize that quotation marks can be used to indicate that a word (or words) is being used "in a special sense" (Hodges & Whitten, 1972, p. 150). What special sense is suggested by the quotation marks around "freedom" in the SDS pamphlet? The most common reaction is that the quotation marks suggest a sense of sarcasm or disbelief. Young Americans were being told that we were fighting in Vietnam to protect their freedom, but by enclosing the word *freedom* in quotation marks, the authors of the SDS pamphlet reaccented the word, attempting to expose the duplicity they perceived in the words and deeds of America's policy elite.

Consider a final example. In his famous "I Have a Dream" speech during the March on Washington in August 1963, Martin Luther King, Jr., described his "dream" that one day his children would "live in a nation where they will not be judged by the color of their skin but by the content of their character." King's statement was stylistically dense.[6] It also has become an object of struggle in the contemporary debate over affirmative action programs. A number of advocates opposed to affirmative action programs have *appropriated* King's statement (either through direct quotation or paraphrase), using it as *evidence* to support their *claim* that affirmative action is inconsistent with both King's understanding of equality and the larger American commitment to equality (King's statement serves as a form of *reluctant testimony*). In appropriating this statement and using it to serve their political interests, affirmative action opponents give it a particular accent. King's words are shaped to make them consistent with the anti-affirmative action position. Many supporters of affirmative action are furious with this process of appropriation and reaccentuation. For example, in a 1996 speech, Jesse Jackson argued,

> We must not allow Newt Gingrich, Bob Dole, Phil Gramm, Pete Wilson, and others to misappropriate Dr. King's quotation about judging people not "by the color of their skin but by the content of their character" as a perverse rationale for eliminating affirmative action. What Dr. King actually said was that he looked forward to the day that such would be the case. We know that day has not yet arrived.

Jackson contested the appropriation and reaccentuation of King's statement by trying to restore its original quality as a speech act. He reminded his audience that King's statement was an expression of hope and not a description of existing conditions. By emphasizing its speech act quality, Jackson reaccentuated King's statement in a way that made it compatible with the policy of affirmative action.[7]

King's discourse illustrates another aspect of the process of accentuation that merits some attention. The examples discussed so far have focused on cases in which single words, phrases, or small clusters of sentences were accented by rhetorical advocates. But in some cases, an entire *idiom* or vocabulary is at the center of the reaccentuation process, and this observation brings us back to King's rhetorical practices. Like many African American advocates before him, King frequently invoked the language of natural rights and natural law.[8] In so doing, he appropriated this idiom and made it work in a particular way; he used it to support the agenda of the civil rights movement. The closely related idioms of natural rights and natural law can be used in different ways. Thomas Jefferson invoked the idiom to support the American colonists' call for independence in 1776. Supreme Court Justice Clarence Thomas summoned the idiom during the 1990s to further the conservative agenda. The idioms of natural rights and natural law are not inherently "progressive," "liberal," or "conservative." In each case, advocates who employ the terms associated with the concepts of natural rights and natural law are engaged in accenting the idiom; they are emphasizing or creating meaning potentials that can be used to advance an agenda or to support a call for action. One task for rhetorical scholars is to heighten our understanding of the specific ways in which idioms such as natural rights and natural law are accented by public advocates.

Detailed analysis of the process of accentuation, as Bakhtin and Voloshinov suggested, requires critics to combine knowledge of context, familiarity with the syntactical and grammatical resources of language, and an understanding of **genres, discursive** conventions, and other discursive resources. Although such analysis can prove difficult given the potential elusiveness of accents and intonations, this approach still can be extremely useful. Discursive accentuation is a crucial part of our public life. When a key **ideograph** such as freedom is appropriated in a commercial jingle (e.g., "Freedom is 7-Eleven"), the only way of recovering a more noble or desirable sense of the term is through redefinition and reaccentuation. Many of the disputes or **controversies** of our public life are, in large part, struggles over the nature and meanings of key terms and expressions. As Morson and Emerson (1990) noted,

> In using a word, speakers may intone the word so as to question the values present in its aura and the presuppositions of its earlier usage. In other words, the word may be "reaccented." . . . This process is an essential factor in shaping a word's evolution. (p. 139)

Accentuation and reaccentuation are important resources in the discursive struggles taking place all around us.

Notes

1. Other Bakhtinian concepts are discussed elsewhere in the book.

2. See also Burke's (1957) rejection of the idea that people ever use a "word in its mere dictionary sense" and his insistence that scholars attend to the "overtones of . . . usage" (p. 31).

3. The entries for **heteroglossia** and **polyphony** describe some of the ways in which "languages" and "voices" are borrowed (or appropriated) for our use.

4. Voloshinov's sense of theme is complex. It resembles Burke's discussion of **motive.**

5. Farrell (1993) described tone as "the degree of ambiguity, clarity, and intensity of pathos within appearances" (p. 31). The Black Panthers' tone can be described as extremely intense.

6. See the discussion of *alliterative antithesis* in the entry for **style.**

7. The struggle to accent another person's words in a particular way is an act of rhetorical interpretation. See the discussion of *hermeneutical rhetoric* in the entry for **hermeneutics and rhetoric.**

8. On the tendency for African American advocates to invoke this idiom, see Condit and Lucaites (1993).

References and Additional Reading

Bakhtin, M. M. (1981). *The dialogic imagination* (M. Holquist, Ed.; C. Emerson & M. Holquist, Trans.). Austin: University of Texas Press.

Burke, K. (1950). *A rhetoric of motives.* New York: Prentice Hall.

Burke, K. (1957). *The philosophy of literary form* (rev. ed.). New York: Vintage.

Byron, G. G. (1991). *Childe Harold's pilgrimage.* New York: Garland. (Original work published 1818)

Condit, C. M., & Lucaites, J. L. (1993). *Crafting equality: America's Anglo-African word.* Chicago: University of Chicago Press.

Farrell, T. B. (1993). *Norms of rhetorical culture.* New Haven, CT: Yale University Press.

Hall, S. (1982). The rediscovery of "ideology": Return of the repressed in media studies. In M. Gurevitch, T. Bennett, J. Curran, & J. Woollacott (Eds.), *Culture, society, and the media.* London: Methuen.

Hodges, J. C., & Whitten, M. E. (1972). *Harbrace college handbook* (7th ed.). New York: Harcourt Brace Jovanovich.

Morson, G. S., & Emerson, C. (1990). *Mikhail Bakhtin: Creation of a prosaic.* Stanford, CA: Stanford University Press.

Murphy, J. M. (1997). Inventing authority: Bill Clinton, Martin Luther King, Jr., and the orchestration of rhetorical traditions. *Quarterly Journal of Speech, 83,* 71-89.

Voloshinov, V. N. (1986). *Marxism and the philosophy of language* (L. Matejka & I. R. Titunik, Trans.). Cambridge, MA: Harvard University Press.

ALLEGORY

Allegory is a central concept in the study of literary narratives. According to Abrams (1993), "An allegory is a narrative in which the agents and action, and sometimes the setting as well, are contrived not only to make sense in themselves but also to signify a second correlated order of persons, things, concepts, or events" (p. 4). Given the increased importance of narrative in contemporary rhetorical studies, allegory as a narrative device merits attention. Abrams identified two common types of allegory. The first is the *historical* or *political* allegory in which the characters and events in the story stand in for or represent historical agents and events. Fliegelman (1982) noted the "crucial relevance of the parable of the prodigal son to the concerns of later eighteenth-century Anglo-American culture" (p. 113). The parable, Fliegelman suggested, functioned allegorically; it helped to rationalize the need for paternal authority over willful children during a time when Great Britain's paternal-political authority was being challenged by its colonial "children." More recently, some commentators have suggested that the film *Fatal Attraction* is an allegory about AIDS. Glenn Close's character, on an allegorical level, represents the medical dangers of unprotected sex. The second type is the allegory of *ideas.* In this form,

> characters represent abstract concepts, and the plot serves to communicate a doctrine or thesis. . . . The central device in the typical allegory of ideas is the personification of abstract entities such as virtues, vices, states of mind, and types of character. (pp. 4-5)

A classic example in English literature is Bunyan's (1678/1978) *The Pilgrim's Progress.* Although not as obvious as Bunyan's allegory, Solomon's (1979) discussion of anti-Equal Rights Amendment rhetoric uncovered its mythic as well as its allegorical grounds. Allegory might not appear with great regularity in public discourse—the traditional province of rhetorical studies—but when it does, it can function in important ways.

References and Additional Reading

Abrams, M. H. (1993). *A glossary of literary terms* (6th ed.). Fort Worth, TX: Harcourt Brace.

Bunyan, J. (1978). *The pilgrim's progress.* Old Woking, UK: Gresham. (Original work published 1678)

Fletcher, A. (1964). *Allegory: The theory of a symbolic mode.* Ithaca, NY: Cornell University Press.

Fliegelman, J. (1982). *Prodigals and pilgrims: The American revolution against patriarchal authority, 1750-1800.* Cambridge, UK: Cambridge University Press.

Solomon, M. (1979). The "positive women's" journey: A mythic analysis of the rhetoric of STOP ERA. *Quarterly Journal of Speech, 65,* 262-274.

AMBIGUITY

Ambiguity traditionally has been considered a defect in language style. It violates the first norm of the CBS (clarity/brevity/sincerity) style guide. The literary critic William Empson and the movement of **new criticism** in literary studies helped to elevate the status of ambiguity in poetic and literary discourse (Empson, 1930); using words or expressions with multiple meanings could be reconceptualized as a source of discursive power or appeal. Thinking about poetic and literary discourse as fundamentally ambiguous also helped to distinguish this form of **discourse** from other discursive realms such as science, business, and the law.[1]

Given that the realm of rhetorical practice has connections to both poetic and various nonpoetic realms of practice, it should not be surprising that ambiguity has an extremely ambivalent status in rhetorical thinking. Although it often is attacked and identified as one of the principal corruptions of language that leads humans into error (Gustafson, 1992), it also is recognized as an inescapable, important, sometimes appropriate, discursive resource and strategy (Depoe, 1991; Foss, 1986; Zarefsky, 1996). For example, Perelman (1982) testified to the inescapability of ambiguity when he wrote, "In natural languages, ambiguity—the possibility of multiple interpretations—would be the rule" (p. 44). Ambiguity often is figured as a *pharmakon* (a Greek term meaning both poison and cure), a potential linguistic poison that prevents understanding and human cooperation that can, in certain circumstances, function as a linguistic cure that enhances the possibility of understanding and cooperation. We can see this pharmakon image playing an important role in the discourse of the American founding period (Jasinski, 1997). For the most part, the founders sought to avoid ambiguity as they crafted the language of the new Constitution, yet on important and potentially divisive topics such as slavery, they took refuge in ambiguous language.

Ambiguity has functioned as a strategic resource in countless contemporary rhetorical performances (Ceccarelli, 1998). Consider the case of Lyndon Johnson's discourse on Vietnam. Commenting on Johnson's speech to the nation in March 1968, Andrews and Zarefsky (1992) wrote, "The genius of this text is in its manipulation of ambiguities. Depending on one's wish, the speech can be read as an indicator of *continuity* or of major *change*" (p. 228). Richard Nixon's Vietnam discourse also exploited the resources of ambiguity as he balanced increasing the bombing of North Vietnam with a plan to end the war in his repeatedly used phrase "win the peace." Like Johnson's discourse, much of Nixon's discourse on Vietnam can be read as strategically ambiguous; it tried to be both pro-war and pro-peace.

Political factions will employ ambiguous words when doing so serves their purposes.

Ronald Reagan attacked congressional Democrats for threatening to "cut" his proposed military buildup when all that the Democrats really wanted was to slow the rate of growth in defense spending. Democrats, of course, will use the same ambiguity when it works to their advantage. For example, Bill Clinton and House leaders assailed Republicans in 1995 for considering "cuts" in social security, as well as in Medicare and Medicaid, when all that the Republicans really proposed to do was slow the rate of growth in these programs. For another example, consider the debate in the Republican party during the spring and summer of 1996 over how abortion should be dealt with in the party's platform. Hard-line pro-life advocates demanded that the party maintain its commitment to a constitutional amendment banning abortion, whereas moderates (including presidential nominee Bob Dole) wanted to include something in the platform that would appeal to potential Republican voters who held a pro-choice position. As the Republican party leaders developed the language of their platform, they inevitably exploited the resources of ambiguity (by including devices such as "tolerance" planks) in trying to satisfy the various wings of the party. Something similar took place in 1991 as George Bush's administration, liberal congressional Democrats, and moderate congressional Republicans crafted compromise civil rights legislation. Virtually all participants in the process agreed that the final bill relied extensively on vague and ambiguous language. No agreement would have been possible without it. In short, practical experience suggests that complete clarity, despite our professed desire to achieve it, is not always the best rhetorical strategy.[2] Finally, we should note that individuals also exploit ambiguity or turn it into a *resource* for negotiating situational *exigences.* For example, Campbell (1995) illustrated how some early 19th-century American women speakers employed ambiguity as a way of negotiating constricting cultural norms.

The concept of ambiguity overlaps in some important ways with another important concept in some contemporary theories of language—*indeterminacy.* The literary theorist Gerald Graff noted,

> Whether the new term means something significantly different from the earlier one is still in dispute, and some observers have argued that new indeterminacy is only old ambiguity by another name. But the critics who have popularized the term "indeterminacy" insist that there are crucial differences. (Graff, 1990, p. 165)

Graff (1990) explained,

> Whereas "ambiguity" stood for a positive and valued attribute of richness in a literary text, "indeterminacy" bespeaks a limitation or failure of [any] text to fulfill its purpose. . . . The concept of indeterminacy proposes that a radical limitation is built into the activity of literary interpretation. (p. 165)

And, we might add, it is built into all human communication. The *indeterminacy thesis* problematizes the activity of making sense of (or understanding) another's discourse. Indeterminacy, its proponents argue, is built into the fabric of language and communication. All efforts to stabilize the meaning-making process (through recourse to a stable context or the stable intentions of an author) are shown to be illusory. All language use—poetic, scientific, or rhetorical—is implicated in a "deceptive gesture" (p. 175) through which it tries, hopelessly, to overcome the inherent insufficiency of language and communication.

Some theorists and critics embrace the indeterminacy thesis. Others reject it outright, maintaining their belief in the possibility of determinate unambiguous meaning. Still others acknowledge that indeterminacy is an interesting linguistic phenomenon that merits attention but are skeptical of the more radical claims that all human discursive practice is inherently indeterminate or ambiguous (Graff seems to fall into this camp). The struggle over linguistic or textual indeterminacy in contemporary rhetorical studies still is in its early phases. It remains to be seen whether (and, if so, how) this concept will reshape disciplinary practices.

Notes

1. Legal and/or **forensic discourse** is an obvious case in which ambiguity clearly is frowned on. After all, how can people enter into "contracts" if their language is ambiguous?

2. Media scholars (e.g., Fiske, 1986) make a similar point when they argue that popularity depends on ambiguity or textual **polysemy.** On the relationship between ambiguity and polysemy in rhetorical studies, see Ceccarelli (1998).

References and Additional Reading

Andrews, J. R., & Zarefsky, D. (1992). *Contemporary American voices: Significant speeches in American history, 1945-present.* New York: Longman.

Bahti, T. (1986). Ambiguity and indeterminacy: The juncture. *Comparative Literature, 38,* 209-223.

Campbell, K. K. (1995). Gender and genre: Loci of invention and contradiction in the earliest speeches by U.S. women. *Quarterly Journal of Speech, 81,* 479-495.

Ceccarelli, L. (1998). Polysemy: Multiple meanings in rhetorical criticism. *Quarterly Journal of Speech, 84,* 395-415.

Depoe, S. P. (1991). Space and the 1960 presidential campaign: Kennedy, Nixon, and "public time." *Western Journal of Speech Communication, 55,* 215-233.

Eisenberg, E. M. (1984). Ambiguity as strategy in organizational communication. *Communication Monographs, 51,* 227-242.

Empson, W. (1930). *Seven types of ambiguity.* London: Chatto and Windus.

Fiske, J. (1986). Television: Polysemy and popularity. *Critical Studies in Mass Communication, 3,* 391-408.

Foss, S. K. (1986). Ambiguity as persuasion: The Vietnam Veterans Memorial. *Communication Quarterly, 34,* 326-340.

Graff, G. (1990). Determinacy/Indeterminacy. In F. Lentricchia & T. McLaughlin (Eds.), *Critical terms for literary study.* Chicago: University of Chicago Press.

Gustafson, T. (1992). *Representative words: Politics, literature, and the American language, 1776-1865.* Cambridge, UK: Cambridge University Press.

Jasinski, J. (1997). Heteroglossia, polyphony, and *The Federalist Papers. Rhetoric Society Quarterly, 27,* 23-46.

Logue, C. M., & Patton, J. R. (1982). From ambiguity to dogma: The rhetorical symbols of Lyndon B. Johnson on Vietnam. *Southern Speech Communication Journal, 47,* 310-329.

Perelman, C. (1982). *The realm of rhetoric* (W. Kluback, Trans.). Notre Dame, IN: University of Notre Dame Press.

Zarefsky, D. (1996). *The roots of American community: The Carroll C. Arnold lecture 1995.* Boston: Allyn & Bacon.

AMBIGUITY (OR PARADOX) OF SUBSTANCE

In *A Grammar of Motives,* Burke (1945) noted, "It is in the areas of ambiguity that transformations take place." Therefore, it is necessary "to study and clarify the *resources* of ambiguity" (p. ix). Burke located one of the key resources of **ambiguity** in the idea of substance.

Burke's understanding of the concept of substance is rather complicated. He observed that the concept remained an important part of contemporary thinking, even though the term *substance* itself fell into disuse. So, he began to think about the word *substance* and its etymology (or the history of the term). He discovered an interesting pattern—a tendency to talk about the idea of substance by talking about something other than substance. Burke (1945) wrote,

> We might point up the pattern as sharply as possible by observing that the word "substance," used to designate what a thing *is,* derives from a word designating something that a thing *is not.* That is, though used to designate something *within* the thing, intrinsic to it, the word etymologically refers to something *outside* the thing, *extrinsic* to it. (p. 23)

Burke's reflection on substance, and its ambiguities or paradox, led him to explore an important discursive dynamic. Essentially, he tried to point out that things are not always as clear-cut (or unambiguous) as they seem. Burke argued that, although the "substance" of a rhetorical situation, an historic event, an individual's past, or a key document might appear clear and unproblematic, there is an element of ambiguity that almost always is available for an advocate or a rhetor to exploit. Ambiguous substance makes possible various forms of rhetorical reversal or transformation. This idea of a rhetorical or discursive transformation through exploiting the ambiguity of substance connects to other concepts in contemporary rhetorical studies such as **definition of situation** and **dissociation.**

Perelman and Olbrechts-Tyteca (1969) discussed a recurrent form of substantive ambiguity under the heading *differences between degree and order* (pp. 345-349). Differences of degree are quantitative; for example, one thing is longer, wider, heavier, or older than something else. But we assume that the two "things" are part of the same general class. Differences of order are qualitative; one thing is an *x*, and another thing is a *y*. Differences of order describe different *types* of things. Perelman and Olbrechts-Tyteca's point was to alert us to the possibilities of transformation of "differences of order into differences of degree" (p. 345). Things that are thought to be radically different in type or order are reconceptualized to reveal merely differences in degree. This type of logic, for example, informs the discourse of 19th-century American feminists such as Elizabeth Cady Stanton. Men and women, Stanton argued, do not belong to different orders; their differences are only matters of degree. The transformation process also works in the reverse direction. As Perelman and Olbrechts-Tyteca noted, "At a given moment, there may be a purely quantitative difference [of degree] that brings about the passage to phenomena of another order" (p. 349). To illustrate their point, Perelman and Olbrechts-Tyteca used a classic example: At what point does a quantitative change (e.g., hair loss) lead to a qualitative change in order (e.g., baldness)? The lack of any absolute fixed point that determines when quantitative changes entail qualitative change creates ambiguity and opens up the possibility for discursive transformations.

Consider some examples. In the debate over his compromise measures in 1850, Senator Henry Clay urged Congress to take no action on the issue of slavery in the newly acquired territories of New Mexico and Utah. But Clay exploited the resources of ambiguity by depicting congressional inaction as a form of positive restraint. Four years later, Senator Stephen Douglas also urged Congress to refrain from action on the subject of slavery in the territories (this time, Kansas and Nebraska). In support of his position, Douglas referred to Congress's lack of action in 1850, but reshaping the ambiguous substance of the prior action, he insisted that it reflected an even more positive principle of "popular sovereignty."

Consider some 20th-century examples. In *1984*, Orwell (1949) described an extreme instance of transformation when "war" becomes "peace." Although the ideas of war and peace would appear to be unambiguous, in the world of the novel, Orwell showed how these ideas can be blurred so that the state of war becomes the condition of peace. Now, consider a less extreme, and real, example. In 1953, Dwight Eisenhower's administration assumed power in the United States. The new administration was not satisfied with the position taken by Harry Truman's administration with respect to the Soviet Union and the cold war. The Truman administration's position, heavily indebted to the thinking of George Kennan, was known as the policy of containment; that is, the United States would work to contain the Soviet Union by responding to every aggressive Soviet move (e.g., a Soviet effort to destabilize an African government) with an appropriate countermove. Eisenhower's secretary of state, John Foster

Dulles, considered this policy defective because it positioned the United States as essentially reactive. Instead of pursuing a proactive policy whereby the United States could effectively "call the shots," the nation was forced into a reactive role that did not comport well with its ideological self-identity. Unfortunately, the most inspiring proactive policy, what Dulles sometimes referred to as the "liberation of captive peoples," was judged to be unrealistic. So, Dulles's dilemma was how to articulate a policy that was proactive, at least on the surface, so as to differentiate the new administration from the past one while being unable to pursue the ideal proactive policy. In a famous speech delivered to the Council on Foreign Relations in January 1954, Dulles developed the policy approach known as massive retaliation. Criticized by some at the time for faulty logic, the speech illustrates how an advocate can exploit the ambiguity of substance to effect a rhetorical transformation. What Dulles managed to do in the speech was to take a policy that remained reactive—the United States would resort to massive retaliation in response to Soviet aggression—but by emphasizing both the degree of U.S. choice and the magnitude of the response, he was able to portray it, or essentially transform it, into something proactive. In a sense, the ultimate quantitative reaction (massive retaliation) became a workable, qualitatively different, proactive policy. As all of the examples illustrate, the ambiguity of substance can be a powerful resource in rhetorical action.

References and Additional Reading

Burke, K. (1945). *A grammar of motives.* New York: Prentice Hall.

Durham, W. B. (1980). Kenneth Burke's concept of substance. *Quarterly Journal of Speech, 66,* 351-364.

Orwell, G. (1949). *1984.* New York: Harcourt Brace.

Perelman, C., & Olbrechts-Tyteca, L. (1969). *The new rhetoric* (J. Wilkinson & P. Weaver, Trans.). Notre Dame, IN: University of Notre Dame Press.

AMPLIFICATION

The rhetorical theorist Richard Weaver stated, "The very task of the rhetorician is to determine what feature of a question is most exigent and to use the power of language to make it appear so" (Weaver, 1971, p. 175). This is how he described the traditional rhetorical principle of **amplification.** The first principle of rhetorical art, for Weaver, is amplification; rhetoric, he wrote, is "an art of emphasis" (p. 173). In "On the Sublime," the classical Greek theorist Longinus (1965) described amplification as "the accumulation of all the small points and incidental topics bearing on the subject matter; it adds substance and strength to the argument by dwelling on it" (p. 117). Amplification is a central part of **invention** in many classical discussions of rhetorical art.[1] More recently, Burke (1950) remarked that amplification is the "most thoroughgoing" of all the traditional rhetorical principles.

> As extension, expatiation, the saying of something in various ways until it increases in persuasiveness by the sheer accumulation, amplification can come to name a purely poetic process of development, such systematic exploitation of a theme as we find in lyrics built about a refrain. (p. 69)

In general, amplification refers to the various linguistic and discursive devices such as repetition, restatement, aggregation (Perelman, 1982), explanation, enumeration, elaboration, elaborate description, magnification, and **iconicity** that can be used to emphasize (or "amplify") a particular point.[2] Although amplification can be found in all of the major rhetorical **genres,** since Aristotle it is most frequently associated with **epideictic discourse.**

Consider a relatively brief example. The *exordium* of Franklin Roosevelt's speech to Congress and the nation asking for a declaration of war against Japan was as follows: "Yesterday, December 7, 1941—a date which will live in infamy—the United States of America was suddenly and deliberately attacked by naval and air forces of the Empire of Japan." Notice, first, the way in which Roosevelt employed restatement (a subtler and more nuanced form of repetition) at the very beginning of the passage. The moment of attack was etched in the audience's mind as Roosevelt moved from the first marker ("yesterday") to the second marker ("December 7, 1941)" and finally closed with the third and most emphatic marker ("a date which will live in infamy"). Notice, also, how Roosevelt's syntax operated as a subtle form of amplification (or emphasis). Rather than employing the more common active voice (Japan attacked the United States), Roosevelt rendered the passage in the passive voice, placing the direct object or entity acted on (the United States) in the position of syntactical prominence. This syntactical positioning added emphasis to Roosevelt's larger claim that the United States was a victim of an unwarranted assault.

Consider a second, more extended example. In her famous address, "The Solitude of Self," delivered in January 1892 in Washington, D.C., 19th-century women's rights advocate Elizabeth Cady Stanton invited her listeners to "think for a moment of the immeasurable solitude of self." Stanton followed this invitation with a wealth of material (e.g., literary allusions, *analogies,* **narrative** accounts of events, *metaphors*) that elaborated (or magnified) her central theme: Despite their social relationships, humans are solitary creatures, only able to depend, in the final analysis, on themselves. As Stanton noted, "We may have many friends, love, kindness, sympathy, and charity to smooth our pathway in everyday life, but in the tragedies and triumphs of human experience, each mortal stands alone." Through the amplification of human solitude, Stanton supported her major **deliberative** claim: Women need to "be fitted for those hours of solitude that come alike to all. . . . As in our extremity we must depend on ourselves, the dictates of wisdom point to complete individual development." (For another elaborate example, see the discussion of Martin Luther King, Jr.'s "Letter From Birmingham Jail" in the entry for **iconicity.**) Perelman and Olbrechts-Tyteca's (1969) discussion of **presence** overlapped considerably with the traditional principle of amplification, as did Osborn's (1986) more recent discussion of *rhetorical depiction* and Farrell's (1998) observations on accumulation and *magnitude.*

Notes

1. On the relationships among invention, amplification, and the doctrine of *copiousness,* see Sloane (1997, pp. 56-79).

2. **Narrative** might be included here as well. Allan (1986) noted, "Narrative form gives dramatic urgency to an account of things and vivid specificity. All the things of my world normally wear a familiar face, for their reality has the same sense as mine. But this reality can be fashioned into a story and thereby brought vividly to consciousness in terms that parallel my most intimate self-understanding" (p. 135).

References and Additional Reading

Allan, G. (1986). *The importance of the past: A meditation on the authority of tradition.* Albany: State University of New York Press.

Burke, K. (1950). *A rhetoric of motives.* New York: Prentice Hall.

Farrell, T. B. (1998). Sizing things up: Colloquial reflection as practical wisdom. *Argumentation, 12,* 1-14.

Lanham, R. (1991). *A handlist of rhetorical terms* (2nd ed.). Berkeley: University of California Press.

Longinus. (1965). On the sublime. In T. S. Dorsch (Trans.), *Classical literary criticism.* New York: Penguin.

Osborn, M. (1986). Rhetorical depiction. In H. W. Simons & A. A. Aghazarian (Eds.), *Form, genre, and the study of political discourse.* Columbia: University of South Carolina Press.

Perelman, C. (1982). *The realm of rhetoric* (W. Kluback, Trans.). Notre Dame, IN: University of Notre Dame Press.

Perelman, C., & Olbrechts-Tyteca, L. (1969). *The new rhetoric: A treatise on argumentation* (J. Wilkinson & P. Weaver, Trans.). Notre Dame, IN: University of Notre Dame Press.

Sloane, T. O. (1997). *On the contrary: The protocol of traditional rhetoric.* Washington, DC: Catholic University of America Press.

Weaver, R. (1971). Language is sermonic. In R. L. Johannesen (Ed.), *Contemporary theories of rhetoric: Selected readings.* New York: Harper & Row.

ANXIETY OF INFLUENCE

American literary critic Harold Bloom's concept of the **anxiety of influence** is the seminal point for a theory of poetic, and more generally literary, production or **invention.** Bloom (1973) sought to counteract what he considered to be "idealistic" accounts of the process of poetic production and poetic influence. Although Bloom's theory is not Marxist in its orientation, it does emphasize one feature typically stressed in Marxist social theory—struggle. Poetic invention, Bloom argued, is a process of struggle.

Who are the participants in poetic struggle, and with whom do they struggle? Part of the answer is obvious; the creative poet is a key participant in the struggle. With whom or what does the poet struggle? This question goes to the core of Bloom's theory. The poet struggles with (a) other "strong poets" from the past and (b) the collective **tradition** of poetry. What is a strong poet? Essentially, a strong poet dominates the discursive field of poetry; he or she speaks in a voice that demands recognition.[1] What is the nature of the struggle? The nature of the struggle is the source of poetic anxiety; the poet is afraid that there is nothing left to say or write and is worried that the strong poets of the past have exhausted the language of poetry. Summarizing Bloom's theory, literary theorist Chris Baldick wrote that the anxiety of influence describes "a poet's sense of the crushing weight of poetic tradition which he [sic] has to resist and challenge in order to make room for his own original vision" (Baldick, 1990, p. 13). By struggling with the strong poets of the past and the poetic tradition, as well as with the poet's fear that he or she does not have anything original to say, the poet discovers his or her own unique voice and reveals an aspiration to become a strong poet in his or her own right.

Bloom's account of the struggle between aspiring strong poets and the poetic tradition drew heavily from Sigmund Freud's discussion of the story of Oedipus. Bloom (1973) viewed the "relations between poets as cases akin to what Freud called the family romance" (p. 8). Gilbert and Gubar (1979) described Bloom's theory as a "literary Oedipal struggle" (p. 47). The strong poets of the past are "fathers," and the aspiring strong poets of the present day are "sons." According to Baldick (1990), the sons embody "the mixed feelings of veneration and envy" (p. 13); they love and respect the fathers, and in many ways they want to be the fathers, but they also are very resentful of the fathers. Poetry, Bloom (1973) suggested, is the working out of these complicated feelings of the sons toward the fathers. For sons to become strong poets, they eventually must overcome or displace the fathers—a form of literary patricide.

How does Bloom's theory of poetic invention and the anxiety of influence contribute to rhetorical studies, an area of study usually (but not always) associated with public and/or political discourse? The struggle that Bloom saw at the heart of poetic creation also can be found in the realm of public discourse; rhetors and advocates, like poets, sometimes are afflicted by the anxiety of influence. Perhaps no period in American history illustrates this idea better than the first half of the 19th century, when Americans struggled to fashion a relationship to their founding "fathers."[2]

In his study of the African American **jeremiad,** Howard-Pitney (1990) remarked, "The Founding Fathers cast a gigantic shadow over future generations, laying on them the burden of measuring up to the fathers' awesome achievements" (p. 10).[3] In Bloom's (1973) terminology, the founders were strong poets, and the aspiring leaders of the early 19th century were their "sons." How did the sons struggle with the legacy (or the achievements) of the founders? We can locate signs of this struggle in countless rhetorical performances. Let us consider some examples as a way of further extending, and clarifying, Bloom's contribution to rhetorical studies. The first example consists of two **epideictic** orations: Daniel Webster's speech commemorating the start of the Bunker Hill monument in 1825 and Abraham Lincoln's 1837 address to the Young Men's Lyceum in Springfield, Illinois. Although the speeches differed in many respects, they also shared some important similarities. Both encouraged their audiences to remember the bravery and virtue of the revolutionary generation, and they urged their audiences to keep the spirit of the founders alive. In effect, then, both speeches asked their audiences to be like the founders (or, in Bloom's terms, to become strong poets). But (and this point is crucial) both speeches also acknowledged in unmistakable terms that it was impossible for the present generation to become strong poets because the work of the strong poets—the revolution and the founding of the new government—was over and done. So, Webster remarked,

> And let the sacred obligations which have devolved on this generation, and on us, sink deep into our hearts. . . . The great trust now descends to new hands. Let us apply ourselves to that which is presented to us as our appropriate object. We can win no laurels in a war for independence. Earlier and worthier hands have gathered them all. Nor are there places for us by the side of Solon, and Alfred, and other founders of states. Our fathers have filled them all.

Lincoln made much the same point in 1837 through an impressive deployment of *metaphor:* "This field of glory is harvested, and the crop is already appropriated." Webster and Lincoln, then, shared an anxiety similar to the anxiety of the aspiring poet: What is left to say and do? Both Webster and Lincoln tried to offer their audiences an "appropriate object" (in Webster's terms), a task that, if fulfilled, would allow their generation to at least equal the accomplishments of the strong poets/founders of the past. For Webster, that task was "defense, preservation, and . . . improvement." For Lincoln, it was "a reverence for the Constitution and laws." By meeting these challenges, Webster and Lincoln suggested, the present generation could negotiate the burden (or the anxiety) of the past.[4]

For a second example of how the anxiety of influence can be extended into rhetorical studies, we can turn to the Declaration of Sentiments of the National Anti-Slavery Society drafted by William Lloyd Garrison in 1833. The declaration functioned as one of the **manifestos** of the abolitionist movement. In it, we see how the abolitionists struggled with the legacy of the founding fathers. Whereas Webster and Lincoln insisted that the present generation could not match the accomplishments of the fathers and had to, in effect, settle for something less, Garrison argued that although the efforts of the founders were noble, those efforts were "incomplete." He continued, "In purity of motive, in earnestness of zeal, in decision of purpose, in intrepidity of action, in steadfastness of faith, in sincerity of spirit, we would not be inferior to them." We see here the aspiring strong poet struggling with the strong poets of the past, refusing to accept a position of inferiority. Garrison then moved into a specific comparison between the fathers and the sons:

> *Their* principles led them to wage war against their oppressors, and to spill human blood like water, in order to be free. *Ours* forbid the doing of evil that good may come and lead us to reject, and to entreat the oppressed to reject, the use of all carnal weapons for deliverance from bondage. . . .
>
> *Their* measures were physical resistance—the marshalling in arms—the hostile array—the moral encounter. *Ours* shall be such only as the opposition of moral purity to moral corruption—the destruction of error by the potency of truth—the overthrow of prejudice by the power of love—and the abolition of slavery by the spirit of repentance.
>
> *Their* grievances, great as they were, were trifling in comparison with the wrongs and sufferings of those for whom we plead. Our

> fathers were never slaves—never bought and sold like cattle—never shut out from the light of knowledge and religion—never subjected to the lash of brutal taskmasters.

Point by point, Garrison tried to establish the superiority of the abolitionists to the founders; that is, the sons overcame their anxiety by displacing the fathers.[5]

Finally, we can turn to a third example to illustrate a specific portion of Bloom's theory as it can relate to public discursive practice. Bloom maintained that one way in which an aspiring strong poet can displace his or her predecessors is through an act of *misreading* and rewriting. That is, Bloom (1973) observed that the poet establishes his or her own "imaginative space" (p. 5) by using the poems of the past as a starting point. But Bloom claimed that the aspiring strong poet misreads and creatively revises the earlier poems.[6] Extending Bloom's insight, we can look for instances where advocates constructed **deliberative** space through a creative misreading of the past. Two cases in 19th-century American public discourse illustrate this process. First, although most abolitionists believed that the Constitution was a corrupt compact with slavery, a group of abolitionist legal scholars (referred to as the "radical constitutionalists") engaged in a form of creative misreading in an effort to open up deliberative space. Men such as Lysander Spooner and Joel Tiffany argued that the Constitution did not support slavery and, in fact, contained clauses that could be used to subvert the institution. As a second example, we can consider Henry Clay's efforts to craft a compromise over slavery in 1850. As Jasinski (1995) argued, Clay's advocacy efforts appealed to a tradition of prudential compromise that could be traced to the Philadelphia constitutional convention. But Jasinski claimed that Clay engaged in a misreading of the founders by ignoring how they balanced compromise with audacity. As Bloom (1973) suggested, the radical constitutionalists and Clay enacted the role of aspiring strong poets through advocacy efforts that relied on creative misreadings of the past.[7]

Bloom's theory of the anxiety of influence has itself been creatively revised by feminist scholars who objected to its masculine fixation and omission or neglect of female voices and practices. Gilbert and Gubar (1979) proposed the concept of *the anxiety of authorship* as a way of understanding a woman's inventional practices. They wrote,

> Thus, the "anxiety of influence" that a male poet experiences is felt by a female poet as an even more primary "anxiety of authorship"—a radical fear that she cannot create, that because she can never become a "precursor," the act of writing will isolate or destroy her. (pp. 48-49)

This anxiety "infects" women's writing, and its traces often shape women's discourse. Women combat the anxiety of authorship—the fear of writing or speaking that a patriarchal culture breeds—in various ways. Gilbert and Gubar noted how women search for "a *female* precursor who, far from representing a threatening force to be denied or killed, proves by example that revolt against patriarchal literary authority is possible" (p. 49).[8] Women writers also employ various strategies of "concealment" (p. 74) and generic subversion (p. 80) as ways of coping with the anxiety of authorship. Over the past two decades, rhetorical scholars began to recover and investigate the discursive strategies and practices of women in the public realm. As this trend continues,[9] the anxiety of authorship, like the anxiety of influence, can be extended into rhetorical studies.

Notes

1. Bloom (1973) identified the English poets John Milton and William Wordsworth as exemplary instances of strong poets.

2. In a way, the struggle with the anxiety of influence during the early 19th century repeated a pattern begun in New England 150 years earlier by second- and third-generation Puritan colonists seeking to forge a connection with their "fathers."

3. On the psychological impact of the founders on their "sons," see especially Forgie (1979).

4. But as Forgie (1979) and others have noted, Lincoln in 1837 was much less sanguine than Webster about meeting these challenges.

5. Travers (1997) detected a similar dynamic at work in what he termed "the 1812 generation." He wrote, "The 'national character' of the 1812 generation was a conceit of their own making, at once an attempt to identify with the revolutionary generation and to proclaim their own autonomy, even superiority: Had they not just completed the process which their parents had only begun?" (p. 207).

6. Making a musical out of a drama, as in the case of *Kiss of the Spider Woman,* is a simple form of creative misreading and rewriting.

7. Bloom's (1973) concept has potential implications both for our understanding of rhetorical invention and for the growing scholarship on the relationship between **hermeneutics and rhetoric.**

8. Along somewhat similar lines, Chevigny (1983) described the act of women biographers writing about their foremothers as one of "retrieval," a remembering of possibilities.

9. For a more detailed discussion, see the entry for **gynocriticism.**

References and Additional Reading

Baldick, C. (1990). *The concise Oxford dictionary of literary terms.* Oxford, UK: Oxford University Press.

Bloom, H. (1973). *The anxiety of influence.* New York: Oxford University Press.

Chevigny, B. G. (1983). Daughters writing: Toward a theory of women's biography. *Feminist Studies, 9,* 357-379.

Forgie, G. B. (1979). *Patricide in the house divided: A psychological interpretation of Lincoln and his age.* New York: Norton.

Gilbert, S. M., & Gubar, S. (1979). *The madwoman in the attic: The woman writer and the nineteenth-century literary imagination.* New Haven, CT: Yale University Press.

Howard-Pitney, D. (1990). *The Afro-American jeremiad: Appeals for justice in America.* Philadelphia: Temple University Press.

Jasinski, J. (1995). The forms and limits of prudence in Henry Clay's (1850) defense of the compromise measures. *Quarterly Journal of Speech, 81,* 454-479.

Travers, L. (1997). *Celebrating the Fourth: Independence day and the rites of nationalism in the early republic.* Amherst: University of Massachusetts Press.

APOCALYPTIC DISCOURSE

O'Leary (1994) noted, "From the beginning of time, humanity has attempted to imagine and predict the end of time" (p. 4). Eschatology, from the Greek word *eschatos* (meaning farthest or last), is the branch of religious or mythological thought concerned with the end of the world and/or human history. Virtually every culture invents a "story"—be it mythical, religious, or secular/scientific—of its own particular origins, but cultures also share stories about the origins of the human race. And with stories of origins come stories of the eschatos or stories about the end. According to Brummett (1984), apocalyptic is "that branch of eschatological discourse which holds that the world will end with a bang" (p. 84). O'Leary (1994) suggested, "Eschatologies offer the doctrine (whether in the form of mythic narrative or theological argument) that history will end at some point in the future, while apocalypticism claims that this end and the manner of its accomplishment are imminent and discernible" (p. 61). Similarly, McGinn (1979) remarked, "General eschatology becomes apocalyptic when it announces details of the future course of history and the imminence of its divinely appointed end" (p. 5). In short, **apocalyptic discourse** is a form of prophesy or **prophetic** speech that predicts when and how the world will end.

Apocalyptic discourse is of interest for at least two reasons. First, it is an incredibly persistent discursive form. Examples of apocalyptic discourse can be found in various cultures throughout history; the Biblical book of Revelation probably is the most well-known example in Western cultures. Intellectual historian Perry Miller noted that there is a strong apocalyptic strand in American Puritanism; the great minister and preacher Jonathan Edwards was, according to Miller (1956), early America's "greatest artist of the apocalypse" (p. 233). From Edwards to present-day survivalists, an apocalyptic **tradition** endures in the United States. Second, as O'Leary (1994) suggested during the mid-1990s, "Fascination with apocalyptic predictions, whether from the Bible, from new interpretations of the writings of ancient seers, or from New Age 'channelers,' seems likely to increase dramatically as the turn of the millennium draws nearer" (p. 3). Apocalyptic discourse, then, is not merely a curiosity of the past but rather a part of our contemporary discursive environment.

Scholars interested in apocalyptic discourse approach it from different perspectives. For example, Brummett (1984) treated apocalyptic discourse as a **genre** that "address[es] one *type* of perceived situational exigence with consistent forms of rhetorical style and substantive argument" (p. 85). For Brummett, "Apocalyptic is always a response to meaninglessness, failure of points of reference, and bewilderment about how to understand the present" (p. 86). Put differently, apocalyptic discourse develops in response to a state of generalized cultural anxiety. Brummett distinguished between two variations in the apocalyptic genre: religious and civil. "At the most basic level," Brummett wrote, "apocalyptic always includes the three main themes of bemoaning the present, expecting the imminent apocalypse, and foreseeing a golden millennium" (p. 87). Functionally, apocalyptic discourse creates a "system of meaning to replace that being lost" (p. 87) and restore the meaningfulness of the world and also builds a sense of community among the adherents of the apocalyptic message through a strategy that Brummett labeled "bipolar dramatization" (p. 91).[1]

O'Leary (1994) developed an alternative strategy for studying apocalyptic discourse. Rejecting the formism at the heart of Brummett's generic approach because it "cannot account for variations in style, substance, and situation" (p. 15), O'Leary proposed to treat apocalyptic discourse as an evolving "textual" (p. 10) or "rhetorical tradition" (p. 196). The virtue of this strategy for O'Leary was that it allows for an appreciation of both the enduring and the dynamic features of apocalyptic discourse. (As discussed in the entry for **genre**, numerous contemporary theorists argue that genre needs to be understood in similar terms.) Attention to processes of "discursive reformulation" (p. 17) is essential because apocalyptic discourse has, at least so far, failed as empirical prophesy, yet such failures have done little to arrest the recurrent appeal of this discursive form.[2]

O'Leary's (1994) detailed and complex presentation makes a short summary of his substantive claims impossible. Briefly, the fundamental exigence addressed by apocalyptic discourse in O'Leary's reading is the "problem of evil" (p. 20); "apocalyptic rhetoric is a symbolic theodicy [i.e., a defense of God in light of the fact of evil and human suffering], a rhetorical solution to the problem of evil that operates on both a rational and a mythic level" (p. 195). Apocalyptic discourse operates on multiple levels and, hence, requires a reading strategy capable of grasping these intertwined aspects. O'Leary's reading strategy combined attention to the **narrative** and **argumentative** dimensions of apocalyptic discourse; his was an effort to study "the argument of apocalyptic drama and the drama of apocalyptic argument" (p. 200). Central to O'Leary's analysis is the transformation of central narrative *themes*—evil, time, and authority—"into characteristic patterns of reasoning or *lines of argument* that together form a structure of proofs in support of the apocalyptic claim" (p. 204). The effect of apocalyptic discourse is both *instrumental* and *constitutive.*[3] Apocalyptic discourse not only works to substantiate specific claims but also can function to reshape how an individual or a community experiences time. O'Leary noted, "As argument, apocalypse seeks to situate its audience at the end of a particular pattern of historical time; to the extent that people adhere to apocalyptic claims, their perception of time is altered." Such altered temporal perception frequently leads to a "conversion experience" as individuals reconstitute their sense of self; they become "believers."[4] The constitution of temporal experience through apocalyptic discourse led O'Leary to suggest the heuristic claim that further study

> enables us to approach an enduring problem, the relationship of time and rhetoric, in a way that accounts for both the effect of time's passage on discourse and the effect of discourse on our phenomenal, social, and historical experiences of time. (p. 13)

Both Brummett and O'Leary called attention to the interpretive dimensions of apocalyptic discourse or how it functions as a form of *hermeneutical rhetoric.* It does so in two different, but interrelated, ways. First, much apocalyptic discourse draws part of its strength from an authoritative or "grounding" text through the "*strategy* of *typology*" (Brummett, 1991, emphasis added). Brummett wrote, "Typology is a way of seeing a grounding text as being *about* the present and future. . . . The strategy of typology is, thus, a strategy of connecting, of linking events and grounding texts, so as to reveal a determined and telic history" (p. 105). This reliance on an authoritative or grounding text creates the first part of the hermeneutic problem. Has the rhetor or advocate interpreted the authoritative text correctly? As O'Leary (1994) remarked, "A credulous audience may require little support for the rhetor's interpretive principles, while a sophisticated audience familiar with hermeneutical problems will exact a more rigorous methodological defense from the rhetor" (p. 204).[5] There is a second way in which apocalyptic discourse functions as a form of hermeneutical rhetoric. Prophets of the apocalypse do not merely read and interpret authoritative texts; they also are actively engaged in "reading" and interpreting the phenomenal events in the world around them, what some scholars refer to as the "social text." Authoritative texts can help to guide how the world is to be read, but the two acts of reading—one directed at the authoritative text and the other directed at the world—are distinct. According to Brummett (1984), a considerable amount of apocalyptic discourse is engaged in "reading . . . the signs of impending doom" (p. 89). In the vision of an apocalyptic rhetor, phenomenal events in the world (e.g., the emergence and spread of AIDS, the birth of a white buffalo) are interpreted as signs that a larger cosmic drama is in motion. *Sign* **arguments** are, then, prominently featured in apocalyptic discourse.

Notes

1. See also Boyer's (1992) sense of apocalyptic as a discursive **style.**
2. On the discursive response to failed prophecy, see Festinger, Riecken, and Schachter (1964) and O'Leary (1997).
3. This distinction is developed in the entry of **effects of rhetorical practice.**
4. See the discussion on **secular conversion.**
5. The entry on **hermeneutics and rhetoric** discusses at greater length the intersection of rhetorical advocacy and textual interpretation.

References and Additional Reading

Ahearn, E. J. (1996). *Visionary fictions: Apocalyptic writing from Blake to the modern age.* New Haven, CT: Yale University Press.

Boyer, P. (1992). *When times shall be no more: Prophecy belief in modern American culture.* Cambridge, MA: Harvard University Press.

Brummett, B. (1984). Premillennial apocalyptic as a rhetorical genre. *Central States Speech Journal, 35,* 84-93.

Brummett, B. (1991). *Contemporary apocalyptic rhetoric.* New York: Praeger.

Festinger, L., Riecken, H. W., & Schachter, S. (1964). *When prophecy fails.* New York: Harper Torchbooks.

Heald, J. C. (1975, Spring). Apocalyptic rhetoric: Agents of the Antichrist from the French to the British. *Today's Speech,* pp. 33-37.

Keller, C. (1996). *Apocalypse now and then: A feminist guide to the end of the world.* Boston: Beacon.

McGinn, B. (1979). *Visions of the end: Apocalyptic traditions in the Middle Ages.* New York: Columbia University Press.

Miller, P. (1956). The end of the world. In P. Miller, *Errand into the wilderness.* Cambridge, MA: Harvard University Press.

Mixon, H., & Hopkins, M. F. (1988). Apocalypticism in secular public discourse: A proposed theory. *Central States Speech Journal, 39,* 244-257.
O'Leary, S. D. (1994). *Arguing the apocalypse: A theory of millennial rhetoric.* New York: Oxford University Press.
O'Leary, S. D. (1997). Apocalyptic argument and the anticipation of catastrophe: The prediction of risk and the risk of prediction. *Argumentation, 11,* 293-313.
O'Leary, S., & McFarland, M. (1989). The political use of mythic discourse: Prophetic interpretation in Pat Robertson's presidential campaign. *Quarterly Journal of Speech, 75,* 433-452.
Reid, R. F. (1983). Apocalypticism and typology: Rhetorical dimensions of a symbolic reality. *Quarterly Journal of Speech, 69,* 229-248.
Weber, E. (1999). *Apocalypses: Prophecies, cults, and millennial beliefs through the ages.* Cambridge, MA: Harvard University Press.
Zamora, L. P. (Ed.). (1982). *The apocalyptic vision in America.* Bowling Green, OH: Bowling Green University Popular Press.

APOLOGIA

Ware and Linkugel (1973) wrote,

> We believe that apologetic discourses constitute a distinct *form* of public address, a family of speeches with sufficient elements in common so as to warrant legitimately generic status. The recurrent theme of accusation followed by apology is so prevalent in our record of public address as to be, in the words of Kenneth Burke, one of those "situations typical and recurrent enough for [individuals] to feel the need of having a name for them." In life, an attack upon a person's character, upon his [sic] worth as a human being, does seem to demand a direct response. The questioning of a man's *moral nature, motives,* or *reputation* is qualitatively different from the challenging of his policies. Witnesses to such a personal charge seem completely and most easily satisfied only by the most personal of responses by the accused. In the case of men and women of position, this response is usually a public speech of self-defense, the apology. Apologia appear to be as important in contemporary society as in years past, despite today's emphasis upon the legal representative and the public relations expert. (pp. 273-274)

Ware and Linkugel helped to break the ground for the contemporary study of apologetic discourse. Building off important work in sociology (e.g., Scott & Lyman, 1968), they divided this **genre** into two elements: postures or overall goals and tactics or particular strategies.

The postures of apologetic discourse are, in effect, discrete sub-genres. They can be thought of as specific types of the larger **apologia** genre. But it is important to recognize that, like all genres, the postures can be combined within a single text or over the course of an apologetic campaign. Postures often are combined due to the double nature of the *exigence* in some apologia situations. For example, certain events (e.g., accusations of malfeasance or discrimination, accidents, explosions) can pose a threat to a corporation's image and often require some form of apologia in response. The problematic event is the first exigence. But the way in which the corporation responds to the event can evolve into a separate exigence shaping its complex **rhetorical situation.** In the well-known case of the Exxon *Valdez* oil spill, the event—the oil spill—was Exxon's first exigence, and the accusations that Exxon's response to the event was inadequate was its second exigence. Exxon adopted different postures in responding to the dual exigences. It sought *absolution* with respect to the first exigence (mixed with some *explanation*), and it sought to *justify* its response as a way of negotiating the second exigence.

Ware and Linkugel (1973) identified four such postures. It may be useful to expand their typology and distinguish five postures or goals:

1. *Seek acquittal.* Acknowledge the charge and respond directly to it with a declaration of "not guilty" or "I didn't do it."
2. *Seek absolution.* Acknowledge the charge and respond with an admission of guilt (or fault, responsibility, etc.) and ask for forgiveness.

3. *Attempt an explanation.* Acknowledge the charge and offer an account of what took place. The objective is to make the audience members less likely to want to condemn the action based on their new knowledge of the circumstances. Explanatory apologias usually are ambivalent on the specific charge of wrongdoing; there is no specific declaration of innocence or admission of guilt.
4. *Seek vindication.* This is an *indirect* response to the charge. In most cases of vindication, the charge never is directly acknowledged or given any legitimacy by the accused. Vindication is accomplished through various strategies of indirection (e.g., attacking the source of the charge as a way of discrediting the charges without addressing them directly).
5. *Justification.* In adopting this posture, the rhetor seeks a major redefinition or transformation of how the entire situation is conceptualized. The objective is to change the act (or acts) in question into something justifiable or even praiseworthy.

Ware and Linkugel (1973) identified four tactics or common strategies in apologetic discourse:

1. *Strategies of denial.* Ware and Linkugel (1973) cautioned that "strategies of denial are not simplistic matters to be lightly passed over" (p. 276). Keeping this warning in mind, we might distinguish among various forms of denial such as (a) *denial of substance* (e.g., "I did not do it"), (b) *denial of intent* (e.g., "I did not mean to do it," "I did not plan for these consequences to occur"), (c) *denial of extent of consequences* (e.g., "The consequences have been exaggerated," "the results are not that bad"), and (d) forms of *indirect denial* (e.g., responding to charges in such a way that the charges never are explicitly acknowledged such as a print advertisement from a car company focusing on the safety of its product functioning as an indirect denial if that message appears while the company is being criticized for safety defects because the message effectively denies the charge—"No, we *do* manufacture safe cars"—without ever publicly acknowledging it).
2. *Bolstering.* This is the process of enhancing the image of a person or an institution under attack by linking the person or institution to abstract values (e.g., liberty, family) or by associating the person or institution with valued objects (e.g., the flag, apple pie).
3. *Differentiation.* This strategy seeks to create necessary distinctions that redefine the questionable act and/or some element of the situational complex (e.g., differentiate or **dissociate** the spirit from the letter of the law to make an act acceptable).
4. *Transcendence.* This strategy tries to effect a significant redefinition or reinterpretation of the questionable act. Often, this will amount to reframing the act by placing it in a different or broader context. A celebrity engages in **transcendence** when he or she responds to charges of immorality by attempting to focus attention on the issue of privacy (Nelson, 1984).

Ware and Linkugel's typology of postures and tactics is useful, but other scholars have proposed alternative conceptualizations of the types of strategies available to rhetors confronted with the task of self-defense or, as some describe it, "image repair." For example, Benoit (1995a) identified five major strategies that overlap slightly with Ware and Linkugel's typology: denial, evasion of responsibility, reduction of offensiveness, corrective action, and **mortification.** Short (1987) noted the way in which a *paranoid style* can function as an apologetic strategy.

Examples of apologetic performances are legion. Some of the more famous instances include John Henry Newman's "Apologia Pro Vita Sua" published in 1864 (where Newman defended his decision to convert from Anglicanism to Catholicism), Eugene Debs' "Address to the Jury" during his 1918 trial on the charge that he violated the Espionage Act, Richard Nixon's 1952 "Checkers" speech in response to charges of political corruption stemming from a previously undisclosed campaign fund, and Bill Clinton's speech to the American people in August 1998 discussing his historic grand jury testimony and admitting his inappropriate sexual relationship with Monica Lewinsky. Countless studies of apologetic discourse have been published over the past 25 years. The Watergate episode ("plumbers," illegal break-ins, the enemies list, obstruction of justice, and the other activities of the Nixon administration) generated a number of interesting studies (Blair, 1984; Harrell, Ware, and Linkugel, 1975; Kahl, 1984; Katula, 1975; Martin, 1976; Wilson, 1976). The rise in sexual harassment charges stimulated the need for apologia responses (Moore, 1996, 1997). Although politicians are the most frequent subject for apologetic study, scholars have begun to extend the categories of apologetic analysis to other cases. For example, Nelson (1984) analyzed the reactions of Billie Jean King and her supporters to the "palimony" lawsuit filed by her former secretary/lover, and Kruse (1981a) investigated apologetic aspects of the discourse of team sports. Finally, one of the most interesting and profitable extensions of apologia can be found in the emerging literature devoted to interest group and "corporate" apologia. As interest groups and corporate practices come under greater public scrutiny, and as accidents and mishaps increase in frequency, interest groups and corporations function as apologetic rhetors seeking forgiveness or public exoneration (Benoit, 1995a, 1995b, 1997b; Benoit & Brinson, 1994; Benoit & Dorries, 1996; Brinson & Benoit, 1996; Hearit, 1994, 1995, 1997; Phillips, 1999).

References and Additional Reading

Benoit, W. L. (1995a). *Accounts, excuses, and apologies: A theory of image restoration strategies.* Albany: State University of New York Press.

Benoit, W. L. (1995b). Sears' repair of its auto service image: Image restoration discourse in the corporate sector. *Communication Studies, 46,* 89-105.

Benoit, W. L. (1997a). Hugh Grant's image restoration discourse: An actor apologizes. *Communication Quarterly, 45,* 251-267.

Benoit, W. L. (1997b). Image repair discourse and crisis communication. *Public Relations Review, 23,* 177-197.

Benoit, W. L., & Brinson, S. L. (1994). AT&T: "Apologies are not enough." *Communication Quarterly, 42,* 75-88.

Benoit, W., & Dorries, B. (1996). *Dateline NBC's* persuasive attack on Wal-Mart. *Communication Quarterly, 44,* 463-477.

Blair, C. (1984). From *All the President's Men* to every man for himself: The strategies of post-Watergate apologia. *Central States Speech Journal, 35,* 250-260.

Brinson, S. L., & Benoit, W. L. (1996). Dow Corning's image repair strategies in the breast implant crisis. *Communication Quarterly, 44,* 29-41.

Downey, S. D. (1993). The evolution of the rhetorical genre of apologia. *Western Journal of Communication, 57,* 42-64.

Harrell, J., Ware, B. L., & Linkugel, W. A. (1975). Failure of apology in American politics: Nixon on Watergate. *Speech Monographs, 42,* 245-261.

Hearit, K. M. (1994). Apologies and public relations crises at Chrysler, Toshiba, and Volvo. *Public Relations Review, 20,* 113-125.

Hearit, K. M. (1995). "Mistakes were made": Organizations, apologia, and crises of social legitimacy. *Communication Studies, 46,* 1-17.

Hearit, K. M. (1997). On the use of transcendence as an apologia strategy: The case of Johnson Controls and its fetal protection policy. *Public Relations Review, 23,* 217-231.

Kahl, M. (1984). *Blind ambition* culminates in *lost honor:* A comparative analysis of John Dean's apologetic strategies. *Central States Speech Journal, 35,* 239-250.

Katula, R. A. (1975, Fall). The apology of Richard M. Nixon. *Today's Speech,* pp. 1-5.

King, R. L. (1985). Transforming scandal into tragedy: A rhetoric of political apology. *Quarterly Journal of Speech, 71,* 289-301.

Kruse, N. W. (1981a). Apologia in team sport. *Quarterly Journal of Speech, 67,* 270-283.

Kruse, N. W. (1981b). The scope of apologetic discourse: Establishing generic parameters. *Southern Speech Communication Journal, 46,* 278-291.

Martin, H. H. (1976). A generic exploration: Staged withdrawal: The rhetoric of resignation. *Central States Speech Journal, 27,* 247-257.

Moore, M. P. (1996). Rhetorical subterfuge and "the principle of perfection": Bob Packwood's response to sexual misconduct charges. *Western Journal of Communication, 60,* 1-20.

Moore, M. P. (1997). Rhetorical subterfuge and "the principle of perfection," Part II: Bob Packwood's Senate resignation. *Southern Communication Journal, 63,* 37-55.

Nelson, J. (1984). The defense of Billie Jean King. *Western Journal of Speech Communication, 48,* 92-102.
Phillips, K. R. (1999). Tactical apologia: The American Nursing Association and assisted suicide. *Southern Communication Journal, 64,* 143-154.
Scott, M. H., & Lyman, S. M. (1968). Accounts. *American Sociological Review, 33,* 46-62.
Short, B. (1987). Comic book apologia: The "paranoid" rhetoric of Congressman George Hansen. *Western Journal of Speech Communication, 51,* 189-203.
Ware, B. L., & Linkugel, W. A. (1973). They spoke in defense of themselves: On the generic criticism of apologia. *Quarterly Journal of Speech, 59,* 273-283.
Wilson, G. L. (1976). A strategy of explanation: Richard M. Nixon's August 8, 1974, resignation address. *Communication Quarterly, 24,* 14-20.

ARCHETYPE

The term **archetype** is used to describe narrative patterns (sometimes described as **myths**), character types, and verbal images that possess a universal (or nearly universal) significance. Abrams (1993) traced the study of archetypes to the fields of comparative anthropology (especially the early work of the British anthropologist James G. Frazer) and Jungian depth psychology. These modes of inquiry share a commitment to uncovering elemental or basic patterns in human thought and behavior that can be found across time and culture. According to Abrams,

> In criticism, the term archetype denotes recurrent narrative designs, patterns of action, character types, or images which are said to be identifiable in a wide variety of works of literature as well as in myths, dreams, and even ritualized modes of social behavior. (p. 224)

Archetypal narrative patterns can be derived from sacred and secular events. Walzer (1985) suggested in *Exodus and Revolution* that the Jewish exodus has become an archetypal event in Western culture; it functions as a template through which oppressed groups can understand their predicament and anticipate their salvation. Rosenberg (1982) described how the various historic "last stands"—ranging from the ancient Spartans guarding the pass at Thermopylae, to the Battle of the Alamo (see also Engelhardt, 1995), to Custer's final battle at Little Big Horn—provide a similar narrative resource. Elaborating on Custer's *symbolic* status in American culture, Rosenberg wrote, "The Custer of our dreams is an archetype of Camus's existential man who rises above the inevitability of his life and of his death by bravely fighting his inescapable fate to his last breath" (p. 110). Myths such as the tale of Prometheus's heroic rebellion and punishment and the story of Icarus chronicling his pride and failure as well as recurrent human experiences (e.g., the quest, the experience of birth/death/rebirth) are frequent sources of archetypal patterns. Abrams (1993) noted that the "death-rebirth theme is often said to be the archetype of archetypes . . . grounded in the cycle of the seasons and the organic cycle of human life" (p. 224). Abraham Lincoln exploited this archetypal pattern to great effect in the "Gettysburg Address" as he moved from national birth, to tragic death, to the promise of rebirth through collective effort.

Archetypal character types (sometimes referred to as archetypal **personas**) can be drawn from the realm of myth and legend (the Arthurian legend furnishes a number of important character types) as well as from secular and sacred history. The Roman general Cincinnatus put down his plow and his peaceful life when the nation was in danger, and when the crisis was resolved, he just as easily put down his sword and returned to his farm. Many Americans, beginning during the late 18th century, saw this pattern repeated in the conduct of their "Cincinnatus," George Washington. America's experience of expansion and the frontier helped to create some culture-specific archetypes such as the "gunslinger," the source of the more contemporary character type—the "hired gun." The biblical character of Moses represents the archetypal persona drawn from sacred history (Ware & Linkugel, 1982).

Archetypal images, drawn from the realm of shared human experience, frequently are used as *metaphorical vehicles.* Images of the sun, imagery based on the light-dark contrast and the seasons, and images of the sea have been the focus of inquiry in contemporary rhetorical studies (Graves, 1983; Osborn, 1967, 1977; Rickert, 1977). *Archetypal metaphors,* Osborn (1967) argued, are marked by three basic characteristics. First, they tend to be stable and resistant to change. Second, they draw on basic human experiences. Third, they appeal to ubiquitous human emotions. Archetypes in all three forms—narrative patterns, character types, and images—are important to rhetorical scholars because they identify key symbols that are part of a community's collective imagination. As such, archetypes tend to possess considerable rhetorical potency.

References and Additional Reading

Abrams, M. H. (1993). *A glossary of literary terms* (6th ed.). Fort Worth, TX: Harcourt Brace.

Chesebro, J. W., Bertelsen, D. A., & Gencarelli, T. F. (1990). Archetypal criticism. *Communication Education, 39,* 257-274.

Engelhardt, T. (1995). *The end of victory culture: Cold war America and the disillusioning of a generation.* New York: Basic Books.

Frentz, T. S., & Rushing, J. H. (1991). Integrating ideology and archetype in rhetorical criticism. *Quarterly Journal of Speech, 77,* 385-406.

Frye, N. (1951). The archetypes of literature. *Kenyon Review, 13,* 92-110.

Frye, N. (1957). Archetypal criticism. In N. Frye, *Anatomy of criticism.* Princeton, NJ: Princeton University Press.

Graves, M. P. (1983). Functions of key metaphors in early Quaker sermons, 1671-1700. *Quarterly Journal of Speech, 69,* 364-378.

Hillbruner, A. (1974). Archetype and signature: Nixon and the 1973 inaugural. *Central States Speech Journal, 25,* 169-181.

Osborn, M. (1967). Archetypal metaphor in rhetoric: The light-dark family. *Quarterly Journal of Speech, 53,* 115-126.

Osborn, M. (1977). The evolution of the archetypal sea in rhetoric and poetic. *Quarterly Journal of Speech, 63,* 347-363.

Rickert, W. E. (1977). Winston Churchill's archetypal metaphors: A mythopoetic translation of World War II. *Central States Speech Journal, 28,* 106-112.

Rosenberg, B. A. (1982). *The code of the West.* Bloomington: Indiana University Press.

Rushing, J. H. (1989). The new frontier in *Alien* and *Aliens:* Patriarchal co-optation of the feminine archetype. *Quarterly Journal of Speech, 75,* 1-24.

Stevens, A. (1983). *Archetypes: A natural history of the self.* New York: Quill.

Walzer, M. (1985). *Exodus and revolution.* New York: Basic Books.

Ware, B. L., & Linkugel, W. A. (1982). The rhetorical *persona:* Marcus Garvey as black Moses. *Communication Monographs, 49,* 50-62.

ARGUMENT

Argument is one of the most fundamental concepts in rhetorical studies. Beginning with Aristotle and other classical Greek rhetoricians, numerous scholars have offered conceptualizations of the nature of argument. We can begin with the model of argument (Figure A.1) developed by Stephen Toulmin (Toulmin, 1958; see also Toulmin, Rieke, & Janik, 1984).[1]

Toulmin's Model

A *claim* expresses a specific position on some doubtful or controversial issue that the arguer wants the audience to accept. When confronting any message, especially a complex one, it is useful to begin by identifying the claims that are made. Claims can be obscured by complex sentence construction where claims and their support often are interwoven. Whereas a rhetorical performance (e.g., a speech, an essay) usually will have one dominant claim (e.g., the prosecuting attorney stating that "the defendant is guilty," the political advocate urging to "vote no on Proposition 182"), most messages will consist of multiple supporting claims (e.g., the defendant had motive, was seen leaving the scene of the crime, and left fingerprints; Proposition 182 will hurt our economy and is unfair to people who have recently moved into the state).

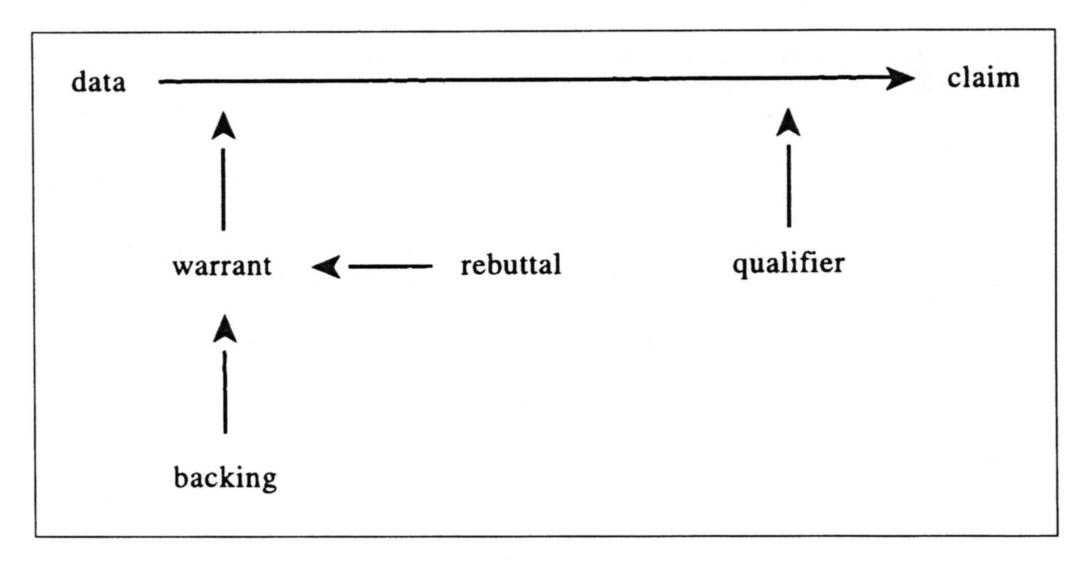

Figure A.1. Toulmin's Model of Argument

Argument scholars commonly identify *three* general types of claims. (Three tends to be a magic number in classical rhetorical theory—three modes of proof, three types of styles, three offices of rhetoric, etc.) The three-claim scheme emerged gradually over the course of the 20th century. The concept of claim as the end point of a specific argument was not discussed in argument texts until after the publication of Toulmin's (1958) *The Uses of Argument.* Prior to Toulmin, the concept of *proposition* was used to describe the end point of an argumentative composition. Most texts at the turn of the 20th century (e.g., Baker & Huntington, 1905) did not distinguish among types of propositions; they limited their attention to the manner in which propositions should be phrased. One exception to this generalization was Alden (1904), who distinguished between "is" propositions of "pure fact" and "ought" propositions of "theory or policy" (p. 10). Alden's framework would become popular as the "fact" (or "truth") versus "policy" distinction became relatively common in argument texts (Hayworth & Capel, 1934; O'Neill, 1921; Shurter & Helm, 1939). One of the first texts (it is unclear whether it was *the* first text) to suggest a third elementary proposition was Wagner's (1936) *Handbook of Argumentation.* Wagner urged argument scholars "to distinguish three main types of propositions, those of fact, of value, and of policy" (p. 15). Over time, this three-claim scheme became the norm in argument studies.

The three common claims in contemporary argumentation theory are discussed next.

Claims of Fact

When someone reports on past or present conditions in the world, that person is making a factual statement. A factual statement becomes a *claim* as soon as someone expresses doubt or disagreement. Factual claims often go unnoticed because we overlook the "fact" that a claim is being made (we assume that the speaker or writer is merely reporting on undisputed conditions in the world).[2] We reestablish a factual claim's status as a claim—not some type of undeniable "truth"—the moment that we cast doubt on the claim. Doubt makes the factual claim controversial; it makes explicit argument necessary. In the final analysis, it seems impossible to establish a factual claim *absolutely* or with complete certainty (witness the continued existence of

"Flat Earth" societies). It always is possible to doubt a factual claim. But over time, based on evidence and argument, countless factual claims become established "beyond a reasonable doubt" and, hence, become generally unproblematic statements.

Factual claims can be further divided into two categories by their *function* and their *temporal orientation.* Each category can then be described more precisely. The functions of factual claims include the following:

1. Establishing the existence or nonexistence of some condition or state (e.g., "Racial discrimination exists in America")
2. Defining or classifying something (e.g., a case of urban unrest is classified as a "revolt" and *not* as a "riot")
3. Establishing a relationship between two or more things (e.g., one of the most common relationships established is that one thing *caused* another thing)

The temporal orientation of factual claims are as follows (see also Rybacki & Rybacki, 1991):

1. Past fact (e.g., "Slavery caused the Civil War")
2. Present fact (e.g., "American white males are angry")
3. Future fact (although it might seem odd, people frequently make "factual" claims, most often in the form of predictions, about the future; e.g., "By the year 2050, people of color will outnumber whites in America")

As the examples should indicate, any factual claim can be categorized in terms of function *and* temporal orientation (claiming that "slavery caused the Civil War" is a past fact of relationship). Of course, claims can be phrased in ways that are ambiguous (e.g., as a **rhetorical question**), making it difficult to identify their function and temporal orientation.

Claims of Value

The relationship between claims of fact and claims of value can be deceptive. Consider the claim often made over the past few years that "major league baseball is racist." Is this a claim of fact or value? The difficulty with this example is the predicate adjective *racist.* Some terms function rather unambiguously as descriptions (they enact the factual functions of existence, classification, or relationship); there is little ambiguity in saying that "the Cubs are *below* the Cardinals in the baseball standings" or that "the color of the sky on a clear day is *blue.*" Other terms reside rather clearly in the realm of evaluation (where they evaluate things based on a standard of good-bad, right-wrong, moral-immoral, etc.), and their use establishes a claim of value. Saying that "*Titanic* is a great movie" is an evaluation or a value claim; saying that "*Titanic* has grossed a billion dollars" establishes the existence of fact.

But, back to the initial example: What about a term such as *racist*? It would seem that some terms are able to *describe* as well as *evaluate,* making a clear differentiation between fact claims and value claims difficult, if not impossible. So, in the case of the statement that "major league baseball is racist," we might ask whether the term *racist* is being used to establish the existence of a condition or to classify the institution of major league baseball *or* whether the term is being used to render a negative evaluation or judgment about the institution of professional baseball. To be able to answer this question usually will entail some form of contextualization or placing the claim in its larger discursive context to better understand its primary force. But it might not always be possible to make these types of distinctions; facts and values, as well as description and evaluation, intersect. So, whereas the realms of fact and value, and of description and evaluation, are different, the way in which we use language frequently complicates the relationship. The intellectual historian and political theorist J. G. A. Pocock affirmed this when he observed that "factual and evaluative statements are inextricably combined in political speech" (Pocock, 1971, p. 17). Rhetorical scholar Richard Lanham echoed this point when he noted that "language is intrinsically value-laden. . . . Every 'fact' comes with values attached" (Lanham, 1993, p. 171).

Claims of Policy

In general, policy claims answer the question "What should we do?" or "What course of action should we take?" Policies, considered broadly, are the courses of action or conduct that we choose for ourselves or, in some cases, have chosen for us. When friends decide how to spend their Saturday night (e.g., "Do we go to the bars, go to a movie, or hang out at home?"), they are engaged in policy deliberation; claims of policy (e.g., "Let's go see a movie"; "No, let's go to the bars") are made, attacked, and defended, and a policy decision is reached. Obviously, the degree of deliberation among friends about how to spend their Saturday night is different from the deliberation in a city council meeting about whether or not to ban smoking in all public facilities or the collective deliberation of a country in deciding whether or not to go to war. But in each case, the central question is deciding on a course of action, and an advocate that defends a course of action—going to a movie or going to war—is making a policy claim.

Policy arguments typically generate a number of specific points of controversy (or **stock topics in policy disputes**). In addition, argument scholars have identified a variety of **case construction strategies** for use in different types of policy controversies. Pubic discourse almost inevitably involves complex chains or networks of claims. Consider a relatively simple example. A policy dispute ("Should we do *x*?") may rest on resolving a separate, potentially complicated factual claim ("Is *x* permissible under the Constitution?"). It often is useful to visualize a complicated text's "network" of claims through a diagram that identifies the main claim and then works back through various levels of subclaims (Inch & Warnick, 1998).

What about the other elements in Toulmin's model? After the claim, we have *data.* Data consist of *uncontested* factual claims (or factual statements), testimony, observations, opinions, statistical generalizations, commonly held values and beliefs, and any other form of evidence that might serve as the starting point for an argument in support of a claim. The key factor is that data are agreed to by other participants in argument and by the audience. Any statement that will be accepted unquestionably by the majority of audience members can function as data. As already noted, because it almost always is possible to doubt data, as arguments evolve over time, it often happens that the data (starting point) for an argument may revert to the status of claim (the point to be established) in subsequent argument. Conversely, once established, the claim can function as data for future argument (e.g., once one accepts the claim that 3% of management-level positions in major league baseball are held by people of color, this claim can function as data to support the subsequent claim that major league baseball is racist).

Despite the commonly used expression, facts or data do not "speak for themselves." That is, the material that functions as data cannot immediately provide support for a claim. Data support, and serve as a reason for accepting, a claim because of the presence of an argument's *warrant.* Anderson and Mortensen (1967) wrote,

> The warrant, unlike the invariant connectives of formal logic, functions as a complex linguistic connective; i.e., it consists of substantive features of both data and claim while providing a lexical and structural link between propositional elements within the argument. (p. 147)

Warrants function to authorize or validate the movement from data to claim.

But the term *presence* can be misleading because arguers frequently do not state warrants explicitly. Warrants often are only implicit (not directly present) in an argument. Anderson and Mortensen (1967) argued that, in many cases of everyday argument, "the meanings of connective terms [warrants] are not clearly specified by the linguistic context of the argument itself" (p. 147).[3] Despite the fact that warrants might not be linguistically present in an argument, they nevertheless serve a crucial function in linking data to claim. For example, if an advocate claims that a voter should vote for Person X in an upcoming election, then the voter might ask why. In response, the advocate could give the voter evidence or provide him or her with data (e.g., all of the voter's friends are going to vote for Person X). The voter might not believe this evidence and so might call all of his or her friends—and, sure enough, they plan to vote for Person X. But the advocate's argument might not persuade the voter. Why not? Probably because the voter is skeptical about the implicit, but very important, warrant. What is it? Roughly put, it amounts to the following "principle": that in *this case* the voter should do what his or her friends are going to do.[4] If, ultimately, the voter instead votes for Person Y, then the voter will have rejected not only the advocate's claim (vote for Person X) but also his or her implicit warrant. The combination of data and warrant often is termed a "line of argument" or an "argument scheme." Some common lines or schemes of argument are described in what follows.

The other three terms in the Toulmin model support and/or modify the three major terms. *Backing* provides additional support for the warrant (it answers the question, "Why should one accept this warrant in this situation?"). In the preceding example, the advocate might try to provide backing for his or her argument in this way: The voter's friends have followed the campaign carefully, they have read the candidates' position statements, and based on this information, they have concluded that Person X is best. In providing this backing, the advocate has tried to answer the question, "In this case, why should the voter follow the lead of his or her friends?" Backing is a fairly common feature of developed arguments and can take the form of a fully developed argument (i.e., the warrant assumes the status of a claim that is supported by supplementary data and a supplementary warrant). *Rebuttal* and *qualifier* appear less frequently. Rebuttal notes the limitations or weakness of the warrant (e.g., the advocate might acknowledge that the voter should not always follow the lead of his or her friends yet still claim that, in this case, it is appropriate to do so), whereas the qualifier provides an overall assessment of the confidence that the arguer has in the argument. Consider the following two sentences from a George Will op-ed piece (dated March 17, 1998) on Bill Clinton's political and legal problems: "If [Kathleen] Willey is truthful, then Clinton is a perjurer. So if she is truthful, [then] he is *probably* not the sort who would flinch from suborning perjury and obstructing justice" (emphasis added). The two sentence have the same basic form (conditional "if-then"). The first sentence is an unqualified conditional; if Willey is telling the truth regarding her White House encounter with Clinton, then the president *is* a liar and a perjurer. But the second sentence contains a key qualifier. Will's "logic" looks something like this:

If Willey is telling the truth,
then Clinton is a perjurer.

If Clinton is a perjurer, then
he *probably* suborned perjury
and obstructed justice.

Will believed Willey. And he was extremely confident in his first claim: Provided that Willey is telling the truth, Clinton *must be* a perjurer. Will believed that Clinton's perjury was data for another claim: that Clinton broke the law and suborned perjury and obstructed justice. But Will realized that this claim (and its supporting argument) is not as strong as the first. The fact that Clinton perjured himself (according to Will) does not automatically lead to the conclusion that he suborned perjury in others. So, Will qualified his claim: Clinton *probably* suborned perjury and obstructed justice.

Brockriede and Ehninger's Typology

In an influential essay that helped to introduce Toulmin's ideas on argument to the community of American rhetorical scholars, Wayne Brockriede and Douglas Ehninger developed a typology of argument schemes. They began by reformulating the classical doctrine of **modes of proof** (**logos, ethos,** and **pathos**) into three different types of warrants that they referred to as *substantive, authoritative,* and *motivational.*

"The warrant of a substantive argument," Brockriede and Ehninger wrote, "reflects an assumption concerning the way in which things are related in the world about us." While acknowledging the possibility of alternative renderings, they suggested that a "commonly recognized . . . six-fold" system of "orderings" manages to describe the key ways in which things are related (p. 48). Each one of the six ways represents a common *substantive* warrant/line of argument.

Cause

Brockriede and Ehninger (1960) wrote,

> In argument from cause, the data consist of one or more accepted facts about a person, object, event, or condition. The warrant attributes to these facts a creative or generative power and specifies the nature of the effect they will produce. The claim relates these results to the person, object, event, or condition named in the data. (p. 48)

In short, doing "A" will cause "B."

In his first address to the American people on the subject of Vietnam in May 1969, Richard Nixon stated, "To abandon them [the South Vietnamese] now would mean a massacre that would shock and dismay everyone in the world who values human life." Nixon's causal argument was that doing "A" (abandoning the South Vietnamese by withdrawing all American troops) would cause "B" (a massacre). Advocates often combine or interweave causal arguments with other argument schemes. For example, Nixon's argument blended into a *pragmatic argument of consequences* (U.S. troops should not be withdrawn from South Vietnam because of the negative consequences that would result). The causal argument supports a claim of future fact (see Brockriede and Ehninger's discussion of the "designative" function of causal arguments); the pragmatic argument supports a policy claim.

Advocates not only reason from cause to effect ("A" will cause "B"); they also reverse the process and reason from effect to cause ("B" has happened, and it is argued that "A" was the cause). Consider how one phenomenon, the purported destruction of the ozone layer, might function as either an effect or a cause (or both). An advocate might reason from cause to effect in arguing that ozone depletion has led to global warming, El Niño, and other atmospheric problems. In a different context, an advocate might argue from effect to cause in suggesting that widespread use of chlorofluorocarbons (CFCs) and other substances has damaged the ozone layer. We can return to Nixon's Vietnam discourse for another example of effect to cause argument. In his November 1969 address on Vietnam, Nixon sought to explain to the American people why there had been no progress in peace negotiations. Lack of progress was the effect (the "B" term); Nixon sought to identify its cause (the "A" term). Nixon argued that North Vietnamese actions (more precisely, their inaction) caused the lack of progress. Effect to cause arguments are common in efforts to establish the **stock topic** of *blame.*

Sign

Brockriede and Ehninger (1960) wrote, "In argument from sign, the data consist of clues or symptoms. The warrant interprets the meaning or significance of these symptoms" (p. 49). The claim indicates the condition to which the clues or symptoms point. A trivial case might be that smoke is a common sign for the presence (the condition) of fire. A common form of sign argument uses *past behavior* as a sign (or an indication) of future behavior. A nation's record of violating treaties and agreements can function as a sign that it probably will violate a new agreement. This is not an instance of causal argument. Past behavior does not *cause* future behavior; it is simply an indicator of likely future behavior (the *cause* of the behavior lies elsewhere). Nor is this example an instance of parallel case argument. We are not dealing with different cases; rather, we are dealing with the behavior of the same group (the same "case") at different points in time. Both parallel case arguments and sign arguments relate past action or events to the present/future, but it is necessary to reconstruct the arguments carefully to determine which warrant or line of argument is at work (because advocates rarely announce how they are reasoning).

In her famous speech at Pennsylvania Hall in 1838, Angelina Grimké relied heavily on sign argument. Early in the speech, she used the presence of protesters outside the hall as a sign that "the spirit of slavery is here" in the North. She continued this sign argument when she claimed, "This opposition shows that slavery has done its deadliest work in the hearts of our citizens." Later in the speech, Grimké used sign reasoning to support her claim that abolitionism had been effective. She noted, "I feel that all this disturbance is but evidence that our efforts are the best that could have been adopted, or else the friends of slavery would not care for what we say and do." Grimké returned to this sign pattern at the very end of her speech when she concluded, "The fact that the South looks with jealousy upon our measures shows that they are effectual." After all, if abolitionists were ineffective, then the South and its northern dough-faced supporters would ignore them. Opposition was a sign of their effectiveness.

Walton (1996a) noted the existence of

> complex cases of argumentation from sign . . . [that] might be called *evidence accumulating arguments,* arguments that proceed through a sequence of signs, each of which only gives a small weight of presumption for the conclusion, but taken together, the whole sequences builds up to quite a plausible argument for the conclusion. (p. 48)

As an example, Walton pointed to an episode from a Sherlock Holmes story in which Holmes, based on a number of signs, concluded that Dr. Watson had recently returned from Afghanistan. In this case, a large number of mutually reinforcing signs supported the claim, overcoming the inherent *ambiguity* of a sign.[5]

Advocates also use sign reasoning as a way of operationalizing abstractions. For example, test scores are used as a "sign" of intelligence (or as a predictor of academic performance), and certain behavior becomes a "sign" of patriotism. This form of sign argument was extremely common in American foreign policy discourse during the cold war. Advocates during this period frequently urged Americans to view certain forms of action (or inaction) as "signs" for an abstract concept. Speaking to the nation in March 1983, Ronald Reagan hoped to rally support for his policy initiatives, particularly his proposed increases in military spending. He told the American people, "If we stop in midstream, we will send a signal of decline, of lessened will, to friends and adversaries alike." Reagan's sign argument (action signals loss of abstract idea of "will") blended into a *pragmatic argument:* Because sending this signal would result in negative consequences, we should "stay the course." George Bush, speaking to the nation about the Persian Gulf crisis in September 1990, employed a similar strategy. The situation in the gulf, Bush asserted, was a "test of our mettle." He continued, "Had we not responded to this first provocation with clarity of purpose, if we do not continue to demonstrate our determination, it would be a signal to actual and potential despots around the world." Like Reagan, Bush emphasized the way in which American actions were a "signal" of an abstraction—our collective "will"—that would be "read" by people around the world. Hence, America had to make sure that it sent the "right" signal. Signs of American "will," American "character," and American "determination" abounded in the discourse of the Vietnam war, other cold war foreign policy issues, and the post-cold war era.

Generalization and Example

These arguments support factual claims about the existence of a condition of some sort. One might claim that "people in Greek letter organizations have successful academic records" and, in support, point to one or two individuals one knows who are "A" students and members of Greek letter organizations (they function as *examples*), or one might report the results of a study he or she conducted that examined the records of a sample of Greek letter students around the country (the sample allows one to make a *generalization* about the larger group).[6] Some generalization arguments simply reason from sample to group (e.g., these Democrats are "tax and spend liberals," all Democrats are "tax and spend liberals"; these Christian fundamentalists are narrow-minded, all Christian fundamentalists are narrow-minded), whereas others proceed from sample, through the group, to an individual (e.g., leading to the claim that this Democratic candidate is or, if elected, will be a "tax and spend liberal" or that this Christian fundamentalist is narrow-minded). In the latter case, generalization has established a general rule or principle that is applied, by way of the argument scheme of *classification,* to the individual case.[7]

Arguments from sign and example can overlap, creating confusion for anyone trying to specify what scheme is being used in a given case. For example, in one of his first abolitionist addresses delivered in Boston on the Fourth of July in 1829, William Lloyd Garrison suggested that American "patriotism" was on the decline. As proof, he pointed out that the celebration of American independence had "degenerated." He then noted various cases of heavy alcohol consumption and other forms of "licentious" behavior on the Fourth of July to support his claim. Was Garrison reasoning from example (by noting specific instances in support of his general claim), or was he reasoning from sign (by pointing out symptoms of an abstract condition)? Or, was he doing both? In this case, *both* might be the most appropriate answer. Garrison supported his claim that American patriotism was on the decline by operationalizing "patriotism," making behavior at Fourth of July festivals a sign of the type and quality of patriotism in America. Garrison then supported his generalization that Fourth of July celebrations have degenerated with specific examples.

In general, arguments from sign support a more limited claim and are more context dependent compared to arguments of example (and generalization), which function to support general statements that are less bound to a specific context. A few simple **expository** examples might help to clarify this point.[8] One observer sees leaves moving quickly past a window one afternoon and concludes, "It's windy today." This conclusion is based on (implicit) sign reasoning; quickly moving leaves usually are a reliable sign that it is windy, just as frost on a window usually is a reliable sign that it is cold outside (both, of course, can be wrong given that someone out of sight might be operating a giant fan to make the leaves move quickly or someone might have etched a frost-like pattern on the glass). Imagine another day when one is looking out the window and, sure enough, there go those leaves moving quickly by again. But this time, one concludes, "We have a lot of windy days in this part of the country." One reaches this conclusion by going beyond sign reasoning ("It's windy today") to use the conditions that one has observed as an example that supports a more general statement ("It's windy in this part of the country" is more general than "It's windy today").

Here is a second example. One witnesses a person jumping into a river to rescue a drowning child. One concludes that the person is brave; he or she is a hero. This conclusion is based on a reasoning process that uses the act as a sign of the person's character.[9] This reasoning might, of course, be flawed; perhaps the person did not voluntarily jump in the river (volition might be considered as an element of fearless action) but rather was pushed in or fell in by accident, and it was not until the person was in the river that he or she decided to help the child. Now consider a slight variation on this scenario. The person that jumped into the river was an off-duty police officer. One still might conclude that the person is brave. But one also might formulate a different conclusion by following another line of reasoning. One might conclude that police officers are brave. This conclusion is based on a reasoning process that employs the combination of the person and his or her act as an example that represents a larger class (police officers). In using the event to claim that police officers are brave, one has moved from reasoning from sign to reasoning from example.

Consider a final example in which the same claim can be reached arguing from sign or example. The claim is, "Racial discrimination exists in City X." One way of supporting this claim might be to point to certain statistics: African Americans constitute 25% of the city's population but make up only 2% of the city's firefighters, 3% of its police officers, and 5% of its city council members. In pointing to these statistics, an advocate would be arguing by way of sign. These figures function as symptoms or as indications of the presence of racial discrimination. Another way of supporting this claim would be to point to specific events or occurrences. An advocate might note that John Doe, an African American applicant for a position on the police force, had the third best score on the police academy entrance examination but was not offered one of the 10 admission slots. When Doe took the city and police department to court, a jury found that Doe was denied a spot due to his race. When used as argumentative data, Doe's case serves as a specific example that supports the asserted existence of racial discrimination.

Parallel Case

The parallel case scheme works through a process of comparison (but should be distinguished from Perelman and Olbrechts-Tyteca's [1969] strategy of "comparison" discussed later). In this instance, the line of argument works through a process of comparing two or more different "cases" that are part of the same general class. Examples include comparing intervention in Vietnam to proposed intervention in Bosnia, comparing the levels of violence in two cities from the same region to different gun control policies, and comparing the number of drunk driving accidents in states with a .08 blood alcohol level limit for legal intoxication to that in states with a .10 limit.[10]

Parallel case argument is quite common in policy deliberation. Advocates supporting a policy urge their communities to adopt courses of action that have been successful in other places. Defending the Equal Rights Amendment, former Indiana Senator Birch Bayh addressed the issue of women serving in the military in April 1977. He claimed that men and women could serve together efficiently. He continued,

> The experience of other countries supports this conclusion. In Israel, women are required to serve in the defense forces just as men. They are not, however, assigned to combat posts, nor are they required to engage in physical combat. . . . Under these circumstances, no significant difficulties have arisen from having men and women serve together.

Defending the claim that allowing gays to serve in the military will not be disruptive, Eric Konigsberg, in the November 1992 issue of *Washington Monthly,* employed a parallel case strategy quite similar to that of Bayh. Konigsberg pointed to cases in which there have been no disruptions in military efficiency when gays are allowed to serve openly (e.g., in the Netherlands, Denmark, and Israel) to warrant his claim that allowing gays to serve openly in the U.S. military would not cause problems.

Advocates opposed to a policy proposal supported by parallel case reasoning often respond by pointing out problems with comparing the different cases. For example, gun control advocates compare Seattle, Washington, and Vancouver, British Columbia, and argue that the gun control measures in place in Canada should be adopted in the United States. Gun control opponents point out that studies comparing Seattle and Vancouver are flawed because of important dissimilarities in the two "cases." At times, a parallel case argument focuses on a specific aspect of one case so as to counteract criticism of a policy. William Bennett used this form of parallel case reasoning to support continuing the criminal approach to drug prevention. In a speech delivered at Harvard University in December 1989, he maintained,

> Twenty-five years ago, no one would have suggested that we must first address the root causes of racism before fighting segregation. We fought it, quite correctly, by passing laws against unacceptable conduct. The causes of racism posed an interesting question, but the moral imperative was to end it as soon as possible and by all reasonable means—education, prevention, the media, and not least of all, the law. So, too, with drugs.

Parallel case arguments function in some typical ways. They can help to support future fact *predictions,* with the future fact predictions also being able to function as negative or positive consequences (e.g., intervention in Bosnia will result in a "quagmire" [as did the similar case in Vietnam], investing in downtown revitalization in City X will lead to economic growth [as it did in the similar case of City Y]). They also can support policy or course of action claims when used as a form of *precedent* (e.g., Jones received a bonus when she won the yearly sales competition, Smith should receive a bonus this year because he won the competition; the city council employed the "standard assessment criteria" when it evaluated last year's grant applications, this year's city council should employ those same criteria when it evaluates the grant applications).

Parallel case reasoning played a key role in the debate over the Panama Canal treaties during the late 1970s. Opponents of the treaty sought to subvert the proposal by comparing the Panama Canal territory with other similar cases of territorial acquisition. "Giving away" the Panama Canal and the canal zone to the Panamanians because they were unhappy with the original deal, argued treaty opponents such as Congressman Philip Crane, would be like giving Alaska back to the Soviet Union because the Soviets did not like the terms under which Russia originally sold Alaska to the United States. Treaty supporters had to counter this parallel case logic (the Panama Canal zone belongs to the United States, just like Alaska does) and did so, in part, by introducing a counter parallel case. Jimmy Carter was a major supporter of the proposed treaties. In a speech to the American people, Carter insisted,

> The canal zone cannot be compared with United States territory. We bought Alaska from the Russians, and no one has ever doubted that we own it. We bought the Louisiana Purchase territories from France, and that's an integral part of the United States. . . . We've never needed to own the Panama Canal zone, any more than we need to own a 10-mile-wide strip of land all the way

> through Canada from Alaska when we build an international pipeline.

Carter attacked the opposition by (a) trying to undercut their parallel case (the canal zone and Alaska are *different* cases) and (b) proposing an alternative parallel case (the canal zone is similar to the Canadian territory on which our pipeline sits).

Analogy

An analogy supports a claim by comparing two things that share some characteristics but are essentially dissimilar (they belong to different classes of things or events).[11] Consider two examples, the first from Michael Moore's book, *Downsize This!* Moore (1996) insisted that Americans should

> prohibit corporations from closing a profitable factory or business and moving it overseas. If they close a business and move it within the [United States], they must pay reparations to the community they are leaving behind. We've passed divorce laws that say that if a woman works hard to put her husband through school, and he later decides to leave her after he has become successful, he has a responsibility to compensate her for her sacrifices that allowed him to go on to acquire his wealth. The "marriage" between a company and [a] community should be no different. If a corporation packs up and leaves, it should have serious alimony to pay. (p. 256)

Moore's claim was one of policy; we should pass laws requiring a corporation to pay reparations when it closes a plant in one community so as to move the plant's operations somewhere else that might be more profitable. His line of argument is analogy. A company's relationship to the community in which it operates is like a marriage; because we require alimony in many divorce cases, we should require something similar in cases of "corporate divorce."

The second example comes from a speech by D. Stanley Eitzen of the University of Colorado at a conference on crime in America in March 1995. In this passage, Eitzen tried to describe the way in which political progressives view the crime control strategies of conservatives. Eitzen suggested,

> Progressives argue that conservative crime control measures are fundamentally flawed because they are "after the fact" solutions. Like a janitor mopping up the floor while the sink continues to overflow, he or she may even redouble the effort with some success, but the source of the flooding has not been addressed.

Two interrelated analogies appeared in the passage; crime was likened to an overflowing sink, and conservative crime control policies were described as "after the fact" mopping up. The analogy speaks to the **stock topic** subissue of *solvency.* Conservative solutions are criticized for failing to address the root of the crime problem.

Classification

This pattern of argument is very common but can be very difficult to discern. Most of Toulmin's examples fall into this scheme of argument. Essentially, in classification arguments, general principles, rules, or cultural values function as a substantive warrant. The process, as Gilbert (1997) noted, has "a distinctly deductive feel" to it (p. 9).[12] Classification arguments can be reconstructed by way of the three-part structure of a *deductive syllogism:* (a) a major premise that states the rule or principle, (b) a minor premise that states the circumstances or conditions of the present case, and (c) the conclusion that is the result of applying the general rule to the present case. In short, classification arguments apply rules and principles to categorize phenomena and/or predict behavior. Brockriede and Ehninger's (1960) example (slightly modified) looks something like this:

Major premise (warrant): Most totalitarian states can make fast decisions in a crisis.
Minor premise (data): The Soviet Union is a totalitarian state.
Conclusion (claim): The Soviet Union can make a fast crisis decision.

Or, consider the general conclusion about windy weather in the discussion of generalization and example earlier. Someone traveling to another part of the country might reason as follows:

Major premise (warrant): It usually is windy in City X.
Minor premise (data): I am going to City X.
Conclusion (claim): I am going to experience some windy days.

And this (future fact) conclusion might then be incorporated into a policy argument: I had better be prepared to deal with the wind.

Here are some additional examples. Steve Kelley, writing in the *Seattle Times* on March 1, 1998, claimed that salary caps in professional sports are a joke. In support, he provided a number of examples. But there was a classification argument at the center of his essay that looked something like this:

Major premise (warrant): Policies that do not deliver on their promises are a "sham."
Minor Premise (data): Salary caps do not deliver on their promises.
Conclusion (claim): Salary caps are a sham.

In a 1992 essay in the *Journal of Contemporary Health Law and Policy,* Kristin Rodgers, an advocate for protecting the rights of abused children, argued that the statute of limitations in cases of child abuse must be expanded. Rodgers (1992) maintained that current restrictions were unfair. How did she support her claim? By way of classification:

Major premise (warrant): The dismissal of "inherently offensive" legal claims is unfair.
Minor premises (data): Child abuse cases are inherently offensive, and existing statute of limitations policies result in the dismissal of claims.
Conclusion (claim): Statute of limitations policies are unfair.

Some people believe that it is a government's responsibility to prevent or reduce the harm that might befall its citizens. This belief is a *political* commitment or principle (see the entry for **ideograph**). It might be incorporated as a major premise or warrant in the following policy argument:

Major premise (warrant): Political principle (government should act to reduce harm).
Minor premises (data): Tobacco products harm individuals, and tobacco products cause additional "social" damages (e.g., Medicaid expense).
Conclusion (claim): The federal government should ban tobacco products.

Classification-like arguments are extremely common in discussions of political "rights." A recurrent warrant or major premise is "rights talk" (e.g., "Anything that might limit a right or be construed as a limitation of a right is a threat"). This major premise or warrant supports policy-specific evaluations such as the following:

Major premise (warrant): Any limit on a right is a threat.
Minor premise (data): The Supreme Court's *Webster* decision might limit a woman's right to an abortion.
Conclusion (claim): The *Webster* decision is a threat to abortion rights.

The same premise also might be used to *subvert* competing "rights" as in the following:

Major premise (warrant): Any limit of a right is a threat.
Minor premise (data): The concept of fetal rights might limit a woman's right to an abortion.
Conclusion (claim): "Fetal rights" are a threat to women's rights.

Finally, abstract and ambiguous cultural **values** can function as classification warrants (Sillars & Ganer, 1982). For example, most Americans believe in the "value" of telling the truth. That value can then warrant a course of action claim:

Major premise (warrant): "Truth" is an important value; people should tell the truth.
Minor premise: One has been asked to express his or her opinion about a friend's new hairstyle.
Conclusion (claim): One should tell the "truth."

Of course, people do not always "tell the truth" or act in accordance with other rules, principles, and values. The application of principles and values to practical questions is a complicated process that often involves competing principles, desires, motives, and so on. But the fact that a given principle or value does not warrant belief or action in *every* case does not mean that it will not function as a warrant in *some* cases. Despite the fact that classification warrants do not command universal assent, they remain a potent resource in practical argument.

The second general class of arguments identified by Brockriede and Ehninger was *authoritative* (see also Walton, 1997). As suggested previously, the idea of authoritative argument is a reformulation of the classical notion of **ethos.** Brinton's (1986, 1987) discussion of "ethotic argument" attempted a similar conceptual move. Brinton (1987) wrote,

> Ethotic argument is argument in which considerations about *ethos* of some person or persons are offered (sometimes together with certain facts about their behavior) as reasons for belief or action. Typically, these are offered as *prima facie* reasons and not as sufficient in themselves. To accept *ethotic* argument is to in one way or another allow ourselves to be influenced by the *ethos* of someone else in the process of belief formation or in choosing courses or policies of action. Typically, something like a transfer of "credibility" from a person to a conclusion is involved. (pp. 251-252)

Consider some examples. In some cases, advocates support claims by relying on the expertise or authority of others. An advocate trying to support the future fact claim that "gas prices will go up" might draw on an essay from the *Wall Street Journal* that quotes an official from the federal energy department. The *Journal* has a strong reputation in the realm of business issues, and officials in the energy department probably have a good feel for trends in gas prices. The authority of both the channel (the *Journal*) and the source of the testimony (the energy department official) warrant the claim. In other cases, advocates rely primarily on their personal **ethos.** Compare two ways of supporting the policy claim, "Vote for Candidate X." The following is Example 1:

Major premise (classification warrant): Good men and women deserve to be in public office.
Minor premise (data): Candidate X is a good person. (Supplementary data support this potentially contestable *evaluative* claim.)
Conclusion (claim): Vote for Candidate X.

The following is Example 2:

Claim: Vote for Candidate X. (Why?)
Data: Because *I know* that Candidate X is a good person.

Warrant (implicit): I am a good judge of character, and you should trust my judgment.

These two arguments might blend together during the period of saturation advertising right before an election. And although they are similar (both make the same claim), they warrant their claims in different ways. The first example is a case of a classification argument. An abstract principle (the belief in meritocracy or government by the most competent and trustworthy) is the major premise or warrant. If an advocate can (a) show his or her audience that this principle is the right standard for **judgment** and (b) show that Candidate X meets this standard, then the advocate will have produced a *potentially* persuasive argument (other factors can intervene to render this argument less effective). In the second example, the advocate makes the same claim and draws on some of the same material (the character of Candidate X). But the potential persuasive force of the second example not only derives from the character of Candidate X but also relies heavily on the character of the advocate advancing the claim. In the second example, the advocate is asking his or her audience members to trust their expertise and their competence as judges of character. We should vote for Candidate X because of the (presumed) authority of the advocate—his or her ability to evaluate candidates for office.

Authority does not always have to be in the form of a specific person (e.g., an official in the energy department, a respected scientist, a distinguished public official). Advocates also may rely on forms of *impersonal authority.* One of the most common forms of impersonal is a respected or revered document. Consider, for example, how often the teachings of the Bible have been, and still are, invoked in practical argument. Should women be ordained as priests? Let us look at what the Bible says. Should gays and lesbians be granted basic civil rights? Let us look at what the Bible says about homosexuality. The Bible is not the only authoritative document or text on which advocates might draw. The U.S. Constitution is a central authoritative document in American public discourse. The use of an authoritative document raises the important question of how a community *interprets* its central texts.[13] Another source of impersonal authority is a culture's **traditions.** An advocate might claim that "we should do *x* because that's the way we have always done things around here" and, in so doing, would be using the culture's traditional practices—the way in which the culture always has done things—to warrant his or her claim. When an advocate appeals to his or her community's tradition, in general, we are in the realm of an authoritative warrant. When an advocate appeals to a specific element of that tradition (e.g., America's commitment to "freedom" or "fairness"), the argument slides into the realm of classification. Some scholars believe that this type of argument is a form of the *ad verecundiam* **fallacy.**[14] The idea of appealing to tradition as an authoritative warrant also resembles Perelman and Olbrechts-Tyteca's (1969) discussion of the *locus of the existent* (discussed later).

Brockriede and Ehninger's third category of argument types is *motivational.* They wrote that in this category, "the warrant provides a motive for accepting the claim by associating it with some inner drive, [personal] value, desire, emotion, or aspiration, or with a combination of such forces" (p. 51). Motivational arguments, as noted previously, are a reformulation of the classical concept of **pathos**—the use of emotions and personal motives to warrant belief and/or action. The range of human emotions—including fear (Walton, 1996b), anger, jealousy, envy, pity (or *empathy*), kindness, and guilt—all can function as an argumentative warrant. Human **motives** (including the desire for security, prosperity, health, personal satisfaction—put broadly, a concern for *self-interest*[15]) can function similarly. For example, a medical report released in November 1998 linked smoking with male impotence. Anti-smoking advocates quickly seized this new information and developed appeals urging males in their teens to quit smoking to protect themselves against this problem. Sex tends to be a powerful motive in human affairs.

As Brockriede and Ehninger (1960) noted, emotions and motives most typically appear in support of value and policy claims. With respect to value claims, they explained, "In motivational argument . . . an item is assigned a value in accordance with its usefulness in satisfying human drives, needs, and aspirations" (p. 53). In other words, people tend to evaluate positively things that satisfy their basic needs. An individual's evaluation of something (e.g., a book, a person, a policy) is based (to at least some degree) on how the item to be evaluated makes the individual feel. If a book makes a person happy, then the feeling of happiness can serve as a warrant in an argument that evaluates the book positively. If a friend's behavior makes one feel guilty, then the feeling of guilt can function as a warrant in a negative evaluation of the friend (or at least a negative evaluation of the action that induces the guilt feeling). If a public policy proposal makes one feel afraid (or if an advocate awakens one's fears and connects them to a proposed policy), then the feeling of fear can work as a warrant in an argument that evaluates the policy negatively (opponents of Clinton's health care proposal exploited fear in their appeals, and Clinton got a bit of revenge when he used fear as a way of attacking Republican budget proposals).

Establishing value claims by way of motivational warrants leads directly to the process of policy **deliberation.** A positive or negative evaluation of a policy becomes a reason for supporting or opposing a policy claim. For example, one person likes a reduction in capital gains taxes for reasons of self-interest (the person will make money), whereas another person dislikes the reduction for reasons that might be described as envy (the person does not want "rich people" getting any more breaks [we should note that a concern with the principle of "fairness" also might be at work here]). One person likes a plan for universal health care for reasons of safety and security (the person believes that he or she will be covered in case of any extraordinary health problems), whereas another person dislikes it because he or she is afraid that "big government" intrusion will lessen the quality of health care. All of these evaluations have the potential to become motivational warrants in policy argumentation.

Perelman and Olbrechts-Tyteca's Argument Schemes

The work of the Belgian legal scholar and argument theorist Chaim Perelman and his research associate L. Olbrechts-Tyteca provides important resources for understanding the nuances of argument strategy. Perelman and Olbrechts-Tyteca (1969) maintained that the end of argument practice is *adherence.* In *The New Rhetoric,* they sought to describe "the discursive techniques allowing us *to induce or to increase the mind's adherence to the theses presented for its assent*" (p. 4).[16] Perelman and Olbrechts-Tyteca's classification of "discursive techniques" or argument schemes is not as easy to grasp as are the categories derived from the Toulmin model. Nevertheless, Perelman and Olbrechts-Tyteca described a range of strategies that are extremely helpful in trying to grasp the discursive moves being made in a text or rhetorical interaction. The following are *some* of the more important strategies or argument schemes that they discussed (see also van Eemeren, Grootendorst, & Henkemans, 1996, pp. 105-119; Walton, 1996a; Warnick, 1996; Warnick & Kline, 1992).

Argument by Comparison

One of the most common ways in which people gain insight into any object (whatever that object might be) is to consider it in terms of something else. We find this process at work in *metaphor,* in *parallel case* arguments, and in *analogies* (argumentative and expository). This process also is at work in comparison arguments. If that is the case, then how does a comparison argument differ from parallel case? In Perelman and Olbrechts-Tyteca's typology, argument by comparison is a strategy for measuring the value of something; it does not provide a way of making predictions or urging action, as is the case with parallel case arguments.[17] When we compare things, we engage in a process of evaluation; one thing is judged better than another, one thing is judged as important as something else, and so on. Ronald Reagan borrowed the argument by comparison strategy from Franklin Roosevelt when in 1980 he asked Americans whether they were better off than they were in 1976. By asking Americans to compare their situations, Reagan hoped that people would conclude that they were worse off in 1980 (and, hence, be inclined to vote against the incumbent president). Comparing present conditions to a supposedly better past is a common argument strategy.

Comparison arguments, as the Reagan example suggests, influence policy decisions indirectly. Consider a second example. During a debate in the U.S. Senate on the war with Mexico in February 1847, Ohio Senator Thomas Corwin remarked, "What is the territory, Mr. President, which you propose to wrest from Mexico? It is consecrated to the heart of the Mexican by many a well-fought battle with his old Castilian master. His Bunker Hills and Saratogas and Yorktowns are there." Corwin enhanced the status of Mexican territory by comparing it to "sacred" locations in the United States. Corwin's reevaluation of the Mexican land led into his larger evaluation (the war was wrong) and policy claim (we needed to halt the war with Mexico).

Perelman and Olbrechts-Tyteca (1969) described a number of important variations of the argument by comparison. In certain cases, an advocate might compare what *has* happened (e.g., the fall of communism) to what *might* have happened (e.g., continued totalitarian rule) as a way of evaluating positively a past policy decision (e.g., the Reagan administration's decision to get tough with the Soviet Union). Perelman and Olbrechts-Tyteca referred to this form of comparison as "the loss not sustained" (p. 245). The basic strategy is comparing the "real" consequences of a past act to what would have happened (hypothetical consequences) *if the past act had not been taken* so as to increase the value of the earlier decision. Martin Luther King, Jr., used this line of argument in his famous "Letter From Birmingham Jail" in April 1963 when he praised the emergence of the civil rights movement by comparing what he believed would have happened (bloodshed) to what had happened (progress through direct action campaigns). King wrote, "If this philosophy had not emerged, I am convinced that by now many streets of the South would be flowing with floods of blood." The emergence of King's philosophy was valorized through the comparison of hypothetical consequences (the bloodshed that would have come about) with the real consequences of the philosophy.

Senator William Fulbright used the same structure in a speech in the U.S. Senate in May 1965. Fulbright wanted to encourage Lyndon Johnson's administration to maintain its policy of restraint in the war in Vietnam. To accomplish this objective, Fulbright praised the Kennedy and Johnson administrations for their past policy of restraint and increased the value of this policy by comparing what might have happened in Vietnam without the policy (a large-scale war) to the lesser consequences that had resulted from the policy of restraint. He remarked, "I believe that President Kennedy and President Johnson have been wise in their restraint and patience, that indeed this patience has quite possibly averted a conflict that would be disastrous for both the Communist countries and for the united States and its associates." Increasing the value of restraint and patience through the loss not sustained strategy helped Fulbright to keep up the pressure on the Johnson administration to resist escalating the war.

Another variation on argument by comparison is the *sacrifice argument.* Perelman and Olbrechts-Tyteca (1969) wrote, "In argumentation by sacrifice, the sacrifice is a measure of the value attributed to the thing for which the sacrifice is made" (p. 248). That is, an advocate can enhance the value of something by showing that people are willing to sacrifice for it. King used this strategy in his "Letter From Birmingham Jail" when he enhanced the value of the civil rights cause by noting people's willingness to sacrifice—"their willingness to suffer and their amazing discipline in the midst of the most inhuman provocation"—on its behalf. Richard Nixon employed the argument of sacrifice in his April 1970 speech to the nation announcing military action into Cambodian territory. Toward the end of the speech, Nixon noted that the new policy might hurt his chances for reelection. But he insisted that it did not matter; he was prepared to sacrifice his chances at reelection to do what he believed was right. Nixon's apparent willingness to sacrifice his political future was an attempt to enhance the value of the policy decision.

In some cases, the process can work in reverse; advocates can diminish the value of something by revealing that people *are not* willing to sacrifice for it. For example, a parent might suggest that a child's desire to go to summer camp cannot be very strong given that the child is not willing to sacrifice something for it. We can find this strategy in an essay on drug policy by P. J. O'Rourke in the November 30, 1989, issue of *Rolling Stone:*

> Maybe the drug laws should be changed. But the drug laws aren't immoral laws. . . . They aren't the laws of an unjust system. . . . Drug laws don't cry out for acts of civil disobedience. I've flipped through Thoreau, Gandhi, and Martin Luther King, and I don't notice any of them going to jail or fasting or getting smacked on the head so mankind can do tootski.[18]

O'Rourke demeaned the idea that drug laws are unfair or unjust by pointing out that, unlike other unjust laws, no one is willing to sacrifice anything to oppose these laws.

Finally, there is another important form of comparison *not* discussed by Perelman and Olbrechts-Tyteca. We can describe this form of comparison as a *middle ground* argument. Middle ground arguments increase the value of something (especially policy proposals) by comparing it to extreme possibilities. Positioning a policy proposal in between two extremes—in the middle ground—is a way of trying to enhance its value. In his famous essay, "Of Mr. Booker T. Washington and Others," early 20th-century civil rights activist W. E. B. Du Bois positioned his preferred course of action in between two undesirable extremes (Du Bois, 1903/1989). At one extreme, Du Bois positioned Washington's policy of passive accommodation to "the will of the greater group," and at the other extreme, Du Bois placed the equally undesirable course of "revolt and revenge." In between the extremes of accommodation and revolt, DuBois placed his recommended action—self-realization and self-development. The middle ground strategy would become a staple in civil rights discourse; King employed it frequently, and even radicals such as Malcolm X used the form.

Middle grounds also are common in foreign policy discourse. In May 1965, J. William Fulbright described our options in Vietnam in these terms:

> It is clear to all reasonable Americans that a complete military victory in Vietnam, though theoretically attainable, can in fact be attained only at a cost far exceeding the requirements of our interest and honor. It is equally clear that the unconditional withdrawal of American support from South Vietnam would have disastrous consequences, including but by no means confined to the victory of the Vietcong in South Vietnam. Our policy therefore has been (and should remain) one of determination to end the war at the earliest possible time

> by a negotiated settlement involving major concessions by both sides.

In this passage, Fulbright painted two unacceptable extremes: complete military victory and withdrawal. His policy, which he believed also had been the nation's policy, resided in the middle and became attractive when compared to the extremes. A similar strategy was employed by Sandy Berger, Bill Clinton's assistant for National Security Affairs, in a speech to the National Press Club shortly after Operation "Desert Fox" in December 1998. Berger broached the question of "where do we go from here?" in relation to Iraq and developed his answer by reviewing the "approaches we [the Clinton administration] reject." He continued, "At one end, some have suggested that we have invested too much for too long in Saddam [Hussein] and that the time has come to downgrade the threat and move on." But Berger insisted that this approach was flawed, and he elaborated on why it would not work. Then he returned to the continuum image: "At the other extreme, most people are so fed up with Saddam's unending deception and defiance that they say we should just get rid of him, now, no matter what the cost." This approach, Berger argued, also was seriously flawed. But the two extremes allowed Berger a frame through which to increase the value of the administration's middle ground—an effort to contain Saddam and support internal reform efforts in Iraq.

Middle ground strategies often set in play a *competition for the middle* among advocates. For example, it is relatively easy to read the Vietnam debate in 1965 and 1966 between Lyndon Johnson and his administration and timid critics of the war, such as Fulbright and George McGovern, as a battle over the middle. Each side tried to position its policy as "in the middle."[19]

Scholars, journalists, and political commentators have long recognized the potency of the middle ground argument strategy. As one political pundit noted in a discussion of the death penalty and the 2000 presidential election, the candidate who manages to occupy the middle ground usually wins national elections.

Pragmatic Argument

Perelman and Olbrechts-Tyteca (1969) wrote,

> We call that argument *pragmatic*, which permits the evaluation of an act or an event in terms of its favorable or unfavorable consequences. . . . The pragmatic argument seems to develop without great difficulty, for the transfer of the value of consequences to the cause comes about by itself. (p. 266).[20]

Pragmatic arguments usually are used to support a policy claim. For example, an advocate might claim that "you should do *x*" based on his or her belief that doing *x* will lead to various positive consequences or tangible benefits. Suffrage advocates argued that women should be granted the right to vote because of the positive consequences that would result from the new policy. For example, suffrage advocates claimed that allowing women the vote would, among other things, help to protect "free institutions" from the pernicious "foreign influence" (according to Olympia Brown in 1889) and help to purify an increasingly corrupt political process. Political leaders during the 1980s and 1990s advocated deficit reduction because of the positive consequences—lower interest rates, greater availability of investment capital for business (as opposed to underwriting the federal budget), and so on—that they believed would follow. Opposition to a policy initiative also can proceed along pragmatic grounds; for example, a tax reform organization argues against a tax increase based on the negative consequences—it would slow economic growth, hamper job creation, and so on—that it believes would follow the adoption of the tax increase. Because pragmatic arguments involve speculation about the future (in the form of claims of future fact), they rely on additional patterns of reasoning (e.g., sign, parallel case, causal) to support the predictive component so as to then defend the overall policy claim (see also Bruner, 1983).

Argument by Division (or Disjunctive Syllogism)

This argument pattern also is used primarily in policy advocacy. The divisional argument begins by reducing the available policy options to two choices: We can do either *a* or *b*. One of the options is then rejected. This will commonly involve a separate argument: In rejecting *b*, the advocate can argue pragmatically (e.g., it costs too much, it will take too long to implement). Once the *b* option is eliminated, the advocate is left with the *a* option as the preferred policy. Richard Nixon defended his Vietnam policy in November 1969 by using this pattern. Nixon maintained,

> My fellow Americans, I am sure you can recognize from what I have said that we really only have two choices open to us if we want to end this war. I can order an immediate precipitate withdrawal . . . or we can persist in our search for a just peace through a negotiated settlement.

Nixon rejected the *a* option, "precipitate withdrawal," leaving the *b* option as the preferred policy. The same pattern was at work in James Madison's famous Essay No. 10 of *The Federalist Papers*. In the essay, Madison reasoned, "There are two methods of curing the mischiefs of faction: the one, by removing its causes; the other, by controlling effects." Madison went on to argue that, because it is impossible to remove the causes of faction, republican governments in the new nation would need to control their effects. Advocates employing this line of argument frequently are criticized for inappropriately reducing the available options; more than two choices exist in a large number of policy situations. But divisional or disjunctive reasoning is effective nevertheless; there is a certain attractive parsimony in being able to reduce complex questions to *either/or* propositions.

Perelman and Olbrechts-Tyteca noted that a frequently used—and, some believe, abused (Hitchens, 1996; Orwell, 1968)—variation of the divisional argument: "the lesser of two evils" (Perelman & Olbrechts-Tyteca, 1969, pp. 237-238). In this version of the strategy, both options are presented as undesirable, but one still is worse than the other. We might not like either of our choices—raising taxes or cutting social services—but if these *are* the only options, then we might argue that raising taxes is the "lesser evil." As Hitchens (1996) noted, people repeatedly excuse the behavior of an elected official by reference to a much worse opponent (e.g., "Clinton might be a jerk, but at least he's better than Dole"). In the version that Hitchens discussed, the argument of lesser evils was combined with *comparison* (e.g., Clinton gains in value through the comparison with Dole).

Residue Arguments

This pattern extends and enlarges the divisional form. Instead of narrowing the focus to options of *a* and *b*, residue arguments try to enumerate all of the available options: "We can do *a, b, c,* or *d*. Each option then receives consideration: "The *a* option costs too much, the conservatives won't go for the *b* option, and we don't have sufficient evidence that the *c* option will work." By subverting the *a, b,* and *c* options, the advocate is left with the *d* option as the residue because it is the least flawed of the four options; the advocate can then claim, "The *d* option deserves our support." Residue arguments[21] sometimes have a negative tone; they do not so much provide positive reasons for the *d* option as they provide reasons for *not* selecting the other options.

For example, in his speech to the nation on civil rights in 1963, John F. Kennedy asserted,

> This is not a sectional issue. Difficulties over segregation and discrimination exist in every city, in every state of the union, pro-

> ducing in many cities a rising tide of discontent that threatens the public safety. Nor is this a partisan issue. In a time of domestic crisis, men of goodwill and generosity should be able to unite regardless of party or politics. This is not even a legal or legislative issue alone. It is better to settle these matters in the courts than on the streets, and new laws are needed [at] every level, but law alone cannot make men see right. We are confronted primarily with a moral issue. It is as old as the scriptures, and it is as clear as the American Constitution.

Kennedy employed the residue process to help him **define the situation.** That is, Americans could not allow the issue of civil rights to be viewed as a sectional problem or legal problem. The residue structure helped Kennedy to show the nation that it confronted a moral dilemma.

Residue and middle ground arguments can overlap. They differ in that middle ground arguments identify "extreme" options, whereas residue arguments simply treat other possible policy alternatives. But the difference between an extreme option and a possible alternative will not always be clear. In a 1961 speech on the growth of radical agitation, Martin Luther King, Jr., identified three ways in which oppressed people have responded to their oppression. King identified one common path as acquiescence or surrender. Throughout history, oppressed people often have given in to their oppressors. Another common path has been violent revolt, but King pointed out that this approach usually creates more problems than it solves. King then identified a third option, the path of nonviolent civil disobedience, that he maintained was being employed by the Student Nonviolent Coordinating Committee in its ongoing protests throughout the South. In this speech, was King following the lead of W. E. B. DuBois, noted earlier, by positioning acquiescence and rebellion as extremes against which nonviolent resistance can be positively evaluated? Or, was he identifying, and rejecting, two largely ineffective historical options as a way of building up to his preferred course of action? The speech seems capable of supporting both readings. Critics and analysts need to pay close attention to the way in which rival "options" are depicted so as to classify the strategy, even if that classification remains tentative.

Residue arguments, like a number of other argument forms, often are encountered in a condensed form. For example, if an advocate claims that "we must go to war because we have no other choice," then there is an implicit residue logic at work supporting the claim. The advocate implies, if not directly stating, that all the other options (e.g., negotiation, economic sanctions) have been tried and have failed. Hence, "we have no other choice." George Bush employed a condensed residue argument in his speech to the nation on January 16, 1991, announcing the beginning of military efforts to force Iraq to withdraw from Kuwait. During the speech, Bush insisted that the United States and its allies had "exhausted all reasonable efforts to reach a peaceful resolution" and had "exhausted every means at our disposal to bring this crisis to a peaceful end." Bush did not itemize every step that had been tried and had failed, as would be the case in a developed residue. He condensed the strategy by eliding the specific measures and emphasizing the conclusion: We have no choice; we must resort to military force.

Or, residue reasoning might be *inverted.* Instead of the basic form of not *a,* not *b,* not *c,* therefore *d,* an advocate might try to subvert the *d* option by maintaining, "There's been a lot of talk lately about *d,* but what about *a,* what about *b,* or what about *c*?" In this case, the advocate tries to broaden the range of possibilities by reintroducing previously excluded options, inverting the common residue pattern.

Relation of a Part to the Whole

This strategy, which Perelman and Olbrechts-Tyteca (1969) also described as "reasoning based on inclusion" (p. 232), is very useful in creating the perception of a problem. Put simply, if a part is threatened, then the whole is threatened. King instantiated this line of argument in a compact form in the "Letter From Birmingham Jail": "Injustice anywhere is a threat to justice everywhere." Kennedy used the strategy to warn America about the problem of religious intolerance in speech to a meeting of Baptists during the 1960 presidential campaign. Kennedy told his audience: "For, while this year it may be a Catholic against whom the finger of suspicion is pointed, in other years it has been, and may someday be again, a Jew, or a Quaker, or a Unitarian, or a Baptist." So long as any religion suffers under the weight of intolerance, Kennedy implied, all religions were in danger. Inclusion of a part in the larger whole was common in cold war foreign policy discourse. During the 1961 Berlin Crisis, Kennedy warned America that the threat to Berlin (part) was a threat to world peace and freedom. Lyndon Johnson employed a similar strategy in February 1966 when he reminded the nation of "how inseparably bound together are Americans' freedom and the freedom of her friends around the world." If one is threatened, Johnson insinuated, all are threatened.

Directional Arguments

The directional argument[22] is predicated on some basic assumptions. We assume that complex events occur in stages; that the stages of complex events are causally related (e.g., Stage 2 leads to Stage 3, Stage 3 leads to Stage 4); and that once the process has been started, once the "threshold" has been crossed and the first stage has begun, it is difficult (if not impossible) to stop. Perelman and Olbrechts-Tyteca (1969) wrote,

> The argument of direction, conjuring up the slippery slope or the toe over the threshold, insinuates that there can be no stopping on the way. . . . [It] implies, then, the existence of a series of stages toward a certain—usually dreaded—end and, with it, the difficulty, if not the impossibility, of crying halt once one has started on the road leading to that end. (p. 284)

For example, John Calhoun in February 1837 urged the U.S. Senate to refuse to even receive petitions on the subject of abolition. Calhoun predicted dire consequences if the Senate chose to receive petitions, even if the Senate then rejected them:

> If we concede an inch, concession would follow concession, compromise would follow compromise, until our ranks would be so broken that effectual resistance would be impossible. . . . If we yield, that will be followed by another, and we will thus proceed, step by step, to the final consummation of the object of these petitions.

Directional reasoning was embodied in the famous "domino" *metaphor* in cold war American foreign policy discourse (once the first country in a region falls to communism, the rest will fall like dominoes) and also is present in much anti-drug advocacy (once one starts smoking pot, it will lead to hard drugs and one will end up a strung-out junkie). George Will used the strategy in an August 1997 editorial column urging voters to reject the idea of medicinal marijuana. Will insisted, "There are few if any uses of marijuana that are good medicine. . . . Legalization for 'medicinal' uses is the thin end of an enormous wedge—legalization, and not just of marijuana, for recreational uses."[23] Directional arguments frequently are used by those advocating the social and political status quo in an effort to reject change; the proposed change is positioned as the first stage in the directional downward slide, and once decline has begun, it is impossible to stop. Opponents of directional arguments work to break the presumed causal link between stages.[24]

The dynamics of directional argument are illustrated in the ongoing struggle over gay marriages. Opponents of gay marriage often will claim that if we redefine marriage to allow gay marriages, then we essentially will cross the threshold and begin a process of uncontrollable redefinition. Charles Krauthammer, in an essay in the July 22, 1996, issue of *Time,* raised this objection: "If marriage is redefined to include two men in love, on what possible grounds can it be denied to three men in love?" The persuasive force of Krauthammer's directional or slippery slope strategy proceeds along two trajectories. First, the strategy dovetails into a motivational argument (urging people to reject gay marriages out of their *fear* of what it will entail). Second, the strategy forces proponents of gay marriages to show that such predicted outcomes will not necessarily result from our crossing the definitional threshold.[25] By forcing proponents to explain how allowing gay marriages will not lead to other predicted outcomes, Krauthammer can then try to attack their reasoning. In his essay, Krauthammer claimed that Andrew Sullivan's explanation (in a June 7, 1996, essay in the *New Republic*) of why gay marriages will not lead to polygamy required Sullivan to create a "moral hierarchy among sexual practices that homosexual advocates decry as arbitrary and prejudiced." In other words, Krauthammer used the directional argument not only to play on people's fears but also to expose an inconsistency in the opposition's position.

Arguments of Waste and Sacrifice

Although they are distinct, the waste and sacrifice argument patterns often overlap. Perelman and Olbrechts-Tyteca (1969) suggested as much when they wrote, "The argument of waste consists in saying that, as one has already begun a task and made *sacrifices* which would be wasted if the enterprise were given up, one should continue in the same direction" (p. 279, emphasis added). Like sacrifice, waste is a useful strategy for increasing or decreasing the value of a policy or course of action. If an advocate can show that a course of action will waste something valuable (e.g., lives, money, time), then he or she can decrease the value of the course of action. Consider a simple case: Someone considers dropping out of school, and a friend counsels that person to stick it out because, otherwise, the person will have wasted his or her previous efforts (see also Walton, 1996a). Nixon defended his Vietnam policy by arguing that "precipitate" withdrawal would waste the lives of all those soldiers who had died in the war (opponents tried to turn the tables by arguing that continuing the war would waste even more lives). Harry Truman argued in 1947 that if Congress did not support the people of Greece and Turkey during their time of need, then it would have wasted America's massive "investment in world freedom and peace."

Extend the Range of an Argument

One way in which an advocate can subvert his or her opponent's position is to criticize its "logic." An advocate can accomplish this form of subversion by *extending* the logic of the opponent's argument,[26] maintaining that if the logic underlying the opponent's argument is extended to more instances of the same case or to other cases, then the results will be disastrous.[27] This strategy is illustrated in a Dilbert cartoon strip from April 1995. The pointy-haired boss announces a plan to rank all of the engineers "from best to worst" so as "to get rid of the bottom 10%." Dilbert's co-worker Wally, included in the bottom 10%, responds that the plan is "logically flawed" and proceeds to extend the range of his boss's argument. Wally asserts that the boss's plan, if made permanent, will mean continual dismissals (there will always be a bottom 10%) until there are fewer than 10 engineers and the boss will "have to fire body parts instead of whole people." The boss's logic will, Wally maintains (with a touch of *hyperbole*), lead to "torsos and glands wandering around unable to use keyboards . . ., blood and bile everywhere!" These horrendous results will be the consequence of *extending* the boss's line of argument; hence, the boss's position should be rejected.[28]

Consider a few more practical examples. In his famous 1750 pamphlet, *A Discourse Concerning Unlimited Submission,* Jonathan Mayhew argued against the then common belief that rulers were to be obeyed in all cases. It was widely feared at the time that any loosening of the reigns of government—any belief in the "right" of resistance—would lead to popular unrest.[29] The right of resistance, Mayhew's critics charged, inevitably would be abused and would lead to anarchy. Anticipating this line of attack (the strategy of *prolepsis*), Mayhew responded by extending the logic of his critics: "According to this way of arguing, there will be no true principles in the world, for there are none what may be wrested and perverted to serve bad purposes, either through the weakness or wickedness of men." The following passage is a more recent example from a 1992 American Civil Liberties Union briefing paper on the subject of abortion and the concept of fetal rights: "Acceptance of that [fetal rights] concept in law could bring about government spying and restrictions on a wide range of behavior in the name of 'fetal protection.'" Although the briefing paper noted possible consequences, this factual prediction was carefully qualified ("could"). The potential argumentative force of the passage derived from the idea that if this concept (fetal rights) were adopted, it would entail a logic (things that might fall under the "fetal protection" banner) that would be extended with disastrous consequences.

Next, consider the following excerpt from Charles Madigan's editorial essay on gun control and gun violence in the August 15, 1993, issue of the *Chicago Tribune:*

> Flawed though the logic may be, they [gun advocates] believe their only protection against an armed criminal is a gun. *Carry that argument to the extreme,* and everyone who goes to McDonald's would be armed, along with all plastic surgeons, all small urban children, anyone who might be somewhere an unhinged gun owner with a gripe might show up. (emphasis added)

The italicized portion of the passage pointed to Madigan's effort to extend the range of the pro-gun argument. Madigan's argument was *not* directional ("If we do this, then this and this and this *will* happen"). Instead, the pro-gun position was subverted by extending its logic, carrying the argument to an extreme. The readers were offered a glimpse of a world organized by the pro-gun logic (just as Wally tried to describe the world organized by his boss's logic in the Dilbert cartoon strip described earlier) so that, Madigan seemed to hope, it would be rejected. This line of argument can be ethically suspect because it involves a process of putting words into the mouths of the opposition. The NRA has not (at least not publicly) advocated arming children. But the strategy can be an effective way for advocates to try shifting the burden of justification back on their opposition.

Finally, in an essay on the North Atlantic Treaty Organization (NATO) and the conflict in Kosovo published in the May 10, 1999, issue of *The Nation,* Benjamin Schwarz and Christopher Layne wrote,

> And as NATO's war against Serbia demonstrates, there is no logical stopping point for U.S. commitments in Europe according to the calculus driving America's European strategy. For example, now that Poland, Hungary, and the Czech Republic have been admitted to NATO, instability arising in the regions to the east of the expanded alliance will threaten those states and ultimately Western Europe, or so it will inevitably be argued. . . . Of course, to *follow this logic* means that the ostensible threats to U.S. security will be nearly endless. (emphasis added)

In this passage, Schwarz and Layne reconstructed the logic (or the argument) guiding U.S. policy in Europe: U.S. policy in Europe should be based on maintaining stability; hence, threats to European stability become threats to U.S. interests and security. But Schwarz and Layne wanted to extend this logic to reveal flaws in the policy that it supports. Because it is easy to discover new "threats" to stability, and it will become even easier as NATO continues to expand, the logic of continually responding to perceived threats will lead to never-ending U.S. involvement in European affairs. Schwarz and Layne warned that Kosovo was only the beginning. They used this subversive effort as a springboard into their constructive argument—greater reliance on existing (United Nations) and new international institutions and procedures.

Loci of Quantity, Quality, and the Existent

Perelman and Olbrechts-Tyteca (1969) discussed a number of loci that describe fairly abstract principles used as premises in argument or argument strategies (Cox, 1980; Secor, 1984).[30] Perelman and Olbrechts-Tyteca wrote that *loci* are ways in which "to establish *values* and *hierarchies* or to intensify the adherence they gain" (p. 83, emphasis added); they are, in short, central to the process of evaluation. For example, an advocate who wants to establish the value of a course of action frequently invokes the locus of *quantity;* more is better than less. If the advocate can show that more people will benefit from one course of action, *x*, as opposed to another course of action, *y*, then that becomes a reason for evaluating *x* positively. This is the logic behind appeals to the "general welfare" in policy debates. The advocate assumes that the "general" (what is more) is superior to the "particular" (what is less). Of course, the way in which the "general interest" is **defined** plays a key role in this type of appeal.

The locus of quantity helps to establish the value of an object or a policy preference by way of consideration of more versus less, the greater versus the lesser, long term versus short term, durability versus fragility, general versus particular, or permanence versus ephemerality. The locus of quantity is present when the first term in these pairs is employed as a way of justifying choice and action. For example, one might argue that the Rolling Stones are the greatest rock band because they have been around for a long time and have outlasted every band from their era. This argument relies on the locus of quantity as a warrant to support one's evaluative claim; the Rolling Stones are great because one has assumed that the durable is better than the fragile and that something that lasts a long time is better than something that does not. Supporters of the North American Free Trade Agreement (NAFTA) employed the locus of quantity when they noted how the proposed treaty would benefit America's "long-term interests." Treaty supporters implied that long-term gains were more important than short-term suffering from job flight because the "long term" is quantitatively superior to the "short term." In arguments between pro-economic development and pro-environment advocates over the wisdom of a proposed shopping mall or dam, those favoring economic development often will blend the locus of quantity into their pragmatic arguments that emphasize more jobs and increased tax revenues. According to this reasoning, the greater the economic benefits, the better the proposed policy.

The locus of *quality* frequently is used to combat claims warranted by way of the locus of quantity. The locus of quality attempts to shift the basis of judgment away from factors such as magnitude and durability and onto other, more qualitative considerations. Consider the following excerpt from a December 24, 1997, essay by nationally syndicated columnist Mona Charen:

> The overall crime rate is dropping. And while that is reassuring news, it does not quiet the concern that the nation is in the grip of a serious moral meltdown. For while the absolute number of crimes is down, the nature of crimes committed, particularly by the very young, continues to shock and dismay.

Charen's strategy? When an appeal to quantity (the number of crimes) does not support one's position (existence of a moral meltdown), switch to the locus of quality (the nature of the crimes committed).

Something fragile is not inherently more or less valuable than something durable. The different loci point us toward *standards* of evaluation. The locus of quality helps us to perceive the fragile as valuable and in need of protection. A piece of fine china can be construed as valuable partly because of its fragility.[31] Some specific aspects, or sub-loci, of the locus of quality discussed by Perelman and Olbrechts-Tyteca include the *unique,* the *irreparable,* and the *precarious.* These loci are widely used in environmental discourse. As Zagacki (1999) observed, "In one fashion or another, all these qualitative loci have long been at the core of environmental rhetoric" (p. 420). For example, an appeal to protect a certain species because "extinction is forever" relies on an implicit sense of the irreparable, on the idea that we must take protective action now because we never will be able to undo the consequences of *not* acting. An argument that we need to protect tropical rainforests because they are "the *sole source* of life-saving medicines" blends the pragmatic with the locus of uniqueness. An appeal that warns that "we are in a breakneck race against time" and that "time is running out" emphasizes the precariousness of the situation, as do appeals that describe the "fragile" or "endangered" state of the environment.[32]

Appeals based on the locus of quality were also common in early American public discourse. William Lloyd Garrison used the locus of the irreparable in an effort to rouse his audience against the evil "monster" of slavery:

> It is often said that the evil of slavery is beyond our control. . . . [But] if we cannot conquer the monster in its infancy, while his cartilages are tender and his limbs powerless, how shall we escape his wrath when he goes forth a gigantic cannibal, seeking whom he may devour?

If we do not act *now,* Garrison warned at the time, then we would not be able to act down the road; the fragility and irreparability of the present was combined with an implicit sense of *waste* (do not waste the opportunity one has been given). This pattern persists into the present. In an April 1998 speech on social security, Bill Clinton urged the nation to "act now with changes that will be far simpler and easier than if we wait until the problem is closer at hand." Like Garrison, Clinton presented the present moment as promising but irreparable; hence, it should not be wasted.

Although the locus of the *existent* received only one paragraph in *The New Rhetoric* (Perelman & Olbrechts-Tyteca, 1969), it merits the attention of argument scholars. This locus exploits the relationship between what exists and what might exist.[33] It directs attention to the existing state of affairs and discourages reflection on what might be. The locus of the existent is a component of what Hariman (1995) referred to as the *realistic style.* It maintains that realism, and not any abstract idealistic standards, must be the locus of decision. For example, in an 1837 speech in the U.S. Senate, Henry Clay discussed the issue of slavery in America:

> If the question [of slavery] were an original question . . ., [then] few, if any, of the citizens of the United States would be found to favor [its] introduction. . . . But that is not the question. The slaves are here. . . . In human affairs, we are often constrained, by the force of circumstances and the *actual state of things,* to do what we would not do if the state of things did not exist. The slaves are here, and here must remain, in some condition. (emphasis added)

What was the basic thrust of Clay's position? Essentially, that no one in America would want slavery introduced into the nation if that decision could be made at the time when Clay spoke. But that was not the question that the nation faced. The issue was not "Do we want slavery to be introduced?" but rather "What do we do about the *existing* institution of slavery?" Clay insinuated that we must adjust our ideals (what we would do if slavery were an "open" question) in light of "the actual state of things." In other words, we must orient our thinking around what currently *exists* and refrain from making decisions based on what might be. In constraining **judgment** by way of the actual state of things, Clay weaved the locus of the existent into his defense of the status quo.

Abraham Lincoln was a great admirer of Clay. In his address at Cooper Union in February 1860, Lincoln echoed Clay in the way in which he used the locus of the existent to justify the Republican party's stance on slavery (prevent expansion into the territories, but leave it alone in the South).[34] In concluding the first section of the speech, Lincoln argued that slavery must be "tolerated and protected [in the South] only because of and so far as its actual presence among us makes that toleration and protection a necessity." Like Clay, Lincoln used the existing state of affairs—slavery's "actual presence among us"—as the locus of decision. Toward the end of the speech, he reiterated this logic when he maintained that Republicans should leave slavery alone where it is "due to the necessity arising from its actual presence in the nation." The nation must accept slavery, at least for the time being, and must adjust its ideals because of its "actual presence" (or its existence).

Here are a few more recent examples. Richard Nixon employed the locus of the existent strategy in his first major speech as president on the war in Vietnam. In May 1969, Nixon stated,

> In weighing alternate courses, we have to recognize that the situation as it exists today is far different from what it was 2 years ago, or 4 years ago, or 10 years ago. One difference is that we no longer have the choice of not intervening. We've crossed that bridge. . . . We can have honest debate about whether we should have entered the war in Vietnam. We can have honest debate about how the war has been conducted. But the urgent question today is what to do now that we are there.

Like Clay and Lincoln, Nixon urged his audience members to orient their thinking to what exists. We were in the war, that was the actual state of things, and now we had to adjust our thinking accordingly. Even if everyone in the nation were to agree that entering the war was a mistake (just as Clay implied that introducing slavery was a mistake), it would not make any difference on the **deliberative** question of what policy we should pursue. Mistake or not, we had "crossed that bridge" and now had to deal with what existed. Like Clay, Nixon employed the locus of the existent to (a) exclude what might be ideal or possible as grounds for making policy decisions and (b) establish the existing state of affairs—more precisely, Nixon's **definition of the situation**—as the proper grounds for judgment.

Finally, we can find the locus of the existent at work in a recent defense of affirmative action programs. An editorial in the *Seattle Post-Intelligencer* on February 22, 1998, maintained,

> Proponents of I-200 [a state initiative that would eliminate affirmative action programs] would present this as a simple case of right and wrong. And were we starting from scratch, assembling a society and an economic structure from the beginning, they would be right. . . . Sadly, the task is not to build a new structure but to repair the flaws in an existing one.

The pattern should be clear. Like Clay, the editorial writers distinguished between "starting from scratch" (Clay's "original question") and responding to the problems of the "existing" situation. And like Clay, they insisted that we must not confuse these questions. They granted that the issue would be "a simple case of right and wrong" if we were "assembling a society and an economic structure from the beginning." But like Clay, Lincoln, and Nixon before them, these editorial writers rejected the ideal or abstract and grounded their pro-affirmative action **judgment** in their understanding of the existing reality.

Developments in Argumentation Theory

The discussion in the entry so far has focused on identifying, explaining, and illustrating a number of common argument forms or patterns. Although the project of explicating the various forms and strategies of argument is critical to argument theory, it does not exhaust the study of argumentation. The realm of argument scholarship and the interests of argument scholars extends beyond the development of argument typologies. The remainder of this entry sketches some key areas in contemporary argumentation theory.[35]

There are a number of relatively distinct programs or traditions in contemporary argumentation scholarship. Some of the more important ones include the Dutch *pragma-dialectical* orientation to argumentation studies (van Eemeren & Grootendorst, 1984, 1992), the still developing tradition of *informal logic* (for early works in this tradition, see Johnson & Blair, 1977; Kahane, 1971; and Thomas, 1973; for more recent works, see Govier, 1985; Hansen, 1990; and Walton, 1989), *social interaction* and *constructivist* approaches (Jackson & Jacobs, 1980; Jacobs & Jackson, 1982, 1989; van Eemeren, Grootendorst, Jackson, & Jacobs, 1993; Willard, 1978, 1983, 1989), and a more inchoate approach that uses the tradition of practical philosophy (especially rhetoric) as a basis for the analysis and criticism of argument (Farrell, 1977; Goodnight, 1982; McKerrow, 1977; Tindale, 1999). Although they are divergent in many respects, the various strands of contemporary argument scholarship address some similar issues and/or questions such as *definition* (What is the object of study?), *reconstruction* (What is the structure of argument?), and *evaluation* (How do scholars and critics evaluate the quality of argumentative practice?). Each issue or question merits some additional attention.

O'Keefe's (1977) essay, "Two Concepts of Argument" (see also Brockriede, 1975; O'Keefe, 1982), helped to inaugurate sustained discussion, especially within the community of American argument scholars, of the following definitional question: What is it that argument scholars study? O'Keefe (1982) sought to distinguish "between two different sorts of things . . . which are . . . referred to by the word 'argument' " (p. 4). He suggested that argument scholars separate the production of a discrete, linguistic, reasoning-giving artifact (referred to as an "argument$_1$") and the activity of exchanging utterances during some type of interpersonal dispute (referred to as an "argument$_2$"). Individuals *produce* an argument$_1$, whereas at least two people are necessary to *engage* in an argument$_2$. Interpreting O'Keefe's distinction as suggesting a product/process dichotomy (an interpretation that O'Keefe [1982] found problematic), Wenzel (1980) identified another sense of argument as procedure in his description of three perspectives or ways of conceptualizing argument: logical, rhetorical, and dialectical.[36]

Scholars who focus on O'Keefe's first sense of argument tend to focus on reconstructing the form of individual argument units as well as the configuration of argument units in a written or oral **text.** A fairly large number of rhetorical scholars share this emphasis with informal logicians. In rhetorical studies, the Toulmin model has enjoyed wide (but not uncontested) popularity, Perelman and Olbrechts-Tyteca's typology has attracted some attention, and the classical concept of the **enthymeme** still retains a following as alternative ways of reconstructing an argument^1. Informal logicians have found Toulmin and Perelman and Olbrechts-Tyteca less helpful in the process of argument reconstruction (van Eemeren et al., 1996, p. 172) and have, consequently, developed alternative methods for reconstructing arguments$_1$. Van Eemeren and colleagues (1996) maintained that the approaches developed by the informal logicians continue "to isolate individual assertions and their relationships in a way that mirrors the practice of logicians tracing deductive entailments" (p. 175). Adherents to the Toulmin model and the enthymeme, as well as many of the informal logicians, continue to depict the form of arguments$_1$ as essentially deductive and syllogistic.

Scholars who, on the other hand, privilege O'Keefe's second sense of argument devote little attention to the form of individual argument units. Pragma-dialecticians and those influenced by the social interaction and constructivist traditions try to reconstruct the structure of interactions through which groups negotiate differences and resolve disputes or disagreements. For Willard (1989), reconstructing argumentative interactions involves, among other things, understanding the dynamics of *adjacency pairs* (defined as "coupled speech acts" [p. 46]), locating *encounter rules* that organize particular types of interaction or specific social spaces (p. 49; cf. Frentz & Farrell, 1976), and describing cognitive *organizing schemes* that provide "typifications . . . such as normal ways to run a meeting or discussion or recipes for behavior in public places . . . and habitual routines for accomplishing regular tasks" (p. 59). Approaching the reconstructive project from a somewhat different perspective, van Eemeren and colleagues (1993) developed a four-stage model that identifies the central phases involved in the process of dispute resolution—confrontation stage, opening stage, argumentation stage, and concluding stage—as well as the common speech act types found in each stage (pp. 25-34).

Whether the focus is on arguments$_1$ or arguments$_2$, argument scholars inevitably confront the challenge of evaluation—how to distinguish superior argumentative practice from inferior argumentative practice. Virtually all contemporary argument scholars agree on one thing: The principles of formal **logic** or the ideals of scientific rationality (complete objectivity, disinterestedness, etc.) cannot and should not be applied unadulterated to the process of evaluating arguments in the real world. But as Cox (1990) noted, the "rejection of formalism" calls into question "the normative dimension of argumentation theory" (p. 2). One pervasive concern in contemporary argumentation theory is to rebuild the grounds for evaluating arguments. But no single approach to the project of argument evaluation has achieved disciplinary hegemony. A few of the more important contemporary approaches to argument evaluation include **fallacy** theory; reliance on the evaluative standards of the **argument field** to which an argument$_1$ or an argument$_2$ belongs; the informal logicians' norms of relevance, sufficiency, and acceptability (van Eemeren et al., 1996); Fisher's (1978, 1980) "logic of good reasons" (consisting of five key questions that can be put to any argument: fact, relevance, consequence, consistency, and transcendent issue); McKerrow's (1977) effort to develop a definition of "rhetorical validity as *pragmatic justification*" (p. 134) that entails principles for the analysis of arguments (see also McKerrow, 1990); and the pragma-dialectical norms—the "Ten Commandments"—of a critical discussion (van Eemeren & Grootendorst, 1992). The quest for definitive normative standards for argument evaluation most likely will remain elusive (on the topic of argument evaluation, see also the essays collected in Schiappa, 1995).

These last few paragraphs only sketch some of the key concerns in contemporary argumentation theory. Readers interested in tracing these and other theoretical issues should consult the numerous journals devoted to argument studies, including *Argument and Advocacy, Argumentation,* and *Informal Logic,* as well as the proceedings of the ten Speech Communication Association/American Forensic Association argument conferences and the four International Society for the Study of Argumentation international argument conferences.

Notes

1. For examples of how Toulmin's model has been evaluated and appropriated by rhetoric, argument, and composition scholars, see Fulkerson (1996); Hart (1973); Kneupper (1978); Manicas (1966); van Eemeren, Grootendorst, and Henkemans (1996); and Willard (1976). Also of interest is Murphy's (1994) extension of Toulmin into the realm of religious discourse.

2. Factual claims also can escape notice because of the language used to express them. See the discussion of **rhetorical question.**

3. See also Windes and Hastings (1965, pp. 160-161).

4. Although warrants always are limited to the case at hand (context or field dependent), the general principles and reasoning patterns that warrants embody can be applied to other cases.

5. The Grimké example illustrates the ambiguous nature of sign argument. Early in the speech, Grimké used northern opposition to abolitionism as a sign that the spirit of slavery had infected the North. But then she shifted and used the "disturbance" outside the hall as "evidence" that abolitionist tactics "are the best that could have been adopted." The same phenomenon—the protesters outside the hall—functioned as a sign of (a) the slave spirit and (b) the effectiveness of abolitionism. The best contemporary illustration of the ambiguity of sign reasoning might be discourse about race relations. Countless bits of information are used as signs to demonstrate either (a) that racial discrimination still exists and continues to be a problem or (b) that America has made great strides to eliminate the problem of racial discrimination. Of course, these two propositions are not mutually exclusive.

6. On the value of combining generalization and example, see Inch and Warnick (1998).

7. For more nuanced discussions of rhetorical examples, see Benoit (1980), Consigny (1976), and Hauser (1968).

8. See Walton (1996a) for a discussion of the *nonargumentative* functions of examples.

9. Perelman and Olbrechts-Tyteca (1969) discussed this type of argument.

10. Note that in the last two examples, a form of causal argument has been intertwined with the parallel cases: It is implied that the gun control laws and legal intoxication limits have a causal impact on violence and drunk driving cases.

11. For more detailed discussions, see Gross (1983), Measell (1985), and Sacksteder (1974).

12. See also Hample (1977) and Trent (1968).

13. On this issue, see the entry for **hermeneutics and rhetoric** as well as the concept of hermeneutic disputes discussed in the entry for **situation, rhetorical.**

14. For a recent discussion of the literature, see Bachman (1995).

15. A classic example of a motivational appeal to self-interest can be found in Booker T. Washington's "Atlanta Exposition Address" in 1895. In that address, Washington solicited economic cooperation from the white South, but his argument was based on an appeal to self-interest: Whites should work with Washington and support his efforts at racial development not because doing so was right or just but rather because they would benefit economically from doing so.

16. For a more detailed treatment of the concept of adherence in Perelman and Olbrechts-Tyteca (1969), see Goodwin (1995).

17. Perelman and Olbrechts-Tyteca (1969) discussed *arguments of reciprocity* that "show that . . . situations are similar" so as to urge that "the same treatment" be given to each (p. 221).

18. King himself briefly addressed the illegitimacy of using civil disobedience to agitate for drug law changes in his October 1966 essay on nonviolence published in *Ebony.*

19. On the search for the middle in Vietnam discourse, see also Bostdorff (1994, pp. 56-91) and Depoe (1988).

20. Pragmatic arguments parallel Weaver's (1953) sense of "argument from consequences."

21. These sometimes are referred to as *expeditio.* See Lanham (1991).

22. Directional arguments often are discussed as the slippery slope **fallacy** in argument and logic texts.

23. Like the domino, the image of a "wedge" is a common indication of directional reasoning.

24. Perelman and Olbrechts-Tyteca (1969, pp. 284-286) discussed ways of responding to directional arguments.

25. For examples of responses to Krauthammer's line of critique, see Stephen Chapman's essay in the January 25, 1996, issue of the *Chicago Tribune* and Andrew Sullivan's essay in the June 7, 1996, issue of the *New Republic.*

26. Many scholars treat this argument strategy as a form of the **fallacy** *reductio ad absurdum.*

27. This strategy resembles the directional argument, but there is a difference. In the directional argument, the focus is on a series of events in the world—the "falling dominoes"—and not on any reasoning process. In extending the range, the focus is on the reasoning employed, with the actual results of applying the reasoning made secondary. Part of the force of extending the consequences strategy depends on its close affiliation with the pragmatic argument scheme.

28. Dilbert creator Scott Adams likes to employ this comic logic. In a recent strip (July 16, 2000), the pointy-haired boss tells Dilbert that his philosophy is, "If it isn't hard, it isn't worth doing," to which Dilbert responds, "That's easy to say. So according to your philosophy, you shouldn't have said it." Dilbert continues, "And it's easy to walk around. Maybe you should hop on one foot." The final panel of the strip reveals the boss hopping around on one foot.

29. This is a form of *directional* argument.

30. Kienpointer (1987) also noted that the *loci* merit attention as argument schemes.

31. On the use of "fragility" in American foreign policy discourse, see Ivie (1987).

32. See Cox (1982) for a discussion of some of the uses and the ontological foundation of the locus of the irreparable.

33. Weaver's (1953) discussion of the "argument from circumstance," an "argument [that] merely reads the circumstances—the 'facts standing around'—and accepts them as coercive or allows them to dictate the decision" (p. 57), covered similar ground.

34. This reading of Lincoln differs from Weaver's (1953) emphasis on definition and principle in Lincoln's rhetoric (pp. 85-114).

35. For more detailed examinations of the state of contemporary argument scholarship, see Cox and Willard (1982); Gilbert (1997); and van Eemeren, Grootendorst, and Henkemans (1996), on which this discussion is largely based.

36. Billig (1996) denied that these two senses of argument are necessarily antithetical. He wrote, "Protagoras's maxim [the *dissoi logoi* which maintained that there are two sides to every controversial issue or question] suggests that these two meanings of argument, the individual and the social meanings, are inherently connected. . . . Any individual argument [O'Keefe's first sense] is actually, or potentially, a part of a social argument" (p. 74).

References and Additional Reading

Alden, R. M. (1904). *The art of debate.* New York: Henry Holt.

Anderson, R. L., & Mortensen, C. D. (1967). Logic and marketplace argument. *Quarterly Journal of Speech, 53,* 143-151.

Bachman, J. (1995). Appeal to authority. In H. V. Hansen & R. C. Pinto (Eds.), *Fallacies: Classical and contemporary readings.* University Park: Pennsylvania State University Press.

Baker, G. P., & Huntington, H. B. (1905). *The principles of argumentation* (rev. ed.). Boston: Ginn.

Benoit, W. L. (1980). Aristotle's example: The rhetorical induction. *Quarterly Journal of Speech, 66,* 182-192.

Billig, M. (1996). *Arguing and thinking: A rhetorical approach to social psychology* (2nd ed.). Cambridge, UK: Cambridge University Press.

Bostdorff, D. M. (1994). *The presidency and the rhetoric of foreign crisis.* Charleston: University of South Carolina Press.

Brinton, A. (1986). Ethotic argument. *History of Philosophy Quarterly, 3,* 245-257.

Brinton, A. (1987). Ethotetic [sic] argument: Some uses. In F. H. van Eemeren, R. Grootendorst, J. A. Blair, & C. A. Willard (Eds.), *Argumentation: Perspectives and approaches.* Dordrecht, Netherlands: Foris Publications.

Brockriede, W. (1975). Where is argument? *Journal of the American Forensic Association, 13,* 129-132.

Brockriede, W., & Ehninger, D. (1960). Toulmin on argument: An interpretation and application. *Quarterly Journal of Speech, 46,* 44-53.

Bruner, M. S. (1983). Argument from a pragmatic perspective. *Journal of the American Forensic Association, 20,* 90-97.

Consigny, S. (1976). The rhetorical example. *Southern Speech Communication Journal, 41,* 121-132.

Cox, J. R. (1980). "Loci communes" and Thoreau's arguments for wilderness in "Walking" (1851). *Southern Speech Communication Journal, 46,* 1-16.

Cox, J. R. (1982). The die is cast: Topical and ontological dimensions of the *locus* of the irreparable. *Quarterly Journal of Speech, 68,* 227-239.

Cox, J. R. (1990). Introduction: Argumentation theory as critical practice. In D. C. Williams & M. D. Hazen (Eds.), *Argumentation theory and the rhetoric of assent.* Tuscaloosa: University of Alabama Press.

Cox, J. R., & Willard, C. A. (1982). Introduction: The field of argumentation. In J. R. Cox & C. A. Willard (Eds.), *Advances in argumentation theory and research.* Carbondale: Southern Illinois University Press.

Depoe, S. (1988). Arthur Schlesinger, Jr.'s "middle" way out of Vietnam: The limits of "technocratic realism" as the basis for foreign policy dissent. *Western Journal of Speech Communication, 52,* 147-166.

Du Bois, W. E. B. (1929). Of Mr. Booker T. Washington and others. In W. E. B. DuBois, *The souls of black folk.* New York: Viking. (Original work published 1903)

Farrell, T. B. (1977). Validity and rationality: The rhetorical constituents of argumentative form. *Journal of the American Forensic Association, 13,* 142-149.

Fisher, W. R. (1978). Toward a logic of good reasons. *Quarterly Journal of Speech, 64,* 376-384.

Fisher, W. R. (1980). Rationality and the logic of good reasons. *Philosophy and Rhetoric, 13,* 121-130.

Frentz, T. S., & Farrell, T. B. (1976). Language-action: A paradigm for communication. *Quarterly Journal of Speech, 62,* 333-349.

Fulkerson, R. (1996). The Toulmin model of argument and the teaching of composition. In B. Emmel, P. Resch, & D. Tenney (Eds.), *Argument revisited, argument redefined: Negotiating meaning in the composition classroom.* Thousand Oaks, CA: Sage.

Gilbert, M. A. (1997). *Coalescent argumentation.* Mahwah, NJ: Lawrence Erlbaum.

Goodnight, G. T. (1982). The personal, technical, and public spheres of argument: A speculative inquiry into the art of public deliberation. *Journal of the American Forensic Association, 18,* 214-227.

Goodwin, J. (1995). Perelman, adhering, and conviction. *Philosophy and Rhetoric, 28,* 215-233.

Govier, T. (1985). *A practical study of argument.* Belmont, CA: Wadsworth.

Gross, A. G. (1983). Analogy and intersubjectivity: Political oratory, scholarly argument, and scientific reports. *Quarterly Journal of Speech, 69,* 37-46.

Hample, D. (1977). The Toulmin model and the syllogism. *Journal of the American Forensic Association, 14,* 1-9.

Hansen, H. V. (1990). An informal logic bibliography. *Informal Logic, 12,* 155-184.

Hariman, R. (1995). *Political style: The artistry of power.* Chicago: University of Chicago Press.

Hart, R. P. (1973). On applying Toulmin: The analysis of practical discourse. In G. P. Mohrmann, C. J. Stewart, & D. J. Ochs (Eds.), *Explorations in rhetorical criticism.* University Park: Pennsylvania State University Press.

Hauser, G. A. (1968). The example in Aristotle's rhetoric: Bifurcation or contradiction. *Philosophy and Rhetoric, 1,* 78-90.

Hayworth, D., & Capel, R. B. (1934). *Oral argument.* New York: Harper.

Hitchens, C. (1996, Fall). Against lesser evilism. *Dissent,* pp. 111-116.

Inch, E. S., & Warnick, B. (1998). *Critical thinking and communication: The use of reason in argument* (3rd ed.). Boston: Allyn & Bacon.

Ivie, R. L. (1987). The ideology of freedom's "fragility" in American foreign policy argument. *Journal of the American Forensic Association, 24,* 27-36.

Jackson, S., & Jacobs, S. (1980). Structure of conversational argument: Pragmatic bases for the enthymeme. *Quarterly Journal of Speech, 66,* 251-265.

Jacobs, S., & Jackson, S. (1982). Conversational argument: A discourse analytic approach. In J. R. Cox & C. A. Willard (Eds.), *Advances in argumentation theory and research.* Carbondale: Southern Illinois University Press.

Jacobs, S., & Jackson, S. (1989). Building model of conversational argument. In B. Dervin, L. Grossberg, B. J. O'Keefe, & E. Wartella (Eds.), *Rethinking communication.* Newbury Park, CA: Sage.

Johnson, R. H., & Blair, J. A. (1977). *Logical self-defense.* New York: McGraw-Hill.

Kahane, H. (1971). *Logic and contemporary rhetoric: The use of reason in everyday life.* Belmont, CA: Wadsworth.

Kienpointer, M. (1987). Towards a typology of argumentative schemes. In F. H. van Eemeren, R. Grootendorst, J. A. Blair, & C. A. Willard (Eds.), *Argumentation: Across the lines of discipline.* Dordrecht, Netherlands: Foris Publications.

Kneupper, C. W. (1978). Teaching argument: An introduction to the Toulmin model. *College Composition and Communication, 29,* 237-241.

Lanham, R. A. (1991). *A handlist of rhetorical terms* (2nd ed.). Berkeley: University of California Press.

Lanham, R. A. (1993). *The electronic word: Democracy, technology, and the arts.* Chicago: University of Chicago Press.

Manicas, P. T. (1966). On Toulmin's contribution to logic and argumentation. *Journal of the American Forensic Association, 3,* 83-94.

McKerrow, R. E. (1977). Rhetorical validity: An analysis of three perspectives on the justification of rhetorical argument. *Journal of the American Forensic Association, 13,* 133-141.

McKerrow, R. E. (1990). The centrality of justification: Principles of warranted assertability. In D. C. Williams & M. D. Hazen (Eds.), *Argumentation theory and the rhetoric of assent.* Tuscaloosa: University of Alabama Press.

Measell, J. S. (1985). Perelman on analogy. *Journal of the American Forensic Association, 22,* 65-71.

Moore, M. (1996). *Downsize this!* New York: Crown.

Murphy, N. C. (1994). *Reasoning and rhetoric in religion.* Valley Forge, PA: Trinity Press International.

O'Keefe, D. J. (1977). Two concepts of argument. *Journal of the American Forensic Association, 13,* 121-128.

O'Keefe, D. J. (1982). The concepts of argument and arguing. In J. R. Cox & C. A. Willard (Eds.), *Advances in argumentation theory and research.* Carbondale: Southern Illinois University Press.

O'Neill, J. M. (1921). *A manual of debate and discussion.* New York: Century.

Orwell, G. (1968). Through a glass, rosily. In S. Orwell & I. Angus (Eds.), *The collected essays, journalism, and letters of George Orwell* (Vol. 4). New York: Harcourt Brace.

Perelman, C. (1982). *The realm of rhetoric* (W. Kluback, Trans.). Notre Dame, IN: University of Notre Dame Press.

Perelman, C., & Olbrechts-Tyteca, L. (1969). *The new rhetoric: A treatise on argumentation* (J. Wilkinson & P. Weaver, Trans.). Notre Dame, IN: University of Notre Dame Press.

Pocock, J. G. A. (1971). *Politics, language, and time: Essays on political thought and history.* New York: Atheneum.

Rodgers, K. (1992). Childhood sexual abuse: Perceptions of tolling the statute of limitations. *Journal of Contemporary Health Law and Policy, 8,* 309-335.

Rybacki, K. C., & Rybacki, D. J. (1991). *Advocacy and opposition: An introduction to argumentation* (2nd ed.). Englewood Cliffs, NJ: Prentice Hall.

Sacksteder, W. (1974). The logic of analogy. *Philosophy and Rhetoric, 7,* 234-252.

Schiappa, E. (Ed.). (1995). *Warranting assent: Case studies in argument evaluation.* Albany: State University of New York Press.

Secor, M. J. (1984). Perelman's loci in literary argument. *PreText, 5,* 97-110.

Shurter, R. L., & Helm, G. D. (1939). *Argument.* New York: Farrar & Rinehart.

Sillars, M. O., & Ganer, P. (1982). Values and beliefs: A systematic basis for argumentation. In J. R. Cox & C. A. Willard (Eds.), *Advances in argumentation theory and research.* Carbondale: Southern Illinois University Press.

Simmons, J. R. (1960). The nature of argumentation. *Speech Monographs, 27,* 348-350.

Thomas, S. (1973). *Practical reasoning in natural language.* Englewood Cliffs, NJ: Prentice Hall.

Tindale, C. W. (1999). *Acts of arguing: A rhetorical model of argument.* Albany: State University of New York Press.

Toulmin, S. E. (1958). *The uses of argument.* Cambridge, UK: Cambridge University Press.

Toulmin, S. E., Rieke, R., & Janik, A. (1984). *An introduction to reasoning* (2nd ed.). New York: Macmillan.

Trent, J. D. (1968). Toulmin's model of argument: An examination and extension. *Quarterly Journal of Speech, 54,* 252-259.

van Eemeren, F. H., & Grootendorst, R. (1984). *Speech acts in argumentative discussions: A theoretical model for the analysis of discussions directed towards solving conflicts of opinion.* Dordrecht, Netherlands: Foris Publications.

van Eemeren, F. H., & Grootendorst, R. (1992). *Argumentation, communication, and fallacies: A pragma-dialectical perspective.* Hillsdale, NJ: Lawrence Erlbaum.

van Eemeren, F. H., Grootendorst, R., & Henkemans, F. S. (1996). *Fundamentals of argumentation theory: A handbook of historical backgrounds and contemporary developments.* Mahwah, NJ: Lawrence Erlbaum.

van Eemeren, F. H., Grootendorst, R., Jackson, S., & Jacobs, S. (1993). *Reconstructing argumentative discourse.* Tuscaloosa: University of Alabama Press.

Wagner, R. H. (1936). *Handbook of argumentation.* New York: Thomas Nelson.

Walton, D. N. (1989). *Informal logic: A handbook for critical argumentation.* Cambridge, UK: Cambridge University Press.

Walton, D. N. (1996a). *Argumentation schemes for presumptive reasoning.* Mahwah, NJ: Lawrence Erlbaum.

Walton, D. N. (1996b). Practical reasoning and the structure of fear appeal arguments. *Philosophy and Rhetoric, 29,* 301-313.

Walton, D. (1997). *Appeal to expert opinion: Arguments from authority.* University Park: Pennsylvania State University Press.

Warnick, B. (1996). Argument schemes and the construction of social reality: John F. Kennedy's address to the Houston ministerial association. *Communication Quarterly, 44,* 183-196.

Warnick, B., & Kline, S. L. (1992). The "new rhetoric's" argument schemes: A rhetorical view of practical reasoning. *Argumentation and Advocacy, 29,* 1-15.

Weaver, R. (1953). *The ethics of rhetoric.* South Bend, IN: Regnery/Gateway.

Wenzel, J. W. (1980). Perspectives on argument. In J. Rhodes & S. E. Newell (Eds.), *Dimensions of argument: Proceedings of the Summer Conference on Argumentation.* Annandale, VA: Speech Communication Association.

Willard, C. A. (1976). On the utility of descriptive diagrams for the analysis and criticism of arguments. *Communication Monographs, 64,* 308-319.

Willard, C. A. (1978). A reformulation of the concept of argument: The constructivist/interactionist foundations of a sociology of argument. *Journal of the American Forensic Association, 14,* 121-140.

Willard, C. A. (1983). *Argumentation and the social grounds of knowledge.* Tuscaloosa: University of Alabama Press.

Willard, C. A. (1989). *A theory of argumentation.* Tuscaloosa: University of Alabama Press.

Windes, R. R., & Hastings, A. (1965). *Argumentation and advocacy.* New York: Random House.

Zagacki, K. (1999). Spatial and temporal images in the biodiversity dispute. *Quarterly Journal of Speech, 85,* 417-435.

ARGUMENT FIELD

In August 1998, Bill Clinton ordered missile attacks against purported Islamic extremist and terrorist Osama bin Laden in retaliation for the bombings of U.S. embassies in Kenya and Tanzania. The Clinton administration claimed that it had proof that bin Laden was the mastermind responsible for the African bombings that killed 224 people. Discussions of the attacks in the media raised a number of issues. One issue had to do with the proof of bin Laden's culpability. Critics suggested that the administration should have submitted its information to the International Court of Justice (or World Court) in The Hague, Netherlands, so that bin Laden could be arrested and tried in a court of law. While pointing to the defects in such a course,[1] supporters of the attacks conceded that the proof of bin Laden's guilt might not have been sufficient to satisfy the standards of international law. But supporters quickly noted that the lack of legal proof did not mean that the Clinton administration was acting blindly; rather, Clinton's defenders relied on an idea that has become familiar to students of argument: Acceptable standards of proof vary from forum to forum or from **argument field** to argument field. Proof that might be satisfactory in the context of administrative deliberations about how to protect national security might not be satisfactory in the context of a court of law. One central point that emerged from this episode is that critics and advocates need to look at the standards or requirements of a particular forum or field when evaluating or criticizing an argument.

The *metaphorical* concept of an argument field was introduced by Stephen Toulmin (1958) in his important book, *The Uses of Argument.* In a discussion of what happens "when we are assessing the merits of . . . different arguments," Toulmin found it "convenient to introduce a technical term," the idea of "a *field* of arguments" (p. 14). As van Eemeren, Grootendorst, and Henkemans (1996) explained,

> [Toulmin's] concept of fields of argument . . . encouraged recognition that the soundness of arguments was not universal and certain but [rather] field-specific and contingent. This belief was another step in undermining the [logical or] analytic ideal and resituating argument within the rhetorical tradition. Instead of asking whether an argument was sound, the questions became "Sound for whom?" and "Sound in what context?" (p. 204)

Toulmin's concept of argument fields would become a key issue in argument scholarship. Dudczak (1989) observed,

> Over fifty papers on argument fields have been presented at the five previous Summer Conferences on Argumentation. Two special issues of the *Journal of the American Forensic Association* have been devoted to the subject in addition to other manuscripts published in its volumes. When combined with the books, convention papers, book chapters, and other manuscripts addressing argument fields, it is clear [that] argumentation fields constitute one of the central interests of argumentation theory. (p. 286)

A central feature of Toulmin's (1958) conception of different fields of argument is a distinction between qualities that are "field invariant" and those that are "field dependent" (p. 15). Reviewing the development of Toulmin's thinking about argument fields, Rowland (1982) maintained that "the force of arguments, their formal structure as revealed by Toulmin's model, and the stages through which arguments develop are invariant." These features can be located in *any* argument, no matter the forum or field in which it might be found. But Rowland continued, "The data and backing, the logical type of the claim and data, and the evaluative criteria appropriate to an argument are field dependent" (p. 229). These features of an argument or the process of argument evaluation vary from field to field. The concept of argument fields, along with the distinction between field-invariant and field-dependent factors, helped to dislodge a "one size fits all" form of argument analysis and criticism. Toulmin directed attention to the particularities of practices in different contexts or fields.

Rowland (1982) asserted, "Despite the importance of the invariance-dependence distinction," in *The Uses of Argument,* Toulmin "does not clearly define the field notion" (p. 229). Recapitulating what has become a lament in argument scholarship, van Eemeren and colleagues remarked, "The idea of argument fields is notoriously vague" (p. 204). Argument scholars have simply been unable to agree on the specific characteristics or defining features of fields of argument. As Rowland and others noted, in later works Toulmin would describe argument fields as "rational enterprises" that were roughly equivalent to academic disciplines. Toward the end of *Human Understanding,* Toulmin (1972) noted his desire to explore "how our disciplinary model might be applied in more detail to rational enterprises outside the sphere of natural science" (p. 364). But as Zarefsky (1982) pointed out, "This approach may well recreate the same error which Toulmin finds in formal logic: selection of an inappropriate paradigm for general argumentation" (p. 196).

Zarefsky's (1982) analysis of the "disciplinary model" is part of a detailed exposition of the more common ways in which argument scholars have tried to specify the nature of argument fields. The disciplinary model of argument fields uses *subject matter* as the defining criterion for determining the nature of argument fields. Zarefsky wrote, "The assumption is that arguments dealing with the same subject are alike in important ways—origins, structural features, validity standards, etc.—and that they differ on those same dimensions from arguments on a different subject" (p. 195). Subject matter, in turn, is one of five different approaches to defining argument fields that Zarefsky identified. Some scholars, such as Toulmin (1958) in *The Uses of Argument,* employ *form* as a defining criterion. As Zarefsky (1982) explained, "If one holds, as Toulmin seemed to in *Uses,* that fields are groups of arguments in which data and conclusions are of the same logical type, it would follow that formal differences would distinguish among fields" (pp. 194-195).[2] A third approach to defining argument fields focuses on **situational** features. Zarefsky suggested, "This approach would seem most useful for researchers investigating arguing as a process, who would be interested in probing the circumstances under which argumentative interactions occur" (p. 196). Zarefsky concluded that there is "a strong tendency" among many argument scholars "to regard 'field' as synonymous with 'situation,' "[3] but this approach has difficulty in "explicat[ing] the ways in which fields differ" (p. 203). Another approach maintains that fields are determined by *purpose.* Zarefsky wrote, "Two arguers are in the same field if they share a common purpose, and—probably because of the shared purpose—the arguments they produce will differ in important ways from arguments which derive from a different purpose" (p. 197). So, the pursuit of justice demarcates the realm of legal argument, whereas the pursuit of knowledge identifies the field of academic argument. But Zarefsky pointed out that not only can "arguers have multiple purposes," they "do not always *know* their purposes" (pp. 197-198), making purpose a suspect criterion for defining fields. A final approach features **audience** as the defining feature of argument fields. Zarefsky stated, "On this view, fields would be distinguished according to the composition of the appropriate audience to evaluate claims" (p. 198). Perelman and Olbrechts-Tyteca's (1969) distinction between *universal* and particular audiences and Goodnight's (1982) tripartite account of personal, technical, and **public spheres** of argument reflect this view.[4] But Zarefsky cautioned that "such immense differences may be found among arguments addressed" to the same audience "as to compel the conclusion that the common audience is an incidental rather than essential feature of the argumentation." He continued, "Moreover, in genuine controversies, often multiple audiences are addressed simultaneously," rendering audience a problematic defining characteristic (p. 198).

Variations among approaches to defining argument fields are based in part, Zarefsky (1982) contended, on "the work which scholars expect the 'field' concept to do" (p. 200). We need to distinguish between *purpose* as a way of defining argument fields and the *purpose* of argument fields as an analytic concept. It appears that there are two broad purposes animating the literature on argument fields. One purpose, consistent with Toulmin's initial introduction of the concept, is *normative.* Starting with Toulmin, scholars became attracted to the field concept because, in Zarefsky's words, "it offers a standard for evaluating arguments." But the specific value of argument fields as a normative concept is its capacity to occupy the *middle ground* between "the absolutism of formal logic and the implications of vicious relativism" (p. 193).

Argument fields offer the hope of defensible localized standards or criteria for judging arguments. An alternative way of conceptualizing the analytic purpose of argument fields focuses on its *descriptive* potential. The concept is useful because it allows scholars to "characterize . . . situations or occasions for arguing" (p. 192) and also provides a basis for "explor[ing] similarities and differences in the arguments which [social] actors produce or . . . identify[ing] recurrent patterns of reasoning by induction from actual arguments" (p. 193). Neither of these two descriptive purposes spills over into the practice of normative evaluation.

Given the variations in analytic purpose and definitional criteria, argument field has remained a somewhat amorphous concept. To combat this situation, some scholars (e.g., Willard, 1982, 1983) advocate greater analytic precision so as to develop different levels or "senses" of the field concept.[5] Willard (1983) began with "two broad rubrics" (p. 169): *disciplinary fields* (which "aim toward improvement—toward expanding and making more precise their knowledge") and *ordinary* or quotidian argument fields (which "are defined by the situated psychological activities of arguers rather than by clearly hewed-to veridical standards" (p. 153). Although both disciplinary and ordinary fields impose *constraints* on those who enter (p. 149), ordinary fields appear to provide social actors with a greater capacity to alter or modify existing roles, practices, or standards than do disciplinary fields. But Willard added that each of the broad rubrics "consist[s] of at least four different senses of 'field,' namely, encounter fields, relational fields, issue fields, and normative fields" (p. 169). *Encounter fields* consist of "the definitions of situation, coorientations, and issue assumptions brought to bear by arguers in a single encounter" (p. 169).[6] Encounter fields are governed by "conventional etiquette" as well as agreements negotiated on the spot (p. 169).[7] *Relational fields* involve "actors united in longer term relationships" where "special conceptual ecologies and background assumptions" have developed over time (p. 170). Willard suggested that there often is an ongoing **dialectic** between the encounter and relational fields. Using legal trials as an exemplary case of relational fields, Willard remarked,

> The relations among legal actors in any particular trial may thus reflect a dialectic between their interaction histories [the relational field] and their definitions of situation in the particular case [the encounter field]. We may take this dialectic to be paradigmatic of the relational bonds undergirding all fields—disciplinary and ordinary alike. (p. 170)

Issue fields, according to Willard, are

> substantive domains . . ., disciplinary issue fields . . ., schools of thought, paradigms, or theoretical orientations. . . . By "ordinary" issue field, I most basically mean the sides a person takes on social and political issues and the interpersonal bonds one builds by virtue of his [sic] positions on issues. (p. 171)

The sense of a disciplinary issue field leads one to expect that particle physicists will argue one way, whereas literary deconstructionists will argue another way. In the realm of ordinary issue fields, we should expect members of Earth First! to argue in similar ways that are different from the ways in which members of the Council on Foreign Relations argue. *Normative fields* are, Willard acknowledged, a "troublesome concept" because "it might turn out that they often collapse into issue fields." But Willard nevertheless attempted to distinguish these last two senses of argument fields. He maintained, "The substance of someone's argument [usually] is drawn from the school of thought [or issue field] deemed relevant to the subject at hand." But in certain cases, "speakers [draw on] . . . broad allegiances which cross issue field boundaries." According to Willard, "The intuitive idea is that, while the issue field—one's school of thought—is a source of *meaning,* a normative field is often a source of general value." "Secular humanism" and the "liberal arts" are examples of what Willard meant by a normative field. He concluded, "Normative fields are general social and professional orientations which affect people's estimation of appropriate behavior" (p. 172).

Delineation of the different senses of argument field proposed by Willard only scratches the surface of his larger theory of argument and argument fields. One of the important conclusions that Willard drew from his preliminary inquiry into argument fields had to do with the nature of *inter*field disputes. Argument scholars "may learn much about fields and their epistemologies," Willard (1983) wrote, by "considering how fields deal with one another" (p. 267). He insisted, "The problem of interfield communication constitutes the core concern of epistemics because it forces consideration of how different substantive domains borrow one another's concepts yet retain differences in the things taken as knowledge" (p. 237). The analytic task, as Willard appeared to conceptualize it, is to explicate the principles that are instantiated in interfield disputes (pp. 268-278) without being tempted to try settling the dispute. The challenges posed by interfield argument have been a principal concern in Willard's subsequent work (e.g., Willard, 1989, 1996).

Interest in the concept of argument fields peaked during the early to mid-1980s. Explicit theoretical and analytic discussion declined during the 1990s, although scholars continued to examine the argumentative practices of various "fields" (e.g., the "law," "medicine," "science").[8] The decline in explicit interest might be attributable to a shift in theoretical paradigms; scholars trained when Toulmin was a cutting-edge thinker speak of fields, whereas those trained during the past decade probably read Foucault and write about **discursive formations.**[9] But the decline in explicit attention also might indicate that argument fields (e.g., related ideas such as the **rhetorical situation**) have become ingrained in the disciplinary consciousness. Whether it is the object of explicit theorizing, the implicit organizing framework of a critical case study, or a taken-for-granted element of the discipline's conceptual ecology, the concept of argument field remains an important topic in contemporary rhetorical studies.

Notes

1. For example, the International Court of Justice has no police force to execute its order.
2. See Willard (1981) for a detailed critique of the "logical type" approach to defining argument fields.
3. Willard (1982) remarked, "We have two different but interrelated projects, using situations to understand fields and using fields to understand situations" (p. 49).
4. See also Willard (1983, pp. 221-222).
5. Wenzel (1982) moved in a similar direction by distinguishing among a *field* ("conceptual and propositional contents of knowledge structures"), a *forum* ("particular disciplinary, professional, and institutional practices [that] . . . organize ways of conducting inquiry"), and a *context* (aspects of the "general environment" that provide a setting for argument).
6. On the idea of "encounter" settings as a force shaping communicative action, see also Frentz and Farrell (1976).
7. Willard (1983) wrote, "We should not be surprised to find arguers explicitly negotiating judgmental standards for purposes of 'getting on with the argument' " (p. 169).
8. See the discussions under the entries for **forensic discourse** and **inquiry, rhetoric of.**
9. Gaonkar's (1982) essay on Foucault anticipated this development.

References and Additional Reading

Benoit, W. L., & Lindsey, J. J. (1987). Argument fields and forms of argument in natural language. In F. H. van Eemeren, R. Grootendorst, J. A. Blair, & C. A. Willard (Eds.), *Argumentation: Perspectives and approaches.* Dordrecht, Netherlands: Foris Publications.

Dudczak, C. A. (1989). Categorizing argument fields: All fields are not created equal. In B. E. Gronbeck (Ed.), *Spheres of argument: Proceedings of the Sixth SCA/AFA Conference on Argumentation.* Annandale, VA: Speech Communication Association.

Frentz, T. S., & Farrell, T. B. (1976). Language-action: A paradigm for communication. *Quarterly Journal of Speech, 62,* 333-349.

Gaonkar, D. P. (1982). Foucault on discourse: Methods and temptations. *Journal of the American Forensic Association, 18,* 246-257.

Goodnight, G. T. (1982). The personal, technical, and public spheres of argument: A speculative inquiry into the art of public deliberation. *Journal of the American Forensic Association, 18,* 214-227.

Newell, S. E. (1984). A socio-pragmatic perspective of argument fields. *Western Journal of Speech Communication, 48,* 247-261.

Perelman, C., & Olbrechts-Tyteca, L. (1969). *The new rhetoric: A treatise on argumentation* (J. Wilkinson & P. Weaver, Trans.). Notre Dame, IN: University of Notre Dame Press.

Prosise, T. O., Mills, J. P., & Miller, G. R. (1996). Fields as arenas of practical discursive struggle: Argument fields and Pierre Bourdieu's theory of social practice. *Argument and Advocacy, 32,* 111-128.

Rowland, R. C. (1982). The influence of purpose on fields of argument. *Journal of the American Forensic Association, 18,* 228-245.

Toulmin, S. E. (1958). *The uses of argument.* Cambridge, UK: Cambridge University Press.

Toulmin, S. (1972). *Human understanding: The collective use and evolution of concepts.* Princeton, NJ: Princeton University Press.

van Eemeren, F. H., Grootendorst, R., & Henkemans, F. S. (1996). *Fundamentals of argumentation theory: A handbook of historical backgrounds and contemporary developments.* Mahwah, NJ: Lawrence Erlbaum.

Wenzel, J. W. (1982). On fields of argument as propositional systems. *Journal of the American Forensic Association, 18,* 204-213.

Willard, C. A. (1981). Argument fields and theories of logical types. *Journal of the American Forensic Association, 17,* 129-145.

Willard, C. A. (1982). Argument fields. In J. R. Cox & C. A. Willard (Eds.), *Advances in argumentation theory and research.* Carbondale: Southern Illinois University Press.

Willard, C. A. (1983). *Argumentation and the social grounds of knowledge.* Tuscaloosa: University of Alabama Press.

Willard, C. A. (1989). *A theory of argumentation.* Tuscaloosa: University of Alabama Press.

Willard, C. A. (1996). *Liberalism and the problem of knowledge: A new rhetoric for modern democracy.* Chicago: University of Chicago Press.

Zarefsky, D. (1982). Persistent questions in the theory of argument fields. *Journal of the American Forensic Association, 18,* 191-203.

ARRANGEMENT

Arrangement (or *dispositio*) is one of the five traditional **canons** or subdivisions of classical rhetorical training.

According to rhetoric and composition scholar Frank D'Angelo, arrangement "is that part of rhetoric concerned with the organization of a discourse" (D'Angelo, 1974, p. 396; see also Winterowd, 1971). Uncovering and describing the structure or economy of discourse is, D'Angelo (1975) asserted, a principal concern of rhetorical scholars. Among other activities, rhetorical scholarship "attempts to discover and to describe grammatical and conceptual patterns in discourse" (p. 18). But progress in this area beyond the vague "an essay has roughly a beginning, a middle, and an end" (D'Angelo, 1974, p. 396) has been meager. D'Angelo (1974) noted, "Despite the countless number of composition and rhetoric texts dealing with arrangement, we know very little about order in composition" and in discourse generally (p. 388).[1]

Classical rhetorical education taught its students the "parts" of an oration. But classical scholars did not always agree on the number of parts that should be taught. In the *Rhetoric,* Aristotle (1954) maintained that "the only necessary parts of a speech are the statement and the argument. These are the essential features of a speech, and it cannot in any case have more than introduction, statement, argument, and epilogue" (1414b7-1414b9). The Roman rhetorician Cicero identified six basic parts: *exordium* (the introduction), *narrative* (a basic **exposition** of events), *partition* (an assessment of the points in dispute and an indication of "the matters which we intend to discuss" [Cicero, 1949, p. 63]), *confirmation* (affirmative proof for the advocate's position), *refutation* (subversion of the antagonistic position), and *peroration* (the conclusion). The same six-part division appears in *Rhetorica ad Herennium* (Anonymous, 1954) and in Quintilian's (1963) *Institutio Oratoria.* During the middle of the 20th century, Burke (1950) summarized the classical position as "rhetorical form in the large" involving the following:

> a progression of steps that begins with an exordium designed to secure the goodwill of one's audience, next states one's own position, then points up the nature of the dispute, then builds up one's own case at length, then refutes the claims of the adversary, and in a final peroration expands and reinforces all points in one's favor while seeking to discredit whatever had favored the adversary. (p. 69)[2]

Few (if any) speeches, essays, or other linguistic compositions today follow the six-part classical dispositional pattern. That does not mean that the classical pattern is irrelevant to contemporary discourse or to discussions of arrangement. Many of its elements have been modified and incorporated as prescriptions or directives in basic composition and public speaking textbooks (e.g., build goodwill in one's introduction, provide one's audience with a preview of the speech). And we can locate some of the classical parts of a speech in specific cases of advocacy. Examples include a newspaper editorial beginning with a partition that identifies the points of dispute in a controversy over where to locate a sewage treatment plant, a student supplying a teacher with a narrative account of recent events in an effort to get an extension on an assignment, and a Supreme Court justice preparing a dissenting opinion that includes a section attacking the reasoning of his or her majority colleagues. Even though its popularity as a method for organizing discourse has all but disappeared, the classical model for arranging a speech still can provide useful information to speakers, writers, and critics alike.

Contemporary rhetorical scholarship on the issue of arrangement usually is suspended between a pedagogical desire to provide instruction that can guide effective performance and a critical-analytic desire to reconstruct and assess the patterns and structures that shape discursive practice. Virtually all basic composition and public speaking textbooks will identify a variety of patterns or structures that can be used to organize an entire discursive performance. Such patterns include *problem-solution* and its variations (these include Monroe's motivated sequence of attention, need, satisfaction, visualization, and action; the John Dewey-inspired pattern of reflective thinking that begins with locating and defining a problem and then moves through the steps of describing and narrowing the problem, suggesting possible solutions, evaluating the solutions, and recommending the strongest solution; and the **stock topics of policy discourse** pattern of *ill, blame, cure,* and *consequences*); *chronology, process,* and **narrative** (events are arranged in a temporal sequence and, in narrative, shaped into a "story" organized around a *plot*); *climactic* or *hierarchical* (elements are arranged from least important to most important); and *topical* (a series of usually linked "points" or "topics"). In addition to these common *main* patterns, textbooks also identify *subsidiary* patterns (those that more typically structure portions of a text rather than the text as a whole) such as *spatial* (mainly used as a way of organizing descriptions) and *elimination* (an elaborate form of *residue* **argument** most often used in the evaluative stage of a reflective structure).

Scholars such as Winterowd (1968) emphasize the interdependence of the processes of **invention** and arrangement. According to Winterowd, "Invention and arrangement are so nearly the same that they are almost indistinguishable; they are basically the same process" (p. 121). D'Angelo (1975) extended this position when he argued that common inventional **topoi** such as "classification, enumeration, exemplification, cause and effect, comparison, contrast, and the like may be considered as formal patterns of arrangement for organizing discourse on almost any level of structure [i.e., sentence, paragraph, section, or entire text]" (p. 57). In other words, decisions about how to develop material (e.g., comparison) entail certain formal structures (e.g., parallelism). McCroskey (1997) reaffirmed the growing consensus when he wrote, "To separate invention and disposition is satisfactory for purposes of description, but it is next to impossible to separate these two mental operations in practice. . . . They are inextricably interwoven" (p. 215).

Just as every text has **style,** every text also has structure (D'Angelo, 1975). Critics focus on describing the economy (or the structure) of a text and its component parts (e.g., paragraphs, sections). But the process of description is complicated by a number of factors. First, as several have noted (e.g., Hart, 1997), few "real-life" messages—speeches, essays, and so on—exhibit the standard patterns collected and taught in basic speech or composition textbooks (pp. 111, 116). Using Richard Nixon's 1952 "Checkers" speech as an illustration, Hart suggested that most instances of public discourse display an amalgam or blend of different structural patterns. Second, patterns of arrangement often exist as a type of subcutaneous "deep structure" in a message. For example, Elizabeth Cady Stanton's speech, "The Solitude of Self," appeared to be a rather disjointed collection of observations concerning its central theme—human solitude.[3] Yet, careful examination reveals a set of structural coordinates. Stanton's reflections on solitude were organized in relation to the span of a human life: We proceed from birth ("we come into this world alone"), through "youth," adolescence ("the girl of sixteen"), and adulthood ("the young wife and mother," "the uneducated woman"), ending "in age, when the pleasures of youth are passed." Stanton's structure was by no means a simple instance of chronological arrangement, but the lack of simplicity does not mean that the speech was formless. As Leff's (1983, 1988) readings of Lincoln's oratory demonstrate, chronological patterns can be varied in complex ways. Critical reconstruction must follow the movement within the text carefully to describe the structure or arrangement pattern. Third, some texts manifest what can best be described as "nonlogical patterns of arrangement." D'Angelo (1975) identified seven such "patterns"—fantasy, hallucination, dream, reverie, vision, trance, and meditation—that develop through specific devices such as free association and stream of consciousness (pp. 58-59).[4] Although they are "difficult to deal with" (p. 59), D'Angelo nevertheless held out the hope that they might be more thoroughly described (on the idea of nonlogical patterns, see also Stevens, 1973).

As the preceding paragraph suggests, describing structure is a complicated and challenging process. What advice or suggestions do practicing critics and theorists provide? We can begin with relatively simple suggestions and then move to those that are more conceptually challenging (illustrating one common structural pattern along the way). Andrews, Leff, and Terrill (1998) suggested that it is "probably best for the critic to organize this phase of analysis by reconstructing a detailed outline of the speech" or text (p. 71). The outline tries to identify the key elements in the text (the main points and the key subpoints). The processes of producing the outline help the critic to identify the relationships among the elements and the patterns in the text. The outline might help the critic to locate a dominant pattern such as problem-solution or a subordinate pattern such as repetition (a text structured topically might repeat the same pattern of development in its discussion of each topic). Andrews and colleagues reminded critics that "the speaker may not *present* the speech in such a way that the pattern is immediately apparent" (p. 72). But a good outline should help the critic to reconstruct the pattern or patterns structuring the message.

Hart (1997) provided a rather thorough discussion of structural analysis. He identified four "probes" (p. 111) that can assist the critic in trying to grasp the structure of a text and assess its potential effects on audiences and/or readers. The first probe focuses on message *design.* Design, in Hart's perspective, refers to the overall pattern or structure that informs the text. The critic's task is to reconstruct this pattern. The second probe focuses on message *emphasis.* Emphasis directs the critic's attention to the way in which the parts of the message function. Is there one dominant pattern that organizes the entire text, or are different patterns combined?[5] How is the reader or listener directed from one section of the text to another?[6] How is the text or message apportioned?[7] How do the parts of the message interact?[8] Hart's third probe into message structure focuses on the idea of *density.* To analyze the density of a text, the critic must uncover the structures or patterns that organize smaller units such as the paragraph. In investigating density, the critic might draw on the literature in composition studies on the "rhetoric of the paragraph" that attempt to uncover recurrent patterns in paragraph construction.[9] One pattern frequently discussed (e.g., Williams, 1990) is the movement from old information to new information. Paragraph structure often reflects a larger objective of rhetorical discourse—trying to use what an audience currently knows and believes to forge a consensus on a controversial issue. We could see a large-scale version of this pattern in Ronald Reagan's 1983 "Star Wars" speech to the National Association of Evangelicals convention. Reagan began the speech by noting the various points on which he and his audience members agreed—their opposition to abortion, support for school prayer, and so on. Reagan's reaffirmation of the old served as a springboard for his discussion of the new and the controversial—the movement for a nuclear weapons freeze. Reagan provided refutative arguments in the latter portion of the speech defending his anti-freeze stand. But the structural pattern of "issues we agree upon—issues that are in dispute" reinforced Reagan's *instrumental* objective. Finally, Hart's fourth probe into message structure emphasizes the idea of *pacing.* An analysis of message pacing might focus on locating interruptions and/or digressions in the message, and other small-scale patterns such as repetition, that disrupt the flow of the text so as to assess their impact on the message's force. Or, it might focus on the size of paragraphs so as to assess how size relates to the relative "speed" with which one moves through the text.

Hart provided some useful directives to help the rhetorical critic describe and analyze text or message structure. More advanced critics might consider drawing on other literatures interested in exploring the shape of prose discourse. Larson (1987) argued, "The most conspicuous and influential developments in the theoretical study of structure in non-literary prose have come . . . in the work of psycholinguists and students of cognitive psychology" (p. 42). This literature explores the relationship between the arrangement or structure of message elements and "readers' comprehension and response" (p. 45). One specific branch of this scholarship is referred to as "text linguistics" (de Beaugrande & Dressler, 1981), and it is worth noting that scholars such as de Beaugrande and Dressler (1981) recognized the link between their project and the traditions of rhetorical inquiry (p. 15). Text linguistics, as they conceived it, explores how texts embody seven central "standards of textuality": cohesion, coherence, intentionality, acceptability, informativity, situationality, and intertextuality (p. 11). Its ultimate goal is to identify models of topical progression that describe the way in which messages develop or the way in which segments or parts of a message relate to each other. Another potentially useful scholarly source for analyzing message structure is the literature focusing on textual *cohesion* and *coherence* (Fahnestock, 1983; Halliday & Hasan, 1976). Larson (1987) remarked, "If attention to any element of structure in non-narrative . . . prose has burgeoned in scholarly inquiry recently, it is attention to the concepts of coherence and cohesion" (p. 66). This line of inquiry poses the following general questions. Why do some texts and/or paragraphs strike readers or listeners as more organized (or more coherent) than others? What features of the text or message contribute to coherence and cohesion? The literature on coherence and cohesion discusses a variety of patterns (e.g., forms of repetition, conjunction, reference) that help to structure a text or hold it together, making it more comprehensible for others.

The concept of coherence opens up additional *interpretive* possibilities for rhetorical criticism. Small-scale patterns of repetition, such as John F. Kennedy's use of *anaphora* in his "Inaugural Address," can be explained in terms of their contribution to the coherence of the discourse. Kennedy's anaphora might lack external significance (it does not appear to address specific generic or situational *exigences* of *constraints*), but it nevertheless has a rhetorical function that can be explicated: It helps to unify and mark off specific segments of the speech as discrete sections (one focusing on the various audiences Kennedy is addressing, the other focusing on the Soviet Union). Both literatures—text linguistics and other variants of psycholinguistics as well as the cohesion and coherence investigations—speak to important and recurrent issues regarding the organization, arrangement, and structure of texts. As such, they may have something to contribute to the critic's effort to comprehend discursive structure.

Notes

1. Writing roughly 10 years later, Larson (1987) appeared to affirm D'Angelo's general claim.
2. On the classical model of an oration, see also Corbett (1971) and Vickers (1988, pp. 67-72).
3. Campbell (1980) argued that speech exhibits a "lyric structure" that is "associative and develops through enumeration" of the central theme (p. 305).
4. See also Lanham's (1983) discussion of the "running style."
5. A problem-solution structure might feature a chronological pattern in the section of the message devoted to describing the problem and explaining how it came into existence. Or, a text might employ chronology within chronology as in Franklin Roosevelt's "War Message" in 1941, where one chronological structure—his enumeration of Japanese attacks—was embedded within a larger past-present-future structure.
6. For example, what *transitional materials* are employed? This question leads into the more complicated issue of *cohesion* and *coherence* to be discussed shortly.
7. For example, are the various sections given equal attention or emphasis, or do one or two of the sections stand out?
8. Do all of the parts support the same end, or are there internal tensions among the parts or sections of the message?
9. Early classic essays in this tradition of research include those of Becker (1965) and Christensen (1965).

References and Additional Reading

Andrews, J. R., Leff, M. C., & Terrill, R. (1998). *Reading rhetorical texts: An introduction to criticism.* Boston: Houghton Mifflin.

Anonymous. (1954). *Rhetorica ad herennium* (H. Caplan, Trans.). London: Heinemann.

Aristotle. (1954). *Rhetoric* (W. R. Roberts, Trans.). New York: Modern Library.

Becker, A. (1965). A tagmemic approach to paragraph analysis. *College Composition and Communication, 16,* 237-242.

Burke, K. (1950). *A rhetoric of motives.* New York: Prentice Hall.

Campbell, K. K. (1980). Stanton's "The Solitude of Self": A rationale for feminism. *Quarterly Journal of Speech, 66,* 304-312.

Christensen, F. (1965). A generative rhetoric of the paragraph. *College Composition and Communication, 16,* 144-156.

Cicero. (1949). *De inventione* (H. M. Hubbell, Trans.). Cambridge, MA: Harvard University Press.

Corbett, E. P. J. (1971). *Classical rhetoric for the modern student* (2nd ed.). New York: Oxford University Press.

D'Angelo, F. J. (1974). A generative rhetoric of the essay. *College Composition and Communication, 25,* 388-396.

D'Angelo, F. J. (1975). *A conceptual theory of rhetoric.* Cambridge, UK: Winthrop.

de Beaugrande, R., & Dressler, W. (1981). *Introduction to text linguistics.* London: Longman.

Fahnestock, J. (1983). Semantic and lexical coherence. *College Composition and Communication, 34,* 400-416.

Halliday, M. A. K., & Hasan, R. (1976). *Cohesion in English.* London: Longman.

Hart, R. P. (1997). *Modern rhetorical criticism* (2nd ed.). Boston: Allyn & Bacon.

Hovland, C. I., Janis, I., & Kelley, H. H. (1957). *The order of presentation in persuasion.* New Haven, CT: Yale University Press.

Lanham, R. A. (1983). *Analyzing prose.* New York: Scribner.

Larson, R. L. (1987). Structure and form in non-narrative prose. In G. Tate (Ed.), *Teaching composition: Twelve bibliographical essays* (rev. ed.). Fort Worth: Texas Christian University Press.

Leff, M. C. (1983). *Rhetorical timing in Lincoln's "House Divided" speech.* Van Zelst lecture, Northwestern University.

Leff, M. (1988). Dimensions of temporality in Lincoln's second inaugural. *Communication Reports, 1,* 26-31.

McCroskey, J. C. (1997). *An introduction to rhetorical communication* (7th ed.). Boston: Allyn & Bacon.

Quintilian. (1963). *Institutio oratoria* (H. E. Butler, Trans.). London: Heinemann.

Stevens, W. (1973). A proposal for non-linear disposition. *Western Speech, 37,* 118-128.
Vickers, B. (1988). *In defense of rhetoric.* Oxford, UK: Clarendon.
Williams, J. M. (1990). *Style: Toward clarity and grace.* Chicago: University of Chicago Press.
Winterowd, W. R. (1968). *Rhetoric: A synthesis.* New York: Holt, Rinehart & Winston.
Winterowd, W. R. (1971). Dispositio: The concept of form in discourse. *College Composition and Communication, 22,* 39-45.

ARTICULATION

The concept of **articulation** has grown in prominence during recent years in cultural, social, and political theory (Grossberg, 1992, pp. 52-61; Hall, 1982, 1986; Laclau & Mouffe, 1985, pp. 105-114; Slack, 1996) and is slowly entering into the conceptual vocabulary of rhetorical studies (Cox, 1994; DeLuca, 1999; Greene, 1998; Jasinski, 1997).[1] Although the concept has a range of meanings in cultural studies theory and analysis, the sense of the term most pertinent to rhetorical scholars holds articulation to be the way in which discourse is used to make connections, establish associations, or build links between different things—different events, different social movements, different ideas, different people, and so on. The type of connection that is made through articulation is different from the connections established through *analogy* or *parallel case* **argument.** Unlike the various forms of argument that support inferences based on similarities and/or dissimilarities, articulations (and the reverse process, disarticulations) shape and reshape our understanding of reality by establishing connections or severing established connections.

Consider the possible relationships between the civil rights movement and the gay rights movement in America. A gay rights advocate might support a *policy claim* such as "we should allow gays to serve in the military" by comparing similar cases (racial integration of the armed forces during the late 1940s with the proposed sexual orientation integration). But an advocate engaged in the process of articulation tries to reshape how we understand different events, people, or movements. In discursive articulation, the cases are not simply parallel or similar to each other; they are fused, combined, and connected. The struggle for gay rights is not simply *like* the struggle for civil rights; it is part of the same struggle. When two ideas become articulated, advocates go beyond pointing out similarities; they establish overt connections.[2]

Articulations occur routinely within a political culture as warranting principles that are successful in one context are articulated to new circumstances. Another example can be found in Rosen's (1993) essay on the subject of gun control. In her essay, Rosen supported gun control by articulating it, on the one hand, to international disarmament (the title of the essay is "Domestic Disarmament") and, on the other, to public health. Like a growing number of activists, Rosen wanted to reorient the debate over firearms. If successful, Rosen's articulations would allow us to look at the issue of gun control in new ways. Gun violence, she and other advocates have asserted, has become a "health" issue, and gun control is not just a public policy option; it is literally a medical "cure." Disarmament no longer is an issue of international relations and foreign policy. Through Rosen's articulation, it enters into the way in which we conceptualize our domestic social relations.

Articulation is a complex process that involves various discursive resources (e.g., argument strategies, figurative resources). It is useful to distinguish two common forms of discursive articulation.

Diachronic Articulation

This process involves forging relationships between things separated by time. Most commonly, elements of the past are connected with elements of the present. American feminists during the 19th century articulated the principles of the Declaration of Independence to their movement for women's rights through the appropriation of the language and form of the 1776 document (Watson, 1997). Similarly, 19th-century abolitionists maintained that they were continuing the struggle begun by the colonists in 1776. During the 20th century, we found pro-life advocates arguing that they were continuing the struggle for civil rights that flourished during the 1960s. This tendency to establish connections between things separated in time helps to explain why arguments over the meaning of the past (what frequently is referred to as *public* **memory**) are so important. Through the process of diachronic articulation, the past constitutes a crucial resource for rhetorical advocacy.

Synchronic Articulation

This process involves establishing connections between different things existing in the present. When Martin Luther King, Jr., was asked how his opposition to the war in Vietnam related to his work on behalf of civil rights, he responded by, in effect, articulating or connecting the two movements. They were not similar struggles, King insisted; they were the *same* struggle.[3] Progressive politicians during the mid-1990s, reacting to attacks on social programs launched by conservatives as well as many moderates, began a campaign to end a range of federal programs that they referred to as "corporate welfare." As a Common Cause solicitation letter explained,

> And what "corporate welfare" boils down to is nothing more than a vast government handout of *our* tax dollars to big business and wealthy special interests. . . . So while members of Congress move boldly to transfer responsibility for social welfare programs to the states, *they have given McDonald's $1.6 million* to help them advertise their fast-food products overseas!

The logic of the appeal is articulation: Federal handouts to McDonald's, defense contractor Martin Marietta, and Walt Disney are not *like* welfare; they *are* a form of welfare. If we are going to phase out one form of welfare, these politicians argued (appealing to the principle of *consistency*), then we should phase out all forms of welfare. A feature story on the topic of corporate welfare in the November 9, 1998, issue of *Time* magazine was a sign that the strategy was having an impact on the nation's political imagination.

The growing popularity of environmentalism makes it a candidate for repeated efforts at synchronic articulation. Cox (1994) uncovered a process of synchronic articulation at work in ongoing efforts to fuse environmentalist and civil rights concerns into a movement for "environmental justice." Mark Hertsgaard, writing in the February 1, 1999, issue of *The Nation,* wanted his readers to appreciate the potential harmony between environmentalism and economic growth. In short, he wanted to create an articulation. He did so, in part, by quoting noted environmental energy specialist Amory Lovins to the effect that "climate change is actually a lucrative business opportunity disguised as an environmental problem." To the degree that Hertsgaard was effective in crafting an articulation, he was able to reshape how people understand the relationship between these two issues. Political scientist Ken Conca detected a potentially problematic articulation between environmentalism and national security. Conca (1998) wrote,

> [Bill Clinton's] administration has undertaken a concerted effort to repackage the environment as a security issue. Although sometimes touted by environmentalists as a way to generate attention and action, the linking of environmental problems to national security and "strategic" American interests is deeply troubling. (p. 40)

Finally, we need to remember that, at times, advocates want to sever rather than establish connections. This is the process of *disarticulation.*[4] Black Power advocates of the late 1960s frequently disarticulated (or separated) their concerns from those of white liberals.

Conceptual disarticulation is a key instance of this general process. Here, concepts that are routinely associated are, in Burke's (1984) terms, "wrenched apart." Anticipating the lyrics to the popular song *Love and Marriage* (they "go together like a horse and carriage"), the early 20th-century radical Emma Goldman sought to sever this connection. In an essay titled "Marriage and Love," Goldman (1917/1969) labored to pull apart these routinely associated ideas, breaking the seemingly "natural" link, as part of an effort to subvert the male-dominated institution of marriage and to empower women. Disarticulation and articulation are potent discursive processes that merit the attention of rhetorical scholars.

Notes

1. See also Hanczor (1997).

2. The articulation-disarticulation pair resembles Perelman and Olbrechts-Tyteca's (1969) argument that association and dissociation are the basic processes underlying argumentative discourse. They wrote, "By processes of association, we understand schemes which bring separate elements together and allow us to establish a unity among them. . . . By processes of dissociation, we mean techniques of separation which have the purpose of dissociating, separating, [and] disuniting elements which are regarded as forming a whole or at least a unified group within some system of thought" (p. 190). Further inquiry is necessary to determine the degree to which Perelman and Olbrechts-Tyteca's discussion of argumentative processes might illuminate the practice of articulation and vice versa.

3. For example, see King's "A Time to Break Silence," a speech he delivered at the Riverside Church in New York City in April 1967. It is worth noting that in this speech, King continued—as he appropriated for subversive ends—a common articulation pattern in cold war America. During this period, it was common in the discourse of moderates (e.g., Dwight Eisenhower) as well as liberals (e.g., Thurgood Marshall) to articulate the problems of civil rights and foreign policy. The fight against communism and the fight for civil rights frequently were linked.

4. As early as *Attitudes Toward History* (originally published in 1937), Burke (1984) discussed "the necessity of wrenching apart . . . associations" as a strategic response to a culture's "tendency towards . . . identification" (p. 77).

References and Additional Reading

Burke, K. (1984). *Attitudes toward history* (3rd ed.). Berkeley: University of California Press.

Conca, K. (1998, Summer). The environment-security trap. *Dissent*, pp. 40-45.

Cox, J. R. (1994). *Re-articulating "environment": Race, class, and the new social movement for environmental justice.* J. Jeffrey Auer lecture, Indiana University.

DeLuca, K. (1999). Articulation theory: A discursive grounding for rhetorical practice. *Philosophy and Rhetoric, 32*, 334-348.

Goldman, E. (1969). Marriage and love. In E. Goldman, *Anarchism and other essays.* New York: Dover. (Original work published 1917)

Greene, R. W. (1998). Another materialist rhetoric. *Critical Studies in Mass Communication, 15*, 21-41.

Grossberg, L. (1992). *We gotta get out of this place: Popular conservatism and postmodern culture.* New York: Routledge.

Hall, S. (1982). The rediscovery of "ideology": Return of the repressed in media studies. In M. Gurevitch, T. Bennett, J. Curran, & J. Woollacott (Eds.), *Culture, society, and the media.* London: Methuen.

Hall, S. (1986). On postmodernism and articulation. *Journal of Communication Inquiry, 10*, 45-60.

Hanczor, R. S. (1997). Articulation theory and public controversy: Taking sides over *NYPD Blue. Critical Studies in Mass Communication, 14*, 1-30.

Jasinski, J. (1997). Rearticulating history in epideictic discourse: Frederick Douglass's "The Meaning of the Fourth of July to the Negro." In T. W. Benson (Ed.), *Rhetoric and political culture in nineteenth-century America.* East Lansing: Michigan State University Press.

Laclau, E., & Mouffe, C. (1985). *Hegemony and socialist strategy: Towards a radical democratic politics.* London: Verso.

Perelman, C., & Olbrechts-Tyteca, L. (1969). *The new rhetoric: A treatise on argumentation* (J. Wilkinson & P. Weaver, Trans.). Notre Dame, IN: University of Notre Dame Press.

Rosen, R. (1993, Fall). Domestic disarmament: A women's issue? *Dissent*, pp. 463-466.

Slack, J. D. (1996). The theory and method of articulation in cultural studies. In D. Morley & K. Chen (Eds.), *Stuart Hall: Critical dialogues in cultural studies.* London: Routledge.

Watson, M. S. (1997). The dynamics of intertextuality: Re-reading the Declaration of Independence. In T. W. Benson (Ed.), *Rhetoric and political culture in nineteenth-century America.* East Lansing: Michigan State University Press.

AUDIENCE

Scholars as diverse in disciplinary affiliation and theoretical orientation as Bakhtin (1986), Bitzer (1968), and Burke (1950) all pointed to the fact that human utterances (**discourse**) always are *addressed* to an **audience.** The growing interest in audience in rhetorical studies and other disciplines should not be surprising to someone familiar with the Aristotelian tradition of rhetoric. Aristotle's rhetorical **genres** were, after all, "determined by the three classes of listeners to speeches" (p. 1358a36). Whereas attention to audience can, then, be traced back at least as far as Aristotle, the range of contemporary scholarship on the concept goes well beyond his more limited *instrumental* outlook.[1]

Audience is at the center of two sometimes conflicting, and sometimes overlapping, areas of inquiry: *rhetorical studies*[2] and *cultural and/or media studies.*[3] One central issue in recent rhetorical theory has been the effort to specify the *nature* of a *rhetorical* audience. Bitzer (1968) argued that for a collection of individuals to constitute a rhetorical audience, two conditions must be met. A rhetorical audience "consists only of those persons who are capable of being influenced by discourse and of being mediators of change" (p. 8). A rhetorical audience, Bitzer maintained, must be "capable of being influenced." People listening to a political speech or reading a persuasive essay who refuse to consider the speaker or writer's arguments and appeals would not satisfy Bitzer's first condition. Individuals must demonstrate a certain basic level of attention and an openness to the speaker or writer's arguments and/or proposals to function as a rhetorical audience. The second, and probably more important, condition of a rhetorical audience is that the group of individuals have the capacity to act as "mediators of change." At times, advocates need to persuade their listeners or readers that they possess such a capacity. In his famous revolutionary pamphlet *Common Sense,* published in early 1776, Thomas Paine went into considerable detail about the raw materials in the colonies to convince his readers that they had a chance against the mightiest nation on the face of the earth. Colonists in 1776 had to be persuaded that they had the capacity to act as agents of change. Civil rights advocates in the South during the 1950s faced a similar problem. They had to show southern blacks that, despite their social and political position, they possessed forms of power and had the ability to mediate change.

In "The Rhetorical Situation," Bitzer (1968) concentrated on describing those factors that transformed an aggregate of individuals into a historically concrete rhetorical audience. Bitzer's rhetorical audience had a material objective existence. It was something that advocates recognized and addressed directly.[4] Shortly after Bitzer's essay was published, his University of Wisconsin colleague, Edwin Black, presented an alternative way of studying audience. In "The Second Persona," Black (1970) wrote,

> It seems a useful methodological assumption to hold that rhetorical discourses, either singly or cumulatively in a persuasive movement, will imply an auditor. . . . The best evidence in the discourse for this implication will be the substantive claims made, but the most likely evidence available will be in the form of stylistic tokens. (p. 112)

Whereas Bitzer (1968) focused on the historically situated audience, Black (1970) urged critics to locate the textual audience so as to find "the auditor implied by a discourse [that is] a model of what the rhetor would have his [sic] real auditor become" (p. 113).[5]

Bitzer and Black's contrasting approaches have evolved into two broad orientations for studying the phenomenon of audience in rhetorical studies. Park (1982) maintained,

> The meanings of "audience" . . . tend to diverge in two general directions: one toward actual people external to a text, the audience whom the writer must accommodate; the other toward the text itself and the audience

> implied there, a set of suggested or evoked attitudes, interests, reactions, [and] conditions of knowledge which may or may not fit with the qualities of actual readers or listeners. (p. 249)

Ede and Lunsford (1984) reached a similar conclusion and described the two contrasting views as the "audience addressed" and the "audience invoked."

Countless critical studies have sought to identify the audience "addressed" by a particular text and to describe the strategies by which the text accommodates this audience. Condit and Greer (1997) reconstructed British sentiments during the early days of World War II to reveal how Winston Churchill's "The War Situation I" speech used *metaphor* to accommodate these feelings. Leff and Mohrmann (1974) identified the primary Republican audience for Lincoln's "Cooper's Union" speech and unpacked his strategies of "ingratiation." Lucas (1989) located the different audiences addressed by the Declaration of Independence to reveal Jefferson's strategies of appeal. In certain cases, the actual audience is less important than the *indirect audience* to whom a speaker or writer appeals. Consider John F. Kennedy's 1960 campaign address to the Baptists in Houston, Texas, or George W. Bush's 2000 address to the National Association for the Advancement of Colored People convention. Each candidate conveyed a message to an indirect audience through the act of addressing the direct audience.

The possibility of *multiple audiences*—or, in Perelman and Olbrechts-Tyteca's (1969) terms, a "composite audience"—merits attention as well. As Perelman and Olbrechts-Tyteca observed, "It often happens that an orator must persuade a composite audience, embracing people differing in character, loyalties, and functions" (p. 21). Critics have, for example, studied the composite or heterogeneous nature of the audience for political convention keynote and acceptance speeches (Henry, 1988; Smith, 1971; Thompson, 1979).[6] As Myers (1999) remarked, "The ability to formulate statements that communicate distinct, and perhaps even incompatible, messages simultaneously to diverse audiences is, therefore, crucial to political success." But Myers added that "relatively little attention has been paid to the techniques of addressing the composite audience" (p. 55). By analyzing the "paper trail" that typically accompanies the production of political discourse, Myers observed that it is possible to uncover "the process of planting appeals to components of the composite audience." Myers wrote,

> By invoking cultural stereotypes, symbols, expressions of commitment, and other "codes" implanted within it, a political speech or act can contain several messages, some of them mutually incompatible, within the framework of a statement crafted by a single author. (p. 58)

Extending the works of sociologist George Herbert Mead and Kenneth Burke, Duncan (1962) developed a typology of audiences based on the mode of address employed. As Duncan explained,

> We can distinguish five types of address in the process of hierarchical appeals. These are determined, as befits a rhetoric based on sociology, by the kinds of audiences we must court. First, there is the general public ("they"); second, there are community guardians ("we"); third, others significant to us as friends and confidants with whom we talk intimately ("you" . . .); fourth, the self we address inwardly in soliloquy (the "I" talking to its "me"); and fifth, ideal audiences whom we address as ultimate sources of social order. (p. 292)

Duncan illustrated the way in which these modes of address or audience types interact in discursive performances. His first example was the master of ceremonies at a stage revue who moves from general audience, to the guardians of the art (other performers and the musicians), to himself or herself, concluding with an appeal that "invokes the spirit of the art in the 'wonderful show.' " His second example was the campaign oration. Duncan wrote,

> In political rallies, the orator greets the good people of the town who make up his [sic] general audience, he turns deferentially to his distinguished guests beside him on the platform, and then addresses his "friends and fellow citizens." During his speech, he breaks off into soliloquy ("When I was a farm boy like your boys here, I said to myself . . ."). He closes his speech with invocations to the great transcendent principles on which the American way of life rests. (p. 293)

In Duncan's view, the **hierarchical** nature of human society and the *rhetoric of courtship* that this entails manifests itself in discourse that continually negotiates multiple audiences.

But texts not only address concrete, historically situated audiences; they sometimes issue invitations or solicitations for auditors and/or readers to adopt a certain perspective for reading or listening. Black's (1970) "Second Persona" essay explored the "form of consciousness" (p. 119) solicited by the "communism is cancer" *metaphor* employed by the radical right during the 1950s and 1960s. Jasinski (1992) described how *The Federalist Papers* constructed a vision of an impartial and "candid" audience that contained specific prescriptions for how the "real" audience should evaluate the arguments being advanced during the constitutional ratification debate. Foss and Foss (1994) probed the way in which Garrison Keillor's monologues on the radio program *A Prairie Home Companion* "creates a preferred spectator position that relies on traditionally feminine competencies" (p. 411).[7]

One specific manifestation of the invoked or constructed audience to receive considerable attention in rhetoric and argumentation studies is Perelman and Olbrechts-Tyteca's (1969) concept of a *universal audience.* They began their account of this concept by noting,

> Argumentation aimed exclusively at a particular audience has the drawback that the speaker, by the very fact of adapting to the views of his [sic] listeners, might rely on arguments that are foreign or even directly opposed to what is acceptable to persons other than those he is presently addressing. (p. 31)

The issue raised here is familiar to students of rhetoric: Rhetorical discourse or rhetorical argument is suspect because it simply panders to audiences, telling them anything so as to be successful.[8] Perelman (1982) recognized this traditional limitation of rhetoric and argumentation when he noted, "The only general advice that a theory of argumentation can give is to ask speakers to adapt themselves to their audiences" (p. 13). But argumentation, although always shaped to some degree by the *instrumental* objectives that mark the real world of human activity, can nevertheless aspire to something beyond accommodation to an addressed audience. The something beyond which argumentation aspires is the agreement of a universal audience. Perelman and Olbrechts-Tyteca wrote, "There exists for each speaker at each moment . . . an audience transcending all others" (p. 30). They continued, "Each individual, each culture has . . . its own conception of the universal audience." An advocate's vision of his or her universal audience is revealed, as Black (1970) suggested, in the substance of the advocate's arguments. Reconstruction of the universal audience invoked through argumentation "would be very instructive," Perelman and Olbrechts-Tyteca (1969) suggested, "as we would learn from it what men [sic], at different times in history, have regarded as *real, true,* and *objectively valid*" (p. 33).[9]

The basic idea that texts invoke or construct audiences leads in a number of additional directions. Abercrombie and Longhurst (1998) nicely summarized two different, but interconnected, directions for thinking about audience in what they termed the *incorporation/resistance paradigm.* The concept of incorporation refers to the ways in which "audience members are incorporated into the dominant ideology by their participation in media activity" (p. 15). In the tradition of rhetorical studies, Charland's (1987) study of the Quebec nationalist movement illustrated a form of incorporation or, as Charland preferred (following Althusser), **interpellation.** Discursive practice, Charland argued, does not simply create an audience; it constitutes the identity—the basic sense of self—of those it encounters. But whereas some scholars have adopted the model of incorporation, other scholars—especially those influenced by the cultural studies movement (e.g., Hall, 1982)—urge a model of audience resistance. Early versions of this position are visible in literary studies (e.g., Fetterley, 1978). Resistant reading emerges more fully in cultural studies scholarship that focuses attention on what readers or audiences actually *do* to or with the texts they encounter. Groundbreaking studies, such as Morley's (1980) analysis of different responses by different audiences to a British television program (see also Morley, 1992) and Fiske's (1986) account of the inherent openness (or **polysemy**) of television "texts," emphasize how audiences and readers can subvert the dominant ideology *inscribed* in a text. Other studies, such as Radway's (1984) examination of the role of romance novels in the lives of the women who read them, straddle the incorporation-resistance continuum by finding aspects of each in the behavior of women readers.

The concept of resistive or oppositional reading is beginning to enter the disciplinary consciousness of rhetorical studies (Rosteck, 1995; Weiler, 1989). In an innovative study, Ceccarelli (1998) wrote, "In public address scholarship, the potential for identifying polysemic 'resistive readings' is high, although it remains largely unrecognized" (p. 400). To illustrate this potential, Ceccarelli proposed a critical strategy that entails the "close reading of reception evidence" (p. 408). She then applied this strategy to some selected cases including Lincoln's "Second Inaugural Address." By unearthing and analyzing southern newspaper responses to Lincoln's 1865 address, Ceccarelli was able to document the way in which many southerners resisted the much more charitable northern reading of the address. Through the Lincoln example as well as other cases, Ceccarelli illustrated how the critical strategy of **close reading** might be used to unpack the reception and circulation of public discourse within different audiences.[10]

Numerous different, sometimes overlapping, sometimes conflicting, perspectives on audience populate the contemporary intellectual landscape. These perspectives have both revitalized and reshaped how rhetorical scholars think about one of the discipline's central concepts—audience (Charland, 1995; Fahnestock, 1995; Scott & Brookey, 1995). This process likely will continue into the foreseeable future.

Notes

1. For brief reviews of audience in the various traditions of rhetorical thought, see Ede (1984) and Porter (1992, pp. 15-28).
2. A large part of the scholarship on audience is centered in the *composition branch* of contemporary rhetorical studies.
3. On the relationship between these two traditions of scholarship, see Rosteck (1995, 1998).
4. Bitzer (1968) did not clearly recognize two important, and sometimes interrelated, phenomena: *composite* or *multiple audiences* (Henry, 1988; Myers, 1999; Thompson, 1979) and *indirect address* (epitomized in the stylistic strategy of *apostrophe*).
5. Black's (1970) essay anticipated themes developed in more detail in works such as Iser (1974) and Ong (1975). Precursors include Gibson (1950).
6. See also Benoit and D'Agostine (1994).
7. Foss and Foss (1994) drew extensively from literature in film and media studies (e.g., Mulvey, 1989; see also Heath, 1981) on spectatorship and viewing positions. The idea that texts from a variety of media work to shape the way in which they are received is an important point of theoretical convergence linking scholarship in rhetoric, literary studies, media studies, and cultural

studies. This convergence might become the point of more detailed examination, especially by students of rhetoric.

8. For example, see Garver's (1987) discussion of "sophistic accommodation."

9. The concept of universal audience has generated a considerable amount of discussion in rhetoric and argumentation. See, for example, Crosswhite (1989), Ede (1981), Golden (1986), Gross (1999), Johnstone (1978), Ray (1978), and Scult (1976, 1985). Leff and Procario (1985) noted that a rough parallel exists between the particular-universal audience relationship in Perelman and Olbrechts-Tyteca (1969) and the audience-public relationship in Bitzer's (1968) work.

10. On the need to link "the moment of production" and "the moment of reception," see Thomas (1991).

References and Additional Reading

Abercrombie, N., & Longhurst, B. (1998). *Audiences: A sociological theory of performance and imagination.* London: Sage.

Allor, M. (1988). Relocating the site of audience. *Critical Studies in Mass Communication, 5,* 217-233.

Aristotle. (1954). *Rhetoric* (W. R. Roberts, Trans.). New York: Modern Library.

Bakhtin, M. (1986). The problem of speech genres. In C. Emerson & M. Holquist (Eds.), *Speech genres and other late essays* (V. W. McGee, Trans.). Austin: University of Texas Press.

Benoit, W. L., & D'Agostine, J. M. (1994). "The Case of the Midnight Judges" and multiple audience discourse: Chief Justice Marshall and *Marbury v. Madison. Southern Communication Journal, 59,* 89-96.

Bitzer, L. (1968). The rhetorical situation. *Philosophy and Rhetoric, 1,* 1-14.

Black, E. (1970). The second persona. *Quarterly Journal of Speech, 56,* 109-119.

Burke, K. (1950). *A rhetoric of motives.* New York: Prentice Hall.

Ceccarelli, L. (1998). Polysemy: Multiple meanings in rhetorical criticism. *Quarterly Journal of Speech, 84,* 395-415.

Charland, M. (1987). Constitutive rhetoric: The case of the *peuple Québécois. Quarterly Journal of Speech, 73,* 133-150.

Charland, M. (1995). The constitution of rhetoric's audience. In S. Jackson (Ed.), *Argumentation and values: Proceedings of the Ninth SCA/AFA Conference on Argumentation.* Annandale, VA: Speech Communication Association.

Condit, C. M., & Greer, A. M. (1997). The particular aesthetics of Winston Churchill's "The War Situation I." In J. M. Hogan (Ed.), *Rhetoric and community: Case studies in unity and fragmentation.* Columbia: University of South Carolina Press.

Crosswhite, J. (1989). Universality in rhetoric: Perelman's universal audience. *Philosophy and Rhetoric, 22,* 157-173.

Duncan, H. (1962). *Communication and social order.* New York: Bedminster Press.

Ede, L. S. (1981). Rhetoric versus philosophy: The role of the universal audience in Chaim Perelman's *The New Rhetoric. Central States Speech Journal, 32,* 118-125.

Ede, L. (1984). Audience: An introduction to research. *College Composition and Communication, 35,* 140-154.

Ede, L., & Lunsford, A. (1984). Audience addressed/audience invoked: The role of audience in composition theory and pedagogy. *College Composition and Communication, 35,* 155-171.

Fahnestock, J. (1995). Audience in *The New Rhetoric* and the formal appeals. In S. Jackson (Ed.), *Argumentation and values: Proceedings of the Ninth SCA/AFA Conference on Argumentation.* Annandale, VA: Speech Communication Association.

Fetterley, J. (1978). *The resisting reader: A feminist approach to American fiction.* Bloomington: Indiana University Press.

Fiske, J. (1986). Television: Polysemy and popularity. *Critical Studies in Mass Communication, 3,* 391-408.

Foss, S. K., & Foss, K. A. (1994). The construction of feminine spectatorship in Garrison Keillor's radio monologues. *Quarterly Journal of Speech, 80,* 410-426.

Garver, E. (1987). *Machiavelli and the history of prudence.* Madison: University of Wisconsin Press.

Gibson, W. (1950). Authors, speakers, readers, and mock readers. *College English, 11,* 265-269.

Golden, J. L. (1986). The universal audience revisited. In J. L. Golden & J. J. Pilotta (Eds.), *Practical reasoning in human affairs: Studies in honor of Chaim Perelman.* Dordrecht, Netherlands: D. Reidel.

Gross, A. (1999). A theory of the rhetorical audience: Reflections on Chaim Perelman. *Quarterly Journal of Speech, 85,* 203-211.

Hall, S. (1982). The rediscovery of "ideology": Return of the repressed in media studies. In M. Gurevitch, T. Bennett, J. Curran, & J. Woollacott (Eds.), *Culture, society, and the media.* London: Methuen.

Heath, S. (1981). *Questions of cinema.* Bloomington: Indiana University Press.

Henry, D. (1988). The rhetorical dynamics of Mario Cuomo's 1984 keynote address: Situation, speaker, metaphor. *Southern Speech Communication Journal, 53,* 105-120.

Iser, W. (1974). *The implied reader: Patterns of communication in prose fiction from Bunyan to Beckett.* Baltimore, MD: Johns Hopkins University Press.

Jasinski, J. (1992). Rhetoric and judgment in the constitutional ratification debate of 1787-1788: An exploration in the relationship between theory and critical practice. *Quarterly Journal of Speech, 78,* 197-218.

Johnstone, H. W. (1978). The idea of a universal audience. In H. W. Johnstone, *Validity and rhetoric in philosophical argument: An outlook in transition.* University Park, PA: Dialogue Press of Man and World.

Leff, M. C., & Mohrmann, G. P. (1974). Lincoln at Cooper Union: A rhetorical analysis of the text. *Quarterly Journal of Speech, 60,* 346-358.

Leff, M. C., & Procario, M. C. (1985). Rhetorical theory in speech communication. In T. W. Benson (Ed.), *Speech communication in the 20th century.* Carbondale: Southern Illinois University Press.

Lucas, S. E. (1989). Justifying America: The Declaration of Independence as a rhetorical document. In T. W. Benson (Ed.), *American rhetoric: Context and criticism.* Carbondale: Southern Illinois University Press.

Lunsford, A. A., & Ede, L. (1996). Representing audience: "Successful" discourse and disciplinary critique. *College Composition and Communication, 47,* 167-179.

Morley, D. (1980). *The nationwide audience: Structuring and decoding.* London: British Film Institute.

Morley, D. (1992). *Television, audiences, and cultural studies.* New York: Routledge.

Mulvey, L. (1989). *Visual and other pleasures.* Bloomington: Indiana University Press.

Myers, F. (1999). Political argumentation and the composite audience: A case study. *Quarterly Journal of Speech, 85,* 55-71.

Ong, S. J. (1975). The writer's audience is always a fiction. *PMLA, 90,* 9-21. (Publication of the Modern Language Association)

Park, D. B. (1982). The meanings of "audience." *College English, 44,* 247-257.

Perelman, C. (1982). *The realm of rhetoric* (W. Kluback, Trans.). Notre Dame, IN: University of Notre Dame Press.

Perelman, C., & Olbrechts-Tyteca, L. (1969). *The new rhetoric: A treatise on argumentation* (J. Wilkinson & P. Weaver, Trans.). Notre Dame, IN: University of Notre Dame Press.

Porter, J. E. (1992). *Audience and rhetoric: An archaeological composition of the discourse community.* Englewood Cliffs, NJ: Prentice Hall.

Radway, J. (1984). *Reading the romance: Women, patriarchy, and popular literature.* Chapel Hill: University of North Carolina Press.

Ray, J. W. (1978). Perelman's universal audience. *Quarterly Journal of Speech, 64,* 361-375.

Rosteck, T. (1995). Cultural studies and rhetorical studies. *Quarterly Journal of Speech, 81,* 386-403.

Rosteck, T. (Ed.). (1998). *At the intersection: Cultural studies and rhetorical studies.* New York: Guilford.

Scott, R. L., & Brookey, R. A. (1995). Audiences argue. In S. Jackson (Ed.), *Argumentation and values: Proceedings of the Ninth SCA/AFA Conference on Argumentation.* Annandale, VA: Speech Communication Association.

Scult, A. (1976). Perelman's universal audience: One perspective. *Central States Speech Journal, 27,* 176-180.

Scult, A. (1985). A note on the range and utility of the universal audience. *Journal of the American Forensic Association, 22,* 83-87.

Smith, C. R. (1971, Fall). Richard Nixon's 1968 acceptance speech as a model of dual audience adaptation. *Today's Speech,* pp. 15-22.

Thomas, B. (1991). *The new historicism and other old-fashioned topics.* Princeton, NJ: Princeton University Press.

Thompson, W. N. (1979). Barbara Jordan's keynote address: Fulfilling dual and conflicting purposes. *Central States Speech Journal, 30,* 272-277.

Weiler, M. (1989). Polysemy and pluralism: The habit of oppositional reading. In B. E. Gronbeck (Ed.), *Spheres of argument: Proceedings of the Sixth SCA/AFA Conference on Argumentation.* Annandale, VA: Speech Communication Association.

BRICOLEUR/BRICOLAGE

The French terms ***bricolage*** (referring to an activity) and ***bricoleur*** (referring to the person who engages in that activity) were introduced into contemporary critical and discourse theory by Levi-Strauss (1966) in his seminal work *The Savage Mind.* In that work, Lévi-Strauss compared the realm of "mythical thought" to the activity of bricolage. He wrote, "Mythical thought is . . . a kind of intellectual 'bricolage' " (p. 17). But what exactly was Lévi-Strauss getting at when he compared mythical thought and bricolage, and how is that relevant for contemporary rhetorical studies?

The *Columbia Dictionary of Modern Literary and Cultural Criticism* describes bricolage as "an improvisatory activity performed by a kind of intellectual jack-of-all-trades." Although the bricoleur is "adept at performing a wide variety of tasks," he or she "must work with a limited stock of materials and tools" (Childers & Hentzi, 1995, p. 34). The early 1990s television character "McGyver" (from the show of the same name) is an example of a bricoleur. McGyver eschews the type of high-tech gadgets made famous in the James Bond movie series. He can escape from any tight spot he might fall into through his skill at improvising with the limited materials that are available. In one episode, he might knock a helicopter out of commission by using popsicle sticks and string. In another, he might elude capture by fashioning a smokescreen from baking soda and bleach.

How is any of this relevant to the realm of contemporary rhetorical studies? The *Columbia Dictionary* suggests that bricolage has become, for some contemporary theorists, an image that embodies the activity of theorizing. "Many contemporary theorists . . . view the practice of theory as itself a form of bricolage performed with concepts and ideas retrieved from the grand theories of the past" (Childers & Hentzi, 1995, p. 34). Charland (1991) illustrated this trend in his essay reflecting on the **critical rhetoric** movement in rhetorical studies. He wrote,

> Thus, instead of being a guerrilla constantly undermining the foundations of any power/knowledge structure in a continued process of negative critique, the critical rhetorician might best be considered as a *bricoleur,* a kind of cultural tinkerer whose art consists of disassembling (deconstructing?) certain formations in order to try out new constructions. (p. 74)

The critical rhetorician, Charland went on to suggest, engages in a "to and fro of assembly and disassembly," taking apart large-scale theories so as to salvage specific concepts for various practical and/or critical tasks (p. 74).

But the interconnected images of the bricoleur and bricolage might have relevance for rhetorical studies beyond providing a model of theoretical practice. Bricolage also might serve as a partial model for the process of rhetorical **invention.** Gaonkar (1993) pointed in this direction when he wrote,

> The rhetor is surrounded by a sea of fragments—bits and scraps of evidence, disembodied arguments, issues and visions—out of which is constructed his or her own fragment. Hence, the rhetor is preeminently an interpreter who attempts to make sense of his or her discursive surrounding in the manner of a bricoleur. (p. 153)

To elaborate a bit on Gaonkar's idea, consider the following passage from Levi-Strauss's (1966) exposition of the nature of bricolage. He wrote,

> [The bricoleur's] first practical step is retrospective. He [sic] has to turn back to an already existent set made up of tools and materials, to consider or reconsider what it contains and, finally and above all, to engage in a sort of dialogue with it and, before choosing between them, to index the possible answers which the whole set can offer to his problem. He interrogates all the heterogeneous objects of which his treasury is composed to discover what each of them could "signify" [in a specific case]. (p. 18)

The bricoleur's most essential task, Levi-Strauss suggested, is to discover the available materials or means for accomplishing some task. This implied definition, some readers will recognize, parallels Aristotle's (1954) famous definition of rhetoric, specifically rhetorical invention, as the discovery of the available means of persuasion in a given case (1355b26). Observing, perceiving, and discovering "how persuasion may be effected" in a given case (Kennedy, 1991, p. 36) is a type of intellectual bricolage. Furthermore, Levi-Strauss's contention that the first step in bricolage is retrospective intersects with recent discussions of the centrality of **tradition** and **hermeneutics** to the process of rhetorical invention (see, e.g., Jasinski, 1997; Leff, 1997). Further exploration of the way in which the image of bricolage and the bricoleur might function as a model for rhetoric invention as a *social process* appears warranted.

References and Additional Reading

Aristotle. (1954). *Rhetoric* (W. R. Roberts, Trans.). New York: Modern Library.

Charland, M. (1991). Finding a horizon and telos: The challenge to critical rhetoric. *Quarterly Journal of Speech, 77,* 71-74.

Childers, J., & Hentzi, G. (Eds.). (1995). *The Columbia dictionary of modern literary and cultural criticism.* New York: Columbia University Press.

Gaonkar, D. P. (1993). Performing with fragments: Reflections on critical rhetoric. In R. E. McKerrow (Ed.), *Argument and the postmodern challenge: Proceedings of the Eighth SCA/AFA Conference on Argumentation.* Annandale, VA: Speech Communication Association.

Jasinski, J. (1997). Instrumentalism, contextualism, and interpretation in rhetorical criticism. In W. Keith & A. Gross (Eds.), *Rhetorical hermeneutics.* Albany: State University of New York Press.

Kennedy, G. (1991). *Aristotle on rhetoric: A theory of civic discourse.* New York: Oxford University Press.

Leff, M. (1997). Hermeneutical rhetoric. In W. Jost & M. J. Hyde (Eds.), *Rhetoric and hermeneutics in our time.* New Haven, CT: Yale University Press.

Lévi-Strauss, C. (1966). *The savage mind* (G. Weidenfeld and Nicolson Ltd., Trans.). Chicago: University of Chicago Press.

BURDEN OF PROOF

In any controversy or disagreement, there are different sides or positions in dispute. Although we sometimes like to think that all sides are treated equally and that no position has a built-in advantage, this is not typically the case. What usually happens is that one side or the other has what is called the **burden of proof.** This means that the side has the greater argumentative or persuasive obligation or challenge. Who has the burden of proof? Generally, whoever proposes something new or different.

For example, in the U.S. criminal justice system, the prosecution *always* has the burden of proof. The defense does not have to *prove* anything because the defendant is innocent until *proven* guilty. The *nature* or *degree* of the burden of proof varies in different legal arenas. When the district attorney seeks a criminal indictment before a grand jury, he or she must establish or prove "probable cause" for the indictment to be handed down. When the matter goes to trial, the prosecuting attorney has a greater burden; he or she must prove the defendant guilty "beyond a reasonable doubt" (meaning that any amount of proof less than this standard is insufficient). In a civil case, the individual or group filing the complaint (e.g., the parents of murder victim Ron Goldman in the O. J. Simpson case) typically need to establish a "preponderance of evidence" to satisfy their burden (Freeley, 1996).

Legal burden of proof can become an object of public controversy. Consider the case of an African American job applicant who accuses a company of racial discrimination in its hiring practices. Who should have the burden of proof? Should the African American applicant be required to prove in some definitive way that the company engages in discriminatory practices (e.g., discovering a memo in which the chief executive officer makes disparaging comments about racial minorities), or should the company have the burden of proving that its hiring practices are racially neutral? Given the history of bigotry and racism in the United States, the Supreme Court during the early 1970s introduced the concept of disparate impact as a way of accounting for unintentional discrimination. In so doing, the court assigned a considerable portion of the burden of proof in discrimination cases to the employer. A plaintiff could establish a prima facie case of discrimination through *sign* **argument** (e.g., showing that only 2% of the company's employees are minorities when minorities constitute 25% of the local workforce), thereby imposing the burden of proof on the company. Under the influence of appointees of Ronald Reagan and George Bush, the Supreme Court altered this approach in its 1989 *Ward's Cove Packing v. Antonio* decision, assigning a more substantial burden of proof to the applicant or employee making the charge. In response, civil rights leaders and other activists lobbied Congress, which then passed the Civil Rights Act of 1990 that, among other things, tried to return the burden of proof in discrimination cases to the pre-*Ward's Cove* or *Griggs v. Duke Power Company* standard. This bill was vetoed by Bush on the grounds that it would force companies to use racial quotas to avoid discrimination lawsuits. Congress and the Bush administration negotiated and eventually crafted a compromise Civil Rights Act that was adopted in 1991.

In social and public controversies, there are no legally sanctioned procedures for assigning the burden of proof. The general rule, as Freeley (1996) noted, is that the one who asserts must prove (p. 43). Rhetoricians over the years, based on their observations of human practice, have described how the burden of proof is normally allocated (one of the most important contributions to the literature is Whately's [1828/1963] *Elements of Rhetoric*). For example, people advocating a *change* in the status quo (e.g., a new law, a new interpretation of an old law, a new procedure) have the burden of proof; they have the responsibility of presenting a compelling case—of providing "good and sufficient reason[s]" (Freeley, 1996, p. 42)—for change. Defenders of the status quo often engage the advocates of change in argument, but they do not share the same argumentative burden. Defenders of the status quo typically have **presumption** on their side. They often can, and do, rely on aphorisms such as "if it ain't broke, don't fix it."[1]

Note

1. On the interaction between burden of proof and presumption, see the entry for **presumption**.

References and Additional Reading

Freeley, A. J. (1996). *Argumentation and debate: Critical thinking for reasoned decision making* (9th ed.). Belmont, CA: Wadsworth.

Rescher, N. (1977). *Dialectics: A controversy-oriented approach to the theory of knowledge.* Albany: State University of New York Press.

Sproule, J. M. (1976). The psychological burden of proof: On the evolutionary development of Richard Whately's theory of presumption. *Speech Monographs, 43,* 115-129.

Whately, R. (1963). *Elements of rhetoric* (D. Ehninger, Ed.). Carbondale: Southern Illinois University Press. (Original work published 1828)

CANON

The term **canon** is derived from the Greek *kanon,* which had two different meanings. Kanon could refer to either a list or a measuring rod. When the term is used to apply to texts and other forms of discursive practice, the two original meanings of the term are fused. Ross (1993) identified "the most familiar current usage of canon" as follows: "a collective term for the totality of the most highly esteemed works in a given culture" (p. 515). Ross's definition reveals the fusion. Canon refers to a list (a "totality of works") that has been measured (the works are "the most highly esteemed") and that then functions as an instrument for measuring (works are compared to, and evaluated against, those thought to reside within the canon).

The contemporary sense of the term began to emerge during roughly the 4th century AD within the Christian church. At that time, church leaders had to determine the "books" that constituted the Holy Scriptures (the Bible). A scriptural canon was created; texts were evaluated, certain texts were selected for inclusion within the scriptural canon (and, as part of the process, other texts were excluded), and an official list of recognized texts was established. Over time, the idea of a canon of texts was secularized and applied to other realms of textual and discursive practice such as literature and rhetoric.[1]

Why is the idea of a canon important? What are its practical implications? The concept of a canon functions in different ways. A **text** that is deemed *canonical* can function as a critical **touchstone.** These texts are used as vehicles for judging other texts, or they are thought to embody certain qualities that can reveal the essential characteristics of a certain type of practice. The idea of a canon of texts functions heuristically. Texts thought to be canonical receive more attention from scholars—they are studied more extensively—compared to noncanonical ones. As Tompkins (1985) pointed out, the canon of American literature focuses scholarly attention on authors such as Hawthorne and Melville and discourages inquiry into the works of other 19th-century authors. Something similar occurs in rhetorical studies. Abraham Lincoln receives more attention than do other 19th-century American presidents such as Franklin Pierce and James Buchanan; Martin Luther King, Jr., is studied more frequently than are Ralph Abernathy and Malcolm X. Perhaps most important, the concept of a canon functions pedagogically. Works thought to reside with a literary or rhetorical canon are taught with greater regularity than is noncanonical material. Canonical works are preserved and disseminated by their inclusion in classroom syllabi; noncanonical works tend to be forgotten.

The notion of a canon of exemplary works has become the subject of extended discussion in literary studies and, to a lesser extent, rhetorical studies over the past few decades. A number of different positions on the topic of canons and canon formation can be identified. Defenders of the idea of a canon subscribe to the "conventional view . . . that the canonicity of a work is established by a consensus of successive generations of readers, critics, and educators as well as by the extent of its influence on later literature" (Ross, 1993, p. 515). Canonical texts, defenders of the concept argue, have stood the proverbial "test of time" (see also Guillory, 1990, p. 236). Defenders of the canon maintain that the approbation of successive generations demonstrates the intrinsic value or quality of a work. The idea of the canon, Bloom (1994) argued, is a way of preserving the autonomy of aesthetic value. But a liberal critic of the canon would point out that this image of successive generations placing their seal of approval on a text is deceptive because it traditionally is the same type of people (predominantly white upper class men) who are doing the judging. The liberal critic finds the ideas of intrinsic aesthetic value and quality or impartial criteria of evaluation to be ideologically tainted. A literary or rhetorical canon does not—and cannot, a liberal critic would argue—embody timeless values and standards; a canon can only embody the values, attitudes, and standards of specific individuals and the social positions that they occupy. In place of problematic ideas such as enduring values, many liberal critics of the canon endorse an ideal of representativeness. A canon of literary or rhetorical works should accurately reflect or represent the culture and time period in question.[2] A third option in the struggle over the canon is outright rejection. Rejection can be defended, more radical critics of the canon maintain, because the basic idea of a canon perpetuates the violence of exclusion. Even the liberal proposal of making the canon more representative will entail a process of exclusion (Thomas, 1991). As Ross (1993) observed, "Some critics have even suggested abandoning the idea of the canon altogether because it is inherently exclusive and elitist" (p. 516).

A problem with outright rejection of the idea of a canon, Ross (1993) noted, "is that it assumes that criticism can do without evaluation when in fact evaluation is implicit in all forms of interpretation" (p. 516).[3] A fourth option with respect to the subject of the canon is to make the process of canon formation itself an object for critical study. Tompkins (1985) noted, "The point [in criticizing the canon] is not that these discriminations [or evaluations] are baseless; the point is that the grounds on which we make them are not absolute and unchanging but [rather] contingent and variable" (p. 193; see also Smith, 1988). Explicitly historicizing literary and rhetorical studies (Guillory, 1990) can open up new avenues of inquiry. Among them would be investigations into the *reception* and *circulation* of texts. Canonical texts, this line of inquiry assumes, are *made* rather than *born*, and the social process of making or creating canonical texts needs to be studied. Tompkins (1985) illustrated this type of inquiry in her chapter on Hawthorne. Rhetorical scholars could adopt a similar approach and study *how* texts by Lincoln and Webster were canonized or *how* previously neglected texts (e.g., a 19th-century text such as Walker's [1829/1995] *Appeal*) are reevaluated. Historicizing the process of canon formation will not end discussions about the value and function of a canon in any particular academic discipline. So long as evaluation is part of the process of critical inquiry, such discussions no doubt will persist.

Notes

1. On the etymology and history of the term, see Guillory (1990) and Ross (1993).

2. This is the position of many feminists in rhetorical studies. See the entry for **gynocriticism** for a discussion of the process of including more women's discourse in the "list" of works that are taught and studied by rhetorical scholars.

3. See the entry for **criticism** for a more extended discussion of the issue of critical *evaluation.*

References and Additional Reading

Bloom, H. (1994). *The Western canon: The books and school of the ages.* Orlando, FL: Harcourt Brace.

Guillory, J. (1990). Canon. In F. Lentricchia & T. McLaughlin (Eds.), *Critical terms for literary study.* Chicago: University of Chicago Press.

Ross, T. (1993). Canon. In I. R. Makaryk (Ed.), *Encyclopedia of contemporary literary theory: Approaches, scholars, terms.* Toronto: University of Toronto Press.

Smith, B. H. (1988). *Contingencies of value.* Cambridge, MA: Harvard University Press.

Thomas, B. (1991). *The new historicism and other old-fashioned topics.* Princeton, NJ: Princeton University Press.

Tompkins, J. (1985). *Sensational designs: The cultural work of American fiction, 1790-1860.* New York: Oxford University Press.

Walker, D. (1995). *Appeal.* New York: Hill & Wang. (Original work published 1829)

CANONS OF RHETORIC

Sometimes referred to as the "parts," "faculties," or "offices" of rhetoric,[1] the five **canons of rhetoric** are the subdivisions of classical rhetorical education. Classical rhetoricians believed that teaching someone to be an effective speaker involved helping him or her to master five constituent activities: **invention** (*inventio*), **arrangement** (*dispositio*), **style** (*elocutio*), **memory** (*memoria*), and delivery. The anonymous author of the classical treatise *Rhetorica ad Herennium* (Anonymous, 1954) usually is credited with articulating these five canons in a relatively clear manner (see, e.g., Vickers, 1988).

Over the centuries, various "parts" of rhetoric were disconnected and linked to other branches of study. For example, during the 16th century it was common to view the province of rhetoric as exclusively style and delivery with the activities of invention and arrangement transferred to the realm of logic. The impact of this gradual shift still can be seen today in the tendency of many European scholars to view rhetoric as the study of *tropes and figures* of speech, disconnected from more substantive concerns such as **argument** (there are, of course, exceptions to this tendency).

The classical canons still play a role in contemporary rhetorical scholarship. Some scholars (e.g., Harper, 1979) view the classical canons as a "paradigm" for all communication theory; hence, they remain present in contemporary thought as an often implicit organizing framework (see also Corbett, 1971; Horner, 1988; Wallace, 1970). But shifts in the nature of rhetorical studies seem to require some rather drastic rethinking of the five traditional canons.[2] As Gaonkar (1993) reminded rhetorical scholars, the foremost concern of classical thinkers writing on the topic of rhetoric was speech production or teaching others how to be more effective public speakers. Whereas the production or performative aspect of rhetoric remains in contemporary thought (primarily in relation to courses in public speaking and composition and the activity of debate), rhetorical studies during the late 20th century became increasingly concerned with the interpretation and criticism of a wide range of discursive or textual phenomena. There is considerable debate in contemporary rhetorical studies as to the value of the classical productionist vocabulary—including the five traditional canons—to the concerns of current scholarship.

Notes

1. This latter term can be confusing because Cicero's use of the term *offices of rhetoric* remains common in classical rhetorical scholarship and is very different from the five traditional parts or canons.

2. This is particularly true with respect to the canon of **memory.**

References and Additional Reading

Anonymous. (1954). *Rhetorica ad Herennium* (H. Caplan, Trans.). London: Heinemann.

Corbett, E. P. J. (1971). *Classical rhetoric for the modern student* (2nd ed.). New York: Oxford University Press.

Gaonkar, D. P. (1993). The idea of rhetoric in the rhetoric of science. *Southern Journal of Communication, 58,* 258-295.

Harper, N. (1979). *Human communication theory: The history of a paradigm.* Rochelle Park, NJ: Hayden.

Horner, W. B. (1988). *Rhetoric in the classical tradition.* New York: St. Martin's.

Kennedy, G. A. (1980). *Classical rhetoric and its Christian and secular tradition from ancient to modern times.* Chapel Hill: University of North Carolina Press.

Vickers, B. (1988). *In defense of rhetoric.* Oxford, UK: Clarendon.

Wallace, K. R. (1970). *Understanding discourse: The speech act and rhetorical action.* Baton Rouge: Louisiana State University Press.

CARNIVALIZATION/ CARNIVALESQUE

Literary and social historians Peter Stallybrass and Allon White observed,

> There is now a large and increasing body of writing which sees carnival not simply as a ritual feature of European culture but as a *mode of understanding,* a positivity, a cultural analytic. "How is it," they ask, "that a festive ritual now virtually eliminated from most of the popular culture of Europe has gained such prominence as an epistemological category?" (Stallybrass & White, 1986, p. 6)

Most scholars who discuss the interrelated concepts of *carnival,* **carnivalization,** or the **carnivalesque,** including Stallybrass and White, identify the Russian philosopher and literary theorist Mikhail Bakhtin as a prime reason for its prominence and popularity. Stallybrass and White maintained,

> The main importance [of Bakhtin's study of the French author François Rabelais] is its broad development of the "carnivalesque" into a potent, populist, critical inversion of *all* official words and hierarchies in a way that has implications far beyond the specific realm of Rabelais studies. (p. 7)

What did Bakhtin mean by carnival? What does it mean to say that literature and other discursive practices have been subjected to a process of carnivalization? How is the concept of carnival and the carnivalesque relevant to contemporary rhetorical studies?

Bakhtin explored the nature of carnival in works such as *Rabelais and His World* (Bakhtin, 1968) and *Problems of Dostoevsky's Poetics* (Bakhtin, 1984). Stallybrass and White (1986) observed,

> Carnival in its widest, most general sense embraced ritual spectacles such as fairs, popular feasts and wakes, processions and competitions . . ., comic shows, mummery and dancing, open-air amusement with costumes and masks, giants, dwarfs, monsters, trained animals, and so forth; it included comic verbal compositions . . . such as parodies, travesties, and vulgar farce; and it included . . . curses, oaths, slang, humour, popular tricks and jokes, scatological forms, in fact all the "low" and "dirty" sorts of folk humour. Carnival is presented by Bakhtin as a world of topsy-turvy, of heteroglot exuberance, of ceaseless overrunning and excess where all is mixed, hybrid, ritually degraded and defiled. (p. 8)

Deloria (1998) noted that carnival, according to Bakhtin,

> represented a second life, a different consciousness that transcended the everyday. In the festive practices of the common people of Europe, [Bakhtin] saw a topsy-turvy, mocking way of being that questioned the rationalized administrative power of the state. As both specific holiday ritual and generalized consciousness, carnival broke

down boundaries, demonstrating the commonalities between upper and lower classes, law and custom, food and flesh, past and present, civilized and savage, birth and death. It replaced all forms of rank and hierarchy with a boundless utopian freedom. Over time, the impact of these different consciousnesses might painstakingly transform the larger structures of society. (pp. 15-16)

Another scholar, Stam (1989), concluded,

> *Carnival*, for Bakhtin, refers to the pre-Lenten revelry whose origins can be traced back to the Dionysian festivities of the Greeks and the Saturnalia of the Romans, but which enjoyed its apogee of both observance and symbolic meaning in the High Middle Ages. In that period, Bakhtin points out, carnival represented an alternative cosmovision characterized by the ludic undermining of all norms. The carnivalesque principle abolishes hierarchies, levels social classes, and creates another life free from conventional rules and restrictions. In carnival, all that is marginalized and excluded—the mad, the scandalous, the aleatory—takes over the center in a liberating explosion of otherness. (p. 86)

As the three long quotations in the previous paragraph illustrate, Bakhtin understood carnival as a complicated and dynamic social and cultural practice. Stallybrass and White (1986) suggested that it might be useful to distinguish between a narrow and more expanded sense of carnival. They wrote,

> On the one hand, carnival was a specific calendrical ritual; carnival proper, for instance, occurred around February each year, ineluctably followed by Lenten fasting and abstinence bound tightly to laws, structures, and institutions which had briefly been denied during its reign. On the other hand, carnival also refers to a mobile set of symbolic practices, images, and discourses which were employed throughout social revolts and conflicts [and other periods of social disturbance]. (p. 15).[1]

Deloria (1998) made a similar point with his distinction between particular holiday **rituals** and a more "generalized consciousness." Bakhtin, most scholars agree, focused on how the elements of the narrower or more particularized practice of carnival spread and come to saturate a social structure.

The passages from Stallybrass and White (1986), Deloria (1998), and Stam (1989) also indicated that Bakhtin found carnival interesting not just because of what it was but also because of what it did—its social *functions.* Bakhtin repeatedly emphasized the liberating and subversive potentiality of carnival. Carnival is decidedly *anti-hierarchical;* put differently, carnival practices overturn or level "social hierarchies" (Stam, 1989, p. 90). Carnival is a practical form of *demystification.* All that is important, official, or sacred within a culture is, during carnival, exposed to ridicule and mockery. Carnival unleashes radical political and cultural potentialities that are repressed by social institutions, procedures, and rules during other times of the year. Bakhtin's evaluation of the transformative potential of carnival almost always is positive. Recent commentators often qualify Bakhtin's exuberance for carnival. For example, Eagleton (1981) remarked, "Carnival, after all, is a *licensed* affair in every sense, a permissible rupture of hegemony, a contained popular blow-off as disturbing and relatively ineffectual as a revolutionary work of art" (p. 148; see also Eco, 1984). Stam (1989) noted how "carnival is . . . susceptible to co-optation" (p. 94) or appropriation by dominant elements of a society (e.g., government, educational and religious institutions, corporations). The result, he suggested, are " 'ersatz' or 'degraded' carnivals" produced by cultural elites and dominant institutions. Stam continued,

> The American mass media are fond of weak or truncated forms of carnival that capitalize on the frustrated desire for a truly egalitarian society by serving up distorted ver-

> sions of carnival's utopian promise: Fourth of July commercial pageantry, jingoistic sing-alongs, authoritarian rock concerts, festive soft drink commercials. (pp. 225-226)

Stallybrass and White (1986) concluded that it is impossible to specify in advance the political valence of carnival forms (whether they are "progressive," "libertory," or "repressive"). They insisted, "The politics of carnival cannot be resolved outside of a close historical examination of particular conjunctures: there is no a priori revolutionary vector to carnival and transgression" (p. 16).

Given this basic understanding of carnival, we can turn to the second key question: What is the relationship between carnival as a specific set of cultural practices and literature and other discursive practices? The key to the relationship is Bakhtin's (1984) idea of *carnivalization*—the "determining influence of carnival on literature" (p. 122; see also Booker, 1991, 1995). According to Stam (1989), "Art becomes carnivalized in those texts which productively deploy the traces, whether absorbed directly, indirectly, or through intermediate links, of carnivalistic folk culture." Carnivalization refers to "a literary, textual echo of the social practice of carnival" (p. 96). The process of carnivalization is first visible, Bakhtin suggested, in the works of the French writer Rabelias and continues to emerge as an important element of the novel. Studies of literary carnivalization abound (see the sources in Booker, 1991, 1995; Stam, 1989).

What influence, if any, does carnival have on more mundane discursive practices? Can we speak of carnivalized rhetoric? Stam (1989) suggested, "The linguistic corollary of carnivalization entails the liberation of language from the norms of good sense and etiquette" (p. 99). What are some instances in which language is so liberated? Rhetorical scholars have noted a few discursive forms that qualify as carnivalized rhetoric. Scholars of protest discourse, such as Bosmajian (1972) and Windt (1972), focus on the use of obscenity and graphic imagery and discuss the way in which these practices purposefully violate or reject established norms of propriety or **decorum.** Recent inquiry into what Deem (1996) described as *scatological rhetoric* also reveals an element of the carnivalesque.[2] Scatology, in its narrowest sense, refers to the study of excrement. The term can be used more broadly to refer to the study of vulgarity and obscenity in language and literature (Burgess, 1992; Sheidlower, 1995). Deem (1996) provided a detailed examination of scatological rhetoric in her study of Valeria Solanis's 1967 SCUM manifesto (SCUM was Solanis's acronym for the Society for Cutting Up Men). Although frequently disparaged as the product of madness, Deem read Solanis's manifesto as an intentionally "indecorous discourse which, through the lushness of bodily excess [an attribute, we can note, of the carnivalesque], deterritorializes language, pushing it to its extremes" (p. 525). The central conceptual question that Deem's study raises, which can be extended to the entire realm of carnivalized rhetoric, is whether scatological rhetoric is merely indecorous or an important form of "the rhetoric of resistance" (Phillips, 1999), understood as a discursive form used to transgress or challenge repressive discursive norms. As these examples indicate, Bakhtin's thinking on carnival might have something to offer rhetorical scholars interested in these issues.

Notes

1. On the ritualistic nature of carnival, see Bell (1997, pp. 126-127).

2. Stam (1989) observed, "By focusing on the shared physiological processes of bodily life—copulation, birth, eating, drinking, defecation—the carnivalesque aesthetic offers a temporary suspension of hierarchy and prohibition. The carnivalesque, for Bakhtin, is designed to transfer all that is spiritual, ideal, and abstract to the material level, to the sphere of earth and the body" (p. 137). On the relationship between carnival and scatology, see also Morson and Emerson (1990).

References and Additional Reading

Bakhtin, M. (1968). *Rabelais and his world* (H. Iswolsky, Trans.). Cambridge, MA: MIT Press.

Bakhtin, M. (1984). *Problems of Dostoevsky's poetics* (C. Emerson, Trans.). Minneapolis: University of Minnesota Press.

Bell, C. (1997). *Ritual: Perspectives and dimensions.* New York: Oxford University Press.

Booker, M. K. (1991). *Techniques of subversion in modern literature: Transgression, abjection, and the carnivalesque.* Gainesville: University of Florida Press.

Booker, M. K. (1995). *Joyce, Bakhtin, and the literary tradition: Toward a comparative cultural poetics.* Ann Arbor: University of Michigan Press.

Bosmajian, H. A. (1972). Obscenity and protest. In H. A. Bosmajian (Ed.), *Dissent: Symbolic behavior and rhetorical strategies.* Boston: Allyn & Bacon.

Burgess, A. (1992). Low-life language. In A. Burgess, *A mouthful of air: Language, languages . . . especially English.* New York: William Morrow.

Castle, T. (1986). *Masquerade and civilization: The carnivalesque in eighteenth-century English culture and fiction.* Stanford, CA: Stanford University Press.

Deem, M. (1996). From Bobbitt to SCUM: Rememberment, scatological rhetorics, and feminist strategies in the contemporary United States. *Public Culture, 8,* 511-537.

Deloria, P. (1998). *Playing Indian.* New Haven, CT: Yale University Press.

Eagleton, T. (1981). *Walter Benjamin or towards a revolutionary criticism.* London: Verso.

Eco, U. (1984). The frames of comic "freedom." In T. A. Sebeok (Ed.), *Carnival!* Berlin: Mouton.

Morson, G. S., & Emerson, C. (1990). *Mikhail Bakhtin: Creation of a prosaics.* Stanford, CA: Stanford University Press.

Phillips, K. R. (1999). Rhetoric, resistance, and criticism: A response to Ono and Sloop. *Philosophy and Rhetoric, 32,* 96-102.

Sheidlower, J. (Ed.). (1995). *The f-word.* New York: Random House.

Stam, R. (1989). *Subversive pleasures: Bakhtin, cultural criticism, and film.* Baltimore, MD: Johns Hopkins University Press.

Stallybrass, P., & White, A. (1986). *The politics and poetics of transgression.* Ithaca, NY: Cornell University Press.

Windt, T. O., Jr. (1972). The diatribe: Last resort for protest. *Quarterly Journal of Speech, 58,* 1-14.

CASE CONSTRUCTION

What general persuasive or argumentative options are available to advocates working as agents of change? What options are open to advocates working as defenders of the present system or status quo? **Case construction** is the term used by argument scholars to describe the general plan or approach that advocates adopt in pursuing their advocacy efforts. Two forms of case construction—*affirmative* (or pro-change) and *negative* (or anti-change)—are discussed in the argumentation and **debate** literature.

Affirmative Case Construction Strategies

Advocates who desire to change the status quo (either by adopting a new policy or course of action or by overturning an existing policy or course of action) need to construct an affirmative case to embody their reasons for change. They need to establish what sometimes is called a *prima facie case* that establishes reasonable grounds for the proposed change. What are their available options? Three affirmative case construction strategies consistently appear in the literature.

The "Needs" Case

The needs case emphasizes the actual or anticipated existence of an *ill* or *problem.* The needs case tries to demonstrate that, unless this ill is remedied, serious consequences will result; hence, a "need" for a remedy exists. Environmental advocates trying to persuade a state legislature to enact new regulations prohibiting the disposal of certain materials in refuse landfills try to establish that there is a need for the new policy by providing evidence of the dangers of current practices (e.g., current dumping practices contribute to the pollution of groundwater). Advocates employing the needs case must establish the existence of the ill; there is no case for change without it. Once the existence of the ill is established, the advocates then show how the current policies (the status quo) are unable to solve or remedy the ill effectively. A new course of action is necessary. This new course of action must be shown to be capable of solving the problem, to be feasible or workable, and to produce no serious detrimental consequences. Essentially, then, the needs case treats each of the **stock issues of a policy dispute** with special emphasis given to the stock issue of ill.

The "Comparative Advantages" Case

As the discussion in the entry for stock issues in policy disputes notes, in certain situations the perceived ill is not a tangible threat to our physical or material safety but rather a perception that things could and, hence, should be better. During discussion at a corporation's stockholders meeting, a stockholder complains that the corporation experienced only 3% growth in the previous fiscal year, so the stockholder's dividend earnings were not what he or she thought they should be. If enough stockholders come to share this perception, then the 3% growth rate becomes an ill that the corporation's board of directors needs to address. In situations where the ill is a felt sense that things could and should be better, advocates of change often employ the case construction strategy of comparative advantages. The first step, as the preceding example indicates, is to create the shared perception that things should be better. Once that perception is shared, the key to the comparative advantages strategy is to show how an alternative course of action will produce more benefits (or more advantages) than retaining current practices. The disgruntled stockholder in the example might propose that the corporation sell off one of its subsidiaries to increase corporate profits and stockholder dividends. In certain situations, selling off a subsidiary might be a response to a threat (e.g., a hostile takeover); hence, advocates most likely would rely on a needs case strategy (we "need" to sell off the subsidiary to fight the takeover). But in the example, there is not a clear need to sell off the subsidiary. The course of action is proposed to accrue more advantages than the status quo provides. Opponents of this course of action would try to argue that more advantages are to be found by retaining the subsidiary and the present course of action (such an argument probably would introduce a *disjunctive* strategy that distinguishes short-term profitability from long-term profitability). The crux of the dispute in this example is which course of action produces the most advantages, and the case construction strategy emphasizes the comparison of advantages produced by the rival courses of action.

Ziegelmueller, Kay, and Dause (1990) suggested that the comparative advantages strategy "should be used when *both* the present system and the affirmative proposal are capable of achieving the primary goal of the proposition or when *neither* the present system nor the affirmative proposal [is] fully capable of achieving the primary goal of the proposition" (p. 186). In other words, in some situations a proposed new policy and the existing policy both are capable of solving a problem or meeting certain goals. Consider current clean air regulations. They appear to be solving the problem of air pollution and helping us to meet our shared goal of clean air. But a new proposal that will mandate the use of electric cars also will help to solve the problem and allow us to meet our goals. Which should we choose—the status quo policy or the new proposal? The decision will turn, most likely, on which plan of action produces the most advantages and the fewest disadvantages. An affirmative plan advocating the new mandates would try to show that it would produce more advantages than the status quo policy and would lead to fewer disadvantages. In other situations, neither the status quo policy nor a new proposal could fully solve the existing ill. Consider the problem of unemployment. Can any plan of action solve it completely? Perhaps not. But we still are faced with choices between competing policies. Which do we choose? Again, the issue comes down to a comparison of advantages and disadvantages. Advocates of a new policy for addressing the problem of unemployment would find the comparative advantages strategy extremely useful.

Finally, we should note that the case construction strategy of comparative advantages also can be used in a supporting role in a needs case. In 1850, America faced a crisis, with slavery seemingly being the root cause. In the U.S. Senate, Henry Clay rose to propose a series of measures that, he believed, would resolve the crisis. In the first part of his famous 2-day speech on February 5-6 of that year, Clay employed the needs case strategy: A threat to the union existed, and he proposed a cure or a way of saving the union. In the latter part of his speech, Clay slipped into the comparative advantages strategy when he analyzed the advantages and disadvantages of his plan in comparison with an earlier plan of regional compromise—the Missouri compromise of 1820. His plan, Clay argued, was superior to the earlier plan; both the North and the South would accrue important advantages and would avoid serious disadvantages by its implementation. Clay was able to provide additional support for his plan of action by supplementing his needs case with the strategy of comparative advantages.

The "Goals" Case

The goals case, also called the "criteria" case, establishes the existence of a shared goal that is then used to evaluate both the status quo and any proposed new policies. As an affirmative construction strategy, the goals case tries to show that the status quo does not meet or satisfy the goal. An advocate seeking to change a nation's interventionist foreign policy could argue that "national self-determination" is an important goal in the area of foreign policy and that the current policy of siding with a particular faction in another country's civil war violates that shared goal. An alternative policy, disengagement from the affairs of the foreign nation, could then be defended as a policy that fits the goal of self-determination. The typical problem with the goals case is that multiple goals often are at stake in any policy dispute, making it difficult to reduce the issue to a single goal or to prioritize the criteria for evaluation and decision.

Negative Case Construction Strategies

Advocates who are opposed to a proposed policy or course of action need to construct a negative case to express their opposition. What options are available? Four negative case construction strategies are widely discussed in the literature.

Direct Refutation

As Ziegelmueller and colleagues (1990) explained, advocates employing the strategy of direct refutation "make no real commitment to either the principles or the mechanisms of the present system" or status quo. In direct refutation, opponents of change

> respond to the claims of the affirmative without assuming the responsibility for defending any alternative policy. . . . In effect, those who argue from this position are saying that they do not know what should be done, but they do know that the affirmative analysis is unsatisfactory. (p. 194)

Opponents of a proposed flat tax, for example, could try to subvert the supporters' claims regarding the existence of an *ill,* attribution of *blame,* the *solvency* and *feasibility* of the plan, or the *consequences* of the new policy. In using the strategy of direct refutation, opponents of the flat tax need not offer arguments in support of the existing tax structure, nor do they need to defend any other alternative. They simply must negate the evidence and/or the lines of argument used by those in favor of the change. Although potentially effective in certain situations, reliance on the strategy of direct refutation opens advocates to an *ad hominem* attack that they are mere obstructionists who are unable to make any positive contribution to ongoing deliberation. This charge can have persuasive force, especially if opponents of change concede that an ill exists. The "negativism" of direct refutation led Ziegelmueller and colleagues to conclude that this strategy tends to be "psychologically unsatisfactory and emotionally unappealing" (p. 194).

Defense of the Status Quo

When confronted with a case for change, opponents of change can rely on the strategy of defending the status quo. Employing this strategy does not commit opponents of change to the belief that present policies are, from an ideal perspective, the best or the most desirable. Defense of the status quo asserts that, given our options at the moment, the status quo is the best course of action. This strategy is, then, a negative version of comparative advantages; it asserts that the status quo, when compared to the affirmative proposal, is the best course of action. Ziegelmueller and colleagues (1990) recommended that this strategy "should be used whenever existing policies can be shown to have considerable success and when alleged failures can either be denied or be shown to be temporary or unavoidable" (p. 192).

Minor Repairs

In many situations, an absolute commitment to the status quo is inadvisable; present policies either are flawed or appear to be flawed, making their defense foolish or extremely difficult. When faced with situations of this type, opponents of the proposed affirmative plan can opt for the strategy of minor repairs. According to Ziegelmueller and colleagues (1990), minor repairs "involves an unqualified commitment to the fundamental principles or basic structure of present policies, but it recognizes that the implementation of those principles can be improved" (p. 193). For example, the 1993 health care proposal of Bill Clinton's administration can be thought of as both an affirmative plan for changing the status quo and a negative strategy of minor repairs in light of calls from some in Congress, as well as various consumer and health care groups, for the United States to institute a national single-payer health plan based on the model of Canada. Clinton's plan, although branded as radical by some, managed to preserve basic principles of the existing health care system (primarily, it left health insurance as a private for-profit enterprise) while rejecting more fundamental changes. Similarly, when faced with calls to dismantle affirmative action programs, Clinton responded with his call to "mend it but don't end it."

Whereas scholars attempt to articulate criteria for judging whether or not repairs should be considered minor, it is important to recognize that the **ambiguity** of the idea of minor repairs can be exploited by advocates. Because it usually is easier to sell the public on minor repairs than to sell the public on radical change, advocates often try to position at least potentially radical or novel proposals as only minor repairs. Critics of Franklin Roosevelt's "New Deal" programs during the 1930s saw them as a major departure from the American traditions of individualism and free enterprise, whereas Roosevelt, in performances such as his 1932 campaign speech at San Francisco's Commonwealth Club, positioned his proposals as consistent with basic American principles; he was merely adjusting those principles to the realities of the 20th century and making minor repairs in policy.[1] What some then saw (and some continue to see) as creeping socialism, Roosevelt depicted as minor repairs to America's basic capitalistic economic system. The Roosevelt example, as well as the previous example of Clinton's health care plan, illustrates another important ambiguity: In certain cases, advocates can position themselves as both agents of change (both Clinton and Roosevelt sought significant changes in existing policies) and agents opposed to change (both Clinton and Roosevelt sought to resist calls for more radical change that were emanating from certain sections of American society). In the abstract, and in many real-world cases, it is relatively easy to determine who is the affirmative advocate of change and who is the negative advocate opposed to change, but in some complex public debates, it can be difficult to place advocates in the affirmative and negative roles because those roles can be reshaped by creative rhetorical performances.

Counterplan

In some situations, advocates opposed to change are unable, for either practical or philosophical reasons, to defend the status quo with or without minor repairs. In these situations, advocates might decide to oppose the call for change by defending a counterplan or an alternative to the affirmative's proposed change as well as to the status quo. As Ziegelmueller and colleagues (1990) suggested, "The counterplan should be used when an advocate feels that there is a third approach that is better than either the present system or the affirmative proposal" (p. 195). The most significant drawback to the counterplan strategy is that advocates give up the **presumption** that typically adheres to the status quo. When selecting the strategy of counterplan, opponents of change assume the same basic **burden of proof** that advocates of change face. The counterplan strategy, like the defense of the status quo, functions as a negative version of comparative advantages. Opponents of change arguing in favor of a counterplan imply that the counterplan, when compared to the affirmative plan, accrues more advantages and fewer disadvantages and, hence, should be adopted.

Note

1. Burke (1950) would term this **casuistic stretching.**

References and Additional Reading

Burke, K. (1950). *A rhetoric of motives.* New York: Prentice Hall.

Freeley, A. J. (1996). *Argumentation and debate: Critical thinking for reasoned decision making* (9th ed.). Belmont, CA: Wadsworth.

Inch, E. S., & Warnick, B. (1998). *Critical thinking and communication: The use of reason in argument* (3rd ed.). Boston: Allyn & Bacon.

Reinard, J. C. (1991). *Foundations of argument: Effective communication for critical thinking.* Dubuque, IA: William C. Brown.

Zarefsky, D. (1969). The "traditional case"—"comparative advantages case" dichotomy: Another look. *Journal of the American Forensic Association, 6,* 12-20.

Ziegelmueller, G., Kay, J., & Dause, C. (1990). *Argumentation: Inquiry and advocacy.* Englewood Cliffs, NJ: Prentice Hall.

CASUISTIC STRETCHING

Casuistry, Burke (1950) wrote in *A Rhetoric of Motives,* is "the application of abstract principles to particular conditions" (p. 155).[1] As contemporary discussions of the traditional concept of **prudence** suggest, the relationship between "principle" or "rule" and local "conditions" or "particular" case is not as simple as the term *application* appears to suggest. Principles are not applied to cases in a mechanistic manner; rather, contemporary theorists speak frequently of the idea of adjusting principles to cases or negotiating the relationship between principle and case. And the particular case must be inspected with the utmost care. As Miller (1996) commented,

> A basic requirement of casuistry is to attend carefully to complex details, the contingencies, and vagaries of human experience. Casuistry demands that we examine the data and interpretations that surround a given case, that we work through appearances in order to find those that are most reliable. (p. 222)

Even in rather mundane situations, the relationship between principle ("always tell the truth," "do not lie") and case (a rather bland dinner at the home of prospective in-laws) can be extremely complex ("Do I tell the truth and risk insulting my future in-laws, or do I violate the principle?"), and this complexity introduces the possibility of modifying or refining the abstract principle. Burke was well aware of this possibility and discussed it under the heading of **casuistic stretching.**

In *Attitudes Toward History,* Burke (1984) defined casuistic stretching as "introducing new principles while theoretically remaining faithful to old principles" (p. 229). For example, Carlson (1992) analyzed the discourse of the 19th-century American Female Reform Society (AFRS), a group devoted to saving women from prostitution, and concluded that "the moral reform movement used skillful casuistic stretching of the feminine ideal to justify taking nontraditional action in the name of traditional values" (p. 17). In Burke's terms, the members of the movement "theoretically" remained faithful to "old principles" (19th-century gender definitions) while introducing new ones (the necessity for women to participate in public deliberation). Casuistic stretching can exact a cost on advocates who employ it. Carlson extended Burke's observation that "casuistic stretching [can] eventually lead to demoralization" (Burke, 1984, p. 229) to the AFRS. Carlson (1992) wrote,

> Casuistry can only "stretch" so far before the guilt created by its violation of hierarchy becomes nearly intolerable. . . . Unable to assuage their guilt, women were prey to their own piety [devotion to the "old" principles] and were soon sent back to their traditional place not made tolerable by comparison. (pp. 29-30)

Another illustration of casuistic stretching, one that reveals the nexus between casuistry and the current revival of interest in prudence, is Franklin Roosevelt's 1932 "Commonwealth Club" address.[2] In the address, Roosevelt made a case for greater governmental intervention in America's economic sphere in the wake of the stock market crash and the nation's economic depression. But what made Roosevelt's strategy an instance of casuistic stretching was his insistence that his "new" proposals were merely an extension or a continuation of America's traditional practices applied to new circumstances. As Roosevelt put it, "We have now to apply the earlier concepts of American government to the conditions of today" that will lead to "the redefinition of these rights in terms of a changing and growing social order." Roosevelt promised to protect "individualism" (the traditional value) through practices that (at least to some of Roosevelt's critics) threatened to destroy individualism. That protection would come in the form of a new "contract" whose "terms . . . are as old as the republic and as new as the new economic order." The artistry of Roosevelt's speech, as Leff's (1991) reading helps to disclose, was his ability to depict American history (e.g., the battle between Hamilton and Jefferson, the rise of industrial titans) in such a way that his innovative proposals were shown to be consistent with traditional values. Or, in Burke's terminology, the traditional values were "stretched" to encompass Roosevelt's political innovations.

Jonsen and Toulmin (1988) wrote, "About casuistical discussion in practical contexts, we may therefore say: 'Everybody depends upon it, even though few people say so explicitly' " (pp. 14-15). Miller (1996) made a similar point: "A careful look at recent events suggests that we all engage in casuistry, if only inchoately" (p. 5). Burke most likely would have agreed with these statements. Casuistry and casuistic stretching seem to saturate language and discourse practices. Burke (1984) concluded,

> The process of casuistic stretching must itself be subjected continually to *conscious* attention. Its own resources . . . must be transcended by the explicit conversion of a method into a methodology. The difference between casuistry as a method and casuistry as a methodology is the difference between mystification and clarification, between the concealing of a strategy (*ars celare artem*) and the description of a strategy (criticism as explanation). (p. 232)

Notes

1. See also Cheney (1991), Jonsen and Toulmin (1988), Miller (1996), and Sunstein (1996).
2. For a **prudential** reading of the address, see Leff (1991).

References and Additional Reading

Burke, K. (1950). *A rhetoric of motives.* New York: Prentice Hall.

Burke, K. (1984). *Attitudes toward history* (3rd ed.). Berkeley: University of California Press.

Carlson, A. C. (1992). Creative casuistry and feminist consciousness: The rhetoric of moral reform. *Quarterly Journal of Speech, 78,* 16-32.

Cheney, G. (1991). *Rhetoric in an organizational society: Managing multiple identities.* Columbia: University of South Carolina Press.

Jonsen, A. R., & Toulmin, S. (1988). *The abuse of casuistry: A history of moral reasoning.* Berkeley: University of California Press.

Leff, M. (1991). Prudential argument and the use of history in Franklin D. Roosevelt's "Commonwealth Club" address. In F. H. van Eemeren, R. Grootendorst, J. A. Blair, & C. A. Willard (Eds.), *Proceedings of the Second International Conference on Argumentation.* Amsterdam: Stichting Internationaal Centrum voor de Studie van Argumentatie en Taalbeheersing (SICSAT).

Miller, R. B. (1996). *Casuistry and modern ethics: A poetics of practical reasoning.* Chicago: University of Chicago Press.

Sunstein, C. R. (1996). *Legal reasoning and political conflict.* New York: Oxford University Press.

CLOSE READING

As Medhurst (1993) noted, one of the ironies in the critical literature of rhetorical studies is that for a discipline associated with the study of human speech, until recently scholars in the field devoted little attention to the study of specific speeches. Detailed attention to specific speeches, as well as other forms of discursive practice such as essays, **public letters,** and declarations, has increased dramatically over the past decade as a new approach to criticism, **close reading,** seized the imagination of many rhetorical critics. Close reading is one of the more important movements in contemporary rhetorical criticism and, as such, demands careful attention.

The strategy of close reading did not emerge overnight, nor is this approach to the practice of criticism unique to the field of rhetorical studies. As early as 1957, Charles Redding lamented the lack of attention to the "intrinsic" characteristics of speech texts (Redding, 1957).[1] G. P. Mohrmann, who (along with Michael Leff) usually is identified as a key figure in the emergence of the close reading approach to criticism, argued in 1980 that the explosion of critical methods that took place in the field during the late 1960s and 1970s did little to help critics analyze the inner workings of rhetorical texts (Mohrmann, 1980). Rhetorical critics, Mohrmann charged, were forever circling the objects of their studies and never entering those objects. Critics interested in digging more deeply into speeches drew some inspiration and advice from the field of literary criticism. The method of **new criticism,** perhaps the dominant model of literary criticism during the middle of the 20th century, encouraged critics to analyze carefully the literary elements of novels and poems (e.g., language, images), whereas the more recent *reader-response* approach to literary criticism encouraged critics to analyze how textual elements shaped and guided the experience of reading.[2] In short, the strategy of close reading did not emerge from a vacuum; trends within rhetorical studies and outside the field contributed to its development.

What are the central principles or guiding assumptions of close reading? Close reading begins in an effort to position the **text**—the specific speech, essay, pamphlet, and so on—at the very center of critical activity. The story of, in Gaonkar's (1989) terms, the "deferral" and subsequent "arrival" of the text in rhetorical studies has become familiar to contemporary rhetoricians. Gaonkar wrote,

> It would seem that the oratorical text has come a long way, journeying through the vicissitudes of our disciplinary consciousness,

> and in the course of that journey, it has been transformed from the fugitive flotsam and jetsam of popular chatter into an autonomous cultural form. (p. 257)

As Gaonkar made clear, the arrival of the text also was the occasion of its transformation. Whereas the text once was understood to be ephemeral, transparent (see the entry for **transparency thesis**), and devoid of substance, critics working in the close reading movement now approach the text—the critical object—in a new way. Close readers tend to conceptualize the text as powerful and extremely complex.

The transformation of the text is most visible in some of the common adjectives used by critics to describe it. Texts possess a "rhetorical texture" (Leff, 1980, p. 339), they embody a certain "integrity and density" (Leff, 1986, p. 381), they are a site of "action" (p. 378), and they are constituted by an "internal dynamic" (Lucas, 1988, p. 253). It might be helpful to unpack these adjectives a bit. To say that a text has "texture" is a way of calling attention to its structure of interacting elements; texts are not a mere collection of words, sentences, and paragraphs but rather an organized composition of various resources (e.g., ideas, images, arguments). To maintain that a text possesses "integrity" is a way of recognizing its wholeness; texts are not mere incoherent scraps of discourse but rather unified or completed discursive products. To write about a text's "density" is a way of acknowledging the wealth of material that is packed within its borders; texts are not empty shells or vessels full of discursive drivel but rather repositories that contain almost endless insights into the particulars of their situations. To describe a text as a site of "action" or to draw attention to a text's "internal dynamics" is a way of emphasizing the interactions among the various elements and forces that constitute and shape the text; texts are not static objects but rather events that unfold, and sometimes mutate, over time.

Leff (1986) summarized this reconfiguration of the text in the following postulate: "*Oratory is an art form*" (p. 381). The rhetorical text possesses the same general type of complexity, nuance, and subtlety found in other art forms (e.g., poetry, painting). But Leff argued that there is one significant difference that complicates the project of close reading. Leff wrote,

> Unlike poetry and other "purer" forms of verbal art, the oration does not call attention to its own status as an art form. Oratory succeeds best when it appears to blend into the context of ordinary experience. It is a genre of discourse that effaces its own constructions. (p. 381)

In short, a rhetorical text appears to hide—to draw attention away from—its constitutive strategies and tactics. Consequently, close readers have to employ some mechanism for piercing the veil that covers the text so as to see how it works.

Some close readers in rhetorical studies have turned to Fish's (1972) account of reader-response criticism as a way of moving through the text's surface appearance of artlessness (the sense that the text is "just" a speech or an essay, nothing as *complicated* as a poem or novel) and into its manner of action. For example, Lucas (1988) wrote,

> The benefit of close textual analysis is that it allows the critic, in essence, to "slow down" the action within the text. . . . To borrow Stanley Fish's analogy about the methods of reader-response literary criticism, "It is as if a slow-motion camera with an automatic stop action effect were recording our linguistic experiences and presenting them to us for viewing." (p. 249)

Lucas's student, Amy Slagell, described her analysis of Abraham Lincoln's "Second Inaugural Address" as a "microscopic" reading of the text. In elaborating this approach to reading, Slagell (1991) also drew on Fish:

> This microscopic perspective offers a new way to account for Lincoln's celebrated mastery. The approach is akin to that of reader-response criticism in literary studies.

> As Stanley Fish notes, "What the method does is *slow down* the reading experience so that 'events' one does not notice in normal time, but which do occur, are brought before our analytical attention." This enables the critic to analyze the developing responses of the reader or listener in relation to the words as they succeed one another in time. (p. 155)

Whether they directly invoke Fish (as did Lucas and Slagell) or not, close readers do employ some method for slowing down their experiences of or encounters with the critical object. The principal object of close reading is to unpack the text. Close readers linger over words, verbal images, elements of **style**, sentences, **argument** patterns, and entire paragraphs and larger discursive units within the text to explore their significance on multiple levels.[3]

This last observation about the different levels of analysis leads into a consideration of the aims of close reading. What do close readers hope to accomplish? As the preceding paragraph suggests, the dominant objective of the close reading movement in rhetorical studies is to unpack texts—to reveal how specific speeches (e.g., Lincoln's "Second Inaugural Address") or essays (e.g., Martin Luther King, Jr.'s "Letter From Birmingham Jail") work. But this homogeneity of aim or purpose is somewhat deceptive. Texts enact multiple functions and work in different ways on different levels. So, although close readers are united in the degree of attention they give to the inner workings of texts, there still are differences within the close reading critical movement when it comes to the appropriate levels of analysis.

Two major trends are discernible in the close reading movement. One trend, represented by the works of Lucas (1988, 1989) and others (Henry, 1988; Iltis, 1992; Slagell, 1991), emphasizes *art* and *strategy.* Lucas (1988) wrote,

> The purpose of the critic is not simply to retell the speech in his or her own words but to apprehend it fully from the inside out—to break down its rhetorical elements so completely as to determine how they function individually and to explain how they interact to shape the text as a *strategic, artistic* response to the exigences of a particular situation. (p. 253, emphasis added)[4]

Although Lucas acknowledged that the close reading approach can operate at different analytic levels, his principal concern was with "the close analysis of individual texts with an eye toward explicating their rhetorical artistry" (p. 254). The level of analysis within this trend is authorial intention[5] and immediate rhetorical situation. The close reader seeks to describe in detail how purpose is realized (at times subconsciously) in particular textual forms and strategies and how these forms and strategies negotiate the various elements in the rhetorical situation (especially *exigences* and *constraints*). Close readings of this sort reveal how art (e.g., grammar, style, structure) and strategy (e.g., purpose, explicit argument) interact in the realization of an *instrumental effect.*

An alternative approach to close reading began to emerge in some of Leff's initial "proto-theoretical formulation[s]" (Gaonkar, 1989, p. 265). The question that shaped Leff's (1980) metacritical essay was as follows: What is the appropriate relationship between theory and critical practice. As Gaonkar (1989) observed, Leff's rejection of the then dominant understanding of the theory-critical practice relationship (where criticism is understood as a process of applying or testing theories) is not a rejection of theory per se but rather an effort "to reconfigure the relationship between rhetorical theory and critical practice" (p. 270). Leff (1980) situated "psychoanalytic interpretation" in an analogous relationship with rhetorical criticism. Leff argued that both practices are united in their concern with particular cases (the psychoanalyst is concerned with his or her patient, the rhetorical critic is concerned with a text) but that each practice also must draw on theoretical principles that are outside the isolated case. In both practices, Leff wrote, "the process [of inquiry] always involves explanation, and the attempt to explain puts the analyst in contact with matters of theoretical interest. . . . The explanation of the specific phenomenon under investigation is itself theoretical." But it is a specific type or "form of theory" (p. 347). Theory in the realms of psychoanalysis and rhetorical criticism, Leff contended, is "inextricably bound up with the particular circumstances the analyst confronts. That is, theoretical precepts attain meaning only as they are vibrated against the particular case and are instantiated in an explanation of it" (p. 347). In his programmatic essay a few years later, Leff (1986) maintained that close reading "eventuates in something we might call theoretical understanding of the particular case" (p. 378).

Close readers who share Leff's interest in what Gaonkar (1989) referred to as a "theory of the case" (p. 266) do not ignore the analytic levels of artistry and strategy. These levels of analysis are fundamental in any version of close reading. But the second trend of close reading in contemporary rhetorical studies consistently pushes beyond the levels of artistry and strategy so as to, as Leff put it metaphorically, "vibrate" theory against text and text against theory. This form of close reading not only leads to a richer understanding of the particular text but also contributes to, in Gaonkar's (1989) terms, "the thickening of [theoretical] concepts through grounded critical readings" (p. 270). Numerous studies in the field illustrate this trend. Leff's (1983) study of Lincoln's "House Divided" address raised the conceptual question of how time is configured in discourse (see also Leff, 1986). The question of how discourse configures or shapes time has appeared in a number of other critical studies (Cox, 1989; Lee, 1991; Stelzner, 1966). Moving in a related direction, Browne (1993b) read Daniel Webster's 1820 "Plymouth Rock Oration" as an instance in the discursive reconstruction of public **memory.** Leff's (1991) analysis of Franklin Roosevelt's 1932 "Commonwealth Club" address thickened our understanding of the traditional concept of **prudence** (see also Browne, 1991; Jasinski, 1995), whereas his study with Rosteck (Rosteck & Leff, 1989) engaged the speech by American anarchist Voltairne de Cleyre, "The Fruit of Sacrifice," as a way of deepening our understanding of the principle of **decorum.** Finally, studies by Browne and Leff (1985) and Farrell (1990) read speeches by Edmund Burke and Fisher Ames, respectively, as instances in the discursive construction of political **judgment.** This discussion of the conceptual trend in close reading, it should be noted, is not exhaustive.

Although close reading has, by some accounts, taken the field of rhetorical studies by storm, it is not without its detractors and critics. For example, Condit (1990) argued that the problem of close reading is that it "pretends that it is reading *the meaning* of a text, when it is only reading the set of experiences that a text enables for a select group" (p. 335). Along similar lines, Warnick (1992) charged that "Leff's approach seeks to mystify and celebrate the discourse of power" (p. 236). What Condit, Warnick, and others emphasize is that close reading encourages an overly formalist, aestheticized approach to the rhetorical text; in short, close reading promotes a type of "rhetoric for rhetoric's sake."[6] These critics suggest that when the text becomes an object for reflection and contemplation, rhetorical critics lose sight of the text's relationship to history (its situatedness) and its role in the perpetuation of the dominant social order (see the entry for **hegemony**). Many scholars who remain skeptical of close reading most likely would agree with the observation of literary scholar F. O. Matthiessen that critics "should realize that we have come to the unnatural point where textual analysis seems an end to itself" (Matthiessen, 1952, p. 5).

Leff (1992) perceived the danger of a "formalism that isolates the text from larger discursive formations and restricts interpretation within the orbit of the text's own construction" (p. 228). If the arrival of the text leads to its historical and cultural isolation, and if textual analysis becomes a formal process of dissecting the text in an effort to catalog its component parts, then close reading is just a pale imitation of literary "new criticism" and eventually will meet the same fate. In Leff's view, the crucial question is as follows: "Is it possible . . . to sustain this concern for the unique integrity of the oratorical text and to remain sensitive to the social and historical dimension of rhetorical practice?" (p. 229). Leff suggested three strategies for negotiating this question.

First, to grasp the relationship between text and **ideology,** Leff introduced the linguistic concept of **iconicity** or the harmony of "form" and "content" (Leff & Sachs, 1990). As Leff and Sachs (1990) acknowledged,

> The effort needed to fathom the intrinsic workings of the text often sponsors an appreciative response and encourages the critic to accept the negotiations effected by it as something more than the construction of a partial and momentary closure. . . . There is a temptation to collapse the context into the text and to lose sight of any larger ideological horizon. (p. 257)

Leff and Sachs suggested that iconicity functions as a way of preserving the integrity of the text as that text is situated within its larger ideological horizon. Iconicity provides the conceptual resource needed to grasp how ideologies are inscribed (or etched) into the *texture* of texts rather than simply present in the "content" of texts. Ideology, they argued, also is "something represented within the tissue of connectives that the text constructs" (p. 269). Close reading need not, then, isolate texts from larger ideological and discursive formations. Instead, it can provide a way of understanding the discursive mechanisms through which ideologies do their cultural and political work.

Second, Leff (1992) suggested that attention to **controversy**—"a sustained activity consisting of particular instances of oppositional discourse"—provides a way of adjusting close reading and render it "more sensitive to intertextual developments" (p. 229). Exploring the pervasive phenomenon of **intertextuality** demands, at a minimum, "attention to the interplay between texts," but such a critical procedure "involves something more than just increasing the number of texts studied" (p. 228). Simultaneous close reading of more than one text, in and of itself, does not allow the critic to engage processes of intertextuality because, as Leff argued, in close reading "the text itself defines the horizon of critical attention. Nothing pushes the critic across intertextual space in the effort to locate and assess the movement of rhetorical strategies and themes" (p. 228). But controversy pushes the critic outside the individual (and potentially isolated) text and forces the critic to engage intertextual dynamics. When a critic approaches texts that are locked in controversy (Leff's examples were Booker T. Washington's "Atlanta Exposition Address" and W. E. B. DuBois's essay, "Of Mr. Booker T. Washington and Others" [DuBois, 1903/1989], but virtually any contemporary controversy [e.g., abortion, animal rights] could be studied in this manner) and reads them closely, "the texts become connected within an intertextual network and with the issues of power and situated interest that inform the whole development [of the controversy], but they retain their integrity as things made by words" (Leff, 1992, p. 230).

Finally, in more recent work, Leff (1997) hinted at another way of pushing the critic into intertextual space. Leff's concept of hermeneutical rhetoric, a reformulation of the relationship between the processes of interpretation and textual production, functions (albeit indirectly) as a theory of textual **invention.** As a theory of invention, hermeneutical rhetoric insists on the commonsense claim that texts are not created in a vacuum; rather, hermeneutical rhetoric understands invention as "a complex process that allows historical texts to serve as equipment for future rhetorical production" (p. 201). Close reading, adjusted to recognize the ubiquity of this inventional process, assumes a Bakhtinian flavor as the critic charts the way in which different languages and voices are borrowed from other texts and subsequently are "orchestrated" or organized in the rhetor's rhetorical performance. Murphy's (1997) study of Bill

Clinton's November 1993 address in Memphis, Tennessee, to a convention of black ministers is an example of this form of close reading. In this essay, Murphy read the speech to uncover the way in which Clinton borrowed, organized, and exploited the rich rhetorical resources of the African American homiletic tradition and, in particular, the work of one of its most outstanding representatives—Martin Luther King, Jr. Through this reading strategy, Murphy pushed beyond the horizon of the individual text in, as Leff (1992) put it, an "effort to locate and assess the movement of rhetorical strategies and themes."[7]

It is too soon to tell whether or not these adjustments to the close reading program will generate a rich body of critical literature that will satisfy its critics. For some rhetorical scholars, close reading is likely to remain a largely formalistic enterprise that describes texts in great detail but leaves them isolated and disconnected from cultural and historical forces.[8] Perhaps rhetorical scholars can find some value in the advice of intellectual historian Dominick LaCapra. LaCapra (1983) wrote, "The obvious problem at present is to learn from formalism without accepting its more extreme claims at face value" (p. 15). One can argue that that is precisely what Leff and other close readers have been trying to do.

Notes

1. But it should be noted that Redding's (1957) proposed solution to this deficiency is drastically different from the practice of close reading.

2. The influence of the early work of Stanley Fish is discussed in more detail shortly.

3. These "levels" include authorial purpose (what Lucas [1988] called the "internal context" of the text), the dynamics of the specific **rhetorical situation**, broader conceptual questions about the nature of language and discursive practice, and the larger political and cultural questions and issues of the times.

4. For a conceptual defense of focusing on the "individuality" of the critical object, see Darsey (1994).

5. See also Leff and Mohrmann's (1974) discussion of "purpose."

6. On the problem posed by the seduction of form, see also Hariman (1989).

7. See also Jasinski's (1997) discussion of "performative traditions" and their relationship to close reading and thick interpretation.

8. The work in the tradition of *critical discourse analysis* (see the entry for **discourse**) might prove instructive in trying to link text and ideological context, close reading, and **critical rhetoric.**

References and Additional Reading

Browne, S. H., & Leff, M. C. (1985). Political judgment and rhetorical argument: Edmund Burke's paradigm. In J. R. Cox, M. Sillars, & G. Walker (Eds.), *Argument and social practice: Proceedings of the Fourth SCA/AFA Conference on Argumentation.* Annandale, VA: Speech Communication Association.

Browne, S. H. (1991). The pastoral voice in John Dickinson's first *Letter From a Farmer in Pennsylvania. Quarterly Journal of Speech, 76,* 46-57.

Browne, S. H. (1993a). *Edmund Burke and the discourse of virtue.* Tuscaloosa: University of Alabama Press.

Browne, S. H. (1993b). Reading public memory in Daniel Webster's *Plymouth Rock Oration. Western Journal of Communication, 57,* 464-477.

Browne, S. (1994). "Like gory spectres": Representing evil in Theodore Weld's *American Slavery as It Is. Quarterly Journal of Speech, 80,* 277-292.

Condit, C. (1990). Rhetorical criticism and audiences: The extremes of McGee and Leff. *Western Journal of Speech Communication, 54,* 330-345.

Cox, J. R. (1989). The fulfillment of time: King's "I Have a Dream" speech. In M. C. Leff & F. J. Kauffeld (Eds.), *Texts in context: Critical dialogues on significant episodes in American political rhetoric.* Davis, CA: Hermagoras Press.

Darsey, J. (1994). Must we all be rhetorical theorists? An anti-democratic inquiry. *Western Journal of Communication, 58,* 164-181.

DuBois, W. E. B. (1989). Of Mr. Booker T. Washington and others. In W. E. B. DuBois, *The souls of black folk.* New York: Viking. (Original work published 1903)

Farrell, J. M. (1990). Fisher Ames and political judgment: Reason, passion, and vehement style in the Jay Treaty speech. *Quarterly Journal of Speech, 76,* 415-434.

Fish, S. (1972). *Self-consuming artifacts.* Berkeley: University of California Press.

Gaonkar, D. P. (1989). The oratorical text: The enigma of arrival. In M. C. Leff & F. J. Kauffeld (Eds.), *Texts in context: Critical dialogues on significant episodes in American political rhetoric.* Davis, CA: Hermagoras Press.

Hariman, R. (1989). Time and the reconstitution of gradualism in King's address: A response to Cox. In M. C. Leff & F. J. Kauffeld (Eds.), *Texts in context:*

Critical dialogues on significant episodes in American political rhetoric. Davis, CA: Hermagoras Press.

Henry, D. (1988). The rhetorical dynamics of Mario Cuomo's 1984 keynote address: Situation, speaker, metaphor. *Southern Speech Communication Journal, 53,* 105-120.

Iltis, R. S. (1992). Textual dynamics of "The New South." *Communication Studies, 43,* 29-41.

Jasinski, J. (1989). Rhetorical force and the unity of political theory and argumentative practice in Madison's *Federalist* #10. In B. E. Gronbeck (Ed.), *Spheres of argument: Proceedings of the Sixth SCA/AFA Conference on Argumentation.* Annandale, VA: Speech Communication Association.

Jasinski, J. (1995). The forms and limits of prudence in Henry Clay's (1850) defense of the compromise measures. *Quarterly Journal of Speech, 81,* 454-478.

Jasinski, J. (1997). Instrumentalism, contextualism, and interpretation in rhetorical criticism. In W. Keith & A. Gross (Eds.), *Rhetorical hermeneutics.* Albany: State University of New York Press.

LaCapra, D. (1983). *Rethinking intellectual history: Texts, contexts, language.* Ithaca, NY: Cornell University Press.

Lee, R. E. (1991). The rhetorical construction of time in Martin Luther King, Jr.'s "Letter From Birmingham Jail." *Southern Communication Journal, 56,* 279-288.

Leff, M. C. (1980). Interpretation and the art of the rhetorical critic. *Western Journal of Speech Communication, 44,* 337-349.

Leff, M. C. (1983). Rhetorical timing in Lincoln's "House Divided" speech. Evanston, IL: Northwestern University Press.

Leff, M. (1986). Textual criticism: The legacy of G. P. Mohrmann. *Quarterly Journal of Speech, 72,* 377-389.

Leff, M. (1991). Prudential argument and the use of history in Franklin D. Roosevelt's "Commonwealth Club" address. In F. H. van Eemeren, R. Grootendorst, J. A. Blair, & C. A. Willard (Eds.), *Proceedings of the Second International Conference on Argumentation.* Amsterdam: Stichting Internationaal Centrum voor de Studie van Argumentatie en Taalbeheersing (SICSAT).

Leff, M. (1992). Things made by words: Reflections on textual criticism. *Quarterly Journal of Speech, 78,* 223-231.

Leff, M. (1997). Hermeneutical rhetoric. In W. Jost & M. J. Hyde (Eds.), *Rhetoric and hermeneutics in our time.* New Haven, CT: Yale University Press.

Leff, M. C., & Mohrmann, G. P. (1974). Lincoln at Cooper Union: A rhetorical analysis of the text. *Quarterly Journal of Speech, 60,* 346-358.

Leff, M., & Sachs, A. (1990). Words the most like things: Iconicity and the rhetorical text. *Western Journal of Speech Communication, 54,* 252-273.

Lucas, S. E. (1988). The renaissance of American public address: Text and context in rhetorical criticism. *Quarterly Journal of Speech, 74,* 241-260.

Lucas, S. E. (1989). Justifying America: The Declaration of Independence as a rhetorical document. In T. W. Benson (Ed.), *American rhetoric: Context and criticism.* Carbondale: Southern Illinois University Press.

Matthiessen, F. O. (1952). *The responsibilities of the critic: Essays and reviews by F. O. Matthiessen* (J. Rackliffe, Ed.). New York: Oxford University Press.

Medhurst, M. J. (1993). The academic study of public address: A tradition in transition. In M. J. Medhurst (Ed.), *Landmark essays on American public address.* Davis, CA: Hermagoras Press.

Mohrmann, G. P. (1980). Elegy in a critical graveyard. *Western Journal of Speech Communication, 44,* 265-274.

Murphy, J. M. (1997). Inventing authority: Bill Clinton, Martin Luther King, Jr., and the orchestration of rhetorical traditions. *Quarterly Journal of Speech, 83,* 71-89.

Redding, W. C. (1957). Extrinsic and intrinsic criticism. *Western Speech, 21,* 96-103.

Rosteck, T., & Leff, M. (1989). Piety, propriety, and perspective: An interpretation and application of key terms in Kenneth Burke's *Permanence and Change. Western Journal of Speech Communication, 53,* 327-341.

Slagell, A. R. (1991). Anatomy of a masterpiece: A close textual analysis of Abraham Lincoln's second inaugural address. *Communication Studies, 42,* 155-171.

Stelzner, H. G. (1966). "War Message," December 8, 1941: An approach to language. *Speech Monographs, 33,* 419-437.

Warnick, B. (1992). Leff in context: What is the critic's role? *Quarterly Journal of Speech, 78,* 232-237.

CONDENSATION SYMBOL

"Black Power," "family values," "male chauvinist," and "welfare queen." What do these terms or slogans have in common? All function as examples of what many scholars have come to term **condensation symbols.** What are condensation symbols? What are their characteristics? How do they function? Scholars in numerous fields have addressed these questions over the past few decades.

Political scientist Doris Graber defined a condensation symbol as "a name, word, phrase, or maxim which stirs vivid impressions involving the listener's most basic values" (Graber, 1976, p. 289). Condensation symbols "are verbal stimuli which evoke multifaceted deeply involving images" in audiences (p. 312). Political theorist Murray Edelman also emphasized the evocative capacity of condensation symbols. They "evoke . . . emotions [and] condense into one symbolic event, sign, or act patriotic pride, anxieties, remembrances of past glories or humiliations, promises of future greatness: some one of these or all of them" (Edelman, 1964, p. 6). Extending the works of linguistic anthropologist Edward Sapir (e.g., Sapir, 1934), Zarefsky (1986) noted how "condensation symbols designate no clear referent but serve to 'condense' into one symbol a host of different meanings and connotations which might diverge if more specific referents were attempted" (p. 11).

Condensation symbols are, then, short and catchy expressions—frequently slogans—that are able to compress (or condense) images, attitudes, reactions, and evaluative judgments into a verbal form. According to Zarefsky (1986), "Condensation symbols are particularly useful when applied to ambiguous situations because they enable an individual to focus on the specific aspects of the situation that are most meaningful" (p. 11). When used skillfully, these compressed verbal forms can evoke, often like a "Pavlovian cue" (Graber, 1976, p. 291), a range of reactions in an audience. Consider a symbolic slogan (e.g., "Remember the Alamo") or a visual image (e.g., a clenched black fist). Each of these condensation symbols evokes different reactions depending on the audience and the situation. An audience's reaction to a condensation symbol frequently is intense and emotionally charged. We often hear people talking about getting someone to act in a certain way by "knowing what buttons to push." Condensation symbols are like those "buttons" except that they are cues for motivating and/or energizing larger groups of people.

Graber (1976) identified three basic characteristics of condensation symbols. First, condensation symbols tend to evoke "rich and vivid" images in an audience (p. 291). But not everyone reacts to a condensation symbol in the same way. The symbol can have different specific functions for different audiences, depending on factors such as race, sex, age or generational affiliation, and political ideology. Consider the slogan "Black Power." This powerful symbol evoked rich and vivid, but different, images from different audiences during the late 1960s. In white audiences, it typically conjured up an image of a black male in a black leather jacket and sunglasses, someone who audience members perceived as potentially violent and a threat and who they consequently feared. In black audiences, the symbol could evoke feelings of pride, solidarity, and empowerment. But not all blacks reacted to the symbol in the same way. Many older blacks during the late 1960s reacted negatively to the symbol, whereas younger blacks, especially those raised in urban areas, tended to react much more positively.[1] Second, condensation symbols possess the "capacity to arouse emotions" (p. 292). The feelings generated by the Black Power symbol made it an "effective mobilizing agent" (p. 292). Third, "condensation symbols supply instant categorizations and evaluations" and help to shape or define our social reality (p. 292).[2] According to Kaufer and Carley (1993), condensation symbols "allow group members to compress their image of the problem at the heart of the issue and solutions to it—often so thoroughly that their decisions about how to decide an issue frequently collapse into their decisions about how to name it" (p. 222). Diffley (1988) suggested that the advantage of a value-laden symbol is that "it insists upon monolithic opposites" (p. 409), thereby shaping how audiences respond to the situation. In other words, when potential condensation symbols such as "reverse discrimination" are used to label a problem, the labels direct how we should think about (or categorize) and evaluate the situation. The condensation symbol names and solves the problem.

Graber's (1976) account of the basic characteristics of condensation symbols led her to suggest some of their more common political and rhetorical functions. Condensation symbols are "economical"; they allow for a type of "shorthand" communication. Using condensation symbols makes it possible for advocates to avoid "the inconvenience and danger of making their reasons explicit" (p. 294). Condensation symbols are a powerful tool for creating and sustaining social solidarity and group identity. They routinely perform a *constitutive* function above and beyond the narrower, and usually more instrumental, objectives of advocates. Finally, condensation symbols play a crucial role in the interrelated processes of definition, socialization, and legitimation. Condensation symbols can help to define the complex events or situations happening in the world, provide a frame of reference for political education, and justify or warrant the exercise of political or state power.[3]

Building off the works of Graber, Edelman, and others, Kaufer and Carley (1993) sought to refine our understanding of the concept of condensation symbols. Based on a multidimensional account of the potency of symbols, they offered a taxonomy of various types of condensation symbols. The first type, *standard symbols,* scored high on all the dimensions of their analytic scale and can be thought of as the most fully developed form of condensation symbols. The other five types that they discussed all placed differently from standard symbols on their analytic scale. Nevertheless, these five types merit attention because it is necessary for a symbol to score high on only one of the scale's three dimensions to merit inclusion in the general category of condensation symbols. The second type of condensation symbol is *buzzwords,* which "name loosely framed goals, aspirations, and ideas that spark excitement but await elaboration and specification" (p. 207). Buzzwords work as "seductive invitations" (p. 214) and try to coax the assent of audiences to ambiguous, loosely defined normative goals. Buzzwords can be found in groups of various sizes. Academic disciplines, multinational corporations, and nations can have various buzzwords that define the current objectives of the groups. Buzzwords can persist through time (e.g., "justice," "equality") or might simply be passing fads (e.g., a corporate manager's fascination with organizational synergy). Their ambiguity makes buzzwords, along with the next two types of condensation symbols, "especially useful for building symbolic bridges" between groups with different belief systems (p. 213).[4] The third type of condensation symbol is *pregnant placeholders,* which "name overarching handles for hot clusters of ideas whose details have yet to be ironed out or agreed upon" (p. 207). So, terms such as "welfare reform" and "balancing the budget" appear to function as pregnant placeholders because "they name concepts that already carry the assumption of having been elaborated . . . without the concomitant assumption that the elaboration has been sorted into strands gaining wide adherence" (p. 207). In other words, it is easy for people to unite behind these condensation symbols because they carry with them the assumption that people agree on exactly *how* to reform welfare or balance the budget. The difference between buzzwords and pregnant placeholders is subtle: "While buzzwords can keep a word 'hot' and in vogue for a period of time, pregnant placeholders can keep entire areas of activity . . . in vogue" (p. 207). The fourth type of condensation symbol well suited for "bridge work" is *allusion,* which provides "nonspecific references that direct a listener or reader's attention to another work, person, place, or event and invite the listener or reader into open-ended exploration" (p. 208). Allusions abound in public discourse as audiences are invited to contemplate the significance of Plymouth Rock, Bunker Hill, Gettysburg, the Declaration of Independence, or Vietnam in the course of their ongoing deliberations. Allusions can function as forms of **articulation** when connections between differing realms are tightly drawn. Kaufer and Carley provided the example of the right-to-life movement's allusion to ecology ("abortion is environmental genocide") that articulates or connects these different movements.

The final two types of condensation symbols—*stereotypes* and *emblems*—have a more **epideictic** function in that they help "sharpen connections within [a] group" (Kaufer & Carley, 1993, p. 219). Stereotypes are common "rallying points" for members of a particular group (p. 219). The colonists during the late 18th century had their "Tories," just as today conservatives have their "liberals." Groups frequently define themselves in opposition to a stereotypically portrayed **enemy** or **other** (Edelman, 1988). Emblems are personal or organizational names used as condensation symbols. Emblems can be positive or negative. Ronald Reagan, or Reaganism, is a positive emblem for contemporary conservatives, whereas the American Civil Liberties Union and Hillary Rodham Clinton are negative emblems. As Kaufer and Carley explained, "What emblematic representations do . . . is turn ordinary words (names) into 'sides' and 'camps' that can efficiently summon friends and foes into battle" (p. 222).

Condensation symbols share important characteristics with other popular concepts in contemporary rhetorical studies. McGee's concept of an **ideograph** and Weaver's notions of "God" and "devil" "ultimate terms" (see the entry for **sermonic, language as**) also try to explore the persuasive force and social power of key words and phrases in our public vocabulary. Explicit attention to symbols was less common in rhetorical studies during the 1990s. This might have been due to the influence of structuralist, poststructuralist, and postmodern theorists and concepts that usually emerge from a *semiotic* (or sign-based) paradigm. One of the ongoing challenges in contemporary rhetorical studies is to discover ways of connecting the more traditional study of discursive symbols with semiotic approaches to the sign and linguistic codes.

Notes

1. On the various meanings of Black Power, see Aberbach and Walker (1970).
2. On this point, see also Bercovitch's (1978) discussion of the "symbol of America" as a force that shapes American consciousness.
3. See also Gustainis (1993, pp. 3-20), Perloff (1998, pp. 123-124), and Pollock (1994).
4. See also the discussion of Burke's idea of *bridging devices*.

References and Additional Reading

Aberbach, J. D., & Walker, J. L. (1970). The meanings of Black Power: A comparison of white and black interpretations of a political slogan. *American Political Science Review, 64,* 367-388.

Bercovitch, S. (1978). *The American jeremiad.* Madison: University of Wisconsin Press.

Diffley, K. (1988). "Erecting anew the standard of freedom": Salmon P. Chase's "Appeal of the Independent Democrats" and the rise of the Republican party. *Quarterly Journal of Speech, 74,* 401-415.

Duncan, H. D. (1968). *Symbols in society.* New York: Oxford University Press.

Edelman, M. (1964). *The symbolic uses of politics.* Urbana: University of Illinois Press.

Edelman, M. (1988). *Constructing the political spectacle.* Chicago: University of Chicago Press.

Graber, D. A. (1976). *Verbal behavior and politics.* Urbana: University of Illinois Press.

Gustainis, J. J. (1993). *American rhetoric and the Vietnam war.* Westport, CT: Praeger.

Kaufer, D. S., & Carley, K. M. (1993). Condensation symbols: Their variety and rhetorical function in political discourse. *Philosophy and Rhetoric, 26,* 201-226.

Perloff, R. M. (1998). *Political communication: Politics, press, and public in America.* Mahwah, NJ: Lawrence Erlbaum.

Pollock, M. A. (1994). The battle for the past: George Bush and the Gulf crisis. In A. Kiewe (Ed.), *The modern presidency and crisis rhetoric.* Westport, CT: Praeger.

Sapir, E. (1934). Symbolism. In E. R. A. Seligman (Ed.), *Encyclopedia of the social sciences.* New York: Macmillan.

Zarefsky, D. (1986). *President Johnson's war on poverty: Rhetoric and history.* Tuscaloosa: University of Alabama Press.

CONFESSIONAL DISCOURSE

In a recent study of the **inventional** struggles of some early U.S. women public speakers, Campbell (1995) discussed the way in which one speaker, Deborah Sampson Gannett (in an address delivered in 1802), incorporated the "familiar" **genre** of "the public confession of a repentant sinner" (p. 480) into her *hybrid* address. The genre of the public confession, a form of **confessional discourse,** has a long history in Western literature. Among some of the more famous examples are Saint Augustine's (1992) *Confessions* and Rousseau's (1928) *Les Confessions.* The literary confession, or confessional, is part of the larger genre of autobiography and typically features intense self-reflection and introspection as the writer confronts and "confesses" his or her flaws and moral defects. As Campbell (1995) noted, the confessional "was a type of discourse in which women had participated for centuries" (p. 480).

Farrell (1998) recently sought to analyze the "rhetorical activity" of public confession. The public confession at times can overlap with the more widely studied genre of **apologia,** but it should not be conflated with it, Farrell argued. A confession is rhetorical, he continued, when "it involves public utterance before an audience at a moment of uncertainty, involving personal diminishment over wrongdoing. Like traditional rhetoric, confessional rhetoric is evocative of judgment; only in this case, the judgment is of the self *by* the self" (p. 3). A rhetorical confession is successful, Farrell suggested, when it fulfills certain performative criteria or *speech act conditions.* First, there must be an explicit admission of wrongdoing. Second, the admission must be true. Third, there must be remorse for the act committed (Farrell referred to this as the "contrition condition"). Fourth, the confession must be made before the appropriate party (either the aggrieved party or an audience/agent empowered to acknowledge and forgive). Finally, the magnitude of the offense must be equal to the effort and burden of confessing (p. 4). These conditions can function as critical **topoi** for analyzing performances such as Bill Clinton's August 1998 speech to the nation following his testimony to the grand jury. For Farrell, Clinton's confession failed primarily because it mismanaged the final condition; it attempted to diminish or "minimize the offense" while simultaneously acknowledging its severity.

Confession is not only a genre of literature and public discourse; it also is an important religious (as in the confession of one's sins), intellectual (Nelson, 1998, pp. 54-61), legal (Brooks, 2000), and social practice. In rhetorical studies scholarship, Scott (1976) observed, "A community may impose its demands quite invidiously by insisting on self-criticism as an instrument of social conformity" (p. 265). And self-criticism, the French historian and social theorist Michel Foucault suggested, is the first step in the social practice of confession. Foucault (1988) drew on the religious model of the confession to demonstrate how the confessional has become one of our principal "technologies of the self"—a form of discursive practice through which individuals help to constitute themselves as **subjects** or help to determine their self-identities. We are, in short, who and what we confess ourselves to be. Foucault (1980) wrote, "Western man has become a confessing animal" (p. 59).[1] Originating primarily as a religious practice,

> the confession has spread its effects far and wide. It plays a part in justice, medicine, education, family relationships and love relationships, in the most ordinary affairs of everyday life, and in the most solemn rites; one confesses one's crimes, one's sins, one's thoughts and desires, one's illnesses and troubles. (p. 59)

He continued, "The confession is a ritual of discourse . . . [that] produces intrinsic modifications in the person who articulates it; it exonerates, redeems, and purifies him [sic], [and] it unburdens him of his wrongs, liberates him, and promises him salvation" (pp. 61-62).[2]

Why has the confessional achieved this prominence in our culture (an afternoon spent watching television talk shows helps to illustrate Foucault's point)? Why has it become such a dominant technology of the self? Dreyfus and Rabinow (1983), in their discussion of Foucault's project, provided a highly plausible answer. The confessional form is so seductive, and so "appealing," because through it we are able to "reveal our deepest selves" (p. 174). We have come to believe that "confession reveals the truth" (p. 175). But Foucault insisted that the "truth" (or knowledge) always is implicated in the exercise of **power** (power over others as well as power over oneself). What Foucault tried to show, Dreyfus and Rabinow argued, is the way in which the confessional functions to merge truth and power. But they observed that this merging of truth and power is difficult to apprehend:

> The conviction that truth can be discovered through the self-examination of consciousness and the confession of one's thoughts and acts now appears so natural, so compelling, indeed so self-evident that it seems unreasonable to posit that such self-examination is a central component in a strategy of power. (p. 175)

But Dreyfus and Rabinow insisted that this is precisely what Foucault tried to reveal. Foucault tried to *demystify* the apparent "naturalness" of the confession. When this is done, the analyst is in a position to examine the consequences of what Dreyfus and Rabinow termed our cultural "incitement to confess" (p. 175).

What are the consequences of this "incitement to confess," and how might rhetorical scholars incorporate Foucault's insights on the confessional in critical practice? Both questions were addressed in Greco's (1999) study of the confessional technologies employed by Alcoholics Anonymous (AA).[3] In the context of the practices of AA, Greco argued, confession both serves a "normalizing" function (confession is a key technique whereby new members internalize the "norms" or standards of acceptable behavior promoted by the group as well as the definition of what is "deviant" or unacceptable behavior) and is instrumental in reconstituting the identity of the individual group member. The person becomes an "alcoholic" through the process of confession. Greco wrote, "Confessional technologies are . . . obvious in the various discourse practices and rituals in which newcomers to AA engage during their initial affiliation with the organization." The most obvious practice is the testimonial, which is a mainstay at AA meetings. Individuals recount their experiences with alcohol, and new or potential members are encouraged to identify their experiences with those related to them. The process culminates with individuals providing their own testimonials beginning with the act of accepting their new identities: "My name is ________, and I am an alcoholic." Through the testimonials, individuals reconstruct their personal or self-**narratives,** thereby consolidating their newfound alcoholic identities. Greco's point, it should be noted, was not to condemn the practices of AA; clearly, the organization has helped countless individuals and families to regain a semblance of control over their lives. But AA practices are, nevertheless, a disciplinary technique or a way of defining and controlling "deviance." As a key disciplinary technique and technology of the self, the practice of the confessional merits continued attention.

Notes

1. On the relationship between the Western concept of the self and confession, see also Brooks (2000).
2. It might be useful to compare Foucault's account of the confessional to Kenneth Burke's discussion of **mortification.**
3. For other examples that explore the function of the confessional in contemporary discursive practice, see Comerford (1997), Felski (1989, pp. 86-121), Sloop (1996), and Supriya (1996).

References and Additional Reading

Brooks, P. (2000). *Troubling confessions: Speaking guilt in law and literature.* Chicago: University of Chicago Press.

Campbell, K. K. (1995). Gender and genre: Loci of invention and contradiction in the earliest speeches by U.S. women. *Quarterly Journal of Speech, 81,* 479-495.

Comerford, L. (1997). Channel surfing for rape and resistance on Court TV. In M. Huspek & G. P. Radford (Eds.), *Transgressive discourse: Communication and the voice of other.* Albany: State University of New York Press.
Dreyfus, H. L., & Rabinow, P. (1983). *Michel Foucault: Beyond structuralism and hermeneutics* (2nd ed.). Chicago: University of Chicago Press.
Farrell, T. B. (1998, November). *Trying truths: The question of magnitude in rhetorical confession.* Paper presented at the meeting of the National Communication Association, New York.
Felski, R. (1989). *Beyond feminist aesthetics: Feminist literature and social change.* Cambridge, MA: Harvard University Press.
Foucault, M. (1980). *The history of sexuality* (Vol. 1, R. Hurley, Trans.). New York: Vintage.
Foucault, M. (1988). Technologies of the self. In L. H. Martin, H. Gutman, & P. H. Hutton (Eds.), *Technologies of the self: A seminar with Michel Foucault.* Amherst: University of Massachusetts Press.
Greco, M. D. (1999). Confessing subjects: Reconstituting the problematic drinker as "alcoholic" through the discourse of Alcoholics Anonymous. In L. S. Eastland, S. L. Herndon, & J. R. Barr (Eds.), *Communication in recovery: Perspectives on Twelve-Step groups.* Cresskill, NJ: Hampton Press.
Nelson, J. S. (1998). *Tropes of politics: Science, theory, rhetoric, action.* Madison: University of Wisconsin Press.
Rousseau, J.-J. (1928). *Les Confessions.* New York: Knopf.
Saint Augustine. (1992). *Confessions.* Oxford, UK: Clarendon.
Scott, R. L. (1976). On viewing rhetoric as epistemic: Ten years later. *Central States Speech Journal, 27,* 258-266.
Sloop, J. M. (1996). *The cultural prison: Discourse, prisoners, and punishment.* Tuscaloosa: University of Alabama Press.
Supriya, K. E. (1996). Confessionals, testimonials: Women's speech in/and contexts of violence. *Hypatia, 11,* 92-106.

CONSPIRACY APPEALS/ ARGUMENTS

Americans traditionally have been fascinated by persuasive appeals exploiting the idea that there is a "conspiracy"—a small band of secretive individuals acting in concert—at work that is ultimately responsible for all of our problems. During the revolutionary period in the American colonies, many people believed that there was a conspiracy in Great Britain to enslave the colonies. During the antebellum period, northerners talked about the "slave power conspiracy," whereas southerners believed that the abolitionists were conspiring to organize slave rebellions (Davis, 1969; Pfau & Zarefsky, 2000). More recently, conspiracy appeals appear to be a significant factor in certain strands of feminist discourse (Fay, 1994),[1] in the "hysterical epidemics" that have been sweeping the nation (Showalter, 1997), in the discourse of Minister Louis Farrakhan (Goldzwig, 1989; Singh, 1997), in the ultraconservative political movements of the mid- to late 20th century (Black, 1970; Johnson, 1983; Lipset & Raab, 1970), in some late-1990s pro-Bill Clinton **apologias,** and in organizing the contemporary anti-government militia movement (Fenster, 1999). And, of course, everyone "knows" that Lee Harvey Oswald could not have killed John F. Kennedy all by himself.

Conspiracy appeals/arguments have an extremely long and rich history (Pipes, 1997). Why are conspiracy appeals so popular and potent? No one knows for sure. Hofstadter (1979) located part of the attractiveness of conspiracy appeals or arguments (an element of what he termed the "paranoid style") in the account of history that they embody (see also Johnson, 1983). According to Hofstadter (1979), advocates relying on this form of argument believe that "history *is* a conspiracy, set in motion by demonic forces of almost transcendent power, and what is felt to be needed to defeat it is not the usual methods of political give-and-take but an all-out crusade" (p. 29). For the dispossessed and the powerless, the view of history embodied in conspiracy appeals often resonates with their own experiences of the world; unseen and malevolent forces exert power over the affairs of the world. Discussing the "Farrakhan phenomenon," Singh (1997) commented,

> Farrakhan's unremitting claims of a conspiracy against black Americans are forged upon a prima facie [case . . . that is] plausible to many African Americans given two

> hundred years of slavery, de jure and de facto segregation, racial discrimination, and prejudice. (p. 238)

But conspiracy appeals are not the exclusive province of social and political outsiders such as the 19th-century nativists or the 20th-century militia movement. Social and political elites can appropriate the discursive form by giving the appeal a new **accent** or inflection. Consider, for example, how often a conservative member of the House or Senate (and hence a member of the political elite) will claim that the nation's problems (e.g., a decline in "values") are the result of a media conspiracy or a conspiracy of 1960s hippies who have taken over the nation's campuses. Like all discursive forms, conspiracy arguments and appeals are attractive because they give voice to, or express the feelings and experiences of, members of a culture.

Hofstadter's discussion of the "demonic forces" with "almost transcendent power" commonly featured in conspiracy appeals points to its frequent imbrication with the **apocalyptic.** Advocates relying on a conspiracy appeal will depict the conspiracy as extremely powerful and suggest that, if it is not thwarted, our civilization or way of life is in grave danger. Conspiracy discourse usually employs some form of *personification;* a specific group of people is identified as the force behind the conspiracy. For example, Lipset and Raab (1970) noted that "the personification of evil in history is another essential element of conspiracy theory" (p. 16). Conspiracy appeals often feature *hyperbole* or exaggeration as well as *hasty generalizations.* A seemingly minor event (e.g., a court ruling, a military exercise) is invested with incredible significance, or an apparently random and isolated event (e.g., an instance of police brutality, a racial slur spray-painted on a wall) becomes the basis for uncovering an insidious pattern. Conspiracy appeals also are notorious for exploiting the ambiguity between correlational relationships (*a* and *b* happen in sequence) and causal relationships (*a* causes *b*). What appears to the uninitiated as a random sequence of events or a series of accidents becomes, for those persuaded by the "logic" of the conspiracy appeal, explicable as part of a larger plan or design (see the discussion of the *post hoc, ergo propter hoc* **fallacy**).

Fenster (1999) argued that conspiracy theories derive much of their appeal from their **narrative** form.[2] He wrote,

> The "classical" conspiracy narrative attempts to unify seemingly disparate, globally significant elements and events within a singular plot, doing so through the traditional logic of conventional popular narratives. . . . The classical conspiracy narrative . . . is composed of certain structural and formal characteristics that individual conspiracy theories, contained in texts that are both fiction and putatively nonfiction, articulate in similar ways. Not quite a specific genre in the formal and social definition of the term, the conspiracy narrative is instead best recognized as putting forth a particular narrative logic that organizes disparate events within a mechanistic, tragic framework. (pp. 108, 111)

The conspiracy narrative is, Fenster continued, commonly organized around a narrative "pivot"—a moment of "convergence" when "opposing forces come into clear focus" (p. 124). Through their pivots, conspiracy narratives aim to produce a type of epiphany or a flash of enlightenment that allows us to see the "real" world behind deceptive appearances.[3]

Extending the work of Creps (1980) and his own study of the Lincoln-Douglas debates of 1858,[4] Zarefsky (1984) offered some tentative inferences about the force and dynamics of conspiracy argument. First, Zarefsky suggested that certain situational or circumstantial factors contribute to the force of conspiracy arguments. These factors include (a) perception of an ambiguous "evil" for which no simple explanation or account is available; (b) perception of a "pattern of anomalies" or "difficult-to-explain events" (p. 72) that, like the perception of evil, lack a clear explanation; (c) an at least nascent **polarization** of attitudes that the conspiracy argument draws on and contributes to; and (d) experience of social liminality or instability where previously accepted values and beliefs have become problematic. Second, Zarefsky identified some of the possible dynamics of conspiracy argument. These features include (a) use of conspiracy arguments to set or control the discursive agenda, (b) use of the *residue* **argument** strategy as way of identifying the nefarious **motives** of the conspirators, (c) importance of speculative inferences in constructing the conspiratorial "plot," and (d) a tendency to respond to charges of conspiracy with a countercharge of conspiracy. Finally, one of the more influential aspects of Zarefsky's account of conspiracy argument was the idea of their "self-sealing" quality (see, e.g., Young, Launer, & Austin, 1990). As Zarefsky (1984) explained,

> Given surface plausibility, the conspiracy argument's 'theory' of events is almost self-sealing. It is virtually impossible to disprove, and even discrepant evidence can be explained easily as the work of the clever conspirator who is trying to cover his [sic] tracks. (p. 72)

This "self-sealing" quality is reinforced by the argumentative dilemma facing someone who would deny the existence of a conspiracy. How does one prove the existence of a negative or prove that something (an alleged conspiracy) does not exist? (p. 74). The inability to disprove further "seals" the case for the existence of a conspiracy.

Notes

1. Commenting on Faludi's (1991) book *Backlash*, Fay (1994) wrote that Faludi "should be seen, as some critics have informally suggested, as a conspiratorial theorist; that is, as someone who sees conspiracy everywhere and uses it to account for otherwise unaccountable phenomena" (pp. 130-131). But Faludi (1991) denied that she was trying to uncover a conspiracy (p. xxi).

2. Fenster (1999) argued that this is the case for both explicitly "fictional" conspiracies (e.g., *The X-Files*) and "real" conspiracies (e.g., the John F. Kennedy assassination).

3. Hence, conspiracy narratives enact a **dissociative** logic.

4. On Lincoln and Douglas's use of conspiracy arguments, see also Kaufer and Butler (1996) and Zarefsky (1990).

References and Additional Reading

Black, E. (1970). The second persona. *Quarterly Journal of Speech, 56,* 109-119.

Creps, E. (1980). *The conspiracy argument as rhetorical genre.* Unpublished dissertation, Northwestern University.

Curry, R. O., & Brown, T. M. (Eds.). (1972). *Conspiracy: The fear of subversion in American history.* New York: Holt, Rinehart & Winston.

Davis, D. B. (1969). *The slave power conspiracy and the paranoid style.* Baton Rouge: Louisiana State University Press.

Davis, D. B. (Ed.). (1971). *The fear of conspiracy: Images of un-American subversion from the revolution to the present.* Ithaca, NY: Cornell University Press.

Faludi, S. (1991). *Backlash: The undeclared war against American women.* New York: Crown.

Fay, E. A. (1994). *Eminent rhetoric: Language, gender, and cultural tropes.* Westport, CT: Bergin & Garvey.

Fenster, M. (1999). *Conspiracy theories: Secrecy and power in American culture.* Minneapolis: University of Minnesota Press.

Goldzwig, S. R. (1989). A social movement perspective on demagoguery: Achieving symbolic realignment. *Communication Studies, 40,* 202-228.

Goodnight, G. T., & Poulakos, J. (1981). Conspiracy rhetoric: From pragmatism to fantasy in public discourse. *Western Journal of Speech Communication, 45,* 299-316.

Hasian, M., Jr. (1997). Understanding the power of conspiratorial rhetoric: A case study of *The Protocols of the Elders of Zion. Communication Studies, 48,* 195-214.

Hofstadter, R. (1979). *The paranoid style in American politics and other essays.* Chicago: University of Chicago Press.

Johnson, G. (1983). *Architects of fear: Conspiracy theories and paranoia in American politics.* Los Angeles: Jeremy P. Tarcher.

Kaufer, D. S., & Butler, B. S. (1996). *Rhetoric and the arts of design.* Mahwah, NJ: Lawrence Erlbaum.

Lipset, S. M., & Raab, E. (1970). *The politics of unreason: Right-wing extremism in America, 1790-1970.* New York: Harper & Row.

Marcus, G. E. (Ed.). (1999). *Paranoia within reason: A casebook on conspiracy as explanation.* Chicago: University of Chicago Press.

Nimmo, D., & Combs, J. E. (1990). *Mediated political realities* (2nd ed.). New York: Longman.

Pfau, M. W., & Zarefsky, D. (2000). Evaluating conspiracy arguments: The case of the Texas annexation controversy. In T. A. Hollihan (Ed.), *Argument at century's end: Reflecting on the past and envisioning the future.* Annandale, VA: Speech Communication Association.

Pipes, D. (1997). *Conspiracy: How the paranoid style flourishes and where it comes from.* New York: Free Press.

Showalter, E. (1997). *Hystories: Hysterical epidemics and modern media.* New York: Columbia University Press.

Singh, R. (1997). *The Farrakhan phenomenon: Race, reaction, and the paranoid style in American politics.* Washington, DC: Georgetown University Press.

Smith, C. A. (1977). The Hofstadter hypothesis revisited: The nature of evidence in politically "paranoid" discourse. *Southern States Communication Journal, 42,* 274-289.

Wood, G. S. (1982). Conspiracy and the paranoid style: Causality and deceit in the eighteenth century. *William and Mary Quarterly, 39,* 401-441.

Young, M. J., & Launer, M. K. (1995). Evaluative criteria for conspiracy arguments: The case of KAL 007. In E. Schiappa (Ed.), *Warranting assent: Case studies in argument evaluation.* Albany: State University of New York Press.

Young, M. J., Launer, M. K., & Austin, C. C. (1990). The need for evaluative criteria: Conspiracy argument revisited. *Argumentation and Advocacy, 26,* 89-107.

Zarefsky, D. (1984). Conspiracy arguments in the Lincoln-Douglas debates. *Journal of the American Forensic Association, 21,* 63-75.

Zarefsky, D. (1990). *Lincoln, Douglas, and slavery: In the crucible of public debate.* Chicago: University of Chicago Press.

CONSTITUTIVE RHETORIC

In his review of the 1984 University of Iowa conference on "The Rhetoric of the Human Sciences," Lyne (1985) maintained that the "constitutive function of rhetoric . . . should probably get more attention in our literature than it does since it helps explain why the study of discourse is important independent of whether it can be demonstrated to have 'caused' events" (p. 68). A constitutive understanding of how discourse functions, Lyne suggested, must move beyond a narrow causal model of influence (e.g., Message X caused Audience Y to act in some specific way). Discursive practice must be understood as producing effects in ways beyond direct causality. Political theorist James Farr and literary theorist Steven Mailloux have made similar points. For example, Farr (1988) distinguished causal relationships that involve a sense of "determination" from "a constitutive relationship" based on "possibility." Farr suggested that discourse functions constitutively when it makes something possible or creates conditions of possibility (e.g., the way in which a *metaphor* makes it possible to conceptualize something in a new way, the way in which a **narrative** makes it possible to see connections among events that previously were unobserved). Mailloux (1991) observed that "rhetorical practices are (at least partly) constitutive of . . . historical categories" such as the social, political, and economic (p. 234). Like Lyne and Farr, Mailloux focused on the way in which discursive practice shapes but does not completely determine the realms of the social, political, and economic.

Over the past decade or so, scholars have begun to explore the constitutive or *constructive* possibilities of discursive practice.[1] For example, legal and literary scholar James Boyd White (e.g., White, 1985) has been investigating the constitutive capacity of a wide range of discursive practices (from novels to legal opinions); **constitutive rhetoric,** in White's view, is the activity and art "of constituting character, community, and culture in language" (p. x).[2] In the discipline of rhetorical studies, Charland's (1987) study of the nationalist movement in Quebec is part of this emerging tradition of critical inquiry. Extending Black's discussion of the way in which discourse creates an image of its **audience,** McGee's (1975) account of the rhetoric of "the people," as well as Burke's focus on rhetorical **identification,** Charland (1987) argued that certain forms of discursive practice function as constitutive rhetoric. Constitutive rhetoric, in Charland's view, does more than create an image of its audience; it generates the conditions of possibility that can structure the identity of those to whom it is addressed. Charland's explanation of this process is indebted to the French philosopher Louis Althusser's discussion of **interpellation** and **ideology.** Charland wrote,

> Interpellation occurs at the very moment one enters into a rhetorical situation, that is, as soon as an individual recognizes and acknowledges being addressed. An interpellated subject participates in the discourse that addresses him [sic]. . . . Note, however, that interpellation does not occur through persuasion in the usual sense, for the very act of *addressing* is rhetorical. . . . In addition, this rhetoric of identification is ongoing, not restricted to one hailing [or one discursive encounter] but usually part of a rhetoric of socialization. (p. 138)

As Charland (1987) explained it, constitutive rhetoric is an ubiquitous force that shapes the identity of its addressees. In the "act of *addressing*" auditors, an advocate's message awakens (or energizes) certain possibilities or a specific identity (or **subject** position) for that audience. In certain cases, Charland noted, this process "is akin more to one of conversion" as audiences come to inhabit a "reconfigured subject position" (p. 142).[3] Consider a relatively simple illustration. A television commercial for toothpaste, for example, manages not only to sell its product but also to energize certain identity possibilities as it positions its audience in the role of "consumers." We *become* consumers, or we are (re)positioned in the role of consumers, as we are addressed by the commercial.

Charland's study of the Canadian "*Québécois*" movement emphasized the way in which **narratives** function in constitutive rhetoric (see also Wald, 1995). Charland (1987) wrote, "Narrative form provides . . . continuity across time" (p. 145); it constructs a history for the collective identity that has been constituted. Whereas the narratives featured in constitutive rhetoric usually are "characterized by a teleological movement" toward some preferred end (p. 144), Charland acknowledged that such narratives, like most rhetorical narratives found in **deliberative** situations,[4] "leave the task of narrative closure to their constituted subjects." In the context of his study of French Canadian constitutive rhetoric, Charland concluded that "it is up to the Québécois of 1980 to conclude the story to which they are identified" and into which they have been interpellated (p. 143).

Subsequent critical scholarship has sought to extend and refine Charland's observations about the nature of constitutive rhetoric. For example, Dow (1994) explored the way in which AIDS activist Larry Kramer's essay, "1,112 and Counting" (Kramer, 1983/1989), exploited **perspective by incongruity** to reorient the collective self-identity of the gay community during the early 1980s; Greene (1993) examined the "social argumentation" of the 1988 Palestinian Declaration of Independence as a type of constitutive rhetoric or a way of creating an identity for the Palestinian people; Sklar (1999) updated the struggle to constitute collective identity in Quebec during the 1990s; and Terrill (2000) uncovered constitutive aspects of the rhetoric of Malcolm X. These case studies of constitutive rhetoric demonstrate that the constitutive function of rhetoric is beginning to receive the attention it would appear to deserve.

Notes

1. See also the discussion under the entry for **effects of rhetorical practice.** The terms *constitutive, constructive,* and *construction* are not synonymous, but they do share (to borrow Wittgenstein's expression) a "family resemblance." On social constructionism, see, for example, Bash (1995) and Shotter (1993).

2. On White's (1985) version of "constitutive rhetoric," see also Freeman (1991). For another "humanistic" account of the constitutive capacity of human language and discourse, see Stewart (1986).

3. See also the discussion of **secular conversion.**

4. On the "openness" of narratives in deliberative discourse, see the discussion in the entry for **narrative.**

References and Additional Reading

Bash, H. H. (1995). *Social problems and social movements: An exploration into the sociological construction of alternative realities.* Atlantic Highlands, NJ: Humanities Press.

Charland, M. (1987). Constitutive rhetoric: The case of the *peuple Québécois. Quarterly Journal of Speech, 73,* 133-150.

Dow, B. J. (1994). AIDS, perspective by incongruity, and gay identity in Larry Kramer's "1,112 and Counting." *Communication Studies, 45,* 225-240.

Farr, J. (1988). Conceptual change and constitutional innovation. In T. Ball & J. G. A. Pocock (Eds.), *Conceptual change and the constitution.* Lawrence: University Press of Kansas.

Freeman, J. (1991). Constitutive rhetoric: Law as a literary activity. *Harvard Women's Law Journal, 14,* 305-325.

Greene, R. W. (1993). Social argumentation and the aporias of state formation: The Palestinian Declaration of Independence. *Argumentation and Advocacy, 29,* 124-136.

Kramer, L. (1989). 1,112 and counting. In L. Kramer, *Reports from the Holocaust: The making of an AIDS activist.* New York: St. Martin's. (Original work published 1983)

Lyne, J. (1985). Rhetorics of inquiry. *Quarterly Journal of Speech, 71,* 65-73.

Mailloux, S. (1991). Rhetorical hermeneutics revisited. *Text and Performance Quarterly, 11,* 233-248.

McGee, M. C. (1975). In search of "the people": A rhetorical alternative. *Quarterly Journal of Speech, 61,* 235-249.

Shotter, J. (1993). *Conversational realities: Constructing life through language.* London: Sage.

Sklar, A. (1999). Contested collectives: The struggle to define the "we" in the 1995 Quebec referendum. *Southern Communication Journal, 64,* 106-122.

Stewart, J. (1986). Speech and human being: A complement to semiotics. *Quarterly Journal of Speech, 72,* 55-73.

Terrill, R. E. (2000). Colonizing the borderlands: Shifting circumference in the rhetoric of Malcolm X. *Quarterly Journal of Speech, 86,* 67-85.

Wald, P. (1995). *Constituting Americans: Cultural anxiety and narrative form.* Durham, NC: Duke University Press.

Wess, R. (1996). *Kenneth Burke: Rhetoric, subjectivity, postmodernism.* Cambridge, UK: Cambridge University Press.

White, J. B. (1985). *Heracles' bow: Essays on the rhetoric and poetics of law.* Madison: University of Wisconsin Press.

CONTINGENCY

In *Norms of Rhetorical Culture,* Farrell (1993) remarked, "Although it is a commonplace among interpreters of Aristotle's *Rhetoric* that the art of rhetoric addresses unsettled matters, few terms within the Aristotelian lexicon are as complex and elusive to contemporary understanding as 'contingency' " (p. 77). The key passages in the *Rhetoric* (Aristotle, 1954) are as follows:

> The duty of rhetoric is to deal with such matters as we deliberate upon without arts or systems to guide us. . . . The subjects of our deliberation are such as seem to present us with *alternative possibilities:* About things that could not have been, and cannot now or in the future be, other than they are, nobody who takes them to be of this nature wastes his [sic] time in deliberation. . . . Most of the things about which we make decisions, and into which therefore we inquire, present us with *alternative possibilities.* For it is about our actions that we deliberate and inquire, and all our actions have a *contingent* character; hardly any of them are determined by necessity. (1357a, emphasis added)

As these two passages indicate, **contingency** is juxtaposed to necessity and impossibility while linked to the unavoidable and potentially unmanageable presence of multiple possibilities (different ways of acting, of organizing social relations, etc.). Or, as Garver (1994) put it in his commentary on the *Rhetoric,* the existence of rhetoric stems from "the complexity and indeterminacy of the world" (p. 109). For Aristotle and the many thinkers who have been influenced by his thought, rhetoric, as an art and a form of discursive practice, has as one of its fundamental concerns the negotiation or management of human contingency—helping people to live in a world where some things are impossible, few things are absolutely necessary, and even fewer things are absolutely certain.[1]

In an important paper on the topic, Gaonkar (1992) argued that the Aristotelian understanding of contingency that has helped to organize contemporary rhetorical thinking in speech communication has "rarely [been] subjected to critical scrutiny" (p. 9). Reflection on the relationship between rhetoric and contingency can proceed along a number of lines. First, consider the implications, highlighted by Gaonkar, that Aristotle's sense of the "realm of the contingent" is a "cunning response to Plato's critique that rhetoric is homeless" (p. 7) or that "rhetoric lacks specificity because it has no subject matter" (p. 4). According to Gaonkar, Aristotle located rhetoric in the realm of the contingent to give it "a domicile, a space within which it can manifest and contain itself" (p. 7). If rhetoric is "about" the contingent (what might happen or things that are uncertain), then it is cut off from the necessary and the impossible.

But it is not clear that Aristotle wanted to sever any relationship between rhetoric and the realms of necessity and impossibility. And it does seem unwise to limit our thinking about rhetoric in this way. For example, rhetorical discourse, by itself, appears incapable of doing anything about the necessary fact that people eventually die. But discursive practices, most commonly those considered as part of the *generic* class of *eulogies,* certainly help people to live with the fact of human finitude. Or, think about the idea of the impossible. Things that once were considered to be impossible now are commonplace, thanks to the advances in science and technology. Our sense of the possible and the impossible flows from our imagination, and imagination is both a product of and a contributor to various forms of discursive practice. When one moves from the realms of science and technology (where we typically think that the relationship between the possible and the impossible is stable but new innovations continue to amaze us) to the social sphere, the issue of what is possible or impossible is even more complicated. There was a time in U.S. history when many of the most enlightened statesman, despite believing that slavery was morally wrong, nevertheless concluded that it was impossible to do anything about it. Not too long ago, many people in America believed that achieving even rough equality between the genders in the workplace was impossible. But in both of these cases, change was possible and discourse played a central role in the process.[2]

Gaonkar's (1992) inquiry into the idea of contingency revealed a second line for further reflection. Gaonkar noted that "Aristotle and those who follow Aristotle do not allow us to peer too deeply into the abyss of the uncertain and the indeterminate" (p. 7).[3] According to Gaonkar, contingency is **domesticated** in the Aristotelian tradition of rhetorical thought: "For Aristotle . . ., the idea of the contingent does not connote a Kafkaesque world of sheer uncertainty and terror but rather a world made familiar by Emily Post—of gamesmanship and good manners displayed by those adept at ideological bricolage" (p. 8).[4] Gaonkar employed contemporary allusions to make his point, but it is useful to translate his claim back into something closer to Aristotle's way of thinking (although admittedly not in Aristotle's technical vocabulary). Think of it along these lines: Contingency exists in specific or local situations (moments where people must choose among various alternative possibilities), but for Aristotle, this local or situational contingency is manageable by recourse to a stable, fixed, and determinate historical horizon.

What is a "historical horizon"? It is a difficult notion to define precisely. The simplest way of proceeding is to describe the historical horizon in relation to what it is *not*—a local situation. A culture's historical horizon consists of those things—values, ideals, ideological beliefs, and social structures are common features of a historical horizon—that transcend or exist beyond particular local situations. It is much easier to speak of the historical horizon of cultures that no longer exist. A term such as "the Renaissance" captures the historical horizon of a period of time for certain European cultures. It connotes a range of values, ideals, ideological beliefs, and structures that gave these cultures a particular shape. Aristotle apparently assumed that a culture's historical horizon was fixed, stable, and shared by all members of the culture. As Farrell (1982) remarked, Aristotle's thinking about rhetorical forms such as the example and the **enthymeme** "required stable and static assumptions about the nature of the world and its possibilities" (p. 126). Two key terms help to describe the fixed historical horizon of Aristotle's Athens. The first is the institutional structure of the *polis* that, Garver (1994) argued, Aristotle believed to be natural and, hence, inevitable and determinative. As Garver noted, "If the polis is as natural as Aristotle says it is, then all such contingencies [that might arise] are satisfied in the polis" (p. 26). The polis provided a structure, a set of practices, and a range of ideological beliefs that, in Gaonkar's terms, allowed local contingencies to be domesticated. The second key term is *telos,* and it signifies the end to which people strive. For Aristotle, the end of human life was happiness, and he believed that most members of his culture shared the same basic ideas of happiness. With happiness understood as the telos or end of human life, the struggle with local contingency was fashioned into a process of selecting the best means for reaching a seemingly predetermined end. This narrowing of the struggle with contingency to the choice of means for reaching a predetermined end was another form of its domestication.

Gaonkar was troubled by some of the baggage that seemed to accompany the appropriation of Aristotelian contingency in contemporary rhetorical thought. The domestication of contingency can be grasped more fully, he argued, by comparing the Aristotelian tradition to trends in contemporary literary theory and philosophy that "radicalize" contingency. This trend can be detected, for example, in the works of literary and legal theorist Stanley Fish (Fish, 1989a, 1989b), the neo-pragmatic philosopher Richard Rorty (Rorty, 1989), and literary theorist Barbara Herrnstein Smith (Smith, 1988). According to Gaonkar (1994), the works of Fish, Rorty, Smith, and others have helped to "deeply destabilize one of the taken-for-granted assumptions of traditional rhetoric" (p. 17). Rather than domesticating contingency—making it safe and manageable—it has come to mean "randomness and indeterminacy" (p. 20), a confrontation with the "abyss" of uncertainty that Aristotle evidently tried to avoid. In Smith's well-known formulation, we face contingency "all the way down." Gaonkar suggested that such a revision of contingency entails a modification in how we conceive of rhetoric. Rhetoric "becomes a contingent achievement as opposed to an art or practice of managing contingency" (p. 21).

Gaonkar's (1994) explication of the shifts in thinking about contingency merits additional attention. First, and most basically, Gaonkar seemed to rely on a *disjunctive* **argument** strategy when he wrote that rhetoric is a "contingent achievement" rather than an "art or practice of managing contingency."[5] But must it be an either/or? It seems possible to conceptualize rhetoric as a contingent achievement at the same time that it is thought of as an art for managing contingency.[6] Along similar lines, Reed (1992) described a "kind of rhetorical criticism" that sought to "constitute a more democratic political realm by pointing out the hidden contingency of dominant claims on the real while acknowledging the necessarily contingent nature of alternative and oppositional claims" (p. 12).

Second, it might be the case that the more recent radical depiction of contingency contains the seeds of a new form of domestication. Consider Fish's (1989b) position in the following passage:

> The acknowledgment that, from the long-run point of view, law is inseparable from force is itself without force, since no one inhabits the long-run point of view. . . . I say this to ward off a conclusion often reached on the left: that a recognition of the temporally contingent nature of our "fundamental" assumptions would lessen their force and make us less likely to surrender to them.

> But the conclusion is possible only if one makes the mistake (which I have called "anti-foundationalist theory hope") of turning the recognition of contingency into a way of avoiding contingency, as if contingency acknowledged were contingency transcended. You may know *in general* that the structure of your convictions is an historical artifact, but that knowledge does not transport you to a place where those convictions are no longer in force. We remain embedded in history even when we know that it is history we are embedded in, and while that knowledge may be satisfying in relation to alternative stories about our convictions . . . in relation to the particular convictions (including itself) by which we are grasped and constituted, it is of no force whatsoever. (pp. 523-524)[7]

What was going on in this important passage on contingency? The radical contingency position reversed, in a sense, the Aristotelian formulation; that is, rather than locating contingency in the local situation against a fixed historical horizon, thinkers such as Fish shifted contingency to the level of the historical horizon (what he termed "the long-run point of view") where our " 'fundamental' assumptions" are revealed as contingent—uncertain and open to alternative possibilities—while making specific local situations seem more fixed and determinate because we are "embedded in history" (subject to a host of institutional and conceptual forces that seriously constrain our possibilities). Rorty's (1989) discussion of cultural change effects a similar reversal; the "logic of contingency" (Gaonkar, 1992, p. 20) functions primarily within the historical horizon, not the local situation.

According to Gaonkar (1992), subscribing to the radical contingency position leads to a more significant confrontation with the abyss of uncertainty and *indeterminacy*—in short, an encounter with what existential philosophers sometimes describe as a type of radical freedom. But is this the case? Fish's position, developed in the preceding passage, suggests otherwise. People might recognize "radical" contingency—the ultimate indeterminacy of the historical horizon—but Fish (1989b) maintained that such recognition is "of no force whatsoever" (p. 524) and has no practical consequences. Radical contingency, in Fish's account, is not very threatening. Located at the level of the historical horizon, radical contingency can be acknowledged, but its impact is domesticated because it has to act through the many more immediate obligations of our daily lives.[8]

In the final analysis, Fish's (1989b) position might not be that different from the Aristotelian tradition. People continually face "practical problems" in their daily affairs and are called on to

> adjudicate between beliefs in the absence of a calculus that is not itself a function of extension of belief. It is a difficulty that cannot be removed, but the fact that it cannot be removed does not condemn us to uncertainty [which would seem to follow from the radical contingency position] and paralysis but [rather] to conflict, to acts of persuasion in which one party attempts to alter the beliefs of another by putting forward arguments that are weighty only in relation to still other beliefs. (p. 522)

Fish's basic point seemed to be that advocates in today's world lack the fixed historical horizon that Aristotle believed they enjoyed in his world. There are no final, fixed, or determinate standards that warrant or justify advocacy. But this does not end or completely disable advocacy; it just makes it more complicated and more important because a greater range of human affairs now is understood to reside in the realm of the contingent.

Literary scholar T. V. Reed and political theorist Anne Phillips addressed the issue of advocacy in a radically contingent world. Reed (1992) maintained,

> To argue that all knowledge is produced historically and subject to relative cultural limits does not preclude judgments about the

> political justness or unjustness of various representations, decisions, or actions within those specific historical conditions or between specific cultures in conflict. (pp. 12-13)

But the judgments produced through advocacy must be recognized as inescapably provisional. Phillips's (1997) discussion of contingency and advocacy emerged by way of a discussion of multiculturalism. Phillips observed that many people are suspicious of multiculturalism because they associate it with the doctrine of *relativism,* which in this context translates into the idea that there are no grounds for making judgments or evaluations of different cultures and their practices. Multiculturalism means, for many of its critics, that anything goes or that the world is random and indeterminate. In short, multiculturalism often is a shorthand expression for the radical contingency position. In such a world, there is no place for political action and public advocacy. But Phillips did not agree with this conclusion; radical contingency in the guise of multiculturalism does not negate the possibility for public **deliberation** and advocacy. She wrote,

> I have to say that I find it deeply puzzling when skeptical self-reflection is said to condemn one to political paralysis. Why should it be so difficult to act on [or *speak* on] what one conceives to be right, even while acknowledging the revisability of one's most cherished ideals? (p. 58)

Our cherished ideals, our culture's most fundamental values and principles, always are revisable; they are contingent. But that fact does not mean that people are unable to act rhetorically or politically. The only thing that radical contingency requires is that "we give up on the extravagant expectation of final proof" (p. 58). Both Reed's and Phillips's conclusions were consistent with Aristotle's vision of public deliberation: We deliberate on matters that are uncertain or about which no "final proof" is possible. Phillips suggested that the practical impact of the contingency of our values, principles, and ideals is to "constrain the certainty with which we affirm our positions, but it does not prevent us from formulating (revisable) principles" for use in public advocacy (p. 59).

The danger of domesticating contingency that Gaonkar (1992) highlighted is real.[9] Garver (1994) provided one possible way of approaching this issue. He argued that it is "a character flaw, not just a logical mistake, to make things appear inevitable when they are not, to make judgment and character seem unnecessary by making the facts seem fully determinative" (p. 183). Garver maintained that character and **ethos** are crucial to avoid the absolute domestication of contingency. The task of practical discourse, although having its range or scope expanded considerably, remains what it was for Aristotle—"to make the practically determinable determinate" (p. 78)[10]—provided that we acknowledge two important qualifications. First, the "practically determinable," no matter how strenuously advocates might insist, never can be "fully determinative" (there is no way of evading **judgment**).[11] Second, the "practically determinable" questions that humans continually confront always are, from Fish's (1989b) "long-run point of view," finally indeterminate. There is no absolute or final way for determining whether our choices were "right"; we simply must muddle along as best we can.

Notes

1. On the importance of contingency and particularity to **prudence** or prudential practical deliberation, see also Kekes (1995) and Miller (1996). The resurgent interest in the concept of contingency in rhetorical studies can be traced, in part, to Scott (1967, 1976).

2. On the relationship between the possible and the impossible in classical rhetorical thought, see Poulakos (1984).

3. Gaonkar is by no means the only rhetorical scholar urging greater reflection on the impact of uncertainty and *indeterminacy* on rhetorical practice. These issues inform *postmodern* inquiry into political and rhetorical **judgment**. See, for example, Sloop and Ono (1997).

4. See also Atwill's (1998) discussion of the tendency in humanist thought to "naturalize contingent social realities" (p. 44).

5. Shusterman (1997, pp. 75-77) made a similar point about Rorty's (1989) explication of contingency.

6. This seems to be the thrust of Farrell's (1993) position in *Norms of Rhetorical Culture.*

7. Fish (1989a) reiterated this point: "The conclusion may seem paradoxical, but it is not: Although a conviction strongly held can affect perception and the experience of fact, the one exception to this generality is the conviction that all convictions are tentative and revisable. The only context in which holding (or being held by) that conviction will alter one's sense of fact is the context in which the fact in question is the nature and status of conviction. In any other context, the conviction of general revisability—the conviction that things have been otherwise and could be otherwise again—will be of no consequence whatsoever" (p. 308).

8. For a more forceful critique of the radical contingency position, see Cole (1994).

9. See discussion under the entry for **mystification.**

10. Kastely (1997) made a similar point about Aristotle's vision of rhetoric. In a discussion of the *Rhetoric,* he wrote, "By rendering the situation determinate, a rhetor also renders an audience temporarily determinate" (p. 12).

11. This point was emphasized by Sloop and Ono (1997) and others.

References and Additional Reading

Aristotle. (1954). *Rhetoric* (W. R. Roberts, Trans.). New York: Random House.

Atwill, J. M. (1998). *Rhetoric reclaimed: Aristotle and the liberal arts tradition.* Ithaca, NY: Cornell University Press.

Bender, J., & Wellbery, D. E. (1990). Rhetoricality: On the modernist return of rhetoric. In J. Bender & D. E. Wellbery (Eds.), *The ends of rhetoric: History, theory, practice.* Stanford, CA: Stanford University Press.

Bernard-Donals, M., & Glejzer, R. R. (Eds.). (1998). *Rhetoric in an antifoundational world: Language, culture, and pedagogy.* New Haven, CT: Yale University Press.

Cole, S. E. (1994). Evading the subject: The poverty of contingency theory. In H. W. Simons & M. Billig (Eds.), *After postmodernism: Reconstructing ideology critique.* London: Sage.

Farrell, T. B. (1982). Knowledge in time: Toward an extension of rhetorical form. In J. R. Cox & C. A. Willard (Eds.), *Advances in argumentation theory and research.* Carbondale: Southern Illinois University Press.

Farrell, T. B. (1993). *Norms of rhetorical culture.* New Haven, CT: Yale University Press.

Fish, S. (1989a). Commentary: The young and the restless. In H. A. Veeser (Ed.), *The new historicism.* New York: Routledge.

Fish, S. (1989b). *Doing what comes naturally: Change, rhetoric, and the practice of theory in literary and legal studies.* Durham, NC: Duke University Press.

Gaonkar, D. (1992, November). *Rhetoric of contingency and contingency of rhetoric.* Paper presented at the meeting of the Speech Communication Association, Chicago.

Garver, E. (1994). *Aristotle's RHETORIC: An art of character.* Chicago: University of Chicago Press.

Kastely, J. L. (1997). *Rethinking the rhetorical tradition: From Plato to postmodernism.* New Haven, CT: Yale University Press.

Kekes, J. (1995). *Moral wisdom and good lives.* Ithaca, NY: Cornell University Press.

Miller, R. B. (1996). *Casuistry and modern ethics: A poetics of practical reasoning.* Chicago: University of Chicago Press.

Phillips, A. (1997, Winter). Why worry about multiculturalism? *Dissent,* pp. 57-63.

Poulakos, J. (1984). Rhetoric, the Sophists, and the possible. *Communication Monographs, 51,* 215-226.

Reed, T. V. (1992). *Fifteen jugglers, five believers: Literary politics and the poetics of social movements.* Berkeley: University of California Press.

Rorty, R. (1989). *Contingency, irony, and solidarity.* Cambridge, UK: Cambridge University Press.

Scott, R. L. (1967). On viewing rhetoric as epistemic. *Central States Speech Journal, 18,* 9-17.

Scott, R. L. (1976). On viewing rhetoric as epistemic: Ten years later. *Central States Speech Journal, 27,* 258-266.

Shusterman, R. (1997). *Practicing philosophy: Pragmatism and the philosophical life.* New York: Routledge.

Sloop, J. M., & Ono, K. A. (1997). Out-law discourse: The critical politics of material judgment. *Philosophy and Rhetoric, 30,* 50-69.

Smith, B. H. (1988). *Contingencies of value: Alternative perspectives for critical theory.* Cambridge, MA: Harvard University Press.

CONTROVERSY

Since the period of Roman antiquity, **controversy** (or *controversiae*) has occupied an important place in rhetorical theory and pedagogy (Clark, 1957; Sloane, 1997). Its basic meaning, seen in the root term *controversus,* is dispute.[1] But as Goodnight (1991) observed, despite the ubiquity of controversies over time, the concept of controversy is marked by an "absence of theoretical reflection" (p. 3). Although countless texts offer advice on how to "deal with" controversial disputes, few (if any) inquire into the nature of the malady they purport to treat (or whether it is even a malady at all). Goodnight attempted to rectify this conceptual gap, first, by trying to locate some of the potential reasons why there has been such a paucity of "reflective discussion of the controversial" (p. 3) and, second, by proposing the outlines of an alternative "orientation" that, in Scott's (1991) judgment, makes "controversy itself . . . the stuff of life" (p. 21).

Goodnight (1991) maintained, "There is good reason to suspect that some, possibly all, orientations of modernity . . . toward controversy have substantially occluded its reflective study" (p. 3). In a survey of three prominent "faces" or orientations of modernity, Goodnight concluded,

> In sum, prominent orientations within modernity leave controversy with only a highly restricted role to play. Idealism discards controversy as dross; dialectical views of society sublate it as opposition waiting for the right moment to be overcome by a higher principle unintentionally at work; and initial proponents of conflict resolution explain it away as either a behavioral problem waiting adjustment or a manifestation of systemic issues waiting for steering corrections. (p. 4)

In other words, most traditions of modern thought find controversy to be something best avoided, transcended, or managed but not in and of itself worthy of sustained study or appreciation. Developments in *postmodern* thought, Goodnight argued, are no more promising for a richer understanding of controversy.

The constructive phase of Goodnight's (1991) discussion began with the delineation of four central categories and four basic characteristics of controversy. Controversies permeate (a) consumer culture, (b) public life, (c) the realm of group and/or special interests, and (d) specialized disciplines. Goodnight's four basic characteristics merited more extended treatment. First, "controversy is a creature of the between" (p. 2) that, following the philosopher/theologian Martin Buber, Goodnight understood "as a social normative realm" of values and practices (p. 9) that both link and separate individuals (see also Arendt, 1958). Every controversy relies on the resources of this social and normative realm but, at the same time, reveals the precariousness or potential inadequacy of these resources. Controversies come into existence through and are resolved by, but also call into question, the values and practices that sustain human communities. Second, "controversy is temporally pluralistic" (Goodnight, 1991, p. 2) in that there is no predetermined length of time for a controversy to exist. Some controversies linger on for centuries, whereas others enjoy their 15 minutes of public attention and then fade from the public agenda. An additional aspect of the temporality of controversies is their tendency to produce "temporal displacements that tangle up memories of historical events" (p. 2). Controversies frequently raise questions about the relationship among the past, present, and future.[2] Third, "controversy pushes the limits of the available means of communication" (p. 2). New technologies frequently expand the possibilities for controversy,[3] whereas controversies invariably enact the dialectic of *affirmation and subversion* as new strategies are generated and old ones are subverted. Fourth, "controversy expands cultural, social, historical, and intellectual arguments" (p. 2). Of the forms of argument expansion Goodnight noted, the most important appears to be in the realm of oppositional argument.

Goodnight (1991) initially defined the expansion of oppositional argument "to include disagreements over the speech acts that implicitly define the parameters of argument contexts and grounds" (p. 5). That is, when oppositional argument is expanded beyond the inspection of specific substantive claims, previously shared **definitions of the situation** are called into question, as are the usually implicit, and sometimes explicit, rules and procedures that organize the "between" and structure argumentative interaction. Goodnight concluded, "When unspoken rules and tacit presumptions are put up for discussion, there are new opportunities and obligations to learn, to decide, [and] to argue" (p. 6). The expansion of oppositional argument pushes discussion beyond the more elemental **stasis** points of fact, definition, and quality and into the less frequently discussed area of procedure and forum. Goodnight elaborated on the nature and importance of oppositional argument in subsequent work with Olson (Olson & Goodnight, 1994). According to this later essay,

> Oppositional arguments work outside and against traditional practices of influence.... Oppositional argument functions to block enthymematic associations and so disrupt the taken-for-granted realm of the uncontested and commonplace. So, oppositional argument unsettles the appropriateness of social conventions, draws attention to the taken-for-granted means of communication . . ., provokes discussion, [and sustains] challenges to communication practices that delimit the proper expression of opinion. (p. 250)

Goodnight's (1991) alternative orientation to controversy emphasized opposition rather than persuasion (p. 6). Opposition is the engine of controversy; it is both a destructive and a constructive force. For example, the fur controversy "demonstrates how social controversy disrupts the assumptions that keep capitalistic society operating in its usual pattern" while also illustrating the potential of oppositional argument to organize a public and revitalize the public sphere (Olson & Goodnight, 1994, p. 272). Oppositional arguments do not emerge in a vacuum; they are not untainted by the social order they wish to disrupt. As Solomon (1991) illustrated, the opposition to the exclusion of women from the public speaking platform relied on many of the resources (e.g., the Bible) that were crucial to the power of the dominant order. Just as the dominant order co-opts opposition to contain potential disruption, oppositional argument appropriates the resources of the dominant order to use as a tool for subversion.

Leff (1992) turned to the domain of controversy as a way of overcoming the problem of "local formalism" that potentially plagued his critical program of **close reading.** Leff suggested that particular controversies might function as the "larger unit" of analysis that allows critics "to sustain th[eir] concern for the unique integrity of the oratorical text and to remain sensitive to the social and historical dimensions of rhetorical practice" (p. 229). Rhetorical scholars, to be sure, have been reading and analyzing controversies for some time (Condit, 1990; Hogan, 1986; Hollihan, 1986; Moore, 1993; Oravec, 1984; Railsback, 1984; Smith & Windes, 1997; Taylor, 1992). But Leff (1992) maintained that this mode of critical practice is "thoroughly analytical. Once a controversy is identified, the critic abstracts recurring issues from the relevant texts and defines the controversy in terms of these issues." Leff's desire to wed close reading with Goodnight's understanding of controversy posited the possibility of conceptualizing "controversy in a different way . . . to stress its fully embodied manifestations [specific texts that function as a representative or paradigm case of the controversy] rather than its persistent themes." Leff continued,

> At this point, the controversy is open to close reading since the critic can deal with [specific] texts in their full complexity and treat them as substantive wholes. A thorough understanding of the intentional construction of the [controversy's] paradigm cases . . . links the critic's effort to differing visions of the social world as they are embodied in controversy. The texts become connected within an **intertextual** network

> and with issues of power and situated interests that inform the whole development, but they [also] retain their integrity as things made by words. (pp. 229-230)

To date, the possibilities for close readings of controversies remain largely unexplored.

Notes

1. One aspect of the traditional doctrine of *controversia* is the need to engage both sides of a dispute. This need is reflected in the pedagogical practice of *in utramque partem* or learning how to argue on both sides of case. In addition to Sloane (1997), see also Kahn's (1985) study of Renaissance rhetoric.

2. On this topic, see also the discussions under **anxiety of influence,** ***diachronic*** **articulation,** and **memory.**

3. For example, the development of the printing press was an important constitutive condition for the religious controversies generally known as the "Protestant Reformation."

References and Additional Reading

Arendt, H. (1958). *The human condition.* Chicago: University of Chicago Press.

Clark, D. L. (1957). *Rhetoric in Greco-Roman education.* New York: Columbia University Press.

Condit, C. M. (1990). *Decoding abortion rhetoric: Communicating social change.* Urbana: University of Illinois Press.

Goodnight, G. T. (1991). Controversy. In D. W. Parson (Ed.), *Argument in controversy: Proceedings of the Seventh SCA/AFA Conference on Argumentation.* Annandale, VA: Speech Communication Association.

Hogan, J. M. (1986). *The Panama Canal in American politics: Domestic advocacy and the evolution of policy.* Carbondale: Southern Illinois University Press.

Hollihan, T. A. (1986). The public controversy over the Panama Canal treaties: An analysis of American foreign policy rhetoric. *Western Journal of Speech Communication, 50,* 368-387.

Kahn, V. (1985). *Rhetoric, prudence, and skepticism in the Renaissance.* Ithaca, NY: Cornell University Press.

Leff, M. (1992). Things made by words: Reflections on textual criticism. *Quarterly Journal of Speech, 78,* 223-231.

Moore, M. P. (1993). Constructing irreconcilable conflict: The function of synecdoche in the spotted owl controversy. *Communication Monographs, 60,* 258-274.

Olson, K. M., & Goodnight, G. T. (1994). Entanglements of consumption, cruelty, privacy, and fashion: The social controversy over fur. *Quarterly Journal of Speech, 80,* 249-276.

Oravec, C. (1984). Conservationism and preservationism: The "public interest" in the Hetch Hetchy controversy. *Quarterly Journal of Speech, 70,* 444-458.

Railsback, C. C. (1984). The contemporary American abortion controversy: Stages in the argument. *Quarterly Journal of Speech, 70,* 410-424.

Rescher, N. (1977). *Dialectics: A controversy-oriented approach to the theory of knowledge.* Albany: State University of New York Press.

Scott, R. L. (1991). Can "controversy" be analyzed to yield useful insights for argument? In D. W. Parson (Ed.), *Argument in controversy: Proceedings of the Seventh SCA/AFA Conference on Argumentation.* Annandale, VA: Speech Communication Association.

Sloane, T. O. (1997). *On the contrary: The protocol of traditional rhetoric.* Washington, DC: Catholic University of America Press.

Smith, R. R., & Windes, R. R. (1997). The pro-gay and anti-gay issue culture: Interpretation, influence, and dissent. *Quarterly Journal of Speech, 83,* 28-48.

Solomon, M. (1991). Contesting the rules of discourse: A case study of women's ascent to public advocacy. In D. W. Parson (Ed.), *Argument in controversy: Proceedings of the Seventh SCA/AFA Conference on Argumentation.* Annandale, VA: Speech Communication Association.

Taylor, C. A. (1992). Of audience, expertise, and authority: The evolving creationism debate. *Quarterly Journal of Speech, 78,* 277-295.

CRITICAL RHETORIC

A common element in the education of most rhetorical scholars is an encounter with Plato's seemingly devastating critique of rhetoric. Plato insisted that rhetoric was no art and that its practice was morally and intellectually bankrupt. Ever since Plato launched his attack, rhetoricians have labored under the shadow it cast. The rehabilitation of rhetoric is a regular feature of nearly all rhetorical thinking.

In his provocative and influential essay, "Critical Rhetoric," McKerrow (1989) suggested that the rhetorician's incessant preoccupation with Plato's critiques has been counterproductive. The "task" of rhetoricians, in McKerrow's view, "is not to rehabilitate rhetoric but to announce it in terms of a critical practice" (p. 91). McKerrow's essay offered "a perspective on rhetoric that explores, in theoretical and practical terms, the implications of a theory that is divorced from the constraints of a Platonic conception" (p. 91). In short, McKerrow wanted to move rhetorical studies out from under Plato's debilitating shadow by refusing to let Plato dictate the terms of the debate. **Critical rhetoric** attempts to establish the "status" of rhetoric—its importance as a form of thinking and a mode of practice—in decidedly non-Platonic terms.

Murphy (1995) noted the "millennial" or quasi-religious quality of McKerrow's account of critical rhetoric.[1] Extending Murphy's insight, the founding constitutive utterance embedded in McKerrow's essay was something like "In the beginning, there was critique" (cf. Eagleton, 1981). Whereas virtually all traditional and contemporary forms of rhetorical theory define the domain of rhetoric by way of topics such as deliberation about matters of public concern, methods of discourse production, and the discovery of available means of persuasion, McKerrow asserted that rhetoric's principal preoccupation is critique; rhetoric is, first and foremost, *critical.*[2]

McKerrow (1989) described two "complementary" phases or moments of critique, with each phase or moment defined by its understanding of **power.** The critique of *domination* understands power as *repressive.* As McKerrow noted, "There is a compelling sense in which power is negative or repressive in delimiting the potential of the human subject" (p. 96). The critique of domination is a continuation of the tradition of **ideology** critique that emerged in the field during the late 1970s and early 1980s. McKerrow claimed that this brand of critique is "a critique of ideologies perceived as rhetorical creations" (p. 92). The purpose of the critique of domination is emancipation or "*freedom from* powers of oppression" (McKerrow, 1991a, p. 75). Domination and oppression can be enacted in various ways (e.g., laws, customary social practices, economic relationships, physical action). Although the critical rhetorician is concerned with these manifestations of domination and oppression, his or her principal focus is "on the *discourse* of power which creates and sustains the social practices which control the dominated" (McKerrow, 1989, p. 92, emphasis added). McKerrow did not reduce all domination to discourse[3]; rather, McKerrow retained the traditional view that discourse is the primary domain of rhetoric while narrowing the scope such that one of the dual foci of critical rhetoric is the discourse of repressive power. Part of the task of critical rhetoric, then, is to unmask or reveal the ways in which discourse helps to create social and/or political oppression, thereby establishing the conditions for emancipation.

Drawing on a range of contemporary social and critical theorists, McKerrow (1989) described some of the modes through which discourse enables repressive power. Beyond some of the more obvious ways in which discourse functions to enact restrictions and rules that regulate who may talk and what may be talked about (p. 93), McKerrow pointed to the process of **hegemony** or the discursive construction of a dominant sense of "the people" as one of the key ways in which discourse effects domination and oppression. McKerrow acknowledged that his discussion did not provide "an exhaustive account of the potential discourses of power which govern social practices" (p. 96). So, as Cloud (1994) noted, Kenneth Burke's interest in the process of **mystification** also is relevant to the project of critical rhetoric. Just as there are multiple ways for discourse to enact repressive power, the discourse of power can emerge from multiple sources, and it is the task of the critical rhetorician to attend to these diverse discursive practices. Oppression and repression are manifest in the speech of the politician justifying a trade agreement that will cost jobs and damage the environment so as to preserve the nation's economic competitiveness, in the press release from a corporation announcing another plant closing because production is being shifted to an overseas plant, in the announcement from the Federal Reserve Board that interest rates will be increased to ward off the danger of inflation even though that will mean fewer new jobs and continued unemployment for millions of Americans, in the television news feature on welfare programs that focuses on a black family even though most recipients of welfare in America are white, in the commentary of the radio talk show host about the rate of illegitimate births in the black community even though the rate of illegitimacy is just as high (if not higher) among white teenagers, and in the magazine article suggesting that women were happier before the rise of the feminist movement or claiming that rape has become a more serious problem since large numbers of women entered the workforce. In different ways, all of these messages contribute to oppression and repression. They place the long-term interests of the upper class over the immediate material needs of American workers, they mystify power, they transform narrow interests into a purportedly national interest, they foster negative and demeaning stereotypes, or they excuse various forms of interpersonal domination and abuse. The critical rhetorician tries to unpack this discourse and reveal what is being concealed or distorted so as to foster the conditions necessary for human emancipation.

But following the work of the French philosopher and historian Michel Foucault, McKerrow (1989) identified a second moment of critique in the critical rhetoric program. A second type of critique is necessary, McKerrow argued, because power is not exclusively repressive. It is necessary because power also is "productive" (p. 98) or constitutive—a "positive force which creates social relations and sustains them" (p. 99)—and domination cannot do justice to this dimension of power. McKerrow labeled this second form of critique the "critique of freedom" (pp. 91, 96-100). A critique of freedom, or a "never-ending skepticism" (p. 96), is necessary because the results of practical political action, no matter how enlightened or disinterested the political actors might be or how pure their motives might be, "are never satisfying . . . [because they] are themselves simply new forms of power and, hence, subject to renewed skepticism" (p. 96). The aim or telos of the critique of freedom is not to overcome explicit domination but rather to overcome the more implicit constraints that subtly, but forcefully, shape human possibilities. Through constant reflection on, and self-scrutiny of, all that we take for granted, the critical rhetorician promotes a positive "*freedom to* pursue other power relations" (McKerrow, 1991a, p. 75). The critique of freedom provides a constant reminder that human existence is radically **contingent.** No values, ideals, or human relationships are natural or inevitable; all are contingent human constructions that must be subjected to constant critical reflection.

McKerrow's (1989) discussion of the two modes of critique constitutes what he described as the "theoretical rationale" (p. 92) for the critical rhetoric project. There is a second component of the project that McKerrow labeled "principles of praxis" (p. 100). McKerrow began his discussion of critical rhetoric as praxis by clarifying its status and identifying its object. In regard to status, McKerrow insisted that critical rhetoric is *not* a methodology "in the narrow sense of formula or prescription" (p. 100). The critical rhetoric project does not stipulate a specific set of research protocols or reading strategies; rather, it offers an "orientation" or a perspective that shapes or guides the critic's interaction with his or her world. McKerrow argued that the critical rhetoric orientation mandates a dramatic reconceptualization of the object of critical practice. According to McKerrow, "The acceptance of a critical rhetoric is premised on the reversal of the phrase 'public address'—we need to reconceptualize the endeavor to focus attention on *that symbolism which addresses publics*" (p. 101). This reversal has important consequences for critical practice in rhetorical studies. First, critical rhetoric challenges certain key assumptions regarding the **text** (e.g., speech, essay) that is central to more mainstream criticism and public address scholarship. Extending Becker's (1971) insights, McKerrow argued in favor of what we can call the *fragmentation thesis:* Rhetorical texts should not be viewed as self-contained units of meaning "with a beginning, [a] middle, and an end"[4]; messages are, in fact, fragments of much larger **discursive formations.** Texts do not reveal their persuasive force in discrete rhetorical situations where a specific audience encounters a specific text; rather, message fragments exert persuasive force, and participate in social and political power relations, as they circulate throughout a culture, migrating from one situation to another, combining and colliding with a host of other fragments. The fragmentation of the text leads to a second key consequence for critical practice. McKerrow argued that the critic is not an interpreter of discrete autonomous texts; instead, the critic is an "inventor" of texts (p. 101; see also McGee, 1990). Critical attention shifts from texts to discursive formations, and the critic's task is "to construct addresses out of the fabric of mediated experience" (p. 101). Critical rhetoric valorizes the role of the critic, whose construction of an object for analysis is as creative as—perhaps more creative than—the inventional acts of message producers. Third, the emphasis on "symbolism which addresses publics" effects a *decentering* of the **subject.** The focus of critical rhetoric is on the symbolism—various fragmented messages—and not on the intentions of the agents that produced these symbols. The critic's attention is *not* directed at how an advocate's *intentions* are realized in various textual strategies; rather, the critic brackets intentions and focuses on the way in which symbolic structures such as narrative and argument function to perpetuate or challenge relations of power.[5] Finally, the emphasis on function leads to a fourth important consequence. McKerrow argued that function, and not any supposedly universal standards of artistic excellence, is the crucial criterion in deciding on what objects to study. As McKerrow noted, " 'Facts of Life' may never aspire to inclusion in the 'canons of oratorical excellence,' but it may have more influence on a teenager's conception of social reality than all the great speeches by long-dead great speakers" (p. 101). Given this emphasis on function, the critical rhetoric project emphasizes **vernacular** cultures and practices over elite cultural practices (Ono & Sloop, 1995).

McKerrow (1989) amplified the orientation of critical rhetoric by outlining eight principles of critical praxis. The first principle, that critique is a practice and not a method, reiterates the point noted previously. Critique is a practice because the process of understanding (what critical "methods" try to systematize) cannot be separated from the act of evaluation (p. 102). Critical rhetoric does not attempt a neutral description of messages or discursive formations; it always is evaluative and, hence, a form of practice actively trying to intervene in the world. McKerrow's second principle is that "the discourse of power is material" (p. 102). This principle, which we can refer to as the *materiality of discourse thesis* (cf. Blair, 1987; Cloud, 1994; Greene, 1998; McGee, 1982), emphasizes the *constitutive* capacity of discursive practice. In essence, discourse does more than describe the world; it creates "what is perceived *as real* to the populace" (p. 103, emphasis added).[6]

The third principle of praxis is that "rhetoric constitutes *doxastic* rather than *epistemic* knowledge" (McKerrow, 1989, p. 103). This principle follows from McKerrow's (1989) attempt to sidestep the Platonic problematic. Plato tried to force rhetoricians to fight on his ground, a ground that would judge practices based on their conformity to universal principles or essential "forms." According to McKerrow, "A more positive approach is to reassert the value of rhetoric's province—*doxa*—and thereby resituate theory and practice in a context far more amenable to its continuance" (p. 104). Such a shift means that "rather than focusing on questions of 'truth' or 'falsity,' " critical praxis can emphasize how "symbols come to possess power—what they 'do' in society as contrasted to what they 'are' " (p. 104). In short, this third principle reveals critical rhetoric to be radically functionalistic; its principal concern is with *how* discursive practice enacts power. McKerrow's recovery of the concept of **doxa,** a concept that emphasizes the concrete over the abstract or universal, is amplified in his fourth principle.[7]

McKerrow's (1989) fourth principle is that "*naming* is the central symbolic act of a *nominalist* rhetoric" (p. 105). Two important points are contained in this principle. First, the principle suggests "a reinterpretation of rhetoric as nominalist" (p. 105). What is involved in this reinterpretation? To answer this question, we need to consider the philosophical concept of *nominalism.* A nominalist stance has been advanced over time by numerous philosophers. For example, in *Leviathan,* the 16th-century English philosopher Thomas Hobbes wrote,

> Of Names, some are *Proper* and singular to only one thing, as *Peter, John, This man, This tree;* and some are *Common* to many things, as *Man, Horse, Tree;* every of which though but one Name is nevertheless the name of diverse particular things; in respect of all which together, it is called a *Universal;* there being nothing in the world Universal but Names; for the things named are every one of them Individual and Singular. (Hobbes, 1994, p. 14)

What was the key point of Hobbes's nominalist observation? Hobbes was skeptical about the existence of abstract universals. People invent words for universal categories (e.g., "table," "tree") and for concepts (e.g., "truth," "justice"), but Hobbes argued that, in reality, all that exists are discrete things or individual human acts.[8] McKerrow's proposed nominalist reinterpretation of rhetoric continued Hobbes's skepticism regarding universals. McKerrow did not deny that advocates routinely employ terms for general categories (e.g., "the poor," "welfare queen") or abstract concepts or **ideographs** (e.g., liberty, equality). The point of the reinterpretation was to insist that these descriptive labels or political principles are *just words.* "The poor" do not exist, only specific individuals to whom the label is applied. There is no "essence" of liberty, only thousands of instances in which the term is used to describe and/or evaluate actual or proposed practices and courses of action (policies). But a nominalist insistence that these terms are just words does not lead to a dismissive conclusion that they are *merely words.* Just because "the poor" does not function as a simple neutral label for a general category does not mean that it is devoid of meaning and significance (see, e.g., Edelman, 1977). Most nominalists recognize that words are extremely powerful political and social weapons. For example, Hobbes clearly perceived how certain words could be "dangerous" and, in light of this fact, recommended a plan for linguistic reform.[9] McKerrow was not a linguistic reformer in the tradition of Hobbes. His nominalist reinterpretation of rhetoric rejected "the universalizing tendencies" (p. 105) of most philosophical systems while emphasizing "the power . . . of naming" (p. 105).

The emphasis on *naming* as the central symbolic act is the second key point and follows from the reinterpretation of rhetoric as nominalist. The process of naming or labeling never is benign or without consequence. The terms we employ in our discursive practices never are merely words. Names and labels are implicated in both senses of power that McKerrow identified—the repressive and the productive. Names and labels can *constrain* as well as *enable* subsequent thought and practice (see also Blair, 1987; Sloop, 1996). When a conservative politician labels a group of federal assistance recipients "welfare queens," that politician has imposed *constraints* on those advocates defending these federal programs (they must deal with the charge in some way) while enabling efforts to reduce or eliminate assistance programs. As McKerrow acknowledged, the emphasis on naming in the critical rhetoric project intersects with a number of other important critical and theoretical programs.[10]

The fifth principle of critical praxis is that "*influence* is not *causality*" (McKerrow, 1989, p. 106). The critical rhetoric project, as McKerrow (1989) elaborated, is part of a larger effort to rethink the idea of discursive or rhetorical effect. Like a number of other contemporary scholars, in rhetoric as well as in other disciplines, McKerrow argued that it is a mistake to reduce rhetorical influence or effect to a principle of causality. Extending Condit's (1987) work, McKerrow argued that causality is based on an idea of rigid determinism: One thing determines or causes another. For example, a speech causes a person to vote in a certain way. But if discursive influence operates in ways that fall outside the model of causal relationships, then this model is of little value to rhetorical scholars. For McKerrow, "To say that a symbol has influence is to claim that it impacts on others" (p. 106), but that impact is not necessarily causal. The task for critical rhetoricians, as it is for many rhetorical scholars, is to try to specify more precisely the noncausal forms of discursive influence.

McKerrow's (1989) sixth principle is that "*absence* is as important as *presence* in understanding and evaluating symbolic action" (p. 107). The basic point of this principle is clear: In many cases, *what* gets said might not be as important as what is *not* said. For example, at a news conference, a politician who is asked a question about reforming social security might respond in such a way that he or she never really answers the question. In this simple case, what gets said (a statement on the need to provide for the nation's senior citizens) is not as important as what is not said (the refusal to deal with the specifics of proposed social security reforms). We might consider absence to exist as a continuum; on one end would be forms of "passive" absence (as in the preceding example), and on the other end would be forms of "active" absence or strategic *elisions.* For example, in a speech about affirmative action policy, a politician might "make present" the concept of equality. But equality is not a simple label or a monodimensional concept; it has multiple meanings or dimensions.[11] In approaching this speech, the critical rhetorician not only can focus on how a certain sense of equality (equality as "equal opportunity") is made present, he or she also can ask how an alternative sense of equality (equality as "equal results") is repressed or elided and how this alternative sense of equality is actively "made absent" through the speech. McKerrow suggested that the absence of an alternative to equality as equal opportunity is crucial to what is happening—how power is being (re)constructed—in this speech.

The seventh principle of critical praxis is that "fragments contain the potential for *polysemic* rather than monosemic *interpretation*" (McKerrow, 1989, p. 107). The concept of **polysemy** maintains that texts contain the possibility of multiple meanings (see, e.g., Fiske, 1986). Whereas many traditional forms of critical practice, in rhetorical studies as well as in other interpretive disciplines, sought *the* essentially monosemic meaning of a text, McKerrow argued that critical rhetoric needs to appreciate the polysemic potential of discursive fragments. According to McKerrow (1989), "A polysemic critique is one which uncovers a subordinate or secondary reading which contains the seeds of subversion or rejection of authority at the same time that the primary reading appears to confirm the power of the dominant cultural norms" (p. 108). For example, a textual fragment (e.g., speech, news broadcast, television program) might initially appear to endorse dominant cultural norms (e.g., ideals of marriage, sanctity of private property), but its polysemic potential allows for a reading "against the grain," so to speak, that reveals how the text might contribute to the subversion of those norms. The inverse also is possible; a text that appears to work subversively (e.g., different forms of comedy) can be read in a way that illustrates its complicity with forms of domination.

The idea of textual polysemy resembles Bakhtin's concept of **heteroglossia.** But Gaonkar (1993b) warned against collapsing the two concepts. He wrote, "While polysemy is susceptible to being reduced to no more than a 'plurality of meanings,' heteroglossia retains its focus on the conflictual and contingent character of the ideological sign" (p. 153). That is, the concept of heteroglossia draws attention to the struggle and/or conflict between different idioms or ideologies that becomes inscribed in the specific word or "sign,"[12] whereas the concept of polysemy draws attention to the apparently inevitable fact that words can have multiple meanings. Although there is some overlap between the discursive effects that each concept tries to describe (multiple meanings), the concepts identify different enabling conditions. Heteroglossia asserts that ideological conflict is the source of multiple meanings, whereas polysemy locates multiple meanings in the inherent ambiguity of language.

McKerrow's (1989) eighth and final principle is that "criticism is a *performance*" (p. 108). The emphasis on the performative dimension of criticism is a final complement to the initial claim that critical rhetoric is a mode of practice and not an analytic method. Criticism is not disinterested inquiry into texts or communicative acts; it is itself a transformative practice. And transformation is crucial to the activity of performance (e.g., when the script of a play is transformed into a theatrical performance). But what gets transformed in critical practice? Whereas some politically motivated critics see it as a vehicle for introducing overt political transformation (e.g., criticism of the debate over health care reform contributing to the creation of a universal, single-payer health care system), McKerrow took "refuge" (p. 108) in a narrower sense of transformation. Borrowing from Foucault and the literary critic Frank Lentricchia, McKerrow (1989) argued that the transformative potential of critical performances can be directed at the specific institutional and disciplinary structures within which the critic operates (see also Lentricchia, 1983). McKerrow acknowledged that critical performances might not be able to change the world, but they can at least modify academic practices. If nothing else, the performance of critical rhetoric might alter the "status" of rhetorical studies within the larger realm of the humanities and the narrower sphere of critical social theory.

The impact of McKerrow's (1989) essay on the field of contemporary rhetorical studies can be seen, in part, in the numerous responses it has evoked. These responses raise a number of issues with respect to McKerrow's initial essay and the critical rhetoric project as a whole. For example, Gaonkar (1993b) found little coherence between McKerrow's "theoretical rationale" and his principles of critical praxis (p. 151), whereas Cloud (1994) found the two moments of critique outlined in the theoretical rationale—the critique of domination and the critique of freedom—to be "mutually contradictory" (p. 155). According to Cloud, "We cannot talk about unmasking repressive, dominating power without some understanding of the reality of oppression" (p. 155), but she continued that McKerrow's turn to Foucault prevents such understanding. Charland (1991) and Ono and Sloop (1992) questioned whether critical rhetoric will lead to an infinitely regressive criticism that disables the critic's ability to make situated **judgments.** Their argument resembles Habermas's (1982) critique of the tradition of social thought that runs from Nietzsche to Foucault. Habermas wrote,

> If . . . all proper claims to validity are devalued and if the underlying value judgments are mere expressions of claims to power rather than validity, according to what standards should critique then differentiate? It must at least be able to discriminate between a power which *deserves* to be esteemed and a power which *deserves* to be disparaged. (p. 27)

Although Charland and Ono and Sloop do not share many of Habermas's concerns, they appear to agree with the point of this passage: Given its radically skeptical stance, critical rhetoric is unable to discriminate between a form of power that should be esteemed and one that should be disparaged. Gaonkar (1993b) and Murphy (1995) questioned McKerrow's dismissal of reason as simply one more element of power and domination. According to Gaonkar (1993b), "It is precisely this stubborn refusal of reason . . . that gives the CR [critical rhetoric] project a distinctly postmodern aura." But Gaonkar found this stubborn refusal problematic:

> Unless McKerrow can show in a convincing fashion that practical reasoning and everyday reasoning are also somehow implicated in erasing situated differences and in universalizing [the] standards of judgment [as is the case with "formal apodeictic reasoning"] . . ., he cannot continue to ignore the simple fact that there are different types of reasoning that are active in different spheres of life. (p. 150)

In a way, Gaonkar accused McKerrow of neglecting his fourth critical principle; that is, McKerrow failed to appreciate the diversity of reasoning practices because he had been seduced by the universal term *reason*. Finally, Hariman (1991) and Murphy (1995) raised questions about how the self or the **subject** was characterized in McKerrow's initial essay. Hariman (1991) argued that despite the postmodern gestures of McKerrow's essay, it presents a picture of a decidedly modernist self or "a stable autonomous subject whose task is to achieve self-determination" (p. 68). Whereas Hariman suggested that McKerrow still is caught in the grip of modernity, Murphy (1995) read McKerrow (especially McKerrow, 1993) as having abandoned the modernist commitment to human sociality in favor of a preoccupation with the self and the body. Murphy (1995) wrote,

> The extent of the change that McKerrow proposes for rhetoric is symbolized by the title of the book he most often offers up as the path to political engagement, [Foucault's] *The Care of the Self.* Whether one accepts or rejects the contours of rhetorical thought from Aristotle to the present, the difference between the sociality of that tradition and a "Care of the Self" is profound. (p. 8)

In subsequent work (see especially McKerrow, 1991a, 1993), McKerrow began to respond to these, and other, criticisms of the critical rhetoric project. Whether the critical rhetoric project will be able to withstand the critiques from its sympathizers and antagonists remains to be seen. For the present moment, at least, critical rhetoric is (along with **close reading**) one of the two dominant orientations in contemporary rhetorical studies. Even if its adherents fail to sustain critical rhetoric as a discrete disciplinary movement, the themes, issues, and questions that the critical rhetoric project has helped to generate—from the materiality of discourse thesis; to the fragmentation thesis; to questions about the nature of human subjectivity, the relationship between discourse and power, and the possibility of judgment—no doubt will continue to provoke sustained discussion and reflection.

Notes

1. On McKerrow's strategy of **exposition,** see also Gaonkar (1993b).

2. On the gradual transformation of rhetoric from a productive practice to an interpretive practice, see Gaonkar (1993a). Eagleton (1981) provided a brief "history" of rhetoric that indirectly supports McKerrow's claim that it has a primarily critical function.

3. But Cloud (1994) argued that this tendency is embedded in the critical rhetoric position.

4. Adherents to the strategy of **close reading** refer to this idea as the *integrity* of the text.

5. As Gaonkar (1993a) pointed out, decentering of agent intentions already is beginning to occur in rhetorical criticism. Jasinski (1995) extended Gaonkar and argued that such decentering is, in fact, an integral part of most conceptually grounded close readings.

6. McKerrow qualified this principle by acknowledging the constitutive force of nondiscursive practices.

7. On the priority of the concrete over the abstract or universal in ancient Greek thought, see Havelock (1963).

8. For a discussion and critique of the philosophical doctrine of nominalism, see Woozley (1967).

9. On the Hobbesian tradition of linguistic reform, see Gustafson (1992).

10. For discussions of the centrality of naming that are compatible with McKerrow's emphasis, see the following entries: **condensation symbols, definition/definition of the situation,** and **ideographs.**

11. The Russian theorist Mikhail Bakhtin would describe it as "internally dialogized" in that different idioms or languages intersect in the word. See discussion under the entry for **heteroglossia.**

12. In the example, the word *equality* is the site or location of struggle between two rival idioms that have certain ideological implications.

References and Additional Reading

Becker, S. (1971). Rhetorical studies for the contemporary world. In E. Black & L. Bitzer (Eds.), *The prospect of rhetoric.* Englewood Cliffs, NJ: Prentice Hall.

Biesecker, B. (1992). Michel Foucault and the question of rhetoric. *Philosophy and Rhetoric, 25,* 351-364.

Blair, C. (1987). The statement: Foundation of Foucault's historical criticism. *Western Journal of Speech Communication, 51,* 364-383.

Charland, M. (1991). Finding a horizon and telos: The challenge to critical rhetoric. *Quarterly Journal of Speech, 77,* 71-74.

Clark, N. (1996). The critical servant: An Isocratean contribution to critical rhetoric. *Quarterly Journal of Speech, 82,* 111-124.

Cloud, D. L. (1994). The materiality of discourse as oxymoron: A challenge to critical rhetoric. *Western Journal of Communication, 58,* 141-163.

Condit, C. (1987). Democracy and civil rights: The universalizing influence of public argumentation. *Communication Monographs, 54,* 1-18.

Eagleton, T. (1981). *Walter Benjamin or towards a revolutionary criticism.* London: Verso.

Edelman, M. (1977). *Political language: Words that succeed and policies that fail.* New York: Academic Press.

Fiske, J. (1986). Television: Polysemy and popularity. *Critical Studies in Mass Communication, 3,* 391-408.

Gaonkar, D. P. (1993a). The idea of rhetoric in the rhetoric of science. *Southern Communication Journal, 58,* 258-295.

Gaonkar, D. P. (1993b). Performing with fragments: Reflections on critical rhetoric. In R. E. McKerrow (Ed.), *Argument and the postmodern challenge: Proceedings of the Eighth SCA/AFA Conference on Argumentation.* Annandale, VA: Speech Communication Association.

Greene, R. W. (1993). Social argumentation and the aporias of state formation: The Palestinian Declaration of Independence. *Argumentation and Advocacy, 29,* 124-136.

Greene, R. W. (1998). Another materialist rhetoric. *Critical Studies in Mass Communication, 15,* 21-41.

Gustafson, T. (1992). *Representative words: Politics, literature, and the American language, 1776-1865.* Cambridge, UK: Cambridge University Press.

Habermas, J. (1982). The entwinement of myth and enlightenment: Re-reading *Dialectic of Enlightenment. New German Critique, 26,* 13-30.

Hariman, R. (1991). Critical rhetoric and postmodern theory. *Quarterly Journal of Speech, 77,* 67-70.

Havelock, E. A. (1963). *Preface to Plato.* Cambridge, MA: Harvard University Press.

Hobbes, T. (1994). *Leviathan.* London: Everyman Library.

Jasinski, J. (1995). The forms and limits of prudence in Henry Clay's (1850) defense of the compromise measures. *Quarterly Journal of Speech, 81,* 454-478.

Lentricchia, F. (1983). *Criticism and social change.* Chicago: University of Chicago Press.

McGee, M. C. (1982). A materialist's conception of rhetoric. In R. E. McKerrow (Ed.), *Explorations in rhetoric: Studies in honor of Douglas Ehninger.* Glenview, IL: Scott, Foresman.

McGee, M. C. (1990). Text, context, and the fragmentation of contemporary culture. *Western Journal of Speech Communication, 54,* 274-289.

McKerrow, R. E. (1989). Critical rhetoric: Theory and praxis. *Communication Monographs, 56,* 91-111.

McKerrow, R. E. (1991a). Critical rhetoric in a postmodern world. *Quarterly Journal of Speech, 77,* 75-78.

McKerrow, R. E. (1991b). Critical rhetoric and propaganda studies. In J. Anderson (Ed.), *Communication yearbook* (Vol. 14). Newbury Park, CA: Sage.

McKerrow, R. E. (1993). Critical rhetoric and the possibility of the subject. In I. Angus & L. Langsdorf (Ed.), *The critical turn: Rhetoric and philosophy in postmodern discourse.* Carbondale: Southern Illinois University Press.

Murphy, J. M. (1995). Critical rhetoric as political discourse. *Argumentation and Advocacy, 32,* 1-15.

Ono, K. A., & Sloop, J. M. (1992). Commitment to telos: A sustained critical rhetoric. *Communication Monographs, 59,* 48-60.

Ono, K. A., & Sloop, J. M. (1995). The critique of vernacular discourse. *Communication Monographs, 62,* 19-46.

Owen, A. S., & Ehrenhaus, P. (1993). Animating a critical rhetoric: On the feeding habits of American empire. *Western Journal of Communication, 57,* 169-177.

Shome, R. (1996). Postcolonial interventions in the rhetoric canon: An "other" view. *Communication Theory, 6,* 40-59.

Sloop, J. M. (1996). *The cultural prison: Discourse, prisoners, and punishment.* Tuscaloosa: University of Alabama Press.

Woozley, A. D. (1967). Universals. In P. Edwards (Ed.), *The encyclopedia of philosophy* (Vol. 8). New York: Macmillan.

CRITICISM IN CONTEMPORARY RHETORICAL STUDIES

Since the revival of rhetorical studies within the field of speech communication during the early part of the 20th century, rhetorical scholars have tried to (a) articulate the nature of rhetorical criticism, (b) identify the object of this form of critical activity, (c) identify specific procedures or methods for practicing criticism, and (d) specify the particular function(s) or purpose(s) of rhetorical criticism. This entry for **criticism in contemporary rhetorical studies** sketches how rhetoricians in speech communication, drawing on a variety of sources including the classical tradition of rhetorical thought, aesthetic theory, literary theory and criticism, and (more recently) various forms of *critical social theory* (Agger, 1998), have sought to accomplish these four objectives. The sketch tries to illuminate points of agreement as well as points of continuing controversy.

What is criticism? What is rhetorical criticism? One way of approaching these questions, as Black (1978) noted, is to "focus on the critic." Black remarked, "Criticism is that which critics do" (p. 4). Black admitted that this approach to the question might appear "suspiciously evasive" (p. 4), but having to start somewhere, he suggested that starting with the critic has considerable heuristic potential. The first problem with Black's approach, of course, is deciding who *is* a critic. One issue in contemporary rhetorical studies has been, to paraphrase Baskerville (1977), whether all rhetoricians must be rhetorical critics as opposed to, say, rhetorical historians.[1] Once we are able to distinguish critics from noncritics, the next problem is trying to uncover the point(s) of convergence in their activity. It might be possible to collect a sufficient sample of critical practice that could be subjected to a type of factor analysis so as to discover the common denominator that links the practices and constitutes the "essence," or the fundamental nature, of criticism. Pursuing such a project would consume a considerable amount of time and be open to charges that the sample of critical work selected failed to adequately represent "that which critics do."

An alternative approach to defining criticism, one that retains the spirit of Black's suggestion, is simply to see how practicing critics have described what they are doing and how they have defined criticism. This approach to the question will at least provide us with a working definition. Here are two definitions notable for their breadth. Abrams (1993) defined criticism, in the context of literary studies, as "the overall term for studies concerned with defining, classifying, analyzing, interpreting, and evaluating works of literature" (p. 39). Bryant (1973) explained the nature of rhetorical criticism in the following terms:

> Rhetorical criticism . . . is directed (1) to discovering and explicating the elements and form of particular discourses; (2) to generalizing particular discourses, or their informative-suasory dimensions, into the wider phenomena of the rhetorical, especially public address; (3) to showing how particular discourses participate in families of didactic and suasory discourse to which they may be related; and finally (4) to supporting value judgments. (pp. 34-35)

Abrams's and Bryant's definitions clearly converge on three key points: Criticism involves analysis (Bryant's first point[2]), it involves *generic* classification (Bryant's third point), and it involves evaluation (Bryant's fourth point). Abrams (1993) included two characteristics or elements of criticism not explicitly included in Bryant's account: definition[3] and interpretation (the issue of interpretation in rhetorical criticism, as the discussion that follows notes, has been a topic of debate in rhetorical studies). Bryant (1973), on the other hand, included one characteristic left out of Abrams's account (his second point). The idea that criticism involves a movement from "particular discourses" to the "wider phenomena of the rhetorical" is important, but this essentially conceptual or theoretical move might more appropriately be considered as one of the functions or purposes of criticism rather than a defining or immanent characteristic of it. So, what this brief review of Abrams's and Bryant's definitions reveals is five crucial characteristics of criticism (see also Hart, 1997, p. 26). All five might not be present in each and every act of criticism, but they nevertheless provide an initial orientation to the nature of criticism. We can deepen our understanding of the nature of criticism by exploring more concretely how these characteristics have helped to shape the practice of rhetorical criticism.

Criticism Defines

Any critical act will, either implicitly or explicitly, define its object as a specific type of thing. A piece of literary criticism will define its object as literature (or as manifesting a significant literary dimension); similarly, any act of rhetorical criticism will define its object as rhetorical (or as manifesting a significant rhetorical dimension). For example, Hart (1997) suggested, "The most basic job of the rhetorical critic is to be able to discover *when* rhetoric is being used in the first place" (p. 11). Gaonkar (1993) identified this characteristic in rhetorical criticism under the label of "recuperation." As Culler (1975) observed, recuperation in literary studies refers to the way in which a critic "make[s] a text intelligible" (p. 159). He also observed that recuperation "stresses the notion of recovery, of putting to use. It may be defined as the desire to leave no chaff, to make everything wheat, to let nothing escape the process of assimilation" (p. 137). In extending this concept from the domain of literary studies into the realm of rhetorical criticism, Gaonkar (1993) argued that rhetorical critics need to engage in acts of recuperation or definition because our culture "lacks resources for spontaneously recognizing what is and what is not 'rhetoric' " (p. 264). Gaonkar explained this need as follows. Members of our culture are unable to identify rhetorical objects (texts and/or practices) because of the general repression of rhetoric that accompanied the rise of modernity. The critic is compelled to engage in a "politics of recognition" (p. 265); he or she must employ recuperative strategies that identify and define the critical object as rhetorical (or as possessing a significant rhetorical dimension).

Gaonkar's discussion of recuperation and *the repression/recognition thesis* highlights the definitional characteristic of criticism. But it also may distort the issue. Gaonkar suggested that recuperation is caught up in the disciplinary status anxieties of contemporary rhetorical studies; rhetorical critics resort to recuperation to gain new intellectual "turf" (new objects, texts, or practices) and thereby enhance their standing within the academy. An implication of this argument is that more established disciplines (e.g., literary studies) do not practice recuperation, so recuperative definition is not a central characteristic of criticism; it is only a strategy forced on rhetorical scholars by the problem of repression and recognition. But this argument overlooks two points. First, as Abrams (1993) suggested, recuperation or definition appears to be an always implicit aspect of criticism. Criticism can proceed only after it has identified the object as a particular type of thing. Second, explicit definition or recuperation by no means is limited to the realm of rhetorical criticism. As Jasinski (1997) pointed out, explicit recuperation tends to be present whenever an object is approached and apprehended in ways that run counter to a discipline's dominant practices. So, a philosopher will have to recuperate a text that he or she believes possesses philosophical significance if that text is not currently granted that status, or a literary scholar will have to recuperate a text like the Constitution if he or she wishes to approach it as a literary object (White, 1984). Although the definitional component of criticism may take on added significance in rhetorical criticism given the broader social context of repression and recognition, this historical fact does not negate the claim that one general characteristic of criticism is that it defines.

As Gaonkar noted, perhaps the most common recuperative or definitional move in rhetorical criticism is to ground discourse within its **situation** (Bitzer, 1968; Bryant, 1973). Criticism becomes rhetorical when it attends to the way in which discourse responds to situational *exigences* and *constraints.* Definition by way of situational grounding is present in countless examples of rhetorical criticism (Condit & Greer, 1997; Hogan, 1989; Leff & Mohrmann, 1974; Lucas, 1989; Nichols, 1954). Another recurrent definitional strategy relies on persuasive intent. Criticism becomes rhetorical through "the positioning of the rhetor as the generating center of discourse . . . [where] the agency of rhetoric is always reducible to the conscious and strategic thinking of the rhetor" (Gaonkar, 1993, p. 275). Although gestures to the historical and/or rhetorical situation and persuasive intention are commonplace in rhetorical criticism, other modes of recuperative definition also are visible. For example, some critics have drawn on Burke's concept of **identification** as a defining feature of rhetoric (Carpenter, 1972; Charland, 1987; Cheney, 1983), whereas other critics have drawn on innovations in philosophy, social theory, or literary theory to aid in the process of defining their object of study (Blair, 1987; Hyde & Smith, 1979; McGuire, 1977). In short, critics have defined their objects of study as rhetorical in numerous ways.

The observation at the end of the preceding paragraph leads to another important point: Critics not only define specific objects as rhetorical or as possessing characteristics that make them ripe for rhetorical analysis; they also engage in defining rhetoric. That is, critical practice in contemporary rhetorical studies frequently contributes to the never-ending conversation about the essence of **rhetoric** (see the introduction to this book for an overview of the dilemmas involved in defining rhetoric).

Criticism Classifies

Beyond defining its object of study as rhetorical, a considerable amount of criticism also will classify its object in specific categories. This characteristic is most prevalent in criticism oriented around the concept of **genre.** Criticism that explicitly evokes generic categories such as **apologia, jeremiad,** and **epideictic** clearly classifies objects as part of the critical process. But classification can be an implicit component of criticism as well. For example, if a critic invokes the **stock topic in policy dispute** in the course of the process of criticism, then he or she is engaging in an act of classification. That is, in invoking the stock topics, the critic classifies the object as an instance of **deliberative** discourse. The critic also can classify by placing an object within a **discursive formation** (Sloop, 1996). By employing concepts associated with various discursive genres or by locating objects within discursive formations, the critic engages in a less obvious process of classification. Although classification can occur in these subtle ways, it should be noted that of the five central characteristics identified by Abrams (1993) and Bryant (1973), classification probably is the one most likely to be absent from any sample of critical studies.

Criticism Analyzes

Critical activity seeks to describe or disclose how an object is put together and how it works. As Bryant (1973) maintained, the critic is an "analytical explicator" (p. 40). Analytical explication involves a careful reconstruction or unpacking of an object's structure, design, and constituent features. Within the once dominant **neo-Aristotelian** perspective, critical analysis featured the five traditional **canons** of classical rhetoric (**invention, arrangement, style, memory,** and delivery) and the three **modes of proof** (**ethos, logos,** and **pathos**). In contemporary rhetorical studies, critical analysis proceeds through a large variety of analytic procedures or *methods* and invokes an equally large body of analytic concepts. The **close reading** movement in rhetorical studies, for example, continues the purported aim of the neo-Aristotelian movement by trying to unpack the internal economy or overall design of an object. This quest typically involves careful attention to a text's modes of appeal, **argument** strategies, style (including **figuration**), and *disposition* or structure (Browne, 1993; Leff & Mohrmann, 1974). Other rhetorical critics have drawn inspiration from the writings of Kenneth Burke, translating Burke's ideas into specific methods (e.g., *pentadic* criticism [Foss, 1996; Ling, 1970]) or appropriating particular concepts that can be used in the process of analytic explication (e.g., **perspective by incongruity, representative anecdote**). Other important bodies of source material from which rhetorical scholars have drawn conceptual insights that are used in the process of critical analysis are contemporary philosophy, literary theory, and social theory.[4]

The precise nature of critical analysis will vary, and these variations are based on a number of factors. For example, the way in which a critic conceptualizes the object of criticism will shape the process of analysis. Traditional neo-Aristotelianism and contemporary close reading typically regard the discrete **text** as the appropriate object of critical inquiry. With this understanding of the object, analysis then proceeds to describe or unpack its specific components and overall design. But the object of criticism can be conceptualized in other ways. Social **movement** scholars, for example, are not interested in unpacking the components of individual texts. They devote their attention to explicating the rhetorical dynamics of the movement as a social phenomenon.[5] A second factor that can shape the nature of analysis is the ultimate objective or purpose of critical activity. Traditional criticism (in both rhetorical and literary studies) usually assumes that its function is to guide or improve taste or to help consumers better appreciate discursive artistry. This understanding of the purpose of criticism leads the critic to emphasize the structural or aesthetic qualities of the critical object. Many contemporary critics, across a number of academic disciplines, view the ultimate purpose of criticism in different terms. Instead of improving the public's taste or determining which objects are granted the status of excellence, these critics believe that the function of their critical work is to intervene or participate in the various processes of public life. A critic who adopts this view of purpose, for example, would be less interested in appreciating the aesthetic qualities of a text as an end in itself and much more interested in probing how the text functions as a form of social or political **power.** Although we can find variations in the process of analysis, there still appears to be a basic unity: Critical analysis aims to explicate or explain what is going on in the critical object.

Criticism Interprets

An understanding of this characteristic of criticism is complicated by the fact that interpretation can mean different things. In its simplest sense, interpretation is a process of decoding or translating. Through interpretation, a confusing or opaque word, phrase, passage, or entire text is made intelligible and its latent meaning is made manifest. Decoding or translating is a common feature in at least some forms of literary criticism. A critic might, for example, try to decode the meaning of "the ship" image in Walt Whitman's "O Captain! My Captain!" (Whitman, 1932/1996) or try to reveal the latent meaning contained in Robert Frost's "Stopping by

Woods on a Snowy Evening" (Frost, 1932/1996). Baskerville (1953) seemed to have something like this more limited sense of interpretation in mind when he noted, "Speeches are seldom abstruse or esoteric. . . . A speech, by its nature, is or should be immediately comprehensible; hence the interpretive function of the critic is seldom paramount" (p. 2). Rhetorical criticism, Baskerville suggested, need not concern itself with the problems of interpretation.

A similar argument was developed by the literary theorist Jonathan Culler. Comparing the process of interpreting political or public discourse with what is involved in interpreting a literary text,[6] Culler (1975) noted,

> To read a political speech, for example, is to submit to a teleology, to take the text as governed by a communicative end which one reconstructs with the help of the conventions of discourse and of the relevant institutions. But literature, foregrounding the text itself, gives freer play to the "essential drift" and autonomous productivity of the language. (pp. 132-133)

According to Culler, the nature of public discourse—its *instrumental* character, institutional embeddedness, and highly *conventional* structure—negates the need for interpretive effort on the part of the critic.

This dismissal of interpretation is an important moment in the development of what Gaonkar (1989, 1990) referred to as the **transparency thesis.** Negotiating the so-called transparency of the text is, as Gaonkar observed, a central preoccupation of the **close reading** movement in rhetorical criticism, prominently featured in the work of one of its principal progenitors, Michael Leff. According to Leff (1980), it is through "the act of interpretation . . . [that] the critic attempts to account for and assign meaning to the rhetorical dimensions of a given phenomenon" (p. 342). Such an account typically emphasizes *external function* (how a specific rhetorical dimension such as argument responds to **situational** factors) but also can focus on an *internal function* (how a specific rhetorical dimension such as **stylistic** *anaphora* helps to generate a sense of unity within one segment of a **text**).

Consider a simple example of interpretation that focuses on external function. In the entry for **style**, the idea of *hypotaxis* is introduced and illustrated through some examples from Martin Luther King, Jr.'s "Letter From Birmingham Jail." Critical analysis reveals King's hypotactic linguistic pattern. But what is the significance of King's hypotaxis, and how does it contribute to the meaning and rhetorical force of the letter? According to Baskerville (1953), the meanings of these passages are, or should be, "immediately comprehensible" and, therefore, require little (if any) interpretive labor. But Leff's approach to criticism encourages the critic to pause and think more carefully about this stylistic phenomenon. Reflection on the phenomenon of hypotaxis that is informed by the literature on prose stylistics (Lanham, 1983) allows the critic to provide a richer account of what it was doing in King's text; King's carefully crafted linguistic subordination signaled to readers that King possessed the capacity of discernment or that he possessed the ability to analyze a situation and make nuanced judgments about the actions and events that have transpired therein. And that is what King was doing in the letter. He was trying to reveal to his critics that they had misread the situation in Birmingham. They had not really considered the plight of black Americans in the South. Lacking the power of discernment, these critics were not appropriate judges of King's conduct, and their criticisms should be discounted. And King's hypotactic style, a style that both enacts and reveals discernment, helped to drive home this point. But without interpretive reflection on the stylistic phenomenon, the critic is unable to provide this account of the text.

This reading of hypotaxis in King's "Letter From Birmingham Jail" retains the sense of interpretation introduced at the outset: Interpretation translates or decodes elements of the critical object and attempts to account for the external function of the elements uncovered during the analytic phase of critical practice (Andrews, Leff, & Terrill, 1998, pp. 75-78). Interpretive decoding is necessary given, in Gaonkar's (1989) terms, "the polysemous character of the oratorical text" (p. 271). But we need to acknowledge, as Gaonkar made clear, "that interpretation cannot fully arrest the natural polysemy of language. Hence, the text is potentially open to alternative readings, and privileged cultural texts can become sites of intense ideological struggle over meaning" (p. 271).[7] But the concept of interpretation in criticism also admits a more expansive meaning. Signs of an expanded sense of interpretation can be detected in Nilsen's (1957) response to Baskerville (1953). Nilsen (1957) began by claiming, "If the meaning of a speech is thought of as the response it explicitly seeks to evoke, then, to be sure, no interpretation is necessary" (p. 70). As the discussion of the King example tries to show, this claim is problematic; interpretation of the particular features of the critical object is an essential part of criticism. But is interpreting particulars the only thing that a critic does? Nilsen spoke directly to this issue: "But if within the meaning of the speech are included the many attendant responses, the more subtle understandings and conceptions evoked by the speech and their possible consequences, then interpretation is a much needed function of the speech critic" (p. 70). The key word in this passage is "understanding." Interpretation can involve more than decoding particular elements of a text or even of entire texts; it can, as the tradition of *hermeneutic philosophy* (Gadamer, 1975) emphasizes, have a much more diffuse objective—understanding. Interpretive understanding within the tradition of philosophical hermeneutics is an extremely challenging idea. Scholars and critics operating within this tradition describe the process differently.[8] At its core, this tradition of thought views the meaning of a critical object to be in a state of flux; it is something that is continually discovered or uncovered rather than decoded. Whereas Baskerville saw interpretation as an inessential characteristic of rhetorical criticism, the scholarship in the tradition of hermeneutic philosophy teaches us that interpretation, as a vehicle for understanding, is an inescapable part of being human.

Leff's (1980) account of the interpretive component of rhetorical criticism emphasized a concern with particulars as well as an interest in theoretical understanding. To bring out both dimensions, he compared rhetorical interpretation with psychoanalytic interpretation; both interpretive processes are "simultaneously particular and theoretical" (p. 347). As Leff explained, psychoanalytic interpretation

> originates in the unique subject, since the relevant motives are discovered in the particular case, and it ends with the particular case, since its results are confirmed in relation to the unique subject. Yet, the process always involves explanation, and the attempt to explain puts the analyst in contact with matters of theoretical interest. (p. 347)

For Leff, interpretation in rhetorical criticism provides insight into particulars (specific passages from King's "Letter From Birmingham Jail" in April 1963) that both draw on and contribute to our understanding of more general theoretical constructs (the concept of hypotaxis). As Leff remarked, through the interpretive component of rhetorical criticism, "theoretical precepts attain meaning . . . as they are vibrated against the particular case and are instantiated in an explanation of it" (p. 347).

Leff's discussion of the nature of interpretation in rhetorical criticism raises a final issue that merits brief consideration: What is the relationship between analysis (critical explication or explanation) and interpretation? The discussion so far suggests that these characteristics of criticism are discrete steps or processes, and the example from King's "Letter From Birmingham Jail" seems to support this view. The critic first analyzes to comprehend issues of style, argument, and/or structure and then moves to the question of interpreting the particulars that have been identified. This bifurcated view of analysis and interpretation has come under fire during recent years. In trying to argue that literary interpretations never are arbitrary, literary critic and theorist Stanley Fish challenged a two-step view of the relationship between analysis and interpretation. Maintaining that critics do not "confer" meanings on texts, Fish (1980) wrote, " 'Confer' is exactly the wrong word because it implies a two-stage procedure in which a reader or hearer first scrutinizes an utterance and *then* gives it a meaning" (p. 310). Fish argued that the problem with this view is that "there is no such first stage" (p. 310) because all analytic description is "interpretation laden"; there never is "a moment when my students 'simply see' a physical configuration of atoms and *then* assign that configuration a significance" or meaning (p. 334). In other words, analysis ("seeing" what is there in a critical object) and interpretation (deciding what it means) are inextricably interwoven.

Space limitations prevent a detailed consideration of Fish's (1980) position. But two points are worth noting. First, Fish raised an important issue in noting the interrelationship between critical analysis and interpretation. Leff's discussion of interpretation and explanation raises a similar issue; the two processes, analysis and interpretation, tend to be mutually reinforcing. As Fish probably would argue, we can recognize the hypotaxis in King's "Letter From Birmingham Jail" only because we already have "interpreted" this object as an instance of prose discourse, thereby making it possible to use the concept of hypotaxis in our analysis/interpretation. But this account of how we approach the letter raises a second point. Fish's "argument" (or, more accurately, my rendering of it) seems to conflate the act of defining something *as something* with the potentially different act of interpreting it *in some specific manner.* Raising this qualification with respect to Fish's position does not lead to the claim that critical analysis or description can proceed in a thoroughly neutral or atheoretical manner. A critic brings to King's text, or any critical object, a host of assumptions, beliefs, theoretical commitments, and political positions that will shape the interconnected processes of analysis and interpretation. The point is that Fish seems to reduce interpretation to a process of decoding meaning. But as the preceding discussion has tried to suggest, the interpretive moment in criticism can exceed this more limited sense of interpretation. Acknowledging the possibility of interpretive excess might be necessary to ensure the possibility of novelty in critical practice.

Criticism Evaluates

As noted earlier, Bryant (1973) viewed the critic as an "analytic explicator." Literary critic Monroe Beardsley provided an (unintentional) variation on Bryant's account when he suggested that criticism involves "analytical appraisal . . . [or an] active concern with desirable and undesirable features." Beardsley (1981) continued, "Analytical appraisal is the characteristic and essential element of criticism in any of its fields of application" (p. 154). There was no doubt in Beardsley's mind that evaluation is a fundamental characteristic of criticism.

Rhetorical critics, like their literary counterparts, who have engaged in the process of evaluation will argue about the appropriate *standards* for critical evaluation. The dominant approach to evaluation for the first half of the 20th century took its cue from Wichelns's (1925/1962) famous observation that "rhetorical criticism . . . is concerned with effect" (p. 209). Thonssen and Baird (1948) would make effect or response the key to rhetorical criticism, as can be seen in this passage:

> The men [sic] who play roles in the making of history—and this includes the orators—are judged finally by their influence upon people and events. In the eventual reckoning, men will be tested in the light of what they did. Orators will be judged by what

> they accomplished, either immediately or in the long run of public affairs. (p. 448)

As Thonssen and Baird and other rhetorical scholars recognized, assessing effectiveness is an extremely challenging enterprise because the concept of effect can be taken to refer to a range of phenomena moving outward from the response of the immediate **audience** to the impact that a message might have on an entire society (on the need to consider social effects, see Nilsen, 1956; Wrage, 1947). Thonssen and Baird (1948) warned the critic: "Rabble-rousers and demagogues hope for instantaneous responses and often get them. Yet the critic of such oratory will not regard the acquisition of the response as a total measure of speech effectiveness" (p. 461). They concluded,

> A speech is effective, therefore, if it achieves an end or response consistent with the speaker's purpose—provided that the purpose is, in turn, consistent with the dictates of responsible judgment and solicitous regard for the positive good of an enlightened society. (p. 461)

The preceding passage illustrates that, at least for many rhetorical scholars, the effects standard never was "pure" in that speeches were not evaluated solely in terms of whether or not they influenced an audience. The effects standard typically was linked to some type of often unarticulated *ethical* standard as the basis for final critical evaluation.[9]

A second common evaluative standard employed by rhetorical critics is *qualitative.* This position was advanced by Parrish (1954) in these terms:

> The critic should not be diverted into an attempt to assess the *result* of a speech except as its effect may help us to judge the quality of the speech itself. Rhetoric, strictly speaking, is not concerned with the *effect* of a speech but with its *quality,* and its quality can be determined quite apart from its effect. (p. 7)

Black (1978) later would subject Parrish's argument to careful reflection. According to Black, qualitative evaluation produces a "formalistic criticism . . . [that] would render a judgment of the discourse as a self-contained unit without regard for any particular audience" (p. 62). Black argued that a formalistic judgment or evaluation can proceed along one of two lines: The judgment will rely on an assessment of the "persuasiveness" of the speech, or the evaluation will rely on a critical **touchstone.**[10] Black maintained that Parrish opted for some version of the first approach: Evaluating quality means assessing the persuasiveness of the speech. The problem with this approach, Black argued, is that it ultimately negates the very distinction that Parrish sought to establish: Quality becomes conflated with effect. As Black explained, in Parrish's version of formalism the critic might evaluate a speech or an essay—judge its "persuasiveness"—in terms of certain precepts or standards derived from classical rhetorical theory. But what Parrish failed to realize is that

> these [classical] standards are sanctioned by the fact that they produced certain desired effects in audiences. . . . When the neo-Aristotelian critic appraises the quality of a discourse in terms of criteria derived from the Aristotelian tradition, the ultimate justification of these criteria is effect. (p. 73)

Black insisted that there is no way of developing qualitative standards of critical evaluation from the classical treatises on rhetoric; any such standard ultimately will collapse into an assessment of effect. But Black's analysis of Parrish's position did not lead to a complete abandonment of qualitative judgment. Black's concluding judgment was that "only when the critic justifies some particular judgment of his [sic] with recourse to a touchstone is he delivering a purely formalistic judgment" (p. 73). A touchstone or analog approach is, for Black, the only way of organizing and justifying qualitative evaluation.

The effects and qualitative standards of evaluation still are retained in some forms of contemporary rhetorical criticism. For example, the qualitative standard is central to some forms of critical **close reading,** and critics still exhibit an interest in effects (but see the entry for **effects of rhetorical discourse** for a discussion of some of the shifts in contemporary scholarship). In some contemporary criticism, the evaluative characteristic of criticism has become severely muted; the critic's primary interest is to analyze and interpret. In other cases, the evaluative characteristic has been combined with the concept of **ideology** to produce a rhetorical form of *ideology critique* (Wander, 1983). But ideologically oriented evaluation—attacking a contemporary message because it perpetuates racial or gender stereotypes or applauding an abolitionist text for its eloquent attack on slavery—is essentially a species of ethical judgment. The principal differences between the evaluative practices of current ideologically oriented critics and an earlier generation of neo-Aristotelians is (a) disconnecting the effects-ethics relationship exemplified in neo-Aristotelians such as Thonssen and Baird and (b) acknowledging the plurality of ethical (as well as political and social) norms that might be introduced as a basis for evaluation. But a lingering issue, identified by Black, remains in place. Black (1978) posed the question of whether it was possible "to call a discourse rhetorically good without referring to its ethical, aesthetic, or logical quality or to its effects" (p. 66). Black's question, in short, was as follows: What is rhetorical quality? Rhetorical critics still are struggling with this question.

Criticism, including rhetorical criticism, involves five common characteristics. This brings us to our second general question: What do critics, especially rhetorical critics, study? Or, to frame the question as it often is discussed within the discipline: What is the *object* of rhetorical criticism? In one sense, the object of criticism of all sorts is quite extensive. For example, Black (1978) wrote,

> Criticism is a humanistic activity.... Criticism is concerned with humanity. . . . The critic . . . studies the products of man [sic]. . . . The subject of criticism is always some harvest of the human imagination.... The subject of criticism consists exclusively in human activities and their results. (p. 5)

But Black did not leave the issue of the object of rhetorical criticism at this level of abstraction. In the first chapter of *Rhetorical Criticism,* he narrowed his focus and articulated a fairly traditional understanding of the object of rhetorical criticism: "The subject matter of rhetorical criticism is persuasive discourse.... Persuasive in this sense refers to intent, not necessarily to accomplishment. Rhetorical discourses are those discourses, spoken or written, which aim to influence men [sic]" (pp. 14-15). Bill Clinton's "Second Inaugural Address," a newspaper op-ed piece, an "advertorial" from Mobil Oil, the BITCH **manifesto,** Martin Luther King, Jr.'s "Letter From Birmingham Jail," Franklin Roosevelt's war message, William Jennings Bryan's "Cross of Gold" speech, Elizabeth Cady Stanton's "Solitude of Self" address, Abraham Lincoln's "Gettysburg Address," Andrew Jackson's "Proclamation to the People of South Carolina," the Virginia and Kentucky resolutions, and the Declaration of Independence all fit Black's definition and are appropriate objects for critical study by rhetorical scholars.

Black's definition of the object of rhetorical criticism displays a considerable degree of confidence based on an assumed disciplinary consensus over the nature of the critical object. But in an important reading of recent work in rhetorical criticism (an instance of **metacriticism**), Gaonkar (1990) detected a significant degree of "anxiety" over the object of rhetorical criticism. Gaonkar's essay traced two rather distinct trajectories in contemporary rhetorical criticism. The first trajectory, running through the works of Wrage (1947), Becker (1971), and McGee (1990), eventuates in the "dissolution" and, especially in McGee's work, the "fragmentation" of the object. Whereas Black's definition assumed the existence of a stable thing—persuasive or rhetorical discourse—McGee's vision of the object was, Gaonkar (1990) argued, one of scraps and fragments. Gaonkar explained that individuals today are "surrounded by a sea of fragments—bits and scraps of evidence, disembodied arguments, issues and visions—out of which is woven the rhetor's own fragment" (p. 307). But as soon as an advocate or a rhetor produces a piece of rhetorical discourse, it quickly dissolves back into the sea of fragments from which it came. Persuasive discourse in Black's sense no longer exists. Critics do not study stable preexisting objects; rather, in the manner of practicing advocates, they assemble discursive artifacts out of the sea of fragments that then functions as their critical object. As McGee (1990) suggested, a critic might combine a few fragments of King's "I Have a Dream" speech with some scraps from the discourses of Malcolm X, John Lewis, John F. Kennedy, George Wallace, and *Time* Magazine in 1963 to fabricate an object—American discourse on race in 1963—for a critical study. But this object is the critic's creation, and it has no more permanence or stability than the fragments from which it is composed. Ultimately, as Gaonkar (1990) pointed out, McGee's dissolution of the critical object revealed rhetoric to be a global ubiquitous material *process* that leaves behind traces or texts (pp. 304-305). McGee suggested that the focus of critical study should be the process and not the trace.

The second trajectory that Gaonkar (1990) identified "springs from a phenomenon" that can be described as "the deferral of the text" (p. 309). Beginning with Redding (1957) and continuing through Mohrmann (1980) and beyond, rhetorical critics have tried to account for a paradox: Why is it that a field of study that professes to be concerned with speeches and other forms of discursive practice has managed to avoid devoting significant attention to the study of specific speech or discursive texts? Following Leff (1986), Gaonkar (1990) identified the **transparency thesis** as the driving force behind the paradox. Rhetorical critics typically deferred their object of study—specific instances of persuasive discourse—because the object was conceptualized as inert; there was no need to study the object carefully because there was nothing of real interest going on in it. No real effort was required to understand what was happening in the average rhetorical text.[11] From Redding's and Mohrmann's "diagnosis" (p. 309) of the problem of deferral, Gaonkar traced the way in which adherents of the **close reading** perspective, especially Leff, have sought to reconceptualize the **text,** endowing it with a density and an "ontological solidity" (pp. 301, 309). But this ontological solidity is not the simple stability found in Black's view of the critical object. For Leff and other close readers, the text is the site of dynamic action, tension, and struggle that requires careful and disciplined reading on the part of the critic.

These two competing characterizations of the object of rhetorical criticism—as a fragment within an undulating sea of fragments and as a dense complex instantiation of discursive artistry—were at the center of disciplinary debate for a good part of the 1990s. But they are not the only objects that can be found in the works of rhetorical critics. Five other objects deserve brief discussion. First, rhetorical critics can focus attention on the discourse constituting a social **movement.** It is the totality of the movement's discursive practices that serves as the object of study. Second, critics can emphasize discursive **controversy.** The object of interest for these critics is the discursive dynamics that shape and animate the practices of advocates confronting pressing public problems. Third, critics can focus attention on the invention, circulation, and transmutation of **fantasy themes.** The way in which specific themes are shaped or reshaped serves as the object of critical inquiry. Fourth, critics can emphasize the development and evolution of discursive **genres.** The object in genre studies might be the specific text, the broader genre, or the relationship between text and genre. Finally, critics can study the texts and practices that constitute a **discursive formation.** The critic's objective is to reconstruct the structure and/or rules that organize and regulate large spheres of human interaction such as the discourses of academic disciplines, the medical community, and the American presidency. Many of these diverse objects still retain something of Black's definition—discourse designed to influence people—but they cannot be reduced to that way of conceptualizing the object of rhetorical criticism.

The third central question to consider is that of what procedures or steps critics, and especially rhetorical critics, follow when they engage in critical practice. Traditionally, one of the first procedural rules that a critic must follow is to adopt a neutral, impartial, objective, or disinterested stance toward the critical object. Writing in the middle of the 19th century, English literary critic Matthew Arnold described conventional thinking when he wrote that the central rule of criticism

> may be summed up in one word: *disinterestedness.* And how is criticism to show disinterestedness? By keeping aloof from what is called "the practical view of things." . . . For what is at present the bane of criticism in this country? It is that practical considerations cling to it and stifle it. (Arnold, 1962, pp. 269-270)

Arnold acknowledged that "by embracing . . . the Indian virtue of detachment and abandoning the sphere of practical life," criticism "condemns itself to a slow and obscure work. Slow and obscure it may be," he concluded, "but it is the only proper work of criticism" (p. 274). The norm of disinterestedness became so entrenched as to allow Black (1978) to write, "The standard of disinterested objectivity in criticism has stood too long and been too widely accepted to require further elaboration here" (p. 18).

During the latter part of the 20th century, the traditional norm of disinterestedness would come under fire in various fields of criticism. In rhetorical studies, one example of this attack can be found in Wander and Jenkins's (1972) essay, "Rhetoric, Society, and the Critical Response." In these authors' view, the idea of objectivity or disinterestedness leads to "the individual [critic] ideally becom[ing] a passive instrument upon which things leave accurate impressions" (p. 442). But they added that "the conceptions of a world of distinct objects periodically bumping into [and leaving impressions on] a properly sensitized critic is, in our view, profoundly misleading" (p. 443). The two key problems that Wander and Jenkins found in the traditional norm were, first, that it "mask[s] the personal quality of the critical act" and, second, that it distorts the complex "relationship of criticism to values" (p. 441). Regarding the first criticism, Wander and Jenkins maintained that the norm of disinterestedness tries to turn the critic into a scientific observer when, in fact, the critic always is a participant in a human world. Forcing the critic to cut himself or herself off from that world distorts what it means to be a human. Regarding the second criticism, Wander and Jenkins suggested that the norm of disinterestedness tries to present itself as completely neutral or valueless when, in fact, all it does is mask the critic's acceptance or tacit endorsement of the status quo. They argued that criticism needs to "strip away the seemingly concrete nature of current reality—to provide us with an option" (pp. 447-448) but that it cannot fulfill this function so long as it remains blindly tethered to a culture's dominant values under the guise of being disinterested. The question of the critic's stance—as disinterested observer or involved participant—remains a central issue in contemporary rhetorical studies (Blair, Jeppeson, & Pucci, 1991). It is one of the points in dispute between adherents of the **close reading** perspective and those who favor the project of **critical rhetoric.**

As important as the struggle over the critic's stance is, it does not really address the narrower question: What are the specific procedures of rhetorical criticism? Critical procedures are commonly referred to as *methods,* so an inquiry into critical procedures leads into a consideration of methods of criticism.[12] Textbooks in rhetorical criticism (e.g., Andrews, 1990; Foss, 1996), as well as theoretical treatises on criticism (e.g., Frye, 1957), insist that criticism is a systematic activity, and the procedures embodied in a critical method often are regarded as one way of making criticism systematic. But textbooks that recognize the importance of method, ironically, devote little (if any) attention to describing the general nature of critical method (most texts describe specific methods) or to specifying how it functions in the process of criticism. Previous generations of rhetorical critics (Baird & Thonssen, 1947; Reid, 1944), for example, understood method as a way of supporting a critic's judgment or evaluation of an object. But this is a rather restrictive view of the function of method in rhetorical criticism. Additional reflection on the idea of method in criticism is warranted.

In broad traditional terms, method is a way of organizing various forms of inquiry including criticism. A method stipulates the research protocols (the steps or the sequence of activity) that should be followed in the process of inquiry. Speaking analogically, a method is like a recipe; it specifies the steps a person needs to follow to achieve a desired result (a recipe tells one how to bake a cake or make ravioli, whereas a critical method tells one how to do criticism). A critical method determines what is significant and directs the critic's perception of the critical object. The rhetorical critic's method tells the critic how to "read" the text. Perhaps most important, method (at least in what we can call its traditional role in scientific inquiry) is seen as a way of guaranteeing that the results of inquiry will be valid; method allows us to have faith in or trust the results of inquiry. We expect that if a person in California and a person in New York each follow the specific steps in a recipe for making an apple tort, then each of them will produce the same thing (discounting insignificant variations). Methods of inquiry—in science and criticism—are supposed to do likewise. If a critic in Florida and a critic in Alaska apply the same method to the same object, then they should reach the same conclusions. To be sure, this traditional sense of method has been the focus of extensive criticism (Bernstein, 1983; Feyerabend, 1975), yet this sense of method helped to shape the practice of rhetorical criticism.[13]

During the middle of this century, criticism in rhetorical studies was dominated by the **neo-Aristotelian** method. Briefly, neo-Aristotelian criticism translated the precepts of classical rhetorical theory into a recipe for reading texts. Critics focused their attention primarily on the five traditional **canons** of rhetoric, the three **modes of proof,** and (to varying degrees) ancillary issues such as the speaker's education and oratorical training, the audience, and the occasion. The overall objective of this method was to uncover and account for the effects of the speech. Critiques of the neo-Aristotelian method began to appear in the scholarly literature during the 1940s and 1950s, and by the 1960s it was on the decline. Black's (1978) *Rhetorical Criticism,* originally published in 1965, usually is credited with delivering the final blow to the neo-Aristotelian method, yet the influence of this method clearly could be found well into the 1970s and beyond (Gaonkar, 1993). With the demise of the neo-Aristotelian method, rhetorical critics during the 1960s and 1970s drew inspiration from various sources in an effort to fashion new methods for organizing their activity. Leff (1980) summarized the pattern as follows:

> For twenty years, a substantial portion of the critical literature enacts the same ritual: Anathematize traditional [neo-Aristotelian] practice and method, sanctify a new theoretical approach (usually borrowed from another discipline), and, if possible, incarnate the newly risen faith by imposing it on some artifact. (p. 339)

The neo-Aristotelian method was replaced by *methodological pluralism;* there appeared to be nearly as many methods as there were critics. The Matlon (1995) *Index to Journals in Communication Studies* identified more than 60 critical methods under the heading for methodology in rhetorical criticism. Among the methods listed were **archetype,** axiological, Burkeian, dialectical, dramatic, ethical, existential, factor analysis, **fantasy theme, genre** studies, historical, inferential, intersubjective, language-action, Marxist, **myth** or mythological, organismic, phenomenological, philosophical, sociolinguistic, structuralist, and symbolic analysis as well as idiosyncratic approaches such as potlach, fugue analogy, game theory, and the panel technique.[14] The structure of many of these critical studies, as Leff (1980) suggested, was the same—a discussion of theoretical sources that eventuated in an articulation of a critical perspective or method (the specific procedures that would be employed) followed by an effort to apply the perspective or method to some object so as to illustrate its analytic, interpretive, and/or evaluative potential.[15]

Ivie's (1974) analysis of presidential war discourse illustrated this pattern. Drawing on the works of sociologists C. Wright Mills and Hugh Duncan as well as Burke's **dramatism,** Ivie constructed a four-step process for uncovering the "vocabularies of motive" in this body of discourse. Each step in the methodology was described, and the results of the analysis were reported in the essay. McGuire's (1977) study of myth in Hitler's (1999) *Mein Kampf* proceeded similarly. In this instance, McGuire borrowed his method from the structuralist anthropology of Claude Levi-Strauss. After summarizing the way in which Levi-Strauss reconstructed the deep structure of myth, McGuire moved on to apply this method so as to uncover Hitler's "rhetorically elaborate myth" (p. 4). We can find this pattern persisting well into the 1980s. Warnick (1987) developed an "approach to rhetorical criticism" (p. 227) out of Paul Ricouer's philosophical hermeneutics. The specific steps entailed by this approach were noted and applied in a reading of Lincoln's "Gettysburg Address." Warnick limited the range of her Ricouerian method, arguing that such an approach is particularly useful for "addresses and essays which endure beyond the immediate situation of their production and reception and are appreciated by subsequent audiences because they express the beliefs and values of a culture" (p. 227). This pattern of theoretical discussion, methodological elaboration, and critical application is especially pronounced in critical studies that are derived from doctoral dissertations because an elaborate discussion of method is an expectation in most dissertations (see also Burgchardt, 1985; Foss, 1979).

Beginning gradually during the early to mid-1980s and continuing into the 1990s, there seemed to be a move away from a preoccupation with explicit methods in rhetorical criticism. Black (1978), in the foreword to the 1978 edition of *Rhetorical Criticism,* anticipated this development when he suggested that the original 1965 edition perhaps devoted too much attention to the issue of method. He now recognized that

> critical method is too personally expressive to be systematized. . . . In consequence of this . . ., it is neither possible nor desirable for criticism to be fixed into a system, for critical techniques to be objectified, for critics to be interchangeable for purposes of replication, or for rhetorical criticism to serve as the handmaiden of quasi-scientific theory. (pp. x-xi)

In short, Black rejected many of the features of the traditional view of method and its function. Critics still employ explicit methods; critical camps or approaches exist within the field of rhetorical criticism; and critics rely on a wide variety of reading strategies or techniques culled from the tradition of rhetorical studies, from the literature on argumentation, from literary and language theory, and from other sources. But the fixation with developing new methods and approaches to criticism that dominated the field during the 1960s and 1970s (but beginning a bit earlier and also lasting a bit longer) appears to be over.[16]

If criticism no longer is methodologically driven or oriented around the development and application of specific methods, then how is it currently organized? How do critics discover or develop their critical procedures? A general answer to the first question is fairly easy. Moving from that answer to the issues raised by the second question is much more difficult. Instead of being preoccupied with the question of method, much of the rhetorical criticism produced today is oriented toward, and organized by, conceptual issues.[17] A brief comparison between a method-driven critical study and one that is more conceptually oriented might be useful to clarify the change.

Burgchardt's (1985) study of the Progressive Era Wisconsin politician Robert La Follette built off Osborn's (1967, 1977) work on **archetypal** *metaphor* to develop a new concept for rhetorical criticism—the "rhetorical imprint" (p. 441). According to Burgchardt, a rhetorical imprint is

> a constant underlying pattern of distinctive verbal characteristics that supports the content of numerous speeches and articles in different contexts. . . . [It] is not simply an isolated recurring element . . . [but rather] an integrated set of rhetorical features . . . [or a] deep structure that governs a range of consonant verbal manifestations on the surfaces of divergent speeches and writings. (p. 441)

Burgchardt explained that his "method for discovering La Follette's rhetorical imprint was to analyze 111 speeches and documents from the period 1879 to 1925." Based on an examination of various "rhetorical aspects" of the texts (defined as "arguments, ideas, themes, techniques, metaphors," etc.), Burgchardt "was able to identify 76 relatively distinct motifs in La Follette's discourse" with "one motif, a distinctive narrative pattern . . ., predominant and constitut[ing] the rhetorical imprint in La Follette's rhetoric" (p. 442). Burgchardt labeled this imprint the "melodramatic scenario," and the bulk of the essay was devoted to explicating its features and demonstrating its persistence across a range of La Follette's texts. The essay concluded with a discussion of "critical applications" or specific ways in which the critic might further analyze rhetorical imprints.[18]

We can detect a shift in critical orientation in rhetorical studies by comparing Burgchardt's (1985) study to Hariman's (1992) reading of Ryszard Kapuscinski's (1983) book *The Emperor,* an account of the demise of the Ethiopian ruler Haile Selassie. At one level, Hariman's and Burgchardt's studies were similar; both identified specific concepts or sets of concepts that would organize their projects. But analysis of the way in which such concepts are deployed reveal some differences in orientation that, although often subtle, are nevertheless important. Burgchardt (1985) was interested in introducing and exploring a new concept that, if proven useful, would expand the repertoire of methods and approaches from which a rhetorical critic might choose. Hariman (1992) was not interested in developing new concepts or in expanding the critic's range of methods. His project was organized around two very traditional concepts: **style** and **decorum.** Hariman was interested in the way in which style and decorum "can be recast as [a] concept for the analysis of political experience" (p. 150), but such an interest did not translate into the development of another new method for critical analysis. Burgchardt's (1985) study was primarily an effort to illustrate a new method or approach to criticism and to establish its value. Hariman's (1992) study was an effort to unpack central terms within the rhetorical tradition in a way that allowed them to speak to issues in contemporary social thought. It represented an example of what Gaonkar (1989) referred to as "the thickening of concepts through grounded critical readings" (p. 270). Hariman (1992) was not illustrating a method (the essay lacks one of the standard features of method-driven criticism, i.e., an articulation of the specific critical procedures that are employed); rather, his study of the court of Haile Selassie advanced a conceptual argument about the relationship among style, decorum, and power or, more specifically, the way in which power is "activate[d]" (p. 165) and "represented and generated" (p. 163) by various manifestations of style and decorum. Hariman did not articulate a method that subsequent critics could try to replicate. His study instead outlined the contours of a "theory of power" (p. 165), a way of thinking about the relationship between power and rhetorical performance, that could serve as the conceptual ground for further critical inquiry. Hariman's essay, in short, did not advance a method to be imitated but rather advanced a conceptual equation in need of additional exploration.

Hariman's (1992) essay illustrated a growing trend in rhetorical criticism—decreased emphasis on questions of critical method and increased emphasis on criticism as a means of engaging questions of conceptual significance.[19] Increasingly, then, rhetorical criticism is organized conceptually as opposed to methodologically. But this shift in orientation does present a major problem. One of the values of methodologically driven criticism is that it is relatively easy to teach. Aspiring critics and students can be taught the steps or central procedures of a specific method that they can then, in turn, employ in the analysis of various objects. Ivie's (1974) method for identifying vocabularies of motive, or Burgchardt's (1985) procedures for uncovering rhetorical imprints, can be applied to nearly any object. For example, a critic might attempt to reconstruct the vocabularies of motive of anti-war advocates or the rhetorical imprint in the discourse of Malcolm X or Rush Limbaugh. Conceptually oriented criticism lacks such fixed procedures. Methodological criticism generally proceeds through a process of deduction; a general method is applied to a specific case or object. Conceptually oriented criticism, on the other hand, proceeds more through a process of *abduction* that can be thought of as a back-and-forth movement between critical object (e.g., text, message) and the concept(s) that is being investigated simultaneously. A critic such as Hariman (1992) would start with an interest in the phenomenon of power and try to understand how it is manifest discursively. This leads to an encounter with a critical object or a series of critical objects. Intermediary concepts such as style and decorum emerge as a way for the critic to organize his or her thinking about the relationship between power and discursive practice. But the concept(s) remains essentially a work-in-progress; our understanding of the concept(s) evolves through the back-and-forth movement between concept and object. Similarly, the critic's understanding of the object grows or develops as conceptual thickening helps to illuminate its diverse qualities. Various specific reading strategies might be employed (emphasizing issues of argument, structure, style, etc.), but in conceptually oriented criticism, these strategies cannot be organized in any a priori fashion. Conceptually oriented criticism proceeds through the constant interaction of careful reading and conceptual reflection.

The fourth and final general question to consider concerns the function(s) and purpose(s) of criticism. What do critics, especially rhetorical critics, hope to accomplish through their critical practice? In some cases, the five characteristics of criticism noted previously (define, classify, analyze, interpret, and evaluate) are ends in themselves. Criticism often functions to define, classify, analyze, interpret, and/or evaluate. But these characteristic features also can contribute to larger purposes. What are some of the common larger purposes that critics hope to accomplish? One recurrent purpose or function of criticism is to shape and/or improve public taste. Writing during the early part of the 20th century, poet and critic T. S. Eliot identified two primary functions of criticism: "the elucidation of works of art and the correction of taste" (Eliot, 1932, p. 13). This same basic idea was reflected in Baskerville's (1953) observation that "competent criticism, based upon sound and significant standards . . ., can do much to guide and improve public taste, to distinguish quality from shoddy, and by so doing can force eventual modifications in practice" (p. 2). Within its various spheres of practice, criticism frequently is seen as a force for educating its audience and helping those audience members to become better judges and/or consumers of various types of practice. Critics, then, often are regarded as the guardians of a culture's standards of value. It is their job to help maintain and enforce a culture's sense of what is good and bad, appropriate and inappropriate, or valuable and inconsequential. This sense of critical purpose often gives rise to the charge that criticism is a conservative elitist activity whose social function is the protection of the status quo or the dominant forces in society.

A second recurrent purpose or function, already alluded to in the previous discussion, is theoretical. Criticism contributes to the development of theory within its respective spheres of practice. For example, Croft (1956) offered a relatively early account of this function in the literature of rhetorical studies. Hart (1986) provided a more recent defense of this function.[20] The theoretical function of rhetorical criticism has given rise to two interrelated tensions in rhetorical studies. First, the concept of a theoretical function is ambiguous. To some scholars in rhetorical studies, it means that criticism should assist in the formulation of "scientific" theories of persuasion (Bowers, 1968), whereas other scholars accept the theoretical function but reject a social science orientation to it. This tension reflects the ongoing struggle to reconceptualize the nature of "theory" in light of intellectual trends such as postmodernism. The second tension concerns the relationship between theoretically or conceptually oriented criticism and that version of rhetorical criticism that is primarily historical in emphasis. Medhurst (1989), for one, rejected the proposition that criticism must contribute to what Hart (1986) called the "conceptual record" (p. 284).[21] Medhurst (1989) contended that such an approach fosters "a narrow standard of scholarly contribution and intellectual importance" (p. 36) that must be resisted. It appears that the "schism" that Lucas (1981) identified in rhetorical studies has been reformulated as a tension between theoretically and historically oriented criticism.

Finally, a growing number of critics, in rhetorical studies as well as in other academic disciplines, believe that criticism must play a role in both exposing and fighting various forms of oppression and injustice in the world. Adherents of this view contend that criticism must be political, must intervene in the practical affairs of society (Eagleton, 1986; in rhetorical studies, see especially McKerrow, 1989, 1991; Wander, 1983). In contemporary rhetorical studies, this position is argued most strenuously by proponents of **critical rhetoric.** Of course, not all critics support the radical politicization of criticism. Reacting to the ferment in literary studies, Fish (1995) argued that criticism is, and must be, constrained by a series of specific institutional structures (e.g., the university, individual disciplines) and their associated traditions that negate the possibility of radically politicized criticism. The call for a radically politicized criticism is, on Fish's interpretation, tantamount to advocating either the dismantling or the abandoning of academic disciplines that specialize in criticism. Fish wrote,

> In the end, the desire for a truly historical criticism, for a truly political criticism, and [for] a truly interdisciplinary criticism is the familiar desire of the academic, and especially of the humanist academic, to be something other than what he or she is. (p. 140)[22]

In response, politically oriented rhetorical critics such as Wander and McKerrow might ask the following question: What is wrong with the academic critic trying to be something other than what his or her disciplinary structure and tradition currently allow the academic critic to be? This question, in short, seems to ask the following: Can an individual be both an academic critic and an engaged political agent *at the same time*? Fish apparently believed that such a fusion is impossible, while politically oriented critics have tried to prove him wrong.

This entry has reviewed four key issues: the nature of criticism (specifically rhetorical criticism), the object of rhetorical criticism, the procedures of rhetorical criticism, and the function(s) or purpose(s) of rhetorical criticism. Criticism is, in many ways, the central activity in the discipline of contemporary rhetorical studies. The continued vitality of the field will depend on the intellectual and creative efforts of the scholars and critics who constitute it.

Notes

1. On the critic-historian "debate," see also Gronbeck (1975), Lucas (1981), and the brief discussion at the end of this entry.

2. For example, Bryant (1973) noted later that "rhetorical criticism . . . is first of all analytical; it discovers how the object is made" (p. 36).

3. But Bryant (1973) did acknowledge this component of criticism when he discussed how the critic must reach a decision on whether an object is essentially poetic, rhetorical, or mixed (p. 35).

4. See the entries for **hermeneutics and rhetoric, anxiety of influence,** and **interpellation,** respectively, for examples of this trend in critical scholarship.

5. The issue of conceptualizing the object of criticism is given greater attention later in this entry.

6. This is a common practice in the tradition of rhetorical studies. See, for example, Hudson (1923).

7. See the entry for **polysemy** for additional treatment of this issue.

8. In rhetorical studies, see Hyde and Smith (1979) and Rosenfield (1974).

9. For a detailed study of ethical criticism, see Booth (1988). Garver (1998) continued this line of inquiry. For examples of an ethical criticism of public oratory, see Antczak (1991, 1993).

10. See also Rosenfield's (1968) discussion of "model" and "analog" as possible sources of norms for critical **judgment.**

11. See the previous discussion of Baskerville's (1953) view of the interpretive characteristic of rhetorical criticism.

12. The discussion in the next few paragraphs draws on Jasinski (in press).

13. On the way in which critical methods fostered the "scientizing of criticism," see Nothstine, Blair, and Copeland (1994, pp. 31-42).

14. For discussion and illustration of many of the enduring methods, see Brock, Scott, and Cheseboro (1990) and Foss (1996).

15. Or, if not an explicit application, then it was a discussion of how the method might be applied (Gregg, 1966; Hyde & Smith, 1979; Lanigan, 1969).

16. But Nothstine and colleagues (1994), writing during the early 1990s, maintained that "method has been and continues to be of prime concern to most critics" (p. 39).

17. This discussion extends Aune's (1989) observation regarding the shift from "method-driven" critical studies to "theory-driven" ones (p. 44).

18. Burgchardt (1985) identified three areas of analysis: "pragmatic, psychological, and historical" (p. 449).

19. For other examples of this tendency, see Browne (1994), Jasinski (1995), Ono and Sloop (1995) and the discussion of theoretically motivated **close reading.** For additional discussions of this growing tendency, see Foss (1990), Henry (1992), and Zarefsky (1989).

20. On the relationship between criticism and rhetorical theory, see the detailed treatment in Nothstine and colleagues (1994) and the literature cited therein.

21. For a different critique of Hart, see Darsey (1994).

22. Rhetorical scholars will recognize similarities between Fish's position and Campbell's (1974) distinction between "ephemeral" criticism (nonprofessional but socially engaged) and academically driven "enduring" criticism.

References and Additional Reading

Abrams, M. H. (1993). *A glossary of literary terms* (6th ed.). Fort Worth, TX: Harcourt Brace.

Agger, B. (1998). *Critical social theories: An introduction.* Boulder, CO: Westview.

Andrews, J. R. (1990). *The practice of rhetorical criticism* (2nd ed.). New York: Longman.

Andrews, J. R., Leff, M. C., & Terrill, R. (1998). *Reading rhetorical texts: An introduction to criticism.* Boston: Houghton Mifflin.

Antczak, F. J. (1991). Differences that unite us: John F. Kennedy's speech to the Houston Ministerial Association and the possibilities of ethical criticism. In V. Aarons & W. A. Salomon (Eds.), *Rhetoric and ethics: Historical and theoretical perspectives.* Lewiston, NY: Edwin Mellon.

Antczak, F. J. (1993). "When silence is betrayal": An ethical criticism of the revolution of values in the speech at Riverside Church. In C. Calloway-Thomas & J. L. Lucaites (Eds.), *Martin Luther King, Jr. and the sermonic power of public discourse.* Tuscaloosa: University of Alabama Press.

Arnold, M. (1962). The function of criticism at the present time. In R. H. Super (Ed.), *The complete prose works of Matthew Arnold: Lectures and essays in criticism* (Vol. 3). Ann Arbor: University of Michigan Press.

Aune, J. A. (1989). Public address and rhetorical theory. In M. C. Leff & F. J. Kauffeld (Eds.), *Texts in context: Critical dialogues on significant episodes in American political rhetoric.* Davis, CA: Hermagoras Press.

Baird, A. C., & Thonssen, L. (1947). Methodology in the criticism of public address. *Quarterly Journal of Speech, 33,* 134-138.

Baskerville, B. (1953). The critical method in speech. *Central States Speech Journal, 4,* 1-5.

Baskerville, B. (1977). Must we all be "rhetorical critics"? *Quarterly Journal of Speech, 63,* 107-116.

Beardsley, M. C. (1981). The name and nature of criticism. In P. Hernadi (Ed.), *What is criticism?* Bloomington: Indiana University Press.

Becker, S. L. (1971). Rhetorical studies for the contemporary world. In L. F. Bitzer & E. Black (Eds.), *The prospect of rhetoric.* Englewood Cliffs, NJ: Prentice Hall.

Bernstein, R. L. (1983). *Beyond objectivism and relativism: Science, hermeneutics, and praxis.* Philadelphia: University of Pennsylvania Press.

Bitzer, L. F. (1968). The rhetorical situation. *Philosophy and Rhetoric, 1,* 1-14.

Black, E. (1978). *Rhetorical criticism: A study in method.* Madison: University of Wisconsin Press.

Blair, C. (1987). The statement: Foundation of Foucault's historical criticism. *Western Journal of Speech Communication, 51,* 364-383.

Blair, C., Jeppeson, M. S., & Pucci, E., Jr. (1991). Public memorializing in postmodernity: The Vietnam Veterans Memorial as prototype. *Quarterly Journal of Speech, 77,* 263-288.

Booth, W. C. (1988). *The company we keep: An ethics of fiction.* Berkeley: University of California Press.

Bowers, J. W. (1968). The pre-scientific function of rhetorical criticism. In T. R. Nilsen (Ed.), *Essays on rhetorical criticism.* New York: Random House.

Brock, B. L., Scott, R. L., & Chesebro, J. W. (Eds.). (1990). *Methods of rhetorical criticism* (3rd ed.). Detroit, MI: Wayne State University Press.

Browne, S. H. (1993). *Edmund Burke and the discourse of virtue.* Tuscaloosa: University of Alabama Press.

Browne, S. H. (1994). "Like gory spectres": Representing evil in Theodore Weld's *American Slavery as It Is. Quarterly Journal of Speech, 80,* 277-292.

Bryant, D. C. (1973). *Rhetorical dimensions in criticism.* Baton Rouge: Louisiana State University Press.

Burgchardt, C. R. (1985). Discovering rhetorical imprints: La Follette, "Iago," and the melodramatic scenario. *Quarterly Journal of Speech, 71,* 441-456.

Campbell, K. K. (1974). Criticism: Ephemeral and enduring. *Speech Teacher, 23,* 9-14.

Carpenter, R. H. (1972). A stylistic basis of Burkeian identification. *Communication Quarterly, 20,* 19-24.

Charland, M. (1987). Constitutive rhetoric: The case of the peuple Québécois. *Quarterly Journal of Speech, 73,* 133-150.

Cheney, G. (1983). The rhetoric of identification and the study of organizational communication. *Quarterly Journal of Speech, 64,* 143-158.

Cohen, J. R. (1998). *Communication criticism: Developing your critical powers.* Thousand Oaks, CA: Sage.

Condit, C. M., & Greer, A. M. (1997). The particular aesthetics of Winston Churchill's "The War Situation I." In J. M. Hogan (Ed.), *Rhetoric and community: Case studies in unity and fragmentation.* Columbia: University of South Carolina Press.

Croft, A. J. (1956). The functions of rhetorical criticism. *Quarterly Journal of Speech, 42,* 283-291.

Culler, J. (1975). *Structuralist poetics: Structuralism, linguistics, and the study of literature.* Ithaca, NY: Cornell University Press.

Darsey, J. (1994). Must we all be rhetorical theorists? An anti-democratic inquiry. *Western Journal of Communication, 58,* 164-181.

Eagleton, T. (1986). Political criticism. In M. A. Caws (Ed.), *Textual analysis: Some readers reading.* New York: MLA of America.

Eliot, T. S. (1932). *Selected essays.* New York: Harcourt Brace.

Feyerabend, P. (1975). *Against method: Outline of an anarchistic theory of knowledge.* London: New Left Books.

Fish, S. (1980). *Is there a text in this class? The authority of interpretive communities.* Cambridge, MA: Harvard University Press.

Fish, S. (1995). *Professional correctness: Literary studies and political change.* Oxford, UK: Clarendon.

Foss, S. K. (1979). The Equal Rights Amendment controversy: Two worlds in conflict. *Quarterly Journal of Speech, 65,* 275-288.

Foss, S. K. (1990). Constituted by agency: The discourse and practice of rhetorical criticism. In G. M. Phillips & J. T. Wood (Eds.), *Speech communication: Essays to commemorate the 75th anniversary of the Speech Communication Association.* Carbondale: Southern Illinois University Press.

Foss, S. K. (1996). *Rhetorical criticism: Exploration and practice* (2nd ed.). Prospect Heights, IL: Waveland.

Frost, R. (1996). Stopping by woods on a snowy evening [poem]. In L. Untermeyer (Ed.), *Treasury of favorite poems.* New York: Barnes & Noble. (Original work published 1932)

Frye, N. (1957). *Anatomy of criticism.* Princeton, NJ: Princeton University Press.

Gadamer, H. G. (1975). *Truth and method* (G. Barden & J. Cumming, Trans.). New York: Crossroad Publishing.

Gaonkar, D. P. (1989). The oratorical text: The enigma of arrival. In M. C. Leff & F. J. Kauffeld (Eds.), *Texts in context: Critical dialogues on significant episodes in American political rhetoric.* Davis, CA: Hermagoras Press.

Gaonkar, D. P. (1990). Object and method in rhetorical criticism: From Wichelns to Leff and McGee. *Western Journal of Speech Communication, 54,* 290-316.

Gaonkar, D. P. (1993). The idea of rhetoric in the rhetoric of science. *Southern Communication Journal, 58,* 258-295.

Garver, E. (1998). The ethical criticism of reasoning. *Philosophy and Rhetoric, 31,* 107-130.

Gregg, R. B. (1966). A phenomenologically oriented approach to rhetorical criticism. *Central States Speech Journal, 17,* 83-90.

Gronbeck, B. E. (1975). Rhetorical history and rhetorical criticism: A distinction. *Speech Teacher, 24,* 309-320.

Hariman, R. (1992). Decorum, power, and the courtly style. *Quarterly Journal of Speech, 78,* 149-172.

Hart, R. P. (1986). Contemporary scholarship in public address: A research editorial. *Western Journal of Speech Communication, 50,* 283-295.

Hart, R. P. (1997). *Modern rhetorical criticism* (2nd ed.). Boston: Allyn & Bacon.

Henry, D. (1992). Text and theory in critical practice. *Quarterly Journal of Speech, 78,* 219-222.

Hitler, A. (1999). *Mein Kampf* (R. Manheim, Trans.). Boston: Houghton Mifflin.

Hogan, M. J. (1989). Managing dissent in the Catholic church: A reinterpretation of the pastoral letter on war and peace. *Quarterly Journal of Speech, 75,* 400-415.

Hudson, H. H. (1923). The field of rhetoric. *Quarterly Journal of Speech Education, 9,* 167-180.

Hyde, M. J., & Smith, C. R. (1979). Hermeneutics and rhetoric: A seen but unobserved relationship. *Quarterly Journal of Speech, 65,* 347-363.

Ivie, R. L. (1974). Presidential motives for war. *Quarterly Journal of Speech, 60,* 337-345.

Jasinski, J. (1995). The forms and limits of prudence in Henry Clay's (1850) defense of the compromise measures. *Quarterly Journal of Speech, 81,* 454-478.

Jasinski, J. (1997). Instrumentalism, contextualism, and interpretation in rhetorical criticism. In W. Keith & A. Gross (Eds.), *Rhetorical hermeneutics.* Albany: State University of New York Press.

Jasinski, J. (in press). The status of theory and method in rhetorical criticism. *Western Journal of Communication.*

Kapuscinski, R. (1983). *The emperor: Downfall of an autocrat* (W. R. Brand & K. Mroczkowska-Brand, Trans.). New York: Vintage.

Lanham, R. A. (1983). *Analyzing prose.* New York: Scribner.

Lanigan, R. L. (1969). Rhetorical criticism: An interpretation of Maurice Merleau-Ponty. *Philosophy and Rhetoric, 2,* 61-71.

Leff, M. C. (1980). Interpretation and the art of the rhetorical critic. *Western Journal of Speech Communication, 44,* 337-349.

Leff, M. (1986). Textual criticism: The legacy of G. P. Mohrmann. *Quarterly Journal of Speech, 72,* 377-389.

Leff, M. C., & Mohrmann, G. P. (1974). Lincoln at Cooper Union: A rhetorical analysis of the text. *Quarterly Journal of Speech, 60,* 346-358.

Ling, D. A. (1970). A pentadic analysis of Senator Edward Kennedy's address to the people of Massachusetts, July 25, 1969. *Central States Speech Journal, 21,* 81-86.

Lucas, S. E. (1981). The schism in rhetorical scholarship. *Quarterly Journal of Speech, 67,* 1-20.

Lucas, S. E. (1989). Justifying America: The Declaration of Independence as a rhetorical document. In T. W. Benson (Ed.), *American rhetoric: Context and criticism.* Carbondale: Southern Illinois University Press.

Matlon, R. J. (Ed.). (1995). *Index to journals in communication studies through 1995.* Annandale, VA: Speech Communication Association.

McGee, M. C. (1990). Text, context, and the fragmentation of contemporary culture. *Western Journal of Speech Communication, 54,* 274-289.

McGuire, M. (1977). Mythic rhetoric in *Mein Kampf:* A structuralist critique. *Quarterly Journal of Speech, 63,* 1-13.

McKerrow, R. E. (1989). Critical rhetoric: Theory and praxis. *Communication Monographs, 56,* 91-111.

McKerrow, R. E. (1991). Critical rhetoric in a postmodern world. *Quarterly Journal of Speech, 77,* 75-78.

Medhurst, M. J. (1989). Public address and significant scholarship: Four challenges to the rhetorical renaissance. In M. C. Leff & F. J. Kauffeld (Eds.), *Texts in context: Critical dialogues on significant episodes in American political rhetoric.* Davis, CA: Hermagoras Press.

Mohrmann, G. P. (1980). Elegy in a critical graveyard. *Western Journal of Speech Communication, 44,* 265-274.

Nichols, M. H. (1954). Lincoln's first inaugural. In W. M. Parrish & M. H. Nichols (Eds.), *American speeches.* New York: Longmans, Green.

Nilsen, T. R. (1956). Criticism and social consequences. *Quarterly Journal of Speech, 42,* 173-178.

Nilsen, T. R. (1957). Interpretive function of the critic. *Western Speech, 21,* 70-76.

Nothstine, W. L., Blair, C., & Copeland, G. A. (1994). *Critical questions: Invention, creativity, and the criticism of discourse and media.* New York: St. Martin's.

Ono, K. A., & Sloop, J. M. (1995). The critique of vernacular discourse. *Communication Monographs, 62,* 19-46.

Osborn, M. (1967). Archetypal metaphor in rhetoric: The light-dark family. *Quarterly Journal of Speech, 53,* 115-126.

Osborn, M. (1977). The evolution of the archetypal sea in rhetoric and poetic. *Quarterly Journal of Speech, 63,* 347-363.

Parrish, W. M. (1954). The study of speeches. In W. M. Parrish & M. H. Nichols (Eds.), *American speeches.* New York: Longman, Green.

Redding, W. C. (1957). Extrinsic and intrinsic criticism. *Western Speech, 21,* 96-103.

Reid, L. D. (1944). The perils of rhetorical criticism. *Quarterly Journal of Speech, 30,* 416-422.

Rosenfield, L. W. (1968). The anatomy of critical discourse. *Speech Monographs, 35,* 50-69.

Rosenfield, L. W. (1974). The experience of criticism. *Quarterly Journal of Speech, 60,* 489-496.

Sloop, J. M. (1996). *The cultural prison: Discourse, prisoners, and punishment.* Tuscaloosa: University of Alabama Press.

Thonssen, L., & Baird, A. C. (1948). *Speech criticism.* New York: Ronald Press.

Wander, P. (1983). The ideological turn in modern criticism. *Central States Speech Journal, 34,* 1-18.

Wander, P., & Jenkins, S. (1972). Rhetoric, society, and the critical response. *Quarterly Journal of Speech, 58,* 441-450.

Warnick, B. (1987). A Ricoeurian approach to rhetorical criticism. *Western Journal of Speech Communication, 51,* 227-244.

White, J. B. (1984). *When words lose their meaning: Constitutions and reconstitutions of language, character, and community.* Chicago: University of Chicago Press.

Whitman, W. (1996). O captain! My captain! [poem]. In L. Untermeyer (Ed.), *Treasury of favorite poems.* New York: Barnes & Noble. (Original work published 1932)

Wichelns, H. A. (1962). The literary criticism of oratory. In A. M. Drummond (Ed.), *Studies in rhetoric and public speaking in honor of James Albert Winans.* New York: Russell and Russell. (Original work published 1925)

Wrage, E. J. (1947). Public address: A study in social and intellectual history. *Quarterly Journal of Speech, 33,* 451-457.

Zarefsky, D. (1989). The state of the art of public address scholarship. In M. C. Leff & F. J. Kauffeld (Eds.), *Texts in context: Critical dialogues on significant episodes in American political rhetoric.* Davis, CA: Hermagoras Press.

DEBATE

In their widely respected text *Decision by Debate,* Ehninger and Brockriede (1969) noted, "The terms 'discussion,' 'debate,' 'public discussion,' 'dialectic,' etc., do not have well-defined meanings in popular discourse and are, in fact, often used so loosely as to be practically interchangeable" (p. 9). The term **debate,** as Ehninger and Brockriede suggested, possesses a range of meanings. Within this range, we will find identifiable patterns in the way in which debate is defined as well as some distinctions among different types or categories of debate.

Perelman and Olbrechts-Tyteca (1969) noted how some definitions are "normative" in nature; they contain directions for evaluating or appraising objects. As an example of a normative definition of debate, consider Branham's (1991) discussion of a "true debate":

> To the popular mind, the term *debate* evokes certain images of a particular form of contest: two or more speakers who appear on the same stage and speak within set time limits on opposing sides of a common question. In fact, however, such exchanges are often not true debates, and many genuine debates . . . are neither formally nor orally transacted. Even in organized oral exchanges, debate is not synonymous with format. (p. 21, emphasis added)

Branham employed a *dissociative definitional* strategy; the realm of debate is divided into two sub-realms. In one sub-realm, we find "true" or "genuine" debate; in the other, we find only the superficial appearance (e.g., a particular "format") that must not be confused with the real thing. The dissociative criteria then become the essence of Branham's definition. Real debate is "the process by which opinions are advanced, supported, disputed, and defended" (p. 22). Absent these characteristics, we have only pseudo-debate. Hence, the definition has a strong normative or evaluative component. By way of contrast, consider the following definition: Debate is "discursive interaction on a specific topic." This definition is much more inclusive and less evaluative.

Definitions also differ in terms of whether or not preparatory or developmental efforts are included as a specific part of the phenomenon being defined. For example, McBurney, O'Neill, and Mills (1951) wrote, "Debate consists of opposing arguments on a given proposition between a supporting affirmative and an opposing negative" (p. 2). The essence of debate, they suggested, is the argument, and the production of that argument (its **inven-**

tion) is not specifically included in the definition. Compare this definition to that of Freeley (1996): "Debate is the process of inquiry and advocacy, a way of arriving at a reasoned judgment on a proposition" (p. 3). Freeley's definition emphasizes both the act of advocacy (argument as a product) and the process leading up to that act (which Freeley described as one of inquiry). Also notice that Freeley included a resulting condition as an element of his definition: Debate produces "reasoned judgment." The implication is that until such a judgment is reached, debate (as an entity) is incomplete.[1] A sense of end state is absent from McBurney and colleagues' (1951) definition; debate is over when the "opposing arguments" have been completed.

Scholars frequently try to distinguish between different forums or fields of debate (sometimes referred to as **argument spheres**) based on the varying organizational procedures, standards of evidence, and other guidelines that regulate the discursive practices in the spheres. At one end of a continuum, we can locate the heavily regulated sphere of *contest* debate (e.g., intercollegiate debate). At the other end, we find minimally regulated *public* debate (e.g., debate over Bill Clinton's health care proposal, debate over the death penalty, debate over the war in Vietnam during the late 1960s and early 1970s). Somewhere in the middle, we find *legislative* debate (e.g., debate in the U.S. Senate over authorizing the use of force in the Persian Gulf in 1990, debate over raising the income tax level to fund elementary education in a state legislature, debate over raising tuition in a university's faculty senate, debate over endorsing assisted suicides at a convention of the American Medical Association), *legal* debate (e.g., interaction between the prosecution and the defense in a trial, clash of opinions in opposing legal briefs in a case before the Supreme Court), and organized *political* debate.[2] Other spheres (e.g., debate over course content standards in a specific academic discipline, debate over the best way of funding municipal public works projects within the ranks of professional public administrators) also can be identified.

The term *debate* refers to a wide range of practices in contemporary rhetorical studies. Most often, the range of the term is fairly broad; debate refers to the processes of inquiry that culminate in rhetorical invention, the exchange of arguments or the argumentative interaction between individuals and/or groups with different positions on the issue in question, and the specific **judgments** that follow from such argumentative exchanges that occur within various fields or spheres.

Notes

1. Compare Ehninger and Brockriede's (1969) definition of debate as leading to "critical decision-making" (p. 10).

2. On the dynamics and strategies of political debates, see Perloff (1998, pp. 378-410).

References and Additional Reading

Branham, R. J. (1991). *Debate and critical analysis: The harmony of conflict.* Hillsdale, NJ: Lawrence Erlbaum.

Ehninger, D., & Brockriede, W. (1969). *Decision by debate.* New York: Dodd, Mead.

Freeley, A. J. (1996). *Argumentation and debate: Critical thinking for reasoned decision making* (9th ed.). Belmont, CA: Wadsworth.

McBurney, J. H., O'Neill, J. M., & Mills, G. E. (1951). *Argumentation and debate: Techniques of a free society.* New York: Macmillan.

Perelman, C., & Olbrechts-Tyteca, L. (1969). *The new rhetoric: A treatise on argumentation* (J. Wilkinson & P. Weaver, Trans.). Notre Dame, IN: University of Notre Dame Press.

Perloff, R. M. (1998). *Political communication: Politics, press, and public in America.* Mahwah, NJ: Lawrence Erlbaum.

DECORUM

The concept of **decorum**, and the cluster of closely related terms that include *appropriateness* or *propriety* (from the Greek *to prepon*) and timing or the "opportune moment" (from the Greek *kairos*), occupies a central place in the history of rhetorical theory. It also has become the object of a considerable amount of contemporary theoretical inquiry (Baumlin, 1984; Deem, 1995; Gronbeck, 1974; Hariman, 1992; Kinneavy, 1986; Leff, 1987, 1990; Rosteck & Leff, 1989).[1] Poulakos (1983) argued that "timeliness and appropriateness," or "rhetorical motifs whose essence cannot be apprehended strictly cognitively and whose application cannot be learnt mechanically" (p. 42), were defining elements of a *sophistic* understanding of rhetoric (see also Poulakos, 1995, pp. 60-64). In the *Rhetoric*, Aristotle (1954) devoted two chapters (Chapters 7 and 8 in Book Three) to the Greek concept of *prepon* (or appropriateness). Trimpi (1983) identified and expanded on the three key aspects of Aristotelian decorum: appropriateness with respect to subject matter, audience and occasion, and the rhetor's character or **ethos.** The topic of decorum received its most elaborate and complicated treatment, many contemporary scholars suggested (e.g., Fantham, 1984; Leff, 1990), in Cicero's (1962) mature work *Orator.* In a famous passage, Cicero wrote, "In an oration, as in life, nothing is harder than to determine what is appropriate. The Greeks call it *prepon;* let us call it *decorum* or 'propriety.' . . . The universal rule, in oratory as in life, is to consider propriety" (pp. 357, 359).

Many of the contemporary efforts to elucidate the concept of decorum use Cicero's discussion in *Orator* as a starting point. Grasping the classical, and more specifically the Ciceronian, sense of decorum is difficult because the term operates on different levels or multiple "dimensions" (Hariman, 1995, p. 180). Leff (1990) explicated two particular dimensions. He wrote,

> On the one hand, decorum sometimes assumes a broad, non-technical (or even anti-technical) function. Here it becomes an architectonic force, the point at which thought and action, form and content, and wisdom and eloquence coalesce. Thus, decorum represents the goal of rhetorical culture—the adaptation of all the available resources to encompass concrete situations. (p. 112)[2]

Leff continued,

> On the other hand, decorum also occupies a technical place within the morphology of the art of rhetoric. Canonized along with purity, clarity, and ornamentation as one of the virtues of style, decorum becomes isolated as a subdivision of one of the main divisions of the art and serves as a heading for a number of seemingly formal precepts. (p. 112)

The second dimension of decorum, what Hariman (1995) referred to as a "set of conventions" for verbal behavior (p. 180), reflects the dominant modern sense of the term. Leff argued that for most modernists, "to act or speak decorously is to yield to appearance, to adhere to the mere surface, and to capitulate to the tyranny of a hollow and artificial social exterior" (p. 108).[3] But the "architectonic" dimension of decorum opens up interesting possibilities for a nuanced examination of situated human action, especially discursive action. Leff acknowledged that, unfortunately, "the first and broader of these conceptions of decorum, precisely because of its radically non-technical character, is difficult to describe or apprehend in theoretical terms" (p. 112). But apprehending and describing this nontechnical sense of decorum is exactly what Leff and other contemporary scholars, such as Hariman and Trimpi, attempted.

Leff (1990) used Todorov's (1982) discussion of decorum as part of the *functionalist* or *instrumental* tradition of rhetoric to help illustrate the difficulty in recovering "a productively complex notion of decorum" (p. 118). Functionalist or instrumental decorum "refers to extrinsic accommodation" (p. 118) or, in Fantham's (1984) words, the "adjustment of thought and style to context and circumstance" (p. 124). Leff (1990) wrote that the key element of such a conceptualization is "accommodation to the circumstances that frame the rhetorical act" (p. 121); the speaker or writer struggles to make his or her discourse "fit" the situation.[4] But Leff, relying in part on Fantham's earlier reading of *Orator,* maintained that "even during the heyday of functionalist rhetoric, propriety was not conceived as solely regulated by the persuasive 'exterior' of discourse" (p. 118). In addition to extrinsic accommodation, Fantham and Leff pointed to a standard of "intrinsic merit" or "aesthetic worth" as an important element in Cicero's sense of decorum. Grasping the external and internal aspects of decorum allows contemporary rhetoricians to view decorum as "a flexible principle that coordinates particular discourses as they simultaneously build internal coherence, refer to a context of facts and circumstances, and stretch outward to alter perception of that context" (Leff, 1990, p. 118).[5]

Within the rhetorical tradition, a nontechnical sense of decorum "articulated not so much a set of rules as a *process of invention*" (Hariman, 1992, p. 181, emphasis added). This inventional process can inform the production of discourse (the traditional province of **invention**) as well as its reception (the practice of **criticism**). But understanding decorum as a nontechnical process of invention raises a difficulty: Can we move beyond intuition and sensibility and articulate some of the flexible norms and principles that constitute a culture's sense of decorum? This is an extremely difficult question to answer. What follows is a provisional attempt to use the classical idea of **topoi**—recurrent lines of argument or analysis—in an effort to elaborate the type of reflection encouraged by the concept of decorum.

The *internal* and *external* distinction (which is, it should be noted, a refinement of the nontechnical dimension of decorum) suggested by Baumlin, Fantham, and Leff points to some possible analytical and critical topoi. These topoi raise a series of questions that might be used to probe the decorousness of discursive action. Internal decorum focuses on what Leff (1990) referred to as "the internal context of the discourse" (p. 121); it seeks to explore the relationship among particular elements or segments of a **text.**[6] These elements or segments might include large semi-autonomous sections within a text, smaller units within these larger sections, specific lines of **argument** or other persuasive appeals, or a range of **stylistic** variables (including **tone** and tropes and figures). Some specific topoi for analyzing internal decorum are described in what follows.

Consistency

Are the various elements or segments of the text (or larger unit of discourse) consistent with each other, or are there contradictions and/or tensions that upset or disrupt harmony? For example, is a dominant *metaphor* (e.g., declaring a "war on poverty") inconsistent with other arguments and appeals? Does a potential incompatibility exist between different metaphor clusters in a text (e.g., metaphors of nature and metaphors of games)? Is the **situation** marked as "urgent" in one part of the message but not marked as urgent in another? Is the *blame* for the social *ill* attributed to one set of factors early in the message but shifted to different factors later in the message? Is the **audience** characterized as "powerless" in one part of the message yet (magically) transformed to "powerful" in a different part of the message? Are principles applied consistently? Assessing consistency is particularly important, and difficult, in dealing with larger discursive units. In the course of a campaign, for example, is the candidate internally consistent with different audiences? How might we deal with potential conflicts between the internal standard of consistency and the external standard of audience?

Proportion

Are the elements of the text balanced, or does one element dominate and disrupt the internal harmony? Does the text devote "equal time" to the various arguments and/or voices that it treats? Does the text emphasize what appears to be the most important issue? Are seemingly important issues addressed superficially while trivial issues receive extensive elaboration (perhaps creating the feeling that the advocate is trying to "sneak something by" the audience)?

Unity or Wholeness

Do the elements of the text cohere into a whole, or do they have the feel of disconnected and unrelated fragments? What strategies does an author or advocate employ to create this feeling? Does a specific image or theme appear regularly in the text? Does the conclusion refer back to the opening images and/or themes? Do the segments of the message all work in the same direction, or do they move in different directions?

The external aspect of nontechnical decorum focuses on the way in which authors and advocates *adjust* their discourse to a variety of situational factors. In Hariman's (1992) terms, the emphasis is on "how we coordinate words, thoughts, acts, and gestures to behave purposively in shifting social circumstances" (p. 155) or, narrowing our focus a bit, the relationship between the text as a whole (or particular elements of the text) and its larger situation. Some important analytic topoi for analyzing external decorum are described in what follows.

Timing

Timing has been a concern of rhetorical thinkers since the ancient Greeks introduced the concept as *kairos* (Atwill, 1998; Gronbeck, 1974; Kinneavy, 1986; Poulakos, 1983, 1995). The earliest teachers of rhetoric tried to instill in their students a sensitivity to opportunities, an ability to seize the moment, or a capacity to perceive the "right time" for action. Many people have had the experience of sensing that the time to speak or act has slipped away (e.g., "If I had only said something then, she wouldn't have left"). Most of us know what it means to miss or waste an opportunity to speak or act. Modern scholarship on the topic of timing focuses on a number of issues such as the following:

The evolution of the rhetorical situation: Given the evolving nature of the situation, when is the right time to speak? To put forth a novel or controversial proposal? To release a damaging report?[7]

Audience expectations: Is the audience ready—is it the right time for audience members—to receive this information or advice? What can I do to make the timing right for the audience?

Strategic shifts: When in the course of an evolving situation is it appropriate to shift strategies? When should an advocate "turn the other cheek" when attacked by opponents, and when might it be appropriate to say "enough is enough" and respond aggressively?

Language, Style, and Imagery

Reflection on the appropriateness or propriety of language dates back to Aristotle and Cicero. Cicero encouraged advocates to adjust their language and style to the subject matter, the audience, and the advocate's character (Fantham, 1984). One might add a fourth factor to Cicero's list—channel and/or occasion. Each of the four factors suggests a cluster of questions that can stimulate further reflection.

Subject: What degree of technical language is appropriate in discussing this issue? What degree of emotionality or intensity is appropriate for this subject? What subjects merit emotional neutrality? When might our language serve to "blow things out of proportion?" That is, when might our language excessively exaggerated the issue being discussed?

Audience: What *idiom* or style is appropriate for this audience? What argumentative or stylistic strategies might be *inappropriate* for this audience?
Source of the message: What idioms or styles might be appropriate for this type of person? Can social or institutional *roles* function as a complicating factor?
Channel and/or occasion: What style or idiom is appropriate for a telephone conversation? For an e-mail note? What style or idiom is appropriate on a first date? For a class lecture? For a job interview?

Message Content

How much information should an oil company release after a pipeline accident? What might constitute too much (or too little) information? How much evidence should an advocate include? Should a utility company disclose every possible outcome following a plant disaster, or can it leave certain things out? How much technical or financial information should a company disclose in response to accusations of inappropriate corporate behavior?

Source

What role does the source choose to occupy? When is it more appropriate for a person to speak as the chief executive officer of a corporation? As a concerned citizen? As a worried parent? How do we determine the appropriate person/role for the persuasive task? What tasks can be handled by the press secretary? What tasks must be performed by the chief executive officer?

Channel and Occasion

Beyond questions regarding idioms and style, we might ask the following. Is a specific message appropriate for a particular occasion? For a particular channel? Can the occasion trivialize the message? When is it appropriate for an advocate to confront a hostile audience or occasion (e.g., John F. Kennedy addressing the Baptists in Houston during the 1960 presidential campaign, Mario Cuomo going to the University of Notre Dame to talk about abortion in 1984)?

Some of the questions raised in the preceding paragraphs will overlap. But this is to be expected given that the elements we are trying to grasp (e.g., message, language, source, channel, occasion) interact in various ways. They can be separated for analytic purposes, but when we get down to specific cases, the elements often resist neat classification. Nor are the answers to these questions beyond dispute once we begin to probe specific practices. One point on which nearly all contemporary scholars agree is that the idea of appropriateness cannot be reduced to fixed unchanging rules or principles. Trimpi (1983) reflected the dominant position when he wrote that decorum "cannot consist of (formal) axioms, (philosophical) propositions, or (rhetorical) sanctions to be codified and transmitted by manuals" (p. 234). Leff (1987) echoed this point when he asserted that decorum "is incapable of being formulated in terms of abstract artistic precepts" (p. 7). Rather than providing us with clear rules that can be applied to any situation (whether one approach that situation as an engaged advocate or as a partially removed critic), the concept of decorum helps to organize how we think and argue about the relationship between discourse and the variable situations to which it is a response.

Notes

1. See also Bitzer's (1968) discussion of the way in which discourse can serve as a "fitting response" to a situation.

2. Leff's (1990) language at the end of this passage, we should note, echoed Burke's (1957) belief that symbolic action consists of "various strategies for the encompassing of situations" (p. 3). Leff's argument here extended Trimpi's (1983) sense of decorum as a continu-

ous process of adjustment through which a speaker or writer attempts to balance the various forces (or energies, impulses, and intentions) arising in the act of verbal composition.

3. Trimpi (1983) noted this tendency as early as Isocrates' idea of decorum as "fixed configurations of stylistic *schemata*" (p. 143).

4. Garver (1987) pointed to an important dilemma of functionalist decorum (a dilemma that also links decorum and another key classical idea, **prudence**) when he observed, "One of the perennial problems of prudence is figuring out how to distinguish . . . a virtuous adaptability to circumstances from sophistic accommodation" (p. 7).

5. On the external-internal distinction, see also Baumlin (1984). He wrote, "Thus decorum, the desire for congruity and proportion, has two related applications to discourse. Writing that is decorous seeks to harmonize with the world it represents—to be a faithful representation. . . . And, considered as a universe in itself, discourse that is decorous shows harmony among its parts—is an organic unity created from the interrelated elements of subject, style, arrangement, purpose, and genre" (p. 175).

6. It seems possible to expand the internal aspect of nontechnical decorum to include larger units such as **discursive formations** and **movements.**

7. See Stewart's (1997) analysis of the rhetoric of Stokely Carmichael for an example of a critical study that explores how an advocate can "seize the moment."

References and Additional Reading

Aristotle. (1954). *Rhetoric* (W. R. Roberts, Trans.). New York: Modern Library.

Atwill, J. M. (1998). *Rhetoric reclaimed: Aristotle and the liberal arts tradition.* Ithaca, NY: Cornell University Press.

Baumlin, J. S. (1984). Decorum, *kairos,* and the "new" rhetoric. *Pre/Text, 5,* 171-183.

Bitzer, L. (1968). The rhetorical situation. *Philosophy and Rhetoric, 1,* 1-14.

Burke, K. (1957). *The philosophy of literary form* (rev. ed.). New York: Vintage.

Cicero. (1962). *Orator* (rev. ed., H. M. Hubbell, Trans.). Cambridge, MA: Harvard University Press.

Deem, M. D. (1995). Decorum: The flight from the rhetorical. In S. Jackson (Ed.), *Argumentation and values: Proceedings of the Ninth SCA/AFA Conference on Argumentation.* Annandale, VA: Speech Communication Association.

Fantham, E. (1984). *Orator* 69-74. *Central States Speech Journal, 35,* 123-125.

Garver, E. (1987). *Machiavelli and the history of prudence.* Chicago: University of Chicago Press.

Gronbeck, B. E. (1974). Rhetorical timing in public communication. *Central States Speech Journal, 25,* 84-94.

Hariman, R. (1992). Decorum, power, and the courtly style. *Quarterly Journal of Speech, 78,* 149-172.

Hariman, R. (1995). *Political style: The artistry of power.* Chicago: University of Chicago Press.

Kinneavy, J. L. (1986). *Kairos:* A neglected concept in classical rhetoric. In J. D. Moss (Ed.), *Rhetoric and praxis: The contribution of classical rhetoric to practical reasoning.* Washington, DC: Catholic University of America Press.

Leff, M. (1987). The habitation of rhetoric. In J. W. Wenzel (Ed.), *Argument and critical practices: Proceedings of the Fifth SCA/AFA Conference on Argumentation.* Annandale, VA: Speech Communication Association.

Leff, M. (1990). Decorum and rhetorical interpretation: The Latin humanistic tradition and contemporary critical theory. *Vichiana,* 1, 107-126. (3a series)

Poulakos, J. (1983). Toward a sophistic definition of rhetoric. *Philosophy and Rhetoric, 16,* 35-48.

Poulakos, J. (1995). *Sophistical rhetoric in classical Greece.* Charleston: University of South Carolina Press.

Rosteck, T., & Leff, M. (1989). Piety, propriety, and perspective: An interpretation and application of key terms in Kenneth Burke's *Permanence and Change. Western Journal of Speech Communication, 53,* 327-341.

Smith, C. R. (1992). Roman decorum as a new praxis for existential communication. *Western Journal of Communication, 56,* 68-89.

Stewart, C. J. (1997). The evolution of a revolution: Stokely Carmichael and the rhetoric of Black Power. *Quarterly Journal of Speech, 83,* 429-446.

Todorov, T. (1982). *Theories of the symbol* (C. Porter, Trans.). Ithaca, NY: Cornell University Press.

Trimpi, W. (1983). *Muses of one mind: The literary analysis of experience and its continuity.* Princeton, NJ: Princeton University Press.

Troyan, S. D. (1994). *Textual decorum: A rhetoric of attitudes in medieval literature.* New York: Garland.

DEFINITION/DEFINITION OF THE SITUATION

In a famous passage from *Alice's Adventures in Wonderland,* Carroll (1946) wrote, " 'The question is,' said Alice, 'whether you can make words mean so many different things.' 'The question is,' said Humpty Dumpty, 'which is to be master—that's all.' " The central issue in this exchange between Alice and

Humpty Dumpty was who determines the meanings or **definitions** of words. Although dictionaries create an illusion of definitional stability and permanence, one need only look at dictionaries from earlier periods of history to see how the definitions of terms change over time. The issue, to rephrase the exchange between Alice and Humpty Dumpty, is not "*which* is to be master"—word or person—but rather *who* is to be master. The person who is able to control the power of definition has a crucial linguistic resource at his or her disposal.

Public advocates often are extremely sensitive to the discursive dynamics of definition. In an essay in the July 24, 1995, issue of *Legal Times* attacking the Clinton administration's support for affirmative action programs, Stuart Taylor wrote,

> The president's implicit redefinition of terms like "discrimination" is typical of the Orwellian semantic dodges long resorted to by advocates of preferences. First, they redefined "quota" to make its meaning so narrow—a rigid numerical target that mandates the hiring of utterly unqualified candidates—that a quota is harder to find than a unicorn. Then they redefined "qualified" to make its meaning so broad as to encompass almost everybody, while tarring as "discriminatory" any measure of qualification that fails to produce racially proportionate results.

The political struggle over affirmative action is, as Taylor recognized, in large part a verbal and rhetorical struggle over how to define key terms such as *quota, qualified,* and *discrimination.* Invoking the image of Orwell's (1949) classic account of definitional subterfuge in *1984,* Taylor lashed out against the deceptive definitions promulgated by the Clinton White House. But were Clinton's definitions instances of Orwellian distortion (as Taylor implied), or were they merely part of an inevitable process of discursive struggle?

In a famous essay, Gallie (1955-1956) suggested that many of the crucial terms or concepts of political life are "essentially contested." The meanings of pivotal terms such as *freedom, democracy, liberty,* and *justice* (or of narrower and more technical terms such as *quota*) are not etched in stone but rather written in sand. For a period of time, the meaning of a pivotal term can be widely, and perhaps universally, shared within a culture, resulting in a state of definitional **hegemony.** But this shared meaning inevitably is a **contingent** achievement. Just as sand is subject to natural forces such as wind and water, the meanings of key concepts are subject to the pressures of discursive force set loose by rhetorical advocates. A growing body of scholarship, both inside and outside the discipline of rhetorical studies, is devoted to unpacking the dynamics of definitional struggle.

The recent career of the term *liberal* in America is fairly well known. Once a "God term" in our political culture, the term has fallen on hard times. Politicians who once rushed to embrace the term now run away from it or try to modify its meaning (see the entry for **accent**) by adding the prefix "neo" (e.g., "Clinton isn't a liberal; he's a neoliberal"). The shift in meaning of the term *liberal* has been orchestrated by conservative politicians over the past decade or so to, not surprisingly, their political advantage. After Republican Barry Goldwater's defeat in the 1964 presidential election, it was difficult to find someone in America who was not liberal; today, few people want to wear the liberal label. But as Rotunda (1986) showed (see also Depoe, 1989; Hamby, 1992), the recent shift in the meaning of liberal is part of a much longer continuing struggle over the meaning of the term. It might be the case that the term *liberal* eventually will fade from our political lexicon,[1] but do not be surprised if it makes a comeback. Similarly, Green (1987) documented the struggle over other key 20th-century terms of American politics such as *progressive* and *individualist.* Other studies of note include Condit and Lucaites's (1993) account of the concept of equality, Rodgers's (1987) examination of the discursive evolution of critical "keywords" in American public discourse, and the essays devoted to concepts such as "constitution" and "republic" collected in the Ball, Farr, and Hanson (1988) and Ball and Pocock (1988) volumes.

While scholars have been devoting increased attention to charting the shifting definitions of key terms in our political culture, less attention has been paid to the particular discursive dynamics—the strategies of definition and redefinition—by which the meanings of words are remade. Condit and Lucaites (1993), working out of the tradition of rhetorical studies, devoted more attention to this issue than do scholars from history or political science, but even they focused more on constructing a broad narrative detailing the "crafting" of equality as opposed to providing an account of the specific definitional strategies employed by different advocates. What are some of the common strategies for defining terms? Perelman and Olbrechts-Tyteca (1969) outlined some of the more common approaches employed by advocates. The first strategy is *stipulative* definition.[2] A stipulative definition provides an operational account of how the term is going to be used in a particular context. For example, suppose that one wants to argue that capital punishment is unconstitutional. One would start with the Constitution's prohibition of "cruel and unusual punishment." But what do these terms mean? One might begin by stipulating one's definition of cruel: Cruelty consists in taking pleasure or satisfaction in the administration of pain to another human. Based on this stipulative definition, one could argue that capital punishment *is* cruel because many Americans take pleasure and/or satisfaction in the administration of pain to, or the execution of, other humans (the movement in many states toward supposedly painless lethal injections complicates this line of argument). One could point to the gatherings held outside prisons by supporters of the death penalty when an execution is scheduled. The behavior of these individuals as they cheer the coming execution illustrates how the death penalty has become a source of pleasure or satisfaction in our society and is, therefore, cruel.

Stipulative definitions, in and of themselves, do not always possess rhetorical or persuasive force. Other definitional strategies might be necessary as either a supplement (functioning as a form of *backing* for the stipulative definition) or a substitute. A second definitional strategy discussed by Perelman and Olbrechts-Tyteca (1969) is the *condensed* definition (p. 211). A condensed definition attempts to locate the "essential elements" that reside in the various common definitions of a term. A condensed definition of cruelty, for example, would review existing definitions (e.g., in dictionaries, in scholarly works) to locate those essential elements that appear in all of the various definitions. These common elements are taken to represent the "essence" of cruelty and serve as the basis for a definition that could either (a) provide backing for the original stipulative definition or (b) function as an alternative. A third definitional strategy is *authoritative.* Authoritative definition establishes the meaning of a term through reference to its meaning for accepted social and/or political authorities (hence, this strategy is a form of the **argument** from *authority*). To develop an authoritative definition of cruelty, an advocate would look to how the term has been used and defined within the American judicial system, which is the relevant authority in the context of the Constitution's "cruel and unusual" clause. A fourth definitional strategy is *etymological.* Etymological definition employs the history of a term's meaning as a resource for defining it in the present. Referencing the history of the term *cruelty* in an argument that capital punishment constitutes cruel and unusual punishment is an appeal to etymological definition.[3] A fifth definitional strategy relies on the argumentative process of **dissociation** (pp. 444-450).[4] A dissociative definition "claims to furnish the real true meaning of the concept as opposed to its customary or apparent usage" (p. 444). For example, Martin Luther King, Jr., frequently used a dissociation by way of appearance and reality to (re)define the concept of peace; King suggested that negative peace, or the "absence of tension," was merely an appearance, whereas positive peace, or the "presence of justice," was real peace. Exploiting the dissociative pair appearance-reality, an advocate could argue that cruelty *really* means taking pleasure and/or satisfaction at someone else's pain while reducing alternative definitions to the *appearance* of cruelty. A sixth definitional strategy is *negation.* In some cases, it might be difficult to specify, in a positive sense, the meaning of a term or concept but relatively easy to identify its antithesis or opposite. So, we then proceed to define the term by reference to its negative. An advocate might not be able to explain with precision his or her idea of "freedom," but the advocate can elaborate on its opposite, thereby indirectly indicating the semantic range of the term *freedom.* Or, consider how scholars define the public. In many cases, they begin with its opposite; that is, they start with what we understand to be "private" and use that as the basis for defining what is "public." In the case of the "cruel and unusual" clause, definition by negation is built into the term *unusual;* we can understand what is "*un*-usual" only by reference to its opposite, what is "usual." Finally, as Lakoff and Johnson (1980) and others demonstrated, we define many of our most important concepts *metaphorically.* Consider Jefferson's famous phrase from the Declaration of Independence, the "pursuit of happiness." Lakoff and Johnson maintained that our understanding of concepts such as "happiness" proceeds by way of *structural metaphors* (p. 118). The metaphorical structuring, or the act of defining, is visible in Jefferson's expression; happiness is something to be pursued or acquired. By unpacking the metaphorical *entailments* of the metaphor "happiness is an acquisition," the dynamic meaning of the concept can be reconstructed.[5]

The various definitional strategies can be combined in different ways. For example, a condensed definition of cruelty can make use of the history of the term's meaning, thereby combining the condensed and etymological strategies. Or, an advocate can appeal to the "original intentions" or the original meaning of the "cruel and unusual" clause for the men who framed it,[6] thereby combining the etymological and authoritative strategies. Or, as Perelman and Olbrechts-Tyteca (1969) noted, an advocate can support a dissociative definition through appeal "to scientific or popular etymology" (p. 448). Lakoff and Johnson (1980), on the other hand, suggested that metaphorical definitions of concepts are widespread. Therefore, we might locate implicit structural metaphors within other definitional strategies.

Another recurrent feature of the dynamic process of establishing and subverting definitions merits attention. Advocates frequently try to show that the use of a particular term by the opposition contributes to the process of **mystification** or distortion. For example, in the third of her "Letters on the Equality of the Sexes," Sarah Grimke (1837) disputed the position taken by a group of congregational ministers in Massachusetts about the propriety of women speaking in public. Advocates opposed to the emerging trend of women speaking in public to audiences of both sexes ("promiscuous" audiences) often appealed to the need to "protect" women from the corrupting influences of public life. These advocates claimed that women could be protected by remaining within the domestic sphere of the home. At the end of her third letter, Grimke took issue with how the ministers and others used the term *protection.* She wrote, "Ah! How many of my sex feel in the dominion, thus unrighteously exercised over them under the gentle appellation of *protection,* that what they have leaned upon has proven to be a broken reed at best, and oft a spear?" For Grimke, the "gentle appellation of *protection*" functioned to mystify—to both justify and obscure—the process of sexual "dominion" or domination. Grimke believed that for women to enter and participate in the **public sphere,** it was necessary to subvert the accepted, and mystifying, meaning of the term *protection.*

Finally, it is important to note that the discursive processes through which terms are defined and redefined are not always explicit. The explicit definitional strategies noted previously do not encompass all of the ways in which discourse is used to define terms and concepts. What are some of the other ways in which advocates and rhetors shape the meanings of terms? Burke (1950), among others, noted how many terms are inherently "dialectical"; that is, their meanings or definitions are established by way of contrasts with what the terms stand against (a variation on the explicit strategy of definition by negation). So, Burke noted that the meaning of capitalism depends on what it is typically contrasted against or viewed in opposition to; capitalism means one thing when contrasted to "feudalism" and means something different when understood in opposition to "socialism" (p. 184). In other cases, the meanings or definitions of terms are crafted through a double contrast. Aristotle, for example, defined the virtues (e.g., courage) as the midpoint between extremes (*middle ground* **argument** as an implicit definitional strategy). Meanings also are established and subverted through a host of subtle discursive moves including forms of inflection, **accent** (Voloshinov, 1986), and "tonalities" (Burke, 1950). In short, the meaning of a term is continually shaped and reshaped by the company it keeps.[7]

Whereas definitions of terms and concepts form a critical part of our discursive practices, there also is a more comprehensive process of definition at work whenever we speak or write. We use language to define entire situations as well as specific terms and concepts. In **defining a situation,** we establish the *perspective* through which we, and others, will look at something, and this perspective largely dictates what can be "seen" or "perceived." As Burke (1984) observed in *Permanence and Change,*

> Stimuli do not possess an *absolute* meaning. . . . Any given situation derives its character from the entire framework of interpretation by which we judge it. . . . We discern situational patterns by means of the particular vocabulary of the cultural group into which we are born. . . . Hence, different frameworks of interpretation will lead to different conclusions as to what reality is. (p. 35; see also Burke, 1966)

Wess (1996), commenting on Burke's thinking, wrote, "Participants in the Burkeian conversation simultaneously share a situation and struggle over its definition" (p. 154). Edelman (1977) echoed Burke's observation when he noted, "It is only in naming situations . . . that they are conceived, communicated, and perceived" (p. 24). A few simple examples can illustrate the importance of discursively shaped perspectives in the definition of situations.

The 16th-century French philosopher Michel Montaigne wrote, "When I play with my cat, who knows if I am not a pastime to her more than she is to me?" Montaigne's (1958) point appeared to be that the meaning of a specific situation—a person playing with his or her cat—depends on perspective. From Montaigne's perspective, the cat was a pastime for him (that is the meaning of the situation). But Montaigne wondered whether the situation might mean something else for the cat. Montaigne did not answer his question. In a Mother Goose and Grimm cartoon strip that appeared in 1995, the cartoonist (Mike Geters) did answer the question. In the first panel of this particular strip, Ma Goose throws a frisbee and tells her dog, "Fetch, Grimmy." In the second panel, Ma is thinking, "I'm teaching him to catch" while Grimmy trots back, frisbee in mouth, thinking, "I'm teaching her to throw." In this example, who is the teacher and who is the student? It depends on the perspective. For Ma

Goose, she is in control and Grimmy is learning to catch. But from a different point of view, Grimmy is teaching Ma to throw. In this case, each of the participants has defined the situation for himself or herself, and each is persuaded that he or she has correctly "sized up" its elements and named the situation (Burke, 1957).

A considerable body of scholarly literature emerged during the 20th century devoted to exploring the nature and dynamics of situational definitions. Thomas and Znaniecki's (1927) study of Polish peasants generally is credited with introducing the terminology "definition of the situation" into scholarly discourse. Since their effort, scholars working in a variety of intellectual traditions and located in various academic disciplines have contributed to the process of conceptual exploration and analysis.[8] In different ways, this body of literature affirms Burke's central insight: People react to their world based on how they have defined it. And this process of defining situations is not exclusively subjective; in most cases, situations are defined collaboratively, with discourse serving as the primary vehicle.

Consider the case of the U.S. budget deficit. Since the early 1980s, the deficit has exploded as the federal government has routinely spent more than $100 billion a year more than it has taken in by way of taxes and other forms of revenue. But what does this situation *mean*? How should we understand (or define) the reality of the deficit? One common approach defines the deficit as a grave public crisis. The deficit is depicted as a drain on the investment capital needed for economic growth. So long as the government continues to pile up massive deficits, the economy will stagnate. The problem—indeed, for many, the immorality—of continued deficit spending is illustrated by comparing the federal government to an average family. According to this line of thinking, the family must make ends meet; family members cannot spend more than they have. It is, therefore, grossly inappropriate to allow the federal government to engage in a practice that, if employed by the average family, would lead the family into economic ruin. Once the deficit is perceived as a crisis, the need for a solution—be it massive spending cuts or tax increases—becomes clear. But the crisis definition is not the only way of defining the situation of the deficit (although alternatives to the crisis perspective do not receive a great deal of media attention). A number of political advocates, including respected economists, dismiss the crisis definition. In their construction of the situation, one that characterizes deficit spending as a routine part of federal policy, they employ alternative **exposition** strategies. The budget deficit is calculated as a percentage of the gross national product (or the gross domestic product) and then is compared to those of other nations (e.g., Canada). In such a comparison, the U.S. deficits no longer appear as huge and no longer seem so threatening. In addition, opponents of the crisis definition contest the family *analogy*. Many families routinely engage in various forms of deficit spending when they pay for merchandise over time or when they take out mortgages to buy homes. Why should the federal government be any different?

This short summary of "deficit discourse" only sketches some of the specific strategies used by those who would define the deficit as a crisis and those who would contest that definition. Similar analyses could be done for many of the other "crises" facing the nation—be it crime, drugs, or moral decline. In all of these cases, one group of public advocates urges the nation to perceive a collection of "brute facts" (e.g., specific events, statistical trends) as a crisis, whereas other advocates contest that definition. Defining certain circumstances as a crisis is only one of the more obvious cases of how situations are defined. Situational definition is ubiquitous. Social actors and public advocates regularly introduce situational definitions in various realms or spheres of action—in politics, where every four years the nation faces a "turning point" or a critical "crossroads"; in the corporate sector, where circumstances present either an opportunity or a threat; in our interpersonal relationships, where we routinely negotiate our perceptions of situations and events (Willard, 1978, 1983); and in our personal lives, when we have to determine, speaking figuratively, if the "glass" of our lives is half empty or half full. How we perceive depends on how we have defined.

Cox (1981) provided some useful insight into the way in which situational definitions are constructed and how these constructed definitions shape perception. Situational definitions emerge through the practices of classification, categorization, and naming. Cox wrote, The "*naming* of objects imbues them with meaning, power, and attraction. Through the naming of social objects, then, actors construct the basis for understanding a situation" (p. 200; see also Edelman, 1977). Situational definitions shape perception along three specific dimensions that Cox (1981) labeled "*closure, counting,* and *coherence*" (p. 200). Closure establishes both a temporal and spatial boundary for a situation; it "defines a 'zone of relevance' " (p. 201) that guides subsequent thinking about the situation. Consider the following passage from Richard Nixon's May 1969 speech to the nation on the war in Vietnam:

> In weighing alternate courses, we have had to recognize that the situation as it exists today is far different from what it was two years ago, or four years ago, or 10 years ago. One difference is that we no longer have the choice of not intervening. We've crossed that bridge. There are now more than half a million American troops in Vietnam, and 35,000 Americans have lost their lives. We can have honest debate about whether we should have entered the war in Vietnam. We can have honest debate about how the war has been conducted. But the urgent question today is what to do now that we are there.

Nixon's defense of administration policy relied on the argument strategy of the *locus of existent* (see the entry for **argument**) that follows from his definitional "closure." How did Nixon impose definitional closure on the Vietnam situation? Figuratively, he imposed closure through the "bridge" *metaphor;* all that happened *before* we "crossed the bridge" was *not* relevant to the nation's current situation. Nixon's metaphor isolated the present moment as the essence of the situation. This temporal isolation was reaffirmed when Nixon turned to the contested issues of the past. Nixon contended that we could debate whether or not the nation should have entered the war, but even if we concluded that entering the war was a mistake, this was a *past fact* that had no relevance to the present situation. Possible mistakes of the past were temporally isolated from Nixon's version of the Vietnam situation.

A closed or bounded situation further shapes perception by "determining 'what counts' as data, that is, what information is germane to actors' decisions" (Cox, 1981, p. 202). Given Nixon's temporal boundary, the past *did not count* as data in policy deliberation on Vietnam. What counted, for Nixon, were factors such as national prestige and the autonomy of the South Vietnamese people. But this autonomy itself was the result of spatial closure in that Nixon defined the South Vietnamese as an independent sovereign nation, whereas most of the opposition considered the "nation" of South Vietnam to be the result of U.S. and French interference in the internal politics of Indochina after the end of World War II. For Nixon and those who supported his administration, the situation in Vietnam was a case of foreign aggression and *not* civil war. This way of naming the situation helped to determine what factors mattered in determining U.S. policy.

Finally, temporal and spatial closure contribute to the third way that situational definitions shape perception. Such definitions create "coherence" by providing "an *organizing* heuristic that provides rules of interpretation for judgments and actions" (Cox, 1981, p. 203). Cox (1981) stated, "Actions which cohere with this 'situation' are interpreted as rational, reasonable, or justified" (p. 205), whereas actions that do not cohere with the definition of the situation become incomprehensible and irrational. Given Nixon's temporal (past mistakes are irrelevant) and spatial (case of foreign aggression) situational boundary, opposition to the war in Vietnam in the United States was incoherent; it just did not "fit" Nixon's understanding of the situation. Because opposition to the war could not appear reasonable given Nixon's definition of the situation, it had to be explained in some other way; opponents either lacked the necessary information to reach the "right" judgment (as Nixon and the "silent majority" had done), or they were the dupes or pawns of the Communist movement that the United States was trying to thwart.

The conflict over the war in Vietnam is only one of countless examples where the definition of the situation was a fundamental issue in public debate. Indeed, as the discussion under the entry for **situation, rhetorical** suggests, defining the situation often is the most fundamental *exigence* faced by advocates. It is virtually impossible to persuade an audience to adopt a policy proposal if audience members do not perceive a need, and the perception of need most often arises when audience members believe they face an *ill* that requires action. Advocates employ a vast array of resources—including lines of argument, metaphors, **narratives,** and the *loci* of **presence**—in their quest to provide a powerful and compelling definition of the situation, one that they hope they can induce their audiences to share. Definitions that become widely shared and taken for granted become **hegemonic.** But no definition is immune from criticism. Advocates seeking to contest, reject, or reorganize established situational definitions will take advantage of various *subversive* strategies (e.g. **perspective by incongruity,** counternarratives).

A final point merits some consideration. The discursive process of defining (and redefining) situations is an obvious case of the *constructive* or **constitutive** potential of rhetorical practice. A constructivist or constitutive perspective on language and discursive practice has become common in the humanities as well as in sectors of the social sciences (Potter, 1996; Wess, 1996). The power or potential of language to construct or constitute selves, communities, and social worlds is a recurrent theme in various academic disciplines. But as Wess (1996) observed, adherents of the constructivist or constitutive perspective need to confront a key question: What is the limit of the constructive power of language and discourse? Have adherents of the constitutive approach to discourse fallen prey to a type of linguistic alchemy, a modern variation of the medieval quest to transform simple substances into gold? In short, can situations be defined in *any* way that an advocate desires, or are there limits on the advocate's power of definition?

Kenneth Burke, whose works have influenced many of the scholars exploring the concept of the definition of the situation, anticipated this type of question. As the previous discussion suggests, Burke viewed the constructive or constitutive potential of language or discourse to be considerable but not limitless. Consider a simple hypothetical. Scientists predict that at some point in the distant future, the sun will collapse and form a dark star and, in the process, extinguish life within the solar system. Could a creative advocate use this scientific prediction as the basis for shaping public perception, creating **presence,** and inducing people to believe that the world faces a grave exigence that must be addressed now? It seems very unlikely. Even the most skilled advocate would have difficulty in making this event appear *urgent* and in need of action. From Burke's perspective, the advocate would be unable to overcome the **recalcitrance** of our existential condition; we are simply unable to conceive of something that will happen millions of years in the future as a problem that requires our immediate attention. Recalcitrance was Burke's way of trying to conceptualize the limits of the constructive potential of discourse. The power of language to shape how we perceive and experience the world is extensive; we all have had the experience of being amazed when someone "buys into" or accepts a situational definition that we believe is problematic. Discursive practice has that potential. But that potential is not without limits. As Emerson (1904) remarked, "You [might be] a very elegant writer, but you can't write up what gravitates down" (p. 131). Scholars interested in studying the constructive or constitutive power of language, whether in the form of situational definitions or some other manifestation, must grapple with Burke's concept of recalcitrance and must struggle to conceptualize the enormous potential of discursive practice as well as the inescapable limits on that potential. Meeting this conceptual challenge will be extremely difficult, but it also might prove to be absolutely necessary.

Notes

1. The term *liberal* might go the way of previous terms such as *whig* and *free soil.* These terms have become, in the words of Russian linguist V. N. Voloshinov, "worn out ideological signs incapable of serving as arenas for the clash of live social accents" (Voloshinov, 1986, p. 23).

2. This is a combination of Perelman and Olbrechts-Tyteca's (1969) discussion of "normative" and "descriptive" (pp. 210-211).

3. An example of etymological definition in public discourse is Elie Wiesel's discussion of "indifference" in his April 1999 lecture, "The Perils of Indifference, delivered at the White House.

4. See also Depoe (1989); Schiappa (1993); Zarefsky (1980, 1986, 1998); and Zarefsky, Miller-Tutzauer, and Tutzauer (1984).

5. See Gronbeck, German, Ehninger, and Monroe (1995) for an alternative typology of definitional strategies.

6. This is a common strategy in hermeneutical rhetoric. See discussion in the entry for **hermeneutics and rhetoric.**

7. For a more detailed effort to examine definitional argument from a Burkeian perspective, see Palczewski (1995).

8. Some examples include the following: in political science, Edelman (1964, 1977) and Graber (1976); in philosophy, Schutz (1945); in sociology, Bernstein (1958), Blumer (1969), and Stebbins (1967); in anthropology, Lincoln (1989); and in rhetoric and argumentation, Cox (1981) and Willard (1978, 1983).

References and Additional Reading

Ball, T., Farr, J., & Hanson, R. L. (Eds.). (1988). *Political innovation and conceptual change.* Cambridge, UK: Cambridge University Press.

Ball, T., & Pocock, J. G. A. (Eds.). (1988). *Conceptual change and the Constitution.* Lawrence: University Press of Kansas.

Bernstein, B. (1958). Some sociological determinants of perception. *British Journal of Sociology, 9,* 159-174.

Blumer, H. (1969). *Symbolic interactionism: Perspective and method.* Englewood Cliffs, NJ: Prentice Hall.

Burke, K. (1950). *A rhetoric of motives.* New York: Prentice Hall.

Burke, K. (1957). *The philosophy of literary form* (rev. ed.). New York: Vintage.

Burke, K. (1966). *Language as symbolic action: Essays on life, literature, and method.* Berkeley: University of California Press.

Burke, K. (1984). *Permanence and change: An anatomy of purpose* (3rd ed.). Berkeley: University of California Press.

Carroll, L. (1946). *Alice's adventures in Wonderland.* Cleveland, OH: World Publishing.

Condit, C. M., & Lucaites, J. L. (1993). *Crafting equality: America's Anglo-African word.* Chicago: University of Chicago Press.

Connolly, W. E. (1974). *The terms of political discourse.* Lexington, MA: D. C. Heath.

Cox, J. R. (1981). Argument and the "definition of the situation." *Central States Speech Journal, 32,* 197-205.

Depoe, S. P. (1989). "Qualitative liberalism": Arthur Schlesinger, Jr. and the persuasive uses of definition and history. *Communication Studies, 40,* 81-96.

Dionisopoulos, G. N., & Crable, R. E. (1988). Definitional hegemony as a public relations strategy: The rhetoric of the nuclear power industry after Three Mile Island. *Central States Speech Journal, 39,* 134-145.

Edelman, M. (1964). *The symbolic uses of politics.* Urbana: University of Illinois Press.

Edelman, M. (1977). *Political language: Words that succeed and policies that fail.* New York: Academic Press.

Emerson, R. W. (1904). Eloquence. In R. W. Emerson, *The complete works of Ralph Waldo Emerson* (Vol. 8). Boston: Houghton Mifflin.

Gallie, W. B. (1955-1956). Essentially contested concepts. *Proceedings of the Aristotelian Society, 56,* 167-198.

Graber, D. A. (1976). *Verbal behavior and politics.* Urbana: University of Illinois Press.

Green, D. (1987). *Shaping political consciousness: The language of politics in America from McKinley to Reagan.* Ithaca, NY: Cornell University Press.

Grimke, S. (1837). Letters on the equality of the sexes. In L. Ceplair (Ed.), *The public years of Sarah and Angelina Grimke: Selected writings, 1835-1839.* New York: Columbia University Press.

Gronbeck, B. E., German, K., Ehninger, D., & Monroe, A. H. (1995). *Principles of speech communication* (12th ed.). New York: HarperCollins.
Hamby, A. (1992). *Liberalism and its challengers: From FDR to Bush.* New York: Oxford University Press.
Lakoff, G., & Johnson, M. (1980). *Metaphors we live by.* Chicago: University of Chicago Press.
Lincoln, B. (1989). *Discourse and the construction of society.* New York: Oxford University Press.
McHugh, P. (1968). *Defining the situation: The organization of meaning in social interaction.* Indianapolis, IN: Bobbs-Merrill.
Montaigne, M. (1958). *The complete essays of Montaigne* (D. M. Frame, Trans.). Stanford, CA: Stanford University Press.
Orwell, G. (1949). *1984.* New York: Harcourt Brace.
Palczewski, C. H. (1995). Definitional argument: Approaching a theory. In S. Jackson (Ed.), *Argumentation and values: Proceedings of the Ninth SCA/AFA Conference on Argumentation.* Annandale, VA: Speech Communication Association.
Perelman, C., & Olbrechts-Tyteca, L. (1969). *The new rhetoric: A treatise on argumentation* (J. Wilkinson & P. Weaver, Trans.). Notre Dame, IN: University of Notre Dame Press.
Potter, J. (1996). *Representing reality: Discourse, rhetoric, and social construction.* London: Sage.
Rodgers, D. T. (1987). *Contested truths: Keywords in American politics since independence.* New York: Basic Books.
Rotunda, R. D. (1986). *The politics of language: Liberalism as word and symbol.* Iowa City: University of Iowa Press.
Schiappa, E. (1993). Arguing about definitions. *Argumentation, 7,* 403-417.
Schutz, A. (1945). On multiple realities. *Philosophy and Phenomenological Research, 5,* 533-574.
Stebbins, R. A. (1967). A theory of the definition of the situation. *Canadian Review of Sociology and Anthropology, 4,* 148-164.
Thomas, W. I., & Znaniecki, F. (1927). *The Polish peasant in Europe and America.* New York: Dover.
Voloshinov, V. N. (1986). *Marxism and the philosophy of language* (L. Matejka & I. R. Titunik, Trans.). Cambridge, MA: Harvard University Press.
Wess, R. (1996). *Kenneth Burke: Rhetoric, subjectivity, postmodernism.* Cambridge, UK: Cambridge University Press.
Willard, C. A. (1978). A reformulation of the concept of argument: The constructivist/interactionist foundations of a sociology of argument. *Journal of the American Forensic Association, 14,* 121-140.
Willard, C. A. (1983). *Argumentation and the social grounds of knowledge.* Tuscaloosa: University of Alabama Press.
Zarefsky, D. (1980). Lyndon Johnson redefines "equal opportunity": The beginnings of affirmative action. *Central States Speech Journal, 31,* 85-94.
Zarefsky, D. (1986). *President Johnson's war on poverty: Rhetoric and history.* Tuscaloosa: University of Alabama Press.
Zarefsky, D. (1998). Definitions. In J. F. Klumpp (Ed.), *Argument in a time of change: Definitions, frameworks, and critiques.* Annandale, VA: National Communication Association.
Zarefsky, D., Miller-Tutzauer, C., & Tutzauer, F. E. (1984). Reagan's safety net for the truly needy: The rhetorical uses of definition. *Central States Speech Journal, 35,* 113-119.

DELIBERATIVE DISCOURSE

Deliberative discourse or political policy discourse is one of the three rhetorical **genres** identified by classical rhetoricians. In the *Rhetoric,* Aristotle (1954) wrote that deliberative discourse and the deliberative or

> political orator offers counsel. . . . He [sic] does not deal with all things, but only with such as may or may not take place. Concerning things which exist or will exist inevitably, or which cannot possibly exist or take place, no counsel can be given. . . . Clearly, counsel can only be given on matters about which people deliberate; matters, namely, that ultimately depend on ourselves and which we have it in our power to set going. (1359a31-1359a39)

Aristotle argued that deliberative discourse is concerned with determining whether a course of action or a policy was useful or harmful (expedient or inexpedient). Aristotle's position—that deliberative discourse offers "counsel" or advice on questions of public policy or "public business" (1359b2), is representative of classical rhetorical thought.

Aristotle (1954) identified five specific issues "on which all men [sic] deliberate and on which political speakers make speeches" (1359b19-1359b20). The five issues are (a) ways and means (taxation and general economic policy), (b) peace and war, (c) national defense, (d) imports and exports (which would include commercial and transportation policies), and (e) legislation (which includes what we refer to today as "constitutional law" as well as issues involving governmental structure and procedures). Although these five issues continue to be the focus of countless speeches in Congress and state legislatures, essays and opinion editorials in newspapers and magazines, letters to the editor, and conversations in bars, barber shops, offices, and grocery stores around the country (and the world), new issues—probably unimaginable to Aristotle, Cicero, and other classical rhetorical theorists—should be added to the list. People deliberate on questions of energy policy (from the "No Nukes" campaign of the 1970s to the U.S. Council on Energy Awareness's "Pro-Nuke" campaign during the late 1980s and 1990s), environmental policy (from campaigns to "save the dolphins" to efforts by logging and timber interests to open up more wooded land for "harvesting"), and telecommunications policy (from the proposal to install "V-chips" in televisions to the efforts to enact a ratings system for television programs). We argue about whether physician-assisted suicides should be legal; whether affirmative action programs should be continued, modified, or abolished; and whether women should be able to file civil rights lawsuits against pornographers. These additions to Aristotle's list do not exhaust the topics of deliberative discourse. Nor are the topics mutually exclusive; certain policy questions bridge the different categories. To take one example, efforts to apply the Fifth Amendment's "takings clause" more widely is both a matter of "legislation" (in Aristotle's sense) and a key issue in environmental policy (because a more rigorous application of the takings clause is seen to endanger many environmental regulations given the new costs that would be incurred).

Deliberative discourse most commonly is oriented toward the future. We deliberate about what we should do tomorrow, next week, next year, or even 10 or 20 years down the road. But in some cases, advocates defend policy choices that already have been enacted. For example, members of Harry Truman's cabinet and his scientific advisers deliberated about whether to use a newly discovered weapon—the atomic bomb—against the Japanese at the end of World War II. They decided that the bomb should be used. But this policy issue did not end with the bombing of Hiroshima and Nagasaki in August 1945. In various corners of American society, voices could be heard questioning the wisdom or necessity of the decision. The criticisms of the decision carried enough weight that individuals involved in the decision-making process emerged to defend it. Karl Compton, president of the Massachusetts Institute of Technology, member of the National Defense Research Committee, and member of Truman's "interim committee," published "If the Atomic Bomb Had Not Been Used" in the December 1946 issue of *Atlantic Monthly.* Two months later, in February 1947, Truman's Secretary of War, Henry Stimson, published "The Decision to Use the Atomic Bomb" in *Harper's* Magazine. Both essays sought to defend the administration's decision to use the bomb; both argued that the bombings of the two Japanese cities were necessary to end the war and save countless American *and* Japanese lives.[1] Discussion of this issue did not end during the late 1940s. Many of the points raised by the critics, as well as by Compton and Stimson, were part of the **controversy** surrounding the Enola Gay exhibit at the Smithsonian Institute and other events marking the 50th anniversary of the bombings. Scholars refer to this type of retrospective or after-the-fact defense of a policy decision as *justification* or *justificatory discourse.*[2]

Numerous concepts in the tradition of rhetorical studies speak to the needs and concerns of deliberative discourse. Perhaps none is as central to the practice of deliberative rhetoric as the idea of **stock topics/issues in policy disputes.** The doctrine of stock topics maintains that policy disputes are organized around a set of recurring topics or issues (*ill, blame* or *cause, cure,* and *consequences*). These topics or issues identify the specific "points" of dispute or disagreement that are possible when considering any potential policy. If deliberative discourse is to be effective, then it must address or engage each of the contested topics/issues. If a topic is not addressed or contested by one's opponents, then it need not be engaged (e.g., if all of the parties in a policy dispute agree that an ill exists, then advocates do not have to prove its existence).

Since Aristotle, rhetoricians generally have insisted that **argument** is the essential ingredient of deliberative discourse. Advocates are believed to be under an obligation to provide reasons, in the form of arguments, for why a policy should or should not be adopted. A number of contemporary scholars have suggested that (a) our understanding of what exactly constitutes an argument has been overly narrow and (b) other discursive forms or strategies may play an important role in deliberative discourse. Considerable attention has been devoted to assessing the role of **narrative** in public and political deliberation (Bass, 1985; Fisher, 1984; Fisher, 1987; Lewis, 1987, Salvador, 1994; Young, 1996, pp. 131-133). The basic thrust of this line of inquiry is to show that people not only make arguments in deliberative discourse but also tell stories and that these stories or narratives embody reasons that can speak for or against particular policies.[3]

Finally, many rhetorical theorists, as well as scholars in related fields such as political theory and philosophy, focus their attention not only on the situated *practice* of deliberative discourse but also on the larger *process* of public or political *deliberation.* If individuals (or, in some cases, groups or organizations) produce deliberative discourse, then communities engage in the process of deliberation; they make decisions. The process of communal decision making or deliberation, its basic nature, its enabling conditions, the factors that disable or constrain it, and its function within a political culture all have emerged as topics for theoretical reflection. In philosophy, scholars frequently return to Aristotle's discussion of intrapersonal deliberation in attempting to unpack its structure and possible significance for contemporary problems (Nussbaum, 1986; Wiggins, 1980). In political theory, unconstrained public deliberation frequently is portrayed as the sine qua non of political legitimacy; a political order (its institutions, practices, and ideals) can be evaluated as illegitimate if it is not rooted in the process of unfettered deliberation (Manin, 1987; see also Knight & Johnson, 1994). Other scholars go a step further in equating democracy and deliberation; a democratic political order simply is one founded on the process of public deliberation.[4] But Bohman (1996) contended that many of these accounts of democratic deliberation leave

> the core of the theory of deliberative democracy relatively unanalyzed. For all their talk about deliberation, few theorists or philosophers describe it at all, and few of those who do [describe it do] so in sufficient detail to make clear why it is democratic, what putting it into practice would mean, or how it is possible under the social conditions of pluralistic and complex societies. (p. 17)[5]

What *is* public deliberation, and what conditions *are* necessary to facilitate this process? These are, quite obviously, exceedingly complex questions. Bohman (1996) offered this definition of public deliberation: "a dialogical process of exchanging reasons for the purpose of resolving problematic situations that cannot be settled without interpersonal coordination and cooperation" (p. 27). As he emphasized, this definition understands public deliberation as "not so much a form of discourse or argumentation [but] as a joint, cooperative activity" (p. 27). He added, "Argumentation is deliberative only when it is dialogical, in the give and take of arguments among speakers" (p. 42). And dialogue, as opposed to a Habermasian sense of discourse, "is the mere give and take of reasons. It does not necessarily aim to produce well-justified claims; rather, it aims to produce claims that are wide enough in scope and sufficiently justified to be accountable to an indefinite public of fellow citizens" (p. 57). Rhetorical scholars likely will find Bohman's account of public deliberation, and the broader trend of which he is a part, of interest. But they might question his valorization of dialogue and his refusal to acknowledge or negotiate the issues and concerns of the traditions of rhetorical scholarship (Ivie, 1998).

In assessing the conditions of deliberation, some scholars in argumentation and rhetorical studies (e.g., Goodnight, 1982), like Bohman, extend on the German philosopher Jürgen Habermas's idea of "distorted communication" so as to locate those conditions (institutions and institutional practices, attitudes, etc.) that effectively disable the process of public deliberation (Habermas, 1970). Consider a simple example. In contemporary society, the production and dissemination of deliberative discourse or the enactment of deliberative dialogue requires an enormous amount of money. The model of an orator on a soapbox speaking to a crowd in a park or of decisions being made at a town meeting does not reflect the realities of our modern political order. Can the public effectively and fully deliberate on an issue when one side in the **debate** controls considerably more resources (especially money) than the other side? Many scholars influenced by the tradition of *critical social theory* would argue that such conditions do not allow for optimal public deliberation and, therefore, need to be altered.[6]

As the conclusion to the preceding paragraph suggests, we not only deliberate about substantive policy issues but also deliberate (in different academic fields as well as in the **public sphere**) about the ways in which we might foster better, more inclusive, and more effective modes of public deliberation. Unfortunately, as Young (1996) noted, most political theorists "typically aim to fulfill the Platonic attempt to distinguish rational speech from mere rhetoric, and in so doing they usually denigrate emotion and figurative language" (p. 130). The "opposition between rational [deliberative] discourse and rhetoric," Young continued, "denigrates both the situatedness of communication and its necessary link to desire" (p. 130). Young suggested that recovering deliberation as a central feature of political life should not come at the expense of important forms of rhetorical strategy (see also Ivie, 1998). Discussion and argument about the processes of public deliberation most likely will continue, and rhetorical scholars should have much to contribute to it.

Notes

1. Stimson, for example, employed the *loss not sustained* strategy to argue that many more Japanese lives would have been lost if the bombings had not taken place.

2. For example, see Cherwitz and Zagacki (1986) and Rasmussen (1973). But note the different sense of the term *justification* as it is used in contemporary **argument** scholarship (e.g., McKerrow, 1990).

3. For an early discussion of the relationship between giving counsel and the practice of storytelling, see Benjamin (1969).

4. On "deliberative democracy," see Benhabib (1996), Bessette (1994), Bohman and Rehg (1997), Chambers (1996), Cohen (1989, 1996), Dryzek (1990), Elster (1997), Fishkin (1991), Ivie (1998), Nino (1996), and Young (1996).

5. See also Habermas (1996).

6. One way of reconstructing the process of deliberation on complex public issues was proposed by Dahl (1997).

References and Additional Reading

Aristotle. (1954). *Rhetoric* (W. R. Roberts, Trans.). New York: Modern Library.

Bass, J. D. (1985). The appeal to efficiency as narrative closure: Lyndon Johnson and the Dominican crisis, 1965. *Southern Speech Communication Journal, 50,* 103-120.

Benhabib, S. (1996). Toward a deliberative model of democratic legitimacy. In S. Benhabib (Ed.), *Democracy and difference: Contesting the boundaries of the political.* Princeton, NJ: Princeton University Press.

Benjamin, W. (1969). The storyteller: Reflections on the works of Nikolai Leskov. In H. Arendt (Ed.), *Illuminations* (H. Zohn, Trans.). New York: Schocken Books.

Bessette, J. M. (1994). *The mild voice of reason: Deliberative democracy and American national government.* Chicago: University of Chicago Press.

Bohman, J. (1996). *Public deliberation: Pluralism, complexity, and democracy.* Cambridge, MA: MIT Press.

Bohman, J., & Rehg, W. (Eds.). (1997). *Deliberative democracy: Essays on reason and politics.* Cambridge, MA: MIT Press.

Chambers, S. (1996). *Reasonable democracy: Jürgen Habermas and the politics of discourse.* Ithaca, NY: Cornell University Press.

Cherwitz, R. A., & Zagacki, K. S. (1986). Consummatory versus justificatory crisis rhetoric. *Western Journal of Speech Communication, 50,* 307-324.

Cohen, J. (1989). Deliberation and democratic legitimation. In A. Hamlin & P. Pettit (Eds.), *The good polity.* Oxford, UK: Oxford University Press.

Cohen, J. (1996). Procedure and substance in deliberative democracy. In S. Benhabib (Ed.), *Democracy and difference: Contesting the boundaries of the political.* Princeton, NJ: Princeton University Press.

Dahl, R. (1997, Summer). On deliberative democracy: Citizen panels and Medicare reforms. *Dissent,* pp. 54-58.

Dryzek, J. (1990). *Discursive democracy: Politics, policy, and political science.* Cambridge, UK: Cambridge University Press.

Elster, J. (Ed.). (1997). *Deliberative democracy.* New York: Cambridge University Press.

Fisher, W. R. (1984). Narration as a human communication paradigm: The case of public moral argument. *Communication Monographs, 51,* 1-22.

Fisher, W. R. (1987). *Human communication as narration: Toward a philosophy of reason.* Columbia: University of South Carolina Press.

Fishkin, J. (1991). *Democracy and deliberation: New directions in democratic reform.* New Haven, CT: Yale University Press.

Goodnight, G. T. (1982). The personal, the technical, and the public spheres of argument: A speculative inquiry into the art of public deliberation. *Journal of the American Forensic Association, 18,* 214-227.

Habermas, J. (1970). On systematically distorted communication. *Inquiry, 13,* 205-218.

Habermas, J. (1996). *Between facts and norms: Contributions to a discourse theory of law and democracy* (W. Rehg, Trans.). Cambridge, MA: MIT Press.

Ivie, R. L. (1998). Democratic deliberation in a rhetorical republic. *Quarterly Journal of Speech, 84,* 491-505.

Knight, J., & Johnson, J. (1994). Aggregation and deliberation: On the possibility of democratic legitimacy. *Political Theory, 22,* 277-296.

Lewis, W. F. (1987). Telling America's story: Narrative form and the Reagan presidency. *Quarterly Journal of Speech, 73,* 280-302.

Manin, B. (1987). On legitimacy and political deliberation. *Political Theory, 15,* 338-368.

McKerrow, R. E. (1990). The centrality of justification: Principles of warranted assertability. In D. C. Williams & M. D. Hazen (Eds.), *Argumentation theory and the rhetoric of assent.* Tuscaloosa: University of Alabama Press.

Nino, C. S. (1996). *The constitution of deliberative democracy.* New Haven, CT: Yale University Press.

Nussbaum, M. C. (1986). *The fragility of goodness: Luck and ethics in Greek tragedy and philosophy.* Cambridge, UK: Cambridge University Press.

Rasmussen, K. (1973). An interaction analysis of justificatory rhetoric. *Western Speech, 37,* 111-117.

Salvador, M. (1994). The rhetorical genesis of Ralph Nader: A functional exploration of narrative and argument in public address. *Southern Communication Journal, 59,* 227-239.

Wiggins, D. (1980). Deliberation and practical reason. In A. E. Rorty (Ed.), *Essays on Aristotle's ethics.* Berkeley: University of California Press.

Young, I. M. (1996). Communication and the other: Beyond deliberative democracy. In S. Benhabib (Ed.), *Democracy and difference: Contesting the boundaries of the political.* Princeton, NJ: Princeton University Press.

DIALECTIC

The term **dialectic,** philosopher Roland Hall acknowledged, possesses a "great variety of meanings" (Hall, 1967, p. 385). Dialectic is derived from the Greek *dialektos,* which can mean (depending on how it is used) discourse, debate, dialogue, or conversation. Aristotle (1954) attributed the invention of the practice of dialectic to the pre-Socratic thinker Zeno of Elea, who was well known for his ability to refute opposing arguments. Dialectic, for Zeno, was a way of subverting "the hypotheses of opponents by drawing unacceptable consequences from those hypotheses" (Hall, 1967, p. 386). Dialectic as a form of rigorous discussion and the collaborative examination of questions played a key role in the thinking of Plato. According to McKeon (1954), in Plato's view, "dialectic simultaneously defines terms, clarifies minds, and discovers truths about things; it occurs in ordinary discussion; it is the method of any science that treats of the nature of things; it is the supreme science which lays the foundations of arts and sciences" (p. 4). For Plato, dialectic and rhetoric generally were antithetical; the former is a genuine method of acquiring knowledge, whereas the latter is a "spurious method" comparable to other forms of sophistry (p. 4).[1]

The relationship between dialectic and rhetoric was characterized differently by Plato's student Aristotle. In the opening passage of the *Rhetoric,* Aristotle (1954) described rhetoric as the "counterpart," or the *antistrophe,* of dialectic (1354a). What was Aristotle getting at when he linked rhetoric and dialectic? This question has engaged rhetoricians for two millennia. In contemporary scholarship, Sloane (1997) suggested that rhetoric and dialectic are "coordinate arts of disputation" (p. 50), whereas Farrell (1993) read Aristotle as claiming that they are "universal arts of the probable constrained by no fixed subject matter" (p. 33). For Sloane and Farrell, an Aristotelian tradition of thought conceptualizes dialectic and rhetoric as discursive "arts" or practices that can be improved through critical reflection. Farrell (1993) emphasized the way in which the arts of dialectic and rhetoric provide methods for dealing with "a world of particulars" (p. 33) or a world that is **contingent** and composed of shifting appearances. Sloane (1997) stressed the "shared intellectual habit" that links dialectic and rhetoric; the "primary mode of 'inquiry' " in each form of practice "proceeds through a given controversy by requiring the arguer to give thought to both sides of the question" (p. 91). Sloane and Farrell highlighted two interrelated features of the Aristotelian tradition of thought on the relationship between dialectic and rhetoric: their usual common *substance* (the probable, the particular, and the contingent) and their characteristic *method* (exploration of a question or issue by considering it from different angles or perspectives).

Although similar in important respects, dialectic and rhetoric remain distinct practices within the Aristotelian imagination. Among the differences, Sloane (1997) noted,

> Dialectic begins in uncertainty and proceeds through inquiry toward more certainty. . . . Rhetoric, however, begins in controversy and proceeds through inquiry to find the means whereby this or that audience . . . may be attracted to a certain resolution of the controversy. (p. 88)

Rhetoric, unlike dialectic, always is "engage[d] with specificity" (p. 96). Another frequently noted difference has to do with the nature of the question or issue under consideration. Farrell (1998) wrote that dialectic "is speculative inquiry over generalized propositions, for instance, definitions of justice, the meaning of the good life, the best sort of political arrangement, and so forth" (p. 3). Farrell (1993) noted that dialectic "tends to move from the alleged facts of particularity to more generalized truths" (p. 33). He contended that rhetoric is practical inquiry over concrete propositions. Are the police officers in the Diallo shooting guilty of murder? Should one's spouse quit his or her job and start his or her own business? Should the nation replace its current structure of political representation with a form of proportional representation? Leff made a similar point by employing the language of Hermagoras and the *Rhetorica ad Herennium* (Anonymous, 1954): "Dialectic deals with the abstract issue or *thesis,* rhetoric with the concrete issue or *hypothesis*" (Leff, 1983b, p. 40, emphasis added).[2]

Distinguishing between the two types of questions—the abstract, acontextual, largely theoretical thesis and the concrete, historically embedded, practical hypothesis—allows Plato's concerns about rhetoric to resurface. From a Platonic perspective, dialectical questions always must precede the rhetorical; their answers must provide the substance of rhetorical practice.[3] One must be able to answer the theoretical/speculative thesis question—What is the good life?—to resolve hypotheses or concrete questions such as the following. Should a person major in business or music? Should a couple have children now or wait a few years until they save up some money? Should a person spend his or her Christmas bonus on a new car or invest it in a retirement account? Later rhetorical thinkers would accept a limited version of this Platonic position. According to Sloane (1997), Cicero maintained that "it's folly to argue an *hypothesis* . . . without giving some thought to the *thesis,* to argue a specific matter without considering the general belief or value . . . which encompasses it" (p. 97). But Sloane pointed out that it is possible to reverse the relationship and give priority to the concrete situation and the rhetorical hypothesis. This appears to have been the position of many Sophists and renaissance humanists. Sloane wrote, "To . . . humanists such as Erasmus, the reverse was not only equally true but even more compelling: Abstract principle becomes important [only] when reduced to cases" (p. 97). The line of thought extending from the Sophists to the humanists suggests that inquiry into a thesis that was not directly connected to a practical, historically grounded case was an idle waste of intellectual energy. The question as to the appropriate relationship between dialectic and rhetoric, or between theses and hypotheses, is part of the historical tension between philosophy and rhetoric.

Aspects of a more Platonic understanding of dialectic persist in certain contemporary approaches to *epistemology* and **argument** theory. Rescher (1977) employed a Platonic and disputational model of dialectic as the basis for a "theory of knowledge," whereas the "formal dialectics" of Barth and Krabbe (1982) and the "pragma-dialectics" of van Eemeren and Grootendorst (1984) and their colleagues at the University of Amsterdam continue the Platonic commitment to a normative, rule-governed dialogic exchange that leads to the critical testing of positions and rational or reasonable decisions.[4] Aspects of the Aristotelian tradition persist in the efforts to understand Aristotle's *antistrophe* claim, in continued interest in the concept of **topoi** or **topics,**[5] and in the effort to explicate the idea of rhetoric as a *method of inquiry* (Farrell, 1993).

But other historically important approaches to dialectic have contributed to the conceptual development of contemporary rhetorical studies. Perhaps the most significant alternative approach to dialectic was developed by the German philosopher Georg Hegel. Hegel's discussion of dialectic was complex, but we can focus on one aspect whose theoretical significance should be explored. Like many of the classical writers on the topic, Hegel believed that dialectic is concerned with antagonistic perspectives, contradictions, and/or clashing opinions and the processes by which these antagonisms or clashes are worked out.[6] But the substance of Hegelian dialectic shifts. According to Rescher (1977): "For Hegel, dialectic addresses itself primarily to *concepts* ('terms') and is concerned to improve their *articulation,* whereas [traditional] dialectic addresses itself primarily to *propositions* ('theses') and is concerned to improve their *substantiation*" (p. 52). Hegel also wanted to show how concepts that are in conflict at one level also are linked at another level. Soll (1969) maintained that Hegel sought to "examine the understanding's pairs of putatively opposed categories and show that these categories, ordinarily thought to be mutually exclusive, really involve each other. They are shown to be one-sided abstractions from a concrete whole to which each belongs" (p. 134).[7]

How does Hegel's insight apply to the development of rhetorical theory? Let us consider some examples. At first glance, the rhetorical processes of *affirmation* and *subversion* appear to be contradictory or antagonistic. Affirming or providing support for a position on a controversial issue is different from attacking or critiquing a position on that issue. Defending affirmative action—providing support for the policy—is not the same as attacking or subverting the arguments of someone who is against affirmative action. Affirmation and subversion appear to be distinct practices. But a dialectical perspective encourages us to see affirmation and subversion as linked in a larger process of advocacy: Almost any instance of **deliberative discourse** will contain affirmative and subversive elements (Cherwitz and Theobald-Osborne,

1990).[8] Hence, rhetoricians might speak of a *dialectic of affirmation and subversion* in deliberative discourse. Terrill (2000) implicitly invoked this dialectic when he argued, "The collective identity Malcolm [X] forges . . . is not *merely* oppositional. Malcolm does not expend all of his energy in negative attack; Malcolm is inventing as well as destroying" (p. 78).

Consider a few more examples of *conceptual dialectics.* **Memory** (or remembering something) and forgetting something are, at least in our commonsense understanding of these concepts, opposites. We either remember an event *or* forget it. The concepts seem to be mutually exclusive. But as a number of scholars suggest (Ehrenhaus, 1989; Sturken, 1997; Whalen, 1993), the relationship between memory and forgetting might be reconceptualized as a dialectic; to remember *x* about an event always involves forgetting other aspects of the event and vice versa. Memory and forgetting then become part of a dialectical whole. Similar dialectical reconceptualizations have been, and are being, performed on a variety of apparent conceptual antagonisms. We generally think that disclosing or *revealing* something about a person (e.g., a secret) is the exact opposite of hiding or *concealing* something. Yet, we find a number of scholars suggesting a more dialectical approach that sees revealing and concealing, or highlighting and suppressing, as "two sides of the same coin" (Cohen, 1998; Lakoff & Johnson, 1980; Leff, 1983a). Revealing and concealing involve each other. For example, a politician reveals aspects of his or her private life through discourse that simultaneously conceals other aspects. As a final example, consider the way in which certain modes of action or social structures simultaneously enable a range of further acts while also constraining other acts. An *enabling-constraining dialectic* is common among scholars influenced by the French historian and philosopher Michel Foucault and the British social theorist Anthony Giddens (Blair, 1987; Montrose, 1989; Sloop, 1996; Stillar, 1998). For example, a text such as John Dickinson's famous *Letters From a Farmer in Pennsylvania* (Dickinson, 1768) can be read as simultaneously enabling British-colonial reconciliation by constraining or narrowing the potential scope of the growing controversy.

This entry has not reviewed all of the significant work on the topic of dialectic that has relevance for contemporary rhetorical studies.[9] But the perspectives that have been discussed—the Platonic, Aristotelian, and Hegelian traditions—have had an important impact on the field of rhetoric. The relationship between rhetoric and dialectic might not receive the attention that it once did, but dialectics as a process of negotiating conceptual tensions, mode of inquiry, and/or form of practice continues to influence the shape of rhetorical thinking.

Notes

1. On Plato, see also González (1998).
2. See also Sloane (1997, pp. 95-96).
3. For more recent defenses of this position, see Natanson (1955) and Weaver (1953).
4. For a somewhat different sense of dialectic and its relationship to argument theory, see Wenzel (1979, 1980).
5. As Sloane (1997) noted, the relationship between rhetoric and dialectic "is nowhere in theory shown more clearly than in their shared use of certain topics" (p. 93).
6. Cornforth (1968) suggested that *contradiction* and *process* are the two central features of dialectical thinking.
7. See also Hook's (1939) discussion of the dialectical principles of "interrelatedness" and "totality."
8. Fisher (1970) detected a "nice relationship between affirmative and subversive rhetorics" (p. 138), and Rosteck and Leff (1989) identified a pattern of subversion and reconstruction in Voltairine de Cleyre's 1895 commemorative oration, "The Fruit of Sacrifice."
9. For one example, see Burke's (1969) discussion of dialectic as "linguistic transformation" (p. 402).

References and Additional Reading

Anonymous. (1954). *Rhetorica ad Herennium* (H. Caplan, Trans.). London: Heinemann.

Aristotle. (1954). *Rhetoric* (W. R. Roberts, Trans.). New York: Modern Library.
Barth, E. M., & Krabbe, E. C. W. (1982). *From axiom to dialogue: A philosophical study of logics and argumentation.* Berlin: Walter de Gruyter.
Blair, C. (1987). The statement: Foundation of Foucault's historical criticism. *Western Journal of Speech Communication, 51,* 364-383.
Burke, K. (1969). *A grammar of motives.* Berkeley: University of California Press.
Cherwitz, R. A., & Theobald-Osborne, J. (1990). Contemporary developments in rhetorical criticism: A consideration of the effects of rhetoric. In G. M. Phillips & J. T. Wood (Eds.), *Speech communication: Essays to commemorate the seventy-fifth anniversary of the Speech Communication Association.* Carbondale: Southern Illinois University Press.
Cohen, J. R. (1998). *Communication criticism: Developing your critical powers.* Thousand Oaks, CA: Sage.
Cornforth, M. (1968). *Materialism and the dialectical method* (4th ed.). New York: International Publishers.
Dickinson, J. (1768). *Letters from a farmer in Pennsylvania.* Boston: Mein and Fleeming.
Ehrenhaus, P. (1989). Commemorating the unwon war: On *not* remembering Vietnam. *Journal of Communication, 39,* 96-107.
Farrell, T. B. (1993). *Norms of rhetorical culture.* New Haven, CT: Yale University Press.
Farrell, T. B. (1998). Sizing things up: Colloquial reflection as practical wisdom. *Argumentation, 12,* 1-14.
Fisher, W. R. (1970). A motive view of communication. *Quarterly Journal of Speech, 56,* 131-139.
González, F. J. (1998). *Dialectic and dialogue: Plato's practice of philosophical inquiry.* Evanston, IL: Northwestern University Press.
Hall, R. (1967). Dialectic. In P. Edwards (Ed.), *The encyclopedia of philosophy* (Vol. 2). New York: Macmillan.
Hook, S. (1939). Dialectic in social and historical inquiry. *Journal of Philosophy, 36,* 365-378.
Lakoff, G., & Johnson, M. (1980). *Metaphors we live by.* Chicago: University of Chicago Press.
Leff, M. (1983a). Topical invention and metaphorical interaction. *Southern Speech Communication Journal, 48,* 214-229.
Leff, M. (1983b). The topics of argumentative invention in Latin rhetorical theory from Cicero to Boethius. *Rhetorica, 1,* 23-44.
McKeon, R. (1954). Dialectic and political thought and action. *Ethics, 65,* 1-33.
Montrose, L. A. (1989). Professing the Renaissance: The poetics and politics of culture. In H. A. Veeser (Ed.), *The new historicism.* New York: Routledge.
Natanson, M. (1955). The limits of rhetoric. *Quarterly Journal of Speech, 41,* 133-159.
Popper, K. R. (1940). What is dialectic? *Mind, 49,* 403-426.
Rescher, N. (1977). *Dialectics: A controversy-oriented approach to the theory of knowledge.* Albany: State University of New York Press.
Rosteck, T., & Leff, M. (1989). Piety, propriety, and perspective: An interpretation and application of key terms in Kenneth Burke's *Permanence and Change. Western Journal of Speech Communication, 53,* 327-341.
Sloane, T. O. (1997). *On the contrary: The protocol of traditional rhetoric.* Washington, DC: Catholic University of America Press.
Sloop, J. M. (1996). *The cultural prison: Discourse, prisoners, and punishment.* Tuscaloosa: University of Alabama Press.
Soll, I. (1969). *An introduction to Hegel's metaphysics.* Chicago: University of Chicago Press.
Stillar, G. F. (1998). *Analyzing everyday texts: Discourse, rhetoric, and social perspectives.* Thousand Oaks, CA: Sage.
Sturken, M. (1997). *Tangled memories: The Vietnam war, the AIDS epidemic, and the politics of remembering.* Berkeley: University of California Press.
Terrill, R. E. (2000). Colonizing the borderlands: Shifting circumference in the rhetoric of Malcolm X. *Quarterly Journal of Speech, 86,* 67-85.
van Eemeren, F. H., & Grootendorst, R. (1984). *Speech acts in argumentative discussions: A theoretical model for the analysis of discussions directed towards solving conflicts of opinion.* Dordrecht, Netherlands: Foris Publications.
Warren, S. (1984). *The emergence of dialectical theory: Philosophical and political inquiry.* Chicago: University of Chicago Press.
Weaver, R. (1953). *The ethics of rhetoric.* South Bend, IN: Regnery/Gateway.
Wenzel, J. W. (1979). Jürgen Habermas and the dialectical perspective on argumentation. *Journal of the American Forensic Association, 16,* 83-94.
Wenzel, J. W. (1980). Perspectives on argument. In J. Rhodes & S. E. Newell (Eds.), *Dimensions of argument: Proceedings of the [First] Summer Conference on Argumentation.* Annandale, VA: Speech Communication Association.
Whalen, S. (1993). The dialectic of memory and forgetting in histories of rhetoric. *Communication Theory, 3,* 157-162.

DISCOURSE

In the not too distant past, students of language—including rhetoricians, literary scholars, philosophers, and social and cultural theorists—worked within a universe of relatively

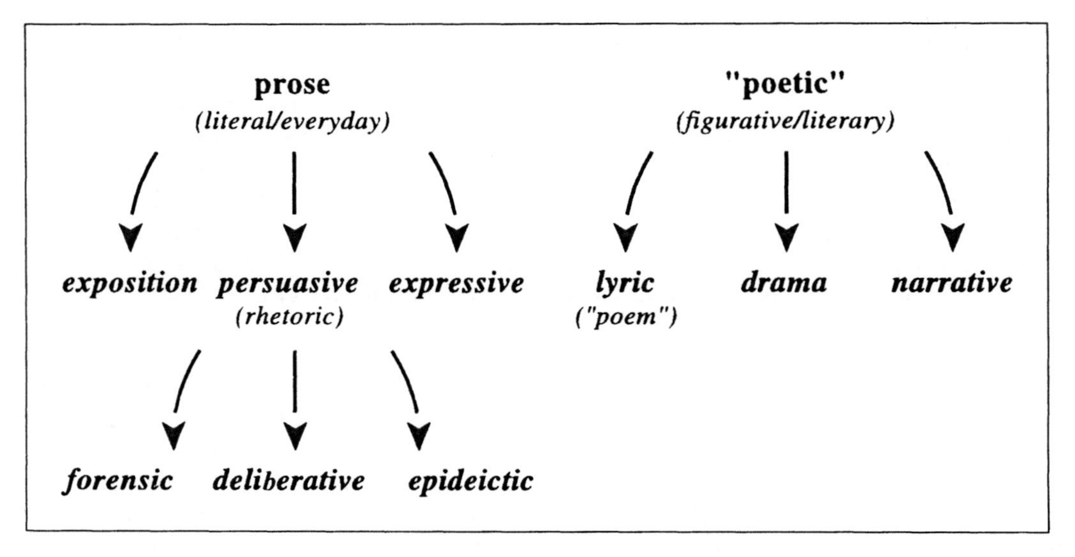

Figure D.1. The Realm of Discourse (traditional version)

stable and autonomous *generic* categories. Scholars might disagree on the precise number of, and boundaries between, **discourse** genres. But there was widespread agreement that literary ("poetic") discourse differed from prose discourse and that the various sub-genres within the two larger divisions were distinct from each other. Figure D.1 illustrates one way of representing the stability and independence of the different forms of discourse.

Over the past few decades, scholars in different fields have begun to question the independence and autonomy of traditional discursive categories. One of the principal contributors to the process, Foucault (1972), wrote, "Can one accept, as such, the distinctions between the major types of discourse, or [those] between such forms or genres as science, literature, philosophy, religion, history, fiction, etc., and which tend to create certain historical individualities?" (p. 22). He insisted, "We must question those divisions or groupings with which we have become so familiar" (p. 22). Foucault's call to question traditional discourse categories has been repeated frequently (e.g., Bové, 1990; Macdonell, 1986). The result has been a new emphasis on the concept of discourse as a general term for referring to linguistic and/or communicative practice. As White (1978) noted, "The conflation of the concepts of poetry and prose within a general theory of *language as discourse* is one of the principal achievements of modern linguistic theory" (p. 104, emphasis added). Scholars now read and analyze novels, poems, scientific papers, scholarly essays, political speeches, everyday conversations at home and at work, newspaper and magazine articles, interoffice memos, self-help books, and judicial opinions (to name only a few specific examples) as instances of discourse or discursive practice.

What exactly is involved in the movement from, as Hall (1997) put it, "language to discourse"? (p. 44). Bové (1990) maintained that essentializing questions such as "What is discourse?" cannot be answered in a definitive sense. He continued,

> An essay [on the topic of discourse] . . . *cannot* provide definitions, nor can it answer what come down to essentializing questions about the "meaning" or "identity" of some "concept" named "discourse." To attempt to do so would be to contradict the logic of the structure of thought in which the term

> "discourse" now has a newly powerful critical function. (p. 53)

Is there any way around the impasse that Bové described? Can we develop an understanding of what scholars mean by "the new sense of 'discourse' " (p. 54) without (at least overly) essentializing it?

One traditional way of thinking about the meaning of discourse is to view it as a specific type of language object with a relation to other taken-for-granted language objects such as clause and sentence. Discourse can then be understood as an organized and/or structured unit of language larger than a sentence. The analytic task is to identify the constituent units of the larger structure and describe the typical ways in which the constituent units are combined to form the larger structure (Harris, 1951; Schiffrin, 1994; Stubbs, 1983). For example, a paragraph fits this definition of discourse. It is an organized and structured language object larger than a sentence. Scholars studying the paragraph attempt to identify its constituent parts and describe how those parts are put together to create the larger language object (Christensen, 1965; Rodgers, 1966). This approach to discourse usually is thought of as "structural" or "formal."[1]

Contemporary thinking about discourse has not abandoned formalism completely, but there has been a steady move away from it over the past few decades. The "new" sense of discourse that Bové alluded to is defined in *functional* terms. Fairclough (1995), for example, maintained that " 'discourse' is use of language seen as a form of social practice" (p. 7). As Schiffrin (1994) summarized, from a functional perspective, discourse is "language in use" (pp. 31-32); as such, it should not be thought of as a type of language object but rather as a language *event* (Johnson, 1990). Focusing on language use introduces factors that are largely absent from formal approaches to discourse. These factors include *purpose* and context. Schiffrin (1994) observed that a "functionalist definition of discourse" emphasizes "the way patterns of talk are put to use for certain purposes in particular contexts" (p. 32). Another central factor in a functionalist approach to discourse is *effect*. For functionalist scholars of discourse, the interesting question is not what a particular language event means but rather what it does. Although purpose is an important factor in thinking about discourse as an event, it does not predetermine the possible effects of a discursive event. Discourse produces multiple effects (Fairclough, 1995; van Dijk, 1997), not all of which (or even most of which) are the result of purpose. A number of scholars emphasize the *constitutive* or *constructive* capacity of discourse. Foucault (1972), for example, observed that although "discourses are composed of signs . . ., what they do is more than use these signs to designate things" (p. 49). What discourses do, among other things, is "systematically form the objects of which they speak" (p. 49). Foucault's observation helps us to understand Bové's (1990) definitional dilemma noted earlier. It is difficult to provide a definition of the "essence" of discourse because one of the things that discourse (in this case, academic discourse) does is to constitute the very "object" or concept of discourse.

Within the prevailing functionalist approach to discourse, we can distinguish three strands of scholarship.[2] The first strand, the Anglo-American strand, tends to emphasize oral interaction and everyday conversation. A variety of labels—*conversational analysis, speech act analysis, language pragmatics,* and *ethnography of speaking* are some examples—are used by the different scholars working within this strand of discourse analysis (for an overview, see Schiffrin, 1994). One common commitment linking these sub-strands is the need to study specific instances of *situated* speech and discursive practice (Coulthard, 1985). Such an emphasis rejected the *structuralist* approach to language analysis that emphasized the abstract and disembodied language system (*langue*) over particular language acts (*parole*). The aim of much of the research within this strand is to reconstruct the rules and structures governing discursive practice. The interests of Anglo-American discourse analysts and rhetorical scholars overlap in a number of areas. For example, the rules of speaking uncovered by ethnographers such as Hymes (1972) have parallels with the more inchoate "rules" of **decorum** that often constrain rhetorical advocates. The shared knowledge that enables conversation (Coulthard, 1985) roughly parallels the **social knowledge** that enables more public **enthymematic** appeals. Some rhetorical scholars (Farrell & Frentz, 1979; Frentz & Farrell, 1976; Sanders, 1978) already have begun to draw on this strand of discourse analysis in their theoretical and critical inquiry. Additional cross-fertilization between the two traditions appears possible. For example, discourse analysts within this tradition already have begun to examine the preferred discursive practice for many rhetorical critics—political discourse (Chilton & Schäffner, 1997; Wilson, 1990). Given that discourse analysts are committed to careful and detailed descriptions of language in use, rhetorical scholars operating within the **close reading** critical perspective might find some useful insights in the Anglo-American strand of discourse analysis.

The second key strand in discourse studies has a European pedigree and is most closely associated with the works of Michel Foucault.[3] Foucault, and the scholars he influenced on the topic of discourse (e.g., Laclau & Mouffe, 1985), tended to be less interested in ordinary language conversation or even routine political discourse. Foucault (1972) recognized that his thinking on the issue of discourse has not always been precise. He acknowledged, "Instead of gradually reducing the rather fluctuating meaning of the word 'discourse,' I believe that I have in fact added to its meanings" (p. 80). Is there, then, a central core to Foucault's analysis of discourse? According to Dreyfus and Rabinow (1983), Foucault restricted his interest to "serious speech acts" or "the plethora of discourse generated by trying to assert truths about objects" (p. 70). Put differently, Foucault's analyses concentrated on **epistemic** discourse—utterances or other linguistic acts participating in the "language game" (to borrow Wittgenstein's phrase) of truth and knowledge. As noted previously, Foucault viewed discourse as a *constitutive* force. He wanted to investigate how discursive practices constitute "objects" of knowledge such as madness and deviant sexuality. Bové noted Foucault's particular interest in *institutional* forms of discourse and/or the discourse of institutions. Foucault, like the Anglo-American strand of discourse analysis, was committed to understanding discourse in its situatedness. His interests centered largely on institutional situations such as hospitals and prisons. But Bové (1990) contended that, in Foucault's view, discourses do not merely exist within institutions. Because of the "materiality of discourse," we need to see that " 'discourse' makes possible disciplines and institutions which, in turn, sustain and distribute those discourses" (p. 57). Discourse, in short, is a mechanism of **power.** It creates knowledge and the institutions and disciplines that protect and perpetuate it.

Foucault's approach to discourse has had a substantial impact on rhetorical and communication studies (Blair, 1987; Foss & Gill, 1987; Gaonkar, 1982; Gemin, 1997; Sloop, 1996).[4] The degree to which these scholars adhered to the details of Foucault's project (or at least the "archaeological" project) is questionable. For example, Blair (1987) tried to remain rigorously faithful to Foucault's archaeological project in her analysis of Lyndon Johnson's September 1967 speech on Vietnam policy in San Antonio, Texas. Sloop's (1996) investigation of "the popular meaning of *prisoners*" (p. 7), on the other hand, was more loosely connected to Foucault's project, or at least its archaeological phase, given that Foucault eschewed the analysis of meaning. Foucault's (1972) archaeological method sought a "pure description" (p. 27) of discursive artifacts; it did not try to uncover their meaning (see also Bové, 1990; Dreyfus & Rabinow, 1983; Gaonkar, 1982). What attracts rhetorical scholars such as Sloop to Foucault's conceptualization of discourse? A few issues seem crucial. First, Foucault encouraged rhetorical critics to broaden their discursive horizons so as to investigate institutionally embedded discursive practices (see also Gaonkar, 1997). Second, Foucault emphasized the analysis of discursive function or discursive power at multiple levels. In so doing, he provided support to those critics who want to challenge the dominant *instrumental* focus of much rhetorical criticism. Finally, as noted previously, Foucault's broadening of discursive function acknowledged a *constitutive* dimension in all discursive practice. Discourse—language in use—does not merely refer to objects; it constitutes phenomena *as* objects that reside within certain institutional/discursive structures (see also Laclau & Mouffe, 1985, p. 108).

The third strand, what is known as "critical discourse analysis," occupies a middle ground between the Anglo-American and continental/Foucaultian perspectives. Critical discourse analysis shares with its Anglo-American relatives an interest in unpacking the micro- and macrostructures of language use. Critical discourse analysis shares with its continental brethren an interest in the relationship between discourse and **power.** Van Dijk (1993), for example, explained that critical discourse analysis explores "the role of discourse in the (re)production and challenge of dominance. Dominance is defined here as the exercise of social power by elites, institutions, or groups that results in social inequality including political, cultural, class, ethnic, racial, and gender inequality" (pp. 249-250; see also Caldas-Coulthard & Coulthard, 1996; Fairclough, 1989; Fairclough, 1995; Fairclough & Wodak, 1997; Riggins, 1997). The interests of many rhetorical scholars, especially those affiliated with the **critical rhetoric** program, overlap with critical discourse analysis, but there has been little in the way of specific influence in research strategies or methods in either direction.

At the midpoint of the 20th century, Bryant (1950) noted that rhetorical critics were shifting their focus from "oratory" to "public address" (p. 331; on the "object" of rhetorical study, see also Gaonkar, 1990). Despite the revitalization of public address scholarship during the 1980s and 1990s, there does seem to be on ongoing reconfiguration of the object of critical attention. More and more, academic courses as well as critical scholarship are embracing the term *public discourse* or, more simply, *discourse.* In so doing, rhetorical scholars are joining an interdisciplinary movement seeking to understand the functions and structures of situated language practice. Rhetorical scholars would seem to have much to contribute to this movement. Practitioners within this movement, in turn, have much to offer rhetorical scholars.

Notes

1. For a review of this approach, see Schiffrin (1994).
2. Compare Barsky (1993), who identified two principal strands.
3. For an overview of this strand, see Bové (1990), Macdonell (1986), and Mills (1997).
4. See also Dryzek's (1997) study of four major "environmental discourses."

References and Additional Reading

Barsky, R. F. (1993). Discourse analysis theory. In I. R. Makaryk (Ed.), *Encyclopedia of contemporary literary theory: Approaches, scholars, terms.* Toronto: University of Toronto Press.

Blair, C. (1987). The statement: Foundations of Foucault's historical criticism. *Western Journal of Speech Communication, 51,* 364-383.

Bové, P. (1990). Discourse. In F. Lentricchia & T. McLaughlin (Eds.), *Critical terms for literary study.* Chicago: University of Chicago Press.

Brown, G. (1995). *Speakers, listeners, and communication: Explorations in discourse analysis.* Cambridge, UK: Cambridge University Press.

Bryant, D. C. (1950). Aspects of the rhetorical tradition: II. Emotion, style, and literary association. *Quarterly Journal of Speech, 36,* 326-332.

Caldas-Coulthard, C. R., & Coulthard, M. (Eds.). (1996). *Texts and practice: Readings in critical discourse analysis.* London: Routledge.

Chilton, P., & Schäffner, C. (1997). Discourse and politics. In T. A. van Dijk (Ed.), *Discourse as social interaction*. London: Sage.

Chimombo, M., & Roseberry, R. L. (1997). *The power of discourse: An introduction to discourse analysis*. Mahwah, NJ: Lawrence Erlbaum.

Christensen, F. (1965). A generative rhetoric of the paragraph. *College Composition and Communication, 16,* 144-156.

Connors, R. J. (1981). The rise and fall of the modes of discourse. *College Composition and Communication, 32,* 444-455.

Coulthard, M. (1985). *An introduction to discourse analysis* (rev. ed.). London: Longman.

Dreyfus, H. L., & Rabinow, P. (1983). *Michel Foucault: Beyond structuralism and hermeneutics* (2nd ed.). Chicago: University of Chicago Press.

Dryzek, J. S. (1997). *The politics of the earth: Environmental discourses*. Oxford, UK: Oxford University Press.

Fairclough, N. (1989). *Language and power*. London: Longman.

Fairclough, N. (1995). *Critical discourse analysis: The critical study of language*. London: Longman.

Fairclough, N., & Wodak, R. (1997). Critical discourse analysis. In T. A. van Dijk (Ed.), *Discourse and social interaction*. London: Sage.

Farrell, T. B., & Frentz, T. S. (1979). Communication and meaning: A language-action synthesis. *Philosophy and Rhetoric, 12,* 215-255.

Foss, S. K., & Gill, A. (1987). Michel Foucault's theory of rhetoric as epistemic. *Western Journal of Speech Communication, 51,* 384-401.

Foucault, M. (1972). *The archaeology of knowledge and the discourse on language* (A. M. Sheridan Smith, Trans.). New York: Pantheon.

Frentz, T. S., & Farrell, T. B. (1976). Language-action: A paradigm for communication. *Quarterly Journal of Speech, 62,* 333-349.

Gaonkar, D. P. (1982). Foucault on discourse: Methods and temptations. *Journal of the American Forensic Association, 18,* 246-257.

Gaonkar, D. P. (1990). Object and method in rhetorical criticism: From Wichelns to Leff and McGee. *Western Journal of Speech Communication, 54,* 290-316.

Gaonkar, D. P. (1997). Close readings of the third kind: Reply to my critics. In A. G. Gross & W. M. Keith (Eds.), *Rhetorical hermeneutics*. Albany: State University of New York Press.

Gemin, J. (1997). Manufacturing codependency: Self-help as discursive formation. *Critical Studies in Mass Communication, 14,* 249-266.

Hall, S. (1997). The work of representation. In S. Hall (Ed.), *Representations: Cultural representations and signifying practices*. London: Sage.

Harris, Z. (1951). *Methods in structural linguistics*. Chicago: University of Chicago Press.

Hymes, D. (1972). Models of the interaction of language and social life. In J. J. Gumperz & D. Hymes (Eds.), *Directions in sociolinguistics*. New York: Holt, Rinehart & Winston.

Johnson, J. (1990). Discourse as event: Foucault, writing, and literature. *Modern Language Notes, 105,* 800-818.

Laclau, E., & Mouffe, C. (1985). *Hegemony and socialist strategy: Towards a radical democratic politics*. London: Verso.

Macdonell, D. (1986). *Theories of discourse: An introduction*. Oxford, UK: Basil Blackwell.

Mills, S. (1997). *Discourse*. London: Routledge.

Riggins, S. H. (Ed.). (1997). *The language and politics of exclusion: Others in discourse*. Thousand Oaks, CA: Sage.

Rodgers, P. C., Jr. (1966). A discourse-centered rhetoric of the paragraph. *College Composition and Communication, 17,* 2-11.

Sanders, R. E. (1978). Utterances, actions, and rhetorical inquiry. *Philosophy and Rhetoric, 11,* 114-133.

Schiffrin, D. (1994). *Approaches to discourse*. Oxford, UK: Basil Blackwell.

Sloop, J. M. (1996). *The cultural prison: Discourse, prisoners, and punishment*. Tuscaloosa: University of Alabama Press.

Stillar, G. F. (1998). *Analyzing everyday texts: Discourse, rhetoric, and social perspectives*. Thousand Oaks, CA: Sage.

Stubbs, M. (1983). *Discourse analysis: The sociolinguistic analysis of natural language*. Chicago: University of Chicago Press.

van Dijk, T. A. (1993). Principles of critical discourse analysis. *Discourse and Society, 4,* 249-283.

van Dijk, T. A. (1997). Discourse as interaction in society. In T. A. van Dijk (Ed.), *Discourse as social interaction*. London: Sage.

White, H. (1978). *Tropics of discourse: Essays in cultural criticism*. Baltimore, MD: Johns Hopkins University Press.

Wilson, J. (1990). *Politically speaking: The pragmatic analysis of political language*. Oxford, UK: Basil Blackwell.

DISCURSIVE FORMATION

In *The Archaeology of Knowledge and the Discourse on Language,* French philosopher and historian Michel Foucault challenged traditional forms of "discursive unity" such as the "book" and the "*œuvre*"—that is, the body of work by a single author (Foucault, 1972, p.

23). Although he challenged these and other traditional ways of organizing or grouping the vast realm of **discourse** (e.g., particular statements, specific utterances), Foucault did not abandon the possibility of systematic relationships among discursive events. Dreyfus and Rabinow (1983) suggested that Foucault sought to develop "a new way to systematize discourse" (p. 59). The concept of a **discursive formation** became Foucault's principal conceptual vehicle for explaining the organization of discursive events.

What did Foucault mean by a discursive formation? Like many of the concepts in *postmodern* or poststructuralist language theory, discursive formation resists neat and easy summarization. Foucault (1972) did provide one relatively simple definition when he wrote, "Discursive formations are, strictly speaking, groups of statements" (p. 115).[1] But on what basis do statements come together to form a "group" or a discursive formation? This question of organization is one of the most critical, and difficult, issues in Foucault's discussion of discursive formations.

On a general level, Foucault's (1972) answer was a bit paradoxical. He wrote,

> Concerning those large groups of statements with which we are so familiar—and which we call *medicine, economics,* or *grammar*—I have asked myself on what their unity could be based. . . . What appeared to me were rather series full of gaps, intertwined with one another, interplays of differences, distances, substitutions, transformations. . . . Hence the idea of describing these dispersions themselves, of discovering whether . . . one cannot discern a regularity [amid the vast field of statements]. (p. 37)

Foucault's idea of "describing dispersions" leads to the paradoxical definition: Discursive formations are characterized as "*systems of dispersion*" (p. 37). As Laclau and Mouffe (1985) remarked, Foucault "makes dispersion itself the principle of unity" in the realm of discourse (p. 105). The statements (the individual discursive events) constituting a formation are, then, both *dispersed* and *systemically connected.* The various discursive events that, from a commonsense perspective, we think of as part of the domain of "medicine" or the "law" lack an immanent logic—something "in" the statements—that holds them together; they exist as dispersed. But these statements are, Foucault (1972) nevertheless maintained, systemically connected. Foucault's great challenge was to describe that systemic connection—to describe the relationships among statements—without falling back onto traditional understandings of discursive unity.

Foucault (1972) established this dispersed systemic connection among discursive events or statements by identifying various "rules of formation" (p. 38) that structure the discursive system. These rules typically cluster into four categories. First, there are rules for how an *object* can emerge or appear within a discursive formation. Second, there are rules regulating *who might speak* and who has **presumption** (on this point, see Dreyfus & Rabinow, 1983, p. 68) within a discursive formation. Third, there are rules governing the development and deployment of *concepts* within a discursive formation. Fourth, there are rules that both constitute and regulate the available *strategies* within a discursive formation. A discursive formation such as "the law" or "education" appears to encompass both a dispersed set of statements and system-generating rules of formation (Foucault, 1972, pp. 40-70; see also Blair, 1987; Dreyfus & Rabinow, 1983).

As the discussion illustrates, Foucault's (1972) idea of a discursive formation was complex. It should not be surprising, then, that rhetorical and communication scholars who have appropriated the concept have done so with differing degrees of fidelity. Some scholars try to remain faithful to Foucault's overarching vision of the discursive formation as a system of dispersion (e.g., Gemin, 1997) or try to reconstruct the rules of particular discursive domains (e.g., Cohen, 1998; Foss & Gill, 1987). Scholars such as Taylor

(1992), in his study of a group of "nuclear texts" (p. 430), appropriate a less complicated version of Foucault's concept, emphasizing function (the production of **power** and knowledge) over nuances of structure.[2] Finally, Sloop's (1996) study of popular discourse about prisoners in America explored the effects of a specific "set of discourses" (p. 7) from a Foucaultian perspective but refrained from explicitly identifying itself as a study of a discursive formation. It might be objected that studies such as Taylor's and Sloop's lack the empirical rigor that Foucault demanded from archaeological investigations of discursive formations. Although these studies might not have reconstructed their discursive systems with the specificity that Foucault apparently desired, they nevertheless disclosed important insights into the discursive dynamics and *constitutive* impact of two significant discursive formations. Scholars following in the critical and conceptual path of Taylor and Sloop will need to continue developing strategies for appropriating Foucault's discussion of discursive formations.[3]

Notes

1. On the concept of statement in Foucault's writing, see Blair (1987).
2. A similar type of appropriation can be found in Hall (1988). See also Grossberg's (1992) discussion of "cultural formations" as "an accumulation or organization of practices" (p. 70).
3. Many historians employ the term *persuasion* in a way that bears some resemblance to Foucault's idea of a discursive formation. Whereas most rhetorical scholars use the term *persuasion* to refer to a process, historians use it to refer to a body of discourse that is held together by recurring thematic (or **ideological**) and strategic elements. See Banning (1978), Kazin (1995), and Meyers (1957).

References and Additional Reading

Banning, L. (1978). *The Jeffersonian persuasion: Evolution of a party ideology.* Ithaca, NY: Cornell University Press.

Blair, C. (1987). The statement: Foundations of Foucault's historical criticism. *Western Journal of Speech Communication, 51,* 364-383.

Cohen, J. R. (1998). *Communication criticism: Developing your critical powers.* Thousand Oaks, CA: Sage.

Dreyfus, H. L., & Rabinow, P. (1983). *Michel Foucault: Beyond structuralism and hermeneutics* (2nd ed.). Chicago: University of Chicago Press.

Foss, S. K., & Gill, A. (1987). Michel Foucault's theory of rhetoric as epistemic. *Western Journal of Speech Communication, 51,* 384-401.

Foucault, M. (1972). *The archaeology of knowledge and the discourse on language* (A. M. Sheridan Smith, Trans.). New York: Pantheon.

Gemin, J. (1997). Manufacturing codependency: Self-help as discursive formation. *Critical Studies in Mass Communication, 14,* 249-266.

Grossberg, L. (1992). *We gotta get out of this place: Popular conservatism and postmodern culture.* New York: Routledge.

Hall, S. (1988). The toad in the garden: Thatcherism among the theorists. In C. Nelson & L. Grossberg (Eds.), *Marxism and the interpretation of culture.* Urbana: University of Illinois Press.

Kazin, M. (1995). *The populist persuasion: An American history.* New York: Basic Books.

Laclau, E., & Mouffe, C. (1985). *Hegemony and socialist strategy: Towards a radical democratic politics.* London: Verso.

Meyers, M. (1957). *The Jacksonian persuasion: Politics and beliefs.* Stanford, CA: Stanford University Press.

Sloop, J. M. (1996). *The cultural prison: Discourse, prisoners, and punishment.* Tuscaloosa: University of Alabama Press.

Taylor, B. C. (1992). The politics of the nuclear text: Reading Robert Oppenheimer's *Letters and Recollections. Quarterly Journal of Speech, 78,* 429-449.

DISSOCIATION

Dissociation is a particular form of **argument** discussed by Perelman and Olbrechts-Tyteca (1969). Its centrality to not only public discourse but also the way in which we think and reason about the world justifies a separate and more extensive entry. We use dissociation arguments to negotiate tensions, inconsistencies, contradictions, "incompatibilities" (Perelman, 1982, p. 126), or what psychologists call "cognitive dissonance." For example, we feel uncomfortable if we believe that a pol-

Figure D.2. Dissociation in Calvin and Hobbes

icy is both good and bad; we tend to want it to be one thing or the other. Dissociation arguments reduce the tension generated by contradictions and inconsistencies in our belief or in our experience of the world. How? Perelman (1982) described how dissociative arguments divide the source of tension into two incompatible parts (the various two-part schemes used in dissociative argument emanate from the fundamental opposition of "appearance" and "reality"), thereby redefining or modifying our experience of the world. The final result is that we can associate our negative feelings with the realm of "appearances" and our positive feelings with the realm of "reality." The policy might appear to be good, but in reality it is bad.

Let us start our investigation of dissociative argument with the Calvin and Hobbes cartoon strip shown in Figure D.2. What tension is Calvin trying to negotiate? He lost the game (in fact, he has lost 165 straight games) but does not consider himself a loser. Losing normally entails loser, so there is an incompatibility at the heart of Calvin's tension. How does he employ a dissociative argument structure to resolve or negotiate his dilemma? Notice Calvin's response in the last two panels. He divides the immediate situation into a realm of appearances (Hobbes's victory is located "in the outward manifestation of this game") and an implicitly more fundamental realm of reality where Calvin's "spirit" remains "unvanquished" and is kicking the spirit of Hobbes's checkers across the room.[1] This is not a simple division of Calvin's world into the either/or form of *disjunctive* arguments. Dissociative arguments not only divide but also redefine or reconstruct. Calvin has used a dissociative structure to reconstruct his world: He is *not* a loser (despite 165 consecutive losses); losing is a mere appearance, and in reality he remains a winner.

Consider the following examples from the realm of public discourse. Ronald Reagan faced a rhetorical problem when he referred to the Soviet Union as an "evil empire" but still called for negotiations with the Soviets on matters such as arms control. Reagan's tension and rhetorical problem: How could he justify negotiating with "evil." Reagan's response, rather common in presidential foreign policy discourse, took the form of a dissociation. The Soviet Union is divided into two components: the government (which is, in the final analysis, only an appearance) and the people (the "real" Soviet Union). We can justify negotiating with "evil" once we realize that evil is only the appearance hiding (or oppressing) the "real" people. We might be talking to the "apparent" Soviet leaders, but in reality we are negotiating with the people of the Soviet Union.

Consider a second example. Martin Luther King, Jr., advocated civil disobedience but insisted that he did not stand for lawlessness. King's tension and rhetorical problem: How could he advocate violating some laws but claim that he still respected "the law" (and wanted other people to respect it as well)? King's dissociative argument, developed most clearly in his "Letter From Birmingham Jail" in April 1963, divided "the law" into two realms: a realm of "unjust" (and hence only apparent) laws and a realm of "just" (and hence real) laws. Again, this was not a simple division but rather a reconstruction of the idea of the law. Based on his dissociation, King could deprive "unjust" laws of the status of the law. Once the idea of law had been reconstructed, King could reconcile the positions that initially seemed at odds. He could maintain that because "unjust" laws were not really laws at all, breaking them was not a sign of disrespect for the law that leads to the general condition of lawlessness (the *directional* argument used by the status quo in the South to critique the civil rights movement); rather, it was in fact (or in "reality") a way of affirming support for "real" laws. The dissociative structure undergirded King's reversal: The apparent lawbreakers were the real supporters of the law. King's conclusion to the dissociative argument made this clear: "I submit that an individual who breaks a law that conscience tells him [sic] is unjust . . . is *in reality* expressing the very highest respect for law" (emphasis added).

The appearance-reality pair is the "Urform" or the "prototype of all conceptual dissociation" (Perelman & Olbrechts-Tyteca, 1969, p. 415). But dissociation arguments can be developed by substituting other pairs for appearance-reality. For example, a common dissociation is between the ideal (as appearance) and the practical (as real). In 1946, Secretary of Commerce Henry Wallace was trying to help shape the direction of postwar American foreign policy. But Wallace had to negotiate a dilemma. On the one hand, he wanted to affirm the sovereignty of all nations, no matter how large or small; every nation should be able to choose its own destiny. On the other hand, he felt compelled to recognize the nature of power politics embedded in the concept of spheres of influence.[2] The two positions—national sovereignty and spheres of influence—were incompatible. To deal with this problem, Wallace resorted to dissociation. In a speech delivered in New York City in August 1946, Wallace maintained,

> And as we build, we must develop fully the doctrine of the rights of small peoples as contained in the United Nations charter. This law should ideally apply as much to Indonesians and Greeks as to Bulgarians and Poles—but practically, the application may be delayed until both the British and Russians discover the futility of their methods.

How did Wallace's dissociation work? He relegated national sovereignty—the "rights of small peoples"—to the realm of the ideal. But this realm was, at least for the time being, equated with the realm of appearance because Wallace subordinated it to the realm of the practical that stood in for the realm of the real. Wallace insisted that, ideally, we should act in this way (respecting rights) but that, being practical, we realized that we could not. In short, we needed to base our policy decisions on what was practical (real) and not on what was merely ideal (appearance).[3]

Two more examples can further illustrate this important dissociative pair. In 1984, New York Governor Mario Cuomo spoke to an audience of faculty and students at the University of Notre Dame on the vexing problem of abortion. The specific focus of Cuomo's speech was whether or not American Catholics should continue their aggressive efforts to overturn the *Roe v. Wade* decision legalizing abortion. Cuomo approached this question in different ways, with one of his more important arguments relying on the ideal-practical dissociation. By reading the history of American Catholics' participation in public moral **controversies** (in particular, the controversy over slavery during the 19th century), Cuomo established a rule of thumb that contained his dissociative strategy. American Catholics, Cuomo insisted, traditionally have "acknowledg[ed] that what is ideally desirable isn't always feasible." Like Wallace, Cuomo relegated ideals to the realm of appearances, thereby questioning whether they can serve as an adequate ground for action. Decisions need to be made in terms of what is practical or feasible—in short, in accordance with the realm of the real.

Here is the second example. One of the many specific questions that helps to constitute America's problem with race relations is whether or not legislative districts should be drawn in such a way as to create "minority-majority" districts (districts in which a minority group is the majority). During the early 1990s, the legality of these minority-majority districts was challenged, and in a number of cases the Supreme Court affirmed the challenges and ordered that such districts be redrawn. Some people supported the court's decisions, whereas others opposed them. An editorial in the June 29, 1993, issue of the *St. Louis Post-Dispatch* criticized one of the court's decisions (in the case of *Shaw v. Reno*) as follows: "Ideally, skin color would not be a determining factor in how [legislative] districts are configured. But that ideal time has not come. Until it does, minorities can only gain the political voice they deserve by concentrating in the same district." The pattern should be familiar. What some called a "color-blind" approach to public policy was recognized as the "ideal" but then relegated to the realm of appearances by the fact that its time had not come. It could not be considered as part of the "real." What did the editorial imply was real? A practical recognition that the only way of guaranteeing adequate minority representation was through minority-majority districts.

Perelman and Olbrechts-Tyteca (1969) identified more than 20 additional terminological pairs that spin out of the basic appearance-reality dissociation. For example, they noted the *theory-practice* pair (e.g., "That sounds nice in theory, but I doubt it will work in practice"), the *verbal-real* pair (e.g., "They might talk a good game, but they never put their money where their mouths are"), the *opinion-knowledge* pair (e.g., "That might be his opinion, but what do we really know about the issue?"), and the *relative-absolute* pair (e.g., "That might be okay for our competitors, but we want to do things the right way"). As Perelman and Olbrechts-Tyteca explained, these various pairs "express a vision of the world" (p. 420) that enables human understanding and action.

One way in which advocates respond to dissociative arguments is through reversals or counter-dissociations. We can see this argumentative dynamic in *hermeneutic disputes* (see discussion of common *exigences* in the entry for **situation, rhetorical**) where advocates argue over the meaning of a text (e.g., the U.S. Constitution). In 1791, George Washington asked his Secretary of State, Thomas Jefferson, for an opinion on whether the proposed national bank was constitutional. Jefferson responded in the negative; the bank was unconstitutional. Jefferson's opinion illustrated what Perelman and Olbrechts-Tyteca (1969) referred to as the *interpretation-letter* pair. According to Jefferson, the (real) meaning of the Constitution could be found in the "letter" of the text—a narrow reading of its specific words, phrases, and clauses. Any other way of construing the meaning of the text was a mere "interpretation" that could only contain the appearance of its meaning. But as Perelman and Olbrechts-Tyteca pointed out, the interpretation-letter pair often will be contested through the *letter-spirit* pair. Advocates relying on this pair, such as Alexander Hamilton in the case of the bank, relegate the letter of a text to the realm of appearances while locating the (real) meaning of the text in its spirit. Here is a clear example of this dissociative strategy. An editorial in the July 3, 1995, issue of the *Chicago Defender* criticizing one of the Supreme Court decisions on minority-majority districts claimed that "the U.S. Supreme Court totally missed the *spirit* of the law. Once again, the court stuck to a strict interpretation of the *letter* of the U.S. Constitution and its amendments." According to the editorial, the (real) meaning of the text resided not in its letter but rather in its spirit.

This dynamic is present in the ongoing abortion controversy. Defenders of abortion rights rely on a rhetorically informed interpretation along these lines: The spirit of the Constitution, found in the "penumbra" shadow of its literal language, establishes the right to privacy, and this right guarantees a woman's freedom of choice. Opponents of abortion rights commonly reject this argument with a reading based on the letter of law: The language of the Constitution is silent on the right to privacy; hence, it does not exist (it is a mere interpretation), and neither does a woman's right to choose abortion.

Dissociations take one of two forms.[4] In a *condensed* dissociation, the advocate (a) does not provide any explicit criteria for distinguishing the realms of "appearance" from "reality" and (b) only explicitly incorporates one of the two dissociative terms in the text or message. Perelman (1982) identified expressions such as "apparent peace" and "true democracy" as examples of dissociations that rely on the presence of only one of the two terms (p. 134). Each expression works by implication. An advocate employing the expression "apparent peace" implies that there is another type of peace—"real peace"—that is to be preferred to its mere appearance. Similarly for the expression "true democracy," an advocate employing these terms implies that there are forms of government masquerading as democracy that need to be recognized as fraudulent.

Let us consider some additional examples in more detail. When Reagan urged cuts in federal domestic spending during the 1980s, he claimed that the "truly needy" would be protected (Zarefsky, Miller-Tutzauer, & Tutzauer, 1984). This is a good example of a condensed dissociation. Condensed dissociations often rely heavily on key modifying terms that do the bulk of the dissociative "work." In Reagan's case, the key modifying term was the adverb *truly.* What did the adverb *do* in this example? It suggested that our current definition of needy was inadequate; supposedly, needy people were cheating the welfare system—and the American taxpayers—out of millions of dollars every year (Reagan was fond of using the anecdote of the "welfare queen" driving around in a Cadillac to illustrate his claim). The adverb contained the seeds of a solution to this problem: Americans need to distinguish the apparently needy (who, given the way dissociations remodel our understanding of the world, now no longer were thought of as needy but rather were thought of as lazy, wasteful, profligate, etc.) from the "real" or "truly needy." On what grounds or criteria was this distinction to be made? Reagan's condensed dissociations did not supply any. The modifying term suggested that such criteria existed (if they did not, then the modifying term would render the dissociative expression meaningless), but the grounds or criteria were not explicit in the message. The force of the dissociation stemmed from the modifying term's ability to suggest the existence of such criteria. Here is a second example. In a televised address to the nation in February 1978, Jimmy Carter urged his audience to support the proposed Panama Canal treaties. Carter insisted that the treaties would enable "real cooperation with Panama." Like Reagan's use of "truly," Carter's condensed dissociation developed out of the key modifying term—real. Carter's dissociation implied that previous relations with Panama, as well as any other type of relationship suggested by treaty opponents, had not been based on real cooperation; rather, they had been based on only the semblance or appearance of cooperation. Carter, like Reagan, provided no explicit criteria for distinguishing real cooperation from apparent cooperation, but the presence of the modifying term *real* implied that such criteria existed.

In *elaborate* dissociations, the criteria for distinguishing between appearance and reality are provided explicitly, and both terms of the dissociation are incorporated into the text or message. King's "Letter From Birmingham Jail" (discussed earlier) advanced specific criteria (e.g., whether the laws apply equally to everyone, whether those to whom the laws apply had an opportunity to participate in the framing of the laws) for distinguishing unjust/apparent laws from just/real laws. In an article in the May 10, 1993, issue of *New Republic,* Jonathan Rauch claimed that gay Americans were not given equal treatment but went on to argue that gays were *not* oppressed (in this case, dissociation worked to support a controversial factual claim). His argument unfolded as an elaborate dissociation: Gays experienced apparent oppression, but based on the criteria that Rauch developed, it was not "real" oppression. Elaborate dissociations derive their argumentative force from audiences' willingness to endorse the criteria supplied by the advocates.

A dissociative argument also can serve as the structural organizing principle of a text (the function that classical scholars described as *disposition* or **arrangement**). For example, in a speech delivered a few days after the North Vietnamese and Vietcong Tet offensive in February 1968, presidential candidate Robert Kennedy employed the illusion-reality dissociative pair to organize his message. In the second paragraph of the text, Kennedy previewed his strategy: "Our enemy, savagely striking at will across all of South Vietnam, has finally shattered the mask of official illusion with which we have concealed our true circumstances, even from ourselves." Kennedy maintained that the nation's task

> is to face the facts. It is to seek out the austere and painful reality of Vietnam, freed from wishful thinking, false hopes, and sentimental dreams. It is to rid ourselves . . . of those illusions which have lured us into the deepening swamp of Vietnam. . . . [We must] confront the grim anguish, the reality, of that battlefield which was once a nation called South Vietnam, stripped of deceptive illusions.

Kennedy then proceeded to examine five specific aspects of the war—the Tet offensive, the nature of the war, America's objective, the issue of interests, and the possible solutions—and applied the illusion-reality pair in each case. So, the claim by Lyndon Johnson's administration that America and South Vietnam had defeated the Tet offensive—that it was a "victory" for our side—was exposed as an illusion. Reinforcing the dissociation through *analogy,* Kennedy remarked that our claiming victory over the offensive "is as if James Madison were able to claim a great victory in 1812 because the British only burned Washington instead of annexing it to the British empire." Over and over, Kennedy invoked the illusion-reality pair in the speech, and in the process, the dissociation worked to organize the address.

Before concluding this entry, it might be helpful to try placing Perelman and Olbrechts-Tyteca's (1969) discussion of dissociation within the broader context of contemporary language theory and *deconstruction* (see also Frank, 1997). As noted by Culler (1975) and others, structuralism and structuralist linguistics posit that all language-based conceptual structures (including the individual text, an author's corpus of work, a philosophical school, a **discursive formation,** or a social **movement**) are organized through binary oppositions or basic *antitheses*—this versus that (e.g., black vs. white, men vs. women, capitalist vs. worker, young vs. old). Culler noted that "structuralists have . . . taken the binary opposition as a fundamental operation of the human mind basic to the production of meaning" (p. 15). Feminist scholar Helene Cixous affirmed and extended this point when she remarked, "Thought has always worked by opposition . . ., by dual hierarchized opposition" (Cixous, 1980, pp. 90-91). Cixous's idea of dual hierarchized opposition is what Perelman and Olbrechts-

Tyteca seemed to be describing with the concept of dissociation—the hierarchical organization of concepts (with the "real" over the "apparent" as the root hierarchy). With respect to the works of philosophers, Perelman and Olbrechts-Tyteca (1969) noted, "The philosopher will establish a *system* that will lead essentially to the relating of various philosophical pairs with each other" (p. 421). They illustrated their point by reconstructing the key dissociations—the central binary oppositions—in works such as Plato's (1961) "Phaedrus" and Spinoza's (1982) "Ethics" (p. 421). Perelman and Olbrechts-Tyteca's discussion of dissociation allows us to understand a little more clearly how hierarchized binary oppositions come into existence and how they might be modified and overturned. Dissociative structures and processes are, in short, a prime mechanism for constituting conceptual structures (Olson, 1995; Schiappa, 1985, 1993).

One of the key issues that separates poststructuralism and deconstruction from the earlier structuralism has to do with the stability of binary oppositions. At the risk of oversimplification, structuralism tends to view binary oppositions as stable, whereas poststructuralism treats them as unstable. The point of a poststructuralist strategy like deconstruction, in the works of writers such as Derrida, is to show how binary oppositions or dissociative strategies, when scrutinized, will collapse or dissolve. King's dissociation of unjust and just laws and Reagan's dissociation of the apparently needy from the truly needy were, at best, **locally stable.** The reading strategy of deconstruction was designed to expose and overcome the "violent hierarchy" (Derrida, 1981, p. 41) inherent in dissociations or binary oppositions. Interestingly, Perelman and Olbrechts-Tyteca (1969) seemed to anticipate the thrust of Derrida's approach when they noted how "contemporary thought strives, in many fields, to abolish [dissociative] pairs" (p. 427). But Perelman and Olbrechts-Tyteca remained skeptical about this possibility. Their discussion of the reversibility of dissociative arguments and the tendency for one dissociative structure to replace another suggested that they believed it is impossible to ever escape from the process of hierarchically organizing binary oppositions through dissociations (Perelman, 1982, pp. 132-133). So long as humans remain valuing and judging creatures, they will rely on dissociations to help carry out these tasks.

At first glance, then, the strategy of deconstruction and the concept of dissociation appear to be at odds. The former looks forward to overcoming violent hierarchies, whereas the latter appears resigned to their inescapability. But Derrida (1981) did seem to appreciate (if indirectly and inadvertently) Perelman and Olbrechts-Tyteca's point about the reversibility within, and the struggle between, dissociations. Derrida wrote that the strategy of deconstruction requires the following:

> We must traverse a phase of *overturning.* To do justice to this necessity is to recognize that in classical philosophical opposition, we are not dealing with peaceful coexistence. . . . One of the two terms governs the other (axiologically, logically, etc.) or has the upper hand. To deconstruct the opposition, first of all, is to overturn the hierarchy at a given moment. To overlook this phase of overturning is to forget the conflictual and subordinating structure of opposition. . . . When I say that this phase is necessary, the word *phase* is perhaps not the most rigorous one. It is not a question of a chronological phase, a given moment, or a page that one day simply will be turned, in order to go on to other things. The necessity of this phase is structural; it is the necessity of an interminable analysis: The hierarchy of dual oppositions always reestablishes itself. . . . The time for overturning is never a dead letter. (pp. 41-42)

In this passage, Derrida recognized the intractability of dissociative arguments. When they are attacked, dissociations are not dissolved once and for all. While some advocates are trying to undermine such dissociative hierarchies as "real over apparent" or "spirit over letter," other advocates are working to reestablish them. The point of this last observation is to suggest that exploring the dynamics of dissociation as part of the strategy of deconstruction might be a fruitful line of inquiry.

Notes

1. Perelman and Olbrechts-Tyteca (1969) discussed how the concept of spirit is a frequent synonym for reality in dissociative arguments.

2. This position maintained that larger nations, because of their size and power, were entitled to certain extra powers over smaller nations residing within their "spheres."

3. Hariman (1995) noted that the ideal-real pair is a common feature of the realist **style** of discourse.

4. The discussion here extends Perelman and Olbrechts-Tyteca's (1969) comments on the "expression of dissociation" (pp. 436-444).

References and Additional Reading

Cixous, H. (1980). Sorties. In E. Marks & I. de Courtivron (Eds.), *New French feminisms* (A. Liddle, Trans.). Amherst: University of Massachusetts Press.

Culler, J. (1975). *Structuralist poetics: Structuralism, linguistics, and the study of literature.* Ithaca, NY: Cornell University Press.

Derrida, J. (1981). *Positions* (A. Bass, Trans.). Chicago: University of Chicago Press.

Frank, D. A. (1997). The new rhetoric, Judaism, and post-Enlightenment thought: The cultural origins of Perelmanian philosophy. *Quarterly Journal of Speech, 83,* 311-331.

Hariman, R. (1995). *Political style: The artistry of power.* Chicago: University of Chicago Press.

Olson, K. M. (1995). The role of dissociation in redeeming knowledge claims: Nineteenth-century shakers' epistemological resistance to decline. *Philosophy and Rhetoric, 28,* 45-68.

Perelman, C. (1982). *The realm of rhetoric* (W. Kluback, Trans.). Notre Dame, IN: University of Notre Dame Press.

Perelman, C., & Olbrechts-Tyteca, L. (1969). *The new rhetoric* (J. Wilkinson & P. Weaver, Trans.). Notre Dame, IN: University of Notre Dame Press.

Plato. (1961). *Plato: The collected dialogues* (E. Hamilton & H. Cairns, Eds.). New York: Pantheon.

Schiappa, E. (1985). Dissociation in the arguments of rhetorical theory. *Journal of the American Forensic Association, 22,* 72-82.

Schiappa, E. (1993). Arguing about definitions. *Argumentation, 7,* 403-417.

Spinoza, B. (1982). *The ethics and selected letters* (S. Feldman, Ed., S. Shirles, Trans.). Indianapolis, IN: Hackett.

Warnick, B. (1996). Argument schemes and the construction of social reality: John F. Kennedy's address to the Houston Ministerial Association. *Communication Quarterly, 44,* 183-196.

Zarefsky, D. (1980). Lyndon Johnson redefines "equal opportunity": The beginnings of affirmative action. *Central States Speech Journal, 31,* 85-94.

Zarefsky, D., Miller-Tutzauer, C., & Tutzauer, F. E. (1984). Reagan's safety net for the truly needy: The rhetorical uses of definition. *Central States Speech Journal, 35,* 113-119.

DOMESTICATION

Here we have an example of how metaphor contributes to the conceptual development of an intellectual tradition. Domesticate is derived from the Latin *domus* and *domesticus* and, like many Latin-based words, sounds sophisticated. Instead of saying "we housebroke the dog," one might say "we domesticated the dog." The basic idea is that one tamed the dog's problematic behavior. This central theme of taming problematic behavior has been extended metaphorically into the realm of rhetorical studies. To domesticate something refers to the discursive process by which something dangerous, threatening, new, and/or problematic is "tamed" and made acceptable or made to appear less dangerous. Historians (Boyer, 1985) and rhetorical critics (Mechling & Mechling, 1995), for example, have described the public relations campaign on behalf of the atom and atomic energy during the late 1940s and 1950s as a process of **domestication.** Through the use of cartoons, *metaphors,* euphemisms, and other discursive strategies, a potentially threatening activity was rendered acceptable to millions of people. Schiappa (1989) analyzed the *idioms* of nuclear discourse, "nukespeak," as a process of rhetorical domestication. Ideas and concepts such as atomic energy and the atom are not the only objects of domesticating discourse. Murphy (1992), for example, illustrated how the response of John F. Kennedy's administration to the 1961 "freedom rides" (a part of the civil rights movement) worked to domesticate the agitation and allow the administration to claim that it was working to both protect "rights" and ensure "order." Hanson (1985) traced the discursive history of the concept of democracy to show how it was domesticated (p. 16). Jasinski (1997) argued that the memory of the American Revolution was domesticated during the first half of the 19th century. Through various rhetorical resources (especially *metaphor* and **narrative**), advocates and rhetors during this period reshaped the revolution into a rather nonrevolutionary, and hence less threatening, event.

References and Additional Reading

Boyer, P. (1985). *By the bomb's early light: American thought and culture at the dawn of the atomic age.* New York: Pantheon.

Hanson, R. (1985). *The democratic imagination in America: Conversation with our past.* Princeton, NJ: Princeton University Press.

Jasinski, J. (1997). Rearticulating history in epideictic discourse: Frederick Douglass's "The Meaning of the Fourth of July to the Negro." In T. W. Benson (Ed.), *Rhetoric and political culture in nineteenth-century America.* East Lansing: Michigan State University Press.

Mechling, E. W., & Mechling, J. (1995). The atom according to Disney. *Quarterly Journal of Speech, 81,* 436-453.

Murphy, J. M. (1992). Domesticating dissent: The Kennedys and the freedom rides. *Communication Monographs, 59,* 61-78.

Schiappa, E. (1989). The rhetoric of nukespeak. *Communication Monographs, 56,* 253-272.

DOXA

Like many of the concepts that constitute the **tradition** of rhetorical thought, **doxa** possesses both a narrow meaning and a set of more expansive meanings. Narrowly, doxa refers to the realm of appearance, ambiguity, fluctuation, becoming, and (most important) *opinion.* Since Plato's attack on the Sophists (in works such as the "Gorgias" [Plato, 1961]), doxa is commonly contrasted to the realm of **episteme**, a realm that emphasizes truth, knowledge, science, certainty, and a fixed reality.[1]

Opinion (or *common opinion*) and *belief* are the terms most often used to translate the Greek doxa. But a number of scholars have observed that thinking about doxa along these narrow lines obscures important issues that merit continued attention. For example, Havelock (1963) described doxa as something more than opinion or belief; it is a "mental condition" or "faculty," a "state of mind," and an array of "psychic habits" associated with the *orality* of the ancient Greek world (pp. 235-239).[2] Havelock suggested that Plato, in attacking doxa, was attacking a specific way of life—the world of an oral culture. What are some of the key elements of a *doxastic* "state of mind"? Havelock argued that someone in this mental condition would tolerate inconsistencies and contradictions that arise within the appearances of the world. As Havelock explained, "In [oral] poetry, antithetical statements are made of the same person, and antithetical predicates are attached to the same subject. He [sic] or it is now good and now bad, now big and now small, depending apparently on the point of view" (p. 246). A doxastic culture, then, contains multiple points of view that are in competition with each other, and this competition is enacted discursively.

Plato's attack on doxa and the doxastic state of mind depicted contradiction as a disease that must be eradicated. The multiple perspectives of the doxastic world were, for Plato, signs of intellectual anarchy. Toleration of inconsistency and contradiction founded on the existence of multiple perspectives had to be replaced by one overarching perspective that could ground inquiry and social existence. But Havelock (1963) noted,

> Contradiction is a disease only if we assume that it is not the immediate events and situations that are real but the isolated abstractions such as greatness and smallness or right and wrong. It is only of these that statements can be made which are never contradictory. . . . In short, the appeal to banish contradiction is another form of the appeal to name and to use and to think about abstracted identities or principles or classes or categories and the like, rather than concrete events and acts of living passionate people. (p. 248)

The tension between abstract and concrete ways of thinking and talking, reflected in Plato's critique of doxa, persists today. As an example, consider an essay on proposals for reforming social security by Trudy Lieberman in the January 27, 1997, issue of *The Nation.* In the essay, Lieberman detailed some of the proposed schemes for "privatizing" social security and critically analyzed the arguments and appeals employed by supporters of privatization. Although Lieberman raised a number of concerns about the ways in which advocates of privatization have advanced their case (e.g., the way in which they have depicted the *ill,* their estimation of likely *consequences*), the general picture that she painted of pro-privatization advocacy was that it is very abstract and bloodless. It focuses on broad principles (e.g., "profit maximization," "economic justice," "the market"), statistics detailing the percentage of the population reaching retirement age over the next 20 years and the percentage of the population that will be in the workforce to support them, abstract "devil terms" ("entitlements"), generalizations about what an average worker might expect if the reform proposals were enacted, and the overall "big picture" of the emerging global economy. What these appeals encourage, Lieberman suggested, is a particular way of thinking about the issue of social security reform. But Lieberman found this way of thinking to be defective, and her animosity emerged most clearly in the final section of the essay under the heading "Forgotten People, Missing Details." In this section, Lieberman eschewed the abstractions of the pro-privatization advocates by focusing on specific cases such as that of Vicki Lawson, a widow supporting two disabled adult children through the social security program; Georgialee Rodgers, a 51-year-old service station manager planning for her future; and Bill Crawford, a victim of cerebral palsy who gets by, in part, on $400 a month from the Supplemental Security Income program administered by the social security system. In so doing, Lieberman crafted a doxastic appeal that emphasized concrete particulars—what Havelock termed "concrete events" and "living passionate people"—as an antidote to the generalizations and abstractions employed by pro-privatization advocates. A similar pattern can be found in other contemporary controversies such as the various "free trade" accords that have been either approved or proposed. Advocates of free trade commonly adopt a rather broad or detached state of mind as they emphasize the economic big picture and the way in which everyone eventually will benefit from economic globalization. Opponents tend to respond with doxastic appeals; they are less interested in what free trade will mean for the gross national product or how it will affect the stock market than in what it will mean, in concrete terms, for their families and communities. Debates such as those on social security reform and free trade agreements not only are about specific details of public policy but also illustrate conflicts between different sets of "psychic habits."

Hariman's (1986) reflections on the concept of doxa also proceed by way of an analysis of its complex etymology in classical Greek. Following the lead of the German philosopher Martin Heidegger, Hariman employed etymological analysis to argue that "*doxa* can be understood better by identifying how it is a complex of the relations of regard, ranking, and concealment" (p. 48). Hariman's reconceptualization of doxa is complex and resists quick summarization. Two points appear essential in his presentation. First, by recovering the connection between doxa and reputation,[3] Hariman disclosed the evaluative or normative dimension of the realm of opinion. Knowing what something (e.g., a person, a speech, an artistic object) *is* or what it *means* depends on the interrelated processes of regard and ranking. A statement about a person, for example, is "both a description of one's *being* and one's *worth*" (p. 49, emphasis added). Hariman referred to this phenomenon as "the reciprocity of substance and status in the verbal world" (p. 49). In the realm of doxa, a thing's "being" or its "substance" is intertwined with its perceived "worth" or "status."

Hariman (1986) suggested that the adherents to one or another of the variations in the *social constructionist* thesis (he used the expression "intersubjective reality") implicitly rely on this way of conceptualizing doxa. Social reality is created or constructed as language is used (in a more or less objective manner) to describe a thing's "substance" at the same time that it (in a more or less subjective manner) is used to attribute "status." Social reality (as an *inter*subjective accomplishment) is then understood as the intersection of substance and status. But this way of thinking about doxa leads to a dilemma that Hariman labeled "the ontological ambiguity of *doxa*" (p. 49). Hariman wrote,

> On the one hand, an opinion is an assertion that something is what it is valued to be (that is, an opinion is inextricably both descriptive and normative), yet, on the other hand, anything ranked seems to possess a being prior to being ranked—there is a separation between its existence and its position—because that thing can also be present in alternative rankings. So *doxa* can exemplify the indivisibility of being and appearance as well as their separation. (p. 49)

Plato responded to this ambiguity by arguing for the "reality" of that "being" that is "prior to being ranked"; everything else, including the realm of doxa, was consigned to the status of appearance. But Hariman's reconstruction of doxa tried to evade Plato's epistemological quagmire, embodied in the traditional opposition of **episteme** and doxa, by emphasizing the linguistic and discursive **dialectic** of *concealing* and *revealing* (pp. 49-50).

No one or no thing, Hariman asserted, is or can be known in his, her, or its entirety. Contra Plato, the epistemic quest for full revelation or "complete disclosure" is impossible. Humans are limited to a world of appearances, a doxastic world (see also Kuypers, 1996; McKerrow, 1989). But the *process* of appearance, especially the way in which language and discourse try to make the world visible, requires attention. Hariman (1986) suggested that the world appears to us "through a process of selecting and deflecting, revealing and concealing" (p. 49). Hariman was echoing Burke's (1945) insight on the nature of language: "Men [sic] seek for vocabularies that will be faithful *reflections* of reality. To this end, they must develop vocabularies that are *selections* of reality. And any selection of reality must, in certain circumstances, function as a *deflection* of reality" (p. 59). Human language, from individual words to elaborate vocabularies or *idioms*, reveals the world through acts of concealment. A linguistic label such as "pro-choice" reveals certain characteristics about a social **movement** (what it "stands for") but also conceals aspects of the world from view (much "pro-life" discourse tries to make visible what the pro-choice label conceals). Therefore, Hariman (1986) maintained that human understanding is the result of "a process of concealing and revealing" (p. 49). Hariman continued, "The dynamic of concealment and unconcealment—of authorizing and marginalizing—is the means by which we determine what we believe" (p. 50). Doxa, then, is more than appearance or opinion as contrasted to knowledge. For Hariman, doxa refers to the way in which the world of appearances becomes manifest through the dynamic interplay of concealment and unconcealment or deflection and selection.

Finally, contemporary rhetorical theorists J. R. Cox and Thomas Farrell invoked the concept of doxa in an effort to describe a fundamental dilemma for rhetorical inquiry and practice. In Cox's (1987) view, rhetorical scholars and practitioners must engage what he termed "the scandal of *doxa*" (p. 7). What did Cox mean by this expression? Simply put, rhetorical discourse often attempts to generate something *new* or something that has not existed before. Virtually every judgment that an advocate solicits from an audience is an effort to create something new.[4] But Cox observed that rhetorical discourse is caught in a bind because its attempt to create or generate something new is constrained by its materials. What materials constrain the advocate, in Cox's view? Doxa. Doxa, for Cox, represents what exists or the common opinions or beliefs of the times. The dilemma is how to use what exists—the doxa of a culture—to bring about what presently does not exist. For example, how might a person living in early 15th-century Europe have argued that the world was round when the existing doxa maintained that it was flat? The solution to the dilemma, Cox suggested, would be to uncover the creative and critical potential of **memory**.

Farrell (1993) posed a similar question. He wrote,

> The question is, may rhetoric be *liberating*? May it, in other words, put us in touch with a range of issues and experience outside our normalized, received opinion, our doxa? And, paradoxically, can it do this *through* received opinion and the traditional resources of rhetoric? (p. 231)

Like Cox, Farrell wanted to know how something new—something "liberating"—can be produced when all that we have to work with are the "received opinions" that presently exist. Based on readings of texts by Jesse Jackson, Betty Friedan, and Václav Havel, Farrell concluded, "Although it [rhetorical practice] always relies on what *appears,* as inflected by received opinions and convention, it may also recombine and individuate these so as to *interrupt* the quotidian of ordinary policy and practice" (p. 273). Farrell suggested that an advocate's ability to use doxa to interrupt or disrupt what is commonly accepted is a critical component of rhetorical art. Although Cox and Farrell differ in how they answered their shared problem, they agreed on a key point: Conceptualizations of rhetorical invention need to engage the "scandal of doxa."[5]

Notes

1. On the contrast, see Havelock (1963) and Ijsseling (1976). For an analysis of Plato's attack on the Sophists, see also Poulakos (1995) and Schiappa (1991).

2. Making a similar point, Swearingen (1991) wrote, "*Doxa* is therefore well chosen as a label not only of the poet's image of reality but of the general image of reality which constituted the content of the Greek mind before Plato" (p. 68).

3. Havelock (1963) made a similar observation (p. 250).

4. A possible exception might be when an appellate court overturns a conviction and orders a new trial. In this instance, the prosecution would be seeking to repeat an earlier accomplishment, but the fact that prosecutors will have to do so with a new jury and, possibly, with certain evidence excluded will make their effort creative and not simply repetitive.

5. For another recent effort that addressed this basic issue, see Campbell (1998). Her primary concern was to disclose how "the principle of rhetorical invention is subversion, using the master's tools to undermine, even sabotage, the master's house" (p. 112).

References and Additional Reading

Burke, K. (1945). *A grammar of motives.* New York: Prentice Hall.

Campbell, K. K. (1998). Inventing women: From Amaterasu to Virginia Woolf. *Women's Studies in Communication, 21,* 111-126.

Cox, J. R. (1987). *Cultural memory and public moral argument.* Van Zelst lecture, Northwestern University.

Farrell, T. B. (1993). *Norms of rhetorical culture.* New Haven, CT: Yale University Press.

Hariman, R. (1986). Status, marginality, and rhetorical theory. *Quarterly Journal of Speech, 72,* 38-54.

Havelock, E. A. (1963). *Preface to Plato.* Cambridge, MA: Harvard University Press.

Ijsseling, S. (1976). *Rhetoric and philosophy in conflict: An historical survey.* The Hague, Netherlands: Martinus Nijhoff.

Kuypers, J. A. (1996). *Doxa* and a critical rhetoric: Accounting for the rhetorical agent through prudence. *Communication Quarterly, 44,* 452-462.

McKerrow, R. E. (1989). Critical rhetoric: Theory and praxis. *Communication Monographs, 56,* 91-111.

Plato. (1961). *Plato: The collected dialogues* (E. Hamilton & H. Cairns, Eds.). New York: Pantheon.

Poulakos, J. (1995). *Sophistical rhetoric in classical Greece.* Columbia: University of South Carolina Press.

Schiappa, E. (1991). *Protagoras and logos: A study in Greek philosophy and rhetoric.* Columbia: University of South Carolina Press.

Swearingen, C. J. (1991). *Rhetoric and irony: Western literacy and Western lies.* New York: Oxford University Press.

DRAMATISM

The term **dramatism** is most commonly used as a label for encompassing the theoretical and critical ideas contained in the works of Kenneth Burke. Burke (1945) first used the term as "the titular word for our own method" (p. xxii) in *A Grammar of Motives* and subsequently expounded on its meaning in a number of works. In his entry for the term in the *International Encyclopedia of the Social Sciences,* Burke (1968) explained, "Dramatism is a method of analysis and a corresponding critique of terminology designed to show that the most direct route to the study of human relations and human motives is via a methodical inquiry into cycles or clusters of terms and their functions" (p. 445). Two aspects of the dramatistic project were identified in this passage. First, dramatism is a "method of analysis" or critical orientation for studying human behavior. Second, dramatism is a "critique" of rival approaches, or alternative "terminologies," to the study of human behavior. Let us consider these two aspects in reverse order.

Like most theoretical innovators, Burke found it necessary to criticize the dominant theoretical positions or paradigms in the social and human sciences so as to create the intellectual space for his dramatistic alternative. Most fundamentally, Burke rejected all theoretical approaches that, either explicitly or implicitly, reduced human behavior to a form of "motion"; he maintained that dramatism focused on human "action." Burke (1966) wrote, "The difference between a thing and a person is that one merely *moves* whereas the other acts" (p. 53). Elsewhere, he wrote, "There can be no action without motion . . ., [but] symbolic action is *not* reducible to terms of sheer motion" (Burke, 1978, p. 814; see also Burke, 1968, p. 447).

Burke's rejection of the terminology of motion (and for him, all theories ultimately were terminologies that could be used when talking about various facets of the world) began in one of his earliest books, *Permanence and Change* (Burke, 1984b). In that work, originally published in 1935, Burke tried to argue in favor of a "poetic metaphor," or a poetic terminology, for studying human behavior (the idea of dramatism evolves out of this earlier idea) as opposed to a "mechanistic metaphor." According to Burke, the mechanistic metaphor was not "wrong"; rather, it was "objectionable . . . because it leaves too much out of account. It shows us merely those aspects of experience which can be phrased with its terms" (p. 261). A poetic or dramatistic terminology is similarly restricted; it can show us only "those aspects of experience which can be phrased with its terms," but ultimately it is superior to terminologies that feature motion as their "titular" term. A poetic terminology is superior because it recognizes that all of human life *is* like an art. Burke emphasized that all of the aspects of life—"either a poem, a social construct, or a method of practical action"—make up a "*composition*" (p. 264)—something that is continually in the process of being made—and that we need a language for talking about life as an ongoing composition.

If dramatism aimed to capture the *compositional* quality of human existence[1] neglected by other terminologies, then it also sought to capture another dimension that Burke believed was missing from the majority of scientific terminologies. In his essay titled "On Human Behavior Considered 'Dramatistically,' "

Burke (1984a) wrote, "By 'dramatistic' terms are meant those that begin in theories of *action* rather than in theories of *knowledge*" (p. 274; see also Burke, 1968, p. 446). The action-knowledge contrast that Burke used to begin this essay resembled the action-motion contrast just discussed, but it also raised an additional issue. If the action-motion contrast helps us to see the "artistic" dimension of human life and the need for a terminology capable of responding to that dimension, then the action-knowledge contrast foregrounds the importance of the "ethical" dimension of life that Burke found absent in most scientific discussions of human conduct. As Burke (1984b) remarked in *Permanence and Change,* "All universe-building is ethical universe-building" (p. 256); the ethical is an inescapable component of human action. He suggested that terminologies for studying human behavior that marginalize or neglect the realm of ethics are, for that reason, severely truncated.

But dramatism is more than a way of criticizing various terminologies; it also is a method (or an interrelated group of methods) of analysis in its own right. Different aspects of Burke's critical and analytic practices frequently are considered part of the method of dramatism,[2] but in the encyclopedia article, Burke (1968) emphasized what he termed the "dramatistic analyses of order" (p. 450; see also Burke, 1984a). This mode of analysis foregrounds "the all-importance of the negative as a specifically linguistic invention" (Burke, 1968, p. 450). But Burke focused on a specific manifestation of the negative; he was less interested in the "propositional negative ('It is not')" and much more concerned with the "moralistic" or "hortatory" form of the negative ("Thou shalt not") (p. 450). Burke maintained that the moralistic negative introduces the principle of "guilt" into any social order. Guilt arises from the inevitable human failure to heed the moralistic negative. He wrote,

> A dramatistic analysis shows how the negativistic principle of guilt implicit in the nature of order combines with the principles of thoroughness (or "perfection") and substitution that are characteristic of symbol systems in such a way that the sacrificial principle of victimage (the "scapegoat") is intrinsic to human congregation. . . . Dramatistic analysis stresses the perennial vitality of the scapegoat principle. (p. 450)

As a method of analysis, dramatism reconstructs the symbolic drama of social redemption, embodied in victimage through **scapegoating,** in "extreme instances like Hitlerite genocide or the symbolic 'cleansings' sought in wars, uprisings, and heated political campaigns" where "the candidate who presents himself [sic] as a spokesman for 'us' can prod his audience to consider local ills primarily in terms of alien figures viewed as the outstanding causes of those ills" as well as those less obvious cases that

> include psychogenic illness, social exclusiveness (the malaise of the "hierarchical psychosis"), "beatnik" art, rabid partisanship in sports, the excessive pollution of air and streams, the "bulldozer mentality" that rips into conditions without qualms, the many enterprises that keep men [sic] busy destroying in the name of progress or profit the ecological balance on which, in the last analysis, our eventual well-being depends, and so on. (p. 451)

This passage illustrates Burke's belief about the wide applicability of dramatistic analysis to various forms of human behavior. What dramatistic analysis allows, Burke believed, is an understanding of the discursive composition of the process of victimage through scapegoating as well as the essentially ethical resources that provide a way of critically subverting the most dangerous and insidious manifestations of the victimage process.[3]

Finally, it should be noted that Burke's writings do not provide *the* definitive statement on dramatism as a perspective for studying human behavior. The writings of scholars in various fields, such as sociologist

Erving Goffman (e.g., Goffman, 1959) and anthropologist Victor Turner (e.g., Turner, 1974), have helped to advance a dramatistic or dramaturgical analytic perspective.[4] The generative dramatistic *metaphor*—life is a drama—has come to occupy a central place in the humanities and interpretive social sciences over the past few decades.

Notes

1. On the importance of "composition" in human action, see also Hariman (1995).

2. Conrad (1984) identified three core "methods" in dramatism: cluster analysis, **representative anecdote,** and pentadic analysis. See the discussion of *pentadic analysis* and *cluster analysis* in the entry for **motive.**

3. See also the entries on **enemies, rhetorical construction of** and **other, rhetorical construction of the.**

4. See also the essays and selections collected in Combs and Mansfield (1976) as well as Gronbeck (1980).

References and Additional Reading

Burke, K. (1945). *A grammar of motives.* New York: Prentice Hall.

Burke, K. (1966). *Language as symbolic action: Essays on life, literature, and method.* Berkeley: University of California Press.

Burke, K. (1968). Dramatism. In D. I. Sills (Ed.), *International encyclopedia of the social sciences* (Vol. 7). New York: Macmillan.

Burke, K. (1978). (Nonsymbolic) motion/(symbolic) action. *Critical Inquiry, 5,* 809-838.

Burke, K. (1984a). On human behavior considered "dramatistically." In K. Burke, *Permanence and change: An anatomy of purpose.* Berkeley: University of California Press.

Burke, K. (1984b). *Permanence and change: An anatomy of purpose.* Berkeley: University of California Press.

Bygrave, S. (1993). *Kenneth Burke: Rhetoric and ideology.* London: Routledge.

Combs, J. E., & Mansfield, M. W. (Eds.). (1976). *Drama in life: The uses of communication in society.* New York: Hastings House.

Comprone, J. J. (1992). Dramatism and dialectic: Kenneth Burke's philosophy of discourse. In C. Sills & G. H. Hansen (Eds.), *The philosophy of discourse: The rhetorical turn in twentieth-century thought.* Portsmouth, NH: Boynton/Cook.

Conrad, C. (1984). Phases, pentads, and dramatistic critical process. *Central States Speech Journal, 35,* 94-104.

Feehan, M. (1979). Kenneth Burke's discovery of dramatism. *Quarterly Journal of Speech, 65,* 405-411.

Goffman, E. (1959). *The presentation of self in everyday life.* New York: Anchor.

Griffin, L. M. (1969). A dramatistic theory of the rhetoric of movements. In W. H. Rueckert (Ed.), *Critical responses to Kenneth Burke 1924-1966.* Minneapolis: University of Minnesota Press.

Gronbeck, B. E. (1980). Dramaturgical theory and criticism: The state of the art (or science?). *Western Journal of Speech Communication, 44,* 315-330.

Hariman, R. (1995). *Political style: The artistry of power.* Chicago: University of Chicago Press.

Overington, M. A. (1977). Kenneth Burke and the method of dramatism. *Theory and Society, 4,* 131-156.

Rueckert, W. H. (1982). *Kenneth Burke and the drama of human relations* (2nd ed.). Berkeley: University of California Press.

Turner, V. (1974). *Dramas, fields, and metaphors: Symbolic action in human society.* Ithaca, NY: Cornell University Press.

Wess, R. (1996). *Kenneth Burke: Rhetoric, subjectivity, postmodernism.* Cambridge, UK: Cambridge University Press.

EFFECTS OF RHETORICAL PRACTICE

The realm of rhetoric, Herbert Wichelns wrote in 1925, is "not concerned with permanence, nor yet with beauty. It is concerned with effect" (Wichelns, 1925/1962, p. 209). These words helped to shape—helped to constitute—the discipline of rhetorical studies. But as Cherwitz and Theobald-Osborne (1990) observed, the concept of effect in contemporary rhetorical studies has been rather limited and one-dimensional. They, along with a number of scholars over the years (Lucas, 1981; Lucaites, 1989; Nilsen, 1956), called for a rethinking of the nature of rhetorical *effect* or the **effects of rhetorical practice** and/or discursive practice.[1] This entry is an exercise in clarifying the concept of effect in rhetorical studies. It outlines three *dimensions* of rhetorical effect.

We can begin with the idea, common in antiquity, that rhetoric is a *productive* art. That is, the application or enactment of the art leads to the production of something. What types of things get "produced" through rhetorical art? We can identify three productive effects of rhetorical practice or three "things" that get produced.[2]

The first thing that gets produced in rhetorical practice is a *text* (e.g., speech, oration, pamphlet, essay). The Greeks used the term *lexis* to refer to the materiality of the text—the shape and *texture* of the words, sentences, and paragraphs that make up the text. The lexis of the text is the locus for the first dimension of effect. We acknowledge this dimension when we say things such as "that speech was moving" and "that essay was powerful." Such expressions may indicate that the listeners or readers have been persuaded to adopt the advocate's point of view or, in Perelman and Olbrechts-Tyteca's (1969) terms, *adherence* has been established between listeners or readers and a proposition. But they need not. What these expressions often indicate is that the listeners or readers were influenced by the *materiality* of the words, sentences, and paragraphs—their physical presence as sound or marks on a page. Chatman (1990) referred to this type of effect as "aesthetic rhetoric." Word choice, discursive rhythm, timing, syntactical patterns, and intonation, among other factors, can have an impact on the consciousness of the listeners or readers. This almost magical power of words to induce feeling and emotion, or to produce a visceral response in an audience, has frightened many people over the years. Plato's opposition to rhetoric stemmed, in part, from the fear he had of the power of speech exhibited by master orators such as Gorgias.[3] Although this dimension of rhetoric might be feared, it seems hard to deny its existence. Rhetorical practice can have a direct impact—can induce movement to feel or experience—through the materiality of language.

As a number of commentators have noted, the last word in Aristotle's (1954) *Rhetoric* is "judgment." We might take this as one of a number of signs pointing to the second thing produced in rhetorical practice and the second dimension of rhetorical effect. Rhetorical practice *helps* to produce or solicit judgments or decisions regarding practical issues and pressing public problems (or *exigences*). The material features of the text discussed previously can contribute to the production of judgment. But more typically, scholars have attributed this effect to the management of proofs within the text. The classical trinity of **modes of proof—ethos, logos,** and **pathos**—has been superseded in more recent scholarship.[4] Scholars still do attend to the construction of **arguments,** but their analytic vocabulary more often is derived from Toulmin or Perelman and Olbrechts-Tyteca rather than from Aristotle or Cicero. In addition, during recent years, scholars have begun to explore the cognitive or judgment-inducing power of discursive forms such as **narrative, myth,** and *metaphor.* Through the management of proofs and other forms of discursive strategy, rhetorical practice fulfills an *instrumental* function as it helps to resolve **situational** exigences and to produce judgments about public issues. This instrumental conceptualization of rhetorical effect has been a dominant force in contemporary rhetorical studies.

The widely noted *linguistic turn* in contemporary humanities and social science scholarship has spun out a number of additional "turns" over the past few years. One of those turns can be termed a *constructivist* or **constitutive** turn that has had a significant impact on rhetorical thinking.[5] When rhetorical practice is approached through the perspective supplied by the constitutive turn, a third productive moment and a third dimension of effect becomes visible. *Simply put, rhetorical practice not only helps to produce judgments about specific issues, it also helps to produce or constitute a social world.* Through all of our different language practices, and especially through that set of practices (however we might draw the boundaries) thought of as rhetorical, we continually create, recreate, and transform our social world—the customs, traditions, values, concepts, shared beliefs, roles, institutions, memories, languages that are our "second" nature. In some cases, this constitutive effect is achieved as an unplanned outcome of instrumental, problem-solving rhetorical practice; it is epiphenomenal. In trying to solve specific practical problems of social security funding, water pollution, or the national debt, advocates will draw on the resources of the social world (e.g., values, traditions, languages) and, in so doing, will contribute to their perpetuation and/or modification.[6] In other cases, advocates will, with at least some degree of intentionality, attempt to produce changes in the larger social world through their rhetorical practice. The classical genre of **epideictic discourse** frequently works in this way. A 19th-century orator at a Fourth of July celebration helped to reproduce the nation's traditions and values just as an advertisement by a large corporation celebrating America's free market system helps to perpetuate and reproduce certain institutions, values, and practices.[7] Of course, some 19th-century orators used a community's Fourth of July celebration not simply as a forum for reproducing the social world but as an opportunity to alter the social world. In abolitionist Fourth of July orations, the instrumental and constitutive dimensions intersected as advocates struggled to modify the traditions and values of the social world as a way of helping them to achieve a specific practical goal—the end of slavery.

It is possible to describe four more specific aspects of the constitutive dimension of rhetorical effect (Jasinski, 1998), as described in the following paragraphs.

The Constitution and Reconstitution of Identity and/or Subjectivity (self as well as others)

As Giddens (1979) observed,

> To study the production of the text is at the same time in a definite sense to study the production of its author. The author is not

> simply "subject" and the text "object"; the "author" helps constitute him- or herself through the text, via the process of production of that text. (pp. 43-44)

Greenblatt (1980), in his study of the process of "self-fashioning" in renaissance textual practice, echoed these assumptions about the constitutive role of discursive practice. Greenblatt identified a characteristic of discursive practice that looms large in contemporary social theory and criticism. Individual and/or group identity frequently is constituted by various strategies of "othering" that secure a privileged identity for an individual or group at the expense of a different group of people who are constituted as negative "other." The constitution of self by way of others (e.g., ethnic/racial minorities, women, individuals from a different socioeconomic position) illustrates the dialectic of enabling and constraining discussed previously. The self-identity of an individual or a group is enabled as the possibilities for those identified as others are constrained. This identity dialectic is visible in Smith-Rosenberg's (1992) study of the constitution of a "new American subject" during the late 18th century. In her study, Smith-Rosenberg traced the emergence of a "privileged middle ground" where the American subject ("republican citizen, American national, middle-class actor") resided, enabled by those excluded and constrained "negative others" ("the white middle-class women, the American Indian warrior, and the enslaved African American"). In multiple ways, rhetorical practice contributes to the production—the formation and transformation—of identity.[8]

The Constitution and Reconstitution of Temporal Experience

In most cultures, temporal experience is organized in terms of the basic categories of past, present, and future. But each of these categories, along with the ever-present experience of temporal flow or the movement of time, can be shaped or constituted in different ways. In some cultures, the past is experienced as a repository of experience that is continually drawn on in the present. In other cultures, the past is experienced as irrelevant (some people believe that this applies to the United States). Not only do our discursive practices help to shape our overall attitude toward the past, but we also use them to constitute and reconstitute the meanings of specific events in the past. In the United States, for example, there has been a 20-year debate over the meaning of the war in Vietnam and a more than 200-year-old tradition of different meanings of the American Revolution (see the entry for **memory**). Probably everyone has had the experience of being somewhere where time seems to drag on and every minute seems like an hour. Or, everyone has had the experience of waiting in anticipation for what the next day will bring. These variable experiences of time are, at least in part, shaped and reshaped through rhetorical practice (Blumenberg, 1987).

For example, Cox's (1989) study of Martin Luther King, Jr.'s "I Have a Dream" speech and Hariman's (1989) rejoinder explore the way in which King's speech helped to shape the nation's experience of time. Cox (1989) emphasized King's metaphoric attack on the ideas of gradualism and inevitability (the beliefs that, with respect to social change, time moves at a naturally slow pace and that social change is inevitable over time) as well as his effort to construct a sense of urgency or a feeling that "the time is now." Hariman (1989), on the other hand, called our attention to King's unstable political position, a position that, Hariman argued, led King to, in effect, reconstitute gradualism. Cox and Hariman showed how, in different ways, rhetorical practice helps to shape how we experience time.[9]

The Constitution and Reconstitution of Political Culture and Political Community

After surveying the works of a number of political thinkers, Smith (1985) concluded that "the preservation of public life is among the most difficult of human projects" (p. xi). A political culture, and the community that inhabits it, continually faces the challenge of "self-maintenance" (Carr, 1986).[10] Political communities and cultures must be preserved and maintained; they must be reconstituted. Communal and cultural reconstitution can take a variety of discursive and symbolic forms (e.g., speeches, essays, novels, films, music) as enduring communal problems of authority, power, bonds of affiliation, meaning, value, and institutional practice are confronted and negotiated.[11] Consider a few simple examples. A presidential inaugural functions, in part, as a *reaffirmation* of American community. A toast at a family celebration functions similarly, albeit on a much smaller scale. A funeral eulogy helps to re-knit a community whose existence is threatened by human mortality. A papal message helps to bolster the community of Roman Catholics. The discursive practices of a feminist collective sustain and perpetuate the community of participants.

The Constitution and Reconstitution of Language (including a society's conceptual realm)

Giddens's (1979) insights on recursivity, introduced earlier in this discussion, are useful here as well. He reminded us that "every instance of the use of language is a potential modification of that language at the same time as it acts to reproduce it" (p. 220). Thinking about language change, and about how linguistic changes contribute to the overall reconstitution of the social world, can be traced back to the ancient Greek historian Thucydides. In his account of the Peloponnesian war, Thucydides observed that the accepted or customary meaning of words changed in the course of political debate. Even more important, Thucydides suggested that these changes contributed to social and political turmoil. Over the centuries, Thucydides' observations about language have been echoed by countless political advocates and social and political theorists. Many followed Thucydides in believing that language change contributed to needless social and political strife. In a satiric poem titled "The True-Born Englishman," the author and political pamphleteer Daniel Defoe complained about the impact of "new-made words" (Defoe, 1997). For many, changes in meanings or the invention of new words represented a harbinger of political and social decay. Others adopted a more disinterested stance toward the phenomenon of linguistic change. An anonymous American writer in 1833 observed, "Questions involving the meaning of political words lie at the very foundation of political society, and accordingly as they are settled in one way or another, the whole fabric must assume a different shape and character." For this author, language change altered the "fabric" of political and social relations, but such changes will not automatically produce civil strife. Finally, we also can find numerous instances where linguistic change was evaluated positively. Thomas Jefferson defended the practice of "judicious neology" (neologism refers to the creation of new words). In a letter to Joseph Milligan in April 1816, Jefferson (1905) wrote,

> Had the preposterous idea of fixing the language been adopted by our Saxon ancestors . . ., the progress of ideas must have stopped with that of the language. On the contrary, nothing is more evident that as we advance in the knowledge of new things, and of new combinations of old ones, we must have new words to express them.

The literary historian Thomas Gustafson coined the term "the Thucydidean moment" to refer to those periods in time when "political and linguistic disorders . . . become one and the same" (Gustafson, 1992, p. 13). As Gustafson illustrated, this Thucydidean moment may be more pronounced at specific points in time,[12] but it is, in essence, ongoing; it never really ends. That is the essence of

Giddens' (1979) recursivity thesis: Every time we use language, we help to both perpetuate it *and* change it. The investigation of language change—the constitution of new words and new idioms and the reconstitution of old words—and its relationship to the larger social world has become an important interdisciplinary area of inquiry. Rhetoricians, political theorists, historians, and literary scholars are attempting to understand the general process of language change as well as particular instances of language change (e.g., shifts in the meanings of words such as *liberty* and *equality,* the introduction of new terms such as *constitution,* the revalorization of words such as *Negro* and *black*) and how these changes help to reconstitute the social world.[13]

One scholar whose work in the area of discursive constitution and reconstitution has been enormously influential is Michel Foucault. Language and discourse practices, Foucault argued, shape the concepts that organize much of our everyday existence. Consider a conceptual phenomenon such as "mental illness." According to Foucault, our understanding of this concept has emerged and changed by way of the productive activity of **discourse.** Foucault (1972) wrote,

> Mental illness was constituted by all that was said in all the statements that named it, divided it up, described it, explained it, traced its developments, indicated its various correlations, judged it, and possibly gave it speech by articulating, in its name, discourses that were to be taken as its own. (p. 32)

Foucault's understanding of the productive and constitutive capacity of discursive practice has had a tremendous impact on rhetorical studies (e.g., Sloop, 1996).[14]

The concept of effect occupies a rather prominent place in rhetorical inquiry. For most of the 20th century, effect was restricted to its instrumental dimension. The most important question for most rhetorical scholars was the following: What observable impact did the message have on its *immediate* audience? But the **hegemony** of the instrumental dimension has been challenged. A number of scholars, often under the mantle of the **close reading** approach to criticism, are devoting significant attention to the lexis or texture of discursive practice. An even larger number of scholars are exploring, in Gaonkar's (1989) terms, "the constitutive power of rhetoric" (p. 273).[15] It seems unlikely that a one-dimensional view of rhetorical effect will again dominate the field in the near future.

Notes

1. For example, Lucaites (1989) wrote, "Rather than to work to develop our understanding of the range of effects which rhetoric can produce, our tendency has been either to ignore the question of rhetorical effect altogether, as if immediate and intentional effects were the only kinds worthy of being studied, or to treat the issue of effect with a tired nod as we turn our vision ever inward to the text itself and to increasingly formalistic analyses" (p. 89).

2. This three-part model of effects might be compared to Hauser's (1991) discussion of rhetoric as product, event, and process. The model also resembles the discussion of the substance of rhetoric in Plato's (1892) "Gorgias." In the early section of the dialogue, Plato had Gorgias advance three different definitions of rhetoric: as an art concerned with words or discourse (pp. 328-330), as an art focused on persuasion (pp. 332-333), and as an art capable of pursuing justice and punishing injustice (pp. 334-335).

3. On Gorgianic *lexis* as magic, see de Romilly (1975).

4. See Gaonkar's (1993) argument that the classical trinity still grips the critical imagination of rhetorical scholars.

5. On the general subject of social constructionism, consult the more than 15 volumes in the Sage series, Inquiries in Social Construction, edited by Kenneth Gergen and John Shotter.

6. Giddens (1979) used the term *recursive* to describe this process of both using a resource and, in the act of using, contributing to the evolution and development of that resource.

7. The corporation's advertisement also might function instrumentally (it is trying to sell a product as well as to reaffirm support for the free market system). In many cases, a single **text** or message can be analyzed with respect to each of the three dimensions of effect.

8. See also the entries for **constitutive rhetoric; other, rhetorical construction of; secular conversion;** and **subject.**

9. See also Depoe's (1991) study of how the "temporal visions" of John F. Kennedy and Richard Nixon helped to construct a sense of "public time" during the 1960 presidential campaign.

10. See also the discussion of *communal exigences* in the entry for **epideictic discourse.**

11. These enduring problems associated with communal maintenance can intersect with the more specific and localized problems or *exigences* that typically inspire instrumentally oriented rhetorical practice.

12. The political, social, and linguistic turmoil of the late 1960s and early 1970s would be one example of a rather pronounced "Thucydidean moment."

13. For example, see the essays collected in Ball, Farr, and Hanson (1988) and Ball and Pocock (1988).

14. Along with Foucault, we should also note the importance of Toulmin's (1972) *Human Understanding* to the project of understanding conceptual development. Toulmin tended to conceptualize this process as *evolutionary,* whereas Foucault's work emphasized discontinuity and rupture.

15. As Leff (1998) noted, the link among many disparate research programs in contemporary rhetorical studies (e.g., **inquiry, rhetoric of; epistemic, rhetoric as; dramatism; fantasy theme analysis, ideology**) is an at least implicit conceptualization of rhetorical practice as a constitutive or generative medium.

References and Additional Reading

Aristotle. (1954). *Rhetoric* (W. R. Roberts, Trans.). New York: Modern Library.

Ball, T., Farr, J., & Hanson, R. L. (Eds.). (1988). *Political innovation and conceptual change.* Cambridge, UK: Cambridge University Press.

Ball, T., & Pocock, J. G. A. (Eds.). (1988). *Conceptual change and the constitution.* Lawrence: University Press of Kansas.

Blumenberg, H. (1987). An anthropological approach to the contemporary significance of rhetoric (R. M. Wallace, Trans.). In K. Baynes, J. Bohman, & T. McCarthy (Eds.), *After philosophy: End or transformation?* Cambridge, MA: MIT Press.

Carr, D. (1986). *Time, narrative, and history.* Bloomington: Indiana University Press.

Chatman, S. (1990). *Coming to terms: The rhetoric of narrative in fiction and film.* Ithaca, NY: Cornell University Press.

Cherwitz, R. A., & Theobald-Osborne, J. (1990). Contemporary developments in rhetorical criticism: A consideration of the effects of rhetoric. In G. M. Phillips & J. T. Wood (Eds.), *Speech communication: Essays to commemorate the seventy-fifth anniversary of the Speech Communication Association.* Carbondale: Southern Illinois University Press.

Cox, J. R. (1989). The fulfillment of time: King's "I Have a Dream" speech (August 28, 1963). In M. C. Leff & F. J. Kauffeld (Eds.), *Texts in context: Critical dialogues on significant episodes in American political rhetoric.* Davis, CA: Hermagoras Press.

Defoe, D. (1997). The true-born Englishman [poem]. In P. N. Furbank & W. R. Owens (Eds.), *The true-born Englishman and other writings.* London: Penguin.

Depoe, S. P. (1991). Space and the 1960 presidential campaign: Kennedy, Nixon, and "public time." *Western Journal of Speech Communication, 55,* 215-233.

de Romilly, J. (1975). *Magic and rhetoric in ancient Greece.* Cambridge, MA: Harvard University Press.

Foucault, M. (1972). *The archaeology of knowledge and the discourse on language* (A. M. Sheridan Smith, Trans.). New York: Pantheon.

Gaonkar, D. P. (1989). The oratorical text: The enigma of arrival. In M. C. Leff & F. J. Kauffeld (Eds.), *Texts in context: Critical dialogues on significant episodes in American political rhetoric.* Davis, CA: Hermagoras Press.

Gaonkar, D. P. (1993). The idea of rhetoric in the rhetoric of science. *Southern Communication Journal, 58,* 258-295.

Giddens, A. (1979). *Central problems in social theory: Action, structure, and contradiction in social analysis.* Berkeley: University of California Press.

Greenblatt, S. (1980). *Renaissance self-fashioning: From More to Shakespeare.* Chicago: University of Chicago Press.

Gustafson, T. (1992). *Representative words: Politics, literature, and the American language, 1776-1865.* Cambridge, UK: Cambridge University Press.

Hariman, R. (1989). Time and the reconstitution of gradualism in King's address: A response to Cox. In M. C. Leff & F. J. Kauffeld (Eds.), *Texts in context: Critical dialogues on significant episodes in American political rhetoric.* Davis, CA: Hermagoras Press.

Hauser, G. A. (1991). *Introduction to rhetorical theory.* Prospect Heights, IL: Waveland.

Jasinski, J. (1998). A conceptual framework for rhetorical historiography: Toward an understanding of the discursive (re)constitution of "constitution" in *The Federalist Papers.* In K. Turner (Ed.), *Doing rhetorical history: Theory and practice.* Tuscaloosa: University of Alabama Press.

Jefferson, T. (1905). *The writings of Thomas Jefferson* (Vol. 14, A. E. Bergh, Ed.). Washington, DC: Thomas Jefferson Memorial Association.

Leff, M. (1998). Cicero's *Pro Murena* and the strong case for rhetoric. *Rhetoric and Public Affairs, 1,* 61-88.

Lucaites, J. L. (1989). Burke's *Speech on Conciliation* as oppositional discourse. In M. C. Leff & F. J. Kauffeld (Eds.), *Texts in context: Critical dialogues on significant episodes in American political rhetoric.* Davis, CA: Hermagoras Press.

Lucas, S. E. (1981). The schism in rhetorical scholarship. *Quarterly Journal of Speech, 67,* 1-20.

Nilsen, T. R. (1956). Criticism and social consequences. *Quarterly Journal of Speech, 42,* 173-178.
Perelman, C., & Olbrechts-Tyteca, L. (1969). *The New Rhetoric: A treatise on argumentation* (J. Wilkinson & P. Weaver, Trans.). Notre Dame, IN: University of Notre Dame Press.
Plato. (1892). Gorgias. In Plato, *The dialogues of Plato* (Vol. 2, 3rd ed., B. Jowett, Trans.). London: Oxford University Press.
Sloop, J. M. (1996). *The cultural prison: Discourse, prisoners, and punishment.* Tuscaloosa: University of Alabama Press.
Smith, B. J. (1985). *Politics and remembrance: Republican themes in Machiavelli, Burke, and Tocqueville.* Princeton, NJ: Princeton University Press.
Smith-Rosenberg, C. (1992). Dis-covering the subject of the "Great National Discussion," 1786-1789. *Journal of American History, 79,* 841-873.
Toulmin, S. (1972). *Human understanding: The collective use and evolution of concepts.* Princeton, NJ: Princeton University Press.
Wichelns, H. A. (1962). The literary criticism of oratory. In A. M. Drummond (Ed.), *Studies in rhetoric and public speaking in honor of James Albert Winans.* New York: Russell and Russell. (Original work published 1925)

EGO-FUNCTION

Richard Gregg's essay, "The Ego-Function of the Rhetoric of Protest" (Gregg, 1971), was part of the rhetorical studies discipline's engagement with the social and political turbulence of the late 1960s and early 1970s. For Gregg, the new and radically different forms of symbolic and discursive practice of the period provided an opportunity for theoretical reflection on the nature of rhetorical practice. Although most of Gregg's terminology has been displaced, many of the themes developed in his essay have been rearticulated in different intellectual idioms that have helped to shape contemporary rhetorical studies.[1]

Gregg began by following the lead of Burks (1970) in extending the domain or sphere of rhetoric. Gregg maintained at the outset that "transaction[s] of self with self may properly be designated 'rhetorical' " (p. 71). This expansion of the domain of rhetoric beyond intentional persuasion of others led Gregg to conclude that "*constituting* selfhood through expression" (p. 74) is an important part of rhetorical action. For Gregg, as for many rhetorical scholars beginning during the 1970s, what discursive practice *did* (as a form of action) was at least as important as what was *said* in practice (as a form of appeal).

Although Gregg's initial focus was on the transaction of "self with self," this intrapersonal perspective expansion of the domain of rhetoric was itself expanded. Gregg (1971) wrote, "We must be aware that at the same time an individual is engaged in a rhetorical act for the primary purpose of establishing his [sic] own identity to himself, he may also, acting as surrogate, aid in the establishment of identities for others" (p. 75). Gregg's thesis, then, was that collective identity, as well as individual identity, is discursively constituted.[2]

Three specific dimensions of **ego-function** occupied Gregg's (1971) attention. The first dimension is *ego-formation.* A concern for ego-formation commonly develops among disenfranchised groups suffering from "ego-deprivation" (p. 81). In disenfranchised groups (Gregg focused on three: black Americans, women, and college students), selfhood is largely imposed on the groups from without. The example of black Americans is clear; their identity as "Negroes" (or even more pejorative *epithets*) was not chosen but rather imposed on them by the dominant white culture. Ego-formation arises as a response to deprivation. Groups construct their own positive sense of identity to replace the identity imposed on them. The expression "black is beautiful" functioned as one element in the constitution of black identity during the 1960s. The second dimension is *ego-maintenance.* Disenfranchised groups not only constitute a new identity but also must invent means for perpetuating that identity. The discursive practices of ego-maintenance function as an **epideictic** celebration of the newly constituted identity. The third dimension is *ego-destruction* and has two separate, but overlapping, trajectories. One part of ego-destruction is directed at the "old" self or identity; as with any form of **secular conversion,** the old self must be destroyed for the new self to emerge. Many of the practices common to conversion experiences (e.g., name changes, reconstruction of the past) are part of this aspect of ego-destruction. The second part of ego-destruction is directed at individuals outside of the group. Gregg explained,

> In the protest movements we are examining, the struggle for a resurrected self seems to be aided by locating other selves, establishing personality typologies among them, and using these as targets for arrows of scorn, ridicule, condemnation, and charges of character defect. This rhetorical identification of personalized enemies enhances establishment of selfhood in several ways. By identifying against an other, one may delineate his [sic] own position—locate himself by contrast. By painting the enemy in dark hued imagery of vice, corruption, evil, and weakness, one may more easily convince himself of his own superior virtue and thereby gain a symbolic victory of ego-enhancement. (pp. 81-82)

In the case of the Black Power movement, enemies included the "Uncle Toms" within the black community who refused to see the emerging Black Power identity as legitimate and most of the white community (from the powerful "the Man" to anxiety-driven "Whitey"). Many contemporary scholars argue that ego-destruction is not merely a tactic of oppressed or marginalized groups; instead, the identity of dominant groups is seen as emerging from a process of "othering."[3] The ego-function of rhetorical practice appears to be as important today as it was when Gregg was writing roughly 30 years ago (Stewart, 1999).

Notes

1. See, for example, Goldzwig (1989), Gresson (1977), and McPhail (1998). See also Lake's (1983) discussion of the *consummatory function* of protest discourse.

2. This issue is treated more extensively in the entry for **effects of rhetorical practice.**

3. See also the discussion in the entries for **other, rhetorical construction of the** and **enemies, rhetorical construction of.**

References and Additional Reading

Burks, D. M. (1970). Persuasion, self-persuasion, and rhetorical discourse. *Philosophy and Rhetoric, 3,* 109-119.

Goldzwig, S. R. (1989). A social movement perspective on demagoguery: Achieving symbolic realignment. *Communication Studies, 40,* 202-228.

Gregg, R. B. (1971). The ego-function of the rhetoric of protest. *Philosophy and Rhetoric, 4,* 71-91.

Gresson, A. D. (1977). Minority epistemology and the rhetoric of creation. *Philosophy and Rhetoric, 10,* 244-262.

Lake, R. A. (1983). Enacting red power: The consummatory function in Native American protest rhetoric. *Quarterly Journal of Speech, 69,* 127-142.

McPhail, M. L. (1998). Passionate intensity: Louis Farrakhan and the fallacies of racial reasoning. *Quarterly Journal of Speech, 84,* 416-429.

Stewart, C. J. (1991). The ego-function of protest songs: An application of Gregg's theory of protest rhetoric. *Communication Studies, 42,* 240-253.

Stewart, C. J. (1999). Championing the rights of others and challenging evil: The ego-function in the rhetoric of other-directed social movements. *Southern Communication Journal, 64,* 91-105.

ELOQUENCE

In a provocative paper, Gaonkar (1989) remarked that "eloquence is one of the most neglected subjects in contemporary rhetoric" (p. 4). This trend is surprising, Gaonkar suggested, because of the centrality of **eloquence** in the history of rhetorical studies. But this centrality, he continued, might be deceptive given that "the idea of eloquence is rarely addressed directly in the classical texts" of Cicero, Quintilian, and the other early rhetorical thinkers (p. 6). Eloquence, in a general sense, is "a recognizable honorific quality" in speech or writing (Farrell, 1993, p. 266); an eloquent (adjective form) address is one that is particularly memorable. But what gives the address that quality? What exactly did the idea of eloquence mean in the traditions of civic oratory that stretch from the classical Greek *polis* to the legislative chambers of 19th-century America? Does the idea of eloquence have any relevance today?

Fortunately, the pattern of neglect that Gaonkar observed is not complete. Bryant (1973), Burke (1968), Cmiel (1990), Condit (1997), Halloran (1978), and Jamieson (1988) all have made important contributions to reconstructing the varied historical meanings of eloquence as well as suggesting possible alternative conceptualizations applicable to the contemporary world. According to Bryant (1973),

> [The] prime components of eloquence through history, with variants of course, tend to be Longinian. . . . The Longinian doctrine embodies the late classical *fusion* of art and nature, of mind and spirit, of substance and form, of rhetoric and poetic, which sustains and legitimates the kinship of the literature of knowledge and the literature of power in the family of eloquence. (p. 122, emphasis added)

Bryant reiterated that eloquence in the dominant Longinian tradition was understood as a "fusion of factors" (p. 122).

Two somewhat different senses of eloquence as fusion can be identified. First, eloquence was something that needed to be combined to or fused with knowledge or wisdom. This sense of fusion was developed by Cicero (1949) in *De Inventione* when he described rhetoric as the union of wisdom and eloquence. But this sense of fusion largely relegates eloquence to aesthetic questions of beauty; wisdom provides the *content* of discursive practice, whereas eloquence provides the *form* or fancy packaging.[1] A second sense of fusion expands the realm of eloquence by conceptualizing it as the *act* of fusion rather than simply as an *element* to be combined with something else. Bryant (1973), for example, illustrated this second sense of fusion when he commented on a particular image in a speech of Winston Churchill: "It effected the fusion of speaker, delivery, matter-at-issue, language, image, occasion, and audience into a live articulation of meaning—into a commanding moment of eloquence" (p. 137). Churchill's image was eloquent because it embodied—it was a discursive instantiation of—the phenomenon of fusion. Condit (1985) echoed Bryant's expanded sense of fusion when she defined eloquence as "the combination of truth, beauty, and power in human speech" (p. 290).

Whereas the Longinian conceptualization of eloquence as fusion may be dominant (as Bryant contended), other strands of thinking also can be detected. Consider, for example, Emerson's (1904) claim that "eloquence is *the power to translate a truth into language perfectly intelligible to the person to whom you speak*" (p. 130). In this passage, Emerson was outlining a sense of eloquence as *adaptation* or a process of *conversion.* Being eloquent means being able to speak or write in a way that will reach a particular audience. Something similar to Emerson's conceptualization informs Burke's (1968) discussion of eloquence as "the result of that desire in the artist to make a work perfect by adapting it in every minute detail to the racial appetites" (p. 41) of an audience. Burke insisted that eloquence "is not showiness" (p. 41); its "primary purpose . . . is to convert life into its most thorough verbal equivalent" (p. 167). These themes of translation, adaptation, and conversion are present in Bryant's (1953) well-known formulation of the function of rhetoric—to adjust ideas to people and to adjust people to ideas. Eloquence resides in the process of adjustment and is visible in the discursive elements in which that process is inscribed.[2]

Conceptualizing eloquence as adaptation or translation pushes it into the orbit of **decorum** and **prudence** given the shared emphasis on *appropriateness.*[3] Gaonkar (1989), in his ruminations on the subject, questioned the wisdom of conflating the spheres of eloquence and prudence. He wrote,

> For eloquence takes us beyond prudence. Most of us are prudent in our own little ways, in saying and doing what is appropriate in a multitude of daily situations that tax our sanity without stirring our imagination, but only the eloquent man [sic] routinely places this cascading stream of particulars into an elevated frame suggestive of what Kant calls an "enlarged mentality." (p. 12)

Gaonkar's reconceptualization of eloquence as a method for verbally encompassing situations—he later referred to eloquence as a "thirst" for "a lyrical summary of our situation" (p. 14)—highlights its cognitive dimension.[4] He suggested that eloquence is the process of comprehending, organizing, and arranging the "stream of particulars" in which we are immersed. Emerson (1890), in a different essay on the subject, also spoke of eloquence in these terms. He wrote,

> The orator possesses no information which his [sic] hearers have not, yet he teaches them to see the thing with his eyes. By the new placing, the circumstances acquire new solidity and worth. Every fact gains consequence by his naming it. . . . His expressions fix themselves in men's memories and fly from mouth to mouth. His mind has some new principle of order. Where he looks, all things fly into their places. . . . By applying the *habits of a higher style of thought* [recall Gaonkar on the idea of an "elevated frame"] to the common affairs of this world, he introduces beauty and magnificence wherever he goes. (p. 76, emphasis added)

More recently, Farrell (1993) echoed Gaonkar and Emerson when he noted that "the inventional power of eloquent rhetoric derives from its ability to subsume particulars within themes and frames of larger generality" (p. 266). What Emerson (in at least one of his essays on the topic), Gaonkar, and Farrell all emphasized is a cognitive orientation that understands eloquence as a power of comprehension manifested in an advocate's ability to organize, in a forceful and compelling manner, the particulars of a given situation.

These three strands—the Longinian emphasis on fusion, the idea of eloquence as effective adaptation, and the cognitive account of eloquence as a method of imaginative comprehension—do not exhaust the various ways in which eloquence has been conceptualized. They do represent three recurrent and still vibrant ways of thinking about this important classical concept. But is the concept of eloquence anything more than a relic from the classical and modern traditions of rhetoric? Does the concept have any significance today? Scholars such as Farrell and Gaonkar demonstrated an interest in revitalizing the traditional concept. Although the specific discursive characteristics that we think of as eloquent might have changed, the ideals embodied in the different strands described in this entry retain their appeal and merit a place in contemporary pedagogy, criticism, and theory.

Approaching the questions from a somewhat different angle, Jamieson (1988) tried to assess the impact of technological and cultural changes on the concept of eloquence. Not only have the discursive characteristics of eloquence changed, but the *metaphors* that help to structure our understanding of the concept also have been fundamentally altered. Jamieson argued that we no longer talk about eloquence by way of metaphors of fire and heat that pervade the thinking of earlier generations. Jamieson maintained that our sense of communicative excellence is decidedly cooler; visual images and a conversational style have displaced the characteristics of previous periods. "Manly" eloquence has been replaced by an "effeminate" style. How to respond to this situation? Some feminist scholars hail the decline of the masculinist ideal of eloquence (see, e.g., the entry for **invitational rhetoric**). New norms and ideals, not tarnished by the masculinist rhetorical tradition, must be developed. Jamieson was less hostile to the "old" ideals of eloquence, but she also recognized that turning back the clock was not an option. For her, the question was whether the old ideals of eloquence might somehow be incorporated (or "fused") into our present practices. Deciding whether to revitalize (and how that might be done) or abandon the concept of eloquence most likely will remain a key issue in rhetorical studies in the near future.

Notes

1. Rhetoric is thereby relegated to the status of a "supplement" (Gaonkar, 1990).

2. The ideas of eloquence as fusion and conversion or adaptation can be combined. Condit (1997) seemed to move in this direction when she suggested that "the fundamental task" of eloquence "is to take an incompletely spoken, fragmentary set of experiences and to articulate those experiences in a coherent set of relationships that nourishes a particular audience in a particular context, perhaps even moving them to new visions for old ones" (p. 107).

3. On the connection between eloquence and decorum, see Cmiel (1990).

4. See also Burke's (1957) discussion of "poetry" and symbolic action generally as "strategies for the encompassing of situations" (p. 3).

References and Additional Reading

Bryant, D. C. (1953). Rhetoric: Its function and its scope. *Quarterly Journal of Speech, 39,* 401-424.

Bryant, D. C. (1973). A concept of eloquence. In D. C. Bryant, *Rhetorical dimensions in criticism.* Baton Rouge: Louisiana State University Press.

Burke, K. (1957). *The philosophy of literary form* (rev. ed.). New York: Vintage.

Burke, K. (1968). *Counter-statement* (3rd ed.). Berkeley: University of California Press.

Caplan, H. (1970). The decay of eloquence at Rome in the first century. In A. King & H. North (Eds.), *Of eloquence: Studies in ancient and medieval rhetoric.* Ithaca, NY: Cornell University Press.

Cicero. (1949). *De inventione* (H. M. Hubbell, Trans.). London: Heinemann.

Cmiel, K. (1990). *Democratic eloquence: The fight over popular speech in nineteenth-century America.* New York: William Morrow.

Condit, C. M. (1985). The functions of epideictic: The Boston Massacre orations as exemplar. *Communication Quarterly, 33,* 284-299.

Condit, C. M. (1997). In praise of eloquent diversity: Gender and rhetoric as public persuasion. *Women's Studies in Communication, 20,* 91-116.

Emerson, R. W. (1890). Eloquence. In R. W. Emerson, *Society and solitude.* Boston: Houghton Mifflin.

Emerson, R. W. (1904). Eloquence. In R. W. Emerson, *The complete works of Ralph Waldo Emerson* (Vol. 8, Concord ed.). Boston: Houghton Mifflin.

Farrell, T. B. (1993). *Norms of rhetorical culture.* New Haven, CT: Yale University Press.

Gaonkar, D. P. (1989, November). *Rhetoric as a vocation: Notes on eloquence.* Paper presented at the meeting of the Speech Communication Association, San Francisco.

Gaonkar, D. P. (1990). Rhetoric and its double: Reflections on the rhetorical turn in the human sciences. In H. W. Simons (Ed.), *The rhetorical turn: Invention and persuasion in the conduct of inquiry.* Chicago: University of Chicago Press.

Halloran, M. S. (1978). Eloquence in a technological society. *Central States Speech Journal, 29,* 221-227.

Jamieson, K. H. (1988). *Eloquence in an electronic age: The transformation of political speechmaking.* New York: Oxford University Press.

ENEMIES, RHETORICAL CONSTRUCTION OF

What do Great Britain, France, Mexico, Spain, Germany, Italy, Japan, North Korea, North Vietnam, the former Soviet Union, Iran, Iraq, and Libya have in common? All, at one time or another, have been either official (via declarations of war) or unofficial *enemies* of the United States. Enemies are not limited to foreign nations. Over the two centuries of American history, the nation has faced numerous internal enemies—Catholics, Jacobins, the "slave power," immigrants, labor agitators, anarchists, Socialists, Communists, gangsters, urban gangs, right-wing reactionaries, and illegal immigrants all have been identified as enemies or groups dangerous to the safety and/or prosperity of the nation.[1] Various social movements wage symbolic war against perceived enemies; radical man-hating feminists, immoral homosexuals, and the liberal elite are favorite targets of conservative public discourse, while liberals and progressives do battle with racist, homophobic reactionaries and greedy, uncaring corporate profit mongers. At times, the enemy is depicted as a social plague, as when the nation metaphorically goes to war against drugs or poverty.

For the most part, enemies can be defined, Edelman (1988) suggested, as "identifiable persons or stereotypes of persons to whom evil traits, intentions, or actions can be attributed" (p. 87). Edelman added, "It is not the [actual] harm that matters but the attribution" (p. 87). By highlighting the process of attribution, Edelman called attention to the **rhetorical construction of enemies** through discourse. To argue that enemies are constructed, as Edelman did, is not to deny that, at specific points in time, various individuals, groups, and/or nations have sought to do harm to either the nation or its citizens. Edelman's point was that the public discourse about enemies is not a simple reflection or **representation** of an unambiguous and objective "reality." Edelman wrote, "Communication about enemies exemplifies the performative nature of language in a striking way; this language is manifestly a form of action, not a tool for describing a situation" (p. 88). We commit a serious mistake if we believe that discourse about enemies simply holds a mirror up to the world, thereby providing us with a wholly accurate and objective picture. Such a belief is mistaken because (a) it is based on a flawed understanding of the way in which language works and (b) it is naive regarding the various functions of discourse about enemies.

To better understand why discourse about enemies is rather common in American society, we need to focus initially on the functions of this discursive practice. For a number of years, both scholars and public advocates have called attention to the relationship between discourse about enemies and communal identity and solidarity. In his famous essay on Hitler's (1999) *Mein Kampf*, Burke (1957) wrote, "Men who can unite on nothing else can unite on the basis of a foe shared by all" (p. 165). Burke extended his observations on Hitler and the discourse of enemies in *A Rhetoric of Motives* (Burke, 1950), where he posited a dialectical relationship between **identification** and division. In what seems to be an almost inevitable pattern with deep religious roots, individuals craft a sense of group unity or identification by dividing themselves from others.[2] Those "others" are then routinely treated as the enemy. Edelman (1988) made similar observations. He wrote, "In constructing . . . enemies, people are manifestly defining themselves and their place in history. . . . To support a war against a foreign aggressor who threatens national sovereignty and moral decencies is to construct oneself as a member of a nation of innocent heroes" (p. 76). Edelman argued that enemies help to "constitute subjectivity. . . . People define themselves in large part in terms of their opposition to other groups they fear and condemn" (p. 82; see also Cheney, 1983; Greene, 1993; Hart, 1998).

One central function of discourse about enemies, then, is the construction of communal identity and solidarity. What other functions are served by the "ubiquitous political rituals through which public enemies are identified, denounced, or cast out from the community" (Kertzer, 1988, p. 91)? Edelman (1988) identified at least four important functions. First, discourse about enemies reinforces various institutional structures. As Edelman noted, "To establish governmental agencies to deal with external or internal security is to guarantee that their top officials will see serious threats to security and so preserve a function, a budget, and careers" (p. 85). The discourse about enemies produced by these government officials creates the public climate necessary for continued funding of their institutions. Second, discourse about enemies produces public anxiety (p. 81) that public officials, in turn, try to alleviate. Edelman remarked, "If [public] yearning for security and protection creates leaders, leaders themselves do more than their share to construct the threats to well-being that keep those aspirations alive" (p. 38). In essence, then, by constructing enemies, leaders make themselves necessary. Edelman's observation here might be applied to the foreign policy discourse during the early years of John F. Kennedy's administration. The continual crises, provoked by our enemies, made Kennedy's dynamic leadership all the more urgent. The question to consider is whether or not Kennedy benefited politically from these various crises. Third, enemies typically function to personify issues, giving concrete form to abstract problems and institutional structures. The discourse of enemies, according to Edelman, enacts a "displacement of resentments onto personified targets" (p. 78). This function of enemy discourse is promoted by those on the political "left" as well as those on the "right." In his discussion of the Italian Marxist Antonio Gramsci's theory of **hegemony,** Aune (1994) noted the recurrent "need to personalize impersonal structure in a hated group or person" (p. 73). Finding cures for the multiple causes of economic decline can be exceedingly difficult, whereas finding an enemy to shoulder the blame is much easier. Which course do many of our politicians choose?[3] Fourth, the discourse of enemies functions as a form of **transcendence,** making it possible for people who are divided on issues to overcome that division through a confrontation with the shared enemy. Discourse about enemies creates, in Kertzer's (1988) terms, "solidarity without consensus" (pp. 67-69).

In addition to understanding the functions of discourse about enemies, it is important to attend to the discursive dynamics through which enemies are constructed. Edelman (1988) argued that **narrative** forms, "stock stories" (p. 71), and **condensation symbols** (e.g., slogans such as "Remember the Alamo," the image of Neville Chamberlain returning from his meeting with Hitler promising peace for Europe) are prime modes of enemy construction. Rhetorical critics have drawn attention to other aspects of the process of enemy construction. Smith (1969) noted the way in which enemies are *vilified* or subject to a process of *vilification;* they are debased, degraded, and portrayed as only partly human (see also Goldzwig, 1989; Vanderford, 1989). Other scholars (e.g., Hogan, 1995; Ivie, 1995) discuss the way in which enemies are *demonized.* Stewart, Smith, and Denton (1989) noted how social movements frequently employ "devil appeals." They wrote, "Every social movement identifies one or more devils and then heaps abuse upon them in the form of name-calling, ridicule, negative associations, and metaphors" (pp. 125-126).[4] Ivie (1980, 1996, 1997) has devoted significant attention to the tendency to construct enemies through images of savagery. Ivie (1980) wrote, "The enemy is portrayed as a savage, i.e., as an aggressor, driven by irrational desires for conquest, who is seeking to subjugate others by force of arms" (p. 281). He argued that this form of depiction supports a sense of American identity as "rational, tolerant of diversity, and pacific" (p. 281). Ivie maintained that the process of constructing the enemy as savage proceeds through a set of **topoi** or stock themes that elaborate on the image of savagery. The construction process functions to "support a claim of reluctant belligerence" (p. 283) on the part of the United States and to construct a positive American identity while also helping to persuade young Americans to kill fellow humans (it seems easier to persuade people that such action is necessary if they think about those to be killed as something less than fully human).[5]

In a study of the discourse of the abortion controversy, Vanderford (1989) observed the seemingly paradoxical tendency of social movement groups to portray their antagonists as both powerful and vulnerable. This "paradoxical view of the enemy" (p. 175) is explainable, Vanderford suggested, because such groups find it desirable to feel "threatened and empowered simultaneously" (p. 176). For example, Planned Parenthood advocacy ads during the late 1980s portrayed right-to-life extremists (those who engage in violence) as a relatively insignificant "small band" of zealots who, nevertheless, possessed significant political influence; they were, in short, both powerless and powerful.

This paradox of enemy construction also can be found in one of the classic documents of the early cold war period, George Kennan's pseudonymously published essay in the July 1947 issue of *Foreign Affairs* titled "The Sources of Soviet Conduct." Kennan's essay articulated and defended a "long-term" policy for dealing with the Soviet Union. Kennan rejected "threats or blustering or superfluous gestures of outward 'toughness' " in favor of a policy of patient and persistent "containment." Careful reading of the essay reveals the paradoxical dynamic that Vanderford uncovered in the discourse of the abortion controversy. On the one hand, Kennan depicted the Soviet Union as crafty, skillful, persistent, ambitious, and (it seemed) powerful. The Soviets' "political action is a fluid stream which moves constantly, wherever it is permitted to move, toward a given goal." The metaphorical comparison of the Soviet Union with a "fluid stream" suggested a considerable degree of power. But Kennan insisted that the Soviet Union also was "tired" and exhausted from its efforts during World War II. In one of the more famous passages in the essay, Kennan compared the Soviet Union to a family in Thomas Mann's novel *Buddenbrooks*. Kennan wrote,

> Observing that human institutions often show the greatest outward brilliance at a moment when inner decay is in reality farthest advanced, he [Mann] compared the Buddenbrook family, in the days of its greatest glamour, to one of those stars whose light shines most brightly on this world when in reality it has long since ceased to exist. And who can say with assurance that the strong light still cast by the Kremlin on the dissatisfied peoples of the Western world is not the powerful afterglow of a constellation which is in actuality on the wane?

How do we explain the paradoxical depiction of the Soviet enemy in Kennan's essay? The Soviets had to be powerful; if they were not, then why should the United States need to invest potentially billions of dollars in a struggle to contain their expansionist drives? But the Soviets also had to be vulnerable; they had to appear like the star that still shines after it has burned out because that satisfied the solvency condition of Kennan's policy argument. The Soviets' vulnerability made the policy work.

Enemy construction remains a key element in contemporary public discourse. The ubiquity of enemies has generated a new rhetorical problem or *exigence*—rehabilitating an "old" enemy. We saw this problem at the end of World War II as former adversaries were transformed into worthy nations in need of assistance. A similar process was under way during the 1990s as the former Soviet Union was transformed with the end of the cold war. The ongoing processes of reconciliation in South Africa and Northern Ireland also involve a degree of enemy *re*construction. Identifying the nuances of enemy construction, as well as enemy rehabilitation, remains on the agenda of rhetorical scholars (e.g., Hart, 1998).

Notes

1. On the idea of the "enemy within," for example, see Diffley (1988, p. 408).
2. See also the entries for **other, rhetorical construction of** and **polarization.**
3. See also Smith's (1969) discussion of *objectification* in radical social **movements.**
4. Other studies that provide insight into what can be called the process of *demonization* include Dower (1986) and Keen (1991).
5. On the *dehumanization* of the enemy, see also Russell (1996).

References and Additional Reading

Aune, J. A. (1994). *Rhetoric and Marxism.* Boulder, CO: Westview.

Burke, K. (1950). *A rhetoric of motives.* New York: Prentice Hall.

Burke, K. (1957). The rhetoric of Hitler's "Battle." In K. Burke, *The philosophy of literary form.* New York: Vintage.

Cheney, G. (1983). The rhetoric of identification and the study of organizational communication. *Quarterly Journal of Speech, 69,* 143-158.

Diffley, K. (1988). "Erecting anew the standard of freedom": Salmon P. Chase's "Appeal of the Independent Democrats" and the rise of the Republican party. *Quarterly Journal of Speech, 74,* 401-415.

Dower, J. (1986). *War without mercy: Race and power in the Pacific war.* New York: Pantheon.

Edelman, M. (1988). *Constructing the political spectacle.* Chicago: University of Chicago Press.

Folena, L. (1989). Figures of violence: Philologists, witches, and Stalinistas. In N. Armstrong & L. Tennenhouse (Eds.), *The violence of representation: Literature and the history of violence.* London: Routledge.

Goldzwig, S. R. (1989). A social movement perspective on demagoguery: Achieving symbolic realignment. *Communication Studies, 40,* 202-228.

Greene, R. W. (1993). Social argumentation and the aporias of state formation: The Palestinian declaration of independence. *Argumentation and Advocacy, 29,* 124-136.

Hahn, D. F., & Gustainis, J. J. (1987). Defensive tactics in presidential rhetoric: Contemporary *topoi.* In T. Windt & B. Ingold (Eds.), *Essays in presidential rhetoric* (2nd ed.). Dubuque, IA: Kendall/Hunt.

Hart, R. P. (1998). Community by negation: An agenda for rhetorical inquiry. In J. M. Hogan (Ed.), *Rhetoric and community: Studies in unity and fragmentation.* Columbia: University of South Carolina Press.

Hitler, A. (1999). *Mein Kampf* (R. Manheim, Trans.). Boston: Houghton Mifflin.

Hogan, J. M. (1995). Demonization, public opinion, and the Gulf War. In S. Jackson (Ed.), *Argumentation and values: Proceedings of the Ninth SCA/AFA Conference on Argumentation.* Annandale, VA: Speech Communication Association.

Hogan, J. M., & Williams, L. G. (1996). Defining "the enemy" in revolutionary America: From the rhetoric of protest to the rhetoric of war. *Southern Communication Journal, 61,* 277-288.

Ivie, R. L. (1980). Images of savagery in American justifications for war. *Communication Monographs, 47,* 279-294.

Ivie, R. L. (1995). Tragic fear in the rhetorical republic: American hubris and the demonization of Saddam Hussein. In S. Jackson (Ed.), *Argumentation and values: Proceedings of the Ninth SCA/AFA Conference on Argumentation.* Annandale, VA: Speech Communication Association.

Ivie, R. L. (1996). Tragic fear and rhetorical presidency: Combating evil in the Persian Gulf. In M. J. Medhurst (Ed.), *Beyond the rhetorical presidency.* College Station: Texas A&M University Press.

Ivie, R. L. (1997). Cold war motives and the rhetorical metaphor: A framework for criticism. In M. J. Medhurst, R. L. Ivie, P. Wander, & R. L. Scott (Eds.), *Cold war rhetoric: Strategy, metaphor, and ideology* (rev. ed.). East Lansing: Michigan State University Press.

Johnson, B. (1975). Images of the enemy in intergroup conflict. *Central States Speech Journal, 26,* 84-92.

Keen, S. (1991). *Faces of the enemy: Reflections of the hostile imagination.* New York: HarperCollins.

Kertzer, D. I. (1988). *Ritual, politics, and power.* New Haven, CT: Yale University Press.

Russell, E. P., III. (1996). "Speaking of annihilation": Mobilizing for war against human and insect enemies, 1914-1945. *Journal of American History, 82,* 1505-1529.

Smith, A. (1969). *Rhetoric of black revolution.* Boston: Allyn & Bacon.

Stewart, C. J., Smith, C. A., & Denton, R. E., Jr. (1989). *Persuasion and social movements* (2nd ed.). Prospect Heights, IL: Waveland.

Vanderford, M. L. (1989). Vilification and social movements: A case study of pro-life and pro-choice rhetoric. *Quarterly Journal of Speech, 75,* 166-182.

ENTHYMEME

The **enthymeme** is, according to classicist William Grimaldi, at the "center" of Aristotle's "analysis of rhetoric" (Grimaldi, 1972, p. 84). In a well-known passage in the *Rhetoric,* Aristotle (1954) remarked that the enthymeme is the essence or "substance of rhetorical persuasion" (1354a15). But what exactly is an enthymeme? This question continues to challenge scholars in a number of academic fields, especially rhetorical studies.

For example, Conley (1984) observed,

> Most of what we read about enthymemes is alarmingly casual about the tangled history of disagreements about just what an enthymeme is. This is true even of attempts to determine the meaning of the term in a single author's *oeuvre*—Aristotle's, for instance, and indeed not the least. (p. 168)

Given the "tangled history" to which Conley alludes, is it possible to introduce any clarity on the topic in the space of a few pages? Fortunately, Conley provided some useful suggestions for how we might proceed.

Following Conley (1984), we can distinguish between two different ways of defining the enthymeme. The first approach, Conley argued, is the dominant understanding of the enthymeme, especially among rhetorical scholars.[1] Although there is not absolute unanimity among adherents to the dominant perspective,[2] Conley identified six widely shared "points of consensus" (p. 168). First, an enthymeme "is a deductive sort of argument" (p. 169). Aristotle (1954) defined the enthymeme as a "rhetorical syllogism" (1356b5), and the enthymeme and the *example* functioned as rhetorical counterparts to the logical processes of deduction and induction. Enthymemes embody a deductive movement from general to specific, whereas examples embody an inductive movement from specific to general (or, in some cases, from specific to specific). An enthymematic argument, like its logical cousin the syllogism, has three basic components (Grimaldi, 1972): two premises and a conclusion. Leff and Hewes (1981) specified that one premise (equivalent to the syllogism's minor premise) functions as a "material base" that supports the argumentative movement toward the conclusion. But the material premise must be combined with another type of premise that possesses inferential or connective potency (pp. 773-774). For example, the conclusion "vote for Candidate X" might be supported through the material premise "Candidate X is an honest person." The material premise supports the conclusion when it is combined with an inferential premise such as "honest people deserve your vote."

Enthymematic form as discussed by Grimaldi (1972), Leff and Hewes (1981), and other scholars (e.g., Jasinski, 1990) is compatible with Toulmin's (1958) data-warrant-claim "model" of practical **argument.** Toulmin now recognizes that his concept of a *warrant* as "general hypothetical statements which can act as bridges [between data and claim] and authorise the sort of step to which our particular argument commits us" (p. 98) was essentially a recovery of the Aristotelian doctrine of **topics** and, along with it, the enthymeme. In a widely cited passage, Toulmin (1983) acknowledged, "Only in retrospect is it apparent that—even though sleepwalkingly—I had rediscovered the topics of the *Topics,* which were expelled from the agenda of philosophy in the years around 1900" (p. 395; see also Bird, 1961). The form and movement of the enthymeme and the Toulmin model are essentially the same—a three-part structure that moves from material premise to a claim by way of an explicit or, in many cases, implicit general premise (Manicus, 1966; Trent, 1968).

The final point in the preceding paragraph—that general premises may at times be only implicit and not actually present in an enthymematic argument—has been a key issue over the years in defining the enthymeme. In the *Rhetoric,* Aristotle (1954) often referred to the enthymeme as truncated (1357a16, 1395b26). A substantial body of textual commentary has arisen that defines the enthymeme as an incomplete or truncated syllogism (for a discussion of this tradition of commentary, see Burnyeat, 1994; Green, 1995). The dominant contemporary view rejects this narrower definition. This was Conley's (1984) second point of consensus. He observed, "An enthymeme is not just a truncated syllogism" (p. 169).

In certain circumstances, an advocate might find it beneficial to condense his or her argument. But as Conley (1984) explained in his third point of consensus, "If an enthymeme should be expressed as a truncated syllogism, it is so expressed for practical reasons, not for formal reasons. In general, one should elide any premise that would be obvious to one's audience or otherwise risk insulting their intelligence" (p. 169). When enthymemes are truncated, or when a premise (usually the general or warranting premise) is omitted, it is up to the audience to supply it. This fourth point in the dominant understanding of the enthymeme was introduced by Bitzer (1959) in his widely read essay, "Aristotle's Enthymeme Revisited." According to Bitzer, scholars must use the expression "incomplete syllogism" carefully when defining the enthymeme. He suggested,

> To say that the enthymeme is an "incomplete syllogism"—that is, a syllogism having

> one or more suppressed premises—means that the speaker does not *lay down* his [sic] premises but lets his audience supply them out of its stock of opinion and knowledge. (p. 407)

He concluded that enthymematic arguments are constructed through the "cooperative interaction" (p. 407) of advocate and audience.[3] As Conley (1984) explained, "In Bitzer's familiar scenario, the rhetor argues A, so C, with the audience filling in the missing B to understand how the connection between A and C could be asserted" (p. 170). For example, an employee might say to his or her employer, "I do good work [A], so I deserve a raise [C]." What does the audience, in this case the employer, have to "fill in"? The employer must accept an implicit premise (B) such as "people who do 'good work' deserve a raise." If the employer does not accept a premise along these lines, believing instead that only people who do exceptional work should get raises, then the employee's enthymeme most likely will fail.

Conley's (1984) fifth and sixth points, like the third and fourth points, qualified and supplemented each other. Each focused on the materials out of which enthymematic premises are generated. According to the fifth point, "The premises of an enthymeme are probabilities, not certainties" (p. 169). As Aristotle (1954) observed, probabilities are one of the four key sources of enthymemes (1402b13). He continued, "Enthymemes based upon probabilities are those which argue from what is, or is supposed to be, usually true. . . . [A] probability is that which happens usually but not always" (1402b15-1402b23). But Conley (1984) quickly pointed out that this fifth point is, itself, not absolute. That is, enthymemes usually are constructed out of probabilities, or statements about what usually happens, but "it should be recognized that enthymemes *may* employ certainties" (p. 169). For example, the fact of human mortality, although a certainty, might have a place in an enthymematic argument over going to war or over the health risks of new technologies.

Finally, Conley's (1984) sixth point further extended the fifth point: "The premises of an enthymeme are not simply statements of probable fact but reflect values and attitudes as well. That is, enthymemes, viewed in their rhetorical context, function not just as *logos* but involve *ethos* and *pathos* as well" (p. 169; see also Grimaldi, 1972; Walker, 1992, 1994, p. 60). This sixth point challenged the long-accepted divisions among the Aristotelian **modes of proof.** The enthymeme traditionally was restricted to the realm of **logos** understood as rational proof or argument. But Conley observed that there was a growing consensus that **ethos** and logos function by way of something very much like enthymematic form. Consider the simple voting example introduced earlier, changing the first material premise. Instead of saying "X is a good person, so vote for Candidate X," an advocate might say "*I think* X is a good person, so vote for Candidate X." Ethos is an issue in both versions, but it functions in an expanded sense in the second case. In the first case, the "missing" premise is something like "good people deserve your vote." Therefore, personal character is introduced as a basis of judgment, but the particular character or ethos of the advocate is not introduced. But in the second case, the advocate relies not only on this general principle but also on his or her specific character or ethos. The "missing" premise in the second case is something like "good people deserve your vote *and* trust my judgment of who is a 'good person.' "[4] The advocate's appeal to his or her personal ethos can be reconstructed as an enthymematic argument.[5]

Conley (1984) summarized the dominant understanding in this way: "First, everyone would agree that an enthymeme is an argument. Second, everyone would agree that it is a deductive argument. Third, it should be viewed 'holistically,' i.e., as involving not just reason but feeling and action as well" (p. 169). But his aim in this essay was not merely to summarize the dominant consensus; he wanted to raise some provocative questions. Is the dominant tradition the only, or the best, way of understanding the enthymeme? Is Aristotle the only classical theorist from whom we can draw insight into the nature and function of enthymemes? Does the dominant consensus (what Conley referred to as the *deductive syllogistic paradigm*) provide an adequate account of the nature of rhetorical argument? The answers to all of these questions, Conley and a few other scholars (e.g., Green, 1995; Walker, 1994), is no. The final question that we need to consider in this entry, then, is the following: What are the key features of an alternative account of the enthymeme?

Conley's (1984) essay concentrated on the limitations of the dominant approach to the enthymeme; it only sketched an alternative. According to Conley, the dominant deductive syllogistic paradigm cannot understand or appreciate much persuasive or argumentative discourse because of its commitment to a three-part structure. He explained,

> It would appear that the success of an argument is dependent on the ability of speakers and audiences to apprehend and interpret connections and differences. It so happens that connections and differences are precisely what syllogisms are about, but only within a very narrow range of allowable predications. But metaphor and simile and abusio and arguments by analogy, even antithesis, anaphora, gradation, and, for that matter, polysyndeton and asyndeton make connections, too; and those ways of making connections are not inherently—i.e., because they do not turn on a middle term—irrational or unreasonable. (p. 182)

The deductive syllogistic account of the enthymeme, based on a three-part structure that emphasizes the "middle term" (Aristotle's "major premise" or Toulmin's "warrant"), is not the essence of persuasion, proof, or argument.

The efforts of Conley, Walker, and others to articulate an alternative, more expansive account of the enthymeme proceeded in part by rereading the history of the term. In short, they argued that Aristotle's account should *not* be privileged as the final word. Inquiry into alternative approaches to the enthymeme in ancient Greece and the subsequent evolution of rhetorical thought allowed Walker (1994) to formulate what he referred to as "a double view of enthymemes" (p. 63). Walker's double view tries to accommodate both Aristotle's view of enthymeme as "intuitive inference . . . that constitutes the substance of an argument" and a more sophistic view of enthymeme as

> a stylistically striking, kairotically opportunistic, argumentative turn that not only presents a claim but also foregrounds an inferential and attitudinal complex, a stance . . ., [and] invokes not only a premise (or warrant) as justification but [also] a "chord" of value-charged, emotively significant ideas to motivate a passional adherence [to] or identification with its stance. (p. 63)

Walker suggested that an enthymeme is the intersection of argument and style informed by the principle of *kairos* (see the entry for **decorum**) that summarizes or "caps" a stretch of discourse (cf. Conley, 1984).

Conley, Walker, and others called our attention to the essentially **polysemic** character of the enthymeme. The term lacks a single unambiguous referent. But there are specific traditions of thought that foreground certain aspects while inevitably leaving other ideas in the background. The approach that a scholar adopts toward the enthymeme probably depends on his or her purpose. The Aristotelian deductive syllogistic approach might not be that useful in teaching public speaking or composition, but it might be a valuable tool for helping to reconstruct the "reasons" embedded in a text. The Aristotelian perspective might not help an advocate *discover* a position, but it might help the advocate to *defend* a position. The sophistic approach to the enthymeme, on the other hand, will helps the rhetorical scholar to dissolve the potentially rigid opposition between the realms of **argument** and **style.** Inquiry into the complicated history of the concept and its relevance for contemporary pedagogy and criticism seems likely to continue.

Notes

1. See also Walker's (1994) discussion of the "prevailing definition" (p. 46).

2. Conley (1984) noted that some scholars "prefer a slightly more rigorous conception," whereas others "prefer an even broader and looser conception" (p. 169).

3. See also Farrell (1976, 1993) and the entry for **social knowledge.**

4. In the Toulmin model, the advocate's personal ethos might be classified as *backing.*

5. For a much more nuanced account of the relationship among enthymemes, argument, and ethos, see Garver (1994).

References and Additional Reading

Aristotle. (1954). *Rhetoric* (W. R. Roberts, Trans.). New York: Modern Library.

Arnhart, L. (1981). *Aristotle on political reasoning.* DeKalb: Northern Illinois University Press.

Bird, O. (1961). The rediscovery of the topics: Professor Toulmin's inference-warrants. *Mind, 70,* 534-539.

Bitzer, L. F. (1959). Aristotle's enthymeme revisited. *Quarterly Journal of Speech, 45,* 399-408.

Burnyeat, M. F. (1994). Enthymeme: Aristotle on the logic of persuasion. In D. J. Furley & A. Nehamas (Eds.), *Aristotle's RHETORIC: Philosophical essays.* Princeton, NJ: Princeton University Press.

Conley, T. M. (1984). The enthymeme in perspective. *Quarterly Journal of Speech, 70,* 168-187.

Cronkhite, G. L. (1966). The enthymeme as deductive rhetorical argument. *Western Journal of Speech Communication, 30,* 129-134.

Farrell, T. B. (1976). Knowledge, consensus, and rhetorical theory. *Quarterly Journal of Speech, 62,* 1-14.

Farrell, T. B. (1993). *Norms of rhetorical culture.* New Haven, CT: Yale University Press.

Fisher, W. R. (1964). Uses of the enthymeme. *Speech Teacher, 13,* 197-203.

Gage, J. T. (1991). A general theory of the enthymeme for advanced composition. In K. H. Adams & J. L. Adams (Eds.), *Teaching advanced composition: Why and how.* Portsmouth, NH: Boynton/Cook.

Garver, E. (1994). *Aristotle's RHETORIC: An art of character.* Chicago: University of Chicago Press.

Green, L. D. (1995). Aristotle's enthymeme and the imperfect syllogism. In W. B. Horner & M. Leff (Eds.), *Rhetoric and pedagogy: Its history, philosophy, and practice—Essays in honor of James J. Murphy.* Hillsdale, NJ: Lawrence Erlbaum.

Grimaldi, W. M. A. (1972). *Studies in the philosophy of Aristotle's RHETORIC.* Wiesbaden, Germany: Franz Steiner Verlag.

Harper, N. (1973). An analytic description of Aristotle's enthymeme. *Central States Speech Journal, 24,* 304-309.

Jasinski, J. (1990). An exploration of form and force in rhetoric and argumentation. In D. C. Williams & M. D. Hazen (Eds.), *Argumentation theory and the rhetoric of assent.* Tuscaloosa: University of Alabama Press.

Lanigan, R. L. (1974). Enthymeme: The rhetorical species of Aristotle's syllogism. *Southern Speech Communication Journal, 39,* 207-222.

Leff, M. C., & Hewes, D. E. (1981). Topical invention and group communication: Towards a sociology of inference. In G. Ziegelmueller & J. Rhodes (Eds.), *Dimensions of argument: Proceedings of the Second Summer Conference on Argumentation.* Annandale, VA: Speech Communication Association.

Manicus, P. T. (1966). On Toulmin's contribution to logic and argumentation. *Journal of the American Forensic Association, 3,* 83-94.

McBurney, J. H. (1936). The place of the enthymeme in rhetorical theory. *Speech Monographs, 3,* 49-74.

Miller, A. B., & Bee, J. D. (1972). Enthymemes: Body and soul. *Philosophy and Rhetoric, 5,* 201-214.

Mudd, C. S. (1959). The enthymeme and logical validity. *Quarterly Journal of Speech, 45,* 409-414.

Poster, C. (1992). A historicist recontextualization of the enthymeme. *Rhetoric Society Quarterly, 22,* 1-24.

Toulmin, S. (1958). *The uses of argument.* Cambridge, UK: Cambridge University Press.

Toulmin, S. (1983). Logic and the criticism of arguments. In J. L. Golden, G. F. Berquist, & W. E. Coleman (Eds.), *The rhetoric of Western thought* (3rd ed.). Dubuque, IA: Kendall/Hunt.

Trent, J. D. (1968). Toulmin's model of argument: An examination and extension. *Quarterly Journal of Speech, 54,* 252-259.

Walker, J. (1992). Enthymemes of anger in Cicero and Thomas Paine. In M. Secor & D. Charney (Eds.), *Constructing rhetorical education.* Carbondale: Southern Illinois University Press.

Walker, J. (1994). The body of persuasion: A theory of the enthymeme. *College English, 56,* 46-65.

Wiley, E. W. (1956). The enthymeme: Idiom of persuasion. *Quarterly Journal of Speech, 42,* 19-24.

EPIDEICTIC DISCOURSE

For all practical purposes, the genre of **epideictic discourse** was invented by Aristotle in his effort to analyze systematically the "art" of rhetoric. As Schiappa and Timmerman (1996) explained, "Prior to Aristotle, the word *epideixis* was used to designate a quality or characteristic of discourse rather than a genre of discourse." Aristotle, in their reading, sought to combine three common and distinct types of oratory into one larger generic category: the *encomium* (speeches of praise or blame for a person or an institution),[1] the *panegyric* (the "festival oration"), and the *epitaphios logos* (the eulogy or funeral oration).[2] For Aristotle, the various particular types of epideictic oratory could be collected under one broad generic heading because they typically (a) were associated with some ceremonial occasion (e.g., funeral, festival, wedding), (b) featured a display of the speaker's mastery of oratorical technique, and (c) focused in some way on the **topics** of praise and/or blame (Aristotle, 1954, 1358b12-1358b13).

Although extremely durable, the epideictic genre also has been the subject of considerable conceptual discussion and theoretical speculation over the centuries. Epideictic was routinely included as one of the three genres of rhetoric in most classical treatises on the subject. These treatises and handbooks emphasized many of the central features of Aristotle's definition, especially the idea of oratorical display and the topics of praise and blame (Chase, 1961). But even during the classical period, more complicated forms of epideictic practice can be located. Poulakos (1987), for example, noted how Isocrates's *Evagoras* was not simply a vehicle for display but also an exercise in civic and/or moral instruction.

Conceptual reflection on the category of epideictic discourse was especially intense during the latter half of the 20th century. Reviewing a number of standard accounts of the subject, Perelman and Olbrechts-Tyteca (1969) concluded, "The epid[e]ictic genre of oratory thus seemed to have more connection with literature than with argumentation" (p. 48), but they went on to attribute this state of affairs to a flawed understanding of the nature of persuasive argument that has prevented scholars from appreciating the important argumentative functions of epideictic discourse. Perelman and Olbrechts-Tyteca maintained that persuasion and argument aim at *adherence.* They wrote, "All argumentation aims at gaining the adherence of minds" (p. 14). Adherence does not, however, immediately result in audience action. For any number of reasons, the time for action may be in the future (e.g., one might listen to a speech by a political candidate and be persuaded to vote for him or her but cannot act because the election is not for two months). According to Perelman and Olbrechts-Tyteca, "the existence of an interval" in time allows complicating factors to weaken adherence. They concluded, "It is in this perspective that epid[e]ictic oratory has significance and importance for argumentation because it strengthens the disposition toward action by increasing adherence to the values it lauds" (pp. 49-50). They continued,

> Unlike the demonstration of a geometrical theorem, which establishes once and for all a logical connection between speculative truths, the argumentation in epid[e]ictic discourse sets out to increase the intensity of adherence to certain values which might not be contested when considered on their own but may nevertheless not prevail against other values that might come into conflict with them [see discussion in the entry for **value hierarchy**]. The speaker tries to establish a sense of communion centered around particular values recognized by the audience, and to this end he [sic] uses the whole range of means available to the rhetorician for purpose of amplification and enhancement. (p. 51)

In short, epideictic discourse reinforces adherence to certain *values* (e.g., liberty, charity, hard work); epideictic reinforcement preserves an existing "disposition toward action"[3] while also establishing a foundation for subsequent **advocacy** based on the reinforced values.

Perelman and Olbrechts-Tyteca's (1969) perspective on the function of epideictic discourse has had a major impact in contemporary rhetorical studies,[4] but it is by no means the only way in which the genre has been reconceptualized in recent scholarship. Like Perelman and Olbrechts-Tyteca, Oravec (1976) emphasized the way in which epideictic discourse reshapes and displays important societal values. She reached her conclusions about the genre by reflecting on what Aristotle meant when he referred to the audience for epideictic oratory as spectators or observers. In addition, Oravec noted how epideictic praise of another also can indirectly enhance the **ethos** of the speaker or writer. Beale (1978) attempted to distinguish epideictic discourse from the other traditional genres by calling attention to its performative character. Whereas **forensic** and **deliberative** discourse refers to or says "something about the world of social action," epideictic discourse engages or participates in "a significant social action in itself" (p. 225). Indirectly, Beale pointed to the important relationship between epideictic performances and the **rituals** in which they often are embedded (e.g., eulogies are an integral part of the funeral ritual, commencement speeches help to constitute the ritual of graduation). Finally, Rosenfield (1980) shed new light on the subject by probing the etymology of the generic term *epideictic.* Epideictic, Rosenfield reminded us, is derived from the Greek *epideixis,* which can be translated as "to shine or show forth. . . . More precisely, the word suggests an exhibiting or making apparent (in the sense of showing or highlighting) what might otherwise remain unnoticed or invisible" (p. 135). The true function of epideictic, therefore, is to reveal or disclose something—to bring new truths out into the open—rather than, as Perelman and Olbrechts-Tyteca argued, to reinforce existing values.[5] Rosenfield suggested that experiencing an authentic epideictic performance is akin to a religious epiphany—a revelation of a divine being. Given this account of the epideictic experience, Rosenfield acknowledged that most of the discursive specimens commonly placed in this generic category are stale and faint echoes of a more primordial form. Authentic epideictic is a rare occurrence.

In a synthetic, and sympathetic, review of much of the extent scholarly literature on this topic, Condit (1985) detected a point of convergence in current thinking about the epideictic genre.[6] The key move in Condit's discussion created two different levels of abstraction or generality for understanding the *function* of epideictic discourse.[7] First, at a very general or abstract level, Condit argued that the epideictic "family" of discourse functions to generate, sustain, or modify a community's existence. Epideictic discourse engages in the process of *communal definition* (p. 291). From micro-communities (e.g., families) to large-scale communities (e.g., nations, institutions), different forms of epideictic discourse help to hold the community together. Consider the toast made by a family member at a holiday gathering or wedding,[8] a discussion of what family members are thankful for before the start of Thanksgiving dinner, or something as simple as a child thanking his or her parents for being there during difficult times. All of these are variations on traditional epideictic themes that help to maintain a community. We see this same broad function in the epideictic discourse of corporate chief executive officers, university presidents, or religious and political leaders; a corporation, a university community, a congregation, or a nation are sustained or held together by this genre of discursive practice.

Why is epideictic discourse so important to the existence of a community, whether it be a community of two people or two million people? Communities suffer from the same problem that afflicts all physical matter—entropy. Put simply, matter disintegrates or degenerates over time, and so do communities. To keep a community together, its members have to *work* at it; few communities will last over time if its members do not act to keep it going. Some of that action is purely instrumental (e.g., maintaining financial solvency, recruiting new members). But some of that action falls into the realm of epideictic (e.g., sharing values, maintaining a common communal identity, passing on customs). Epideictic discourse helps communities to overcome the natural processes of degeneration and decay.

Is it possible to identify with more precision some of the problems that threaten communities and contribute to the inevitable problem of entropy? Condit (1985) did not address this issue directly. But one way of approaching this question seems promising. Bitzer (1968) argued that every **rhetorical situation** is shaped by some type of *exigence.* Many, and perhaps most, of the exigences that a community faces are practical questions of policy that need to be resolved through deliberative discourse. Do we raise taxes, restrict immigration, abolish social security, decriminalize certain forms of drugs, and so on? But there is another class of problems that can afflict a community, problems that are not directly resolvable through any clear policy resolution. Extending and synthesizing Bitzer and Condit, we might refer to this class of problems as *communal exigences* (see also Murphy, 1990).

What are some common types of communal exigences? One recurrent communal exigence is *value.* Communities face a problem when their core values are (or are thought to be) threatened. Contemporary public discourse in America is saturated with "values talk." Different individuals and groups see substantial threats to the nation's moral standards, our attitudes regarding the centrality of the family, and our commitment to personal responsibility. Whereas policy proposals are developed to help curb these problems, we also encounter a substantial amount of epideictic discourse—from speeches by the president to sermons at our local churches and synagogues—that encourages a *reaffirmation* of core values. Of course, any reaffirmation almost always will involve an element of definition; a community can agree on an abstract value but still run into difficulty when it comes to a more precise understanding of the value in question.

Another communal problem concerns *meaning* and *understanding.* Most communities share a *worldview* that helps its members to "make sense" of the different events in the world. Worldviews can be predominantly religious or secular, or they can combine aspects of the two. Political **ideology** might be a key factor in shaping the worldview of a particular community. Whatever its sources, a community's worldview enables its members to understand the meaning of the events that surround them. But troubling events can and do occur; such events might include natural disasters, economic catastrophes, acts of political or social violence, or dramatic shifts in the behavior of individuals or groups.[9] When these events are not explicable within the framework of the reigning worldview, they might be denied or reconstructed in ways that are conformable to the dictates of the worldview. The process of denial or reconstruction often can occur by way of epideictic discourse (e.g., a priest or minister trying to explain how an event is part of God's plan, a president trying to make sense of an economic depression). In some cases, members of the community might be identified and held responsible for a problematic event. Epideictic discourse reaffirming the worldview then merges with the process of **scapegoating.** But in some cases, denial and reconstruction are inadequate, and the worldview is called into question. In many cases, the process of questioning the existing worldview is facilitated by an emerging rival worldview (e.g., the conflict between "faith" and "science" that marked the transition from the Middle Ages to the Renaissance and modernity) and ushers in a period of discursive turmoil as adherents of the rival worldviews seek converts to their respective positions.

A third common communal exigence is *identity.* Members of a community see themselves as possessing certain characteristics or as being a particular type of "people." But this communal identity can come under attack. For example, Americans like to see themselves as a righteous people. We are not oppressors who take advantage of other people. We act out of principle and with a concern for what is right. But this self-understanding can be threatened by reflection on the nation's past history (e.g., treatment of Native Americans during the 19th century) or more recent history (e.g., our involvement in the war in Vietnam). What exactly is it that "we"—as a people—stand for? What does it mean to be an American? These are recurring questions in epideictic discourse. As Condit (1985) noted, in epideictic discourse "we constitute ourselves as good (necessarily) by ranging ourselves against 'the bad' " (p. 291). In so doing, we create an identity for our community through a process of exclusion, creating a stereotypical **other** or an **enemy** whose primary purpose is to illuminate "our" virtues. We know who "we" are in opposition to "them"; we are not like them. Similarly, what Charland (1987) referred to as **constitutive rhetoric** can be considered as a form of epideictic discourse concerned with the problem of communal identity.

Finally, communities confront the problem of *authority.* Burke (1984) argued that **hierarchy** is part of human social existence. No matter how egalitarian they might claim to be, societies or communities have some type of social structure that divides and ranks their members. Those near the top of any social hierarchy are commonly considered to be authorities, and their words carry extra force within the community (the traditional rhetorical principle of **ethos**). But hierarchies are not etched in stone; they are fluid and subject to change. When the social hierarchy is stable, the problem of authority is less likely to arise. People know who they should listen to and whose words they should respect. But during periods of flux, social authority is destabilized and it is not clear whose words should command the most respect. Doctors, lawyers, business leaders, teachers, religious leaders, social activists, celebrities, and politicians (to name a few of the relevant categories) all make claims at various times, and on various issues, to the status of authority. Past accomplishments and achievements certainly contribute in the construction of social authority. But communal authority *is* constructed, and epideictic discourse plays an important role in that process. Through epideictic discourse, a community learns who to listen to, who to respect, who to look up to as role models, and who to imitate. And community members also learn who they should not listen to and who they should not emulate.

This typology of four types of communal exigences is not exhaustive. Other recurrent problems that threaten the existence of a community can be identified. Nor are the four types described in the preceding paragraphs mutually exclusive. Problems of value, meaning/understanding, identity, and authority can overlap and combine in multiple ways. It seems likely that if a problem arises in one of these four realms, then it will have a rippling effect in the others. What the typology does is specify a bit more precisely the circumstances that make the general function of communal definition through epideictic discourse such a common practice.

Beyond the general function of communal definition, Condit (1985) also identified another level at which epideictic discourse operates. She contended, through her synthesis of the literature, that there are three more specific functions manifested in epideictic discourse. Through these more particularized functions, advocates respond to the various communal exigences and enact the broader function of communal definition. Condit described the specific functions from the perspectives of both the advocate (the speaker or writer) and the audience. The first specific function Condit labeled as "definition and understanding" (p. 288); epideictic advocates seek to define and "audiences actively seek and invite speech that performs this epideictic function when some event, person, group, or object is confusing and troubling" (p. 288). This particular epideictic function responds most directly to the communal problems of meaning/understanding and identity, but as Condit noted, enacting this function also confers "definitional authority" (p. 288) on the advocate, thereby suggesting a secondary link to the problem of authority. The second specific function is "shaping and sharing" (pp. 289-290); epideictic advocates seek to "shape" communal values that are "shared" with an audience. Through this function, "the community renews its conception of itself and of what is good" (p. 289). This particular function speaks most directly to the communal problem of value, but because this function is "interlaced" with the first function (definition/understanding), it also contributes in the areas of identity and meaning/understanding. The third specific function is "display and entertainment" (pp. 290-291); epideictic advocates seek to display "eloquence," and "the audience is 'entertained' by such a speech in a most humane manner. They [audience members] are allowed to stretch their daily experiences into meanings more grand, sweet, noble, or delightful" (p. 290). This particular function responds most directly to the communal problem of authority. Through the display of eloquence, an advocate positions himself or herself as someone to whom the community should listen.

Condit (1985) illustrated the larger process of communal definition and the more specific functions through a reading of the discourse that was part of a key ritual in colonial Boston—the Boston Massacre orations. As further illustration, consider John F. Kennedy's acceptance speech at the 1960 Democratic Convention. Acceptance speeches, like inaugural addresses (Campbell & Jamieson, 1990; Fields, 1996), are largely epideictic in nature. They tend to emphasize a candidate's "vision" for the national community (and are not focused on deliberative or policy issues). In short, they are a prime example of the general epideictic function of communal definition. And Kennedy's 1960 speech was no exception. His definition of the American community was encapsulated in the central *metaphor* of the "new frontier." But to appreciate the way in which the metaphor works, we need to consider the range of communal exigences that Kennedy identified. All four exigences noted previously surfaced during the speech. With respect to the problem of value, Kennedy noted the "slippage . . . [of] moral strength . . ., the payola mentality, the expense account way of life, [and] the confusion between what is legal and what is right." In terms of the problem of meaning/understanding, Kennedy itemized the numerous changes—literal and metaphoric "revolutions"—taking place around the world and at home with which Americans had to come to grips. With respect to the problem of identity, Kennedy noted how "too many Americans have lost their way, their will, and their sense of historic purpose"—in short, their sense of what it meant to be an American. Finally, given its role in a political campaign, Kennedy's speech very explicitly raised the issue of authority: To whose vision—his or Richard Nixon's—should the American people listen?

Although Kennedy's speech addressed these problems in different ways, for illustration purposes, we can concentrate on the "new frontier" metaphor and how it enacted the narrower epideictic functions of define/create understanding and shaping/sharing. First, the metaphor transformed a world of troubling changes into a new challenge for Americans to master. As Kennedy noted, "The new frontier of which I speak is not a set of promises—it is a set of challenges." Second, the metaphor restored a sense of identity. Kennedy called on Americans to become "new pioneers on that new frontier." Third, the metaphor authorized an *antithetical* structure through which Kennedy privileged certain values (e.g., sacrifice, the common good) while disparaging others (e.g., complacency, the status quo). Finally, Kennedy insisted that to conquer the new frontier, Americans had to be "young in heart, regardless of age." As part of the struggle for social authority, Kennedy linked Nixon with the past and what was old (thereby "de-authorizing" Nixon) while linking himself with the frontier spirit of youth and vigor. The metaphor (along with the countless other aspects of the "display" function) enacted Kennedy's eloquence and established his authority.

The traditional category of epideictic discourse, as the preceding discussion demonstrates, remains an object of theoretical and conceptual dispute. What seems equally clear is that even though scholars might not have reached a clear consensus on how to define it, epideictic practices continue to flourish. So long as that remains the case, the category of epideictic discourse will occupy an important place in contemporary rhetorical studies.

Notes

1. See also Schiappa (1995).
2. On funeral oratory, see also Loraux (1986). On the various types of ceremonial or epideictic oratory in ancient Greece, see Burgess (1902) and Kennedy (1963).
3. Social scientists sometimes refer to this as an *inoculation effect*.
4. For example, Crable and Vibbert (1983) and Bostdorff and Vibbert (1994) extended it into the realm of corporate discourse.
5. On a somewhat similar note, Sullivan (1993) concluded that the experience of "true epideictic discourse" occurs "when rhetor and audience enter the timeless, consubstantial space carved out by their mutual contemplation of reality" (p. 128).
6. It is worth noting that Condit's (1985) argument is an illustration of a *condensed* **definition.**
7. On the idea of different levels of abstraction or generality, see the entry for **genre.**
8. The ancient Greeks even had a term for a speech at a wedding—*gamelion.*
9. Campbell (1984) suggested that human mortality is an "ultimate" exigence (p. 236).

References and Additional Reading

Aristotle. (1954). *Rhetoric* (W. R. Roberts, Trans.). New York: Modern Library.

Beale, W. H. (1978). Rhetorical performative discourse: A new theory of epideictic. *Philosophy and Rhetoric, 11,* 221-245.

Bitzer, L. (1968). The rhetorical situation. *Philosophy and Rhetoric, 1,* 1-14.

Bostdorff, D. M., & Vibbert, S. L. (1994). Values advocacy: Enhancing organizational images, deflecting public criticism, and grounding future argument. *Public Relations Review, 20,* 141-158.

Burgess, T. C. (1902). *Epideictic literature* (Studies in Classical Philology, No. 3). Chicago: University of Chicago Press.

Burke, K. (1984). *Permanence and change: An anatomy of purpose* (3rd ed.). Berkeley: University of California Press.

Campbell, J. A. (1984). A rhetorical interpretation of history. *Rhetorica, 2,* 227-266.

Campbell, K. K., & Jamieson, K. H. (1990). *Deeds done in words: Presidential rhetoric and the genres of governance.* Chicago: University of Chicago Press.

Charland, M. (1987). Constitutive rhetoric: The case of the *peuple Québécois. Quarterly Journal of Speech, 73,* 133-150.

Chase, J. R. (1961). The classical conception of epideictic. *Quarterly Journal of Speech, 47,* 293-300.

Condit, C. M. (1985). The functions of epideictic: The Boston Massacre orations as exemplar. *Communication Quarterly, 33,* 284-299.

Crable, R. E., & Vibbert, S. L. (1983). Mobil's epideictic advocacy: "Observations" of Prometheus-bound. *Communication Monographs, 50,* 380-394.

Fields, W. (1996). *Union of words: A history of presidential eloquence.* New York: Free Press.

Kennedy, G. (1963). *The art of persuasion in ancient Greece.* Princeton, NJ: Princeton University Press.

Loraux, N. (1986). *The invention of Athens: The funeral oration in the classical city* (A. Sheridan, Trans.). Cambridge, MA: Harvard University Press.

Murphy, J. M. (1990). "A time of shame and sorrow": Robert F. Kennedy and the American jeremiad. *Quarterly Journal of Speech, 76,* 401-414.

Oravec, C. (1976). "Observation" in Aristotle's theory of epideictic. *Philosophy and Rhetoric, 9,* 162-173.

Perelman, C., & Olbrechts-Tyteca, L. (1969). *The new rhetoric: A treatise on argumentation* (J. Wilkinson & P. Weaver, Trans.). Notre Dame, IN: University of Notre Dame Press.

Poulakos, T. (1987). Isocrates's use of narrative in the *Evagoras:* Epideictic rhetoric and moral action. *Quarterly Journal of Speech, 73,* 317-328.

Rosenfield, L. W. (1980). The practical celebration of epideictic. In E. E. White (Ed.), *Rhetoric in transition: Studies in the nature and uses of rhetoric.* University Park: Pennsylvania State University Press.

Schiappa, E. (1995). Gorgias' Helen revisited. *Quarterly Journal of Speech, 81,* 310-324.

Schiappa, E., & Timmerman, D. (1996, November). *Aristotle's disciplining of epideictic.* Paper presented at the meeting of the Speech Communication Association, San Diego.

Sullivan, D. L. (1993). The ethos of epideictic encounter. *Philosophy and Rhetoric, 26,* 113-133.

EPISTEME

The Greek term **episteme** usually is translated as either "knowledge" (Ijsseling, 1976; Kennedy, 1991) or "science" (Havelock, 1963). Beginning with Plato, the idea of episteme was juxtaposed to the idea of **doxa.** This contrast was one of the key means by which Plato fashioned his powerful critique of rhetoric (Ijsseling, 1976; Hariman, 1986). For Plato, episteme was an expression of, or a statement that conveys, *absolute certainty* (Havelock, 1963, p. 34; see also Scott, 1967) or a means for producing such expressions or statements. Doxa, on the other hand, was a decidedly inferior expression of opinion or probability.

In the dialogue "Gorgias," Plato (1892) advanced the contrast between episteme and doxa and used this contrast to support his condemnation of sophistic rhetoric (for a review of some of the different readings of Plato's critique of rhetoric, see Black, 1958). In his well-known analogies, Plato likened rhetorical practice to cookery and cosmetics, or sham or pseudo-arts, in comparison to "real" arts such as medicine and gymnastics. As Hariman (1986) observed, there is a **dissociative** logic embedded in Plato's critique that arranges episteme and doxa in a hierarchy. Doxa, and with it rhetoric, gets relegated to the inferior realm of *appearances,* whereas episteme, and with it Plato's vision of the philosophic life, is placed in the superior position associated with *reality.*

As many scholars have noted, Plato's critique of rhetoric has posed a continuing challenge for the tradition of rhetorical studies. The key question, as scholars such as Hariman (1986) and Scott (1967) have suggested, is the following: What possibilities for rhetoric—as both a theory and the practice of discourse—might exist in a world committed to the Platonic ideal of episteme? Scott argued that the possibilities for rhetoric in such a world are rather "limited" (p. 10). A world committed to the ideal of episteme is a world of clear and fixed truth, absolute certainty, and stable knowledge. The only possibility for rhetoric in such a world would be to "make truth effective" (see also Weaver, 1953). A radical gulf is presumed to exist between *discovering* truth (the province of philosophy or science) and the lesser task of *disseminating* it (the province of rhetoric). Conceptualizing rhetoric as a collection of devices for "dressing up" truth and knowledge, or making it more interesting for an audience, guarantees rhetoric's status as a "supplement" to philosophy (on the tradition of conceptualizing rhetoric as a supplement, see Gaonkar, 1990).

Do we live in a world committed to a Platonic ideal of episteme, or have we abandoned the quest for absolute certainty? It is impossible to provide any "absolute" answer to this question. The general drift in rhetorical studies parallels the broader movement in areas such as philosophy and the philosophy of science (Brummett, 1976; Rorty, 1979). As Bernstein (1983) observed,

> The confusion and uncertainty in philosophy exhibits and reflects a phenomenon that is characteristic of our intellectual and cultural life. In the entire range of the human and social sciences, we have witnessed the playing out of bold attempts to secure foundations and the elaboration of new methods that promise genuine knowledge, followed by a questioning that reveals cracks and crevices in what had been taken to be solid and secure. There seems to be almost a rush to embrace various forms of relativism. (p. 3)

Most rhetorical scholars would follow Scott (1967) in "rejecting prior and enabling truth as the epistemological basis for rhetoric" (p. 12). In rejecting episteme, "genuine knowledge," and the Platonic critique of rhetoric, contemporary rhetorical scholarship appears to have joined the rush to embrace relativism (Croasmun & Cherwitz, 1982). But this rejection also can be viewed as a quest to identify and conceptualize the positive and constructive possibilities of rhetoric in a world no longer organized by the ideal of episteme. Instead of seeing rhetoric as governed by episteme, most rhetorical scholars now subscribe to some version of the idea of rhetoric as **epistemic.**

References and Additional Reading

Bernstein, R. J. (1983). *Beyond objectivism and relativism: Science, hermeneutics, and praxis.* Philadelphia: University of Pennsylvania Press.

Black, E. (1958). Plato's view of rhetoric. *Quarterly Journal of Speech, 44,* 361-374.

Brummett, B. (1976). Some implications of "process" or "intersubjectivity": Postmodern rhetoric. *Philosophy and Rhetoric, 9,* 21-51.

Croasmun, E., & Cherwitz, R. A. (1982). Beyond rhetorical relativism. *Quarterly Journal of Speech, 68,* 1-16.

Gaonkar, D. P. (1990). Rhetoric and its double: Reflections on the rhetorical turn in the human sciences. In H. W. Simons (Ed.), *The rhetorical turn: Invention and persuasion in the conduct of inquiry.* Chicago: University of Chicago Press.

Hariman, R. (1986). Status, marginality, and rhetorical theory. *Quarterly Journal of Speech, 72,* 38-54.

Havelock, E. A. (1963). *Preface to Plato.* Cambridge, MA: Harvard University Press.

Ijsseling, S. (1976). *Rhetoric and philosophy in conflict: An historical survey* (P. Dunphy, Trans.). The Hague, Netherlands: Martinus Nijhoff.

Kennedy, G. A. (1991). *Aristotle, on Rhetoric: A theory of civic discourse.* New York: Oxford University Press.

Plato. (1892). Gorgias. In Plato, *The dialogues of Plato* (Vol. 2, 3rd ed., B. Jowett, Trans.). London: Oxford University Press.

Rorty, R. (1979). *Philosophy and the mirror of nature.* Princeton, NJ: Princeton University Press.

Scott, R. L. (1967). On viewing rhetoric as epistemic. *Central States Speech Journal, 18,* 9-17.

Weaver, R. (1953). *The ethics of rhetoric.* South Bend, IN: Regnery/Gateway.

EPISTEME (IN FOUCAULT)

The French historian and theorist Michel Foucault appropriated the Greek word for knowledge, *episteme,* and deployed it as a central concept in his *archaeological* method of **discourse** analysis (for an overview of this method, see Dreyfus & Rabinow, 1983). As Dreyfus and Rabinow (1983) and others have noted, the concept of **episteme** figured prominently in Foucault's analysis of the discourse of the human sciences (in *The Order of Things* [Foucault, 1970]). But it was in *The Archaeology of Knowledge* (Foucault, 1972) that Foucault provided an explicit definition.

Foucault developed his definition tentatively. After acknowledging that his project involved "the analysis of the *episteme,*" Foucault (1972) wrote,

> This episteme may be suspected of being something like a worldview, a slice of history common to all branches of knowledge, which imposes on each one the same norms and postulates, a general stage of reason, a certain structure of thought that the men [sic] of a particular period cannot escape—a great body of legislation written once and for all by some anonymous hand. (p. 191)

This *approximate* definition begins to provide readers with a sense of the concept, but the approximation is flawed. In what way? Foucault himself was not explicit, but commentators (e.g., O'Quinn, 1993) have provided a potential explanation. Conceptualizing episteme along the lines of a worldview (an English translation of the German term *Weltanschauung*) suggests a type of unity, something like a "spirit of the age" or "spirit of the culture," that Foucault found problematic. Foucault was looking for order or structure, but he wanted to differentiate his sense of it from, in his view, the more traditional ideas of unity or a definitive center. His more precise account of episteme helped him to do that.

Foucault's (1972) language shifted as he began his more precise definition (the shift to a more abstract and rather technical idiom, compared to the approximate definition, might reflect his desire to develop a detached and autonomous method).[1] He wrote,

> By *episteme,* we mean, in fact, the total set of relations that unite, at a given period, the discursive practices that give rise to epistemological figures, sciences, and possibly formalized systems. . . . The episteme is not a form of knowledge or type of rationality which, crossing the boundaries of the

> most varied sciences, manifests the sovereign unity of a subject, a spirit, or a period; it is the totality of relations that can be discovered, for a given period, between the sciences when one analyzes them at the level of discursive regularities. (p. 191)

Dreyfus and Rabinow (1983) summarized Foucault's definition of episteme as an "epistemic system" (p. 18). Foss and Gill (1987) wrote that "an episteme . . . is a characteristic order that defines the discourse for a period" (p. 386). Blair and Cooper (1987) described it as "the historical epistemologies that characterize discursive formations" (p. 164). What makes the concept difficult to grasp, in part, is its somewhat *oxymoronic* quality; an episteme is the order or structure that lies underneath a plethora of discursive practices, but this order or structure lacks any ultimate unity. An episteme is a type of "decentered center" that shapes, or enables and constrains, the discourse of a period.

Foucault's concept of episteme emerged as part of an effort to study the discourse of science, especially the human sciences such as psychology, sociology, and linguistics. Its relevance to rhetorical studies is, in part, in the way that it buttresses the growing disciplinary movement that views rhetoric or discourse practice as **epistemic** (the implications of Foucault's thinking on this topic were explored by Foss & Gill, 1987). Scientific discourse establishes, enacts or reenacts, and (in some cases) challenges or subverts the reigning "epistemic system" or episteme.[2] Foucault's (1972) account of scientific discourse acknowledged, if only indirectly, its rhetorical character. More broadly, Foucault's discussion of the episteme, and related concepts such as "rules of exclusion" and "rules serving to control discourse" (discussed in the essay, "The Discourse on Language," reprinted in *The Archaeology of Knowledge* [Foucault, 1972]), highlights the various forces that both enable and constrain discursive practice. Even if, as Dreyfus and Rabinow (1983) argued, Foucault's later analyses were "no longer systematized in terms of the formation rules of the episteme" (p. 199), something of its "spirit" (for lack of a better term) remained in Foucault's interest in understanding the forces that shape and structure discursive practice. Concepts such as the episteme challenge rhetorical scholars to come to grips with the range of forces that enable and constrain situated discursive practice, even if these forces cannot be systematically described and interrelated (see, e.g., Blair, 1987).

Notes

1. On this point, see Dreyfus and Rabinow's (1983) discussion of "the methodological failure of archaeology" (p. 79).

2. Foucault's conceptualization of the structure and dynamics of epistemic systems resembles, as Dreyfus and Rabinow (1983) and others have noted, Kuhn's (1970) ideas about *paradigms* and their role in organizing scientific enterprises.

References and Additional Reading

Blair, C. (1987). The statement: Foundation of Foucault's historical criticism. *Western Journal of Speech Communication, 51,* 364-383.

Blair, C., & Cooper, M. (1987). The humanist turn in Foucault's rhetoric of inquiry. *Quarterly Journal of Speech, 73,* 151-171.

Dreyfus, H. L., & Rabinow, P. (1983). *Michel Foucault: Beyond structuralism and hermeneutics* (2nd ed.). Chicago: University of Chicago Press.

Foss, S. K., & Gill, A. (1987). Michel Foucault's theory of rhetoric as epistemic. *Western Journal of Speech Communication, 51,* 384-401.

Foucault, M. (1970). *The order of things: An archaeology of the human sciences.* New York: Pantheon.

Foucault, M. (1972). *The archaeology of knowledge* (A. M. Sheridan Smith, Trans.). New York: Pantheon.

Kuhn, T. S. (1970). *The structure of scientific revolutions* (2nd ed.). Chicago: University of Chicago Press.

O'Quinn, D. (1993). Episteme. In I. R. Makaryk (Ed.), *Encyclopedia of contemporary literary theory: Approaches, scholars, terms.* Toronto: University of Toronto Press.

EPISTEMIC, RHETORIC AS

To paraphrase Scott (1993), in one form or another, the question of rhetoric's **epistemic** status has haunted the tradition of rhetorical studies for two and a half millennia (p. 122). To understand how the tradition of rhetorical studies has been haunted by this question and to appreciate the way in which contemporary scholars have responded to this predicament, we need to be clear about the question: What do scholars mean when they talk about "rhetoric's epistemic status"? Let us begin with the term *epistemic,* an adjective derived from the noun *epistemology.*

What is epistemology? Hamlyn (1967) wrote,

> Epistemology, or the theory of knowledge, is that branch of philosophy which is concerned with the nature and scope of knowledge, its presuppositions and basis, and the general reliability of claims to knowledge. . . . Epistemology differs from psychology in that it is not concerned with why men [sic] hold the beliefs that they do or with the ways in which they come to hold them. . . . The epistemologist . . . is concerned not with whether or how we can be said to know some particular truth but with whether we are justified in claiming knowledge of some whole class of truths [e.g., scientific] or, indeed, whether knowledge is possible at all. (pp. 8-9)

The final subordinate clause alerts us to an important issue. As Hamlyn noted, epistemology becomes necessary as a response to skepticism about the possibility of knowledge. He wrote,

> It is no coincidence that epistemology began in the context of a form of the Sophists' general skepticism about knowledge, for until such doubts had been raised, the possibility of knowledge was bound to be taken for granted. Once the doubts had been raised, they had to be answered. (p. 9)

Why is epistemology a relevant concern for rhetorical scholars? To answer this question, we need to return to the historical context that helped to generate rhetorical and philosophical thinking or rhetorical and philosophical ways of living in the world. The Sophists' skepticism, noted by Hamlyn, was connected to their advocacy of rhetoric; many key Sophists (e.g., Gorgias) were teachers and practitioners of the emerging "art" of rhetoric. At the risk of oversimplification, the sophistic attitude might be summed up as follows: People cannot, in any ultimate sense, determine knowledge or truth, but they can make determinations about what is better or worse for them and their community. Rhetoric became crucial for the Sophists because it was a means for making determinations of what was better and what was worse.[1] Plato's attack on the Sophists in works such as the "Gorgias" (Plato, 1892) focused heavily on their skeptical or relativistic approach to knowledge. Plato argued that rhetorical practice was dangerous precisely because it was based on **doxa** (unreliable opinion) and not **episteme** (truth or knowledge). As Hariman (1986) noted, "The division central to the conflict between philosophy and rhetoric has been that between *episteme* and *doxa,* knowledge and opinion" (p. 48).[2] Over time, the terms might have changed, but the conflict remains essentially unchanged. Bernstein (1983) affirmed this point when he remarked, "The *agon* between objectivists and relativists has been with us ever since the origins of Western philosophy or at least from the time of Plato's attack on the Sophists and on Protagoras's alleged relativism" (p. 8).[3] (The terms *objectivist* and *relativist* are important to the disciplinary **debate** over rhetoric's epistemic status and will be discussed more fully later in the entry.)

Plato's "victory" in the ancient Greek "culture wars" shaped the dominant **tradition** of Western thought with respect to rhetoric's epistemic status.[4] In the context of this dominant tradition, rhetoric had no epistemic status. Rhetorical practice did not proceed from, nor did it produce, reliable knowledge. Rhetorical theory was, similarly, epistemically bankrupt; rhetoric was not a true art but rather just a knack or a randomly organized collection of techniques. Over the centuries, defenders of rhetoric had to adjust to the dominant tradition. That adjustment is captured, Scott (1967) suggested, in the idea that rhetoric's function is to "make the truth effective" (p. 10). Weaver (1953) endorsed such a view when he wrote, "What rhetoric accomplishes is to take any dialectically secured position . . . and show its relationship to the world of prudential conduct" (pp. 27-28). Perelman (1982) detected this tendency as well. He maintained that philosophers "grant, at best, only a rhetoric which serves to propagate the truths guaranteed to speakers through intuition or self-evidence" (p. 7). Having no epistemic status, rhetoric exists as the handmaiden, or the supplement (Gaonkar, 1990), of truth and knowledge. It is tolerated because it promises to help those with access to knowledge lead the ignorant or the unenlightened. But toleration does not translate into a positive evaluation of rhetoric; it was considered, at best, a necessary evil.

The dominant "objectivist" tradition inaugurated by Plato has, over the past few decades, been subjected to increasing criticism. What are the central tenets of the objectivist, or "modern" (Leff, 1978), tradition? Bernstein (1983) provided the following summary:

> By "objectivism," I mean the basic conviction that there is or must be some permanent, ahistorical matrix or framework to which we can ultimately appeal in determining the nature of rationality, knowledge, truth, reality, goodness, or rightness. . . . Objectivism is closely related to foundationalism and the search for an Archimedean point. The objectivist maintains that unless we can ground philosophy, knowledge, or language in a rigorous manner, we cannot avoid radical skepticism [or relativism]. (p. 8)

Bernstein acknowledged that there are many "species" of objectivism (as he opted to use the term). Consequently, individual philosophers or philosophical positions that differ in many respects are gathered together under his definition. Bernstein suggested that the thread connecting this diverse group is the quest for certainty (see also Scott, 1967) and the desire to locate an ultimate ground that will guarantee knowledge.

The objectivist tradition is being challenged, Bernstein argued, by an emerging form of intellectual relativism (with deep historic roots). He wrote,

> [Its] basic conviction [is] that when we turn to the examination of those concepts that philosophers have taken to be the most fundamental—whether it is the concept of rationality, truth, reality, right, the good, or norms—we are forced to recognize that in the final analysis all such concepts must be understood as relative to a specific conceptual scheme, theoretical framework, paradigm, form of life, society, or culture.... For the relativist, there is no substantive overarching framework or single metalanguage by which we can rationally adjudicate or univocally evaluate competing claims of alternative paradigms. (p. 8)

Whereas the objectivist either sees or searches for a fixed ground or a firm place to stand so as to determine what is true or what is good, the relativist sees constant motion, variation, and perpetual **contingency**. The emergence of the rhetoric as epistemic position must be understood in terms of both the founding conflict between **episteme** and **doxa** and its more recent manifestation in the struggle between objectivism and relativism.

The idea that rhetoric might possess epistemic status in some important way is, Leff (1978) wrote, "a radical break from the modern tradition" of rhetorical theory and philosophy (p. 77). In Scott's (1967) groundbreaking essay, the path to epistemic status begins with a rejection of "prior and enabling truth as the epistemological basis for a rhetoric" (p. 12). In rejecting episteme, Scott thereby rejected the traditional role of rhetoric as a handmaiden for truth and knowledge. Rhetorical practice *does more* than dress up truth and knowledge in fancy clothes. Scott wrote that rhetoric "may be viewed not as a matter of giving effectiveness to truth but of creating truth" (p. 13; see also Scott, 1976, 1993). If truth is "created" and not merely discovered, then it must be "contingent" (Scott, 1967, p. 16). Scott (1993) insisted, "Rhetoric is epistemic, then, if one takes truth as existing in time and, as such, is like all that exists in time, changing, becoming in some way different" (p. 128).

Important theoretical formulations in any academic discipline tend to generate controversy. The introduction of the idea that "rhetoric is epistemic" illustrates this general rule. Existing reviews of the literature (e.g., Bineham, 1990; Leff, 1978) have identified a number of nuanced positions in the disciplinary contest over rhetoric's epistemic status. Most participants and reviewers tend to agree that the controversy centers on a basic opposition between *objectivist* and *consensus* camps, with these camps being variations on the historical episteme-doxa tension and the more recent objectivist-relativist tension just noted. We need to probe the particular positions of each of these camps to develop an adequate understanding of the epistemic debate.

Scott's reversal of rhetoric's traditional "status" (Hariman, 1986) maintained that rhetoric is a vehicle for creating truth. Once rhetoric is understood as a creative force in human affairs, its creative energy can be expanded; rhetoric not only creates truth, it also creates "reality." This position was argued most clearly by one of Scott's students, Barry Brummett, in his influential essay, "Some Implications of 'Process' or 'Intersubjectivity' " (Brummett, 1976). Brummett (1976) maintained that "reality is meaning" (pp. 29-31). Where does meaning come from? One traditional answer is from sense experience, but Brummett subverted this view claiming that "sensation alone is *meaningless*" (p. 28). So, "if things do not take meaning from an objective reality [that stimulates our senses], then they must take meaning from other components in the system of which they are a part" (p. 29). Reality is not fixed and immutable; it is not a ground for truth or knowledge. Reality is in flux, or in a "process" of becoming, and it is temporarily fixed, or made understandable and meaningful, through human effort. For Brummett, reality is one of the most significant ways in which humans make reality meaningful. Brummett concluded, "While rhetoric may be defined in many ways and on many levels, it is in the deepest and most fundamental sense the *advocacy of realities*" (p. 31).[5]

Brummett's (1976) position was part of a larger intellectual development often referred to as *social constructionism.*[6] Constructivists such as Brummett want to place their views in a *middle ground* between a rigid commitment to objectivity (where knowledge or truth is determined by an objective reality) and an essentially solipsistic subjectivity (where isolated individuals determine their own truth and reality). That middle ground is contained in Brummett's idea of *intersubjectivity.* We do not experience reality as isolated individuals (even if we are lost in a forest by ourselves); rather, we experience it as part of a human community. Brummett insisted that reality is *shared.* He continued, "The shared nature of this reality is quite important. Participation in shared meanings [is a requisite] for participation in society; madness is by definition an inability to share conventional meanings" (p. 31). Reality is constructed or created through discourse *within a community.* In the final analysis, it is the community that endows reality with meaning. Truth, knowledge, and reality all are a matter of communal consensus. The emphasis on communal consensus gives rhetoric a double function; discourse not only "works up" descriptions of reality (Potter, 1996) but also solicits agreement from a community. Brummett (1976) concluded, "A worldview in which truth is agreement *must* have rhetoric at its heart, for agreement is gained in no other way" (p. 35).

The constructivism inherent in Scott's initial essay (Scott, 1967) and more explicitly present in Brummett (1976) can be, and has been, criticized in different ways (e.g., Orr, 1978). Potter (1996) labeled one common objection the "furniture argument" (p. 7).[7] Variations on this argument are employed by those in the objectivist camp against Brummett's claims (Cherwitz, 1977; Cherwitz & Hikins, 1983, 1986; Croasmun & Cherwitz, 1982). What Potter (1996) referred to as the furniture argument runs something like this. An advocate either points to (in the context of a public forum such as a seminar or lecture) or makes reference to an ordinary item of furniture (e.g., a desk, a chair) and demands that the supporters of the constructionist position explain how discourse has constructed or created that specific physical object (walls work nicely as well in this argument, as objectivists are fond of challenging constructivists to alter the composition of a wall linguistically so that they can walk through it). Although the furniture argument might appear simplistic, it raises a number of important issues. One of the key points that objectivists make against the consensus or constructivist position is that constructivists typically confuse or inappropriately conflate epistemology (extended to include questions of understanding and meaning) and ontology (the study of the nature of reality). Croasmun and Cherwitz (1982), for example, remarked that "the meaning we attach to an object does not, in any sense, change the *ontological character of that object*" (p. 6). In short, we can talk all we want about, and assign whatever meaning we want to, the wall or the table, but our talk will not alter the "ontological character"—the "reality"—of those material objects.

Croasmun and Cherwitz's (1982) discussion of the "impingement of reality" (pp. 4-6) raised an important issue that, Wess (1996) suggested, constructivists have not focused on sufficiently: What are the limits of the constructive powers or the creative capacity of language and discursive practice? Burke (1984), in his discussion of the idea of **recalcitrance,** is one thinker with constructionist tendencies who tried to engage this problem. Brummett (1982) appealed to Burke's notion in his response to Croasmun and Cherwitz's (1982) critique of his consensus position. Brummett (1982) wrote, "Consensus theorists *postulate* that [it is] reality = meaning + something else that causes recalcitrance. It is convenient to refer to that something else as the physical component of reality" (p. 425). Although one might bump into a "physical component of reality" or have a "physical component of reality" hit him or her in the head, one cannot know anything about that physical component (what Croasmun & Cherwitz [1982] referred to as its "ontological characteristics") "except through symbolic mediation." Brummett (1982) argued, "Even a blow to the head will be instantly strained through a symbolic net; the victim will *make something of it*" (p. 425). Along similar lines, Railsback (1983) responded to Croasmun and Cherwitz's point about the "impingement of reality" by arguing that "the fact that objective reality 'exists' does not entail the existence of objective truths" (p. 353). Many constructivists will follow Burke in recognizing the way in which material conditions (Railsback) or physical components (Brummett) can function as *constraints* on human discourse without granting the objectivists' claim that material conditions or physical components completely determine truth or what we can know about the objects in the world.

Although objectivists such as Cherwitz, Hikins, and Croasmun have strived for precision in the development of their critiques of constructionism, there is a degree of slippage in the way in which they formulated their views that has resulted in some confusion. For example, Cherwitz and Hikins (1983) offered the "independence of reality" as a central postulate of their position on rhetoric's epistemic status (from a different ideological perspective, see also Cloud, 1994). They wrote, "In experience there is presented to us, directly, a world of phenomena largely independent of our attitudes, beliefs, and values. This postulate . . . is sustained by the overwhelming persistence of the belief that reality exists independent of our consciousness of it" (p. 251, emphasis removed from original). As this passage reads, the thesis that (a) objects in the world are presented directly to consciousness is made equivalent to the thesis that (b) reality exists independent of consciousness. Reality might exist independent of consciousness, but it does not follow that reality therefore presents itself *directly* to consciousness. Brummett (1982) wrote,

> We perceive the sun, earth, rocks, and trees through meanings and symbols that produce these "objects" *as* animate or inanimate, hiding places of the gods or profane objects, threatening or beneficial or neutral in their effects upon us, of greater or lesser value than other "objects" in the world. (p. 426)

Brummett took a self-confessed "agnostic stand towards an independent, objective reality" (p. 425), although we might wonder about how "agnostic" he would be when hit on the head by a rock. But the rock that hits Brummett on the head is nevertheless inextricably intertwined in a web of symbols and communal meanings; although the rock might land on his head, it does not present itself *directly* to his consciousness. The rock exists independently of Brummett's consciousness, but it does not present itself directly to his consciousness.

A similar view was articulated by the postmodern political theorists Ernesto Laclau and Chantel Mouffe. They wrote,

> The fact that every object is constituted as an object of discourse has *nothing to do* with whether there is a world external to thought or with the realism/idealism opposition. An earthquake or the falling of a brick is an event that certainly exists in the sense that it occurs here and now, independently of my will. But whether their specificity as objects is constructed in terms of "natural phenomena" or "expressions of the wrath of God" depends upon the structuring of a discursive field. What is denied is not that such objects exist externally to thought but the rather different assertion that they could constitute themselves as objects outside any discursive condition of emergence. (Laclau & Mouffe, 1985, p. 108)

This point might be summarized as follows: Objects external to the individual and community exist, and they impose *constraints* to a greater or lesser degree on human action and decision making, but such objects enter consciousness—the individual's as well as that inchoate idea of the public consciousness—through discourse, language, and rhetorical practice (see also Hasian, 1996).

One of the **argument** strategies employed by objectivists such as Cherwitz, Hikins, and Croasmun is to deny the viability of the *middle ground* that consensus scholars try to occupy. Cherwitz and Hikins (1983), for example, removed the middle ground by reducing the idea of *intersubjectivity* to the narrower notion of *subjectivity.* They wrote,

> The problem with the [consensus] view . . . is that it is inherently *solipsistic.* In the absence of any account establishing the *objective* existence of *other subjects,* intersubjectivity collapses altogether. . . . In sum, *inter*subjectivity reduces to solipsism and hence to subjectivity, for if meaning determines reality, [then] it is just as likely that the world is a product of the *intra*personal communication within *a* mind (subjectivity) as it is of *inter*personal communication among several minds (intersubjectivity). (p. 254)

Eminent rhetorical advocates such as Abraham Lincoln seemed to understand that middle grounds are unstable and precarious. Cherwitz and Hikins exploited the precariousness of intersubjectivity to argue that the consensus position is untenable.

Cherwitz and Hikins (1983) acknowledged that there are qualified or restricted versions of the consensus position. Some scholars, such as Carleton (1978), argue a nonrestricted position: All knowledge is discursively constituted through rhetorical practice. But other scholars, most notably Farrell (1976, 1978) in his idea of **social knowledge,** restrict the constructionist thesis. Farrell distinguished between *technical knowledge* of external objects produced through the procedures of science and *social knowledge* of *human reality* (the realm of values, ideals, etc.) produced through rhetorical practice. But Cherwitz and Hikins (1983) found the distinction between two realms to be problematic and labeled Farrell's project as a form of "mitigated subjectivism" that did not escape the problem of solipsism (pp. 254-255). Cherwitz and Hikins insisted that

> all objects of experience, including the objects of scientific inquiry as well as such characteristics as "good," "bad," "justice," "virtue," and the like, are endowed with a similar *ontological* status; they all *exist* and are all *entities* in the world of nature. (p. 258)

Cherwitz, Hikins, and Croasmun expended considerable effort to reveal the subjectivist and, in their view, solipsistic implications of the consensus position. They did so to warn scholars of the dangers inherent in the *relativism* of consensus or constructivist thinking. The question of relativism is perhaps the most important issue in the rhetoric as epistemic debate. Scott seemed to perceive the importance of this issue from the outset. His initial essay (Scott, 1967) dealing with rhetoric's epistemic status concluded with a lengthy discussion of the ethical prescriptions that follow from abandoning rhetoric's role as handmaiden to truth. And the ethical dimension remained a key issue in Scott's later essays on the subject (Scott, 1976, 1993). But as Hariman (1986) noted, in the process Scott shifted his focus from epistemology to ethics (p. 47). The *status* of these ethical or communicative norms (what Cherwitz, Hikins, and Croasmun might describe as their "ontological character" or nature) remains a recurrent issue in much contemporary scholarship.

In the end, Cherwitz, Hikins, and Croasmun used the issue of relativism to undercut what seems to be one of the core objectives of the consensus camp—to elevate the status of rhetoric in society. The problem, according to Croasmun and Cherwitz (1982), is that the attempt to elevate rhetoric by investing it with the capacity to construct knowledge, truth, and reality actually disables reasoned argument and judgment. They wrote,

> Intersubjectivity involves a comparison of subjective beliefs and a choice of a consensus viewpoint. One of two things must then be true. [Notice the reliance on the *disjunctive* argument that eliminates alternatives or a middle ground.] Either this intersubjective choice is rooted in something, or it is arbitrary. In other words, there must be some *reason* why one subjective view should be consensually validated and the other rejected. . . . Otherwise, people would have no cause to change their interpretations. One could never say to another, "My interpretation of this phenomenon is superior to yours, and you should therefore believe." The most obvious retort would be, "My interpretation is true for me. Since there can be multiple truths and multiple realities, we can both hold our current views and still be right. So, why should I reject my conception of reality in favor of yours?" (pp. 4-5)

For choice or **judgment** to be "rooted," there must be some "common ground" or some fixed standard to which all parties can appeal. Lacking a common ground or fixed standard, there is no way in which to assess "rival theories and beliefs" (p. 6). The result is arbitrariness, irrationalism, and all of the other commonly cited "dangers of relativism" (p. 6). Consensus theory and constructionism accept the thesis that reality, or at least social reality, is radically **contingent** or "precarious."[8] Nothing is fixed or stable; everything is in flux. But ironically, given the aims of the consensus camp, the objectivists maintain that advocacy is impossible under these conditions. Cherwitz and Hikins (1986) maintained that the rehabilitation of rhetoric can best be achieved by embracing objectivity, certainty (at least the quest for certainty as a way of organizing the pursuit of knowledge), and an essentially facilitative (but not constructive) role for rhetoric in epistemic matters (pp. 109-111).

Some central questions emerge. Does *radical contingency* or relativism disable rhetorical practice? Can argument and persuasion function in a world lacking any stable ground or fixed standard for determining knowledge or truth? These questions, critical to the disciplinary debate over rhetoric's epistemic status, echo the historical argument between Plato and the Sophists and are part of the ongoing objectivist-relativist struggle that Bernstein (1983) reconstructed. How do consensus theorists respond to the charges? One response is a counterattack. If a constructivist view of reality raises the specter of relativism, then consensus theorists charge that appeals to fixed or immutable standards often lead to the greater problem of dogmatism (Scott [1967] suggested this in his initial essay on the epistemic issue). A second response is to deny that radical contingency, relativism, or sophistry makes argument, persuasion, and decision making completely arbitrary and groundless. Sloane (1997), for example, maintained that "a self-confessed adherence to sophistry does not make advocacy impossible" (p. 13). In fact, he continued, one key objective of the sophistic tradition was to enhance a person's advocacy skills. Echoing Toulmin's (1958) discussion of *warrant-using* versus *warrant-establishing* arguments, Scott (1976) approached the problem from a different angle. He wrote, "Relativism [only] indicates circumstances in which standards have to be established cooperatively and renewed repeatedly" (p. 264); it does not mean that standards are nonexistent. Advocates appeal to *warrants*, principles, values, and other standards in their discursive practice. But as Scott suggested, these standards are not fixed and immutable; they, like the decisions or judgments they help to generate, ultimately are contingent. A third response is to question the *idea* of a "ground" for argument practices. Philosopher Richard Rorty, for example, wrote,

> The practice of argumentation . . ., [which is] the practice of playing sentences off against one another in order to decide what to believe . . ., no more requires a "ground" than [does] the practice of using one stone to chip pieces off another stone to make a spear-point. (Rorty, 1991, p. 125)

The effort to ground social practices is, Rorty suggested, both incomprehensible and fruitless.

One might ask, doesn't an advocate need to know, or at least firmly believe in, the truth of his or her position so as to advocate it effectively? If an advocate shares Scott's views and considers all standards of argument as well as all evidence, facts, testimony, and the like to be contingent, then can he or she engage in advocacy? If an advocate must practice "toleration" (as Scott insisted repeatedly), then can he or she ever *oppose* anything? Wouldn't the advocate always have to say, "Well, I guess I have to tolerate that injustice because my standard of justice is contingent, and consequently, I have no grounds for argument." Perhaps Croasmun and Cherwitz are right; without fixed standards and immutable grounds, advocacy is impossible.

At least two responses to this way of looking at the issues of relativism, contingency, and argument are possible. One is practical and the other is more theoretical or conceptual. Practically, one can point to the realm of legal or **forensic discourse** as an example of a **discursive formation** or **argument field** where effective advocacy routinely takes place in the absence of certainty. Standards, rules, and conventions of practice exist and help to structure the interactions in the legal sphere, but these elements can and do change over time. Lawyers work with the available materials and (usually) do the best jobs that they can for their clients despite the fact that they face contingency and uncertainty. Our legal practices might not be perfect, and mistakes are made (at least in some people's view), but the system seems to embody the type of relativism and toleration that Scott endorsed in a generally successful way.[9]

The conceptual or theoretical response to this dilemma was suggested by the literary theorist (and, more recently, legal theorist) Stanley Fish. Fish (1989) was keenly interested in the consequences of relativism and contingency in our everyday practices or at least in the practices of literary critics and lawyers. The thrust of Fish's argument was that, although we might recognize contingency as a fact of our human existence, we do not, and cannot, live lives that are dominated by contingency. We might know that, in the long run, our standards, values, and beliefs are contingent, but Fish insisted that "no one inhabits the long-run point of view" (p. 523). He continued, "You may know *in general* that the structure of your convictions is an historical artifact [i.e., contingent], but that knowledge does not transport you to a place where those convictions are no longer in force" (p. 524). Fish suggested that the fears of contingency and relativism that permeate the writings of objectivists such as Cherwitz, Hikins, and Croasmun are unwarranted. The recognition of contingency as a general fact of human existence will not, indeed cannot, alter the real (if nevertheless mutable) structures that organize human existence.

Fish (1989) observed,

> We still are faced with the difficulty of adjudicating between beliefs in the absence of a calculus that is not itself a function or extension of belief. It is a difficulty that cannot be removed, but the fact that it cannot be removed does not condemn us to uncertainty and paralysis but [rather] to conflict, acts of persuasion in which one party attempts to alter the beliefs of another by putting forward arguments that are weighty only in relation to still other beliefs. By definition, the career of persuasion is unpredictable and theoretically interminable. (p. 522)

Rhetoric itself is contingent; its existence is precarious. The continual challenge for practitioners, critics, and theorists is to make the possibilities of rhetoric "come alive," even though we know that nothing is permanent and that the possibilities always will be threatened. But wouldn't it be nice if we could, once and for all, establish rhetoric (both its status and its substance) on firm foundations? Something like this type of wish has seemed to surface in the works of the rhetorical objectivists (given Bernstein's definition discussed earlier, we can say that it is this type of wish that makes objectivists *objectivists*). Croasmun and Cherwitz (1982) remarked, "Our point is that to embrace the full ontological implications of the contention that rhetoric creates situations (reality) is to base the art upon a precarious, if not ethically dubious, stance" (p. 12). At the margins of their comment, there seems to be an unspoken wish or a desire for a firm foundation on which to base the art of rhetoric. In reply, someone representing the loose tradition that links Brummett, Farrell, Fish, Scott, and many others might reply that rhetoric, like social reality, might simply be a contingent and precarious practice. Firm or absolute foundations for this type of practice are merely the theorists' or philosophers' dream.[10] But we should recognize that, since Plato, it has been a very powerful dream.

The discussion in this entry has not covered all of the issues that have arisen in the epistemic debate in rhetorical studies.[11] One final point does merit discussion. In one of his recent essays on the epistemic question, Scott (1993) acknowledged that his effort to appropriate and reaccentuate the term *epistemic* might have been a mistake from the start. He wrote, "Ironically enough, my attempts for more than 20 years to establish a non-Platonic starting point may themselves be severely flawed by my choice of *epistemic* as a titular term" (p. 132). Scott's attempt to, as he put it in his initial essay (Scott, 1967), "philosophize about rhetoric" (p. 10) focused on rhetoric's relationship to knowledge and truth. But in so doing, Scott realized in 1993, he had allowed Plato—and the objectivist tradition—to dictate the terms of the debate. Reflection on rhetoric's epistemic status is problematic, Scott suggested, because it is an effort to play Plato's game or, to extend the metaphor, because it gives Plato and the objectivists "home court advantage." McKerrow's (1989) recent efforts to describe a **critical rhetoric**—"a theory that is divorced from the constraints of a Platonic conception" (p. 91) of truth, knowledge, language, and discursive practice—is one effort to change the nature of the game and the terrain on which it is played. Following Hariman's (1986) reconceptualization of **doxa,** McKerrow (1989) argued that rhetoric is *doxastic* or concerned with the process of how the elements in the world are revealed and concealed through language (see the entry for **representation**), rather than epistemic. McKerrow argued, "Rather than focusing on questions of 'truth' or 'falsity,' a view of rhetoric as doxastic allows the focus to shift to how the symbols come to possess power—what they 'do' in society as contrasted to what they 'are' " (p. 104). Echoing Gorgias, McKerrow maintained that language and discursive practice is primarily a form of **power** and not a mechanism for faithfully and accurately mirroring the world.

The debate over rhetoric's epistemic status was a major issue in the discipline throughout much of the 1970s and 1980s. Explicit attention to the epistemic question began to decline during the 1990s.[12] The question of rhetoric's epistemic status might no longer organize the disciplinary conversation in the way it once did, but the issues and questions raised in that debate—such as relativism and advocacy, the nature of contingency, language and social constructionism, and the nature and scope of rhetoric—remain matters of interest for rhetorical scholars. The conversation about language, discourse, and knowledge begun long ago by Plato and Gorgias continues.

Notes

1. For more detailed accounts of the Sophists' views on knowledge and their relevancy for rhetoric, see Enos (1972), Schiappa (1991), and Segal (1962).

2. For a survey of the conflict, see Ijsseling (1976).

3. Compare Fish's (1989) observation that "the debate [between philosophy and rhetoric or between *homo seriosus* and *homo rhetoricus*] continues to this very day, and . . . its terms are exactly those one finds in the dialogues of Plato and the orations of the Sophists" (p. 485).

4. There were, of course, some notable exceptions to this dominant tradition, a point emphasized by Brummett (1982).

5. See also Vatz (1973).

6. For recent discussions and critiques, see Gergen (1994), Grace (1987), Peters and Rothenbuhler (1989), Potter (1996), Searle (1995), and Slezak (1994).

7. For an overview of the anticonsensus or anticonstructionist arguments, see Cherwitz and Hikins (1986, pp. 116-123).

8. Croasmun and Cherwitz (1982, p. 6) cited Berger and Luckmann (1966) on this point.

9. These characteristics might be why so many scholars—from Cicero, to Toulmin and Perelman, to James Boyd White—turn to the legal sphere when writing about rhetoric and argument.

10. On the problem of "theory hope," see Fish (1989).

11. A review of the literature identified in the References will help to familiarize interested readers with some of the other important issues at stake.

12. For a discussion of this trend, see the short essays by Brummett (1990), Cherwitz and Hikins (1990), and Farrell (1990) in the February 1990 issue of the *Quarterly Journal of Speech.*

References and Additional Reading

Berger, P. L., & Luckmann, T. (1966). *The social construction of reality: A treatise in the sociology of knowledge.* Garden City, NY: Doubleday.

Bernstein, R. J. (1983). *Beyond objectivism and relativism: Science, hermeneutics, and praxis.* Philadelphia: University of Pennsylvania Press.

Bineham, J. L. (1990). The Cartesian anxiety in epistemic rhetoric: An assessment of the literature. *Philosophy and Rhetoric, 23,* 43-62.

Brinton, A. (1982). William James and the epistemic view of rhetoric. *Quarterly Journal of Speech, 68,* 158-169.

Brummett, B. (1976). Some implications of "process" or "intersubjectivity": Postmodern rhetoric. *Philosophy and Rhetoric, 9,* 21-51.

Brummett, B. (1982). On to rhetorical relativism. *Quarterly Journal of Speech, 68,* 425-430.

Brummett, B. (1990). A eulogy for epistemic rhetoric. *Quarterly Journal of Speech, 76,* 69-72.

Burke, K. (1984). *Permanence and change: An anatomy of purpose* (3rd ed.). Berkeley: University of California Press.

Carleton, W. A. (1978). What is rhetorical knowledge? A response to Farrell—and more. *Quarterly Journal of Speech, 64,* 313-328.

Cherwitz, R. (1977). Rhetoric as a "way of knowing": An attenuation of the epistemological claims of the "new rhetoric." *Southern Speech Communication Journal, 42,* 207-219.

Cherwitz, R. A., & Hikins, J. W. (1982). Toward a rhetorical epistemology. *Southern Speech Communication Journal, 47,* 135-162.

Cherwitz, R. A., & Hikins, J. W. (1983). Rhetorical perspectivism. *Quarterly Journal of Speech, 69,* 249-266.

Cherwitz, R. A., & Hikins, J. W. (1986). *Communication and knowledge: An investigation in rhetorical epistemology.* Columbia: University of South Carolina Press.

Cherwitz, R. A., & Hikins, J. W. (1990). Burying the undertaker: A eulogy for the eulogists of rhetorical epistemology. *Quarterly Journal of Speech, 76,* 73-77.

Cloud, D. L. (1994). The materiality of discourse as oxymoron: A challenge to critical rhetoric. *Western Journal of Communication, 58,* 141-163.

Croasmun, E., & Cherwitz, R. A. (1982). Beyond rhetorical relativism. *Quarterly Journal of Speech, 68,* 1-16.

Enos, R. L. (1972). The epistemology of Gorgias' rhetoric: A re-examination. *Southern Speech Communication Journal, 38,* 27-38.

Farrell, T. B. (1976). Knowledge, consensus, and rhetorical theory. *Quarterly Journal of Speech, 62,* 1-14.

Farrell, T. B. (1978). Social knowledge II. *Quarterly Journal of Speech, 64,* 329-334.

Farrell, T. B. (1990). From the Parthenon to the bassinet: Death and rebirth along the epistemic trail. *Quarterly Journal of Speech, 76,* 78-84.

Fish, S. (1989). *Doing what comes naturally: Change, rhetoric, and the practice of theory in literary and legal studies.* Durham, NC: Duke University Press.

Gaonkar, D. P. (1990). Rhetoric and its double: Reflections on the rhetorical turn in the human sciences. In H. W. Simons (Ed.), *The rhetorical turn: Invention and persuasion in the conduct of inquiry.* Chicago: University of Chicago Press.

Gergen, K. J. (1994). *Realities and relationships: Soundings in social construction.* Cambridge, MA: Harvard University Press.

Grace, G. W. (1987). *The linguistic construction of reality.* London: Croom Helm.

Gregg, R. B. (1984). *Symbolic inducement and knowing: A study in the foundations of rhetoric.* Columbia: University of South Carolina Press.

Hamlyn, D. W. (1967). History of epistemology. In P. Edwards (Ed.), *The encyclopedia of philosophy* (Vol. 3). New York: Macmillan.

Hariman, R. (1986). Status, marginality, and rhetorical theory. *Quarterly Journal of Speech, 72,* 38-54.

Hasian, M. A., Jr. (1996). *The rhetoric of eugenics in Anglo-American thought.* Athens: University of Georgia Press.

Hikins, J. W. (1981). Plato's rhetorical theory: Old perspectives on the epistemology of the new rhetoric. *Central States Speech Journal, 32,* 160-176.

Ijsseling, S. (1976). *Rhetoric and philosophy in conflict* (P. Dunphy, Trans.). The Hague, Netherlands: Martinus Nijhoff.

Laclau, E., & Mouffe, C. (1985). *Hegemony and socialist strategy: Towards a radical democratic politics.* London: Verso.

Leff, M. C. (1978). In search of Ariadne's thread: A review of the recent literature on rhetorical theory. *Central States Speech Journal, 29,* 73-91.

Lyne, J. R. (1981). Rhetoric and everyday knowledge. *Central States Speech Journal, 32,* 145-152.

McKerrow, R. E. (1989). Critical rhetoric theory and praxis. *Communication Monographs, 56,* 91-111.

Orr, C. J. (1978). How shall we say: "Reality is socially constructed through communication"? *Central States Speech Journal, 29,* 263-274.

Perelman, C. (1982). *The realm of rhetoric* (W. Kluback, Trans.). Notre Dame, IN: University of Notre Dame Press.

Peters, J. D., & Rothenbuhler, E. W. (1989). The reality of construction. In H. W. Simons (Ed.), *Rhetoric in the human sciences.* London: Sage.

Plato. (1892). Gorgias. In Plato, *The dialogues of Plato* (Vol. 2, 3rd ed., B. Jowett, Trans.). London: Oxford University Press.

Potter, J. (1996). *Representing reality: Discourse, rhetoric, and social construction.* London: Sage.

Railsback, C. C. (1983). Beyond rhetorical relativism: A structural-material model of truth and objective reality. *Quarterly Journal of Speech, 69,* 351-363.

Rorty, R. (1991). Is Derrida a transcendental philosopher? In R. Rorty, *Essays on Heidegger and others: Philosophical papers* (Vol. 2). Cambridge, UK: Cambridge University Press.

Schiappa, E. (1991). *Protagoras and logos: A study in Greek philosophy and rhetoric.* Columbia: University of South Carolina Press.

Scott, R. L. (1967). On viewing rhetoric as epistemic. *Central States Speech Journal, 18,* 9-16.

Scott, R. L. (1976). On viewing rhetoric as epistemic: Ten years later. *Central States Speech Journal, 27,* 258-266.

Scott, R. L. (1993). Rhetoric as epistemic: What difference does that make? In T. Enos & S. C. Brown (Eds.), *Defining the new rhetorics.* Newbury Park, CA: Sage.

Searle, J. R. (1995). *The social construction of reality.* New York: Free Press.

Segal, C. (1962). Gorgias and the psychology of the logos. *Harvard Studies in Classical Philology, 66,* 99-155.

Slezak, P. (1994). The social construction of social constructionism. *Inquiry, 37,* 139-157.

Sloane, T. O. (1997). *On the contrary: The protocol of traditional rhetoric.* Washington, DC: Catholic University of America Press.
Toulmin, S. (1958). *The uses of argument.* Cambridge, UK: Cambridge University Press.
Vatz, R. E. (1973). The myth of the rhetorical situation. *Philosophy and Rhetoric, 6,* 154-161.
Weaver, R. (1953). *The ethics of rhetoric.* South Bend, IN: Regnery/Gateway.
Wess, R. (1996). *Kenneth Burke: Rhetoric, subjectivity, postmodernism.* Cambridge, UK: Cambridge University Press.

ETHOS

Like many of the ideas in Aristotelian rhetorical theory, **ethos** is at once relatively simple and exceedingly complex. As Farrell (1993) observed, ethos is "one of the most enigmatic concepts in the entire lexicon" (p. 80). Ethos is commonly translated as "character" and was used by Aristotle to refer to the ways in which the perceived attributes of a speaker, manifest in discourse, are persuasive. Aristotle (1954) noted, in a widely quoted passage from the *Rhetoric,* that character or ethos "may almost be called the most effective means of persuasion" (1356a13). Ethos is particularly important, Aristotle maintained, "where exact certainty is impossible and opinions are divided" (1356a8). Aristotle went on to discuss how "there are three things which inspire confidence in the orator's own character—the three, namely, that induce us to believe a thing apart from any proof of it: good sense [*phronesis* or practical wisdom], good moral character [*arete* or virtue], and goodwill [*eunoia*]" (1378a6). Aristotle believed that when these qualities are manifest or made present in the speech, and not merely beliefs that an audience has about the speaker, the speech will be persuasive.

This basic sense of ethos has generated discussion among scholars interested in rhetoric and persuasion for centuries. Among the many topics that have stimulated discussion, one specific concern is Aristotle's limitation of ethos as proof to the manner in which character is made manifest in the speech. Scholars have suggested that attributes of a speaker's character *not* present in the speech—say, the speaker's reputation for donating to charity—will have an impact on his or her ability to persuade an audience. Why did Aristotle limit ethos to what goes on *in* the speech itself? One answer to this question—we might refer to it as the aesthetic answer—is that Aristotle was concerned with identifying an "art" of rhetoric. Elements of character not in the speech are *inartistic* and, consequently, not of interest for someone describing the constituents of an art. A more complicated, sociologically grounded answer to this question was suggested in the work of Arendt (1959). In her discussion of the Greek *polis* (the term *polis* generally is used to describe the overall structure of Greek political and civic life), Arendt argued that the ancient Greeks managed to create an artificial "space" where all participants in action and deliberation were considered to be equal despite the fact that, outside the space of the polis, individuals had different degrees of wealth, power, knowledge, and the like. Arendt wrote, "The *polis* was distinguished from the household in that it knew only 'equals' " (p. 30); it established "an equality of unequals" (p. 192). To insist, as Aristotle did, that ethos be limited to what is manifest in the speech can be considered, following Arendt's suggestions, as a way of maintaining the integrity of the polis. That is, Aristotle sought to exclude from the polis those aspects of character that might break down or destroy the artificial space of equality. The fact that someone was rich or famous might give that person a degree of power in the Greek city, but that power, if allowed into the polis, might destroy it as a space of equality. So, Aristotle's exclusion of inartistic aspects of character helped to protect the polis; the polis remained a space of equality where all that mattered was artistic persuasion. In the polis and through the resources of speech, an individual could fashion "*ethos* without identity" (a phrase suggested by Maurice Charland); the specific features of one's identity (e.g., gender, race, social class) would be irrelevant, with the only relevant factor being the character, or the ethos, created in and through a discursive performance.[1]

The point just discussed has troubled a number of commentators on the *Rhetoric.* It seems to some that Aristotle's (1954) discussion of ethos obscures the important distinction between "real" character and artistically produced character. According to Yoos (1979), "Aristotle's emphasis on portrayal . . . lays a foundation for dissimulation" (p. 45). Put more simply, Aristotle did not appear concerned about the fact that his theory of rhetoric seemed to encourage people to distort the truth about their character. For Yoos, this lack of concern was especially problematic because it removed the "ethical" dimension from ethos. We return to this issue later when we review Garver's recent reconstruction of Aristotelian ethos.

In late 20th-century scholarship, the idea of ethos frequently was displaced by the concept of *source credibility.* Scholars have identified a variety of attributes that, when present in the perceptions of the audience (and not, as Aristotle maintained, manifest in the speech), might affect the process of persuasion. The early work of Hovland, Janis, and Kelley (1953), for example, focused on three attributes—the perception of the advocate's intentions, expertness, and trustworthiness—that loosely parallel Aristotle's three central characteristics. Some rhetorical critics, such as Hart (1997), have expanded the list of relevant factors—identifying power, competence, trustworthiness, goodwill, idealism, and similarity to audience (or **identification**) (pp. 292-293)—and encouraged critics to note how advocates try to elicit these perceptions from an audience. Yoos (1979) argued that the "influence of operationalism on experimental studies" of source credibility has led to "a further blurring of the concept of *ethos*" (p. 47). Yoos contended that the "measuring procedures used in . . . experimental investigations" of ethos or credibility impose blinders on scholars and consequently limit our understanding of the phenomenon of ethos.

Yoos and a number of other scholars (e.g., Corder, 1978/1994) have encouraged rhetoricians to renew reflection on the idea of ethos. The work now being done by scholars is extremely diverse.[2] In the remainder of this entry, the focus is on four themes in contemporary scholarship: (a) efforts to rethink or reconceptualize the basic nature of ethos or human character, (b) efforts to articulate the relationship between character and discourse, (c) efforts to better comprehend the role of ethos in persuasion, and (d) efforts to restore the ethical dimension to the concept of ethos.

Reflection on the basic idea of human character or ethos leads to complex issues on the nature of selfhood and human personality. As Alcorn (1994) observed, "A theory of *ethos* needs to be grounded in a relatively clear, but also a relatively complex, understanding of the self" given the presumed relationship between character and selfhood (p. 4). At the risk of oversimplification, we can identify two dominant models of self in contemporary scholarship that, interestingly enough, seem to parallel a division in ancient Greek thinking about ethos (on this parallel, see Davis & Gross, 1994). Let us start with the division in Greek thought and then turn to its contemporary variation. Discussing the etymology or history of the term *ethos,* Sattler (1947) detected two traditions of thought. The first tradition approaches ethos as personal character, whereas the second understands ethos as custom or habit. The two traditions are interrelated in that ethos in the first sense would refer to the character of an individual, whereas ethos in the second could be used to identify the character of a culture or community; that is, the ethos of, say, a sports team or a corporation would refer to the customs or habits that are embodied in the group's practices. For example, a sports team might have a hard-working ethos or one marked by unsportsmanlike behavior, whereas a corporation's ethos might be conservative and resistant to change.[3]

Although the two senses of ethos are interrelated, they also seem to suggest two different models of self—models that are central in various forms of contemporary critical and social theory including rhetoric. Ethos as character points in the direction of what sometimes is called a Cartesian (after the French philosopher Rene Descartes) model of self, a model predicated on the idea of a "sovereign individual" (Baumlin, 1994). The individual self is conceptualized as a unified, coherent, stable, basically unchanging, self-directing, and autonomous entity. Ethos as custom or habit points in a different direction, toward what might be called a post-Cartesian or, more commonly, postmodern understanding of the self. In this model, the self is understood as a thoroughly social creature or a creature that lacks any enduring essence but, rather, consists of a shifting array of social roles, conventions, customs, and habits. To put the difference as starkly as possible, the Cartesian self possesses or "owns" certain attributes or habits of character,[4] whereas the postmodern self is nothing but a **contingent,** frequently conflicted or divided collection of roles, habits, and conventions. Culler (1981) described the postmodern sense of self in this way: "As the self is broken down into component systems, deprived of its status as source and master of meaning, it comes to seem more and more like a construct: a result of systems of convention" (p. 33). (Some of the important implications of postmodern thinking on the topic of the self are further developed in the entry for **subject.**)

The two different models of self, Cartesian and postmodern, shape and/or inform contemporary theorizing about ethos. We can detect the influence of the models on a range of issues. For illustration purposes, we can concentrate on how the models suggest different approaches to the second theme noted earlier—how to understand the relationship between discourse and character. The Cartesian model of self depicts discourse as the embodiment or reflection of preexisting character traits; public speeches or essays reflect the types of persons we are. Audiences both judge and are potentially persuaded by the character we exhibit in our discursive practices. A war hero's bravery is embodied in his or her discourse, thereby contributing to the individual's persuasive power. The postmodern model depicts discourse as a force that constructs or *constitutes* the self; we compose or create our character—our ethos—through the countless choices we make in every discursive performance.[5] From the postmodern perspective, there simply is no "real" or "essential" character that can be embodied in rhetoric; we continually create and recreate ourselves, or engage in an ongoing process of "self-fashioning" (Greenblatt, 1980), through our discursive practice. The two models of self, and the different ways in which they conceptualize the relationship between discourse and self, also have important implications for how the process of **invention,** or the creation of messages, is understood.

The Cartesian and postmodern models of self do not play a major role in the third theme outlined earlier—comprehending the role of ethos in persuasion. The persuasive power of ethos has been characterized in contemporary theory in different ways. One approach emphasizes the connection between ethos and *authority.* Farrell (1993), for example, wrote, "Authority may be considered as a variation of ethos, a grounded entitlement to offer a perspective on appearances based on some claim to a constituency" (p. 290). Contra Arendt, who viewed authority as destructive of the conditions of argument and deliberation, Farrell posited a productive role for authority and "its characteristic mode of address . . ., the command" (p. 290). Farrell's project involved investigating the "conditions" and "grounds" for authority in modern society, always recognizing that authority might "be challenged, disputed, and even disobeyed" (p. 291). From a Burkeian perspective, ethos was conceptualized as part of the process of **identification.** As Burke (1950) explained in a well-known passage from *A Rhetoric of Motives,* "You persuade a man [sic] only insofar as you can talk his language by speech, gesture, tonality, order, image, attitude, [and] idea, *identifying* your ways with his." This process of identification, Burke continued, is an extension of Aristotle's and

Cicero's idea of the rhetor being able "to display the appropriate 'signs' of character needed to earn the audience's goodwill" (pp. 55-56). In a way, Burke's emphasis on identification made ethos the central component of rhetorical art and strategy.

The centrality of ethos also was a key thesis in Garver's (1994) recent rereading of Aristotle's *Rhetoric.*[6] Garver's subtitle made this clear; rhetoric, at least for Aristotle, was "an art of character." Garver's complex argument, seeking to establish both the centrality of ethos and the compatibility of art and character, resists easy summary. Like Farrell, who saw authority as "a form of argument" (p. 291), Garver understood the persuasive power of ethos to be a result of its embodiment in argument.[7] Garver wrote, "We make our discourse ethical by making our *ethos* argumentative. . . . the best displays of character are argumentative" (pp. 194-195). But ethos, in Garver's rendering, is not something that is added to an argument; we do not select arguments for our position (e.g., why our audience should oppose the death penalty) and then determine how we can make those arguments possess more ethos. Ethos saturates rhetorical practice in a more fundamental sense. For Garver, "in rhetoric and practical judgment . . ., *ethos* is necessary for finding and formulating arguments and not just presenting them" (p. 191). Advocates need ethos, or need "ethical perception" (p. 191), because it is the foundation for the choices that make deliberation and advocacy possible.

Whereas Garver (1994) emphasized the integration of ethos and argument, he also explained why ethos is more powerful and more persuasive than simply "logical argument" in deliberation about practical matters. Argument, in itself, cannot speak to the complex of factors that make up a **rhetorical situation.** We all know this from our own experience; a perfectly "sound" or "valid" argument might, in certain circumstances, be unpersuasive. Even Mr. Spock, in the former *Star Trek* television series, had a difficult time in relying solely on logic. He had to place his faith and trust in his friends; he had to rely on their ethos, and they had to rely on his. As Garver explained, rhetoric can accomplish its task of making the "practically indeterminate" or **contingent** situations of life determinate—it can help to choose and defend courses of action—"only because character can go where logic itself cannot" (p. 92). Ethos ultimately is persuasive not merely because it is embodied in argument but also because it speaks to *humans* or creatures with complex minds that sometimes are beyond the reach of even the most rigorous logic.

Finally, the fourth theme in contemporary investigations of ethos is the need to restore the link between ethos and ethics. The principal issue in this line of inquiry is the problem of dissimulation or of advocates pretending to possess qualities that they do not, in fact, possess. In Garver's (1994) terms, the issue was the distinction between "real" and "artful" or "apparent" ethos (pp. 193-197). Garver's strategy was, in effect, to dissolve the **dissociation** between appearance and reality that is at the heart of the problem. Garver agreed with Arendt (1962) when she wrote, "In politics, more than anywhere else, we have no possibility of distinguishing between being [the "real"] and appearance. In the realm of human affairs, being and appearance are indeed one and the same" (p. 94). Arendt and Garver appeared to share the same fear: If members of the polis or public emphasize the appearance-reality division, then they will introduce a suspicious mood to public life that will destroy the polis as a space of appearances.

One scholar who found the potential distinction between artful or apparent ethos and real ethos to be important and in need of exploration was Yoos. As noted earlier, Yoos was concerned about the problem of deception or those cases in which advocates employ art or strategy to create a false or misleading picture of their character. Yoos's (1979) concern was to "put ethics back into 'ethical appeal' " (p. 54). Yoos attempted to identify the central "attributes or qualities" that make something an "ethical appeal" (p. 50). His investigation revealed four factors that he labeled as the

"A," "R," "E," and "V" factors. First, an ethical appeal will exhibit an attempt by the advocate to reach "mutual agreement" with his or her audience (the A factor). An ethical appeal does more than try to persuade an audience; it tries to find "common ground" with the audience and relies on "mutually accepted premises" (pp. 50-51). Second, an ethical appeal recognizes the "rational autonomy" of the audience (the R factor). To satisfy this condition, "the speaker must therefore display the attitude that the listener's decision as to what is rational is the ultimate rhetorical ground of persuasion" (p. 52). The advocate might question or doubt the validity of the audience's standards for determining what is rational, but nevertheless, the advocate "must accept the further obligation, as an aspect of his [sic] ethical appeal, to convince his audience [members] that their standards are irrational" (p. 52). Third, an ethical appeal displays an advocate's commitment to being equal to or on par with his or her audience (the E factor). Yoos explained that "the speaker cannot adopt a superior role toward his [sic] audience unless the audience concedes that role" (p. 52). This condition seems to, in effect, restore the sense of equality that Arendt saw as essential to the Greek polis. Fourth, an ethical appeal recognizes the "intrinsic worth" of the audience's desires, ends, and values (the V factor). The advocate need not, and probably should not, make a blanket promise to help the audience members realize their needs and values. In an ethical appeal, the advocate "commits himself [sic] to openness and to a full consideration of the worth of what listeners want or hope for" (p. 53).

Yoos's account of the conditions of ethical appeal have attracted considerable attention, not all of it positive. Writing from a feminist perspective, Jarratt and Reynolds (1994) contended, "Yoos seems to want to bracket off the embodied speaker, with all the confusing emotions and desires that he or she arouses, from judgments about ethics" (p. 41). They believed that this bracketing is evidence of "Yoos's investment in a theory of the autonomous, self-aware individual created by Plato, reborn in the Enlightenment, and more at home in a liberal philosophy than with some feminisms and with rhetoric" (p. 43). Jarratt and Reynolds' critique of Yoos returns us to the first theme in contemporary reflection on ethos—the nature of the self. The value of the concept of ethos, for Jarratt and Reynolds, was that it "theorizes the positionality inherent in rhetoric—the speaker having been created at a particular site within the contingencies of history and geography" (p. 47). If the theoretical value of the idea of ethos for Jarratt and Reynolds is the way in which it can help us to recognize that we are "positioned" and positioning creatures, or that all of our discourse emerges from a particular but constantly changing "site" that is the contingent essence of who we "are," then its practical value as "an ethical political tool" consists of the way in which it encourages us to take "responsibility for our positions in the world, for the ways we see, [and] for the places from which we speak" (p. 52).

Notes

1. Ober's (1989, 1996) reconstruction of ancient Greek political life lends some support to an Arendtian account of the relationship between ethos and the fictional equality of the polis.

2. See, for example, the Baumlin and Baumlin (1994) collection of essays.

3. On the need for rhetorical scholars to expand how they conceptualize corporate or collective rhetors, see Cheney (1992).

4. The idea of self-as-owner is an important theme in much postmodern critical thought. See, for example, Wald (1995).

5. On the constitutive dimension of discursive practice, see the discussion in the entry for **effects of rhetorical practice.**

6. On Aristotle's view of ethos, see also Fortenbaugh (1996).

7. On the relationship between ethos and argument, see also Willard (1989, pp. 131-142).

References and Additional Reading

Alcorn, M. W. (1994). Self-structure as a rhetorical device: Modern *ethos* and the divisiveness of the self. In

J. S. Baumlin & T. F. Baumlin (Eds.), *Ethos: New essays in rhetorical and critical theory.* Dallas, TX: Southern Methodist University Press.

Arendt, H. (1959). *The human condition.* New York: Anchor.

Arendt, H. (1962). *On revolution.* New York: Viking.

Aristotle. (1954). *Rhetoric* (W. R. Roberts, Trans.). New York: Modern Library.

Baumlin, J. S. (1994). Introduction: Positioning *ethos* in historical and contemporary theory. In J. S. Baumlin & T. F. Baumlin (Eds.), *Ethos: New essays in rhetorical and critical theory.* Dallas, TX: Southern Methodist University Press.

Baumlin, J. S., & Baumlin, T. F. (Eds.). (1994). *Ethos: New essays in rhetorical and critical theory.* Dallas, TX: Southern Methodist University Press.

Burke, K. (1950). *A rhetoric of motives.* New York: Prentice Hall.

Cheney, G. (1992). The corporate person (re)presents itself. In E. L. Toth & R. L. Heath (Eds.), *Rhetorical and critical approaches to public relations.* Hillsdale, NJ: Lawrence Erlbaum.

Corder, J. W. (1994). Varieties of ethical argument, with some account of the significance of ethos in the teaching of composition. In R. E. Young & Y. Liu (Eds.), *Landmark essays on rhetorical invention in writing.* Davis, CA: Hermagoras Press. (Original work published 1978)

Culler, C. (1981). *The pursuit of signs: Semiotics, literature, deconstruction.* Ithaca, NY: Cornell University Press.

Davis, R. C., & Gross, D. S. (1994). Gayatri Chakravorty Spivak and the *ethos* of the subaltern. In J. S. Baumlin & T. F. Baumlin (Eds.), *Ethos: New essays in rhetorical and critical theory.* Dallas, TX: Southern Methodist University Press.

Farrell, T. B. (1993). *Norms of rhetorical culture.* New Haven, CT: Yale University Press.

Fortenbaugh, W. W. (1996). Aristotle's account of persuasion through character. In C. L. Johnstone (Ed.), *Theory, text, context: Issues in Greek rhetoric and oratory.* Albany: State University of New York Press.

Garver, E. (1994). *Aristotle's RHETORIC: An art of character.* Chicago: University of Chicago Press.

Garver, E. (1998). The ethical criticism of reasoning. *Philosophy and Rhetoric, 31,* 107-130.

Greenblatt, S. (1980). *Renaissance self-fashioning: From More to Shakespeare.* Chicago: University of Chicago Press.

Halloran, S. M. (1982). Aristotle's concept of *ethos,* or if not his, somebody else's. *Rhetoric Review, 1,* 58-63.

Hart, R. P. (1997). *Modern rhetorical criticism* (2nd ed.). Boston: Allyn & Bacon.

Hovland, C. I., Janis, I. L., & Kelley, H. H. (1953). *Communication and persuasion.* New Haven, CT: Yale University Press.

Jarratt, S. C., & Reynolds, N. (1994). The splitting image: Contemporary feminisms and the ethics of *ethos.* In J. S. Baumlin & T. F. Baumlin (Eds.), *Ethos: New essays in rhetorical and critical theory.* Dallas, TX: Southern Methodist University Press.

May, J. M. (1988). *Trials of character: The eloquence of Ciceronian ethos.* Chapel Hill: University of North Carolina Press.

Miller, C. R. (1978). Technology as a form of consciousness: A study of contemporary ethos. *Central States Speech Journal, 29,* 228-236.

Ober, J. (1989). *Mass and elite in democratic Athens: Rhetoric, ideology, and the power of the people.* Princeton, NJ: Princeton University Press.

Ober, J. (1996). *The Athenian revolution: Essays on ancient Greek democracy and political theory.* Princeton, NJ: Princeton University Press.

Rosenthal, P. I. (1966). The concept of ethos and the structure of persuasion. *Speech Monographs, 33,* 114-126.

Sattler, W. M. (1947). Conceptions of *ethos* in ancient rhetoric. *Speech Monographs, 14,* 55-65.

Wald, P. (1995). *Constituting Americans: Cultural anxiety and narrative form.* Durham, NC: Duke University Press.

Walton, D. (1997). *Appeal to expert opinion: Arguments from authority.* University Park: Pennsylvania State University Press.

Willard, C. A. (1989). *A theory of argumentation.* Tuscaloosa: University of Alabama Press.

Yoos, G. E. (1979). A revision of the concept of ethical appeal. *Philosophy and Rhetoric, 12,* 41-58.

EULOGISTIC COVERING

Kenneth Burke derived his concept of **eulogistic covering** from the writings of the late 18th- and early 19th-century British philosopher Jeremy Bentham. In Bentham's (1952) *Handbook of Political Fallacies* and other works, he discussed the problem of "eulogistic" and "dyslogistic" (or "disparaging") terms. Bentham believed that it was "reasonable to think that originally all terms expressive of any of these objects ["pains, pleasures, desires, emotions, motives, affections, propensities, dispositions and other moral entities"] were neutral" (p. 140). That is, the term simply named or stood for the thing being represented. But "by degrees [terms] acquired, some of them a eulogistic, some a disparaging, cast" (p. 140). In other words, terms began to do more than merely represent the things they represented; they began to convey feelings or attitudes about their objects. One example that Bentham used in his discussion of fallacies was the term *innovation.* Its restricted meaning is simply "something new," but in England and America during Bentham's lifetime, the term had a dyslogistic or disparaging connotation. To label something an "innovation" (as anti-Federalists tried to do in the debate over the ratification of the American Constitution during 1787-1788) was to do more than refer to a proposal; it was an implicit act of criticism (p. 142). In Bentham's judgment, eulogistic and dyslogistic terms introduced confusion into public discussion. Consequently, Bentham believed that political life could be greatly improved by reforming public discursive practices. Such reforms would include the elimination of eulogistic and dyslogistic terms.[1]

Burke shared Bentham's interest in uncovering the way in which certain terms, phrases, or *epithets* functioned to convey attitudes and feelings about the objects to which they pointed, but he did not share Bentham's desire for radical linguistic reform. Bentham thought that language originally was neutral; Burke rejected this view. In his essay, "The Philosophy of Literary Form," Burke (1957) explained,

> The magical decree is implicit in all language, for the mere act of naming an object or situation decrees that it is to be singled out as such-and-such rather than as something other. Hence, I think that an attempt to *eliminate* magic, in this sense, would involve us in the elimination of vocabulary itself as a way of sizing up reality. (p. 5)

In *A Rhetoric of Motives,* Burke (1950) continued his critique of Bentham's desire for a neutral vocabulary. Burke wrote, "Where inducement to action is concerned, a genuinely neutral vocabulary would defeat its own ends, for there would be no act in it" (p. 96). For Burke, language was a form of action, and action never is "neutral."[2]

In *Attitudes Toward History,* Burke (1984) introduced the idea of eulogistic covering in a discussion of various stances that a critic can take toward analyzing **motives** and human action. Burke was concerned that critics not be misled into thinking that all human behavior could be explained by way of a transcendent "scheme of motives" (i.e., that all behavior is a realization of abstract principles such as "honor" and "duty"); to fall prey to this scheme of motives was to be deluded by a eulogistic covering (p. 92). At the same time, Burke cautioned against the opposite critical vice—"the antithetical scheme"—that reduced all behavior to self-interest or "utilitarian motives." Constant "debunking" was as problematic as being blinded by eulogistic coverings.

Burke (1950) returned to the idea of eulogistic covering in his discussion of Bentham and Karl Marx in *A Rhetoric of Motives.* The crucial link between Bentham and Marx that Burke explored was **mystification.** He wrote that ideological mystification in Marx was "what Bentham would have called 'eulogistic coverings' " (p. 108). Burke suggested that both Bentham and Marx "admonish us to look for 'mystification' at any point where social divisiveness caused by property and the division of labor is obscured by unitary terms" (p. 108). These unitary terms—patriotism, national interest, and union—are eulogistic coverings that gloss over the "reality" of social divisions. The challenge, Burke maintained, is to introduce "the clarity of division terms" to replace the "fog of merger terms" (p. 109).

This last observation about how critics and advocates alike can respond to the mystification promoted by eulogistic coverings and merger terms raises a central issue in rhetorical and critical theory generally. How can a critic or an advocate argue that one set of terms—one form of verbal "magic"—is any better than another set of terms? No language—no set of terms—is, in an ultimate or final sense, inherently better than another; none can ever reflect reality simply, clearly, and without distortion. All language—every set of terms—is partial, partisan, and parochial. How do we choose? How do we decide that one is better than another? In one way or another, all of the important trends in contemporary critical thought—Derridian deconstruction, Habermasian critical theory, cultural studies, and rhetorical theory—negotiate this question. How did Burke respond to it? We can get a sense of Burke's response to this dilemma by returning to the passage from "Philosophy of Literary Form" discussed earlier. Picking up the paragraph where we left off, Burke (1957) continued, "Rather, what we may need is *correct* magic, magic whose decrees about the naming of real situations is the closest possible approximation to the situation named (with the greater accuracy of approximation being supplied by the 'collective revelation' of testing and discussion)" (p. 5). Burke was appealing to traditional standards—correctness and accuracy—with which critics and advocates could combat the apparent distortions of eulogistic coverings and other forms of verbal mystification. But as the final parenthetical observation appears to suggest, Burke recognized that these standards are themselves eulogistic coverings given that there is no (final) way in which to judge what is correct or what is accurate. The world that Burke described is absolutely—some might say fabulously—rhetorical; we appeal to standards and norms of various types, but these standards and norms are themselves constituted and reconstituted through our discursive practices. There is no way out. All we can do, as critics and advocates, is enter the contest or, to use the image that Burke (1950) employed at the end of *A Rhetoric of Motives,* descend into the street (p. 294). Through our discursive practices, we cover and uncover incessantly, continually "testing" our various languages, *idioms,* and sets of terms.

Notes

1. On the tradition of language reform of which Bentham was a part, see Gustafson (1992).

2. For further discussion of some of the issues of language raised here, see the entries for **definition** and **representation.**

References and Additional Reading

Bentham, J. (1952). *Handbook of political fallacies* (H. A. Larrabee, Ed.). Baltimore, MD: Johns Hopkins University Press.

Burke, K. (1950). *A rhetoric of motives.* New York: Prentice Hall.

Burke, K. (1957). The philosophy of literary form. In K. Burke, *The philosophy of literary form* (rev. ed.). New York: Vintage.

Burke, K. (1984). *Attitudes toward history* (3rd ed.). Berkeley: University of California Press.

Gustafson, T. (1992). *Representative words: Politics, literature, and the American language, 1776-1865.* Cambridge, UK: Cambridge University Press.

EXHORTATION

In *Rhetorical Criticism,* Black (1978) argued that the appropriation of classical rhetorical theory under the critical banner of **neo-Aristotelianism** was unable to respond productively to certain forms of discursive practice. Black labeled one of these forms "exhortative discourse."[1] He maintained that **exhortation** aims at "the evocation of an emotional response" (p. 138); it operates by way of the passions or emotions (see the entry for **pathos**). Robertson (1995) made a similar point when he wrote, "Hortatory rhetoric was a cry of 'Fire!' in the theater. It linked the audience in an immediate, emotional way to events, principles, or policies, mostly real, often exaggerated, sometimes illusory" (p. 11). A passage from African American abolitionist Henry Garnet's 1843 "Address to the Slaves" illustrates Robertson's point. Garnet exhorted his audience as follows[2]:

> Look around you and behold the bosoms of your loving wives, heaving with untold agonies! Hear the cries of your poor children!

> Remember the stripes your fathers bore. Think of the torture and disgrace of your noble mothers. Think of your wretched sisters, loving virtue and purity, as they are driven into concubinage and are exposed to the unbridled lusts of incarnate devils. Think of the undying glory that hangs around the ancient name of Africa—and forget not that you are native born American citizens. . . . Think how many tears you have poured out upon the soil which you have cultivated with unrequited toil and enriched with your blood, and then go to your lordly enslavers and tell them plainly that you are determined to be free.

Garnet's strong use of the *imperative mood* in this passage is an important sign of the presence of exhortation.[3]

If exhortation aims at inducing an emotional response in an audience or in readers, then it "finds its end in radical conversion" (Black, 1978, p. 142). Exhortation, given Black's account, is an important force in the process of **secular conversion.** Because exhortation aims at radical change, the exhorter faces a serious challenge. As Black (1978) explained,

> We interpret . . . new experiences by some relatively stable frame of reference that, in its essential characteristics, usually remains unaltered throughout our adult lives. The exhorter means to change the frame of reference from top to bottom. How can he [sic] convey his meaning? His is, after all, not an ordinary message, since it would revise the very presuppositions by which ordinary messages are understood. (p. 142)

In short, the exhorter faces a heightened or amplified version of a basic rhetorical problem—how to use what the audience currently accepts or believes in such a way that it leads audience members to accept or believe something new—something at odds with their current "frame of reference."[4]

Drawing on material from the 18th-century preacher Jonathan Edwards and the 19th-century abolitionist William Lloyd Garrison, Black (1978) argued that there are "two attributes of the style of exhortation" (p. 143) that help a person to revise his or her frame of reference, thereby promoting radical conversion. First, exhortation commonly features a language of "concrete description" given that "abstractions do not have the power to move one to a new conviction" (p. 143).[5] Black wrote, "We would unhesitatingly acknowledge our disapproval of hunger and starvation, but this disapproval would be of a concept merely. We must apprehend specific cases of starvation, either directly, imaginatively, or through the medium of descriptive language, before we experience a strong affective response" (p. 143). Second, exhortation features "the frequent substitution of *is* or *will be* [copula] for *should* or *should be* [moral imperative]" (p. 143). Black suggested that the use of the copula ("what *is* the case") as opposed to the moral imperative ("what *ought to be* or *should be* the case") gives to exhortation "the tone of prophesy" (p. 144); exhortation often is a form of "prophetic utterance" (p. 144), with the speaker or writer assuming a **prophetic ethos.** In addition, Robertson (1995) suggested that hortatory rhetoric traffics in frequent use of *antithesis* (pp. 29, 40-43) and **conspiracy arguments** or appeals (pp. 33-34).

Notes

1. Some scholars describe this **style** as *hortatory* rhetoric. See, for example, Robertson (1995).

2. Garnet's immediate audience members were free northern blacks and some white abolitionists. Hence, his "address" to the slaves and his use of exhortation are a form of *apostrophe.*

3. For another example, see Holland's (1953) discussion of Wendell Phillips' famous address, "The Murder of Lovejoy," delivered in Boston in December 1837.

4. On this problem, see also the discussion of the *paradox of* **doxa.**

5. For alternative accounts of the force of "abstract nouns," see the discussions of **condensation symbols** and **ideographs.**

References and Additional Reading

Black, E. (1978). *Rhetorical criticism: A study in method.* Madison: University of Wisconsin Press.

Holland, V. (1953). Rhetorical criticism: A Burkeian method. *Quarterly Journal of Speech, 39,* 444-450.

Lazenby, W. (1971). Exhortation as exorcism: Cotton Mather's sermons to murders. *Quarterly Journal of Speech, 57,* 50-56.

Robertson, A. W. (1995). *The language of democracy: Political rhetoric in the United States and Britain, 1790-1900.* Ithaca, NY: Cornell University Press.

EXPOSITION

Rhetoric is most commonly identified with the theory and practice of *persuasive* **discourse.** But the focus on persuasion was not absolute in the history of rhetorical thought. For example, the Roman rhetorician Quintilian (1920) implicitly (if not explicitly) broadened the focus of inquiry when he defined rhetoric as the "knowledge of speaking well" (p. 315). In his effort to mediate pagan rhetorical theory (principally Cicero's doctrine of the "duties" of the orator) and the cultural norms of Christianity, Saint Augustine (1958) hypothesized that orators attempted to do three things: teach, delight, and move an audience. Perhaps the most influential departure from the "rhetoric = persuasion" equation was proposed by the 18th-century British theorist George Campbell.[1] Invoking Quintilian in the first paragraph of *The Philosophy of Rhetoric,* Campbell (1963) defined rhetoric as the "art or talent by which the discourse is adapted to its end" (p. 1). Extending the logic of *faculty psychology*[2] into rhetoric, Campbell went on to identify four dominant ends: "to enlighten the understanding, to please the imagination, to move the passions, or to influence the will" (p. 1). The first end that Campbell identified—to enlighten the understanding—would serve as the springboard for developing a method of *expository* prose discourse.

Explicit attention to the **genre** of **exposition** emerged during the 19th century, primarily in composition textbooks. Crowley (1990) credited Alexander Bain's *English Composition and Rhetoric* with providing "a definitive and influential" discussion of exposition and expository discourse. Bain (1871) defined exposition as "the mode of handling applicable to knowledge or information," primarily in the realm of science (p. 185). Subsequent definitions emphasized the epistemic or informative thrust identified by Bain. Baldwin (1909) described exposition as "the succinct and orderly setting forth of some piece of information" (p. 40). Scott and Denney (1897) viewed it as "the kind of discourse in which the writer's aim is to make others see the meaning of some idea as clearly as he himself [sic] sees it; its subject matter is general ideas, laws, or principles" (p. 302). Fulton (1920) defined exposition as "that kind of writing which has as its primary function the impartial unfolding of any phenomenon, hypothesis, or generalization to the understanding of the reader" (p. xx). Richards (1936) maintained that exposition was "concerned to state a view, not to persuade people to agree or to do anything more than examine it" (p. 24). Finally, according to a more recent textbook, "Exposition refers to prose whose primary purpose is giving information" (Wyrick, 1993, p. 179). These definitions do not provide a consistent account of exposition. But they do suggest that the realm of expository prose is broad. Given the definitions and descriptions just noted, exposition includes a scientific report, a newspaper account of a recent homicide, a corporate earnings statement, a cookbook, a biography, a philosophical treatise, an insurance policy declaration of coverage, a computer operating manual, a tourist guidebook, a magazine article about the eruption of Mount St. Helens, and informative speeches in a public speaking class or an English 101 composition class (see also Conners, 1985).[3]

Many of the strategies of expository prose discussed in the textbook literature either overlap with or are closely related to common

argument strategies. The strategies, like the genres, differ with respect to intention and purpose. Some common expository strategies include use of *example,* describing a *process,* noting *cause and effect,* relating things by way of *comparison* and *contrast,* providing a **definition** or engaging in *classification,* and employing *division* and *classification* (Conners, 1981; Wyrick, 1993). Other strategies include *statistical quantification* and *testimony.*[4] Identification and elaboration of expository strategies often intersects with the traditional rhetorical principle of **amplification** and Perelman and Olbrechts-Tyteca's (1969) discussion of **presence.**

Developments in contemporary literary and critical theory have led many scholars to question the autonomy of the expository genre.[5] If, as a number of scholars maintain, language is *not* a transparent medium or a mechanism for replicating reality precisely, and if, as many of those same scholars contend, our discursive practices are saturated with attitudes, perspectives, biases, and prejudices, then a "pure" genre of neutral disinterested information dissemination is impossible. The human world is populated with discourses—with an *undifferentiated textuality*—that shape and structure the world in multiple ways. The task is to study carefully how purportedly "factual" or "informative" discursive practices produce effects and/or solicit beliefs and actions from readers and listeners (Winterowd, 1990).[6] But does the demise of faculty psychology and the lack of generic purity mean that genres such as exposition should be abandoned? Probably not. Even if humans are not the complete masters of their purposes and intentions, there are times when the aim(s) or end(s) of expository prose is paramount in a specific **rhetorical situation.** Contemporary policy questions such as health care reform, international monetary fund contributions, and the privatization of social security demand efforts at careful explanation and explication if reasoned public decision making is going to be possible. Individuals, and the community as a whole, *can* benefit from continued training in the techniques of effective exposition that they receive in the composition and public speaking classrooms.

Notes

1. Corbett (1971) wrote, "What was Campbell's peculiar contribution to the art of rhetoric? For one thing, he ventured the notion that rhetoric could have an end other than to persuade" (p. 623).

2. Proponents of faculty psychology held that the human mind was divided into different properties, capacities, or "faculties." *Reason* and *emotion* usually were identified as the two most basic faculties, but in some versions of faculty psychology, a number of discrete mental properties were identified. Golden, Berquist, and Coleman (1997, pp. 109-110) discussed the basic elements of faculty psychology as it relates to Campbell's (1963) *The Philosophy of Rhetoric.*

3. Expository or "informative" discourse was incorporated into the domain of 20th-century rhetorical studies in Bryant's (1953) well-known definition of rhetoric as "the *rationale of informative and suasory discourse*" (p. 404).

4. See Hart's (1997) discussion of "clarification devices" (pp. 88-89).

5. The entries for **discourse, representation,** and **sermonic, language as** discuss some of these developments.

6. See also the discussions of **epistemic, rhetoric as** and **inquiry, rhetoric of.**

References and Additional Reading

Bachelor, J. M., & Haley, H. L. (1947). *The practice of exposition.* New York: Appleton-Century.

Bain, A. (1871). *English composition and rhetoric: A manual* (rev. ed.). New York: D. Appleton.

Baldwin, C. S. (1909). *A college manual of rhetoric* (2nd ed.). New York: Longmans.

Brown, H. (1966). *Prose style: Five primary types.* Minneapolis: University of Minnesota Press.

Bryant, D. C. (1953). Rhetoric: Its functions and its scope. *Quarterly Journal of Speech, 39,* 401-424.

Campbell, G. (1963). *The philosophy of rhetoric* (L. F. Bitzer, Ed.). Carbondale: Southern Illinois University Press.

Conners, R. J. (1981). The rise and fall of the modes of discourse. *College Composition and Communication, 32,* 444-455.

Conners, R. J. (1985). The rhetoric of explanation: Explanatory rhetoric from 1850 to the present. *Written Communication, 2,* 49-72.

Corbett, E. P. J. (1971). *Classical rhetoric for the modern student* (2nd ed.). New York: Oxford University Press.

Crowley, S. (1990). *The methodical memory: Invention in current-traditional rhetoric.* Carbondale: Southern Illinois University Press.

Fulton, M. G. (1920). *Expository writing.* New York: Macmillan.

Golden, J. L., Berquist, G. F., & Coleman, W. E. (1997). *The rhetoric of Western thought* (6th ed.). Dubuque, IA: Kendall/Hunt.

Hart, R. P. (1997). *Modern rhetorical criticism* (2nd ed.). Boston: Allyn & Bacon.

Kinneavy, J. (1971). *A theory of discourse.* Englewood Cliffs, NJ: Prentice Hall.

Martin, H. C. (1957). *The logic and rhetoric of exposition.* New York: Rinehart.

Quintilian. (1920). *Institution oratoria* (H. E. Butler, Trans.). London: Heinemann.

Perelman, C., & Olbrechts-Tyteca, L. (1969). *The New Rhetoric: A treatise on argumentation* (J. Wilkinson & P. Weaver, Trans.). Notre Dame, IN: University of Notre Dame Press.

Richards, I. A. (1936). *The philosophy of rhetoric.* New York: Oxford University Press.

Saint Augustine. (1958). *On Christian doctrine* (D. W. Robertson, Jr., Trans.). Indianapolis, IN: Bobbs-Merrill.

Scott, F. N., & Denney, J. V. (1897). *Composition-rhetoric, designed for use in secondary schools.* Boston: Allyn.

Willis, H. (1964). *Structure, style, and usage: A guide to expository writing.* New York: Holt, Rinehart & Winston.

Winterowd, W. R. (1990). *The rhetoric of the "other" literature.* Carbondale: Southern Illinois University Press.

Wyrick, J. (1993). *Steps to writing well: A concise guide to composition* (5th ed.). Fort Worth, TX: Harcourt Brace.

FALLACY

For more than 2,000 years, scholars have struggled to identify and describe forms of faulty or defective reasoning used in persuasion and argumentation. This tradition of thought goes back at least as far as Aristotle's discussion of apparent **enthymemes** in the *Rhetoric* (Aristotle, 1954) and his work *Sophistical Refutations* (Aristotle, 1955). The term commonly used to label defective arguments is **fallacy**.

Since Aristotle, scholars have compiled descriptive lists of the various fallacies. One of the first questions to be considered is whether there are different forms or categories of fallacies and, if so, where to classify specific fallacies. Aristotle, for example, distinguished between fallacies dependent on language and those not dependent on language (Hamblin, 1970, p. 13). Aristotle's distinction is at the root of the modern distinction between fallacies of clarity or ambiguity and fallacies of relevance (see, e.g., Fogelin, 1987). A variation on the Aristotelian and modern two-part scheme can be found in Whately's (1848) distinction between "formal" (defective reasoning) and "informal" (problematic verbal strategy) fallacies. In recent scholarship, Kahane (1995) employed a three-part scheme for organizing and classifying fallacies (questionable premise, suppressed evidence, and invalid inference), and Finocchiaro (1987) proposed a six-part classificatory scheme (formal, explanatory, presuppositional, positive, semantical, and persuasive).

Just as there is disagreement on the question of the number of categories, there also is disagreement on the total number of fallacies. Aristotle's original list contained 13 fallacies, and according to Hamblin (1970), Aristotle's discussion remains the basis for many modern expositions. Contemporary scholars have identified a list of 18 to 20 prominent fallacies (Hansen & Pinto, 1995, p. 199), although some (e.g., Kahane, 1995) have discussed as many as 25 different types of fallacies. Given the lack of any definitive number of categories or types, the following discussion is somewhat idiosyncratic and not exhaustive. Three categories of fallacies—of reasoning, of relevance, and of clarity—are briefly described and illustrated.

Fallacies of Reasoning

The particular instances that can be classified in this category are cases where a commonly accepted pattern of reasoning or line of argument is employed in a manner that is defective. Specific instances of this category include the following.

Hasty Generalization (or secundum quid)

If someone claims that everyone who belongs to a fraternity is a drunk and uses as evidence his or her direct observations of four individuals who belong to a fraternity, then that person is guilty of the fallacy of hasty generalization. The person has tried to warrant a claim or conclusion based on an insufficient and unrepresentable sample.

False Cause (or post hoc, ergo propter hoc)

In this type of fallacy, a sequential relationship is mistaken for a causal relationship. Politicians employ subtle forms of this fallacy with regularity. For example, a politician might claim that the economic recovery program that he or she championed, and that subsequently was adopted, has led to the economic upturn that the nation is experiencing at the present time (and so, of course, voters should reelect that politician). But can we be sure that two things with a sequential relationship (first the recovery program was approved and then the economy improved) also have a causal relationship? Did the program cause the economic recovery? How do we know that the politician was not simply the beneficiary of good fortune? Or that the economic recovery was not simply a recurrent cycle of economic activity? We cannot be sure. That is why the attribution of causal status (even if only indirectly) is problematic.

Another fallacy that exploits causal reasoning is the *single cause.* Given the way in which social, economic, and political forces tend to interact (see entry for **overdetermined, discourse as**), it usually is problematic to try to identify a single cause for any complex event. The hypothetical example of the politician taking credit for reviving the economy also is an example of the single cause fallacy in that one cause—the economic recovery program—is assumed to be *the* cause of a very complex event.

Finally, another commonly discussed fallacy, the *slippery slope,* can be included here as a type of causal fallacy. The slippery slope strategy exploits our understanding of causal relations by constructing a type of "chain reaction" such that once one thing happens, or once a certain threshold is crossed, it sets off a causal process that produces a number of other, usually undesirable consequences.[1] The famous "domino" metaphor of cold war foreign policy (once one nation in a region fell to communism, the rest would fall like dominoes) and some forms of anti-drug persuasion (where advocates suggest that once a person tries one drug, it will set off a chain reaction leading downhill to addiction) are good examples of the slippery slope.[2]

False Dilemma

In certain situations, an individual might have only two options available to him or her. If a teacher is assigning final grades for a course and comes across a borderline case, then the teacher must choose either the higher or the lower of the grades. There do not appear to be any other legitimate options. But we frequently encounter advocates who frame issues in clear *disjunctive* terms (e.g., we must either raise taxes or cut spending) that obscure alternatives that might not fit neatly into the disjunctive opposition. In these cases, the disjunctive line of argument can be attacked as a false dilemma.

False Analogy

Because all analogies are, at some level, false (to use one of Ronald Reagan's examples, cutting the federal budget is not the same thing as a person going on a diet), this often is a very slippery type of fallacy. The force of analogy, like the force of *metaphor,* arises from its ability to help us look at something in a new way. As Kenneth Burke recognized in his discussion of **perspective by incongruity**, there are times when maximum incongruity is a necessary way of helping us to escape from habitual modes of thought. Nevertheless, it seems sensible to suggest that, in certain circumstances, an analogy might go too far; it might impede our ability to think about and decide among various courses of action. Did Reagan's analogy between cutting the budget and going on a diet go too far? One probably could make a good argument that it did—that the analogy distorted the complex factors involved in cutting the budget. But the question of whether a particular analogy goes too far often is, like beauty, in the eye of the beholder.

Fallacies of Relevance

Most discussions of relevance focus on the so-called "*ad* fallacies." The ad fallacies are patterns of argument used in ways that are considered inappropriate in that they introduce issues that are not germane to the questions under consideration. The most common ad fallacies include the following.

Argument ad hominem

In the *ad hominem* fallacy, the person making an argument, rather than the substance of his or her argument, is the object of attack. If one responds to someone's argument in favor of cutting the defense budget by referring to the person as a miserable, draft-dodging coward, then one is engaging in an ad hominem attack rather than responding to the person's specific arguments for cutting the defense budget.[3]

Argument ad verecundiam

The *ad verecundiam* strategy is an appeal to authority in the form of a specific person (e.g., "Newt Gingrich believes that we should . . ."), role or office (e.g., "The surgeon general says . . ."), the past (e.g., "We should follow the advice of Lincoln and . . ."), tradition (e.g., "This is the way we have always done things . . ."), institutions (e.g., "The scientific thing to do is . . ."), or shared values (e.g., "If you support the family, then you will . . ."). This type of fallacy is most obvious when the authority appealed to has no expertise regarding, or no clear relevance to, the issue under discussion. The pope might be against all forms of birth control, but what does that have to do with the question of whether condoms should be available in public high schools (Walton, 1997a)?

Argument ad populum

The *ad populum* strategy is an appeal to popular opinion. We encounter this appeal with regularity in advertising and politics. When a television commercial informs the viewer that three out of four people surveyed preferred Soft Drink X over Soft Drink Y, it invites the inference that the viewer will prefer what is popular. But will the viewer do so? Maybe. Clearly, some of our preferences are shaped by popular opinion (e.g., one might buy and wear a certain brand of jeans because it is fashionable and popular), but in many cases popular opinion is not relevant to the various choices people have to make or the questions and decisions they confront. Consider a "Snapshot" from the November 20, 1997, issue of *USA Today.* It reported that 33% of the American public believe that terrorist groups represent the most significant nuclear threat to the nation. As a bit of information, the statistic is relatively harmless. But it exemplifies the type of meaningless statistics on which the ad populum strategy thrives. Does the American public's *opinion* on what constitutes the greatest threat have any relevance to questions about national security policy? Little, if any. But one should not be surprised if a statistic like this shows up (perhaps in a slightly altered form) in a message advocating increased security measures.

Argument ad baculum

The Latin word *baculum* means "stick," and the *ad baculum* strategy is commonly considered an appeal by way of some type of threat. Elements of **ambiguity** enter into this strategy because it often is difficult to distinguish between a *threat* and a *warning* (e.g., when the local bully mentions that a boy might have an "accident" if he does not hand over his lunch money, is that person threatening the boy or simply warning him about the dangers of walking home from school?). Although we do not usually think of threats as a legitimate strategy, they nevertheless play a crucial role in many situations. Woods (1995), for example, suggested that they are inevitable in many negotiation situations (e.g., employees threatening to strike if their wage demands are not met).[4]

Argument ad crumenam

The *ad crumenam* strategy is an appeal "to the purse" or to monetary and/or material interests. This strategy is quite common in debates over taxes where politicians appeal directly to voters' pocketbooks. The ad crumenam strategy enters the realm of fallacy when an advocate argues, for example, that the military base in his or her district cannot be closed because closing the base would damage the local economy. Closing the base might very well hurt the local economy, but is that relevant to the question of where military bases should be located?

Argument ad misericordiam

Literally an appeal to "pity," the term *ad misericordiam* often is used to apply to emotional appeals of all types. See the discussion in the entry for **pathos** on the issue of the *appropriateness* of emotional appeals (see also Walton, 1992a, 1997b).

Argument ad ignorantium

In the *ad ignorantium* appeal, advocates use a lack of knowledge or a lack of certainty (ignorance) as a way of proving something. For example, a person might argue that the lack of evidence about life on other planets—no one, after all, has proven that there is not life on other planets—is a reason to believe that life does exist on other planets. But the problem of relevance arises when one considers how the lack of knowledge or certainty helps to establish the claim that life does exist on other planets.

Fallacies of Clarity

Arguments can be defective because they are phrased in ways that make them **ambiguous** or unclear. The two most common fallacies of clarity discussed in the literature are *equivocation* (where a word is used with more than one meaning) and *amphiboly* (where lack of clarity is due to syntax or sentence construction). Equivocation often comes into play in syllogistically structured **arguments** when the term that appears in both the major and minor premises is equivocal. For example, here is a reconstructed syllogism from the Ronald Reagan administration's defense of the Strategic Defense Initiative (SDI or "Star Wars"):

> The United States needs to feel safe.
> The SDI provides safety.
> The United States needs the SDI.

But "feeling safe" and "safety" are not necessarily the same thing. Hence, the reconstructed argument is a form of equivocation. Amphiboly can appear in premise/data statements or in claims. In either case, a lack of clarity arises from the way in which the sentence is constructed as in this example from Copi (1961): "Save soap and waste paper" (cited in Hamblin, 1970, p. 16).

There has been a figurative explosion in scholarship on the topic of fallacies during the past 15 years. Most contemporary scholars credit Hamblin (1970) with revealing the shallowness and artificiality of the literature on fallacies. Numerous issues mark the contemporary resurgence in work on fallacies, but one in particular stands out. Among the problems that Hamblin detected in the "standard account" of fallacies was the tendency to seek a simple formula for determining whether a specific expression was or was not a fallacy. The literature on fallacies took on a rather mechanical feel as classification, rather than explication, became the dominant task. A new approach to fallacies was suggested by Walton (1992b) when he wrote, "We need to rethink the concept of fallacy, redefining a fallacy as a basically reasonable type of argument which has been used in a bad or corrupted way in a given instance" (p. 27). Adler

(1997) labeled this new approach the " 'F not f' thesis," which is short for stating that a fallacy is not always fallacious (p. 33). The project of rethinking the "traditional account" of fallacies, as Walton and others have recognized, must abandon the rather disembodied approach of the standard account and turn to actual cases of language use in context (Willard, 1995). Whereas the traditional account of fallacies tended to make blanket condemnations of various patterns of argument and appeal without inquiring into their possible appropriateness in specific contexts, contemporary inquiry focuses on the situated use of language and probes the situational norms of communication that can help to determine whether or not a specific strategy is problematic. To take one example, Woods's (1995) analysis of the ad baculum, discussed earlier, considered numerous cases where the appeal to force or threat was present to determine the types of conditions that lend the appeal legitimacy. Similarly, Bachman (1995) concluded his analysis of the ad verecundiam by suggesting, "The formulation of fixed rules concerning when the appeal to an authority is legitimate or fallacious is misleading because strategies for assessing answers and oracles are dependent in part upon the inquirer's specific situation and purposes" (p. 286).

The same type of analysis can be extended throughout the realm of fallacies. Fallacy then becomes a label used for describing various forms of inappropriate discourse, recognizing that the idea of situational appropriateness is itself often highly contested. The emphasis on situational appropriateness in much current work on fallacies helps to link the more "logical" and "persuasive" forms of argumentation scholarship under the traditional concept of **decorum.**

Notes

1. See also Perelman and Olbrechts-Tyteca's (1969) discussion of the *directional* argument.

2. For a much more nuanced and detailed analysis, see Walton (1992b).

3. For various reinterpretations and reappraisals of ad hominem, see Brinton (1995), Cragan and Cutbirth (1984), Johnstone (1952, 1978), and Walton (1998).

4. See also Wreen (1989).

References and Additional Reading

Adler, J. E. (1997). Fallacies not fallacious: Not! *Philosophy and Rhetoric, 30,* 333-350.

Aristotle. (1954). *Rhetoric* (W. R. Roberts, Trans.). New York: Modern Library.

Aristotle. (1955). *Sophistical refutations* (E. S. Forster, Trans.). Cambridge, MA: Harvard University Press.

Bachman, J. (1995). Appeal to authority. In H. V. Hansen & R. C. Pinto (Eds.), *Fallacies: Classical and contemporary readings.* University Park: Pennsylvania State University Press.

Bentham, J. (1952). *Handbook of political fallacies* (H. A. Larrabee, Ed.). Baltimore, MD: Johns Hopkins University Press.

Brinton, A. (1995). The ad hominem. In H. V. Hansen & R. C. Pinto (Eds.), *Fallacies: Classical and contemporary readings.* University Park: Pennsylvania State University Press.

Copi, I. M. (1961). *Introduction to logic* (2nd ed.). New York: Macmillan.

Cragan, J. F., & Cutbirth, C. W. (1984). A revisionist perspective on political ad hominem argument: A case study. *Central States Speech Journal, 35,* 228-237.

Finocchiaro, M. A. (1981). Fallacies and the evaluation of reasoning. *American Philosophical Quarterly, 18,* 13-22.

Finocchiaro, M. A. (1987). Six types of fallaciousness: Toward a realistic theory of logical criticism. *Argumentation, 1,* 263-282.

Fogelin, R. J. (1987). *Understanding arguments: An introduction to informal logic* (3rd ed.). Orlando, FL: Harcourt Brace Jovanovich.

Hamblin, C. L. (1970). *Fallacies.* London: Methuen.

Hansen, H. V., & Pinto, R. C. (Eds.). (1995). *Fallacies: Classical and contemporary readings.* University Park: Pennsylvania State University Press.

Johnstone, H. W., Jr. (1952). Philosophy and *argumentum ad hominem. Journal of Philosophy, 49,* 489-498.

Johnstone, H. W., Jr. (1978). "Philosophy and *argumentum ad hominem*" revisited. In H. W. Johnstone, Jr., *Validity and rhetoric in philosophical argument: An outlook in transition.* University Park, PA: Dialogue Press of Man and World.

Kahane, H. (1995). *Logic and contemporary rhetoric: The use of reason in everyday life* (7th ed.). Belmont, CA: Wadsworth.

Massey, G. (1981). The fallacy behind fallacies. *Midwest Journal of Philosophy, 6,* 489-500.
Perelman, C., & Olbrechts-Tyteca, L. (1969). *The new rhetoric: A treatise on argumentation* (J. Wilkinson & P. Weaver, Trans.). Notre Dame, IN: University of Notre Dame Press.
van Eemeren, F. H., Grootendorst, R., & Henkemans, F. S. (1996). *Fundamentals of argumentation theory: A handbook of historical and contemporary developments.* Mahwah, NJ: Lawrence Erlbaum.
Walton, D. (1992a). *The place of emotion in argument.* University Park: Pennsylvania State University Press.
Walton, D. (1992b). *Slippery slope arguments.* Oxford, UK: Clarendon.
Walton, D. (1995). *A pragmatic theory of fallacy.* Tuscaloosa: University of Alabama Press.
Walton, D. (1997a). *Appeal to expert opinion: Arguments from authority.* University Park: Pennsylvania State University Press.
Walton, D. (1997b). *Appeal to pity: Argumentum ad misericordiam.* Albany: State University of New York Press.
Walton, D. (1998). *Ad hominem arguments.* Tuscaloosa: University of Alabama Press.
Whately, R. (1848). *Elements of logic* (9th ed.). London: Longmans.
Willard, C. A. (1995). Failures of relevance: A rhetorical view. In H. V. Hansen & R. C. Pinto (Eds.), *Fallacies: Classical and contemporary readings.* University Park: Pennsylvania State University Press.
Woods, J. (1995). Appeal to force. In H. V. Hansen & R. C. Pinto (Eds.), *Fallacies: Classical and contemporary readings.* University Park: Pennsylvania State University Press.
Wreen, M. J. (1989). A bolt of fear. *Philosophy and Rhetoric, 22,* 131-140.

FANTASY THEME ANALYSIS

One of the seminal intellectual developments during the 20th century was the rise of various forms of *constructivist* or *constitutive* theories of language and human communication. Burke (1966), one of the many thinkers associated with the constructivist turn, raised the central issues through a series of questions:

> Can we bring ourselves to realize . . . just how overwhelmingly much of what we mean by "reality" has been built up for us through nothing but our symbol systems? Take away our books, and what little do we know about history, biography, even something so "down to earth" as the relative position of seas and continents? What is our "reality" for today (beyond the paper-thin line of our own particular lives) but all this clutter of symbols about the past combined with whatever things we know mainly through maps, magazines, newspapers, and the like about the present? . . . And however important to us is the tiny sliver of reality each of us has experienced firsthand, the whole overall "picture" is but a construct of our symbol systems. (p. 5)

On this subject, Wess (1996) observed, "Constructionist theorists may disagree sharply; some render constructions visible by historicizing them, others by deconstructing them. But they come together in agreeing that there is a constructive ingredient in our 'realities' " (p. 4). In short, a considerable body of contemporary social, linguistic, and literary theory posits that language, symbols and symbol systems, and discursive practice(s) shape, and in many cases create, the sense of reality that humans experience.

The constructivist or constitutive turn has had a significant impact on contemporary rhetorical studies.[1] This impact is evident in that body of critical scholarship commonly referred to as **fantasy theme analysis.** The fantasy theme method of criticism was pioneered by Ernest Bormann (1972, 1973, 1977, 1982b, 1985a, 1985b; see also Bormann, Cragan, & Shields, 1996) and was extended and refined in the works of a number of his students and disciplinary colleagues (Chesebro, 1980; Cragan & Shields, 1977; Doyle, 1985; Foss, 1979; Hensley, 1975; Ilkka, 1977; Nimmo & Combs, 1982; Putnam, Van Hoeven, & Bullis, 1991). Fantasy theme analysis has proven to be one the most popular methods of rhetorical criticism over the past 25 years.

Bormann's (1972) initial formulation of the fantasy theme method analogically extended on the work of psychologists studying group behavior (Bales, 1970). The key insight that Bormann (1972) derived from Bales's work was "*the dynamic process of group fantasizing*" (p. 396) present in small group interaction. Extending this insight, Bormann argued that "Bales provides the [rhetorical] critic with an account of how dramatizing communication creates social reality for groups of people and with a way to examine messages for insights into a group's culture, motivation, emotional style, and cohesion" (p. 396). Bormann (1985a) argued, "Much of what has commonly been thought of as persuasion can be accounted for on the basis of group and mass fantasies" (p. 9). The fantasy theme method functions as a way for rhetorical critics to examine the discursive and symbolic processes by which "social reality" is constructed and within which specific acts of persuasion occur.

What exactly is "group fantasizing"? Imagine a group of students sitting around in a classroom before the start of class or a group of factory workers sitting at a table in the break room toward the end of the lunch hour. One person in the student group might comment that "this class really bites," or one of the factory workers might comment that "this job sucks." Another student might follow up the first comment by describing what he or she would rather be doing (perhaps something like sitting in the bleachers at Wrigley Field with a cold beer). Then another student might follow up that comment by extending the basic idea (describing the warm sun, the cool breeze coming off Lake Michigan, the sound of the various vendors, etc.). The group members have begun to exercise their imaginative capacity; they have begun to fantasize. This fantasy might continue to develop or might be interrupted. Perhaps a woman in the group might offer an alternative idea (fantasizing about an afternoon in Wrigley Field is, after all, a rather "male" thing to do). Perhaps her fantasy is winning the lottery and how she might spend the money. Other students might join in and describe what they would do if they won the lottery. And so, a new fantasy develops. Consider the case of the factory workers. Imagine that one of the factory workers follows up the comment about how much the job sucks by blurting out that the factory owner is an "S.O.B." Another person might follow up that comment by describing what he or she would do to the owner if that person encountered him alone in a dark alley. Then someone else might describe a more painful way of exacting his or her frustrations and hostilities on the factory owner. Soon, the discussion resembles a scene from the movie *9 to 5* when the characters (played by Lily Tomlin, Jane Fonda, and Dolly Parton) fantasize about what they would do to their sexist boss (played by Dabney Coleman). One of the workers might interrupt this fantasy by trying to focus the group members' attention on what they realistically might do to better their working conditions. But their supposedly more realistic discussion—perhaps they should unionize the factory—also involves the process of group fantasizing as the workers begin to make plans to seize the means of production (a Marxist fantasy) or as they imagine various heroic acts they might take on behalf of their new cause (a "Norma Rae" fantasy).[2]

Bormann (1972) described the outward manifestations of group fantasizing in these terms: "The tempo of the conversation would pick up. People would grow excited, interrupt one another, blush, laugh, [and] forget their self-consciousness" (p. 397). The conversation "would become lively, animated, and boisterous" as the individuals began to participate in the fantasizing process. But Bormann was most interested in the "manifest content of a group fantasy" (p. 397); he wanted to be able to describe specific fantasy episodes with some precision while also being able to make generalizations about the communication practices that characterize the fantasizing process. He took his cue from Bales's observation that group fantasizing proceeds by way of "dramatizing communication" (p. 396) and provided the following initial account: "The content consists of characters, real or fictitious, playing out a dramatic situation in a setting removed in time and space from the here-and-now transactions of the group" (p. 397). In short, when groups fantasize, they collaboratively construct stories, **narratives**, or dramas. The students in the preceding example first create a "taking the day off" story that is followed by a "strike it rich" story (relatively common plots in popular culture narratives). The factory workers initially develop a story of revenge that is followed by one focusing on worker solidarity.

Fantasy communication dramatizes or tells a story. The elements that make up the story—details concerning the characters, the setting, and the lines of action pursued by the characters (or the plot)—are referred to as *fantasy themes* (Bormann, 1972, p. 401; Foss, 1996, p. 123). In an effort to provide a more precise definition, Bormann (1985a) wrote,

> The technical meaning for fantasy [within fantasy theme analysis and symbolic convergence communication theory] is the creative and imaginative interpretation of events that fulfills a psychological or rhetorical need. . . . Rhetorical fantasies may include fanciful and fictitious scripts of imaginary characters, but they often deal with things that have actually happened to members of the community or that are reported in authenticated works of history, in the news media, or in the oral history and folklore of the group. The content of the dramatizing message . . . is called a *fantasy theme*" (p. 5)

Once a fantasy theme is introduced into a group (the worker's comment about wanting to meet the factory owner in a dark alley is an example of theme that combines elements of setting, character, and lines of action), it can become the focal point for what fantasy theme critics describe as a *chaining* process. Chaining refers to the way in which a specific theme, or a group of themes, is appropriated, circulated, revised, and/or elaborated by other members of the group; it is the active and dynamic process at the center of group fantasizing. Both of the preceding examples described limited forms of chaining in that a specific theme was collaboratively developed within a small group. But given that fantasy theme criticism wants to analyze both public and group communication, how does chaining occur within larger discursive communities? Let us consider two examples. First, in his acceptance speech at the 1960 Democratic Convention, John F. Kennedy introduced a rather famous *metaphor* that fantasy theme critics would interpret as a setting theme—the new frontier. To study the process of chaining, the critic would need to review as much discursive material as possible subsequent to Kennedy's speech. Do the news media pick up and circulate the fantasy theme? Do other politicians appropriate it for their purposes? Do rival politicians contest the theme? Do average citizens (e.g., as reflected in letters to the editor of newspapers) adopt, as well as adapt, the theme? In short, what do the other members of the national "group" *do* with the theme? Do they ignore it (as with Bill Clinton's 1992 theme of the "new covenant"), or does it help to structure the national "conversation"? Signs of "frontier talk" during the fall of 1960 and beyond would serve as evidence that Kennedy's theme had begun to "chain out" among the population (and that Americans had begun to "chain in" to an emerging vision).

For a second example, consider a topic that appears to have chained out in our society—crime. Despite statistical evidence suggesting a drop in crime rates in most parts of the country, surveys and opinion polls suggested that Americans during the late 1990s remained quite concerned about crime. Might the social reality of crime be a discursive or rhetorical fantasy? To be sure, a murder, rape, or armed robbery is a "real" event, and the lives of countless "real" people are harmed or destroyed because of these acts. But what is the "reality" of crime for the millions of Americans who never have been victims? This question returns us to Burke's observation quoted at the beginning of this entry—the degree to which our reality is built by symbols. Most Americans have not experienced violent crime. What they have experienced is countless television reports, newspaper accounts, and ordinary conversations on that topic. What they "know" about the reality of crime is, as Burke suggested, a discursive and symbolic construction. News reports, fictional television shows, conversations, and other forms of communication function as mechanisms through which certain emotions (e.g., fear) can chain out through society.

Fantasy themes, then, constitute dramatic stories that shape a group's experience of social reality. The world becomes a little different as a fantasy chains out to larger and larger numbers of people. According to Bormann (1972),

> The dramatizations which catch on and chain out in small groups are worked into public speeches and into the mass media and, in turn, spread out across larger publics, serve to sustain the members' sense of community, to impel them strongly to action . . ., and to provide them with a social reality filled with heroes, villains, emotions, and attitudes. The composite dramas which catch up large groups of people in a symbolic reality . . . [can be thought of as] a "rhetorical vision." . . . A rhetorical vision is constructed from fantasy themes that chain out in face-to-face interacting groups, in speaker-audience transactions, in viewers of television broadcasts, in listeners to radio programs, and in all the diverse settings for public and intimate communication in a given society. (p. 398)

A rhetorical vision, Bormann (1985a) wrote, "is a unified putting-together of the various scripts which gives the participants a broader view of things" (p. 8). Although some *postmodern* scholars (e.g., Lyotard) discuss the decline of *metanarratives* (grand encompassing stories that help to define and motivate a community), fantasy theme critics insist that such metanarratives or rhetorical visions remain alive and well. As one grand rhetorical vision such as the "cold war" dissolves (Bormann et al., 1996), another vision such as George Bush's "new world order" emerges (Stuckey, 1995).

Investigating rhetorical visions provides insight into human motivation because, as Bormann (1972) maintained, "the rhetorical vision of a group of people contains their drives to action. . . . When a person appropriates a rhetorical vision, he [sic] gains with the supporting dramas constraining forces which impel him to adopt a lifestyle and to take certain action" (p. 406). Although Bormann distinguished his approach to uncovering *motivation* from that developed by Burke, there appear to be important similarities between fantasy theme analysis and **dramatism** on this subject (cf. Foss, 1979). Consistent with Burke, Bormann insists that motives are "embedded in the rhetorical vision rather than hidden in the skulls and viscera of people" (p. 407). He argued, "Motives do not exist to be expressed in the communication but rather arise in the expression itself and come to be embedded in the drama of the fantasy themes that generated and serve to sustain them." In short, "motives are in the messages" (p. 406).

Bormann (1982a) acknowledged that fantasy theme critics initially

> tended to label all dramatizing content as fantasy themes no matter its scope or level of abstraction. This imprecision led to research difficulties. As we studied these problems, we discovered interrelated sets of fantasy themes of broad scope, [and] we used the term *rhetorical vision* to indicate these integrated symbol systems. . . . Subsequently, we found material of middle range abstraction and scope which led to the refinement of the concept I label *fantasy type*. (p. 294)

Fantasy types are, then, the recurrent stories that are constructed from fantasy themes. Bormann (1985a) argued, "A *fantasy type* is a stock scenario repeated again and again by the same characters or by similar characters" (p. 7). In the preceding examples, "taking the day off" and revenge fantasy narratives are recurrent enough in our society to merit the label fantasy type. Another common example

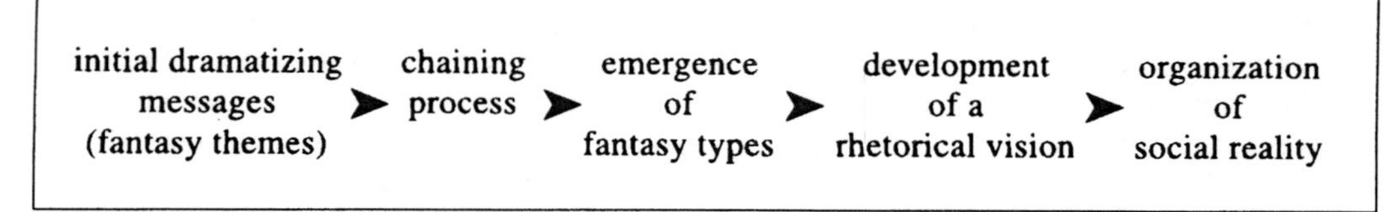

Figure F.1. The Process of Group Fantasizing

that Bormann (1985a) discussed is "the Pauline conversion fantasy" type, a recurrent scenario frequently embedded in the discourse of **secular conversion.**

Fantasy themes, fantasy types, and rhetorical visions are the central analytic concepts of the fantasy theme method, but they are not the only concepts employed. Fantasy theme critics also will borrow concepts such as **persona** (Bormann, 1973) from literary and dramatic theory. The method presumes an unfolding process of development that can be represented in the visual model depicted in Figure F.1. Critical analysis can emphasize different stages in the process. A number of fantasy theme studies, often focused on social **movements,** concentrate on the right side of the visual representation in their effort to reconstruct the rhetorical vision developed in movement rhetoric (Foss, 1979; Hensley, 1975). Other studies emphasize the chaining process or "the relationship between dramatizing messages in public channels of communication and the way people" ignore, reject, or appropriate the messages (Bormann, 1982a, p. 298; see also Bormann, Koester, & Bennett, 1978; Cragan & Shields, 1977).

Bormann's (1972, 1977, 1985a) studies of colonial New England Puritans illustrated both the process and value of fantasy theme criticism.[3] Bormann (1972) wrote, "Huddled in unheated, crude, and undecorated meeting houses in the wilderness in the early years of the Massachusetts Bay Colony . . ., the Puritans of colonial New England led an internal fantasy life of mighty grandeur and complexity" (p. 402). Colonial Puritans patterned their vision after the biblical drama of the Jewish exodus from Egypt. "They participated in a rhetorical vision that saw the migration to the new world as a holy exodus of God's chosen people" (p. 402). Bormann continued,

> The Puritan rhetorical vision saw them as conquering new territories for God, saving the souls of the natives, and, most importantly, as setting up in the wilderness a model religious community, a new Israel, patterned after the true meaning of the scriptures to light the way for the reformation still to be accomplished in old England and in all of Europe. (p. 402)

How did this vision develop? Bormann (1985a) explained,

> The rhetoricians who broke away from the established Anglican traditions of sixteenth-century England and began to generate the new vision chained into dramas provided by the adherents of John Calvin. The fantasies that emerged in their small group discussions and subsequently in their sermons featured an everyman persona who was a lowly mean creature, tainted with the guilt of Adam's sin. In all scenarios, man [sic] was universally and completely dependent upon God. He had not the ability to determine his own salvation. The God persona was a just, beneficent, stern, and awesome character who was under no obligation to provide eternal life for any of the unworthy human beings who populated the vision. (p. 40)

But the Puritans believed that God did grant salvation to a fortunate few. These various fantasy themes (characterizations of God, humanity, etc.) fused to create the "central fantasy type . . . of election to sainthood" (p. 40).

But this fantasy type, "the mighty drama of individual salvation" (p. 41), is only one of the stories that constituted the Puritan vision. Another key fantasy type that Bormann (1985a) noted was the "scenario . . . of God giving His chosen people a time of troubles as a warning for the evil of their ways in turning out of ignorance away from Him" (p. 43). This fantasy type was bifurcated; it could lead to a happy ending, or it could culminate in destruction. He added, "In the scenarios with a happy ending, the chosen people used God's time of troubles as a spur to an understanding of their sin. . . . When they found God's way again, the result was a glorious happy ending, a time of regeneration and rebirth" (p. 43). Bormann argued that the various fantasy themes and fantasy types, and the encompassing rhetorical vision, created the social reality of the colonial Puritans. Their vision was a source of motivation, a way of maintaining communal identity, and a framework for understanding events in the world. It is impossible to understand the Puritans, Bormann intimated, without taking account of their rhetorical fantasies and vision.

As is the case with most established programs or movements in criticism, fantasy theme analysis has generated controversy and opposition. Mohrmann (1982a, 1982b) offered perhaps the most sustained **metacritical** assault on the fantasy theme method. Mohrmann raised a number of questions and problems. Some of the more important ones include the following. First, Mohrmann (1982a) argued that the analytic categories and concepts introduced by Bormann invite "mechanical application" (p. 119). In Mohrmann's view, the result too often is unimaginative criticism. The first difficulty is compounded by a second difficulty—that the "basic definitions lack precision. . . . Consider, first, fantasy themes. Monumentally various, they range from a snippet of information in a television newscast to the entirety of John F. Kennedy's appearance before the Houston Ministerial Association, and they reach to almost every imaginable phenomenon" (pp. 119, 125). The problem, for Mohrmann, was conceptual slippage caused by ambiguity. How can we categorize and analyze elements of a text with any confidence when the conceptual categories are poorly defined? As an example, consider how Bormann shifted conceptual categories in his studies of the Puritans. In his 1972 essay, the migration to the new world was identified as the Puritans' underlying rhetorical vision, whereas in *The Force of Fantasy* (Bormann, 1985a), the Puritan migration was recategorized as a "fantasy type" (p. 44). But Bormann provided no clear or explicit explanation for the shift.[4] Third, Mohrmann (1982a) questioned whether fantasy theme critics have delivered the promised goods. He noted, for example, that "we might expect . . . a charting of concatenation, but if so, we would be disappointed because none appears, no instance in which a critic attempts to follow the chaining sequence from one communication context to another" (p. 120). From Mohrmann's perspective, one of the more promising aspects of the fantasy theme method remained unexplored. Finally, Mohrmann (1982a) suggested that fantasy theme criticism is little more than an exercise in relabeling or "a naming of parts [as] its own raison d'etre" (p. 125). As an example, Mohrmann considered Bormann's (1973) use of the concept **persona** and found it to be of little value. As another example, consider the case of Kennedy's use of "the new frontier" discussed earlier. For Mohrmann, there appeared to be little gained by relabeling the metaphor as a fantasy theme. In sum, Mohrmann (1982a) wrote, "The assumptions about social reality, the restricted view of drama, the delimited vocabulary, and the flaccidly developed hierarchy are coalescent features that become an impediment against, rather than a bridge to, understanding and discrimination in criticism" (p. 128).

Despite critiques by Mohrmann and others, fantasy theme criticism has remained a central method in rhetorical studies. Its popularity has declined from the peak period of fantasy theme studies (roughly 1975-1985), reflecting the general trend away from fixed methods in rhetorical **criticism.** Another factor that might have contributed to its declining fortunes was the rise in prominence of the closely related concept of **narrative** and narrative analysis (e.g., Fisher, 1987). Both approaches to criticism—fantasy theme and narrative analysis—try to uncover the sometimes explicit, often implicit stories that saturate and undergird public discourse. Are there any significant differences between the two, or are they essentially the same approaches clothed in different terminology? No doubt, scholars will differ on how they answer this question. But one difference, a key element in Bales's research program that had such an influence on Bormann, seems important. Narrative analysis tends to approach discourse *synchronically.* The narrative usually is understood as complete or fully developed, and the critic's tasks include analytic reconstruction, interpretation, and/or critical evaluation. Fantasy theme analysis tends to approach discourse, at least in theory if not always in critical practice, *diachronically.* The social drama or story emerges over time through the process of chaining. The fantasy theme critic tries to describe the collaborative process through which the story comes into existence. Ideally, this would mean locating the initial fantasy themes, charting the chaining process by which multiple advocates or social agents contribute to the development of the emerging story, noting the way in which the developing story circulates within a culture and describing how that process of circulation introduces additional modifications to the story, and culminating in an account of a rhetorical vision that reveals how at least one segment of the culture defines its social reality. The central concerns of the fantasy theme critic—collaborative development, dynamic process of emergence, and ongoing circulation—are largely absent in synchronically oriented narrative analysis. These concerns connect with other recent developments in humanities scholarship. Although the fit is not exact, a number of the concerns of the fantasy theme critic overlap with the important trend in literary studies that goes under the label "new historicism." So, despite Mohrmann's critique, fantasy theme analysis still might have much to contribute to contemporary rhetorical studies.[5]

Notes

1. For an overview, see the discussion of constitutive effects under the entry for **effects of rhetorical practice.**
2. For another fictional example, consider the scene in the film *Big* when Josh (played by Tom Hanks) criticizes the toy designed by his rival—a building that turns into a robot. Hanks's character introduces an alternative—a bug that turns into a robot. The rest of the group then picks up on Hanks's idea, and the process of group fantasizing is under way.
3. See also Bercovitch's (1993) discussion of the American "fantasy of Puritan origins" (p. 6) as well as Miller's (1956) pioneering work on the Puritans and Bercovitch's (1978) earlier study.
4. Bormann might have argued, however, that the concept of fantasy type had not been formulated in 1972. But once it had been introduced, it could then be employed as a more appropriate way of understanding the migration fantasy.
5. Berlant's (1991) use of the concept of fantasy has potential relevance for contemporary rhetorical studies and might be read in the context of fantasy theme analysis.

References and Additional Reading

Bales, R. (1970). *Personality and interpersonal behavior.* New York: Holt, Rinehart.

Bercovitch, S. (1978). *The American jeremiad.* Madison: University of Wisconsin Press.

Bercovitch, S. (1993). *The rites of assent: Transformations in the symbolic construction of America.* New York: Routledge.

Berlant, L. (1991). *The anatomy of national fantasy: Hawthorne, utopia, and everyday life.* Chicago: University of Chicago Press.

Bormann, E. G. (1972). Fantasy and rhetorical vision: The rhetorical criticism of social reality. *Quarterly Journal of Speech, 58,* 396-407.

Bormann, E. G. (1973). The Eagleton affair: A fantasy theme analysis. *Quarterly Journal of Speech, 59,* 143-159.

Bormann, E. G. (1977). Fetching good out of evil: A rhetorical use of calamity. *Quarterly Journal of Speech, 63,* 130-139.

Bormann, E. G. (1982a). Fantasy and rhetorical vision: Ten years later. *Quarterly Journal of Speech, 68,* 288-305.

Bormann, E. G. (1982b). A fantasy theme analysis of the television coverage of the hostage release and the Reagan inaugural. *Quarterly Journal of Speech, 68,* 133-145.

Bormann, E. G. (1985a). *The force of fantasy: Restoring the American dream.* Carbondale: Southern Illinois University Press.

Bormann, E. G. (1985b). Symbolic convergence theory: A communication formulation. *Journal of Communication, 35,* 128-138.

Bormann, E. G., Koester, J., & Bennett, J. (1978). Political cartoons and salient rhetorical fantasies: An empirical analysis of the '76 presidential campaign. *Communication Monographs, 45,* 317-329.

Bormann, E. G., Cragan, J. F., & Shields, D. C. (1996). An expansion of the rhetorical vision component of the symbolic convergence theory: The cold war paradigm case. *Communication Monographs, 63,* 1-28.

Burke, K. (1966). *Language as symbolic action: Essays on life, literature, and method.* Berkeley: University of California Press.

Chesebro, J. W. (1980). Paradoxical views of "homosexuality" in the rhetoric of social scientists: A fantasy theme analysis. *Quarterly Journal of Speech, 66,* 127-139.

Cragan, J. F., & Shields, D. C. (1977). Foreign policy communication dramas: How mediated rhetoric played in Peoria in campaign '76. *Quarterly Journal of Speech, 63,* 274-289.

Doyle, M. V. (1985). The rhetoric of romance: A fantasy theme analysis of Barbara Cartland novels. *Southern Speech Communication Journal, 51,* 24-48.

Fisher, W. R. (1987). *Human communication as narration: Toward a philosophy of reason, value, and action.* Columbia: University of South Carolina Press.

Foss, K. A., & Littlejohn, S. W. (1986). The Day After: Rhetorical vision in an ironic frame. *Critical Studies in Mass Communication, 3,* 317-336.

Foss, S. K. (1979). The Equal Rights Amendment controversy: Two worlds in conflict. *Quarterly Journal of Speech, 65,* 275-288.

Foss, S. K. (1996). *Rhetorical criticism: Exploration and practice* (2nd ed.). Prospect Heights, IL: Waveland.

Hensley, C. W. (1975). Rhetorical vision and the persuasion of a historical movement: The disciples of Christ in nineteenth century American culture. *Quarterly Journal of Speech, 61,* 250-264.

Ilkka, R. J. (1977). Rhetorical dramatization in the development of American communism. *Quarterly Journal of Speech, 63,* 413-427.

Koester, J. (1982). The Machiavellian princess: Rhetorical dramas for women managers. *Communication Quarterly, 30,* 165-172.

Lyotard, J. F. (1984). *The postmodern condition: A report on knowledge.* Minneapolis: University of Minnesota Press.

Miller, P. (1956). *Errand into the wilderness.* Cambridge, MA: Harvard University Press.

Mohrmann, G. P. (1982a). An essay on fantasy theme criticism. *Quarterly Journal of Speech, 68,* 109-132.

Mohrmann, G. P. (1982b). Fantasy theme criticism: A peroration. *Quarterly Journal of Speech, 68,* 306-313.

Nimmo, D., & Combs, J. E. (1982). Fantasies and melodramas in television network news: The case of Three Mile Island. *Western Journal of Speech Communication, 46,* 45-55.

Nimmo, D., & Combs, J. E. (1990). *Mediated political realities* (2nd ed.). New York: Longman.

Porter, L. W. (1976). The White House transcripts: Group fantasy events concerning the mass media. *Central States Speech Journal, 27,* 272-279.

Putnam, L. L., van Hoeven, S., & Bullis, C. A. (1991). The role of rituals and fantasy themes in teachers' bargaining. *Western Journal of Speech Communication, 55,* 85-103.

Smith, C. A. (1986). Leadership, orientation, and rhetorical vision: Jimmy Carter, the "new right," and the Panama Canal. *Presidential Studies Quarterly, 16,* 317-328.

Stuckey, M. E. (1995). Competing foreign policy visions: Rhetorical hybrids after the cold war. *Western Journal of Communication, 59,* 214-227.

Wess, R. (1996). *Kenneth Burke: Rhetoric, subjectivity, postmodernism.* Cambridge, UK: Cambridge University Press.

FEMININE STYLE

According to Campbell (1989), a **feminine style** emerged in 19th-century America as woman speakers sought "to cope with the conflicting demands of the podium" (p. 12). The podium, a *synecdoche* for the **public sphere**, had throughout history been the province of men. As women advocates and rhetors began to tear down the barriers of custom that had excluded them from public life and to assume the role of public advocates, they faced a critical problem: *How* should they speak and write? One option would be to try and imitate the male orators of the day. But choosing this option would, in all likelihood, mean abandoning the rhetorical resources contained in social attitudes toward women (e.g., the idea that women possessed a moral sense superior to that of men) and in women's specific social experiences (e.g., child rearing). In addition, as Campbell noted, if a woman chose to imitate male speech, "she was likely to be judged masculine, unwomanly, aggressive, and cold" (p. 12). But if speaking in the dominant male style was not a live option for the increasing number of female advocates, women still had to find ways of making their case. As Campbell wrote, "A woman had to meet all the usual requirements of speakers, demonstrating expertise, authority, and rationality in order to show her competence and make herself credible to audiences" (p. 12). The bind of a woman advocate, in short, was how to speak in a way that was as persuasive as male speakers without becoming a "male" speaker—without abandoning her "femininity."

Campbell (1989) traced the development of a feminine style to the processes of "craft learning" that were an essential element of women's lived experience in 19th-century America. The essence of craft learning was that the imparted "skills cannot be expressed in universal laws; one must learn to apply them contingently, depending upon conditions and materials" (p. 13).[1] As a model for rhetorical **invention,** craft learning

> produces discourse with certain characteristics. Such discourse will be personal in tone . . ., relying heavily on personal experience, anecdotes, and other examples. It will tend to be structured inductively. . . . It will invite audience participation, including the process of testing generalizations or principles against the experiences of the audience. Audience members will be addressed as peers, with recognition of authority based on experience . . ., and efforts will be made to create identification with the experiences of the audience and those described by the speaker. The goal of such rhetoric is empowerment. (p. 130)[2]

In some cases, women rhetors further feminized their discourse and the role of public speaker by speaking through the **personas** of wives, mothers (Tonn, 1996), daughters, and/or sisters (p. 91).

Whereas Campbell introduced the idea of feminine style to help explain the practices of 19th-century women's rights advocates in America, the concept was further refined and extended to 20th-century cases. For example, Dow and Tonn (1993) employed the concept of feminine style in their analysis of former Texas Governor Ann Richards. Beyond illustrating that the central attributes of the feminine style were present in Richards' discourse, Dow and Tonn argued that shifting attention away from the discourse of "feminist social reform" to the "context of public political discourse" provides a mechanism for further conceptual development. They argued that in the context of Richards' discourse, "feminine style can be interpreted as . . . creating alternative grounds for political judgment" (p. 298). Dow and Tonn wrote,

> The synthesis of formal qualities of feminine style evident in Richards' rhetoric (use of narrative, concrete examples, analogies, and anecdotes as primary evidence sources; personal tone; and encouragement of audience participation) with an alternative political philosophy reflecting feminine ideals of care, nurturance, and family relationships functions as a critique of traditional political reasoning that offers alternative grounds for political judgment. (p. 289)

Dow and Tonn's (1993) essay illustrated nicely the way in which critical practice in rhetorical studies can generate conceptual reflection and refinement. But further reflection on their discussion of the relationship between feminine style and political **judgment** may yield intriguing results. Their argument is built on a contrast between "male" public discourse and political judgment, characterized as "abstract, hierarchical, dominating, and oriented toward problem-solving" (p. 288), and an alternative discursive form, the feminine style, that entails a different model or standard of judgment. A similar contrast, without the gender inflections, was at the heart of political theorist Ronald Beiner's book, *Political Judgment* (Beiner, 1983). The idea of political judgment, Beiner argued, is situated in a tension between two traditions of thought: a Kantian tradition that emphasizes "formal principles" (principles that overlap at a number of points with Dow and Tonn's account of male political judgment) and an Aristotelian tradition that emphasizes "substantive principles" (principles such as empathy and personal experience that overlap with Dow and Tonn's account of the manner of political judgment solicited by Richards' feminine style). Reading Dow and Tonn's discussion of the relationship between feminine style and political judgment through Beiner's framework suggests a potentially provocative hypothesis. In an effort to counteract the modern Enlightenment standards of the male public sphere, the feminine style developed by 19th-century women's rights advocates and continued by contemporary women rhetorical actors might be an unconscious recuperation of classical practical philosophy. Space limitations prevent a thorough discussion of this hypothesis here, but a few additional observations might help to establish its heuristic potential. First, consider Dow and Tonn's (1993) discussion of "nurturing" as an effort to "constantly negotiate the balance between authority and independence" (p. 297) in light of recent efforts to recover a sense of **prudence** as a balance between stability and innovation (Garver, 1987; Leff, 1991). The balancing process that Dow and Tonn saw at the heart of nurturing might be understood as a variation on the traditional model of prudence or *phronesis* (practical wisdom). Second, consider Dow's (1995) claim that the feminine style "facilitates experiential reasoning" (p. 108) in terms of Farrell's (1976) account of **social knowledge.** In Farrell's rehabilitation of Aristotelian doctrine, all argument that relies on social knowledge engages in a mode of experiential reasoning because social knowledge is the concrete discursive manifestation of collective experience. For Farrell, the contrast is not between experiential reasoning and "male" reasoning but rather between reasoning based on social knowledge and patterns of reasoning that draw on technical knowledge. This possible line of inquiry is not meant to suggest that the concept of feminine style can or should be reduced to, or dismissed as, another effort to resurrect classical rhetoric. There *are* differences between feminist rhetorical thought and the dominant tradition of rhetorical thought (e.g., much feminist theory argues for the need to redistribute power, whereas much traditional rhetorical thinking was directed at how to achieve power). The point of this brief discussion is only to draw attention to some *possible* parallels between the efforts of women advocates struggling to dismantle a male-dominated public sphere and the efforts of scholars in various fields to recover elements of the tradition of practical philosophy as an antidote to the problems produced by modernist visions of instrumental rationality.[3]

The concept of feminine style raises the question of whether or not this style is the exclusive province of women. Campbell (1989) was clear that, in her view, "it was not, and is not today, a style exclusive to women" (p. 12).[4] But as Dow (1995) noted, "The argument that women face unique rhetorical situations has been transmuted into the argument that the rhetoric itself is intrinsically unique and that this uniqueness is linked to gender" (p. 108). Viewing feminine style as unique to women—a result of the differences in male and female socialization—creates conceptual problems. As Dow argued, when gender is privileged as the only relevant difference, other important differences (e.g., race, economic status) tend to be ignored. Reflection on the problem of difference led Dow to refine the concept of feminine style. She wrote, "Feminine style is as much a product of *power* as it is a product of *gender*" (p. 109). That is, the experience of *powerlessness,* along with the experiences associated with female socialization, is a critical element shaping the feminine style ignored in previous scholarship. By factoring in the element of power, critics will be able to identify relative variations within women's discourse. For example, the feminine style of college-educated white women is not the same as the feminine style displayed in the discourse of working class women or women of color. This point is illustrated in Tonn's (1996) study of labor activist "Mother" Jones.[5]

Finally, rhetorical scholarship on feminine style intersects with a number of lines of inquiry in the humanities and social sciences. For example, scholars trained in the tradition of sociolinguistics also investigate the different characteristics of women's discourse (Kramarae, 1981; Kramer, 1974), whereas psychologists focus on the relationship between gender and reasoning (Gilligan, 1982). Perhaps the clearest intersection is with the idea of *écriture féminine* introduced by the French feminist philosopher and critic Hélène Cixous (e.g., Cixous, 1980). According to Cixous, écriture féminine is a mode of writing (speaking receives little attention) that seeks to subvert or overturn the structures of oppression that are "built in" (so to speak) to male-dominated language. Green and LeBihan (1996) explained,

> *Écriture féminine* is a discourse which is written out of a concern with subjectivity, sexuality, and language. It maintains the belief that whatever symbolic systems currently exist—the most prominent of these systems being language—they are not adequate; they relentlessly place women within a restrictive system in which it is impossible for them to be active subjects. (p. 243)

Cixous suggested that even basic features of language use such as grammatical or syntactic conventions are forms of male domination because they perpetuate the dominant masculinist or patriarchal bias. Écriture féminine is, then, an inchoate form of practice that disrupts patriarchal hierarchies as it gives voice to the unique experiences of historically situated women. In comparison to the more moderate functions of feminine style, écriture féminine is an inherently radical mode of discursive practice.

Notes

1. As Campbell (1989) noted, this account of craft learning closely parallels one version of the classical tradition of rhetorical pedagogy.
2. Compare Blankenship and Robson (1995) on the central characteristics of a feminine style.
3. For a more detailed discussion of the relationship between feminist theory and the traditions of rhetoric, see Condit (1997).
4. See also Jamieson (1988) and Parry-Giles and Parry-Giles (1996).
5. On the contrast between masculine and feminine style, see also Campbell's (1998) comparison of Hillary Rodham Clinton and Elizabeth Hanford Dole.

References and Additional Reading

Beiner, R. (1983). *Political judgment.* Chicago: University of Chicago Press.

Blankenship, J., & Robson, D. C. (1995). A "feminine style" in women's political discourse: An exploratory essay. *Communication Quarterly, 43,* 353-366.

Campbell, K. K. (1989). *Man cannot speak for her: A critical study of early feminist rhetoric* (Vol. 1). New York: Greenwood.

Campbell, K. K. (1998). The discursive performance of femininity: Hating Hillary. *Rhetoric and Public Affairs, 1,* 1-19.

Cixous, H. (1980). The laugh of the Medusa. In E. Marks & I. de Courtivron (Eds.), *New French feminisms.* Amherst: University of Massachusetts Press.

Condit, C. M. (1997). In praise of eloquent diversity: Gender and rhetoric as public persuasion. *Women's Studies in Communication, 20,* 91-116.

Dow, B. J. (1995). Feminism, difference(s), and rhetorical studies. *Communication Studies, 46,* 106-117.

Dow, B. J., & Tonn, M. B. (1993). "Feminine style" and political judgment in the rhetoric of Ann Richards. *Quarterly Journal of Speech, 79,* 286-302.

Farrell, T. B. (1976). Knowledge, consensus, and rhetorical theory. *Quarterly Journal of Speech, 62,* 1-14.

Garver, E. (1987). *Machiavelli and the history of prudence.* Madison: University of Wisconsin Press.

Gilligan, C. (1982). *In a different voice: Psychological theory and women's development.* Cambridge, MA: Harvard University Press.

Green, K., & LeBihan, J. (1996). *Critical theory and practice: A coursebook.* London: Routledge.

Jamieson, K. H. (1988). *Eloquence in an electronic age: The transformation of political speechmaking.* New York: Oxford University Press.

Kramarae, C. (1981). *Men and women speaking: Frameworks for analysis.* Rowley, MA: Newbury House.

Kramer, C. (1974). Women's speech: Separate but unequal. *Quarterly Journal of Speech, 60,* 14-24.

Leff, M. (1991). Prudential argument and the use of history in Franklin D. Roosevelt's "Commonwealth Club Address." In F. H. van Eemeren, R. Grootendorst, J. A. Blair, & C. A. Willard (Eds.), *Proceedings of the Second International Conference on Argumentation.* Amsterdam: Stichting Internationaal Centrum voor de Studie van Argumentatie en Taalbeheersing (SICSAT).

Mattina, A. F. (1994). "Rights as well as duties": The rhetoric of Leonora O'Reilly. *Communication Quarterly, 42,* 196-205.

Parry-Giles, S. J., & Parry-Giles, T. (1996). Gendered politics and presidential image construction: A reassessment of the "feminine style." *Communication Monographs, 63,* 337-353.

Sheckels, T. F. (1997). The rhetorical use of double-voiced discourse and feminine style: The U.S. Senate debate over the impact of Tailhook '91 on Admiral Frank B. Kelso II's retirement rank. *Southern Communication Journal, 63,* 56-68.

Tonn, M. B. (1996). Militant motherhood: Labor's Mary Harris "Mother" Jones. *Quarterly Journal of Speech, 82,* 1-21.

Zurakowski, M. M. (1994). From doctors and lawyers to wives and mothers: Enacting "feminine style" and changing abortion rights arguments. *Women's Studies in Communication, 17,* 45-68.

FIGURE/FIGURATION

Historian and theorist of rhetoric Richard Lanham defined **figure** as "any device or pattern of language in which meaning is enhanced or changed" (Lanham, 1991, p. 178). Figures, or figurative language, occur in different shapes and sizes; individual words, short phrases, patterns of words that extend over a number of sentences or paragraphs, and even an entire text (e.g., essay, short story) can manifest the figurative functions of enhancing or altering meaning. A list of a large number of common figures (including examples) is included in the entry for **style.**

Over the centuries, rhetoricians have tried to classify and categorize the range of figures found in discursive practice. One common form of categorization noted by Lanham (1991) divides figures into *tropes* and *schemes.*[1] The term *trope* is used narrowly to refer to any figure that changes the normal, literal, or conventional meaning of a word or a series of words. *Metaphors,* such as "he is a pig" and "she is a fox," are common examples; in both examples, the common meaning of the terms *pig* and *fox* are modified in the act of *predication* (the act of linking the terms to the pronouns *he* and *she*). When the metaphor "he is a pig" is used to describe one's roommate, this does not imply that the roommate has four legs, a curly tail, and a snout nose; instead, it means that the roommate exhibits certain behaviors that can be associated with the animal labeled with the term *pig.* But as Lanham and countless scholars have noted, our ideas of normal, literal, and conventional meanings are not as unproblematic as the terms *normal* and *conventional* suggest. The distinction between normal meaning and a trope's "abnormal" meaning is not always clear or precise. Many scholars favor abandoning the literal or normal versus nonliteral or abnormal distinction as the basis for defining tropes, but the distinction continues to persist (in part because other ways of defining trope do not offer the clarity, albeit deceptive clarity, of the normal-abnormal distinction). The term *scheme* is used to refer to "a figure in which words preserve their literal meaning but are placed in a significant arrangement of some kind" (p. 178). Figures such as *anaphora* (repetition of a word at the beginning of a series of phrases, clauses, or sentences) and *alliteration* (repetition of consonant sounds) are examples of figurative schemes.

Another way of classifying or categorizing figures can be found in Quinn's (1982) *Figures of Speech.* Quinn categorized figures in terms of the specific strategies that they embody. Anaphora and alliteration are figures of *arrangement.* Metaphor is a figure of *substitution* (where the nonliteral meaning is substituted for the literal one).[2] *Asyndeton* (the deletion of conjunctions as in "I came, I saw, I conquered") is a figure of *omission,* whereas *polysyndeton* (the liberal use of conjunctions) is a figure of *addition.* But combinations are possible. The figure of *metaplasmus* (purposeful misspelling of a word), for example, can be accomplished by altering the normal arrangement of letters in a word (e.g., "Friday" becomes "Firday"), by substituting one letter for another (e.g., Jacque Derrida's use of the term *differance* substitutes an *a* for an *e*), by deleting a letter or letters (e.g., "I am" becomes the contraction "I'm"), and by the addition of letters (e.g., a person disliking the college Greek system might refer to "sororitities" and "fraterniraties"). Or, the types can be combined; as Quinn observed, "If we wish to emphasize the sounds of a dialect, we might misspell God as Gawd" (p. 19), substituting the *a* for the *o* and adding the *w*. Like all category systems, Quinn's has a number of advantages, but like the various systems that have been proposed over the years, slippage and ambiguity are inescapable when it comes to rhetorical figures.

The second term to be considered in this entry, **figuration,** is itself a type of rhetorical figure—*polyptoton* (where a new word is derived from the root of the old word). We can begin to understand the concept of figuration by exploring the suffix used to derive it from the term *figure* (through a process of addition). The suffix "ion" denotes both an act or a process and the result of an act or a process. Both of these senses apply to the term *figuration*.[3] For example, the philosopher Owen Barfield used the term *figuration* to describe the "work of construction" by which "mere sensations must be combined and constructed by the percipient mind into the recognizable and nameable objects we call 'things' " (Barfield, 1988, p. 24). Barfield's definition emphasized figuration as a process of mental "work" that produces a certain type of result, namely the "objects we call 'things.' " Process and product or result are blended together in this definition.

Barfield was interested in describing human consciousness, perception, and cognition, and the idea of figuration played a key role in his account. But Barfield was not interested in examining the relationship among human consciousness, perception, and cognition and the root from which his term *figuration* is derived—figure. Other scholars, in some cases explicitly using the concept of figuration and in other cases relying on different terminology, are exploring the way in which rhetorical figures and figurative language help to shape human consciousness, perception, and cognition. Within this diverse tradition of scholarship, figuration refers to the act or process of shaping or structuring human perception and cognition through rhetorical figures as well as the structures of thought and perception that are the result (or product) of this process. To unpack this definition, we can turn to two specific examples of contemporary scholarship.

In their highly influential book, *Metaphors We Live By*, linguist George Lakoff and philosopher Mark Johnson did not employ the term *figuration*. But the overall thrust of their book amplified the definition provided in the previous paragraph. As the title of the book indicates, Lakoff and Johnson (1980) were interested in exploring the central rhetorical figure of metaphor. But how do we "live by" metaphors? According to Lakoff and Johnson, "Human *thought processes* are largely metaphorical. . . . The human conceptual system is metaphorically structured and defined" (p. 6). We "live by" metaphors because they are essential to how we think; metaphors structure the conceptual systems (the clusters of specific concepts) by which we apprehend the world and through which we act in the world.

Metaphors We Live By is full of examples that illustrate the way in which metaphors *prefigure* or shape our experience of the world. Lakoff and Johnson (1980) began the book by introducing a number of concepts such as argument, time, and love and asking how it is that we come to understand these concepts. The answer, they argued, is that we come to understand these and countless other concepts by learning the dominant metaphors that give shape and structure to these concepts. In our everyday talk about argument, for example, Lakoff and Johnson discovered an underlying *structural metaphor:* Argument is war. We tend to think about argument in terms of war, and they argued that thinking about one thing *in terms of* something else is the "essence of metaphor" (p. 5). What about an inchoate concept such as time? Reviewing some of the standard ways in which people talk about time, Lakoff and Johnson identified three interrelated structuring metaphors: Time is money, time is a resource, and time is a valuable commodity. These three metaphors form a system because "in our society, money is a limited resource, and limited resources are valuable commodities. These subcategorization relationships characterize entailment relationships between the metaphors. TIME IS MONEY entails that TIME IS A LIMITED RESOURCE, which entails that TIME IS A VALUABLE COMMODITY" (p. 9). Does this metaphorical system, connected through the process of "metaphorical entailment" or implication, completely circumscribe how we think about time? No, it does not; we talk and think about time in ways that escape the dominant "time is money" metaphor. But we do not escape the process of metaphorical figuration. What we discover are degrees of coherence and conflict among the metaphors we use to think and talk about concepts. Consider the concept of love. As Lakoff and Johnson noted, our talk about love reveals a variety of structuring metaphors: Love is a physical force (as in "his whole life *revolves* around her"), love is a patient (as in "their relationship is *dead*"), love is madness (as in "he's *crazy* about her"), love is magic (as in "she *cast a spell* on him"),[4] and love is war (as in "she *retreated* from his *advances*" or "she is *besieged* by suitors"). Careful analysis would reveal degrees of coherence among the various metaphors (e.g., the physical force, madness or illness, and magic metaphors all prefigure love as something that exceeds our ability to remain in control of the situation). But the different metaphors also allow for conflict in how we think, talk, and act with respect to the concept of love. A person who talks about love in terms of the patient metaphor might seek "treatment" when a relationship "turns sour" (a different type of metaphor), whereas someone accustomed to talking about love as madness might not see or feel the same need.

Consider a concrete example of how metaphor can structure or shape the way in which people think and act. In comments quoted in the May 31, 1999, issue of *The Nation,* Ron Hampton, executive director of the 4,000-member National Black Police Association, remarked,

> This militarization of police work started a long time ago. It began with the use of terms like "war on crime" and "war on drugs." . . . When police officers are inundated with this kind of military training and language, they go out thinking they're soldiers, that they are the line between civilization and anarchy. Pretty soon, you're bringing your war to traffic stops and minor arrests.

Hampton did not employ the theoretical vocabulary common in rhetorical studies and other disciplines, but his central point affirmed the claims advanced by scholars such as Lakoff and Johnson. Like many Americans, Hampton was troubled by the growing aggressiveness that *some* police officers bring to the job and the overall militarization of police work. Although the reasons behind this development no doubt are complex, Hampton asserted that at least part of the problem is a result of how we *talk* about crime in urban America. If we talk about fighting crime as a "war," he indicated, then we will begin to *act* like we are fighting a war and formulate policies for prosecuting a war. Hampton concluded, "After a while, we were talking as if we were fighting a war in our inner cities when there isn't any war there."

The discussion in the past few paragraphs merely scratched the surface (more metaphors at work here) of Lakoff and Johnson's (1980) discussion. Hopefully, it illustrated how Lakoff and Johnson, without using the term *figuration,* were nevertheless exploring the way in which figures structure human perception and cognition. The second example of contemporary scholarship that explores the process of figuration came from the works of historian, critic, and language theorist Hayden White. In a number of books and essays (e.g., White, 1973, 1978), he probed the figurative or "tropical element in all discourse" (White, 1978, p. 1). Like Lakoff and Johnson, White (1978) saw discourse as providing clues to the way in which people think. He wrote, "Discourse is itself a kind of model of the processes of consciousness" (p. 5). And like Lakoff and Johnson, White viewed figuration as the junction or point of intersection between how people talk and write and how people think. He wrote that the "process of understanding proceeds by the exploitation of the principal modalities of figuration, identified in post-Renaissance rhetorical theory as the 'master tropes' (Kenneth Burke's phrase) of metaphor, metonymy, synecdoche, and irony" (p. 5). Where White differed from Lakoff and Johnson was in his contention that there is "an *archetypal* pattern" (p. 5, emphasis added) in the process of figuration—a movement in both thought and verbal expression from metaphor, through metonymy and synecdoche, to irony. Each trope or figure, for White, provides a different way of shaping or structuring human understanding and thinking.

White's writings are too nuanced and complex to allow for quick summarization. The point that needs emphasis is White's (1978) belief that figuration or "tropics is the process by which all discourse *constitutes* the objects which it pretends only to describe realistically and to analyze objectively" (p. 2). The purported **transparency** of language—the ability to *see through* words so as to *get at* reality—is, for White, a figurative achievement; however detached, objective, or neutral a piece of prose discourse seems, its ability to describe or **represent** events, objects, or people is based on the figurative or tropical resources of language. White's position is consistent with the *constructivist* or *constitutive* approach to language and discourse that has had such a profound impact on contemporary rhetorical studies. As he noted, "Discourse is intended to *constitute* the ground whereon to decide *what shall count as fact* in the matters under consideration and to determine *what mode of comprehension* is best suited to the understanding of the facts thus constituted" (p. 3). In the works of White, Lakoff and Johnson, and many other scholars, rhetorical figures are not mere verbal ornaments added to our writing and our talk to "dress it up."[5] Rhetorical figures are constantly implicated in processes of rhetorical and discursive figuration that shape our perception of the world and structure our capacity to think about and act in the world.

Notes

1. The terms *figure* and *trope* often are considered to be synonymous despite their different denotations in the history of rhetorical thought.

2. As the discussion in the entry for **style** notes, the *substitution* view of metaphorical meaning has been challenged in recent scholarship.

3. Some scholars add a prefix to the mix and speak of prefigure or prefiguration (e.g., White, 1978), but the prefix does not seem to alter the sense of the new term substantially. See White's (1978) essentially synonymous use of prefiguration and figuration (pp. 105-106).

4. Feminist scholars would remind us, with good reason, that this example also prefigures women as witches, revealing the way in which different structuring metaphors can overlap in the same expression.

5. Consider how often we talk about language and discourse with clothing metaphors and how that tendency might shape how we think about these topics.

References and Additional Reading

Barfield, O. (1988). *Saving the appearances: A study in idolatry* (2nd ed.). Middletown, CT: Wesleyan University Press.

Burke, K. (1969). Four master tropes. In K. Burke, *A grammar of motives.* Berkeley: University of California Press.

Lakoff, G., & Johnson, M. (1980). *Metaphors we live by.* Chicago: University of Chicago Press.

Lanham, R. (1991). *A handlist of rhetorical terms* (2nd ed.). Berkeley: University of California Press.

Paul, A. M. (1970). Figurative language. *Philosophy and Rhetoric, 3,* 225-248.

Quinn, A. (1982). *Figures of speech.* Salt Lake City, UT: Peregrine Smith.

White, H. (1973). *Metahistory: The historical imagination in nineteenth-century Europe.* Baltimore, MD: Johns Hopkins University Press.
White, H. (1978). *Tropics of discourse: Essays in cultural criticism.* Baltimore, MD: Johns Hopkins University Press.

FORENSIC DISCOURSE

The origins of rhetorical studies are shrouded in the mists of Greek antiquity. Kennedy (1980) offered one version of the invention of rhetoric:

> In Syracuse in Sicily [a Greek "colony" at the time] . . ., democracy on the Athenian pattern was introduced suddenly in 467 BC. Citizens found themselves involved in litigation over the ownership of property or other matters and [were] forced to take up their own cases before the courts. Nowhere in Greece did the profession of lawyer, advocate, or patron at the bar exist. . . . A few clever Sicilians developed simple techniques . . . for effective presentation and argumentation in the law courts and taught these to others for a price. According to later tradition, the two leading teachers were Corax . . . and a slightly younger, better known teacher . . . named Tisias. (pp. 18-19; on the Corax/Tisias legend, see also Hinks, 1940)

According to this account, a rudimentary form of rhetorical studies emerged as a response to the popular need for training in legal affairs. The first "teachers" of rhetoric provided instruction in the various techniques of legal advocacy.

Aristotle identified legal discourse, specifically the presentation of a case to a jury, as one of the three **genres** of rhetoric. The traditional term for this rhetorical genre is **forensic discourse.** Training in forensic rhetoric would remain a central part of rhetorical education for centuries. The **stasis** doctrine, usually credited to Hermagoras, was developed as a way of systematically analyzing legal cases. Cicero (1949) incorporated the doctrine into his handbook, *De Inventione,* and it would reappear in numerous technical treatises on rhetoric and public speaking in the coming centuries. As Kennedy (1980) observed, throughout the Middles Ages and into the Renaissance, "rhetorical theory remained tied to judicial oratory" (p. 183).

The link among rhetorical studies, judicial or forensic oratory, and legal education would persist for some time (for a brief overview of the relationship, see Rieke, 1982). Schuetz and Snedaker (1988) noted,

> When the first law school in the United States opened at Harvard [University] in 1756, the curriculum featured the study of Aristotle's *Rhetoric* and Cicero's *De Oratore.* Many famous legal advocates, including Daniel Webster, Rufus Choate, and William Ewarts, studied rhetoric as a preparation for their distinguished legal careers. (p. ix; see also Ferguson, 1984)

As late as 1893, a Yale University law professor, William C. Robinson, was publishing *Forensic Oratory: A Manual for Advocates* (Robinson, 1893; see also Rieke, 1982). But this link would gradually erode. Schuetz and Snedaker (1988) continued, "As schools of law became more specialized . . ., rhetoric gradually disappeared from the curriculum" (p. ix). A conceptual nexus that had persisted for more than 2,000 years was broken.

Over the past few decades, scholars in rhetorical studies and other disciplines (including political science, literary studies, and the law itself) have begun to reforge a new link among the law, legal advocacy, and rhetoric. The scholarship that falls within this interdisciplinary movement is extremely diverse. One line of inquiry continues the Ciceronian emphasis on legal advocacy by providing strategic advice to advocates (Rieke & Stutman, 1990). Following a research project begun by Perelman (1963, 1980), other scholars use the discourse of the law as material for exploring key conceptual issues within the tradition of rhetoric and argumentation (e.g., Makau,

1984). Other scholars challenge preconceived ideas about the nature of legal discourse by uncovering a central **narrative** (Bennett, 1978, 1979; Bennett & Feldman, 1981; La Rue, 1995; Sarat, 1994; see also most of the essays collected in Brooks & Gewirtz, 1996) or *metaphorical* dimension (Bosmajian, 1992) in legal discourse. Another line of inquiry explores the rhetorical dynamics of particular legal cases or judicial opinions (Bartanen, 1987; Hariman, 1990; Hasian, 1997, 2000; Sanbonmatsu, 1971; Schuetz & Snedaker, 1988).

Two specific scholarly movements, emerging within the sphere of legal studies but also having a significant impact on related fields, merit brief consideration. The first is referred to as the *critical legal studies* movement (Kelman, 1987; Unger, 1983). Lucaites (1990) surveyed some of the key elements of this movement as they relate to the concerns of contemporary rhetorical studies and concluded that both critical legal studies and rhetorical scholars share an interest in *demystifying* the discourse of the law, revealing the extent to which this discourse is a rhetorical *and* **ideological** formation. Lucaites suggested that the task is to explore in more concrete detail how "the law"—conceptualized as a series of institutional procedures and relationships, a collection of discursive practices, and a set of normative commitments—functions within a larger "rhetorical culture." Hasian, Condit, and Lucaites (1996) began this analytic process in their study of the *Plessy v. Ferguson* and *Brown v. Board of Education* decisions (see also Hasian & Croasmun, 1996).

The second specific movement that has had a wide impact on contemporary humanities scholarship usually is referred to as the *law and literature* movement. The phrase "law and literature" is somewhat misleading. As Thomas (1991) observed, "If the reasons for the law and literature revival could be put in a nutshell, it is the increased acknowledgment in legal circles that the law has been and remains intricately tied up with rhetoric" (p. 523). In addition, White (1984) wrote that the law is "an art essentially literary and rhetorical in nature" (p. xi). So, a more accurate characterization of this second movement might be law, literature, *and rhetoric* (Scallen, 1995).[1]

But as Thomas (1991) acknowledged, invoking rhetoric creates additional problems given that "there is no issue so thorny . . . as what we mean by rhetoric" (p. 523).[2] At least two senses of rhetoric are invoked by practitioners in the law, literature, and rhetoric movement. On the one hand, literary theorist Steven Mailloux saw the realm of rhetoric as a way of overcoming the perennial problem of interpretive method. Lawyers, like literary scholars, spend a considerable amount of time reading and interpreting **texts.** This being the case, the issue of interpretive method is as central to the practice of law as it is in literary studies. According to Mailloux (1989), the quest for the "right" or "correct" method of interpretation is futile. The process of interpretation, in law as in literature, is rhetorical; whether one is reading a contract, a constitution, a poem, or a novel, interpretation is a process of constructing **arguments** and the meaning of a text emerges through rhetorical interaction. Interpretive methods or strategies function, Mailloux argued, like traditional rhetorical **topics;** they are "places" or resources to which one turns when trying to construct an argument about the meaning of a text. Rhetoric, then, is an inescapable part of the law because (a) interpretation is a central activity within legal practice and (b) interpretation is fundamentally a process of rhetorical interaction.[3]

When Mailloux turned to rhetoric, he was turning to a particular sense of rhetoric—what scholars have come to call *instrumental.*[4] Rhetoric, for Mailloux, is the intentional use of strategies in an effort to persuade an audience. A different sense of rhetoric can be found in the seminal work of James Boyd White. White, a professor of law, literature, and the classics at the University of Michigan, is considered by many to be the "father" of the law and literature movement. In an impressive series of books (White, 1973, 1984, 1985, 1990, 1994; for an overview of White's works, see also Dellapenna & Farrell, 1991), he outlined a *constitutive* model of language and discourse that he then applied to the realms of politics, the law, and literature. Although White did not deny that people use language for instrumental purposes, he insisted that whenever we perform with language we also are constituting (and/or reconstituting) a sense of self or character (see the entry for **subject**), a community, and the linguistic medium within which we are acting. For White, law is rhetorical not because trial lawyers use various techniques to persuade a jury and not because lawyers and judges employ different strategies in their interpretive work; rather, law is rhetorical because, through its various practical performances (e.g., trial advocacy, preparing appeals, producing judicial opinions), a culture of argument is continually reenacted or recreated. The task for the scholar and critic is to describe *how* legal language—or any language—is used to create, perpetuate, and/or overturn a culture and to assess the quality of the culture so constituted.[5]

Notes

1. See also the essays collected in Brooks and Gewirtz (1996) and Sarat and Kearns (1994).

2. For a more detailed discussion of the complicated issue of defining rhetoric, see the entry for **effects of rhetorical practice.**

3. For more on Mailloux's (1989) idea of *rhetorical hermeneutics,* see the discussion in the entry for **hermeneutics and rhetoric.**

4. On the presence of an instrumental understanding of rhetoric in the law/literature movement, see Thomas (1991). On the general topic of rhetoric as an instrumental activity, see the discussion in the entry for **effects of rhetorical practice.**

5. For White's influence on rhetorical scholarship, see Sullivan and Goldzwig (1995).

References and Additional Reading

Bartanen, K. M. (1987). The rhetoric of dissent in Justice O'Conner's *Akron* opinion. *Southern Speech Communication Journal, 52,* 240-262.

Bennett, W. L. (1978). Storytelling in criminal trials: A model of social judgment. *Quarterly Journal of Speech, 64,* 1-22.

Bennett, W. L. (1979). Rhetorical transformations of evidence in criminal trials: Creating grounds for legal judgment. *Quarterly Journal of Speech, 65,* 311-323.

Bennett, W. L., & Feldman, M. S. (1981). *Reconstituting reality in the courtroom: Justice and judgment in American culture.* New Brunswick, NJ: Rutgers University Press.

Bosmajian, H. (1992). *Metaphor and reason in judicial opinions.* Carbondale: Southern Illinois University Press.

Brooks, P., & Gewirtz, P. (Eds.). (1996). *Law's stories: Narrative and rhetoric in the law.* New Haven, CT: Yale University Press.

Cicero. (1949). *De inventione* (H. M. Hubbell, Trans.). London: Heinemann.

Dellapenna, J. W., & Farrell, K. (1991). Law and the language of community: On the contributions of James Boyd White. *Rhetoric Society Quarterly, 21,* 38-58.

Ferguson, R. A. (1984). *Law and letters in American culture.* Cambridge, MA: Harvard University Press.

Ferguson, R. A. (1990). The judicial opinion as a literary genre. *Yale Journal of Law and the Humanities, 2,* 201-219.

Fish, S. (1989). *Doing what comes naturally: Change, rhetoric, and the practice of theory in literature and legal studies.* Durham, NC: Duke University Press.

Goodrich, P. (1987). *Legal discourse: Studies in linguistics, rhetoric, and legal analysis.* New York: St. Martin's.

Hariman, R. (Ed.). (1990). *Popular trials: Rhetoric, mass media, and the law.* Tuscaloosa: University of Alabama Press.

Hasian, M., Jr. (1994). Critical legal rhetorics: The theory and practice of law in a postmodern world. *Southern Communication Journal, 60,* 44-56.

Hasian, M., Jr. (1997). Judicial rhetoric in a fragmentary world: "Character" and storytelling in the Leo Frank case. *Communication Monographs, 64,* 250-269.

Hasian, M., Jr. (2000). Jurisprudence as performance: John Brown's enactment of natural law at Harper's Ferry. *Quarterly Journal of Speech, 86,* 190-214.

Hasian, M., Jr., Condit, C. M., & Lucaites, J. L. (1996). The rhetorical boundaries of "the law": A consideration of the rhetorical culture of legal practice and the case of the "separate but equal" doctrine. *Quarterly Journal of Speech, 82,* 323-342.

Hasian, M., Jr., & Croasmun, E. (1996). Rhetoric's revenge: The prospect of a critical legal rhetoric. *Philosophy and Rhetoric, 29,* 384-399.

Hinks, D. A. G. (1940). Tisias and Corax and the invention of rhetoric. *Classical Quarterly, 34,* 59-69.

Kahn, V. (1989). Rhetoric and the law. *Diacritics, 19,* 21-34.

Kelman, M. (1987). *A guide to critical legal studies.* Cambridge, CA: Harvard University Press.

Kennedy, G. A. (1980). *Classical rhetoric and its Christian and secular tradition from ancient to modern times.* Chapel Hill: University of North Carolina Press.

Klinger, G. D. (1994). Law as *communicative praxis:* Toward a rhetorical jurisprudence. *Argument and Advocacy, 30,* 236-247.

La Rue, L. H. (1995). *Constitutional law as fiction: Narrative in the rhetoric of authority.* University Park: Pennsylvania State University Press.

Levinson, S., & Mailloux, S. (Eds.). (1988). *Interpreting law and literature: A hermeneutic reader.* Evanston, IL: Northwestern University Press.

Lewis, W. (1994). Of innocence, exclusion, and the burning of flags: The romantic realism of the law. *Southern Communication Journal, 60,* 4-21.

Lucaites, J. L. (1990). Between rhetoric and "the law": Power, legitimacy, and social change. *Quarterly Journal of Speech, 76,* 435-449.

Mailloux, S. (1989). *Rhetorical power.* Ithaca, NY: Cornell University Press.

Makau, J. M. (1984). The Supreme Court and reasonableness. *Quarterly Journal of Speech, 70,* 379-396.

Makau, J. M., & Lawrence, D. (1994). Administrative judicial rhetoric: The Supreme Court's new thesis of political morality. *Argument and Advocacy, 30,* 191-205.

McDorman, T. F. (1997). Challenging constitutional authority: African American responses to *Scott v. Sandford. Quarterly Journal of Speech, 83,* 192-209.

O'Rourke, S. P. (1994). Cultivating the "higher law" in American jurisprudence: John Quincy Adams, neoclassical rhetoric, and the *Amistad* case. *Southern Communication Journal, 60,* 33-42.

Perelman, C. (1963). *The idea of justice and the problem of argument* (J. Petrie, Trans.). London: Routledge and Kegan Paul.

Perelman, C. (1980). *Justice, the law, and argument* (J. Petrie, Trans.). Boston: D. Reidel.

Posner, R. A. (1988). *Law and literature: A misunderstood relation.* Cambridge, MA: Harvard University Press.

Rieke, R. D. (1982). Argumentation in the legal process. In J. R. Cox & C. A. Willard (Eds.), *Advances in argumentation theory and research.* Carbondale: Southern Illinois University Press.

Rieke, R. D., & Stutman, R. K. (1990). *Communication and legal advocacy.* Columbia: University of South Carolina Press.

Robinson, W. C. (1893). *Forensic oratory: A manual for advocates.* Boston: Little, Brown.

Sanbonmatsu, A. (1971). Darrow and Rourke's use of Burkeian strategies in *New York v. Gitlow* (1920). *Speech Monographs, 38,* 36-48.

Sarat, A. (1994). Speaking of death: Narratives of violence in capital trials. In A. Sarat & T. R. Kearns (Eds.), *The rhetoric of law.* Ann Arbor: University of Michigan Press.

Sarat, A., & Kearns, T. R. (Eds.). (1994). *The rhetoric of law.* Ann Arbor: University of Michigan Press.

Scallen, E. A. (1994). Judgment, justification, and junctions in the rhetorical criticism of legal texts. *Southern Communication Journal, 60,* 68-74.

Scallen, E. A. (1995). American legal argumentation: The law and literature/rhetoric movement. *Argumentation, 9,* 705-717.

Schuetz, J., & Snedaker, K. H. (1988). *Communication and litigation: Case studies of famous trials.* Carbondale: Southern Illinois University Press.

Srader, D. (1994). Spanning ideological chasms: The response to conceptual segregation in *Bowers v. Hardwick. Argument and Advocacy, 30,* 206-219.

Sullivan, P. A., & Goldzwig, S. R. (1995). A relational approach to moral decision-making: The majority opinion in *Planned Parenthood v. Casey. Quarterly Journal of Speech, 81,* 167-190.

Thomas, B. (1991). Reflections on the law and literature revival. *Critical Inquiry, 17,* 510-539.

Tiersma, P. (1999). *Legal language.* Chicago: University of Chicago Press.

Unger, R. M. (1983). *The critical legal studies movement.* Cambridge, MA: Harvard University Press.

White, J. B. (1973). *The legal imagination.* Boston: Little, Brown.

White, J. B. (1984). *When words lose their meaning: Constitutions and reconstitutions of language, character, and community.* Chicago: University of Chicago Press.

White, J. B. (1985). *Heracles' bow: Essays on the rhetoric and poetics of law.* Madison: University of Wisconsin Press.

White, J. B. (1990). *Justice as translation: An essay in cultural and legal criticism.* Chicago: University of Chicago Press.

White, J. B. (1994). *Acts of hope: Creating authority in literature, law, and politics.* Chicago: University of Chicago Press.

Wiethoff, W. E. (1996). *A peculiar humanism: The judicial advocacy of slavery in high courts of the old South, 1820-1850.* Athens: University of Georgia Press.

GENERATION/ GENERATIONAL ARGUMENT

Beginning in Book II, Chapter 12, of the *Rhetoric,* Aristotle (1954) offered some observations on the "character" of individuals during different periods of life (at different "ages"). So, people during the period of "youth" are "changeable and fickle in their desires" (1389a6), are "excessive" (1389b3), and "think they know everything and are always quite sure about it" (1389b7). The elderly are "distrustful" (1389b21) and "cowardly" (1389b30); "they lack confidence in the future" (1390a4) and "live by memory rather than hope" (1390a6). People in the prime of life, occupying the middle that Aristotle valued, are "free from the extremes" of youth and old age (1390a30). "To put it generally," Aristotle wrote, "all the valuable qualities that youth and age divide between them are united in the prime of life, while all their excesses or defects are replaced by moderation and fitness" (1390b7-1390b9).

Aristotle's (1954) discussion in these chapters provided a rudimentary sociological analysis of the phenomenon of generations. Following the German sociologist Karl Mannheim, the concept of a generation is a way of grouping or classifying people based on their location in time. Mannheim (1952) wrote,

> Generation location is based on the existence of biological rhythm in human existence—the factors of life and death, a limited span of life, and aging. Individuals who belong to the same generation, who share the same year of birth, are endowed, to that extent, with a common location in the historical dimension of the social process. (p. 290)

Aristotle's interest in the three "ages" or generations was practical; he assumed that advocates need to know something about the typical characteristics of the different generations so as to persuade them. Recent inquiry into the concept of generation eschews Aristotle's narrow *instrumental* focus and approaches the idea of generation as a heuristic tool for conceptual and critical inquiry.

One of the crucial differences that separate Aristotle from thinkers such as Mannheim is the way in which they understand the notion of temporal location. For Aristotle, what mattered was how old a person was; age determined the generation (young, middle age, elderly) of which the person was a part. Aristotle assumed that societies remained stable over time. Mannheim and most modern scholars understand temporal location a bit differently. A distinguishing feature of modern thought is that history, or the unfolding of time, is a force of change. This assumption led Mannheim to focus on a different sense of temporal location—when a person was born. Date of birth functions as a type of anchor that helps to shape the experience and character of individuals who fall into this temporal location.

Goodnight's (1987) study of *generational argument* was premised on a modernist understanding of history. He wrote, "To study how reason *enters into history* . . ., the generational potentialities of argumentation itself must be discussed" (p. 134, emphasis added). Because reason and argumentation are themselves historical and temporal phenomena, this historical and temporal quality also must be investigated. Goodnight suggested that the concept of **generation** or **generational argument** provides one way of doing so.

Goodnight's (1987) discussion of the heuristic potential of generation is organized around three dominant *spheres* or *fields* of **argument.** Of particular interest is Goodnight's account of generations within technical spheres of argument. He drew on Marías' (1968) hypothesis that four generations are "coexistent" at any particular point in time.[1] These four generations are (a) "survivors" of a time that is quickly passing away, (b) the dominant generation that is in power, (c) the rising generation that is beginning to challenge the dominant generation, and (d) the new generation that has not yet begun to enter the various domains (e.g., economic, technical, political) of practice. Goodnight argued that if we understand Marías's position "metaphorically, as an illustration of the potential stances toward the practices of reasoning, then the potentialities of argumentative positions in time may be discovered" (p. 137). Discursive interaction and conflict among representatives of the four generations might provide a way of understanding the argumentative dynamics of particular argument fields.[2] A similar process of generational interaction and conflict marks the argumentative practice of the **public sphere.** Goodnight argued that each generation possesses "an animating sentiment" that functions as a "generative" or **inventional** ground of argument (p. 141). The argument practices of the public sphere are marked by "the struggle to fashion arguments which create continuity among generations yet are authentic to the unique experience of one's contemporaries" (p. 141).[3]

The generative quality or inventional capacity of generational experience is best illustrated if we think in terms of generational "paradigms." Paradigms are events that seem to impose themselves on the thought processes of a generation; they are anchors or reference points to which members of a generation continually return as they struggle to make sense of the changing world. Paradigms might be construed as **condensation symbols** for specific generations. Argumentatively, paradigms function as a *model* or *anti-model* (Perelman & Olbrechts-Tyteca, 1969) that not only "establish[es] or illustrate[s] a general rule but also . . . incite[s] [people] to . . . action" (p. 362). Whereas different generational paradigms can be a source of argumentative conflict, it also is possible for members of the same generation to argue over the meaning or **definition** of a paradigmatic event.

A few examples can help to illustrate the notion of generational paradigms. For the generation that fought World War II, British Prime Minister Neville Chamberlain's performance at Munich in 1938 became an anti-model paradigm. Chamberlain's effort to secure "peace for our time" through a policy of appeasement embodies an enduring negative lesson for this generation. The image of Chamberlain, umbrella in hand, returning from Munich was burned into the minds of this generation. As one encyclopedia entry noted, "British and American cartoonists made Chamberlain, with his ever-present umbrella, the symbol of the Munich Agreement and of appeasement" (Palmer, 1968, p. 768). Both the symbolism of appeasement and its status as an anti-model for this generation can be detected in the foreign policy discourse of American presidents. Consider, for example, how prominent the anti-model of appeasement, as well as the condensation symbols of "Munich" and "Hitler," was in the public discourse of George Bush regarding how America should respond to Iraq's invasion of Kuwait (Perloff, 1998, pp. 123-124). Although we cannot know for certain, it is interesting to speculate on whether the Munich/appeasement symbol would have been featured as prominently if the American president at that time had *not* been a member of the World War II generation.[4]

On the domestic scene, one of the antimodels for this generation was Wisconsin Senator Joseph McCarthy. Even during the late 1990s, members of a different generation invoked the symbol of McCarthy in efforts to delegitimize certain forms of political discourse. In the debate over "Monicagate" during the fall of 1998 and spring of 1999, a number of Bill Clinton supporters such as law professor Alan Dershowitz attacked the growing intrusion into the private lives of public figures as a type of "sexual McCarthyism," thereby demonstrating that McCarthy remains a potent inventional resource. For many Americans of the World War II generation, Franklin Roosevelt's "New Deal" programs served as a positive paradigmatic model. Roosevelt's New Deal functioned as a symbol that encapsulated, for this generation, a new understanding of both the responsibility of the federal government to address domestic problems and the possibilities for government action to address and rectify these problems. Although the election of Ronald Reagan in 1980 helped to dismantle the New Deal political coalition, Reagan was careful in the way in which he criticized New Deal social welfare policies.[5] Reagan, Bush, and Dan Quayle more often would identify Lyndon Johnson and his Vietnam-era "Great Society" programs as an object of ridicule. While members of the World War II generation—Democrats as well as Republicans—were in office, one of the centerpieces of the New Deal, social security, was untouchable. With the passing of this generation, we find a growing chorus for efforts to "reform," or in some cases "privatize," the once untouchable social security program.

What are some of the paradigmatic events of the post-World War II generation, the so-called "baby boomers"? Whereas numerous events (e.g., Watergate, the civil rights movement, feminism) have had an impact, the most obvious would have to be the nation's experience with the war in Vietnam. But Vietnam also illustrates the potential for events to engender intragenerational definitional conflict. Not only is there considerable disagreement about the lessons or the meaning of Vietnam between generations, but the baby boomers themselves argue over the meaning of this episode and its potential lessons. The nation's ongoing negotiation of the Vietnam experience suggests the possibility of analyzing how members of each of the four generations that Marías identified respond to this paradigmatic event and use it as an inventional resource.

And what of the post-baby boomers, frequently referred to as members of "Generation X." What events are shaping their generational consciousness? Will this generation find any value in the paradigmatic events of the "surviving" generation (the World War II generation)? One event from that earlier time that appears to retain its enduring significance, thanks in part to the efforts of the post-World War II generation, is the Holocaust. But how will this event function in the arguments of the new generation? Will members of Generation X find any value in the paradigmatic events of the baby boomer generation? Will they accept, contest, or reject the generational reference points of their parents? Will the arguments between their parents over the meaning of these paradigmatic events have any impact on the new generation, or will these arguments incline members of the new generation to cynicism and skepticism? What new events and experiences will become reference points for members of this generation, and how will their parents' generation respond to these new generational paradigms? How will generational dynamics shape deliberation about pressing public concerns?[6] As these questions suggest, the heuristic potential of concepts such as generation, generational argument, and generational paradigms is considerable. In various ways, the discussion and questions included here speak to Goodnight's (1987) quest to understand how "rhetorical invention" functions "to translate historical experience into reasoned argument about the nature of present choice" (p. 141).

Notes

1. See also Marías (1970).

2. As Harris (1991) noted, in the analysis of scientific practice, scholars refer to the "Max Planck Effect, the phenomenon whereby the clash between competing paradigms—one emerging, one established—divides rather neatly along generational lines" (p. 286).

3. On the difficulty of intergenerational conversation in the modern world, see Laslett (1979).

4. Bush's successor, Bill Clinton, was not a member of the World War II generation. Some of Clinton's arguments regarding Iraq policy throughout the crisis during the fall and early winter of 1998 resemble Bush's arguments. But the appeals to appeasement that were central in Bush were not present in Clinton's discourse.

5. For detailed discussions, see Weiler (1992) and Weiler and Pearce (1992).

6. For an example of analysis along these lines, see Wallach (1997).

References and Additional Reading

Aristotle. (1954). *Rhetoric* (W. R. Roberts, Trans.). New York: Modern Library.

Goodnight, G. T. (1987). Generational argument. In F. H. van Eemeren, R. Grootendorst, J. A. Blair, & C. A. Willard (Eds.), *Argumentation: Perspectives and approaches.* Dordrecht, Netherlands: Foris.

Harris, R. A. (1991). Rhetoric of science. *College English, 53,* 282-307.

Kertzer, D. I. (1983). Generation as a sociological problem. *Annual Review of Sociology, 9,* 125-149.

Laslett, P. (1979). The conversation between generations. In P. Laslett & J. Fishkin (Eds.), *Philosophy, politics, and society* (5th series). Oxford, UK: Basil Blackwell.

Mannheim, K. (1952). The problem of generations. In P. Kecskemeti (Ed.), *Essays on the sociology of knowledge.* London: Routledge and Kegan Paul.

Marías, J. (1968). Generations. In D. L. Sills (Ed.), *International encyclopedia of the social sciences.* New York: Macmillan.

Marías, J. (1970). *Generations: A historical method* (H. C. Raley, Trans.). Tuscaloosa: University of Alabama Press.

Palmer, N. D. (1968). Munich Agreement. In *The World Book encyclopedia.* Chicago: Field Enterprises Educational Corporation.

Perelman, C., & Olbrechts-Tyteca, L. (1969). *The new rhetoric* (J. Wilkinson & P. Weaver, Trans.). Notre Dame, IN: University of Notre Dame Press.

Perloff, R. M. (1998). *Political communication: Politics, press, and public in America.* Mahwah, NJ: Lawrence Erlbaum.

Spitzer, A. B. (1973). The historical problem of generations. *American Historical Review, 78,* 1353-1385.

Wallach, G. (1997). *Obedient sons: The discourse of youth and generations in American culture, 1630-1860.* Amherst: University of Massachusetts Press.

Weiler, M. (1992). The Reagan attack on welfare. In M. Weiler & W. B. Pearce (Eds.), *Reagan and public discourse in America.* Tuscaloosa: University of Alabama Press.

Weiler, M., & Pearce, W. B. (1992). Ceremonial discourse: The rhetorical ecology of the Reagan administration. In M. Weiler & W. B. Pearce (Eds.), *Reagan and public discourse in America.* Tuscaloosa: University of Alabama Press.

GENRE

The term **genre** ultimately is derived from the Latin word for "kind" or "class." When used in rhetorical or literary studies (where the term is most common), genre refers to the various types, classes, or categories of discursive practice that can serve as objects of study. Consider some common contemporary literary genres such as science fiction, fantasy, mystery, and romance. Referring to each of these different classes of literature as a genre assumes that the works we would classify in each category (e.g., novels by Arthur C. Clarke, Isaac Asimov, and Philip K. Dick usually are located in the science fiction section of bookstores) share certain basic characteristics (e.g., plot, setting, character) that allow the specific works to be collected under the general heading. In rhetorical studies, common characteristics or discursive conventions relating to **style, argument,** structure, and **situation** have allowed scholars to identity a range of generic classes or categories. **Apologias,** inaugural addresses, eulogies, defiant concessions, and scientific reports are just some of the genres studied by contemporary rhetorical scholars.

Because locating the essential characteristics that every work within a genre would share with every other is difficult, some scholars have adopted the philosopher Ludwig Wittgenstein's concept of *family resemblances* as a way of explaining how a group of texts coalesces into a genre. Wittgenstein's basic point is that just as every member of a family does not share all the characteristics of the others (e.g., hair color, eye color, body shape), we should not expect every work or text to exhibit the full range of characteristics that constitute its genre. Rather, just as in an extended family we will find different characteristics linking some members of the family to each other but not to all members of the family (but there are enough similarities to hold the group, as a whole, together), in the realm of discursive practice there are particular characteristics that link together some texts but not others. And the network of links allows us to talk about a generic "family" held together by a set of common characteristics that are not always shared by every member of the group (Condit, 1985; Fishelov, 1993; Mandelbaum, 1965). Genres understood along the lines of the idea of family resemblance allow us to see both the uniformity (common characteristics) and diversity (different characteristics) within the specific works that make up a generic category.

Of course, it is possible to think more broadly and see specific classes of literature as part of a more inclusive common category or genre (e.g., the novel) that is different from other broader categories of literary practice (e.g., poetry, drama). Or, we can move in the other direction and further divide specific literary classes into sub-categories or sub-genres (e.g., the historical romance, "high tech" or "hard" science fiction). In locating genres of discourse, we continually confront what Simons (1978) referred to as multiple "level[s] of abstraction" (p. 33) or what Fisher (1980) termed different "levels of generality" (p. 292). All genre scholarship has to negotiate the problems of abstraction and generality. Do we learn more about a specific text by locating it within a broad or narrow genre? What can we learn about a domain of discursive practice (e.g., the domain of "literature," the domain of "rhetoric") by trying to identify its various sub-genres? If not always directly considered, these questions are central issues in generic thinking.

Given this rather basic introduction to the concept of genre, we can consider another question. Why have theorists engaged, either explicitly or implicitly, in the process of generic thinking? Why is the history of literary and rhetorical studies riddled with various generic schemes and typologies? A number of scholars have answered these interrelated questions by invoking a type of essential human nature. For example, Jamieson (1973) wrote, "When a critic compares a contemporary critical object to great specimens of that type, he [sic] is merely formalizing a natural process. . . . The human need for a frame of reference lures the mind to generic classification" (p. 167; cf. Fisher, 1980; Miller, 1984). Although it might not be verifiable in an absolute sense, the basic assumption guiding most genre scholarship is that humans are inherently categorizers or classifiers. Whenever we encounter an object in the world (e.g., a rock, another person, a text), our apprehension of the object at some point will involve locating it within some larger class or category. We are able to identify an object as a "rock" because we understand and can apply the category criteria that distinguish rocks from golf balls, sea shells, or pieces of tree bark. The fact that making this type of distinction seems to us to be a matter of common sense (we usually do not spend a lot of time thinking about whether an object is or is not a rock) does not negate the claim. It simply means that we have internalized countless categories (and their defining criteria) and use them without much conscious effort. As Kamberelis (1995) observed with respect to discursive genres, "Part of the effectiveness of genre lies in their capacity to 'naturalize' what they index" (p. 147). The common genres that we employ and in which we participate in our daily lives (from asking a question in a class to ordering food at a restaurant) have become so obvious to us—so "natural"—that we lose sight of the fact that we are dealing with a **contingent** discursive form. So, as Jamieson suggested, thinking in terms of categories, classes, or genres does seem to be part of the human condition.

In the tradition of rhetorical studies, the emergence of generic thinking or generic theory usually is associated with Aristotle's (1954) *Rhetoric.* Classical scholar George Kennedy noted,

> Up until Aristotle's time, it had been recognized that there were various species of oratory, including prosecutions, defenses, funeral orations, and others, but these had not been classified into genres, and as far as we know Aristotle originated the concept of the three kinds of oratory, which became a permanent part of rhetorical theory. (Kennedy, 1980, p. 72)

Aristotle (1954) introduced his generic classification of types of oratory or rhetoric in Chapter 3 of Book I:

> Rhetoric falls into three divisions, determined by the three classes of listeners to speeches. For of the three elements in speech-making—speaker, subject, and person addressed—it is the last one, the hearer, that determines the speech's end and object. The hearer must be either a judge, with a decision to make about things past or future, or an observer. . . . From this, it follows that there are three divisions of oratory—(1) political, (2) forensic, and (3) the ceremonial oratory of display. (1358a36-1358b8)

Garver (1994) noted that "the kinds of rhetoric are defined by their purposes and ends, by their practical and conventional contexts, and by the methods they usually employ to accomplish those ends" (p. 55). The chart shown in Figure G.1, derived from Hill (1995), summarizes Aristotle's reconstruction of the **deliberative, forensic,** and **epideictic** genres.

Although the three genres are discrete, Aristotle recognized that it was possible to blend or combine elements from different genres in a specific speech or written text. Contemporary scholars refer to the result of this process as a *generic hybrid.*[1] One type of hybrid that Aristotle (1954) discussed involves the merging of deliberative and epideictic elements within a text (1367b36). Consider the following hypothetical example. A politician delivers a speech at a ceremony commemorating the 50th anniversary of an important piece of legislation. In typical epideictic fashion, the politician praises the legislative act as well as the wisdom, energy, and determination of all those individuals who fought to get it enacted. Now, imagine that members of the opposing political party do not like the legislation that was passed 50 years ago, and they believe that public opinion might have shifted enough that they can get the legislation overturned. Given this contextual wrinkle, would we want to label the politician's speech as purely epideictic? Probably not. As Aristotle recognized, an advocate can shift from epideictic praise to deliberative advocacy, or can blend the two, by means of increased emphasis and other strategies. In praising the work that was done 50 years ago, the politician is (if only indirectly) rallying the public to protect what the earlier generation had accomplished. The politician suggests that if the public fails to act, then the sacrifice of that earlier generation will have been in vain.[2]

In their discussion of generic hybrids, Jamieson and Campbell (1982) focused on the introduction of deliberative appeals in a ceremonial eulogy—a *deliberative eulogy.* Such hybrids, they suggested, are most common in the cases of well-known public figures but are not necessarily restricted to these cases. When a small child falls victim to gang violence, the priest or minister may use the occasion of the funeral eulogy to encourage public policy changes designed to stem the tide of urban decay. Eulogies also may be fused with other genres. Consider the situation of the British royal family after the death of Princess Diana. Accused by the press and public of indifference to the nation's grief, Queen Elizabeth made a rare appearance on national television, and her speech to the na-

RHETORICAL GENRES IN ARISTOTLE'S *RHETORIC*

RHETORICAL GENRE	deliberative	forensic (legal)	epideictic
AUDIENCE ORIENTATION	participant/ judge	participant/ judge	spectator
TEMPORAL ORIENTATION	future	past	present
DOMINANT DISCURSIVE STRATEGY	example; special topoi concerning the good	enthymeme; universal topoi concerning wrong doing; accusation/ defense	amplification; praise/blame
SUBJECT MATTER	public policy	questions of guilt or innocence	human character and habits
OBJECTIVE	determining what is advantageous/ disadvantageous; expedient/ inexpedient; and/or useful/harmful	determining what is just/unjust; legal/illegal	determining what is noble/ shameful and/or honorable/ dishonorable

Figure G.1. Rhetorical Genres in Aristotle's *Rhetoric*
SOURCE: Adapted from Hill (1995; see also Aristotle, 1954).

tion both eulogized Diana and defended the royal family. The speech combined elements of the eulogy with some of the strategies of the **apologia**.

Another hybrid possibility recognized by Aristotle, on which Garver (1994) sheds important light, is the interaction between the deliberative and forensic genres.[3] In Garver's assessment of this relationship, more is involved than an attorney using the occasion of a trial to advance his or her political ambitions (a common sub-plot in John Grisham novels). According to Garver, Aristotle admitted the "intertranslation between utility and justice"—the ends of deliberative and forensic discourse—because it "assures that deliberative reason [will] not be reduced to instrumental reason" (p. 67). There is, it seems, a tendency for deliberative discourse, concerned as it is with matters of expediency, to narrow into what Garver termed "instrumental reason" or what others might call utilitarian calculation (the doctrine of "what is good for the greatest number is good"). The fact that the forensic concern with justice can be introduced into the deliberative process provides a way of destabilizing instrumental reason or utilitarian calculation. Policy decisions cannot be made solely in terms of these criteria; they also can be subjected to forensic scrutiny.

An issue that engaged the attention of a number of classical thinkers concerned the relative status of the different genres. Put simply, were all of them co-equal or was one more important than the others? Aristotle seemed to place priority on deliberative discourse (Garver, 1994). Isocrates, the Greek Sophist, emphasized the value of epideictic discourse through his own discursive practices. Cicero, the Roman theorist and practitioner, devoted considerable attention to forensic discourse. Leff (1986) provided a reading of Cicero's *De Oratore* that reveals the way in which classical genre theory intersected with the broader pedagogical question of how individuals learn the principles of oratory. According to Leff, not only did Aristotle and Isocrates emphasize different genres, they also advanced different models of rhetorical pedagogy. Aristotle believed rhetoric to be a "systematic art," whereas Isocrates conceived it as a "synthetic practice" (p. 323). Leff argued that Cicero's innovation was to try to synthesize these rival perspectives and that Cicero's synthetic medium was a conceptualization of forensic oratory as a "paradigm genre." According to Leff,

> Cicero argues that the generic system [found in Aristotle] cannot achieve its own technical goal . . . [and that] it cannot generate an exhaustive and coherent typology. But Cicero does not simply discard the generic method. Instead, he exploits its imperfection in order to redefine and redeem it. Once seen as incomplete at the theoretical level, genre can be conceived in less systematic and more empirical terms—it can be used to demarcate and describe a particular sphere of action without any pretensions that the particular category reflects a grand theoretical structure. Restrained in this fashion, the generic apparatus can now do its analytical work since the divisions it generates refer only to a paradigm type and cannot claim authority over the whole field. (p. 323)

In sum, Cicero found Aristotle's generic scheme to be too abstract and unable to account for the particularities of rhetorical practice. But instead of abandoning the generic approach (in favor of an exclusive emphasis on the particular), Cicero narrowed his focus to the forensic genre. Cicero believed that would-be advocates, by learning the requirements of this genre, would be prepared to proceed analogically to other spheres of practice. Cicero, on Leff's reading, was engaging a fundamental issue for generic thinking—how to conceptualize the relationship between particular practices and the larger generic classes or categories in which they participate. This question remains central in contemporary genre theory.

Contemporary approaches to genre theory in rhetorical studies have not abandoned Aristotle's approach; rather, scholars have sought to extend, elaborate, and refine Aristotle's methodology. As Jamieson (1973) noted,

> For centuries, the discipline of rhetoric anchored itself in the generic distinctions of

> Aristotle, who classed rhetoric as deliberative, forensic, or epideictic. The Aristotelian taxonomy must strain to account for the sermon, however, and fractures when confronted by the data with which the contemporary critic must deal. (p. 162)

One of the key conceptual moves in contemporary genre theory is to expand Aristotle's three elements of speech making (speaker, subject, and person addressed) by including the **rhetorical situation.** Indeed, situation often is considered as the primary element in genre scholarship. Bitzer (1968), in a passage frequently cited in generic scholarship, remarked, "From day to day, year to year, comparable situations occur, prompting comparable responses; hence, rhetorical forms are born and a special vocabulary, grammar, and style are established" (p. 13). As Campbell and Jamieson (1978) explained, "situational requirements" (p. 20) lead to the production of a discursive response that contains specific stylistic and substantive elements. As similar situations recur, discourse with similar stylistic and substantive elements also will be present. But Campbell and Jamieson cautioned that "a genre does not consist merely of a series of acts in which certain rhetorical forms recur" (p. 21). They argued that a genre exists when situational requirements, stylistic choices, and substantive elements (e.g., strategic choices, lines of argument) combine or are "fused into an indivisible whole" (pp. 20-21). The fusion of elements, based on an "internal dynamic" (p. 21) present in the different discursive responses, is the crucial characteristic of a genre.[4]

What are the important tasks facing genre scholars in rhetorical studies? According to Harrell and Linkugel (1978), "One initial task of generic critics . . . is to discover a compensatory schema which will allow the systematic classification of rhetorical discourse" (p. 263). This task involves engaging the issue of levels of abstraction or generality noted previously. Harrell and Linkugel identified four common logics or principles of classification operating in generic scholarship: *de facto* (classification based on superficial similarities), *structural* (classification based on recurrent patterns of language, style, and argument), *motivational* (classification based on the motivational state of the speaker or writer), and *archetypal* (classification based on the presence of "deeply embedded" images [p. 264]). But these authors acknowledged that identifying various logics or principles leads to a key issue: Which logic or principle should be used to organize generic inquiry? De facto classification based on subject matter (e.g., the rhetoric of war, the rhetoric of dissent) can be useful (and is routinely used as a basis for rhetorical pedagogy), but it does not offer much in the way of analytic precision. De facto classification does not yield insight into the nuances of a group of texts. This logic seems more appropriate in trying to grasp more loosely structured classes of practices often described as a **discursive formation. Archetypal** classification allows access to specific nuances[5] of discursive practice but typically ignores the relationship between practice and situation.[6] Structural and motivational logics (or some combination thereof) dominate contemporary rhetorical genre scholarship. Harrell and Linkugel argued for the superiority of the motivational principle, but as Miller (1984) observed, "The description of motives in terms of the possible effects of discourse on ideas does not reflect the way human motivation is engaged by particular rhetorical situations. . . . Motives describe more about human nature than they do about rhetorical practice" (p. 154). Harrell and Linkugel (1978) suggested that a consensus among rhetorical scholars on the logic or principle of classification is necessary to organize systematic inquiry. But the quest for systematic scholarship, propelled by a quasi-social science view of rhetorical scholarship, might disable critical creativity and innovation.[7]

A second task noted by Harrell and Linkugel (1978) is the need to identify the "basic operations" (p. 274) or specific objectives of generic scholarship. They identified three operations or objectives: (a) *generic description,* which entails "mapping" (p. 274) the genre by way of an investigation of a broad sample of discourse (mapping uncovers the basic features of the generic class and "strives to generate theoretical constructs" [p. 275] that can guide subsequent inquiry into the genre); (b) *generic participation,* which "consists of determining what speeches participate in which genres" (p. 275) (participatory inquiry seeks to establish whether a specific text is or is not a member of the generic class); and (c) *generic application,* which employs the previously "mapped" elements of a genre as "standards or norms" (p. 276) that can be used to render a judgment about a particular text or practice (the process of application tries to determine whether or not a text or practice is a "good" instance of the genre). Harrell and Linkugel's tripartite description of the objectives of generic inquiry has become a mainstay of critical pedagogy (e.g., Foss, 1996).

The prominence of generic inquiry during the 1970s and 1980s produced, as might be expected, a critical backlash from skeptical scholars who called into question the assumptions and aims of the movement. For example, Conley (1986; see also Benoit, 2000; Conley, 1979; Patton, 1976) questioned whether or not purported generic characteristics can be used as a "normative measure" (p. 76) for evaluating specific practices or texts. According to Conley, "Making speeches fit into classificatory schemes involves radical abridgment" (pp. 71-72). The result is that generic inquiry "may, in fact, obfuscate more than it illuminates" (p. 71). Conley suggested that there is a "dialectical" relationship (p. 65) between "the particular actuality of a work" and "the class or category of which it may be a member" (p. 59). Conley suggested that, given generic inquiry's fixation with identifying and explicating fixed generic categories, it fails to recognize or appreciate this relationship. The net result is unimaginative criticism that fails to comprehend the dynamics of discursive practice. But numerous genre critics do attempt to blend an interest in uncovering generic categories with a concern for the particularities of individual texts and practices.[8] The issue that separates Conley from genre scholars is a variation on the dilemma that Leff uncovered in classical thought: Is rhetorical practice best characterized by way of systematic models (which genre theory provides) or by an emphasis on synthetic practices (which Conley, like Isocrates, appeared to endorse)? Something like Conley's conception of a dialectical relationship between genre and practice, which speaks to this recurrent tension in rhetorical studies, is an element in more recent generic inquiry.

Scholarly inquiry into the concept of genre is by no means limited to the realm of rhetorical studies. Genre is a topic of interdisciplinary interest, and work in related academic fields (e.g., sociolinguistics, literary studies) merits the attention of rhetorical scholars. In a survey of this interdisciplinary literature, Kamberelis (1995) detected a "sociocultural view of genre" (p. 125) that moves beyond the formalist fixation with static categories and generic classification. Drawing on a wide variety of works on genre (Bakhtin, 1986; Hanks, 1987; Rosmarin, 1985; Swales, 1990; Todorov, 1990), including those done by scholars in rhetorical studies, Kamberelis (1995) outlined some of the major conceptual implications of a sociocultural approach to genre. Kamberelis observed that the work that he drew on "redirects our attention away from textual forms and toward the people, institutions, purposes, thematic content, rhetorical situations, social contexts, specific text-making practices, and historical trajectories that together constitute genres and are, in turn, constituted by genres" (p. 119). In short, it appears that the sociocultural approach to genre expands on the text-genre-situation nexus that constituted one of the basic insights of contemporary work in rhetorical studies.

Rethinking genre from a sociocultural perspective involves, most essentially, a move away from defining genre primarily as a class or category. A sociocultural view, Kamberelis (1995) suggested, emphasizes two interrelated definitional issues. First, genres are not merely categories for placing texts; they are forms of action or modes of activity.[9] For example, a eulogy is not only a type of speech delivered when someone dies; it is a mode of communal action. A community grieves, remembers, and prepares for the future through the activities embedded in the eulogy. Second, genres function as "cultural models" (p. 119), "frames," or "structures" that "provide rough templates" for organizing discursive practice (p. 159). This second point extends the relatively common observation made by rhetorical scholars that genres function as *constraints* on rhetorical action. The two issues were integrated when Kamberelis suggested that "genres are human activity structures" (p. 159) or ways of organizing human behavior. A sociocultural definition of genre redirects the objectives of generic inquiry. From a sociocultural point of view, generic inquiry is not directed at describing generic categories, testing to see whether a particular text fits the description, or providing a normative assessment of a specific work that falls into a generic class; rather, generic inquiry strives to uncover the multiple ways in which genres, as "activity structures," function in human communicative practice. The sociocultural perspective is, first and foremost, highly functional in its approach to generic inquiry.

A sociocultural approach to genres, Kamberelis (1995) argued, emphasizes their durability as well as their dynamism (pp. 125-140). Generic structures exist over time, yet they are continually mutating; they constrain practitioners but also can serve as a resource for discursive innovation. The intersection of the "general" and the "specific" in particular practices is a key concern for scholars adopting a sociocultural perspective.[10] Few texts or discursive practices ever simply reduplicate a generic structure. There is a "co-constituting" or "mutually constituting" relationship (p. 122) between practices and genres that must be acknowledged. Kamberelis wrote, "Genres are at least partially created in their continual enactment" (p. 133). As such, genres are "continually open to reconfiguration" (p. 135) and modification. Generic innovations are the result of both individual "genius or exceptionality" (a romantic model of **invention**) and "more quotidian enactments" (p. 137). Rather than simply mapping the contours of a fixed genre, the sociocultural approach encourages inquiry into the essentially dialectical relationship between durability and dynamism that is continually enacted in discursive practice.[11]

A sociocultural approach to genre also emphasizes the relationship between genres and **ideology.** Kamberelis (1995) observed, "Genres are primary carriers of ideologies" (pp. 146, 148). The process of learning, or being socialized into, an ideology is coextensive with one's immersion in generic frames or structures. Academic disciplines illustrate this process. Kamberelis argued that disciplinary genres not only organize or structure a range of practices but also contain and disseminate ideological commitments. Specific practices, structured by way of the reigning genre(s), "rearticulate collective ideologies" (p. 146). But given the inherent possibility of innovation noted previously, the rearticulation of ideology by way of generically organized practices is "never [a] simple reflection of these ideologies" (p. 146). Kamberelis insisted that the relationship between ideology and genre is complicated; genres "carry" ideologies but do so in a "partial and refracted fashion" (p. 146). Learning a genre is equivalent to learning an ideology; generic enactments rearticulate ideologies. But learning a genre also is a lesson in how to contest or disrupt an ideology. Generic enactments refract or *reaccentuate* ideologies, modifying the ideology along with the genre.

This brief discussion of Kamberelis's (1995) essay only scratches the surface of his discussion of a sociocultural approach to genre. The point that needs to be underscored is that such an approach is not a complete rejection or repudiation of the formalist perspective that emphasizes generic categories or classes. Rather, just as modern genre scholarship refined and expanded many of the key points developed in classical genre theory, the sociocultural perspective refines and expands on many of the issues raised in the formalist tradition of genre scholarship. It also should be noted that contemporary genre scholarship in rhetorical studies is not purely formalist in nature; many of the issues that Kamberelis discovered in the sociocultural approach to genres also are raised (if not explored as fully) in the literature of rhetorical studies. What does seem clear, as critics of genre scholarship point out, is that exercises in constructing abstract generic typologies or in classifying specific works in terms of such typologies is of limited value. Just as genres themselves evolve over time, so too does genre scholarship. The next phase of genre scholarship in rhetorical studies might be on the horizon.

Notes

1. See Jamieson and Campbell (1982).
2. This is a form of what Perelman and Olbrechts-Tyteca (1969) termed the *argument from sacrifice.*
3. See, for example, Carlson's (1985) analysis of John Quincy Adams' address in the *Amstad* slave revolt case.
4. See also Miller's (1984) constructive critique of the "demand-response vocabulary" (p. 152) underpinning the Campbell and Jamieson perspective.
5. See Osborn's (1967, 1977) studies of **archetypal** metaphors.
6. See Condit and Greer's (1997) discussion of archetypal metaphors and Winston Churchill's "War Situation I" address delivered to the House of Commons in August 1940.
7. See, for example, Jamieson's (1973) suggestive comments about how generic categories might be used as a type of **perspective by incongruity** in critical practice.
8. See, for example, Jamieson's (1973, 1975) discussions of antecedent genres and their impact on responses to novel situations, Jamieson and Campbell's (1982) work on generic hybrids, and Olson's (1993) effort to link "generic embodiment" and history.
9. On this issue, Kamberelis (1995) acknowledged the importance of Miller's (1984) discussion of genre as action.
10. This concern seems to acknowledge Conley's point, discussed earlier, about the dialectic between the "work" and the larger "class or category."
11. For works in rhetorical studies along these lines, see Browne (1990) and works inspired by Jamieson and Campbell's (1982) idea of generic hybrids such as Carlson (1985).

References and Additional Reading

Aristotle. (1954). *Rhetoric* (W. R. Roberts, Trans.). New York: Modern Library.

Bakhtin, M. M. (1986). *Speech genres and other late essays* (C. Emerson & M. Holquist, Eds., V. W. McGee, Trans.). Austin: University of Texas Press.

Benoit, W. L. (2000). Beyond genre theory: The genesis of rhetorical action. *Communication Monographs, 67,* 178-192.

Berkenkotter, C., & Huckin, T. N. (1995). *Genre knowledge in disciplinary communication: Cognition/culture/power.* Hillsdale, NJ: Lawrence Erlbaum.

Bitzer, L. F. (1968). The rhetorical situation. *Philosophy and Rhetoric, 1,* 1-14.

Browne, S. H. (1990). Generic transformation and political action: A textual interpretation of Edmund Burke's *Letter to William Elliot, Esq. Communication Quarterly, 38,* 54-63.

Campbell, K. K., & Jamieson, K. H. (1978). Form and genre in rhetorical criticism: An introduction. In K. K. Campbell & K. H. Jamieson (Eds.), *Form and genre: Shaping rhetorical action.* Falls Church, VA: Speech Communication Association.

Campbell, K. K., & Jamieson, K. H. (1986). Introduction [to special issue on genre criticism]. *Southern Speech Communication Journal, 51,* 293-299.

Campbell, K. K., & Jamieson, K. H. (1990). *Deeds done in words: Presidential rhetoric and the genres of governance.* Chicago: University of Chicago Press.

Carlson, A. C. (1985). John Quincy Adams' "Amistad Address": Eloquence in a generic hybrid. *Western Journal of Speech Communication, 49,* 14-26.

Clark, T. D. (1977). An exploration of generic aspects of contemporary American Christian sermons. *Quarterly Journal of Speech, 63,* 384-394.

Condit, C. M. (1985). The functions of epideictic: The Boston Massacre orations as exemplar. *Communication Quarterly, 33,* 284-299.

Condit, C. M., & Greer, A. M. (1997). The particular aesthetics of Winston Churchill's "The War Situation I." In J. M. Hogan (Ed.), *Rhetoric and community: Case studies in unity and fragmentation.* Columbia: University of South Carolina Press.

Conley, T. M. (1979). Ancient rhetoric and modern genre criticism. *Communication Quarterly, 27,* 47-53.

Conley, T. (1986). The Linnaean blues: Thoughts on the genre approach. In H. W. Simons & A. A. Aghazarian (Eds.), *Form, genre, and the study of political discourse.* Columbia: University of South Carolina Press.

Fishelov, D. (1993). *Metaphors of genre: The role of analogy in genre theory.* University Park: Pennsylvania State University Press.

Fisher, W. R. (1980). Genre: Concepts and applications in rhetorical criticism. *Western Journal of Speech Communication, 44,* 288-299.

Foss, S. K. (1996). *Rhetorical criticism: Exploration and practice* (2nd ed.). Prospect Heights, IL: Waveland.

Garver, E. (1994). *Aristotle's RHETORIC: An art of character.* Chicago: University of Chicago Press.

Hanks, W. (1987). Discourse genres in a theory of practice. *American Ethnologist, 14,* 668-692.

Harrell, J., & Linkugel, W. A. (1978). On rhetorical genre: An organizing perspective. *Philosophy and Rhetoric, 11,* 262-281.

Hill, F. I. (1995). The *Rhetoric* of Aristotle. In J. J. Murphy (Ed.), *A synoptic history of classical rhetoric* (2nd rev. ed.). Davis, CA: Hermagoras Press.

Jamieson, K. M. H. (1973). Generic constraints and the rhetorical situation. *Philosophy and Rhetoric, 6,* 162-170.

Jamieson, K. M. (1975). Antecedent genre as rhetorical constraint. *Quarterly Journal of Speech, 61,* 406-415.

Jamieson, K. M., & Campbell, K. K. (1982). Rhetorical hybrids: Fusion of generic elements. *Quarterly Journal of Speech, 68,* 146-157.

Kamberelis, G. (1995). Genre as institutionally informed social practice. *Journal of Contemporary Legal Issues, 6,* 117-171.

Kennedy, G. (1980). *Classical rhetoric and its Christian and secular tradition from ancient to modern times.* Chapel Hill: University of North Carolina Press.

Leff, M. (1986). Genre and paradigm in the second book of *De Oratore. Southern Speech Communication Journal, 51,* 308-325.

Mandelbaum, M. (1965). Family resemblances and generalization concerning the arts. *American Philosophical Quarterly, 2,* 219-228.

Miller, C. R. (1984). Genre as social action. *Quarterly Journal of Speech, 70,* 151-167.

Olson, K. M. (1993). Completing the picture: Replacing generic embodiments in the historical flow. *Communication Quarterly, 41,* 299-317.

Osborn, M. (1967). Archetypal metaphor in rhetoric: The light-dark family. *Quarterly Journal of Speech, 53,* 115-126.

Osborn, M. (1977). The evolution of the archetypal sea in rhetoric and poetic. *Quarterly Journal of Speech, 63,* 347-363.

Patton, J. H. (1976). Generic criticism: Typology at an inflated price. *Rhetoric Society Quarterly, 6,* 4-8.

Perelman, C., & Olbrechts-Tyteca, L. (1969). *The new rhetoric: A treatise on argumentation* (J. Wilkinson & P. Weaver, Trans.). Notre Dame, IN: University of Notre Dame Press.

Rosmarin, A. (1985). *The power of genre.* Minneapolis: University of Minnesota Press.

Simons, H. W. (1978). "Genre-alizing" about rhetoric: A scientific approach. In K. K. Campbell & K. H. Jamieson (Eds.), *Form and genre: Shaping rhetorical action.* Falls Church, VA: Speech Communication Association.

Swales, J. (1990). *Genre analysis.* Cambridge, UK: Cambridge University Press.

Todorov, T. (1990). *Genres in discourse.* Cambridge, UK: Cambridge University Press.

GYNOCRITICS/GYNOCRITICISM

In a discussion of the impact of feminism on rhetorical studies, Dow (1995) noted that "rhetorical scholars have sometimes too easily conflated criticism of feminist rhetoric with feminist criticism in rhetorical studies" (p. 106). The conceptual imprecision that Dow found is not unique to contemporary rhetorical studies. A similar predicament led feminist literary scholar Elaine Showalter to offer a "taxonomy" of the "varieties" of feminist criticism in literary studies (Showalter, 1985b, p. 128). According to Showalter, one type of feminist criticism focuses on the "woman as reader." She described this type of critique as

> a historically grounded inquiry which probes the ideological assumptions of literary phenomena. Its subjects include the images and stereotypes of women in literature [e.g., Gilbert & Gubar's (1979) discussion of women as "angel" and "monster" in Western literature], the omissions of and misconceptions about women in criticism, and the fissures in male-constructed literary history. (p. 128)

A second type of feminist criticism focuses on the "woman as writer." It treats subjects such as "the psychodynamics of female creativity; linguistics and the problem of a female language; the trajectory of the individual or collective literary career; literary history; and, of course, studies of particular writers and works" (p. 128). Showalter labeled this second mode of inquiry as "gynocriticism."

The term **gynocritics** or **gynocriticism** has not been adopted by scholars in rhetorical studies despite the fact that, as Showalter used the term, it describes the dominant trajectory of feminist scholarship in the field (for an exception, see Miller, 1997). The most prominent practitioner of a form of gynocriticism in rhetorical studies has been Karlyn Kohrs Campbell. In a series of important agenda-setting critical studies (Campbell, 1973, 1980, 1986, 1989a, 1995, 1998; see also Campbell, 1989b, 1991), she sought "to rescue the works of great women speakers from the oblivion to which most have been consigned" (Campbell, 1989a, p. 15). Her works sought to recover the artistry and creativity—the "inventional skill" (Campbell, 1995, p. 479)—of women advocates and rhetors. Working within the dominant *instrumentalist* framework, Campbell focused on the unique problems or *exigences* that women advocates have had to confront[1] and reconstructed the strategies that women have employed over time to gain access to the sphere of rhetorical deliberation and promote gender equality. Whereas Campbell has called attention to the problems that women faced in gaining access to the public sphere, another aspect of her scholarly project has been to reveal the way in which women's voices also have been excluded from the study of rhetoric in the public realm (Campbell, 1985; see also Vonnegut, 1992). Campbell's works have, both directly and indirectly, contributed to a growing number of gynocritical studies of 19th-century American women advocates.[2]

In both literary and rhetorical studies, the practice of gynocriticism has raised a number of questions demanding further critical and conceptual reflection. According to Warren (1987), gynocriticism has "raised nagging questions about the possibility and prudence of drawing generalizations across and beyond particular texts and authors" (p. 105). In rhetorical studies, one of Campbell's (1989a) generalizations was the idea of a **feminine style** in the public discourse of women advocates. According to Campbell, "That style emerged out of their experiences as women and was adapted to the attitudes and experiences of female audiences" (p. 12). Although Campbell qualified her claim by noting that this style was not "exclusive to women" (p. 12), critical generalizations such as feminine style are open to charges of overgeneralization and *essentialism.* That is, concepts such as feminine style seem to assume that there are essential differences between men and women that shape the way in which they think and communicate. But as Dow (1995) acknowledged, although the idea of essential differences might be useful for "explaining the experiences of some women, they can unwittingly elide differences *among* women, falsely universalizing women's experience according to a model based on the lives of white, middle-class women" while also exaggerating the differences between women and men (p. 109). In response to this issue, Dow argued that gynocritics making generalizations about "women's writing" or "women's rhetoric" should be "more careful about the limitations of how we make claims in the name of woman" (p. 114).

A second question broached in the literature is the relationship between gynocriticism and critical theory. As Warren (1987) noted, there is a hostility toward what is perceived as male-dominated domain of critical theory among many literary practitioners of gynocriticism. For example, Showalter (1985a) remarked, "No theory, however suggestive, can be a substitute for the close and extensive knowledge of women's texts which constitutes our essential subject" (p. 266).[3] At first glance, this aversion to theory does not seem as common among rhetorical gynocritics. For example, Campbell (1989b) concluded, "In the end, a feminist critique of rhetorical studies is not simply a demand for the inclusion of materials by and about women; it is a challenge to rethink fundamental assumptions in our theory, criticism, and pedagogy" (p. 214; see also Foss & Griffin, 1992). Given Campbell's (1989b) understanding of the relationship between theory and critical practice

(p. 213), the critic's encounter with "the sound of women's voices" cannot be atheoretical; rather, theory is generated through critical practice, and theoretical concepts are "refined or abandoned" on the basis of subsequent critical studies. But given Campbell's (1993) critical response to Biesecker's (1992) theoretical challenge, it appears that a gulf remains between at least *certain forms* of theorizing and the practices of rhetorical gynocritics.

A third question raised about the project of gynocriticism is whether or not it contributes to "female tokenism." As Spitzack and Carter (1987) noted, although the addition of women writers and orators into the classroom and into the critical **canon** "lends richness and balance to research" and is "unquestionably valuable," it "can easily support the presumption that the *majority* of women cannot rival male accomplishments. Great women are presumed to be atypical" (p. 405). Biesecker (1992) reiterated this position when she wrote, "The inclusion of particular texts spoken by women serve, albeit unwittingly, to perpetuate the damaging fiction that most women simply do not have what it takes to play the public rhetorical game" (p. 142).[4] But for Biesecker, the problem of possible female tokenism was only the tip of the proverbial iceberg. The real problem that she located in Campbell's gynocritical program, and by extension the works of other gynocritics in rhetorical studies, is the way in which it reinforces a pernicious "ideology of individualism" that binds the dynamics of discursive practice to authorial intentions. Biesecker's provisional solution to the problem of *intentionalism*[5] was to focus on the "collective rhetorical practices" that "have been the most common form of women's intervention in the public sphere" along with a rigorous rethinking of the origins of "the speaking subject" (p. 144). But as Campbell (1993) noted, Biesecker provided no examples of what she meant by "collective rhetorical practices" and ignored the fact that such practices already have been the object of critical inquiry.

The problem of possible female tokenism is addressed more directly by scholars who urge a turn away from the discourse of elite (mainly white) women in the public sphere and toward the **vernacular** or everyday practices of women. In their collection of materials devoted to exploring the "eloquence of women's lives," Foss and Foss (1991) rejected the assumption—which they contended is common in rhetorical studies—that significant communication occurs only in the public realm. While acknowledging that "scholarship in the area of *public* address [a traditional component of most rhetorical studies curricula] is supposed to deal with public rather than private discourse," they argued that "the delineation of a realm of study confined to *public* discourse unnecessarily limits the kinds of knowledge that can be generated about communication" (p. 13). Foss and Foss's call to expand the parameters of public address scholarship in rhetorical studies so as to better appreciate the diverse forms of women's rhetoric reaffirmed an ongoing trend in the field. Their contention that the study of public discourse "unnecessarily limits" communication inquiry was potentially more problematic. It is not apparent from their discussion *how* rhetorical inquiry into public discourse blocks or impedes other modes of analysis. In the end, Foss and Foss appeared to be leveling a "fails to" indictment against contemporary rhetorical studies. That is, they were criticizing the field for failing to be something else (e.g., interpersonal communication, family communication, small group communication).

Finally, some feminist scholars wonder whether the emphasis on vernacular practices, with its "overreliance on the personal voice" of women, might actually be doing a disservice to women and feminism. Stimpson (1996), for example, noted "the admirable desire to help each woman develop her voice" but wondered whether this emphasis on the vernacular "has had an unintended consequence: neglecting to teach our students how to move effectively in the rhetorical spaces between autobiography and wild overgeneralization, between saying 'I hate my father' and 'All men are hateful' " (p. 71). Stimpson suggested that appreciation of, and inquiry into, the vernacular practices of women should not lead feminists to turn their backs on more traditional rhetorical forms and spaces. Condit (1993) made a similar point when she wrote, "For feminists to abandon the study of rhetoric is to abandon an important arena of power" (p. 215).

The questions that have been raised, either directly or indirectly, about gynocriticism as a critical program no doubt will continue to generate scholarly discussion. Although the terminology may vary from one academic discipline to another, and although the specifics of the critical program no doubt will shift over time, gynocriticism—the study of women's discourse and the study of women as producers of discourse—will continue for some time to come.

Notes

1. During the 19th century, for example, the most pressing problem was the fact that women were excluded from the **public sphere.**

2. See, for example, Carlson (1992, 1994), Dow (1991), Japp (1985), Thompson (1995), Tonn (1996), and Wertheimer (1997).

3. Showalter's aversion to abstract critical theory and her emphasis on engaging women's texts and practices resemble, in some respects, the antipathy to theory found among some practitioners of **close reading** in contemporary rhetorical studies.

4. For Campbell's response to this possibility, see Campbell (1993, pp. 154-155).

5. In Biesecker's (1992) diagnosis of this problem, she anticipated Gaonkar (1993).

References and Additional Reading

Biesecker, B. (1992). Coming to terms with recent attempts to write women into the history of rhetoric. *Philosophy and Rhetoric, 25,* 140-161.

Campbell, K. K. (1973). The rhetoric of women's liberation: An oxymoron. *Quarterly Journal of Speech, 59,* 74-86.

Campbell, K. K. (1980). Stanton's "The Solitude of Self": A rationale for feminism. *Quarterly Journal of Speech, 66,* 304-312.

Campbell, K. K. (1985). The communication classroom: A chilly climate for women. *ACA Bulletin, 51,* 68-72. (Association for Communication Administration)

Campbell, K. K. (1986). Style and content in the rhetoric of early Afro-American feminists. *Quarterly Journal of Speech, 72,* 434-445.

Campbell, K. K. (1989a). *Man cannot speak for her: A critical study of early feminist speakers* (2 vols.). Westport, CT: Greenwood.

Campbell, K. K. (1989b). The sound of women's voices. *Quarterly Journal of Speech, 75,* 212-220.

Campbell, K. K. (1991). Hearing women's voices. *Communication Education, 40,* 33-48.

Campbell, K. K. (1993). Biesecker cannot speak for her either. *Philosophy and Rhetoric, 26,* 153-159.

Campbell, K. K. (1995). Gender and genre: Loci of invention and contradiction in the earliest speeches by U.S. women. *Quarterly Journal of Speech, 81,* 479-495.

Campbell, K. K. (1998). Inventing women: From Amaterasu to Virginia Woolf. *Women's Studies in Communication, 21,* 111-126.

Carlson, A. C. (1988). Limitations on the comic frame: Some witty American women of the nineteenth century. *Quarterly Journal of Speech, 74,* 310-322.

Carlson, A. C. (1992). Creative casuistry and feminist consciousness: A rhetoric of moral reform. *Quarterly Journal of Speech, 78,* 16-32.

Carlson, A. C. (1994). Defining womanhood: Lucretia Coffin Mott and the transformation of femininity. *Western Journal of Communication, 58,* 85-97.

Condit, C. M. (1993). Opposites in an oppositional practice: Rhetorical criticism and feminism. In S. P. Bowen & N. Wyatt (Eds.), *Transforming visions: Feminist critiques in communication studies.* Cresskill, NJ: Hampton Press.

Dow, B. J. (1991). The "womanhood" rationale in the woman suffrage rhetoric of Francis E. Willard. *Southern Communication Journal, 56,* 298-307.

Dow, B. J. (1995). Feminism, difference(s), and rhetorical studies. *Communication Studies, 46,* 106-117.

Fabj, V. (1993). Motherhood as political voice: The rhetoric of the mothers of Plaza de Mayo. *Communication Studies, 44,* 1-18.

Foss, K. A., & Foss, S. K. (1991). *Women speak: The eloquence of women's lives.* Prospect Heights, IL: Waveland.

Foss, S. K., & Griffin, C. L. (1992). A feminist perspective on rhetorical theory: Toward a clarification of boundaries. *Western Journal of Communication, 56,* 330-349.

Gaonkar, D. P. (1993). The idea of rhetoric in the rhetoric of science. *Southern Communication Journal, 58,* 258-295.

Gilbert, S. M., & Gubar, S. (1979). *The madwoman in the attic: The woman writer and the nineteenth-century literary imagination.* New Haven, CT: Yale University Press.

Gubar, S. (2000). *Critical condition: Feminism at the turn of the century.* New York: Columbia University Press.

Japp, P. M. (1985). Esther or Isaiah? The abolitionist-feminist rhetoric of Angelina Grimké. *Quarterly Journal of Speech, 71,* 335-348.

Kendall, K. E., & Fisher, J. Y. (1974). Frances Wright on women's rights: Eloquence versus ethos. *Quarterly Journal of Speech, 60,* 58-68.

Lunsford, A. A. (Ed.). (1995). *Reclaiming rhetorica: Women in the rhetorical tradition.* Pittsburgh, PA: University of Pittsburgh Press.

Marston, P. J., & Rockwell, B. (1991). Charlotte Perkins Gilman's "The Yellow Wallpaper": Rhetorical subversion in feminist literature. *Women's Studies in Communication, 14,* 58-72.

Miller, D. H. (1997). The future of feminist rhetorical criticism. In M. M. Wertheimer (Ed.), *Listening to their voices: The rhetorical activities of historical women.* Charleston: University of South Carolina Press.

Showalter, E. (1985a). Feminist criticism in the wilderness. In E. Showalter (Ed.), *The new feminist criticism: Essays on women, literature, and theory.* New York: Pantheon.

Showalter, E. (1985b). Toward a feminist poetics. In E. Showalter (Ed.), *The new feminist criticism: Essays on women, literature, and theory.* New York: Pantheon.

Showalter, E. (1993). American gynocriticism. *American Literary History, 5,* 109-128.

Smith-Rosenberg, C. (1985). Hearing women's words: A feminist reconstruction of history. In C. Smith-Rosenberg, *Disorderly conduct: Visions of gender in Victorian America.* New York: Oxford University Press.

Spitzack, C., & Carter, K. (1987). Women in communication studies: A typology for revision. *Quarterly Journal of Speech, 73,* 401-423.

Stimpson, C. R. (1996, Winter). Women's studies and its discontents. *Dissent,* pp. 67-75.

Sullivan, P. A. (1993). Women's discourse and political communication: A case study of Congressperson Patricia Schroeder. *Western Journal of Communication, 57,* 530-545.

Thompson, J. M. (1995). Incarcerated souls: Women as individuals in Margaret Fuller's *Woman in the Nineteenth Century. Communication Quarterly, 43,* 53-63.

Tonn, M. B. (1996). Militant motherhood: Labor's Mary Harris "Mother" Jones. *Quarterly Journal of Speech, 82,* 1-21.

Vonnegut, K. S. (1992). Listening for women's voices: Revisioning courses in American public address. *Communication Education, 41,* 26-39.

Warren, H. B. (1987). "The truth lies somewhere between the two": Feminist formulations on critical theory and practice. In J. B. Wenzel (Ed.), *Argument and critical practices: Proceedings of the Fifth SCA/AFA Conference on Argumentation.* Annandale, VA: Speech Communication Association.

Wertheimer, M. M. (Ed.). (1997). *Listening to their voices: The rhetorical activities of historical women.* Charleston: University of South Carolina Press.

HEGEMONY

Aune (1994) noted that "no term from the Marxist tradition retains as much currency among leftists as 'hegemony' " (p. 68). Associated most closely with the work of Italian theorist Antonio Gramsci, **hegemony** is a key concept in contemporary *critical theory.* Gramsci's views on this topic have been widely discussed (Adamson, 1980; Eagleton, 1991; Laclau & Mouffe, 1985; Lears, 1985; Mouffe, 1979; Williams, 1977), but as Femia (1987) concluded, "Despite the huge and ever-growing pile of secondary literature, there remains to this day remarkably little general agreement about what Gramsci really said" on the topic of hegemony (p. 8).

Carragee (1993) asserted that Gramsci employed the concept of hegemony "to explain the failure of European socialist movements in the early twentieth century" (p. 330). For Gramsci, the power exercised by the dominant class was not primarily a form of physical coercion or repression.[1] Instead, Gramsci emphasized the way in which the bourgeoisie dominated the minds of the people. Gramsci's concept of hegemony, Gitlin (1994) wrote, described the "bourgeois domination of the thought, the common sense, the life-ways, and everyday assumptions of the working class. . . . [It] called attention to the routine structures of everyday thought—down to 'common sense' itself—which worked to sustain class domination and tyranny" (p. 517). Williams (1977) noted how the concept of hegemony conceptualizes the process of domination

> as in effect a saturation of the whole process of living—not only of political and economic activity . . . but of the whole substance of lived identities and relationships. . . . Hegemony is a whole body of practices and expectations, over the whole of living: our senses and assignments of energy, our shaping of perceptions of ourselves and our world. . . . It thus constitutes a sense of reality for most people in the society, a sense of absolute because experienced reality beyond which it is very difficult for most members of the society to move, in most areas of their lives. (p. 110)

Cloud (1996) contended that hegemony is "the process by which a social order remains stable by generating consent to its parameters through the production and distribution of ideological texts that define social reality for the majority of the people" (p. 117). Similarly, Eagleton (1991) wrote,

> We might define hegemony as a whole range of practical strategies by which a dominant power elicits consent to its rule from those [it] subjugates. To win hegemony . . . is to establish moral, political, and

> intellectual leadership in social life by diffusing one's own "worldview" throughout the fabric of society as a whole, thus equating one's own interests with the interests of society at large. (pp. 115-116)

Hegemony is both an achieved condition (e.g., masculinist hegemony) and the process—the interaction of "strategies"—that produces the condition (Williams, 1977). Although it overlaps with a Marxist or neo-Marxist understanding of **ideology,** hegemony refers to a more encompassing set of cultural practices. Eagleton (1991) explained,

> Hegemony . . . is not just some successful kind of ideology, but may be discriminated into its various ideological, cultural, political, and economic aspects. Ideology refers specifically to the way power struggles are fought out at the level of signification [discourse]; and though such signification is involved in all hegemonic processes, it is not in all cases the *dominant* level by which rule is sustained. . . . Hegemony is also carried in cultural, political, and economic forms—in non-discursive practices as well as in rhetorical utterances. (p. 113)

As Eagleton and others noted, hegemony emerges in virtually every sphere of life. It is like a giant web woven by elites in which the public is caught and by which the elite perpetuate their rule.[2] Whereas numerous practices help to weave this web, a culture's communication practices are of critical importance. Rhetorical and communication scholars have seized the concept of hegemony and begun to explore the way in which communication helps to generate this condition. A considerable amount of attention has been devoted to the hegemonic nature of the new media.[3] One group of scholars focus their attention on masculinist hegemony in popular television programs (Dow, 1990; Hanke, 1990; see also Trujillo, 1991). Murphy (1992) examined the interconnection between hegemony and **domestication** in the response of John F. Kennedy's administration and the mass media to the civil rights "freedom rides" of the early 1960s. Cloud (1996) explored the way in which popular biographies of Oprah Winfrey help to perpetuate the "hegemony of liberal individualism" (p. 117). Other scholars are investigating the process of hegemony creation and perpetuation in a variety of cultural spheres and discursive practices (Bineham, 1993; Clair, 1993; Conrad, 1988; Dionisopoulos & Crable, 1988; Lewis, 1992; Sloop, 1994, 1996). Rhetorical and communication scholars are not only appropriating the concept of hegemony but also contributing to its theorization or conceptual refinement. Condit (1994), for example, suggested ways of adjusting the concept to the realities of late 20th-century American society and illustrated the utility of her approach through an analysis of the emergence of hegemony in the context of reproductive technology.[4]

Whereas scholars frequently depict hegemony as a pervasive and ubiquitous force in a society, most also note that hegemony never is complete. Murphy (1992), for example, noted that no society or culture is "*completely* dominated by a single set of beliefs" (p. 64). Hegemonic forces always are at work to "bring recalcitrant rhetors 'into the fold' " (p. 64).[5] But these forces (associated with the dominant media, governmental institutions and agencies, the corporate sector, mainstream interest groups, etc.) cannot bring everyone "into the fold"; they cannot eliminate all oppositional voices. As Williams (1977) pointed out, "A specific and complex hegemonic process . . . is in practice full of contradictions and of unresolved conflicts" (p. 118). More specifically, Williams argued that any society not only will manifest a dominant or hegemonic culture but also will be the home of "residual" and "emergent" cultures (pp. 121-127). Williams wrote,

> What has really to be said, as a way of defining important elements of both the residual and the emergent and as a way of understanding the character of the dominant, is that *no mode of production, and therefore no dominant social order, and therefore no dom-*

> *inant culture, ever in reality includes or exhausts all human practice, human energy, and human intention.* (p. 125)

Residual cultures (e.g., rural communities, small farmers, some environmentalists) and emergent cultures (e.g., a new "generation" or new group that establishes an alternative and independent self-identity) can exploit the contradictions and conflicts of the hegemonic culture,[6] challenge the values and practices of the dominant culture, and serve as a recurrent source of social and political **controversy.**[7]

Those individuals and groups that challenge the dominant and hegemonic culture do not seek—in fact cannot seek—an end to hegemony. Like Michel Foucault's sense of **power,** there is no escape from hegemony. But the inability to escape hegemony should not lead to frustration or political quiescence. For Gramsci, hegemony was a two-way street (Aune, 1994; Laclau & Mouffe, 1985). People opposed to the dominant order fight back by developing a "counter-hegemony" (Aune, 1994). The problem with how critical scholars have appropriated the concept, Aune (1994) suggested, is that they have seized on the negative moment (hegemony as domination) and too often have ignored its positive potential (hegemony as a political strategy for change). Aune pointed out that hegemony implies "leadership" (pp. 69-70) and advocacy. Regrettably, he noted, "the policy successes of the [Ronald] Reagan and [George] Bush administrations might lead an observer to think that it has actually been only the *right* that reads Gramsci" (p. 72).[8] Aune acknowledged that part of the problem lies in the fact that Gramsci "was unable to theorize systematically (either in an abstract or a concrete way) how moments of counter-hegemony are made"; he was unable to describe "what specifically will 'spark' a decisive change in popular consciousness" (p. 73). Aune seemed to hint that Gramsci's conceptual powers might have been limited by his attitude toward rhetoric (p. 164). In fact, in his famous *Prison Notebooks,* Gramsci (1971) spoke rather critically of the tradition of rhetoric. During a discussion of education, he noted "the need to combat the habits formed in public speaking—prolixity, demagogy, and paralogism" (p. 29). A few pages later, Gramsci expressed the fear that, without reform, "we will have rhetorical schools, quite unserious, because the material solidity of what is 'certain' will be missing and what is 'true' will be a truth only of words: that is to say, precisely, rhetoric" (p. 36). Gramsci's sense that rhetoric produces a false "truth"—truth only in the domain of words—positioned him among the long line of critics going back to Plato who maintained that rhetoric was a sham art and practice. A positive sense of hegemony as a political strategy for social change most likely will remain undeveloped so long as scholars retain Gramsci's anti-rhetorical prejudices.

Notes

1. Given that Gramsci spent a good part of his adult life as a political prisoner in Italy, he recognized that physical repression was one of the ways in which the dominant order retained its power.
2. In an often-quoted passage, Gitlin (1994) noted how accounts of hegemony often depict it as "a sort of immutable fog that has settled over the whole of public life" (p. 517).
3. For a survey of the literature, see Carragee (1993).
4. Condit's (1994) perspective was criticized by Cloud (1996), and their disagreement was further developed in Condit (1996, 1997) and Cloud (1997). On the utility of hegemony, see also Aune (1994).
5. For a different approach to this issue, see Sloop (1994).
6. See, for example, Aune's (1994) discussion of the contradictions in the ideal of the free and open "market" (p. 72).
7. For an analysis of American political culture that tries to counter the limitations of strong hegemony theory, see Ellis (1993).
8. George (1997) echoed Aune's (1994) lament.

References and Additional Reading

Adamson, W. L. (1980). *Hegemony and revolution: A study of Antonio Gramsci's political and cultural theory.* Berkeley: University of California Press.

Aune, J. A. (1994). *Rhetoric and Marxism*. Boulder, CO: Westview.

Bineham, J. L. (1993). Theological hegemony and oppositional interpretive codes: The case of evangelical Christian feminism. *Western Journal of Communication, 57,* 515-529.

Carragee, K. M. (1993). A critical evaluation of debates examining the media hegemony thesis. *Western Journal of Communication, 57,* 330-348.

Clair, R. P. (1993). The use of framing devices to sequester organizational narratives: Hegemony and harassment. *Communication Monographs, 60,* 113-136.

Cloud, D. L. (1996). Hegemony or concordance? The rhetoric of tokenism in "Oprah" Winfrey's rags-to-riches biography. *Critical Studies in Mass Communication, 13,* 115-137.

Cloud, D. L. (1997). Concordance, complexity, and conservatism: Rejoinder to Condit. *Critical Studies in Mass Communication, 14,* 192-197.

Condit, C. M. (1994). Hegemony in a mass-mediated society: Concordance about reproductive technologies. *Critical Studies in Mass Communication, 11,* 205-230.

Condit, C. M. (1996). Hegemony, concordance, and capitalism: A reply to Cloud. *Critical Studies in Mass Communication, 13,* 382-384.

Condit, C. M. (1997). Clouding the issues? The ideal and the material in human communication. *Critical Studies in Mass Communication, 14,* 197-200.

Conrad, C. (1988). Work songs, hegemony, and illusions of self. *Critical Studies in Mass Communication, 5,* 179-201.

Dionisopoulos, G. N., & Crable, R. E. (1988). Definitional hegemony as a public relations strategy: The rhetoric of the nuclear power industry after Three Mile Island. *Central States Speech Journal, 39,* 134-145.

Dow, B. J. (1990). Hegemony, feminist criticism, and *The Mary Tyler Moore Show. Critical Studies in Mass Communication, 7,* 261-274.

Eagleton, T. (1991). *Ideology: An introduction*. London: Verso.

Ellis, R. J. (1993). *American political cultures*. New York: Oxford University Press.

Fairclough, N. (1995). *Critical discourse analysis: The critical study of language*. London: Longman.

Femia, J. V. (1987). *Gramsci's political thought: Hegemony, consciousness, and the revolutionary process*. Oxford, UK: Clarendon.

George, S. (1997, Summer). How to win the war of ideas: Lessons from the Gramscian right. *Dissent*, pp. 47-53.

Gitlin, T. (1994). Prime time ideology: The hegemonic process in television entertainment. In H. Newcomb (Ed.), *Television: The critical view* (5th ed.). New York: Oxford University Press.

Gramsci, A. (1971). *Selections from the prison notebooks* (Q. Hoare & G. N. Smith, Eds. and Trans.). New York: International Publishers.

Hanke, R. (1990). Hegemonic masculinity in *Thirtysomething. Critical Studies in Mass Communication, 7,* 231-248.

Laclau, E., & Mouffe, C. (1985). *Hegemony and socialist strategy: Towards a radical democratic politics*. London: Verso.

Lears, T. J. J. (1985). The concept of cultural hegemony: Problems and possibilities. *American Historical Review, 90,* 567-593.

Lewis, C. (1992). Making sense of common sense: A framework for tracking hegemony. *Critical Studies in Mass Communication, 9,* 277-292.

Martin-Barbero, J. (1993). *Communication, culture, and hegemony: From the media to mediations* (E. Fox & R. A. White, Trans.). London: Sage.

Mouffe, C. (1979). Hegemony and ideology in Gramsci. In C. Mouffe (Ed.), *Gramsci and Marxist theory*. London: Routledge and Kegan Paul.

Mumby, D. K. (1997). The problem of hegemony: Rereading Gramsci for organizational communication studies. *Western Journal of Communication, 61,* 343-375.

Murphy, J. M. (1992). Domesticating dissent: The Kennedys and the freedom rides. *Communication Monographs, 59,* 61-78.

Perloff, R. M. (1998). *Political communication: Politics, press, and public in America*. Mahwah, NJ: Lawrence Erlbaum.

Sloop, J. M. (1994). "Apology made to whoever pleases": Cultural discipline and the grounds of interpretation. *Communication Quarterly, 42,* 345-362.

Sloop, J. M. (1996). *The cultural prison: Discourse, prisoners, and punishment*. Tuscaloosa: University of Alabama Press.

Trujillo, N. (1991). Hegemonic masculinity on the mound: Media representations of Nolan Ryan and American sports culture. *Critical Studies in Mass Communication, 8,* 290-308.

Williams, R. (1977). *Marxism and literature*. Oxford, UK: Oxford University Press.

HERMENEUTICS (AND RHETORIC)

In Greek mythology, Hermes was the messenger of the gods. The ancient Greeks used the name of their mythological avatar to develop a word—*hermeneus*—for another type of messenger. A hermeneus in ancient Greece was an *interpreter* or someone who could translate a message in a foreign language and/

or explain the meaning of an ambiguous or cryptic message.

Hermeneutics, as this brief etymology suggests, is concerned with *interpretation* and usually is defined as the practice and/or art of interpretation. What, more precisely, do scholars mean by the term *interpretation*? Exploring the nature of this concept, Mailloux (1990) wrote, "Reading words on walls. Explicating poems in classrooms. Making sense of treaties in Congress. Reading, explicating, making sense; these are three names given to the activity of 'interpretation' " (p. 121). Interpretation, he continued, is inherently a mediating process; the interpreter (or hermeneus) is positioned between a text or message and an audience and serves as an intermediary between the two. Interpretation, then,

> conveys the sense of a translation pointed in two directions simultaneously: *toward* a text to be interpreted and *for* an audience in need of the interpretation. That is, the interpreter mediates between the translated text and its new rendering *and* between the translated text and the audience desiring the translation. (p. 121)

Consistent with its ultimate mythological origins, the concept of interpretive hermeneutics initially focused on discovering the meaning of the word of God as it was inscribed in the Bible. Hermeneutics originally was the art and practice of biblical exegesis—a procedure for uncovering the frequently complicated meaning of the Scriptures. Basic principles of biblical exegesis began to emerge early in the third century. Origen, who Kennedy (1980) argued is "the greatest Christian thinker between Paul and Augustine," introduced the idea that "just as a man consists of body, soul, and spirit, so does the Scripture have three similar levels, arranged intentionally by God for man's [sic] salvation" (p. 138). Kennedy explained that these levels proceeded from the corporeal or literal level, continued through the moral level, and culminated in the theological level, where the interpreter/priest recognized the "essential truths of Christianity" (p. 138).

The tradition of biblical hermeneutics is both extensive and complicated. But the nuances of this tradition are not essential to a general examination of the concept of hermeneutics and its relationship to rhetoric. The larger conceptual significance of hermeneutic thinking began to emerge in the works of the German theologian and philosopher Friedrich Schleiermacher. Writing during the late 18th and early 19th centuries, Schleiermacher was an early proponent of broadening the focus of hermeneutics. According to Kerby (1993), "Schleiermacher was the first scholar to seek a general theory of interpretation, one applicable not only to religious texts" (p. 90).[1] Schleiermacher's most enduring contribution to hermeneutic theory, most contemporary scholars agree, was the concept of the *hermeneutic circle.* The hermeneutic circle was Schleiermacher's term for describing a seeming paradox or tension at the heart of the process of interpretation. Contemporary scholar Bernhard Radloff described the circle in these terms:

> Interpretation moves in a circle. In order to understand the word, the sentence must be understood and vice versa; striving to understand an author's work, we attempt to unfold it sentence by sentence, but the sentence remains opaque unless we have already grasped, by a leap in advance, its rhetorical function in the whole of the work. (Radloff, 1993, p. 550)

Consider the opening sentence to Abraham Lincoln's "Gettysburg Address": "Fourscore and seven years ago, our fathers brought forth on this continent a new nation, conceived in liberty and dedicated to the proposition that all men [sic] are created equal." How do we interpret or uncover the meaning of this utterance? According to Schleiermacher and those influenced by his description of the circular nature of interpretation, we can understand only the *part* (specific word, phrase, clause, sentence, etc.) in relation to a larger *whole* (sentence, paragraph, text, œuvre, etc.) while being able to understand the whole only through its accumulating parts. The phrase "fourscore and seven years ago" that opened the address acquires its meaning when we grasp (at some level of awareness) its adverbial function; it locates an event (whose identity remains to be disclosed) in time. Absent an understanding of how the phrase was functioning in the sentence, our understanding of the phrase will remain incomplete. The meaning of the possessive pronoun-noun combination "our fathers" emerges when we see it in relationship to the action of the sentence. We are then able to perceive that the pronoun "our" referred to all Americans and "fathers" was a *metaphorical vehicle* that referred to the signers of the Declaration of Independence. Our knowledge of practical aspects of language such as grammar, discursive conventions, and *generic* formulas allows us to "leap" ahead and formulate a tentative sense of the "whole" so that we might understand the specific parts of Lincoln's oration.

But as the parts accumulate, one's sense of the whole becomes sharper, and sometimes this will lead to modifying one's initial sense of the whole while also inviting a reappraisal of the earlier parts. For example, imagine that a person goes to see a movie. The person does not know anything about the film other than that it stars Jim Carrey. So, the person thinks, "Jim Carrey . . ., okay, this is going to be a comedy." And then the film begins. The viewer approaches each early scene in the film in relation to the comedy genre (the whole) and expects to be amused. But as the parts accumulate, the viewer might think, "This isn't what I expected. . . . It's nothing like *Dumb and Dumber*." This revised sense of the whole (the viewer's sense of the type of film that he or she is watching) then begins to guide how the viewer understands the parts and might lead him or her to go back and revisit the initial parts (the early scenes) of the film and alter how to understand them. Something similar might take place with the "Gettysburg Address." The full title (an address "delivered at the dedication of the cemetery at Gettysburg") and the first two paragraphs provided a sense of a whole (ceremonial oratory) that guided the understanding of the parts. But then, in the third paragraph, Lincoln disrupted this frame when he announced that it was impossible to accomplish the task—dedicating the ceremony—in which he and his audience had been engaged. The disruption invites a rereading of the early sections in light of an altered sense of the whole while also requiring the listener or reader to posit a new whole so as to understand the remainder of the speech.

Schleiermacher's concept of the hermeneutic circle tries to describe the basic conditions that make it possible to interpret, or understand, any linguistic object. The point is simply that all interpretation involves this continual oscillation between part and whole; the circle is inescapable. But the concept of a hermeneutic circle does not specify any specific procedure that an interpreter should follow in trying to understand a text. Subsequent philosophers and theorists, such as Wilhelm Dilthey, would become much more normative and stipulative as they formulated *methods* or strategies for interpreting various linguistic objects. Hermeneutics gradually evolved into a mode of epistemological reflection focused on humanistic or interpretive inquiry (what is known in German as the *Geisteswissenschaften*). Hermeneutic thinking tried to answer the question: What is the best or most appropriate way of studying or comprehending human action, especially human linguistic or discursive action?[2]

One line of hermeneutic thought identifies distinct models or methods of interpretive inquiry. For example, the French philosopher Paul Ricoeur distinguished between interpretive methods based on the interpreter's *stance* or *mood*. According to Ricoeur (1970), it is possible to distinguish between "interpretation as a recollection of meaning" and "interpretation as [an] exercise of suspicion" (pp. 28-36) or between a *hermeneutics of appreciation* (or *faith*) and a *hermeneutics of suspicion*. Practitioners of a hermeneutics of appreciation search for the meaning that is embedded in human linguistic action, whereas practitioners of a hermeneutics of suspicion (Ricoeur believed that Marx, Nietzsche, and Freud were the three original "masters of suspicion") seek to bring to light all that is repressed and/or distorted by human linguistic action. The tension between these rival hermeneutic postures has been an aspect of contemporary literary and social theory and criticism for at least the past 30 years. The so-called Gadamer-Habermas "debate" is one fairly well-known moment in this rivalry. Efforts to blend or balance the two stances sometimes are referred to as *critical hermeneutics* (Huspek, 1991; Thompson, 1981).

Not surprisingly, we can locate these rival hermeneutic stances in the realm of rhetorical criticism. Extending the hermeneutic theorizing of Martin Heidegger, Rosenfield (1974) argued that the proper stance of the rhetorical critic is appreciative; his or her objective is to attend to, and help bring to light, the processes of disclosure that are manifest in the text. Unless the critic is open to these processes, it will be impossible to fully grasp the way in which the text reveals the world. Wander (1983) rejected Rosenfield's call to attend to the textual processes of disclosive revelation. Wander suggested that rhetorical practice is most commonly an instrument of **power** and domination. Hence, the critic's task is to expose the processes of domination and repression that are manifested in the text (the critic engages in *ideology critique*), and the most appropriate hermeneutic stance for this task is one of suspicion. Traces of the appreciation-suspicion dichotomy also are visible in the more recent tensions between the **close reading** and **critical rhetoric** movements. Many close readers subscribe to the postulate that "oratory is an art form" (Leff, 1986) and, therefore, attempt to reconstruct the artistry of the rhetorical text. Artistry tends to be most visible when the critic adopts an appreciative stance. Most critical rhetoricians, on the other hand, subscribe to Wander's dictum that discourse is an instrument of power. The operation of power in and through the text tends to be most visible when the critic engages the text by way of a suspicious stance.

The appreciation-suspicion contrast is not the only way of organizing and clarifying competing hermeneutic methods and theories. But as a number of scholars have argued recently, hermeneutics has more relevance to rhetorical studies than as a source for interpretive models or methods or as a mode of methodological self-reflection. Three specific strands of scholarship merit additional attention: Hyde and Smith's (1979) ontological account of the relationship between hermeneutics and rhetoric, Mailloux's (1985, 1989, 1991) rhetorical intervention into the interpretive theory debates in literary studies, and Leff's (1997) revision of the relationship between textual production (**invention**) and interpretation to illuminate what he referred to as *hermeneutical rhetoric.*

Hyde and Smith's (1979) project was indebted to the expansion of hermeneutic reflection developed in the works of Heidegger and his student Hans-Georg Gadamer. Heidegger and Gadamer maintained that hermeneutic thinking could do more than offer insight into how to interpret a text; it possessed ontological significance. They insisted that hermeneutic reflection could provide insight into the nature of human existence. For Heidegger and Gadamer, humans exist in a linguistically saturated world. Because of this feature of the world, interpretation is not something that humans do occasionally; it is a basic fact of human existence. Humans are engaged in a never-ending quest to "understand" the world through interpretive/hermeneutic practice.[3] In much of their writings, Heidegger and Gadamer tried to explore this ontological dimension of hermeneutics (e.g., Gadamer, 1976, 1982; Heidegger, 1962).

Working within this expanded sense of hermeneutics, Hyde and Smith (1979) sought to reconstruct the ontological or "primordial" relationship (p. 347) between rhetoric and hermeneutics. Humans exist in a world of almost infinite "linguistic possibilities." Human *reality* (what we know or what we comprehend) comes into existence as the massive

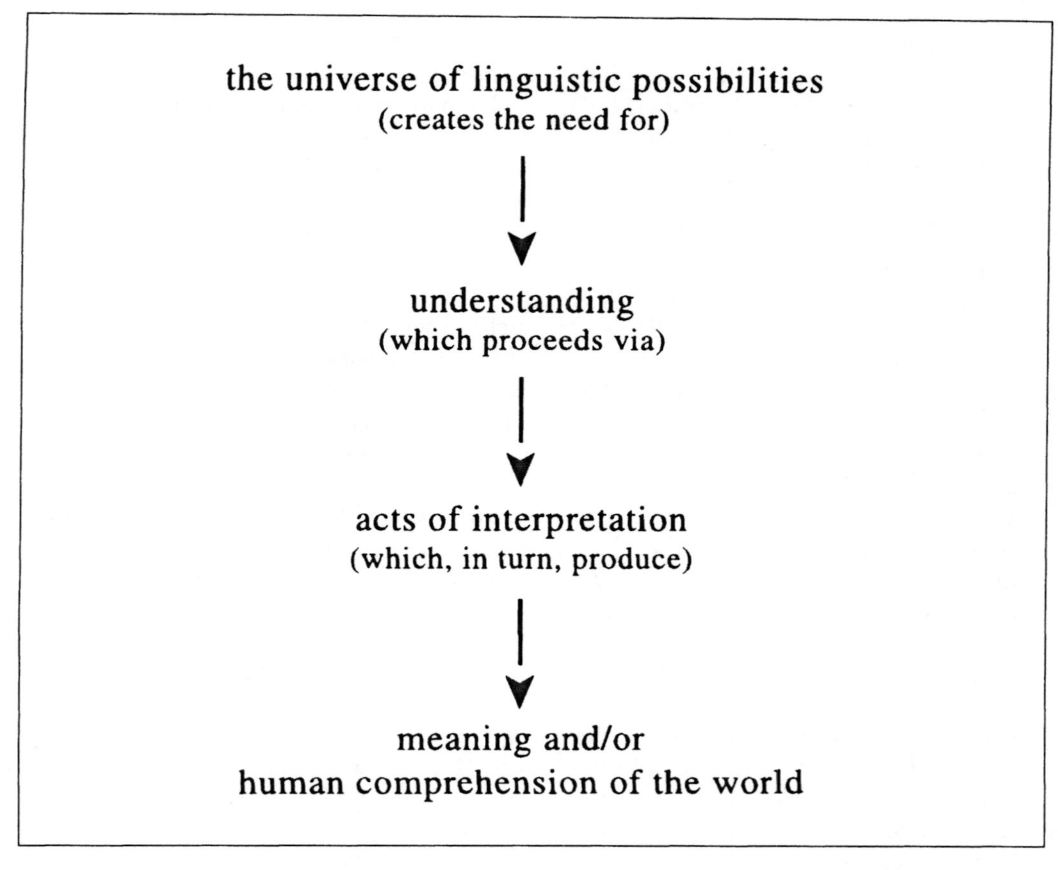

Figure H.1. The Hermeneutic Situation (traditional account)

realm of linguistic possibilities is narrowed and structured. The critical challenge, Hyde and Smith suggested, is to describe the process through which the realm of linguistic possibilities is structured and a meaningful world is created. What might be termed the standard account of this process looks something like the diagram depicted in Figure H.1. As Hyde and Smith explained, "Interpretation develops understanding . . ., [and] understanding becomes meaningful when interpretation shows it 'as something' " (p. 353). But they intimated that this standard account of the structuring of linguistic possibilities is incomplete; there is a rhetorical component to the process that requires recognition. Their alternative account can be visualized along the lines of the diagram depicted in Figure H.2. Hyde and Smith maintained that rhetoric has an ontological or primordial function, and that is "to 'make known' meaning both *to oneself and to others*" (p. 348). They elaborated later in the essay,

> Rhetoric's ontological relationship with hermeneutics occurs when understanding becomes meaningful, when interpretation shows it "as something." This showing of understanding by interpretation, such that meaning is made known, is rhetoric in the purest sense; it is how rhetoric originates as a fundamental condition of human existence. Ontologically speaking, *rhetoric shows itself in and through the various ways understanding is interpreted and made known.* What the "as" of a perceived is selected to be when a linguistic possibility (or possibilities) is actualized within a herme-

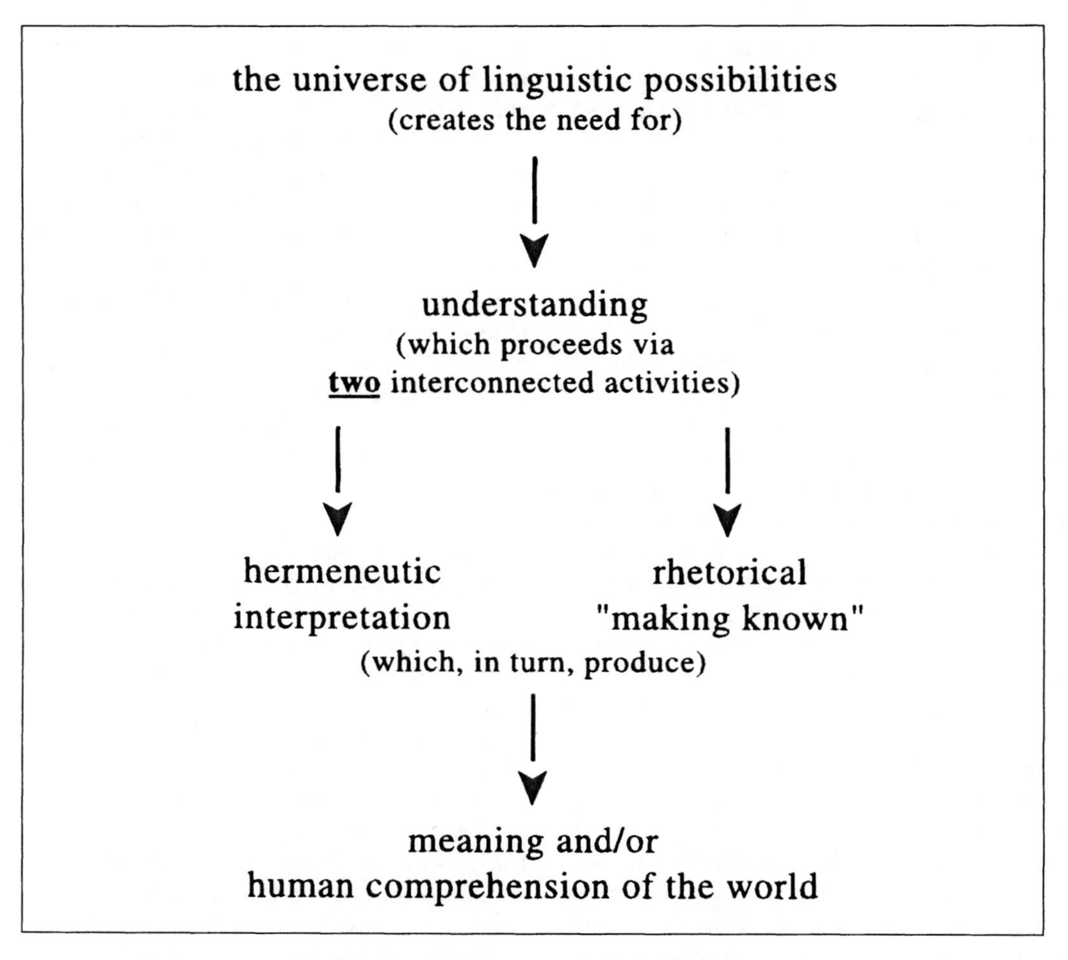

Figure H.2. The Hermeneutic Situation (Hyde and Smith's revised account)

neutic situation marks the presence of rhetoric. (p. 354)

Hyde and Smith's (1979) ontological account of rhetoric and its relationship to hermeneutics is dense and difficult to illustrate. Their account might be thought of as an elaborate gloss on a remark made by Burke (1950) in *A Rhetoric of Motives:* "Wherever there is persuasion, there is rhetoric. And wherever there is 'meaning,' there is 'persuasion' " (p. 172). Like Hyde and Smith, Burke appeared to suggest that rhetoric is present wherever meaning is being produced. Consider a simple case. Imagine that a person goes to work and that his or her boss calls the worker into her office. She then tells the worker a story about an ant and an anteater. As the worker listens, he or she is thinking, "What's her *point*? What is she trying to tell me with this story? What does it *mean*?" The worker is faced with a very quotidian example of the ubiquitous hermeneutic situation. The worker begins to consider various interpretive possibilities (e.g., "Maybe I'm the ant and my boss is the anteater," "My boss wants me to be an anteater with the other 'ant' employees"). Each reading of the story contains a different message; one appears to be a warning, whereas the other is a form of indirect encouragement to be more aggressive at work. For Hyde and Smith, rhetoric exists in the making known of meaning; it arises in the worker's struggle to determine the point of the boss's story. They wrote, "Without rhetoric, the latent meaning housed in the hermeneutical situation could never be actualized"; they maintained that rhetoric "*is the selecting tool for making known . . . meaning*" (p. 354). Rhetoric comes into existence as the worker struggles with the story; its specific mission is to reveal a linguistic possibility "as" something.

Hyde and Smith's (1979) description of rhetoric was a marked departure from traditional conceptualizations (discussed in the introduction to this book). One of the most common definitions holds rhetoric to be *public* discourse—something that is relatively easy for different people to experience. But Hyde and Smith argued that this definition is an *ontic* account (part of the observable world) and not an *ontological* account (concerned with ultimate essences) of rhetoric. Rhetoric is not a thing; it is a process that exists, in its purest form, *within* an individual rather than *between* individuals. Hyde and Smith wrote, "Rhetoric's function shows itself originally in a person's thinking about existence, in a person's *intra*personal domain" (p. 354). The public text might contain traces of this internal process, but Hyde and Smith suggested that we should not mistake the ontic product for the ontological process.

Mailloux's intervention into the debates about interpretive method in literary theory has some parallels to Hyde and Smith's (1979) project. Both Mailloux and Hyde and Smith tried to explore the relationship between rhetoric and hermeneutics. But Mailloux's focus was decidedly ontic rather than ontological. He was not interested in looking inside an individual person as that person grapples with the universe of linguistic possibilities; he wanted to examine how a group of readers, in particular literary critics, reach an agreement or a consensus on the meaning of a text. Like Hyde and Smith, Mailloux found flaws in the standard account of this process. The standard account holds that readers, such as literary critics, employ an interpretive method or a hermeneutic theory to discover the meaning of a text. Given their importance, literary scholars devote considerable attention to the adequacy (or lack thereof) of specific interpretive methods and hermeneutic theories. The basic idea is that if scholars can uncover the "right" method/theory, then reaching agreement on the meaning of texts will be a matter of correctly applying the theory to the text. But Mailloux contended that the effort to ground specific interpretive acts in an abstract account of the general process of interpretation (a hermeneutic theory) is a futile endeavor (e.g., Mailloux, 1989, pp. 4-14).[4] Mailloux (1989) asserted that literary critics need to "stop doing theory" (p. 14).

How, if not through theory, do literary critics (and potentially other groups of readers) reach agreement on the meanings of texts? Mailloux's answer to this question is *through rhetoric.* Mailloux (1998) wrote, "Hermeneutics and rhetoric are intertwined" (p. 16). The best way of studying the process of literary interpretation, then, is what Mailloux (1985, 1989, 1991, 1998) referred to as *rhetorical hermeneutics.* All "interpretive work always involves rhetorical action [and] attempts to convince others of the truth of explications and explanations" (Mailloux, 1998, p. 15). The "foundations of meaning" are not to be found in hermeneutic theory. Nor are they to be found in the primordial making-known function of rhetoric. Hyde and Smith's ontological account of hermeneutics and rhetoric is, Mailloux implied, simply one more general theory of interpretation that should be rejected. Mailloux (1998) argued that the "foundations of meaning" can be found only within "rhetorical exchanges" and "practices" (p. 16). In his perspective, interpretive theory functions "as historical sets of topics, arguments, tropes, ideologies, and so forth which determine how texts are established as meaningful through rhetorical exchanges" (p. 15). Mailloux recommended that literary scholars abandon the quest for *the* definitive general theory of interpretation and instead turn their attention to the historical struggle over the meanings of specific texts.

And that struggle proceeds by way of an ontic rhetoric of **arguments** and other persuasive strategies and appeals.

Mailloux's approach to the relationship between hermeneutics and rhetoric can help the rhetorical critic to better understand the dynamic of *hermeneutic disputes.*[5] For example, in the conclusion to *Rhetorical Power,* Mailloux (1989) turned his attention away from the rhetorical struggle over the meaning of literary texts such as *Huckleberry Finn* and directed it toward the realm of public politics. Mailloux examined how Ronald Reagan's administration tried to defend the proposed "Star Wars" missile defense system from attacks that it violated the provisions of the 1972 Anti-Ballistic Missile (ABM) Treaty with the Soviet Union (as well as the 1958 Space Act). In examining the interpretive or hermeneutic dispute over the meaning of the ABM Treaty, Mailloux found traditional interpretive theories (e.g., that the meaning of a text can be located in the literal meaning of the words, that it can be located by reading one part of a text in terms of other parts of a text, that it can be discovered in the intentions of the text's authors) functioning as "rhetorical resources" (p. 175).[6]

But someone might reply that the Reagan administration's interpretation of the ABM Treaty was illogical and unsound. We *need* interpretive *theory*—we need a final ground for meaning—to get people to see this point. Mailloux (1989) considered this issue and wrote that, to dispute the Reagan administration's interpretation of the treaty, "one simply and rigorously argues for a counter-interpretation, making such rhetorical moves as pointing to the text, citing the authors' intentions, noting the traditional reading, and invoking the consensus" (p. 180). But there is no, and Mailloux believed that there can be no, final or ultimate ground that proves, once and for all, what the treaty means. The only thing that both sides of the treaty debate can turn to is rhetoric. But Mailloux noted that a rhetorically grounded interpretation always is **contingent** and open to subsequent reinterpretation.

The final position to review briefly is Leff's (1997) concept of a hermeneutical rhetoric. As the wording suggests, his idea is a variation on Mailloux's discussion of rhetorical hermeneutics (a point acknowledged by Leff in the opening pages of his essay). The difference, Leff maintained, is a matter of emphasis. In rhetorical hermeneutics, rhetoric is rendered as an *adjective* that modifies the dominant *noun* hermeneutics. Leff wrote that Mailloux "works through rhetoric to generate a more sophisticated conception of the hermeneutic enterprise" (p. 197). Leff proposed to reverse the adjective-noun relationship so as to focus on rhetoric. But what exactly does this involve? Leff explained that the "focal interest" of a hermeneutical rhetoric

> centers on rhetorical practice as manifested in texts that directly and overtly engage political circumstances. And this change in focal object also suggests a different motive—a shift from how rhetoric constrains understanding of texts to how interpretive processes become inventional resources in texts that purport to address extraverbal reality. To put the point simply: Where Mailloux asks how rhetorical strategies enter into hermeneutic activity, I ask how hermeneutic strategies enter into the production of political rhetoric. (pp. 197-198; cf. McGee, 1990)

The reversal of the adjective-noun relationship and Leff's (1997) explanation present a neat and clear picture of the differences between the two concepts: rhetorical hermeneutics and hermeneutical rhetoric. But Leff acknowledged that the relationship between the two concepts might be much more complicated. He wrote, "In critical practice, the two orientations are not easily separated, and whoever begins with one almost inevitably becomes entangled with the other" (p. 198). Why? In his initial account of the differences between his position and Mailloux's position, Leff presented discourse *production* (the rhetorical **canon of invention**) and textual *interpretation* as separate and distinct activities.

But Leff admitted that this might not be an accurate depiction of the production-interpretation relationship.[7] He developed his argument through a careful reconstruction of the program for classical rhetorical education, but the main point can be summarized in this way:

> Simple distinctions between production and interpretation give way to an analysis that reveals how the processes blend in the communicative context. . . . From a broader perspective, we might say that all interpretive work involves participation in rhetorical exchange, and every rhetorical exchange involves some interpretive work. (p. 198)

Like Mailloux, Leff was interested in ontic manifestations of rhetoric. But his account of the relationship between textual interpretation and discursive production paralleled Hyde and Smith's ontological description of the relationship between hermeneutics and rhetoric. The theme that links Hyde and Smith, Mailloux, and Leff is that the practices of hermeneutics and rhetoric, of textual interpretation and discourse production, or (on an even more basic level) of reading and writing are not as distinct as was commonly assumed. All of these authors insisted that these practices must be seen as intertwined.

Finally, we might ask the question: Do these theoretical discussions have any practical value? The common thread in the works of Hyde and Smith, Mailloux, and Leff might lead in a couple of directions. First, as Leff explored most fully, the thread suggests that interpretation and *imitation* might profitably be introduced into discussions of rhetorical invention. Second, the thread outlines an agenda for critical scholarship. Numerous disputes in public life are hermeneutic in nature. Does the Second Amendment prohibit a ban on handguns? Does the Bible demand that wives submit to their husbands? Do Microsoft's commercial practices violate the agreement the company had previously entered into with the Department of Justice? These all are questions that illustrate how matters of interpretation frequently saturate the process of public argument. As critics study these and similar pubic controversies, they might explore the "seen but unobserved" link between hermeneutics and rhetoric.

Notes

1. For a general introduction to Schleiermacher's theory, see Palmer (1969).
2. For an example of hermeneutic reflection on interpretive inquiry, see Hoy (1978).
3. Hyde and Smith (1979) wrote that language use is the "experiential form of understanding" (p. 351).
4. Mailloux's (1989) argument drew on Knapp and Michaels' (1982) provocative essay.
5. See the discussion of exigence types in the entry for **situation, rhetorical.**
6. See also Compier's (1999) extension of Mailloux's (1989) argument into the realm of theology.
7. On this point, see Eden (1997).

References and Additional Reading

Bineham, J. L. (1995). The hermeneutic medium. *Philosophy and Rhetoric, 28,* 1-16.

Bleicher, J. (1980). *Contemporary hermeneutics: Hermeneutics as method, philosophy, and critique.* London: Routledge and Kegan Paul.

Burke, K. (1950). *A rhetoric of motives.* New York: Prentice Hall.

Chen, K. H. (1987). Beyond truth and method: On misreading Gadamer's praxical hermeneutics. *Quarterly Journal of Speech, 73,* 183-199.

Compier, D. H. (1999). *What is rhetorical theology? Textual practice and public discourse.* Harrisburg, PA: Trinity Press International.

Deetz, S. (1978). Conceptualizing human understanding: Gadamer's hermeneutics and American communication studies. *Communication Quarterly, 26,* 12-23.

Eden, K. (1997). *Hermeneutics and the rhetorical tradition: Chapters in the ancient legacy and its humanist reception.* New Haven, CT: Yale University Press.

Gadamer, H. G. (1976). On the scope and function of hermeneutical reflection. In D. E. Linge (Ed.), *Philosophical hermeneutics* (D. E. Linge, Trans.). Berkeley: University of California Press.

Gadamer, H. G. (1982). *Truth and method* (G. Barden & J. Cumming, Trans.). New York: Crossroad.

Heidegger, M. (1962). *Being and time* (J. Macquarie & E. Robinson, Trans.). New York: Harper & Row.

Hoy, D. C. (1978). *The critical circle: Literature, history, and philosophical hermeneutics.* Berkeley: University of California Press.

Huspek, M. (1991). Taking aim on Habermas's critical theory: On the road toward a critical hermeneutics. *Communication Monographs, 58,* 225-233.

Hyde, M. J., & Smith, C. R. (1979). Hermeneutics and rhetoric: A seen but unobserved relationship. *Quarterly Journal of Speech, 65,* 347-363.

Kennedy, G. A. (1980). *Classical rhetoric and its Christian and secular tradition from ancient to modern times.* Chapel Hill: University of North Carolina Press.

Kerby, A. (1993). Hermeneutics. In I. R. Makaryk (Ed.), *Encyclopedia of contemporary literary theory: Approaches, scholars, terms.* Toronto: University of Toronto Press.

Knapp, S., & Michaels, W. B. (1982). Against theory. *Critical Inquiry, 8,* 723-742.

Leff, M. (1986). Textual criticism: The legacy of G. P. Mohrmann. *Quarterly Journal of Speech, 72,* 377-389.

Leff, M. (1997). Hermeneutical rhetoric. In W. Jost & M. J. Hyde (Eds.), *Rhetoric and hermeneutics in our time: A reader.* New Haven, CT: Yale University Press.

Mailloux, S. (1985). Rhetorical hermeneutics. *Critical Inquiry, 11,* 620-641.

Mailloux, S. (1989). *Rhetorical power.* Ithaca, NY: Cornell University Press.

Mailloux, S. (1990). Interpretation. In F. Lentricchia & T. McLaughlin (Eds.), *Critical terms for literary study.* Chicago: University of Chicago Press.

Mailloux, S. (1991). Rhetorical hermeneutics revisited. *Text and Performance Quarterly, 11,* 233-248.

Mailloux, S. (1998). *Reception histories: Rhetoric, pragmatism, and American cultural politics.* Ithaca, NY: Cornell University Press.

McGee, M. C. (1990). Text, context, and the fragmentation of contemporary culture. *Western Journal of Speech Communication, 54,* 274-289.

Palmer, R. E. (1969). *Hermeneutics: Interpretation theory in Schleiermacher, Dilthey, Heidegger, and Gadamer.* Evanston, IL: Northwestern University Press.

Radloff, B. (1993). Hermeneutic circle. In I. R. Makaryk (Ed.), *Encyclopedia of contemporary literary theory: Approaches, scholars, terms.* Toronto: University of Toronto Press.

Rickman, H. P. (1981). Rhetoric and hermeneutics. *Philosophy and Rhetoric, 14,* 100-111.

Ricoeur, P. (1970). *Freud and philosophy: An essay on interpretation* (D. Savage, Trans.). New Haven, CT: Yale University Press.

Rosenfield, L. W. (1974). The experience of criticism. *Quarterly Journal of Speech, 60,* 489-496.

Thompson, J. B. (1981). *Critical hermeneutics: A study in the thought of Paul Ricoeur and Jürgen Habermas.* Cambridge, UK: Cambridge University Press.

Wander, P. (1983). The ideological turn in modern criticism. *Central States Speech Journal, 34,* 1-18.

HETEROGLOSSIA

Russian literary theorist Mikhail Bakhtin introduced the term **heteroglossia** to describe the nature of language as it appears in prose discourse. For Bakhtin, the prose text (e.g., a novel, a speech, a newspaper essay, a short story) is made up of numerous languages, vocabularies, lexicons, or idioms. Bakhtin argued that the general language of a culture is "internally stratified" or divided into a large number of specific sub-languages or idioms. These sub-languages or idioms separate themselves from the general national language through a process of appropriation that provides words with idiom-specific meanings (e.g., the word *blitz* has a specific meaning in the idiom of American football that is different from what the word means when used to describe military strategy) that, in turn, enact a variety of functions.[1] Particular words can function as a part of a number of different idioms; each idiom imparts to the word subtle shades of meaning (as do the *accentuations* of particular speakers and writers).

Bakhtin (1981) maintained that "the internal stratification of any single national language" can be seen in

> social dialects, characteristic group behavior, professional jargon, generic languages, languages of generations and age groups, tendentious languages, languages of the authorities, [languages] of various circles and of passing fashions, languages that serve the specific sociopolitical purposes of the day [and] even of the hour. (pp. 262-263)

Countless factors, then, contribute to the stratification or segmentation of any "national language." We can add factors to Bakhtin's list that further describe the way in which contemporary American society is linguistically divided. In addition to the sub-languages or idioms noted by Bakhtin, Americans employ sub-languages of gender, race, religion, region, and social class. Most Americans speak the same general language (American English), but that general language is itself divided into multiple idioms or sublanguages. Bakhtin used the term *heteroglossia* to refer to the overall segmentation of language within any culture.

Bakhtin also employed the term *heteroglossia* to refer to the interaction of idioms or sub-languages within specific prose texts. In some cases, a specific piece of prose discourse will feature one primary idiom. For example, a lawyer preparing an appeal will speak or write in the idiom of the law, a doctor preparing an article for a medical journal will write in the idiom of medical science (or perhaps one of the even more specialized areas of medicine), a tax consultant will speak in the idiom of tax law, a television sports commentator will speak in the idiom of the particular sport being televised (we would be surprised if the commentator used the idiom of football to describe the performance of a figure skater), or a minister delivering a sermon will speak in the specific idiom (e.g., Roman Catholic, Episcopalian) of his or her religion. But in a large number of cases, we have what Bakhtin (1981) termed a "social dialogue among languages" (p. 263) within the prose text. Consider some relatively simple examples. When Thurgood Marshall argued the National Association for the Advancement of Colored People's case against school segregation before the Supreme Court during 1952-1953, he relied heavily (as we would expect) on the language of constitutional law. But Marshall also employed evidence from psychological studies on the effects of segregation on the human personality. In introducing these studies into his argument, Marshall was combining the *language* of social science with the language of constitutional law. When a conservative politician quotes the Bible during the course of a speech on a policy proposal, he or she intermingles the *language* of religion with the language of policy **deliberation** (a language and **genre** that more commonly features appeals to expedience, utility, and comparative advantages). Of course, conservatives are not the only public advocates who draw on the language of religion in their advocacy efforts. The language of religion was a key resource in the discourse of the civil rights movement during the 1950s and 1960s. As a variety of scholars have noted (Bercovitch, 1978; Bonomi, 1986; Strout, 1974), the interanimation of the language(s) of religion and politics is a crucial aspect in the history of American public discourse.

The examples in the preceding paragraph are illustrative but basic. Bakhtin's central point was that the process of rhetorical **invention** or the production of prose texts consists of the selection and organization of different idioms and voices (on voice, see the entry for **polyphony**). Whenever we speak or write, we borrow and/or appropriate (make our own) elements from the various vocabularies and idioms to which we have been exposed (Kamberelis & Scott, 1992; Knoeller, 1998).[2] This process can be quite intentional (e.g., when a student writes a paper that employs the idiom of an academic discipline for the first time, when a white politician borrows the vocabulary of the civil rights movement when speaking to a black audience), but it also can be very unreflective and unintentional. People are like language sponges; we absorb bits and pieces of the various idioms and vocabularies to which we are exposed, and we then employ them in our discourse. Satirist P. J. O'Rourke, in an essay about America's drug problem in the November 30, 1989, issue of *Rolling Stone,* noted how many of his baby boomer friends with teenage children had absorbed the language of the criminal justice system. O'Rourke commented that these individuals had learned to speak a language that once was limited to prosecuting attorneys, public defenders, and the police as a result of having to deal with the drug problems of their children. When these individuals related their tales of woe to O'Rourke, they slipped into the idiom of criminal justice as easily, it seemed, as they might have slipped into other idioms that they used in their daily lives (idioms of sports, work, hobbies, etc.).

But as we slide from one idiom to the next and weave idioms into our conversations and our more polished prose compositions, we often do so unintentionally and unreflectively. Bakhtin suggested that speaking and writing simply is a process of weaving or combining languages and voices.

Following Bakhtin's insight into the heteroglot nature of a culture's language and the process of text production, rhetorical critics now are devoting considerable effort to unpacking the play of languages within specific texts and trying to describe the process of "orchestration" that Bakhtin saw as basic to prose composition and rhetorical invention (Jasinski, 1997a; Murphy, 1997; Zulick, 1992). Trying to describe the play of language within a text—the process of "appropriating" a language and harnessing its resources—is a complicated task. One prerequisite for this type of analysis is a familiarity with the various idioms and vocabularies that together constitute both a culture's stratified general language and the resources for rhetorical invention. For example, Bakhtin's (1984) analysis of the novels of Dostoevsky depended on his own deep immersion into the languages and voices of Russian culture (e.g., philosophical, religious, popular, political). Put simply, the critic needs to know a language so as to detect its presence within a text (Jasinski, 1997b; Pocock, 1987). And Jasinski (1997b) argued that such knowledge can be gained only through "the concrete engagement of texts and performative traditions" (p. 218).

Perceiving the play of idioms within a text also is facilitated by an understanding of the common forms of language and voice appropriation. Put differently, how do people, both intentionally and unintentionally, borrow and incorporate different idioms, vocabularies, or voices into their written and/or spoken communication? A typology of language appropriation techniques developed by Kamberelis and Scott (1992) provides some important insight into answering this question. They identified five primary forms or techniques of language appropriation.

Direct Quotation

In *direct quotation,* the act of appropriation is "explicitly marked" or recognized by the author or advocate (usually through placing borrowed material in quotation marks). Most often, we quote from languages considered to be authoritative (e.g., the language of science, the language of medicine, the language of religion, the language of a political ideology).

Adoption or Imitation

In *adoption* or *imitation,* the author or advocate borrows a language and, in a sense, internalizes it or makes it his or her own. We see this most often in the process of socialization where initiates to a new speech community (e.g., law students, new converts to a religion) learn to "speak the language" of the community.

Stylization

Stylization is a type of middle ground between direct quotation and adoption. It is a form of paraphrasing another language without quoting directly from other speakers or writers but also not really internalizing the language. The language of rhetorical stylistics provides some clear examples of stylization such as *prosopopoeia* or speaking in the voice and language of someone absent (e.g., a widow saying to her young son, "If your father was here, I know he'd say . . ."; a coach exhorting her team at halftime with the words of the absent injured star player). In his 1967 anti-war speech at the Riverside Church in New York, Martin Luther King, Jr., tried to speak for those who, like the people of Vietnam, he believed were voiceless in the debate over U.S. Vietnam policy. In so doing, King did not directly quote any Vietnamese, nor did he internalize their language; instead, he tried to voice their concerns and present their perspective on events, stylizing his language to make it sound something like the language of the people of Vietnam.

Parody

Parody is a form of language appropriation that ridicules or pokes fun at the language that has been borrowed. For example, a conservative politician might introduce the language of contemporary American liberalism (through direct quotation of a famous liberal such as Ted Kennedy or through stylized paraphrase) in a speech to a gathering of Republicans so as to make fun of that language. The recent best-seller *Politically Correct Bedtime Stories* (Garner, 1994) is a good example of parody as the language strategies associated with the political correctness movement are used to retell traditional stories so as to reveal (at least from the authors' perspective) the foolishness of that language.[3]

Polemic

Polemical language appropriation tends to be used for partisan purposes. This very important method of appropriation can take a number of particular forms such as *prolepsis* (voicing the anticipated language and arguments of the opposition so as to refute them), *reluctant testimony* (using the language of a member of the opposition, typically in the form of a direct quote, against the opposition's position), and *epitrope* (an ironic form of appropriation in which an opponent's language and arguments are affirmed, only to be rejected later in the text). We find polemical language appropriation in instances such as conservatives "borrowing" the "language of choice" used by feminists to defend abortion and employing it on behalf of a different proposition (e.g., attacking government regulation) and feminists adopting the "language of the family" typically associated with contemporary conservatives to combat attacks on their movement. Family has become something of a contested **ideograph** in contemporary political debate. There does not appear to be a single "language" of family (although conservatives, no doubt, believe that they are speaking for, and in the typical idiom of, the American family). Instead, a number of idioms have emerged through which various advocates can speak for and to "family matters."

Consider another example. In April 1964, Malcolm X delivered one of his most well-known speeches—"The Ballot or the Bullet"—to an audience in Cleveland, Ohio. This speech followed King's famous "I Have a Dream" speech by roughly seven months, and it can be read as a response to King's speech. Reading "The Ballot or the Bullet" as a response to King (or reading it **intertextually**) reveals the way in which Malcolm X polemically appropriated a number of images from the "I Have a Dream" speech that were then used against King and the moderate civil rights movement. Where King held onto his American "dream," Malcolm X perceived an American "nightmare." Where King demanded that America make good on the "check" it *gave* to African Americans, Malcolm X demanded that African Americans be repaid for their "investment" in American prosperity. In Malcolm X's polemical response, white America did not *give* anything to black America; rather, black America built white America through its investment of blood and sweat. Finally, where King defended nonviolent civil disobedience and its method of appealing to the conscience of the nation, Malcolm X responded that the nation's conscience was "bankrupt" (another image that he "borrowed" from King).

Burke (1984) anticipated the idea of polemical voice appropriation a number of years ago in his short discussion of the "stealing back and forth of symbols." Burke described the process in this way:

> The divine right of kings was first invoked by *secular* interests combating the authority of the theocrats. It held that God appointed the king, rather than the church authorities, to represent the secular interests of "the people." Later, when the church made peace with established monarchs, identifying its interests with the interests of the secular authorities, *the church* adopted the doctrine as its own. (p. 328, emphasis added)

The basic point of this form of polemic is that symbols and languages developed by one group for one set of purposes can be appropriated by other groups and used for different purposes.

The Kamberelis and Scott (1992) typology is not necessarily exhaustive, nor are the five categories just discussed mutually exclusive. But the Kamberelis and Scott typology does provide a way of exploring the way in which language appropriation and orchestration functions in textual production. The typology, along with the specific examples of practical criticism in rhetorical studies that appropriate Bakhtinian insights, provides some indication of how Bakhtin's concept of heteroglossia can inform contemporary rhetorical studies.

Notes

1. See also Hart's (1997) discussion of the various functions of "code" words.
2. See also Newcomb (1984) for an extension of Bakhtin's insights into the realm of the mass media.
3. See also Wertsch's (1991) discussion of parody in George Bush's 1988 acceptance speech.

References and Additional Reading

Bakhtin, M. M. (1981). *The dialogic imagination* (M. Holquist, Ed., C. Emerson & M. Holquist, Trans.). Austin: University of Texas Press.

Bakhtin, M. M. (1984). *Problems of Dostoevsky's poetics* (C. Emerson, Ed. and Trans.). Minneapolis: University of Minnesota Press.

Bercovitch, S. (1978). *The American jeremiad.* Madison: University of Wisconsin Press.

Bonomi, P. U. (1986). *Under the cope of heaven: Religion, society, and politics in colonial America.* New York: Oxford University Press.

Burke, K. (1984). *Attitudes toward history* (3rd ed.). Berkeley: University of California Press.

Fairclough, N. (1995). *Critical discourse analysis: The critical study of language.* London: Longman.

Garner, J. F. (1994). *Politically correct bedtime stories.* New York: Macmillan.

Hart, R. P. (1997). *Modern rhetorical criticism* (2nd ed.). Boston: Allyn & Bacon.

Jasinski, J. (1997a). Heteroglossia, polyphony, and *The Federalist Papers. Rhetoric Society Quarterly, 27,* 23-46.

Jasinski, J. (1997b). Instrumentalism, contextualism, and interpretation in rhetorical criticism. In A. G. Gross & W. M. Keith (Eds.), *Rhetorical hermeneutics.* Albany: State University of New York Press.

Kamberelis, G., & Scott, K. (1992). Other people's voices: The co-articulation of texts and subjectivities. *Linguistics and Education, 4,* 359-403.

Knoeller, C. (1998). *Voicing ourselves: Whose words we use when we talk about books.* Albany: State University of New York Press.

Lemke, J. L. (1988). Discourses in conflict: Heteroglossia and text semantics. In J. Benson & W. Greaves (Eds.), *Systemic functional approaches to discourse.* Norwalk, NJ: Ablex.

Murphy, J. M. (1997). Inventing authority: Bill Clinton, Martin Luther King, Jr., and the orchestration of rhetorical traditions. *Quarterly Journal of Speech, 83,* 71-89.

Newcomb, H. (1984). On the dialogic aspects of mass communication. *Critical Studies in Mass Communication, 1,* 34-50.

Pocock, J. G. A. (1987). The concept of language and the *metier d'historien:* Some considerations on practice. In A. Pagden (Ed.), *The languages of political theory in early-modern Europe.* Cambridge, UK: Cambridge University Press.

Strout, C. (1974). *The new heavens and new earth: Political religion in America.* New York: Harper & Row.

Wertsch, J. V. (1991). *Voices of the mind: A sociocultural approach to mediated action.* Cambridge, MA: Harvard University Press.

Zulick, M. D. (1992). The agon of Jeremiah: On the dialogic invention of prophetic ethos. *Quarterly Journal of Speech, 78,* 125-148.

HIERARCHY/ HIERARCHICAL PSYCHOSIS

Hierarchy, and its neurotic "perfection" in **hierarchical psychosis,** is one of the central concepts in Kenneth Burke's **dramatistic** conceptualization of human society. The centrality of hierarchy in Burke's thought is reflected in his "definition of man [sic]" initially formulated in 1961 in the original publication of *The Rhetoric of Religion* (Burke, 1970) and revised in *Language as Symbolic Action* (Burke, 1966). According to Burke (1970),

> Man [sic] is
> (1) the symbol-using animal,
> (2) inventor of the negative,

> (3) separated from his natural condition by instruments of his own making, [and]
> (4) goaded by the spirit of hierarchy. (p. 40)

Burke (1966, p. 15; 1970, p. 42) would extend the fourth clause to read "or moved by a sense of order." For Burke, order and hierarchy are inseparable.

Human social life, Burke suggested, involves the perpetual struggle to create, maintain, and overturn an economic-political order (see also Griffin, 1969). Whereas order might be the pivotal term in Burke's (1970) theory of human relations (see also Rueckert, 1982), hierarchy is its substance or "structural principle" (Brock, 1980; see also Duncan, 1962). As Burke (1984) observed, social

> "order" is not just "regularity." It also involves a distribution of *authority.* And such mutuality of rule and service, with its uncertain dividing line between loyalty and servitude, takes roughly a pyramidal or hierarchical form (or, at least, it is like a ladder with "up" and "down"). (p. 276)

According to Burke, the quest for order produces authority, and the distribution of authority introduces the "spirit" of hierarchy that infuses most human societies. Burke (1950) wrote in *A Rhetoric of Motives* that "hierarchy is inevitable," but he quickly qualified his point by noting that this "is not to say that any particular hierarchy is inevitable; the crumbling of hierarchies is as true a fact about them as their formation" (p. 141).

Burke's concept of hierarchy might be thought of in two ways. First, hierarchies have a corporeal or material existence in various "social differentiations and stratifications [that are] due to the division of labor and to corresponding distinctions in the possession of property" (Burke, 1966, p. 41). The person who drives a BMW has higher status than the person who drives a Ford (just ask a real estate agent if you want to move into a neighborhood full of Fords or BMWs). Ivy League schools are more prestigious than regional state universities, and their graduates typically find jobs with greater ease and make more money. Wealthy individuals charged with committing crimes are convicted much less frequently than are those with less wealth, and when wealthy individuals are convicted, they usually receive lighter penalties (e.g., when the sons or daughters of wealthy persons are busted for drugs, they usually are sent off to the Betty Ford center or some other "rehab" center, whereas children of the less well off more often do time in jail for their mistakes). These are just a few of the ways in which egalitarian American society is hierarchically structured. Race, ethnicity, gender, class, and region are some of the raw materials out of which hierarchies are constructed. If this first sense is materialistic, then we also can find a second, more idealistic inflection in Burke's discussions of hierarchy. Hierarchy is a pervasive "spirit" or "principle" operating in human social existence. It is inescapable. Ranking, grading, comparing, and evaluating one thing (e.g., an idea, a person) against another appear to be ubiquitous features of "social thinking" (Hariman, 1986) and illustrate Burke's contention that humanity is "goaded" by the spirit of hierarchy. As Burke (1950) observed, "The hierarchic principle is indigenous to all well-rounded human thinking" (p. 141).

If the quest for order (e.g., economic, political, conceptual) produces hierarchy, then we might ask what the results of the quest for hierarchy are. What are some of the important implications of our being "goaded" by a hierarchical spirit? In his essay, "On Human Behavior Considered 'Dramatistically,'" Burke (1984) employed a common hierarchical image to make an important point about the impact of hierarchy on human life: "Pyramidal magic is inevitable in social relations" (p. 279). What did Burke mean by "pyramidal magic"? For Burke, communication that bridges different levels of hierarchy (as when someone at the top tries to induce cooperation from those below or when someone toward the bottom solicits the assistance of someone near the top) is a significant accomplishment that he likened to magic. For Burke (1950), overcoming the "social estrangement" or divisions of hierarchy is best thought of as a type of social "courtship" (pp. 208-212). Burke's ideas on courtship and hierarchical address received extended discussion in Duncan (1962, pp. 288-301). A second important implication of the spirit of hierarchy is the way in which it can enhance the conditions of *mystery* (difference and otherness) and **mystification.**[1] As Duncan (1962) noted, "Those on top tend to deny or cloak division, difference, and disorganization" (p. 256). Anyone attempting to oppose "those on top" must find a way of subverting the hierarchical address (in this case, the appeal from a superior to an inferior or, perhaps, to someone with roughly equal social standing), but this task is made more difficult given that the hierarchy has been rendered obscure through linguistic mystification. A third point to note is that because hierarchy is inescapable, it will infect anyone or any group that manages to displace the reigning structure. Griffin (1969), for example, noted how the **persona** of the movement advocate attempting to displace the status quo will necessarily shift if the movement is successful. The advocate who begins as "prophet" (preaching impiety and urging a rejection of the dominant order and its hierarchy) becomes a "priest" (preaching a new piety or orthodoxy—a new order—with a new hierarchy).

Burke portrayed hierarchy as a social and conceptual phenomenon that is inescapable but always materially **contingent.** That is the central point in the passage from *A Rhetoric of Motives* (Burke, 1950) quoted earlier. But in some cases, people lose the ability (or perhaps never possessed the ability) to recognize the contingency of any particular hierarchy and insist that the existing particular hierarchy must be preserved at (almost) any cost. Burke referred to this obsession as hierarchical psychosis (Burke, 1966, p. 19; 1985, p. 279). Duncan (1962) provided a useful gloss on this concept. He wrote, "When the enactment of hierarchy becomes so dogmatic and the stages of development so rigid that doubt, question, or creation of new hierarchies are no longer possible and, indeed, are *punishable,* we enter the realm of hierarchical psychosis" (p. 122). Hierarchical psychosis, Burke argued, is problematic because of the tendency of those under its spell to turn to **scapegoating** as a means of maintaining order and preserving the status quo.

Note

1. See Burke (1950) on " 'mystifications' that cloak the state of division" (p. 141). See Duncan (1962) on "hierarchical mystification" (p. 255; see also Smith, 1973).

References and Additional Reading

Brock, B. L. (1980). Rhetorical criticism: A Burkeian approach. In *Methods of rhetorical criticism* (2nd ed., B. L. Brock & R. L. Scott, Eds.). Detroit, MI: Wayne State University Press.

Burke, K. (1950). *A rhetoric of motives.* New York: Prentice Hall.

Burke, K. (1966). *Language as symbolic action: Essays on life, literature, and method.* Berkeley: University of California Press.

Burke, K. (1970). *The rhetoric of religion: Studies in logology.* Berkeley: University of California Press.

Burke, K. (1984). On human behavior considered "dramatistically." In K. Burke, *Permanence and change: An anatomy of purpose* (3rd ed.). Berkeley: University of California Press.

Carlson, A. C. (1999). "You know it when you see it": The rhetorical hierarchy of race and gender in *Rhinelander v. Rhinelander. Quarterly Journal of Speech, 85,* 111-128.

Duncan, H. D. (1962). *Communication and social order.* London: Oxford University Press.

Griffin, L. M. (1969). A dramatistic theory of the rhetoric of movements. In W. H. Rueckert (Ed.), *Critical responses to Kenneth Burke.* Minneapolis: University of Minnesota Press.

Hariman, R. (1986). Status, marginality, and rhetorical theory. *Quarterly Journal of Speech, 72,* 38-54.

Rueckert, W. H. (1982). *Kenneth Burke and the drama of human relations* (2nd ed.). Berkeley: University of California Press.

Smith, J. M. (1973, Spring). Erik H. Erikson's sex role theories: A rhetoric of hierarchical mystification. *Today's Speech,* pp. 27-31.

ICONICITY

Iconicity is a linguistic concept (Haiman, 1985) that has been introduced into rhetorical criticism during recent years (Daughton, 1995; Leff & Sachs, 1990). Iconicity refers to a harmony between the semantic ("content") and syntactical ("form") levels of an utterance. Consider a simple example. In the sentence, "He is very, very, very big," the length of the sentence (its syntax) reinforces its semantic or propositional content (a comment on size).

Now consider a more complex example. In his "Letter From Birmingham Jail" in April 1963, Martin Luther King, Jr., was trying to explain to his readers why black Americans have difficulty in accepting the white moderates' admonition to "wait." He wrote,

> I guess it is easy for those who have never felt the stinging darts of segregation to say, "Wait." But when you have seen vicious mobs lynch your mothers and fathers at will and drown your sisters and brothers at whim; when you have seen hate-filled policemen curse, kick, brutalize, and even kill your black brothers and sisters with impunity; when you see the vast majority of your twenty million Negro brothers smothering in an airtight cage of poverty in the midst of an affluent society; when you suddenly find your tongue twisted and your speech stammering as you seek to explain to your six-year-old daughter why she can't go to the public amusement park that has just been advertised on television, and see tears welling up in her little eyes when she is told that Funtown is closed to colored children, and see the depressing clouds of inferiority begin to form in her little mental sky, and see her begin to distort her little personality by unconsciously developing a bitterness toward white people; when you have to concoct an answer for a five-year-old son asking in agonizing pathos: "Daddy, why do white people treat colored people so mean?"; when you take a cross-country drive and find it necessary to sleep night after night in the uncomfortable corners of your automobile because no motel will accept you; when you are humiliated day in and day out by nagging signs reading "white" and "colored"; when your first name becomes "nigger" and your middle name becomes "boy" (however old you are) and your last name becomes "John," and your wife and mother are never given the respected title "Mrs."; when you are harried by day and haunted by night by the fact that you are a Negro, living constantly at tiptoe stance and never quite knowing what to expect next, and plagued with inner fears and outer resentments; when you are forever fighting a degenerating sense of "nobodiness"; then

> you will understand why we find it difficult to wait.

What happened in this passage? King was trying to describe the conditions of black Americans in 1963. His account painted a picture of unrelenting segregation and oppression. The sentence **amplified** King's claim regarding the unremitting horror of racial segregation. But notice also the structure of the sentence (it was by far the longest sentence in the letter). The sentence itself, apart from its "content," was unrelenting; it went on, and on, and on (through an elaborate pattern of *dependent clauses*). Like black oppression, it seemed to never end. The readers, waiting for the end of the sentence (waiting for an *independent clause*), now knew something about King's frustration at being told to "wait." The form of the sentence tried to communicate the experience of black Americans; King wanted white America to know what it meant to be black and to be told to wait. And this knowledge was imparted through the iconic merger of form and content in the sentence.[1]

Ironic forms of iconicity also are possible. In these cases, there is a tension or a discordancy between *what* is being said and *how* it is being said. Weaver (1953) noted how a certain "friction" can develop "whenever a given unit of the system of grammar is tending to say one thing while the semantic meaning and the general organization are tending to say another" (p. 116). For example, a writer might try to describe a scene of intense action but could frustrate that effort by employing a sentence structure that is passive and static (e.g., the *noun style* discussed in the entry for **style**). In this case, the syntax—*how* something is said—ironically subverts what the author is trying to accomplish. The critical perspective commonly known as deconstruction emphasizes discursive self-subversion of this sort.

But ironic iconicity can be quite complex. Consider this example from Abraham Lincoln's 1860 speech at Cooper's Union:

> Let all who believe that "our fathers, who framed the government under which we live, understood this question just as well, and even better than we do now," speak as they spoke, and act as they acted upon it. . . . As those fathers *marked it,* so let it be again *marked,* as an evil not to be extended, but to be tolerated and protected only because of and so far as its actual presence among us makes that toleration and protection a necessity. (emphasis added)

What was Lincoln doing in this passage? Functionally, the passage is an *epitrope* (an appropriation of the words of his opponent, Stephen Douglas, that are used against Douglas); Lincoln was urging the nation to follow the path that the founding fathers "marked" with respect to slavery. But notice the presence, in the portion of the passage that is highlighted, of *chiasmus* (the pattern of A-B, B-A reversal). Through the chiasmus, Lincoln ironically subverted his call to follow the path of the founders; the content says "continue," whereas the style and syntax says "reverse." But the passage is complex. On a broader level, the passage can be read as iconic. How? There was a tension in the passage between the content and the form—the call to continue and the **figure** of reversal. But this tension might not, in fact, be self-subversive; it might emphasize or reaffirm the tension that Lincoln was experiencing as he struggled with the dilemma of slavery in America. The tension between form and content has an iconic relationship—a relationship of harmony—with Lincoln's experience; it is a textual sign of the tensions that Lincoln was trying to negotiate as he confronted this critical moral dilemma. Or, the chiasmus might be read in another way. The chiasmus could be interpreted as Lincoln's acknowledgment that the only way for his generation to *return* to the founders' moral vision was to *reverse* their current policies with respect to slavery. This passage from Lincoln illustrates the complex ways in which substance and syntax, or content and form, can interact. The concept of iconicity tries to map that complicated interaction.

Note

1. For additional insight into this passage, see Mott (1975).

References and Additional Reading

Daughton, S. M. (1995). The fine texture of enactment: Iconicity as empowerment in Angelina Grimké's Pennsylvania Hall address. *Women's Studies in Communication, 18,* 19-43.

Haiman, J. (Ed.). (1985). *Iconicity in syntax.* Amsterdam: John Benjamins.

Leff, M., & Sachs, A. (1990). Words most like things: Iconicity and the rhetorical text. *Western Journal of Speech Communication, 54,* 252-273.

Mott, W. T. (1975). The rhetoric of Martin Luther King, Jr.: *Letter From Birmingham Jail. Phylon, 36,* 411-421.

Weaver, R. (1953). Some rhetorical aspects of grammatical categories. In R. Weaver, *The ethics of rhetoric.* South Bend, IN: Regnery/Gateway.

IDENTIFICATION

In an essay published shortly after *A Rhetoric of Motives* (Burke, 1950) appeared, Burke (1951) wrote,

> If I had to sum up in one word the difference between the "old" rhetoric and the "new," . . . I would reduce it to this: The key term for the "old" rhetoric was "persuasion," and its stress was upon deliberate design. The key term for the "new" rhetoric would be "identification," which can include a partially unconscious factor in appeal. (p. 203)[1]

Burke (1950) first introduced the concept of **identification** in *A Rhetoric of Motives* in the company of two other terms that help to shape its meaning: *consubstantiality* and *division.*[2]

Let us start with division. In *A Rhetoric of Motives,* Burke (1950) maintained,

> Identification is affirmed with earnestness [as the first principle of rhetoric] precisely because there is division. Identification is compensatory to division. If men [sic] were not apart from one another, there would be no need for the rhetorician to proclaim their unity. If men were wholly and truly of one substance, absolute communication would be of man's very essence. (p. 22)

He continued exploring this theme on the next page: "For one need not scrutinize the concept of 'identification' very sharply to see, implied in it at every turn, its ironic counterpart: division." He concluded, "Rhetoric is concerned with the state of Babel after the fall" (p. 23). Identification, then, is the "flip side" of division. The two are interconnected like day and night; each principle needs the other to exist.

Identification also intersected with another of Burke's conceptual preoccupations—the concept of substance. We can glimpse this intersection in one of the passages in the preceding paragraph where Burke linked identification to substance. If humanity shared a common substance, then absolute communication—and identification—would be our essence. But the human essence, it seems, is negative; people are divided from each other and must use language, or rhetoric, to promote identification or overcome division. Burke (1950) suggested that we are able to share substance only momentarily and always incompletely. He explained the process in a frequently quoted passage:

> A is not identical with his colleague, B. But insofar as their interests are joined, A is *identified* with B. Or he may *identify himself* with B, even when their interests are not joined, if he assumes that they are or is persuaded to believe so. . . . In being identified

> with B, A is "substantially one" with a person other than himself. Yet at the same time, he remains unique, an individual locus of motives. Thus he is both joined and separate, at once a distinct substance and consubstantial with another. . . . To identify A with B is to make A "consubstantial" with B. (pp. 20-21)

Identification always is provisional and incomplete because people never can completely share substance (e.g., interests, motives). But they can become consubstantial, which might be thought of as a type of mixed ontological state in which people are "both joined and separate" or part of a community of shared interests while remaining autonomous individuals.[3] So, as this brief discussion has tried to indicate, identification, division, and consubstantiality form an interrelated network of terms.

Soon after Burke (1950) published *A Rhetoric of Motives,* rhetorical scholars were at work extending, applying, and qualifying his discussion of identification. Hochmuth (1952) was quick to note how identification functions as both a *means* and an *end.* She wrote that "at its simplest level," identification

> may be a deliberate device, or a means, as when a speaker identifies his [sic] interests with those of his audience. But *identification* can also be an "end," as "when people earnestly yearn to identify themselves with some group or another." (p. 136)

Conceptualizing identification as a "means" typically led scholars to look for *strategies* of identification. An early effort in the search for strategies of identification can be found in Holland (1953). Some notable examples of inquiry in this trajectory include Carpenter's (1972) effort to unpack the significance of *syntactical* and **stylistic** patterns for the process of identification,[4] Crable's (1977) examination of identification and argument in Dwight Eisenhower, Sanbonmatsu's (1971) discussion of identification strategies in **forensic discourse,** and Trent's (1971) comparative content analysis of Richard Nixon's 1960 and 1968 presidential campaigns. A more recent and highly influential discussion of Burkeian identification can be found in the work of Cheney (1983b; see also Cheney, 1983a, 1991; Cheney & Tompkins, 1987). Cheney not only extended the range of practices to which Burkeian theory can be applied, he focused attention on three key strategies of identification: (a) a *common ground* technique focusing on shared interests and/or values; (b) *identification through antithesis,* which focuses on uniting in the face of a shared **enemy;** and (c) forms of **transcendence** such as the collective "we," which "often goes unnoticed as an appeal to identification between parties who may have little in common" (Cheney, 1983b, pp. 148-149).[5]

Cheney (1983b) noted a paradoxical aspect of analyses focusing on identification as means/strategy: Strategy often suggests conscious intention, yet Burke shifted away from the traditional term *persuasion* and toward the principle of identification because he wanted to move beyond the constraints of *intentionality* and incorporate "unconscious" aspects of symbolic appeal into his account of rhetoric.[6] Yet, scholars who have sought to explore the link between identification and the unconscious have noted its difficulty (Wright, 1993). Wright's (1993) study of Jonathan Edwards' famous sermon, "Sinners in the Hands of an Angry God" (originally delivered in New England in July 1741), provides the best example of a rhetorical critic trying to reveal the unconscious aspects of a speech's appeal. Wright focused on Edwards' unconscious *cluster* of images that are linked to primordial sensations (e.g., falling, shrinking, heat). Wright argued that these images would be able to evoke a type of preconscious emotional response (e.g., feelings of fear and terror) in an early 18th-century audience. Wright's analysis suggested that the unconscious or preconscious operates as a factor in the process of **invention** as well as **audience** *reception.*[7]

Charland (1987) and Wess (1996) suggested a possible way of bridging Burke's sense of unconscious identification with identification functioning as the end state or goal of rhetorical practice. Following Burke, many contemporary rhetorical scholars have endorsed the idea that discursive action not only aims at overt persuasion but also solicits identification between advocates and audiences. But both Charland and Wess pointed out that identification not only is an end or a strategy but also is the precondition of rhetorical interaction. Extending Charland's earlier synthesis of Burke's notion of identification and Althusser's idea of **interpellation,** Wess (1996) wrote, "By constituting subjects as participants in a distinctive culture, identifications on a sub- or unconscious level make possible the activity of persuasion on a conscious level" (p. 200). Charland and Wess argued that identification does more than function as an *instrumental* strategy or instrumental objective. It serves a **constitutive** *function* that merits the continuing attention of rhetorical scholars.

Notes

1. Burke could be ambiguous on the relationship between the old and new rhetorics. In *A Rhetoric of Motives,* Burke (1950) insisted that his idea of identification "is decidedly not meant as a substitute . . . but [only as] an accessory to the standard lore" of persuasion (p. x). But later, Burke hinted at a different relationship when he wrote, "We are proposing that our rhetoric be reduced to this term of wider scope [identification], with the term of narrower scope being treated as a species of it" (p. 20). It is not completely clear what "term of narrower scope" Burke had in mind.

2. Kastely (1997) suggested that Burke's idea of human interaction as a form of *courtship* needs to be included in this cluster of concepts. He wrote, "If difference was a source of rhetoric, community, in the form of identification, was one of its goals, and the way to achieve community was through courtship" (p. 235). For Burke's discussion of courtship as a model for analyzing persuasive appeals, see *A Rhetoric of Motives* (Burke, 1950, pp. 208-212, 221-233).

3. See Wess (1996) for a more detailed treatment of Burke's (1950) struggle with "individualistic orthodoxy" (p. 194) in *A Rhetoric of Motives.*

4. Carpenter was extending Duncan's (1962) observation that "style is a social identification, and we are dependent on skilled creators of forms for our symbols of identification" (pp. 274-275). Lischer's (1995) study of Martin Luther King, Jr.'s style as a form of identification is part of this scholarly trajectory.

5. Other useful studies of identification strategies include Payne (1989) and Stuckey and Antczak (1994).

6. The role of intentionality in criticism remains a contested issue in contemporary rhetorical studies. This topic is addressed in more detail in the entry on **subject.**

7. On Burke's effort to integrate identification and the unconscious, see also Ambrester (1974) and Wright (1994).

References and Additional Reading

Ambrester, R. (1974). Identification within: Kenneth Burke's view of the unconscious. *Philosophy and Rhetoric, 7,* 205-216.

Burke, K. (1950). *A rhetoric of motives.* New York: Prentice Hall.

Burke, K. (1951). Rhetoric—Old and new. *Journal of General Education, 5,* 203-205.

Carpenter, R. H. (1972, Winter). A stylistic basis of Burkeian identification. *Today's Speech,* pp. 19-24.

Charland, M. (1987). Constitutive rhetoric: The case of the *peuple Québécois. Quarterly Journal of Speech, 73,* 133-150.

Cheney, G. (1983a). On the various and changing meanings of organizational membership: A field study of organizational identification. *Communication Monographs, 50,* 342-362.

Cheney, G. (1983b). The rhetoric of identification and the study of organizational communication. *Quarterly Journal of Speech, 69,* 143-158.

Cheney, G. (1991). *Rhetoric in an organizational society: Managing multiple identities.* Columbia: University of South Carolina Press.

Cheney, G., & Tompkins, P. K. (1987). Coming to terms with organizational identification and commitment. *Central States Speech Journal, 38,* 1-15.

Crable, R. (1977). Ike: Identification, argument, and paradoxical appeal. *Quarterly Journal of Speech, 63,* 188-196.

Day, D. G. (1960). Persuasion and the concept of identification. *Quarterly Journal of Speech, 46,* 270-273.

Duncan, H. D. (1962). *Communication and social order.* London: Oxford University Press.

Hochmuth, M. (1952). Kenneth Burke and the "new rhetoric." *Quarterly Journal of Speech, 38,* 133-144.

Holland, V. (1953). Rhetorical criticism: A Burkeian method. *Quarterly Journal of Speech, 39,* 444-448.

Kastely, J. L. (1997). *Rethinking the rhetorical tradition: From Plato to postmodernism.* New Haven, CT: Yale University Press.

Lischer, R. (1995). *The preacher King: Martin Luther King, Jr. and the word that moved America.* New York: Oxford University Press.

Payne, D. (1989). *The Wizard of Oz:* Therapeutic rhetoric in a contemporary media ritual. *Quarterly Journal of Speech, 75,* 25-39.

Sanbonmatsu, A. (1971). Darrow and Rourke's use of Burkeian strategies in *New York v. Gitlow* (1920). *Speech Monographs, 38,* 36-48.

Stuckey, M. E., & Antczak, F. J. (1994). The battle of issues and images: Establishing interpretive dominance. *Communication Quarterly, 42,* 120-132.

Trent, J. C. (1971, Fall). Richard Nixon's methods of identification in the presidential campaigns of 1960 and 1968: A content analysis. *Today's Speech,* pp. 23-30.

Wess, R. (1996). *Kenneth Burke: Rhetoric, subjectivity, postmodernism.* Cambridge, UK: Cambridge University Press.

Wright, M. H. (1993). Identification and the preconscious. *Communication Studies, 44,* 144-156.

Wright, M. H. (1994). Burkeian and Freudian theories of identification. *Communication Quarterly, 42,* 301-310.

IDEOGRAPH

Since the late 1970s, rhetorical scholars have exhibited a keen interest in the topic of **ideology.** Recurrent questions confronting rhetorical scholars have included the following. What is the relationship between public discourse and ideology? If public discourse contributes to the creation and preservation of ideology, then *how* is this effect accomplished? How should rhetorical *theory* be modified to accommodate the concern with ideology? Michael McGee's 1980 essay, "The 'Ideograph': A Link Between Rhetoric and Ideology" (McGee, 1980a), was an early and highly influential attempt to address these and other questions regarding the relationship between rhetoric as theory and practice and ideology.

McGee (1980a) opened his essay on the **ideograph** by reflecting on the antithetical virtues and vices of two modes of thought: idealist/symbolist and materialist/Marxist. The opening reflections led McGee to a conclusion: There is a need for a synthetic

> theoretical model which accounts for both "ideology" [materialist thought] and "myth" [idealist thought], a model which neither denies human capacity to control "power" through the manipulation of symbols nor begs Marx's essential questions regarding the influence of "power" on creating and maintaining political consciousness. (p. 4)

For McGee, such a model must be predicated on the assumption that, at least in the realm of politics, truth and falsity (and the possibilities for **power** or "social control" that follow) always are illusions or, in a Foucaultian sense, "fictions" that are a "product of persuasion" (pp. 4, 6).[1] Persuasion emerges as McGee's point of synthesis; his new "theoretical model" ultimately is a new model of persuasion. He continued, "Since the clearest access to persuasion . . . is through the discourse used to produce it, I will suggest that ideology in practice is a *political language,* preserved in documents, with the capacity to dictate decision and control public belief and behavior" (pp. 4-5, emphasis added). But political language is not a precise enough locus of analytic attention, and McGee asserted that the more traditional focus of rhetorical studies on **argument** is "a mistake" (p. 6). He seemed to ask the following questions. What is the substance of political language? What is the source of its persuasive force or power? How does political language function as a mechanism of social control? His answer to these questions was the concept of *ideographs.*

McGee (1980a) wrote, "The political language which manifests ideology seems characterized by slogans, a vocabulary of 'ideographs' easily mistaken for the technical terminology of political philosophy" (p. 5). Later in the essay, he offered the following, more elaborate account: "An ideograph is an ordinary-language term found in political discourse. It is a high-order abstraction representing collective commitment to a particular but equivocal and ill-defined normative goal" (p. 15). Ideographs "signify and 'contain' a unique ideological commitment. . . . [They] are one-term sums of an orientation" (p. 7). Two of McGee's students, Celeste Condit and John Lucaites, observed, "Ideographs represent in condensed form the normative, collective commitments of the members of a public, and they typically appear in public argumentation as the necessary motivations or justifications for action performed in the name of the public" (Condit & Lucaites, 1993, pp. xii-xiii). Robertson (1995), acknowledging the influence of McGee, defined ideographs as "political slogans or labels that encapsulate ideology in political discourse" (p. 93).

What are some examples of ideographs? In his essay, McGee (1980a) identified a large number including liberty (see also McGee, 1980c), property, law or the rule of law, religion, right of privacy, freedom of speech, and popular sovereignty.[2] As the first passage in the preceding paragraph demonstrated, McGee distinguished the way in which these terms are used in "technical" political philosophy (where scholars try to discover the essence, or the "real" meaning, of key terms in a culture's political vocabulary) from the way in which they are used in public discourse. Public discourse, for McGee, ranges from "formal" documents such as the American Declaration of Independence and Constitution to the more ephemeral products of legislators, presidents, political activists, and other rhetorical advocates. According to McGee, ideographs have no disembodied fundamental meaning. What we have, as an empirical fact, are countless uses—countless texts and other discursive performances where we find "liberty" and "property" residing. One of McGee's principal objectives was to urge rhetorical scholars to study concrete, situationally bound ideographic manifestations.

How do we distinguish ideographs from other labels, terms, or words that appear regularly in public discourse? No absolute test for determining what is or is not an ideograph can be found in the literature. It appears that ideographs are defined, in large part, through their function. McGee (1980a) wrote that ideographs are "agencies of social control" (p. 6) and "agents of political consciousness" (p. 7). In other words, ideographs exert social control by shaping political consciousness (see also Green, 1987). McGee qualified his account of how ideographs exert control; they do not operate mechanistically or in accordance with the model of classical conditioning. According to McGee, "Human beings are 'conditioned,' not directly to belief and behavior but [rather] to a vocabulary of concepts that function as guides, warrants, reasons, or excuses for behavior and belief" (p. 6). Ideographs are, then, those recurrent words, labels, or expressions that guide and warrant behavior and belief; a culture's ideographs are its dominant "vocabulary" of **motives** (pp. 5, 7).[3] Ideographs are more than popular expressions such as "where's the beef?" They are different from the labels we give to political **controversies** (e.g., abortion, gun control, crime, poverty). They are not the jargon of political insiders and media spin doctors. Nor are they simply the latest *neologized* "buzzwords" or "trendspeak." Ideographs constitute a structure of "public motives" (p. 5); they are the terms we use to impart value (McGee & Martin, 1983, p. 50), justify decisions, motivate behavior, and **debate** policy initiatives.

McGee (1980a) acknowledged the affinity between his concept of ideographs (p. 7) and Weaver's (1953) idea of "ultimate terms" (see also Burke, 1950, pp. 187-189). Weaver (1953) defined *ultimate terms* as "rhetorical absolutes" or "terms to which the very highest respect is paid" (p. 212). McGee's (1980a) discussion of the different categories or "vocabularies" of ideographs—those that "unite" and those that "separate" (p. 8)—was an extension of Weaver's (1953) distinction between "God" and "devil" terms. God terms are those that we unite around such as *liberty* and *freedom.* Devil terms usually are used to characterize those who are different from "us" (the **other**); they are what we use to distinguish between "us" and "them" (e.g., "*We* stand for freedom; *they* practice tyranny").

Condit and Lucaites (1993) noted that a "key feature of ideographs" is "their flexibility as cultural signifiers." Ideographs are "abstractions" and, therefore, "lack any rigidly defined meaning" (p. xiii). Ideographs are, in short, **ambiguous.** The ambiguity of ideographs provides advocates with a considerable, but not absolute, degree of latitude. The meaning of ideographs, Condit and Lucaites maintained, is not "totally arbitrary or absolutely polysemous" (p. xiii). The flexibility of ideographs is manifest through the process of **articulation.** For example, members of the American public might not have considered the ability to choose any doctors they wanted as an indispensable prerequisite for the good life prior to the organized campaign against the health care plan of Bill Clinton's administration in 1993. But that campaign articulated, or connected, doctor choice and personal "freedom." The meaning of freedom was subtly modified as the ideograph was extended to a new topic.

But flexibility also sets the stage for conflict and struggle. Many key ideographs are marked by long histories of discursive conflict. For example, does "equality" refer to a condition where all people have the same opportunities (which some people, due to their effort and hard work, manage to exploit better than others), or can it also refer to a condition where social resources (e.g., money, land, power) are distributed uniformly to all or proportionally to different groups? The "equal opportunity" meaning tends to be dominant in American history. But there almost always have been voices contesting its meaning. Those voices have included radicals such as Malcolm X, who challenged the equal opportunity meaning in April 1964 with his "diner analogy" in "The Ballot or the Bullet" speech, and moderate mainstream politicians such as Lyndon Johnson, who also used analogy to challenge a narrow equal opportunity understanding of the term in his 1965 speech at Howard University (for a detailed treatment of the ideograph *equality,* see Condit & Lucaites, 1993). Consider another example. Does liberty refer to a condition in which individuals are able to act free from governmental supervision or regulation? Or, might liberty also refer to a political system that not only allows but also insists on maximum citizen participation in political decision making? Given the potential for conflict, critics might seek to chart ideographic struggle among various factions in a political controversy, or they might examine the way in which a single text excludes one sense of liberty at the same time that it privileges another sense.

Finally, we need to consider the contribution that the concept of the ideograph makes to contemporary rhetorical scholarship. McGee appeared to sense that the ideograph might be used in rather dull and pedestrian forms of criticism where all the critics do is label particular terms as ideographs and leave it at that. Clearly, McGee envisioned the ideograph generating a more substantial mode of criticism. About halfway through his essay, McGee (1980a) asked, "What do we describe with the concept 'ideograph,' and how do we actually go about doing the specific cultural analysis promised by conceptually linking rhetoric and ideology?" (p. 7). McGee projected a manner of analysis that did more than toss around the label "ideograph." He demanded that critics attend to specific uses—that they study the *situational function* of ideographs. McGee did not believe that locating ideographs in specific discursive practices was a challenging task; he wrote that "there is no trick in gleaning from public documents the entire vocabulary of ideographs that define a particular collectivity" (p. 11).[4] Gleaning ideographs in a text is one thing; unpacking their function—understanding how they shape consciousness or enable and constrain decision and action—is a much more difficult and complicated project.

Exhaustive ideographic analysis entails a *diachronic* component as well as a *synchronic* component. Diachronic analysis examines the *history* of uses: How does this advocate's use of Ideograph Y at Time X continue or contest prior uses? To understand what Ideograph Y is doing at Time X, it must be located within its "diachronic structure" (Condit & Lucaites, 1993). To understand a particular use of "freedom of speech," a critic needs to place the utterance within a diachronic structure that

> spans the distance from its original and minimalist articulation by the framers of the U.S. Constitution as protection for "political speech," to its most recent [uses] as the defense for a much more widely defined "freedom of expression" that includes nude photography and dancing. (p. xiii)

An ideograph always carries traces of past uses that shape its meaning in the present.

Synchronic analysis, on the other hand, focuses on how an ideograph used at Time X gains at least part of its meaning from its interaction with other terms in the public's ideographic vocabulary. McGee (1980a) noted the way in which Richard Nixon expanded the meaning of "confidentiality" by "attempting to alter its 'standing' among other ideographs" circulating at the time (p. 13). Condit and Lucaites (1993) noted how the meaning of "freedom of speech" changes as it moves from one context (where it collides with the ideograph "national security") to another (where its meaning is shaped by its relationship to "privacy" and "liberty") (pp. xiii-xiv). The meaning and function of an ideograph always will depend on its relationship to other terms residing, for example, in the text that contains the ideograph in question, in the discourse of the opposition, or in the culture at large.

A number of innovative ideographic critical studies have appeared in the literature (Cloud, 1998; Delgada, 1995; Edwards and Winkler, 1997; Miller, 1999; Moore, 1993, 1994, 1997), but few critical projects have attempted the manner of rigorous diachronic and synchronic ideographic analysis described here. The notable exception to this generalization is Condit and Lucaites's (1993) study of the evolution of "equality" in American public discourse.[5] Concentrating primarily on equality in the context of race relations and drawing on an enormous amount of discursive material, these authors tried to unpack both the diachronic and synchronic structures that shape the potential meanings of equality. As they argued, to "understand the meanings of equality as a foundation of American political life . . ., [scholars must devote] careful attention to its continuing dynamic genealogy within American public discourse from its inception in the 1760s to the present" (p. xvii). Most likely, Condit and Lucaites's study will remain the model for ideographic analysis for some time to come.

Notes

1. On the concept of fiction, see the discussion of the Greek term *apate* in the entry for **mystification.**
2. Some scholars suggest that, at times, the name of a *person* can function like an ideograph. See, for example, Leff (1997).
3. McGee, like Burke, adhered to a "vocabulary" view of motives as opposed to a "psychological" one. See Hauser (1991, p. 129).
4. See also the discussion of the "transparent" **text.**
5. On the subject of equality, see also the essays collected in Devins and Douglas (1998).

References and Additional Reading

Burke, K. (1950). *A rhetoric of motives.* New York: Prentice Hall.

Cloud, D. L. (1998). The rhetoric of <family values>: Scapegoating, utopia, and the privatization of social responsibility. *Western Journal of Communication, 62,* 387-419.

Condit, C. M., & Lucaites, J. L. (1993). *Crafting equality: America's Anglo-African word.* Chicago: University of Chicago Press.

Delgada, F. P. (1995). Chicano movement rhetoric: An ideographic interpretation. *Communication Quarterly, 43,* 446-454.

Devins, N., & Douglas, D. M. (Eds.). (1998). *Redefining equality.* New York: Oxford University Press.

Edwards, J. L., & Winkler, C. K. (1997). Representative forms and the visual ideograph: The Iwo Jima image in editorial cartoons. *Quarterly Journal of Speech, 83,* 289-310.

Green, D. (1987). *Shaping political consciousness: The language of politics in America from McKinley to Reagan.* Ithaca, NY: Cornell University Press.

Hasian, M. A., Jr. (1996). *The rhetoric of eugenics in Anglo-American thought.* Athens: University of Georgia Press.

Hauser, G. A. (1991). *Introduction to rhetorical theory.* Prospect Heights, IL: Waveland.

Leff, M. C. (1997). Lincoln among the nineteenth-century orators. In T. W. Benson (Ed.), *Rhetoric and political culture in nineteenth-century America.* East Lansing: Michigan State University Press.

Martin, M. A. (1983). Ideologues, ideographs, and "the best men": From Carter to Reagan. *Southern Speech Communication Journal, 49,* 12-25.

McGee, M. C. (1980a). The "ideograph": A link between rhetoric and ideology. *Quarterly Journal of Speech, 66,* 1-16.

McGee, M. C. (1980b). The "ideograph" as a unit of analysis in political argument. In J. Rhodes & S. Newell (Eds.), *Proceedings of the [First] Summer Conference on Argumentation.* Annandale, VA: Speech Communication Association.

McGee, M. C. (1980c). The origins of "liberty": A feminization of power. *Communication Monographs, 47,* 22-46.

McGee, M. C., & Martin, M. A. (1983). Public knowledge and ideological argumentation. *Communication Monographs, 50,* 47-65.

Miller, M. L. (1999). Public argument and legislative debate in the rhetorical construction of public policy: The case of Florida midwifery legislation. *Quarterly Journal of Speech, 85,* 361-379.

Moore, M. P. (1993). Constructing irreconcilable conflict: The function of synecdoche in the spotted owl controversy. *Communication Monographs, 60,* 258-274.

Moore, M. P. (1994). Life, liberty, and the handgun: The function of synecdoche in the Brady Bill debate. *Communication Quarterly, 42,* 434-447.

Moore, M. P. (1997). The cigarette as representative ideograph in the debate over environmental tobacco smoke. *Communication Monographs, 64,* 47-64.

Robertson, A. W. (1995). *The language of democracy: Political rhetoric in the United States and Britain, 1790-1900.* Ithaca, NY: Cornell University Press.

Weaver, R. (1953). Ultimate terms in contemporary rhetoric. In R. Weaver, *The ethics of rhetoric.* South Bend, IN: Regnery/Gateway.

IDEOLOGY

During the decade from 1978 to 1988, the concept of **ideology** was a recurring theme in rhetorical studies (Balthrop, 1984; Brown, 1978; Jasinski, 1988; Kneupper, 1985; McGee, 1978, 1980; McGee & Martin, 1983; McKerrow, 1983; Moore, 1988; Wander, 1983). Explicit attention to the concept of ideology faded somewhat during the subsequent decade,[1] but this should not be taken as a sign that interest has waned. A more plausible explanation of the place of ideology in rhetorical studies over the subsequent decade is that it was refracted through a number of other concepts, especially the idea of **critical rhetoric.**[2] Before reviewing some key trends in rhetorical thought with respect to ideology, it will be useful to provide a sense of the historical context of the concept.

Giddens (1979) wrote, "The concept of ideology had its origins in the Enlightenment critique of tradition and prejudice; rational, grounded knowledge was to replace the mystifications of preexisting modes of thought" (p. 182). Ideology, according to Antoine Destutt de Tracy (the late 18th-century French intellectual commonly credited with coining the term), was a "*science des idées*" that "will describe the natural history of the mind, that is, the manner in which our thoughts are formed" (cited in Lichtheim, 1965, p. 167). The goal of this mode of inquiry was to analyze a society's "ideas"—its core beliefs and values—scientifically. The science of ideas envisioned by de Tracy and other leading Enlightenment figures would free society from the tyrannical reign of religious superstition and metaphysical speculations such as the idea of a "great chain of being" that was used to justify a rigid social hierarchy.

The evolution of the concept of ideology during the 19th and 20th centuries is a complex story (for relatively short accounts, see Giddens, 1979; Lichtheim, 1965). Amid the complex history of the concept, two dominant traditions of thought can be identified. First, emerging from Marx and Engels' (1964) *The German Ideology* and the later writings of Engels and Lenin was the idea of ideology as *false consciousness* (Eyerman, 1981). In the Marxist tradition, the normative and critical component of the earlier uses of the term are emphasized as the term ideology takes on a decidedly pejorative connotation. An ideology can be likened to a mental infection that distorts a person's ability to think and perceive the world around him or her. Ideologies have an insidious function. By hampering a person's capacity to employ his or her cognitive abilities—by presenting a distorted picture of the world—ideologies contributed to the **mystification** of **power** and domination. A nationalist or religious ideology inhibited or prevented members of the working class from perceiving the pervasiveness of class oppression and exploitation. Members of the working class were deluded into thinking that they were contributing to God and country when, in fact, their labor was being stolen from them by the capitalist economic system. The antidote to false consciousness was true consciousness (often characterized in the Marxist tradition as "class consciousness" or historical consciousness); Marxist thinkers during the late 19th and early 20th centuries frequently depicted the results of their intellectual efforts as scientific truths that revealed the falsity of ideology.

The second trend in thinking about ideology downplayed the normative and critical dimension prominent in Marxism by emphasizing the neutral descriptive aspect of the term (although, to be sure, the normative often was smuggled in through the back door, so to speak). Ideology, in this second tradition, is understood as a "belief system" (Sartori, 1969; for a related use, see Geertz, 1973). The basic assumption guiding this mode of thinking is that beliefs typically cluster together to form systems whose characteristics can then be studied. "Secular humanism" and "atheism" both are ideologies in the second tradition of use in that both are labels for more or less organized systems or structures of belief. The two traditions are not inherently antagonistic. A belief system such as liberal capitalism also can function as a mode of false consciousness. The difference between the traditions is primarily one of emphasis; the Marxist tradition considers ideology as an object of critique or something that needs to be overcome, whereas the belief system tradition views ideology as an object of disinterested analysis or something that needs to be studied.

Both senses of ideology can be found in the literature of rhetorical studies. The belief system perspective, McKerrow (1983) noted, leads the critic "to uncover the argumentative premises of [an] ideology" (p. 192).[3] McKerrow suggested that the belief system approach to ideology proceeds "on the assumption that the borrowed term [i.e., ideology] remains essentially unchanged by its linkage to rhetoric" (p. 192). This leads to studies that focus on the rhetoric of this or that belief system or ideology. Developments in the Marxist tradition of ideology have contributed to what Wess (1996) termed "the rhetoricizing of ideology" (p. 7), an extension of Burke's (1950) observation that "ideology cannot be deduced from economic considerations alone. It also derives from man's [sic] nature as a 'symbol-using animal' " (p. 146). McKerrow (1983) made much the same point when he argued for the "creation of a specialized rhetorical understanding" of ideology that "begins with the premise that an ideology is a rhetorical construct having no existence apart from its expression as a symbol system" (p. 192). As the inclusion of "system" in the passage from McKerrow acknowledged, a "systemic" approach to ideology is not entirely rejected. Ideologies are systems of symbols, words (especially, as McGee [1980] suggested, **ideographs**), conventional expressions, "disparate rhetorical idioms" that are stitched together (Aune, 1994, p. 142), root *metaphors,*[4] narratives, and recurrent argument patterns that are *constituted* and *reconstituted* through a variety of discursive and symbolic practices (e.g., public speeches, journalistic practices, novels, films, **rituals,** advertisements, slogans). The discursive and symbolic practices that sustain ideological systems produce effects that not only must be understood but, in many cases, must be opposed or fought against as well (e.g., consider the widely shared belief in the need to combat the ideology of racism). The rhetoricizing of ideology discussed by Wess, McKerrow, and others continues as it refines the Marxist tradition's emphasis on ideology as a process of **mystification** that requires sustained critical reflection.

What are the *effects* of discursively produced ideological systems, and *how* do discursive and symbolic practices that constitute these structures produce these effects? These are two of the central theoretical questions that engage the attention of critically oriented scholars in rhetorical studies and other academic disciplines. In terms of the problem of identifying effects, at least two relatively distinct strands of thinking can be located. The first strand extends the thinking of French Marxist philosopher Louis Althusser's "conception of ideology as the interpellation of subjects" (Wess, 1996, p. 7). For Althusser, ideology is essentially a process of socialization or, more accurately, of subjectification; ideology creates **subjects,** or particular types of people, out of physical bodies. In an often-quoted passage, Althusser (1971) wrote,

> Ideology "acts" or "functions" in such a way that it "recruits" subjects among the individuals [in a society]. . . . [It] "transforms" the individuals into subjects (it transforms them all) by that very precise operation which I have called *interpellation* or hailing and which can be imagined along the lines of the most commonplace everyday police (or other) hailing: "Hey, you there!" (p. 174)

The process of ideological **interpellation** creates or enables possibilities (forms of thinking and modes of acting) while constraining other possibilities. This **dialectic** of *enabling* and *constraining* establishes the subject positions (the various "roles" we occupy such as citizen, student, gender identity, and sexual identity) that our bodies occupy. Althusser contended that the creation of subject positions is the principal effect of ideology (see also Charland, 1987; Therborn, 1980).

British social theorist Anthony Giddens emphasized a different category of ideological effects. Giddens's (1979) sense of ideology as "structures of signification" (p. 188) is consistent with the rhetoricization of ideology already noted. The function or effect of these structures is "to legitimate the sectional interests of hegemonic groups" (p. 188) in ways that conceal their social domination. This sense of function or effect is consistent with the traditional Marxist emphasis on ideology as a mystification of power. Giddens identified three more specific aspects of the way in which ideological structures conceal domination and legitimate interests. First, ideological structures depict "sectional interests as universal ones" (p. 193). Nations often go to war for the "national interest," but who gets to define *national* in these cases? Many critical scholars would argue that appeals to national interest are what Burke termed **eulogistic covers** that conceal the particular interests that are at stake. Second, ideological structures deny or transmute contradictions (p. 194). For example, Bell (1976) and others have tried to point out the contradiction in the capitalist ideological structure between the need for self-discipline and the deferral of gratification and the need for massive commodity consumption. In essence, capitalist consumers need to *save* and *spend* for the system to thrive, yet our leading political figures continue to gloss over this fundamental inconsistency through their perpetual reconstitution of the capitalist ideology. Third, ideological structures naturalize or *reify* the existing status quo. This process of *reification* is a central ideological effect. As Giddens explained, "Forms of signification which 'naturalize' the existing state of affairs, inhibiting recognition of the mutable historical character of human society, thus act to sustain [the] interests" of dominant groups (p. 195). Ideological structures present the status quo as possessing a "fixed and immutable character" (p. 195) by effectively denying **contingency** and alternative possibilities. The ongoing debate over sexual orientation presents a rather clear case of reification. Heterosexuality frequently is portrayed as "natural" and homosexuality as deviant. The institution of (heterosexual) marriage does not possess a mutable historical character; it simply is a reflection of the natural order, and any possible changes (e.g., legal recognition of gay marriages) become a threat to that order.

How are these various ideological effects discursively constituted? That is the central question with which ideologically oriented rhetorical scholars continually must grapple. Virtually every significant discursive element, form, or strategy (e.g., individual words, syntactical patterns, narratives, lines of argument) can contribute to the production of ideological effects.[5] Argument strategies (e.g., the *locus of the existent*) are a key discursive mechanism for reifying the status quo, whereas narratives are a prime discursive mode of subjectification (on ideology and narration, see Charland, 1987). The challenge for rhetorical scholars is to expand and deepen our understanding of the various ways in which discursive and symbolic practices produce ideological effects so as to establish the conditions necessary for reflective consideration of alternative possibilities.

Notes

1. But the continued presence of the concept of ideology was demonstrated in a special issue (Spring 1993) devoted to the topic in the *Western Journal of Communication.*
2. But see Cloud's (1994) argument against collapsing ideology critique into critical rhetoric.
3. See, for example, Hirschman (1991) and Weiler (1984, 1987).
4. See, for example, Kramnick's (1990) discussion of the centrality of the "race" metaphor in classical liberalism.
5. On the ideological implications of syntactical patterns, see Kress and Hodge (1979) and the growing tradition of *critical discourse analysis.*

References and Additional Reading

Althusser, L. (1971). Ideology and ideological state apparatuses. In L. Althusser, *Lenin and philosophy and other essays* (B. Brewster, Trans.). New York: Monthly Review Press.

Aune, J. A. (1994). *Rhetoric and Marxism.* Boulder, CO: Westview.

Balthrop, V. W. (1984). Culture, myth, and ideology as public argument: An interpretation of the ascent and demise of "southern culture." *Communication Monographs, 51,* 339-352.

Bell, D. (1976). *The cultural contradictions of capitalism.* New York: Free Press.

Brown, W. R. (1978). Ideology as communication process. *Quarterly Journal of Speech, 64,* 123-140.

Burke, K. (1950). *A rhetoric of motives.* New York: Prentice Hall.

Charland, M. (1987). Constitutive rhetoric: The case of the Peuple Québécois. *Quarterly Journal of Speech, 73,* 133-150.

Cloud, D. L. (1994). The materiality of discourse as oxymoron: A challenge to critical rhetoric. *Western Journal of Communication, 58,* 141-163.

Eagleton, T. (1991). *Ideology: An introduction.* London: Verso.

Eyerman, R. (1981). *False consciousness and ideology in Marxist theory.* Atlantic Highlands, NJ: Humanities Press.

Geertz, C. (1973). Ideology as a cultural system. In C. Geertz, *The interpretation of cultures.* New York: Basic Books.

Giddens, A. (1979). *Central problems in social theory.* Berkeley: University of California Press.

Hirschman, A. O. (1991). *The rhetoric of reaction.* Cambridge, MA: Harvard University Press.

Jasinski, J. (1988). Ideology, reflection, and alienation in rhetorical and argumentative practice. *Journal of the American Forensic Association, 24,* 207-217.

Kneupper, C. W. (1985). Rhetoric, public knowledge, and ideological argumentation. *Journal of the American Forensic Association, 21,* 183-195.

Kramnick, I. (1990). *Republicanism and bourgeois radicalism: Political ideology in late eighteenth-century England and America.* Ithaca, NY: Cornell University Press.

Kress, G., & Hodge, R. (1979). *Language as ideology.* London: Routledge and Kegan Paul.

Lichtheim, G. (1965). The concept of ideology. *History and Theory, 4,* 164-195.

Marx, K., & Engels, F. (1964). *The German ideology* (S. Ryazanskaya, Ed. and Trans.). Moscow: Progress Publishers.

McGee, M. C. (1978). Not men but measures: The origins and import of an ideological principle. *Quarterly Journal of Speech, 64,* 141-154.

McGee, M. C. (1980). The "ideograph": A link between rhetoric and ideology. *Quarterly Journal of Speech, 66,* 1-16.

McGee, M. C., & Martin, M. A. (1983). Public knowledge and ideological argumentation. *Communication Monographs, 50,* 47-65.

McKerrow, R. E. (1983). Marxism and a rhetorical conception of ideology. *Quarterly Journal of Speech, 69,* 192-205.

Moore, M. P. (1988). The rhetoric of ideology: Confronting a critical dilemma. *Southern Communication Journal, 54,* 74-92.

Sartori, G. (1969). Politics, ideology, and belief systems. *American Political Science Review, 63,* 398-411.

Therborn, G. (1980). *The ideology of power and the power of ideology.* London: Verso.

Thompson, J. B. (1984). *Studies in the theory of ideology.* Berkeley: University of California Press.

Thompson, J. B. (1990). *Ideology and modern culture: Critical social theory in the age of mass communication.* Stanford, CA: Stanford University Press.

Wander, P. (1983). The ideological turn in modern criticism. *Central States Speech Journal, 34,* 1-18.

Weiler, M. (1984). The rhetoric of neo-liberalism. *Quarterly Journal of Speech, 70,* 362-378.

Weiler, M. (1987). Neo-conservatism: A study of ideological argument. *Journal of the American Forensic Association, 24,* 37-47.

Wess, R. (1996). *Kenneth Burke: Rhetoric, subjectivity, postmodernism.* Cambridge, UK: Cambridge University Press.

INQUIRY, RHETORIC OF

The movement in contemporary scholarship referred to as the **rhetoric of inquiry** (some scholars prefer the label "rhetoric of science") is the most recent rejoinder in a centuries-old "debate" or "discussion" about the nature of—and the relationship among—knowledge, language, human discourse, and reality. The traditional home for this discussion has been that branch of philosophy known as *epistemology.* According to Hamlyn (1967), epistemology

> is concerned with the nature and scope of knowledge, its presuppositions and basis, and the general reliability of claims to knowledge . . . [as well as] the attempt to justify the claim that knowledge is possible and to assess the part played by the senses and reason in the acquisition of knowledge. (pp. 8-9)

Philosophical interest in epistemological matters emerged during the 5th century BC when, according to Hamlyn, "human practices and institutions came under critical examination for the first time" (p. 9). The fact that the emergence of epistemology coincided with the sophistic movement in Greek thought (a movement that devoted considerable attention to language and rhetoric) is not a coincidence; in many of his writings, Plato, "who can be said to be the real originator of epistemology" (Hamlyn, 1967, p. 9), sought to refute sophistic skepticism about knowledge and challenge the prominence given to language and rhetoric in sophistic thought. Nelson, Megill, and McCloskey (1987) suggested that it was no accident that the rise of epistemology in philosophy and science coincided with "the denigration of rhetoric" (p. 7). Rhetorical practice, language, and knowledge typically have been positioned in an antagonistic relationship throughout history. At the risk of oversimplification, the contemporary rhetoric of inquiry movement can be understood as an effort to rethink and reconsider the nature of this relationship.

As Nelson and colleagues (1987) indicated, the intellectual roots of the rhetoric of inquiry can be located in the thought of a diverse group of thinkers who, despite widespread disagreements on a host of issues, jointly questioned the epistemological project of philosophy—providing an absolute ground for knowledge. Membership in this group of thinkers, whose rejection of the quest for certainty "point[ed] toward rhetoric of inquiry" (p. 7), includes the German philosophers Friedrich Nietzsche, Martin Heidegger, and Hans-Georg Gadamer; the American pragmatist John Dewey; the French intellectuals Michel Foucault and Jacques Derrida; and the Austrian philosopher Ludwig Wittgenstein. To this list, we might add the names of scholars affiliated with the rhetoric as **epistemic** movement in rhetorical studies (beginning with Scott, 1967; see also Scott, 1993). Scott (1976), for example, remarked,

> In the common intersubjective devices of science, we see at least dimly the epistemic role of rhetoric, for all of these depend on communities of experience and commitment that do not exist automatically "in nature," so to speak, but are formed as all communities are formed, by the interactions of people. (p. 262)[1]

Among contemporary philosophers, the works of American neo-pragmatist Richard Rorty have provided considerable inspiration to the rhetoric of inquiry movement. For example, Rorty (1979) argued that traditional "epistemology is the attempt to see the patterns of justification within normal discourse as *more* than just such patterns. It is the attempt to see them as hooked onto something which demands moral commitment—reality, truth, objectivity, [and] reason" (p. 385). Rorty's basic point—that it is fruitless to try to find or invent something beyond the common "patterns of justification" (e.g., arguments, reasons, appeals) that we use to defend our claims—undergirds much of the thinking in the rhetoric of inquiry movement. If there are no final or absolute scientific methods or procedures that can be used to guarantee the claims to knowledge made by practitioners in the various academic fields of inquiry, then we are left with only one thing—the way in which scholars or scientists talk (to each other and with other audiences). Once we look through the important conceptual and epistemological issues that are at stake in the rhetoric of inquiry movement, what we find is a group of scholars devoted to the careful description and analysis of scientific and academic discourse.[2]

Although the participants in the rhetoric of inquiry movement probably would agree with Simons's (1990) summary claim that "there is no escape from rhetoric" (p. 16), there are some differences of opinion regarding how deeply rhetoric penetrates the processes of academic and intellectual inquiry. Within the broad rhetoric of inquiry movement, it is possible to identify weaker and stronger versions of the inescapability of rhetoric thesis (Ginev, 1999). Toward the weaker end of a weak-strong continuum (a type of "lite" rhetoric of inquiry) is the basic proposition that, as Nelson and colleagues (1987) put it, "scholars write rhetorically" (p. 3). Following the lead of Kuhn's (1970) discussion of paradigm shifts in the sciences (e.g., the shift from Newtonian to Einsteinian physics), Simons (1990) noted that "it is generally acknowledged that scientific discourse is inherently rhetorical at the point of paradigm clash and, furthermore, that scholars have no choice but to rely on rhetorical appeals and arguments in the forging of a discipline" (p. 8). But the discovery of rhetorical dimensions in scientific prose, in paradigm disputes, and in the formation of an academic discipline does not necessarily lead to the stronger claim that all scientific and intellectual inquiry is, in some basic sense, rhetorically grounded or constituted. Adherents to a weak form of rhetoric of inquiry might focus on the rhetorical aspects of interfield disputes (e.g., how scientists from different academic fields might argue with each other about a common topic), generic and stylistic characteristics in scientific discourse (Bazerman, 1987), or the role of **ethos** in scientific discourse (Prelli, 1989a). But studies such as these do not position rhetoric as central to the process of inquiry; although it is important, rhetoric occupies its more traditional role as a *supplement* to a substantive field of study (Gaonkar, 1990, 1993).

Stronger versions of the rhetoric of inquiry find rhetorical dimensions at the very center of intellectual and scientific activity. But as Lyne (1985) noted, there is not a single unified sense of rhetoric in the rhetoric of inquiry movement. Consequently, positioning rhetoric at the center of inquiry can mean different things to different people. As Lyne observed, one way in which inquiry is seen as inescapably rhetorical is by defining rhetoric as a process of **figuration** or "configuration" (p. 69). Lyne noted that there is "a spreading interest in the ways academics mount their knowledge claims on figurative scaffolding" (p. 69). For example, Carlston (1987) and Klamer (1987) illustrated the way in which *metaphors* help to constitute the central concepts of different fields of inquiry (see also McCloskey, 1985). Both Carlston and Klamer argued that metaphors are not mere window dressing in academic prose; rather, they are part of the conceptual deep structure—the set of taken-for-granted assumptions—that organizes different academic fields and guides specific practices of inquiry.

The basic differences between strong and weak versions of the rhetoric of inquiry are visible in relation to what sometimes is called the *undifferentiated textuality* thesis. Adherents to a strong version of the rhetoric of inquiry tend to endorse this thesis (e.g., Nelson, 1998). These scholars recognize that particular discursive practices will have different functions (literary, political, and scientific discourses try to accomplish different things), but they will not allow these different functions to lead to rigid categorical distinctions among types of discourse. When all is said and done, scientific talk is no different from political or literary talk; scientific talk cannot be differentiated in any final or absolute sense. Nor can the discursive "substance" of scientific talk be firmly distinguished from its modes of presentation (its "form" or "style"); there is, as Nelson and colleagues (1987) recognized, an ongoing "interaction of style and substance" in the discourse of inquiry (p. 17). Consequently, the concepts, critical methods, and analytic procedures that have been developed for studying political and literary discourse can be used to shed light on the practices of the sciences. Adherents to a weaker version of the rhetoric of inquiry tend to be a bit more ambivalent about the undifferentiated textuality thesis. These scholars see considerable value in studying certain rhetorical aspects, or the rhetorical dimension, of scientific discourse, but they are not as quick to collapse the distinctions among the different fields or spheres of discursive practice. Scientific discourse might possess a logic (a conceptual structure) of its own, and although rhetorical analysis might help to clarify and illuminate that logic, the autonomy of that logic—its difference from the logics of literature and politics—should be maintained.

As with any social or political movement, the intellectual movement of the rhetoric of inquiry is not without opposition (e.g., Hikins & Zagacki, 1988; Keith & Cherwitz, 1989). Focusing on the realm of psychoanalysis, Spence (1994) maintained,

> Unless . . . the power of rhetoric [is] diminished, the fate of psychoanalysis as a creative enterprise would seem [to be] in jeopardy. . . . The time has come to call attention to the rhetorical voice of psychoanalysis before it can do further damage and before more evidence is displaced by unsupported assumptions. (pp. 4-5)

Spence and other critics have questioned the contention, advanced by Rorty and others, that the modernist epistemological project has collapsed. In defending some refurbished form of traditional epistemology that clearly differentiates "fact" or the "evidential voice" (pp. 87-91) from "persuasion" and its "rhetorical voice," opponents of the rhetoric of inquiry have added yet another voice to the continuing discussion about the relationship among knowledge, language, and rhetoric. No doubt, the larger conceptual debate will continue, as it has for more than 2,000 years. Every neo-sophistic movement seems to call forth its neo-Platonic antagonist. But in the end, the rhetoric of inquiry is not simply an abstract discussion about the possibility of grounding claims to knowledge. As Nelson and colleagues (1987) cautioned, "Rhetoricians of inquiry must not make the same mistake [as do logicians of inquiry]. They must not seek an abstracted and autonomous field. Their work must arise from practice" (p. 16). Their work also must begin "with texts" (p. 14; cf. Gaonkar, 1990). The future of the rhetoric of inquiry movement depends on the quality of the critical scholarship it produces. So long as it continues to produce studies that shed light on the practices of various academic disciplines in ways that help to enhance the actual process of inquiry and advance our understanding of the nature of language and discourse practice, it most likely will continue to thrive.[3]

Notes

1. Advancing a similar claim, van Eemeren, Grootendorst, and Henkemans (1996) noted, "Although not specifically intended by Scott, one consequence of the rhetoric-as-epistemic perspective has been to foster studies of rhetoric within academic disciplines" (p. 208).

2. In addition to the scholarship that explicitly links itself to the rhetoric of inquiry movement, see also works such as Martin and Veel (1998) and McRae (1993).

3. On the "ends" of the rhetoric of inquiry, see also McCloskey (1985), Nelson and colleagues (1987), and Simons (1990).

References and Additional Reading

Bazerman, C. (1987). Codifying the social scientific style: The APA *Publication Manual* as a behavioristic rhetoric. In J. S. Nelson, A. Megill, & D. N. McCloskey (Eds.), *The rhetoric of the human sciences: Language and argument in scholarship and public affairs.* Madison: University of Wisconsin Press.

Bazerman, C. (1994). *Constructing experience.* Carbondale: Southern Illinois University Press.

Brown, R. H. (1987). *Society as text: Essays on rhetoric, reason, and reality.* Chicago: University of Chicago Press.

Carlston, D. E. (1987). Turning psychology on itself: The rhetoric of psychology and the psychology of rhetoric. In J. S. Nelson, A. Megill, & D. N. McCloskey (Eds.), *The rhetoric of the human sciences: Language and argument in scholarship and public affairs.* Madison: University of Wisconsin Press.

Ceccarelli, L. (2001). *Shaping science with rhetoric: The cases of Dobzhansky, Schrödinger, and Wilson.* Chicago: University of Chicago Press.

Gaonkar, D. P. (1990). Rhetoric and its double: Reflections on the rhetorical turn in the human sciences. In H. W. Simons (Ed.), *The rhetorical turn: Invention and persuasion in the conduct of inquiry.* Chicago: University of Chicago Press.

Gaonkar, D. P. (1993). The idea of rhetoric in the rhetoric of science. *Southern Communication Journal, 58,* 258-295.

Ginev, D. (1999). From a strong hermeneutics of science to a strong rhetoric of science. *Philosophy and Rhetoric, 32,* 247-281.

Gross, A. G. (1990). *The rhetoric of science.* Cambridge, MA: Harvard University Press.

Hamlyn, D. W. (1967). History of epistemology. In P. Edwards (Ed.), *The encyclopedia of philosophy* (Vol. 3). New York: Macmillan.

Harris, R.A. (1991). Rhetoric of science. *College English, 53,* 282-307.

Hikins, J. W., & Zagacki, K. S. (1988). Rhetoric, philosophy, and objectivism: An attenuation of the claims of the rhetoric of inquiry. *Quarterly Journal of Speech, 74,* 201-228.

Keith, W. M., & Cherwitz, R. A. (1989). Objectivity, disagreement, and the rhetoric of inquiry. In H. W. Simons (Ed.), *Rhetoric in the human sciences.* London: Sage.

Klamer, A. (1987). As if economists and their subjects were rational. In J. S. Nelson, A. Megill, & D. N. McCloskey (Eds.), *The rhetoric of the human sciences: Language and argument in scholarship and public affairs.* Madison: University of Wisconsin Press.

Kuhn, T. S. (1970). *The structure of scientific revolutions* (2nd ed.). Chicago: University of Chicago Press.

Lyne, J. (1985). Rhetorics of inquiry. *Quarterly Journal of Speech, 71,* 65-73.

Martin, J. R., & Veel, R. (Eds.). (1998). *Reading science: Critical and functional perspectives on discourses of science.* London: Routledge.

McCloskey, D. M. (1985). *The rhetoric of economics.* Madison: University of Wisconsin Press.

McRae, M. W. (Ed.). (1993). *The literature of science: Perspectives on popular scientific writing.* Athens: University of Georgia Press.

Nelson, J. S. (1998). *Tropes of politics: Science, theory, rhetoric, action.* Madison: University of Wisconsin Press.

Nelson, J. S., Megill, A., & McCloskey, D. N. (1987). Rhetoric of inquiry. In J. S. Nelson, A. Megill, & D. N. McCloskey (Eds.), *The rhetoric of the human sciences: Language and argument in scholarship and public affairs.* Madison: University of Wisconsin Press.

Potter, J. (1996). *Representing reality: Discourse, rhetoric, and social construction.* London: Sage.

Prelli, L. J. (1989a). The rhetorical construction of scientific ethos. In H. W. Simons (Ed.), *Rhetoric in the human sciences.* London: Sage.

Prelli, L. J. (1989b). *A rhetoric of science: Inventing scientific discourse.* Columbia: University of South Carolina Press.

Roberts, R. H., & Good, J. M. (Eds.). (1993). *The recovery of rhetoric: Persuasive discourse and disciplinarity in the human sciences.* Charlottesville: University Press of Virginia.

Rorty, R. (1979). *Philosophy and the mirror of nature.* Princeton, NJ: Princeton University Press.

Scott, R. L. (1967). On viewing rhetoric as epistemic. *Central States Speech Journal, 18,* 9-17.

Scott, R. L. (1976). On viewing rhetoric as epistemic: Ten years later. *Central States Speech Journal, 27,* 258-266.

Scott, R. L. (1993). Rhetoric is epistemic: What difference does that make? In T. Enos & S. C. Brown (Eds.), *Defining the new rhetorics.* Newbury Park, CA: Sage.

Simons, H. S. (1990). Introduction: The rhetoric of inquiry as an intellectual movement. In H. W. Simons (Ed.), *The rhetorical turn: Invention and persuasion in the conduct of inquiry.* Chicago: University of Chicago Press.

Spence, D. P. (1994). *The rhetorical voice of psychoanalysis: Displacement of evidence by theory.* Cambridge, MA: Harvard University Press.

van Eemeren, F. H., Grootendorst, R., & Henkemans, F. S. (1996). *Fundamentals of argumentation theory: A handbook of historical backgrounds and contemporary developments.* Mahwah, NJ: Lawrence Erlbaum.

INTERPELLATION

What is the relationship between **ideology** and concrete individual humans? This question was posed by the French philosopher and Marxist theorist Louis Althusser in his important essay, "Ideology and Ideological State Apparatuses" (Althusser, 1971). In this essay, Althusser tried to show that, whatever additional effects it might produce, the central function of ideology is to produce and reproduce humans as **subjects.** He contended, "All ideology has the function (which defines it) of 'constituting' concrete individuals as subjects" (p. 171) or, as some scholars might phrase it, of placing individuals into *subject positions.* The initial question of relationship then gives way to the question of means: *How* does ideology produce or "constitute" subjects? Althusser answered this question by introducing the concept of **interpellation.**

What did Althusser (1971) mean by interpellation? In a widely quoted passage, he wrote,

> I shall then suggest that ideology "acts" or "functions" in such a way that it "recruits" subjects among the individuals (it recruits them all) or "transforms" the individuals into subjects (it transforms them all) by that very precise operation which I have called *interpellation* or hailing and which can be imagined along the lines of the most commonplace everyday police (or other) hailing: "Hey, you there!" (p. 174)

In this passage Althusser compared interpellation with the process of *hailing* or being called on. When a person is called on (e.g., by a teacher in a class, by a judge during a legal proceeding), he or she is being addressed by someone with authority. And the act of addressing the person does something; it *positions* the person in a certain way. When the person recognizes or acknowledges that he or she is being called on, the person comes to occupy that position; the person is "recruited" (to use Althusser's terminology) into the position of "student" or is "transformed" into the position of "defendant," "plaintiff," or "juror." Although Althusser illustrated the process of interpellation through the specific act of hailing or calling on someone, we need to recognize that interpellation, like ideology, is ubiquitous and operates through a variety of mechanisms and institutions (Charland, 1987, p. 138). One challenge for critical theorists is to identify these mechanisms and institutions.

Althusser's explanation of interpellation posited a central role for human **discourse.** As Wess (1996) pointed out, Althusser's theories of ideology and interpellation described "the discursive construction of the subject" (p. 10). But Wess suggested that Althusser avoided identifying the discursive process as *rhetorical;* Althusser "speaks rhetorically when he comes to his key concept of interpellation," but rhetoric, as a practice or a theory of practice, remained absent (p. 10). One scholar to draw on both Althusser and the tradition of rhetorical scholarship is Maurice Charland. In his essay, "Constitutive Rhetoric: The Case of the *Peuple Québécois,*" Charland (1987) developed a conceptual perspective that he termed "the rhetoric of interpellation" (p. 137). This perspective emerged as Charland explored "the radical edge of [Kenneth] Burke's identificatory principle" (p. 137). Burke's discussion of the way in which discourse constantly constructs and overturns **identifications** among individuals and groups, and his emphasis on how, in Charland's words, "our being is significantly constituted by our symbolicity," prompted Charland to "consider the textual nature of social being" (p. 137). Althusser's theory of interpellation functioned for Charland as a logical extension of Burke's positions on identification and human symbolicity.[1] Just as Burke sought to displace *persuasion* with the concept of identification, Charland insisted that "interpellation does not occur through persuasion in the usual sense" (p. 138). He argued that the discursive process of interpellation is "part of a rhetoric of socialization" or an "ongoing" immersion into a culture or subculture. Following Althusser, Charland maintained that ideological or rhetorical force[2] is instantiated in "the very act of *addressing*" an audience (p. 138). Charland's project, then, was not an effort to study the persuasive efforts of the Québécois **movement**; instead, he was trying to understand the discourse that created this new subject position and, therefore, made the political movement possible. There can be no political or social movement until a common identity has been fashioned, and Charland suggested that this common identity can emerge only through a rhetoric of interpellation.

Notes

1. For a somewhat different approach to interpellation and identification, see Berger (1995).
2. On the conflation of rhetorical and ideological, see Wess (1996).

References and Additional Reading

Althusser, L. (1971). Ideology and ideological state apparatuses (notes towards an investigation). In L. Althusser, *Lenin and philosophy and other essays* (B. Brewster, Trans.). New York: Monthly Review Press.

Aune, J. A. (1994). *Rhetoric and Marxism.* Boulder, CO: Westview.

Berger, A. A. (1995). *Cultural criticism: A primer of key concepts.* Thousand Oaks: Sage.

Charland, M. (1987). Constitutive rhetoric: The case of the *peuple Québécois. Quarterly Journal of Speech, 73,* 133-150.

King, R. (1993). Interpellation. In I. R. Makaryk (Ed.), *Encyclopedia of contemporary literary theory: Approaches, scholars, terms.* Toronto: University of Toronto Press.

Wess, R. (1996). *Kenneth Burke: Rhetoric, subjectivity, postmodernism.* Cambridge, UK: Cambridge University Press.

INTERTEXTUALITY

Still and Worton (1990) observed that it is possible to locate "theories of intertextuality wherever there has been discourse about texts" (p. 2). But *explicit* discussion of the phenomenon of **intertextuality** is a relatively recent development in literary and critical theory. Many scholars (e.g., Culler, 1981; Godard, 1993) credit French theorist Julia Kristeva (e.g., Kristeva, 1980, 1984) with formulating the broad contours of the concept. But locating an "origin" for the concept of intertextuality is both difficult and ironic. It is difficult because, as Still and Worton (1990) demonstrated, the idea of intertextuality has a complex conceptual genealogy; they uncovered antecedents in, for example, the ancient Roman rhetorical doctrine of transformative *imitation* (see the entry for **invention**) and Mikhail Bakhtin's *dialogic* theory of prose discourse.[1] The effort to locate an origin for the concept of intertextuality is ironic because, at least for many scholars, one central principle of intertextuality is to eschew the search for origins. As Roland Barthes, an early exponent of intertextuality, remarked, "Intertextuality, the condition of any text whatsoever, cannot, of course, be reduced to a problem of sources or influences; the intertext is a general field of anonymous formulae whose origin can scarcely ever be located" (Barthes, 1981, p. 39). Extending on Barthes' insights, Culler (1981) argued that texts are, in fact, "cut off from origins." He continued, "Doubtless, the signs and grammatical rules of English have origins in some sense, but a pursuit of their origins would never yield an event that could truly count as an origin" (pp. 102-103).

The concept of intertextuality lacks a clear origin (as in "inventor") and has a complex conceptual genealogy. But what *is* intertextuality? How does it alter more traditional assumptions about the nature of the literary or rhetorical **text**? Probably the most important aspect of recent writing on the topic is a resounding rejection of the concept of an autonomous, autotelic, or self-sufficient text. Proponents of what we can call an intertextual thesis (as Barthes [1981] put it, intertextuality as the condition of any text whatsoever) insist that texts cannot be conceived or understood in isolation. A text or an utterance always exists and, hence, must be studied and/or understood in relation to *other* texts and utterances. Culler (1981) wrote that intertextuality "calls our attention to the importance of prior texts, insisting that the autonomy of texts is a misleading notion and that a work has the meaning it does only because certain things have previously been written" or spoken (p. 103). Consider a simple example. A person is in a conversation with someone else. They produce an utterance. What does it mean? We answer this question not by isolating the utterance but by locating it in relation to the unfolding episode of interaction. If we understand the episode to be one of joking or fooling around, then we most likely will interpret an utterance as consistent with that pattern (the utterance is understood as a tease or joke). But if previous utterances have produced episodes marked by tension, then we most likely will consider a new utterance in relation to that pattern (so that what might be a joke in one context now appears as a veiled threat).

Minimally, then, the concept of intertextuality calls our attention to the way in which a *linguistic context* (a set of prior texts or utterances) conditions or shapes the meaning of a discursive element (e.g., a text, an utterance, a single word) that might enter its domain. But intertextuality often involves much more. In the simple example from the preceding paragraph, meaning emerges from the relationships between utterances; Utterance A will shape the meanings of the utterances that follow. But in this example, the utterances still are considered as discrete entities; Utterance A is different from Utterance B and so on. But it is possible that utterances in a conversation, or the texts circulating in a culture, have a more complex relationship with each other. Utterances and texts not only will share topics or themes (or be about the same thing) but often will share structure, style, and/or substance as well. The concept of intertextuality points out the way in which utterances and texts intermingle with each other as well as the way in which one text frequently is derived from another text. Commenting on the works of literary scholar Joseph Riddel, Leitch (1983) noted that "prior texts reside in present texts" and, hence, "no text itself is ever fully self-present, self-contained, or self-sufficient; no text is closed, total, or unified" (p. 98). Elaborating on Riddel's works, Leitch concluded that intertextuality resides in the way that every literary text is "irreducibly infiltrated by previous texts. . . . [Literary texts] are uncontrollably permeated with previous texts" (p. 98).

The difference between Culler's initial account of intertextuality and Leitch's more elaborate view is subtle but important. Culler (1981) called our attention to the external relationship between utterances and texts; Text A is understood in relationship to Text B. Leitch (1983), following Riddel, emphasized a more internal relationship between utterances and texts; Text A consists of bits or *fragments* of Texts B, C, D, and so on. Intertextuality in this second sense refers to the way in which any text is composed of pieces (e.g., structural patterns, metaphorical images, arguments) from previous texts. The difference between these two accounts of intertextuality is a matter of emphasis. Still and Worton (1990) described this difference as the two "axes of intertextuality" (p. 2). One axis of intertextuality (the dimension emphasized by Leitch) focuses on *text production* or

invention. Still and Worton explained that every writer or speaker "is a reader of texts (in the broadest sense) before s/he is a creator of texts, and therefore the work of art is inevitably shot through with references, quotations, and influences of every kind" (p. 1).[2] For example, we can assume that Geraldine Ferraro, the Democratic congresswoman and vice presidential nominee in 1984, had at some point been exposed to John F. Kennedy's "Inaugural Address." So, we should not have been surprised to see *traces* of Kennedy's speech in the most important speech of Ferraro's career—her address at the Democratic Convention on July 19, 1984. We saw Kennedy's influence when Ferraro constructed a variation of Kennedy's famous *chiasmus,* as "Ask not what your country can do for you but what you can do for your country" was transformed into "The issue is not what America can do for women but what women can do for America." Readers familiar with Kennedy's text might detect other traces in Ferraro's speech (e.g., the *anaphora* pattern of repetition at the beginning of paragraphs).

Appreciation of the intertextual relationship between the Kennedy and Ferraro addresses depends on a familiarity with both texts; one cannot "see" or perceive the traces of Kennedy if one is not familiar with his "Inaugural Address." This issue of familiarity leads to the second axis of intertextuality noted by Still and Worton (1990). This axis (emphasized by Culler, 1981) focuses on the reception and *interpretation* of texts. Still and Worton (1990) explained that "a text is available only through some process of reading; what is produced at the moment of reading is due to the cross-fertilization of the packaged textual material (say a book) by all the texts which the reader brings to it" (pp. 1-2). For example, suppose that a person is very conversant in classical music. The person brings his or her knowledge of all those "texts" to any encounter with contemporary music. The person's reception of a contemporary pop ballad is filtered because of the cross-fertilization of texts; he or she can hear the chord progressions of the contemporary ballad in relation to the common patterns in the tradition of classical music. The person is able to "hear" things—repetition of, or variation on, a classical pattern—that other listeners without the same stock of knowledge are unable to perceive.

Further reflection on the productive axis reveals a lingering tension in the way that intertextuality is operationalized as a critical heuristic. In Morgan's (1989) discussion of the concept, she situated intertextuality in relation to more traditional literary "theories of influence" (p. 246). Early exponents such as Kristeva (1984) attempted a clear demarcation between a "banal sense of 'study of sources' " (p. 60) or efforts to locate the forces influencing the creation of particular text and a more elaborate sense of the intermingling or "transposition" of texts.[3] But can the study of influences and the analysis of the larger phenomenon of intertextuality be distinguished this easily? Morgan (1989) raised some doubts. Examining one of Kristeva's intertextual analyses, she wrote,

> When Kristeva goes on to point out that we must verify which edition of Pascal's *Pensées* Lautréamont used for his parody, one cannot escape the uncanny feeling that we are back with Brower [a literary critic during the 1950s], trying to reconstruct a historically accurate picture of the life and literary times of Alexander Pope by figuring out which editions of Dryden and Horace he read. The twin problems of intentionality and influence thus return, thinly disguised under the poststructuralist "productive" subject. (p. 261)

Culler (1981) also noticed the tension. Early in his essay, he stressed the difference between the study of influence and intertextual analysis: "The study of intertextuality is thus not the investigation of sources and influences as traditionally conceived; it casts its net wider to include anonymous discursive practices, codes whose origins are lost, that make possible the signifying practices of later texts" (p. 103). But as Culler proceeded in his exposition, the difference between locating sources and engaging in intertextual analysis became more difficult to specify. Commenting on a passage in Kristeva (1984) where she discussed the importance of locating the correct edition (a passage similar to the one that Morgan [1989] identified), Culler (1981) wrote,

> The point is not that such questions [of identifying the correct sources] are uninteresting or insignificant but only that a situation in which one can track down sources with such precision cannot serve as the paradigm for a description of intertextuality if intertextuality is the general discursive space that makes a text intelligible. (p. 106)

The tension, Culler went on to point out, is that critics can access the "general discursive space" only through particular cases. He continued,

> Kristeva's procedure is instructive because it illustrates the way in which the concept of intertextuality leads the critic who wishes to work with it to concentrate on cases that put in question the general theory. A criticism based on the contention that meaning is made possible by a general anonymous intertextuality tries to justify the claim by showing how in particular cases "a text works by absorbing and destroying at the same time the other texts of the intertextual space" and is happiest or most triumphant when it can identify particular pretexts with which the work is indubitably wrestling. (pp. 106-107)

The general point, then, is that intertextual analysis aims to be something more than locating the sources or the influences on the focal text, but it can do this only by engaging in the study of particular sources and influences. Hence, the continuing question is as follows: Is the concept of intertextuality, and the mode of analysis it generates, radically different from an older tradition of historical criticism or influence studies?

One way in which much intertextual analysis is significantly different from tracking down historical sources was suggested by Morgan's (1989) brief discussion of the "productive subject." Whereas most "historical" inquiry into sources and influences assumes the stability of the human self, the critique of the autonomous text in intertextual theory encourages a similar critique of the autonomous human **subject** (Clayton & Rothstein, 1991). For theorists such as Kristeva, intertextuality as a discursive or linguistic phenomenon is linked to ongoing revisions in the idea of the human self or subject. Kristeva (1989) explained,

> The discovery of intertextuality at a formal level leads us to an intrapsychic or psychoanalytic finding . . . concerning the status of the "creator," the one who produces a text by placing himself or herself at the intersection of this plurality of texts on their different levels. . . . This leads me to understand creative subjectivity as a kaleidoscope, a "polyphony" as Bakhtin calls it. (p. 281)

According to Kristeva, individual subjects, like texts, are composed or created through a process of splicing together or *grafting* (Culler, 1982) bits and pieces of different languages and voices (see also the discussion of **polyphony**). This principle was illustrated nicely in Kamberelis and Scott's (1992) discussion of the "co-articulation of texts and subjectivities." What these authors demonstrated, consistent with Kristeva's observation, was that there is considerable overlap between the process of composing a text and the fashioning of subjectivity.

This short discussion does not exhaust the intricacies in the concept of intertextuality. But before concluding the entry, we need to turn our attention to the way in which the concept of intertextuality has influenced contemporary rhetorical scholarship. Intertextuality appears in rhetorical criticism in both an implicit and an explicit manner. In his discussion of John Campbell's critical analyses of Charles Darwin, Gaonkar (1993) argued that, over time, Campbell deemphasized Darwin's purpose or intentions and began to locate Darwin's texts, especially *On the Origin of Species* (Darwin, 1964), within "an intertextual space of notebooks, letters, and abandoned works" (p. 281). Gaonkar suggested that Campbell's shift from an *instrumental* reading strategy to an intertextual one was not an explicit embrace of the intertextuality thesis. Campbell's turn to intertextuality remained implicit. But other rhetorical critics have explicitly embraced intertextuality as a critical heuristic. Rosteck (1994), for example, argued that Bill Clinton's 1992 campaign film, *The Man From Hope,* was "quintessentially intertextual" (p. 243). Rosteck argued that "any audience seeking to make sense" of the film "is likely to do so by actively reading it as part of three dominant intertextual relationships: text and history, text and narrative, [and] text and myth" (p. 230). Rosteck's analysis appeared to privilege the reception axis of intertextuality described earlier; although he did not ignore the process of production, Rosteck foregrounded the audience in his analysis. He maintained that the meaning of the text for an audience emerged in the reverberations between textual elements (e.g., words, visual images) and the realms of history, narrative structure, and mythical ideals.

Another rhetorical critic to emphasize intertextuality was Martha Solomon Watson, who took issue with McGee's (1990) claim that "contemporary fragmentation of culture has altered rhetorical roles." Watson (1997) continued,

> In contrast to McGee, I will demonstrate that historically rhetors have been interpreters of texts to their own strategic ends. In my view, rhetors have often construed the meaning of previous texts to their own advantage by constructing public discourse that draws upon those texts. (p. 92)[4]

Watson's disagreement with McGee over whether intertextuality is a response to cultural fragmentation or a recurrent form of textual production parallels debates in contemporary literary theory (for overviews, see Morgan, 1989; Still & Worton, 1990). Watson (1997) illustrated her thesis with an analysis of "the process by which rhetors deliberately use previous texts as the model and basis for their own rhetorical action" (p. 93). Her specific illustration focused on the impact of the 1776 American Declaration of Independence on the founding texts of the abolitionist and women's rights movements during the 19th century. Stressing the productionist axis of intertextuality, Watson traced how abolitionists and women's rights advocates appropriated the language of the Declaration of Independence and how, in turn, these 19th-century appropriations helped to reconstruct the meaning and significance of the 1776 text. Watson argued that there was an "interanimation" among these texts that merits critical attention (p. 103; cf. Solomon, 1993).

Watson (1997) raised some important issues that can serve as the final discussion points in this entry. Watson maintained that her "analysis will demonstrate and expand on McGee's rejection of our discipline's traditional iconic approach to texts" (p. 93). One issue in need of more reflection is Watson's claim that the "iconic" (self-sufficient or autonomous) approach to texts has been the tradition in rhetorical studies. Scholars such as Medhurst (1993) will dispute this claim and argue that the emphasis on texts found in the **close reading** movement is a very recent, and still precarious, development in rhetorical scholarship. More important was Watson's (1997) suggestion that intertextual analysis is antithetical to the close reading of specific texts. Are intertextual analysis and close reading inherently antagonistic critical practices? Rosteck (1994) did not believe this to be the case. Close readers tend to focus on the *instrumental* quality of the text, whereas an intertextual analysis is less concerned with assessing the impact of a discrete text. But Rosteck argued that Clinton's *The Man From Hope* film is a case of a discrete text whose instrumental force was derived from the intertextual relations it generated. He concluded, "However we may want to distinguish between the discrete text and the intertextual 'text,' in this case, the intertextual relationships may well account for the function of the discrete text as a discourse set in a specific time and place" (p. 243).

Jasinski (1997) approached the relationship between close reading and intertextuality on the plane of critical theory. Drawing on Bakhtin, he suggested a form of reconstructive analysis that attends to both the dynamics *in* the text and the languages and voices that *surround* the text. He asserted,

> Reconstructing the appropriation and diffusion of, and play among, performative traditions [e.g., idioms, voices, generic conventions] moves rhetorical criticism beyond a formalist recounting of discursive techniques [Watson's critique of the iconic approach]. It seeks to provide a thick description of the organic emergence of text from its performative context, recognizing the radical multiplicity of the text's context. (p. 216)

Rosteck and Jasinski provided two different ways of responding to Watson's suggestion that close reading and intertextual analysis are opposed. This tension, like the larger modern versus postmodern antagonism of which it is a part, will continue to engage rhetorical scholars in the future.

Notes

1. Kristeva (1980) discussed the importance of Bakhtin in her essay, "Word, Dialogue, and Novel."

2. Compare this position with Leff's (1997) discussion of the relationship between interpretation and production in "hermeneutical rhetoric."

3. Distinguishing influence from intertextuality is a key issue in contemporary literary theory. See, for example, Clayton and Rothstein (1991), Frow (1990), and Godard (1993).

4. Watson's (1997) point was similar to Leff's (1997) account of "hermeneutical rhetoric."

References and Additional Reading

Barthes, R. (1981). Theory of the text. In R. Young (Ed.), *Untying the text: A post-structuralist reader.* London: Routledge and Kegan Paul.

Clayton, J., & Rothstein, E. (1991). Figures in the corpus: Theories of influence and intertextuality. In J. Clayton & E. Rothstein (Eds.), *Influence and intertextuality in literary history.* Madison: University of Wisconsin Press.

Culler, J. (1981). Presupposition and intertextuality. In J. Culler, *The pursuit of signs: Semiotics, literature, deconstruction.* Ithaca, NY: Cornell University Press.

Culler, J. (1982). *On deconstruction: Theory and criticism after structuralism.* Ithaca, NY: Cornell University Press.

Darwin, C. (1964). *On the origin of species.* Cambridge, MA: Harvard University Press.

Frow, J. (1990). Intertextuality and ontology. In M. Worton & J. Still (Eds.), *Intertextuality: Theories and practices.* Manchester, UK: Manchester University Press.

Gaonkar, D. P. (1993). The idea of rhetoric in the rhetoric of science. *Southern Communication Journal, 58,* 258-295.

Godard, B. (1993). Intertextuality. In I. R. Makaryk (Ed.), *Encyclopedia of contemporary literary theory: Approaches, scholars, terms.* Toronto: University of Toronto Press.

Jasinski, J. (1997). Instrumentalism, contextualism, and interpretation in rhetorical criticism. In A. G. Gross & W. M. Keith (Eds.), *Rhetorical hermeneutics: Invention and interpretation in the age of science.* Albany: State University of New York Press.

Kamberelis, G., & Scott, K. D. (1992). Other people's voices: The co-articulation of texts and subjectivities. *Linguistics and Education, 4,* 359-403.

Kristeva, J. (1980). Word, dialogue, and novel. In L. S. Roudiez (Ed.), *Desire in language: A semiotic approach to literature and art* (T. Gora, A. Jardine, & L. S. Roudiez, Trans.). New York: Columbia University Press.

Kristeva, J. (1984). *Revolution in poetic language* (M. Waller, Trans.). New York: Columbia University Press.

Kristeva, J. (1989). An interview with Julia Kristeva. In P. O'Donnell & R. C. Davis (Eds.), *Intertextuality and contemporary American fiction.* Baltimore, MD: Johns Hopkins University Press.

Leff, M. (1997). Hermeneutical rhetoric. In W. Jost & M. J. Hyde (Eds.), *Rhetoric and hermeneutics in our time: A reader.* New Haven, CT: Yale University Press.

Leitch, V. B. (1983). *Deconstructive criticism: An advanced introduction.* New York: Columbia University Press.

Long, B. W., & Strine, M. S. (1989). Reading intertextually: Multiple mediations and critical practice. *Quarterly Journal of Speech, 75,* 467-475.

McGee, M. C. (1990). Text, context, and the fragmentation of contemporary culture. *Western Journal of Speech Communication, 54,* 274-289.

Medhurst, M. J. (1993). The academic study of public address: A tradition in transition. In M. J. Medhurst (Ed.), *Landmark essays on American public address.* Davis, CA: Hermagoras Press.

Morgan, T. (1989). The space of intertextuality. In P. O'Donnell & R. C. Davis (Eds.), *Intertextuality and contemporary American fiction.* Baltimore, MD: Johns Hopkins University Press.

Rosteck, T. (1994). The intertextuality of "The Man From Hope." In S. A. Smith (Ed.), *Bill Clinton on stump, state, and stage: The rhetorical road to the White House.* Fayetteville: University of Arkansas Press.

Solomon, M. (1993). The things we study: Texts and their interactions. *Communication Monographs, 60,* 62-67.

Still, J., & Worton, M. (1990). Introduction. In M. Worton & J. Still (Eds.), *Intertextuality: Theories and practices.* Manchester, UK: Manchester University Press.

Watson, M. S. (1997). The dynamics of intertextuality: Re-reading the Declaration of Independence. In T. W. Benson (Ed.), *Rhetoric and political culture in nineteenth-century America.* East Lansing: Michigan State University Press.

INVENTION

Philosopher and classicist Richard McKeon observed, "Invention is the art of discovering new arguments and uncovering new things by argument. . . . [It] extends from the construction of formal arguments to all modes of enlarging experience by reason as manifested in awareness, emotion, interest, and appreciation" (McKeon, 1987, p. 59). As McKeon suggested, **invention,** one of the five traditional parts or **canons of rhetoric,** ranges from the analysis of case, through the selection of arguments, to the enhancement of experience through language.[1] But from the classical period to the present day, questions persist as to whether or not invention can be described and systematized, what is the precise nature of the process of invention, and what exactly is the scope and function of inventional activity. Leff and Procario (1985) noted that invention is "an amorphous and unwieldy concept" in contemporary rhetorical theory (p. 11). Lauer (1984) observed that, over time, the various strands within the large tradition of rhetorical studies have produced several "divergent conceptions of invention" (p. 127). At the risk of oversimplification, we can identify four historically recurring conceptions: romantic, systematic, imitative, and social.

In Kennedy's (1963) study of rhetoric in ancient Greece, he described three different explanations of "creativity" (pp. 332-333) or, by extension, rhetorical invention. The first of these is the Platonic ideal of *inspiration* (p. 75). LeFevre (1987) echoed this view when she suggested that "a Platonic view of invention" places the "accent on the isolated writer seeking inspiration within" (pp. 17-18). Platonic inspiration is an early manifestation of a broader conception of invention that can be labeled "romantic." LeFevre wrote, "Romanticism holds that the writer is inspired from within, as Coleridge claims to have written 'Kubla Khan' in a trance, or as Wordsworth made poems that were a 'spontaneous overflow of emotion recollected in tranquillity.' " (p. 17).[2] She continued,

> In the romantic tradition, the inspired writer is apart from others and wants to keep it that way, either to prevent himself [sic] and his creations from being corrupted by society or to maintain a necessary madness (in the style of Poe) that is thought to be, at least in part, the source of art. (p. 17)

D'Angelo (1975) described a recent trend in composition and invention theory that continues the romantic emphasis on inspiration. He labeled this new trend the "new romanticism" (e.g., Miller, 1972, 1974). D'Angelo (1975) argued that new romantics believe that the process of invention is "relatively free of control and direction" (p. 159). Miller (1974) suggested that the romantic pedagogical process must emphasize "liberation" and not rigid adherence to rules or norms (p. 367). The romantic conceptualization of invention that runs from Plato to recent work in composition theory also has links to the tradition of thought that Gadamer (1982) referred to as "the aesthetics of genius." Excellence in expression is understood to arise out of a mysterious process that takes place within the imaginations of a small group of gifted individuals. The only thing that the rest of us can do is wait for our muse.

The second approach to rhetorical creativity that Kennedy (1963) identified consists of *systematic* rules or procedures for composing discourse. Classical rhetorical theorists developed a number of systematic analytic procedures that could be used to generate persuasive messages. Lauer (1984) observed that **stasis** theory is "the earliest art governing the genesis of discourse" (p. 129). The more recently developed analytic scheme of **stock topics** continues this systematic approach to invention. But the most widely recognized systematic approach to the composition process is the doctrine of **topoi** or **topics.** As Corbett (1971a) noted,

> The method that the classical rhetoricians devised to aid the speaker in discovering matter [for the speech] . . . was the *topics. Topics* is the English translation of the Greek word *topoi* and the Latin word *loci.* Literally, *topos* or *locus* meant "place" or "region." . . . In rhetoric, a topic was a place or store or thesaurus to which one resorted in order to find something to say on a given subject. (p. 35)

As Sloane (1997) explained, "The purpose of any topic is simply to suggest a fundamental mode of inquiry" (p. 92). Topics remain popular in contemporary composition and invention theory and instruction (Hudson, 1921; Wallace, 1972). McCroskey (1993), for example, included an extensive discussion of different topical systems and justified the discussion by observing,

> The only way to be certain that you have the best arguments [in your message] is to make sure that you have *all* the arguments available. You will probably never generate all the available arguments, but some system is needed that will enable you to approach that desirable goal. (p. 187)

Topics provide that systematic procedure for generating arguments and reasoned discourse.

Imitation is the third approach to creativity in classical rhetorical theory that Kennedy (1963) noted. It was central to the thought of numerous ancient teachers and theorists including Isocrates, Longinus, Cicero, Quintilian, and Dionysious of Halicarnassus.[3] Winterowd (1970) remarked, "One of the great constants in rhetoric is the doctrine of imitation" (p. 161). Drawing on the corpus of classical scholarship, Copeland (1991) explored one of the paradoxical aspects of the concept of imitation: When serving as a vehicle for rhetorical invention, can imitation be more than "a barren act" (p. 27) or a mindless re-creation of the model being copied? Can imitation of what exists produce novelty or lead to creativity? Leff (1997a; see also 1997b, 1997c) continued this line of inquiry in his recent discussion of *hermeneutical rhetoric.* According to Leff (1997a),

> *Imitatio* is not the mere repetition or mechanistic reproduction of something found in an existing text. It is a complex process that allows historical texts to serve as equipment for future rhetorical production. . . . Through a process similar to Kenneth Burke's "casuistic stretching," imitation of the structure and language of an old text may help introduce radically new ideas. (pp. 201, 203)[4]

Imitation, in Leff's reading, responds to a dilemma in the rhetorical tradition that Cox (1987) described as the "scandal of doxa" (see the entry for **doxa**). According to Leff (1997a),

> As the embodied utterances of the past are interpreted for current application, their ideas and modes of articulation are reembodied, and old voices are recovered for use in new circumstances. [Imitation] . . . is at once a mechanism for technical production [or invention] and a vehicle for achieving what J. Robert Cox calls the invention of usable traditions. (p. 203)[5]

Unlike the romantic and, at least to a certain extent, systematic approaches to invention, the imitative model locates speakers and writers in a world of *other texts and voices* that help to shape the generation of discourse.[6] Recent scholarship in composition theory (LeFevre, 1987) and linguistics (Kamberelis & Scott, 1992) called our attention to the centrality of these other texts and voices to the process of inventing discourse. In so doing, this scholarship illustrated a fourth approach—the *social*—to rhetorical invention. The image of the rhetor or advocate, from a social perspective, is similar to the idea of a **bricoleur**—a person who acts by making do or improvising with the limited materials that are available in a particular situation. The rhetor is a language "tinkerer" pasting together bits of linguistic material and persuasive strategy to meet the demands of the occasion.

For LeFevre (1987), human language serves "as a foundation for a view of invention as a social act" because language itself is "the result of an ongoing social process" (pp. 95-96). Invention must be conceptualized as a social process, LeFevre argued, because its raw material—language—is a social phenomenon, not an individual one. She asserted that a social approach to rhetorical invention

> asks us to look at the inventing writer [or speaker] as part of a community, a socioculture, a sphere of overlapping (and sometimes conflicting) collectives. It draws our attention to social contexts, discourse communities, [and] political aims. It reminds us that writers invent not only in the study but also in the smoke-filled chamber, not only alone but with others with whom they must work or with whom they choose to think, and not in utter isolation even when they are alone, but [also] by means of inner conversations carried on with internalized others. (p. 93)[7]

Kamberelis and Scott (1992) also emphasized the centrality of language in the process of text production (LeFevre drew inspiration from the philosopher Ernst Cassirer, whereas Kamberelis & Scott took their cues from the works of Russian theorist and critic Mikhail Bakhtin). They wrote,

> We seldom, if ever, create our own language styles and texts anew. Rather, we use the styles and texts of other individuals and groups with whom we wish to be affiliated, have power over, or resist. . . . All speakers and writers borrow and adapt the language of others in the process of constructing their own texts. (p. 363)

Any text is an **intertextual** product, in Still and Worton's (1990) terms, because it inevitably is "shot through with references, quotations, and influences of every kind" (p. 1).[8]

A scholar's decision to adopt the social conceptualization of invention often will entail or lead to other theoretical commitments. For example, Kamberelis and Scott (1992) suggested that a social approach to invention can be extended to the realm of the individual self or human **subject.** They described a process of "co-articulation" whereby the various social languages and voices that create a text also function to constitute an individual's sense of self-identity. They argued that the process of constructing a text "is simultaneously the forging of subjectivity" (p. 373). Adopting a social approach to rhetorical invention helps to *decenter* or destabilize a romantic or autonomous vision of the self as the origin of action. Gaonkar (1993) described this decentering when he wrote, "In the formation of discourse [or the process of invention], the rhetor is no longer the seat of origin but a point of intersection" (p. 153).

As Leff and Procario (1985) noted, reflection on the concept of invention has been on the decline in the speech communication trajectory of rhetorical studies. Much more attention is devoted to the topic in the literature of composition studies (e.g., Sloane, 1989; Young & Liu, 1994). Perhaps the social turn advanced by LeFevre, Kamberelis and Scott, and others, or a recuperation of the classical idea of imitation discussed by Leff, will help to rejuvenate this central theoretical concept.

Notes

1. On the range of activities included in the orbit of invention, see also Lauer (1984) and Sloane (1997).
2. Wordsworth's idea of "recollecting" his poems bears a resemblance to Plato's doctrine of *anamnesis* or recollection.
3. On the classical concept of imitation, in addition to Kennedy (1963, 1972), see Clark (1951), Corbett (1971b), Fantham (1978), and especially McKeon's (1936/1952) groundbreaking essay. For a general discussion of the topic, see Todorov (1982).
4. See also Campbell's (1998) argument that "the principle of rhetorical invention is subversion" (p. 112).
5. On the imitative or hermeneutic model of rhetorical invention, see also Sloane (1997, pp. 28-57).
6. Some scholars (e.g., Still & Worton, 1990) see a relationship between the concept of imitation in rhetorical studies and recent developments in literary theory and the concept of **intertextuality.**
7. On the concept of internalized others, see the discussion of George Herbert Mead in the entry for **subject.**
8. For another example of a social approach to invention, see Benoit's (1994) Burkeian-inspired account of the "genesis of rhetorical action."

References and Additional Reading

Benoit, W. L. (1994). The genesis of rhetorical action. *Southern Communication Journal, 59,* 342-355.

Campbell, K. K. (1998). Inventing women: From Amaterasu to Virginia Woolf. *Women's Studies in Communication, 21,* 111-126.

Clark, D. L. (1951). Imitation: Theory and practice in Roman rhetoric. *Quarterly Journal of Speech, 37,* 11-22.

Copeland, R. (1991). *Rhetoric, hermeneutics, and translation in the Middle Ages.* Cambridge, UK: Cambridge University Press.

Corbett, E. P. J. (1971a). *Classical rhetoric for the modern student* (2nd ed.). New York: Oxford University Press.

Corbett, E. P. J. (1971b). The theory and practice of imitation in classical rhetoric. *College Composition and Communication, 22,* 243-250.

Cox, J. R. (1987). *Cultural memory and public moral argument.* Van Zelst lecture, Northwestern University.

Crowley, S. (1990). *The methodical memory: Invention in current-traditional rhetoric.* Carbondale: Southern Illinois University Press.

D'Angelo, F. J. (1975). *A conceptual theory of rhetoric.* Cambridge, UK: Winthrop.

Fantham, E. (1978). Imitation and evolution: The discussion of rhetorical imitation in Cicero's *De Oratore* 2.87-97 and some related problems of Ciceronian theory. *Classical Philology, 73,* 1-16.

Gadamer, H. G. (1982). *Truth and method* (G. Barden & J. Cumming, Eds. and Trans.). New York: Crossroad.

Gaonkar, D. P. (1993). Performing with fragments: Reflections on critical rhetoric. In R. E. McKerrow (Ed.), *Argument and the postmodern challenge: Proceedings of the Eighth SCA/AFA Conference on Argumentation.* Annandale, VA: Speech Communication Association.

Hudson, H. H. (1921). Can we modernize the study of invention? *Quarterly Journal of Speech Education, 7,* 325-334.

Kamberelis, G., & Scott, K. D. (1992). Other people's voices: The coarticulation of texts and subjectivities. *Linguistics and Education, 4,* 359-403.

Kellogg, R. T. (1994). *The psychology of writing.* New York: Oxford University Press.

Kennedy, G. (1963). *The art of persuasion in Greece.* Princeton, NJ: Princeton University Press.

Kennedy, G. (1972). *The art of rhetoric in the Roman world.* Princeton, NJ: Princeton University Press.

Lauer, J. M. (1984). Issues in rhetorical invention. In R. J. Conners, L. S. Ede, & A. A. Lunsford (Eds.), *Essays on classical rhetoric and modern discourse.* Carbondale: Southern Illinois University Press.

LeFevre, K. B. (1987). *Invention as a social act.* Carbondale: Southern Illinois University Press.

Leff, M. (1997a). Hermeneutical rhetoric. In W. Jost & M. J. Hyde (Eds.), *Rhetoric and hermeneutics in our time.* New Haven, CT: Yale University Press.

Leff, M. (1997b). The idea of rhetoric as interpretive practice: A humanist's response to Gaonkar. In A. G. Gross & W. M. Keith (Eds.), *Rhetorical hermeneutics: Invention and interpretation in the age of science.* Albany: State University of New York Press.

Leff, M. C. (1997c). Lincoln among the nineteenth-century orators. In T. W. Benson (Ed.), *Rhetoric and political culture in nineteenth-century America.* East Lansing: Michigan State University Press.

Leff, M. C., & Procario, M. O. (1985). Rhetorical theory in speech communication. In T. W. Benson (Ed.), *Speech communication in the twentieth century.* Carbondale: Southern Illinois University Press.

McCroskey, J. C. (1993). *An introduction to rhetorical communication* (7th ed.). Boston: Allyn & Bacon.

McKeon, R. (1952). Literary criticism and the concept of imitation in antiquity. In R. S. Crane (Ed.), *Critics and criticism* (abridged ed.). Chicago: University of Chicago Press. (Original work published 1936)

McKeon, R. (1987). The methods of rhetoric and philosophy: Invention and judgment. In M. Backman (Ed.), *Rhetoric: Essays in invention and discovery.* Woodbridge, CT: Ox Bow Press.

Miller, J. E., Jr. (1972). *Word, self, reality: The rhetoric of imagination.* New York: Dodd, Mead.

Miller, J. E., Jr. (1974). Rediscovering the rhetoric of imagination. *College Composition and Communication, 25,* 360-367.

Ochs, D. J. (1989). Cicero and philosophic *inventio. Rhetoric Society Quarterly, 19,* 217-227.

Sloane, T. O. (1989). Reinventing *inventio. College English, 51,* 461-473.

Sloane, T. O. (1997). *On the contrary: The protocol of traditional rhetoric.* Washington, DC: Catholic University of America Press.

Still, J., & Worton, M. (1990). Introduction. In J. Still & M. Worton (Eds.), *Intertextuality: Theories and practices.* Manchester, UK: Manchester University Press.

Todorov, T. (1982). *Theories of the symbol* (C. Porter, Trans.). Ithaca, NY: Cornell University Press.

Wallace, K. R. (1972). *Topoi* and the problem of invention. *Quarterly Journal of Speech, 58,* 387-395.

Winterowd, W. R. (1970). Style: A matter of manner. *Quarterly Journal of Speech, 66,* 161-167.

Young, R. (1987). Recent developments in rhetorical invention. In G. Tate (Ed.), *Teaching composition: Twelve bibliographic essays* (rev. ed.). Fort Worth: Texas Christian University Press.

Young, R. E., & Liu, Y. (Eds.). (1994). *Landmark essays on rhetorical invention in writing.* Davis, CA: Hermagoras Press.

INVITATIONAL RHETORIC

In some recent essays, Foss and Griffin (1995) noted an emerging trend in feminist rhetorical scholarship—efforts to "explicate the ways in which standard theories of rhetoric embody patriarchal perspectives" (p. 2; see also Foss & Griffin, 1992). For example, they argued that, extending Gearhart's (1979) earlier analysis, the traditional "definition of rhetoric as persuasion" conceals a "patriarchal bias" (Foss & Griffin, 1995, p. 2). That bias becomes visible when we consider that the essence of persuasion is a "desire to effect change" (p. 2) and that "embedded in efforts to change others is a desire for control and domination, for the act of changing another establishes the power of the change agent over that other" (p. 3). Foss and Griffin (1995) wrote, "The traditional conception of rhetoric is characterized by efforts to change others and thus gain control over them. . . . This is a rhetoric of patriarchy, reflecting its values of change, competition, and domination" (pp. 3-4).[1]

Once the purportedly universal veil of persuasion/domination is lifted, it is possible to construct an alternative "rhetorical system" based on the principles and values of "equality, immanent value, and self-determination" (Foss & Griffin, 1995, p. 4). Foss and Griffin (1995) labeled this alternative **invitational rhetoric.** An invitational rhetoric

> offers an invitation to understanding—to enter another's world to better understand an issue and the individual who holds a particular perspective on it. Ultimately, its purpose is to provide the basis for the creation and maintenance of relationships of equality. Its primary communicative options are offering perspectives and the creation of external conditions of safety, value, and freedom that enable audience members to present their perspectives to the rhetor. (p. 13)

As Foss and Griffin (1995) explained, the communicative practice of "offering perspectives" is "the giving of expression to a perspective without advocating its support or seeking its acceptance. . . . In offering, rhetors tell what they currently know or understand; they present their vision of the world and show how it looks and works for them" (p. 7). Such offerings at times can resemble other, more traditional rhetorical forms such as **narrative,** but Foss and Griffin insisted that these forms can be distinguished. In traditional rhetoric, narratives function "as a form of support for a rhetor's position," but an offering employs the devices of narrative (e.g., character, plot) "for the purpose of articulating a viewpoint but not as a means to increase the likelihood of the audience's adherence to that viewpoint" (p. 7). Offerings, then, evade the "dichotomy of cause and effect" (p. 7); they are ends in themselves. Offerings solicit *understanding* from an audience of self as well as of the issue under discussion; understanding, and not persuasion, is the *telos* or the end of invitational rhetoric.[2]

Invitational rhetoric, Foss and Griffin (1995) maintained, involves more than the adoption of particular communicative forms by a speaker or writer. Invitational rhetoric "involves not only the offering of the rhetor's perspective but the creation of an atmosphere in which audience members' perspectives also can be offered" (p. 10). Three conditions are necessary for the creation of full-fledged invitational rhetoric. First, audience members should be made to feel safe, and they must believe that they will be treated with "respect and care" (p. 10). Second, audience members must be valued and encouraged to feel that they "have intrinsic or immanent worth" (p. 11). Third, audience members must experience the condition of freedom; in invitational rhetoric, "participants can bring any and all matters to the interaction for consideration; no subject matter is off limits, and all presuppositions can be challenged" (p. 12).

Foss and Griffin (1995) described invitational rhetoric as a "feminist rhetoric" (p. 4), but the feminist roots of their proposal are somewhat ambiguous. On the one hand, they insisted that "we are not suggesting that only feminists have dealt with and developed [invitational rhetoric's] various components or that only feminists adhere to the principles on which it is based" (p. 5). But later in the same paragraph, they wrote, "What makes [invitational rhetoric] feminist is not its use by a particular population of rhetors but rather the grounding of its assumptions in feminist principles and theories" (p. 5). The ambiguity lies in the fact that in the first passage, the principles of invitational rhetoric were not described as uniquely feminist (people other than feminists "have dealt with and developed its various components"), but in the second passage, invitational rhetoric appeared to be derived from uniquely feminist "principles and theories." The relationship between the principles of invitational rhetoric and feminist theory is not as clear as it could be. It *might* be the case that not much is gained by positioning invitational rhetoric as a distinctly *feminist* project (see also Dow, 1995).

Many of the assumptions and ideas embedded in Foss and Griffin's concept of invitational rhetoric can be traced to different philosophical traditions. The idea that persuasion is a form of domination that robs people of their independence is, Smith (1999) argued, a key feature of Enlightenment rationalism in both Europe and the United States. More specifically, their discussion of the way in which traditional rhetoric inhibits audience freedom and autonomy, or how it "infringe[s] on others' rights to believe as they choose and to act in ways they believe are best for them" (Foss & Griffin, 1995, p. 3), is consistent with 18th-century German philosopher Immanuel Kant's contention that rhetoric deprives audiences of their freedom as it moves them like machines to a judgment (Kant, 1951, pp. 171-172). Kant's (1951) critique of traditional rhetoric is extended in the works of the contemporary German philosopher and social theorist Jürgen Habermas. Habermas (e.g., Habermas, 1979), like Foss and Griffin, posited a fundamental distinction between two modes of discursive action: action oriented toward understanding and action oriented toward strategic success. The Kantian and Habermasian projects, like Foss and Griffin's proposal, were predicated on the assumption that individual autonomy or freedom and the strategic exercise of power are radically incommensurable. In effect, all of these projects assume the existence of "pure" forms of freedom (e.g., invitational rhetoric) that are uncontaminated by power and "pure" forms of power (e.g., strategic persuasion) that are untouched by the quest for understanding. But following the insights of the French philosopher and historian Michel Foucault (e.g., Foucault, 1980), we might question this assumption of pure freedom and power and, instead, focus critical and analytical attention on the complicated ways in which freedom and power, the quest for understanding, and the pursuit of strategic advantage are imbricated or interlaced in all discursive practice.[3] Literary critic and theorist Wayne Booth provided a potentially useful perspective on an issue at the center of Foss and Griffin's discussion—the question of what it means to *influence* another person. Foss and Griffin suggested that to be influenced means giving up what makes each of us unique individuals—our freedom and autonomy (see also Condit, 1997). But Booth approached the issue of human essence from the other direction. Booth (1988) suggested that we "accept influences as the very source of . . . being" or, put differently, that we see being influenced as the very condition of being human (p. 265). Such a reconceptualization allows for a shift in human energy; instead of "a futile cursing of my fate as an essentially conditioned creature," an individual can engage in "a very careful appraisal of particular invitations" to be influenced (p. 265). Rather than treating invitation as a model for a specific type of rhetoric,[4] Booth saw invitation as a useful metaphor for all literary and rhetorical practice. From Booth's perspective, all texts issue invitations to see the world in a certain way or to adopt particular perspectives on people and events. The critic's and audience's challenge "is not . . . to learn how to resist the inhibiting influence of others in an opposition always implicitly doomed; rather, it is to winnow, from among the myriad narrative advisors, those whose seductive plot suggestions are acts of genuine friendship" (p. 290).

Condit (1997) raised some parallel concerns about the concept of invitational rhetoric. She suggested that the invitational rhetoric concept is too *essentialistic;* it does not adequately acknowledge the way in which gender and other categories are inevitably *constructed* through discursive practice. Condit also objected to Foss and Griffin's "reductive account" of the history of rhetoric, an account that tends to link rhetoric with a quest for domination. Condit's complaint about reductiveness was similar to a point made by philosopher Richard Burke when he wrote, "The difficulty of drawing the line in borderline cases—manipulative advertising, religious cults, etc.—should not lead us to draw the fallacious inference that all persuasion, or even all irrational persuasion, is a form of coercion" (Burke, 1982, p. 45).

Foss, Griffin, and Foss (1997) responded that their perspective is not based on an essentialistic understanding of gender. They wrote that they "see gender not as an essential pre-given quality but as a social construction" (p. 120). But they pointed out that "some features tend to characterize women's and men's realms and the communication that occurs in those realms" (p. 120). Male communication, and rhetorical practice in general, tends to be more aggressive and competitive than female communication. Reflection on this type of practice—in the form of rhetorical theory—contains a "*patriarchal bias*" (p. 122). The nature and consequences of that bias, Foss and colleagues contended, need to be exposed so that the bias may be overcome.

The exchange between Condit and Foss and colleagues briefly summarized in the preceding two paragraphs raised a host of important issues for rhetorical scholars. The idea of an invitational rhetoric most likely will continue to foster critical insights and conceptual explorations during the coming years.

Notes

1. Compare Foss and Griffin's (1995) position to Barris's (1996) argument against defining rhetoric as a mode of persuasion, Czubaroff's (2000) contrast between instrumental and dialogical rhetoric, Rosenfield's (1980) discussion of what he called the "agonistic paradigm" in most rhetorical theory, Sloop and Ono's (1997) observation that many **discursive formations** contain "an imperial impulse" (p. 51), Trebilcot's (1988) account of the violence of persuasion, and Warren's (1988) examination of patriarchy and *critical thinking.*

2. Compare Foss and Griffin's (1995) account of "offering" to Rosenfield's (1980) discussion of the revelatory and disclosive functions of **epideictic discourse** and Spinosa, Flores, and Dreyfus's (1997) sense of "interpretive speaking" as a way for people to exchange experiences.

3. See also the discussion in the entry for **sermonic, language as** and Condit's (1997) description of the persuasive character of discursive practice.

4. Foss and Griffin at times seemed to do this (e.g., Foss & Griffin, 1995, p. 16).

References and Additional Reading

Barris, J. (1996). The foundation in truth of rhetoric and formal logic. *Philosophy and Rhetoric, 29,* 314-328.

Booth, W. (1988). *The company we keep: An ethics of fiction.* Berkeley: University of California Press.

Burke, R. J. (1982). Politics as rhetoric. *Ethics, 93,* 45-55.

Condit, C. M. (1997). In praise of eloquent diversity: Gender and rhetoric as public persuasion. *Women's Studies in Communication, 20,* 91-116.

Czubaroff, J. (2000). Dialogical rhetoric: An application of Martin Buber's philosophy of dialogue. *Quarterly Journal of Speech, 86,* 168-189.

Dow, B. J. (1995). Feminism, difference(s), and rhetorical studies. *Communication Studies, 46,* 106-117.

Foss, S. K., & Griffin, C. L. (1992). A feminist perspective on rhetorical theory: Toward a clarification of boundaries. *Western Journal of Communication, 56,* 330-349.

Foss, S. K., & Griffin, C. L. (1995). Beyond persuasion: A proposal for an invitational rhetoric. *Communication Monographs, 62,* 2-18.

Foss, S. K., Griffin, C. L., & Foss, K. A. (1997). Transforming rhetoric through feminist reconstruction: A response to the gender diversity perspective. *Women's Studies in Communication, 20,* 117-135.

Foucault, M. (1980). *Power/Knowledge: Selected interviews and other writings, 1972-1977* (C. Gordon, Ed., C. Gordon, L. Marshall, J. Mepham, & K. Soper, Trans.). New York: Pantheon.

Gearhart, S. M. (1979). The womanization of rhetoric. *Women's Studies International Quarterly, 2,* 195-201.

Habermas, J. (1979). *Communication and the evolution of society* (T. McCarthy, Trans.). Boston: Beacon.

Kant, I. (1951). *The critique of judgment* (J. H. Bernard, Trans.). New York: Hafner Press.

Rosenfield, L. W. (1980). The practical celebration of epideictic. In E. E. White (Ed.), *Rhetoric in transition: Studies in the nature and uses of rhetoric.* University Park: Pennsylvania State University Press.

Sloop, J. M., & Ono, K. A. (1997). Out-law discourse: The critical politics of material judgment. *Philosophy and Rhetoric, 30,* 50-69.

Smith, K. K. (1999). *The dominion of voice: Riot, reason, and romance in antebellum politics.* Lawrence: University Press of Kansas.

Spinosa, C., Flores, F., & Dreyfus, H. L. (1997). *Disclosing new worlds: Entrepreneurship, democratic action, and the cultivation of solidarity.* Cambridge, MA: MIT Press.

Trebilcot, J. (1988). Dyke methods. *Hypatia, 3,* 1-13.

Warren, K. J. (1988). Critical thinking and feminism. *Informal Logic, 10,* 31-44.

JEREMIAD

The term **jeremiad** is derived from the name of the Hebrew prophet Jeremiah. Jeremiah lived in the late 7th and early 6th centuries BC. In his prophecies, he warned ancient Israel of its impending doom at the hands of the Babylonians and urged the nation to repent for its sins so that it could be restored to God's good grace. The term jeremiad has been in use since at least the late 18th century to describe a particular form of public discourse that echoes the key themes of Jeremiah's prophecy.

The jeremiad is part of the somewhat loosely organized **epideictic** genre. One of the foremost students of the jeremiad, literary historian Sacvan Bercovitch, described it as a "political sermon" popularized by 17th-century Puritan immigrants to Great Britain's North American colonies (Bercovitch, 1978). The jeremiad "might be called the state-of-the-covenant address, tendered at every public occasion (on days of fasting and prayer, humiliation and thanksgiving, at covenant renewal and artillery company ceremonies, and, most elaborately and solemnly, at election day gatherings)" observed by the Puritan colonists (p. 4). Given its ubiquity at public ceremonies, the jeremiad became an important part of Puritan social and political **rituals.**

What was the substance of the Puritan jeremiad? Howard-Pitney (1990) argued that it had three key elements (see also Murphy, 1990, p. 403). First, the jeremiad rearticulated God's promise to the Puritans. The 17th-century Puritans "believed God had chosen them as the historic instrument of his will. America was destined to be a beacon to the world, lighting and leading the way to the millennium" (Howard-Pitney, 1990, p. 7). The Puritans saw themselves as a special and peculiar people. It was their mission—their "errand"—to keep their covenant with God and to show the world how to live and how to love God. If they kept their part of the bargain, then God would keep his promise and grant the Puritans eternal salvation. Second, the jeremiad criticized members of the Puritan community for their failures, their weaknesses, and their inability to live according to their covenant with God. The jeremiad served as a form of public lamentation, or a way of expressing sorrow and regret, for what was happening to the Puritan community. What was happening, Puritans were told over and over again, was a process of *decline* or a falling away from the terms of the promise. The end result of this element of the jeremiad, Bercovitch (1978) maintained, was to instill a sense of anxiety in the community. The third element of the Puritan jeremiad was "a resolving *prophecy* that society will shortly complete its mission and redeem the promise" (Howard-Pitney, 1990, p. 8). The jeremiad routinely transformed calamities (e.g., outbreaks of disease, crop failures, Indian attacks) into signs that reaffirmed the Puritans' special status as God's chosen people. God had not forsaken them.[1] For the promised redemption to occur, the Puritans had to rededicate or recommit themselves to the terms of their covenant with God. The ultimate end sought by the jeremiad through its blending of promise, decline, and redemption was "cultural revitalization" (Bercovitch, 1978, p. 179).

If the jeremiad remained a unique feature of 17th-century Puritan life, then it would merit the attention of historians and public address scholars but be of little interest to students of rhetoric generally. As numerous scholars have documented, the elements of the Puritan jeremiad have exerted considerable influence on American public discourse. Over time, beginning during the late 18th century, the jeremiad was secularized. This process of secularization should not be surprising given that the jeremiad never was a *purely* religious mode of address. As Bercovitch's (1978) description of it as a "political sermon" would suggest, the jeremiad traditionally straddled the boundary between the secular world of politics and public affairs and the private world of religious experience. Bush (1999) explained, "The major burden of jeremiadic speech is to engender repentance among listeners and exhort them toward fulfillment of their destinies as dictated by the American civil religion" (p. 81).

Two dimensions of the jeremiad's secularization merit brief comment. First, the idea that the Puritans were the chosen people was replaced by the idea that the American people (or, more abstractly, America) were somehow special. As Howard-Pitney (1990) noted, "No belief has been more central to American civil religion than the idea that Americans are in some important sense a chosen people with a historic mission to save and remake the world" (p. 6). Through this substitution or replacement, "America" becomes a **condensation symbol**—a verbal cue that embodies our most basic beliefs and values—and the promise contained in the Puritans' covenant with God becomes our collective promises to each other embodied in the idea of the "American Dream." Second, the Bible and the lives of the saints were replaced by new texts and new heroes—the Declaration of Independence, the Constitution, Jefferson, Washington, Lincoln, and so on—as the sources from which secular Jeremiahs could draw to instruct their audiences on the appropriate policies and practices for realizing America's special role in the world.

Numerous scholars have tracked the various trajectories of the secularized jeremiad. Bercovitch (1978) traced its influence through 19th-century literature and public discourse. Buehler (1998) and Opie and Elliot (1996) detected its presence in environmental discourse.[2] Bell (1993), Bush (1999, pp. 33-51), Howard-Pitney (1990), Hubbard (1986, 1994), and Moses (1982) described how the secularized jeremiad helped to shape the public discourse of America's African American community during the 19th and 20th centuries. Consider, for example, Martin Luther King, Jr.'s famous "I Have a Dream" speech in August 1963. We could see the three elements of the jeremiad rather clearly in this speech. King began by noting the promises that had been made to the black community, directly in the Emancipation Proclamation and indirectly in the Constitution and Declaration of Independence. Then he moved to a vivid depiction of America's fallen state—its unwillingness to "cash the check" and redeem its promises. He concluded, with an almost paradigmatic form of prophesy, his "dream" of what America would be like if only we rededicated ourselves to the terms of our mutual promises—our national covenant. But the jeremiad is not limited to environmentalists or the tradition of African American protest. Murphy (1990) detailed the way in which the secular jeremiad helps to structure Robert Kennedy's discourse in the aftermath of

King's assassination in 1968. Johannesen (1986) described the persistence of the jeremiad in the discourse of Ronald Reagan.

One final example can illustrate the enduring significance of the jeremiad on American public discourse. During the summer of 1979, the American nation was in the throes of a crisis that, although certainly different from those calamities that befell the 17th-century Puritans, managed to induce a significant degree of anxiety. The Organization of Petroleum Exporting Countries (OPEC) seemed to have the nation over a barrel (so to speak); interest rates were skyrocketing; inflation had risen to double digits; and the approval ratings of the incumbent president, Jimmy Carter, had plummeted and appeared to be heading for single digits. Carter clearly faced a policy *exigence* as well as a personal crisis of leadership. His response to the situation came in a nationally televised address on July 15 (after having canceled a scheduled speech to the nation 10 days earlier). If we listened carefully, we could hear echoes of two centuries of "calamity howlers" (a term sometimes used to describe modern Jeremiahs) in Carter's address. Unlike the example of King, Carter did not begin with any explicit references to our collective promises or our national covenant (although he did refer to his personal promise to the American people when he campaigned for office in 1976). In moving into the substance of the nation's problems, Carter briefly assumed the **persona** of the prophet who had been wandering in the wilderness looking for divine guidance. In Carter's case, his wilderness was largely the presidential retreat at Camp David, although he did wander by helicopter to the homes of "average" Americans in Carnegie, Pennsylvania, and Martinsburg, West Virginia. Carter returned from his retreat prepared to report on what he had discovered. And what he discovered was very disturbing. Carter maintained that America faced "a crisis that strikes at the very heart and soul and spirit of our national will." Americans were losing their faith (or their confidence) in themselves, in progress, and in the future. Carter then moved into a more detailed account of the problems facing the nation, and here the echoes of the jeremiad probably were most clear. Carter complained that "too many" Americans "now tend to worship self-indulgence and consumption." We had replaced our spiritual goods with material goods, only to realize that they "cannot fill the emptiness of lives which have no confidence or purpose." The nation was suffering from deep "wounds" left by the legacies of the war in Vietnam and the Watergate scandal. And the government, in the face of this growing crisis, had been "isolated" and incompetent. Carter ended his litany of the signs of decline by noting that the only thing that most Americans could see was "paralysis and stagnation and drift." His performance provided a vivid example of the modern Jeremiah lamenting the pattern of decline that afflicted the community.[3]

Carter devoted the final third of his speech to specific recommendations regarding energy policy, but this section was rather anticlimactic. The real thrust of the speech was to "regain national unity" and "restore" national "faith." Both of these goals were consistent with the jeremiad's tendency to focus more on matters of moral and spiritual restoration than on specific details of public policy.[4] Carter's method of remedying the nation's crisis was a form of what Kenneth Burke called **mortification** or a way of acting very much in keeping with the spirit of the jeremiad. Carter's speech is an interesting case study, in part, because it generally was considered a failure; it did little to restore Americans' confidence in their government, their president, or themselves. A question to consider is whether Carter's apparent failure was the result of his instantiation of the **tradition** of the jeremiad or whether it might speak to the declining force and appeal of the discursive form.

Finally, issues that have arisen in the scholarly literature on the jeremiad intersect with other concepts and issues in contemporary rhetorical studies. Two examples can illustrate this point. First, as Bercovitch (1978) recognized, the jeremiad sought to reconcile the potentially antagonistic ideas of "progress" and "continuity" (p. 71). Practitioners within the jeremiad tradition asserted the possibility of progressing beyond our current state by acting in ways that established continuity with the past. If this seems paradoxical (how do we go beyond something while still maintaining continuity with it?), then it is a paradox very similar to what some scholars find at the center of the idea of practical wisdom or **prudence.** If prudence is understood as "stable innovation," then it might be the case that one of its paradigmatic manifestations is in the jeremiad tradition. Second, the nature of the jeremiad lends support to those critics and theorists who argue that the practices of most modern social formations contain or render impotent any subversive forces that might arise within it. Building off of Bercovitch's discussion of the way in which the jeremiad contributes to cultural **hegemony,** Murphy (1990) made this point clear in his study of Robert Kennedy. According to Murphy,

> The jeremiad limits the scope of reform and the depth of social criticism . . . [because] jeremiadic strategies function to transform dissent and doubt about American society into a rededication to the principles of American culture. . . . The jeremiad deflects attention away from possible institutional or systemic flaws and toward considerations of individual sin. (p. 402)

Containment by way of a deflection away from systemic problems was visible in Carter's 1979 address. Rooted within the jeremiad tradition, Carter appeared incapable of understanding the problem of, for example, rampant materialism as a systemic feature of a capitalist economic system. Instead, consistent with Murphy's observation, Carter defined the problem as a flaw in our individual and collective moral constitutions. Further reflection and critical investigations are necessary to determine whether or not the jeremiad as a discursive form is capable of articulating a significant challenge to, or merely reinforcing the hegemony of, the "symbol of America" or the American Dream.[5]

Notes

1. As Darsey (1997) noted, "The putative view of the jeremiad as a speech of woe notwithstanding, prophetic religion is profoundly optimistic" (p. 114).

2. On the link between the jeremiad and environmental discourse, see also Ellis (1993, pp. 171-172).

3. Hahn (1980) noted the religious themes and the motif of rebirth in the speech but failed to appreciate the way in which these elements come together in the jeremiad.

4. In this regard, see Murphy's (1990) analysis of Robert Kennedy's eschewal of policy goals in the aftermath of King's assassination.

5. See Ellis (1993, pp. 170-174), Howard-Pitney (1990, p. 186), and Jasinski (1997, p. 89; 1999).

References and Additional Reading

Bell, B. W. (1993). The African American jeremiad and Frederick Douglass' Fourth of July 1852 speech. In P. Goetsch & G. Hurm (Eds.), *The Fourth of July: Political oratory and literary reactions, 1776-1876.* Tübingen, Germany: Gunter Narr Verlag.

Bercovitch, S. (1978). *The American jeremiad.* Madison: University of Wisconsin Press.

Bormann, E. (1977). Fetching good out of evil: A rhetorical use of calamity. *Quarterly Journal of Speech, 63,* 130-139.

Buehler, D. O. (1998). Permanence and change in Theodore Roosevelt's conservation jeremiad. *Western Journal of Communication, 62,* 439-458.

Bush, H. K., Jr. (1999). *American declarations: Rebellion and repentance in American cultural history.* Urbana: University of Illinois Press.

Darsey, J. (1997). *The prophetic tradition and radical rhetoric in America.* New York: New York University Press.

Diffley, K. (1988). "Erecting anew the standard of freedom": Salmon P. Chase's "Appeal of the Independent Democrats" and the rise of the Republican party. *Quarterly Journal of Speech, 74,* 401-415.

Dionisopoulos, G. N., Gallagher, V. J., Goldzwig, S. R., & Zarefsky, D. (1992). Martin Luther King, the American Dream, and Vietnam: A collision of rhetorical trajectories. *Western Journal of Communication, 56,* 91-107.

Ellis, R. J. (1993). *American political cultures.* New York: Oxford University Press.

Griffin, C. J. G. (1982). Sins of the fathers: The jeremiad and the Franco-American crisis in the fast day ser-

mons of 1798. *Southern Speech Communication Journal, 47,* 389-401.
Hahn, D. (1980). Flailing the profligate: Carter's energy sermon. *Presidential Studies Quarterly, 10,* 583-587.
Howard-Pitney, D. (1990). *The Afro-American jeremiad: Appeals for justice in America.* Philadelphia: Temple University Press.
Hubbard, D. (1986). David Walker's *Appeal* and the American Puritan jeremiadic tradition. *Centennial Review, 30,* 331-346.
Hubbard, D. (1994). *The sermon and the African American literary imagination.* Columbia: University of Missouri Press.
Jasinski, J. (1997). Rearticulating history in epideictic discourse: Frederick Douglass's "The Meaning of the Fourth of July to the Negro." In T. W. Benson (Ed.), *Rhetoric and political culture in nineteenth-century America.* East Lansing: Michigan State University Press.
Jasinski, J. (1999, February). *Martin Luther King's "A Time to Break Silence" and the American jeremiad tradition.* Paper presented at the meeting of the Western Communication Association, Vancouver, British Columbia.
Johannesen, R. L. (1985). The jeremiad and Jenkin Lloyd Jones. *Communication Monographs, 52,* 156-172.
Johannesen, R. L. (1986). Ronald Reagan's economic jeremiad. *Central States Speech Journal, 37,* 79-89.
Moses, W. J. (1982). *Black messiahs and Uncle Toms: Social and literary manipulations of a religious myth.* University Park: Pennsylvania State University Press.
Murphy, J. M. (1990). "A time of shame and sorrow": Robert F. Kennedy and the American jeremiad. *Quarterly Journal of Speech, 76,* 401-414.
Opie, J., & Elliot, N. (1996). Tracking the elusive jeremiad: The rhetorical character of American environmental discourse. In J. G. Cantrill & C. L. Oravec (Eds.), *The symbolic earth: Discourse and our creation of the environment.* Lexington: University Press of Kentucky.
Ritter, K. W. (1980). American political rhetoric and the jeremiad tradition: Presidential nomination acceptance addresses, 1960-1976. *Central States Speech Journal, 31,* 153-171.
Smith, C. A. (1994). The jeremiadic logic of Bill Clinton's policy speeches. In S. A. Smith (Ed.), *Bill Clinton on stump, state, and stage: The rhetorical road to the White House.* Fayetteville: University of Arkansas Press.

JUDGMENT

Discussing Aristotle's (1954) *Rhetoric,* Grimaldi (1980) wrote, "The rhetorical methodology so constituted has one primary objective: to enable the person to whom the spoken or written word is addressed to make a judgment" (p. 350). **Judgment,** Grimaldi suggested, is the end of rhetorical practice (see also Farrell, 1993). Rhetorical scholar Edwin Black, commenting on *Rhetoric* 1377b21-1377b22 where Aristotle (1954) discussed the relationship between rhetoric and judgment, raised a provocative question: "What can it mean to say that 'the object of rhetoric is judgment'?" (Black, 1978, p. 103). In posing this question, Black was one of the first contemporary rhetorical scholars to make the concept of judgment an explicit object of theoretical reflection. Drawing on Black as well as scholarship outside the field, a number of scholars have contributed to this line of theoretical inquiry.

We can begin this survey of recent work on the concept of judgment by considering how Black answered his own query. Black (1978) approached his question by positing a distinction between coming to a judgment and coming to a belief. He wrote,

> Our standards for evaluating judgments differ patently from our standards for evaluating convictions or beliefs, so that judgment and belief are not synonymous terms. . . . The most crucial difference between judgment and belief is that a judgment is supposed to follow from a definitively systematized procedure of adjudication, but the procedures for acquiring or coming to hold beliefs vary so considerably, according to the subject of the belief, that the same procedural standards are not applicable. (p. 110)

Black was insistent on this difference:

> While there is a certain procedure that one is supposed to follow in coming to a judgment, there is no particular procedure that one is supposed to follow in coming to hold a conviction. Unlike *belief* or *conviction,* the term judgment entails a procedural norm in its very usage. (p. 110)

These reflections on the difference between belief and judgment allowed Black to respond to his question: "A rhetorical theory worked out on the assumption that the end of rhetoric is judgment would differ from one that assumed that the end of rhetoric was belief" (p. 111). Positing judgment as the end of rhetoric leads to a narrow, overly prescriptive, overly rationalistic theory of rhetoric. That is what it means to say that judgment is the end of rhetoric. Black's analysis of judgment as the end or object of rhetoric serves as one of his arguments for rejecting Aristotelian theory.

A very different answer to Black's question, and a different reading of Aristotle's (1954) *Rhetoric,* can be found in Beiner's (1983) book *Political Judgment.* Somewhat like Black, Beiner found contrast a useful way of proceeding. But whereas Black contrasted belief and judgment, Beiner focused on contrasting Aristotle's discussion of rhetoric and judgment to the account of this relationship found in the work of one of the key figures of Enlightenment philosophy, Immanuel Kant. What Black saw as inherent to the idea of judgment—that it entails a formal systematized procedure—Beiner viewed as a legacy of Kantianism. Beiner argued that the tradition of rhetoric, and Aristotle's writing on the subject, provides a different understanding or conceptualization of judgment. According to Beiner, "Rhetoric expresses this sense of community by accommodating itself to the particular substantive beliefs and desires of the listeners it addresses rather than holding to abstract or formal principles of judgment" (p. 101). In effect, Beiner's reflections on judgment dissolved the opposition between judgment and belief that is central to Black's position. Without that opposition, Black's skepticism about judgment being the end or object of rhetoric is unfounded. Beiner insisted that rhetoric constitutes one of the "substantive conditions of political life and of political judgment" (p. 101).

Beiner's linkage of rhetoric and judgment, inspired by his alternative reading of Aristotle, has encouraged a line of conceptually oriented criticism in rhetorical studies concerned with the relationship between rhetoric and judgment. Among the critical studies exploring this relationship are Browne and Leff's (1985) analysis of Edmund Burke's speech in 1780 to the electors in Bristol, England; Farrell's (1990) and Manolescu's (1998) explorations of Fisher Ames's speech in the U.S. House of Representatives regarding the Jay Treaty in 1796; Jasinski's (1992) investigation of the constitutional ratification debate of 1787-1788; and Browne's (1993) extended reading of key performances by Burke.

What tentative conclusions and directions for further inquiry emerge from this line of critical scholarship? First, political judgment, like rhetoric, is understood as a human faculty or capacity. The faculty of judgment mediates or negotiates political flux and political principle. As Browne and Leff (1985) explained, political judgment is "the meeting ground between the flux of political circumstance and the reflexive principles that guide our sense of continuity in the public world" (p. 198). What is the "flux of political circumstance"? We can think of political flux as the constantly shifting concrete particulars that saturate our public world. The concrete particulars of politics include specific political personalities (e.g., Ross Perot, Jesse Jackson, Newt Gingrich), economic and ideological interests (and the various organizations that represent and advocate these interests), policy proposals, the cycle of elections, the practices of the news media, disruptive events and national disasters (e.g., bombings, scandals, stock market crashes, heat waves) for which some type of response is expected, and the overall economic and social conditions of society. What are the "reflexive principles" that help to organize political life? These include the guiding doctrines inscribed in foundational texts, such as the Declaration of Independence and the Constitution (e.g., liberty, equality, legitimate authority), and the normative ideals embodied in widely shared **ideographs** (e.g., freedom, property rights, honesty). To assert, as Browne and Leff did, that these principles are a source of continuity is not to say that they are timeless and unchanging; clearly, our understanding of the normative principles of political life change over time and can be intensely contested at any point in time. But the continual recourse to these principles, despite contestation and change, allows them to function as a source of stability in political life. Judgment, then, is the "meeting ground"—the mode of practical conduct—where principles and particulars intersect and interact. Farrell (1993) observed, "By judging, we help to perform the virtues of public life" (p. 75).

Second, rhetorical practice both enacts and shapes or guides the practice of judgment. Advocates implicitly, and at times quite explicitly, display standards or modes of judgment, or ways of reconciling principles and particulars, that help to structure their advocacy efforts (on this point, see especially Browne, 1993). The standards or modes of judgment displayed by an advocate, in turn, function as a way of guiding or shaping the judgment of addressed audiences. Jasinski (1992), for example, focused on how the standards of judgment displayed in Federalist and anti-Federalist advocacy worked as modes of inducing the desired judgment from the public.

Third, the "space" of judgment[1] is divided or internally bifurcated. Put differently, the practice or activity of judgment is marked by certain tensions that must be negotiated, and temporarily resolved, by those engaging in this mode of action. Reflecting on the different investigations of judgment, Farrell (1990) noted "a constant rhetorical negotiation in the deliberative sphere over the proper attitude and 'distance' for rendering legitimate political judgment" (p. 431). Because the internal bifurcation of judgment presents the greatest opportunity for further investigations of the relationship between rhetoric and judgment, it merits further elaboration.

Extending Beiner's (1983) theoretical account of the nature of political judgment, Jasinski (1991) offered a possible way of unpacking the internal tensions or divisions marking the space/activity of judgment. Jasinski began his account by suggesting that the divided space of judgment is an extension on a division implicit in the act of advocacy. He argued that advocates solicit an audience's judgment with respect to (a) a specific instrumental goal (e.g., a policy proposition, an evaluative claim, a declaration of guilt or innocence) and (b) the validity (soundness) and legitimacy (appropriateness) of argumentative form (see also Jasinski, 1990). In most instances of advocacy, the two dimensions of this division —the instrumental and the formal—are so intertwined as to become conceptually indistinct. Jasinski tried to clarify and illustrate the division in the act of advocacy by way of the practice of concurrent opinions in jurisprudence. Probably the most well-known examples of the practice of concurrent opinions are found in the decisions of the Supreme Court. When a justice in the majority issues a concurrent opinion, it indicates that he or she agrees with the course of action (the instrumental dimension) that has been selected but disagrees with the grounds or reasons (the formal dimension) that have been adduced. In effect, Jasinski inscribed Browne and Leff's tension between the particulars and principles at stake in any judgment in the practice of advocacy itself.[2]

More important, Jasinski (1991) maintained that the interaction of the instrumental and formal dimensions of advocacy—particulars and principles—initiates a play of "antagonistic orientations" that "constitutes the existential space of political judgment as a structured field of tension" (p. 192). These orientations and the structured field or space of judgment are summarized in Figure J.1.

The antagonistic role orientations of actor and spectator were at the center of Beiner's (1983) and Bernstein's (1986) reflections on political judgment. These two positions indicate the basic stances that people have available for relating to the social world and from which they might judge actions and events in that world. Adopting the role orientation of actor or participant enables the individual to focus strategically on the specific choices that are available for achieving instrumental ends and purposes, whereas the more withdrawn

STRUCTURAL ANTAGONISMS CONSTITUTING THE SPACE OF JUDGMENT

ROLE ORIENTATION	COMMUNITY ORIENTATION	POLITICAL ORIENTATION	TEMPORAL ORIENTATION
actor	particular	partisan advocate	synchronic
spectator	universal	impartial citizen	diachronic

Figure J.1. Structural Antagonisms Constituting the Space of Judgment

stance of the spectator allows individuals to appreciate the significance of the events that are occurring around them and provides them with the opportunity to organize their perceptions and determine the meanings of events. Some form of communal orientation or affiliation is essential to the faculty of judgment. Beiner (1983), for example, wrote, "Judgment implies a community that supplies common grounds or criteria by which one attempts to decide" (p. 143). At various moments in their lives, individuals orient themselves by way of a number of different particular communities—nation-state, workplace, profession or occupation, class, religion, racial/ethnic background, gender, neighborhood, **generation**, and so on. Each of these specific communities provides principles, values, and goals on which individuals can draw in the interrelated processes of advocacy and judgment. The idea of a universal community is more abstract but, nonetheless, is a powerful source of principles, values, and goals. Individuals frequently affiliate themselves with goals of the universal community such as "human rights" or with seemingly universal principles such as being "civilized" and being "reasonable." The third orientation, political, refers to the attitude or stance that individuals adopt toward political affairs. Each specific political orientation entails a different vision of the political process. The political partisan generally believes that politics is a process of adjusting competing interests and ambitions in an inherently competitive and pluralistic environment, whereas the impartial citizen sees politics as the pursuit of the general or public interest in an environment of mutual cooperation and public sacrifice. Finally, we find contrasting temporal orientations. The synchronic orientation focuses primarily on the immediate or short-term temporal horizon, whereas the diachronic orientation adopts a broader, enlarged, or expanded approach to one's situatedness in time. This enlarged temporal outlook applies to both the past and the future.

How might this account of the internal bifurcation of judgment (viewed as a structured field of tensions) contribute to our understanding of the relationship between rhetorical practice and the faculty of judgment? Essentially, the antagonistic orientations provide recurrent resources that advocates can employ for constructing standards or modes of judgment for themselves as well as for their audiences. When engaged in the activity of judgment or the practice of advocacy leading to the judgment of an audience, an individual must respond to the pull of the antagonistic orientations. Should the individual judge/advocate from the position of actor or spectator? In judging/advocating a judgment, should the individual orient himself or herself to a particular community or to an idealized universal community? Should the individual judge/advocate from the standpoint of a political partisan or a disinterested citizen? In judging/advocating a judgment, should the individual focus on the demands of the immediate moment (synchronic) or adopt a more long-term outlook (diachronic)? The individual's negotiation of these antagonistic orientations does not always lead to a *disjunctive* either/or choice. Instead of choosing between actor and spectator—between synchronic and diachronic—the individual might try to craft a standard of judgment that blends or balances the conflicting positions. "In this case," an advocate might argue, "the way to proceed is to be both an actor and a spectator."

Critical analysis of rhetorical performances might then focus on how advocates discursively negotiate (through arguments, stylistic vehicles, and other strategies) this field of tensions—how they depict specific orientations as appropriate for the issue at hand, how they reject or subvert rival orientations as inappropriate, how they combine aspects of the different orientations (role, community, political, and temporal), or how they attempt to craft a stable standard of judgment within one of the antagonistic orientations. Consider some recent controversies and how the orientations might provide entry points for further critical analysis. The debate over the North American Free Trade Agreement (NAFTA) involved the antagonism between the two temporal orientations. Supporters of the treaty adopted, and urged audiences to adopt, a more diachronic orientation through *pragmatic arguments.* They focused on the "big picture"—the shift in the global economy and the need for the United States to remain competitive for the long haul. If that meant some temporary sacrifices in the short term, so be it, because in the long run the United States would benefit. Opponents of the treaty focused on the immediate loss of jobs that they believed the treaty would produce. They were extremely reluctant to adopt the diachronic vision of the treaty's supporters. For many treaty opponents, a standard of judgment fashioned from the diachronic orientation (in combination with other orientations) was a sham; they tried to subvert this orientation by revealing how it functioned as a **eulogistic covering** for the protection and enhancement of the material interests of the dominant class. As a second example, consider the public debate in the aftermath of the O. J. Simpson murder trial verdict. Many Americans (predominantly white) did not believe that there was "reasonable doubt" in this case; Simpson, in their judgment, was guilty. But the largely African American jury found reasonable doubt and acquitted Simpson. Many who disagreed with the jury's verdict suggested that jury members had failed to adopt a universal community orientation—that they failed to implement the legal standard of reasonable doubt in a manner consistent with its nature as a universal (at least for the United States) legal principle. Critics charged that the jury members were too invested in their particular communal attachments and that those attachments clouded their judgment. Those defending the jury's verdict (although perhaps not its instrumental decision) maintained that the idea of a universal standard of reasonable doubt is, to a large extent, a fiction; all the jury could do was understand reasonable doubt within the context of their particular communal orientations. If the standards of reasonableness differ between white and black Americans, then that might be a sign that the problems of race relations in America are far from resolved.

Judgment is one of a number of "mid-level" theoretical concepts currently receiving significant attention in rhetorical studies. The crucial challenge is to deepen our understanding of the nature of judgment and the relationship between rhetorical practice and the faculty of political judgment. Understanding judgment as marked by an internal bifurcation that is discursively negotiated and renegotiated might present one avenue for further reflection and critical analysis. Another potentially fruitful path is suggested by the growing efforts to theorize judgment from a *postmodern* perspective (Sloop & McDaniel, 1998; Sloop & Ono, 1997).[3] Reflection on, and examination of, the processes of judgment most likely will constitute an important avenue of inquiry in rhetorical studies in the foreseeable future.

Notes

1. Thinking about judgment as occurring in a space was suggested by Browne and Leff's (1985) "meeting ground" *metaphor* as well as by Sloop and Ono's (1997) discussion of judgment as arising within "an imaginary space" that is discursively constructed (p. 64).

2. Approaching the issue of judgment from a *postmodern* perspective, Sloop and Ono (1997) reached a similar conclusion. They wrote that "in addition to resolving the conflict," the decision on the instrumental plane "affirms the idiom" or argument form "in which the phrase is spoken" (p. 55).

3. Although there are important differences between the "Aristotelian-Beinerian" (for lack of a better term) strand of inquiry and the emerging postmodern perspective, points of convergence nevertheless exist. For example, each mode of inquiry emphasizes the need to engage judgment as a concrete, situated, and discursively animated practice, what Sloop and Ono (1997) described as "a materialist's conception of judgment" (p. 54).

References and Additional Reading

Aristotle. (1954). *Rhetoric* (W. R. Roberts, Trans.). New York: Modern Library.

Beiner, R. (1983). *Political judgment.* Chicago: University of Chicago Press.

Bernstein, R. J. (1986). Judging—The actor and the spectator. In R. J. Bernstein, *Philosophical profiles: Essays in a pragmatic mode.* Philadelphia: University of Pennsylvania Press.

Black, E. (1978). *Rhetorical criticism.* Madison: University of Wisconsin Press.

Browne, S. H. (1993). *Edmund Burke and the discourse of virtue.* Tuscaloosa: University of Alabama Press.

Browne, S. H., & Leff, M. C. (1985). Political judgment and rhetorical argument: Edmund Burke's paradigm. In J. R. Cox, M. Sillars, & G. Walker (Eds.), *Argument and social practice: Proceedings of the Fourth SCA/AFA Conference on Argumentation.* Annandale, VA: Speech Communication Association.

Farrell, J. M. (1990). Fisher Ames and political judgment: Reason, passion, and vehement style in the Jay Treaty speech. *Quarterly Journal of Speech, 76,* 415-434.

Farrell, T. B. (1993). *Norms of rhetorical culture.* New Haven, CT: Yale University Press.

Grimaldi, W. M. A. (1980). *Aristotle RHETORIC I: A commentary.* New York: Fordham University Press.

Jasinski, J. (1990). An exploration of form and force in rhetoric and argumentation. In D. C. Williams & M. D. Hazen (Eds.), *Argumentation theory and the rhetoric of assent.* Tuscaloosa: University of Alabama Press.

Jasinski, J. (1991). Argument, judgment, and the problem of alienation. In F. H. van Eemeren, R. Grootendorst, J. A. Blair, & C. A. Willard (Eds.), *Proceedings of the Second International Conference on Argumentation.* Amsterdam: Stichting Internationaal Centrum voor de Studie van Argumentatie en Taalbeheersing (SICSAT).

Jasinski, J. (1992). Rhetoric and judgment in the constitutional ratification debate of 1787-1788: An exploration in the relationship between theory and critical practice. *Quarterly Journal of Speech, 78,* 197-218.

Lucaites, J. L., & Taylor, C. A. (1993). Theorizing the grounds of rhetorical judgment. *Informal Logic, 15,* 29-40.

Manolescu, B. I. (1998). Style and spectator judgment in Fisher Ames's Jay Treaty speech. *Quarterly Journal of Speech, 84,* 41-61.

Ruderman, R. S. (1997). Aristotle and the recovery of political judgment. *American Political Science Review, 91,* 409-420.

Sloop, J. M., & McDaniel, J. P. (Eds.). (1998). *Judgment calls: Rhetoric, politics, and indeterminacy.* Boulder, CO: Westview.

Sloop, J. M., & Ono, K. A. (1997). Out-law discourse: The critical politics of material judgment. *Philosophy and Rhetoric, 30,* 50-69.

Steinberger, P. J. (1993). *The concept of political judgment.* Chicago: University of Chicago Press.

Whedbee, K. (1998). Authority, freedom, and liberal judgment: The "presumptions" and "presumptuousness" of Whately, Mill, and Tocqueville. *Quarterly Journal of Speech, 84,* 171-189.

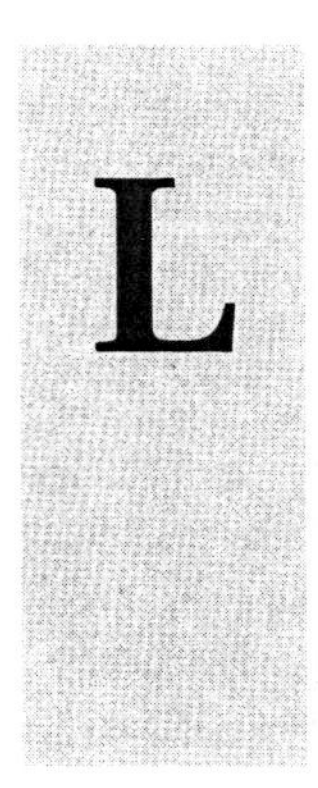

LOCAL STABILITY

In their contribution to the 1990 *Western Journal of Speech Communication* symposium on rhetorical criticism, Michael Leff and Andrew Sachs introduced the concept of **local stability** as a way of negotiating the conceptual challenges that the ideas of **contingency** (lack of certainty and necessity in human affairs) and *indeterminacy* (lack of a final or foundational meaning in human discourse) pose for rhetorical practice (Leff & Sachs, 1990). Traditional thinking on rhetoric often is read as advocating a mastery or **domestication** of contingency (Gaonkar, 1992) and as advancing the possibility of fixed or determinate meaning. This traditional line of thought, it often is argued, makes rhetorical theory decidedly "modern" and, hence, vulnerable to criticism from the growing trends in postmodern theory and criticism.[1]

Leff and Sachs (1990) did not address the modern-postmodern theoretical impasse directly in their essay. Their position emerged from reflection on the "form/content dichotomy" (p. 255) that they found to be persistent in rhetorical criticism. They argued that the dichotomy has helped to produce a division in critical practice between methods that desire to move into texts but lack the conceptual resources to do so and methods that "take us more deeply into the [larger realm of] symbolic process[es]" (p. 255) but that eschew interest in particular discursive texts or performances. The approach to criticism that they defended emphasizes "the situated character of rhetorical discourse and its function as a practical mode of encompassing concrete social and political issues" (p. 255).[2] Such an approach to criticism "views the rhetorical work not as a mirror of reality but as a field of action unified into a functional and *locally stable* product" (p. 255, emphasis added).[3]

Something close to Leff and Sachs's (1990) sense of "local stability" can be located in Laclau and Mouffe's (1985) postmodern account of **discourse.** They wrote, "Any discourse is constituted as an attempt to dominate the field of discursivity, to arrest the flow of differences, to construct a centre" (p. 112). In short, discourse fixes meaning. But like Leff and Sachs, Laclau and Mouffe emphasized the "partial" or incomplete nature of discursively constituted meaning. Discursive or rhetorical practice cannot completely "arrest the flow of differences"; it cannot fully "encompass" or organize the contingent features of the world. Ivie (1998) also developed an account of rhetorical **deliberation** that resembles Leff and Sachs's sense of local stability. Ivie wrote that "participation in a rhetorical culture" enables advocates and audiences "to arrive at temporary closures in particular situations." He continued, "Public advocacy addresses the problems of identification and division through configurations of meaning that require an audience's ratification in order to prevail *momentarily* over alternative frames of acceptance and rejection" (p. 409, emphasis added). All of these scholars suggested that discursive practice is capable of crafting incomplete, but locally stable, configurations of meaning.

Although Leff and Sachs's (1990) discussion was not addressed directly to the problems of contingency and *indeterminacy,* their idea of local stability, along with Laclau and Mouffe's (1985) sense of partial fixation of meaning and Ivie's (1998) idea of temporary closure, spoke to these issues. The task of rhetorical discourse is to organize or "encompass" the particulars of a **situation.** These particulars vary from situation to situation but generally will include people, motives, interests, accounts of events, public opinion (**doxa**), definitions of key terms and principles (or **ideographs**), inherited **traditions,** formal and informal institutional structures, and forms of political and social power. The contingency thesis maintains that the configuration of these particulars rarely (if ever) is certain and necessary.[4] Situations *are* contingent and unstable; they are constantly in a state of flux. And even when a situation seems to remain stable over time and appears to be "natural," that appearance ultimately is an illusion. As a simple example of the point, consider the aftermath of the tragic bombing in Oklahoma City, Oklahoma, in 1995. The initial configuration of particulars created a situation of foreign terrorism reaching into the heartland of America. Over time, through the agency of various forms of public discourse, the particulars of the situation were reorganized. A new menace—domestic militant reactionaries—was uncovered and used as the organizing focus of the particulars. But is this the only way in which the particulars can be configured, encompassed, or organized? Do we now have a final, fixed, determinate meaning for the event? No. Over time, the nature and meaning of this event undoubtedly will change. This is one of the basic insights of postmodern thought.

Leff and Sachs's (1990) idea of local stability does not deny a strong sense of contingency or indeterminacy. What it does is suggest that discursive practice has the capacity to arrest (if only temporarily) our fluctuating condition of contingency and indeterminacy so as to make collective deliberation, decision, and action possible. As Garver (1994) noted, the function of rhetoric is "to make the practically determinable" (yet ultimately indeterminate) "determinate" (p. 78). Few (if any) texts or discursive performances are constructed in a way that fully eradicates contingency and indeterminacy. When "pushed," or when subjected to careful analysis and scrutiny, any text can be made to deconstruct. For example, an advocate might *warrant* a policy claim by recourse to an appeal to principle (e.g., liberty, freedom, democracy). But does this warrant have absolute power? Does it function as a permanent foundation for all future decision and action? No. Following Leff and Sachs and the other scholars discussed in this entry, we should conclude that it is, and only can be, "locally stable." The appeal, if effective, creates a momentary or temporary finality.[5] It is possible for subsequent advocates to appropriate such appeals, thereby creating a state of social and cultural **hegemony** that makes the appeal to principle part of a totalizing **discursive formation.** The critical question, frequently raised by postmodern thinkers, is whether the act of advocacy ultimately is a totalizing gesture. Does rhetorical advocacy inherently function to deny or repress contingency and indeterminacy? The answer that Leff and Sachs seemed to imply is that although advocacy, as a collective process, may result in totalizing discursive formations, public advocacy as a practice does not, in any necessary sense, entail totalization at the level of the local situation. Rhetorical advocacy crafts points of stability that allow decision and action, but these points eventually dissolve back into the flux of contingency and indeterminacy that constitutes our human condition.[6]

When extended in the manner outlined here, Leff and Sachs's (1990) idea of local stability points in the direction of a nonfoundational, nontotalizing form of *contingent advocacy.* There is, at the center of this conceptualization of public discourse, a tension that would seem to be present in all advocacy efforts—a tension between the drive toward "stability" and all that it entails (e.g., permanence, determinate meaning) and an appreciation of, and respect for, the "local" and all that it entails (e.g., change, flux). This tension, then, might be a recurrent focal point for critical analysis. Critics could try to describe how particular texts and performances negotiate this tension.[7] What the idea of contingent advocacy, emerging from the concept of local stability, provides is a way of responding to the postmodern indictment of rhetoric and advocacy as a type of dangerous "general persuasion" (on this indictment, see Rooney, 1989).

Notes

1. Kastely (1997) offered a different reading of traditional rhetorics—one very close to the thrust of Leff and Sachs's (1990) concept of local stability—when he wrote, "Traditional rhetorics see any determinate closure as inherently situational, temporary, and capable of being undone" (p. 197).

2. The term *encompass* was borrowed from Burke's (1957) discussion of the way in which literary works are "strategies for the encompassing of situations" (p. 3).

3. On the metaphor "field of action," see the discussion in the entry for **text.** See also Leff's discussion of the idea of "local integration" as a way of theorizing propriety or **decorum** (Rosteck & Leff, 1989), Leff's (1990) reading of Cicero's concept of decorum as an effort "to discover points of local stasis where function, form, and subject interact harmoniously" (p. 126), and Leff's (1997) discussion of the text as "a point of local closure."

4. See also Laclau and Mouffe (1985) on the discursive *construction* of necessity.

5. The use of the figure of *oxymoron* here—the incompatible ideas of "temporary" and "final"—is intentional. The figure of the oxymoron appears frequently in many forms of contemporary theory. Its recurrent presence suggests that it is a suitable **representative anecdote,** in Burke's terms, for the paradoxical human condition. For two recent examples of theoretical oxymora that, like Leff and Sachs's (1990) idea of local stability, acknowledge the precariousness of rhetorical action, see Ono and Sloop's (1995) discussion of "conditional essentialism" and Wess's (1996) discussion of "contingent hierarchization."

6. This description of rhetorical advocacy in many respects parallels Sunstein's (1996) account of the way in which "incompletely theorized agreements" enable legal argumentation.

7. See, for example, Hart's (1990) effort at deconstructing a speech by Gerald Ford that explored this tension in a somewhat indirect way.

References and Additional Reading

Burke, K. (1957). *The philosophy of literary form* (rev. ed.). New York: Vintage.

Gaonkar, D. (1992, November). *Rhetoric of contingency and contingency of rhetoric.* Paper presented at the meeting of the Speech Communication Association, Chicago.

Garver, E. (1994). *Aristotle's RHETORIC: An art of character.* Chicago: University of Chicago Press.

Hart, R. (1990). *Modern rhetorical criticism.* Glenview, IL: Scott, Foresman.

Ivie, R. L. (1998). Democratic deliberation in a rhetorical republic. *Quarterly Journal of Speech, 84,* 491-505.

Kastely, J. L. (1997). *Rethinking the rhetorical tradition: From Plato to postmodernism.* New Haven, CT: Yale University Press.

Laclau, E., & Mouffe, C. (1985). *Hegemony and socialist strategy: Towards a radical democratic politics.* London: Verso.

Leff, M. (1990). Decorum and rhetorical interpretation: The Latin humanistic tradition and contemporary critical theory. *Vichiana, 1,* 107-126. (3a series)

Leff, M. C. (1997). Lincoln among the nineteenth-century orators. In T. W. Benson (Ed.), *Rhetoric and political culture in nineteenth-century America.* East Lansing: Michigan State University Press.

Leff, M., & Sachs, A. (1990). Words the most like things: Iconicity and the rhetorical text. *Western Journal of Speech Communication, 54,* 252-273.

Ono, K. A., & Sloop, J. M. (1995). The critique of vernacular discourse. *Communication Monographs, 62,* 19-46.

Rooney, E. (1989). *Seductive reasoning: Pluralism as the problematic of contemporary literary theory.* Ithaca, NY: Cornell University Press.

Rosteck, T., & Leff, M. (1989). Piety, propriety, and perspective: An interpretation and application of key terms in Kenneth Burke's *Permanence and Change. Western Journal of Speech Communication, 53,* 327-341.

Sunstein, C. R. (1996). *Legal reasoning and political conflict.* New York: Oxford University Press.

Wess, R. (1996). *Kenneth Burke: Rhetoric, subjectivity, postmodernism.* Cambridge, UK: Cambridge University Press.

LOGIC

A standard textbook definition of **logic** defines it as "the study of the methods and principles used in distinguishing correct from incorrect reasoning" (Copi, 1968, p. 3). To appreciate fully Copi's (1968) definition, we need to consider what is meant by the concept of *reasoning.* Kirwan (1995) asserted, "The word 'reasoning' describes two associated *processes:* searching for . . . reasons (often cooperatively) and giving them when you or somebody else has found them" (p. 748). Kirwan suggested that we search for reasons when confronted by practical, theoretical, or response problems.[1] He said that "searching for reasons involves cogitation" or a process of "thinking things through" (p. 748). But as Copi (1968) noted, reasoning does not refer to—and, hence, logic is not concerned with—simply "*any* process that occurs in people's minds. . . . All reasoning is thinking, but not all thinking is reasoning" (p. 4). Copi continued, "Reasoning is a special kind of thinking in which inference takes place or in which conclusions are drawn from premises" (p. 5). Reasoning, in short, is a process of producing reasons for action, belief, and evaluation. It is a mode of thought whereby we search for and, eventually, arrive at solutions to practical, theoretical, or response problems.

Kirwan (1995) observed,

> Giving reasons is setting them out, to oneself or someone else. This too is a process. . . . Since it can be rehearsed and repeated, it is likely to be more orderly than the search was. And since it is useful for persuading people and necessary for transmitting knowledge . . ., there is a motive for making it as orderly and lucid as possible. Even if you are not going public, reason-giving is a way of checking for yourself that a search has been conducted properly—that you have reasoned well. (p. 749)

Logic is, then, essentially a process for testing or evaluating particular reasons and the larger process of reasoning. It is a way of determining whether one has "reasoned well." It works on and with the discursive manifestations of the process of reason giving—**arguments.** According to Kirwan, logic "proposes rules and principles that good arguments must observe" (p. 749). But "good," in the context of logic, has a specific meaning. It does not mean effective with a particular audience or useful as a way of responding to an interlocutor. Logically good means *valid* or *sound.* The premise statements of a valid argument provide, in Copi's (1968) terms, "conclusive evidence for its conclusion" (p. 21).[2]

Given that the fields of logic and rhetoric both are concerned with argument and the process of reason giving, it should not be surprising that the scope and methods of these two fields have generated some controversy. Over the years, many scholars understood the study of argument practice as an "applied logic" (Cox & Willard, 1982). Anderson and Mortensen (1967) asserted,

> Critics of argument have relied almost without exception upon the critical tools of the philosopher-logician as a method of ascertaining the logical worth of rhetorical argument. The logician, according to the prevailing view, offers the appropriate critical apparatus for determining under what linguistic conditions one proposition may be said to follow from another. (p. 143; see also Mortensen and Anderson, 1970)

Logic supplies the standards for valid inference or connection between premises (Simmons, 1960) and also provides a handy typology of defective arguments—the **fallacies.** Students of public discourse need only apply these standards to their specific objects of inquiry.

Beginning during the middle of the 20th century, a number of scholars (e.g., Perelman & Olbrechts-Tyteca, 1969[3]; Toulmin, 1958) began to attack the accepted traditional view of the logic-rhetoric relationship (see also Cox & Willard, 1982, pp. xxii-xxv). As Anderson and Mortensen (1967) argued, "Given the full powers of language, much rhetorical argument may be simply beyond logic" (p. 143). Many scholars became convinced that the rules of logic were artificial and, therefore, extremely limited. The rules of logic could not make a substantial contribution to the study of either quotidian interaction or public discourse. Traditional concepts in logic such as validity needed to be reconceptualized if they were to have any relevance for inquiry in rhetoric and argumentation (Farrell, 1977; McKerrow, 1977). The process of reasoning in everyday discourse and public argument did not enact context-invariant logical rules or principles. Wallace (1963) argued that the substance of rhetorical practice was simply "good reasons." But most rhetorical scholars came to believe that the process of locating and evaluating "good reasons" required the rejection of traditional logic and its complete reliance on *form* as the measure of *validity* or *soundness.*

The rejection of traditional or formal logic became widespread in rhetorical studies during the latter part of the 20th century. But not every rhetorical scholar agrees with this development. Bybee (1993) argued that the field of logic continues to have relevance for rhetorical scholarship. He maintained,

> Those structures [that] logic identifies . . . are artifacts of our noetic lives. In other words, these structures *describe* (not "prescribe") how we "go" from some bits of information to others—"go" in both directions, either from something we know to some new thing we did not know (logical inference—the syllogism) or from something we believe to the grounds we have for believing it (rhetorical justification—the enthymeme). (pp. 185-186)[4]

According to Bybee, both logic and rhetoric attempt to describe and evaluate the process of human reason giving; hence, they are "intimately and intricately intertwined—and ultimately inseparable" (p. 185). Bybee's perspective, and the emerging tradition of *informal logic,* might offer a middle ground between the "tyranny" of logic over rhetoric (Kneupper, 1984) and their absolute disjunction.

Notes

1. Kirwan's (1995) three-part scheme of problems—practical (what should I do?), theoretical (what is the truth on this matter?), and response (how should I feel?)—parallels the common distinction in **argument** scholarship among *policy, fact,* and *value claims.*

2. As Copi (1968) noted, a strong sense of validity—validity as "conclusive" proof—usually is limited to the process of *deduction.*

3. *The New Rhetoric* originally was published in 1958.

4. Bybee's (1993) defense of logic appeared to turn it into a branch of psychology; logic "describes" the process of reasoning. Scholars such as Copi expended considerable effort in trying to distinguish logic from psychology.

References and Additional Reading

Anderson, R. L., & Mortensen, C. D. (1967). Logic and marketplace argument. *Quarterly Journal of Speech, 53,* 143-151.

Bybee, M. D. (1993). Logic in rhetoric—and vice versa. *Philosophy and Rhetoric, 26,* 169-190.

Copi, I. M. (1968). *Introduction to logic* (3rd ed.). New York: Macmillan.

Cox, J. R., & Willard, C. A. (1982). Introduction: The field of argumentation. In J. R. Cox & C. A. Willard (Eds.), *Advances in argumentation theory and research.* Carbondale: Southern Illinois University Press.

Farrell, T. B. (1977). Validity and rationality: The rhetorical constituents of argumentative form. *Journal of the American Forensic Association, 13,* 142-149.

Gottlieb, G. (1968). *The logic of choice.* New York: Macmillan.

Kirwan, C. (1995). Reasoning. In T. Honderich (Ed.), *The Oxford companion to philosophy.* Oxford, UK: Oxford University Press.

Kneupper, C. W. (1984). The tyranny of logic and the freedom of argumentation. *Pre/Text, 5,* 113-121.

McKerrow, R. E. (1977). Rhetorical validity: An analysis of three perspectives on the justification of rhetorical argument. *Journal of the American Forensic Association, 13,* 133-141.

Mortensen, C. D., & Anderson, R. L. (1970). The limits of logic. *Journal of the American Forensic Association, 7,* 71-78.

Perelman, C., & Olbrechts-Tyteca, L. (1969). *The new rhetoric: A treatise on argumentation* (J. Wilkinson & P. Weaver, Trans.). Notre Dame, IN: University of Notre Dame Press.

Simmons, J. R. (1960). The nature of argumentation. *Speech Monographs, 27,* 348-350.

Toulmin, S. (1958). *The uses of argument.* Cambridge, UK: Cambridge University Press.

Wallace, K. R. (1963). The substance of rhetoric: Good reasons. *Quarterly Journal of Speech, 49,* 239-249.

LOGOS

One of the most complex terms that contemporary rhetorical studies has inherited from classical Greek thinking, **logos,** has been translated in multiple ways. Within the tradition of **neo-Aristotelian** scholarship in 20th-century rhetorical studies, logos most commonly has been defined as one of the three central **modes of proof** employed in rhetorical practice. As a mode of proof, logos is understood as rational **argument** or appeals based on reason as opposed to appeals to the emotions or to the character of the speaker or writer.

But the Greek idea of logos is more complicated and nuanced than the typical neo-Aristotelian reduction to rational argument or appeal to reason recognizes. Roochnik (1990) wrote, "Word, sentence, talk, speech, explanation, language, discourse, story, argument, rational account—all these function at different times as the proper translation of 'logos.' . . . 'Logos' thus comprehends virtually all that is verbal and rational within us" (p. 12). Kerferd (1981) offered the following account of what logos means:

> first of all, the area of language and linguistic formulation, hence speech, discourse, description, statement, arguments (as expressed in words), and so on; secondly, the area of thought and mental processes, hence thinking, reasoning, accounting for, explanation . . ., etc.; thirdly, the area of the world, that about which we are able to speak and to think, hence structured principles, formulae, natural laws, and so on. (p. 83)[1]

Roochnik and Kerferd both focused on the duality of logos; it could refer to both language or discursive practice and the intellectual capacity or power to formulate ideas linguistically and employ language as a means to specified ends.

Given that the Greek concept of logos refers broadly to the realm of "language and linguistic formulation," an important point then follows. As the Greeks altered their understanding of language, they also modified the concept of logos (and with it, the interrelated idea of rhetoric). Discussing the "transition [that] took place in early Greek philosophy," Cassirer (1944) observed,

> The magic function of the word was eclipsed and replaced by its semantic function. The word is no longer endowed with mysterious powers; it no longer has an immediate physical or supernatural influence. . . . The decisive feature is not its physical but its logical character. (p. 111)

In Cassirer's view, a sense of logos language as magical force with the power to shape the world[2] gradually was displaced by a sense of logos language as a semantic tool (see the entry for **representation**) and medium for logical calculation. The shift in conceptualizations of logos is relatively easy to perceive in retrospect, but the struggle between these two different accounts of logos language helped to shape the course of much philosophical and rhetorical thought in ancient Greece.

Political historian Paul Rahe argued that a more restrained sense of logos-as-argument was a central, if not *the* central, assumption of

Greek social and political thought. According to Rahe (1994),

> For Aristotle, *logos* is something more refined than the capacity to make private feelings public: It enables the human being to perform as no other animal can; it makes it possible for him [sic] to perceive and make clear to others through reasoned discourse the difference between what is advantageous and what is harmful, between what is just and what is unjust, and between what is good and what is evil. (p. 21)

Rahe maintained that the ancient Greeks placed enormous "trust" in the capacity of logos (p. 195). He concluded, "At no time in human history has a people displayed so complete a commitment to the principle that man is by nature a political animal blessed with a capacity for *logos* enabling him [sic] to discern and make clear to others what is advantageous, just, and good" (p. 194; see also Roochnik, 1990, pp. 23-45).

But as Rahe (1994) also noted, at least some Greek thinkers understood and appreciated that the magical power of logos could not be easily restrained and that, consequently, logos was a "double-edged sword" (pp. 41, 209). The human ability to employ logos—to think, reason, and speak—could bring people together, but it also could drive them apart. Gorgias, the ancient Greek Sophist, recognized this duality when he referred to logos or language as a *pharmakon*—a drug that could be either a remedy or a poison depending on the circumstances (on this issue, see also Derrida, 1981). This double-edged or ambivalent quality encouraged a degree of skepticism regarding the capacity of logos to guide human affairs. Rahe (1994) located the roots of this skepticism in early modern thinkers such as Machiavelli (p. 215), but it can be argued that they run much deeper. Gustafson (1992) noted, "From Thucydides and Plato to Orwell and beyond, we can find writers commenting upon (or constructing) a pattern of political and linguistic corruption" (p. 87). The corruption of logos—its degeneration from the ideal of logical calculation into an ability to manipulate and deceive—is a recurrent source of anxiety in much Western philosophy and rhetorical theory.

Notes

1. See also Schiappa (1991), Swearingen (1991), and Wardy (1996).
2. See also de Romilly (1975) and Segal (1962).

References and Additional Reading

Cassirer, E. (1944). *An essay on man: An introduction to a philosophy of human culture.* New Haven, CT: Yale University Press.

de Romilly, J. (1975). *Magic and rhetoric in ancient Greece.* Cambridge, MA: Harvard University Press.

Derrida, J. (1981). Plato's pharmacy. In J. Derrida, *Dissemination* (B. Johnson, Trans.). Chicago: University of Chicago Press.

Gustafson, T. (1992). *Representative words: Politics, literature, and the American language, 1776-1865.* Cambridge, UK: Cambridge University Press.

Kerferd, G. B. (1981). *The sophistic movement.* Cambridge, UK: Cambridge University Press.

Rahe, P. A. (1994). *Republics ancient and modern: The ancien régime in classical Greece.* Chapel Hill: University of North Carolina Press.

Roochnik, D. (1990). *The tragedy of reason: Toward a Platonic conception of logos.* New York: Routledge.

Schiappa, A. E. (1991). *Protagoras and logos.* Charleston: University of South Carolina Press.

Schiappa, E. (1999). *The beginnings of rhetorical theory in classical Greece.* New Haven, CT: Yale University Press.

Segal, C. (1962). Gorgias and the psychology of the *logos.* *Harvard Studies in Classical Philology, 66,* 99-155.

Swearingen, C. J. (1991). *Rhetoric and irony: Western literacy and Western lies.* New York: Oxford University Press.

Wardy, R. (1996). *The birth of rhetoric: Gorgias, Plato, and their successors.* London: Routledge.

MANIFESTO

"A spectre is haunting Europe—the spectre of communism." This was the opening sentence from perhaps the most famous **manifesto** in history—Marx and Engels's (1965) *Communist Manifesto.* As Farrell (1993) noted, "Manifestos of nationalism, revolution, and religious reform were prominent forms of expression from the seventeenth century" (p. 164). Yet as literary scholar Janet Lyon observed, "This genre that has played so decisive a role in the history of radical democracy and dissent has received little theoretical [and, we might add, critical] attention in this country" (Lyon, 1991, p. 101). Given the centrality of the manifesto to social and political **movements**—Farrell (1993) described the manifesto as a "movement genre" (p. 163)—this discursive **genre** or form merits the attention of rhetorical scholars.

The term manifesto is derived from the Latin *manifestus,* which means "hit by the hand." A manifesto, then, is a type of verbal or linguistic slap directed at unjust and oppressive social conditions. It is a mode of public denunciation aimed at those who perpetuate social oppression and injustice (e.g., the object of scorn in *The Communist Manifesto* is the "bourgeoisie"). First and foremost, a manifesto is vituperative and vitriolic.

What other functions does the manifesto typically manifest, and what are some of its recurrent characteristics? First, as Lyon (1992) suggested, a manifesto "textualizes the otherwise ephemeral moment of a group's emergence" (p. 101); it tries to establish a sense of group "identity" (Farrell, 1993, p. 162). According to Lyon (1991), "The manifesto's characteristic pronoun [is] 'we,' " and this pronominal tactic "seeks to create an ideal audience, in part by *assuming* this audience" (p. 104). Whereas the manifesto directs its "slap" at the perpetrators of social oppression and injustice, it does so in the name of a collective "we" that the manifesto seeks to *constitute* or bring together as one of its common functions.[1] A second function, one that contributes indirectly to the first, is *differentiation.* Lyon (1991) noted that the manifesto "is governed by its need to position itself against and *make itself intelligible to* the dominant culture" (p. 104; see also Farrell, 1993, p. 162). By positioning itself against, or differentiating itself from, the dominant culture, the manifesto can help to reinforce the emerging group identity ("we" know who "we" are through "our" opposition to those **others**). Through differentiation, the manifesto contributes to social and political **polarization.**[2] Differentiation also appears in the manifesto in another sense. As Marx and Engels's attack on other oppositional movements in the third part of *The Communist Manifesto* illustrated, the manifesto seeks differentiation not only from the dominant culture but from other emerging or existing groups or organizations. What differentiates one group from another is found in the third function of the manifesto—to articulate principles and a program of action. Manifestos routinely announce the concrete goals of movements and inscribe such movements' guiding principles.

What are some of the other recurrent characteristics of the manifesto? Consistent with the term's etymology, manifestos often incorporate various forms of the *argument ad baculum* (see the entry for **fallacy**)—an appeal to force or threats. For example, Lyon (1991) noted the presence of "veiled threat" (p. 112) in *The Communist Manifesto.* Stylistically, manifestos frequently are **exhortative** (Farrell, 1993, p. 172) and appropriate modes of **prophetic** discourse (Lyon, 1991, p. 104). Lyon (1991) elaborated on three recurrent "rhetorical strategies" found in the manifesto:

> First, a foreshortened, impassioned, and highly selective history chronicles the oppression leading to the present moment; second, a forceful enumeration of grievances or proposals politicizes this oppression; and third, an epigrammatic, declarative style directly challenges the oppressor. (p. 104)

The label "manifesto" has not been as common in America as it has in Europe. For example, the expression "declaration of sentiments" was used by the founders of the American Anti-Slavery Society in 1833 and by the women who gathered at Seneca Falls, New York, in 1848 to label the texts produced at their inaugural meetings. In form and function, these texts are part of the genre of the manifesto despite the absence of the term. Texts explicitly labeled manifestos have played an important role in movements protesting various forms of oppression in the United States. It has been an important discursive vehicle in the opposition to racial oppression, beginning with Robert Alexander Young's "Ethiopian Manifesto" in 1829 and continuing with W. E. B. DuBois's "Manifesto of the Second Pan-African Congress" in 1921 and James Forman's "Black Manifesto" in 1969. The manifesto was featured prominently in the resurgence of the women's movement during the latter part of the 20th century in America. Among some of the notable manifestos produced were the "SCUM Manifesto" in 1967, the "Witch Manifesto" in 1968, the "Bitch Manifesto" in 1970, and the "Redstockings Manifesto" in 1970.

There have been a limited number of critical studies of the manifesto genre and specific examples of the manifesto. Bosmajian's (1963) **neo-Aristotelian** analysis of *The Communist Manifesto* unpacked many of its basic rhetorical strategies but did not speak to the larger issue of genre. Farrell's (1993) study of art manifestos during the early 20th century emphasized the relationship between manifesto and movement and offered some useful directives for critical extensions. Pearce (1999) focused on the process of "generic appropriation" (p. 307) in second-wave feminist manifestos. Lyon's (1991, 1992) studies of primarily feminist manifestos devoted the most attention to questions of genre and raised a variety of important questions for further critical reflection.[3] One example will have to suffice for the purpose of illustration. Lyon (1991) wanted to probe "the rhetorical tensions that make manifesto[s] both functional and problematic" (p. 101). For example, one of these tensions is between "the manifesto's inflated and catachrestic rhetoric," which frequently is interpreted as "the very discursive model of the lunatic" (p. 101), and the manifesto's concrete political agenda. The manifesto, then, emerges in a precarious space "between lunacy and social praxis" (p. 121). One possible task for critics would be to chart *how* particular manifestos negotiate this generic tension.

Notes

1. Lyon's account of this process drew, in part, on Althusser's concept of **interpellation**. From a different

theoretical perspective, the manifesto's objective could be described as **secular conversion** or the **ego-function** of protest discourse.

2. See Farrell (1993, p. 175), Lyon (1991, p. 102), and Pearce (1999, p. 314).

3. See also Lyon (1999).

References and Additional Reading

Bosmajian, H. A. (1963). A rhetorical approach to the *Communist Manifesto. The Dalhousie Review, 43,* 457-468.

Farrell, T. B. (1993). Manifesting perspectives: Rhetoric in the movements of modern art. In D. Zarefsky (Ed.), *Rhetorical movement: Essays in honor of Leland M. Griffin.* Evanston, IL: Northwestern University Press.

Lyon, J. (1991). Transforming manifestoes: A second-wave problematic. *Yale Journal of Criticism, 5,* 101-127.

Lyon, J. (1992). Militant discourse, strange bedfellows: Suffragettes and vorticists before the war. *Differences: A Feminist Journal of Cultural Studies, 4,* 100-132.

Lyon, J. (1999). *Manifestoes: Provocations of the modern.* Ithaca, NY: Cornell University Press.

Marx, K., & Engels, F. (1965). *Communist manifesto* (J. Katz, Ed., S. Moore, Trans.). New York: Washington Square Press.

Pearce, K. C. (1999). The radical feminist manifesto as generic appropriation: Gender, genre, and second wave resistance. *Southern Communication Journal, 64,* 307-315.

MEMORY

Edward P. J. Corbett, in one of the early texts in the contemporary revival of classical rhetoric, made the following observation:

> Of all the five parts [or **canons**] of rhetoric, *memoria* [memory] was the one that received the least attention in the rhetoric books. The reason for the neglect of this aspect of rhetoric is probably that not much can be said, in a theoretical way, about the process of memorizing. (Corbett, 1971, p. 38)

Corbett's account of this element of the traditional canon is common; the concept of **memory** usually is taken to refer to the way in which a speaker memorized a speech for presentation. Although scholars have demonstrated that the concept and practice of memory during the classical period and beyond was more complicated and nuanced than Corbett's account suggested,[1] the association of memory with memorization has persisted. But during the past decade, rhetorical scholars have begun to reconceptualize this traditional concept. Two research trajectories merit attention: first, the emergence of interest in the ideas of collective, popular, and public memory (as well as the relationship between rhetoric and the process of *memorialization*); and, second, renewed interest in the relationship among memory, **invention,** and social critique.

Within an emerging interdisciplinary research tradition, the terms *collective, cultural, popular, social,* and *public* memory can take on specific and divergent meanings. For example, Morris (1997) distinguished "public memory" from "cultural memory" as follows:

> Cultural memory reflects the particularized worldview and ethos of the members of a *particular* culture, [whereas] public memory is perhaps best conceived as an *amalgam* of the current hegemonic bloc's cultural memory and bits and pieces of cultural memory that members of other cultures are able to preserve and protect. (p. 26; see also Sturken, 1997)

For Morris, cultural memory is the result of **vernacular** practices, whereas public memory is the product of political institutions and institutionalized practices. Although this distinction, and others that can be located in the literature, may be important, the various forms of memory noted in the preceding paragraph *can* be viewed as roughly synonymous in the way that they all distinguish between an individual's memory (memory as a subjective phenomenon) and memory as an intersubjective and interactive phenomenon (memory as something that exists among a group of people). In the course of this discussion, the expression *public* memory is used as a covering term for this shared sense of intersubjective memory.

How can we define the concept of public memory, and what is its relevance for contemporary rhetorical studies? Scholars in various fields have begun to address the definitional question. Social historian John Bodnar defined public memory as "a body of beliefs and ideas about the past that help a public or society understand both its past [and] present, and by implication, its future" (Bodnar, 1992, p. 15). Intellectual and cultural historian Michael Kammen described public memory as "a slowly shifting configuration of traditions" that is both "selective" and "contested" (Kammen, 1991, p. 13). In rhetorical studies, Stephen Browne offered the following definition of public memory: "a shared sense of the past, fashioned from the symbolic resources of community and subject to its particular history, hierarchies, and aspirations" (Browne, 1995, p. 248). These three efforts at definition by no means exhaust the scholarly literature on the subject. They do provide an initial orientation to the phenomenon in question.

We can gain a more precise understanding of public memory and begin to appreciate its significance to contemporary rhetorical studies by noting certain recurrent characteristics that appear in the literature on the subject.[2] The first characteristic concerns the genesis of memory. Bolles (1988), for example, noted the tradition of thought that approached personal memory "as a passive file cabinet for things past" (p. 15). The *metaphor* of file cabinet or warehouse suggests that memory begins in a process of storage and culminates in an act of retrieval. The passive view of memory began to be challenged during the early 20th century. In pioneering work, psychologist Frederick Bartlett began to reconceptualize memory as an active process rather than a passive one—a matter of construction as opposed to reproduction (Bartlett, 1932). The assumption that memory—personal as well as public—is constructed is widely shared by contemporary scholars. The genesis of public memory can be found in an active process of social interaction; through various forms of social interaction (including, but not limited to, public discourse), members of a community or society construct the "body of beliefs and ideas about the past" that is the substance of public memory.

Browne (1995) asserted, "Public memory lives as it is given expressive form" (p. 248). Browne's observation reaffirmed the first characteristic of public memory—constructed through social interaction—while gesturing toward a second one. Public memory is *made public* when specific acts of memory are given "expressive form." What does it mean to give an act of memory (e.g., an individual's recollections of American life during the 1960s) expressive form? It means, at a minimum, that the act of memory is performed for others who witness the performance as an audience (e.g., a person might recount certain stories about his or her childhood for an audience of other people). The performative dimension of public memory is embodied most clearly in the numerous **rituals** and ceremonies that shape and reshape the "body of beliefs and ideas about the past." More important for rhetorical scholars, the expressive form of public memory is commonly textual as acts of memory are inscribed or incorporated into texts. Philosopher Edward Casey noted that "communal remembering" relies on the "agency of a text." Different forms of textual practice—novels, poems, speeches, essays, public letters, and so on—function as "vehicles" of public memory (Casey, 1987, pp. 217-218). As Browne (1995) emphasized, public memory has a *texture*—a discursive structure and shape—that demands the attention of rhetorical scholars.

Before turning to various efforts to read the texture of public memory, it will be useful to note two additional characteristics of public memory: its contested nature and its multifunctionality. A number of scholars have employed a pair of antithetical terms to highlight the contested and conflicted nature of public memory. For Bodnar (1992), the contest is between the memories constructed by an "official culture" that often conflict with the memories that arise from the practices of "vernacular cultures." Kammen (1991) noted, with some reservations, how "collective memory" often is used to describe "what is remembered by the dominant civic culture" and how "popular memory" is used to describe what "ordinary folks" remember. Whether or not specific terms are introduced to represent the various sides in the struggle, scholars generally agree that public memory never is completely **hegemonic.** The texture of public memory frequently is marked by intense struggle over *how* and *what* to remember. Consider some examples. In an editorial from the *Chicago Tribune* on July 16, 1995, Darrell Fasching noted how different **generations** have different memories of the emergence of the atomic age in August 1945 when the United States dropped two atomic bombs on Japan. Fasching maintained that members of his "father's generation" (those who fought and died during World War II) remember the bomb "as a miraculous deliverance" from the horrors of war. Fasching went on to note how members of his own generation (the infamous baby boomers), although they did not experience the event firsthand, nevertheless have memories of the emergence of the atomic age that conflict with those of his father's generation. For Fasching's generation, "their first memories of the bomb are of air raid drills and hiding under their desks." In short, Fasching suggested that, for his generation, the bomb was the beginning of horror, not the end. These different, conflicting memories play themselves out in a variety of **controversies.**[3] For a more recent example, consider the question of the meaning of the war in Vietnam. How do we remember Vietnam? Was it a fundamentally misguided effort on the part of the United States to impose its will on a foreign nation, or was it a noble effort at preventing the domination of one group of people by another? Clearly, our memories of Vietnam, like many public memories, are contested.[4]

In noting the contested character of public memory, scholars do not suggest that what is needed is greater attention to the "facts." Although it seems possible to focus on the degree of accuracy of a particular public memory (e.g., attempts by some to deny that the Holocaust took place are met by intense resistance that points to the factual or documentary record of Nazi atrocities), most scholars believe that it is impossible to remember *everything* about the past. Memory always, and inevitably, is partial and selective. As Sturken (1997) observed, "All memories are 'created' in tandem with forgetting. (p. 7) . . . Memory and forgetting are co-constitutive processes; each is essential to the other's existence" (p. 2; see also Ehrenhaus, 1989). Beyond the inherent selectivity of memory—its structural dependence on forgetting—many scholars note that "getting the past right" is not one of the principal functions of public memory. Geographer and historian David Lowenthal affirmed this point when he wrote, "The prime function of memory is not to preserve the past but to adapt it so as to enrich and manipulate the present" (Lowenthal, 1985, p. 210).

Lowenthal's observation leads to the final issue—the functions of public memory. How is public memory used as a social, cultural, and political resource? Existing scholarship points to a number of different functions. Irwin-Zarecka (1994), for example, maintained that public memory "is one of the most important symbolic resources we have . . . for mobilizing action and legitimating it" (p. 67). Public memory is a source of power and authority. During the 19th century, for example, American abolitionists and many of their more moderate opponents found public memory to be a useful resource for mobilizing and legitimating action. But each group appealed to a different memory of the past. Moderates such as Henry Clay called on the nation to remember the compromises of the Philadelphia Constitutional Convention of 1787 as a way of mobilizing and legitimating compromise on the issue of slavery in 1850. Radical abolitionists such as William Lloyd Garrison called on the nation to remember the revolutionaries of 1776 who scoffed at the notion of compromise with Great Britain as a way of mobilizing and legitimating continued abolitionist agitation. Fentress and Wickham (1992) suggested that public memory "tells us who we are" (p. 201), whereas Wolin (1989) maintained that its "most important function is to fix collective identity in the present" (p. 3).[5] In short, public memory contributes substantially to the constitution of collective identity. What it means to be an American is determined, in part, by what we remember (and what we are encouraged to remember) about our past.

If who we are as a people is shaped by our memories of the past, then it follows that who we are also is determined by what we inevitably *forget.* Public memory not only preserves some "beliefs and ideas," it also eliminates or discards others. The importance of this function of public memory needs emphasis. Ronald Reagan both helped to create and appealed to public memory when he urged the nation to support the Contras and their effort to overthrow the Sandanista-dominated government of Nicaragua during the 1980s. Reagan crafted a **narrative** that related the history of the relationship between Nicaragua and the United States. But Reagan chose to begin his story in 1979, shortly after the Sandanista revolution. Reagan's version of the story—his textualization of public memory—forgot the decades of U.S. support for the dictator who ruled Nicaragua prior to the revolution. In so doing, Reagan implied that such information was irrelevant to the policy question that the nation faced.[6]

Over the past decade, rhetorical critics have begun to explore both the texture and functions of public memory. Dionisopoulos and Goldzwig (1992) examined the efforts of George Schultz (then secretary of state) to recraft the meaning of the war in Vietnam. Stuckey (1992) noted the persistence of World War II and Vietnam in George Bush's discourse on the Gulf War. Browne (1993) read Daniel Webster's 1820 "Plymouth Rock Oration" as "a symbolic bulwark against cultural change" (p. 469). Webster's story of birth and subsequent growth of New England functioned, Browne argued, as a reaffirmation of dominant values, especially the value of "property." Goodnight (1996) analyzed how the memory of the war in Vietnam, specifically the "lessons" that Americans attempted to derive from the experience, shaped debate over Central American policy during the 1980s. Jasinski (1997) explored the way in which Frederick Douglass's 1852 Fourth of July oration (actually delivered on July 5) functioned to contest the dominant meaning of the American Revolution.[7] By focusing on Douglass's subversion of generic *constraints* and his appropriation of common *metaphors,* Jasinski described how Douglass tried to give the revolution a new expressive form that legitimated his call for emancipation. Finally, a considerable body of scholarship has emerged devoted to detailing the struggle over the meaning, and the memory, of the war in Vietnam.[8] Critical analysis of the texts and texture of memory most likely will remain an important part of the agenda of rhetorical critics during the coming years.

The second strand of scholarship engaged in the process of reconceptualizing the traditional canon of memory focuses on how this concept can contribute to our thinking about the practices of invention and social critique. Composition theorists have led the way in reclaiming memory as part of the process of discursive invention. Summarizing the literature in rhetoric and composition, Reynolds (1993) outlined four "approaches to memory in modern composition studies" (p. 7). First, memory as "mnemonics" (devices for facilitating retention and recall) has led to various writing strategies and pedagogical exercises that make written discourse easier to remember. Second, memory as "memorableness" focuses on ways of making writing memorable. Third, memory as "databases" explores ways of tapping into personal and cultural memory as a source for discourse production. Finally, memory as "psychology" has stimulated thinking about how cognitive processes can be used to generate approaches to the compositional process.

Rhetorical theorist and critic J. R. Cox launched an important research program devoted to exploring the relationship between memory and social critique.[9] Cox (1990) wanted to theorize memory as a "mode of invention" (p. 2), similar to the work of composition theorists. But he was interested in a very specific form of discursive practice—social critique. Cox (1987b) attempted to "discover loci for social critique in cultural memory" (p. 6) or to unpack how "remembrance [functions] as an emancipatory agency" (Cox, 1990, p. 3). What did he mean by social critique, and how can memory contribute to this mode of discursive practice? To understand Cox's project, we need to begin with the social conditions that, according to Cox, make critique urgently needed. In one sense, the conditions are obvious—injustice, oppression, economic insecurity, environmental degradation, and so on. But what makes social critique so problematic, and hence so necessary, is not simply the material existence or the "facticity" of these conditions. The root of the problem is that people seem unable to really perceive these conditions *as* a problem; they seem unable to imagine that there is any alternative to the conditions and the practices of our world. The way things are is simply the way things *always have been;* our conditions and practices appear to us as inevitable or "natural." Early in the 20th century, the Marxist philosopher Georg Lukács referred to this *second* condition (the belief that our present conditions and practices are inevitable or natural) as *reification.*[10] So, to summarize, critique is necessary not only as a way of addressing and redressing various problematic conditions and practices but also to break the "spell" (to speak metaphorically) of reified consciousness and mystification.

How is memory related to the problem of reification or mystification? Cox (1990) noted an observation made by another Marxist philosopher, Theodor Adorno, that "every reification is a forgetting" (cited on p. 3). But what exactly does the process of reification make us forget? Is it, like the example of Reagan's discourse on Central America introduced earlier, a case where audiences are encouraged to forget specific events or practices? Not exactly; the kind of forgetting that critics such as Adorno have in mind is different from cases where particular items are elided from the realm of public memory. According to Adorno and a long tradition of critical theorists (e.g., Giddens, 1979), the conditions and practices of our world appear to be inevitable or "natural" because people have been encouraged to forget not particular events but rather the **contingency** of human life. Forgetting the contingency of human existence means that we cannot remember the host of circumstances that gave rise to or enabled the emergence of our present conditions and practices. And through this forgetting or *domesticating* of contingency, people gradually have lost the ability to seriously imagine alternative possibilities. The horizon of our lives has become severely contracted, with our choices reduced to which brand of blue jeans we should buy or what deodorant we should use.

The antidote to reification and forgetfulness is a certain type of memory—a *critical* memory. Critical memory is much more than being able to recall the words to the *Gilligan's Island* theme song or the first names of the Marx brothers. It is more than being able to remember the words to the preamble of the Declaration of Independence or the arguments used to justify the North American Free Trade Agreement (NAFTA). Cox developed his account of *critical* memory through the works of the German philosopher Martin Heidegger and the Marxist philosopher Herbert Marcuse. From Heidegger, Cox (1987b) recovered the distinction between **tradition** and heritage. Like Kammen (discussed earlier), Heidegger understood traditions to be the "stuff" of public memory. In America, we have countless traditions regarding the sanctity of private property, individual rights and liberty, freedom of expression, and so on. Traditions, for Heidegger, are the actual structure of possibilities handed down to us by the past. But heritage represents the much broader range of possibilities that existed in the past, only some of which have been given expressive form by entry into a tradition. Clearly, some aspects of the past—our collective heritage—are best left in the past. When we recall practices such as slavery and the Salem witch trials, it is to remember the horrors of those episodes and to maintain our commitment to never allow them to occur again. But are there possibilities that have been lost—beliefs, goals, ideals, and so on—whose recovery might be of some value? Following Heidegger, Cox argued that this is the case. Critical memory is, first and foremost, an act of recovery.

Sometimes the possibilities contained in a culture's historical heritage have been polluted or damaged.[11] Critical memory aims not only at recovery but also at a "*re*-collecting [of] ideals that were ideologically deformed" (Cox, 1990, p. 5; see also Cox, 1987a). Cox (1987a, 1990) argued that ideological deformation is overcome through a **dissociation** process that uncovers the possibilities[12] repressed by dominant traditions of thought and argument. In his essays, Cox illustrated this process by way of theological and feminist argument practices. Let us consider another example. The writings of the British philosopher John Locke often are invoked as a philosophical foundation, or a *warrant,* for capitalist economic practices, the ideal of private property, and the **ethos** of acquisition. Locke maintained that humankind has a natural right to property including the fruits of individual labor. This belief in the right to property functions as a cornerstone of America's economic and political traditions. For example, if a person is the sole proprietor of *his or her* property, then that person has no obligations to anyone else for how he or she disposes of the property and must give his or her consent whenever the property is taken from that person by the government (the doctrine of popular consent). Critics have, over the years, objected to Locke's philosophy for its apparent lack of regard to the collective welfare and its atomization of society. But perhaps, following Cox, we might ask whether Locke's ideas have been subjected to "ideological deformation." Are there ideas and/or ideals in Locke's writings worth recovering? Consider the following passage from Locke's (1988) famous *Two Treatises of Government:*

> Though the Earth and all inferior Creatures be common to all Men [sic], yet every Man has a *Property* in his own *Person.* This no Body has any Right to but himself. The *Labour* of his Body, and the *Work* of his Hands, we may say, are properly his. Whatsoever then he removes out of the State that Nature hath provided and left it in, he hath mixed his *Labour* with, and joyned to it something that is his own, and thereby makes it his *Property.* It being by him removed from the common state Nature placed it in, hath by this *Labour* something annexed to it, that excludes the common right of other Men. For this *Labour* being the unquestionable Property of the Labourer, no Man but he can have a right to what is once joyned to, at least where there is enough, and as good left in common for others.

The beginning of this passage was the Locke of our tradition; an individual makes nature his or her own through labor, and once that is done, no one else has a right to what is produced (the "property"). There are no exceptions except those to which the individual consents (people have no obligation to help the poor given Locke's perspective, but an individual might, for pragmatic or philanthropic reasons, consent to be taxed for welfare programs). But notice the very end of this passage, where Locke explicitly noted an exception to his doctrine of a natural right to property; it holds only "where there is enough, and as good left in common for others." This condition might have held for 19th-century America; land was cheap, and if a person did not like what was going on in New Jersey, then the person always could pick up his or her "property" (or body), move west, and begin the scramble for property all over again. But then something happened. America ran out of land (what the historian Frederick Jackson Turner referred to as the closing of the American frontier). There no longer was "enough, and as good left in common for others." But as the Lockean tradition was perpetuated in America, this qualification was forgotten. The scramble of everyone for himself or herself is the way that things are, and always have been, and we just have to go on and keep scrambling. Or do we? Perhaps when there is not enough, or as good left, for everyone, we need to rethink or reimagine the necessity of the scramble. Perhaps Locke's defense of the right of property provides a way of criticizing the practices of acquisition and capitalism (e.g., plant closings, job flight) in the late 20th and early 21st centuries. Matthews (1995) indicated that this is the case. He wrote, "These apparently innocent-looking limitations on human appropriation in Locke . . . contain the potential of a radical critique of the very institution of property that they originally helped to justify" (pp. 118-119).[13] Using Locke against the regime of private property and unlimited acquisition that he helped to establish is an example of what Cox (1990) meant by a "subverting use of history" (p. 10) where memory of what has been forgotten, repressed, or deformed functions as a way of overcoming reification and imagining alternative possibilities.

Notes

1. See, for example, Caplan (1970), Carruthers (1990), and Yates (1966).

2. In addition to the Bodnar, Browne, and Kammen studies noted previously, other key sources on the characteristics of public memory include Bolles (1988), Connerton (1989), Fentress and Wickham (1992), Irwin-Zarecka (1994), Lipsitz (1990), Morris (1997), and Sturken (1997).

3. Fasching's essay was in response to the controversy that stemmed from the Smithsonian Institute's attempt to construct an exhibit that would "remember" the dropping of the atomic bomb and the end of World War II.

4. The literature on "remembering Vietnam" is quite extensive. See, for example, Ehrenhaus (1989), Goodnight (1996), Isaacs (1997), Lembcke (1998), and Sturken (1997). Of course, Vietnam is not the only war whose memory is contested. For a discussion of the contested memory of the Civil War, see Blight (1989).

5. On the issue of memory and identity, see the essays collected in Gillis (1994).

6. On the role of narrative in recovering forgotten "origins" or "essences," see Kraig (1997).

7. On Douglass and the struggle over the memory of the American Revolution, see also Waldstreicher (1997).

8. In addition to the sources already cited, see Blair, Jeppeson, and Pucci (1991) and Morris and Ehrenhaus (1990).

9. See, for example, Cox (1987a, 1987b, 1990).

10. Lukács' thinking on this subject bears some similarity to the concept of **mystification.**

11. See, for example, Baker's (1994) discussion of the way in which the memory of Martin Luther King, Jr., has been appropriated by conservatives. Baker's response was, in his words, a "sharp resistance to nostalgia" (p. 31).

12. This is what Perelman and Olbrechts-Tyteca (1969) referred to as the "real."

13. Ashcraft (1986) also discussed the "radical" side of Locke's political theory.

References and Additional Reading

Ashcraft, R. (1986). *Revolutionary politics and Locke's Two Treatises of Government.* Princeton, NJ: Princeton University Press.

Baker, H. A., Jr. (1994). Critical memory and the black public sphere. *Public Culture, 7,* 3-33.

Bartlett, F. C. (1932). *Remembering.* Cambridge, UK: Cambridge University Press.

Blair, C., Jeppeson, M. S., & Pucci, E., Jr. (1991). Public memorializing in postmodernity: The Vietnam Veterans Memorial as prototype. *Quarterly Journal of Speech, 77,* 263-288.

Blight, D. W. (1989). "For something beyond the battlefield": Frederick Douglass and the struggle for the memory of the Civil War. *Journal of American History, 75,* 1156-1178.

Bodnar, J. (1992). *Remaking America: Public memory, commemoration, and patriotism in the twentieth century.* Princeton, NJ: Princeton University Press.

Bolles, E. B. (1988). *Remembering and forgetting: An inquiry into the nature of memory.* New York: Walker.

Boyarin, J. (1994). Space, time, and the politics of memory. In J. Boyarin (Ed.), *Remapping memory: The politics of TimeSpace.* Minneapolis: University of Minnesota Press.

Browne, S. H. (1993). Reading public memory in Daniel Webster's *Plymouth Rock Oration. Western Journal of Communication, 57,* 464-477.

Browne, S. H. (1995). Reading, rhetoric, and the texture of public memory. *Quarterly Journal of Speech, 81,* 237-250.

Browne, S. H. (1999). Remembering Crispus Attucks: Race, rhetoric, and the politics of commemoration. *Quarterly Journal of Speech, 85,* 169-187.

Caplan, H. (1970). Memoria: Treasure-house of eloquence. In A. King & H. North (Eds.), *Of eloquence: Studies in ancient and medieval rhetoric.* Ithaca, NY: Cornell University Press.

Carruthers, M. (1990). *The book of memory: A study of memory in medieval culture.* Cambridge, UK: Cambridge University Press.

Casey, E. S. (1987). *Remembering: A phenomenological study.* Bloomington: Indiana University Press.

Connerton, P. (1989). *How societies remember.* Cambridge, UK: Cambridge University Press.

Corbett, E. P. J. (1971). *Classical rhetoric for the modern student* (2nd ed.). New York: Oxford University Press.

Cox, J. R. (1987a). Argument and usable traditions. In F. H. van Eemeren, R. Grootendorst, J. A. Blair, & C. A. Willard (Eds.), *Argumentation: Across the lines of discipline.* Dordrecht, Netherlands: Foris Publications.

Cox, J. R. (1987b). *Cultural memory and public moral argument.* Evanston, IL: Northwestern University.

Cox, J. R. (1990). Memory, critical theory, and the argument from history. *Argument and Advocacy, 27,* 1-13.

Dickinson, G. (1997). Memories for sale: Nostalgia and the construction of identity in Old Pasadena. *Quarterly Journal of Speech, 83,* 1-27.

Dionisopoulos, G. N., & Goldzwig, S. R. (1992). "The meaning of Vietnam": Political rhetoric as revisionist cultural history. *Quarterly Journal of Speech, 78,* 61-79.

Ehrenhaus, P. (1989). Commemorating the unwon war: On *not* remembering Vietnam. *Journal of Communication, 39,* 96-107.

Fentress, J., & Wickham, C. (1992). *Social memory.* Oxford, UK: Basil Blackwell.

Giddens, A. (1979). *Central problems in social theory: Action, structure, and contradiction in social analysis.* Berkeley: University of California Press.

Gillis, J. R. (Ed.). (1994). *Commemorations: The politics of national identity.* Princeton, NJ: Princeton University Press.

Goodnight, G. T. (1996). Reagan, Vietnam, and Central America: Public memory and the politics of fragmentation. In M. J. Medhurst (Ed.), *Beyond the rhetorical presidency.* College Station: Texas A&M University Press.

Gronbeck, B. E. (1998). The rhetorics of the past: History, argument, and collective memory. In K. J. Turner (Ed.), *Doing rhetorical history: Concepts and cases.* Tuscaloosa: University of Alabama Press.

Hutton, P. (1987). The art of memory reconceived: From rhetoric to psychoanalysis. *Journal of the History of Ideas, 48,* 371-392.

Irwin-Zarecka, I. (1994). *Frames of remembrance: The dynamics of collective memory.* New Brunswick, NJ: Transaction Publishers.

Isaacs, A. R. (1997). *Vietnam shadows: The war, its ghosts, and its legacy.* Baltimore, MD: Johns Hopkins University Press.

Jasinski, J. (1997). Rearticulating history through epideictic discourse: Frederick Douglass's "The Meaning of the Fourth of July to the Negro." In T. W. Benson (Ed.), *Rhetoric and political culture in nineteenth-century America.* East Lansing: Michigan State University Press.

Jorgensen-Earp, C. R., & Lanzilotti, L. A. (1998). Public memory and private grief: The construction of shrines at the site of public tragedy. *Quarterly Journal of Speech, 84,* 150-170.

Kammen, M. (1991). *Mystic chords of memory: The transformation of tradition in American culture.* New York: Knopf.

Kammen, M. (1997). Some patterns and meanings of memory distortion in American history. In M. Kammen, *In the past lane: Historical perspectives on American culture.* New York: Oxford University Press.

Katriel, T. (1994). Sites of memory: Discourses of the past in Israeli pioneering settlement museums. *Quarterly Journal of Speech, 80,* 1-20.

Kraig, R. A. (1997). The narration of essence: Salmon P. Chase's Senate oration against the Kansas-Nebraska Act. *Communication Studies, 48,* 234-253.

Lembcke, J. (1998). *The spitting image: Myth, memory, and the legacy of Vietnam.* New York: New York University Press.

Lipsitz, G. (1990). *Time passages: Collective memory and American popular culture.* Minneapolis: University of Minnesota Press.

Locke, J. (1690, 1988). *Two treatises of government* (P. Laslett, Ed.). Cambridge, UK: Cambridge University Press.

Lowenthal, D. (1985). *The past is a foreign country.* Cambridge, UK: Cambridge University Press.

Matthews, R. K. (1995). *If men were angels: James Madison and the heartless empire of reason.* Lawrence: University Press of Kansas.

Middleton, D., & Edwards, D. (Eds.). (1990). *Collective remembering.* London: Sage.

Morris, R. (1997). *Sinners, lovers, and heroes: An essay on memorializing in three American cultures.* Albany: State University of New York Press.

Morris, R., & Ehrenhaus, P. (Eds.). (1990). *Cultural legacies of Vietnam: Uses of the past in the present.* Norwood, NJ: Ablex.

Pennebaker, J. W., Paez, D., & Rimé, B. (Eds.). (1997). *Collective memory of political events: Social psychological perspectives.* Mahwah, NJ: Lawrence Erlbaum.

Perelman, C., & Olbrechts-Tyteca, L. (1969). *The new rhetoric: A treatise on argumentation* (J. Wilkinson &

P. Weaver, Trans.). Notre Dame, IN: University of Notre Dame Press.

Pollock, M. A. (1994). The battle for the past: George Bush and the Gulf crisis. In A. Kiewe (Ed.), *The modern presidency and crisis of rhetoric.* Westport, CT: Praeger.

Reynolds, J. F. (1993). Memory issues in composition studies. In J. F. Reynolds (Ed.), *Rhetorical memory and delivery: Classical concepts for contemporary composition and communication.* Hillsdale, NJ: Lawrence Erlbaum.

Spillman, L. (1997). *Nation and commemoration: Creating national identities in the United States and Australia.* Cambridge, UK: Cambridge University Press.

Stuckey, M. (1992). Remembering the future: Rhetorical echoes of World War II and Vietnam in George Bush's public speech on the Gulf War. *Communication Studies, 43,* 246-256.

Sturken, M. (1997). *Tangled memories: The Vietnam war, the AIDS epidemic, and the politics of remembering.* Berkeley: University of California Press.

Waldstreicher, D. (1997). *In the midst of perpetual fetes: The making of American nationalism, 1776-1820.* Chapel Hill: University of North Carolina Press.

Wolin, S. (1989). *The presence of the past.* Baltimore, MD: Johns Hopkins University Press.

Yates, F. (1966). *The art of memory.* Chicago: University of Chicago Press.

Young, J.E. (1993). *The texture of memory: Holocaust memorials and meaning.* New Haven, CT: Yale University Press.

Zelizer, B. (1992). *Covering the body: The Kennedy assassination, the media, and the shaping of collective memory.* Chicago: University of Chicago Press.

Zelizer, B. (1995). Reading the past against the grain: The shape of memory studies. *Critical Studies in Mass Communication, 12,* 214-239.

METACRITICISM

As the prefix "meta" suggests,[1] **metacriticism** is criticism of **criticism.** Take a simple example. An essay or a book about the oratory of Abraham Lincoln is an example of criticism; an essay or a book about the criticism of Lincoln's oratory is an instance of metacriticism. Nothstine, Blair, and Copeland (1994) described metacriticism in rhetorical studies as "scholarly and textbook materials describing, prescribing, and justifying the particular character of critical practices within rhetorical criticism" (p. 30).

Metacriticism has played an important role in the emergence and development of contemporary rhetorical studies. Wichelns's (1925/1962) classic essay, "The Literary Criticism of Oratory," is commonly considered one of the founding texts of the field. The essay is principally a work of metacriticism; Wichelns wrote that its "chief aim is to know how critics have spoken of oratory" (p. 182). By reading the existing critical studies of oratory critically, Wichelns discerned a variety of discrete emphases. But most of the criticism that Wichelns surveyed tended to treat oratory as a species of literature; these critics "are all, in various ways, interpreters of the permanent and universal values they find in the works of which they treat" (p. 209). But some of the examples of criticism proceeded differently. And in these examples, Wichelns uncovered the essence of a rhetorical approach to oratory or rhetorical criticism. This form of criticism "regards a speech as a communication to a specific audience and holds its business to be the analysis and appreciation of the orator's method of imparting his [sic] ideas to his hearers" (p. 209). The practice of modern rhetorical criticism emerged from Wichelns's metacritical reflections.

Metacriticism remains an important form of rhetorical scholarship.[2] In some cases, rhetorical scholars will combine moments of criticism and metacriticism in the scope of an elaborate scholarly project. For example, in *Rhetorical Criticism,* Black (1978) blended metacritical reflection on key examples of rhetorical criticism (e.g., readings of Marie Hochmuth's critique of Lincoln's "First Inaugural Address" and Ernest Wrage's study of Henry Clay) with an original reading of John Jay Chapman's previously overlooked "Coatesville Address" as a way of advancing his claims on the nature of rhetorical criticism. Other scholars use metacriticism as a point of departure to address more abstract questions of critical method and theory. Rosenfield (1968), for example, used two different critiques of a speech by General Douglass MacArthur in 1951 as a jumping-off point for his effort to describe the "anatomy" of critical discourse. Metacriticism also can be employed to reconstruct the often implicit guiding assumptions of critics. Gaonkar (1993), perhaps the field's most prominent metacritic, read the criticism produced under the auspices of the *rhetoric of science* movement to tease out lingering vestiges of **neo-Aristotelianism** and reveal implicit assumptions about the nature of the human **subject**.

Critical activity invites metacritical reflection, much like an assertion invites a rejoinder. By analyzing the conceptual assumptions, methods, and procedures that guide critics and critical practice, metacriticism provides a vehicle for challenging existing orthodoxies, modifying embedded assumptions and procedures, and proposing innovative approaches to the practice of rhetorical criticism. Metacriticism, in short, helps to keep the conversation among rhetorical critics going.

Notes

1. Among other things, the prefix is used to designate a type of reflective practice.
2. Gaonkar (1989) observed, "The lament is the dominant genre of metacritical discourse in our field" (p. 258).

References and Additional Reading

Black, E. (1978). *Rhetorical criticism: A study in method.* Madison: University of Wisconsin Press.

Gaonkar, D. P. (1989). The oratorical text: The enigma of arrival. In M. C. Leff & F. J. Kauffeld (Eds.), *Texts in context: Critical dialogues on significant episodes in American political rhetoric.* Davis, CA: Hermagoras Press.

Gaonkar, D. P. (1993). The idea of rhetoric in the rhetoric of science. *Southern Communication Journal, 58,* 258-295.

Nothstine, W. L., Blair, C., & Copeland, G. A. (1994). *Critical questions: Invention, creativity, and the criticism of discourse and media.* New York: St. Martin's.

Rosenfield, L. W. (1968). The anatomy of critical discourse. *Speech Monographs, 35,* 50-69.

Wichelns, H. A. (1962). The literary criticism of oratory. In A. M. Drummond (Ed.), *Studies in rhetoric and public speaking in honor of James Albert Winans.* New York: Russell and Russell. (Original work published 1925)

MODES OF PROOF

In the *Rhetoric,* Aristotle (1954) identified three "modes of persuasion" or **modes of proof** (*pistis* or *pisteis*) that operate in rhetorical discourse. According to Aristotle, "the first kind depends on the personal character of the speaker [**ethos**]; the second on putting the audience into a certain frame of mind [**pathos**]; the third on the proof, or apparent proof, provided by the words of the speech itself [**logos**]" (1356a). (For additional details, see the entries for each of these topics.)

The three modes of proof described by classical rhetoricians have become a recurrent feature of many contemporary public speaking texts, and it is in this context that most people encounter them. But the modes of proof also can be applied in more creative and analytic ways. Covino (1998) found the classical modes of proof to be useful for discussing a variety of persuasive practices including legal discourse, Jane Austen's novel *Emma,* and Spike Lee's film *Do the Right Thing.* Darsey (1997) employed the classical trinity as a vehicle for unpacking the dynamics of *prophetic rhetoric.* Both Covino and Darsey provided potential models that other scholars might use in trying to adapt the classical modes of proof to the demands of contemporary rhetorical scholarship.

Some contemporary scholars suggest that a fourth mode of proof can be found in ancient theories of rhetoric and in contemporary rhetorical practice. That fourth mode of proof is *mythos*—**myth** or **narrative** (Baumlin & Baumlin, 1994; Osborn, 1986).

References and Additional Reading

Aristotle. (1954). *Rhetoric* (W. R. Roberts, Trans.). New York: Modern Library.

Baumlin, J. S., & Baumlin, T. F. (1994). On the psychology of the *pisteis:* Mapping the terrains of mind and rhetoric. In J. S. Baumlin & T. F. Baumlin (Eds.), *Ethos: New essays in rhetorical and critical theory.* Dallas, TX: Southern Methodist University Press.

Braet, A. C. (1992). Ethos, pathos, and logos in Aristotle's *Rhetoric:* A re-examination. *Argumentation, 6,* 307-320.

Conley, T. M. (1990). *Rhetoric in the European tradition.* New York: Longman.

Covino, W. A. (1998). *The elements of persuasion.* Boston: Allyn & Bacon.

Crowley, S., & Hawhee, D. (1999). *Ancient rhetorics for contemporary students* (2nd ed.). Boston: Allyn & Bacon.

Darsey, J. (1997). *The prophetic tradition and radical rhetoric in America.* New York: New York University Press.

Fisher, W. (1987). *Human communication as narration: Toward a philosophy of reason, value, and action.* Columbia: University of South Carolina Press.

Herrick, J. A. (1998). *The history and theory of rhetoric: An introduction.* Boston: Allyn & Bacon.

Osborn, M. (1986). Rhetorical depiction. In H. W. Simons & A. A. Aghazarian (Eds.), *Form, genre, and the study of political discourse.* Columbia: University of South Carolina Press.

MORTIFICATION

One of Kenneth Burke's most important insights was his appreciation of the linkages between rhetoric or public discourse and **ritual.**[1] Rituals, and the discourse that helps to sustain them, fulfill numerous functions. One common function, and type, of ritual is that of *purification* and/or *redemption.* Although these types of ritual are not exactly the same, they share some basic similarities. Rituals of purification respond to the perceived "pollution" or desecration of either a person's body or some "sacred" site (e.g., a church).[2] Redemption rituals also aim for a type of purification, but the problem or threat to which they respond is one concerning the social order. Redemption tries to resolve a problem of cultural "pollution." Cultural pollution can have numerous causes such as action that is impious or disrespectful toward social and cultural norms and values, rejection of established authority, and "failure or threats of failure in social organization" (Duncan, 1962, p. 125; see also Burke, 1970; Rueckert, 1982).

The problem of cultural pollution, and the uneasiness, anxiety, and *guilt* that it creates, was a recurrent theme in Burke's works. He discussed at great length the process of *redemption* through *victimage* and its key principal strategy, **scapegoating** (Burke, 1950, 1957, 1966, 1970, 1984). But Burke (1984) also tried to identify what he termed "variants of victimage" (p. 289). One important variant is **mortification.** In a narrow sense, mortification is "a scrupulous and deliberate clamping of limitation upon the self" (p. 289) or "the deliberate slaying of appetites and ambitions" (Burke, 1970, p. 135). Duncan (1962) described it as a "ritual of renunciation" (p. 362).[3] But how does self-denial, self-discipline, or "self-control" (Burke, 1970, p. 190) help to generate a ritual of redemption?

Mortification, in Burke's view, is not merely a personal lifestyle choice; rather, it is woven into the fabric of human social relations. Burke (1970) wrote, "The principle of mortification is basic to the pattern of governance" (p. 200); mortification is an essential feature of social order (p. 201). Burke's observations about the broader social function of mortification suggest that it is a productive principle or **motive;** mortification helps to structure and guide collective human behavior. As a motive, mortification promotes cultural purification or redemption through a dual process of internalization and repression. A culture or social group infused by the motive of mortification enacts the role of secular sinner. Pollution is removed and redemption is achieved as individuals accept personal responsibility for the culture's problems.[4] Brummett (1981) wrote that mortification "involves open confession of one's 'sins' and actual or symbolic punishment of them" (p. 256). It is, Duncan (1968) observed, a "victimization of self" (p. 147). Rather than searching for an external scapegoat, the motive of mortification transforms the self into a scapegoat (Burke, 1970, p. 248). If the self—or parts of it—is "sacrificed"—if its problematic drives, impulses, or appetites are repressed—then the self, and the social order, can be redeemed. This is, in broad strokes, the "logic" of mortification that Burke reconstructed.

Perhaps the best illustration of mortification as a motive informing the discourse of a community and structuring its social world is the Puritan **jeremiad** and its secularized variations. As Bercovitch (1978) and other scholars have noted, the jeremiad is a prime discursive vehicle for communal redemption. And as the example of Jimmy Carter's speech to the nation on energy policy in July 1979 illustrated,[5] it is a **genre** infused with the spirit (or motive) of mortification. Carter's speech exhibited the two processes noted previously: the interrelated moments of internalization and repression. Carter acknowledged in the speech that the nation was threatened; it was suffering from "a crisis of confidence." Who or what was to blame? What was causing our collective uneasiness and anxiety? Carter did identify specific events such as the assassinations of John F. Kennedy, Robert Kennedy, and Martin Luther King, Jr., as well as the "shock of Watergate." But he seemed to emphasize how America's problems were *our* responsibility; *we* were to blame. We had lost confidence in ourselves and in our future. We now tended to "worship self-indulgence and consumption." We were allowing "a growing disrespect for government and for churches and for schools, the news media, and other institutions." We were the ones tempted by "the path that leads to fragmentation and self-interest," and we were seduced by the idea that it is "right to grasp for ourselves some advantage over others." Carter appeared to suggest in the speech that we must acknowledge our responsibility for the nation's plight. How were we to solve our collective problems? Carter drew on the common generic themes of returning to our roots and restoring American values. But there also was a healthy dose of repression in Carter's cure. When he turned to the specific issue of energy policy, Carter called for self-sacrifice. He called on the nation:

> And I'm asking you for your good and for your nation's security to take no unnecessary trips, to use carpools or public transportation whenever you can, to park your car one extra day per week, to obey the speed limit, and to set your thermostats to save fuel. Every act of energy conservation like this is more than just common sense—I tell you, it is an act of patriotism.

Carter's last sentence was a rather clear illustration of Burke's thesis about the relationship between mortification and governance in that self-sacrifice is equated with love for one's country.[6]

Burke probably was not surprised that Carter failed in his reelection bid in 1980. Mortification, Burke sensed, is a difficult motive to induce. Burke (1970) wrote that the mortified, or those who we would make mortified, tend to experience "the urgent incentive to be 'purified' by 'projecting' his [sic] conflict upon a scapegoat, by 'passing the buck,' by seeking a sacrificial vessel upon which he can vent, as from without, a turmoil that is actually within" (pp. 190-191). One could argue that this is the strategy that Ronald Reagan followed in the 1980 campaign. Reagan countered Carter's strategy and motive of mortification with redemption through victimage, transforming Carter and the doctrine of political liberalism into scapegoats who must be "sacrificed" for the health of the nation.[7] Sacrifice, whether of the self or of other varieties, is a recurrent ritual frequently energized by public discourse. We might do well to follow Burke's (1970) advice: "Let us be on guard ever, as regards the subtleties of sacrifice, in their fundamental relationship to governance" (p. 235).

Notes

1. See Burke (1957). For discussions of Burke's insights on rhetoric and ritual, see Hoban (1980) and Kertzer (1988).

2. On the pollution-purification ritual process, see Kertzer (1988) and Lincoln (1989).

3. In its narrower manifestations, mortification functions as a Foucaultian "disciplinary technology" or "technology of **power**." For an overview of Foucault's

thought on these subjects, see Dreyfus and Rabinow (1983).

4. See also the entry for **confessional.**

5. For background on the speech, see the discussion in the entry for **jeremiad.** See also Check's (2000) analysis of mortification in an earlier Carter speech on energy policy.

6. Martin Luther King, Jr.'s anti-war speech delivered at Riverside Church in New York in April 1967 is another example of the link between the jeremiad and the motive of mortification. One should pay particular attention to the final section of the speech.

7. For a different reading of mortification and scapegoating in the 1980 election, see Brummett (1981).

References and Additional Reading

Bercovitch, S. (1978). *The American jeremiad.* Madison: University of Wisconsin Press.

Brummett, B. (1981). Burkean scapegoating, mortification, and transcendence in presidential campaign rhetoric. *Central States Speech Journal, 32,* 254-264.

Burke, K. (1950). *A rhetoric of motives.* New York: Prentice Hall.

Burke, K. (1957). *The philosophy of literary form* (rev. ed.). New York: Vintage.

Burke, K. (1966). *Language as symbolic action: Essays on life, literature, and method.* Berkeley: University of California Press.

Burke, K. (1970). *The rhetoric of religion: Studies in logology.* Berkeley: University of California Press.

Burke, K. (1984). On human behavior considered "dramatistically." In K. Burke, *Permanence and change: An anatomy of purpose* (3rd ed.). Berkeley: University of California Press.

Chandler, R. C., Hobbs, J. D., King, A. S., & Walts, C. (2000). Scapegoating, transcendence, mortification, and forgiveness: Compensatory arguments of blame after Littleton. In T. A. Hollihan (Ed.), *Argument at century's end: Reflecting on the past and envisioning the future.* Annandale, VA: National Communication Association.

Check, T. (2000). "The moral equivalent of war": Jimmy Carter's use of metaphor and mortification in the energy speech of April 18, 1977. In T. A. Hollihan (Ed.), *Argument at century's end: Reflecting on the past and envisioning the future.* Annandale, VA: National Communication Association.

Dreyfus, H. L., & Rabinow, P. (1983). *Michel Foucault: Beyond structuralism and hermeneutics* (2nd ed.). Chicago: University of Chicago Press.

Duncan, H. D. (1962). *Communication and social order.* London: Oxford University Press.

Duncan, H. D. (1968). *Symbols in society.* New York: Oxford University Press.

Hoban, J. L., Jr. (1980). Rhetorical rituals of rebirth. *Quarterly Journal of Speech, 66,* 275-288.

Kertzer, D. I. (1988). *Ritual, politics, and power.* New Haven, CT: Yale University Press.

Lincoln, B. (1989). *Discourse and the construction of society: Comparative studies of myth, ritual, and classification.* New York: Oxford University Press.

Payne, D. (1986). Adaptation, mortification, and social reform. *Southern Speech Communication Journal, 51,* 187-207.

Rueckert, W. (1982). *Kenneth Burke and the drama of human relations* (2nd ed.). Berkeley: University of California Press.

Tonn, M. B. (1996). Donning sackcloth and ashes: *Webster v. Reproductive Health Services* and moral agony in abortion rights rhetoric. *Communication Quarterly, 44,* 265-279.

MOTIVE/MOTIVATION

During the middle of the 20th century, Walter (1955) remarked, "For over two thousand years, rhetoricians have attempted to develop an understanding of the forces that impel the human being to act. Various concepts of 'emotion,' 'drive,' 'need,' 'desire,' and 'motive' have been evolved" (p. 271). What exactly have rhetoricians meant by the term **motive or motivation,** and how is the concept relevant to rhetorical inquiry? These are the two key questions addressed in this entry. What readers will discover is that motive is conceptualized in different ways and that, given these alternative ways of understanding motive, its contribution to, or place in, rhetorical studies is variable.

We can begin with a very common way of understanding motives: Motives reside *in* people and function to guide behavior. Here is a more formal presentation of this view by McClelland (1987): A motive is "a recurrent concern for a goal state based on a natural incentive—a concern that energizes, orients, and selects behavior" (p. 590). What did McClelland mean by "concern"? A concern is something that we "think about" (this expression was repeated a number of times in McClelland's discussion [pp. 590-591]). Motives do not "refer to fleeting or occasional thoughts, since nearly every eventuality occurs to everyone once in a while" (p. 590).

Concerns are not fleeting; they do not come and go like moods. They are a key element that define an individual's identity. But McClelland made it clear that concerns are not always "conscious"; motives "are not necessarily part of a person's conscious self-image" (p. 592). Motives are, then, psychological phenomena—they are part of our mental infrastructure—that may be more or less conscious and that possess varying degrees of strength. McClelland also distinguished motives from other aspects of human psychology. Motives are not the same as "cognitive desires" (p. 591) or personal "values" (p. 592), and they are more diffuse than a "specific and limited" intent or purpose (p. 593). Motives are grounded in human nature or what McClelland referred to as "natural incentives." Motives are "in" people. It is possible to reinforce, and hence develop, these natural incentives, but motives are not acquired or learned in the same way as are values and other "purely cognitive wish[es]" (p. 591).

Like many other social scientists, McClelland (1987) wanted to identify basic categories or "systems" of interconnected motives. Based on his reading of the literature, McClelland identified four major systems: *achievement, power, affiliation,* and *avoidance.* The achievement motive "represents a recurrent concern about the goal state of doing something better," leading McClelland to remark that "it might better have been named the *efficiency motive*" (p. 595). Achievement or efficiency is a crucial motive "characteristic" in "successful entrepreneurs." McClelland noted, "It turned out that the achievement motive has been a major factor in the economic rise and fall of ancient and modern civilizations" (p. 595). The power motive "represents a recurrent concern to have impact certainly on people and perhaps on things as well" (p. 596). It is "associated with many competitive and assertive activities and with an interest in attaining and preserving prestige and reputation" (p. 596). It is reflected in a need to be dominant or in control. The affiliative motive is exemplified in "the recurrent concern . . . for the goal state of *being with* another" (p. 597). Individuals with well-developed affiliative motives "are interested in establishing and maintaining warm interpersonal relationships" (p. 598). Unlike the first three systems, avoidance motives "involve negative incentives" (p. 593). Avoidance motives operate through our "fears" (of failure, rejection, etc.) and our "anxieties."

Motives, along the lines discussed by McClelland, frequently are characterized as central components of **argument** or persuasive appeals by rhetorical scholars. In their overview and analytic illustration of the Toulmin model, Brockriede and Ehninger (1960) recharacterized appeals to **pathos** (one of the three classical **modes of proof**) as "motivational arguments." A motive, which they defined as "some inner drive, value, desire, emotion, or aspiration" (p. 51), can function argumentatively as a *warrant.* It can supply "link" between *data* and *claim;* it can function as a "reason" justifying belief or action. Similarly, Jasinski (1990) discussed how appeals to "self-interest" function as a motivational warrant or line of argument. Discussions of motivational arguments or appeals are common in introductory public speaking textbooks.[1]

But other senses of motive can be found in contemporary rhetorical scholarship. Fisher (1970), for example, fused the concepts of motive and **rhetorical situation.**[2] According to Fisher, there are four fundamental varieties of rhetorical situation, and each variety can be identified by a fundamental motive or purpose.[3] The motive arising out of some situations is *affirmation* or the need to affirm or endorse a policy proposal or a proposition of value or fact. In other situations, the underlying motive is *reaffirmation* or the need to reaffirm or resuscitate a discredited policy or a forgotten ideal. A third type of situation is organized around the motive of *purification* or the need to purify or cleanse a policy or image that has come under attack (see the entry for **apologia**). Finally, Fisher speculated that a fourth type of situation exists that is the dialectical twin of the first. In the fourth case, the situation is structured by the motive of *sub-*

version or the need to subvert or undermine an existing or proposed policy or proposition. Affirmation and subversion are **dialectically** *interconnected.* Messages that affirm something (a proposition or a policy) almost always engage in some subversion, and subversive messages typically contain an affirmative component. For example, in speeches such as "The Ballot and the Bullet" (delivered in Cleveland, Ohio, in April 1964), Malcolm X sought to subvert the objectives and strategies of the moderate mainstream civil rights movement, but he coupled the subversive element with an affirmation of the policy of "black nationalism." Subversion and affirmation frequently are intertwined in public discourse.

Perhaps the most significant sense of motive in contemporary rhetorical theory and criticism can be found in the works of Kenneth Burke. Beginning with Burke's (1984) book *Permanence and Change,* originally published in 1935, motive would remain a central concept in Burke's thinking. According to Hauser (1991), Burke "changes motive from a *psychological* concept that must be inferred to a *vocabulary* concept that can be observed" (p. 129). We need to explore the nature of this shift to grasp Burke's contribution to the literature on motives.

Burke (1984) opened his discussion of motives in *Permanence and Change* by contrasting the ideas of "real motive" and "pure rationalization" (p. 19). But he expressed considerable doubt about the adequacy of this contrast and, in so doing, questioned the idea that real motives are something residing inside an individual. Burke wrote that motives "are distinctly linguistic products" (p. 35). Motives do not reside in people; they are "not some fixed thing, like a table, which one can go and look at" (p. 25). Motives instead reside in various "terminologies" or "vocabularies" of motives (pp. 20-21). Dismissing a person's "vocabulary of motives" in the quest to uncover his or her "real" motives made no sense to Burke. He wrote, "To explain one's conduct by the vocabulary of motives current among one's group is about as self-deceptive as giving the area of a field in the accepted terms of measurement. One is simply interpreting with the only vocabulary he [sic] knows" (p. 21). Scholars within and outside of rhetorical studies later would take up Burke's concept of vocabularies of motive (Allen & Tompkins, 1996; Campbell, 1991; Hopper, 1993; Ivie, 1974; Mills, 1940).

From 1935 onward, Burke was clear that motives are a linguistic phenomenon. But what exactly was Burke referring to when he used the term *motive*? What did motive mean for Burke? Commenting on some of the initial efforts to incorporate Burkeian concepts into rhetorical studies, Crable and Makay (1972) concluded, "The Burkeian idea of motive, so crucial to understanding Burke's thinking, needs further clarification" (p. 13). Unfortunately, Crable and Makay's discussion of motives as "forces acting upon the agent" (p. 13) did not provide much clarification. Burke's sense of motive remains elusive.

Here is one possible way of understanding Burke's position on motive. In *Permanence and Change,* Burke (1984) discussed motive in the context of two other key concepts: *orientation* and *situation.* Let us try to see how these two ideas might shed some light on Burke' sense of motive. First, there is the idea of orientation. At the end of the passage quoted earlier where Burke was describing how a "vocabulary of motives" is roughly equivalent to "accepted terms of measurement," he connected motive and orientation. He wrote, "One is simply interpreting with the only vocabulary he [sic] knows. One is stating his orientation, which involves a vocabulary of ought and ought-not, with attendant vocabulary of praiseworthy and blameworthy" (p. 21). A vocabulary of motives is, for Burke, part of an "orientation"—a "system of interpretation" (p. 3) or a "schema" (p. 21)—that makes our world comprehensible and meaningful. We do not, and indeed cannot, perceive the world in some type of neutral or objective manner devoid of any orientation; our understanding of the world is derived from our orientation in the same way that the length of something is derived from the system of measurement used by a culture (e.g., a piece of string measured in the United States will be 6 inches long, whereas the same piece will measure 15.2 centimeters in Canada). Motives, then, are simply a shorthand way of saying, "In this culture, here's how we see the world, and as a result, here's how we do things."

A few pages after Burke (1984) talked about motives in the context of orientation, he shifted gears and approached the concept from the perspective of the situation. He wrote that "words for motive are in reality words for situation" (p. 31). This theme was reintroduced toward the end of the book, where Burke suggested that

> man's [sic] words for motives are merely a shorthand description of *situations.* One tends to think of a duality here, to assume some kind of breach between situation and a response. Yet the two are identical. . . . The situation was our motive, and our word for the motive characterizes the situation. (pp. 220-221)

But we need to recall that people do not encounter situations in a vacuum; they encounter situations through established orientations. Burke was setting up a dialectical interaction between orientation and situation; orientations allow us to understand situations, and situations shape and reshape orientations. And motive? Motives, it seems, arise from and operate within the interaction between orientations and situations. Motives exist in the vocabularies that we use for grasping situations and formulating responses to situations. Motives, in short, appear to be cultural principles embodied in vocabularies that shape and guide human perception and action.

Is this reconstruction of Burke's sense of motives fundamentally at odds with the position of someone such as McClelland? The answer to that question is probably yes and no. The answer is no when we look to the issue of function. There seems to be a broad consensus among scholars interested in the topic that motives are a force shaping human behavior. Differences arise when we look more closely at *how* motives operate, the ontic status of motives, and how scholars gain access to motives. Burke suggested that motives not only guide behavior but also influence perception. Hence, the relationship between perception and action needs close scrutiny. In Burke's view, motives do not exist *in* someone's head; they generally exist in vocabularies and in situations. But motives ultimately reside in the language people use to talk about the world of problems, events, and relationships as well as their behavior in it. And because people frequently speak in more than one *idiom* (**heteroglossia**), motives tend to get jumbled together; human motivation rarely is "pure" or singular. Motives do not exist "behind" our action; rather, motives saturate or suffuse our action. The key is learning how to "read" or interpret action, especially linguistic or symbolic action. Burke's *methods* for uncovering motives have had a substantial impact on the realm of rhetorical criticism.

One of the central methods that Burke (1945) developed for studying motivation is the *pentad* of *act, scene, agent, agency,* and *purpose.* In a well-known passage from the "Introduction" to *A Grammar of Motives,* Burke remarked, "Any complete statement about motives will offer *some kind of* answers to these five questions: what was done (act), when or where it was done (scene), who did it (agent), how he [sic] did it (agency), and why (purpose)" (p. xv). The five terms of the pentad are the substance out of which human motives are fashioned. Each pentadic element might be thought of as a summational term for a basic or fundamental vocabulary of motives. The motives embedded *in* verbal action can be read by reconstructing the play among the various manifestations of the pentadic elements in a text (which element is dominant and how the elements interact are crucial questions to consider). The play of pentadic elements will, Burke argued, be "present in systematically elaborated metaphysical structures, in legal judgments, in poetry and fiction, in political and scientific works, in news, and in bits of gossip offered at random" (p. xv). In short, wherever and whenever we find verbal action (a **text**), we will find a play of vocabularies that reveals the motives guiding or organizing the action.

Two different ways of applying the pentad have emerged in the works of rhetorical critics. Some critics have used the pentad to try to discover the motive *of* a specific text or verbal act. Crable and Makay (1972), for example, used the pentad to examine George Wallace's symbolic 1963 stand in the doorway at the University of Alabama. According to Crable and Makay, Wallace was the *agent,* his defiance of a court order was the *act,* the television cameras covering the event were the *agency,* blocking integration was Wallace's *purpose,* and "the total physical and psychological environment" was the *scene* (p. 15). Only by apprehending the motivational forces that emerge within each element, and in the interaction of elements, can the critic reconstruct the motivation of the "rhetorical act" (p. 15) or "rhetorical event" (p. 17). But there is some irony in Crable and Makay's analysis. To uncover the forces motivating the act, they had to ignore the *verbal* act (in the language of contemporary rhetorical **metacriticism,** they "deferred the text"). Despite the fact that the final word in their essay was "discourse" (p. 17), Crable and Makay said nothing about Wallace's discourse while standing in the schoolhouse door. Their application of the pentad was *external* or "extrinsic" (Cohen, 1998); they identified agents, acts, scenes, agencies, and purposes as they exist in the world and tried to reconstruct the motive *of* from these sources.

But another approach that appears more in keeping with the spirit of Burke's discussion is possible. Instead of trying to uncover externally the motive *of* a verbal act (a process that usually leads to the deferral of the text), the critic can proceed *internally* and investigate the motive *in* the verbal act. This process involves treating the material substance of the text as its own miniature "world" with acts, agents, and the other pentadic elements. Consider a text such as Elizabeth Cady Stanton's "The Solitude of Self" speech delivered in Washington, D.C., in January 1892. If approached by way of Crable and Makay's (1972) external form of pentadic analysis, then Stanton would be the likely *agent;* the place where she delivered the speech (e.g., the suffrage convention, the U.S. Congress) would be the *scene;* the presentation of the speech would be the *act;* her voice, language, and diction likely would be the *agency;* and the drive for women's suffrage would be the *purpose.* But if we adopt the second approach and seek the motives *in* the verbal act, then the analysis would proceed much differently. The critic would begin by identifying the agents that appear *in* the text (e.g., the little girl all alone at Christmas time, the young mother trying to cope with her life, the women prisoners saving the sailors during the storm) and then move to the scenes that are depicted, the particular acts that are reported, the means used to perform these acts, and the ostensible purposes behind these acts. This way of applying the pentad is, admittedly, much more complicated; the critic needs to proceed with care in his or her effort to reconstruct, first, the play among pentadic elements and, then, the motives that such a play of elements suggests. Although more difficult, the internal form of analysis is the method at work in most of the more interesting versions of pentadic criticism such as Ling's (1970) reading of Ted Kennedy's speech to the people of Massachusetts after the accident at Chappaquiddick; Birdsell's (1987) study of Ronald Reagan's address to the American public on October 27, 1983, regarding the bombing in Lebanon and the American invasion of Grenada; and Tonn, Endress, and Diamond's (1993) analysis of the debate in Maine following the accidental shooting of a young mother by a local hunter.[4]

Burke also suggested another way in which critics might unearth the motives in a text. This approach generally is known as *cluster analysis.* Burke explained and illustrated this approach in the long essay, "The Philosophy of Literary Form" (Burke, 1957), as well as in the shorter essay "Fact, Inference, and Proof in the Analysis of Literary Symbolism" (Burke, 1964). In widely quoted passage from the long essay, Burke (1957) wrote,

> Now, the work of every writer contains a set of implicit equations. He [sic] uses "associational clusters." And you may, by examining his work, find "what goes with what" in these clusters—what kinds of acts and images and personalities and situations go with his notions of heroism, villainy, consolation, despair, etc. And though he [may] be perfectly conscious of the act of writing . . ., he cannot possibly be conscious of the interrelationships among all these equations. Afterward, by inspecting his work "statistically," we or he may disclose by objective citation the structure of motivation operating here. There is no need to "supply" motives. The interrelationships themselves *are* his motives. . . . The motivation out of which he writes is synonymous with the structural way in which he puts events and values together when he writes; and however consciously he may go about such work, there is a kind of generalization about these interrelations that he could not have been conscious of, since the generalization could be made by the kind of inspection that is possible only *after the completion* of the work. (p. 18)

Motives, Burke here again emphasized, never are fully present or fully formed *prior* to verbal action; motives inform verbal action at the same time as the verbal action gives the motives a concrete existence. The critic can access the motives in verbal action by reconstructing the "clusters." In the long essay, Burke illustrated this approach in an analysis of Clifford Odets' play, "Golden Boy." The play is structured, Burke argued, around two *antagonistic* clusters summarized by the images of "prize-fight" and "violin." The motivation of the play simply *is* the antagonism disclosed through a careful reconstruction of the associational clusters. Berthold (1976) and Brummett (1979) illustrated how the cluster method has been appropriated by rhetorical critics.[5]

The concept of motive in Burke's writing is central but elusive. Burke emphasized a linguistic view of motives (motives are *in* vocabularies and verbal action) as opposed to a psychological one (motives are *in* people). But this insistence on the linguistic nature of motives is not always appreciated by rhetorical scholars engaged in the process of appropriating Burke's work and transforming it into a critical method. Interest in the concept of motive or motivation is on the decline in rhetorical studies. Many scholars influenced by postmodern theory have abandoned the idea of motivation (in whatever form) as too "modern" or too subject centered and have replaced it with concepts such as *desire.*[6] But one thing has continued—the rhetorician's quest to understand "the forces that impel the human being to act."

Notes

1. Walter made this observation in 1955. For recent examples, see Beebe and Beebe (1997) and Gronbeck, German, Ehninger, and Monroe (1995).

2. For an earlier effort to link motivation and situation, see Walter (1955).

3. On Fisher's conflation of motive and purpose, see Crable and Makay (1972).

4. On the internal/external distinction, see also Cohen (1998, p. 96) and Foss (1989, pp. 338-339).

5. In Brummett's (1979) case, his critical strategy is best described as a blend of pentadic and cluster analysis.

6. Burke probably would argue that desire is simply the titular term for a new or refurbished vocabulary of motives.

References and Additional Reading

Allen, B. J., & Tompkins, P. K. (1996). Vocabularies of motives in a crisis of academic leadership. *Southern Communication Journal, 62,* 322-331.

Beebe, S. A., & Beebe, S. J. (1997). *Public speaking: An audience-centered approach* (3rd ed.). Boston: Allyn & Bacon.

Berthold, C. A. (1976). Kenneth Burke's cluster-agon method: Its development and application. *Central States Speech Journal, 27,* 302-309.

Birdsell, D. S. (1987). Ronald Reagan on Lebanon and Grenada: Flexibility and interpretation in the application of Kenneth Burke's pentad. *Quarterly Journal of Speech, 73,* 267-279.

Brock, B. L. (1990). Rhetorical criticism: A Burkeian approach revisited. In B. L. Brock et al. (Eds.), *Methods of rhetorical criticism* (3rd ed.). Detroit, MI: Wayne State University Press.

Brockriede, W., & Ehninger, D. (1960). Toulmin on argument: An interpretation and application. *Quarterly Journal of Speech, 46,* 44-53.

Brummett, B. (1979). A pentadic analysis of ideologies in two gay rights controversies. *Central States Speech Journal, 30,* 250-261.

Burke, K. (1945). *A grammar of motives.* New York: Prentice Hall.

Burke, K. (1957). The philosophy of literary form. In K. Burke, *The philosophy of literary form* (rev. ed.). New York: Vintage.

Burke, K. (1964). Fact, inference, and proof in the analysis of literary symbolism. S. E. Hyman (Ed.), *Terms for order.* Bloomington: Indiana University Press.

Burke, K. (1984). *Permanence and change: An anatomy of purpose* (3rd ed.). Berkeley: University of California Press.

Campbell, C. (1991). Reexamining Mills on motive: A character vocabulary approach. *Sociological Analysis, 52,* 89-97.

Cohen, J. R. (1998). *Communication criticism: Developing your critical powers.* Thousand Oaks, CA: Sage.

Conrad, C. (1984). Phases, pentads, and dramatistic critical process. *Central States Speech Journal, 35,* 94-104.

Crable, R. E., & Makay, J. J. (1972, Winter). Kenneth Burke's concept of motives in rhetorical theory. *Today's Speech,* pp. 11-18.

Fisher, W. R. (1970). A motive view of communication. *Quarterly Journal of Speech, 56,* 131-139.

Foss, S. K. (1989). *Rhetorical criticism: Exploration and practice.* Prospect Heights, IL: Waveland.

Gronbeck, B. E., German, K., Ehninger, D., & Monroe, A. H. (1995). *Principles of speech communication* (12th ed.). New York: HarperCollins.

Hauser, G. A. (1991). *Introduction to rhetorical theory.* Prospect Heights, IL: Waveland.

Hochmuth, M. (1952). Kenneth Burke and the "new rhetoric." *Quarterly Journal of Speech, 38,* 133-144.

Hopper, J. (1993). The rhetoric of motives in divorce. *Journal of Marriage and the Family, 55,* 801-813.

Ivie, R. L. (1974). Presidential motives for war. *Quarterly Journal of Speech, 60,* 337-345.

Jasinski, J. (1990). An exploration of form and force in rhetoric and argumentation. In D. C. Williams & M. D. Hazen (Eds.), *Argumentation theory and the rhetoric of assent.* Tuscaloosa: University of Alabama Press.

Ling, D. (1970). A pentadic analysis of Sen. Edward Kennedy's address to the people of Massachusetts, July 25, 1969. *Central States Speech Journal, 21,* 81-86.

McClelland, D. C. (1987). *Human motivation.* Cambridge, UK: Cambridge University Press.

Mills, C. W. (1940). Situated actions and vocabularies of motive. *American Sociological Review, 5,* 904-913.

Peterson, T. R. (1986). The will to conservation: A Burkeian analysis of Dust Bowl rhetoric and American farming motives. *Southern Speech Communication Journal, 52,* 1-21.

Tonn, M. B., Endress, V. A., & Diamond, J. N. (1993). Hunting and heritage on trial in Maine: A dramatistic debate over tragedy, tradition, and territory. *Quarterly Journal of Speech, 79,* 165-181.

Walter, O. M. (1955). Toward an analysis of motivation. *Quarterly Journal of Speech, 41,* 271-278.

MOVEMENTS

The classical treatises on rhetoric provided advice to advocates on how to be persuasive. The focus of these works was highly individualistic; a rhetorical encounter commonly was conceptualized as a contest between rival combatants, with each individual struggling to defeat his or her opponent. This individualistic emphasis became even more prominent as legal oratory emerged as the main focus of rhetorical handbooks.

During the early part of the 20th century, rhetorical scholars in newly created academic departments of speech appropriated the insights and ideas of classical theorists as part of their effort to establish a modern discipline of rhetorical studies. Just as the classical handbooks offered advice to individual practitioners and advocates, modern rhetorical critics initially directed their attention to individual speakers. The focus on the individual practitioner might be appropriate for certain types of legal oratory such as the rhetorical battles between rival orators/lawyers (e.g., Clarence Darrow and William Jennings Bryant), but advocates for change as well as defenders of the status quo rarely are isolated individuals. Although we might occasionally find an advocate howling in the wilderness, more often advocates are part of a larger collective effort either to alter or overturn the existing economic, social, and/or political order or to defend that order. These larger collective efforts to change or defend the status quo to which advocates devote their considerable talents and energies typically are referred to as social or rhetorical **movements.** Thousands of advocates have appeared on the American public stage. William Lloyd Garrison, Susan B. Anthony, Tom Hayden, Stokely Carmichael, and Pat Buchanan are just some of the more famous practitioners of public advocacy. Although these advocates might have sought personal gain such as fame or electoral success at various times, each was a participant in a broader movement; each was part of a larger collective effort to alter the nature of American society.

During the late 1940s and early 1950s, rhetorical scholars began to recognize the centrality of movements in American public life (Crandell, 1947; Griffin, 1951). They were not alone. Sociologists and historians, to name two of the most obvious examples, also began to explore the dynamics of social movements. Drawing inspiration from the works in other fields as well as from the tradition of rhetorical studies, many rhetorical scholars made the movement, and not the individual advocate, the primary object of inquiry. Rhetoricians sought to define the central characteristics or features of a social movement, understand the patterns of temporal evolution that are common in movements (often referred to as the *life cycle* of a movement), and describe and analyze the persuasive strategies employed by the participants in specific movements.

A considerable amount of research on social movements has emerged over the past few decades in contemporary rhetorical studies.[1] One way of sorting through the research is to invoke the distinction between *means* and *ends.* Much of the research considers a social movement to be a means to a specified end. The abolitionist movement was a means to the end of slavery, whereas the pro-life movement is a means to the end of the practice of abortion. Within this branch of means-oriented movement scholarship, other subdivisions can be identified. One of the most common forms of movement scholarship attempts to analyze the dominant strategy or strategies employed by the members of a movement to accomplish its end. For example, Cox (1974) investigated the efforts of reformers to change child labor laws during the early 20th century, Erlich (1977) examined the rhetorical strategies of the populist movement in late 19th-century America, Campbell (1973) uncovered a central discursive feature of the women's liberation movement of the late 1960s, and Conrad (1983) found a significant recurrent form in the rhetoric of the moral majority. Some movement scholarship focuses attention on a particular part or segment of a larger movement. For example, Kennicott (1970) investigated the strategies and practices of black abolitionists, Yellin and Van Horne (1994) analyzed the efforts of female abolitionists, and Yoder (1969) looked at the efforts of the clergy in the Vietnam antiwar movement. Although the bulk of rhetorical scholarship has focused on movements for change, some scholars have analyzed the efforts of movements that are resisting change. For example, Solomon (1978, 1979) uncovered key strategies and discursive forms in the discourse of the anti-Equal Rights Amendment movement, Hillbruner (1960) examined southern responses to abolitionism during the 19th century, and Murphy (1992) traced mainstream responses to civil rights agitation during the early 1960s. Finally, there is a strand of means-oriented movement scholarship that attempts to identify and analyze particular innovative or novel strategies that may be employed by the members of a movement. Critical attention has been devoted to song (Knupp, 1981), slogans (Denton, 1980), obscenity (Rothwell, 1971), civil disobedience (Ritchie, 1970), and riots Doolittle (1976).

For a movement to function as a means to an end, the movement itself must at times be the *end* of discourse. If a movement falls apart, splinters into competing factions, or starts to "backslide" (a process whereby members return to pre-movement habits of thought), then the movement no longer will be an effective force for social change. Consequently, although the energies of the movement are constantly directed toward the larger end to which it is a means—whether that end be the abolition of slavery, the adoption of the Equal Rights Amendment, or an alteration in civil law to allow same-sex marriages—some energy or attention must be devoted to the functional tasks of creating, organizing, sustaining, and expanding the movement. Whereas social movements usually begin in opposition to established institutions and their practices, most sustained movements develop their own institutional structures that must then be sustained through rhetorical action.[2] When scholars investigate the ways in which a movement uses discourse to resolve the common problems or *exigences* that it faces, the movement is conceptualized as an end in itself as well as a means to some larger programmatic goal.

What common functional exigences do social movements face that threaten the continued viability of the movement, hence calling into question the movement's ability to accomplish its substantive goal? No list of movement exigences can be exhaustive, but the following are some of the more common ones (see also Jurma, 1982). First, movements inevitably encounter setbacks and frustrations (e.g., a court injunction prohibiting an important rally or march, the arrest of key movement leaders, lack of money). Severe setbacks and frustrations might threaten the continued existence of the movement and, consequently, must be addressed if the movement is to continue working toward its larger goal. Critical attention is devoted to the discursive strategies that movement advocates employ to lessen the potential severity of the setbacks. For example, a setback might be *redefined* into an opportunity or a critical test that the movement must pass. Advocates might rely on **conspiracy** appeals as a way of explaining the presence of setbacks or might depict the opposition as **enemies** that are powerful yet vulnerable if only the movement stays on target.

Second, history demonstrates rather clearly that movements tend to fragment or splinter over time. The history of the Protestant reformation is a case in point. Fragmentation can result from a variety of factors. The slow pace of change leads some members of a movement to adopt more aggressive tactics, differences of opinion can emerge with respect to movement objectives, and incidents can occur that have the potential to divide movement members against each other.[3] When movements splinter, valuable energy often is redirected away from trying to change the dominant social order and instead is spent on fighting against rival splinter factions. When Martin Luther King, Jr., delivered his famous speech during the March on Washington in August 1963, the civil rights movement was in danger of splintering into different factions. Part of King's rhetorical challenge, then, was not only to urge the adoption of the movement's agenda but also to maintain the unity of the movement. One strategy for establishing unity within a movement is the use of **condensation symbols.** As Graber (1976) noted, "Social movements which seek to generate strong ties among their followers may take painstaking care to create effective condensation symbols; without such symbols, the movement may fail or grow at an unduly slow pace" (p. 319). A related strategy for maintaining unity is **transcendence** or an attempt to move beyond narrower, and hence trivial, differences by focusing attention on broader, more abstract goals and values (Burkholder, 1989). Effective condensation symbols allow the members of a movement to overcome or transcend their differences by focusing on the more inclusive values cued by the condensation symbol.

Third, participants in a movement are, in effect, converts to a cause; they undergo a process of **secular conversion** that often involves the adoption of a new identity or a new sense of self. For example, a woman who joined the women's liberation movement of the 1960s assumed a new identity or became a new person. But the new sense of self always is threatened or challenged by the "old" self. The liberated woman of the 1960s was surrounded by messages from numerous sources celebrating the "old" habits and ways of thinking that she was trying to leave behind. Temptation is not merely a problem in religious conversion; it also exists in secular conversion experiences. Consequently, a movement must continue to reinforce the new identity or new self that helps to sustain the movement and give it direction. Gregg (1971) described this important task as the **ego-function** of movement rhetoric; if a movement fails to satisfy this need, then it runs the risk of having its members backslide and return to their pre-movement identities. As noted earlier, these three movement exigences do not exhaust the functional tasks that movements face, but they do indicate some of the more common rhetorical problems that movements must grapple with if they are to be an effective force in public life.

Movement scholarship has been on the decline in rhetorical studies, at least quantitatively, over the past decade.[4] Part of the decline can be attributed to the growing prominence of *close textual analysis* in contemporary rhetorical criticism that emphasizes the artistry and dynamics of specific texts and practices over the broader patterns that mark the rhetoric of social movements. Part of the decline also might be attributed to the emergence of alternative conceptual categories such as **discursive formation, argument field,** and the **public sphere** that provide critics with different resources and tools for talking about the ways in which particular texts and practices can be organized into larger units for analysis. Although movement scholarship might be waning, its central thrust remains in place. Contemporary rhetorical scholarship still is marked by an interest in, and a concern for, the discursive practices of variously organized groups and collectives that function as a major force in public deliberation.

Notes

1. For an overview of trends, methods, and approaches, see Stewart, Smith, and Denton (1989).

2. On the functional approach to movements, see Stewart (1980, 1983) and Simons (1970).

3. As an example of the last source of fragmentation, consider the difficulties that feminists had to negotiate in responding to Bill Clinton's sex scandals in 1998.

4. Movement scholarship continues in other fields in response to developments such as the decline of political parties, the rise of identity politics, the growth of "new" social movements, and the emergence of a "postindustrial" society. See, for example, Bash (1995); Habermas (1981); Jasper (1997); Johnston and Klandermans (1995); Laraña, Johnston, and Gusfield (1994); McAdam and Snow (1997); Morris and Mueller (1992); Reed (1992); and Tarrow (1994). The Twayne series, *Social Movements: Past and Present* (edited by Robert D. Benford), contains more than 25 volumes and ranges over a large number of significant movements in American history. For exceptions to this general trend in rhetorical studies, see Hauser and Whalen (1997), Palczewski (1995), Stewart (1997), and Whalen and Hauser (1995).

References and Additional Reading

Bash, H. H. (1995). *Social problems and social movements: An exploration into the sociological construction of alternative realities.* Atlantic Highlands, NJ: Humanities Press.

Boggs, C. (1986). *Social movements and political power.* Philadelphia: Temple University Press.

Burkholder, T. R. (1989). Kansas populism, woman suffrage, and the agrarian myth: A case study in the limits of mythic transcendence. *Communication Studies, 40,* 292-307.

Campbell, K. K. (1973). The rhetoric of women's liberation: An oxymoron. *Quarterly Journal of Speech, 59,* 74-86.

Conrad, C. (1983). The rhetoric of the moral majority: An analysis of romantic form. *Quarterly Journal of Speech, 69,* 159-170.

Cox, J. R. (1974). The rhetoric of child labor reform: An efficacy-utility analysis. *Quarterly Journal of Speech, 60,* 359-370.

Crandell, S. J. (1947). The beginnings of a methodology for social control studies in public address. *Quarterly Journal of Speech, 33,* 36-39.

Denton, R. E. (1980). The rhetorical functions of slogans: Classifications and characteristics. *Communication Quarterly, 28,* 10-18.

Doolittle, R. J. (1976). Riots as symbolic: A criticism and approach. *Central States Speech Journal, 27,* 310-317.

Erlich, H. S. (1977). Populist rhetoric reassessed: A paradox. *Quarterly Journal of Speech, 63,* 140-151.

Graber, D. (1976). *Verbal behavior and politics.* Urbana: University of Illinois Press.

Gregg, R. B. (1971). The ego-function of the rhetoric of protest. *Philosophy and Rhetoric, 4,* 71-91.

Griffin, L. M. (1951). The rhetoric of historical movements. *Quarterly Journal of Speech, 38,* 184-188.

Griffin, L. M. (1969). A dramatistic theory of the rhetoric of movements. In W. H. Rueckert (Ed.), *Critical responses to Kenneth Burke.* Minneapolis: University of Minnesota Press.

Habermas, J. (1981). New social movements. *Telos, 49,* 33-37.

Hauser, G. A., & Whalen, S. (1997). New rhetoric and new social movements. In B. Kovacic (Ed.), *Emerging theories of human communication.* Albany: State University of New York Press.

Hillbruner, A. (1960). Inequality, the great chain of being, and antebellum southern oratory. *Southern Speech Journal, 25,* 172-189.

Hillbruner, A. (1978). The theory of the avant-garde: Some *topoi* for the study of movements. *Central States Speech Journal, 29,* 251-262.

Jasper, J. (1997). *The art of moral protest: Culture, biography, and creativity in social movements.* Chicago: University of Chicago Press.

Johnston, H., & Klandermans, B. (Eds.). (1995). *Social movements and culture.* Minneapolis: University of Minnesota Press.

Jurma, W. E. (1982). Moderate movement leadership and the Vietnam moratorium committee. *Quarterly Journal of Speech, 68,* 262-272.

Kennicott, P. C. (1970). Black persuaders in the antislavery movement. *Speech Monographs, 37,* 15-24.

Knupp, R. E. (1981). A time for every purpose under heaven: Rhetorical dimensions of protest music. *Southern Speech Communication Journal, 46,* 377-389.

Lucas, S. E. (1980). Coming to terms with movement studies. *Central States Speech Journal, 31,* 255-266.

Laraña, E., Johnston, H., & Gusfield, J. R. (Eds.). (1994). *New social movements: From ideology to identity.* Philadelphia: Temple University Press.

McAdam, D., & Snow, D. A. (Eds.). (1997). *Social movements: Readings on their emergence, mobilization, and dynamics.* Los Angeles: Roxbury.

Melucci, A. (1989). *Nomads of the present.* Philadelphia: Temple University Press.

Morris, A. D., & Mueller, C. M. (Eds.). (1992). *Frontiers in social movement theory.* New Haven, CT: Yale University Press.

Murphy, J. M. (1992). Domesticating dissent: The Kennedys and the freedom rides. *Communication Monographs, 59,* 61-78.

Palczewski, C. H. (1995). Definitional argument: Approaching a theory. In S. Jackson (Ed.), *Argumentation and values: Proceedings of the Ninth SCA/AFA Conference on Argumentation.* Annandale, VA: Speech Communication Association.

Reed, T. V. (1992). *Fifteen jugglers, five believers: Literary politics and the poetics of American social movements.* Berkeley: University of California Press.

Ritchie, G. (1970, Winter). The sit-in: A rhetoric of human action. *Today's Speech,* pp. 22-25.

Rothwell, J. D. (1971). Verbal obscenity: Time for second thoughts. *Western Speech, 35,* 231-242.

Sillars, M. O. (1980). Defining movements rhetorically: Casting the widest net. *Southern Speech Communication Journal, 46,* 17-32.

Simons, H. W. (1970). Requirements, problems, and strategies: A theory of persuasion for social movements. *Quarterly Journal of Speech, 56,* 1-11.

Simons, H. W., Mechling, E., & Schreier, H. (1984). Functions of communication in mobilizing for action from the bottom up: The rhetoric of social movements. In C. C. Arnold & J. W. Bowers (Eds.), *Handbook on rhetorical and communication theory.* Boston: Allyn & Bacon.

Solomon, M. (1978). The rhetoric of STOP ERA: Fatalistic reaffirmation. *Southern Speech Communication Journal, 44,* 42-59.

Solomon, M. (1979). The "positive woman's" journey: A mythic analysis of the rhetoric of STOP ERA. *Quarterly Journal of Speech, 65,* 262-274.

Stewart, C. J. (1980). A functional approach to the rhetoric of social movements. *Central States Speech Journal, 31,* 298-305.

Stewart, C. J. (1983). A functional perspective on the study of social movements. *Central States Speech Journal, 34,* 77-80.

Stewart, C. J. (1997). The evolution of a rhetoric: Stokely Carmichael and the rhetoric of Black Power. *Quarterly Journal of Speech, 83,* 429-446.

Stewart, C. J., Smith, C. A., & Denton, R. E. (1989). *Persuasion and social movements* (2nd ed.). Prospect Heights, IL: Waveland.

Tarrow, S. (1994). *Power in movement: Social movements, collective action, and politics.* Cambridge, UK: Cambridge University Press.

Whalen, S., & Hauser, G. A. (1995). Identity arguments in new social movement rhetoric. In S. Jackson (Ed.), *Argumentation and values: Proceedings of the Ninth SCA/AFA Conference on Argumentation.* Annandale, VA: Speech Communication Association.

Yellin, J. F., & Van Horne, J. C. (Eds.). (1994). *The abolitionist sisterhood: Women's political culture in antebellum America.* Ithaca, NY: Cornell University Press.

Yoder, J. (1969, September). The protest of the American clergy in opposition to the war in Vietnam. *Today's Speech*, pp. 51-59.

MYSTIFICATION

In *A Rhetoric of Motives*, Burke (1950) observed that there appear to be two types of **mystification:** "a special kind and a general kind" (p. 179). What did Burke mean by these two types of mystification? The special type of mystification, he wrote, is "simple but ubiquitous" and is based on the fact that "language can be used to deceive" (p. 178). One type of mystification, then, is a process of verbal and symbolic deception; linguistic or symbolic mystification obscures or covers up (or covers over) the world that supposedly is being described. Extending on Burke's discussion, and drawing on more recent scholarship, we can note a number of specific forms of this type of special mystification.

First, mystification exists in the process of naming or **definition.** *Euphemisms* are a common example of this form of mystification. When an advocate labels a new missile system a "peacekeeper," when an international agreement limiting the number of new strategic weapons that can be produced is referred to as an "arms reduction treaty," or when corporate executives describe the growing number of workers displaced from full-time employment by ongoing corporate restructuring as "contingent workers," we are in the presence of this form of mystification. Consider the word *security.* We associate the word with safety or being free from danger. But how safe is an investment in the *securities* market? Does the naming strategy subtly mystify the process of economic speculation? Borrowing a concept from British philosopher Jeremy Bentham, Burke (1950) referred to mystifying euphemisms and vague "unitary terms" such as *country* and *fatherland* as **eulogistic coverings** (p. 108). Such terms function to insulate or protect and confer a strategic advantage on those who employ them.[1]

Burke believed that economic factors, such as "private property and the division of labor," are important sources of mystification (p. 107; see also Burke, 1984). Social historian Stuart Ewen explored a particular form of mystification operating in America's culture of consumer capitalism. Extending on the work of French critic Roland Barthes, Ewen (1976) argued that a key aspect of America's consumer **ideology** is the "mystification of the production process" (p. 105). Ewen explained, "The success of consumerization depended on the ability to obfuscate the work process, to create an understanding of the industrial world which avoided any problematic reference to production altogether" (p. 79). Ewen argued that during the early 20th century, American business leaders attempted to

> eradicate the productive process from the ideology that surrounded the products. . . . The reality of life within the factory only tended to cast aspersions on the visions of happiness projected by consumer ideology, and it was an essential principle of commercial propaganda that depiction of this reality be avoided at all costs. (p. 78)

The eradication or elision of the productive process can be both simple and subtle. In its simpler forms, eradication is accomplished through silence. For example, readers should ask themselves when was the last time that they saw an ad for Nike products that mentioned the working conditions in Third World sweatshops where the products are produced (the same question could be asked about almost any personal apparel products). In its subtler forms, we find a more pronounced effort to mystify the conditions of production. For example, a television ad for fish sticks depicts a solitary fisherman (wearing the stereotypical yellow rain slicker) unloading the day's catch from his rather dinky and very modestly equipped boat. The voice-over states something to the effect that the fish go from the fisherman's boat to the consumer's plate. Does the ad portray the reality of commercial fishing? Although there still might be a few independent fishermen (and women) who sell their daily catches to commercial processors, the vast majority of commercial fishing is done aboard tanker-size vessels with front ends that open up and suck thousands of fish into their hulls at a time. But depicting this process would not make the fish sticks very attractive, so the process is romanticized or mystified. An even more extreme case is the Wendy's ad that reveals the "secret" behind its hamburger patties. The on-screen picture depicts an elderly grandmother-type figure shaping the hamburger patties by hand. So, now we know why the Wendy's hamburgers do not look or taste like the ones at Burger King or McDonald's. In this ad, as in the fish sticks commercial, the reality of product production is distorted and the process of production is mystified (see also Leiss, Kline, & Jhally, 1990).

Another common form of mystification is closely related to Ewen's (1976) observations about the obfuscation of the conditions of production. Organizations, especially corporations, routinely produce messages that, instead of eradicating the conditions of productions, elide the material conditions of their existence. Corporations are profit-making operations; they exist to make money for their stockholders (in the *idiom* of the corporate world, the corporation has a "fiduciary responsibility" to the stockholders). But consider the now common *image* ads that are disseminated by the corporate sector. Do these ads acknowledge the material realities of profit motivation? Rarely. Instead, these ads extol the virtues of particular corporations—their contributions to the community, their records as friends of the environment, their commitment to central communal values, and so on. Corporate image ads can function in multiple ways,[2] and one of those functions often will be to mystify the realities of the corporate world.

Burke stressed that mystification is a response to the reality of social **hierarchy** and inequality; through forms of mystification, the institutions, structures, and practices that maintain hierarchy and inequality tend to be obscured.[3] Anthropologist David Kertzer echoed these Burkeian concerns. Kertzer (1988) wrote that mystification is the "symbolic representation of the political order in a way that systematically differs from the actual power relations found in the society" or, put differently, is the "symbolic misrepresentation of the nature of power in the society" (p. 48). Through typical democratic mystifications such as the widespread belief that "people are all equal . . . , inequalities are legitimated" and "political stability" is promoted (pp. 48, 50). Kertzer was particularly interested in the way in which language and political **ritual** interact to produce mystification. He argued that one example is "the ritual of 'free elections.' . . . In the United States, elections foster the illusion that American government is the result of the free, informed choice of the entire citizenry and that all are equal in deciding questions of public policy" (p. 49). What election rituals obscure, Kertzer suggested, is the reality of Wall Street investment bankers and the other obscure individuals who shape public policy. Did Kertzer's claim that elections function as a mystification ritual mean that they never can produce "real" change? No, because rituals, like language and other symbolic forms, can be appropriated and made to work against the intentions of those who initially set them in motion. As one example, Kertzer noted the Philippine election of 1986 (p. 50). Ferdinand Marcos, who had been "successful in stage-managing" previous elections, was unable to replicate his past successes; his opponents, in effect, had turned the election into a vehicle for demystifying Marcos.

One more Burkeian theme can be extended to reveal a fourth basic form of mystification. Burke (1950) observed that "universal or generic motives" often are used to conceal "specific motives" and argued that this process is a form of mystification (p. 110). This observation can be expanded. When matters that are **contingent** (the result of specific choices, luck, accident, individual effort, etc.) are rendered or depicted as natural, inevitable, or universal, we are in the presence of mystification. Put differently, mystification makes the contingent appear natural or inevitable. Barthes (1972) made a similar point; in his view, mystification can be understood as the process that "transforms petit-bourgeois culture into a universal nature" (p. 9).[4] Kertzer (1988) also affirmed this point. He wrote,

> We feel uncomfortable in recognizing our society as merely the arbitrary product of cultural history, environmental adaptation, and political struggle. Instead, we attribute cosmological meaning to our political order, believing that our society has somehow been divinely ordained, that it reflects some higher purpose. (p. 37)

Such attributions of divine meaning mystify by transforming the contingent into the inevitable or the preordained. A vivid illustration of this process can be found in the 19th-century American discourse of "manifest destiny." Finally, Marxist scholars often refer to this process of "inevitablizing the contingent" as *reification*. Giddens (1979), for example, described reification as "forms of signification which 'naturalize' the existing state of affairs, inhibiting recognition of the mutable historical character of human society" (p. 195). Whether we use the Marxist term *reification* or the Burkeian term *mystification*, the underlying idea is the same: Both concepts point to the way in which language can be used to obscure or distort the contingent nature of our social practices and institutions and the central events that shape our public and political culture.[5]

Burke (1950) observed that "rhetorical analysis should always be ready to expose mystifications" (p. 178). Burke's observation suggests an important function for **criticism**—*de*mystification. Demystifying criticism explores the way in which a message or text *conceals* certain things while it *reveals* other things.[6] This function is central to critical approaches such as **ideology** criticism and the **critical rhetoric** movement in contemporary rhetorical studies. As McKerrow (1989) maintained, "A critical rhetoric serves a demystifying function" (p. 92) in its attempt to uncover the ways in which discourse conceals and/or distorts the effects of **power**. Burke noted that criticism of this type typically will encounter considerable obstacles. A critic "may have no great difficulty" in detecting various forms of mystification, but "it may be hard to spread the glad tidings of [the critic's] discovery since there is usually powerful social organization behind the errors [he or she] would clear away" (p. 179). These "powerful social organization[s]" (e.g., the media, educational institutions, government agencies) that Burke noted are external obstacles to critical demystification. Although they might be difficult to overcome, a persistent and talented critic still might be able to point out the errors, or the mystifications, under which a community is laboring. The critic also might celebrate texts and practices that engage in a form of demystification. For example, social critics (e.g., Stallybrass & White, 1986) influenced by Bakhtin's concept of **carnival** pointed to its "persistent *demystifying* potential" (p. 18). Locating the *carnivalesque* elements in cultural practice can then contribute to the larger project of demystification.

But Burke raised the possibility that there also might be a type of internal obstacle to critical demystification. And this possibility leads us back to the second (or general) sense of mystification identified by Burke and noted at the outset of the entry. As McKerrow and many other contemporary rhetorical scholars have noted, the critic engaged in demystification is an advocate attempting to persuade an audience to see and/or read certain parts of the social world (e.g., a **text**, a **controversy**, a type of practice) in a specific way. Critics do not have access to some type of ultimate truth that they can then share with their audience. Critics provide reasons for, and argue on behalf of, a certain way of looking at the world and the things in it. Criticism is, at its root, a persuasive activity. How is this discussion of the persuasive nature of demystifying criticism (any form of criticism, for that matter) relevant to Burke's discussion of a general sense of mystification? It is relevant because Burke thought that it was possible that "there may be a profounder kind of mystification . . . implicit in the very act of persuasion itself" (p. 178). Burke insisted that this "profounder" or "general" kind of mystification "cannot be cleared away by a mere debunker's reduction" (p. 179). The first (or special) type of mystification, whose various forms were described earlier, can be confronted and, with effort, overcome; community members can begin to "see through" various naming strategies or acknowledge the **contingency** of their social structures. But the general or "profounder" sense of mystification cannot be escaped. An element of mystification is present in all persuasion; it is "the 'logical conclusion' of the persuasive principle" (p. 179).

Burke's concept of a "profounder" type of mystification contains echoes of a doctrine expounded many centuries ago by the Greek sophistic thinker Gorgias, who was a radical epistemological skeptic; he had grave doubts about humanity's ability to ever truly or fully know anything about the world or about ourselves. Gorgias maintained that to live without the possibility of ultimate knowledge, people had to be deceived (the important Greek term is *apate*) so that they would accept certain things as "true." And the instrument of that process of psychological deception was rhetoric. Kennedy (1980), summarizing a substantial body of scholarship on Gorgias's position,[7] described his view in this way:

> Since the truth cannot be known rationally, the function of an orator is not logical demonstration so much as emotional presentation which will stir the audience's will to believe. Thus for Gorgias the power of persuasion involves deceiving "the emotional and mental state of listeners by artificially stimulating sensory reactions through words." (p. 31)[8]

Gorgias and Burke both pointed in a similar direction: All persuasion involves an element of deception or mystification.[9] As much as we might want to confront and overcome mystification, we also seem to depend on it. The enduring questions for rhetorical scholars, and society as a whole, include the following. Can the deceptive or mystifying moment in persuasion ever be controlled? Can the deceptive **representation** be clearly distinguished from the accurate one? How do we judge between or among competing mystifications, deceptions, or fictions (especially if there is no ground of "truth" to which one can appeal)? Burke's discussion of the "profounder kind of mystification" opened up some of the most vexing problems in the tradition of rhetorical thought.

Notes

1. On the relationship between political language and mystification, see also Edelman (1988) and Rodgers (1987). On the importance of "naming," see McKerrow (1989) and the entry for **critical rhetoric.**

2. They could be analyzed, for example, as forms of **epideictic discourse.**

3. On "hierarchical mystification," see Duncan (1962, p. 255). See also Smith (1973).

4. On the process of negative **hegemony,** see also Aune (1994, p. 72).

5. See also Shils's (1981) discussion of the way in which **traditions** establish a " 'natural way' to do things" (p. 200).

6. On the play between concealing and revealing, see the entry for **representation.**

7. This scholarship includes de Romilly (1975), Enos (1976), Rosenmeyer (1955), and Segal (1962).

8. Kennedy (1980) was quoting Enos in the last portion of the passage. On Gorgianic deception, see also Verdenius (1981).

9. For other contemporary views that emphasize the creation of fictions through discourse, see Foucault's (1979) discussion of the inevitability of "fiction" and McGee's (1975) account of the "people."

References and Additional Reading

Aune, J. A. (1994). *Marxism and rhetoric.* Boulder, CO: Westview.

Barthes, R. (1972). *Mythologies* (A. Lavers, Trans.). New York: Hill & Wang.

Blankenship, J. (1989). "Magic" and "mystery" in the works of Kenneth Burke. In H. W. Simons & T. Melia (Eds.), *The legacy of Kenneth Burke.* Madison: University of Wisconsin Press.

Burke, K. (1950). *A rhetoric of motives.* New York: Prentice Hall.

Burke, K. (1984). On human behavior considered "dramatistically." In K. Burke, *Permanence and change: An anatomy of purpose* (3rd ed.). Berkeley: University of California Press.

Cerling, L. R. (1989). The discursive construction of the physician: The death of dialogue. In B. E. Gronbeck (Ed.), *Spheres of argument: Proceedings of the Sixth SCA/AFA Conference on Argumentation.* Annandale, VA: Speech Communication Association.

de Romilly, J. (1975). *Magic and rhetoric in ancient Greece.* Cambridge, MA: Harvard University Press.

Duncan, H. D. (1962). *Communication and social order.* London: Oxford University Press.

Edelman, M. (1988). *Constructing the political spectacle.* Chicago: University of Chicago Press.

Enos, R. L. (1976). The epistemology of Gorgias' rhetoric: A re-examination. *Southern Speech Communication Journal, 42,* 35-51.

Erikson, K., & Fleuriet, C. A. (1991). Presidential anonymity: Rhetorical identity management and the mystification of political reality. *Communication Quarterly, 39,* 272-289.

Ewen, S. (1976). *Captains of consciousness: Advertising and the social roots of the consumer culture.* New York: McGraw-Hill.

Foucault, M. (1979). Interview with Lucette Finas. In M. Morris & P. Patton (Eds.), *Michel Foucault: Power, truth, strategy.* Sydney, Australia: Feral Publications.

Giddens, A. (1979). *Central problems in social theory: Action, structure, and contradiction in social analysis.* Berkeley: University of California Press.

Kennedy, G. A. (1980). *Classical rhetoric and its Christian and secular tradition from ancient to modern times.* Chapel Hill: University of North Carolina Press.

Kertzer, D. I. (1988). *Ritual, politics, and power.* New Haven, CT: Yale University Press.

Leiss, W., Kline, S., & Jhally, S. (1990). *Social communication in advertising: Persons, products, and images of well-being* (2nd ed.). New York: Routledge.

McGee, M. C. (1975). In search of "the people": A rhetorical alternative. *Quarterly Journal of Speech, 61,* 235-249.

McKerrow, R. E. (1989). Critical rhetoric: Theory and praxis. *Communication Monographs, 56,* 91-111.

Rodgers, D. T. (1987). *Contested truths: Keywords in American politics since independence.* New York: Basic Books.

Rosenmeyer, T. G. (1955). Gorgias, Aeschylus, and *apate. American Journal of Philology, 76,* 225-260.

Segal, C. (1962). Gorgias and the psychology of the logos. *Harvard Studies in Classical Philology, 66,* 99-155.

Shils, E. (1981). *Tradition.* Chicago: University of Chicago Press.

Smith, J. M. (1973, Spring). Erik H. Erikson's sex role theories: A rhetoric of hierarchical mystification. *Today's Speech,* pp. 27-31.

Stallybrass, P., & White, A. (1986). *The poetics and politics of transgression.* Ithaca, NY: Cornell University Press.

Verdenius, W. J. (1981). Gorgias' doctrine of deception. In G. B. Kerferd (Ed.), *The Sophists and their legacy: Proceedings of the Fourth International Colloquium on Ancient Philosophy.* Wiesbaden, Germany: Steiner Verlag.

Woodward, G. C. (1975). Mystifications in the rhetoric of cultural dominance and colonial control. *Central States Speech Journal, 26,* 298-303.

MYTH

Literary theorists René Wellek and Austin Warren noted that the concept of **myth** "is not easy to fix; it points today at an 'area of meaning' [or an issue of concern] . . . shared by religion, folklore, anthropology, sociology, psychoanalysis, and the fine arts" (Wellek & Warren, 1956, pp. 190-191). Many contemporary scholars in rhetorical studies would add their discipline to Wellek and Warren's (1956) list. Myth often is considered to be a key element in rhetoric and public discourse. Hart (1997), for example, wrote, "Virtually all rhetoric depends on myth for its effect. . . . Even if a rhetor does not retell a mythic tale in full, he or she will use some device (a quick allusion, a metaphor) to invite the audience's remembrance of that tale" (pp. 242-243).

Hart (1997) defined myths as "master stories describing exceptional people doing exceptional things and serving as moral guides to proper action" (p. 234). Wellek and Warren's (1956) definition is a bit different from, but not inconsistent with, Hart's definition.

They defined myths in this way: "But, in a wider sense, myth comes to mean any anonymously composed storytelling of origins and destinies: the explanations a society offers its young of why the world is and why we do as we do, its pedagogic images of the nature and destiny of man [sic]" (p. 191). Cultural historian Richard Slotkin wrote,

> Myths are stories drawn from a society's history that have acquired through persistent usage the power of symbolizing that society's ideology and of dramatizing its moral consciousness—with all the complexities and contradictions that consciousness may contain. . . . Myths are formulated as ways of explaining problems that arise in the course of historical experience. (Slotkin, 1992, pp. 5-6)

Myths, in short, are **narratives** that report the struggles and heroic exploits from a community's past; frequently, mythic stories draw on **archetypal** images (particular characters, events, etc.) that transcend the boundaries of a specific community. Like dreams, myths "are complex mixtures of archetypal and cultural elements" (Rushing & Frentz, 1995, p. 45).[1]

Myths function as reference points or cognitive coordinates for the members of a culture or community. They explain the world and suggest ways of coping with it. Doty (1986) explained,

> Myths are normative in supporting particular types of behavior and association and rejecting other *exampla;* they are educative and heuristic in highlighting adaptive and adjustive patterns. They provide social cohesion by creating a shared symbolic articulation of social patterns and relations, by leading to a releasing of tensions . . ., and by blocking nonapproved explorations of relationship or behavior or inquiry. (p. 29)

More simply, Weiss (1969) suggested that myths "condition the way men [sic] view the world and understand their experience" (pp. 3-4). For example, the ancient Greeks understood their world and their place in it through reference to a pantheon of Gods (e.g., Zeus, Apollo) and their exploits. Although science and rationality have displaced mythic Gods as a source for explaining most natural events, myths nevertheless continue to exist in different forms and exert considerable influence. Kertzer (1988) noted,

> Each society has its own mythology detailing its origins and sanctifying its norms. Some of these revolve around great men (in Western society female cultural heroes are less common), while others revolve around notable events that, whether having a historical basis or not, are defined through a web of symbolically constructed meaning. In the United States, children grow up learning about the Puritans, the Indians, the slaves, life on the plantation, the melting pot, George Washington, Abraham Lincoln, Daniel Boone, John Kennedy, and Martin Luther King. Indeed, their conceptions of society are in good part based on understandings passed on through such symbols. They learn both what are valued norms of conduct and what are the criteria of success. More to the point here, these [mythic] symbols provide a way to understand such abstract political entities as the nation and a means (indeed the compulsion) of identifying with them. (pp. 12-13; see also Bennett, 1980; McGee, 1975)

Hart (1997) identified four characteristic types of myths based on their different functions. *Cosmological* myths explain "why we are here, where we came from, [and] what our ancestors were like" (e.g., the story of Adam and Eve). *Societal* myths offer instruction on "the proper way to live" (e.g., the story about George Washington and the cherry tree, the novels of Horatio Alger). *Identity* myths provide the members of a community with a story that serves as the basis for their sense of who they are as a collectivity (e.g., the myth of American innocence that came under attack during the debate over the war in Vietnam).

Eschatological myths (see also the entry for **apocalyptic discourse**) "help a people know where they are going [and] what lies in store for them" in the future (e.g., the promise of heaven or the threat of hell in various Christian religions) (p. 242). If myths are elaborate with respect to the characters and events contained within them, then they may fulfill numerous functions (e.g., the story of the American Revolution). When incorporated into public discourse, myths can produce *instrumental* as well as *constitutive* effects.[2]

Consider the narrative or story of Moses leading the children of Israel out of Egyptian bondage. Some Christians might object to labeling this story as a myth because the term often suggests something completely fictitious. But the exodus story is a myth; it is a story of great events and people who provided a community with an understanding of its origins. And it has had a profound impact on Western societies. Walzer (1985) noted,

> Since late medieval or early modern times, there has existed in the West a characteristic way of thinking about political change, a pattern that we commonly impose upon events, a story that we repeat to one another. The story has roughly this form: oppression, liberation, social contract, political struggle, [and] new society. . . . This isn't a story told everywhere; it isn't a universal pattern; it belongs to the West, more particularly to Jews and Christians in the West, and its source, its original version, is the exodus of Israel from Egypt. (p. 133)

As Walzer suggested, the exodus myth helps to shape the way in which members of various cultures think about political struggle. We find its imprint in all types of public discourse. At the beginning of his study of the role of narratives or stories in **forensic** or judicial discourse, LaRue (1995) provided a reading of Supreme Court Justice Hugo Black's opinion in the 1947 case of *Everson v. Board of Education,* a key moment in the evolution of American jurisprudence with respect to the separation of church and state. The opinion, LaRue argued, was shaped by an underlying narrative—the story of exodus. LaRue noted,

> As one reads, the Book of Exodus seems to hover in the background. . . . The story begins with the "early settlers" fleeing the "bondage" and the "persecutions" that characterized the European experience. . . . Like the ancient Israelites fleeing from Egypt, the "early settlers" must suffer in the desert [before they are finally delivered to the "promised land"]. (pp. 20, 22)

As numerous scholars have noted (Miller, 1993; Osborn, 1989; Rosteck, 1992; Smylie, 1970; Snow, 1985), the exodus myth was an important resource in the discourse of the civil rights movement; it helped to shape or structure the experience of many black Americans and provided them with the courage to continue with their struggle. The exodus myth was especially prominent in Martin Luther King, Jr.'s famous speech, "I've Been to the Mountaintop," delivered the evening before his assassination in Memphis, Tennessee, in 1968.

The story of the exodus of the Jews from Egypt is just one of the countless myths that continue to inhabit our public discourse. Slotkin (1992), for example, noted,

> The myth of the frontier is our oldest and most characteristic myth, expressed in a body of literature, folklore, ritual, historiography, and polemics produced over a period of three centuries. According to this myth-historiography, the conquest of the wilderness and the subjugation or displacement of the Native Americans who originally inhabited it have been the means to our achievement of a national identity, a democratic polity, an ever-expanding economy, and a phenomenally dynamic and "progressive" civilization. (p. 10)[3]

Slotkin suggested that the myth of the frontier helps to explain the connection between progress and expansion in American thought. The continual repetition of the myth encourages Americans to understand progress as the result of a recurring cycle—from initial (but decaying) civilization, through an encounter with the wilderness frontier, to progress and a new revitalized civilization. For example, John F. Kennedy's famous address to the Democratic Convention in 1960 evoked this myth as it encouraged Americans to strike out and conquer their "new frontier." A related, and equally popular, mythic form is the *agrarian myth* organized around the heroic exploits of the "yeoman farmer" (Burkholder, 1989; Hofstadter, 1955; Smith, 1950).

Consider a final example. Since the birth of the tool, humanity has been plagued by the fear that its technological creations might someday turn against humans. This cultural anxiety has been the source of countless stories, perhaps receiving its most exemplary expression in Mary Shelley's *Frankenstein* (Small, 1972). Although the "Frankenstein myth" (as it sometimes is termed) can be considered as a distinct or autonomous transcultural story, it also might be understood as an evolutionary moment or phase in what Rushing and Frentz (1995) described as the "myth of the hunter." Humans, especially men, continually engage in the quest for identity, and Rushing and Frentz argued that this quest is at the root of the hunter myth. Drawing on works in anthropology (e.g., Campbell, 1949), Rushing and Frentz (1995) maintained that the young hunter gains his or her identity through participation in this *initiation* **ritual.** The repetition of variations on this basic story line embody and perpetuate the quest for identity. But modern society has witnessed the "technologization" (p. 7) of the hunter/hero; the "quest for identity" has been transformed into "a search for power" (p. 72). Victor Frankenstein was the "prototype" (p. 70) of the technological hunter, only now the roles were reversed; the technological hunter was as much the hunted (by the technological creations that humans had invented in their quest for power) as the hunter. Rushing and Frentz suggested that the logic of the technological hunter can be found in various discursive and cultural products, from Ronald Reagan's concept of the Strategic Defense Initiative (SDI or "Star Wars") to popular films such as *Blade Runner* and *The Terminator.*

Despite the advances of science and the proliferation of the scientific method, myths persist. They appear to be inescapable. Scholars uncover myths or mythic elements in a variety of sources; they can be found in political communication (Bass & Cherwitz, 1978; Bennett, 1980; Dorsey, 1997; Edelman, 1971; Fisher, 1973; Gustainis, 1989; Klope, 1986; McGee, 1975; Nimmo & Combs, 1980; O'Leary & McFarland, 1989; Rosteck, 1994; Rushing, 1986b), agricultural policy debates (Peterson, 1991; Peterson & Horton, 1995), popular films (Rushing, 1986a, 1989), commercial advertising (Berger, 1997; Leymore, 1975), and even the discourse of corporations (Crable & Vibbert, 1983). It is little wonder, then, that myth has become an important concept in contemporary rhetorical studies.

Notes

1. On the need to define myth narrowly, see Rowland (1990) and the responses by Brummett (1990), Osborn (1990), Rushing (1990), and Solomon (1990).

2. On this distinction, see the entry for **effects of rhetorical practice.**

3. See also Rushing (1986a, 1989) and Slotkin (1973, 1985).

References and Additional Reading

Barthes, R. (1972). *Mythologies* (A. Lavers, Trans.). New York: Hill & Wang.

Bass, J. D., & Cherwitz, R. (1978). Imperial mission and manifest destiny: A case study of political myth in rhetorical discourse. *Southern Speech Communication Journal, 43,* 213-232.

Bennett, W. L. (1980). Myth, ritual, and political control. *Journal of Communication, 30,* 166-179.

Berger, A. A. (1997). *Narratives in popular culture, media, and everyday life.* Thousand Oaks, CA: Sage.

Brummett, B. (1990). How to propose a discourse: A reply to Rowland. *Communication Studies, 41,* 128-135.

Burkholder, T. R. (1989). Kansas populism, woman suffrage, and the agrarian myth: A case study in the limits of mythic transcendence. *Communication Studies, 40,* 292-307.

Campbell, J. (1949). *The hero with a thousand faces.* New York: Pantheon.

Cassirer, E. (1946). *Language and myth* (S. K. Langer, Trans.). New York: Harper.

Crable, R. E., & Vibbert, S. L. (1983). Mobil's epideictic advocacy: "Observations" of Prometheus-bound. *Communication Monographs, 50,* 380-395.

Dorsey, L. G. (1997). Sailing into the "wondrous now": The myth of the American navy's world cruise. *Quarterly Journal of Speech, 83,* 447-465.

Doty, W. G. (1986). *Mythography: The study of myths and rituals.* Tuscaloosa: University of Alabama Press.

Edelman, M. (1971). *Politics as symbolic action.* Chicago: Markham.

Fisher, W. R. (1973). Reaffirmation and subversion of the American Dream. *Quarterly Journal of Speech, 59,* 160-167.

Fulmer, H. W. (1990). Southern clerics and the passing of Lee: Mythic rhetoric and the construction of a sacred symbol. *Southern Communication Journal, 55,* 355-371.

Gustainis, J. J. (1989). John F. Kennedy and the green berets: The rhetorical use of the hero myth. *Communication Studies, 40,* 41-53.

Hart, R. P. (1997). *Modern rhetorical criticism* (2nd ed.). Boston: Allyn & Bacon.

Hofstadter, R. (1955). *The age of reform: From Bryan to F.D.R.* New York: Knopf.

Kertzer, D. I. (1988). *Ritual, politics, and power.* New Haven, CT: Yale University Press.

Klope, D. C. (1986). Defusing a foreign policy crisis: Myth and victimage in Reagan's 1983 Lebanon/Grenada address. *Western Journal of Speech Communication, 50,* 336-349.

LaRue, L. H. (1995). *Constitutional law as fiction: Narrative in the rhetoric of authority.* University Park: Pennsylvania State University Press.

Leymore, V. L. (1975). *Hidden myth: Structure and symbolism in advertising.* New York: Basic Books.

Lincoln, B. (1989). *Discourse and the construction of society: Comparative studies of myth, ritual, and classification.* New York: Oxford University Press.

Marsden, M. (1978). The American myth of success: Visions and revisions. In J. Nachbar, D. Weiser, & J. L. Wright (Eds.), *The popular culture reader.* Bowling Green, OH: Popular Press.

McGee, M. C. (1975). In search of "the people": A rhetorical alternative. *Quarterly Journal of Speech, 61,* 235-249.

Miller, K. D. (1993). Alabama as Egypt: Martin Luther King, Jr. and the religion of slaves. In C. Calloway-Thomas & J. L. Lucaites (Eds.), *Martin Luther King, Jr. and the sermonic power of public discourse.* Tuscaloosa: University of Alabama Press.

Moore, M. P. (1991). Rhetorical criticism of political myth: From Goldwater legend to Reagan mystique. *Communication Studies, 42,* 295-308.

Nimmo, D. D., & Combs, J. E. (1980). *Subliminal politics: Myths and mythmakers in America.* Englewood Cliffs, NJ: Prentice Hall.

O'Leary, S., & McFarland, M. (1989). The political use of mythic discourse: Prophetic interpretation in Pat Robertson's presidential campaign. *Quarterly Journal of Speech, 75,* 433-452.

Olson, K. M. (1991). Expanding the horizon of justification: The role of myth in cultural transformation. In D. W. Parson (Ed.), *Argument in controversy: Proceedings of the Seventh SCA/AFA Conference on Argumentation.* Annandale, VA: Speech Communication Association.

Osborn, M. O. (1989). "I've been to the mountaintop": The critic as participant. In M. C. Leff & F. J. Kauffeld (Eds.), *Texts in context: Critical dialogues on significant episodes in American political discourse.* Davis, CA: Hermagoras Press.

Osborn, M. (1990). In defense of broad mythic criticism: A reply to Rowland. *Communication Studies, 41,* 121-127.

Peterson, T. R. (1991). Telling the farmers' story: Competing responses to soil conservation rhetoric. *Quarterly Journal of Speech, 77,* 289-308.

Peterson, T. R., & Horton, C. C. (1995). Rooted in the soil: How understanding the perspectives of landowners can enhance the management of environmental disputes. *Quarterly Journal of Speech, 81,* 139-166.

Rosteck, T. (1992). Narrative in Martin Luther King's *I've Been to the Mountaintop. Southern Communication Journal, 58,* 22-32.

Rosteck, T. (1994). The intertextuality of "The Man From Hope." In S. A. Smith (Ed.), *Bill Clinton on stump, state, and stage: The rhetorical road to the White House.* Fayetteville: University of Arkansas Press.

Rowland, R. C. (1990). On mythic criticism. *Communication Studies, 41,* 101-116.

Rushing, J. H. (1983). The rhetoric of the American western myth. *Communication Monographs, 50,* 14-32.

Rushing, J. H. (1986a). Mythic evolution of the new frontier in mass mediated rhetoric. *Critical Studies in Mass Communication, 3,* 265-296.

Rushing, J. H. (1986b). Ronald Reagan's "Star Wars" address: Mythic containment of technical reasoning. *Quarterly Journal of Speech, 72,* 415-433.

Rushing, J. H. (1989). Evolution of "the new frontier" in *Alien* and *Aliens:* Patriarchal co-optation of the feminine archetype. *Quarterly Journal of Speech, 75,* 1-24.

Rushing, J. H. (1990). On saving mythic criticism: A reply to Rowland. *Communication Studies, 41,* 136-149.

Rushing, J. H., & Frentz, T. S. (1995). *Projecting the shadow: The cyborg hero in American film.* Chicago: University of Chicago Press.

Slotkin, R. (1973). *Regeneration through violence: The mythology of the American frontier, 1600-1860.* Middletown, MA: Wesleyan University Press.

Slotkin, R. (1985). *The fatal environment: The myth of the frontier in the age of industrialization, 1800-1890.* New York: Atheneum.

Slotkin, R. (1992). *Gunfighter nation: The myth of the frontier in twentieth-century America.* New York: Atheneum.

Small, C. (1972). *Ariel like a harpy: Mary Shelley's Frankenstein—Tracing the myth.* Pittsburgh, PA: University of Pittsburgh Press.

Smith, H. N. (1950). *Virgin land: The American West as symbol and myth.* Cambridge, MA: Harvard University Press.

Smylie, J. H. (1970). On Jesus, pharaohs, and the chosen people: Martin Luther King as biblical interpreter and humanist. *Interpretation: A Journal of Bible and Theology, 24,* 74-91.

Snow, M. (1985). Martin Luther King's "Letter From Birmingham Jail" as Pauline epistle. *Quarterly Journal of Speech, 71,* 318-334.

Solomon, M. (1979). The "positive women's" journey: A mythic analysis of the rhetoric of STOP ERA. *Quarterly Journal of Speech, 65,* 262-274.

Solomon, M. (1990). Responding to Rowland's myth or in defense of pluralism: A reply to Rowland. *Communication Studies, 41,* 117-120.

Sutton, D. (1997). On mythic criticism: A proposed compromise. *Communication Reports, 10,* 211-217.

Sykes, A. J. M. (1970). Myth in communication. *Journal of Communication, 20,* 17-31.

Walzer, M. (1985). *Exodus and revolution.* New York: Basic Books.

Weiss, R. (1969). *The American myth of success: From Horatio Alger to Norman Vincent Peale.* New York: Basic Books.

Wellek, R., & Warren, A. (1956). *Theory of literature* (3rd ed.). New York: Harcourt Brace.

NARRATIVE

More and more over the past few decades, scholars have noted the ubiquity of stories or **narratives** in human experience. Martin (1986) wrote,

> We need not go to school to understand the importance of narrative in our lives. News of the world comes to us in the form of "stories" told from one or another point of view. The global drama unfolds every twenty-four hours—split up into multiple story lines that can be reintegrated only when they are understood from the perspective of an American (or Russian or Nigerian), a Democrat (or Republican, or monarchist, or Marxist), a Protestant (or Catholic, or Jew, or Muslim). . . . Narrative, considered as a form of entertainment when studied as literature, is a battleground when actualized in newspapers, biography, and history. (pp. 7-8)

Narratives no longer are confined to novels, short stories, films, and children's bedtime stories; narratives permeate journalism, legal and **forensic discourse,** scholarly books and monographs, conversational interaction, and the various forms of public discourse.

The relationship between narrative or storytelling and rhetoric or public discourse has received considerable attention during the past two decades thanks, in part, to the works of Walter Fisher (e.g., Fisher, 1984, 1987). This resurgence in interest has sparked theoretical debates over the relationship between narrativity and rationality and the idea that narrative might serve as a "paradigm" for human communication (Rowland, 1987, 1989; Warnick, 1987). Library shelves are filled with books on the general subject of narrative[1] and on the relationship between narrative and various aspects of human life.[2] Given the tremendous volume of thinking on the subject, this entry is limited to discussion of four basic tasks. The first task is *definitional* (what do we mean by "narrative"?), the second is *functional* (what common functions do narratives fulfill and, more specifically, how do narratives work rhetorically?), the third is *formal* (in what forms or shapes do we typically encounter narrative in public discourse?), and the fourth is *evaluative* (how might critics, as well as audiences in the public realm, judge the narratives they encounter in public discourse?). Although the answers provided to these questions introduce a number of important issues in contemporary rhetorical studies, they are only a preliminary discussion of the interrelated topics of narrative, narrative theory, and narrative in public discourse.

What is a narrative? The range of practices falling under this label is extremely broad. Literary critic Wayne Booth, describing this range of practices, wrote,

> My subject must be all narratives, not only novels, short stories, epics, plays, films, and

> TV dramas but all histories, all satires, all documentaries, all gossip and personal anecdote, all biography and autobiography, all "storied" ballets and operas, all mimes and puppet shows, all chronicles—indeed, every presentation of time-ordered or time-related experience that in any way supplements, re-orders, enhances, or interprets unnarrated life. (Booth, 1988, p. 14)

Booth continued and affirmed a point noted previously (that narratives seem to be everywhere): "Even the life we think of as primary experience—that is, events like birth, copulation, death, plowing and planting, getting and spending—is rarely experienced without some sort of mediation in narrative" (p. 14). Given the range of practices that fall under the narrative label, finding a common denominator that captures the essence of narrative can be difficult.

The passage from Booth just quoted identifies a common thread that frequently is considered to be the root or essence of narrative—ordering events or experiences in a time sequence (cf. Scholes & Kellogg, 1966, p. 207). Many rhetoricians echo Booth in their definitions of narrative. For example, Foss (1996) wrote that "a narrative involves a sequence of some kind so that at least two events or states are organized sequentially" (p. 400; cf. Fisher, 1987, p. 58). Although the definition's abstractness helps to preserve its validity, its generality does not really help get to the heart of the issue. The thrust of the definition is that narratives establish relationships between or among things (e.g., events, states, situations) over time (sequentially). How? The traditional Aristotelian answer to this question, sometimes overlooked in recent rhetorical thinking on narrative, is *plot.*[3] Narratives do more than relate things sequentially (first this happened, then this happened, then this happened, etc.). White (1981), writing on the topic of the transformation of "real" events into narratives, wrote, "Events must be not only registered within the chronological framework of their original occurrence but narrated as well, that is to say, revealed as possessing a structure, an order of meaning, which they do *not* possess as mere sequence" (p. 5). Plot transforms a sequence into a narrative; it is, as Martin (1986) suggested, "formed from a combination of temporal succession and causality" (p. 81).

Plot, then, is simply *a structure of actions.* Consider a typical (heterosexual) romance. A boy meets a girl. They fall in love. Some type of complication arises (e.g., the boy spends too much time at work, the girl has unresolved feelings for an old flame, the boy and girl discover that they might actually be long lost siblings). The complication threatens the relationship, but eventually it is resolved. They live happily ever after. The events in this story follow a very conventional structure: introduction of characters, rising action and introduction of complication, development of complication, climax or discovery of how the complication can be overcome, and *denouement* or final resolution of the complication. This basic structure was first discussed by Aristotle (1954a) in the *Poetics* (often referred to as the *principle of wholeness*) and was refined during the 19th century by the German critic Gustav Freytag. Freytag's description of this common structure is known as "Freytag's pyramid." Aristotle also argued that the elements of the narrative (the actions or events that it describes) should be "so closely connected that the transposal or withdrawal of any one of them will disjoin and dislocate the whole. For that which makes no perceptible difference by its presence or absence is no real part of the whole" (1451a33-1451a35). Plot establishes both wholeness and unity of action; the elements of the story are interconnected, and they develop or progress toward a satisfying conclusion. The notion of a satisfying conclusion led Martin (1986) to add an another component to the concept of plot:

> To temporality and causality we must add a third factor if our inventory of the conditions necessary for narrative is to be complete. . . . It is human interest that deter-

> mines whether events and causes fit together in a plot with beginning and end. . . . The shapes of narrative are then instances of general cultural assumptions and values—what we consider important, trivial, fortunate, tragic, good, evil, and what impels movement from one to another. (p. 87)

The structure of a narrative—its plot—may follow the conventional formula noted previously, but if it fails to reflect the assumptions and values of its culture, then it most likely will be judged unsatisfactory. For example, one of the plot complications introduced in the illustration—that the boy and the girl might come to believe that they are long lost siblings—was relatively common during earlier time periods but does not reflect the assumptions of our contemporary world.

Do all narratives have a pyramidal plot structure? No. Aristotle (1954a) recognized alternatives (although he judged them to be inferior modes of structuring a story). For example, he discussed the idea of an *episodic* plot that recounts the exploits of its focal character in various situations. But Aristotle found the episodic plot wanting because "there is neither probability nor necessity in the sequence of its episodes" (1451b34-1451b35). But an episodic structure is not the only alternative to the unified coherent plot. Contemporary theorists such as Martin (1986) have noted both the persistence and the growing popularity of an open or fractured narrative structure that resists closure (e.g., the "plot" in a typical music video)—in other words, "the disappearance of traditional plots" (p. 83).[4] Unified and coherent narratives still remain the dominant structural form and are relatively easy to recognize. Examples include parents describing to their children how they met, fell in love, and got married; historians describing the coming of the Civil War or the end of feudalism; prosecuting attorneys describing the commission of a crime for the jury; and novelists describing the consequences of characters' tragic flaws. But music videos, experimental novels, and even some Hollywood films (e.g., *Pulp Fiction*) challenge the traditional idea of a unified and coherent narrative structure.

What should rhetorical scholars make of the process of narrative fragmentation? This is a complex question. For some contemporary rhetorical scholars (e.g., McGee, 1990), fragmentation is the norm; the disappearance of traditional plots is the counterpart to the dissolution of the oratorical model of public discourse. Fragmented discourse and fractured plots simply shift the burden of meaning making; as McGee (1990) argued, "Text construction is now something done more by the consumers than by the producers of discourse" (p. 288). A counterargument to the fragmentation position could maintain that narrative plots cannot completely disappear from public rhetorical discourse so long as that discourse has some business to transact. Consider narratives in the context of legal or **forensic discourse.** So long as prosecuting attorneys try to win convictions and defense attorneys attempt to secure acquittals, the narratives they employ will be—indeed *must* be—coherent and unified. Each attorney must construct a unified plot that is coherent and accounts for all of the relevant details in the case. But, as will be discussed a bit more later in the discussion of narratives in **deliberative discourse,** there are cases when the narratives found in public rhetorical discourse might, in fact, gain force or persuasiveness from a certain degree of openness or a lack of closure.

One final question merits some consideration. Who imposes structure on the events contained in the narrative? The answer to this question introduces one of Scholes and Kellogg's (1966) distinguishing characteristics of narrative: All narratives are marked by the presence of a narrator or storyteller (p. 4). The narrator or storyteller can select, edit, organize, arrange, and (in some cases) alter or fabricate actions, events, and situations. As Scholes and Kellogg remarked, "In the relationship between the teller and the tale, and

[in] that other relationship between the teller and the audience, lies the essence of narrative art" (p. 240). We will return to the relationship between narrator and audience later.

There is a second broad question to consider: How do narratives function and, more particularly, what are at least some of their key rhetorical functions? For Aristotle (1954a), the function of narrative is to imitate reality. He wrote at the beginning of the *Poetics* that the literary arts are "modes of imitation" (1447a16); this sense of function frequently is described as *mimetic.* Aristotle's mimetic approach to narrative function would remain influential for centuries (Auerbach, 1946). The Romantic revolution of the 19th century displaced imitation as the primary function and substituted the idea that the primary function of literary art is personal expression (Abrams, 1953). The Aristotelian-Romantic tension—the question of whether literary art (and all discursive practice, for that matter) functions primarily to imitate or reflect the world or to express or evoke the inner world of the author—remains a topic in aesthetic and discursive theory.

More recent approaches to narrative function approach the question in a broader, more abstract manner. A common theme in the literature is that narratives function as a way for humans to organize various aspects of their existence. Riessman (1993) wrote that "narratives structure perceptual experience [and] organize memory" (p. 2). Carr (1986) maintained that "narrative is our primary . . . way of organizing our experience of time" (pp. 4-5). Mumby (1993a) asserted that "narratives function to construct the social reality that constitutes the lived world of social actors" (p. 5). Ricoeur (1984-1988) suggested that narrative " 'grasps together' and integrates into one whole . . . multiple and scattered events" (p. x). Foss (1996), surveying the literature on narrative theory, argued that "narratives help us impose order on the flow of experience so that we can make sense of events and actions in our lives" (p. 399). Above and beyond specific functions such as imitating reality, expressing inner feelings, and entertaining an audience (a function that achieves prominence in our modern age), narratives are a way through which people make sense of the various elements of their lives, a vehicle for ordering and organizing experiences, and a mechanism for both comprehending and constituting the social world. Narratives, in short, fulfill a range of basic human needs, leading scholars such as MacIntyre (1981) to conclude that a human is a "storytelling animal" (p. 201; cf. Fisher, 1987).

Given the extensive functions of narrative just noted, is it possible to speak about specific rhetorical functions? Identifying the rhetorical functions of narrative depends on how the term *rhetoric* is defined. One approach to locating the rhetorical functions of narrative is to employ the three **effects of rhetorical practice**—the aesthetic or visceral, the instrumental, and the constitutive—as an organizing framework so as to unpack *how* narratives induce these effects in audiences.

In *The Rhetoric of Fiction,* Booth (1983) began by suggesting that the author of a narrative attempts to "impose his [sic] fictional world upon the reader" (p. xiii). Extending on Booth's approach to narrative rhetoric, Chatman (1990) labeled the author's effort to control or shape the reader's (or audience's) response as "aesthetic rhetoric" (p. 189). According to Chapman, aesthetic rhetoric "refers to a fiction's suasion that its unfolding *form* be accepted" (p. 188). He added, "The end of aesthetic rhetoric is verisimilitude, the creation and maintenance and . . . the intensification of the illusion," or the "world" that is called into being by the narrative (pp. 189-190). When a critic approaches a narrative in terms of its aesthetic function, he or she investigates how specific techniques (e.g., point of view, plot construction, characterization) contribute to the narrative's ability to create a world for the reader or audience and to, in Booth's words, "impose" that world on the reader or audience. Using Mark Twain's *Huckleberry Finn* as an illustration, Chatman suggested, "Aesthetic rhetoric addresses such questions as 'Why does the choice of first-person narrative voice make Huck's story plausible, viable, [and] [a]esthetically whole?' " (p. 192). In short, the key question in analyzing aesthetic rhetoric in a narrative is "how [authorial] choices function toward aesthetic ends" (p. 193), with the idea of "aesthetic ends" understood in a Boothian manner.

Consider a novel or film that has made a strong impression on its audience. It could be anything from the film *Titanic,* to the film *Sling Blade,* to the latest Stephen King novel, to the novel *The Great Gatsby.* In Booth's (1983) terms, the author or filmmaker has managed to "impose" his or her vision or world on the audience; the author or filmmaker has been able to control the audience's response. Both Booth and Chatman maintained that this accomplishment is a form of persuasion or rhetoric.[5] The audience has been persuaded to accept, at least for a period of time, the vision or world created by the narrative. The challenge is to uncover *how* the narrative was able to shape or control the audience's response. The specific techniques will vary with the medium used to construct the narrative. As Chatman observed, film narratives can employ not only language (e.g., character dialogue, voice-over narration) but also visual imagery (ranging from camera angles to the latest innovations in computer graphics) and sound, whereas novels and short stories are more limited in their strategic choices. But certain narrative techniques transcend the materiality of the medium and can be employed as a way of pulling the reader or audience into a narrative world. In one case, it might be the visual and sound effects of a film that produce a visceral response; in another case, it might be the particular mode of narration that is employed by an author that invites the reader into the author's world. But when a narrative "works," it functions aesthetically to create a vivid, memorable, and compelling world for the reader or audience.

Chatman (1990) contrasted the idea of aesthetic rhetoric with a second rhetorical function that narratives can enact; he termed this second function "ideological rhetoric" (p. 189). Chatman added an additional level of complication by another distinction; he wrote that "it is important to distinguish between the implication of an ideology and the urging of a thesis" (p. 11). This distinction, between the narrower function of narrative as **argument** and the broader function whereby narratives implicate or "radiate" an ideology (p. 197), roughly corresponds to the difference between the *instrumental* and *constitutive* effects of rhetoric. Narratives function in an instrumental manner when they are used to respond to *exigences* in a **rhetorical situation** and manifest direct or indirect arguments and persuasive appeals. Narratives function constitutively when they help to shape and transform how a community understands its world and when they offer inducements to create, recreate, or transform the social world. Each of these functions merits further attention.

The instrumental function of narrative in explicit persuasive discourse has been discussed by rhetorical theorists since Aristotle (1954b) devoted a chapter to the subject in the *Rhetoric* (Book III, chap. 16). As Kennedy (1991) pointed out, in Greek and Latin rhetorical theory, the term *narrative* referred to (a) a specific part of the speech (see the entry for **arrangement**) as well as (b) any sequentially organized account of events (pp. 268-269). According to Aristotle (1954b), narrative played an important role in **epideictic** and **forensic discourse;** in both speech types, character is an important topic and narrative is an effective mode for depicting character. Aristotle believed that narrative played a much less important role in political oratory or **deliberative discourse** (1417b13-1417b14). But contemporary scholarship challenges this assertion.[6] Contemporary scholars also extend the scope of rhetorical narrative well beyond the scope imagined by Aristotle. Brown (1998), for example, uncovered narrative in an unlikely place—scientific discourse.

Literary scholars, like their rhetorical counterparts, have long recognized the instrumental rhetorical or persuasive potential of narrative (e.g., Coste, 1989, pp. 297-333).

The common term used to describe instrumental narratives in literary studies is *didactic* (from the Greek verb *didaskein*, meaning "to teach or instruct"). Didactic narratives, in Chatman's terms, urge a thesis or convey a clear moral or point; they endeavor to do more than mimetically reflect the world, express the inner feelings of an author, or serve as a source of pleasure. We can find examples of didactic narratives in different literary **genres.** For example, George Orwell's **allegorical** novel, *Animal Farm* (Orwell, 1946), warned against the dangers of totalitarianism, whereas Harriet Beecher Stowe's sentimental novel, *Uncle Tom's Cabin* (Stowe, 1994), and Upton Sinclair's realistic novel, *The Jungle* (Sinclair, 1906), attack the evils of slavery and the problems in America's meatpacking industry, respectively, at the beginning of the 20th century. This instrumental or didactic function can be manifested in various ways—in a narrator's explicit comments on characters and their behavior, through the speech or revealed thoughts of a character (Chatman, 1990, p. 14), or through the various events depicted in (and the overall structure of) the narrative.

When employed instrumentally, narratives respond to perceived situational exigences. Consider some common exigences routinely encountered by public advocates (for more detailed explication of these exigences, see the entry for **situation, rhetorical**). Advocates face the problem of affirming or rejecting policy proposals or courses of action; in Chatman's terms, they must defend or attack a thesis. Dalton Trumbo's novel, *Johnny Got His Gun* (the story of a soldier severely wounded and disfigured during World War I), advanced a clear anti-war thesis (Trumbo, 1988). During the war in Vietnam, advocates on both sides of the dispute employed narratives to defend their positions. Supporters of American involvement in the war told the story of North Vietnamese Communist aggression against the peaceful nation of South Vietnam, whereas opponents of the war countered with the story of South Vietnamese corruption and oppression leading to a civil war. Another recurrent rhetorical exigence is the need to define the situation (see also the entry for **definition/definition of situation**).[7] In a study of Martin Luther King, Jr.'s final public speech during the 1968 sanitation workers' strike in Memphis, Tennessee, Rosteck (1992) noted the way in which King employed the narrative (or **myth**) of the Jewish exodus "to shape an otherwise inchoate situation" (p. 23) and give it meaning; the exodus narrative functioned, in short, "to define the situation for that audience and to 'tell' that audience how [it] must act" (p. 29). The competing narratives of the war in Vietnam defended a thesis (either support the war or oppose the war) through the ways in which they defined the situation; in one story, the situation was a war of aggression, whereas in the other, it was an internal civil war. Consider one final example. Recent scholarship on **epideictic discourse** suggests the existence of what we can term *communal exigences* (Condit, 1985; Murphy, 1990)—recurrent problems that threaten a community's ability to maintain and perpetuate itself over time. Narratives function as an important resource in combating the range of communal exigences that might plague any particular community. We can see how narrative worked in this manner in the epideictic oratory of Daniel Webster during the first half of the 19th century. Webster's epideictic speeches frequently recounted key events in American history (e.g., the founding of the New England colonies by the Puritans, the American revolutionary struggle), and like most historiography, these efforts to preserve events from the past took a narrative form. In numerous epideictic addresses, Webster told the story of the great Puritan migration to America or the story of the colonies' struggle against British oppression. In memorializing and preserving these events in the nation's collective **memory,** Webster also was addressing his sense of the communal problems—issues of value, identity, meaning, and authority—plaguing the young nation (Browne, 1993).

As noted earlier, the instrumental function can be actualized through different discursive means (e.g., narrator commentary, character dialogue). But how specifically do these various discursive elements of a narrative function instrumentally? How are they persuasive? Prado (1984) observed, "If [narrative] fiction does enrich us, it must somehow operate as does descriptive assertive discourse. That is, it must operate by presenting or 'intimating' content to which we can assent. The content must be propositional, if only indirectly or implicitly" (p. 88).[8] Prado appeared to be suggesting that, for narratives to function instrumentally, they must be able to present (directly or indirectly) propositions to which an audience can assent; in other words, they must argue. In raising the issue of propositional content, Prado called attention to a key issue: How do narratives *argue*?

Pursuing the question of how narratives argue can lead in different directions. For example, Chatman (1990) noted, "One fruitful sort of inquiry . . . would be to outline or taxonomize the technical means by which film [as a narrative medium] *could* argue in ways correspondent to formal verbal arguments" (p. 58). Do narratives instantiate or embody common **argument** forms? Fisher (1987) answered this question with a somewhat qualified yes. He stated,

> Aesthetic proofs function outside the realm of regular argumentation in that they are neither general principles that become the bases for deduction nor real examples that are used as bases for induction. Aesthetic proofs are representations of reality that fall somewhere between analogies and examples. . . . Dramatic and literary works move by suggestion rather than "logical" direction. (p. 162)

For Fisher, narrative arguments resemble the common argument forms of analogy and example but still are different from such "formal argumentative structures" (p. 162). Chatman (1990), on the other hand, answered the question with an unqualified yes. Analyzing the opening of Henry Fielding's 18th-century novel *Joseph Andrews,* Chatman located "a classical . . . chain of enthymemes" proceeding from major premise, through minor premise, to conclusion, with the conclusion of one enthymeme serving as the major premise for the next (pp. 12-13). The difference between Fisher's and Chatman's views might not ultimately be that significant; whether narrative arguments resemble common argument forms or actually contain and enact such forms is not as important as the underlying idea that it is useful to think about the instrumental function of narratives in terms of argument.

What are some examples of common argument forms embodied in narrative discourse? One of the most common is the argument of *example.* In his study of biblical parables, Kirkwood (1985) noted the way in which such stories function to illustrate or exemplify desirable courses of action. By way of the argument of example, narratives instruct audience members on how they should act, what they should find valuable, and/or what types of situations they should avoid. Narratives also can argue inductively or by way of *generalization.* Fisher (1987) described how Arthur Miller's *Death of a Salesman* accumulated examples to establish its thesis: "The play argues narratively, piling up incidents and bits of discourse that coherently, through narrative time, suggest the thesis over and over in different terms and in relation to different characters" (p. 168). Another common narrative argument is *analogy.* Allegories such as Orwell's (1946) *Animal Farm* argue in this manner, inviting the reader or audience to see one situation in terms of another. Lewis (1987) observed the way in which narrative anecdotes in Ronald Reagan's discourse functioned as "practical analogies . . . [that] explain and . . . justify his policy choices" (p. 293). Reagan's anecdotes (e.g., cutting the federal government's "allowance") depicted "unfamiliar events and complex situations" in terms that rendered them "simple and familiar" (p. 293). Narratives can enact *pragmatic* arguments. As Perelman and Olbrechts-Tyteca (1969) explained, a pragmatic argument "permits the evaluation of an act or event in terms of its favorable or unfavorable consequences" (p. 266). Narratives provide a vivid way for advocates to depict the possible future consequences of an act or event. For example, an episode of the "new" *Outer Limits* television show speculates on what might happen if human genetic engineering were to become available through a type of "high-tech black market." In the episode, a young couple come to believe that the only way in which their unborn child can compete in the emerging brave new world is if they have the fetus genetically enhanced. But as the story unfolds, the couple discover that their next-door neighbors underwent the procedure before their son was born. The child, who was presumed dead, actually is alive and suffering from a new man-made malady—genetic deformity syndrome. This "unfavorable consequence" supports the argument and moral of the tale: Don't mess with "Mother Nature." Narratives also can argue by way of *comparison* and *disjunction* (Green, 1984). In his examination of the film *The Big Chill,* Jasinski extended the works of Burke (1957) and White (1984) in maintaining that the film

> enacts a complex disjunctive argument in which alternative "persuasive communities" . . . are constructed and juxtaposed. Through narrative exposition, crosscutting, and montage sequences, the film establishes and then compares and contrasts the norms (the guiding values, beliefs, and actions) of the constructed communities. (Jasinski, 1993, pp. 467-468)

The result of the process of juxtaposition and comparison, Jasinski claimed, is a narrative argument that rejects one model of communal life (*eros* or intimacy) while endorsing an alternative model (*philia* or friendship). The complex disjunctive argument that Jasinski described also might be considered as a form of *middle ground* argument in that the film situates its preferred model of communal life (friendship) in between two unacceptable extremes (communities based on intimacy and the essentially anti-community model of estrangement).

Either/or disjunctive arguments typically play a prominent role in deliberative narratives. Cox's (1989) reconstruction of the "temporal movement"—the basic narrative sequence—of Martin Luther King, Jr.'s "I Have a Dream" speech in August 1963 can serve as an initial illustration. According to Cox, King began the speech in the past, describing the "promises of democracy" that were made to black Americans. The speech then moved to the present time in the famous "check" metaphor section, showing how the promises remained unfulfilled. Cox argued that the present opened up onto two possible futures: The nation could "make real the promises of democracy," or it could take the "tranquilizing drug of gradualism." Although King urged the first path (employing pragmatic arguments to reject the "drug" option), the future—and the conclusion of the narrative—was left up to members of the audience; it was their choice. Another example can be found in Franklin Roosevelt's "Commonwealth Club" address during the 1932 presidential campaign. Roosevelt constructed a narrative that charted the emergence and development of democratic government in Western Europe and the United States. Exploiting important parallels within the story to steer the audience in a particular direction, Roosevelt concluded the speech disjunctively: Americans could choose "economic oligarchy" or "enlightened administration" as the next phase (or chapter) in the evolution of democracy.

It might be possible to extend this description of the disjunctive choice embedded in the King and Roosevelt narratives into an account of the basic structure and argumentative mode of deliberative narratives. Most historical or literary narratives are closed; the complications or conflicts energizing the plots are wrapped up, and the stories are brought to (hopefully) satisfying conclusions (e.g., the couple get married, the villain is punished). Closure is achieved primarily through the decisions and choices of the characters; what they do determines the outcomes.[9] Deliberative narratives typically are not closed; they remain unfinished or incomplete. Deliberative narratives culminate with the pivotal kernels—the key choices that must be made to determine how the stories will end. But in deliberative narratives, the agent of choice usually is the audience. In essence, deliberative narratives position their audience as key characters in the still unfolding narratives (cf. Lewis, 1987, pp. 284-285). The conclusion of the deliberative narrative depends on which of the paths the audience chooses. An advocate, as a deliberative narrator, can try to influence the audience's choice by describing the probable impact of each option. But the choice remains the audience's to make. Deliberative narratives illustrate Farrell's (1993) claim that "rhetoric helps to define and . . . constitute . . . a culture . . . by inviting audiences to think figuratively about their own place and conduct in unfolding historical episodes" (p. 213).[10]

One foreign policy controversy, the **debate** over the Panama Canal treaties during the late 1970s, can provide further illustration of the openness of deliberative narratives.[11] To keep the discussion brief, we can focus on two of the key participants in the debate: President Jimmy Carter (arguing that the treaties should be adopted) and Congressman Philip Crane (arguing that they should be rejected). Both Carter and Crane told the American people a story. In Carter's story, America had treated the much smaller nation of Panama unfairly in the past. Now that smaller nation was expressing legitimate discontent with America. The people of Panama were asking Americans to treat them fairly, and Carter maintained that the treaties did just that while also protecting America's legitimate security interests. In Crane's story, America had made a shrewd and legal bargain to acquire the Panama Canal zone. Now the people of Panama were demonstrating childish ingratitude, ignoring all of the things that America has done for them over the previous 75 years. Crane contended that the treaties would give away the Panama Canal to a nation that was basically a banana republic. Carter's and Crane's narrative depictions of the past and present differed dramatically, and their projections for the future also were very different. But in each story, the future remained open; the final chapter still had to be written. The American people—the audience—were confronted with a choice; they would decide how the story would end.

But Carter and Crane framed the audience's choice in different ways given their projections for the future. For Carter, failure to ratify the treaties would frustrate the legitimate aspirations of the Panamanian people and weaken America's position in Central America. In a nationally televised address on the issue, Carter told the American people that "nothing could strengthen our competitors and adversaries in this hemisphere more than for us to reject this agreement." But Carter predicted that if the nation ratified the treaties, it would result in a bright future—a "new era of friendship and cooperation" brought about by America's moral strength. For Crane, defeating the proposed treaties would demonstrate that third-rate nations could not push America around anymore and would ensure regional stability through America's material strength. Ratifying the treaties—or, as the title of Crane's (1978) book on the issue termed it, *Surrender in Panama*—"would appear not as a noble act of magnanimity but as the cowardly retreat of a tired, toothless paper tiger" (p. 112). Carter and Crane both projected two possible futures—one negative and one positive—as the culmination of their respective narratives. In each story, the final chapter would be written by the audience members in their choice to either support or oppose the treaties.[12]

Consider one final example of narrative argument. In his reading of Shakespeare's *Julius Caesar*, Burke (1957) noted a problem that Shakespeare had to confront. Burke wrote, "We cannot profitably build a play around the horror of a murder if you do not care whether the murdered man lives or dies. So we had to do something for Caesar" (p. 281). What did Shakespeare do? Burke's reconstruction of the "argument" (whose function here, it should be noted, was principally aesthetic and not instrumental) resembled the form that Perelman and Olbrechts-Tyteca (1969) described as "transitivity." Transitivity, in their account, enacts a fourth figure syllogistic pattern: A → B, B → C, therefore A → C. In the case of Shakespeare's play, Burke suggested the following instantiation of the pattern: The audience "loves" Anthony, Anthony loves Caesar, therefore the audience should love Caesar as well. Shakespeare solved his aesthetic problem by embedding a transitive argument pattern into the dramatic structure of *Julius Caesar.*[13]

Narrative discourse also fulfills a third rhetorical function. All narratives, whether they are explicitly didactic or not, manifest what Chatman (1990) referred to as "ideological-rhetorical force" (p. 198); they implicate an **ideology.** Chatman's sense of an ideological-rhetorical force emanating from narrative discourse parallels the idea of a *constitutive* function for discursive practice discussed in contemporary rhetorical, social, and literary theory (Charland, 1987; White, 1984). Whereas the instrumental function of a narrative includes efforts to solve problems, urge a thesis, or promote action, the idea of constitutive or ideological-rhetorical force refers to the way in which a narrative relates or positions itself with respect to a culture's social world (its customs, traditions, values, shared beliefs, roles, institutions, memories, and language that become a type of "second" nature to the members of that culture). Instrumental and constitutive narrative functions are not mutually exclusive; at times, they can intersect and overlap. For example, in his "I Have a Dream" speech, King sought to negotiate a number of *exigences* including the need to generate support for the John F. Kennedy administration's civil rights bill and the problem of increasing fragmentation in the civil rights movement. In the course of his unfinished deliberative narrative, King addressed these instrumental concerns. But in the process, King challenged the pervasive belief that time flows slowly or gradually; the ideological-rhetorical force of the address helped to reshape, or reconstitute, how Americans thought about time.

The nature of constitutive or ideological-rhetorical force in narrative discourse can be conceptualized as a continuum. At one end, narratives function to reaffirm or perpetuate the status quo; they reinforce common assumptions about the world and how it works. For example, a heterosexual love story helps to reaffirm the naturalness of heterosexuality. A "rags to riches" biography helps to reaffirm dominant attitudes about individualism, hard work, equal opportunity, and the American economic system. At the other end of the continuum, narratives function to challenge or subvert the reigning ideological beliefs and values. For example, a gay or lesbian love story implicitly, if not explicitly, subverts the cultural norm of heterosexuality. A story about corporate greed (anything from Oliver Stone's fictitious film *Wall Street* to Michael Moore's "documentary" exposé *The Big One*) challenges reigning attitudes about the benefits of American capitalism. In between the two ends of the continuum is a large middle ground consisting of various mixtures of *affirmation and subversion;* in this middle ground, the constitutive or ideological-rhetorical force of narratives can simultaneously affirm some cultural norms (e.g., individualism, hard work) while subverting other elements of the culture (e.g., racism, sexism). It must be noted that the constitutive or ideological-rhetorical force of a narrative will not be the same for every reader or every member of an audience. Many contemporary scholars emphasize that audiences and readers are not necessarily passive receivers of messages; they can, at times, work as *resistant* readers or audience members (Fetterley, 1978).[14] Discussion of a narrative's constitutive or ideological-rhetorical function must be qualified to acknowledge that other readings of the text are possible. It has become relatively common in literary criticism, while remaining less common in rhetorical studies, for the critic to try to show how a narrative that appears to be emitting subversive ideological-rhetorical force is, in fact, subtly reaffirming or reconstituting central cultural norms (Michaels, 1987).

In the entry for **effects of rhetorical practice,** four specific aspects of the constitutive dimension of rhetoric were identified. Those four aspects—the constitution of identity and **subjectivity**, the constitution of time and temporal experience, the constitution of community and political culture, and the constitution of language—organize this overview of the ideological-rhetorical or constitutive function of narrative. First, narratives help to shape or constitute identity and subjectivity. Carr (1986) suggested that the self might be understood as a "unity of experiences and actions" (p. 149), with narrative serving as "the manner in which our experiences and actions are organized over time" (p. 73). The stories that we tell about ourselves, and the way in which we organize, edit, and revise those stories, help to shape our identity—our sense of who we are as persons. In a sense, an individual is a constantly unfolding story; events, experiences, and feelings are continually being integrated into (or deleted from) the plots of our lives.[15] Narratives play a particularly important role in cases of **secular conversion** or those instances in which individuals attempt drastic revisions in their narrative selves. An individual who undergoes a major religious, political/ideological, or lifestyle conversion almost inevitably has to reconstruct his or her personal narrative. Events and experiences that previously were unimportant or inexplicable might now be woven into a new life story while other events or experiences are revised, reinterpreted, or deleted to create a coherent narrative—a story that reaches a type of mini-climax in the conversion experience.[16]

Second, narratives help to shape or constitute a person's or culture's experience of time. For illustration purposes, consider how the members of a culture experience the culture's past. To a large degree, the meaning and significance of the past will be shaped by the narratives told about it. One recent case of conflicting narratives of the past emerged during the 1995 anniversary of the end of World War II. Some of the events that were commemorated (e.g., the defeat of fascism) caused little discussion, but other events (e.g., America's use of atomic weapons against the Japanese cities of Hiroshima and Nagasaki) generated considerable public debate. As Americans debated the appropriate way of remembering the bombings, they produced conflicting narratives of the end of the war with Japan. For some, the bombings at Hiroshima and Nagasaki were moments of American military and technological triumph that saved the lives of millions of American and Japanese soldiers whose lives would have been lost if the Allies had been forced to invade the Japanese mainland. For others, the story of America's decision to use atomic weapons against Japan was more tragic than triumphant. This story emphasized America's stubborn unwillingness to clarify the terms under which it would accept Japan's surrender, its desire to avenge the attack against Pearl Harbor, and its hope that U.S. possession of the atom bomb would be a constant warning to the Soviet Union. Cultures routinely face the question of what to remember about the past, and the answer is contained in the stories through which we preserve the past. Similar observations could be made about the other central components of temporal experience. We use narratives to understand the present, to envision possible futures, and to remember the past.

Third, narratives help to shape or constitute political community and culture. Carr (1986) drew a parallel between the way in which narratives shape individual identity and the way in which they constitute a community's identity and sustain its institutions, practices, and values. Carr wrote,

> [A] group's temporally persisting existence as a community, and as a social subject of experience and action, is not different from the story that is told about it; it too is constituted by a story *of* the community, of what it is and what it is doing, which is told, acted out, and received and accepted in a kind of self-reflective social narration. (pp. 149-150)

The importance of narrative to communal identity has been noted in a number of critical studies. Charland (1987), for example, noted the way in which narrative functions within the Quebec nationalist movement to constitute a "*peuple Québécois*" or a unified and sovereign people. Peterson (1991) uncovered the way in which narrative structures the values of America's farmers. Rosteck (1992) disclosed the way in which King's use of the "exodus" narrative helped to constitute the identity of African Americans during the late 1960s. Wald (1995) described the way in which the American "nation-builders" during the 19th century used narratives to "instantiate their visions of the union and define what the United States Constitution called 'we the people' " (p. 2). But as Wald pointed out, the "official stories" of nation-builders exist in an uneasy relationship to those individuals and groups left out of these stories. The stories of those left out or marginalized by the dominant culture are alternative stories that can challenge, disrupt, or severely qualify the depictions contained in official stories. Rhetorical scholars need to recognize the ideological-rhetorical force that narratives exert to shape a community while also acknowledging the potential of alternative stories to challenge or redirect a community's stock of key stories.

Finally, narratives help to shape a culture's language including, but not limited to, its key terms of value, motive, understanding, and desire (see also the entry for **ideograph**). As White (1984) noted, whenever we speak or write, "we struggle to make our words work as we wish, to redefine them to meet our needs, and doing this we remake, in ways however small, our language and our world" (p. 4).[17] White argued that our relationship to language is "deeply reciprocal. . . . For while a person acts both with and upon the language that he [sic] uses, at once employing and reconstituting its resources, his language at the same time acts upon him" (p. 8). White's critical investigations explored in considerable detail the ways in which discourse functions to "constitute and reconstitute language, character, and community" (the subtitle of his 1984 book). His critical gaze frequently turned to narrative discourse. For example, White read Jane Austen's novel *Emma* as a case of remaking language. White maintained that Austen "can be said to make out of her inherited materials a moral language of extraordinary range, discrimination, and coherence and to teach her reader how to make it his [sic] own so that he may use it in his own life as an instrument of perception and judgment" (p. 163). White argued that, over the course of the novel, Austen revealed that Emma Woodhouse's language was "highly defective" (p. 165). The problem with Emma's language was that "it ha[d] no internal opposition, no tension to give it life and to make meaning possible"; it was essentially a language of "daydream" (pp. 166-167). But as the novel unfolded, and as Emma confronted or was made to confront her flaws, she began to glimpse the key terms of a "new" language. White wrote that friendship, kindness, and generosity were remade and became core terms of value in Emma's reconstituted language. *Emma* illustrated nicely the way in which narratives can function to shape and reshape language.

So far, the discussion has not addressed the question of how narratives appear in public discourse. This question has not received much explicit attention in the literature (for an exception, see Lewis, 1987), but it merits brief consideration so as to introduce a bit of clarity into our critical investigations. In what forms do we encounter narratives in public discourse? *Form* here does not refer to the traditional genres of narrative (e.g., comedy, tragedy, epic); rather, it refers to the ways in which narratives might exist for our public inspection and interaction. Three such forms can be identified.

First, narratives can exist, and be encountered, as self-contained, autonomous discursive or textual acts.[18] Most of the examples discussed in this entry are of this type. A novel such as *Emma* or *Uncle Tom's Cabin*, a film such as *The Big Chill*, and a play such as *Death of a Salesman* all are self-contained or autonomous. They exist independently or set apart from other texts or discursive practices. But this idea of textual independence or autonomy needs to be qualified. As many contemporary critics and theorists argue, texts are shaped or influenced by a web of other texts that have preceded them (see the entry for **intertextuality**). The idea of an autonomous narrative does not deny the inevitability of intertextuality. Various traces (relating to characters, images, plots, etc.) of other texts can be found in any self-contained narrative. Autonomy or independence refers to the external relationship among texts and not to their substantive interconnections. A group of narrative texts can cohere at various levels (e.g., genre, theme) while remaining discrete textual artifacts. Autonomy means only that a narrative's external appearance is not dependent on another text.

Second, narratives can exist, and be encountered, as elements inserted into or embedded within other discursive practices. In some cases, texts may be littered with embedded narratives. For example, Russell Conwell's famous speech, "Acres of Diamonds" (delivered well over 1,000 times during the late 19th century), weaved together a variety of embedded narratives—brief stories, anecdotes, and accounts of notable individuals beginning with the opening tale of Al Hafed's tragic quest for diamonds and continuing with the story about the farmer in Pennsylvania who sold his farm to go search for oil, the story of how John Jacob Astor became rich in the millinery business, and the story of the woman in Connecticut who invented a new "snap button" for women's clothing.[19] Elizabeth Cady Stanton's speech, "The Solitude of Self" (delivered in Washington, D.C., in January 1892), not only had a loose narrative structure (the progression from childhood to old age and death) but also contained a number of brief embedded narratives such as the story of the young girl at Christmas, an account of how Russia's Prince Krapotkin survived imprisonment, and the story of how women prisoners formed a human chain to save drowning sailors in the Bay of Biscay. An embedded narrative might function as the core of a speech or other discursive text. In Franklin Roosevelt's address to the Commonwealth Club in 1932, his "story" of the emergence and development of central government, beginning in feudal Europe and continuing to present-day America, was the dominant component of the speech. But this story was not autonomous; it was embedded within the larger framework of the speech.

Third, narratives can exist, and be encountered, as underlying structural presences that shape or inform a number of seemingly unconnected messages.[20] Lewis (1987) identified the presence of an underlying **myth**, or narrative, that structured the discourse of Reagan (see also Fisher, 1987, pp. 146-147). As Lewis (1987) noted, "Reagan never tells the whole of his American story at any one time," but such a story still undergirded much of his public discourse. Lewis described the essence of the story in these terms:

> Reagan portrays American history as a continuing struggle for progress against great obstacles imposed by economic adversity, barbaric enemies, or big government. It is a story with great heroes—Washington, Jefferson, Lincoln, Roosevelt—with great villains—the monarchs of pre-revolutionary Europe, the Depression, the Communists, the Democrats—and with a great theme—the rise of freedom and economic progress. It is a story that is sanctified by God and validated by American experience. All the themes of Reagan's rhetoric are contained in this mythic history—America's greatness, its commitment to freedom, the heroism of the American people, the moral imperative of work, the priority of economic advancement, the domestic evils of taxes and government regulation, and the necessity of military strength.... Reagan repeatedly tells his audiences that if they choose to participate in the story, they will become a part of America's greatness. (pp. 282-283)

A structural narrative can inhabit the discourse of a single person,[21] or it can shape the messages produced by a group, organization, or social **movement**. For example, a critic might uncover the underlying narrative that shapes the discourse of organized labor or, like Peterson (1991), focus on the "story" of American farmers. Once a structural narrative is uncovered, the critic can investigate its instrumental and/or constitutive function(s) and persuasive potential.

The final question to consider is how critics, as well as public audiences, can evaluate narrative discourse. Critics can and do apply some of the general standards of critical evaluation (e.g., effects, quality) to narrative discourse (on these standards, see the entry for **criticism**). Beyond these standards, are there standards particularly appropriate for evaluating narratives? Booth (1988) and Fisher (1987) identified evaluative stances that they indicated are well suited for the study of narrative discourse.

Booth (1988) described his approach to narrative appraisal as a form of *ethical criticism*. For Booth, narratives invite readers and audience to enter into a relationship—to establish a type of friendship. Like any interpersonal relationship, a reader's relationship with a narrative will involve certain forms of activity; Booth suggested that a narrative will invite its reader to enter into a relationship based on particular types of activity. Booth's exploration of the friendship *metaphor* led him to identify seven specific topics that a critic can use to assess the invitations that a narrative makes and the activities in which it asks us to engage. These include (a) the *quantity* of invitations contained in a narrative, (b) the relationship established between narrator and reader (how reciprocal the relationship is), (c) the degree of intimacy in the relationship, (d) the intensity of engagement that a narrative demands from its reader, (e) the coherence of the world created in the narrative, (f) the distance between the world of the narrative and the world of the reader (the degree of familiarity or strangeness of the narrative world), and (g) the specific types of activities that a narrative invites, suggests, or demands (pp. 179-180). Booth indicated that these topics are essentially the same ones that we use to establish and assess our relationships with "our living friends" (p. 180). He suggested that an ethical approach to narrative evaluation attempts to "use the vocabulary of friendship to appraise the patterns of desire that narratives ask us to share" (p. 198).

Fisher (1987) viewed his approach to narrative evaluation as an extension of a reconstructed narrative rationality. He maintained that narrative rationality or logic has two "essential components": *probability* or coherence and *fidelity* or truthfulness and reliability (p. 47). Like Booth (and a large number of narrative critics), Fisher insisted that probability or coherence is an essential criterion for evaluating narratives. He suggested that coherence can be broken down and assessed in three more specific ways: (a) *structural coherence* (similar to Aristotle's idea that a narrative must manifest unity), (b) *material coherence* (the relationship between what Chatman [1978, p. 19] termed the *what* and *how* or the "story" [the "raw" events related in the narrative] and the "discourse" [the way in which the narrator depicts those events]), and (c) *characterological coherence* (the degree of compatibility among a character's "actional tendencies" [Fisher, 1987, p. 47]). Probability, in short, aims to assess how well a narrative "hangs together" (p. 47).

Assessing fidelity involves inquiring into the reliability or suitability of the narrative's "equipment for living" (Burke, 1957). In Fisher's (1987) terms, "Does [the narrative] provide a reliable guide to *our* beliefs, attitudes, values, [and] actions? . . . Are the central conclusions of [the narrative] reliable/desirable guides for one's own life?" (pp. 175-176). Like Booth and the many critics he has influenced (e.g., James Boyd White), Fisher seemed to emphasize the need to evaluate the invitations that a narrative offers to its reader or audience. As White (1984) remarked, a narrative inevitably will "ask its reader to become someone" (p. 15), to assume a certain type of character and identity, and to act in a particular way. White's example was a racist joke; a reader might not realize it, but when he or she is told such a "story," that story is asking the reader to become a certain type of person. This leads to the key question: Does the reader want to become that type of person? This manner of evaluation can be extended to virtually any narrative that an individual encounters. Consider an episode of the television show *NYPD Blue*. A viewer could ask himself or herself the question: What type of person are these stories asking me to become? As another example, consider the John Grisham novel (and film version) *A Time to Kill*. What type of person is Grisham's story asking the reader or viewer to become? Someone who endorses an individual's taking the law into his or her own hands? Someone who sympathizes with a father whose daughter has been savagely raped? Someone who will acknowledge and work to overcome racial injustice? Once the reader or viewer identifies the type of person the narrative is asking him or her to become, the individual has to grapple with the even more difficult question: Does (or should) he or she want to become that type of person? Booth, Fisher, and White stressed a similar point, albeit in different ways: Evaluating a narrative entails identifying and assessing the type of person that it is asking the reader or audience to become.

Notes

1. See, for example, Chatman (1978), Coste (1989), Martin (1986), Mitchell (1981), and Scholes and Kellogg (1966).

2. See, for example, Berger (1997), Carpenter (1995), Carr (1986), Danto (1985), MacIntyre (1981), Morson (1994), Mumby (1993b), Polkinghorne (1988), Ricoeur (1984-1988), Schectman (1996), and Schram and Neisser (1997).

3. Plot was one of the six parts of tragic narrative identified by Aristotle. The other five parts were spectacle (in general terms, the setting), character, thought, diction, and melody.

4. Booth (1988) suggested that the contemporary fascination with fragmentation can be traced to the influence of aesthetic and literary romanticism.

5. But as Chatman (1990) noted, it is different from the more commonplace equation of rhetoric and public persuasion in politics and the law.

6. The nature and form of narrative in deliberative discourse is addressed a bit later in this entry.

7. On the use of narrative in **deliberative discourse**, see also Kraig (1997).

8. See also Hart's (1997) claim that narratives can constitute "depropositionalized argument" (p. 93).

9. See Chatman's (1978) discussion of narrative *kernels*—moments of choice that determine the direction of the story.

10. This account of deliberative narrative parallels Charland's (1987) discussion of narrative in **constitutive rhetoric**. Charland observed, "While classical narratives have an ending, constitutive rhetorics leave the task of narrative closure to their constituted subjects" (p. 143).

11. On the competing narratives in the Panama Canal treaty debate, see also Hollihan (1986); Smith (1986); and Stewart, Smith, and Denton (1989).

12. A final qualification is necessary. Narratives introduced in a deliberative situation will be open when they are created or generated by advocates and/or social **movements**. In some cases, advocates will appropriate existing narratives and introduce them into deliberative contexts, as King did with the "exodus" narrative in Memphis in 1968. In a case such as this, advocates urge their audience to follow the course of action set down in the existing narrative. The audience members still are faced with a choice—to either abandon their role in the narrative or fulfill the obligation laid out for them in the existing narrative.

13. It is important to emphasize that these specific types of narrative arguments are illustrative and not an exhaustive account of the topic. Additional critical inquiry might be able to produce a taxonomy of narrative arguments, describing how narrative elements work to instantiate the different patterns and providing additional insight into the instrumental function of narrative discourse.

14. For a review of the relevant literature, see Abercrombie and Longhurst's (1998) discussion of the "incorporation/resistance paradigm" of **audience** research.

15. See also Schectman's (1996) discussion of "narrative self-constitution."

16. For a critical study that explores the relationship between narrative and personal identity, see Carlson (1995).

17. On the struggle to make "words work as we wish," see the entry for **accent**.

18. See Brummett's (1994) discussion of "discrete" texts as "clearly distinct and separate in time and space, surrounded by clear boundaries" (p. 40).

19. On Conwell's use of narrative, see Carlson (1989).

20. See Brummett's (1994) discussion of "diffuse" texts as "a collection of signs working for the same or related rhetorical influence that [are] not discretely separated from [their] context" (p. 64).

21. Examples would include the cases of Reagan and Webster (Erickson, 1986).

References and Additional Reading

Abercrombie, N., & Longhurst, B. (1998). *Audiences: A sociological theory of performance and imagination.* London: Sage.

Abrams, M. H. (1953). *The mirror and the lamp: Romantic theory and the critical tradition.* Oxford, UK: Oxford University Press.

Aristotle (1954a). *Poetics* (I. Bywater, Trans.). New York: Modern Library.

Aristotle. (1954b). *Rhetoric* (W. R. Roberts, Trans.). New York: Modern Library.

Auerbach, E. (1946). *Mimesis: The representation of reality in Western literature* (W. R. Trask, Trans.). Princeton, NJ: Princeton University Press.

Bal, M. (1985). *Narratology: Introduction to the theory of narrative* (C. van Bohhmen, Trans.). Toronto: University of Toronto Press.

Berger, A. A. (1997). *Narratives in popular culture, media, and everyday life.* Thousand Oaks, CA: Sage.

Booth, W. C. (1983). *The rhetoric of fiction* (2nd ed.). Chicago: University of Chicago Press.

Booth, W. C. (1988). *The company we keep: An ethics of fiction.* Berkeley: University of California Press.

Brooks, P., & Gewirtz, P. (Eds.). (1996). *Law's stories: Narrative and rhetoric in the law.* New Haven, CT: Yale University Press.

Brown, R. H. (1998). *Toward a democratic science: Scientific narration and civic communication.* New Haven, CT: Yale University Press.

Browne, S. H. (1993). Reading public memory in Daniel Webster's *Plymouth Rock Oration. Western Journal of Communication, 57,* 464-477.

Brummett, B. (1994). *Rhetoric in popular culture.* New York: St. Martin's.

Burke, K. (1957). *The philosophy of literary form* (rev. ed.). New York: Vintage.

Carlson, A. C. (1989). Narrative as the philosopher's stone: How Russell H. Conwell changed lead into diamonds. *Western Journal of Speech Communication, 53,* 342-355.

Carlson, A. C. (1995). Character invention in the letters of Maime Pinzer. *Communication Quarterly, 43,* 408-419.

Carpenter, R. H. (1995). *History as rhetoric: Style, narrative, and persuasion.* Columbia: University of South Carolina Press.

Carr, D. (1986). *Time, narrative, and history.* Bloomington: Indiana University Press.

Charland, M. (1987). Constitutive rhetoric: The case of the *peuple Québécois. Quarterly Journal of Speech, 73,* 133-150.

Chatman, S. (1978). *Story and discourse: Narrative structure in fiction and film.* Ithaca, NY: Cornell University Press.

Chatman, S. (1990). *Coming to terms: The rhetoric of narrative in fiction and film.* Ithaca, NY: Cornell University Press.

Condit, C. M. (1985). The functions of epideictic: The Boston Massacre orations as exemplar. *Communication Quarterly, 33,* 284-299.

Coste, D. (1989). *Narrative as communication.* Minneapolis: University of Minnesota Press.

Cox, J. R. (1989). The fulfillment of time: King's "I Have a Dream" speech. In M. C. Leff & F. J. Kauffeld (Eds.), *Texts in context: Critical dialogues on significant episodes in American political rhetoric.* Davis, CA: Hermagoras Press.

Crane, P. (1978). *Surrender in Panama: The case against the treaty.* New York: Dale Books.

Czarniawska, B. (1997). *Narrating the organization: Drama of institutional identity.* Chicago: University of Chicago Press.

Danto, A. C. (1985). *Narration and knowledge.* New York: Columbia University Press.

Erickson, P. D. (1986). *The poetry of events: Daniel Webster's rhetoric of the Constitution and union.* New York: New York University Press.

Farrell, T. B. (1993). *Norms of rhetorical culture.* New Haven, CT: Yale University Press.

Fetterley, J. (1978). *The resisting reader: A feminist approach to American fiction.* Bloomington: Indiana University Press.

Fisher, W. R. (1984). Narration as a human communication paradigm: The case of public moral argument. *Communication Monographs, 52,* 1-22.

Fisher, W. R. (1987). *Human communication as narration: Toward a philosophy of reason, value, and action.* Columbia: University of South Carolina Press.

Foss, S. K. (1996). *Rhetorical criticism: Exploration and practice* (2nd ed.). Prospect Heights, IL: Waveland.

Green, L. D. (1984). "We'll dress him up in voices": The rhetoric of disjunction in *Troilus and Cressida. Quarterly Journal of Speech, 70,* 23-40.

Hart, R. P. (1997). *Modern rhetorical criticism* (2nd ed.). Boston: Allyn & Bacon.

Hollihan, T. A. (1986). The public controversy over the Panama Canal treaties: An analysis of American foreign policy rhetoric. *Western Journal of Speech Communication, 50,* 368-387.

Jasinski, J. (1993). (Re)constituting community through narrative argument: *Eros* and *philia* in *The Big Chill. Quarterly Journal of Speech, 79,* 467-486.

Kennedy, G. A. (1991). *Aristotle on rhetoric: A theory of civic discourse.* New York: Oxford University Press.

Kirkwood, W. G. (1985). Parables as metaphors and examples. *Quarterly Journal of Speech, 71,* 422-440.

Kraig, R. A. (1997). The narrative of essence: Salmon P. Chase's Senate oration against the Kansas-Nebraska Act. *Communication Studies, 48,* 234-253.

Lewis, W. F. (1987). Telling America's story: Narrative form and the Reagan presidency. *Quarterly Journal of Speech, 73,* 280-302.

MacIntyre, A. (1981). *After virtue: A study in moral theory.* Notre Dame, IN: University of Notre Dame Press.

Martin, W. (1986). *Recent theories of narrative.* Ithaca, NY: Cornell University Press.

McGee, M. C. (1990). Text, context, and the fragmentation of contemporary culture. *Western Journal of Speech Communication, 54,* 274-289.

Michaels, W. B. (1987). *The gold standard and the logic of naturalism.* Berkeley: University of California Press.

Mitchell, W. J. T. (Ed.). (1981). *On narrative.* Chicago: University of Chicago Press.

Morson, G. S. (1994). *Narrative and freedom: The shadows of time.* New Haven, CT: Yale University Press.

Mumby, D. K. (1993a). Introduction: Narrative and social control. In D. K. Mumby (Ed.), *Narrative and social control.* Newbury Park, CA: Sage.

Mumby, D. K. (Ed.). (1993b). *Narrative and social control: Critical perspectives.* Newbury Park, CA: Sage.

Murphy, J. M. (1990). "A time of shame and sorrow": Robert F. Kennedy and the American jeremiad. *Quarterly Journal of Speech, 76,* 401-414.

Newton, A. Z. (1995). *Narrative ethics.* Cambridge, MA: Harvard University Press.

Orwell, G. (1946). *Animal farm.* New York: Harcourt Brace.

Perelman, C., & Olbrechts-Tyteca, L. (1969). *The new rhetoric: A treatise on argumentation* (J. Wilkinson & P. Weaver, Trans.). Notre Dame, IN: University of Notre Dame Press.

Peterson, T. R. (1991). Telling the farmers' story: Competing responses to soil conservation rhetoric. *Quarterly Journal of Speech, 77,* 289-308.

Polkinghorne, D. E. (1988). *Narrative knowing and the human sciences.* Albany: State University of New York Press.

Prado, C. G. (1984). *Making believe: Philosophical reflections on fiction.* Westport, CT: Greenwood.

Prince, G. (1982). *Narratology: The form and functioning of narrative.* New York: Mouton.

Ricoeur, P. (1984-1988). *Time and narrative* (3 vols., K. McLaughlin & D. Pellauer, Trans.). Chicago: University of Chicago Press.

Riessman, C. K. (1993). *Narrative analysis.* Newbury Park, CA: Sage.

Rosteck, T. (1992). Narrative in Martin Luther King's *I've Been to the Mountaintop. Southern Communication Journal, 58,* 22-32.

Rowland, R. C. (1987). Narrative: Mode of discourse or paradigm? *Communication Monographs, 54,* 264-275.

Rowland, R. C. (1989). On limiting the narrative paradigm: Three case studies. *Communication Monographs, 56,* 39-54.

Rowland, R. C., & Strain, R. (1994). Social function, polysemy, and narrative-dramatic form: A case study of *Do the Right Thing. Communication Quarterly, 42,* 213-228.

Schectman, M. (1996). *The constitution of selves.* Ithaca, NY: Cornell University Press.

Scholes, R., & Kellogg, R. (1966). *The nature of narrative.* New York: Oxford University Press.

Schram, S. F., & Neisser, P. T. (Eds.). (1997). *Tales of the state: Narrative in contemporary U.S. politics and public policy.* Lanham, MD: Rowman & Littlefield.

Sinclair, U. (1906). *The jungle.* New York: Doubleday, Page.

Smith, C. A. (1986). Leadership, orientation, and rhetorical vision: Jimmy Carter, the "new right," and the Panama Canal. *Presidential Studies Quarterly, 16,* 317-328.

Stewart, C. J., Smith, C. A., & Denton, R. E., Jr. (1989). *Persuasion and social movements* (2nd ed.). Prospect Heights, IL: Waveland.

Stowe, H. B. (1994). *Uncle Tom's cabin* (E. Ammons, Ed.). New York: Norton.

Stuckey, M. E. (1995). Competing foreign policy visions: Rhetorical hybrids after the cold war. *Western Journal of Communication, 59,* 214-227.

Trumbo, D. (1988). *Johnny got his gun.* New York: Bantam Books.

Wald, P. (1995). *Constituting Americans: Cultural anxiety and narrative form.* Durham, NC: Duke University Press.

Warnick, B. (1987). The narrative paradigm: Another story. *Quarterly Journal of Speech, 73,* 172-182.

Weiler, M. (1990). Arguments in fiction. In D. C. Williams & M. D. Hazen (Eds.), *Argumentation theory and the rhetoric of assent.* Tuscaloosa: University of Alabama Press.

Wells, S. (1996). *Sweet reason: Rhetoric and the discourses of modernity.* Chicago: University of Chicago Press.

White, H. (1981). The value of narrativity in the representation of reality. In W. J. T. Mitchell (Ed.), *On narrative.* Chicago: University of Chicago Press.

White, J. B. (1984). *When words lose their meaning: Constitutions and reconstitutions of language, character, and community.* Chicago: University of Chicago Press.

NEO-ARISTOTELIANISM

Speech communication scholars and students use the term **neo-Aristotelianism** to describe a program or method of criticism that was extremely popular in rhetorical studies especially during the 1940s and 1950s.[1] The origins of the term are unclear. Edwin Black, in his important critique of the program originally published in 1965 (Black, 1978), might have been the first to employ the label explicitly. But he noted that Brigance (1943), in the preface to the first volume of *A History and Criticism of American Public Address,* referred to the "Aristotelian pattern" found in many of the essays in the volume (p. x).[2] The precise origins of the term are unimportant. Our concern is with the contours of the critical program that the label indexed and with the reasons why that program was abandoned during the 1960s.[3]

A number of scholars (e.g., Brock, Scott, & Chesebro, 1989; Foss, 1996) have suggested that three texts are crucial to understanding the neo-Aristotelian program: Wichelns's (1925/1962) essay, "The Literary Criticism of Oratory," the three-volume collection *A History and Criticism of American Public Address,*[4] and Thonssen and Baird's (1948) text, *Speech Criticism.* As the title of his essay suggests, Wichelns (1925/1962) was interested chiefly in how students of literature and history approached the subject of oratory. Although Wichelns found some scholarship that was, in his judgment, appropriate for its object of analysis, he argued that extant treatments of oratory were, for the most part, off target. They did not focus on the essence of the oratorical object[5] or the oratorical act. What, in Wichelns' opinion, would be an adequate account of oratory? Two elements of his response to this question are important. First, he emphasized the *instrumental* character of the oratorical object; speeches exist to influence audiences. The task of *rhetorical* criticism, Wichelns argued, is to understand in detail how speech influences an audience. In a famous passage, Wichelns wrote that rhetorical criticism "is concerned with effect. It regards a speech as a communication to a specific audience and holds its business to be the analysis and appreciation of the orator's method of imparting his [sic] ideas to his hearers" (p. 209). Second, Wichelns outlined a list of analytic topics that might be useful in helping the rhetorical critic to study the instrumental nature of oratory and specific oratorical performances. These topics included knowledge of the audience; an understanding of the speaker's ideas, personality, and "public character"; a description of the speaker's "proofs," "mode of arrangement," "mode of expression," "habit of preparation," "manner of delivery"; and an assessment of "the effect of the discourse on its immediate hearers" (pp. 212-213; see also Medhurst, 1993, pp. xvi-xvii). Writing more than 30 years later, Wichelns' student, Donald Bryant, remarked that Wichelns' essay "set the pattern and determined the direction of rhetorical criticism for more than a quarter of a century and has had a greater and continuous influence upon the development of the scholarship of rhetoric and public address than any other single work published in this century" (p. 5).

The neo-Aristotelian program that Wichelns helped to introduce did not produce studies that were exact replications of each other. The neo-Aristotelian method functioned less as a fixed procedure to which all critics adhered and more as a set of critical topics or issues that were mixed in different ways by different critics. The mixture of topics is visible in the essays collected in the *History and Criticism of American Public Address* volumes edited by Brigance (1943) and Hochmuth (1955). Some authors emphasize an individual's education and training in the areas of debate, literature, foreign language, or the classics and try to assess the influence of that training on the person's oratory (a process often labeled as *rhetorical biography*), whereas other scholars devote little or no attention to these issues. Some scholars devote significant attention to the manner in which an individual composed and/or developed his or her speeches (e.g., describing the drafting and revising process, charting the evolution of key passages over the course of various versions of a speech), whereas other authors (perhaps partly because of inaccessible materials) ignore this topic. Some authors structure a speaker's career into distinct periods, whereas others do not.

But some analytic topics appear with greater frequency than do others. These topics constitute the core of the neo-Aristotelian program. They include an analysis of the speaker's **modes of proof** (according to the classical division of **ethos, logos,** and **pathos**), a description of the way in which a speaker employed the five **canons of rhetoric** (**inven-**

tion, arrangement, delivery, **style,** and **memory**), an assessment of the speaker's efforts in terms of the classical **genres** of rhetoric (**deliberative, forensic,** and **epideictic**), and identification of the **effects** produced by the speaker's discourse. These topics, along with a reconstruction of the speaking *occasion,* were prominently featured in Thonssen and Baird's (1948) *Speech Criticism* and became the dominant critical *loci* in rhetorical studies. They were exemplified in, for example, Aly's (1941) study of Alexander Hamilton, Nichols's (1954) "Lincoln's First Inaugural," and countless master's theses and doctoral dissertations.

Black's (1978) *Rhetorical Criticism* generally is credited with driving a stake through the heart of the neo-Aristotelian program of rhetorical criticism.[6] Black's critique can be organized into two categories: the problems that result from the flawed assumptions of the neo-Aristotelian program and the limitations of the neo-Aristotelian program when evaluated in terms of "the generic functions of criticism" (p. 36). The first assumption that Black identified was "the comprehension of the rhetorical discourse as tactically designed to achieve certain results with a specific audience on a specific occasion" (p. 33).[7] The problem with this assumption, Black argued, is that it limits the critic to seeing "only one direction of movement" (p. 35). Consequently, "neo-Aristotelians ignore the impact of the discourse on rhetorical conventions, its capacity for disposing an audience to expect certain ways of arguing and certain kinds of justifications in later discourses that [audience members] encounter, even on different subjects" (p. 35). The second assumption in neo-Aristotelianism was "the close relationship between rhetoric and logic." The problem that Black identified with respect to this assumption was "the tendency of neo-Aristotelian critics to concentrate on discourses that approach logical demonstration and to eschew the explication of discourses that do not have a demonstrative form" (p. 34). The final assumption that Black noted was "the tendency to assume the rationality of audiences." The result is a type of critical distortion as "even 'emotional appeals,' which appears to be the rubric for persuasive discourse not susceptible to logical explanation, are often conceived of as a type of proof" (p. 34).[8]

Following the lead of aesthetician Thomas Greene, Black (1978) identified three "generic functions of criticism": historical, re-creative, and judicial (p. 36). In Black's analysis, neo-Aristotelianism came up short in each function. With respect to the historical function, he argued that neo-Aristotelianism suffers from "a restricted view of context" (p. 39) that, in turn, leads the critic to a truncated understanding of the purpose and/or intention of the advocate being studied (pp. 41-42). Black argued that, in terms of the re-creative function (where the critic directly encounters and engages the object being studied), the neo-Aristotelian critic does not really engage his or her object, the oratorical or rhetorical **text.** He maintained that the neo-Aristotelian critic is preoccupied with the attempt "to make an estimate of the historical factual effects of the discourse on its relatively immediate audience" (p. 48). The tendency of neo-Aristotelianism is to "substitute historical reconstruction for re-creative criticism" (p. 75). Finally, when it comes to the judicial function, Black uncovered two problems with the neo-Aristotelian program. First, neo-Aristotelianism "limits judicial criticism to the evaluation of immediate effects" (p. 75) and is, therefore, incapable of a nuanced appraisal of the object. The ability to render a judgment about the object is further hampered, Black argued, by the way in which the neo-Aristotelian critic defers to the rhetor whose work is being studied. He wrote that "the neo-Aristotelian critic adopts the rhetor's ends as adequate to an assessment of the discourse," but in so doing, the critic abdicates at least part of his or her judicial responsibility (p. 78).

Whereas neo-Aristotelian (Hill, 1972) and "neo-classical" (Leff & Mohrmann, 1974) criticism would appear in print after the publication of *Rhetorical Criticism,* Black's (1978) critique ushered in the end of neo-Aristotelian critical **hegemony** and the beginning of an era of critical pluralism. Or did it? In a provocative and controversial essay, Gaonkar (1993) argued that "what this pluralist critical stance actually concealed is the persistence and the recuperation of classical rhetoric" (p. 263). Despite the proliferation of new methods and an expansion in the objects of study, Gaonkar maintained that "our critical studies are sustained by the vocabulary of classical rhetoric, a vocabulary primarily fashioned for directing performance rather than facilitating understanding" (p. 263). In short, Gaonkar claimed that, despite all the renunciations, neo-Aristotelianism lives on. But Gaonkar should not be misunderstood. The Aristotelian influence that he wanted to track in the critical practices of the 1980s and 1990s is not the same as the cluster of analytic topics that emerged in the wake of Wichelns. Gaonkar was not claiming that critics have resurrected the neo-Aristotelian "cookie-cutter."[9] Instead, Gaonkar was suggesting that there are close parallels between the way in which contemporary critics are "recuperating" rhetoric[10] and the assumptions undergirding the neo-Aristotelian project beginning with Wichelns. From Wichelns to the present, Gaonkar detected a persistent "model of intentional persuasion"—an *instrumental* paradigm—that positions "the rhetor as the generating center of discourse" and attributes the design of the text to "the conscious and strategic thinking of the rhetor" (p. 275). Gaonkar argued that this model remains firmly in place despite the demise of the neo-Aristotelian program. He suggested that the future of rhetorical criticism depends on how critics negotiate between the intentional and **intertextual** models of rhetoric and rhetorical **invention.**[11]

Notes

1. The use of the term in speech communication must be distinguished from its use in literary studies to label the work of a group of scholars associated with the University of Chicago that included Richard McKeon, Elder Olson, and R. S. Crane. See, for example, Crane (1952).

2. See also Thonssen and Baird's (1948) comments about the "Aristotelian standards of criticism" embodied in this volume (p. 285).

3. For a brief account of the historical development of rhetorical criticism, see Medhurst (1993). For a less inclusive and more analytic account, see Gaonkar (1990).

4. The first two volumes were published in 1943 and edited by William Norwood Brigance. The third volume was published in 1955 and edited by Marie Hochmuth.

5. On the importance of defining the object in Wichelns, see Gaonkar (1990).

6. But as Medhurst (1993) and others have noted, evidence of dissatisfaction with neo-Aristotelianism can be found in the discipline during the 1940s and 1950s.

7. It should be noted that Black (1978) was not questioning the *instrumental* orientation emphasized by Wichelns. Black, like Wichelns, defined the object of rhetorical criticism as "discourses, spoken or written, which aim to influence men [sic]" (p. 15).

8. The movement to conceptualize emotional appeals as reasonable and argumentative is not limited to neo-Aristotelian critics. On this issue, see the entry for **pathos.**

9. "Cookie-cutter" is a common pejorative expression that refers to the way in which critics unimaginatively applied neo-Aristotelian analytic topics to different discursive objects.

10. See the discussion of *recuperation* in the entry for **criticism.**

11. On intentionality and human agency as issues in contemporary rhetorical studies, see also the entry for **subject.**

References and Additional Reading

Aly, B. (1941). *The rhetoric of Alexander Hamilton.* New York: Columbia University Press.

Black, E. (1978). *Rhetorical criticism: A study in method.* Madison: University of Wisconsin Press.

Brigance, W. N. (Ed.). (1943). *A history and criticism of American public address* (2 vols.). New York: McGraw-Hill.

Brock, B. L., Scott, R. L., & Chesebro, J. W. (1989). *Methods of rhetorical criticism: A twentieth-century perspective* (3rd ed.). Detroit, MI: Wayne State University Press.

Bryant, D. C. (1958). Introduction. In D. C. Bryant (Ed.), *The rhetorical idiom: Essays in rhetoric, oratory, language, and drama.* Ithaca, NY: Cornell University Press.

Crane, R. S. (Ed.). (1952). *Critics and criticism: Ancient and modern.* Chicago: University of Chicago Press.

Foss, S. K. (1996). *Rhetorical criticism: Exploration and practice* (2nd ed.). Prospect Heights, IL: Waveland.
Gaonkar, D. P. (1990). Object and method in rhetorical criticism: From Wichelns to Leff and McGee. *Western Journal of Speech Communication, 54,* 290-316.
Gaonkar, D. P. (1993). The idea of rhetoric in the rhetoric of science. *Southern Communication Journal, 58,* 258-295.
Hill, F. (1972). Conventional wisdom—traditional form: The president's message of November 3, 1969. *Quarterly Journal of Speech, 58,* 373-386.
Hochmuth, M. K. (1955). *A history and criticism of American public address* (Vol. 3). New York: Longmans, Green.
Leff, M. C., & Mohrmann, G. P. (1974). Lincoln at Cooper Union: A rhetorical analysis of the text. *Quarterly Journal of Speech, 60,* 346-358.
Medhurst, M. J. (1993). The academic study of public address: A tradition in transition. In M. J. Medhurst (Ed.), *Landmark essays on American public address.* Davis, CA: Hermagoras Press.
Nichols, M. H. (1954). Lincoln's first inaugural. In W. M. Parrish & M. H. Nichols (Eds.), *American speeches.* New York: Longmans, Green.
Thonssen, L., & Baird, A. C. (1948). *Speech criticism: The development of standards for rhetorical appraisal.* New York: Ronald Press.
Wichelns, H. A. (1962). The literary criticism of oratory. In A. M. Drummond (Ed.), *Studies in rhetoric and public speaking in honor of James Albert Winans.* New York: Russell and Russell. (Original work published 1925)

NEW CRITICISM

The term **new criticism** stems from a book by the literary critic John Crowe Ransom published in 1941 with this title. Although Ransom's (1941) book might have introduced the label that would be used to characterize the dominant tendency in literary criticism during the middle of the 20th century, the seeds of this practice had been planted a few decades earlier. During the first few decades of the century, critics such as T. S. Eliot and I. A. Richards complained that literary study focused too much on inessential matters such as biographical details about an author and the historical context in which a work was produced. Both Eliot (1932) and Richards (1925, 1929) urged critics to pay more attention to the literary work—especially the poem—as a product of literary art. The thinking of Eliot and Richards would be highly influential on successive generations of American literary critics[1] and, more indirectly, on contemporary rhetorical studies.

Commentators (Abrams, 1993; Childs, 1993; see also Elton, 1951) have identified a number of basic elements in the practice of new criticism. Perhaps first and foremost, the new criticism movement held the literary work to be self-sufficient, autonomous, and *autotelic* (from the Greek *auto* and *telos,* meaning self-directed or self-governed). As such, intrinsic methods of analysis and evaluation, methods that respected the autonomy and self-sufficiency of literature, needed to be developed. The principal method of analysis employed by new critics was **close reading;** as Richards (1929) remarked, "All respectable poetry invites close reading" (p. 203). Abrams (1993) described close reading as "the detailed and subtle analysis of the complex interrelations and ambiguities . . . of the components within a work" (p. 247). The exploration of paradox (Brooks, 1947) and **ambiguity** (Empson, 1930) emerged as principal concerns of new critical analysis. Close reading also sought to disclose the action within the literary text, in particular what Childs (1993) described as the "ironic competition of meanings" (p. 121) within the work (e.g., the conflict between various images and/or themes within a poem). Although new criticism understood the literary text as a structure of internal tensions, most new critics nevertheless maintained that specific works achieved a form of unity—a balancing or reconciliation of tensions—that needed to be described and analyzed.

Opposition to new criticism could be found throughout the 1940s and 1950s (e.g., Kenneth Burke's works reflected both his opposition to and his agreement with key elements of the new criticism program) but flourished beginning during the late 1950s (Lentricchia, 1980). Although new criticism has been displaced in literary studies, some of its principal concerns have been incorporated into other modes of literary study through various transmutations (Childs, 1993). One area where a transmuted new criticism resurfaced is the close reading movement in contemporary rhetorical studies. Mohrmann's (1980) lament that rhetorical critics too often circled their object instead of delving into it echoed the complaints of literary critics during the early part of the century. Leff's (1986) conceptualization of the text as a "field of action" seemed to be part of the intellectual trajectory of new criticism (with a strong dose of Burke), as did his focus on the "integrity" of the rhetorical text. But it probably would be a mistake to reduce the close reading movement in rhetorical studies during the 1980s and 1990s to an imitation of literary new criticism. Although there are some significant points of convergence between these modes of close reading, there are equally important points of divergence that need to be recognized.

Note

1. See, for example, Brooks (1947) and Wimsatt (1954). On the continuing influence of new criticism in literary studies, see also Brooks and Warren (1938, 1959) and Wellek and Warren (1984).

References and Additional Reading

Abrams, M. H. (1993). *A glossary of literary terms* (6th ed.). Fort Worth, TX: Harcourt Brace.

Brooks, C. (1947). *The well wrought urn: Studies in the structure of poetry.* New York: Harcourt Brace.

Brooks, C., & Warren, R. P. (1938). *Understanding poetry.* New York: Henry Holt.

Brooks, C., & Warren, R. P. (1959). *Understanding fiction* (2nd ed.). New York: Appleton-Crofts.

Childs, D. J. (1993). New criticism. In I. R. Makaryk (Ed.), *Encyclopedia of contemporary literary theory: Approaches, scholars, terms.* Toronto: University of Toronto Press.

Eliot, T. S. (1932). The function of criticism. In T. S. Eliot, *Selected essays.* London: Faber.

Elton, W. (1951). *A guide to the new criticism* (rev. ed.). Chicago: Modern Poetry Association.

Empson, W. (1930). *Seven types of ambiguity.* London: Chatto and Windus.

Leff, M. (1986). Textual criticism: The legacy of G. P. Mohrmann. *Quarterly Journal of Speech, 72,* 377-389.

Lentricchia, F. (1980). *After the new criticism.* Chicago: University of Chicago Press.

Mohrmann, G. P. (1980). Elegy in a critical graveyard. *Western Journal of Speech Communication, 44,* 265-274.

Ransom, J. C. (1941). *The new criticism.* Norfolk, VA: New Directions.

Richards, I. A. (1925). *The principles of literary criticism.* New York: Harcourt Brace.

Richards, I. A. (1929). *Practical criticism: A study of literary judgment.* New York: Harcourt Brace.

Wellek, R., & Warren, A. (1984). *Theory of literature* (3rd ed.). Orlando, FL: Harcourt Brace Jovanovich.

Wimsatt, W. K. (1954). *The verbal icon: Studies in the meaning of poetry.* Lexington: University of Kentucky Press.

OTHER, RHETORICAL CONSTRUCTION OF

Critical discourse analyst Stephen Riggins observed, "The word *other* is an elliptic pronoun or a deictic category that can refer to practically anything, depending on the context or situation" (Riggins, 1997, p. 4). Although the term **other** (and closely related concepts such as *alterity* and *difference*) has multiple meanings, it has developed a relatively stable meaning and achieved a position of some importance in critically oriented scholarship over the past few decades. Attesting to its importance, Hall (1997) remarked, "From many different directions, and within many different disciplines, this question of 'difference' and 'otherness' has come to play an increasingly significant role" (p. 238).

But what stable sense of the other has emerged in contemporary critical scholarship, and what is meant by the **rhetorical construction of the other**? Hall (1997) identified four "different levels of analysis" in current work: linguistic, social, cultural, and psychic (p. 238). But he pointed out that these levels are not mutually exclusive; they overlap and intersect in different ways. The level that Hall labeled the psychic one has attracted a considerable amount of attention and is of particular interest to rhetorical scholars. A psychic understanding of the other begins with a central premise of *postmodern* thinking about the human **subject**—the lack of a central or essential core "self" or identity. Humans gain their individual identities or sense of self through social interaction. But it seems that a very specific type of human interaction is crucial in the formation of identity—interaction with people who are different. Blumenberg (1987), for example, noted that "man [sic] comprehends himself only by way of what he is not" (p. 456; see also Greenblatt, 1980). Blumenberg suggested that individuals create and/or discover their identities through their interactions with "what they are not" or people who are different—people who are "other." This insight into the development of personal identity often is transposed into the broader realm of cultural identity. Said (1994) illustrated this tendency when he wrote,

> We are dealing with the formation of cultural identities understood not as essentializations . . . but as contrapuntal ensembles, for it is the case that no identity can ever exist by itself and without an array of opposites, negatives, oppositions: Greeks always require barbarians, and Europeans Africans, Orientals, etc. (p. 52)

Like its closely related strategic "cousins," the **enemy** and the **scapegoat**, the other is increasingly recognized by critical scholars as a central vehicle in forms of **constitutive rhetoric** or those discourses that create individual and group identity (JanMohamed, 1985; Kornfeld, 1995; Mills, 1997; Riggins, 1997; Smith-Rosenberg, 1992). As Smith-Rosenberg (1992) explained, "Internally fragmented subjectivities assume a coherence . . . by being juxtaposed to multiple others—especially negative (feared or hated) others" (p. 846). In short, "we" gain our sense of self through opposition; we "know" who we are because "we're not like them." And we justify our **power** over others through the process of othering. As Armstrong and Tennenhouse (1989) suggested, "[A] class of people cannot produce themselves as a ruling class without setting themselves off against certain others" (p. 24).

Riggins (1997) described the discourse used by dominant groups to describe, or generally talk about, those who are different as the "rhetoric of *othering*." The idea of a rhetoric of othering, or what Hall (1997) referred to as "repertoires of representation" (p. 225), called attention to the fact that the others who help to constitute the identities of members of a dominant culture are themselves discursively constituted and/or *socially constructed*. The discourse of a dominant group fashions the other, endows them with certain characteristics and habits, and thereby allows them to function as a contrast to the dominant group. For example, "we" know that we are hard-working because (a) "those people" (the other) are lazy (the discourse of our group says that this is true) and (b) we know that we are not like "them."

Others are, then, at least partially constituted through the discourse of dominant groups. What are some of the specific characteristics of this rhetoric of othering? At least four can be identified in the extant literature. First, the discourse of dominant groups tends to erase any internal differences within the group selected to serve as other. Describing the discursive practices of European colonialism (often viewed as a paradigmatic example of the rhetoric of othering), JanMohamed (1985) noted how the colonial subject—the other—is "perceived as a generic being that can be exchanged for any other native (they all look alike, act alike, and so on)" (p. 83). JanMohamed added that the colonial native "is considered too degraded and inhuman to be credited with any specific subjectivity" (p. 85). In her account of travel literature (another prime example of the rhetoric of othering), Pratt (1985) noted how "the people to be othered are homogenized into a collective 'they' " (p. 139); collective attributes are all that matter, not individual ones. When popularized and disseminated among the dominant group(s), these attributes of the other are commonly referred to as *stereotypes.*[1] Once constructed, stereotypes of the other remain a cultural force for a long period of time, as Bogle (1973) illustrated in his study of African American images in motion pictures.

A second characteristic extends out of the first. The homogenized attributes of the other often are *essentialized*. JanMohamed (1985) argued that the colonial writer "transform[s] social and historical dissimilarities into universal, metaphysical differences" (p. 87). Pratt (1985) made a similar observation when she noted how the actions of the other are characterized "not as a particular historical event but as an instance of a pre-given custom or trait" (p. 139). Kornfeld (1995) noted the way in which the rhetoric of othering constructs "categories of identity . . . [that] are taken to be divinely ordained, immutable, or natural, determined by biological or psychological heredity" (p. 288). Therefore, the behavior and attributes of the other, as depicted in the discourse of the dominant group, are not contingent on or in need of historical or situational analysis. Rather, the rhetoric of othering presents the actions and attributes of the other as something "natural" or as part of the other's essential nature (see also Shome, 1996a).

The rhetoric of othering frequently is marked by a profound *ambivalence*, and this is its third characteristic. Riggins (1997) noted the ubiquitous blend of "derision and desire" (p. 9) found in the rhetoric of othering; others are both valued (most often for their "exotic" qualities) and *de*valued (p. 5). In the paradigmatic case of European colonization, the discourse of the dominant Europeans reveals a simultaneous attraction to and revulsion toward colonial natives. Kornfeld (1985) observed a similar tension in her analysis of white discourse about Indians in late 18th-century America. She wrote, "The other must seem not only terrible or inferior but also alluring. The other attracts as well as repels" (p. 289; see also Bhabha, 1986; Smith-Rosenberg, 1992). The rhetoric of othering is, then, internally inconsistent and unstable.

A final characteristic of the rhetoric of othering concerns the **persona** of the author. Pratt (1985) observed how "a great deal of travel writing in the last century, especially the literature of exploration . . ., effaces the speaking self" (p. 143). The narrator in this discourse maintains a "distanced and self-effaced stance" (p. 143). European authors enacted such a stance through a common syntactic device—agent or subject deletion through passive sentence structures (Morenberg, 1997). According to Pratt (1985), Europeans are only indirectly present in the travel and exploration discourse; they exist in the text as "deleted subjects of passive verbs" (p. 143). By removing or distancing themselves from the action in the text, European narrators help to fashion the native other as both an object of knowledge and a subject in need of supervision and administration (see also Mills, 1991; Spurr, 1993).

The discussion so far has focused on some basic characteristics of the rhetoric of othering. What are some of its common generic forms and its typical social functions? Some of the most common generic forms have already been noted; travel literature (see also Pratt, 1992), reports of exploration, the literature of the colonial imperialism, initial encounters between different cultures, and the literature of emerging nationalisms are some of the common forms examined by scholars. But the rhetoric of othering is not limited to these forms. Other discursive forms receiving increased attention include advertising (Hoechsmann, 1997; O'Barr, 1994), historiography (Hartog, 1988, pp. 212-259), contemporary political discourse (Folena, 1989; Van Dijk, 1997), and mass media discourse (Hall, 1997; Riggins, 1997; Said, 1981). The function of othering discussed with great frequency is the constitution of identity for *both* the dominant and subordinate groups. But identity construction and **power** maintenance often go hand in hand. As Armstrong and Tennenhouse, JanMohamed, and other critics have emphasized, the creation of others often is the first step toward their subordination. The rhetoric of othering reveals the imbrication of collective identity and political power.

Let us consider a final example in a bit more detail to reveal another function of othering. In September 1957, Dwight Eisenhower addressed the American people in an effort to justify his decision to use federal troops to help quell disturbances in Little Rock, Arkansas, that arose out of efforts to desegregate one of its high schools. In that address, Eisenhower attributed the problems in Little Rock to the presence of "outsiders" determined to thwart the orders of the federal court. Eisenhower implied that the people of Little Rock, the South, and the entire nation were basically good; our problem consisted entirely of these outsiders who threatened to unleash anarchy on America. The outsider is a rather common image of the other in American history (it can be traced back to the revolutionary period), and it would become a staple of political discourse during the 1960s (embodied in the recurrent expression "outside agitator"). We can consider the outsider or outside agitator as a type of *domestic* othering. How did the outsider as other appear in Eisenhower's address, and perhaps more important, how did it function? Eisenhower's address did not exhibit many of the general characteristics of the rhetoric of othering discussed earlier (it did not erase the internal differences among the individuals gathered in the category). But what it did do was help the nation to constitute its identity, especially with respect to the increasingly difficult issue of race. The key question with which many Americans struggled was whether or not "we" (the majority of Americans) were racists (as Soviet "propaganda" at the time suggested). Eisenhower's rhetoric of othering worked to absolve the general public ("us" as opposed to those outsiders) of any responsibility for America's race problem. Eisenhower's othering strategy basically told the nation not to worry and that the vast majority of Americans were good people who had not done anything wrong and who did not need to do anything special or different except to follow the law; all of our nation's problems with race were due to the work of those outsiders. In effect, Eisenhower's address reconstituted the ideal of American innocence and, with it, the belief that average Americans were innocent when it came to matters of race relations. Consequently, there was no need for Americans to reflect on or discuss the race question; denial and evasion of racial issues would remain as the nation's order of the day.

Attention to the phenomenon of othering already has begun in rhetorical scholarship. This attention is visible, for example, in Wander's (1984) discussion of the "third persona." The third persona refers to individuals who are "negated" in discourse, groups that are made "alien" or "equated with disease," or people who are objectified and deprived of fully human status (pp. 209-210). Wander explained, "The potentiality of language to commend being [or selfhood] carries with it the potential to spell out being unacceptable, undesirable, [and] insignificant" (p. 209). Writing around the same time that scholars in other disciplines began to examine the idea of the other, Wander appeared to anticipate this emerging line of thought as he urges rhetorical scholars to examine the way in which discourse is used to negate humans or to transform "some group, or class, or sex, or race into an 'it' " or into an other (p. 216). Rhetoric and communication scholars are beginning to examine the issues raised by Wander and other scholars. Shome (1996b), for example, extended the analysis of othering from colonial literature to contemporary Hollywood cinema in her analysis of the film *City of Joy*. What she found was the common pattern that associates "whiteness with progress and civilization, and natives with primitivity and chaos" (p. 507). Crenshaw (1997) identified another part of the dynamic of race discourse in her study of the Jesse Helms-Carol Mosley Braun debate over the symbolic value of the Confederate flag. Crenshaw argued that Helms illustrated a form of othering in which "people of color" are depicted "as having the characteristic of race while simultaneously assuming that white people are somehow not 'raced' " (p. 264). White America continues to define itself—without seemingly recognizing the process—against a racial other (see also Nakayama & Krizek, 1995). Influenced by **ideology** critique and **critical rhetoric,** more and more rhetorical scholars are examining the rhetoric of othering.

Women, native Africans, African slaves and their descendants, Jews, Irish immigrants, Polish immigrants, Italian immigrants, Asian immigrants, Mexican immigrants, native American Indians, hippies and "freaks," Hispanics, illegal aliens, the poor, the disabled, gays and lesbians, outsiders—these are just some of the others who have occupied, at one time or another, a prominent place in American public discourse (this list expands considerably when America is connected to a larger pattern of neocolonial othering). Given Burke's (1957) observations about the human tendency to create unity and identity through opposition, it is highly unlikely that the process of othering will disappear anytime soon. As Shome (1996a) noted, "When the rhetoric of cultural 'othering' is manifest in almost every aspect of public discourse, it is unfortunate that rhetorical scholars have not done much to expose and decry the neocolonial strategies through which such discourse operates" (p. 51).

Note

1. See, for example, Bhabha (1986), Gilman (1985), Hall (1997), and Wodak (1997).

References and Additional Reading

Armstrong, N., & Tennenhouse, L. (1989). Introduction: Representing violence, or "how the West was won." In N. Armstrong & L. Tennenhouse (Eds.), *The violence of representation: Literature and the history of violence.* London: Routledge.

Bhabha, H. K. (1986). The other question: Difference, discrimination, and the discourse of colonialism. In F. Barker, P. Hulme, M. Iversen, & D. Loxley (Eds.), *Literature, politics, and theory: Papers from the Essex Conference, 1976-84.* London: Methuen.

Blumenberg, H. (1987). An anthropological approach to the contemporary significance of rhetoric (R. M. Wallace, Trans.). In K. Baynes, J. Bohman, & T. McCarthy (Eds.), *After philosophy: End or transformation.* Cambridge, MA: MIT Press.

Bogle, D. (1973). *Toms, coons, mulattoes, mammies, and bucks: An interpretive history of blacks in American films.* New York: Viking.

Burke, K. (1957). The rhetoric of Hitler's "Battle." In K. Burke, *The philosophy of literary form* (rev. ed.). New York: Vintage.

Crenshaw, C. (1997). Resisting whiteness' rhetorical silence. *Western Journal of Communication, 61,* 253-278.

Folena, L. (1989). Figures of violence: Philologists, witches, and Stalinistas. In N. Armstrong & L. Tennenhouse (Eds.), *The violence of representation: Literature and the history of violence.* London: Routledge.

Gilman, S. L. (1985). Black bodies, white bodies: Toward an iconography of female sexuality in late nineteenth-century art, medicine, and literature. In H. L. Gates, Jr. (Ed.), *"Race," writing, and difference.* Chicago: University of Chicago Press.

Greenblatt, S. (1980). *Renaissance self-fashioning.* Chicago: University of Chicago Press.

Hall, S. (1997). The spectacle of the "other." In S. Hall (Ed.), *Representations: Cultural representations and signifying practices.* London: Sage.

Hartog, F. (1988). *The mirror of Herodotus: The representation of the other in the writing of history* (J. Lloyd, Trans.). Berkeley: University of California Press.

Hoechsmann, M. (1997). Beneton culture: Marketing difference to the new global consumer. In S. H. Riggins (Ed.), *The language and politics of exclusion: Others in discourse.* Thousand Oaks, CA: Sage.

JanMohamed, A. R. (1985). The economy of Manichean allegory: The function of racial difference in colonialist literature. In H. L. Gates, Jr. (Ed.), *"Race," writing, and difference.* Chicago: University of Chicago Press.

Kornfeld, E. (1995). Encountering "the other": American intellectuals and Indians in the 1790s. *William and Mary Quarterly, 52,* 287-314. (3rd series)

Mills, S. (1991). *Discourses of difference: An analysis of women's travel writing and colonialism.* London: Routledge.

Mills, S. (1997). *Discourse.* London: Routledge.

Morenberg, M. (1997). *Doing grammar* (2nd ed.). New York: Oxford University Press.

Nakayama, T. K., & Krizek, R. L. (1995). Whiteness: A strategic rhetoric. *Quarterly Journal of Speech, 81,* 291-308.

O'Barr, W. (1994). *Culture and the ad: Exploring otherness in the world of advertising.* Boulder, CO: Westview.

Pratt, M. L. (1985). Scratches on the face of the country: Or, what Mr. Barrow saw in the land of the bushmen. In H. L. Gates, Jr. (Ed.), *"Race," writing, and difference.* Chicago: University of Chicago Press.

Pratt, M. L. (1992). *Imperial eyes: Travel writing and transculturalism.* London: Routledge.

Riggins, S. H. (1997). The rhetoric of othering. In S. H. Riggins (Ed.), *The language and politics of exclusion: Others in discourse.* Thousand Oaks, CA: Sage.

Said, E. W. (1981). *Covering Islam: How the media and the experts determine how we see the rest of the world.* New York: Pantheon.

Said, E. W. (1994). *Culture and imperialism.* New York: Vintage.

Shome, R. (1996a). Postcolonial interventions in the rhetoric canon: An "other" view. *Communication Theory, 6,* 40-59.

Shome, R. (1996b). Race and popular cinema: The rhetorical strategies of whiteness in *City of Joy. Communication Quarterly, 44,* 502-518.

Smith-Rosenberg, C. (1992). Dis-covering the subject of the "great constitutional discussion," 1786-1789. *Journal of American History, 79,* 841-873.

Spurr, D. (1993). *The rhetoric of empire: Colonial discourse in journalism, travel writing, and imperial administration.* Durham, NC: Duke University Press.

Todorov, T. (1984). *The conquest of America: The question of the other* (R. Howard, Trans.). New York: Harper & Row.

Van Dijk, T. A. (1997). Political discourse and racism: Describing others in Western parliaments. In S. H. Riggins (Ed.), *The language and politics of exclusion: Others in discourse.* Thousand Oaks, CA: Sage.

Wander, P. (1984). The third persona: An ideological turn in rhetorical theory. *Central States Speech Journal, 35,* 197-216.

Wodak, R. (1997). *Das Ausland* and anti-Semitic discourse: The discursive construction of the other. In S. H. Riggins (Ed.), *The language and politics of exclusion: Others in discourse.* Thousand Oaks, CA: Sage.

OVERDETERMINED, DISCOURSE AS

In *The German Ideology,* Marx and Engels (1947) wrote,

> Conceiving, thinking, [and] the mental intercourse of men [sic], appear at this stage as the direct efflux of their material behavior. The same applies to mental production as expressed in the language of politics, laws, morality, religion, metaphysics, etc., of a people. . . . We set out from real, active men, and on the basis of their real life-process we demonstrate the development of ideological reflexes and echoes of this life-process. . . . Life is not *determined* by consciousness, but consciousness by life. (pp. 14-15, emphasis added)

A central element in the Marxist tradition of *materialism* is the concept of *determination.* As the preceding passage from *The German Ideology* indicates, all "mental production"—including the various forms of discursive practice that might fall within the realm of rhetoric—is determined by a culture's "material behavior." As the British literary theorist and critic Raymond Williams observed, "A Marxism without some concept of determination is in effect worthless" (Williams, 1977, p. 83). But note Williams's subtle qualification—"*some* concept of determination." For Williams and many other thinkers influenced by Marx and the Marxist tradition of social theory, revising what appeared to be a rather mechanistic and reductive sense of determination (reflected in the "economic base determines ideological superstructure" model) was a key theoretical challenge. One of the revisions proposed is the concept of *overdetermination* and, more specifically, the way in which discursive practice is **overdetermined.**

The roots of the concept of overdetermination can be found in the psychological theories of Sigmund Freud. Zetzel and Messner (1973) wrote, "Freud himself introduced the notion of overdetermination, meaning that a particular psychic event or set of psychic events could be explained in terms of more than one set of determining factors" (p. 59). For example, Freud argued that a specific dream was not caused or determined by a *single* factor (a specific anxiety or phobia); rather, it was overdetermined or was the result of a number of factors that collectively determined the substance of the dream. The concept of overdetermination was incorporated into the works of social and critical theory largely through the efforts of the French philosopher Louis Althusser. Rejecting the rigid base/superstructure model, Althusser (1969) argued *analogically* that historical events or episodes are similar to dreams. Just as dreams have multiple determining factors, the same can be said for the elements of history. Any particular event or episode (e.g., the 1963 March on Washington, the civil rights movement) is the site of numerous (and at times conflicting) economic, ideological, social, cultural, and individual (e.g., personality) forces. Althusser's reconstruction of the concept of determination (with the assistance of Freud) emphasized, first, the need to eschew monocausal explanations of historical occurrences and, second, the necessity of focusing on the multiple forces that determine historical events and episodes.

The concept of overdetermination, and its particular relevance to the study of public discourse, has begun to have an impact on contemporary rhetorical studies (e.g., McGee, 1990). Among other things, the idea of overdetermination problematizes dominant disciplinary assumptions such as the **rhetorical situation.** Whereas Bitzer (1968) argued that discourse is determined by its situation (in particular, *exigence* and *constraints*) much like an answer is determined by the question posed, contemporary social theory inspired by Althusser maintains that it is impossible to locate *the* situation or *the* exigence to which discourse is a response. Contemporary social theorists argue that there simply are too many forces at work in the world—forces that shape the discourse we produce—to make a monocausal account of discursive practice workable. At a minimum, the concept of overdetermination requires the reformulation of situational theory in such a way as to make multiple exigences the norm. In addition, the concept of overdetermination contributes to the process of conceptualizing the discipline's dominant object of study—the **text.** The text, like any historical event, is a site where multiple forces intersect, collide, combine, and so on. At a minimum, the concept of overdetermination requires a way of conceptualizing the text that acknowledges its nature as a site of historical forces (see the discussion on the prominence of the **metaphor** of the *field* as a way of describing the text) and encourages modes of analysis that pay special attention to the way in which advocates and rhetors negotiate multiple forces in their discursive practice.

References and Additional Reading

Althusser, L. (1969). Contradiction and overdetermination. In L. Althusser, *For Marx* (B. Brewster, Trans.). New York: Pantheon.

Bitzer, L. (1968). The rhetorical situation. *Philosophy and Rhetoric, 1,* 1-14.

Freud, S. (1965). *The interpretation of dreams* (J. Strachey, Ed. and Trans.). New York: Avon Books.

Marx, K., & Engels, F. (1947). *The German ideology* (R. Pascal, Ed.). New York: International Publishers.

McGee, M. C. (1990). Text, context, and the fragmentation of contemporary culture. *Western Journal of Speech Communication, 54,* 274-289.

Williams, R. (1977). *Marxism and literature.* Oxford, UK: Oxford University Press.

Zetzel, E., & Messner, W. W. (1973). *Basic concepts of psychoanalytic psychiatry.* New York: Basic Books.

PASTORAL

Two senses of the term **pastoral** have relevance in rhetorical studies. Both are derived from the Latin root *pastoralis,* which means shepherd or pertaining to the life of a shepherd (Alpers, 1996). The first, and narrowest, sense of pastoral refers to a **public letter** written by a bishop, often characterized metaphorically as the shepherd for a flock, to be read to his (and, in some faiths, her) congregation. Cheney (1991) described the pastoral letter as "a traditional form of communication between bishops and the faithful; it is designed as moral guidance or teaching, but not as binding rule or law" (p. 125). Rhetorical critics have focused attention on significant instances of this discursive form. One example that has generated some critical debate is the American National Conference of Catholic Bishops' pastoral letter on war and peace published in 1983 during the height of antinuclear advocacy in the United States and Western Europe (see also Goldzwig and Cheney, 1984; Hogan, 1989).

The second sense of pastoral refers to a poetic **genre** and/or certain literary conventions initially associated with the genre. Abrams (1993) described the earliest forms of pastoral poetry (also referred to as *idyllic*) as "a deliberately conventional poem expressing an urban poet's nostalgic image of the peace and simplicity of the life of shepherds and other rural folk in an idealized natural setting" (p. 141). The range of poetic practices falling within the domain of the pastoral grew over time as specific conventions and themes were employed by poets in various ways. Cuddon (1991) remarked,

> Fundamentally, this is what pastoral is about: It displays a nostalgia for the past, for some hypothetical state of love and peace which has somehow been lost. The dominating idea and theme of most pastoral is the search for the simple life away from the court and town, away from corruption, war, strife, the love of gain, away from "getting and spending." In a way, it reveals a yearning for a lost innocence, for a pre-fall paradis[ic]al life in which man [sic] existed in harmony with nature. . . . [It is] a potent longing for things past. (p. 689)

Discursive practices—poetic and prosaic—that embody these various themes exhibit signs of the pastoral.

Rhetorical scholars have sought to understand the role and function of pastoral themes or appeals in public discourse. One of the first scholars to pursue this issue was Kenneth Burke. In *A Rhetoric of Motives,* Burke (1950) discussed the work of English literary critic William Empson on the pastoral (Empson, 1935). Burke (1950), extending but also subverting some of Empson's ideas, argued that pastoral appeals are "profoundly concerned with the rhetoric of courtship between contrasted social classes" (p. 123). Pastoral themes and appeals, in Burke's view, function as part of the symbolic process of **mystification** that reinforces social hierarchy (pp. 124-127). For example, Ronald Reagan's reelection campaign in 1984 featured numerous pastoral appeals to simplicity, lost innocence, and a longing for things past. These appeals were exemplified in the television commercials that linked Reagan to the idea of "morning in America." From Burke's perspective, the pastoralism of the Reagan campaign could be analyzed to uncover in more detail the way in which pastoral themes and appeals mystify class relationships and economic inequity, thereby protecting the social hierarchy.[1]

More recently, Browne (1990) used the pastoral as a way of probing a key text of the American pre-revolutionary period, John Dickinson's *Letters From a Farmer in Pennsylvania* (Dickinson, 1768). Browne argued that Dickinson exploited key pastoral themes (e.g., removal from urban life, simplicity of manners, nostalgia for the past) to construct an **ethos** that grounds the letters' call to action. Focusing on the first letter in the series, Browne maintained that Dickinson's conservative "pastoral *ethos*" qualified his potentially radical argument questioning the authority of Parliament over the colonies. The first letter worked to create a space for political deliberation and action in between public "quiescence" and a passionate expression of public outrage at the recent British actions (pp. 51-52). Browne argued that this balancing of conservative and radical discursive forces reveals the standard of **judgment** that was enacted within the text. That standard depended on the interaction of value-laden pastoral themes such as "distance, reflection, and disinterest" (p. 54) with ideas of civic responsibility and political experience, generating a "tension" that was the essence of Dickinson's "persuasive appeal" (p. 54).

What other critical projects might rhetorical scholars pursue that could draw on the concept of the pastoral? Buell (1989, 1995) suggested one possibility when he noted the connection between literary pastoralism and *environmental advocacy.*[2] Pastoralism has remained an important ideological and aesthetic—in other words, rhetorical—resource for combating the excesses of industrialization and urbanization. Buell (1995) concluded that "pastoralism is sure to remain a luminous ideal and to retain the capacity to assume oppositional forms for some time to come" (p. 51).[3]

Notes

1. Conrad's (1983) analysis of moral majority "romantic rhetoric [that] describes an idyllic world" (p. 162) provides another example of this process.

2. The connection between pastoralism and environmental discourse is an important theme in the growing *ecocriticism* movement. See Love (1992). Scholars in rhetoric and allied fields have begun to engage discourses focusing on the environment. For examples and reviews of this trend, see Cantrill and Oravec (1996), Depoe (1998), and Killingsworth and Palmer (1992).

3. See also Lindsay (1996) and Marx (1986).

References and Additional Reading

Abrams, M. H. (1993). *A glossary of literary terms* (6th ed.). Fort Worth, TX: Harcourt Brace.

Alpers, P. (1996). *What is pastoral?* Chicago: University of Chicago Press.

Browne, S. H. (1990). The pastoral voice in John Dickinson's first *Letter From a Farmer in Pennsylvania. Quarterly Journal of Speech, 76,* 46-57.

Buell, L. (1989). American pastoral ideology reappraised. *American Literary History, 1,* 1-29.

Buell, L. (1995). *The environmental imagination: Thoreau, nature writing, and the formation of American culture.* Cambridge, MA: Harvard University Press.

Burke, K. (1950). *A rhetoric of motives.* New York: Prentice Hall.

Cantrill, J. G., & Oravec, C. L. (Eds.). (1996). *The symbolic earth: Discourse and our creation of the environment.* Lexington: University of Kentucky Press.

Cheney, G. (1991). *Rhetoric in an organizational society: Managing multiple identities.* Columbia: University of South Carolina Press.

Conrad, C. (1983). The rhetoric of the moral majority: An analysis of romantic form. *Quarterly Journal of Speech, 69,* 159-170.
Cuddon, J. A. (1991). *The Penguin dictionary of literary terms and literary theory* (3rd ed.). London: Penguin.
Depoe, S. P. (1998). Talking about the earth: On the growing significance of environmental communication studies. *Rhetoric and Public Affairs, 1,* 435-448.
Dickinson, J. (1768). *Letters from a farmer in Pennsylvania.* Boston: Mein and Fleeming.
Empson, W. (1935). *Some versions of pastoral.* London: Chatto and Windus.
Ettin, A. V. (1984). *Literature and the pastoral.* New Haven, CT: Yale University Press.
Goldzwig, S., & Cheney, G. (1984). The U.S. Catholic bishops on nuclear arms: Corporate advocacy, role definition, and rhetorical adaptation. *Central States Speech Journal, 35,* 8-23.
Hogan, J. M. (1989). Managing dissent in the Catholic church: A reinterpretation of the pastoral letter on war and peace. *Quarterly Journal of Speech, 75,* 400-415.
Killingsworth, M. J., & Palmer, J. S. (1992). *Ecospeak: Rhetoric and environmental politics.* Carbondale: Southern Illinois University Press.
Lindsay, C. (1996). *The rhetoric of modern American pastoral.* Unpublished Ph.D. dissertation, University of Oregon.
Love, G. A. (1992). *Et in arcadia ego:* Pastoral theory meets ecocriticism. *Western American Literature, 27,* 195-207.
Marx, L. (1964). *The machine in the garden: Technology and the pastoral ideal in America.* New York: Oxford University Press.
Marx, L. (1986). Pastoralism in America. In S. Bercovitch & M. Jehlen (Eds.), *Ideology and classic American literature.* Cambridge, UK: Cambridge University Press.
Patterson, A. (1987). *Pastoral and ideology: Virgil to Valery.* Berkeley: University of California Press.
Toliver, H. E. (1971). *Pastoral forms and attitudes.* Berkeley: University of California Press.

PATHOS

Scholars have long puzzled over Aristotle's discussion of this **mode of proof.** There is widespread agreement on the meaning of this term; **pathos** is defined as an appeal to the *emotions* or *passions* of an audience. But Aristotle's discussion of this mode of proof was rather inconsistent. In the first chapter of the *Rhetoric,* Aristotle (1954) criticized previous thinkers who "deal mainly with nonessentials." The first example of an inessential issue that Aristotle provided was emotion. He wrote, "The arousing of prejudice, pity, anger, and similar emotions has nothing to do with the essential facts, but is merely a personal appeal to the man [sic] who is judging the case" (1354a15-1354a19). Aristotle concluded this opening condemnation of emotional persuasion with a famous *metaphor:* "It is not right to pervert the judge by moving him [sic] to anger or envy or pity—one might as well warp a carpenter's rule before using it" (1354a24-1354a26). The metaphor implied that emotional appeals are as valid and reliable as a bent ruler; just as one would not want his or her house built by someone using a defective measuring instrument, one would not want someone to judge a case using a defective mode of proof.

But in the second chapter, Aristotle's (1954) attitude toward emotional appeals shifted. Here, he identified pathos as one of the three essential modes of proof and told readers that it is necessary "to understand the emotions—that is, to name them and describe them, to know their causes and the way in which they are excited" (1356a24-1356a25). Aristotle's seeming inconsistency is a puzzle. Perhaps his opening indictment of emotional appeals was directed at their use in the **genre** of forensic or legal oratory. More likely, Aristotle's indictment was directed at a particular understanding of emotional appeals, one that took them to be a form of "enchantment" that allowed advocates to "overcome" their audience. Fortenbaugh (1974), for example, pointed out that for the Sophist Gorgias, "being overcome by emotion is analogous to rape" (p. 232). As opposed to this almost magical view of emotions and emotional appeal, Aristotle tried to provide a systematic, or artful, approach to the subject.

According to Fortenbaugh (1974), Aristotle's systematic approach to emotional appeals "depends upon correctly understanding the nature of individual emotions, upon knowing the conditions favorable to, the objects of, and the grounds for individual emotions" (p. 209). The first step, then, is to identify and define the nature of each emotion. All emotions, Aristotle (1954) told us, involve either "pain or pleasure" (1378a21). He then proceeded to itemize the emotions, defining each and indicating its affiliation with pain or pleasure. Aristotle specified 14 emotions or emotional states: anger, calmness, enmity, friendship, fear, confidence, shame, shamelessness, kindness, unkindness, pity, indignation, envy, and emulation. Each emotion was defined. For example, the emotional state of fear was defined as "a pain or disturbance due to a mental picture of some destructive or painful evil in the future" (1382a21-1382a22), pity as "a feeling of pain caused by the sight of some evil, destructive or painful, which befalls one who does not deserve it" (1385b13-1385b14), and envy as "pain at the sight of . . . good fortune" (1387b23). In addition to listing and defining each emotion, Aristotle analyzed each in three ways. For each emotion, Aristotle identified the type of people who typically experience the emotion (their "state of mind" [1378a24]), the "objects" in the world that stimulate the emotion, and the "grounds" for the emotion (see also Fortenbaugh, 1974, p. 209). In short, for each emotion, Aristotle focused on *who, toward what,* and *why.* All three points are essential. Aristotle insisted, "It is not enough to know one or even two of these points; unless we know all three, we shall be unable to arouse anger in anyone. The same is true of the other emotions" (pp. 1378a26-1378a28). With a systematic understanding of emotions—what they are, what causes them, and so on—Aristotle believed that advocates would be in a position to either "produce" appropriate emotions in their audiences or "dissipate" inappropriate ones (p. 1388b29). We return to Aristotle's discussion shortly when we consider how it has shaped contemporary thinking on the subject.

Few writers on rhetoric have discussed emotional appeals as systematically as did Aristotle. The 18th-century scholar George Campbell's *Philosophy of Rhetoric* came close.[1] Like Aristotle, Campbell (1963) considered whether appeals to the passions or emotions were "an unfair method of persuasion" (p. 77). Based on a set of assumptions that contemporary scholars have described as "faculty psychology," Campbell believed that for an advocate to persuade, the advocate had to reach both the mind (the "understanding") and the heart (the "will") of the audience. Campbell maintained that passion was necessary to influence the heart or will; it is "the mover to action" (p. 78). Campbell did not identify and define the specific passions or emotions that advocates routinely tried to stimulate or control. His principal question was as follows: "How is a passion or disposition that is [favorable] to the design of the orator to be excited in the hearers?" (p. 81). In keeping with the psychological assumptions of the time, Campbell held that immediate sense experience was most important; he wrote that "a passion is most strongly excited by sensation" (p. 81). After sensation, memory has the greatest impact on the passions, and after memory comes imagination. He wrote,

> Now, as it is this power of which the orator must chiefly avail himself [sic], it is proper to inquire what those circumstances are, which will make the ideas he summons up in the imaginations of his hearers resemble, in lust[er] and steadiness, those of sensation and remembrance. (p. 81)

Campbell (1963) identified seven specific "circumstances" that have a significant impact on the passions. The first is *probability* or "an expedient for enliving passion" (p. 81). Probability functions to make something questionable seem more certain. If we are trying to use a fear appeal on an audience (in the context of trying to alter audience members' sexual behavior in light of the dangers of AIDS), then we enhance the feeling of fear—increase its *intensity*—by showing the high probability of contracting HIV during unsafe sex. The second circumstance is *plausibility.* Campbell acknowledged a "relation" between these first two circumstances but insisted on the importance of the distinction. Plausibility, Campbell wrote, "[arises] chiefly from the consistency of the narration, from its being what is commonly called natural and feasible" (p. 82). In the example just introduced, we might try to induce fear in an audience by relating the story of someone who contracted HIV. From Campbell's perspective, the value of the story depends on its plausibility. Does it strike the listeners as realistic or true to life? If it does, then the story can contribute to the intensity of the emotional experience. The third circumstance is *importance.* Campbell suggested that importance derives largely from consequences. In a fear appeal regarding AIDS, itemizing the consequences—for the individual, their loved ones, and so on—functions as a way of establishing the importance of the topic and the intensity of the emotional response. The fourth circumstance is *proximity in time,* and it works both retrospectively (in relation to the past) and prospectively (in relation to the future). A story about someone contracting AIDS gains force by its being recent. Regarding the future, Campbell observed that "an event that will probably soon happen [has] greater influence upon us than what will probably happen a long time hence" (p. 87). As Campbell's comments acknowledged, an appeal to prospective proximity in time commonly works in conjunction with the first circumstance (probability). The fifth circumstance is *connection of place.* In his discussion of this circumstance, Campbell remarked, "With how much indifference, at least with how slight and transient emotion, do we read in newspapers the accounts of the most deplorable accidents in countries distant and unknown!" (p. 88). In this passage, he emphasized a simple point: People think and feel more deeply and intensely about things that happen close to home. We may be curious about a disease afflicting people thousands of miles away, but it is unlikely that we would become afraid. Fear is the result of the disease striking close to home. The sixth circumstance is *relation to the persons concerned,* and it extends the fifth circumstance in that "it is the persons, not the place, that are the immediate objects of the passions" (p. 89). We feel and care more about things that happen close to home than about those that occur on a distant continent. We feel even more intensely about things that happen to people who we know and care about—family, friends, co-workers, and so on. Finally, the seventh circumstance is *interest in the consequences.* This circumstance extends the third circumstance. It is necessary not only to show the general importance of something but also to establish its importance *for the audience*—to show why audience members should be interested in the consequences. The consequences of the AIDS epidemic are not simply of general importance (e.g., cost of health care, research and development of new drugs); they are of vital personal interest. Showing that personal interest enhances an emotional appeal on the topic.

The writings of Aristotle and Campbell represent two accounts of pathos, or emotional appeals, that have shaped the tradition of rhetorical thought. We also need to consider the state of contemporary research into the emotions and their relationship to rhetorical studies. A large body of literature has emerged on the topic of the emotions during the past few decades. It is impossible to review all of this material here. Three themes or questions will organize the remainder of the discussion. First, what is the basis or nature of emotional experience? Is it a cognitive response to stimuli (one that relies on human thought processes to at least some degree) or a physiological and/or behavioral phenomenon? What is the difference between these contrasting accounts of emotions for rhetorical reflection on the issue? Second, what is the relationship between emotions and argument? Between emotions and reason? Are we dealing with, as Campbell believed, two rather different dimensions of a human—the emotional versus the rational—or is there a greater connection between the emotions and reason than thinkers such as Campbell were able to perceive? Third, what type of persuasive function or effect results from emotional appeals? Do emotional appeals have only an *instrumental* function, or might they produce

effects beyond the instrumental objectives of advocates?

The first two issues, or sets of questions, overlap to a degree and can be treated together. The issues overlap in that if one answers the first question by arguing that emotions have a cognitive basis—that they are the result of a form of intellectual reflection—then one already has begun to argue, with respect to the second question, that emotions are *not* radically different from what we think of as the capacity to reason. Claiming that the emotions have a cognitive dimension does not deny that there is no physiological component to emotional experience. Virtually all of us have felt—physically—an intense emotional experience. But numerous contemporary scholars argue (see, e.g., de Sousa, 1987) that it is inaccurate to reduce every emotional experience to a physiological or conditioned response that bypasses the mind's ability to think, reflect, and reason about the situation that induces the emotional response. There is a growing consensus in the scholarly literature that (a) emotions are partly the result of cognitive processes and (b) there is a complex relationship between emotion and reason.[2]

A number of scholars interested in exploring the cognitive and reason-based element in emotional experience have turned to Aristotle's discussion as a point of departure. Fortenbaugh's reading of Aristotle's (1954) *Rhetoric* illustrates this trend. According to Fortenbaugh (1974), "The *Rhetoric* makes clear that emotions can be reasonable and that all emotional appeal need not be a matter of charms and enchantments" (pp. 205-206). He contended, "Instead of viewing emotions simply as particular kinds of inner (mental) feelings or sensations that impel a man [sic] to behave in certain characteristic ways, Aristotle . . . includes cognition within his conception of emotions" (p. 212). Fortenbaugh concluded, "Cognition is not simply concurrent with emotional response. It is essential to and the cause of emotional response" for Aristotle (p. 215). Fortenbaugh suggested that Aristotle's cognitive account of emotional experience leads to understanding emotions as "reasonable" responses to stimulation; Aristotle "makes clear that emotions are not blind impulses. When a man [sic] responds emotionally, he is not the victim of some automatic reflex. On the contrary, he is acting according to his judgment" (p. 216). Fortenbaugh used Aristotle's discussion of anger as an illustration. A person gets angry, and takes revenge, because he or she feels "insulted." The perceived insult is the source of the emotional response. But it is possible, Fortenbaugh concluded from Aristotle's discussion, for the emotional response to be "unreasonable"; a person might "think" that he or she has been insulted when that is not the case. In this situation, "anger is unreasonable and criticized as unjustified" (p. 216). Fortenbaugh's argument did not claim that the person does not feel or experience anger; rather, the argument was that the person's anger is based on a misguided cognitive appraisal of the situation and can be judged as unreasonable. Something similar occurs with respect to emotional persuasion. As Fortenbaugh explained,

> When an orator demonstrates that danger is imminent, he [sic] is arousing fear in the audience. His reasoned arguments lead the audience to conclude that danger threatens. . . . Their fear is based upon a reasoned consideration of the situation and so is reasonable. . . . [But] further deliberation may convince the hearers that danger is not imminent and so lead them to abandon their fear and become confident. (p. 216)[3]

Fortenbaugh's account of the reasonable nature of emotional experience is important to understanding the way in which emotional persuasion works. But it does not present a complete picture of the process. Consider the following hypothetical example. A U.S. president goes on national television to report that a foreign nation has shot down a U.S. airplane flying in international airspace. In supplying the details of the attack, the president makes the audience angry. And reflection on this situation convinces the audience that the anger in this case is reasonable. Now, suppose that our hypothetical president tries to use the audience's experience of anger as a *warrant* or as a way of justifying a particular course of action. The president reports that U.S. planes have been ordered to shoot down the first plane they find from this nation in retaliation. Does the reasonable experience of anger serve to justify this course of action? If the audience members conclude that, however reasonable their experience of anger might be, it does not justify the type of response that the president is asking them to validate, then they are acknowledging that there is an additional element in the process of emotional persuasion. That missing element, according to Garver (1994), is appropriateness. That is, beyond the implicit claim to being reasonable, an emotional appeal also makes an implicit claim to being an appropriate justification for a specific line of action. As Garver explained, "I cannot simply refer to [a] passion in justification" for a particular action. "I do not offer the emotion as reason for my decision—that would be to admit that emotion corrupts judgment—but [rather] the *appropriateness* of the emotion as the reason" (p. 137). Emotional persuasion works by inducing a *reasonable* emotional response in an audience that also is an *appropriate* warrant for action.[4]

The account of reasonableness and appropriateness just provided supplies the raw materials for a more precise way of conceptualizing the process of emotional persuasion in public advocacy. The diagram in Figure P.1 highlights the key elements. The first thing to note is that the diagram does *not* describe the structure or **arrangement** of a message containing an emotional appeal. Rather, the diagram attempts to describe how emotional appeals work on an audience.

We can start by following Hauser's (1986) extension of Solomon (1976) that identifies two steps in the process of emotional persuasion: experience and judgment. The first step, what Hauser termed experience, raises the claim of reasonableness discussed by Fortenbaugh. The second step, what Hauser termed judgment, raises the claim of appropriateness noted by Garver. The next level of the model tries to break down the two primary steps into their separate components. Initially, let us begin with a nondiscursive, nonrhetorical example to illustrate how the model might help us to understand emotions and persuasion (in this nondiscursive example, we are dealing with a case of self-persuasion). Imagine that an individual is walking down a street in a large city. It is late at night, the street is not lit very well, and there are no other pedestrians in sight. Suddenly, the individual hears footsteps behind him or her. The footsteps function as the primary *cue* in this situation, with the other details discussed serving as relevant secondary cues. How does the individual respond to the cue? What emotion might it stimulate? This leads into the next part of the model—*application.* Application refers to the cognitive element in emotional experience that Fortenbaugh emphasized. In the application process, we can distinguish between ways that the cue might be *minimized* and ways that the cue might be *maximized.* If the individual is a 6-foot 4-inch male weightlifter who is skilled in self-defense and just happens to be carrying a concealed weapon, then the odds are good that he will not be frightened by the sound of footsteps—startled perhaps, but not frightened. But most likely, the individual would not be able to use these attributes to minimize the cue. Instead, he or she would engage in forms of maximization. Campbell's discussion of how orators are able to make emotional experience more intense can help us to understand what might be going on inside the individual's head. The individual might recall acquaintances who have been mugged, remember that muggings have occurred in this area before, remind himself or herself that most muggings occur at night, and/or think about the fact that he or she never has been mugged before even though the odds of being mugged in this particular city at some point are one in five. So, in thinking about the cue, the individual becomes afraid and, at some level, probably concludes that most people in a similar situation also would be afraid. The emotional response is reasonable.

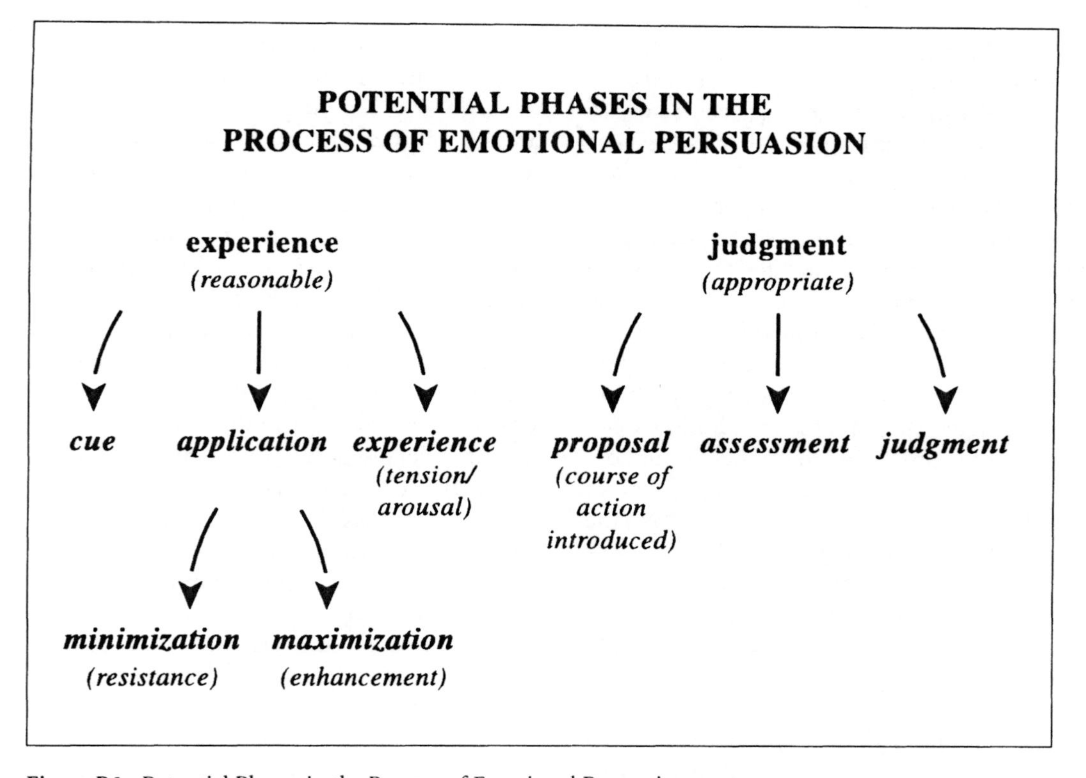

Figure P.1. Potential Phases in the Process of Emotional Persuasion

That leads to the second phase of the process. What does the individual do? In public discourse, this next step usually involves consideration of some proposal from an advocate. In this case, the individual starts to consider the possible courses of action available to him or her. Should the individual walk faster, cross the street, or start to run? This *assessment* of the possible courses of action depends on the individual's sense of the threat involved as well as on the level of emotional intensity. In general, we seek courses of action that correspond to the levels of intensity that we experience (and the levels of intensity can be assessed, like the basic emotional experience, in terms of their reasonableness), and in this situation, most of us probably would conclude (or *judge*) that some sort of precautionary measures would be an appropriate response to the level of emotional arousal and the perception of the threat. Suppose, instead, that the individual decided that the best course of action would be to start screaming for help. Or, imagine that the individual was carrying a concealed firearm and that he or she decided to turn around and open fire. Would these responses be considered appropriate? Probably not. The individual might defend the decision by emphasizing his or her high level of emotional arousal. The individual's action might be appropriate to that level of intensity, but then we return to the initial issue of whether that high level was reasonable in this situation. Of course, people might disagree on the issues of reasonableness and appropriateness, but that is precisely the point. We argue, internally as well as in various public forums, about the claims to reasonableness and appropriateness that are "built in," so to speak, to the process of emotional persuasion.

The various aspects of the model of emotional persuasion suggest numerous lines of inquiry. For example, Solomon (1990) criticized what he described as "a stubborn, infantile insistence on blocking out the nastiness of the world" (p. xv) that is making people less likely to respond to the problems of poverty, disease, and oppression in the world today. In terms of the model, Solomon was calling into question the forms of minimization that help make people immune to emotional persuasion. Is minimization necessarily a bad thing? Undoubtedly, a persistent pattern of emotional minimization—an unwillingness to consider the claims advanced by the disadvantaged or the destitute—might be taken as a sign of cultural decline. But a degree of minimization also seems necessary for our mental health. Consider the range of emotional appeals to which a person is routinely subjected, from parental "guilt trips" to the appeals of countless well-intentioned and necessary humanitarian agencies. If the person responded to each one of the emotional appeals by experiencing the desired emotional state and level of arousal, then he or she might wind up a rather high-strung emotional basket case. Some degree of emotional minimization seems necessary. But what degree? And when? These clearly are matters for continued reflection and deliberation.

The model also might be used to gain insight into specific persuasive performances. Consider the following hypothetical. A student in a public speaking class is giving a speech on the general topic of automobile safety. Through the use of statistics, statistical probability, vivid narrative description, and the other strategies that Campbell recommended, the student paints a picture that makes driving on our streets and highways look like something out of the *Mad Max* movies; crashes, twisted metal, and body parts are everywhere. The student has provided dramatic cues, worked to overcome any audience resistance through minimization, and used strategies to help the audience to maximize the emotional experience. The student has induced what appears to be a reasonable level of fear in the audience. What does the student propose as a course of action? Wearing seat belts. How might the audience react? The audience might be dissatisfied with this performance. Why? Audience dissatisfaction is explainable by considering the point noted earlier: There needs to be some congruence, or some fit, between the level of emotional arousal and the proposed course of action to satisfy the condition of appropriateness. In this hypothetical case, the student was able to induce a considerable degree of emotional arousal, but that arousal could not find relief in the recommended plan of action. The student was successful in producing an emotional experience, but that experience was inappropriate for the proposed course of action. The induced emotional experience seems to suggest the need for a more radical plan of action—reengineering cars for greater safety, proposing new laws that punish bad drivers or lessen the chance of accidents, and so on.

This same line of analysis might be applied to the discourse of the nuclear freeze movement during the early 1980s. Vivid cues detailing the horrific consequences of nuclear war appeared in books, magazine articles, and other media. New terms such as "nuclear winter" were coined to describe the consequences of nuclear conflict. What course of action did these advocates recommend? The ultimate goal, of course, was the elimination of the threat—the destruction of nuclear weapons. But what specific actions did these advocates try to elicit from members of the public audience? Typically, the actions were things such as writing the president or their congressional representatives and engaging in symbolic acts (e.g., having their cities declared as "nuclear-free zones"). Do these specific actions fit the level of emotional arousal generated by the discourse? Perhaps for some they do, but some of the dissatisfaction with the discourse of the nuclear freeze movement (Hogan, 1987, 1994) might be reinterpreted along the lines suggested by the model of emotional persuasion. The problem with freeze discourse was not that it was "emotional" and not "rational" (as the preceding discussion has tried to show, this dichotomy is problematic); rather, the problem was that the degree of emotional arousal was inappropriate for the specific actions it recommended.

The discussion of emotional persuasion has focused on its instrumental utility in public advocacy. In satisfying the conditions or claims of reasonableness and appropriateness, advocates are able to use emotional appeals as a way of responding to situational *exigences.* But are emotional appeals limited to an instrumental function? Might they also function in a more *constitutive* manner? This issue returns us to the third and final theme/question introduced earlier. In recent essays, Michael Hyde and Craig Smith (Hyde & Smith, 1993; Smith & Hyde, 1991) combined elements of Aristotle's account of emotional persuasion with the works of the German philosopher Martin Heidegger. They argued that this conceptual synthesis helps to disclose a broader function for emotional appeals in public life. Specifically, Hyde and Smith argued that emotional appeals not only warrant specific courses of action (instrumental function) but also help to create and sustain the tissue of relations that is the basis of a community or a public. Their argument suggested that emotions produce different rhetorical effects that can function *instrumentally* as well as *constitutively.*

Since Aristotle, emotions and emotional appeals have been a key element in the tradition of rhetorical studies. Given that humans are, to at least some extent, emotional creatures, inquiry into both the form and function of emotional appeals most likely will continue.

Notes

1. On Campbell's (1963) account of the passions, see also Walzer (1999).

2. On these issues, see also Elster (1999), Greenspan (1988, 1995), and Turski (1994).

3. On the argumentative or enthymematic nature of appeals to emotions such as anger, see Walker (1992).

4. On the role of appropriateness in emotional appeals and argument in general, see Booth (1974, pp. 158-164), Jasinski (1990), and McGee (1998).

References and Additional Reading

Aristotle. (1954). *Rhetoric* (W. R. Roberts, Trans.). New York: Modern Library.

Booth, W. C. (1974). *Modern dogma and the rhetoric of assent.* Chicago: University of Chicago Press.

Campbell, G. (1963). *The philosophy of rhetoric* (L. F. Bitzer, Ed.). Carbondale: Southern Illinois University Press.

Cronkhite, G. L. (1964). Logic, emotion, and the paradigm of persuasion. *Quarterly Journal of Speech, 50,* 13-18.

Denzin, N. K. (1984). *On understanding emotion.* San Francisco: Jossey-Bass.

de Sousa, R. (1987). *The rationality of the emotions.* Cambridge, MA: MIT Press.

Elster, J. (1999). *Alchemies of the mind: Rationality and the emotions.* Cambridge, UK: Cambridge University Press.

Fortenbaugh, W. W. (1974). Aristotle's *Rhetoric* on emotions. In K. V. Erickson (Ed.), *Aristotle: The classical heritage of rhetoric.* Metuchen, NJ: Scarecrow Press.

Fortenbaugh, W. W. (1975). *Aristotle on emotion: A contribution to philosophical psychology, rhetoric, poetics, politics, and ethics.* New York: Barnes & Noble.

Garver, E. (1994). *Aristotle's* Rhetoric: *An art of character.* Chicago: University of Chicago Press.

Greenspan, P. S. (1988). *Emotions and reasons: An inquiry into emotional justification.* New York: Routledge.

Greenspan, P. S. (1995). *Practical guilt: Moral dilemmas, emotions, and social norms.* New York: Oxford University Press.

Hauser, G. (1986). *An introduction to rhetorical theory.* New York: Harper & Row.

Hogan, J. M. (1987). Apocalyptic pornography and the nuclear freeze movement: A defense of the public. In J. W. Wenzel (Ed.), *Argument and critical practice: Proceedings of the Fifth SCA/AFA Conference on Argumentation.* Annandale, VA: Speech Communication Association.

Hogan, J. M. (1994). *The nuclear freeze campaign: Rhetoric and foreign policy in the telepolitical age.* East Lansing: Michigan State University Press.

Hyde, M. J. (1984). Emotion and human communication: A rhetorical, scientific, and philosophical picture. *Communication Quarterly, 32,* 120-132.

Hyde, M. J., & Smith, C. R. (1993). Aristotle and Heidegger on emotion and rhetoric: Questions of time and space. In I. Angus & L. Langsdorf (Eds.), *The critical turn: Rhetoric and philosophy in postmodern discourse.* Carbondale: Southern Illinois University Press.

Jasinski, J. (1990). An exploration of form and force in rhetoric and argumentation. In D. C. Williams & M. D. Hazen (Eds.), *Argumentation theory and the rhetoric of assent.* Tuscaloosa: University of Alabama Press.

Katz, J. (1999). *How emotions work.* Chicago: University of Chicago Press.

McGee, B. R. (1998). Rehabilitating emotion: The troublesome case of the Ku Klux Klan. *Argumentation and Advocacy, 34,* 173-188.

Nussbaum, M. C. (1996). Aristotle on emotions and rational persuasion. In A. O. Rorty (Ed.), *Essays on Aristotle's RHETORIC.* Berkeley: University of California Press.

Smith, C. R., & Hyde, M. J. (1991). Rethinking "the public": The role of emotion in being-with-others. *Quarterly Journal of Speech, 77,* 446-466.

Solomon, R. C. (1976). *The passions.* Garden City, NY: Anchor.

Solomon, R. C. (1990). *A passion for justice: Emotions and the origins of the social contract.* Reading, MA: Addison-Wesley.

Turski, W. G. (1994). *Toward a rationality of emotions: An essay in the philosophy of mind.* Athens: Ohio University Press.

Walker, J. (1992). Enthymemes of anger in Cicero and Thomas Paine. In M. Secor & D. Charney (Eds.), *Constructing rhetorical education.* Carbondale: Southern Illinois University Press.

Walton, D. (1992). *The place of emotion in argument.* University Park: Pennsylvania State University Press.

Walton, D. (1997). *Appeal to pity: Argumentum ad misericordiam.* Albany: State University of New York Press.

Walzer, A. E. (1999). Campbell on the passions: A rereading of the *Philosophy of Rhetoric. Quarterly Journal of Speech, 85,* 72-85.

PERSONA

The term **persona** is of Latin origin and originally was used to refer to masks worn by actors in theatrical productions in ancient Greece.[1] In contemporary literary and rhetorical studies, the term is used to identify a human presence that saturates a **text** (e.g., poem, novel, essay, speech). The concept of persona often is a central feature in **fantasy theme** analysis (Bormann, 1973; Rarick, Duncan, Lee, & Porter, 1977). Literary scholars sometimes refer to this presence as an "implied author" (Booth, 1983), a "second self" (Tillotson, 1959), or an authorial *voice* (for more on voice, see the entry for **polyphony**). Students of the mass media (e.g., Fiske, 1986) describe a similar presence as "the author-in-the-text" (p. 394). In rhetorical studies, scholars such as Hart (1997) employ the concept of *role* as a way of explaining the human presence in a text and do so, in part, by drawing on literature devoted to the concept of persona. What these terms share in common is the idea that there is a consciousness that organizes, controls, and directs what appears in the text and that is manifested in the text in different ways. A persona is, in short, both a type of controlling consciousness *behind* the text (so to speak) and an image of a person speaking or writing that surfaces *in* the text (on the presence of a persona in the text, see Gibson, 1969). In some cases (e.g., certain types of literary narration, the pseudonymous authorship of a political pamphlet), the presence of a constructed persona is very obvious. But personae can appear in more subtle forms as well.

When scholars speak of the presence of a persona in a text, they usually use the term in a way that clearly distinguishes what it represents from the "real" author or speaker. As Abrams (1993) noted, the idea that the author or speaker is somehow present in a text is an aspect of the rhetorical tradition and the doctrine of **ethos**. But ethos, understood as the speaker's character as it appears in the speech, and the real character of an author or speaker is different from the persona that organizes and appears in a text. Talking specifically about persona in rhetorical performances, Ware and Linkugel (1982) wrote that "the rhetorical *persona* is not the rhetor *qua* person" (p. 51). They continued, "We draw a sharp distinction here between the rhetor's personal ethos and the ethos represented by the rhetorical *persona* the speaker assumes" (p. 51). Whether we are dealing with a poem, an anonymous political pamphlet, or a public speech, the persona present in each of these texts, and the ethos or persuasive character that the persona may exhibit, is distinct from the ethos and character of the person who produced the text. But is there *any* relationship between the persona and the person? This remains a hotly contested issue. Elliott (1982), for example, concluded, "To what degree the mask [or the persona] is equivalent to the true person—or whether 'true person' has any meaning in this context—is unresolved" (p. 13).

The space between textual persona and real person raises the possibility of unethical deception (Yoos, 1979). Can we, as an audience, trust the persona exhibited by a political candidate? Can we, or should we, depend on the persona of the disinterested scientist recommending a solution to a pressing public problem? In general, how can we *evaluate* textual personae? The problem of deception is more acute in the realm of rhetoric than in that of literature. One way of approaching the issue is to probe the assumptions on which it based. For example, many of us are comfortable making a judgment about someone based on his or her "real" character rather than any persona (or role) the person might choose to inhabit or play. Persona is something artificial or fabricated, whereas we think of character as something that is "real" and merely revealed by a person. But we could look at this question of what is fabricated and what is revealed from a different perspective. Garver (1994) argued that, according to Aristotle, "ethos is artificial" (p. 197). If that is an accurate way of understanding Aristotle and the concept of ethos, then we are left with a situation in which ethos and persona, although not identical, are similar in that both are constructed. We can, as Ware and Linkugel urged, distinguish between the rhetor's personal ethos and the ethos associated with a particular mask, role, or persona, but not on the basis that one (personal ethos) is more real or authentic than the other. Both are constructed by way of language and action. The key difference is that textual personae emerge within a culture as a result of the efforts of multiple actors and agents, whereas personal ethos is more idiosyncratic or the result of individual decisions (which, to be sure, are influenced by cultural norms and values).[2]

How does this discussion relate to the question of judging or evaluating textual personae? Can we trust the politician with an attractive persona? Or, should we try to uncover the "real" politician lurking behind the persona? If we adopt the *constructivist* position outlined in the preceding paragraph, then we need to give up the attempt to look behind or underneath the persona that appears in a text. Why? Because what is behind is no different from what is in the text; it is something constructed. How can we evaluate the politician? We might adapt the standard that Booth (1983) endorsed for assessing literary personae—"harmony" or consistency (p. 75). Does the individual present a harmonious or consistent pattern of self-representations or self-images? As Garver (1994) noted, the lack of consistency is not *always* a reliable *sign* of ethical or moral failure; individuals need to conduct and construct themselves differently in different situations. Although harmony and consistency cannot function as absolute standards for **judgment,** they can serve as a *topos* for argument and critical reflection when it comes to questions of persona and ethos.

Although the concept of persona, when applied to the realm of rhetorical performance, introduces some complex evaluative questions, its primary impact in both literary and rhetorical studies is in analytic critical practice. Persona analysis or criticism (or what Hart [1997] called "role criticism") tries to, among other things, identify recurrent personae, trace the emergence and evolution of these personae, describe the essential discursive characteristics (e.g., argumentative, stylistic) of the personae, describe how specific individuals might manage multiple personae (**polyphony**), and assess the impact of particular personae in particular situations. Consider a few examples. Wright (1960) examined the personae present in the poetry of T. S. Eliot, W. B. Yeats, and Ezra Pound, Walker (1991a) identified and analyzed a set of personae that appeared in women's poetry during the early 20th century (e.g., the "androgynous persona," the "passionate virgin persona," the "woman warrior persona").

Gilbert (1994) traced the emergence and evolution of the personae of female comics (identifying discrete personae such as the "bawd," the "whiner," and the "bitch"). Lake (1990) explored the "warrior" persona in Native American advocacy. Dow and Tonn (1993) identified a "nurturing persona" as part of the **feminine style** of rhetorical production. Tonn (1996) uncovered a "militant" variation on the more common "maternal persona" in the public speeches of labor activist Mary Harris "Mother" Jones. Hogan and Williams (2000) reconstructed the "charismatic" persona in Tom Paine's revolutionary era pamphlet, *Common Sense.* In one of the classic analyses of persona in rhetorical studies, Ware and Linkugel (1982) examined the way in which early 20th-century black activist Marcus Garvey enacted an **archetypal** persona derived from the biblical character Moses. Campbell (1975) suggested the possibility of analyzing the personae present in scientific discourse, inaugurating a line of inquiry that Lessl (1989) continued in his investigation of the way in which scientists appropriate the personae and voices of priests. In a different sphere of discursive practice, Browne (1990) examined the way in which colonial leader John Dickinson created the persona and voice of a "farmer" in his famous *Letters From a Farmer in Pennsylvania.*

Finally, rhetorical scholars not only have employed the concept of persona in their practical criticism but also have suggested ways of extending the concept. Two examples of this trend are particularly noteworthy. Black's (1970) essay, "The Second Persona," extended Booth's discussion of personae and implied authors by identifying a "second" persona present in a text—its implied auditor or **audience.** Black reasoned that if a text contains traces of an implied author or persona, then it most likely also contains traces of "the audience it implies" or the one for which it is "appropriate" (p. 112). He continued,

> It seems a useful methodological assumption to hold that rhetorical discourses, either singly or cumulatively in a persuasive movement, will imply an auditor, and that in most cases the implication will be sufficiently suggestive as to enable the critic to link this implied auditor to an ideology. (p. 112)

Black suggested that a text, through its second persona or its subtle shaping of the audience, will exert an **ideological** influence.[3]

Fourteen years after Black's essay, Wander (1984) extended Black's thinking by proposing a "third" persona that required the attention of rhetorical scholars. Wander wrote,

> There is . . . implied, through certain features of the discourse entailing specific characteristics, roles, actions, or ways of seeing things for one who can use the language, a "you" or a second persona. But, just as the discourse may be understood to affirm certain characteristics, it may also be understood to imply other characteristics, roles, actions, or ways of seeing things to be avoided. What is negated through the second persona forms the silhouette of a third persona—the "it" that is not present, that is objectified in a way that "you" and "I" are not. (p. 209)

In essence, the third persona refers to who is "negated," who is elided, or who and what we are "told to avoid becoming" (p. 210) in a text.[4] For example, the discourse of most mainstream politicians during the middle of the 19th century negated or elided African slaves; slavery *as an institution* frequently was discussed, but few politicians talked about the material existence of slaves. The slaves were, in Wander's terms, "negated" in most public discourse.[5] Consider a contemporary case. A person of the pro-life persuasion might detect a third persona in the discourse of abortion rights activists: The fetus-as-human is deleted, elided, or negated; abortion rights discourse does not recognize or does not include the fetus as something worthy of discursive attention. Conversely, a person of the pro-choice persuasion might detect a third persona in abortion opponents: The woman-as-autonomous, self-determining, and rights-bearing individual is conspicuously absent; anti-abortion discourse might talk frequently about women as mothers or wives but typically elides or ignores women as autonomous agents.

Notes

1. On the etymology of the term, see Elliott (1982, pp. 19-32).

2. For more detailed treatment of the issues of personal identity raised here, see the entries for **ethos** and **subject.**

3. See also Charland's (1987) discussion of the relationship between Black's (1970) idea of the "second" persona and his sense of **constitutive rhetoric.**

4. See also the entry for **other, rhetorical construction of.**

5. Their plight was, of course, prominently featured in abolitionist discourse, but even that discourse engaged in its own subtle form of silencing (Browne, 1994).

References and Additional Reading

Abrams, M. H. (1993). *A glossary of literary terms* (6th ed.). Fort Worth, TX: Harcourt Brace.

Black, E. (1970). The second persona. *Quarterly Journal of Speech, 56,* 109-119.

Booth, W. C. (1983). *The rhetoric of fiction* (2nd ed.). Chicago: University of Chicago Press.

Bormann, E. G. (1973). The Eagleton affair: A fantasy theme analysis. *Quarterly Journal of Speech, 59,* 143-159.

Browne, S. H. (1990). The pastoral voice in John Dickinson's first *Letter From a Farmer in Pennsylvania. Quarterly Journal of Speech, 76,* 46-57.

Browne, S. (1994). "Like gory spectres": Representing evil in Theodore Weld's *American Slavery as It Is. Quarterly Journal of Speech, 80,* 277-292.

Campbell, P. N. (1975). The *personae* of scientific discourse. *Quarterly Journal of Speech, 61,* 391-405.

Carpenter, R. H. (1994). The stylistic persona of Bill Clinton: From Arkansas and Aristotelian Attica. In S. A. Smith (Ed.), *Bill Clinton on stump, state, and stage: The rhetorical road to the White House.* Fayetteville: University of Arkansas Press.

Charland, M. (1987). Constitutive rhetoric: The case of the *peuple Québécois. Quarterly Journal of Speech, 73,* 133-150.

Dow, B. J., & Tonn, M. B. (1993). "Feminine style" and political judgment in the rhetoric of Ann Richards. *Quarterly Journal of Speech, 79,* 286-302.

Elliott, R. C. (1982). *The literary persona.* Chicago: University of Chicago Press.

Fiske, J. (1986). Television: Polysemy and popularity. *Critical Studies in Mass Communication, 3,* 391-408.

Garver, E. (1994). *Aristotle's RHETORIC: An art of character.* Chicago: University of Chicago Press.

Gibson, W. (1969). *Persona: A style study for readers and writers.* New York: Random House.

Gilbert, J. (1994). *Performing marginality: Humor, gender, and social control.* Unpublished Ph.D. dissertation, University of Texas at Austin.

Hart, R. P. (1997). *Modern rhetorical criticism* (2nd ed.). Boston: Allyn & Bacon.

Hogan, J. M., & Williams, L. G. (2000). Republican charisma and the American Revolution: The textual persona of Thomas Paine's *Common Sense. Quarterly Journal of Speech, 86,* 1-18.

Lake, R. A. (1990). The implied arguer. In D. C. Williams & M. D. Hazen (Eds.), *Argumentation theory and the rhetoric of assent.* Tuscaloosa: University of Alabama Press.

Lessl, T. M. (1989). The priestly voice. *Quarterly Journal of Speech, 75,* 183-197.

Morris, C. E., III. (1996). Contextual twilight/critical liminality: J. M. Barrie's *Courage* at St. Andrews, 1922. *Quarterly Journal of Speech, 82,* 207-227.

Pauley, J. L. (1998). Reshaping public persona and the prophetic *ethos:* Louis Farrakhan at the Million Man March. *Western Journal of Communication, 62,* 512-536.

Rarick, D. L., Duncan, M. B., Lee, D. G., & Porter, L. W. (1977). The Carter persona: An empirical analysis of the rhetorical visions of Campaign '76. *Quarterly Journal of Speech, 63,* 258-273.

Sloan, T. O. (1965). The persona as rhetor: An interpretation of Donne's *Satyre III. Quarterly Journal of Speech, 51,* 14-27.

Tillotson, K. (1959). *The tale and the teller.* London: R. Hart-Davis.

Tonn, M. B. (1996). Militant motherhood: Labor's Mary Harris "Mother" Jones. *Quarterly Journal of Speech, 82,* 1-21.

Walker, C. (1991a). *Masks outrageous and austere: Culture, psyche, and persona in modern women poets.* Bloomington: Indiana University Press.

Walker, C. (1991b). Persona criticism and the death of the author. In W. H. Epstein (Ed.), *Contesting the subject: Essays in the postmodern theory and practice of biography and biographical criticism.* West Lafayette, IN: Purdue University Press.

Wander, P. (1984). The third persona: An ideological turn in rhetorical theory. *Central States Speech Journal, 35,* 197-216.

Ware, B. L., & Linkugel, W. A. (1982). The rhetorical *persona:* Marcus Garvey as Black Moses. *Communication Monographs, 49,* 50-62.

Wright, G. T. (1960). *The poet in the poem: The personae of Eliot, Yeats, and Pound.* Berkeley: University of California Press.

Yoos, G. E. (1979). A revision of the concept of ethical appeal. *Philosophy and Rhetoric, 12,* 41-58.

PERSPECTIVE BY INCONGRUITY

Rhetorical critics Thomas Rosteck and Michael Leff suggested that Burke's (1984b) elaborate discussion of the concept of *piety* in *Permanence and Change* represents a way of conceptualizing or theorizing "order within a relativistic universe" (Rosteck & Leff, 1989, p. 328). The term *piety* traditionally has been used to describe the feelings of fidelity to one's family or a person's religious devotion. Burke wanted to retain this sense of fidelity and/or devotion as he expanded or secularized the idea of piety. Burke (1984b) wrote that piety is "merely the sense of what goes with what. . . . it involves the putting together of experiences" (p. 76). Burke's adverbial qualifier "merely" is deceptive; although the essence of piety—"what goes with what"—might be simple, the social function that he attributed to piety is of fundamental importance. Piety preserves order (including conceptual as well as political order) when it functions as a way of organizing or governing our perceptions and cognitive processes. Piety assumes the ontic status (or exists in the concrete form) of conceptual schemata, frames, or orientations, thereby becoming the plural *pieties.* Rosteck and Leff (1989) argued that these conceptual schemata, frames, or orientations function "as stable frames of reference which direct human perception and determine our judgments about what is proper in a given circumstance" (p. 329). Pieties shape the way in which we think and act across the broad spectrum of human interaction. Specific pieties exist with respect to sexuality, politics, economics, race, gender, **generations,** and various subcultures that constitute our heterogeneous social world. Burke (1984b) maintained that the principle or process of piety "extends through all the texture of our lives but has been concealed from us because we think we are so thoroughly without religion and think that the 'pious process' is confined to the sphere of churchliness" (p. 75).[1]

In short, the principle of piety (embodying the human need for order and stability) and the specific pieties that organize a culture are mechanisms for maintaining social order in a **contingent** world (see also Baumlin, 1984). But what does the concept of piety have to do with the idea of **perspective by incongruity?** The relationship between these two ideas in Burke's thought goes something like this. If social existence were static and unchanging, then an established piety would continue indefinitely and our world would be structured by the pieties that organized ancient Greek and Roman civilizations. But Burke (along with countless other social theorists) maintained that change is a constant. Perspective by incongruity, or planned incongruity, is a principal mechanism of change—a way of disrupting and reorganizing existing pieties to allow for the possibility of new ways of thinking about and perceiving the world (perspective by incongruity is, then, intimately related to the continued negotiation of **definitions of the situation**). Burke (1984b) wrote,

> Planned incongruity should be deliberately cultivated for the purpose of experimentally wrenching apart all those molecular combinations of adjective and noun, substantive and verb, which still remain with us. It should subject language to the same "cracking" process that chemists now use in their refining of oil. (p. 119)

Elsewhere, Burke (1984a) described perspective by incongruity as

> a method for gauging situations by verbal "atom cracking." That is, a word belongs by custom to a certain category—and by ratio-

> nal planning you wrench it loose and metaphorically apply it to a different category.... "Perspective by incongruity" carries on the same kind of enterprise [as metaphors and puns] in linking hitherto unlinked words. ... It is "impious" as regards our linguistic categories established by custom. (308-309)

Rosteck and Leff (1989) concluded that perspective by incongruity "is the wedge that pries apart established linkages" (p. 330), thereby making change and innovation possible.[2]

Rhetorical scholars have adapted and extended Burke's idea of perspective by incongruity in two ways. First, perspective by incongruity can function as a (usually implicit) *critical heuristic.* That is, a scholar can approach a particular text from a perspective that is incongruous with its usual or typical associations. The critic's perspective by incongruity breaks the established linkages and allows for a new reading of the text. For example, Stelzner (1971) disrupted the common ways of reading a **deliberative** oration by approaching Richard Nixon's November 1969 speech on the war in Vietnam from the perspective of an **archetypal** quest. (As a point of clarification, not all instances of archetypal criticism exemplify a critical perspective by incongruity; perspective by incongruity functions as a critical heuristic when archetypal analytic schemes are employed outside their customary frame of application.) Similarly, Gregg and Hauser (1973) disturbed conventional deliberative analysis when they read Nixon's April 1970 address on the invasion of Cambodia from the perspective of a specific Indian tribal ceremony (the "Potlach" ceremony of confrontation). The authors of these critical studies did not explicitly invoke Burke's idea of perspective by incongruity in developing their analyses, but nevertheless, something like Burke's idea of disrupting conventional associations to enable a new outlook on events was embedded in these critical performances.

The second, and more common, way in which rhetorical critics have adapted and extended Burke's idea of perspective by incongruity has been to consider it as an *inventional resource* exploited in the process of advocacy. Extending Burke's insight into the relationship between *metaphor* and perspective by incongruity, a number of scholars have examined the use of radical metaphor (or *catachresis*) as a way of generating perspective by incongruity. Solomon (1988), for example, noted the radical metaphors employed by the anarchist agitator Emma Goldman in her discussions of religion and politics. Goldman also employed radical metaphors in her discussion of the institution of marriage; in her 1917 essay, "Marriage and Love," Goldman (1917/1969) wrote that "the institution of marriage makes a *parasite* of woman" (emphasis added). Radical metaphors for marriage would become quite common in feminist advocacy during the late 1960s and early 1970s. In her "Sexual Politics: A Manifesto for Revolution," Kate Millet disrupted the common associations of marriage with happiness, security, and love by considering it in economic terms. According to Millet (1973), women were forced into the practice of "the *sale* of their sexuality in marriage," thereby hinting that marriage was merely a legalized form of prostitution. In a 1970 essay, "Marriage," Sheila Cronin continued the process of disruption by equating marriage with *slavery* (Cronin, 1970/1973). (Cronin, in all likelihood, would have denied that she was speaking metaphorically; she wanted to show her readers that marriage *is* slavery.) In all of these instances, radical metaphors functioned as a disruptive perspective by incongruity, subjecting society's conception of marriage to an extremely impious "cracking" process so as to alter its dominant conceptual frame.

Perspective by incongruity appears to be a potent discursive resource for advocates of change. Foss (1979), for example, located the process in efforts of feminists to challenge dominant attitudes of the Catholic church. Dow (1994) found perspective by incongruity to be a critical part of the discursive strategy of AIDS activist Larry Kramer's essay, "1,112 and Counting" (Kramer, 1983/1989). Dow

(1994) further extended our understanding of the possible functions of perspective by incongruity by arguing that it does more than reconfigure a community's understanding of specific situations, events, and/or institutions. Kramer's discursive "process of existential disruption" (p. 231) functioned to instigate a *reconstitution* of gay self-identity. Perspective by incongruity also could be found in the discourse of the student movement during the 1960s. In his December 1964 speech at the University of California, Berkeley, Mario Savio used the radical metaphor of the university as a *factory* to disrupt accepted pieties about higher education and to provide his audience with a new way of seeing the university in the context of modern American society. Students of social protest and dissent need to be particularly sensitive to the way in which various discursive impieties (e.g., radical metaphor or *catachresis, hyperbole, irony,* sarcasm) generate perspective by incongruity.

Notes

1. Burke's suggestion that piety saturates human existence anticipated Foucault's discussion of the ubiquity of **power**.
2. Burke's thinking on perspective by incongruity bore some similarity to the literary technique of *defamiliarization* described by Russian literary theorists such as Viktor Shklovsky during the early 20th century. This resemblance was briefly discussed by Stacy (1977). In rhetorical studies, see Ekdom Vande Berg (1989).

References and Additional Reading

Baumlin, J. S. (1984). Decorum, *kairos,* and the "new" rhetoric. *Pre/Text, 5,* 171-183.

Burke, K. (1984a). *Attitudes toward history* (3rd ed.). Berkeley: University of California Press.

Burke, K. (1984b). *Permanence and change: An anatomy of purpose* (3rd ed.). Berkeley: University of California Press.

Bygrave, S. (1993). *Kenneth Burke: Rhetoric and ideology.* London: Routledge.

Cronin, S. (1973). Marriage. In A. Koedt, E. Levine, & A. Rapone (Eds.), *Radical feminism.* New York: Quadrangle. (Original work published 1970)

Dow, B. J. (1994). AIDS, perspective by incongruity, and gay identity in Larry Kramer's "1,112 and Counting." *Communication Studies, 45,* 225-240.

Ekdom Vande Berg, L. R. (1989). Dramedy: *Moonlighting* as an emergent generic hybrid. *Communication Studies, 40,* 13-28.

Foss, S. K. (1979). Feminism confronts Catholicism: A study in the uses of perspective by incongruity. *Women's Studies in Communication, 3,* 7-15.

Goldman, E. (1969). Marriage and love. In E. Goldman, *Anarchism and other essays.* New York: Dover. (Original work published 1917)

Gregg, R. B., & Hauser, G. A. (1973). Richard Nixon's April 30, 1970 address on Cambodia: The "ceremony" of confrontation. *Communication Monographs, 40,* 167-181.

Kramer, L. (1989). 1,112 and counting. In L. Kramer, *Reports from the Holocaust: The making of an AIDS activist.* New York: St. Martin's. (Original work published 1983)

Levasseur, D. G. (1993). Edifying arguments and perspective by incongruity: The perplexing argumentative method of Kenneth Burke. *Argument and Advocacy, 29,* 195-203.

Millet, K. (1973). Sexual politics: A manifesto for revolution. In A. Koedt, E. Levine, & A. Rapone (Eds.), *Radical feminism.* New York: Quadrangle.

Rosteck, T., & Leff, M. (1989). Piety, propriety, and perspective: An interpretation and application of key terms in Kenneth Burke's *Permanence and Change. Western Journal of Speech Communication, 53,* 327-341.

Shklovsky, V. (1965). Art as technique. In L. T. Lemon & M. J. Reis (Ed. and Trans.), *Russian formalist criticism.* Lincoln: University of Nebraska Press.

Solomon, M. (1988). Ideology as rhetorical constraint: The anarchist agitation of "Red Emma" Goldman. *Quarterly Journal of Speech, 74,* 184-200.

Stacy, R. H. (1977). *Defamiliarization in language and literature.* Syracuse, NY: Syracuse University Press.

Stelzner, H. G. (1971). The quest story and Nixon's November 3, 1969 address. *Quarterly Journal of Speech, 57,* 163-172.

POLARIZATION

In *A Rhetoric of Motives,* Burke (1950) proposed that **identification,** rather than persuasion, be considered the master term for rhetorical studies. But Burke was quick to point out that the idea of identification, a type of symbolic joining together, should not blind critics and scholars to "the presence of strife, enmity, [and] faction as a characteristic motive of rhetorical expression"; these motives, and the particular discursive forms in which they are manifest, must be kept "clearly in view" (p. 20). The concept of **polarization** is one way in which rhetorical critics have tried to follow Burke's advice.

In its most basic sense, polarization is the creation and/or intensification of fundamental divisions and differences within a group of people. A group (e.g., a sports team, a fraternity, an academic department, a political party, a nation) is polarized when personal antagonisms or more substantive conflicts (e.g., ideological, philosophical, religious) evolve into a schism that divides the group into rival "camps." King and Anderson (1971) provided the following more formal definition: "Polarization, as a rhetorical phenomenon, may be defined as the process by which an extremely diversified public is coalesced into two or more highly contrasting, mutually exclusive groups sharing a high degree of internal solidarity" (p. 244). Polarizing discourse is the concrete linguistic expression of a type of Manichean "we/they" or "us/them" way of thinking. It depicts a world of clear-cut absolutes without any gray areas or ambiguity.

Scholars have identified a number of common characteristics of polarizing rhetoric. First, polarizing discourse seeks to create a strong sense of unity or identification *within one segment* of a larger social collective. This sense of unity or identity frequently is achieved by way of opposition to a discursively constructed **enemy**. As Burke (1957) noted, "Men [sic] who can unite on nothing else can unite on the basis of a foe shared by all" (p. 165). King and Anderson (1971), for example, illustrated the creation of group unity in Richard Nixon's elaboration of the idea of a "silent majority" that must join together in opposition to the radical minority that Nixon believed was threatening the fabric of American society.[1] Second, polarizing discourse paints a vivid picture of the threat posed by the identified "enemy." It is common for polarizing discourse to elide the differences between a group and those to whom its members are opposed. Enemies are portrayed as "monolithic,"[2] or all of the various groups to whom one group is opposed are linked to their most extreme elements.[3] Third, polarizing discourse routinely features *antithesis* along with *disjunctive* or *divisional* arguments (King & Anderson, 1971; Raum & Measell, 1974; Stewart, 1997). Finally, advocates engaged in the strategy of polarization often seek out dramatic confrontations to further their efforts at amplifying social divisions. For example, Nixon and George Wallace campaign staffers regularly admitted protesters and hecklers into overcrowded speaking venues so as to provide human "props" that could be exploited for polarizing purposes. But as Bowers and Ochs (1971) argued, strategies of polarization are not limited to social and political elites; in many cases, protesters and agitators make use of the various strategies of polarization.[4]

The study of polarizing rhetoric declined along with the social and political turbulence of the late 1960s and early 1970s. But forms of polarization continue to appear in American public discourse. Perhaps the best example during the 1990s could be found in the political oratory of former Nixon speechwriter Patrick Buchanan. Buchanan's attacks on illegal immigrants and his description of the nation's ongoing "cultural war" demonstrated the persistence of this form of practice.

Notes

1. See also Gustainis (1993) and Newman (1970).

2. See Davis's (1969, pp. 32-61) study of the antebellum slavery dispute as well as Raum and Measell's (1974) study of Wallace.

3. King and Anderson (1971) demonstrated this strategy in both Nixon and Spiro Agnew. Another example would be efforts to discredit contemporary feminism by linking the movement as a whole with its more extreme factions.

4. Also relevant here is Jensen's (1977) discussion of how the "family" *metaphor* contributed to the polarization of British and colonial attitudes during the 1770s. Jensen suggested that metaphors are an often recognized

polarizing force. This certainly seems to be the case with "war" metaphors.

References and Additional Reading

Bowers, J. W., & Ochs, D. J. (1971). *The rhetoric of agitation and control.* Reading, MA: Addison-Wesley.

Burke, K. (1950). *A rhetoric of motives.* New York: Prentice Hall.

Burke, K. (1957). The rhetoric of Hitler's "Battle." In K. Burke, *The philosophy of literary form* (rev. ed.). New York: Vintage.

Davis, D. B. (1969). *The slave power conspiracy and the paranoid style.* Baton Rouge: Louisiana State University Press.

Goldzwig, S. R. (1989). A social movement perspective on demagoguery: Achieving symbolic realignment. *Communication Studies, 40,* 202-228.

Gustainis, J. J. (1993). *American rhetoric and the Vietnam war.* Westport, CT: Praeger.

Jensen, J. V. (1977). British voices on the eve of the American Revolution: Trapped by the family metaphor. *Quarterly Journal of Speech, 63,* 43-50.

King, A. A., & Anderson, F. D. (1971). Nixon, Agnew, and the "silent majority": A case study in the rhetoric of polarization. *Western Journal of Speech Communication, 35,* 243-255.

Newman, R. P. (1970). Under the veneer: Nixon's Vietnam speech of November 3, 1969. *Quarterly Journal of Speech, 56,* 168-178.

Raum, R. D., & Measell, J. S. (1974). Wallace and his ways: A study in the rhetorical genre of polarization. *Central States Speech Journal, 25,* 28-35.

Stewart, C. J. (1997). The evolution of a revolution: Stokely Carmichael and the rhetoric of Black Power. *Quarterly Journal of Speech, 83,* 429-446.

POLYPHONY

In a narrow sense, Russian literary theorist Mikhail Bakhtin's concept of **polyphony** described a very special type of prose writing (exemplified by the Russian author Fyodor Dostoevsky) in which an author creates a number of independent and equal voices, or consciousnesses, that engage in dialogue with each other. But polyphonic dialogue has a special quality arising from the nature of the voices that appear in the text; although the author *creates* the dialogue (in the sense that he or she writes down the words on paper), the author does not *control* the dialogue. Commenting on Dostoevsky, Bakhtin (1984) wrote, "What unfolds in his works is not a multitude of characters and fates in a single objective world, illuminated by a single authorial consciousness; rather, *a plurality of consciousnesses, with equal rights and each with its own world,* combine but are not merged in the unity" of the work (p. 6). It might be more accurate to say that the polyphonic author *records* voices, and the consciousnesses from which they emerge, rather than creates them. Discursive artistry then becomes a process of organizing, or orchestrating (a musical metaphor that Bakhtin liked to employ), these independent voices.

We also might approach polyphony from a broader perspective and consider it as the vocal counterpart to Bakhtin's concept of linguistic **heteroglossia.**[1] He suggested that all spoken or written discourse is generated or produced through a process of language appropriation (heteroglossia) and *voice appropriation* (polyphony).[2] These forms of appropriation can be distinguished conceptually, but in practice they overlap to a considerable degree. For example, to speak the language of expertise usually entails speaking in the voice of an "expert" (see also the entry for **persona**). That voice will become more specific as a particular expert language is appropriated (e.g., one speaks in the voice of a scientist when making predictions or that of a doctor when rendering a diagnosis for a complex problem). Specific language communities are marked by different voices.[3] For example, the language community of medicine consists of the positions/voices of doctor, nurse, hospital and health insurance administrators, and patient, whereas the language community of the judicial system consists of the positions/voices of judge, defendant, prosecuting and defense attorneys, and witness (to name some of the more obvious positions/voices in these two communities).

In addition to the various manifestations of the voice of the expert, other voices that are appropriated with regularity in public advocacy include the *prophetic voice* (see the entry for **prophetic ethos**), the *priestly voice* (Lessl, 1989; Zagacki, 1996), the *voice of the martyr* (usually implicit in an *argument from sacrifice*), the *confessing voice* (found in some forms of public **apologia** or in **confessional** discourse), the *voice of the teacher,*[4] and the *voice of experience.*[5] In addition to appropriating and speaking in various *types* of voices, advocates often will appropriate specific or individualized voices. The discourse of U.S. presidents provides numerous examples. In both his convention acceptance speech and inaugural address, John F. Kennedy echoed the language—and the voice—of Abraham Lincoln. In his speech to the nation following Kennedy's assassination, Lyndon Johnson crafted not only a *generic hybrid* (the combination of eulogy and deliberation) but also a vocal hybrid by speaking in ways that would remind his audience of the dead president (the vocal hybrid quality of the speech was due, in large part, to the fact that Johnson had one of his speechwriters work with one of Kennedy's on the speech). Ronald Reagan was fond of quoting Franklin Roosevelt (to the chagrin of Democrats); in so doing, he invoked the presence and voice of Roosevelt.[6] In January 1997, Bill Clinton's second inaugural fell on the Martin Luther King, Jr., holiday, and during his "Second Inaugural Address," Clinton recognized the overlapping occasions by appropriating King's voice.[7]

Finally, we should note that advocates will, on occasion, speak or write in an explicitly fictitious or contrived voice. It was a common practice during the 18th and 19th centuries for advocates to publish political essays or pamphlets under pseudonyms, with the pseudonyms not only functioning as fictitious authorial **personas** (e.g., "A Patriot," "A Mechanic," "A Farmer") but also creating distinctive (if contrived) voices for the authors (authors who signed their essays "Vox Populi," which is Latin for "voice of the people," rarely were typical members of the public). The layering of voices in a text could be quite complex. In one of his essays in *The Federalist Papers,* James Madison not only employed the pseudonymic persona of "Publius" but also created another voice, "one of our southern brethren" and let that voice deal with one of the more notorious constitutional compromises—the provision that counted a southern slave as three fifths of a person for determining representation in the House of Representatives (Jasinski, 1997). The practice of pseudonymous authorship is not as prevalent today as it once was (although examples such as George Kennan's famous cold war essay, "The Sources of Soviet Conduct" [published under the name "X" in the July 1947 issue of *Foreign Affairs*], and the more recent political novel/exposé, *Primary Colors* [published anonymously], still can be found), but less elaborate variations still are present in public discourse. For example, in contemporary journalism, we frequently encounter anonymous or pseudonymous "voices" such as the unnamed but quoted "senior administration official" and "state department representative." Occasionally, the anonymous voices of contemporary journalism appear with regularity and, hence, acquire stable pseudonymous "names" (e.g., "Deep Throat" during the Watergate episode). Another example can be found in the use of the stylistic device of *prosopopoeia* or where a speaker or writer creates a fictitious voice and then incorporates what that voice "says" into the text. For example, an advocate supporting American intervention in Bosnia might create the voice of one of the thousands of Bosnians executed as part of the policy of "ethnic cleansing" and then speak through that voice, letting this fictitious dead Bosnian describe the consequences of our inaction (speeches from the dead are a fairly common form of poetic prosopopoeia). King used a weak form of prosopopoeia in his 1967 antiwar speech, "A Time to Break Silence," when he gave voice to the feelings and needs of the common people of Vietnam. In all of its various manifestations, voice creation and appropriation merits the careful attention of rhetorical scholars.

Notes

1. But not all theorists would agree with this broader characterization. Compare Morson and Emerson (1990, pp. 232) and Zulick (1992, pp. 144).

2. See also Booth (1982, pp. 52-53) and Knoeller (1998, pp. 13-22).

3. Foucault (1972) referred to these as speaking or **subject** positions.

4. See, for example, Gustafson's (1992) discussion of Noah Webster as the nation's "schoolmaster."

5. An example would be the former soldier who speaks from experience on the question of war and peace, as John Kerry did during the debate in the U.S. Senate on authorizing force in the Persian Gulf.

6. This example raises the question of whether all direct quotation involves individualized voice appropriation. The answer is probably not. When an advocate includes expert testimony in a speech or an essay, he or she most likely is invoking the voice of expertise rather than the individualized voice of the specific expert who is quoted. Individualized voice appropriation seems limited to cases (e.g., Reagan) in which the advocate wants to invoke the memory or **presence** of the individual being quoted.

7. On Clinton's appropriation of King in a different context, see Murphy (1997). On King's recurrent use of "voice merging," see Miller (1992).

References and Additional Reading

Bakhtin, M. M. (1984). *Problems of Dostoevsky's poetics* (C. Emerson, Trans.). Minneapolis: University of Minnesota Press.

Booth, W. C. (1982). Freedom of interpretation: Bakhtin and the challenge of feminist criticism. *Critical Inquiry, 9,* 45-76.

Foucault, M. (1972). *The archaeology of knowledge* (A. M. Sheridan Smith, Trans.). New York: Pantheon.

Fowler, R. (1989). Polyphony in *Hard Times.* In R. Carter & P. Simpson (Eds.), *Language, discourse, and literature: An introductory reader in discourse stylistics.* London: Unwin Hyman.

Gustafson, T. (1992). *Representative words: Politics, literature, and the American language, 1776-1865.* Cambridge, UK: Cambridge University Press.

Jasinski, J. (1997). Heteroglossia, polyphony, and *The Federalist Papers. Rhetoric Society Quarterly, 27,* 23-46.

Knoeller, C. (1998). *Voicing ourselves: Whose words we use when we talk about books.* Albany: State University of New York Press.

Lessl, T. M. (1989). The priestly voice. *Quarterly Journal of Speech, 75,* 183-197.

Miller, K. D. (1992). *Voice of deliverance: The language of Martin Luther King, Jr. and its sources.* New York: Free Press.

Morson, G. S., & Emerson, C. (1990). *Mikhail Bakhtin: Creation of a prosaics.* Stanford, CA: Stanford University Press.

Murphy, J. M. (1997). Inventing authority: Bill Clinton, Martin Luther King, Jr., and the orchestration of rhetorical traditions. *Quarterly Journal of Speech, 83,* 71-89.

Wertsch, J. V. (1991). *Voices of the mind: A sociocultural approach to mediated action.* Cambridge, MA: Harvard University Press.

Zagacki, K. S. (1996). The priestly voice of neoconservatism. *Western Journal of Communication, 60,* 168-187.

Zulick, M. D. (1992). The agon of Jeremiah: On the dialogic invention of prophetic ethos. *Quarterly Journal of Speech, 78,* 125-148.

POLYSEMY

Consider the following hypothetical situation. The president of the United States delivers a speech that argues for new and more stringent controls on both the advertising and sales of tobacco products. Mass media pundits describe the speech as a political ploy designed to boost the president's sagging approval ratings. The tobacco lobby protests the president's implication that cigarette manufacturers are vultures that prey on the nation's youth. The White House press secretary replies that the president is simply trying to do what is best for the nation and its young people.

In this situation, whose interpretation of the president's speech is correct? What did the speech *really* mean? Who controlled the meaning of the speech? Some scholars (e.g., Hirsch, 1967) have maintained that a text has only one correct meaning and that it is the job of critics or interpreters to locate it. The idea that a text possesses one and only one meaning—that it is *monosemic*—has been challenged over the past few decades. More and more, scholars are focusing on textual **ambiguity,** *indeterminacy,* or **polysemy** to draw attention to the existence of multiple meanings in a text. Rather than conceptualizing meaning as singular and as something residing "in" the text, many scholars argue that a text's meaning emerges through a contested process of interpretation and **argument** (Mailloux, 1989). The president's speech might very well be both a valiant effort to protect the health of the nation's youth *and* an act of self-interested political preservation.

In its most rudimentary sense, polysemy simply means multiple meanings; the term comes from the prefix *poly* (meaning many or several) and the Greek term *sema* (meaning sign). As Gaonkar (1989) observed, "The idea of polysemy . . . is making its way into the lexicon of rhetorical criticism" (p. 271). In contemporary critical scholarship, discussions of polysemy branch out in at least two different but interrelated directions.[1] First, polysemy is used as a way of characterizing a basic feature of all **texts.** According to Fiske (1986), polysemy refers to the "unresolved contradictions" (p. 392), the "gaps" (p. 398), or the "fissures" (p. 402) that mark texts, especially texts that aim to be popular. Every society is marked by struggles among its various subcultures (e.g., class, gender, ethnic), and Fiske argued that these struggles are inscribed in every social text; "the structure of meanings in a text is a miniaturization of the structure of subcultures in society" (p. 392). In Fiske's view, a text has a **representational** or *mimetic* function, but because what is being represented (the society) is itself fractured and divided, the text will contain fractures and divisions. These fissures and gaps make the text unstable, thereby generating considerable "semiotic excess" (p. 403) or "meaning potential" (p. 394). Fiske, following the lead of the semiotician Umberto Eco, insisted that a text is fundamentally "open" (p. 392). Authors, advocates, or speakers usually will try to limit the semiotic play of a text or narrow its meaning potential into a "preferred reading" (p. 400). In the hypothetical example, for example, the president would prefer that the speech be read as a valiant effort at health promotion. But authors, advocates, or speakers cannot completely control the reading process. Fiske wrote that authorial authority "attempts to impose itself but is met with a variety of variously successful strategies of resistance or modification that change, subvert, or reject the authoritatively proposed meanings" (p. 394). Fiske's polysemic conceptualization of the text raises a fundamental challenge to those who argue that mainstream texts (e.g., political discourse, television shows) always perpetuate a **hegemonic** dominant **ideology.**

In the last passage from Fiske's (1986) essay, we saw the emergence of the second branch of thinking associated with the concept of polysemy. The concept not only refers to certain characteristics of a text (e.g., semantic excess, openness, fissures) but also gestures in the direction of the capacity of readers to generate "polysemic readings" (p. 394). The polysemic nature of the text is closely associated with a reconceptualization of the **audience.** As Fiske made clear, audience members are not dupes, nor are they "powerless" (p. 399). The openness of the polysemic text enables the subversive practice of *resistant reading* (see also Weiler, 1989). Resistant readers reject the author's effort to promote a preferred reading and exploit the semiotic excess of the text. The result is a reading of the text that (a) undermines its ability to perpetuate the dominant ideology and/or (b) uses the text to promote practices and values that run counter to those endorsed by the dominant culture.

It should be noted that scholars adopt different approaches to the process of resistant reading. For Fiske, it is the polysemic openness of the text that makes resistant reading possible. For Judith Fetterly, an early promoter of the concept, resistant readers confront "a closed system [that] cannot be opened up from within but only from without. It must be entered into from a point of view which questions its values and assumptions and which has its investment in making available to consciousness precisely that which the literature wishes to keep hidden" (Fetterly, 1978, p. xx). In Fetterly's view, resistant reading emerges from a confrontation with a closed text, not an open one. Gaonkar

(1993) spoke to this issue when he wrote, "If language is fundamentally and ineradicably polysemic, then language itself furnishes the last line of defense against the historically grounded attempt at linguistic closure. . . . Polysemy is [then] an ally of the oppressed" (p. 153). But Gaonkar noted that this view might be "unduly optimistic" (see also Condit, 1989). Gaonkar (1993) continued,

> The proponents of CR [**critical rhetoric**] might find it profitable [to] think of the ideological sign . . . in terms of heteroglossia rather than polysemy. While polysemy is susceptible to being reduced to no more than a "plurality of meanings," heteroglossia retains its focus on the conflictual and contingent character of [the] ideological sign. (p. 153)

Condit (1989) raised similar questions about the efficacy of polysemy as an explanatory concept (see also Cloud, 1992; Sloop, 1994). Whereas Fiske (1986) qualified his stance by stating that "the television text is not anarchically open" (p. 392), Condit (1989) apparently found this to be insufficient. Her position was that audience-oriented scholarship overstates its case regarding the openness of the text to multiple readings and understates the "substantial limits to the polysemic potential of texts and decodings" (p. 105).[2] Condit suggested that scholars distinguish between polysemy and *polyvalence.* She wrote,

> Polyvalence occurs when audience members share understandings of the denotations of a text but disagree about the valuation of those denotations to such a degree that they produce notably different interpretations [of the text]. In this case, it is not a multiplicity or instability of textual meanings but rather a difference in audience evaluations of shared denotations that best accounts for [divergent interpretations of a text]. (p. 106)[3]

Condit did not deny that some texts are open or "internally polysemous" (p. 108); rather, she questioned whether this textual phenomenon is as ubiquitous as some suggest.

In the works of scholars such as Fiske and McKerrow, the concept of polysemy encourages a valorization of discursive openness; texts that allow for multiple and resistant readings can be considered as superior to (or at least more interesting than) those that are "closed." Rowland and Strain (1994) suggested that radically polysemous texts such as the Spike Lee film, *Do the Right Thing,* are valuable because they are able to "enact contradictory truths" (p. 217) through a both/and logic that "may provide symbolic tools for minimizing social conflict" (p. 215). Radical polysemy, in Rowland and Strain's formulation, is the modern, frequently **narrative** equivalent of the ancient sophistic concept of *dissoi logoi* or the discursive technique of constructing two opposed but equally compelling arguments for a disputed question (Kerferd, 1981). The textual play and openness that Fiske, McKerrow, Rowland and Strain, and many others locate and celebrate can function as an important antidote to cultural domination. But rhetorical scholars also might ponder the implications of this position.[4] The valorization of openness seems to fosters a disdain for any type of pragmatic or interpretive closure; the challenge seems to be to keep every situation or text open to new readings. But the practice of advocacy (whether pragmatic or interpretive) seeks at least temporary closure or **local stability.** In a **rhetorical situation,** advocates cannot endlessly defer choice so as to keep things open; at some point, a choice must be made.[5] The issue that rhetorical scholars might need to confront more directly is whether a commitment to the concept of polysemy and textual openness frustrates the traditional connection between rhetoric and public advocacy.

Notes

1. Ceccarelli (1998) identified three distinct strands of thought in rhetorical criticism: resistive reading, strategic ambiguity, and hermeneutic depth.

2. See also Raymond Williams' (1977) discussion of "the finite but significant openness" in cultural texts.

3. Compare Condit's (1989) discussion of polysemy and polyvalence and Hirsch's (1967) account of the difference between "meaning" and "significance."

4. The problems of valorizing polysemy also were noted by Ceccarelli (1998).

5. But it should be acknowledged that our recognition of the moment of choice is itself usually a discursive accomplishment.

References and Additional Reading

Ceccarelli, L. (1998). Polysemy: Multiple meanings in rhetorical criticism. *Quarterly Journal of Speech, 84,* 395-415.

Cloud, D. (1992). The limits of interpretation: Ambivalence and the stereotype in *Spenser: For Hire. Critical Studies in Mass Communication, 9,* 311-324.

Condit, C. M. (1989). The rhetorical limits of polysemy. *Critical Studies in Mass Communication, 6,* 103-122.

Fetterley, J. (1978). *The resisting reader: A feminist approach to American fiction.* Bloomington: Indiana University Press.

Fiske, J. (1986). Television: Polysemy and popularity. *Critical Studies in Mass Communication, 3,* 391-408.

Fiske, J. (1987). *Television culture.* London: Metheun.

Gaonkar, D. P. (1989). The oratorical text: The enigma of arrival. In M. C. Leff & F. J. Kauffeld (Eds.), *Texts in context: Critical dialogues on significant episodes in American political rhetoric.* Davis, CA: Hermagoras Press.

Gaonkar, D. P. (1993). Performing with fragments: Reflections on critical rhetoric. In R. E. McKerrow (Ed.), *Argument and the postmodern challenge: Proceedings of the Eighth SCA/AFA Conference on Argumentation.* Annandale, VA: Speech Communication Association.

Hirsch, E. D., Jr. (1967). *Validity in interpretation.* New Haven, CT: Yale University Press.

Kerferd, G. B. (1981). *The sophistic movement.* New York: Cambridge University Press.

Mailloux, S. (1989). *Rhetorical power.* Ithaca, NY: Cornell University Press.

McKerrow, R. E. (1989). Critical rhetoric: Theory and praxis. *Communication Monographs, 56,* 91-111.

Rowland, R. C., & Strain, R. (1994). Social function, polysemy, and narrative-dramatic form: A case study of *Do the Right Thing. Communication Quarterly, 42,* 213-228.

Sloop, J. M. (1994). "Apology made to whoever pleases": Cultural discipline and the grounds of interpretation. *Communication Quarterly, 42,* 345-362.

Solomon, M. (1993). The things we study: Texts and their interactions. *Communication Monographs, 60,* 62-68.

Solomon, M. M., & McMullen, W. J. (1991). *Places in the Heart:* The rhetorical force of an open text. *Western Journal of Speech Communication, 55,* 339-353.

Weiler, M. (1989). Polysemy and pluralism: The habit of oppositional reading. In B. E. Gronbeck (Ed.), *Spheres of argument: Proceedings of the Sixth SCA/AFA Conference on Argumentation.* Annandale, VA: Speech Communication Association.

Williams, R. (1977). *Marxism and literature.* Oxford, UK: Oxford University Press.

POWER

Power has been a topic for philosophers and social theorists since antiquity. Many contemporary social theorists would agree with Giddens's (1984) remark that power is one of the "primary concepts" in social theory (p. 283) or with Wartenberg's (1990) comment that power has a "central role in social theory" (p. 4). Although power generally is accorded a place on the contemporary intellectual agenda in the humanities and social sciences, its exact nature remains a matter of some dispute. Ball (1988), for example, noted that power has been at the center of a "continuing conceptual controversy" (p. 80) for some time. Two clusters of questions organize the present discussion of power. First, how has power been conceptualized or theorized during the past 40 or so years? How has the debate about the nature of power evolved? What are the prime issues at stake in the debate? Second, why should rhetorical scholars be concerned with the issue of power? How have rhetorical scholars appropriated work on the issue of power for their critical projects? How have those projects contributed to its explication?

Reflection on the nature of power has emerged from many sources. We can begin this general summary of the way in which power has been conceptualized by reviewing the "faces" of power debate that developed largely within the academic field of political science beginning during the 1950s (for overviews of this debate, see Ball, 1988; Isaac, 1987; Wartenberg, 1990). Wartenberg (1990) suggested that "the power debate is a particular discussion of social power that stems from certain criticisms of C. Wright Mills's seminal work, *The Power Elite*" (p. 53). Mills's (1956) neo-Marxist thesis, put simply, was that a small group of individuals occupy key political and economic positions in American society that grant them considerable power to make decisions that will affect the lives of average Americans.[1] Numerous scholars responded to Mills's analysis, and these responses developed two interrelated points. First, power in America is distributed more widely than Mills recognized. Second, Mills's conceptualization of power was flawed. In a number of influential essays, Robert Dahl (e.g., Dahl, 1957, 1968) developed what often is referred to as a "behavioral" model of power (see also Ball, 1988; Wartenberg, 1990).

Dahl (1957) offered what he acknowledged is an "intuitive" definition of power: "A has power over B to the extent that he [sic] can get B to do something that B would not otherwise do" (pp. 202-203). Three important points are embedded in this rather simple definition. First, power is primarily a relational phenomenon; it exists or is manifest in particular relationships between individuals (e.g., a teacher and a student), between groups (e.g., men and women), or between an individual and a group (e.g., a police officer and a group of inner-city Latinos). Second, a power relationship is something that is explicit and observable (it can, therefore, be studied in "behavioral" terms). Ball (1988) summarized Dahl's position in this way: "Thus an exercise of power can be said to have occurred only if A makes an *observable* attempt to cause B to do what A intends but what B would not otherwise do" (p. 88, emphasis added). Third, a power relation is essentially oppressive in that one person (or group) is able to control the will or decision-making capacity of another person or group. The paradigmatic instance of a power relationship for Dahl, according to Ball, is that between a police officer and a motorist, and the discursive mechanism through which power is exercised is the *speech act* of the *command.*

But is the command that is obeyed the only, or the most common, way in which power is exercised? This question is at the center of Bachrach and Baratz's (1962) essay, "Two Faces of Power" (see also Bachrach & Baratz, 1970). Bachrach and Baratz (1962) maintained that Dahl's conceptualization is defective because his model "takes no account of the fact that power may be, and often is, exercised by confining the scope of decision-making to relatively 'safe' issues" (p. 948). They continued,

> Of course power is exercised when A participates in the making of decisions that affect B. But power is also exercised when A devotes his [sic] energies to creating reinforcing social and political values and institutional practices that limit the scope of the political process to public consideration of only those issues which are comparatively innocuous to A. (p. 948)

According to Dahl, power exists in a direct relationship of one person or group over another. Bachrach and Baratz countered that power can exist when one person or group shapes the political agenda and eliminates issues or topics that might threaten that person's or group's interests or desires. Consider the case of Bill Clinton's health care reform plan. Did the insurance industry exert any power on the issue? Bachrach and Baratz suggested that Dahl's model allows power to exist only if we can clearly observe A (the insurance industry) dictating or commanding the behavior of B (Congress). Absent that direct observation, we cannot conclude that a power relationship was manifest in the situation. But Bachrach and Baratz suggested that perhaps power also works indirectly. Wartenberg (1990) summarized their view as follows: "An agent can also exercise power, according to Bachrach and Baratz, by keeping something from happening—for example, by keeping an issue that affects the welfare of the other agent from coming up for political decision" (p. 57). Issues can be suppressed through explicit actions as well as through implicit or unconscious behavior. Bachrach and Baratz's (1962) basic point was as follows: "To the extent that a person or group—consciously or unconsciously—creates or reinforces barriers to the public airing of policy conflicts, that person or group has power" (p. 949). So, the fact that Clinton's health care proposal never came up for a decision might be a sign that power was at work in the situation. The insurance industry, through a variety of discursive forms (e.g., the famous "Harry and Louise" television commercials), helped to remove health care from the arena of public deliberation. And this issue is a rather public instance of non-decisions as a medium of power; for every case like health care, there are countless examples of power relationships coming into existence as potential public issues are removed from the public *agenda.*[2]

Bachrach and Baratz's central idea—that power can be manifest in "non-decisions" (Wartenberg, 1990, p. 57) or through the manipulation of the public agenda, is an important yet ultimately minor modification of Dahl's behavioral model of power. That appears to be the argument of Lukes (1974) in his monograph *Power.* Lukes's objective in this work was to introduce a third dimension or "face" to the idea of power. One of the major problems that Lukes found in Bachrach and Baratz's second face of power is its continued "association of power with actual, observable conflict. . . . This insistence on actual conflict as essential to power will not do, for at least two reasons" (pp. 22-23). The first (and less important) reason is that it is inconsistent with Bachrach and Baratz's analysis (p. 23). But the second (and more important) reason is that such a view unnecessarily restricts our understanding of power because of its behaviorist assumptions. Lukes maintained,

> To put the matter sharply, A may exercise power over B by getting him [sic] to do what he does not want to do, but he also exercises power over him by influencing, shaping, or determining his very wants. Indeed, is it not the supreme exercise of power to get another or others to have the desires you want them to have—that is, to secure their compliance by controlling their thoughts and desires? . . . The trouble seems to be that both Bachrach and Baratz and the pluralists [e.g., Dahl] suppose that because power, as they conceptualize it, only shows up in cases of actual conflict, it follows that actual conflict is necessary to power. But this is to ignore the crucial point that the most effective and insidious use of power is to prevent such conflicts from arising in the first place. (p. 23)

Lukes (1974) made a second related critique of Bachrach and Baratz. In their view "non-decision-making power only exists where there are grievances which are denied entry into the political process. . . . If the observer can uncover no grievances, then he [sic] must assume there is a 'genuine' consensus on the prevailing allocation of values" (p. 24). Again, Lukes found this approach to power to be unsatisfactory and developed his critique in the form of a **rhetorical question:**

> Is it not the supreme and most insidious exercise of power to prevent people, to whatever degree, from having grievances by shaping their perceptions, cognitions, and preferences in such a way that they accept their role in the existing order of things, either because they can see or imagine no alternative to it, or because they see it as natural and unchangeable, or because they value it as divinely ordained and beneficial? (p. 24)

Lukes's third face or dimension of power introduced the issues of **ideology** and interests (see also Isaac, 1987). Whenever people fail to recognize their own objective interests (due to factors such as ideological **mystification**), power is at work. Lukes (1974) wrote, "A exercises power over B when A affects B in a manner contrary to B's interests" (p. 34). As Wartenberg (1990) observed, "Central to

Lukes's concern are exercises of power in which the subordinate agent does not even recognize the fact that power has been exercised over her [sic]" (p. 60). Clearly, Lukes's neo-Marxist approach expanded the idea of power well beyond Dahl's more restrictive liberal account of explicit commands and acquiescent responses.

An effort to expand our understanding of power can develop along two different lines. First, we can expand our understanding of *who* wields power. Second, we can expand our understanding of *how* power operates. Let us briefly consider an example of each. First, let us consider the issue of who wields power. Republican Representative J. C. Watts was selected by his party to respond to Clinton's "State of the Union" address in January 1997. In his speech, Watts raised a number of themes that have helped the Republican party to wrest control of Congress away from the Democrats. One of those has to do with the way in which power is allocated in America. According to Watts, the Republicans' mission was to "limit the claims and demands of Washington—to limit its call for more power, more authority, and more taxes. Our mission is to return power to your home, to where mothers and fathers can exercise it according to their beliefs." Watts's comments are interesting because they illustrate a tendency to *narrow* our thinking about who wields power, a tendency that was criticized by scholars such as Lukes. Watts framed the subject of power in America *disjunctively;* power either resides "in Washington" or resides in individual families "where mothers and fathers can exercise it." But is this an adequate account of *who* exercises power in contemporary America? Probably not given that it fails to mention one of the more powerful forces in society—the corporate sector. When a corporation decides that downsizing is in its interests, the lives of individuals and entire communities can be radically altered. But an excessively narrow focus on "political" power obscures the way in which corporations dominate contemporary life (e.g., when a corporation exacts concessions from a union after threatening to close down a plant and move its operations to another country). In fact, Watts's disjunctive depiction of power was itself an instance of power in both Bachrach and Baratz's and Lukes's terms. Watts's disjunction removed corporate power from public view in a way that, in Bachrach and Baratz's (1962) terms, "reinforces barriers to the public airing of policy conflicts" (p. 949).

Just as an expanded sense of who exercises power helps us to appreciate certain elements in Watts's appeal, we also can focus on an expanded sense of *how* power is actualized. Consider the dilemma facing southern slaveholders in Congress during the 1830s as abolitionists submitted petition after petition requesting the elimination of slavery in the District of Columbia. How should they respond? Some southerners, such as John C. Calhoun in the Senate and James Henry Hammond in the House of Representatives, advocated the complete unqualified rejection of not only the substance but also the form of the petitions; Congress should not even "receive" the petitions and, instead, should firmly and clearly slam the door in the faces of the abolitionists and their sympathizers. In the opinion of Calhoun and Hammond, Congress should do whatever it could to repress and eradicate abolitionist sentiment including suppressing free speech and the public mail (for a recent account of this episode in American history, see Miller, 1996). Henry Clay of Kentucky was a more moderate southerner, a slaveholder who believed that slavery was wrong (a tension that could be found in many southern political leaders including Thomas Jefferson). Clay agreed with Calhoun that abolitionist agitation was dangerous and that acting in a way that would lead to its decline was in the best interests of the nation. The question, for Clay, was what method of action would be best for stamping out abolitionism. Should he support Calhoun's hardline stance, or was there a different way that power over the abolitionists might be exercised? Clay opted to oppose Calhoun and advocate a "softer" approach to the problem. Clay concluded a speech in the Senate in January 1838 with an *analogy.* "In private life, if a wife pouts, and frets, and scolds," how should the husband respond? Clay considered the husband's options (a form of *residue* argument) and rejected those that called for harshness or threats. Instead, Clay urged the husband to "approach the lady with kind and conciliatory language and apply those natural and more agreeable remedies, which never fail to restore domestic harmony." Did Clay suggest that the husband give up his power and give in to the demands of his wife? Of course not. Nor did Clay accept any of the abolitionists' proposals about banning the interstate slave trade or outlawing slavery in the District of Columbia. What Clay sensed was that the husband could exercise his power over his wife less harshly or aggressively; he could say a few sweet things, calm her down, and then get back to living his life the way in which he wanted. Congress, Clay reasoned, could treat the abolitionists the same way. But a vigorous exercise of power only made it likely that Congress would create martyrs for subsequent abolitionist exploitation. Power in the form of a bare fist or a gloved hand (to use a different analogy)—that was the way in which Clay saw the dispute with Calhoun. Clay's perception of the situation illustrates that power can be exercised in different ways.

Many of the nuances of the "faces of power" debate have been left out of this general account (they are treated in detail in the secondary sources cited earlier). Although different in crucial respects, the liberal perspectives of Dahl and Bachrach and Baratz and the neo-Marxist approach of Lukes are nevertheless linked in some important ways (these links are discussed in greater detail by Wartenberg, 1990, pp. 63-69). Perhaps the most important similarity in their works is the shared conceptualization of power as "power-over" or power as a source of constraint and/or restraint.[3] Power is presented as a type of "necessary evil"; it must exist to create social order, but it must be watched carefully because its existence threatens human autonomy. This depiction of power suggests the existence of two different realms or zones of human action: one that is completely outside of or exempt from the effects of power (a zone protected by "privacy rights" or other legal barriers to power) and one in which individuals may be subjected to power. Specific relations or instantiations of power in the zone where it is allowed are not automatically granted or accepted; efforts to exercise power can and should be evaluated. There is, then, an important normative dimension in the works of Dahl, Bachrach and Baratz, and Lukes; they suggest that distinguishing between legitimate (sanctioned by law) and illegitimate (usurped) instances of power is a crucial aspect of social and political critique.

This basically negative account of power—power as "power-over" others—informs a wide range of studies that seek to establish clearer distinctions among the various manifestations of power such as domination (Airaksinen, 1992), oppression (Young, 1992), coercion, force, and influence and manipulation (Lukes, 1974; Wartenberg, 1990). Such typologies and sub-typologies of power try to shed additional light on the specific ways in which power is exercised in the contemporary world.

As a matter of classification, we might label all of the various negative accounts of power (the sense of power as power-over that runs from Mills and Dahl through Lukes) as modern so as to distinguish them from two other approaches to defining the nature of power. The first alternative, articulated in the works of philosopher Hannah Arendt, sometimes is referred to as a "communication" or "communicative" (Ball, 1988; Habermas, 1977) or "consensual" (Wartenberg, 1990) theory of power, but Arendt's project also might be thought of as an effort to recover important elements of a premodern understanding of power. The second alternative, developed at some length in the works of historian and philosopher Michel Foucault, rejects the "repressive hypothesis" and "force model" that undergirds the modernist idea of power-over and, hence, might be considered as a postmodern account of power.

Arendt also found the modernist account of power to be defective. In her essay, "On Violence," Arendt (1972) remarked, "If we turn to discussions of the phenomenon of power, we soon find that there exists a consensus among political theorists from left to right to the effect that violence is nothing more than the most flagrant manifestation of power" (p. 134). Arendt argued that this view of power is predicated on a "command-obedience relationship" or model (p. 139); power exists and is exercised through the performance and execution of commands. She argued that this understanding of power leads to a particular understanding of politics and public affairs—a reduction of "public affairs to the business of dominion" or domination where the "most crucial political issue is . . . the question of who rules whom?" (pp. 142-143).

But Arendt (1972) observed that "there exists another tradition and another vocabulary" for conceptualizing power and its role in political affairs. Turning to the era of classical Greece and Rome, Arendt argued that the political thinkers and citizens of these worlds possessed "a concept of power and law whose essence did not rely on the command-obedience relationship and which did not identify power and rule or law and command" (p. 139). What exactly was entailed in this premodern and noncoercive conceptualization of power, particularly political power? (Wartenberg [1990] argued that Arendt's account of power is limited to the realm of political affairs and does not offer a general theory of "social power.") Arendt (1972) began her reconstruction by examining the etymology of the word. The term *power* is derived from the French *pouvoir,* which stems from the Latin *potentia* (pp. 142-143; see also Arendt, 1959, p. 179; Ball, 1988, p. 81). Power needs to be understood as a form of potentiality or as a capacity or ability to do something. But power is a rather unique form of potentiality.

Arendt (1972) provided a brief summary of her understanding of power in "On Violence." She wrote that power

> corresponds to the human ability not just to act but to act in concert. Power is never the property of an individual; it belongs to a group and remains in existence only so long as the group keeps together. When we say of somebody that he [sic] is "in power," we actually refer to his being empowered by a certain number of people to act in their name. The moment the group, from which the power originated to begin with . . . , disappears, "his power" also vanishes. (p. 143)

Elsewhere, Arendt (1959) wrote,

> Power springs up between men [sic] when they act together and vanishes the moment they disperse. . . . The only indispensable material factor in the generation of power is the living together of people. Only where men live so close together that the potentialities of action are always present can power remain with them. (pp. 179-180)

Arendt's paradigmatic instance of political power was radically different from the police officer issuing a command. A group of people living and acting together, such as in the ancient Greek city-states through the mechanism of the *polis,* was her conceptualization of the essence of power.

Some key elements in Arendt's account of power include the following. First, power is not the possession or "property" of an individual; it belongs to the group that brings it into existence. Second, power is not primarily a relationship of one person or group with another; it is a capacity or potential that resides within a group (Lukes, 1974, p. 31). Third, power is not primarily an instrument that can be used to dominate a specific group or an entire people (power-over); it is a (potential) resource (power-to) that a group brings into existence to protect its members and expand the realm of action (thereby enhancing freedom and liberty). Fourth, power is not manifested discursively in the command or its derivatives (e.g., threats) or in physical force or violence; it emerges in cooperative human activity and is manifested through mechanisms that harness public consent (e.g., public opinion, voting) or dissent (ranging from passive resistance to revolt). Fifth, power is not governed by the process of inertia (where something that is brought into existence continues to exist unless overt action is taken against it); it continues to exist only so long as people remain unified and act together. For Arendt, power and popular action are mutually constitutive. Arendt (1959) wrote, "What keeps people together after the fleeting moment of action has passed (what we today call 'organization') and what, at the same time, they keep alive through remaining together is power" (p. 180). Sixth, power should not be equated with force, strength, manipulation, coercion, or any of the other processes that theorists have treated as variations of it; true power[4] is a positive force in human life.

Arendt's conceptualization of power has been dismissed by many social scientists and political theorists as rather idiosyncratic and anachronistic (for a review of the critiques, see Wartenberg, 1990). In a generally sympathetic discussion, Habermas (1977) faulted Arendt for attempting to resurrect "an Aristotelian theory of action" (p. 15). Luban (1979) developed a vigorous defense of Arendt's understanding of power, action, and communication against Habermas's critique. Luban provided a useful summary (Figure P.2) that compared their respective views on a number of key issues (p. 93). For Luban, Arendt's view of power merits attention as (at the very least) a normative model given its underlying vision of radical democracy founded in the process of political debate.

Like Arendt, Foucault rejected the modernist account of power. In an interview published in *Power/Knowledge*, Foucault (1980) acknowledged that in his earliest works he

> accepted the traditional conception of power as an essentially judicial mechanism, as that which lays down the law, which prohibits, which refuses, and which has a whole range of negative effects: exclusion, rejection, denial, obstruction, occultation, etc. Now I believe that conception to be inadequate. (p. 183)

What Foucault rejected is a "purely negative conception of power" (p. 184) that mirrors Arendt's sense of the command-obedience model. But Foucault did not turn, as Arendt did, to the classical Greek polis and the Aristotelian idea of praxis for a model of a different type of power; instead, Foucault confronted the phenomenon of the contemporary prison. He stated,

> The case of the penal system convinced me that the question of power needed to be formulated not so much in terms of justice as in those of technology, of tactics and strategy, and it was this substitution for a judicial and negative grid of a technical and strategic one that I tried to effect in *Discipline and Punish* [and other recent works]. (p. 184)

What exactly did Foucault have in mind when he discussed power in terms of technology and strategy?

Foucault's extensive discussions on the topic of power have attracted considerable attention and are difficult to summarize (among the relevant secondary literature, see Digester, 1992; Dreyfus and Rabinow, 1983; Fraser, 1989; Harstock, 1990; Honneth, 1991; Hoy, 1986; McCarthy, 1990; Rouse, 1994; Said, 1986; see also Ball, 1988; Wartenberg, 1990; Wolin, 1988). Foucault's position inhabits a type of precarious middle ground between the negative sense of power-over and Arendt's positive reconstruction of power as power-to. Foucault (1983) made this point when he considered the role of "violence" and "consent" in the "bringing into play of power relations." He stated that "the use of violence" and the "obtaining of consent" are not excluded from the field of power; "no doubt the exercise of power can never do without one or the other, often both at the same time. But even though consensus and violence are the instruments or the results, they do not constitute the principle or the basic nature of power" (p. 220). So, what is the principle or the basic nature of power according to Foucault?

	Habermas	Arendt
Concept of communication	dialogue	political debate
Relationship of science and politics	process of translation	unbridgeable gap
Role of truth in politics	guarantees rationality	invites tyranny
Civic participation as communication	idealized dialogue that leads to a rational consensus	political debate that produces persuasion amidst plurality

Figure P.2. Habermas and Arendt on Power

For Foucault, power is not primarily negative repression or positive empowerment; it is a normatively neutral mechanism or technology of production. Foucault (1980) argued that power "needs to be considered as a productive network which runs through the whole social body, much more than as a negative instance whose function is repression" (p. 119). He suggested that power not only functions as a negative constraint but (in a manner somewhat similar to that of Arendt) also can be a positive or enabling force.[5] In Foucault's view, power is a type of ligature that binds every element of the social structure (from the nation-state to the various public and private institutions with which we interact and in which we exist); power has worked itself into all of the "cracks" and "joints" of the social structure and, in so doing, effectively holds the structure, as well as the humans who inhabit it, together. Foucault suggested that power is the dynamic force in human society.

Before turning our attention to the question of *what* power produces and other important implications of Foucault's shift to a postmodern productive model, we still need to probe *how* productive power comes into existence. Foucault suggested that productive power exists as a process of structuring human action; wherever human actions are organized and structured, power is at work. Foucault (1983) wrote that power

> is a total structure of actions brought to bear upon possible actions; it incites, it in-

> duces, it seduces, it makes easier or more difficult; in the extreme, it constrains or forbids absolutely; it is nevertheless always a way of acting upon an acting subject or acting subjects by virtue of their acting or being capable of action. A set of actions upon other actions. . . . The exercise of power consists in guiding the possibility of conduct and putting in order the possible outcomes. . . . The exercise of power [is] a mode of action upon the actions of others. (pp. 220-221)

One of the first implications of Foucault's productive account of power is that it dismantled the modernist opposition between freedom and power. There is no zone or realm of action free of power; as Fraser (1989) put it, "Power is everywhere" (p. 26). Foucault (1983) replaced the modernist *disjunction*[6] with a sense of the "more complicated interplay" between freedom and power. Foucault wrote, "There is no face-to-face confrontation of power and freedom which is mutually exclusive [because] freedom must exist for power to be exerted" (p. 221). Power and freedom exist in a state of "permanent provocation" (p. 220). No structure, however complete, can fully eradicate the possibility of resistance.

Foucault's works move in two different, but not necessarily antagonistic, directions with respect to the question of what power produces. On the one hand, power produces **subjects** through "the mechanisms of subjection" (Foucault, 1980, p. 97; 1983, p. 213; see also Butler, 1997). At the beginning of his essay, "The Subject and Power," Foucault (1983) noted that his primary intellectual "objective . . . has been to create a history of the different modes by which, in our culture, human beings are made into subjects" (p. 208). His interest in power stemmed from this goal. Later in the essay, he discussed

> a form of power which makes individuals subjects. . . . This form of power applies itself to immediate everyday life which categorizes the individual, marks him [sic] by his own individuality, attaches him to his own identity, [and] imposes a law of truth on him which he must recognize and which others have to recognize in him. (p. 212)

A variety of mechanisms or technologies have emerged to carry out the process of subjection. In very broad terms, Foucault (1980) described the way in which various disciplines and institutions (e.g., medical, mental health, criminal justice) and the practices they have spawned have created a "*society of normali[z]ation*" (p. 107). The creation and dissemination of various models and standards that specify what is "normal" (in behavior, physical appearance, fashion, etc.) function as mechanisms of subjection; these models and standards are structures that shape (both enabling and constraining) subsequent conduct. A second important mechanism or technology of subjection is surveillance. Dreyfus and Rabinow (1983) observed, "The act of looking over and being looked over will be a central means by which individuals are linked together in a disciplinary space. . . . On a broad scale, the model of the military camp provided control through hierarchy and observation" (pp. 156-157). Individuals' possibilities for action, as well as their sense of who they are, will be structured when they are the subject of the various technologies of surveillance. Another important mechanism or technology of subjection is the **confessional,** a technology that is, in essence, internalized surveillance. Individual subjectivity is structured as individuals are taught and encouraged to keep themselves under surveillance and to confess their "sins."[7]

On the other hand, power also is implicated in the production of knowledge and truth. Foucault's account of the relationship between power and knowledge and/or truth dismantled another modernist disjunction. Truth and knowledge do not stand opposed to power, and power does not suppress the truth. Truth and/or knowledge is an effect of power, and power is brought into existence by way of the production of knowledge. Foucault (1980) remarked, "What makes power hold good, what makes it accepted, is simply the fact that it doesn't only weigh on us as a force that says no, but it traverses and produces things, it induces pleasure, *forms knowledge,* [and] produces discourse" (p. 119, emphasis added). He continued,

> The important thing here . . . is that truth isn't outside power or lacking in power; contrary to a myth whose history and functions would repay further study, truth isn't the reward of free spirits, the child of protracted solitude, or the privilege of those who have succeeded in liberating themselves. Truth is a thing of this world; it is produced only by virtue of multiple forms of constraint. And it induces regular effects of power. (p. 131)

And finally, " 'Truth' is linked in a circular relation with systems of power which produce and sustain it and to effects of power which it induces and which extend it" (p. 133; see also Dreyfus & Rabinow, 1983).

Although the ideas of truth and knowledge (and their relationship to power) can be intimidating, Foucault's essential point might be rather simple. That point is this: No discourse (e.g., text, utterance) is ever "pure"—outside of or disconnected from the workings of power. For example, an utterance that purports to express the "truth" about something or that advances a knowledge claim is not, as Foucault put it, "outside power." The knowledge or truth claims advanced by economists, psychologists, criminologists, or authorized representatives of any discipline (the process of disciplinary authorization is itself part of the enveloping network of power relations operating in a society) cannot erase or remove all of the marks of the world, and the narrower situation, in which it was produced. The claims of experts and specialists always are implicated in the concrete practices of the world; they serve interests and pursue objectives beyond the "disinterested" and "objective" quest for truth and knowledge (the work of scientists funded by the tobacco industry probably is an extreme example of this phenomenon). Foucault's point, it seems, was not to automatically reject the claims of experts and specialists but rather to analyze their utterances more carefully and develop ways of better uncovering the way in which power and knowledge interact in **epistemic** discourse.[8]

The corollary of the preceding point also would seem to be true; if no epistemic utterance can escape the taint of power, then no utterance attempting to exercise or wield power is completely devoid of epistemic significance (or, in Habermas's terminology, of raising claims to validity).[9] As Foucault (1979) observed, "There is no power relation without the correlative constitution of a field of knowledge, nor [is there] any knowledge that does not presuppose and constitute at the same time power relations" (p. 27). Even the command, that paradigmatic example of repressive power, raises claims of intelligibility, sincerity, and truth (Habermas, 1979). Every utterance is implicated in what Foucault (1980) termed a " 'regime' of truth"—"a system of ordered procedures for the production, regulation, distribution, circulation, and operation of statements" (p. 133).[10] Every utterance functions as one more node in the network of power that regulates truth and knowledge. Foucault not only dismantled the traditional opposition between freedom and power, he also challenged the tendency to oppose truth or knowledge and power. He called our attention to the way in which knowledge and power continually intersect or overlap in discursive practice.

Foucault's apparent conflation of truth and power and the sense that power is everywhere have troubled some of his readers. If, for example, any command that restricts behavior is part of the network of power, then how do we make decisions about what forms of power are desirable and what forms we would like to avoid? Did Foucault provide any grounds or resources that might help to justify a decision to use one form of power over another? Or a decision to refuse a command? From Foucault's perspective, are *all* commands accorded the same status, or did he provide a way of identifying some commands as legitimate and others as illegitimate (the concern with legitimacy, as noted earlier, is one of the central features of the various modernist accounts of power)? Or, to put the issue in the broadest terms possible, if power is everywhere—if it is inescapable—then do we lose the ability to render **judgments** about particular instantiations? Commenting on the tradition of "totalizing critique" and its conflation of "power and validity claims"—a tradition that runs from Nietzsche, through the later works of the German critical theorists Horkheimer and Adorno, to Foucault—Habermas (1982) wrote,

> If, however, all proper claims to validity [i.e., claims to truth or knowledge as well as claims to legitimacy or appropriateness] are devalued, and if the underlying value judgments are mere expressions of claims to power rather than validity, according to what standards should critique then differentiate? It [a critical theory or a theory of power] must at least be able to discriminate between a power which *deserves* to be esteemed and a power which *deserves* to be disparaged. (p. 27)

Habermas suggested that Foucault's account of power cannot be used to make these necessary distinctions. Fraser (1989), a more sympathetic critic, made a similar point. She concluded, "Clearly, what Foucault needs, and needs desperately, are normative criteria for distinguishing acceptable from unacceptable forms of power" (p. 33). The tension between the positions of Habermas and Fraser and that of Foucault is part of the larger tension in contemporary scholarship between modernism and *postmodernism*.[11]

The discussion so far has tried to sketch some of the main currents in scholarship on the concept of power. But how is this concept relevant to rhetorical inquiry, and what have rhetorical scholars been doing with the concept of power? It is possible to argue that power has been at the center of rhetorical scholarship since its rebirth in the United States during the first decades of the 20th century. When Wichelns (1925/1962) wrote that rhetoric and rhetorical criticism "is concerned with effect" (p. 209), he was (indirectly) grounding rhetorical scholarship in the study of power (see also Lucaites, 1989), for what is discursive effect if it is not the result of a type of discursive or rhetorical power? So, a concern with questions relating power and discourse is not something alien that has been grafted onto contemporary rhetorical scholarship; it is an issue that is immanent to the discipline's self-understanding.[12]

But explicit attention to the questions of discourse and power is a more recent development.[13] Reflection on the relationship between discourse and power is visible in the **ideological** turn in criticism beginning during the late 1970s. And this issue is at the center of the emerging **critical rhetoric** program. Drawing heavily on Foucault for his theoretical formulations, McKerrow (1989) stipulated that one of the aims of a critical rhetoric is to reclaim "the status . . . of centrality in the analysis of a discourse of power" (p. 92). McKerrow continued, "The task of a critical rhetoric is to undermine and expose the discourse of power" as well as the power of discourse given that "discourse is the tactical dimension of the operation of power" (p. 98). The relationship between discourse and power in Foucault's thought is somewhat complicated. On the one hand, Foucault (1983) insisted that "power relations" could not be reduced to "relationships of communication" (pp. 217-218). On the other hand, Foucault did seem to accord discourse and communication a significant role in the generation of power. In one of the lectures reprinted in *Power/Knowledge,* Foucault (1980) maintained, "In any society, there are manifold relations of power which permeate, characteri[z]e, and constitute the social body, and these relations of power cannot themselves be established, consolidated, or implemented without the production, accumulation, circulation, and functioning of a discourse" (p. 93).[14]

Critical studies of discourse and power, drawing on Foucault and/or extending the critical rhetoric program, have begun to appear over the past decade. Cooper and Makay (1988) employed Foucault to help analyze the constitution of a power/knowledge nexus in a series of lectures by Sigmund Freud. Jasinski (1987) tried to use Foucault's work on power to develop a critical framework for studying rhetoric and power. Jasinski illustrated the framework through a broad survey of key public conflicts during the Jacksonian era. A subsequent study (Jasinski, 1993) extended McGee's (1980) discussion of the "feminization of power" by analyzing the role of feminine *metaphors* for liberty in the reconstitution of power and authority during the period after the American Revolution. Ono and Sloop (1995) examined the operation of power and the constitution of subjectivity in **vernacular** discourse. Sloop (1996) continued this general line of inquiry in his investigation of the discourse through which inmates in America's criminal justice system are represented and disciplined. Finally, Blair, Brown, and Baxter (1994) and Bach, Blair, Nothstine, and Pym (1996) extended Foucault's interest in the way that power operates in various institutions and "disciplines" to the practices of the rhetorical and speech communication communities. These provocative studies, in turn, examined the way in which a masculinist **ideology** turns the practices of the speech communication field into "ideological mechanisms" that "seek to ensure that the masculinist paradigm represents the exclusive thematic directive for professional work in the discipline" (Blair et al., 1994, p. 397) and the way in which disciplinary publishing practices reconstitute the "militantly conventionalizing aspects of the disciplinary community's authority structure, sense of history, material conditions of labor, and socialization patterns" (Bach et al., 1996, p. 399). These essays remind us that power structures not only political action but also the practices of an academic discipline.

Perhaps the most innovative critical study focusing on the relationship between discourse and power was Hariman's (1992) reading of the courtly practices in Ethiopia under its emperor, Haile Selassie. In trying to understand "how power is composed" (p. 151) through discourse, Hariman turned to the realm of **style** and argued that style has been neglected by scholars interested in the topic of discourse and power. For Hariman, style is a crucial resource in the composition of power. But personal discursive style never is random or idiosyncratic; it always is organized and ordered by principles of **decorum** or rules of propriety and appropriateness. Hariman concluded by suggesting that "decorum should be reactivated as a concept for the analysis of power." Such an approach is sensible because "power is both represented and generated by particular rules of appropriateness." Discursive style, the location where principles of decorum interact with individual interests and desires, is an important "apparatus of power" (p. 163). Hariman's study concretely illustrates a point made earlier: An interest in power appears inherent to rhetorical thinking.

Notes

1. Mills's (1956) analysis of corporate influence in American life should be distinguished from a somewhat similar argument advanced by conservative politicians and commentators who, for the past 30 or so years, have been warning the nation about the dangers of the "liberal" power elite.

2. For an account of some of the dynamics of the public issue agenda, see the entry for **situation, rhetorical.**

3. On this essential feature of power, see also Wartenberg (1990).

4. Arendt relied on an embedded **dissociative** argument.

5. On the *enabling/constraining* **dialectic** of power, see also Blair (1987), Giddens (1979), Montrose (1989), and Sloop (1996).

6. Where freedom and power are mutually exclusive, a person cannot be free or autonomous if he or she is a victim of power relations.

7. On the discursive constitution of subjectivity, see also the entries for **constitutive rhetoric** and **interpellation.**

8. On Foucault's account of power/knowledge as a resource for **criticism,** see also Cooper and Makay (1988) and Foss and Gill (1987).

9. Something close to Foucault's position was developed in rhetoric and argumentation theory by Charles Willard. Willard (1983) based his theory on "the assumption that arguments have epistemic effects" (p. 170). All argument, which Willard defined broadly as "a kind of interaction in which two or more people maintain what they construe to be incompatible positions" (p. 21) or, in other words, all strategic social interaction, has epistemic significance.

10. See also the entry for Foucault's use of the term **episteme.**

11. In rhetorical studies, this tension is manifest in discussions over the status of **critical rhetoric.**

12. Eagleton (1981) made a similar observation in his somewhat unconventional reading of the history of rhetoric. He suggested that one of the initial impulses guiding the emergence of rhetorical theory was to "theorize the articulation of discourse and power" (p. 101).

13. See also the work being done on this topic in the field of critical linguistics (e.g., Fowler, 1985).

14. On this subject, see also Jasinski (1993, p. 160).

References and Additional Reading

Airaksinen, T. (1992). The rhetoric of domination. In T. E. Wartenberg (Ed.), *Rethinking power.* Albany: State University of New York Press.

Arendt, H. (1959). *The human condition.* Garden City, NY: Anchor.

Arendt, H. (1972). On violence. In H. Arendt, *Crises of the republic.* New York: Harcourt Brace Jovanovich.

Bach, T. E., Blair, C., Nothstine, W. L., & Pym, A. L. (1996). How to read "How to Get Published." *Communication Quarterly, 44,* 399-422.

Bachrach, P., & Baratz, M. S. (1962). Two faces of power. *American Political Science Review, 56,* 947-952.

Bachrach, P., & Baratz, M. S. (1970). *Power and poverty: Theory and practice.* New York: Oxford University Press.

Ball, T. (1988). The changing face of power. In *Transforming political discourse: Political theory and critical conceptual history.* Oxford, UK: Basil Blackwell.

Blair, C. (1987). The statement: Foundation of Foucault's historical criticism. *Western Journal of Speech Communication, 51,* 364-383.

Blair, C., Brown, J. R., & Baxter, L. A. (1994). Disciplining the feminine. *Quarterly Journal of Speech, 80,* 383-409.

Butler, J. (1997). *The psychic life of power: Theories in subjection.* Stanford, CA: Stanford University Press.

Clegg, S. R. (1989). *Frameworks of power.* London: Sage.

Cooper, M., & Makay, J. J. (1988). Knowledge, power, and Freud's Clark Conference lectures. *Quarterly Journal of Speech, 74,* 416-433.

Dahl, R. A. (1957). The concept of power. *Behavioral Science, 2,* 201-215.

Dahl, R. A. (1968). Power. In D. L. Sills (Ed.), *International encyclopedia of the social sciences* (Vol. 12). New York: Macmillan.

Digester, P. (1992). The fourth face of power. *Journal of Politics, 54,* 977-1007.

Dreyfus, H. L., & Rabinow, P. (1983). *Michel Foucault: Beyond structuralism and hermeneutics* (2nd ed.). Chicago: University of Chicago Press.

Eagleton, T. (1981). *Walter Benjamin or towards a revolutionary criticism.* London: Verso.

Fairclough, N. (1989). *Language and power.* London: Longmans.

Foss, S. K., & Gill, A. (1987). Michel Foucault's theory of rhetoric as epistemic. *Western Journal of Speech Communication, 51,* 384-401.

Foucault, M. (1979). *Discipline and punish: The birth of the prison* (A. Sheridan, Trans.). New York: Vintage.

Foucault, M. (1980). *Power/Knowledge: Selected interviews and other writings, 1972-1977* (C. Gordon, Ed., C. Gordon et al., Trans.). New York: Pantheon Books.

Foucault, M. (1983). The subject and power. In H. L. Dreyfus & P. Rabinow, *Michel Foucault: Beyond structuralism and hermeneutics* (2nd ed.). Chicago: University of Chicago Press.

Fowler, R. (1985). Power. In T. A. van Dijk (Ed.), *Handbook of discourse analysis* (Vol. 4). San Diego: Academic Press.

Fraser, N. (1989). Foucault on modern power: Empirical insights and normative confusions. In N. Fraser, *Unruly practices: Power, discourse, and gender in contemporary social theory.* Minneapolis: University of Minnesota Press.

Giddens, A. (1979). *Central problems in social theory: Action, structure, and contradiction in social analysis.* Berkeley: University of California Press.

Giddens, A. (1984). *The constitution of society.* Berkeley: University of California Press.

Habermas, J. (1977). Hannah Arendt's communications concept of power. *Social Research, 44,* 3-24.

Habermas, J. (1979). *Communication and the evolution of society* (T. McCarthy, Trans.). Boston: Beacon.

Habermas, J. (1982). The entwinement of myth and enlightenment: Re-reading *Dialectic of Enlightenment. New German Critique,* No. 26, pp. 13-30.

Hariman, R. (1992). Decorum, power, and the courtly style. *Quarterly Journal of Speech, 78,* 149-172.

Harstock, N. (1990). Foucault on power: A theory for women? In L. Nicholson (Ed.), *Feminism/Postmodernism.* London: Routledge.

Honneth, A. (1991). *The critique of power: Reflective stages in a critical theory* (K. Baynes, Trans.). Cambridge, MA: MIT Press.

Hoy, D. C. (1986). Power, repression, progress: Foucault, Lukes, and the Frankfurt school. In D. C. Hoy (Ed.),

Foucault: A critical reader. Oxford, UK: Basil Blackwell.

Isaac, J. C. (1987). *Power and Marxist theory: A realist view.* Ithaca, NY: Cornell University Press.

Jasinski, J. (1987). Liberty and power in nineteenth century public argument: A Foucaultian analysis of Jacksonian rhetoric. In J. W. Wenzel (Ed.), *Argument and critical practices: Proceedings of the Fifth SCA/AFA Conference on Argumentation.* Annandale, VA: Speech Communication Association.

Jasinski, J. (1993). The feminization of liberty, domesticated virtue, and the reconstitution of power and authority in early American political discourse. *Quarterly Journal of Speech, 79,* 146-164.

Kramarae, C., Schulz, M., & O'Barr, W. M. (Eds.). (1984). *Language and power.* Beverly Hills, CA: Sage.

Luban, D. (1979). On Habermas on Arendt on power. *Philosophy and Social Criticism, 6,* 81-95.

Lucaites, J. L. (1989, November). "*. . . at the boundaries of politics and literature": Reading the "public" in Herbert A. Wichelns' "The Literary Criticism of Oratory."* Paper presented at the meeting of the Speech Communication Association, San Francisco.

Lukes, S. (1974). *Power: A radical view.* London: Macmillan.

McCarthy, T. (1990). The critique of impure reason: Foucault and the Frankfurt school. *Political Theory, 18,* 437-469.

McGee, M. C. (1980). The origins of "liberty": A feminization of power. *Communication Monographs, 47,* 23-45.

McKerrow, R. E. (1989). Critical rhetoric: Theory and practice. *Communication Monographs, 56,* 91-111.

Miller, W. L. (1996). *Arguing about slavery: The great battle in the United States Congress.* New York: Knopf.

Mills, C. W. (1956) *The power elite.* Oxford, UK: Oxford University Press.

Montrose, L. A. (1989). Professing the Renaissance: The poetics and politics of culture. In H. A. Veeser (Ed.), *The new historicism.* New York: Routledge.

Ono, K. A., & Sloop, J. M. (1995). The critique of vernacular discourse. *Communication Monographs, 62,* 19-46.

Rouse, J. (1994). Power/Knowledge. In G. Gutting (Ed.), *The Cambridge companion to Foucault.* Cambridge, UK: Cambridge University Press.

Said, E. (1986). Foucault and the imagination of power. In D. C. Hoy (Ed.), *Foucault: A critical reader.* Oxford, UK: Basil Blackwell.

Sloop, J. M. (1996). *The cultural prison: Discourse, prisoners, and punishment.* Tuscaloosa: University of Alabama Press.

Wartenberg, T. E. (1990). *The forms of power: From domination to transformation.* Philadelphia: Temple University Press.

Wichelns, H. A. (1962). The literary criticism of oratory. In A. M. Drummond (Ed.), *Studies in rhetoric and public speaking in honor of James Albert Winans.* New York: Russell and Russell. (Original work published 1925)

Willard, C. A. (1983). *Argumentation and the social grounds of knowledge.* Tuscaloosa: University of Alabama Press.

Wolin, S. S. (1988). On the theory and practice of power. In J. Arac (Ed.), *After Foucault: Humanistic knowledge, postmodern challenges.* New Brunswick, NJ: Rutgers University Press.

Young, I. M. (1992). Five faces of oppression. In T. E. Wartenberg (Ed.), *Rethinking power.* Albany: State University of New York Press.

PRESENCE

In *The New Rhetoric,* Perelman and Olbrechts-Tyteca (1969) commented that "all argumentation [indeed, all discursive **invention**] is selective" (p. 119). The inevitability of selection makes the idea of an exact impartiality or neutrality in our use of language an "illusion" (p. 120). As Weaver (1953) insisted, language is **sermonic.**[1]

An important question follows from this initial observation: What implicit rules guide the selection process? What exactly is going on when people invent messages? Scholars in different traditions address this basic question. Focusing on the realms of rhetoric and argumentation, Perelman and Olbrechts-Tyteca (1969) argued,

> One of the preoccupations of a speaker [or writer] is to make present, by verbal magic alone, what is actually absent but what he [sic] considers important to his argument or, by making them more present, to enhance the value of some of the elements of which one has actually been made conscious. (p. 117)

In later work, Perelman (1982) elaborated on the importance of **presence:** "The techniques of presentation which create presence are essential above all when it is a question of evoking realities that are distant in time and space" (p. 35). For Perelman and Olbrechts-Tyteca (1969), achieving presence is a rule that guides the process of selection; we choose words, phrases, figurative images, and other discursive strategies to either (a) make something absent "present" to our audience[2] or (b) increase the presence of something that already has been brought to the audience's attention. An example of the latter sense would be the way in which an orator, in a patriotic Fourth of July oration during the 19th century, would try to increase the presence of the spirit of the founding fathers.

These two aspects of presence are not mutually exclusive; in fact, they frequently overlap. An advocate might begin by trying to make something absent present to an audience and then work to increase the presence of that item (whatever it might be). As Murphy (1994) noted, the idea of presence is a conceptual *metaphor;* when presence is achieved, what initially was absent "almost seems to be in the room" with the audience (p. 5). Presence, then, is a discursive effect; through the effect of presence, some phenomenon, idea, concept, process, or person is made vivid, tangible, and/or proximate to an audience. The basic meaning of presence was summarized by Karon (1976) as follows:

> First, it is a felt quality in the auditor's consciousness. This quality, created by the rhetor's "verbal magic," enables him [sic] to impress upon the consciousness of his audience whatever he deems important. Second, presence fixes the audience's attention while altering its perceptions and perspectives. Third, its strongest agent is the imagination. Fourth, its purpose is to initiate action or to dispose the audience toward an action or judgment. Fifth, it is created chiefly through techniques traditionally studied under the headings of style, delivery, and disposition. (p. 97)

The concept of presence is important for a number of reasons. Perelman and Olbrechts-Tyteca (1969) emphasized its strategic or *instrumental* value as a "technique of argumentation." They were less interested in presence as "a philosophical formulation" (p. 119). Other scholars have extended their discussion into the realms of philosophy and theory. Mader (1973), for example, explored the ontological dimension of presence (how it speaks to certain aspects of our experiential existence) to uncover its persuasive potential. Karon (1976) probed the epistemological dimension of presence (how the concept is part of a theory of knowledge). Murphy (1994) questioned the value of this type of extension, suggesting that Perelman, through the concept of presence, "sought to evade questions of epistemology" (p. 14). The concept of presence also speaks to another enduring conceptual issue in rhetorical studies—the relationship between discursive form and substantive content (Leff, 1983, 1987). Perelman and Olbrechts-Tyteca (1969) refused to "separate the form of a discourse from its substance" (p. 142); they argued that "questions of form and questions of substance are intermingled in order to achieve presence" (p. 120). Like Leff and Sachs's (1990) discussion of **iconicity**, the concept of presence provides a way for scholars to conceptualize the interdependence of a text's form and its content (see also Murphy, 1994). Finally, presence assumes that an active, practically conscious agent is the source of a message and that this agent has an interpretive relationship to his or her world. Put more simply, to select and make something present in discourse, the advocate or rhetor must be able to "read" or interpret the world around him or her. The advocate or rhetor's interpretive relationship to the world allows him or her to determine the meaning and significance of events, processes, ideas, concepts, and the like that are to be given presence in a particular message. The concept of presence is, then, connected to the growing interest in the **hermeneutics and rhetoric** relationship.

What are some of the specific ways in which presence is achieved in discursive practice? Perelman and Olbrechts-Tyteca (1969) identified numerous strategies that can help to produce the effect of presence. Some of the strategies they discussed (e.g., repetition [p. 144]) are part of the traditional doctrine of **amplification** (pp. 175-176). They suggested that illustrations are particularly useful "to increase [the] presence . . . [of] an abstract rule . . . by means of a particular case" (p. 360). For example, when Mario Cuomo sought to invoke the potentially abstract idea of **prudence** in his speech on abortion, religion, and politics at the University of Notre Dame in 1984, he was able to give the idea added presence through a concrete illustration—an account of the practices of the U.S. Catholic church with respect to slavery during the 19th century. Through the illustration, Cuomo hoped to show his audience more clearly what the "rule" of prudence would imply in his particular case. Accumulation of material and evocative details are two additional discursive strategies that Perelman and Olbrechts-Tyteca recommended (p. 145). Finally, they noted how various syntactical, **figurative,** and/or **stylistic** strategies are useful for producing presence (pp. 160-163, 171-179; see also Leroux, 1992). Critical extensions of the concept have explored how specific devices such as metaphor (Kauffman & Parson, 1990) and *analogy* (Murphy, 1994) contribute to the effect of presence.

In public advocacy, the concept of presence has special relevance to the idea of **stock issues.** A central task in advocacy is to make the problem or *ill* that one wants to address present to the audience. As Perelman and Olbrechts-Tyteca (1969) acknowledged (p. 118), George Campbell's discussion of the "circumstances" that make emotional appeals more effective (see the entry for **pathos**) can be extended to identify certain *loci*—common themes or lines of appeal—that are useful for creating presence. Perelman and Olbrechts-Tyteca discussed four—time, place, relation, and personal interest—and their discussion can be adjusted slightly to identify five key loci of presence that may be used for making an exigence more present or more vivid for an audience:

1. *Urgency:* Can the advocate show that the problem or exigence will have an immediate impact on the audience?
2. *Duration:* Can the advocate show that the problem and/or its effects will persist for a long period of time?
3. *Proximity:* Can the advocate establish that the effects of the problem will "hit close to home" or touch the lives of people who members of the audience know?
4. *Magnitude:* Can the advocate show that the effects of the exigence are, or will be, felt by a large number of people or that there has been, or will be, substantial property damage (or other quantifiable signs of the exigence's impact)?
5. *Severity:* Can the advocate show that, even if the exigence is lacking in terms of magnitude, those affected by the problem have suffered great hardship or had their lives disrupted in an extreme way?

By tapping into the common themes or loci that are relevant in the particular case, the advocate can increase the presence of an exigence or problem for his or her audience.

Notes

1. In a well-known passage, Burke (1969) observed, "Men [sic] seek for vocabularies that will be faithful *reflections* of reality. To this end, they must develop vocabularies that are *selections* of reality. And any selection of reality must, in certain circumstances, function as a *deflection* of reality" (p. 59).

2. The absence can be either *physical* (as when an anti-war advocate tries to make the horror of war present to audience members who have not experienced the physical reality directly) or *conceptual* (as when an advocate of a balanced budget amendment tries to make the somewhat abstract fact of the "budget deficit" present to an audience).

References and Additional Reading

Burke, K. (1969). *A grammar of motives.* Berkeley: University of California Press.

Karon, L. A. (1976). Presence in *The New Rhetoric. Philosophy and Rhetoric, 9,* 96-111.

Kauffman, C., & Parson, D. W. (1990). Metaphor and presence in argument. In D. C. Williams & M. D. Hazen (Eds.), *Argumentation theory and the rhetoric of assent.* Tuscaloosa: University of Alabama Press.

Leff, M. (1983). Topical invention and metaphorical interaction. *Southern Speech Communication Journal, 48,* 214-229.

Leff, M. (1987). The habitation of rhetoric. In J. W. Wenzel (Ed.), *Argument and critical practices: Proceedings of the Fifth SCA/AFA Conference on Argumentation.* Annandale, VA: Speech Communication Association.

Leff, M., & Sachs, A. (1990). Words the most like things: Iconicity and the rhetorical text. *Western Journal of Speech Communication, 54,* 252-273.

Leroux, N. R. (1992). Perceiving rhetorical style: Toward a framework for criticism. *Rhetoric Society Quarterly, 22,* 29-44.

Mader, T. F. (1973). On presence in rhetoric. *College Composition and Communication, 24,* 375-381.

Murphy, J. M. (1994). Presence, analogy, and *Earth in the Balance. Argumentation and Advocacy, 31,* 1-16.

Perelman, C. (1982). *The realm of rhetoric* (W. Kluback, Trans.). Notre Dame, IN: University of Notre Dame Press.

Perelman, C., & Olbrechts-Tyteca, L. (1969). *The new rhetoric: A treatise on argumentation* (J. Wilkinson & P. Weaver, Trans.). Notre Dame, IN: University of Notre Dame Press.

Weaver, R. (1953). *The ethics of rhetoric.* South Bend, IN: Regnery/Gateway.

PRESUMPTION

Presumption is the counterpart to the concept of **burden of proof.** Whately (1963) defined presumption as "a *preoccupation* of the ground . . . [that] implies that it must stand good [until] some sufficient reason is adduced against it" (p. 112). To enjoy presumption is, as Whately's *metaphor* suggests, to occupy "ground"; no one else is entitled to that ground until (and unless) that person provides "sufficient reason" for it to be awarded to him or her. In the case of the U.S. criminal justice system (introduced in the entry for **burden of proof**), the defendant enjoys presumption and the prosecution has the burden of proof; the defendant is *presumed* innocent until *proven* guilty. As Whately observed, "If you have the 'presumption' on your side and can but *refute* all the arguments brought against you, you have, for the present at least, gained a victory" (p. 113).

Whately (1963) identified a number of sources of presumption. Perhaps most important, existing institutions (or the status quo) enjoys presumption (p. 114). Inertia is a powerful force in human affairs; people tend to continue doing what they have traditionally or habitually done. Advocates who want to change the status quo have the burden; they have to prove that (a) there is a problem with the way we currently are doing things and (b) there is a better way to do things. Advocates of change commonly satisfy their burden of proof, and overcome the initial presumption in favor of the status quo, by addressing the **stock issues of policy disputes.** Despite the fact that some of Whately's sources of presumption have been overturned,[1] presumption remains a potent force in social life and public discourse.

As Whately recognized, the initial configuration of presumption and burden of proof can be altered. Perhaps the best example in American history occurred during the debate over the ratification of the U.S. Constitution. During the summer of 1787, representatives of most of the 13 states met in Philadelphia to deliberate and recommend revisions to the existing governance charter, the Articles of Confederation. But the delegates, many of whom desired a much stronger central government than that provided for by the articles, opted to recommend an entirely new system of government for the new nation. At times, advocates of the proposed Constitution emphasized the degree of continuity between the provisions of the Articles of Confederation and the provisions of the new

Constitution, thereby exploiting the **ambiguity** between *minor repairs* and a *counterplan*[2] and making the new plan seem like less of a radical departure from the status quo. Given the nature of burden of proof and presumption, advocates of the new plan had the burden of proof, and those who were opposed to the new plan (and who wanted to defend, at least in some fashion, the status quo) enjoyed presumption. But this initial configuration was altered rather quickly. Through a variety of strategies, including **definition of the situation** and using the labels "federal" and "anti-federal" as **condensation symbols,** the "federalist" supporters of the new Constitution discharged their burden of proof and seized the "ground" of presumption. They insisted that the new plan was absolutely essential to the preservation and health of the new nation, and they forced their opponents to accept the burden of proof. The "anti-federalist" opponents of the Philadelphia proposal were put in the position of having to adduce reasons *against* the change rather than being able to simply *refute* the federalists' reasons for change (Einhorn, 1990). As this episode illustrates, the burden of proof and presumption are not necessarily fixed and instead can be dynamic evolving forces within the life of a society.

Notes

1. See, for example, Whately's (1963) discussion of "deference" (pp. 118-119).
2. See the discussion of **case construction strategies.**

References and Additional Reading

Cronkhite, G. (1966). The locus of presumption. *Central States Speech Journal, 17,* 270-276.

Einhorn, L. L. (1990). A twist of principles: Presumption and burden of proof in the Virginia ratification debates on the federal Constitution. *Southern Communication Journal, 55,* 144-161.

Lee, R., & Lee, K. K. (1985). Reconsidering Whately's folly: An emotive treatment of presumption. *Central States Speech Journal, 36,* 164-177.

Liu, Y. (1997). Authority, presumption, and invention. *Philosophy and Rhetoric, 30,* 413-427.

McKerrow, R. E. (1975). Probable argument and proof in Whately's theory of rhetoric. *Central States Speech Journal, 26,* 259-266.

Rescher, N. (1977). *Dialectics: A controversy-oriented approach to the theory of knowledge.* Albany: State University of New York Press.

Sproule, J. M. (1976). The psychological burden of proof: On the evolutionary development of Richard Whately's theory of presumption. *Speech Monographs, 43,* 115-129.

Whately, R. (1963). *Elements of rhetoric* (D. Ehninger, Ed.). Carbondale: Southern Illinois University Press.

Whedbee, K. (1998). Authority, freedom, and liberal judgment: The "presumptions" and "presumptuousness" of Whately, Mill, and Tocqueville. *Quarterly Journal of Speech, 84,* 171-189.

PROPHETIC ETHOS/ PROPHETIC SPEECH

Long of interest to biblical scholars, the discursive or rhetorical performance of prophesy or prophetic speech, and with it the central idea of **prophetic ethos,** has received attention of late in the rhetorical studies literature. Recent works by Darsey (1988, 1997), Pauley (1998), and Zulick (1992) shed important light on this phenomenon.[1] As Darsey (1997) observed, "At the center of prophetic rhetoric is the prophetic *ethos*" (p. 29).

The speech act of prophecy is a form of prediction that is sanctioned by some form of (usually divine) inspiration or compelling insight. The act of prophecy figures prominently in **apocalyptic discourse** (Brummett, 1991) and in the **jeremiad** (Bercovitch, 1978) but is not restricted to these discursive forms. Aspects of prophetic speech and prophetic ethos appear in a variety of situations and discursive forms. Weaver (1953), much like Emerson (1904), went so far as to suggest that prophecy is an essential ingredient of all rhetoric when he wrote that "true rhetoric is concerned with the potency of things" and "all prophecy is about the tendency of things" (p. 20). The following two basic questions are central to gaining some understanding of prophetic speech and prophetic ethos. What are some of the common characteristics of prophetic speech? How do these characteristics help to constitute the **persona** or ethos of the prophet?

Prophecy might best be characterized as a *vision* one has experienced that is rendered accessible to others through a linguistic translation. This translation process can be difficult, and the struggle to make the vision comprehensible to others helps to explain the frequent presence of *aporia* and **ambiguity** in prophetic speech.[2] A fictional example can help to illustrate the visionary quality of prophecy. In a recent fantasy novel, *Stone of Tears* (Goodkind, 1995), a young Sister of the Light presses the prophet Nathan about the nature of prophesy. Nathan responds,

> Would you like to be really frightened? Would you like me to *show* you a prophecy? Not tell you the words, but show it to you? Show it to you the way it was meant to be passed on? I have never shown a sister before. You all study them and think you can decipher their meaning from the words, but you don't understand. That is not the true way they work.

The author of this novel, Terry Goodkind, represented the process of prophesy with considerable fidelity to the way in which it often is portrayed; prophecy begins in an overwhelming vision that is then translated into words.

Prophetic visions and the prophetic speech that represents them do not argue; put differently, argument is subordinated to vision in prophetic speech. Prophetic visions reveal truths; they remove blindness and replace it with clarity. Discussing the prophetic ethos of the radical agitator Eugene Debs, Darsey (1988) wrote, "Debs understood clearly the claims he was making to supranormal vision. He denies the gift of charisma, yet he sees something more than is seen by the human eye" (p. 441). One mark of prophetic ethos, then, is the claim to a special capacity to perceive truth and reveal it to others. An individual who enacts a prophetic persona can see things clearly while others are constrained by blinders.

How do prophets gain the gift of special sight or the ability to see the world clearly? They commonly do so by undergoing, in Darsey's (1988) words, "an extraordinary rebirth or conversion" (p. 439).[3] Darsey (1988) quoted a passage from Debs's explanation of his conversion to socialism that links the process of conversion with the attainment of the capacity to see the truth clearly: "At this juncture there was delivered, from wholly unexpected quarters, a swift succession of blows that blinded me for an instant and then opened wide my eyes—and in the gleam of every bayonet and the flash of every rifle *the class struggle was revealed*" (p. 439). A second element of prophetic ethos is the experience of a profound conversion that awakens the person's capacity to see the truth (Darsey, 1997).

The gift of prophetic vision exacts a cost from the person who would exercise it. The Bible is full of examples of prophets who ended up martyrs because they insisted on the veracity of their vision and their "commission" (Darsey, 1988, p. 436) to communicate that vision to others. Two additional aspects of prophetic ethos come into view. First, in a somewhat ironic reversal, prophetic ethos is attained through the effacement of self or individual ego. In religious prophesy, it is not the prophet's voice but rather God's voice that we hear; the prophet no longer possesses an ethos of his or her own but rather gives it up to be the vessel for God's word. The effacement of self in prophetic ethos also is visible in the fact that an individual rarely, if ever, chooses to serve as the vehicle for prophesy. More commonly, prophetic vision is depicted as a burden or a calling that one is compelled to accept. Both Darsey and Zulick noted the persistence of the biblical description of the prophet as a "suffering servant." So, prophetic ethos is marked by a heavy emphasis on duty or on obedience to a calling from some higher source (be it God, history, class solidarity, sisterhood, etc.).

The effacement of self and the adoption of the *role* (or **persona**) of the suffering servant reveals an additional aspect of prophetic ethos. Prophets are not reluctant martyrs. A mark of prophetic ethos is the acceptance of the reality that one most likely will be misunderstood and persecuted for remaining faithful to the prophetic calling. The prophet might lament this reality, but he or she accepts it; it is part of the burden of prophecy. The willingness of the prophet to accept persecution, and in many cases throughout history death, introduces an important argumentative function to prophetic ethos. This last aspect of prophetic ethos functions as a type of literal *enactment* of what Perelman and Olbrechts-Tyteca (1969) referred to as the *argument of sacrifice.* The truth or validity of the prophet's vision is reinforced through a prophetic ethos that embraces persecution and suffering; the prophet's willingness to suffer demonstrates the nobility of his or her cause and calling.

It is a mistake to see prophesy, prophetic speech, and prophetic ethos as a relic of the world of the Old Testament. As Zulick (1992) noted, "Prophecy, both as stylized speech and as dramatized public character, is an enduring deep source of American rhetorical consciousness that taps into the wellsprings of our religious and social imagination" (p. 126; see also Boyer, 1992). We find prophetic ethos present in the colonial origins of the nation. Commenting on John Winthrop's famous sermon, "A Model of Christian Charity" (delivered aboard the *Arabella* to the first wave of Puritan colonists in 1630), Arch (1994) noted Winthrop's "self-conscious posing as a prophet in the tradition of Moses and David and Ezekiel" (p. 19).[4] Browne (1996), Japp (1985), and Tonn (1996) explored, in varying degrees, the feminine appropriation of prophetic ethos. Prophetic speech and prophetic ethos also play a central role in the discourse of America's African American community, from Marcus Garvey (Ware & Linkugel, 1982) to Louis Farrakhan (Pauley, 1998). Darsey (1997) uncovered prophecy and prophetic ethos as a recurring feature in the history of American radicalism. The nature and function of prophetic speech and prophetic ethos merit continued exploration by rhetorical scholars.

Notes

1. See also Bush's (1999) discussion of "prophetic revivalism" and "prophetic voice" among African American orators and women's rights activists during the 19th century.
2. For more detailed consideration of a "prophetic style," see Brown (1966).
3. See also the discussion of **secular conversion.**
4. Arch's (1994) observation illustrates a final element of prophetic ethos—a conscious effort on the part of the advocate to position himself or herself within a prophetic tradition.

References and Additional Reading

Arch, S. C. (1994). *Authorizing the past: The rhetoric of history in seventeenth-century New England.* DeKalb: Northern Illinois University Press.

Bercovitch, S. (1978). *The American jeremiad.* Madison: University of Wisconsin Press.

Boyer, P. S. (1992). *When time shall be no more: Prophecy belief in modern American culture.* Cambridge, MA: Harvard University Press.

Brown, H. (1966). *Prose styles: Five primary types.* Minneapolis: University of Minnesota Press.

Browne, S. H. (1996). Encountering Angelina Grimké: Violence, identity, and the creation of radical community. *Quarterly Journal of Speech, 82,* 55-73.

Brueggemann, W. (1978). *The prophetic imagination.* Philadelphia: Fortress Press.

Brummett, B. (1991). *Contemporary apocalyptic rhetoric.* New York: Praeger.

Bush, H. K., Jr. (1999). *American declarations: Rebellion and repentance in American cultural history.* Urbana: University of Illinois Press.

Darsey, J. (1988). The legend of Eugene Debs: Prophetic *ethos* as radical argument. *Quarterly Journal of Speech, 74,* 434-452.

Darsey, J. (1997). *The prophetic tradition and radical rhetoric in America.* New York: New York University Press.

Emerson, R. W. (1904). Eloquence. In R. W. Emerson, *The complete works of Ralph Waldo Emerson* (Vol. 8). Boston: Houghton Mifflin.

Goodkind, T. (1995). *Stone of tears.* New York: TOR/Tom Doherty Associates.

Japp, P. M. (1985). Esther or Isaiah? The abolitionist-feminist rhetoric of Angelina Grimké. *Quarterly Journal of Speech, 71,* 335-348.

Pauley, J. L. (1998). Reshaping public persona and the prophetic *ethos:* Louis Farrakhan at the Million Man March. *Western Journal of Communication, 62,* 512-536.

Taylor, R. (1911). *The political prophecy in England.* New York: Columbia University Press.

Tonn, M. B. (1996). Militant motherhood: Labor's Mary Harris "Mother" Jones. *Quarterly Journal of Speech, 82,* 1-21.

Ware, B. L., & Linkugel, W. A. (1982). The rhetorical *persona:* Marcus Garvey as Black Moses. *Communication Monographs, 49,* 50-62.

Weaver, R. (1953). *The ethics of rhetoric.* South Bend, IN: Regnery/Gateway.

Zulick, M. D. (1992). The agon of Jeremiah: On the dialogic invention of prophetic ethos. *Quarterly Journal of Speech, 78,* 125-148.

PRUDENCE/PHRONESIS

Comedian Dana Carvey spent a considerable amount of time during the late 1980s and early 1990s imitating George Bush. One of the signature lines of Carvey's impersonation, "it wouldn't be prudent," poked fun at Bush's image as a rather unimaginative and overly cautious politician. The phrase is more than humorous; it accurately reflects the dominant common meaning of the term **prudence:** A prudent person generally is considered to be careful, cautious, and circumspect. Pieper (1959) noted, "In colloquial use, prudence always carries the connotation of timorous, small-minded self-preservation, of a rather selfish concern about oneself" (pp. 14-15). Similarly, Nelson (1992) commented,

> According to a common modern view, prudence has to do with the self-interested calculation of costs and benefits. We tend to think of prudence as a kind of calculating carefulness, an ability to anticipate consequences.... In fact, we often view prudence negatively and associate it with people who know what is right but refrain from doing it because of their concern for the expected costs. (p. 78)

But as Pieper, Nelson, and others (e.g., Maritain, 1954) have argued, this common-sense view of prudence is a pale reflection of a once vibrant concept. A considerable amount of intellectual energy has been devoted over the past few decades, in rhetorical studies and other academic disciplines, to recovering and deploying a more robust, and less timorous, understanding of prudence.

We can start with the following two basic questions. What is the genealogy of a robust sense of prudence? Why has the concept generated such a resurgence of interest? Prudence occupied an important place in Aristotle's ethical theory and also received significant attention in the works of Cicero, Aquinas, and many of the leading thinkers of the Renaissance (Kahn, 1985; Westberg, 1994). For many scholars, recovering a more robust understanding of prudence involves, to at least some degree, a rigorous encounter with Aristotle's discussion of **phronesis** and its subsequent development. But why are so many scholars returning to Aristotle and the larger tradition of prudence? Hariman (1991) suggested that the concept is particularly appealing to scholars who reject the modern tradition of empiricism and are dissatisfied with "modern conceptions of rationality" (p. 26). Dunne (1993) explained how his interest in the concept emerged from an uncomfortable encounter with *technical reasoning.* Prudence or phronesis has attracted attention because it (at least potentially) offers an alternative account of how reason might inform human action for those who are dissatisfied with modernity's regimes of rationality but who also are suspicious of the seeming arationality or even irrationality of the broad intellectual movement that goes under the heading of *postmodernism.* To appreciate how prudence might provide such an alternative, we need to return briefly to its Aristotelian genealogy and review its ongoing recovery in contemporary scholarship.

An extensive body of commentary has arisen around the Aristotelian concept of phronesis (Beiner, 1983, pp. 72-82; Dunne, 1993, pp. 275-314; MacIntyre, 1988, pp. 124-145; Nussbaum, 1986, pp. 290-317; Reeve, 1995, pp. 67-98; Tessitore, 1996, pp. 42-50). The reconstructive task is complicated by the fact that "Aristotle's definitions of phronesis had a marked uncertainty about them" (Gadamer, 1982, p. 287) and his discussion of the topic often proceeded in "a fragmentary and unsystematic fashion" (Dunne, 1993, p. 245). Scholars generally agree on the way in which Aristotle differentiated the practice of prudence from other spheres of human life or other forms of human behavior. Phronesis differs from Platonic "wisdom" (*sophia*) and sophistic "cleverness"; it is neither a "science" (an *episteme*) nor an "art" (a *techne*) (see the discussion in Aristotle's "Nicomachean Ethics" [Aristotle, 1973]). Prudence is not concerned with abstract knowledge or with an ability to make or produce something. Neither science nor art illuminates the realm of human action (or *praxis*), and according to Aristotle (1973), "practical wisdom is concerned with action" (1141b22). Aristotle told his readers that prudence also is "concerned with the ultimate particular fact" (1142a25); to be prudent is to be perceptive or insightful (Dunne, 1993, pp. 301-302). In addition, prudence involves an ability to "deliberate well" about matters that are variable, indeterminate, or **contingent** (Aristotle, 1973, 1141b10).

Given that, on Aristotle's account, prudence is manifest in sound or thoughtful deliberation, it should not be surprising that its relationship to rhetoric has been a recurring theme in the humanities (Brownstein, 1974; Farrell, 1993; 1998; Kahn, 1985; Self, 1979). But do Aristotle's observations about the nature of prudence add up to a coherent "theory" or account of its essence? That depends on how one defines *theory.* Traditionally, theory articulates the essential principles that can describe and explain a phenomenon. For example, economic theory contains "laws" that explain what happens to product prices as demand for the product increases, the theory of evolution explains the emergence of *homo sapiens,* and Sigmund Freud's theory of the unconscious provides a way of explaining certain forms of behavior. Probably the essential point in Aristotle's discussion of phronesis, emphasized by most commentators, is that not every aspect of human existence, especially the realm of choice and action, can be neatly subsumed by theoretical principles (or reduced to an **episteme**). Commenting on Aristotle's account of phronesis, Nussbaum (1986) wrote,

> Principles . . . fail to capture the fine detail of the concrete particular, which is the subject matter of ethical choice. . . . General rules are . . . criticized . . . both for lack of concreteness and for lack of flexibility. "Perception" can respond to nuance and fine shading, adapting its judgment to the matter at hand in a way that principles set up in advance have a hard time doing. (pp. 300-301)

Dunne (1993) made a similar observation: "In the sphere of phronesis . . ., practical-moral universals cannot unproblematically cover or include particular cases because they contain in themselves an element of indeterminateness which is removed only through confrontation with the particular case" (p. 311). Prudence is, therefore, not a simple process of applying principles or rules to cases that leaves the principles or rules unchanged; in prudential practice, there is a negotiation between the case and the principle that allows *both* to gain in clarity (see also Nelson, 1992; Westberg, 1994).

Nussbaum and Dunne revealed prudence to be a deliberative process (both intra- and interpersonal in nature) through which general principles and "particular" cases are brought into contact to reach judgments about courses of action.[1] But can this prudential or phronetic process be systematized? Can it be codified into a limited number of theoretical principles? The answer, all commentators would agree, is no. Nelson (1992) noted, "Although there are practical principles and rules of thumb reflecting the accumulated moral wisdom of a community or culture to which one can look for guidance in moral decision-making, one does not become prudent by memorizing a set of principles" (pp. 79-80). Gadamer (1982) argued that prudence emerges through the *application* of principles and rules of thumb to specific situations but that the process of application itself never can be reduced to following a rule.[2] It is in the process of application that the negotiation of principles and cases takes place. Dunne (1993) explained the dilemma of a "theory" of prudence: "Aristotle's ethical 'theory' is one that disabuses us of theory . . . by showing us that the ethical agent must give up the kind of attachment to generalized knowledge that prevails, legitimately, in theoretical fields" (p. 313). Garver (1987, 1994) observed that prudence cannot be codified into theoretical precepts; it can only be embodied in personal character (or **ethos**).

If ethical scholars, and by extension rhetorical scholars, cannot produce a traditional "theory" of prudence, and if they cannot specify what principles to apply in what situations, then what can they do? How might the *capacity* of prudence be enhanced in individual moral agents or rhetorical advocates? One way of proceeding, consistent with the classical tradition of rhetorical education, is through an engagement with what Nussbaum (1986) termed "complex examples" (p. 313).[3] Let us turn to an example to try to illustrate this sense of prudence as the mediation of universal/general principles and concrete/particular situations.

In the fall of 1984, then New York Governor Mario Cuomo was invited to speak at the University of Notre Dame on the broad theme of religion and public morality. At the time, Cuomo and other Catholic politicians (particularly Democratic vice presidential nominee Geraldine Ferraro) were coming under attack from the Catholic hierarchy for their "pro-choice" votes and decisions. For a variety of reasons, Cuomo elected to use his Notre Dame forum to address the problem that abortion posed for Catholic politicians (on this speech, see also Farrell, 1993, pp. 213-229). The key issue that Cuomo confronted was the following: What obligations do Catholics (given Catholic doctrine that abortion is murder) have to change public abortion policy? As Cuomo put it, "When should I argue to make my religious value your morality? My rule of conduct your limitation?" This question is, it appears, rather simple for the Catholic hierarchy to answer. Catholic bishops practice a version of what is referred to variously as *categorical rule ethics* or *apodictic reasoning.* The basic idea in these forms of decision making is that general principles should dictate or govern human action, regardless of the situation. For the bishops, the doctrine that abortion is murder/immoral entails that (a) Catholics *must not* engage in the practice of abortion *and* (b) Catholics *must* act politically, in the public realm, to end the practice of abortion in the United States.

Cuomo, it seemed, was willing to endorse the first point—that individual Catholics, in their own lives, must not practice abortion. But he was unwilling to accept the second point; he did not agree that Catholic doctrine should have the power to dictate public or political action. In effect, Cuomo sought to destabilize—but not destroy (on this distinction, see Garver, 1987)—the relationship between principle (Catholic doctrine) and particular case (the political decisions of Catholic politicians). He sought what he termed a "latitude of judgment" when it came to how and when Catholic politicians would attempt to convert others to Catholic moral beliefs. Cuomo insisted that the public application of moral principles "is not a matter of doctrine." He explained,

> There is no inflexible moral principle which determines what our *political* conduct should be. . . . There is no church teaching that mandates the best political course for making our belief everyone's rule. . . . There is neither an encyclical nor a catechism that

spells out a political strategy for achieving legislative goals.

Echoing the Aristotelian position outlined earlier, Cuomo maintained that the relationship between principle and particular case—Catholic doctrine and political practice—"is a matter of prudential political judgment." He continued, "The Catholic trying to make moral and prudent judgments in the political realm must discern which, if any, of the actions one could take would be best." And the decision would be reached only after taking into account all, or as many as possible, of the "particulars"—the "opportunities and limitations" (Dunne, 1993, p. 311)—of each decision-soliciting situation.

Did Cuomo's performance at Notre Dame—his effort to both recover *and* enact the classical prudential method—solve the problem of abortion in America? Of course not. Did it resolve the dilemma facing Catholic politicians? Not really. Did it change the minds of the many Catholic priests in attendance? Probably not. If these assessments of the speech are accurate, then should we judge it, and the prudential process it illustrates, a failure? Not necessarily. If we judge the speech a failure because it did not solve the moral dilemmas of abortion policy or permanently resolve the dilemma of Catholic politicians, then we would be applying standards of certainty and maximum effectiveness that belong more appropriately to the practices of *episteme* and *techne.* But Aristotle insisted that prudence could not be reduced to episteme or techne; its methods of enactment and standards of evaluation are not identical to those of the other intellectual virtues.[4] Did Cuomo address head-on some of the key issues raised by his critics? Did he articulate a thoughtful, cogent, and perspicacious position (one that might be thought of as **locally stable**) on these controversial issues? Did his speech invite and encourage further reflection and argument? Did it help to shape or direct subsequent conversation? Did it help to improve the quality of deliberation on this vexing issue? If we answer these questions with at least a tentative yes, then we might judge Cuomo's speech to be successful. Although it fails to meet the rigorous standards of episteme and techne, it does appear to satisfy the more modest expectations of the prudential method.

Cuomo's Notre Dame speech illustrates the "flexible movement back and forth between particular and general" that Nussbaum (1986, p. 316) found in Aristotle's conceptualization of prudential deliberation. But does the negotiation or adjustment of general principle and particular case exhaust the scope of prudence? Not necessarily. Another type of situation that invites prudential deliberation, Aristotle recognized, is one involving *incommensurable values.* Nussbaum noted that Aristotle recognized that "the values that are constitutive of a good human life are plural and incommensurable" (p. 294; see also Stocker, 1990). How, then, do humans adjudicate between *competing* values or decide *which* values, rights, or principles should prevail in a particular situation? Consider the case in Northern Ireland during the summer of 1998. The Protestant and Catholic disputants reached a historic settlement that offered the conflicted region the possibility of peace. But tensions remain. Shortly after the peace accord was signed, the Protestant Orange Order sought to hold its annual commemorative march through a largely Catholic neighborhood. Catholics in the area resisted and appealed to the new authorities for assistance. The case was widely viewed, as one observer remarked, as a struggle over whose rights should prevail—those of the radical Protestant Orangemen or those of Garvaghy Road's militant Catholics? Whose rights—whose values—*should* prevail? Was there any fixed permanent standard (an episteme) that could resolve this dispute between incommensurable values? There did not appear to be any. Conflicts such as this might be thought of as recurrent **situational** exigences—*prudential dilemmas* or disputes. In this type of situation, advocates struggle to construct viable, but ultimately **contingent, value hierarchies.** It might not be possible, in the abstract, to determine what rights or whose values are most important. An example is the ongoing struggle between "equality" and "liberty" in American culture. But it might be possible, through reasoned deliberation, to reach a decision that, in this particular case, liberty outweighs equality or the value of truth outweighs that of consideration for the feelings of others.

Garver's (1987) study of Machiavelli further probed the nature and scope of prudence. One of his central contributions to the ongoing recovery of prudence was his analysis of the relationship between prudence and moderation. Acknowledging the Aristotelian tradition, Garver asserted that prudence is "an inferential relation between rules and cases" (p. 12). Continuing a theme developed by Aristotle, Garver located prudence in a *middle ground;* it is "halfway between an ethics of principles, in which those principles univocally dictate action . . ., and an ethics of consequences, in which the successful result is all" (p. 12). Aristotle's discussion of virtue as an "intermediate" often has been used to valorize moderation and compromise as the essence of prudence. But Garver echoed Aristotle's (1973) observation that "it is no easy task to find the middle" (1109a24) when he wrote, "Prudence is not simply the middle ground between two extremes, the middle that any reasonable person should adopt just because extremes are bad" (Garver, 1987, p. 19; see also Dunne, 1993). Valorizing moderation, it seems, turns it into a fixed principle, but as noted earlier, adhering to fixed principles (even the supposedly prudent principle of moderation) leaves a person incapable of responding to a situation and its nuances and particulars. Garver (1987) argued that the Aristotelian tradition of prudence does not demand moderation as the key to virtuous action; rather, the tradition entails a "transformation of moderation" (p. 163) that destabilizes it, rendering it a flexible situational norm.

While anchored in the Aristotelian tradition, Garver used Machiavelli's writings (primarily *The Prince* and *Discourses on Livy*) to expand the realm of prudential action beyond negotiating the relationship between principles and particular cases or the relationship between competing values and principles. A prudential process of reasoning, unlike other forms such as "algorithmic" (or principle-driven) and "heuristic" (or consequence-driven) reasoning, is rooted in a political community. This fact, according to Garver, raises specific practical and prudential problems that communities must negotiate such as "how to combine stability . . . and innovation . . ., how to make stability a function, as much as possible, of active ability" and "how imitation can lead to autonomy rather than dependence" (p. 23). At first glance, these problems are abstract, so a concrete example is in order. Leff's (1991) reading of Franklin Roosevelt's 1932 address to the Commonwealth Club in San Francisco extended Garver's discussion and illustrated how an advocate might negotiate the problem of stability and innovation.

When Roosevelt, the Democratic nominee for president, spoke to his California audience, the nation had been mired in an economic depression for more than 2 years. The Republicans and incumbent president, Herbert Hoover, promised that if the nation remained true to its traditional ideal of "rugged individualism," it would pull itself out of its economic plight. Roosevelt believed otherwise; aggressive action on the part of the federal government was necessary. This very brief overview of the situation helps to clarify the nature of Roosevelt's (and the nation's) practical prudential problem. Roosevelt was convinced that federal action was necessary, but such action would be viewed by many in the nation as a potentially dangerous form of innovation—a drastic departure from the traditional principles that were the cornerstone of American stability. Roosevelt's rhetorical, and prudential, challenge was to combine innovation and stability by making his economic proposals consistent with American ideals of liberty and individualism.

Garver (1987) argued that Machiavelli provided a model for how a political leader might negotiate the tension between stability and innovation. Machiavelli realized (if only intuitively) that "stability is continuing innovation" (p. 35), or phrased as an *oxymoronic* norm, Machiavelli illustrated that prudence resides in a process of "stable innovation." Leff (1991) argued that Roosevelt's performance at the Commonwealth Club enacted this prudential norm. American history, in Roosevelt's **narrative** reconstruction, became an ongoing process of adjusting principles to circumstances. Given this narrative context, Roosevelt's economic proposals were not a departure from, but rather a continuation of, America's founding ideals. By presenting potentially novel ideas as an extension of traditional practices, Roosevelt combined or blended innovation with stability in a form of prudential rhetorical action. There is considerable evidence that this Machiavellian paradigm of stable innovation is quite ubiquitous. There are countless examples of American reform organizations and movements—and in some cases even radical ones—linking (or **articulating**) their innovative goals and objectives to a stable American tradition. Women's rights advocates, labor organizers, and civil rights activists are just some of the political innovators who have presented their causes as both a continuation and an extension of the work of America's founders. American political innovators are not the only advocates to adopt the paradigm. Anderson (1991) noted how countless nationalist movements around the world legitimate their objective (the novel act of creating new nations) by invoking "an historical tradition of serial continuity" (p. 195). Anderson suggested that nationalists negotiate the contingency of nation building by rediscovering something that had been lost.

The preceding paragraphs reviewed some of the significant works in the ongoing project of recovering prudence.[5] Rhetorical scholars are active participants in this project, branching off in more theoretical as well as more analytic or critical directions. Hariman (1991) represented the theoretical trajectory of prudential inquiry in rhetorical studies. His work explicated two strands in the history of prudence: the *cognitive* (or *calculative*) and the *performative.*[6] In focusing on the latter strand, Hariman reminded us that decision making, often the focus for discussions of prudence, is invariably enacted or performed. He wrote, "Prudent conduct will be conduct that relies on shared expectations regarding how and how well one might act out one's decision" (p. 27). Ultimately, "prudential conduct includes both an act of calculation and a politically consequential performance" (p. 32).[7] Focusing on the often neglected performative dimension places qualities such as an "aesthetic sensibility," "imitation of a performative ideal," and "improvisation upon conventions of presentation" (pp. 28-29) at the core of prudential action and prudential theory. To better appreciate Hariman's distinction, consider a simple example. A person has decided to break off an ongoing relationship (it may be a business or professional relationship, a romantic relationship, or some other form). We may assume that the decision to end the relationship is based on some type of calculation; various criteria were employed in assessing the situation and in determining that the relationship should be terminated. But *does* the decision actually end the relationship? Not really. Hariman called our attention to the performative element in calculative decision making: To enact the decision, we have to engage in some form of relationship-breaking behavior, and in this example nonaction (e.g., the person stops going to work or avoids his or her former significant other) still is a form of performative enactment. The needs of performance consequently enter into the process of decision calculation. Even in this simple example, the manner in which the decision might be performed can have profound consequences for each of the participants. Performance, then, needs to be better integrated into our accounts of prudential action.

A number of rhetorical scholars follow a somewhat different path and deploy prudence as an analytic strategy. Extending the works of Garver and others, Jasinski (1995, in press) developed an "idiomatic" or vocabulary-based approach to reconstructing prudence in public **controversies.** This approach tries to identify recurrent public idioms or vocabularies (and interrelated argumentative and stylistic strategies) that have been invented and deployed as part of humanity's ongoing efforts to negotiate problems of incommensurable values, contingency, and temporal finitude. The two key idioms that Jasinski identified—organized around the central ideals of *audacity* and *accommodation*—parallel observations made by Bricker (1980). The tension that Bricker pointed to when he wrote, "Prudence directs: Make the world conform to your preferences! On the other hand, prudence [also] directs: Make your preferences conform to the world!" (p. 401), mirrors the tension that Jasinski uncovered in both Renaissance political theory and antebellum public discourse. Levasseur (1997) examined one of the acknowledged masters of prudential political action, the English politician and philosopher Edmund Burke.[8] His study also located a central tension—between "rhetorical prudence" and "rhetorical heroism." In the case of Burke, Levasseur argued that there was a tendency to view situations as a "battleground" requiring heroic action rather than as an opportunity for accommodation. Consequently, he suggested that Burke's reputation for prudence might be overrated. Finally, Wilson (1998) resisted "approach[ing] prudence as a stable even *a priori* reflection of cultural expectations" (p. 133). In so doing, Wilson treated prudence as a type of **ideograph** or an "essentially contested concept"; it is "a contested space that political actors struggle to control through discourse. . . . [It] is a coveted space of legitimacy that [public advocates] attempt to occupy by discursively controlling its meaning" (p. 133). Such a project would seem to require the critic to focus on discourse where the concept of prudence is explicitly present. Wilson, however, sought to reconstruct "the forms of prudence implicated by . . . textual contexts" (p. 133). As a case study, Wilson examined the debate in Congress during the early 1870s over Senator Charles Sumner's "Supplementary Civil Rights Bill." Wilson's investigation uncovered a contest between "the principle of expediency" (p. 138) and the "ideal of justice" (p. 140) suggesting, at least indirectly, that the diachronic tradition of prudence (reconstructed by scholars such as Garver) contributes substantially to the meanings that might emerge in the "contested space" of prudence.

Prudence, phronesis, practical reason—these roughly synonymous terms try to name an intellectual capacity and/or performative sensibility that has provoked the imagination of thinkers, decision makers, and practicing public advocates since the days of Aristotle. It frequently is *defined by negation;* it most often is understood as a way of guiding action through deliberation and reflection that must be differentiated from an ethics of principles and consequences, algorithmic and heuristic rules, or the intellectual practices of episteme and techne. Like the related concept of **decorum,** prudence seems to mandate careful reflection on the context of action and the relevant norms of propriety and appropriateness. But the concept of prudence often is frustrating because it resists the systemitization and precise explication that constitute our modern standards of intellectual rigor. Prudence seems to be a hopelessly inchoate and incomplete method for dealing with the problems and dilemmas of our world. Perhaps that is its most notable similarity to the tradition of rhetoric; both appear indispensable, yet both provoke discomfort because of their lack of precision and specificity.

Notes

1. See also the entry for Burke's (1984) concept of **casuistic stretching.**

2. See also Günther's (1993) elaborate examination of the issue of application as well as Risser's (1997) discussion of Gadamer and the "problem of application" (p. 107).

3. See the discussion of *imitation* in the entry for **invention** as well as the discussions of prudence and *improvisation* in Hariman (1991) and Nussbaum (1986).

4. As Garver (1987) pointed out, "Prudential reasoning yields conclusions that are always open to further debate because it yields conclusions that are always open to further action, and for that reason prudential reasoning will always appear [to be] a weak kind of reasoning measured against standards of theoretical reasoning [or techne]" (p. 16). Garver added, "The conclusion of a prudential method is always open to further debate, and so its evaluation is always a comparative judgment—not this conclusion is true and this inference valid, but this conclusion is better than some alternative" (p. 34).

5. See also Hargrove's (1998) discussion of prudence and presidential leadership.

6. In more recent work (Hariman & Beer, 1998), Hariman has identified three "modes" of prudence: *normative, calculative,* and *performative.* On the idea of a performative account of prudence, see also Schwarze (1999).

7. Although Hariman (1991) distinguished the calculative from the performative, he was not trying to erect a rigid dichotomy. His claim was essentially that they are (to use a somewhat overworked image) two sides of the same coin. The challenge that Hariman presented to theorists and critics alike was to not only recognize the analytic distinction but also locate how these two dimensions merge or overlap in practice.

8. Burke's prudential skills were discussed in Browne (1993, in press) and Chapman (1967).

References and Additional Reading

Anderson, B. (1991). *Imagined communities: Reflections on the origins and spread of nationalism* (rev. ed.). London: Verso.

Aristotle. (1973). *Introduction to Aristotle* (2nd ed., R. McKeon, Ed.). Chicago: University of Chicago Press.

Beiner, R. (1983). *Political judgment.* Chicago: University of Chicago Press.

Bricker, P. (1980). Prudence. *Journal of Philosophy, 77,* 381-401.

Browne, S. H. (1993). *Edmund Burke and the discourse of virtue.* Tuscaloosa: University of Alabama Press.

Browne, S. H. (in press). Burke's *Letter to the Sheriffs of Bristol* and the texture of prudence. In R. Hariman (Ed.), *The discourses of prudence.*

Brownstein, O. L. (1974). Aristotle and the rhetorical process. In W. R. Fisher (Ed.), *Rhetoric: A tradition in transition.* East Lansing: Michigan State University Press.

Burke, K. (1984). *Attitudes toward history* (3rd ed.). Berkeley: University of California Press.

Chapman, G. W. (1967). *Edmund Burke: The practical imagination.* Cambridge, MA: Harvard University Press.

Dunne, J. (1993). *Back to the rough ground: Practical judgment and the lure of technique.* Notre Dame, IN: University of Notre Dame Press.

Farrell, T. B. (1993). *Norms of rhetorical culture.* New Haven, CT: Yale University Press.

Farrell, T. B. (1998). Sizing things up: Colloquial reflection as practical wisdom. *Argumentation, 12,* 1-14.

Gadamer, H. G. (1982). *Truth and method* (G. Barden & J. Cumming, Trans.). New York: Crossroad.

Garver, E. (1987). *Machiavelli and the history of prudence.* Madison: University of Wisconsin Press.

Garver, E. (1994). *Aristotle's RHETORIC: An art of character.* Chicago: University of Chicago Press.

Günther, K. (1993). *The sense of appropriateness: Application discourses in morality and law* (J. Farrell, Trans.). Albany: State University of New York Press.

Hargrove, E. C. (1998). *The president as leader: Appealing to the better angels of our nature.* Lawrence: University Press of Kansas.

Hariman, R. (1991). Prudence/Performance. *Rhetoric Society Quarterly, 21,* 26-35.

Hariman, R. (Ed.). (in press). *The discourses of prudence.*

Hariman, R., & Beer, F. A. (1998). What would be prudent? Forms of reasoning in world politics. *Rhetoric and Public Affairs, 1,* 299-330.

Jasinski, J. (1995). The forms and limits of prudence in Henry Clay's (1850) defense of the compromise measures. *Quarterly Journal of Speech, 81,* 454-478.

Jasinski, J. (in press). The idioms of prudence in three antebellum controversies: Revolution, Constitution, and slavery. In R. Hariman (Ed.), *The discourses of prudence.*

Kahn, V. (1985). *Rhetoric, prudence, and skepticism in the Renaissance.* Ithaca, NY: Cornell University Press.

Leff, M. (1991). Prudential argument and the use of history in Franklin D. Roosevelt's "Commonwealth Club" address. In F. H. van Eemeren, R. Grootendorst, J. A. Blair, & C. A. Willard (Eds.), *Proceedings of the Second International Conference on Argumentation.* Amsterdam: Stichting Internationaal Centrum voor de Studie van Argumentatie en Taalbeheersing (SICSAT).

Levasseur, D. G. (1997). A reexamination of Edmund Burke's rhetorical art: A rhetorical struggle between prudence and heroism. *Quarterly Journal of Speech, 83,* 332-350.

MacIntyre, A. (1988). *Whose justice? Which rationality?* Notre Dame, IN: University of Notre Dame Press.

Maritain, J. (1954). *Creative intuition in art and poetry.* London: Harvill Press.

Miller, R. B. (1996). *Casuistry and modern ethics: A poetics of practical reasoning.* Chicago: University of Chicago Press.

Nagel, T. (1970). *The possibility of altruism.* Oxford, UK: Clarendon.

Nelson, D. M. (1992). *The priority of prudence: Virtue and natural law in Thomas Aquinas and the implica-*

tions for modern ethics. University Park: Pennsylvania State University Press.
Nussbaum, M. C. (1986). *The fragility of goodness: Luck and ethics in Greek tragedy and philosophy*. Cambridge, UK: Cambridge University Press.
Pieper, J. (1959). *Prudence* (R. Winston & C. Winston, Trans.). New York: Pantheon.
Reeve, C. D. C. (1995). *Practices of reason: Aristotle's NICOMACHEAN ETHICS*. Oxford, UK: Clarendon.
Risser, J. (1997). *Hermeneutics and the voice of the other: Re-reading Gadamer's philosophical hermeneutics*. Albany: State University of New York Press.
Schwarze, S. (1999). Performing *phronesis:* The case of Isocrates' *Helen. Philosophy and Rhetoric, 32*, 78-95.
Self, L. S. (1979). Rhetoric and *phronesis:* The Aristotelian ideal. *Philosophy and Rhetoric, 12*, 130-145.
Stocker, M. (1990). *Plural and conflicting values*. Oxford, UK: Clarendon.
Tessitore, A. (1996). *Reading Aristotle's ETHICS: Virtue, rhetoric, and political philosophy*. Albany: State University of New York Press.
Westberg, D. (1994). *Right practical reason: Aristotle, action, and prudence in Aquinas*. Oxford, UK: Clarendon.
Wiggins, D. (1980). Deliberation and practical reason. In A. O. Rorty (Ed.), *Essays on Aristotle's ETHICS*. Berkeley: University of California Press.
Wilson, K. H. (1998). The contested space of prudence in the 1874-1875 civil rights debate. *Quarterly Journal of Speech, 84*, 131-149.

PUBLIC LETTER

The letter, and with it the activity of letter writing, emerged as an important **discursive formation** during the late Medieval period in Europe. Secular and religious leaders needed a way of training officials in this new craft. Creative scholars turned to the tradition of rhetoric as a resource, and the *ars dictaminis*—the art of letter writing—was born.[1] The practice of letter writing, directly and indirectly shaped by the tradition of rhetoric, grew and spread throughout European and Western society during the centuries that followed. By the 18th century, various **genres** of letter writing could be identified such as the *didactic letter* (commonly written by parents to children) and the *personal* or *familiar letter*. Anderson and Ehrenpreis (1966) identified the 18th century as "the great age of the personal letter" (p. 269; see also Redford, 1986). As the letter became an established cultural institution, it began to influence other modes of discourse.

In the realm of literature, epistolary narratives (stories told through a series of letters) became quite common beginning during the late 17th century and continuing throughout the 18th century (this phenomenon is widely discussed in literary studies such as Day, 1966). In the realm of politics and public affairs, the popularity of letter writing helped to generate a new discursive *hybrid*—the **public letter.** Favret (1993) commented,

> In the mind of late eighteenth-century Europe, the letter fused the world of epistolary romance, the domestic tragedies of *Clarissa* or *Julie*, with the world of political revolution. . . . The letter had, in fact, become a phenomenally useful political tool, available to anyone with a pen. (pp. 7, 9)

Favret concluded, "The genre of the familiar epistle, from its roots in classical rhetoric, had emerged at the end of the [18th] century as the medium of collective political activity" (p. 30). Similarly, Warner (1990) observed, "In the [American] colonial period, by far the most popular genres for political debate were the epistolary pamphlet and the dialogue" (p. 40). Despite the pervasiveness of the public letter, it has not received extensive scholarly attention (Favret, 1993).

Given its political agenda and persuasive function, the public letter is an important rhetorical form. Scholars in rhetorical studies have, to some degree, begun to address its particular dynamics and characteristics (Browne, 1988, 1990; Fulkerson, 1979; Hammerback & Jensen, 1999; Vonnegut, 1995). The public letter tends to appear as one of two types: a letter explicitly addressed "to the public" or a letter addressed to a specific correspondent that is then *made* public (e.g., printed in a newspaper or as a pamphlet). In some cases, a letter is made public without the permission of the author, but in many cases the author intends to address a larger public but does so through the "fiction" of a familiar letter (Favret, 1993). In this latter case, the mode of address functions as a variation on the **stylistic** device of *apostrophe*. The correspondent, to whom the letter is ostensibly addressed, serves as an apostrophic frame through which the letter writer addresses a larger public audience.[2] Favret (1993) suggested that the public letter is "promiscuous" (p. 23) in the way that it addresses multiple audiences.[3]

Given the lack of scholarly attention to this discursive form, it is difficult to generalize about its dynamics and characteristics. Browne (1988), for example, noted how the "protean" nature of the "epistolary form" provides letter writers such as Edmund Burke "the opportunity to range across a spectrum of themes, [to] invoke a variety of styles of voices, and to transcend the limits of conventional rhetorical genres" (p. 219). The public letter, as Browne suggested, is a hybrid form uniting elements of the familiar letter (e.g., conversational quality, spontaneity, candor), the biblical epistle (e.g., the discursive conventions contained in the letters of St. Paul[4]), and the didactic epistle (and its effort to exercise authority and give instruction) with the characteristics of political orations and pamphlets. The hybrid public letter creates a type of space—a *middle ground* of sorts—between the vehemence and passion of many political orations and the detached or disinterested quality of the typical political treatise. Browne (1988, 1990) argued that this discursively constructed space provides readers with a place to stand, as well as standards, for enacting political **judgment.** Scholars generally agree that the public letter mediates or bridges the domains of private and public life. The letter form makes it possible (as a matter of **decorum** or *propriety*) for personal experiences to be made public. It appears that the public letter helped to enable the personalization of political life that had become commonplace by the late 20th century. As Browne (1988) noted in the case of Burke, one of the common functions of the public letter is the exoneration and/or rehabilitation of personal character; as such, many cases of the public letter incorporate elements of the **apologia.**

Existing scholarship suggests some possible lines of inquiry on this topic. For example, numerous scholars have discussed the gradual shift from a predominantly oral culture to a print culture and how this shift influenced public discourse (e.g., Robertson, 1995; Warner, 1990). What role did the public letter play in this shift? We might speculate that the public letter was such a popular discursive mode during this time period because the form was able to retain some of the intimacy of the spoken word while also taking advantage of the resources of print. Another line of inquiry, explored in the context of European culture by Favret (1993), is the relationship between the letter form and gender. If, as Favret argued, the familiar letter was seen by many during the 18th century as a decidedly feminine mode of communication, then what was the impact of its appropriation for use in the **public sphere**? Did the public letter contribute to the feminization of American public culture (on this contested issue, see Douglas, 1977)? What are the implications, if any, of the public letter on the process of gender construction in American society?

The public letter reached its apogee in American culture during the late 18th and 19th centuries. The form was widespread throughout the political **debates** of the revolutionary, constitutional, and early national periods. It remained extremely important well into the 19th century. For example, John Calhoun employed the form to announce that he was rejoining the Democratic party (in what is known as the "Edgefield letter"), and Henry Clay used the public letter as a vehicle for discussing his views on the question of Texas annexation during the 1844 presidential election (the "Raleigh letter"). Clay subsequently published two additional letters on the issue (the "Alabama letters") that qualified his earlier views, and a number of historians believe that the Alabama letters might have cost Clay the presidency in 1844. The public letter was not a discursive form limited to social elites and those with access to political authority. Dissenting advocates regularly made use of the public letter during the 19th century. Abolitionist Angelina Grimké's 1836 "Appeal to the Christian Women of the South" was cast in the form of a public letter, and her sister Sarah also relied on the form in her "An Epistle to the Clergy of the Southern States" published during the same year.

Given the emphasis on the 18th and 19th century in extant scholarship, the following would be a fair question: Does the concept of the public letter have any contemporary relevance? Although the use of the form clearly has declined, it nevertheless remains an avenue for rhetorical expression. Perhaps the most famous 20th-century instance of the form was Martin Luther King, Jr.'s "Letter From Birmingham Jail" in April 1963 (Fulkerson, 1979). Public letters have become part of the public relations arsenal of many U.S. corporations. The form is used with some frequency by corporations when dealing with threats to their images; it has, in short, become a staple of the modern subgenre of the *corporate* **apologia.** But it might be the case that technological developments, so important in the historical evolution of the public letter, will breathe new life into the form. Lanham (1991) observed,

> It might perhaps be argued that the role played in the classical period by the formal speech . . ., as the central pattern for educated utterance, was taken over in the Middle Ages by the formal letter, and that this yielded to the essay in the Renaissance, only to be giving way, today, to a new form of electronic on-line exchange which is part speech, part conversation, part essay, and part letter. (p. 22)

From its origins as a hybrid composed from elements of the familiar letter and the public oration, the public letter now might be mutating into a new hybrid form, thanks to computer technology and the Internet.

Notes

1. For an overview, see Kennedy (1980).
2. See Fulkerson's (1979) discussion of Martin Luther King, Jr.'s use of the eight white ministers as a frame for his "Letter From Birmingham Jail" in April 1963 and White's (1984) observations on Edmund Burke's use of the "very young gentleman at Paris" as a frame for his *Reflections on the Revolution in France* (pp. 195-197).
3. On the "promiscuous" audience in 19th-century America, see Zaeske (1995).
4. For a discussion of how King relied on these conventions in the letter, see Snow (1985).

References and Additional Reading

Anderson, H., & Ehrenpreis, I. (1966). The familiar letter in the eighteenth century: Some generalizations. In H. Anderson, P. B. Daghlian, & I. Ehrenpreis (Eds.), *The familiar letter in the eighteenth century.* Lawrence: University Press of Kansas.

Browne, S. H. (1988). Edmund Burke's *Letter to a Noble Lord:* A textual study in political philosophy and rhetorical action. *Communication Monographs, 55,* 215-229.

Browne, S. H. (1990). The pastoral voice in John Dickinson's first *Letter From a Farmer in Pennsylvania. Quarterly Journal of Speech, 76,* 46-57.

Day, R. A. (1966). *Told in letters: Epistolary fiction before Richardson.* Ann Arbor: University of Michigan Press.

Douglas, A. (1977). *The feminization of American culture.* New York: Knopf.

Favret, M. A. (1993). *Romantic correspondence: Women, politics, and the fiction of letters.* Cambridge, UK: Cambridge University Press.

Fulkerson, R. P. (1979). The public letter as a rhetorical form: Structure, logic, and style in King's "Letter From Birmingham Jail." *Quarterly Journal of Speech, 65,* 121-136.

Hammerback, J. C., & Jensen, R. J. (1999). History and culture as rhetorical constraints: Cesar Chavez's Letter From Delano. In K. J. Turner (Ed.), *Doing rhetorical history: Concepts and cases.* Tuscaloosa: University of Alabama Press.

Kennedy, G. A. (1980). *Classical rhetoric and its Christian and secular tradition from ancient to modern times.* Chapel Hill: University of North Carolina Press.

Lanham, R. A. (1991). *A handlist of rhetorical terms* (2nd ed.). Berkeley: University of California Press.

Redford, B. (1986). *The converse of the pen: Acts of intimacy in the eighteenth-century familiar letter.* Chicago: University of Chicago Press.

Robertson, A. W. (1995). *The language of democracy: Political rhetoric in the United States and Britain, 1790-1900.* Ithaca, NY: Cornell University Press.

Snow, M. (1985). Martin Luther King's "Letter From Birmingham Jail" as Pauline epistle. *Quarterly Journal of Speech, 71,* 318-334.

Vonnegut, K. S. (1995). Poison or panacea? Sarah Moore Grimké's use of the public letter. *Communication Studies, 46,* 73-88.

Warner, M. (1990). *The letters of the republic: Publication and the public sphere in eighteenth-century America.* Cambridge, MA: Harvard University Press.

White, J. B. (1984). *When words lose their meaning: Constitutions and reconstitutions of language, character, and community.* Chicago: University of Chicago Press.

Zaeske, S. (1995). The "promiscuous audience" controversy and the emergence of the early women's rights movement. *Quarterly Journal of Speech, 81,* 191-207.

PUBLIC SPHERE

In 1962, a young German philosopher and social theorist, Jürgen Habermas, published *Strukturwandel der Oeffentlichkeit* (*The Structural Transformation of the Public Sphere*), which helped him to establish a reputation as one of Germany's leading public intellectuals (Habermas, 1962/1989). According to Hohendahl (1974),

> *Strukturwandel der Oeffentlichkeit* soon became a standard work which was to help shape the political consciousness of the emerging [German] New Left in the 1960s. The book remained in the center of discussion even after 1968, when many leftist students broke with the Frankfurt school with which Habermas was also identified. (p. 45)

What did Habermas write in 1962 that had such an impact on the German New Left? Even more important, what significance might this work have for students of rhetoric?

Structural Transformation (the English translation of Habermas's [1962/1989] work appeared in 1989), like many works of a historical nature, told a story (Dahlgren, 1995). But Habermas's (1962/1989) interest in social theory was visible in the story's main "character." Habermas did not tell a story about individual social actors; he did not focus on princes or presidents or on poets or popes. Nor did his story focus on a collective agent such as a heroic proletariat, an enlightened "public," or a mythical "people." The central character in his tale was an *institution* that he labeled the **public sphere;** more specifically, he concentrated on the European *bourgeois* public sphere. The "plot" of Habermas's story was rather familiar. *Structural Transformation* employed the common "rise-and-fall," or constitution-disintegration, plot structure. Habermas traced the gradual emergence of his main character in late 17th and early 18th-century Europe and described the way in which it functioned to mediate between the "state" (most specifically, the executive power of a nation) and "society" (private economic activity), noted its most salient features and accomplishments, and then described its demise and transformation during the 20th century. Habermas's tale of social disintegration, and his call (however muted) to recover the critical potential of the public sphere, resonated with many young Germans during the 1960s who, like their French and American counterparts, were growing increasingly frustrated with the overall direction of their society.

Before proceeding to unpack the concept further, we might pause briefly to consider one of the questions already raised: Why is the concept of the public sphere of interest or importance to rhetorical scholars? A preliminary answer to this question might run something like this. Rhetorical practice always is *situated;* it regularly comes into existence in certain physical places or settings (see also the entry for **argument field**). In ancient Greece, for example, rhetorical practice most frequently occurred within the *polis* (the political system of the city-state). The norms, customs, and traditions of the polis exerted a powerful influence on rhetorical advocates acting within it. Habermas (1962/1989) suggested that the European bourgeois public sphere is a descendent of the ancient Greek polis (p. 3). The public sphere can be thought of as the common (albeit not exclusive) realm or arena in which public discourse is produced. Arato and Cohen (1998) reiterated this idea when they described the "civil public sphere" as "the domain that informs the electorate about issues and choices, promotes discussion that can lead to democratic demands, and brings popular concerns to the attention of decision makers" (p. 61). Public discourse and political **deliberation** are, then, essential features of virtually any public sphere. Given the mutually reinforcing relationship between rhetorical practice and the public sphere, the attention devoted to the concept by rhetorical scholars should not be surprising.

But *how* have scholars in rhetorical studies and other fields characterized the public sphere? Most contemporary discussions of the concept are, directly or indirectly, indebted to Habermas's groundbreaking work. We need to outline its key arguments before turning our attention more directly to work in rhetorical studies.[1] According to Habermas, the public sphere is both *real* and *ideal;* put differently, it is both a *descriptive* and *normative* concept. We need to be clear about this distinction because the tension between these two "sides" of the concept can cause problems.

As a descriptive concept, the public sphere tries to identify and characterize a range of historically real political and social conditions that both *enable* and *constrain* public discourse within a given society. A specific public sphere (e.g., America during the late 20th century, England during the late 18th century) consists of (a) *institutions* and their particular structures, norms, and discursive practices (e.g., coffeehouses, public squares, newspapers and other ideologically grounded periodicals, the television industry, labor unions, political parties, political action committees); (b) established legal rights, constraints, and proscriptions (e.g., rights to free speech and assembly, definitions of citizenship, laws regarding libel or regulating commercial speech); and (c) cultural values and traditions that inform institutional norms and structures and that provide an important part of a culture's *common sense* or **social knowledge.** Working with these and other analytic directives, scholars can produce rigorous descriptions of the institutions and practices of culturally specific public spheres (Landes, 1988; Ryan, 1990; Warner, 1990).

As a normative concept, the public sphere, according to Habermas, tries to identify norms and ideals with enduring value that, while only incompletely realized in a specific public sphere, can function as a ground (or *warrant*) for social critique (on the normative dimension of the public sphere, see also Taylor, 1995). For example, Habermas argued that the liberal or bourgeois public sphere that emerged in Europe revealed the possibility that rational-critical discourse could function as a way of testing *claims* to the general or "national" interest. Claims that could not withstand the critical scrutiny (or "publicity") of the public sphere would necessarily be withdrawn. As Calhoun (1992b) observed, Habermas labored to recover this "valuable critical ideal from the classical bourgeois public sphere" (p. 29). Consider a second example. Habermas (1962/1989) argued that the European bourgeois public sphere incorporates the ideal of open or "universal" access; "a public sphere from which specific groups would be *eo ipso* excluded was less than merely incomplete, it was not a public sphere at all" (p. 85; see also Hauser, 1987). Yet, groups were routinely denied access to the public sphere. Doesn't this contradiction between ideal and practice invalidate the entire concept of the bourgeois public sphere? Habermas's answer was no; the principle of universal access to the public sphere still can have a normative function—it can be deployed in social and political critique—despite its only partial realization in the historical practices that constituted the bourgeois public sphere.

The first half of *Structural Transformation* (Habermas, 1962/1989) described the emergence of "a public that critically debated political issues" (p. 67) in different European nations.[2] Within the bourgeois public sphere, citizens gathered and, both orally and in print, argued about the pressing issues of the day. Habermas argued that in the bourgeois public sphere, individual social status or rank did not matter; only the force of the better argument could prevail (p. 36).[3] Unconstrained argument is, in many respects, the essence of the bourgeois public sphere, in Habermas's view (this early interest in critical argument eventually would be developed into a normative theory of communicative action). Through the practice of critical argument in the public sphere, citizens produced rationally grounded public *opinion* that became an important source of **power** in 17th and 18th-century Europe. Habermas (1974) contended, "Public opinion refers to the tasks of criticism and control which a public body of citizens . . . practices *vis-à-vis* the ruling structure organized in the form of a state. . . . [It] can by definition only come into existence when a reasoning public is presupposed" (pp. 49-50).

In the latter part of *Structural Transformation,* Habermas (1962/1989) charted the decline of the bourgeois public sphere. Whereas a number of factors are involved, one issue that received significant attention is the displacement of public argument by processes of cultural *consumption.* Habermas wrote,

> When the laws of the market governing the sphere of commodity exchange and of social labor also pervade the sphere reserved for private people as a public, rational-critical debate had a tendency to be replaced by consumption, and the web of public communication unraveled into acts of individuated reception, however uniform in mode. (p. 161)

In other words, the growth of a market mentality has turned public discourse into a commodity; as a number of contemporary political commentators have observed, in America we "sell" our presidents in the same way as we sell soap or deodorant. The capacity for critical reflection atrophies.[4]

A number of Habermas's descriptive and normative insights into the bourgeois public sphere have been incorporated into the works of rhetorical scholars. Conceptually, Hauser (1999) extended Habermas's discussion when he defined a public sphere as

> a space in which strangers discuss issues they perceive to be of consequence for them and their group. Its rhetorical exchanges are the bases for shared awareness of common issues, shared interests, tendencies of extent and strength of difference and agreement, and self-constitution as a public whose opinions bear on the organization of society. (p. 64)

We can see further evidence of Habermas's influence, both directly and indirectly, in Fabj and Sobnosky's (1995) discussion of AIDS activism and the public sphere, Goodnight's (1982) reconstruction of three central spheres of argument practice, Hauser's (1995) reading of the Meese Commission report on pornography, and Jasinski's (1986) analysis of the U.S. constitutional ratification debate during 1787-1788. Whereas Habermas's work on the public sphere has influenced scholars both in and outside the field of rhetorical studies, it also has been the object of criticism (in rhetorical studies, see Griffin, 1996; Phillips, 1996). Among the objections that have been raised (Calhoun, 1992b), some of the more prominent include the following. First, Habermas presented the bourgeois public sphere as too monolithic. There is a need to study "nonliberal, nonbourgeois, competing public spheres" that might be described as "subaltern counterpublics" (Fraser, 1992, pp. 115, 123; see also Felski, 1989, pp. 164-174), "nested public spheres" (Taylor, 1995), or "enclaved publics" (Zulick & Laffoon, 1991).[5] Second, Habermas idealized the operation of the bourgeois public sphere, ignoring the various institutions and practices that might challenge its normative potential. Third, Habermas exaggerated the decline of the public sphere by not devoting sufficient attention to important phenomena such as social **movements**.[6]

Whatever the precise nature of its defects,[7] Habermas's discussion of the public sphere opened up new avenues of theoretical reflection and critical inquiry in a variety of academic fields. As Calhoun (1992b) noted, Habermas's public sphere project was an attempt to recover "an institutional location for practical reason in public affairs" (p. 1). Among its many guises, rhetoric sometimes is thought of as the art and practice of *practical reason* (see the entry for **prudence**). For scholars who envision a relationship between situated rhetorical practice and the performative ideal of practical reason, the continued relevance of the public sphere, as both a descriptive category and a normative concept, should be clear.

Notes

1. For useful summaries of Habermas's formulation, see Calhoun (1992b) and Hohendahl (1979).

2. On the related concept of a public, see Bitzer (1978), Dewey (1927), Lippmann (1925), McGee (1975), and McGee and Martin (1983).

3. Compare Habermas's discussion of the suspension of rank in the bourgeois public sphere and the idea of "ethos without identity" introduced in the entry for **ethos.**

4. Arato and Cohen (1998) suggested that the demise of the public sphere in the United States might be exaggerated. They located evidence of its vitality in an unlikely place—the 1998-1999 Bill Clinton sex scandal. They asserted, "It seems to us, however, that the relationship between the media and public opinion in the Clinton crisis shows that obituaries for a thinking and critical civil public have been premature. In fact, we might be witnessing a trend in the opposite direction" (pp. 61-62).

5. See also the studies collected in the Black Public Sphere Collective (1995).

6. For additional critiques of Habermas's public sphere project, see also Negt and Kluge (1993) and a number of the essays in Robbins (1993).

7. Habermas (1992) acknowledged that *Structural Transformation* (Habermas, 1961/1989) was a flawed work.

References and Additional Reading

Arato, A., & Cohen, J. (1998, Summer). Politics by other means? Democracy and the Clinton crisis. *Dissent,* pp. 61-66.

Bitzer, L. F. (1978). Rhetoric and public knowledge. In D. M. Burks (Ed.), *Rhetoric, philosophy, and literature: An exploration.* West Lafayette, IN: Purdue University Press.

Black Public Sphere Collective. (Ed.). (1995). *The Black Public Sphere: A public culture book.* Chicago: University of Chicago Press.

Calhoun, C. (Ed.). (1992a). *Habermas and the public sphere.* Cambridge, MA: MIT Press.

Calhoun, C. (1992b). Introduction: Habermas and the public sphere. In C. Calhoun (Ed.), *Habermas and the public sphere.* Cambridge, MA: MIT Press.

Dahlgren, P. (1995). *Television and the public sphere.* London: Sage.

Dewey, J. (1927). *The public and its problems.* New York: Henry Holt.

Fabj, V., & Sobnosky, M. J. (1995). AIDS activism and the rejuvenation of the public sphere. *Argumentation and Advocacy, 31,* 163-184.

Felski, R. (1989). *Beyond feminist aesthetics: Feminist literature and social change.* Cambridge, MA: Harvard University Press.

Fraser, N. (1992). Rethinking the public sphere: A contribution to the critique of actually existing democracy. In C. Calhoun (Ed.), *Habermas and the public sphere.* Cambridge, MA: MIT Press.

Goodnight, G. T. (1982). The personal, technical, and public spheres of argument: A speculative inquiry into the art of public deliberation. *Journal of the American Forensic Association, 18,* 214-227.

Goodnight, G. T. (1997). Opening up "The Spaces of Public Dissension." *Communication Monographs, 64,* 270-275.

Goodnight, G. T., & Hingstman, D. B. (1997). Studies in the public sphere. *Quarterly Journal of Speech, 83,* 351-370.

Griffin, C. L. (1996). The essentialist roots of the public sphere: A feminist critique. *Western Journal of Communication, 60,* 21-39.

Habermas, J. (1974). The public sphere: An encyclopedia article (1964) (S. Lennox & F. Lennox, Trans.). *New German Critique,* No. 3, pp. 49-55.

Habermas, J. (1989). *Strukturwandel der Oeffentlichkeit* (The structural transformation of the public sphere: An inquiry into a category of bourgeois society) (T.

Burger, Trans.). Cambridge, MA: MIT Press. (Original work published 1962)

Habermas, J. (1992). Further reflections on the public sphere. In C. Calhoun (Ed.), *Habermas and the public sphere.* Cambridge, MA: MIT Press.

Hauser, G. A. (1987). Features of the public sphere. *Critical Studies in Mass Communication, 4,* 437-441.

Hauser, G. A. (1995). Constituting publics and reconstituting the public sphere: The Meese Commission report on pornography. In E. Schiappa (Ed.), *Warranting assent: Case studies in argument evaluation.* Albany: State University of New York Press.

Hauser, G. A. (1997). On publics and public spheres: A response to Phillips. *Communication Monographs, 64,* 275-279.

Hauser, G. A. (1998). Civil society and the principle of the public sphere. *Philosophy and Rhetoric, 31,* 19-40.

Hauser, G. A. (1999). *Vernacular voices: The rhetoric of publics and public spheres.* Charleston: University of South Carolina Press,

Hauser, G. A., & Blair, C. (1982). Rhetorical antecedents to the public. *Pre/Text, 3,* 139-167.

Hohendahl, P. (1974). Jürgen Habermas: "The Public Sphere" (1964) (P. Russian, Trans.). *New German Critique,* No. 3, pp. 45-48.

Hohendahl, P. U. (1979). Critical theory, public sphere, and culture: Jürgen Habermas and his critics (M. Silberman, Trans.). *New German Critique,* No. 16, pp. 89-118.

Jasinski, J. (1986). *Rhetorical practice and its visions of the public in the ratification debate of 1787-1788.* Unpublished Ph.D. dissertation, Northwestern University.

Landes, J. B. (1988). *Women and the public sphere in the age of the French Revolution.* Ithaca, NY: Cornell University Press.

Lippmann, W. (1925). *The phantom public.* New York: Harcourt Brace.

McGee, M.C. (1975). In search of "the people": A rhetorical alternative. *Quarterly Journal of Speech, 61,* 235-249.

McGee, M. C., & Martin, M. A. (1983). Public knowledge and ideological argumentation. *Communication Monographs, 50,* 47-65.

Negt, O., & Kluge, A. (1993). *The public sphere and experience: Toward an analysis of the bourgeois and proletarian public sphere* (P. Labanyi, J. O. Daniel, & A. Oksiloff, Trans.). Minneapolis: University of Minnesota Press.

Phillips, K. R. (1996). The spaces of public dissension: Reconsidering the public sphere. *Communication Monographs, 63,* 231-248.

Robbins, B. (Ed.). (1993). *The phantom public sphere.* Minneapolis: University of Minnesota Press.

Roberts, P. (1998). Habermas's rational-critical sphere and the problem of criteria. In M. Bernard-Donals & R. R. Glejzer (Eds.), *Rhetoric in an antifoundational world: Language, culture, and pedagogy.* New Haven, CT: Yale University Press.

Ryan, M. P. (1990). *Women in public: Between banners and ballots.* Baltimore, MD: Johns Hopkins University Press.

Strum, A. (1994). A bibliography of the concept of *öffentlichkeit. New German Critique,* No. 64, pp. 161-202.

Taylor, C. (1995). Liberal politics and the public sphere. In C. Taylor, *Philosophical arguments.* Cambridge, MA: Harvard University Press.

Warner, M. (1990). *The letters of the republic: Publication and the public sphere in eighteenth-century America.* Cambridge, MA: Harvard University Press.

Zulick, M. D., & Laffoon, E. A. (1991). Enclaved publics as inventional resources: An essay in generative rhetoric. In D. W. Parson (Ed.), *Argument in controversy: Proceedings of the Seventh SCA-AFA Conference on Argumentation.* Annandale, VA: Speech Communication Association.

RECALCITRANCE

In his recent book on Kenneth Burke and postmodernism, Wess (1996) wrote,

> In the constructionist theme in current theoretical discussion, one sees rhetoric transform itself upwards from the pejorative "mere rhetoric" into a discursive "worldview" with considerable power, one that a generation of theorists has put on the historical map. . . . Perhaps, however, the time has arrived to force constructionism to interrogate itself more rigorously. . . . *Discourse constructs, but what is the limit of its constructive power?* (p. 5, emphasis added)

Long before the *constructivist* or *constitutive* nature of language and discourse practice was put on the historical map, Burke sensed the need to engage the question raised by Wess: What is the limit of the constructive or constitutive power of our discursive practices? Burke's answer to this question is contained in his concept of **recalcitrance.**

In *Permanence and Change,* Burke (1984) wrote that "to say 'I am a bird'" is to have produced a "pseudo-statement." He maintained, "When we attempt to extend our pseudo-statements into the full complexity of life, we meet with considerable recalcitrance" (p. 255). He added,

> The factor of recalcitrance may force us to alter our original strategy of expression greatly. And in the end, our *pseudo-statements* may have been so altered by the revisions which the recalcitrance of the material has forced upon us that we can now more properly refer to them as *statements.* (p. 255)

Burke deployed his idea of recalcitrance as a defense against the charge commonly made against adherents to a constructivist orientation: Their position is radically idealist, subjectivist, or solipsistic. As Burke explained his idea of recalcitrance, he noted that the universe appears differently depending on one's point of view. He wrote,

> Such a position does not involve us in subjectivism or solipsism. It does not imply that the universe is merely the product of our interpretations [and, we should add, our talk about those interpretations]. For the interpretations themselves must be altered as the universe displays various orders of recalcitrance to them. (p. 256)

Burke's idea of recalcitrance—the sense that our words *must* conform to the nature of reality—can give the impression that he was backing away from his constructivist focus on language practice as a form of *action* that effectively constitutes the human world and returning to a traditional mimetic, reflective, or realistic model of verbal **representation.** But this is not a wholly accurate reading of Burke's position on this topic (Crable, 1998; Wess, 1996). Rather, he appeared to be charting a course that leads, to borrow the title from Bernstein's (1983) book, "beyond objectivism and relativism." Wess (1996) suggested that Burke's thinking on this issue struggled with a paradox—"the paradox of rhetorical realism, which insists on the real even while subscribing to the constructionist thesis that we are always already inside constructions that bring something into being 'for the first time' " (p. 109). Burke's "orders of recalcitrance" were partly aspects of brute physical reality (e.g., "laws" of physics, the materiality of the world), but for the most part Burke wanted to focus on the recalcitrance that inheres in all human communities (on this point, see Brummett, 1982, p. 426). The failure to consider the orders of recalcitrance present in any society is to run the risk of being incomprehensible and, consequently, ineffective.

Burke (1984) used the example of a "visionary" engaged in "cosmological speculation." He argued,

> But as one goes farther afield, new aspects of recalcitrance arise. One strategically alters his [sic] statements, insofar as he is able, to shape them in conformity with the use and wont of his group. At this stage, his message is taken up and variously reworked by many different kinds of men—and by the time they have fitted it to the recalcitrance of social relationships, political exigences, economic procedures, etc., transferring it from the private architecture of a poem into the public architecture of a social order, those who dealt with it in its incipient or emergent stages could hardly recognize it as having stemmed from them. (p. 258)

As the preceding passage suggests, Burke's primary interest was in the recalcitrance of our various "social orders"—the beliefs, values, **traditions,** practices, and institutions that structure (*enabling* and *constraining*) human existence. The "orders of recalcitrance" themselves change over time. For example, the recalcitrance experienced by religious skeptics during the 17th century (and the verbal strategies they used to negotiate this recalcitrance) is different from the orders of recalcitrance that surround the practice of religion in contemporary America. Crable (1998) summarized, "Recalcitrance both limits our ability to construct 'reality' and motivates us to change our existing interpretations and constructions" (p. 311).

Something like Burke's idea of recalcitrance has become commonplace in contemporary rhetorical theory.[1] Bitzer's (1968) discussion of *constraints* (see the entry for **situation, rhetorical**) and Croasmun and Cherwitz's (1982) discussion of how reality "impinges" on the production of discourse illustrate this tendency. Orders of recalcitrance, constraints, impinging reality, circumstances directly encountered—all of these formulations attempt to grasp the fluid, constantly shifting, yet constantly present limits on the constructive power of discursive practice.[2]

Notes

1. It is explicitly discussed in Brummett (1982), Charland (1987), Consigny (1974), and Crable (1998).
2. See also the discussions under the entries for **definition/definition of the situation; epistemic, rhetoric as,** and **representation.**

References and Additional Reading

Bernstein, R. J. (1983). *Beyond objectivism and relativism: Science, hermeneutics, and praxis.* Philadelphia: University of Pennsylvania Press.

Bertelsen, D. A. (1993). Kenneth Burke's conception of reality: The process of transformation and its implications for rhetorical criticism. In J. W. Chesebro (Ed.), *Extensions of the Burkeian system.* Tuscaloosa: University of Alabama Press.

Bitzer, L. (1968). The rhetorical situation. *Philosophy and Rhetoric, 1,* 1-14.

Brummett, B. (1982). On to rhetorical relativism. *Quarterly Journal of Speech, 68,* 425-430.

Burke, K. (1984). *Permanence and change* (3rd ed.). Berkeley: University of California Press.
Charland, M. (1987). Constitutive rhetoric: The case of the *peuple Québécois. Quarterly Journal of Speech, 73,* 133-150.
Consigny, S. (1974). Rhetoric and its situations. *Philosophy and Rhetoric, 7,* 175-186.
Crable, B. (1998). Ideology as "metabiology": Rereading Burke's *Permanence and Change. Quarterly Journal of Speech, 84,* 303-319.
Croasmun, E., & Cherwitz, R. A. (1982). Beyond rhetorical relativism. *Quarterly Journal of Speech, 68,* 1-16.
Wess, R. (1996). *Kenneth Burke: Rhetoric, subjectivity, postmodernism.* Cambridge, UK: Cambridge University Press.

RECURSIVE/RECURSIVITY

The adjective **recursive** and the noun **recursivity** are derived from the Latin *recurrere,* meaning "to run back." Recursive has a technical meaning in mathematics, but its more commonplace meaning is "indefinite repetition."[1] The term has a prominent place in Anthony Giddens's social theory and has been appropriated by some rhetorical scholars as a way of describing certain complex relationships.

The larger contours of Giddens's theory of *structuration*—which, like the social theories developed by Habermas, Foucault, and others, has some broad implications for students of contemporary rhetoric—need not detain us. Recursivity plays a specific role with respect to a phenomenon that Giddens described as the *duality of structure.* Giddens (1979) argued that the concept of duality of structure is designed to help overcome problematic dualisms such as "action" (or "agency") and "structure" (or free will and determinism) that plague social theory. Giddens wrote, "In place of each of these dualisms, the theory of structuration substitutes the central notion of the duality of structure." He continued, "By the duality of structure, I mean the essential recursiveness of social life, as constituted in social practices: Structure is both medium and outcome of the reproduction of practices" (p. 5). Later, Giddens wrote that the "duality of structure . . . relates to the fundamentally recursive character of social life . . . [and acknowledges] that the structural properties of social systems are both the medium and the outcome of the practices that constitute those systems" (p. 69).[2]

What exactly was Giddens driving at in these passages? What does it mean to say that social life is "recursive"? How does the idea of duality of structure extend and/or modify the basic fact of recursivity? Social life is recursive because it is repetitive. For example, every workweek begins with Monday (with some exceptions, of course), and the school term ends with exams. We tend to follow the same path in traveling from one destination to another. Our lives, both individually and collectively, are rather routinized; they consist of patterns of behavior that are repeated over and over again, with degrees of variation. But does repetition perpetuate "sameness," or do things change over time? What is the relationship between repetition and change? Giddens argued that repetition or recursivity is a central aspect of our lives, but so is change. Duality of structure, as a concept, tries to accommodate both recursivity and modification—repetition and change—as facts of life.

Duality of structure is a property or characteristic of complex systems. A complex system can be anything from an individual person to a family, a network of friends, a discursive **genre** or **discourse formation,** a social institution (e.g., a church, a corporation), a social **movement,** or an entire society. The concept of duality of structure specifies that when "properties" or elements of the system (e.g., beliefs, rules, resources) are employed in practice, those properties will be both the *medium* of practice and an *outcome* or *result* of practice. Giddens (1981) used the example of a language "system" to illustrate his point. He wrote,

> The structural properties of language, as qualities of a community of language speakers (e.g., syntactical rules), are drawn upon

> by a speaker in the production of a sentence. [The syntactical rules function here as a medium for the practice of producing a sentence.] But the very act of speaking that sentence contributes to the reproduction of those syntactical rules as enduring properties of the language. (p. 19)

So, the rules are both a medium for producing a sentence and the outcome or result of someone having produced a sentence; they are both medium and outcome.

This account of duality of structure has demonstrated the basic recursiveness of social life as a process of reproduction. Language (as a system) is reproduced every time someone (consciously or unconsciously) employs linguistic rules to produce discourse; the rules are both the medium of situated action (producing a sentence) and the outcome of that action (employing rules revitalizes them and continues their existence, thereby reproducing the system that the rules structure). But language changes; old rules are discarded, new meanings for words are introduced, and so on. This fact must be taken into account and incorporated into a theory of how it is reproduced. White (1984), for example, captured this dynamic aspect of language when he wrote that "a person acts both with and upon the language that he [sic] uses, at once employing and reconstituting its resources" (p. 8).

Giddens (1979) elaborated on this dynamic by using the concept of duality of structure to modify a more limited understanding of recursivity.[3] In a conceptual move that resembles the way in which Derrida (1977a; see also LaCapra, 1983) linked iteration and alteration, Giddens wanted to use recursivity to encompass repetition and mutation within the process of social reproduction so as to recognize the interconnection of continuity and change. In Giddens' recursive view of action or practice, the act of producing a sentence (or more complicated rhetorical acts) combines repetition and modification; no act can ever be an *exact* repetition or reproduction of a previous act or any abstract rule. Every utterance contains an element of repetition that is combined with an element of change or modification; it perpetuates and alters the system (or systems) of which it is a part. In this way, Giddens' sense of recursivity exceeds the narrower meaning of indefinite repetition.

How have rhetorical scholars drawn on Giddens's ideas of recursivity and duality of structure? Condit (1987) did so in her attempt to explain how "moral terms" (from the most abstract terms such as *good* and *evil* or *right* and *wrong* to the more specific ones such as *justice* or *fairness*) operate in public discourse. To say simply that such terms are used recursively—that they are repeated—is insufficient. Condit argued that moral terms are constantly repeated in public discourse, but drawing on Giddens, she maintained that the process of repetition introduces change. Like Giddens's example of the sentence and linguistic rules, the moral terms employed in public discourse are both a medium of **argument** (functioning frequently as argumentative *warrants*) and the outcome of discursive action (p. 82). Public discourse recursively reproduces and modifies a community's moral vocabulary. Jasinski (1988) invoked the concept of recursivity to explain the relationship between **ideology** and public discourse. He argued that ideological "belief systems" are recursive; they are both the medium and the outcome of discursive practice. Advocates draw on specific elements of an ideological belief system (e.g., the image of the "marketplace" that, with some relatively minor differences, is a fixture of contemporary liberalism and conservatism) as a medium of action, and through the process of action the element (and system) is reproduced as an outcome.

Jasinski also suggested that something like Giddens's sense of recursivity undergirds Leff's (1978) reading of Farrell's (1976) **social knowledge** thesis. Leff (1978) argued that Farrell was able to "circumvent" the traditional dualistic opposition between rhetoric as "process" and rhetoric as "substance" by (at least implicitly) characterizing social knowledge as both product and substance

(p. 89). Social knowledge, in other words, can be thought of as a recursive system marked by the duality of structure. Social knowledge, in Farrell's (1976) view, is the medium of rhetorical action (it makes rhetorical argument possible) as well as the outcome of rhetorical action. Social knowledge is employed in, and reproduced (and modified) through, discursive practice. As these examples illustrate, the concept of recursivity, along with the duality of structure, may help rhetorical scholars to negotiate or circumvent vexing conceptual dualisms.

Notes

1. Recursivity is similar to the term *iterable* or *iteration* that appears with some frequency in the deconstructionist writings of Derrida (1977a, 1977b) and those influenced by him (e.g., Butler, 1993; LaCapra, 1983). LaCapra's (1983) idea of "repetition with variation over time" (p. 44) roughly parallels Giddens's sense of recursivity.

2. On the "duality of structure" as a resource for **discourse** analysis, see Stillar (1998).

3. See, in particular, Giddens' (1979) "revision" of a passage from the French social theorist Pierre Bourdieu (p. 217).

References and Additional Reading

Butler, J. (1993). *Bodies that matter: On the discursive limits of "sex."* New York: Routledge.

Condit, C. M. (1987). Crafting virtue: The rhetorical construction of public morality. *Quarterly Journal of Speech, 73,* 79-97.

Derrida, J. (1977a). Limited Inc. In S. Weber (Ed.), *Glyph* (Vol. 2). Baltimore, MD: Johns Hopkins University Press.

Derrida, J. (1977b). Signature event context. In S. Weber (Ed.), *Glyph* (Vol. 1). Baltimore, MD: Johns Hopkins University Press.

Farrell, T. B. (1976). Knowledge, consensus, and rhetorical theory. *Quarterly Journal of Speech, 62,* 1-14.

Giddens, A. (1979). *Central problems in social theory: Action, structure, and contradiction in social analysis.* Berkeley: University of California Press.

Giddens, A. (1981). *A contemporary critique of historical materialism.* Berkeley: University of California Press.

Jasinski, J. (1988). Ideology, reflection, and alienation in rhetorical and argumentative practice. *Journal of the American Forensic Association, 24,* 207-217.

LaCapra, D. (1983). *Rethinking intellectual history: Texts, contexts, language.* Ithaca, NY: Cornell University Press.

Leff, M. C. (1978). In search of Ariadne's thread: A review of the recent literature on rhetorical theory. *Central States Speech Journal, 29,* 73-91.

Stillar, G. F. (1998). *Analyzing everyday texts: Discourse, rhetoric, and social perspectives.* Thousand Oaks, CA: Sage.

White, J. B. (1984). *When words lose their meaning: Constitutions and reconstitutions of language, character, and community.* Chicago: University of Chicago Press.

REPRESENTATION

What happens, or what is going on, when someone uses language to communicate with someone else? This is an important question, and it (or some variation on it) can be found at the heart of numerous academic disciplines including rhetorical studies. But it is a rather vague and abstract question, so let us approach it through a mundane example that will start to introduce the topics of language, communication, and **representation.** Imagine that it is early in the morning. An individual has stumbled into the bathroom and begun his or her morning ritual. The individual begins to consider what clothes to wear that day and realizes that he or she had forgotten to watch the weather forecast the night before or to look outside on the way to the bathroom. But the individual hears a roommate in the kitchen, so he or she calls out, "What's it like outside?"

In this example, the individual has asked the roommate to use language in a very specific way; what is wanted is a report on, or a description of, the weather. And the individual also is assuming that language has the capacity to accomplish these functions or that it is capable of reflecting or referring to things in the world clearly and accurately. When something reflects, refers to, or stands in for something else, we can describe this as a process of representation. Before continuing the discussion, we should note that language is not the only medium or material that can initiate a representational process and enact a representational function. American philosopher C. S. Peirce described three types or forms of representation. Perhaps the most common form of representation is what Peirce (1960) termed *symbolic.* Symbolic representation proceeds by way of shared agreements (e.g., essentially arbitrary sounds or handwritten/typographic marks on a page are understood to refer to or stand in for something). In the example, the roommate might reply, "It's sunny and about 65 degrees." Because of our culture's shared agreements, the individual knows what meteorological condition "sunny" and "65 degrees" refer to, so he or she can dress accordingly. There is nothing inherent in the word *sunny* that necessitates its reference; we understand the word to refer to a cloudless blue sky as a matter of cultural agreement. But using language to effect symbolic representation is not the only option available to the roommate. He or she might, for example, shove a drawing under the bathroom door. The drawing depicts a yellow object that looks like the sun surrounded by a field of blue. In Peirce's terms, the roommate has employed an *iconic* form of representation. The drawing looks like or resembles the conditions outside, allowing the individual to conclude that the sun is shining and it is a pleasant day. There is a third representational possibility as well. Imagine that the roommate opens the bathroom door and throws wet leaves on the floor. What might this represent? According to Peirce, we can represent things *indexically* by relying on established causal connections (e.g., smoke represents or is a sign for the presence of fire). The wet leaves on the bathroom floor can represent inclement weather outside because the individual can figure out that the wet leaves (probably) are the result of rain.

Representation, in all of its forms but especially in its symbolic or linguistic form, often is considered the sine qua non of being human. Mitchell (1990), for example, observed, "Man, for many philosophers both ancient and modern, is the 'representational animal,' *homo symbolicum,* the creature whose distinctive character is the creation and manipulation of signs—things that 'stand for' or 'take the place of' something else" (p. 11). Therefore, representation is considered by many to be the essence of all human communication—including aesthetic[1] and rhetorical modes of action—and its paradigmatic characteristic. When people communicate through the spoken or written word, through visual imagery, or through material objects (e.g., leaves), they are engaged in the process of representing conditions that exist in the world. Mitchell also noted that "the long tradition of explaining literature and the other arts in terms of representation is matched by an equally long tradition of discomfort with this notion" (p. 14). One of the first and best expressions of this discomfort can be found in Plato's philosophical dialogues. As Mitchell explained, Plato maintained that linguistic and other forms of symbolic representation "are mere substitutes for the things themselves; even worse, they may be false or illusory substitutes that stir up antisocial emotions (violence or weakness), and they may represent bad persons and actions, encouraging imitation of evil" (pp. 14-15). Consequently, Plato advocated placing careful restrictions on the process of representation in much the same way as contemporary advocates urge restrictions on violence in television programming. So far as he was concerned, poets and rhetorical advocates should be banned from the ideal political community.

Plato did not deny the centrality of representation to human existence; he just thought it was dangerous and that, in Mitchell's (1990) words, it should be "carefully controlled by the state" (p. 15). Mitchell also directed our attention to a wide range of intellectual and philosophical movements that, in different ways, challenge the primacy accorded to the process of representation.[2] One source of challenge can be located in the broad intellectual and aesthetic movement known as *romanticism.* Fliegelman (1993) suggested that romanticism developed "a new model of representation that defines truth as truthfulness to feelings rather than to facts" (p. 60). The romantic movement did not deny that aesthetic and everyday discourse engages in the process of representation; rather, the adherents to this movement typically maintained that the objects represented in discourse do not reside *in the material or external world* but rather could be located in the *psychic world* of artists, writers, and speakers. This perspective, Fliegelman wrote, can be considered as an "emotive theory of representation." As an example, Fliegelman cited Paul Revere's print depicting the Boston Massacre. Considered from the traditional or realistic view of representation, Revere's print might be criticized "as a propagandistic misrepresentation of an incident in which, in fact, British soldiers were sorely provoked and no clear order to fire was issued" (p. 76). But when viewed from the emerging emotive or romantic perspective, Revere's "misrepresentation of the event serves to make possible the accurate representation of an emotion or emotions that otherwise could not be represented" (p. 76). Revere's iconic image still represents something, but that something is the emotional outrage felt by the people of Boston and not the "reality" of the event.

Other intellectual movements have developed more extensive critiques of the traditional doctrine of representation. *Structuralism,* for example, rejects the idea that the meaning of a sign or symbol is synonymous with the object it represents. In the structuralist tradition, the task is not discovering or uncovering what a specific sign or symbol (e.g., a word such as *sunny,* the image of a yellow circle in a field of blue) refers to or represents; rather, attention is directed to the relationship between sign or symbol and the larger system of which it is a part. Meaning depends on the interaction of sign or symbol with other signs or symbols rather than on the relationship between a sign or symbol and a referent.[3] A different approach to the issue of language, communication, and representation was developed within the *speech act* movement in contemporary philosophy. One of the founders of the movement, J. L. Austin, began with the observation that whereas some types of communicative behavior are compatible with a representational model of language use, other types of communicative behavior are not. In the earlier example, Austin (1962) would label the roommate's response to the question about the weather as a "constative"—an utterance that describes or reports some aspect of the world and that can be evaluated by way of the criteria of truth and falsehood. But Austin was troubled by the fact that constative utterances often were used as the standard model for understanding how language functions in human communication. Turning to a variety of examples of language in use, Austin observed numerous cases in which speakers and writers were doing things other than reporting or stating facts; they were engaging in routine acts such as making promises and getting married. Austin concluded that instead of thinking about language use as a process of representation, it might be more appropriate to conceive it as a mode of performance. Instead of using the representational criteria of truth and falsity as standards of evaluation, *performatives* can be analyzed in terms of "felicity conditions" that assess the quality of the performative act.[4]

Challenges to the representational model of language use come from other intellectual traditions as well.[5] Perhaps the most radical challenge to the idea of language use as a form of representation can be found in the somewhat overlapping traditions of poststructuralism and *postmodernism* (the expression "somewhat overlapping" tries to indicate that some points of convergence exist between these traditions of thought while still acknowledging that poststructuralism and postmodernism are not synonymous intellectual movements). Theorist and critic Paul de Man credited the German philosopher Friedrich Nietzsche with introducing the main lines of this critique; de Man (1979) argued that Nietzsche affirmed that "the paradigmatic structure of language is rhetorical rather than representational or expressive of a referential proper meaning" (p. 106). Another literary scholar, Brook Thomas, described "the poststructuralist critique of representation" in these terms:

> Emphasizing the gap in any effort to represent, poststructuralists remind us that the desire for full representation is linked to an impossible to achieve dream of presence. Constituted by both a temporal and spatial gap, representation is structurally dependent on misrepresentation. Since by definition representation can never be full, all acts of representation produce an "other" that is marginalized or excluded. . . . [Poststructuralism reveals] the inevitability of partial representation. (Thomas, 1991, pp. 27-28)

Thomas's (1991) account employed concepts central to Derridian deconstruction (e.g., the "dream of presence," the "spatial and temporal gap") that cannot be pursued in detail here. To get at the thrust of his observation, it might be useful to compare the preceding passage with an often quoted passage from Burke's (1969) *A Grammar of Motives:* "Men [sic] seek for vocabularies that will be faithful *reflections* of reality. To this end, they must develop vocabularies that are *selections* of reality. And any selection of reality must, in certain circumstances, function as a *deflection* of reality" (p. 59).

What do the passages from Thomas and Burke have in common? Both note a recurrent desire to use language "to get things right." For Burke this meant finding a vocabulary that accurately reflects or represents reality, whereas Thomas developed this idea by invoking the Derridian notion of presence. Both suggested that this desire to embody reality fully and completely in language inevitably is frustrated. Burke explained the frustration as a result of the need to employ vocabularies that always are only a selection of reality. He argued that every vocabulary is limited to a specific perspective or position.[6] Thomas again followed Derrida and explained the frustration as a result of "gaps" that are embedded in language use. Finally, both suggested that any act of linguistic or symbolic representation always will be partial or incomplete; in short, the ability to represent things with language actually is accomplished through *mis*representation. Burke noted that, in at least some circumstances (given this qualification, his critique of representation appears to be more restricted than the poststructuralist critique), when we reflect or represent a part of reality, we do so by deflecting attention away from other parts of reality; Wess (1996) remarked that, for Burke, every "linguistic act . . . [is] both reflection and deflection" (p. 120). Thomas made a similar point when he observed that in any act of linguistic representation, we always will exclude or marginalize certain things, turning these aspects of reality into unspeakable "others." One key theme, then, in the poststructuralist critique of representation, which a comparison to Burke's thought helps to highlight, is the symbiotic relationship between representation and misrepresentation. Representational acts, whatever the specific medium that is employed (words, visual images, or a combination of both), *reveal* as well as *conceal.* Traditional thinking about representation has focused almost exclusively on the process of revealing; the poststructuralist critique of representation calls attention to the process of concealment and makes this process an equal object for analytical and critical attention.

Consider a simple example that illustrates the interconnection or imbrication of revealing and concealing in the act of representation. Given the prominence of welfare policies in political debate, the news media have been devoting significant attention to this issue. A newspaper or television report typically will recount the cases of particular individuals whose lives are in some way connected to the issue of welfare. Given the reigning standards of journalistic objectivity, we assume that the individual cases presented in these reports are representative or that they are an accurate reflection of the people and problems that cluster together to constitute the welfare issue. But *are* the cases presented in the news media representative? Some critics argue that the news media typically feature African American women in reports about welfare, thereby creating the false impression that they are the principal beneficiaries of welfare policies. The poststructuralist perspective directs attention to the inherency of concealment—what Burke referred to as deflections—in the process of symbolic representation. The poststructuralist wants to know what gets concealed in representations about welfare policy (e.g., typical representations of African American women in welfare discourse might conceal the continued existence of sexism and racism in American society). In certain cases, we might attribute the high proportion of African American women in news accounts of welfare to the intentional and willful distortion on the part of the social elites who control the media and label this representative practice as **mystification.** But the poststructuralist will remind us that concealment or deflection is an inevitable part of symbolic representation. Even the most "accurate" news report on the issue of welfare—one that seems to reveal the issue in all its complexity—will nevertheless exclude and conceal.

The traditional model of representation evaluates specific acts of representation according to the standards of truth or falsity. But the imbrication of representation and misrepresentation challenges the adequacy of these standards. If all representations are partial—if they are selections and not simple reflections of reality—then the idea of representational truth or accuracy, and the ideas commonly associated with it such as neutrality, impartiality, and objectivity, is untenable. Defenders of the traditional account of representation argue that the poststructuralist critique of representation leads to vicious *relativism* and an inability to evaluate competing representations of reality.[7] To illustrate the problem, consider the way in which issues of race are represented in America. Has America overcome the problem of race, or are we still mired in race prejudice? Do we represent race as a problem that we have put behind us or as a challenge that we must continue to confront? The way that we talk about, or represent, the issue will help to shape the stance we take on **deliberative** questions such as affirmative action policy. The key theoretical or conceptual question, then, is what standards might be used in evaluating competing representations of reality.

The question as to what standards can be employed for evaluating competing representations once the traditional criterion of truth is displaced is exceedingly complex. Burke provided one way of approaching the problem. At the end of the paragraph from *A Grammar of Motives* quoted earlier, Burke (1969) wrote that a vocabulary's "scope and reduction become a deflection when the given terminology, or calculus, is not suited to the subject matter which it is designed to calculate" (p. 59). What exactly was Burke suggesting here? The traditional view of representation judges a vocabulary, or any act of representation, in terms of its truth (is it an accurate reflection of reality?). But Burke did not believe that vocabularies or representations could simply reflect reality; Wess (1996) made this point clear when he wrote that, for Burke, "representations of reality are never simply reproductions of reality without any intervention on our part" (pp. 149-150). Representation is *human* activity and, as such, cannot escape or evade human purposes, interests, or values (see also Eldridge, 1996b; Railsback, 1983, p. 359). What we might do, Burke suggested, is try to incorporate human attributes such as purpose and interest into our evaluations of representational action. Burke incorporated interest and purpose into his account when he wrote that a vocabulary is a deflection, and hence problematic, when it is not *suited* to the subject matter that it is trying to represent. Instead of evaluating the truth value of a representation, Burke wanted to judge its suitability. But the only way in which we can judge the suitability of a representation or vocabulary is to consider its purpose, or what it is designed to do, in relation to other purposes. A vocabulary such as "cost-benefit analysis," like all modes of representation, is a selection and, hence, a reduction of reality. But when might this vocabulary be a problematic deflection or a type of mystification? Should it be used, for example, in debates over environmental policy? Burke's response, it seems, would be that it is unsuitable or inappropriate when it negates or denies other relevant purposes or interests (purposes such as environmental protection).

Burke's approach did not really solve the problem of evaluating competing representations; instead, he shifted the location or plane of struggle. Judging competing representations of reality involves an evaluation of the purposes embedded in the representational practices. And there is no final arbiter of human purposes and their underlying **motives.** Wess (1996) affirmed this point when he wrote, "For Burke, the issue of circumference [or the issue of selecting a vocabulary] is resolved through the rhetorical struggle of the cultural conversation, not through an epistemological judgment of truth and falsity" (p. 150). Public discourse contains an ongoing struggle of perspectives and positions, a rhetorical or persuasive battle between competing vocabularies and modes of representation.

The idea that misrepresentation is a central feature of all acts of representation is one of the central themes in the poststructuralist and postmodern critique of representation. Another important theme is the fictitiousness of representation. Laclau and Mouffe (1985) maintained, "Every relation of representation is founded on a fiction, that of the presence at a certain level of something which, strictly speaking, is absent from it" (p. 119). In this passage, Laclau and Mouffe were speaking primarily about the process of *political* representation (the way in which one person or group represents or stands in for a larger collection of people), but their observation can be extended to cover the range of representational relationships including political, symbolic, and linguistic relationships.[8] The assertion of the fictional quality of representation taps into the etymology of the word (Pitkin, 1967); the Latin term *repraesentare* was "used . . . to mean the literal bringing into presence of something previously absent" (p. 3). Representation is fictional, in a narrow sense, in that what is literally absent can be made to appear present; in the example used at the beginning of the entry, the roommate makes the literally absent environmental conditions present to the individual in the bathroom through various representational tactics (e.g., words, visual images, wet leaves).

The view that representation is a fiction, or that it involves some element of creative activity, has a broader meaning as well. To assert that linguistic or symbolic representation is fictional is not necessarily the same as claiming that linguistic or symbolic practice can conjure things out of thin air and make them "real" (see the entry for **recalcitrance**). But the assertion does recognize the *constitutive* or *constructive* capacity of language, symbolic action, and discursive practice.[9] There is a long tradition in rhetorical thought that emphasizes the capacity of language and discourse to shape the way in which humans experience the world. The Sophist Gorgias, for example, believed that rhetorical practice was a verbal equivalent of magic (de Romilly, 1975) that allowed humans to overcome the anxieties caused by their inability to know anything about the world with certainty (Segal, 1962). Rhetorical discourse and linguistic representation, for Gorgias, were a necessary fiction or an inescapable mode of deception (*apate*) that made human existence possible. Echoes of Gorgias's thinking could be heard in Burke (1957), who wrote, "The magical decree is implicit in all language, for the mere act of naming an object or situation decrees that it is to be singled out as such-and-such rather than as something-other" (p. 5). The poststructuralist critique of representation extends the tradition of thought that stretches from Gorgias to Burke. It reminds us that linguistic or symbolic representation never is a neutral reflection of reality; rather, the process of representation possesses a fictional or magical quality that gives speakers and writers the ability, within certain always shifting and ill-defined limits, to shape how audiences or readers experience the world.

The concept of representation and the poststructuralist or postmodern critique, although central to many of the ongoing discussions and controversies in contemporary rhetorical, literary, and social theory, can be rather abstract and difficult to grasp. To help better grasp its importance, let us consider how the concept has been put to use in critical practice. In his study of Theodore Weld's 1839 abolitionist pamphlet, *American Slavery as It Is*, Browne (1994) focused on Weld's problem of "representing evil." According to Browne, Weld and the abolitionist movement faced the critical problem of "chronic apathy" (p. 282) within their northern audiences. Their solution was to fashion "a more dramatic and compelling mode of representing the 'peculiar institution' " of slavery (p. 284). The mode of representation that Weld employed in *American Slavery* would "combine testimony with detail" (p. 284); the nature of southern slavery would be represented to readers in the North by way of the testimonies of actual slaveholders (the material was culled from newspaper articles and advertisements, published and unpublished letters, handbills circulated in the effort to recover fugitive slaves, etc.). Browne was particularly interested in probing the effects of *American Slavery*'s mode of representation. One specific effect noted by Browne had to do with the impact of the pamphlet on those who it sought to help—southern slaves. Browne argued that Weld "discovered a means to represent slavery to maximum effect even as he virtually silenced its victims" (p. 286). Weld's representational strategies illustrate a recurrent dilemma that often "besets discourses of reform: In speaking for the oppressed, we speak instead of the oppressed"; *American Slavery* sacrificed "slavery's voice for its image" (p. 286).[10] Put in the terms used earlier in this entry, Weld revealed the evil of slavery by, ironically, concealing or silencing its victims.[11]

Browne (1994) introduced a second consequence of the text's representational strategies when he noted "the lingering anxiety which permeate[d] *American Slavery*" (p. 288). How is anxiety linked to the issue of representation? Anxiety is the effect of the imbrication of representation and misrepresentation discussed previously. Although explicit recognition of, and reflection on, this phenomenon is one of the principal contributions of poststructuralist theory, critics can detect its traces in the texts and practices of different historical periods. Anxiety, as inscribed in a text or practice, is an inchoate expression of the inadequacy of representation or of the inability of a speaker or writer to make his or her subject fully present to an audience or reader (a variation on the stylistic device of *aporia*). The critic's task is to uncover evidence of anxiety in the text—signs that the speaker or writer was beset by doubts about the representative medium or his or her representative strategies—and then try to describe the ways in which the speaker or writer negotiated his or her typically unconscious or semiconscious anxiety. In the case of *American Slavery*, Browne identified possible signs of anxiety and argued that "the overwhelming emphasis on the slave's body and its brutal violation" functioned as "a site onto which anxieties of self and culture [and, it seems fair to add, anxieties about representation] could be projected" (p. 289). The end result, Browne suggested, is "an enduring mode of representation" that has become "a dangerous precedent for representing race relations" (pp. 289-290).[12]

The issues raised by the poststructuralist or postmodern critique of representation have begun to make an impact on contemporary rhetorical studies (e.g., Browne, 1994). But there appears to be a tendency in the discipline to resist poststructuralist and postmodern insights. Hariman (1997) provided a tentative explanation while also articulating a challenge for the rhetorical studies community. Hariman wrote,

> The problem is that poststructuralist linguistic theory runs directly against the grain of vernacular speech. Ordinary people prove to be poor theorists, even when they are politically creative and effective, for they believe in direct statement, verbal representation, and artistic excellence. Whether engaging in the vernacular economics of buying a car, or the vernacular politics of serving on a library board, or the vernacular rhetoric of writing a letter to the editor, they persist in thinking that words can clearly communicate intentions, that descriptions can be accurate or misleading, and that some deals and decisions and texts are more beautifully crafted than others. Poststructuralists know better, of course, for they can prove that these beliefs rely on naive ideas about language and reality while they perpetuate misleading assumptions regarding individual subjectivity. . . . My point is not that the poststructuralist critique of modernist ideas of representation, subjectivity, and culture is wrong; in fact, I think it largely correct and rightly influential, but this philosophical achievement is largely irrelevant at many important moments in the conduct of inquiry. (pp. 169-170)

Poststructuralist insights on representation have not made a substantial impact on rhetorical studies, Hariman suggested, because the discipline deals mainly with practical (and often quotidian) discourse, and in that realm practitioners persist in thinking that words can adequately represent their thoughts and feelings and external reality. Hariman acknowledged that poststructuralist insights such as the imbrication of representation and misrepresentation and the fictionality of representative practice are an important philosophical achievement but concluded that they are, nevertheless, largely irrelevant in the conduct of inquiry. Hariman's unstated challenge for the discipline, it seems, was to determine when poststructuralist insights on matters of representation or **subjectivity** *are* relevant for rhetorical inquiry. The discipline will, in all likelihood, continue to confront this challenge during the coming years.

Notes

1. In aesthetic theory, representation often is referred to as *mimesis* or *imitation.*

2. On some of the various "attitudes" taken toward representational symbols, see also Aune (1983).

3. Structuralism is a complex intellectual movement. For discussions of some of its basic principles, see Culler (1975), Hawkes (1977), and Scholes (1974).

4. For more detailed discussions of speech act philosophy, see Austin (1962) and Searle (1969).

5. See, for example, the essays collected in Eldridge (1996a) and Stewart (1996).

6. The unstated premise here is that no vocabulary can represent reality fully or completely, a point made by Burke (1957) when he wrote, "A completely accurate chart [or vocabulary] would, of course, be possible only to an infinite, omniscient mind" (p. 8). On humanity's desire for a final God-like vocabulary for representing the world, see Rorty (1979). For a discussion of "positionality" in Burke's thinking, see Wess (1996).

7. For an overview of the objectivist-relativist "debate," see Bernstein (1983).

8. On some of the potential connections between political and linguistic representation, see Gustafson (1992) and Pitkin (1967).

9. The *constitutive* nature of rhetoric is discussed more fully in the entry for **effects of rhetorical practice.** On the idea of the *social construction of reality* through discourse, see Potter (1996) and Shotter (1993).

10. On the "silence of the image," see Norton (1993, pp. 166-169).

11. The issue of representation and "the problem of speaking for others" received extended treatment in Alcoff (1991). On the potential violent effects and productive **power** of representation, see the essays collected in Armstrong and Tennenhouse (1989).

12. On the continuing influence of the representational pattern described by Browne, see Lewis (1996).

References and Additional Reading

Alcoff, L. (1991). The problem of speaking for others. *Cultural Critique,* No. 20, pp. 5-32.

Armstrong, N., & Tennenhouse, L. (Eds.). (1989). *The violence of representation: Literature and the history of violence.* London: Routledge.
Aune, J. A. (1983). Beyond deconstruction: The symbol and social reality. *Southern Speech Communication Journal, 48,* 255-268.
Austin, J. L. (1962). *How to do things with words* (J. O. Urmson & M. Sbisa, Eds.). Cambridge, MA: Harvard University Press.
Bernstein, R. J. (1983). *Beyond objectivism and relativism: Science, hermeneutics, and praxis.* Philadelphia: University of Pennsylvania Press.
Browne, S. (1994). "Like gory spectres": Representing evil in Theodore Weld's *American Slavery as It Is. Quarterly Journal of Speech, 80,* 277-292.
Burke, K. (1957). *The philosophy of literary form* (rev. ed.). New York: Vintage.
Burke, K. (1969). *A grammar of motives.* Berkeley: University of California Press.
Culler, J. (1975). *Structuralist poetics.* London: Routledge and Kegan Paul.
de Man, P. (1979). *Allegories of reading: Figural language in Rousseau, Nietzsche, Rilke, and Proust.* New Haven, CT: Yale University Press.
de Romilly, J. (1975). *Magic and rhetoric in ancient Greece.* Cambridge, MA: Harvard University Press.
Eldridge, R. (Ed.). (1996a). *Beyond representation: Philosophy and poetic imagination.* Cambridge, UK: Cambridge University Press.
Eldridge, R. (1996b). Introduction: From representation to *poiesis.* In R. Eldridge (Ed.), *Beyond representation: Philosophy and poetic imagination.* Cambridge, UK: Cambridge University Press.
Fliegelman, J. (1993). *Declaring independence: Jefferson, natural language, and the culture of performance.* Stanford, CA: Stanford University Press.
Gustafson, T. (1992). *Representative words: Politics, literature, and the American language, 1776-1865.* Cambridge, UK: Cambridge University Press.
Hall, S. (1982). The rediscovery of "ideology": Return of the repressed in media studies. In M. Gurevitch, T. Bennett, J. Curran, & J. Woollacott (Eds.), *Culture, society, and the media.* London: Methuen.
Hall, S. (1997). The work of representation. In S. Hall (Ed.), *Representations: Cultural representations and signifying practices.* London: Sage.
Hariman, R. (1997). Afterward: Relocating the art of public address. In T. W. Benson (Ed.), *Rhetoric and political culture in nineteenth-century America.* East Lansing: Michigan State University Press.
Hawkes, T. (1977). *Structuralism and semiotics.* Berkeley: University of California Press.
Laclau, E., & Mouffe, C. (1985). *Hegemony and socialist strategy: Towards a radical democratic politics.* London: Verso.
Lewis, W. (1996, September). *Race-ing the democratic imagination.* Paper presented at the Fifth Biennial Public Address Conference, Champaign, IL.
Mitchell, W. J. T. (1990). Representation. In F. Lentricchia & T. McLaughlin (Eds.), *Critical terms for literary study.* Chicago: University of Chicago Press.
Norton, A. (1993). *Republic of signs: Liberal theory and American popular culture.* Chicago: University of Chicago Press.
Peirce, C. S. (1960). *Collected papers of Charles Sanders Peirce* (Vols. 1-2, C. Hartshorne & P. Weiss, Eds.). Cambridge, MA: Harvard University Press.
Pitkin, H. F. (1967). *The concept of representation.* Berkeley: University of California Press.
Potter, J. (1996). *Representing reality: Discourse, rhetoric, and social construction.* London: Sage.
Railsback, C. C. (1983). Beyond rhetorical relativism: A structural-material model of truth and objective reality. *Quarterly Journal of Speech, 69,* 351-363.
Rorty, R. (1979). *Philosophy and the mirror of nature.* Princeton, NJ: Princeton University Press.
Scholes, R. (1974). *Structuralism in literature: An introduction.* New Haven, CT: Yale University Press.
Searle, J. R. (1969). *Speech acts: An essay in the philosophy of language.* Cambridge, UK: Cambridge University Press.
Segal, C. (1962). Gorgias and the psychology of the logos. *Harvard Studies in Classical Philology, 66,* 99-155.
Shotter, J. (1993). *Conversational realities: Constructing life through language.* London: Sage.
Stewart, J. (1986). Speech and human being: A complement to semiotics. *Quarterly Journal of Speech, 72,* 55-73.
Stewart, J. (Ed.). (1996). *Beyond the symbol model: Reflections on the representational nature of language.* Albany: State University of New York Press.
Thomas, B. (1991). *The new historicism and other old-fashioned topics.* Princeton, NJ: Princeton University Press.
Wess, R. (1996). *Kenneth Burke: Rhetoric, subjectivity, postmodernism.* Cambridge, UK: Cambridge University Press.

REPRESENTATIVE ANECDOTE

In *A Grammar of Motives,* Burke (1969) described his "search" for a "representative anecdote" that would enable the study of human relations and human motivation (pp. 59-61, 323-325). What exactly did Burke mean by the concept **representative anecdote**? What is its purpose? And how has the concept been appropriated by scholars in rhetorical studies?

An anecdote, Burke (1969) suggested, is something around which an analytic vocabulary is "constructed" (p. 59). An anecdote "contains *in nuce* the terminological structure that is evolved in conformity with it" (p. 60). Burke insisted, "A terminology of conceptual analysis must be constructed in conformity with a representative anecdote" (p. 510). His initial example was a scientific behaviorist who employs "experiments with the conditioned reflex as the anecdote about which to form his [sic] vocabulary for the discussion of human motives" (p. 59). The conditioned reflex functions for the behaviorist as the initial building block or the starting point in the quest to understand human behavior. The behaviorist's technical vocabulary of analytic concepts (e.g., stimulus, response, impulse, drive) evolves out of this anecdote. But is the behaviorist's anecdote representative? Does it support inquiry into the complexities of human behavior? Burke indicated that the answer to each of these questions is no. He argued that a representative anecdote for studying human behavior "must have a strongly linguistic bias" and "must be supple and complex enough to be representative of the subject matter it is designed to calculate" (pp. 59-60). And he maintained that the subject matter of human behavior and human relations requires an extraordinarily supple anecdote that can ground further inquiry.

In *A Grammar of Motives,* Burke (1969) introduced *two* representative anecdotes. The first (and most obvious) anecdote is the idea of **dramatism.** Burke wrote,

> By selecting drama as our representative, or informative, anecdote . . ., the vocabulary developed in conformity with this form can possess a systematically interrelated structure while at the same time allowing for the discussion of human affairs and the placement of cultural expressions in such typically human terms as personality and action [with personality and action being terms that evolve from the dramatistic anecdote]. (p. 60)

Dramatism, for Burke, is an apt anecdote because it contains the "strongly linguistic bias" that characterizes human behavior and relations. But Burke continued,

> In selecting drama as our anecdote . . ., we discover that we have made a selection in the realm of *action,* as against scientific reduction to sheer *motion.* And we thereupon begin to ask ourselves: What would be "the ultimate act" or "the most complete act"? That is, what would be the "pure" act, an act so thoroughly an act that it could be considered the form or prototype of all acts? . . . Such a paradigm or prototype of action, the concept of an ultimate or consummate act, is found in the theologians' concern with the act of Creation. (p. 61)

Burke surveyed a number of possible anecdotes or prototypes of creative action (e.g., magic, money) but, as Wess (1996) suggested, did not settle on a paradigm for action until the third part of his book when its focus shifted to the U.S. Constitution. Wess wrote, "In theorizing the constitutive act Burke, draws his terminology from his representative anecdote, the U.S. Constitution" (p. 143). Burke (1969) himself noted that, with

> a book on human relations being, by the nature of its subject, to a large extent "idealistic" (since such a book should feature the relationships typical of *agents*), it is obvious that our analytic instruments must be shaped in conformity with representative idealist anecdotes. . . . And a constitution would be an "idealistic anecdote" in that its structure is an enactment of human wills. (p. 323)[1]

How are Burke's two representative anecdotes, dramatism and the Constitution, related? Speaking figuratively, the two anecdotes might be thought of as two sides of the same coin. The idea of dramatism acknowledges, in more abstract terms, the centrality of symbolic or constitutive action in human existence, whereas the Constitution (its development and continued operation) provides a tangible or substantial case of constitutive action. The dramatism anecdote evolves into the analytic terminology of the *pentad* (act, scene, agent, agency, and purpose), whereas the Constitution anecdote serves as the paradigmatic or prototypical case of constitutive action. As Wess (1996) remarked, "The Constitution and the pentad ultimately seem to entail one another" (p. 180).

How has Burke's thinking on the representative anecdote been appropriated in rhetorical studies? The concept has either been described as or served as the *critical method* for countless convention papers and published essays.[2] These critical appropriations appear to share an underlying characteristic—a creative misreading of Burke's writings on the subject. As the previous discussion tried to demonstrate, in Burke's work the representative anecdote is part of the process of developing or generating an analytic terminology or a critical method (see also Crable, 2000). But it does not seem to be the case that Burke conceived of the representative anecdote *as itself* a critical method. In appropriating the concept, rhetorical scholars have creatively misread Burke and, in the process, transformed the representative anecdote into a method for analyzing specific texts. Madsen (1993) illustrated the transformation when he wrote, "The critic uses the anecdote as a methodological procedure" (p. 209). Burke's concern with "selecting" an anecdote that adequately represents a specific subject matter (e.g., human relations) is reworked into a method for "detecting" (Brummett, 1984b, p. 4) anecdotes that "will fully represent the text" (Madsen, 1993, p. 209) or the body of discourse (e.g., **discursive formation**) being analyzed. Observing the creative misreading involved in the appropriation of the concept of representative anecdote does not demean the value of the critical studies that have been produced through that process; instead, it illustrates Bloom's (1973) point that *misprision,* or misreading, is an important source of creativity in both the aesthetic and critical spheres.

Following a suggestion made by Williams (1986), Madsen argued that a textual representative anecdote might be either (a) a specific act (e.g., one text [as an act] can represent a larger group of texts, one act [an *illocutionary performative*] within a text can represent the entire text) or (b) a discursive form (e.g., a *metaphor,* an embedded **narrative**). Brummett, Madsen, and others suggested that the value of anecdotal analysis is its ability to aid the critic in disclosing the **motives** embedded in a text. Madsen (1993) maintained, "The identification of an anecdote sums up the essence of a text" (p. 208).

A sense of representative anecdote much closer to Burke's explication of the concept can be found, albeit only implicitly, in Owen and Ehrenhaus's (1993) discussion of useful metaphors for "animating" the **critical rhetoric** project. They wrote,

> We have come to see the value of three related metaphors for informing our critical understanding of the relations among rhetoric, social forms, and social processes (and thus, among text, context, and culture); moreover, these metaphors establish a vocabulary and imagery through which critical commentary can find a place in the broader community beyond academe. (p. 170)

Owen and Ehrenhaus's three metaphors—American culture as an empire, imperialistic growth as feeding, and feeding as a form of pornography—function along similar lines as Burke's use of dramatism and the Constitution in that they are linguistic constructions developed by the critic for "calculating" or comprehending a complex subject matter. Owen and Ehrenhaus were rather explicit on this point: "These master metaphors enable the critic to locate coherence and continuity among seemingly distinct and disparate actions, themes, textual fragments, and discourse practices" (p. 170). The metaphors of empire, feeding, and pornography are, in short, potential representative anecdotes of our postmodern world.[3]

Notes

1. We should note Wess's (1996) observation that in Burke's later works, especially *The Rhetoric of Religion* (Burke, 1970), Burke shifted from the secular back to the sacred in his use of the biblical story of Genesis as his more substantial "representative anecdote."

2. See, for example, Brummett (1984a, 1984b), Conrad (1984), and Madsen (1993).

3. See, for example, Alpers' (1996) use of the representative anecdote as a strategy for defining the **pastoral** and Bush's (1999) discussion of the Declaration of Independence as a representative anecdote of America's political culture.

References and Additional Reading

Alpers, P. (1996). *What is pastoral?* Chicago: University of Chicago Press.

Bloom, H. (1973). *The anxiety of influence.* New York: Oxford University Press.

Brummett, B. (1984a). Burke's representative anecdote as a method in media criticism. *Critical Studies in Mass Communication, 1,* 161-176.

Brummett, B. (1984b). The representative anecdote as a Burkean method, applied to evangelical rhetoric. *Southern Speech Communication Journal, 50,* 1-23.

Burke, K. (1969). *A grammar of motives.* Berkeley: University of California Press.

Burke, K. (1970). *The rhetoric of religion: Studies in logology.* Berkeley: University of California Press.

Bush, H. K., Jr. (1999). *American declarations: Rebellion and repentance in American cultural history.* Urbana: University of Illinois Press.

Conrad, C. (1984). Phases, pentads, and dramatistic critical process. *Central States Speech Journal, 35,* 84-93.

Crable, B. (2000). Burke's perspectives on perspectives: Grounding dramatism in the representative anecdote. *Quarterly Journal of Speech, 86,* 318-333.

Madsen, A. (1993). Burke's representative anecdote as a critical method. In J. W. Chesebro (Ed.), *Extensions of the Burkeian system.* Tuscaloosa: University of Alabama Press.

Owen, A. S., & Ehrenhaus, P. (1993). Animating a critical rhetoric: On the feeding habits of American empire. *Western Journal of Communication, 57,* 169-177.

Wess, R. (1996). *Kenneth Burke: Rhetoric, subjectivity, postmodernism.* Cambridge, UK: Cambridge University Press.

Williams, D. C. (1986, November). *"Drama" and "nuclear war" as representative anecdotes of Burke's theories of ontology and epistemology.* Paper presented at the meeting of the Speech Communication Association, Chicago.

RHETORICAL QUESTION

A **rhetorical question** is commonly defined as a query posed by an advocate for which a response is not expected. In advocacy situations, the question form provides for a sense of openness (because multiple answers *are* possible), but in many cases the situated force of the utterance seriously undermines the veracity of any answer other than the one implied by the advocate. Understood in this way, rhetorical questions can be seen as a way of making *indirect* assertions or *claims* (Fogelin, 1987). Commenting on a passage from the famous Greek orator Demosthenes, the ancient rhetorician Longinus (1965) elaborated on the potential impact of rhetorical questions:

> If this had been given as a bald statement, it would have been completely ineffective; but as it is, the inspired rapidity in the play of question and answer, together with the device of meeting his own objections as though they were someone else's [*prolepsis*], has not only added to the sublimity of his words but also given them greater conviction. (p. 128)

Let us consider a more contemporary example. In an essay arguing against gays in the military, a writer might pose a rhetorical question such as "Do the proponents of gays in the military believe that heterosexual soldiers will accept gays without a fight?" In this context, the rhetorical question does a few things. First, it puts words in the mouths of gay rights supporters by suggesting that their view of the way in which the military operates is unrealistic. Second, it in effect makes the claim that heterosexual soldiers will openly resist the inclusion of acknowledged gays in the military, but because this claim is made indirectly, the writer is not under any obligation to provide support for the assertion. Finally, the indirectness of the assertion distances it from the writer, thereby allowing the writer to avoid taking a stand on the legitimacy of the predicted action.

Many of these functional aspects are at work in the following example as well. In an editorial in the February 1, 1998, issue of the *Seattle Times* supporting affirmative action and arguing against a proposed state initiative that would ban it, James Gregory noted a growing trend in California for conservative groups to monitor the hiring and/or admissions practices of public institutions. The purpose of such monitoring, Gregory maintained, was to make sure that all vestiges of affirmative action would be demolished. Given this scrutiny, he then posed the rhetorical question: "How long will it be before some employers are thinking twice about hiring or promoting a minority candidate?" Gregory asserted, indirectly, a claim about the consequences of banning affirmative action and enforcing such a ban through zealous legal scrutiny. Fewer minority candidates will be hired and/or promoted because employers will want to avoid legal challenges emanating from conservative groups. Only obviously superior minority candidates will be hired, promoted, or admitted. In cases where a white candidate and a minority candidate have roughly equal qualifications, employers will want to avoid even a hint of lingering affirmative action by hiring, promoting, or admitting the white applicant. These claims were some of the more important entailments spinning out from Gregory's rhetorical question. Rhetorical questions, as these examples have tried to demonstrate, merit careful attention from the critic of public discourse.

References and Additional Reading

Fogelin, R. J. (1987). Some figures of speech. In F. H. van Eemeren, R. Grootendorst, J. A. Blair, & C. A. Willard (Eds.), *Argumentation: Across the lines of discipline.* Dordrecht, Netherlands: Foris Publications.

Longinus. (1965). On the sublime. In *Classical literary criticism* (T. S. Dorsch, Trans.). New York: Penguin.

RITUAL

There is no single definition of **ritual** on which all scholars agree. The meaning of the concept of ritual is contested (Bell, 1997; Leach, 1968; Schechner, 1993). Increasingly, scholars are acknowledging that rituals are "not a fact of nature" (Leach, 1968, p. 521); rather, they are "an analytic category that helps us [scholars in particular] deal with the chaos of human experience and put it into a coherent framework" (Kertzer, 1988, p. 8). In an effort to sort out the potential confusion, Grimes (1990) distinguished between a *rite* and a *ritual.* A rite or rites are "specific enactments located in concrete times and places" (p. 9). Rites are particular, historically situated actions or performances in which people and/or entire communities and cultures engage. A ritual, on the other hand, is "the general idea of which a rite is a specific instance" (p. 10). Rituals are abstractions, or "analytic categories," formulated by observers to help understand specific instances of human practice. They exist only in concrete instantiations (on the definition of ritual, see also Bell, 1997).

What types of human practices or performances are commonly identified with the label "ritual"? Here again, we find disagreements among scholars. As noted by Leach (1968), among others, many scholars interested in the issue of ritual seek to distinguish two spheres of life. One sphere is the realm of the everyday, the ordinary, the common, or the *secular,* whereas the other is the realm of the mysterious or mystical, the unusual or nonrational, the religious, or the *sacred.* Given this division of the world, one way of defining ritual behavior is to locate it within the realm of the sacred. Ritual practices are then defined as "a body of custom specifically associated with religious performance" (p. 521). Other scholars challenge the stability of these two realms and, in particular, disagree with relegating ritual to the realm of the religious or the sacred. This line of scholarship argues that ritual action or behavior permeates all realms of human existence. The realm of the everyday or the ordinary is saturated with behaviors and practices that might be understood as rituals or, at least, as ritual*istic.*[1]

Given the discussion in the preceding paragraph, we need to address a key question: Is the quest for a definition of ritual a hopeless pursuit? A number of ritual scholars, while acknowledging the lack of definitional consensus, have labored to develop working definitions. Grimes (1990), for example, suggested that instead of overly dense "formal definitions" of ritual, scholars should locate a cluster of "qualities" that constitute "the nature of ritual." He wrote,

> A better way to get at the nature of ritual is to identify its "family characteristics," expecting only some of them to show up in specific instances. This approach keeps us from thinking of activities as if they either are or are not ritual. It allows us to specify in what respects and to what extent an action is ritualized. Ritual is not a "what," not a "thing." It is a "how," a quality, and there are "degrees" of it. (p. 13)

Grimes identified 15 common qualities of ritual behavior (p. 14); other scholars focus on a smaller number. Most "cluster of qualities" definitions include the following: Ritual behaviors and practices are *enacted* (and not simply thought about) and tend to be *formalized* or *stylized* (the nuances of practice are therefore extremely important), *repetitive* or *redundant* (they occur with some frequency and often in regular temporal patterns), *communal* and/or *institutional* (rather than idiosyncratic), and *multidimensional* (they work on different levels and accomplish multiple goals).

Do ritualized behaviors or practices themselves cluster into groups or "genres" (Bell, 1997)? What is the relevance of the concept of ritual for rhetorical studies? These are extremely important questions. Let us start with the second one. The most obvious answer is that rituals are important because they communicate. Leach (1968) made the point when he wrote that "all customary [ritualized] behavior is a form of speech, a mode of communicating information" (p. 523; see also Bell, 1997, pp. 15-16). But as countless scholars in rhetoric and other disciplines have come to recognize, information dissemination and/or exchange is not an appropriate paradigm for conceptualizing the nature of human communication.[2] Nor is ritual communication merely *instrumental* in nature. Although a specific rite might have an ostensible instrumental purpose (e.g., the desire for purification manifested in the American Indian ghost dance during the 19th century), ritual action is multidimensional. Ritual behavior, like all linguistic and communicative practice, has a *constitutive* component. As Lincoln (1989) observed during the late 1980s,

> For over the course of the last two decades, it has gradually become clear that ritual, etiquette, and other strongly habituated forms of practical discourse and discursive practice do not just encode and transmit messages, but they play an active and important role in the construction, maintenance, and modification of the borders, structures, and hierarchic relations that characterize and constitute society itself. (p. 75)

Similarly, Berlant (1991) noted the importance of ritual in the constitution of political identity when she wrote, "Participation in national celebration connects the citizen to a collective subjectivity constituted by synchronous participation in the same national rituals" (p. 29). Rituals, in short, serve important instrumental and constitutive functions.

Rituals frequently are communicative and, given the inevitable slant or perspective woven into communication, rhetorical as well. Rituals function instrumentally and function as part of the process of *social construction* or constitution. But ritual practices are connected to the realm of rhetoric and rhetorical studies in at least two additional ways. First, relatively circumscribed ritual behaviors can be appropriated and transformed into secular rhetorical strategies. Perhaps the most obvious example of this process is the strategy of **scapegoating.** The strategy of scapegoating reveals how sacrificial rituals, enacted in different ways within numerous cultures, evolve into primarily discursive devices for purifying the community, building communal solidarity, and/or saving face (and deflecting responsibility for negative outcomes). Second, speech (and, in a number of cases, formal oratorical performance) often is a key ingredient in the overall composition of a rite. For example, a funeral rite most likely would appear incomplete or defective without the inclusion of a *eulogy.* Eulogistic speech is a critical component of the funeral ritual.[3]

We can gain further insight into both the broad communicative function of ritual and the way in which speech forms are incorporated into ritual performances by returning to the first question introduced earlier: What are some common genres of ritual action? Bell (1997) noted the variety of answers to this question proposed by various scholars. She settled on "six categories of ritual action [that] are a pragmatic compromise between completeness and simplicity" (p.94). Bell emphasized that these categories are not mutually exclusive. The principle of *generic hybridity*—the recurrent mixture or interaction between **genres**—applies to ritual genres as well as discursive ones.

The first category noted by Bell (1997) consists of "rites of passage," which probably are one of the most common and most discussed ritual forms. Bell described them as "ceremonies that accompany and dramatize such major events as birth, coming-of-age initiations for boys and girls, marriage, and death. Sometimes called 'life-crisis' or 'life-cycle' rites, they culturally mark a person's transition from one stage of social life to another" (p. 94). Bell noted that the elements of rites of passage "provide some of the most basic models and metaphors for all sorts of ritual processes" (p. 95). Beginning with van Gennep (1908/1960), many scholars have identified three phases in rites of passage: (a) an initial phase where the individual is *separated* from his or her original group; (b) an intermediate or *liminal* stage where the individual is, in essence, "between" groups or identities; and (c) a final phase or *re-incorporation* where the individual is integrated into a new group or comes to occupy a new position, a new status, or a new role. An enormous body of literature has been generated on the topic of rites of passage. Some of the important studies and discussions include Eliade's (1958) work on rebirth imagery and religious initiation, La Fontaine's (1985) study of initiation rituals, Shorter's (1987) discussion of initiation rituals for women, and Turner's (1974) examination of "pilgrimage processes" (p. 166) and the reconstitution of identity.[4] Rhetorical scholars such as Jorgensen-Earp and Lanzilotti (1998) have used the idea of rites of passage to explore the rhetorical and ritual dimensions of public mourning, whereas Hoban (1980) explored the ways in which this literature might inform investigations of presidential inaugurals (see also Campbell & Jamieson, 1990), eulogies for public figures, and other "transformations of identity" (Hoban, 1980, p. 281). What Hoban termed "rituals of rebirth" often play a central role in the process of **secular conversion.**

Bell's (1997) second category encompasses various "calendrical rites" that "give socially meaningful definitions to the passage of time, creating an ever-renewing cycle of days, months, and years" (p. 102). Calendrical rites can be subdivided into *seasonal* and *commemorative* celebrations (p. 103). According to Bell, "Seasonal celebrations are rooted in the activities of planting and harvesting for agriculturists or grazing and moving the herd for pastoralists" (p. 103). What repetitive seasonal activities have supplanted those essentially premodern festivals "dependent upon the fecundity of the land" (p. 103)? End of fiscal year spending binges, pig roasts at the beginning of a new school year, and Super Bowl parties seem to share some of the qualities of seasonal rites. Bell suggested that commemorative rites include "activities that explicitly recall important historical events," either secular or religious, in the life of the community (p. 104). Typically, "rites that evoke secular events long past attempt to involve participants in experiencing and affirming a set of values seen as rooted in those events" (pp. 107-108). Of special importance are "founding events" whose celebration "is able to generate a meaningful, mythic, and cyclical sense of time, a temporal sense in which it is as if the original events are happening all over again" (p. 108). Celebrations of founding events often are thought to "release something of their original transformative power" (p. 108). Rhetorical scholars, among others, have been particularly interested in the way that the discourse associated with commemorative rites such as Fourth of July celebrations, Memorial Day, and the landing of the Puritans at Plymouth Rock function to construct and reconstruct public **memory** and a sense of community (Browne, 1993; Travers, 1997; Waldstreicher, 1997).

The third category identified by Bell (1997) consists of rites of exchange and communion. These rites specifically concern "human-divine interaction" but typically function to promote "social organization" (p. 109). One of the most common forms of human-divine interaction is the *sacrifice;* as Bell noted, "When defined in very general terms, some form of sacrifice can be found in almost all societies" (p. 112). Rhetorical and communication scholars have exhibited a keen interest in the way that the "logic" of the sacrifice has been inscribed in the strategy of **scapegoating** (e.g., Burke, 1957) as well as how political elections meld "themes of sacrifice and regeneration" into a "regenerative ritual" that "re-creates" or renews the community (Marvin, 1994, p. 263). Other communication scholars are exploring ritual features of secular exchanges such as bargaining practices (e.g., Putnam, Van Hoeven, & Bullis, 1991).

Bell's (1997) fourth category consists of "rites of affliction." The rites included in this category "seek to mitigate the influence of spirits thought to be afflicting human beings with misfortune. . . . Rituals of affliction attempt to rectify a state of affairs that has been disturbed or disordered; they heal, exorcise, protect, and purify" (p. 115). Bell noted that "healing rituals are particularly ubiquitous" (p. 116); they often are interwoven with the practice of **confession** (p. 115). Bell observed, "Purification is a major theme within rites of affliction, although it can be understood in a variety of ways. It can involve freeing a person from demonic possession, disease, sin, or the karmic consequences of past lives" (p. 118). Rites of affliction and the processes for purifying what has been polluted have received detailed treatment in classic studies by Douglas (1966) and Turner (1967).

The fifth ritual genre described by Bell (1997) consists of "feasting and fasting rites" and the associated realm of "festival" practices. Feasting and fasting rites place "a great deal of emphasis on the public display of religiocultural sentiments"; they are a public expression of a culture's "commitment and adherence to basic religious values" (p. 120). Bell reminded her readers that "shared participation in a food feast is a common ritual means for defining and reaffirming the full extent of the human and cosmic community." She added, "While feasting seems to celebrate the consubstantial unity of creation, fasting seems to extol fundamental distinctions, lauding the power of the spiritual realm while acknowledging the subordination and sinfulness of the physical realm" (p. 123). Thanksgiving celebrations in the United States and Lenten fasting among Christians are examples of this type of ritual activity.

Although rhetorical scholars exhibit little interest in the specifics of feasting and fasting, they are concerned with the broader function of this ritual category—communal cohesion. Rituals that affirm and/or legitimate communal or group identity can be considered, following Kertzer (1988), as "rites of social communion." Kertzer wrote,

> Through these rites, the boundaries of the social group, the group of people to whom

> the individual feels allegiance, are defined. Ritual activity is not simply one possible way of creating group solidarity; it is a necessary way. Only by periodically assembling together and jointly participating in such symbolic action can the collective ideas and sentiments be propagated. . . . Social solidarity is . . . a requirement of society, and ritual [is] an indispensable element in the creation of that solidarity. (p. 62)

We see a concern for "rites of social communion" in Braithwaite's (1990, 1997) studies of the ritual behaviors of veterans of the war in Vietnam and in Frank's (1981) analysis of the Israeli peace movement.

The third element in this category—festival—also plays a crucial role in group and/or community definition. A substantial body of literature has emerged focusing on the **carnival** as a ritual festival. Bell (1997) observed, "Carnival traditions are considered particularly ritualistic because they draw together many social groups that are normally kept separate and create specific times and places where social differences are either laid aside or reversed for a more embracing experience of community" (p. 126). Carnival festivals feature "standard ritual inversions" such as the "appointment of a jester or king of fools to serve as a burlesque parody of institutional power and order" (p. 126). Scholars disagree on the degree to which carnival festivals support or subvert communal order. Scholars such as Gluckman (1962) and Shaw (1981) have described the appropriation of festival practices and their transformation into potent "rituals of rebellion." Commenting on Gluckman's discussion of rituals of rebellion, Balandier (1970) observed, "The supreme ruse of power is to allow itself to be contested *ritually* in order to consolidate itself more effectively" (p. 41).

The discussion of rituals and **power** in the preceding paragraph makes for an easy transition into the final category of ritual identified by Bell—"political rites." Of all the categories of ritual, this is the one to which rhetorical and communication scholars have devoted the most attention (e.g., Rothenbuhler, 1998). Bell (1997) suggested that political rituals can be defined as "those ceremonial practices that specifically construct, display, and promote the power of political institutions . . . or the political interests of distinct constituencies and subgroups" (p. 128). Kertzer (1988) noted that it is important to remember that "ritual is used to constitute power, not just reflect power that already exists" (p. 25).

Rituals constitute and display political power in different ways. In addition to ceremonial rites such as presidential inaugurals, the juridical administration of the death penalty,[5] and the symbolism of the courtroom, a number of other political rituals that constitute and display power were described by Edelman (1971, 1977) and Bennett (1977, 1980, 1981). For example, Edelman (1977) argued that "most formal procedures [in politics] are instances of ritual, not of policy making, in the sense that they influence popular beliefs and perceptions while purporting, usually falsely, to be directly influencing events and behaviors" (pp. 122-123). In other words, institutionally prescribed procedures such as legislative committee hearings, fact-finding trips, and bipartisan commissions are the political equivalents of "rain dances." Their general function, according to Edelman, is legitimation; they induce "general acquiescence in power arrangements" (p. 123).[6] Bennett's analyses have moved in a similar direction. Bennett (1980) argued that rituals "establish the dominance of authorities and perpetuate the submissiveness of the powerless" (p. 174). But political rituals not only display power but also "display the social principles" on which the social order is based. Bennett suggested, "Elections are the most sweeping and important rituals in American politics" (p. 174). They function "to create the appearance that grand choices face the voters" (p. 177). Elections, committee hearings, and other political rituals all are ways in which political power is manifested and often **mystified** (on the ritual mystification of power, see also Kertzer, 1988, pp. 48-50).

Bennett's and Kertzer's discussions of election rituals illustrate the way in which power struggles often are ritualized; political conflict can be contained as it is ritualized.[7] But as was noted earlier under the rubric of "rituals of rebellion," rituals also can serve as a vehicle for *contesting* power. Bell (1997), for example, pointed out that "rituals meant to establish a particular power relationship are not invulnerable to being challenged, inverted, or completely thwarted by counteractions" (p. 132). Lukes (1975) reminded us that there are "other contemporary rituals which express alternative and non-official attitudes and values. Consider, for example, the alternative Memorial Day parades staged in recent years in protest against the Vietnam war" (p. 299).[8] Ritual, then, is not simply a vehicle for the powerful or a tool of repressive **hegemony.** It is a multidimensional, multifunctional mode of human conduct. Rhetorical scholars have only begun to explore the relationships between discourse and ritual performance.

Notes

1. See, for example, Bell (1997, pp. 138-169), Firth (1972), Goffman (1967), and Grimes (1990).
2. For one example, see the entry for **sermonic, language as.**
3. The relationship between rhetorical forms and ritual performance, especially political ritual, was explored further in Bloch (1975) and Paine (1981).
4. See also Gluckman (1962); Kett (1977); Lincoln (1991); the essays collected in Mahdi, Christopher, and Meade (1996); and Vizedom (1976).
5. On the ritual dimensions of the death penalty, see Bell (1997, pp. 132). See also Masur (1989) and Purdum and Paredes (1989).
6. On rituals and acquiescence, see also Lukes (1975). On legitimation rituals in politics, see also Farrell (1978).
7. On this point, see also Nieburg's (1970) idea of "rituals of conflict."
8. African Americans in Boston during the mid-19th century illustrated this process when they appropriated the symbolism associated with the Boston Massacre and transformed it into Crispus Attucks Day. For an analysis of this discourse, see Browne (1999).

References and Additional Reading

Balandier, G. (1970). *Political anthropology* (A. M. Sheridan Smith, Trans.). London: Penguin.

Bell, C. (1992). *Ritual theory, ritual practice.* New York: Oxford University Press.

Bell, C. (1997). *Ritual: Perspectives and dimensions.* New York: Oxford University Press.

Bennett, W. L. (1977). The ritualistic and pragmatic bases of political campaign discourse. *Quarterly Journal of Speech, 63,* 219-238.

Bennett, W. L. (1980). Myth, ritual, and political control. *Journal of Communication, 30,* 166-179.

Bennett, W. L. (1981). Assessing presidential character: Degradation rituals in presidential campaigns. *Quarterly Journal of Speech, 67,* 310-321.

Berlant, L. (1991). *The anatomy of national fantasy: Hawthorne, utopia, and everyday life.* Chicago: University of Chicago Press.

Bloch, M. (Ed.). (1975). *Political language and oratory in traditional society.* New York: Academic Press.

Braithwaite, C. A. (1990). Cultural communication among Vietnam veterans: Ritual, myth, and social drama. In R. Morris & P. Ehrenhaus (Eds.), *Cultural legacies of Vietnam: Uses of the past in the present.* Norwood, NJ: Ablex.

Braithwaite, C. A. (1997). "Were YOU There?": A ritual of legitimacy among Vietnam veterans. *Western Journal of Communication, 61,* 423-447.

Browne, S. H. (1993). Reading public memory in Daniel Webster's *Plymouth Rock Oration. Western Journal of Communication, 57,* 464-477.

Browne, S. H. (1999). Remembering Crispus Attucks: Race, rhetoric, and the politics of commemoration. *Quarterly Journal of Speech, 85,* 169-187.

Burke, K. (1957). *The philosophy of literary form: Studies in symbolic action* (rev. ed.). New York: Vintage.

Burke, K. (1984). General nature of ritual. In K. Burke, *Attitudes toward history.* Berkeley: University of California Press.

Campbell, K. K., & Jamieson, K. H. (1990). *Deeds done in words: Presidential rhetoric and the genres of governance.* Chicago: University of Chicago Press.

Douglas, M. (1966). *Purity and danger: An analysis of concepts of pollution and taboo.* New York: Praeger.

Edelman, M. (1971). *Politics as symbolic action: Mass arousal and quiescence.* New York: Academic Press.

Edelman, M. (1977). *Political language: Words that succeed and policies that fail.* New York: Academic Press.

Eliade, M. (1958). *Birth and rebirth: The religious meanings of initiation in human culture* (W. R. Trask, Trans.). New York: Harper.

Farrell, T. B. (1978). Political conventions as legitimation ritual. *Communication Monographs, 45,* 293-305.

Finkelstein, L., Jr. (1981). The calendrical rite of the ascension to power. *Western Journal of Speech Communication, 45,* 51-59.

Firth, R. (1972). Verbal and bodily rituals of greeting and parting. In J. S. La Fontaine (Ed.), *The interpretation of ritual: Essays in honor of A. I. Richards.* London: Tavistock.

Frank, D. A. (1981). "*Shalom Achshav*": Rituals of the Israeli peace movement. *Communication Monographs, 48*, 165-182.

Gluckman, M. (1962). Les rites de passage. In M. Gluckman (Ed.), *Essays on the ritual of social relations*. Manchester, UK: Manchester University Press.

Goffman, E. (1967). *Interaction ritual: Essays on face-to-face behavior*. Garden City, NY: Anchor.

Grimes, R. L. (1990). *Ritual criticism: Case studies in its practice, essays on its theory*. Columbia: University of South Carolina Press.

Herbeck, D. A. (1994). Presidential debate as political ritual: Clinton vs. Bush vs. Perot. In S. A. Smith (Ed.), *Bill Clinton on stump, state, and stage: The rhetorical road to the White House*. Fayetteville: University of Arkansas Press.

Hoban, J. L., Jr. (1980). Rhetorical rituals of rebirth. *Quarterly Journal of Speech, 66*, 275-288.

Jorgensen-Earp, C. R., & Lanzilotti, L. A. (1998). Public memory and private grief: The construction of shrines at the sites of public tragedy. *Quarterly Journal of Speech, 84*, 150-170.

Kertzer, D. I. (1988). *Ritual, politics, and power*. New Haven, CT: Yale University Press.

Kett, J. F. (1977). *Rites of passage: Adolescence in America, 1790 to the present*. New York: Basic Books.

La Fontaine, J. S. (1985). *Initiation*. Manchester, UK: Manchester University Press.

Lake, R. A. (1990). The implied arguer. In D. C. Williams & M. D. Hazen (Eds.), *Argumentation theory and the rhetoric of assent*. Tuscaloosa: University of Alabama Press.

Leach, E. R. (1968). Ritual. In D. L. Sills (Ed.), *International encyclopedia of the social sciences* (Vol. 13). New York: Macmillan.

Lincoln, B. (1989). *Discourse and the construction of society: Comparative studies of myth, ritual, and classification*. New York: Oxford University Press.

Lincoln, B. (1991). *Emerging from the chrysalis: Rituals of women's initiations* (rev. ed.). New York: Oxford University Press.

Lukes, S. (1975). Political ritual and social integration. *Sociology, 9*, 289-308.

Mahdi, L. C., Christopher, N. G., & Meade, M. (Eds.). (1996). *Passages: The quest for contemporary rites of passage*. Chicago: Open Court.

Marvin, C. (1994). Fresh blood, public meat: Rituals of totem regeneration in the 1992 presidential race. *Communication Research, 21*, 264-292.

Marvin, C., & Ingle, D. W. (1999). *Blood sacrifice and the nation: Totem rituals and the American flag*. Cambridge, UK: Cambridge University Press.

Masur, L. P. (1989). *Rites of execution: Capital punishment and the transformation of American culture, 1776-1865*. New York: Oxford University Press.

Nieburg, H. L. (1970). Agonistics: Rituals of conflict. *Annals of the American Academy of Political and Social Science, 391*, 56-73.

Paine, R. (Ed.). (1981). *Politically speaking: Cross-cultural studies of rhetoric*. Philadelphia: Institute for the Study of Human Issues.

Philipsen, G. (1993). Ritual as a heuristic device in studies of organizational discourse. In S. Deetz (Ed.), *Communication yearbook* (Vol. 16). Newbury Park, CA: Sage.

Purdum, E. D., & Paredes, J. A. (1989). Rituals of death: Capital punishment and human sacrifice. In M. I. Radelet (Ed.), *Facing the death penalty: Essays on a cruel and unusual punishment*. Philadelphia: Temple University Press.

Putnam, L. L., Van Hoeven, S. A., & Bullis, C. A. (1991). The role of rituals and fantasy themes in teachers' bargaining. *Western Journal of Speech Communication, 55*, 85-103.

Rothenbuhler, E. (1998). *Ritual communication: From everyday conversation to mediated ceremony*. Thousand Oaks, CA: Sage.

Schechner, R. (1993). *The future of ritual: Writings on culture and performance*. London: Routledge.

Shaw, P. (1981). *American patriots and the rituals of revolution*. Cambridge, MA: Harvard University Press.

Shorter, B. (1987). *An image darkly forming: Women and initiation*. London: Routledge and Kegan Paul.

Travers, L. (1997). *Celebrating the Fourth: Independence Day and the rites of nationalism in the early republic*. Amherst: University of Massachusetts Press.

Turner, V. (1967). *The forest of symbols: Aspects of Ndembu ritual*. Ithaca, NY: Cornell University Press.

Turner, V. (1969). *The ritual process*. Chicago: Aldine.

Turner, V. (1974). Pilgrimages as social processes. In V. Turner, *Dramas, fields, and metaphors: Symbolic action in human society*. Ithaca, NY: Cornell University Press.

van Gennep, A. (1960). *The rites of passage* (M. B. Vizedom & G. L. Caffee, Trans.). Chicago: University of Chicago Press. (Original work published 1908)

Vizedom, M. (1976). *Rites and relationships: Rites of passage and contemporary anthropology*. Beverly Hills, CA: Sage.

Waldstreicher, D. (1997). *In the midst of perpetual fetes: The making of American nationalism, 1776-1820*. Chapel Hill: University of North Carolina Press.

Weaver, R. A. (1982). Acknowledgment of victory and defeat: The reciprocal ritual. *Central States Speech Journal, 33*, 480-489.

S

SCAPEGOATING

Over the course of his long career, Kenneth Burke frequently turned his attention to the phenomenon of the *scapegoat,* the process of **scapegoating,** and their roles as the driving force in the sacrificial **ritual** of *redemption* through *victimage.* The scapegoat and scapegoating were a "recurring theme" (Wess, 1996, p. 199) in Burke's work.[1] We can begin an overview of the concept by reviewing the development of the scapegoating theme in Burke's thought.

One of Burke's (1984b) first discussions of scapegoating appeared in his book *Permanence and Change,* originally published in 1935. In that early work, he discussed the scapegoat as "an error in interpretation" that seemingly could be corrected (p. 14). As Wess (1996) noted, Burke's later discussions of scapegoating tended to depict it as inescapable or "as inevitable as death and taxes" (p. 199). But Burke's basic account of the "scapegoat mechanism" remained rather consistent over time; Burke (1984b) wrote in *Permanence and Change* that scapegoating is "in its purest form the use of a sacrificial receptacle for the ritual unburdening of one's sins" and that it functions within society as a "technique of purification" (p. 16). Burke's (1957a) long essay, "The Philosophy of Literary Form," continued his interest in the topic. He wrote that the scapegoat is "the 'representative' or 'vessel' of certain unwanted evils, the sacrificial animal upon whose back the burden of these evils is ritualistically loaded" (p. 34). Burke noted in this essay the importance of finding a sacrificial vessel that is "worthy" of sacrifice. This idea of worthiness, or "perfecting" the scapegoat, was pursued in Burke's (1957b) frequently reprinted essay on Adolph Hitler, "The Rhetoric of Hitler's 'Battle.' " He suggested that Hitler's treatment of the Jews is a paradigmatic instance of scapegoating; following Burke, Duncan (1962) argued that it is a "classical example" (p. 127). Burke's interest in the topic continued in his groundbreaking studies of human **motives,** *A Grammar of Motives* (Burke, 1945) and *A Rhetoric of Motives* (Burke, 1950). In *A Grammar of Motives,* Burke (1945) identified the **dialectical** structure of the scapegoating process when he wrote,

> All told, note what we have here: (1) *an original state of merger,* in that the iniquities are shared by both the iniquitous and their chosen vessel; (2) *a principle of division,* in that the elements shared in common are being ritualistically alienated; (3) *a new principle of merger,* this time in the unification of those whose purified identity is defined in dialectical opposition to the sacrificial offering. (p. 406, emphasis added)[2]

Burke's (1984a) essay, "On Human Behavior Considered 'Dramatistically' " (originally written in 1951 and published as an appendix to the 1984 edition of *Permanence and Change*), extended his earlier efforts so as to provide a more systematic account of " 'redemption' through victimage" (p. 284) and the process of "perfecting" the sacrificial victim or scapegoat (pp. 286-289). In *The Rhetoric of Religion* (originally published in 1961), one of Burke's (1970) final works, he provided a verse summary of his view of human history and society and the place of victimage within it:

Here are the steps

In the Iron Law of History

That welds Order and Sacrifice:

Order leads to Guilt

(for who can keep commandments!)

Guilt needs Redemption

(for who would not be cleansed!)

Redemption needs a Redeemer

(which is to say, a Victim!).

Order

Through Guilt

To Victimage

(hence: Cult of the Kill) . . . (4-5)

Given that Burke's discussion of scapegoating spanned a period of nearly 30 years and was developed in the context of different projects, is it possible to identify a set of core ideas that articulate the essence of the concept? Perhaps. The first thing that should be noted is that Burke did not invent the concept of scapegoating; in his work, he drew on a tradition of scholarship that has explored the concept.[3] As Burke's writing on the topic evolved, scapegoating was associated with the inevitable presence of **hierarchy** in human society (Burke, 1966, p. 19) and with the problem of maintaining order and stability in a hierarchical society. Burke (1950) seemingly believed in the inevitability of hierarchy (p. 141) as well as a persistent drive to disrupt hierarchical order (via the linguistic invention of the "negative"). Humanity, in Burke's reading, seems to possess a rabble-rousing streak; we *want* order, but we also need or desire to break the rules, rock the boat, march to a different drummer, or engage in forms of unconventional behavior. In his earliest writings on scapegoating, he described the impetus behind the process as "sin" (in *Permanence and Change* [Burke, 1984b]) or "evil" (in "The Philosophy of Literary Form" [Burke, 1957a]). In his later writings, he offered a less theologically charged term—"guilt"—to describe the seeds of the scapegoating process. Guilt arises from disruptions to, or violations of, the social order or from threats to the social order. Burke suggested that guilt might be manifested in a variety of ways—social tensions; anxieties; and feelings of uneasiness, uncertainty, or decline. In whatever form it might appear, guilt has a debilitating impact on the society. Consequently, there emerges a need to "cure" the social order—to cleanse it of guilt and achieve a state of social redemption.

Burke maintained that a society might be redeemed or purified, and its guilt removed, in one of two ways. One strategy is **mortification** or self-victimization in which the members of a society internalize the "sins" that threaten the social order and engage in other behavioral reforms. The other strategy for achieving social redemption is victimage or scapegoating. Scapegoating develops through the principle of externalization. Some individual or group is selected, and all of the society's problems—its sins—are blamed on the chosen individual or group. An "us versus them" *antithesis* is established.[4] The selected individual or group then begins to function, as Burke wrote, as a "sacrificial receptacle" or "vessel" for all that is wrong with the society. In many cases, the scapegoat is symbolically slain (through artistic images or as part of a ritual religious or cultural event) or banished from the society. Through such an act, the society restores or redeems itself. But in some cases (most notably, the Jews in Hitler's Germany), the scapegoat is literally exterminated. We also might encounter a combination. For example, some people today believe that illegal immigrants are serving as a scapegoat for the nation's economic anxieties. When politicians bash illegal immigrants, they are symbolically slaying their scapegoat, and when they vote to cut off medical care or educational benefits, their actions begin to slide toward the literal. But politicians voting to cut off aid are, nevertheless, less literal in their scapegoating than are the Skinhead gangs that go out and beat up Mexican Americans in an effort to "protect" America.[5]

A number of rhetorical critics have turned to Burke's discussion of scapegoating and redemption through victimage as a way of explaining the dynamics of individual texts or an interactive rhetorical episode (Brummett, 1980, 1981; Cloud, 1998; Duffy, 1984; Ivie, 1980; Klope, 1986; Leff, 1973; Mackey-Kallis & Hahn, 1994; Ryan, 1979). Leff (1973), for example, read Cicero's "Catilinarian Orations" (speeches by Cicero attacking the rival political figure Lucius Sergius Catiline) as an exercise in "redemptive identification." Leff began his analysis by noting a perplexing aspect of Cicero's speeches—a peculiar pattern of exaggeration or *hyperbole* (pp. 158-159). The task that Leff set for himself was to explain this rhetorical phenomenon, and to do that he turned to Burke's writings on scapegoating and victimage. Leff reconstructed an ancient Roman empire in the throes of anxiety and beset by "a sense of impending disaster" (p. 163). Roman society needed to be redeemed. This reconstruction of the situation allowed Leff to read Cicero's speeches on two levels or dimensions: *instrumentally* (Cicero's speeches set out to identify a tangible threat to society and urge a specific course of action in response) and *symbolically* or *constitutively* (Cicero's speeches transformed Catiline into the epitome of evil so that his destruction would help redeem or reconstitute Roman society). Leff summarized his analysis as follows:

> We see that Cicero's hyperbole functions to change Catiline from a man representing a specific external threat to the government to a symbol representing an internal threat to the integrity of society. In other words, Catiline becomes a scapegoat. The use of exaggeration is necessary because the real Catiline is neither powerful enough nor dangerous enough to serve as a victim in this sacrificial drama. (p. 171)

Leff argued, following Burke, that Cicero's pattern of exaggeration "perfected" Catiline and made him a suitable "receptacle" for the guilt—the tensions and anxieties—of Roman society.

Let us use Leff's (1973) analysis as a type of model to consider a more contemporary instance of scapegoating. After World War II, America was a proud nation. But it also was a nation beset by doubts, insecurities, and anxieties.[6] We can heed Leff's warning about the danger in drawing "analogies between one society and another" (p. 163) but still observe that there appear to be some similarities between Cicero's Rome and postwar America. The text for our analysis is a speech made by New York Judge Irving Kaufman on April 5, 1951, in which he sentenced convicted spies Ethel and Julius Rosenberg to death. We can begin our analysis in the same way as did Leff—by noting an interesting pattern of exaggeration in Kaufman's speech. For example, at one point in the speech, Kaufman claimed,

> Your crime is worse than murder. Plain deliberate contemplated murder is dwarfed in magnitude by comparison with the crime you have committed. . . . In your case, I believe [that] your conduct in putting into the hands of the Russians the A-bomb years before our best scientists predicted Russia would perfect the bomb has already caused the Communist aggression in Korea with the resultant casualties exceeding 50,000

> Americans, and who knows but that millions more of innocent people may pay the price of your treason. Indeed, by your betrayal you have undoubtedly altered the course of history to the disadvantage of our country.

The question of the Rosenbergs' guilt or innocence has been debated by historians and others since their eventual execution in 1953. Although a consensus seems to be emerging that they were in fact Soviet spies, few argue that they were anything more than amateurs who had little (if any) impact on Soviet atomic research (to say nothing of North Korean and Chinese Communist behavior). So, we have a question similar to that posed by Leff: How do we explain the pattern of exaggeration in Kaufman's speech?

The answer is, no doubt in part, a cultural one. Kaufman was a creature of cold war America, and he shared most of its feelings and beliefs (e.g., the belief in monolithic communism directed from Moscow). But was something more going on in the speech? Perhaps. This is not the place for a full analysis of Kaufman and the Rosenbergs episode. But an analysis along the lines of Leff's account of Cicero is possible once we use the cultural situation to open the text and perceive its multiple levels or dimensions. Instrumentally, Kaufman had to justify his sentencing decision, and his **amplification** of the despicable character of the Rosenbergs and their loathsome actions contributed to that task. Yet, might Kaufman's decision to sentence them to death itself have had a symbolic dimension that, combined with the nature of the situation, invites a broader reading of the text and episode? Might the Rosenbergs (along with the countless other Americans persecuted during the Joe McCarthy era) have functioned, like Catiline, as scapegoats or vessels on whom the sins, guilt, anxieties, and/or tensions of the period were loaded? Kaufman's attribution of blame for the war in Korea then might be read as an instance of rhetorically perfecting the victim, and his discussion of how Ethel and Julius "profited from our system of free higher education" could be taken as a sign of the "original state of merger" (see also Leff, 1973, p. 171) from which they have been removed. Like Catiline in Cicero's orations, Kaufman could be interpreted as transforming the Rosenbergs from a minor external threat to a major internal threat to the integrity of society. The speech would then reveal the logic of the scapegoat process: The Rosenbergs must be executed so that America can be preserved.

The Rosenbergs may or may not have functioned as scapegoats during the early 1950s; that point is open for debate. But Burke's most important point left little room for debate: The scapegoating process appears to be ubiquitous; we are surrounded by it. Scapegoating is not only an implicit aspect of public discourse revealed by discerning rhetorical critics. Political advocates also use scapegoating as a label to critique the strategies of their opponents. For example, during the debate over the proposed Civil Rights Act in June 1991, California Congressman Ron Dellums accused his opponents of "engaging in the politics of scapegoating." Dellums elaborated,

> White America believes that they are losing their jobs, that this [bill] threatens them. Mr. Chairman, what we should be doing is addressing that human misery, not attempting to sell white America, steeped in poverty and unemployment, that in some way blacks, browns, reds, yellows, and women, attempting to redress their historical injustice, are in some way threatening them. Mr. Chairman, to couple these issues . . . is indeed dangerous. . . . When white America is feeling pain, and we suddenly attempt to join these issues at the hip, we are playing a frightening and dangerous, exploitative and manipulative, game. It is called scapegoating politics.

Dellums revealed one possible strategy for confronting scapegoating—public exposure. But the use of scapegoating in contemporary discussions of race in America underscores

Burke's central point: Scapegoating is an ubiquitous discursive strategy. Rhetorical scholars still must struggle with the question: What are we going to do about it?

Notes

1. For extended discussions of the centrality of scapegoating in Burke's thought, see Carter (1996) and Duncan (1962).

2. On the way in which personal and communal identity is shaped through opposition to other individuals and groups, see the entries for **enemies, rhetorical construction of** and **other, rhetorical construction of.**

3. See, in particular, Frazer's (1922) classic study and, more recently, studies by Girard (1982) and Douglas (1995).

4. As Burke (1966) noted, "Antithesis helps reinforce unification by scapegoat" (p. 19).

5. Scapegoating is a complex process. Attentive readers might notice that Skinheads were used as scapegoats in the previous example in that many of the evils of American society are placed on their shoulders as they are held up for ridicule and symbolic banishment.

6. On the anxieties of postwar America, see Rose (1999).

References and Additional Reading

Brummett, B. (1980). Symbolic form, Burkean scapegoating, and rhetorical exigency in Alioto's response to the "Zebra" murders. *Western Journal of Speech Communication, 44,* 64-73.

Brummett, B. (1981). Burkean scapegoating, mortification, and transcendence in presidential campaign rhetoric. *Central States Speech Journal, 32,* 254-264.

Burke, K. (1945). *A grammar of motives.* New York: Prentice Hall.

Burke, K. (1950). *A rhetoric of motives.* New York: Prentice Hall.

Burke, K. (1957a). The philosophy of literary form. In K. Burke, *The philosophy of literary form: Studies in symbolic action* (rev. ed.). New York: Vintage.

Burke, K. (1957b). The rhetoric of Hitler's "Battle." In K. Burke, *The philosophy of literary form: Studies in symbolic action* (rev. ed.). New York: Vintage.

Burke, K. (1966). *Language as symbolic action: Essays on life, literature, and method.* Berkeley: University of California Press.

Burke, K. (1970). *The rhetoric of religion: Studies in logology.* Berkeley: University of California Press.

Burke, K. (1984a). On human behavior considered "dramatistically." In K. Burke, *Permanence and change: An anatomy of purpose* (3rd ed.). Berkeley: University of California Press.

Burke, K. (1984b). *Permanence and change: An anatomy of purpose* (3rd ed.). Berkeley: University of California Press.

Carter, C. A. (1996). *Kenneth Burke and the scapegoat process.* Norman: University of Oklahoma Press.

Chandler, R. C., Hobbs, J. D., King, A. S., & Walts, C. (2000). Scapegoating, transcendence, mortification, and forgiveness: Compensatory arguments of blame after Littleton. In T. A. Hollihan (Ed.), *Argument at century's end: Reflecting on the past and envisioning the future.* Annandale, VA: National Communication Association.

Cloud, D. L. (1998). The rhetoric of <family values>: Scapegoating, utopia, and the privatization of social responsibility. *Western Journal of Communication, 62,* 387-419.

Douglas, T. (1995). *Scapegoats: Transferring blame.* London: Routledge.

Duffy, B. K. (1984). The antihumanist rhetoric of the new religious right. *Southern Speech Communication Journal, 49,* 339-360.

Duncan, H. D. (1962). *Communication and social order.* London: Oxford University Press.

Frazer, J. G. (1922). *The golden bough: A study in magic and religion.* New York: Macmillan.

Girard, R. (1982). *The scapegoat* (Y. Freccero, Trans.). Baltimore, MD: Johns Hopkins University Press.

Heyns, M. (1994). *Expulsion and the nineteenth-century novel: The scapegoat in English realist fiction.* Oxford, UK: Clarendon.

Ivie, R. L. (1980). Images of savagery in American justifications for war. *Communication Monographs, 47,* 279-291.

Klope, D. C. (1986). Defusing a foreign policy crisis: Myth and victimage in Reagan's 1983 Lebanon/Grenada address. *Western Journal of Speech Communication, 50,* 336-349.

Leff, M. C. (1973). Redemptive identification: Cicero's Catilinarian orations. In G. P. Mohrmann, C. J. Stewart, & D. J. Ochs (Eds.), *Explorations in rhetorical criticism.* University Park: Pennsylvania State University Press.

Mackey-Kallis, S., & Hahn, D. (1994). Who's to blame for America's drug problem? The search for scapegoats in the "war on drugs." *Communication Quarterly, 42,* 1-20.

Perera, S. B. (1986). *The scapegoat complex: Toward a mythology of shadow and guilt.* Toronto: Inner City Books.

Rose, L. A. (1999). *The cold war comes to Main Street: America in 1950.* Lawrence: University Press of Kansas.

Ryan, H. R. (1979). Roosevelt's first inaugural: A study of technique. *Quarterly Journal of Speech, 65,* 137-149.

Vickery, J. B., & Sellery, J. M. (Ed.). (1972). *The scapegoat: Ritual and literature.* Boston: Houghton Mifflin.

Wess, R. (1996). *Kenneth Burke: Rhetoric, subjectivity, postmodernism.* Cambridge, UK: Cambridge University Press.

SECULAR CONVERSION

The term *conversion* typically refers to the process by which individuals alter their religious affiliations. A common prototype or paradigm of religious conversion is the case of Saul of Tarsus. After experiencing God's presence, he converted to Christianity, changing his name to Paul and eventually becoming one of the first saints of the Catholic church.[1] Rhetorical scholars have studied the rhetoric of religious conversion from two perspectives: discourse that functions to generate conversion within an audience or to *reaffirm* a process of conversion[2] and discourse produced by individuals *after* experiencing conversion that functions to authenticate, justify, and extend the conversion process.[3] Conversion rhetoric stands as an example of how the *constitutive* dimension of rhetorical effect, specifically the constitution or reconstitution of identity, sometimes can serve as an *instrumental* objective.

Postconversion discourse often assumes a **narrative** form, leading scholars to coin the expression "conversion narrative." Smith (1999) noted,

> Conversion narratives . . . came into use in America in the early 1600s and were soon required by most Puritan churches of anyone who wished to join. Their primary purpose was to demonstrate to the church, represented either by the congregation or by an audience of church leaders, that the petitioner had undergone a genuine conversion. (p. 227; see also Caldwell, 1983)

Smith (1999) argued that religious conversion narratives had a profound impact on abolitionist discourse during the 19th century.

In *Permanence and Change,* Burke (1984) suggested that the experience of religious reaffiliation might be generalized to the secular (nonreligious) world and introduced the term **secular conversion** as a label for the process. Burke believed that the practice of psychoanalysis was a prime instance of secular conversion. He maintained that psychoanalysis "effects its cures by providing a new perspective that dissolves the system of pieties lying at the roots of the patient's sorrows or bewilderments. . . . [It offers] a fresh terminology [or vocabulary] of motives to replace the patient's painful terminology of motives" (p. 125). For Burke, then, the psychoanalytic "cure" is roughly the same as a religious conversion; the patient's recovery is predicated on the dissolution of the "old self" (along with the "pieties" and *vocabulary of motives* that sustain the old self) that allows the emergence of a "new self." The "trick" to psychoanalysis, Burke argued, is a process he termed "exorcism by misnomer." As Burke explained, "One casts out demons by a vocabulary of *conversion,* by an *incongruous* naming" (p. 133).[4] Sometimes, as the case of Saul/Paul illustrates, the trick is for the individual to change his or her name (reinforcing the shift in identity that marks the conversion process). In other cases, as Burke's idea of exorcism by misnomer suggests, the trick is to redefine or rename the nature of the problem.

Consider how Burke's ideas might be applied to the increasingly popular recovery and self-help movements. Addicts of all sorts are undergoing a process of secular conversion. They are abandoning their old vocabularies and old pieties in exchange for new ones. Along the way, they become "new" people. For example, the "recovering alcoholic" takes responsibility for things that the (old) alcoholic might have done, but the recovering alcoholic is a different person. Or, consider how the process of renaming someone as "co-dependent" enacts something like Burke's idea of *exorcism by misnomer.* The person resolves his or her difficulties by accepting the new label and, along with it, the new identity. Or, in perhaps an unlikely extension, Brown (1998) discovered "narratives of conversion" functioning as "logics of discovery" in scientific discourse. Brown argued that foundational texts of modern rationalism such as Descartes' *Discourse on Method* function as conversion narratives that support a change in self and perspective.[5]

Something quite similar to Burke's idea of secular conversion was developed in the works of sociologists Peter Berger and Thomas Luckmann. In *The Social Construction of Reality,* Berger and Luckmann (1967) described how individuals modify their "subjective reality" and labeled this process "alteration." Like Burke, they took religious conversion as paradigmatic, noting that "the historical prototype of alteration is religious conversion" (p. 158). Berger and Luckmann focused on the way in which reinterpretations of the past work to help secure the individual's new reality and new identity. At times, "this involves a reinterpretation of past biography *in toto,* following the formula 'Then I *thought* . . ., now I *know*' " (p. 160). The person's prealteration or preconversion past is rejected; "prealteration biography is typically nihilated *in toto* by subsuming it under a negative category occupying a strategic position in the new legitimating apparatus" (p. 160). For example, a converted Marxist might reject his or her past by claiming that he or she was ensnared by "bourgeois consciousness"; a woman converted to feminism might reread her past as a time when she was a victim of male patriarchy; and former 1960s radical David Horowitz might describe his youth, as he did in his autobiography *Radical Son* (Horowitz, 1997), as a period of confusion. In each of these examples, the individual rejects his or her past as a period of "false consciousness" that is now comprehensible given the person's experience of secular conversion (pp. 64-92).

In other cases, Berger and Luckmann (1967) noted, the process of reinterpretation is not so radical. Instead of completely rejecting the past, the person reinterprets specific events in ways that make the old events conform to the new person. Old events now are understood as steps leading up to the change in identity. As Berger and Luckmann noted, "Since it is relatively easier to invent things that never happened than to forget those that actually did, the individual may fabricate and insert events wherever they are needed to harmonize the remembered with the reinterpreted past" (p. 160). Ronald Reagan can be used to illustrate the processes of reinterpretation and fabrication. Many scholars and commentators have noted Reagan's problem with recalling historical events, both those that he was directly involved in and those that took place outside his range of personal experience. Wallace (1987), among others, noted Reagan's tendency to engage in the "whiting out of inconvenient memories" and "retrospective tidying up of the past" (p. 17). These practices were used both with respect to broader historical events and with respect to Reagan's own past. Comparing Reagan with America's quintessential myth maker, Walt Disney, Wallace noted,

> It is interesting that both Disney and Reagan fudged their *own* histories, bathing fairly wretched childhood experiences in a Norman Rockwell glow. . . . Reagan's early years were shadowed by his father's alcoholism, unemployment, and constant relocation, years that got gauzed over in his official recollections. (p. 17)

Some of his critics charged Reagan with mendacity. And the charge has some merit; it seems to be an accurate way of characterizing Reagan's claim that he assisted in the liberation of Nazi concentration camps at the end of World War II (p. 16). But we also should recall that Reagan underwent a profound political conversion. A one-time New Deal Democrat and committed follower of Franklin Roosevelt, he would end up leading what many believe is a fundamental conservative reorientation of American politics. What remains to be explored is the relationship between Reagan's secular political conversion and his practice of historical reinterpretation and fabrication.[6]

Humans have a tendency to change aspects of their existence. Sometimes, these alterations are purely physical (e.g., changes in hair style or color, a shift from glasses to contacts, a new fashion look). At other times, the changes are more psychological and more fundamental to an individual's sense of who and what he or she is. So long as this human tendency persists, the process of conversion—both religious and secular—will remain an object for critical study.

Notes

1. See Bormann's (1985) discussion of the "Pauline conversion fantasy."

2. See, for example, White's (1972) study of the "morphology [structure] of conversion" in Puritan rhetoric and Kertzer's (1988) discussion of how initiation rituals or "rites of induction" function to help "get the recruit to redefine his [sic] identity" (p. 17).

3. See, for example, Griffin's (1990) study of former Richard Nixon adviser Charles Colson's account of his experience of being "born again" and McGee's (1998) study of the "conversion" of Louisiana politician David Duke. These cases, and many others, demonstrate how the *metaphor* of (re)birth is a common trope in conversion rhetoric.

4. As Burke (1984) acknowledged later in the chapter, secular conversion or metaphorical "rebirth and **perspective by incongruity** are thus seen to be synonymous, a process of conversion" (p. 154, emphasis added).

5. Smith (1999) quoted 19th-century University of Vermont professor Calvin Pease to illustrate that "the practice of conversion narratives . . . wasn't confined to religious discourse" but also can account for "the persuasive power of scientific discourse" (pp. 228-229).

6. On the relationship between narrative and conversion, see also Fabj (1998) and Griffin (1990). On the broader issue of narrative and identity, see Carr (1986) and the entry for **subject**.

References and Additional Reading

Berger, P. L., & Luckmann, T. (1967). *The social construction of reality: A treatise in the sociology of knowledge.* Garden City, NY: Anchor.

Bormann, E. G. (1985). *The force of fantasy: Restoring the American dream.* Carbondale: Southern Illinois University Press.

Brown, R. H. (1998). *Toward a democratic science: Scientific narration and civic communication.* New Haven, CT: Yale University Press.

Burke, K. (1984). *Permanence and change: An anatomy of purpose.* Berkeley: University of California Press.

Caldwell, P. (1983). *The Puritan conversion narrative.* Cambridge, MA: Harvard University Press.

Carr, D. (1986). *Time, narrative, and history.* Bloomington: Indiana University Press.

Fabj, V. (1998). Intolerance, forgiveness, and promise in the rhetoric of conversion: Italian women defy the Mafia. *Quarterly Journal of Speech, 84,* 190-208.

Golden, J. L., Berquist, G. F., & Coleman, W. E. (1989). Secular and religious conversion. In J. L. Golden, G. F. Berquist, & W. E. Coleman, *The rhetoric of Western thought* (4th ed.). Dubuque, IA: Kendall/Hunt.

Griffin, C. J. G. (1990). The rhetoric of form in conversion narratives. *Quarterly Journal of Speech, 76,* 152-163.

Hawkins, A. H. (1985). *Archetypes of conversion: The autobiographies of Augustine, Bunyan, and Merton.* Lewisburg, PA: Bucknell University Press.

Horowitz, D. (1997). *Radical son: A generational odyssey.* New York: Free Press.

Kertzer, D. I. (1988). *Ritual, politics, and power.* New Haven, CT: Yale University Press.

McGee, B. R. (1998). Witnessing and *ethos:* The evangelical conversion of David Duke. *Western Journal of Communication, 62,* 217-243.

Smith, K. K. (1999). *The dominion of voice: Riot, reason, and romance in antebellum America.* Lawrence: University Press of Kansas.

Wallace, M. (1987). Ronald Reagan and the politics of history. *Tikkun, 2,* 13-18, 127-131.

White, E. E. (1972). *Puritan rhetoric: The issue of emotion in religion.* Carbondale: Southern Illinois University Press.

SENTIMENTALISM/ SENTIMENTAL STYLE

In contemporary rhetorical studies, the term **sentimentalism** or **sentimental style** is most closely associated with Black's (1978) study of Daniel Webster and 19th-century American oratory. Black claimed that Webster was "an acutely sonorous representative" (p. 78) of a ubiquitous discursive style. Black's interest in the essay was not with the surface manifestations or the outward "symptoms" of sentimentality (its specific discursive texture) but rather with "the *function* of these symptoms" (p. 78). The important question for Black was what sentimental discourse does to its audience and its culture, not what sentimental discourse looks like.

Black's (1978) functional emphasis led him to conceptualize sentimentality as a "form of consciousness" (p. 85). What Black emphasized about this style was "the detail with which it shapes one's responses. No scintilla of reaction is left for the auditor's own creation. . . . What this sort of style seeks is a total control over the consciousness [of the audience]" (p. 78). Black argued that sentimentalism is "excessively didactic" (p. 79) and highly manipulative. Sentimentalism manipulates a particular aspect of human consciousness—emotional experience. Through "emotional expression," the sentimental style "elicits affective experiences but also defines and delimits them. It enables the emotions to be given a re-creation under sanctioned auspices" (p. 78). It was common during the 19th century for public leaders to speak of emotional "enthusiasm," in religion as well as in politics, as dangerous; the sentimental style spoke to that fear by producing a type of "sanitized" emotional experience in audiences. The problematic emotions are **domesticated.**

For Black (1978), sentimentalism, as a style and as a form of consciousness, remains a symptom; it is "a symptom of disquiet and unease, of a subtly gnawing conscience and a tacit agreement to repress" (p. 80). The cultural function of sentimentalism is "the subordination of moral to aesthetic considerations" (pp. 81, 83). In a wonderful sound pun, Black elaborated on the cultural function of sentimentalism by terming it "an aesthetic anesthetic" (p. 81). Sentimentalism dominated consciousness through a process of aesthetic numbing; troubling ideas and issues could be rendered harmless by an overwhelming, but tightly controlled, emotional and aesthetic assault on the consciousness of the audience. The end result, for Black, was a form of massive cultural repression; sentimentalism was a coping mechanism (p. 82) for a culture that refused to confront its contradictions and paradoxes, most notably the horror of slavery in the land of liberty.[1] Black likely would agree with White's (1984) observation that "sentimentality is thus a political as well as an aesthetic vice" (p. 18).

Black (1978) acknowledged that the "discursive" elements of the sentimental style (left largely unenumerated in his essay) were at that time "unfashionable" (p. 86). But he did suggest that the "epistemic function" of sentimentalism, the subordination of moral considerations to aesthetic ones, remained an issue with which contemporary critics and advocates had to reckon. Black's reconstruction of the 19th-century sentimental style, and its potential rearticulation in the contemporary **public sphere,** revoiced a continuing issue in the history of rhetoric—the role of the aesthetic dimension in our discursive practices.

The type of reconstruction of sentimentalism that Black provided has been critiqued in recent literary scholarship. Tompkins (1985), for example, questioned many of the assumptions that had led to the critical dismissal of much literary sentimentalism during the 19th century. Tompkins shared Black's view that sentimentalism is more than a narrowly conceived style; she agreed that sentimentalism is a form of consciousness or a "framework for the ordering of experience" (p. 154). But whereas Black saw sentimentalism as a repressive aesthetic anesthetic, Tompkins reconstructed sentimentalism as a form of empowerment. To be sure, the sense of **power** that Tompkins located in the sentimental tradition of literature and pulpit oratory was not the sense of power commonly equated with political activity in the public sphere. Tompkins's analysis centered on Harriet Beecher Stowe's *Uncle Tom's Cabin,* which (like Black's example of Daniel Webster) was one of the most popular texts of the period. What Black might consider aesthetic repression was described by Tompkins as "a conception of the world that is now generally regarded as naive and unrealistic" (p. 132). But whereas Black found the naïveté of sentimentalism as a retreat or a way of hiding from the ugly reality of the world, Tompkins saw sentimentalism as a way of trying to reconfigure or alter the world. Tompkins wrote,

> Because most modern readers regard such political and economic facts as final, it is difficult for them to take seriously a novel that insists on religious conversion as the necessary precondition for sweeping social change. . . . Reality, in Stowe's view, cannot be changed by manipulating the physical environment; it can only be changed by conversion in the spirit because it is the spirit alone that is finally real. (pp. 132-133)

Tompkins suggested that sentimentalism provided a different way for advocates to engage the problems they perceived in America's social order.[2]

It might not be necessary to choose between Black's and Tompkins's reconstructions of sentimentalism.[3] Black's contention that sentimentalism functions as a type of cultural narcotic, numbing audiences into a stupor that prevents them from confronting the contradictions in their world, can be reconciled with Tompkins's reading if we approach the issue dialectically. When we hide or repress something, we also reveal or illuminate something else. Perhaps this dialectic is at work in sentimentalism and the sentimental style. If nothing else, the contrast between Black's and Tompkins's readings suggests the need to refine our critical vocabulary and explore different forms of sentimentalism and their various functions, both in the past and in the ways that this form of consciousness is discursively enacted and manifested in the present.

Notes

1. On the limitations of sentimentalism, see also Brown (1940) and Douglas (1977). On sentimentalism as a way of negotiating constraints experienced by members of the abolitionist movement, see Browne (1994).

2. For other reappraisals of sentimentalism, see the essays collected in Samuels (1992).

3. Black (1992) reviewed Tompkins' reading of sentimentality in such a way as to reaffirm most of his earlier critique while modifying the hypothesized relationship between 19th-century sentimentalism and slavery.

References and Additional Reading

Black, E. (1978). The sentimental style as escapism, or the devil with Dan'l Webster. In K. K. Campbell & K. H. Jamieson (Eds.), *Form and genre: Shaping rhetorical action.* Falls Church, VA: Speech Communication Association.

Black, E. (1992). Authoritarian fiction. In E. Black, *Rhetorical questions: Studies of public discourse.* Chicago: University of Chicago Press.

Brown, H. R. (1940). *The sentimental novel in America, 1789-1860.* Durham, NC: Duke University Press.

Browne, S. (1994). "Like gory spectres": Representing evil in Theodore Weld's *American Slavery as It Is. Quarterly Journal of Speech, 80,* 277-292.

Douglas, A. (1977). *The feminization of American culture.* New York: Knopf.

Samuels, S. (Ed.). (1992). *The culture of sentiment: Race, gender, and sentimentality in nineteenth-century America.* New York: Oxford University Press.

Tompkins, J. (1985). *Sensational designs: The cultural work of American fiction, 1790-1860.* New York: Oxford University Press.

White, J. B. (1984). *When words lose their meaning: Constitutions and reconstitutions of language, character, and community.* Chicago: University of Chicago Press.

SERMONIC, LANGUAGE AS

Speculative inquiry into the nature and essential function(s) of language has become a (nonexclusive) part of the domain of rhetorical thinking over the past half century.[1] This form of inquiry often is organized through opposition or contrast; one way of understanding language is illuminated by juxtaposing it to an alternative (typically inferior or partial) conceptualization (on this tendency, see Hariman, 1986). Such is the case with Weaver's (1971) lecture/essay, "Language Is Sermonic."

Like many recent rhetorical theorists (cf. Burke, 1966), Weaver (1971) developed his "sermonic" sense of language, or **language as sermonic,** through a contrast with a "scientistic" conceptualization (p. 165). Scientism, for Weaver, "denotes the application of scientific assumptions to subjects which are not wholly comprised of naturalistic phenomena" (p. 165). With respect to language, scientism envisions language as a neutral instrument capable of an accurate and disinterested representation of reality. As Burke (1966) observed, "A 'scientistic' approach begins with questions of *naming* or *definition*" (p. 44). Weaver and Burke both found scientistic assumptions to be problematic with respect to the nature and function of language. For Weaver (1971), "As long as man [sic] is a creature responding to purpose, his linguistic expression will be a carrier of tendency" (p. 177). He maintained that our language *always* carries within it attitudes, feelings, beliefs, and other human "tendencies." Weaver continued,

> Language, which is thus predicative [inherently a practice of "classifying"], is for the same reason sermonic. We are all of us preachers in private or public capacities. We have no sooner uttered words than we have given impulse to other people to look at the world, or some part of it, in our way. (p. 178)

In *Permanence and Change,* Burke (1984) made a similar observation:

> Speech in its essence is not neutral. Far from aiming at suspended judgments, the spontaneous speech of a people is loaded with judgments. It is intensely moral. . . . Such speech is profoundly *partisan.* . . . [It is] not a naming at all but a system of attitudes, of implicit exhortations. (pp. 176-177)

He repeated the point in later works: "There is, *implicit in language itself,* the act of persuasion" (Burke, 1950, p. 274) and "The power of language to define and describe may be viewed as derivative, and its essential function may be treated as attitudinal or hortatory" (Burke, 1966, p. 44).

Another major figure in the 20th-century revival of rhetoric, Chaïm Perelman, reiterated the sermonic thesis. In an essay for the inaugural issue of the journal *Philosophy and Rhetoric,* Perelman (1968) wrote,

> The choice of a linguistic form is neither purely arbitrary nor simply a carbon copy of reality. . . . The form is not separable from the content; language is not a veil which one need only discard or render transparent in order to perceive the real as such; it is inextricably bound up with a point of view, with the taking of a position. When an author does not express himself [sic] after the fashion of a mathematician . . ., he adopts, with respect to all those points which he has not explicitly modified, the classifications and evaluations that the language carries with it. (pp. 17-18)

The challenge for rhetorical scholarship, in the tradition of Burke, Perelman, and Weaver, is to enhance our understanding of *how* various linguistic and discursive elements (e.g., specific words, lexical codes, syntactical patterns, **argument** strategies, **narrative** patterns) embody attitudes or tendencies and *why* different elements are persuasive in particular situations.

Notes

1. For an overview, see the entry for **representation.**
2. On this tendency, see Hariman (1986).

References and Additional Reading

Burke, K. (1950). *A rhetoric of motives.* New York: Prentice Hall.

Burke, K. (1966). *Language as symbolic action: Essays on life, literature, and method.* Berkeley: University of California Press.

Burke, K. (1984). *Permanence and change: An anatomy of purpose* (3rd ed.). Berkeley: University of California Press.
Hariman, R. (1986). Status, marginality, and rhetorical theory. *Quarterly Journal of Speech, 72,* 38-54.
Perelman, C. (1968). Rhetoric and philosophy. *Philosophy and Rhetoric, 1,* 15-24.
Weaver, R. (1971). Language is sermonic. In R. L. Johannesen (Ed.), *Contemporary theories of rhetoric: Selected readings.* New York: Harper & Row.

SITUATION, RHETORICAL

Since its publication during the late 1960s, Bitzer's (1968) essay, "The Rhetorical Situation," has been at the center of a lively conversation in contemporary rhetorical studies. More than three decades after its initial presentation, the idea of a **rhetorical situation** still occupies a significant place in both the rhetoric classroom and scholarly discourse. This entry cannot review in detail the three decades of discussion that has focused on this concept. Its aim is to both introduce some key issues in the situational conversation and make a modest contribution to that conversation.

Bitzer's (1968) now classic formulation held that

> rhetorical discourse comes into existence as a response to a situation, in the same sense that an answer comes into existence in response to a question. . . . A rhetorical situation must exist as a necessary condition of rhetorical discourse, just as a question must exist as a necessary condition of an answer. (pp. 5-6)

After analogically developing the idea of a rhetorical situation, Bitzer offered a definition that brings it to life. He wrote,

> Rhetorical situation may be defined as a complex of persons, events, objects, and relations presenting an actual or potential exigence that can be completely or partially removed if discourse, introduced into the situation, can so constrain human decision or action as to bring about the significant modification of the exigence. (p. 6)

Out of this "complex," three factors stand out and are, according to Bitzer, the primordial "constituents" of a rhetorical situation: *exigence,* **audience,** and *constraints* (p. 6). Each merits additional attention.

An exigence, Bitzer (1968) asserted, is "an imperfection marked by urgency; it is a defect, an obstacle, something waiting to be done, a thing which is other than it should be" (p. 6). In other words, an exigence is a pressing problem in the world, something to which people must attend.[1] The exigence functions as the "organizing principle" of a situation; the situation develops around its "controlling exigence" (p. 7). But not every problem is a rhetorical exigence. Bitzer explained,

> An exigence which cannot be modified is not rhetorical; thus, whatever comes about of necessity and cannot be changed—death, winter, and some natural disasters, for instance—are exigences to be sure, but they are nonrhetorical. An exigence is rhetorical when it is capable of positive modification and when positive modification *requires* discourse or can be *assisted* by discourse. (pp. 6-7, emphasis added)

Racism is an example of the first type of exigence, one where discourse is *required* to remove the problem. Bitzer seemed to assume that the only way in which people will alter behavior that demeans people of a different race is if they are persuaded to do so. Therefore, persuasive discourse is required to modify the exigence of racism.[2] As an example of the second type—an exigence that can be modified by the *assistance* of rhetorical discourse—Bitzer offered the case of air pollution. He wrote, "The pollution of air is also a rhetorical exigence because its positive modification—reduction of pollution—strongly invites the assistance of discourse producing public awareness, indignation, and action of the right kind" (p. 7). This example can help to clarify the relationship between exigence and the related concept of *ill* (although Bitzer did not take his discussion in this direction). The physical presence of hazardous particles in the air—the phenomenon of air pollution—is an ill or a condition that threatens human health. Discourse by itself cannot make air pollution go away. But discourse can assist in the elimination of air pollution when it is used to persuade legislators to pass a new law requiring drastic reductions in the quantity of hazardous emissions from automobiles and other sources of air pollution. The exigence then becomes one of getting the legislators to take action; that is, the exigence in this case is the problem of *policy advocacy* or the need to induce a legislative body to take action against the ill of air pollution. Finally, we should note that problems have a way of resurfacing or of coming back to life after it appears that they have been eradicated. Consequently, most rhetorical scholars believe that rhetorical exigences typically are *resolved* through deliberation and action; rarely (if ever) are they *solved* or eliminated in a final sense.

Not every collection of individuals who happen to listen to a speech in person, watch one on television, or read an essay in a newspaper or magazine constitute a rhetorical audience. Bitzer (1968) argued that a *rhetorical audience* must meet two conditions: It must consist "only of those persons who are capable of being influenced by discourse and of being mediators of change" (p. 8). The first condition of a rhetorical audience is that its members are "capable of being influenced." A group of individuals who refuse to consider an advocate's arguments and appeals or who are completely closed to alternative perspectives do not, in Bitzer's judgment, constitute a rhetorical audience. For an individual to be part of a rhetorical audience or for a group of people to function as a rhetorical audience, they must demonstrate a certain minimum level of attention and a willingness to consider the advocate's arguments and/or proposals. The second condition of a rhetorical audience is that its members can function as "mediators of change." At times, an advocate might need to awaken his or her listeners or readers to their capacity to act as agents of change (e.g., Henry Garnet's efforts during the 19th century to show African slaves that they had the power to change their condition). At other times, a group of people might not possess the capacity to make the final decision but might possess an ability to influence others with final decision-making power. Bitzer's condition of capacity might then be divided into (a) an audience capable of making the final decision and (b) an audience capable of influencing those with final decision-making authority (on this distinction, see Crable & Vibbert, 1985). In short, a rhetorical audience is open to, and interested in, the discourse *and* possesses the capacity to act as a mediator of change (see also Hauser, 1986).

Constraints are the third constituent of a rhetorical situation.[3] In an often quoted passage from *The Eighteenth Brumaire of Louis Bonaparte,* Marx (1967) wrote, "Men [sic] make their own history, but they do not make it just as they please; they do not make it under circumstances chosen by themselves, but under circumstances directly encountered, given, and transmitted from the past." To simplify Marx's point a bit and blend it with Bitzer's idea of the rhetorical situation, people "make history" by confronting exigences. They craft discourse to help resolve those exigences. But in so doing, they encounter "circumstances" that they did not choose, and quite possibly if they had a choice would not have chosen, but with which they must cope. For example, a defense attorney would not recommend that his or her client sign a confession, but if the client did, then it would be a circumstance that the attorney must negotiate. These circumstances can include history (e.g., past events, traditions); people; present events; recognized facts, values, and beliefs; discursive conventions; written documents (e.g., contracts, letters); authoritative documents (e.g., the Bible, the U.S. Constitution); physical location; and other important economic, social, and cultural factors (Bitzer,

1968, p. 8). Constraints, then, are circumstances that interfere with, or get in the way of, an advocate's ability to respond to an exigence. A politician's negative image is a constraint on his or her effort to run for higher office. Conflicting opinions in the scientific community are a constraint on those who want to use scientific testimony to support a policy position. The arguments of the opposition are a constraint that hampers any policy initiative. Circumstantial constraints are, in effect, mini-exigences; they are secondary problems that an advocate must negotiate or deal with to resolve the dominant exigence. When circumstances provide material that can work to the advocate's advantage, those circumstances are *resources* that the advocate tries to exploit. A male politician's attractive wife might be a resource on the campaign trail. An advocate's firsthand experiences in a foreign country might serve as a resource in an effort to win approval for a military appropriation on the country's behalf. An advocate's prior history with an audience might be a resource in trying to win its members' support of a local tax referendum. Both constraints and resources are critical components of any rhetorical situation.

Situations are not "born" fully developed; they evolve over time. Bitzer (1980) described four stages of development.[4] The first consists of *origin* and *development.* During this stage, "an exigence comes into existence" and "we assume that someone recognizes it" (p. 34). But audience, constraints, and resources either are unclear or have not developed fully. During the second stage, *maturity,* "the exigence is present and perceived, often by speaker and audience; the audience is capable of modifying the exigence and can be easily addressed; [and] operative constraints are available." Bitzer noted that "the duration of this stage may be no more than a moment" (p. 34), or it may continue indefinitely. The third stage is *deterioration.* During this stage, the configuration of constituents "changes in ways that make modification of the exigence significantly more difficult" (p. 35). The fourth and final stage is *disintegration.* During this stage, the configuration of constituents dissolves; the audience disappears, the exigence no longer has **presence,** resources have been exhausted, and/or constraints become overwhelming. An advocate who persists in addressing a disintegrated situation is a lone voice howling in the wilderness. But as demonstrated by continued "status" fluctuation (Crable & Vibbert, 1985) of issues such as health care and the resurgence of feminism during the 1960s, no situation must remain dormant forever.

One of the issues in Bitzer's situational formula that has attracted the most attention and criticism is its purported *objectivism.* Bitzer (1968) observed,

> The exigence and the complex of persons, objects, events, and relations which generate rhetorical discourse are located in reality, are objective and publicly observable historic facts in the world we experience, [and] are therefore available for scrutiny by an observer or critic who attends to them. To say the situation is objective . . . means that it is real or genuine. . . . Real situations are to be distinguished from sophistic ones in which, for example, a contrived exigence is asserted to be real; from spurious situations in which the existence or alleged existence of constituents is the result of error or ignorance; and from fantasy in which exigence, audience, and constraints may all be the imaginary objects of a mind at play. (p. 11)

Bitzer's claim that the situation is an "objective" phenomenon—that it exists as a real thing apart from human perception, recognition, or interaction—was challenged in different ways by a number of scholars (Brinton, 1981; Consigny, 1974; Hunsaker & Smith, 1976; Miller, 1972; Vatz, 1973). In one of the earliest critiques of the *situational objectivity thesis,* Vatz (1973) insisted, "No situation can have a nature independent of the perception of its interpreter or independent of the rhetoric with which he [sic] chooses to characterize it" (p. 154). For Vatz and many other rhetorical scholars, advocates not only *respond* to situations, they also help to *create* and/or *define* situations.[5] Rhetorical discourse on this view is not merely *instrumental;* it also possesses a *constructive* or *constitutive* capacity. When a theorist recognizes the constructive or constitutive potential of discourse, it does not mean that the theorist believes that discourse creates the physical particles that pollute the atmosphere. The constructive or constitutive hypothesis suggests, instead, that physical objects such as pollutants, or social objects such as crime and poverty, are made intelligible or comprehensible in and through discourse.[6]

The issues separating Bitzer and his critics should not be framed as a mutually exclusive *disjunction.* It is not a question of whether discourse either responds to or creates situations. Most rhetorical scholars believe that it does both. Patton (1979), for example, noted how "the meaning of rhetorical situations is a dual process, partly a matter of recognition, i.e. clarity and accuracy of perception, and partly a matter of intentional, artistic, human action" (p. 49). Bitzer (1980) modified the rigid objectivism of his initial formulation by admitting human "interests" into the process of exigence formation. He wrote, "A rhetorical exigence consists of a factual condition plus a relation to some interest. . . . An exigence exists when a factual condition and an interest are joined" (p. 28). For example, grade school students' test scores are a factual condition; the tests were administered, they were scored, and the raw results can be reported. But Bitzer acknowledged that this factual condition can become an exigence only when it is connected to human interests. "The addition of interests," according to Bitzer, makes a factual condition "something other than it should be, a defect, a matter to be altered" (p. 28). Test scores reveal a problem that must be addressed when they are connected to human interests in things such as *success, prosperity,* and *achievement.* Low test scores can be perceived as a threat to these interests. When they are so perceived, an exigence comes into existence.

In a sense, every situation is unique; the cluster of events that constitute a situation do not occur twice in *exactly* the same way. But situations can have similar structures and characteristics. Bitzer (1968) wrote, "From day to day, year to year, comparable situations occur, prompting comparable responses" (p. 13). This observation was an important stimulus in the development of **genre** scholarship in contemporary rhetorical studies (e.g., Jamieson, 1973). Bitzer's observation also might be extended in another direction. The existence of situational similarities can support the development of a *typology* of situational exigences that addresses the question: What are some of the recurrent problems that organize rhetorical situations and to which advocates respond? In certain cases, the different problems discussed in what follows dominate and organize a situation; as such, they function as primary exigences. In other cases, certain problems are subsidiary elements in the quest to resolve the dominant exigences; in these cases, the problems can be viewed as either secondary exigences or constraints that must be negotiated or overcome to resolve the dominant exigences. Some common exigences/constraints in rhetorical situations are described in what follows.

Define the Situation

In a sense, this is the most basic or fundamental exigence, and it plays a role in every rhetorical situation. Advocates need to create a particular understanding of the world, or some part of it, that can be shared with the audience. They need to render the world, or some part of it, intelligible or understandable; they have to make confusing or troubling events meaningful for their audience. Public discourse often centers on specific questions such as the following. What has happened or is happening? How should we characterize what is going on around us? What elements within the situational "complex" should be given special emphasis (**presence**)? Does a problem exist? Is it urgent?[7] Who is to blame?

Our position on policy questions such as national health care will be shaped by our understanding of the present situation. Does a health care "crisis" exist? How adequate is our health care system? If there are problems with health care, then who is to blame? Although advocates will rely on various "facts" and statistics to establish the "reality" of their situational definition, we are nevertheless dealing with matters of perception. A public problem exists to the degree that the public perceives a state of affairs *as* a problem. And as Bitzer's critics pointed out with regularity, perception always is subject to persuasive influence.

Advocates not only try to define the immediate situation but, in many cases, also strive to establish the meaning of previous events that may be related to present circumstances. For example, as advocates debate the possibility of U.S. military intervention in various "crises" around the world (e.g., Central America during the mid-1980s, the Persian Gulf during the early 1990s, Bosnia during the mid-1990s), they frequently invoke the memory of the war in Vietnam. But what *was* the war in Vietnam? A noble failure? A misguided effort? An attempt to halt the spread of communism? An attempt to protect U.S. economic interests?[8] The "lessons" we learn from the past depend on how we understand past events. Hence, the meaning of the past often is a point of intense rhetorical controversy.

Create an Audience/Build Solidarity Among the Audience/Overcome Divisions Within the Audience

Advocates need to find people who will listen or, in effect, need to persuade people that they must or should listen; they must convince audience members that they have the power or capacity to institute change; and, frequently, they must instill a sense of group identity or solidarity among heterogeneous audiences. Many social reform advocates have spent their entire public careers searching for audiences and trying to persuade people to listen. Throughout history, advocates have struggled to convince attentive audiences that they have the capacity to change the status quo. One of the remarkable features of Thomas Paine's famous pamphlet, *Common Sense* (published in 1776), was its attention to practical issues such as the colonies' shipbuilding capacity. Paine's attention to these details was an effort to solve a key problem—convincing the colonists that they had a chance against what was, at the time, the world's greatest military force. Similarly, during the early 1960s, black nationalist activist Malcolm X had to convince African Americans that they had the capacity to effect change. Given the similarity in exigences, it is not surprising that Paine and Malcolm X relied on some similar strategies. Both employed a form of **dissociation** that showed how the supposedly subordinate group—the colonists for Paine and African Americans for Malcolm X—actually was responsible for the material power of the dominant group.

Advocates routinely strive to reconstitute audiences' sense of identity.[9] During national emergencies, for example, advocates invoke patriotic themes to remind members of their audiences that they all are "Americans." This process is visible in smaller communities as well. A collection of women *become* sorority sisters through discourse that encourages this type of group **identification.** A group of workers *become* members of a united working class, imbued with "class consciousness," through the discursive appeals of labor leaders. A congregation of worshipers *become* Roman Catholics, Baptists, or Methodists through the appeals embedded in the sermons delivered by their priest or minister. One common strategy for crafting group identity is to contrast the group to a stereotypical **other** or **enemy.**

Advocates face the challenge not only of constituting group identity but also of *maintaining* or *reinforcing* group identity. Consider the case of the United Parcel Service (UPS) strike during the late summer of 1997. The Teamsters Union faced the problem of maintaining union solidarity in the face of company efforts to divide UPS drivers from the rest of the Teamsters (the company proposed a separate pension for UPS drivers to which it would contribute instead of continuing its contribution to the Teamster-administered pension fund). The company offered the drivers an attractive proposal, but it meant that the drivers would have to (at least implicitly) reorient their identity; accepting the company's offer would make them UPS drivers first and Teamsters second. The union's exigence was to reinforce the drivers' group identity; the drivers were Teamsters first and foremost, and their positions as UPS drivers were secondary. Given the multiplicity of *subject positions* that people regularly occupy, this exigence occurs with some regularity.

Get the Audience to Take Action

In some rhetorical situations, the chief objective for an advocate—the "problem" that must be solved—is to get an audience to take action. The specific forms of action urged by advocates vary with the needs of specific situations. Among other things, advocates urge audiences to vote for particular candidates, write their representatives expressing their opinions on policy matters, donate time and/or money to support the actions of some groups, engage in some valued behavior (e.g., recycling, donating blood), boycott certain products or companies, and (in extreme cases) revolt against the established structures of power and authority. One task for rhetorical scholars is to try to identify the common **topoi** or themes that advocates employ to energize and activate audiences.

Establish and/or Rehabilitate the Advocate's Ethos

A newcomer to the civic or public forum needs to establish a sense of character or **ethos.** When Ross Perot emerged from the corporate sector in 1992 to become a significant public advocate, one of his challenges was the creation of an ethos with which average Americans could identify. Relatively obscure politicians tabbed to run for vice president face a similar problem (e.g., Geraldine Ferraro, Dan Quayle).

In other situations, advocates need to repair their public images or the images of the groups they represent. Corporations spend large amounts of money to persuade the American public that they are not greedy and uncaring institutions but rather are, in fact, concerned about the environment, education, and so on. Hollywood personalities caught with their pants down, so to speak, make the round of television talk shows to rehabilitate their ethos. Sociologists study a similar process through the concept of "face saving" (e.g., Goffman, 1967). "Face work" consists of the various ways in which we respond to threats to our face or image. Politicians accused of unethical or improper behavior give speeches, issue press releases, hold press conferences, and/or give interviews in hopes of restoring their reputations. Rhetorical scholars who study this type of discourse refer to it as **apologia.** Among the common *posture* strategies of apologetic discourse, we can find *denial* ("I didn't do it"), *denial of intent* ("I didn't mean to do it"), claim *justification* ("They had it coming to them" or "I'm allowed to blow off steam every once in a while"), and *redefinition* ("It's no big deal—everybody does it").

Explain Failure (sometimes combined with ethos rehabilitation)

Events do not always turn out the way that advocates originally had hoped or predicted. Consequently, advocates need to explain what went wrong (often by finding **scapegoats** to blame). Consider what happens when a sports team fails to perform up to the level of its preseason hype. The coaches and owners face a rhetorical problem; they have to account for the failure or the team's inability to achieve expected success. Similarly, experts who predict disasters that fail to materialize must explain why the disasters did not occur (O'Leary, 1997). One way in which advocates try to prevent this problem from developing is to deflate expectations in advance of important events. For example, to avoid the appearance of failure at a summit conference, presidential advisers will appear on the Sunday morning talk shows before the conference and say that not much is expected to happen.

Defend or Attack a Specific Policy Proposal

When we are persuaded that an ill or a problem exists, we often will search for a course of action that will serve as a remedy or antidote. A course of action designed to remove an ill (e.g., restrict emissions of greenhouse gases to diminish the ill of global warming, establish evening basketball leagues in urban areas as a way of combating crime) creates a specific rhetorical task: We must persuade people to adopt *our* course of action or proposed policy. Advocates need to persuade their audience that a certain course of action (e.g., restricting abortions, legalizing drugs) should be adopted, while other advocates reject the policy (typically offering one of their own). At times, advocates attempt to refurbish (or "purify" [Fisher, 1970]) a previously discredited policy (e.g., George Bush's decision to accept a tax increase after his "read my lips" pledge against tax increases). In other cases, the task is not to defend a *proposed* policy but rather to *justify* a course of action that already has been taken (e.g., Richard Nixon on the decision to "invade" Cambodia in 1970).[10] When policies are entrenched, advocates face the complex task of *finding a language* through which they can register their opposition. This often can involve appropriating the language originally used to justify a policy so as to use it against the policy. Opponents of affirmative action are engaged in this type of language appropriation.

Restore Public Confidence or Restore Adherence to Declining Values

Advocates might face a situation in which large numbers of people believe that they have lost control of their lives. The cause might be a natural disaster (e.g., a flood) or a social problem (e.g., crime). The advocates' task is to restore meaning and hope, making people believe that things will turn out okay in the long run (a variation on the **epideictic** exigence of *meaning* and *understanding*). The problem of a lack of faith or confidence often is encountered in the aftermath of a tragic and/or senseless death.[11] Ronald Reagan's response to the *Challenger* explosion in 1986 and Bill Clinton's responses to the tragedies in Jonesboro, Arkansas, in 1998 and in Littleton, Colorado, in 1999 are examples of how the president tries to shore up communities' faith and confidence in themselves and their futures. In other situations, the task is to restore the audience's commitment to declining values, institutions, and figures of authority (versions of the **epideictic** or *communal exigences* of *value* and *authority*). Conservative politicians over the past decade or so have devoted considerable energy to *reaffirming* (Fisher, 1970) a cluster of values lumped together under the label of "family values." Many progressive activists (e.g., gay rights advocates) contest the particular *connotations* (or **accent**) that conservatives give to words such as *family*. Hence, the continuing discussion of family values reveals overlapping exigences; advocates not only try to reaffirm specific values, they also are engaged in the process of shaping the meaning of key value terms.

Institutions and authority figures also face the problem of *reaffirmation*. As the value of institutions declines (e.g., banks after a wave of bank failures, the savings and loan industry after its government bailout, higher education in the wake of various exposés, journalism as a result of a media feeding frenzy over the latest sex scandal), or as the value of authority figures declines (e.g., Catholic priests, lawyers), advocates struggle to restore audiences' faith and confidence in these institutions and authority figures. The discourse of individuals associated with these institutions (e.g., a representative of the savings and loan industry testifying before a congressional hearing, a university president addressing a local chamber of commerce) or these roles (e.g., a Supreme Court justice delivering a commencement address) often can be read as a response to the critiques and a reaffirmation of the role and function of the institution or authority figure.

Create and/or Remove Distinctions

Advocates often need to make their ideas and proposals appear to be different from those of their opponents or predecessors when, viewed from a different perspective, they appear quite similar. For example, to enhance his chances of being elected president in 1988, Bush had to create the impression that there was some difference between his positions and those of Reagan. But Bush had to be careful not to introduce too many differences that might cost him the votes of Reagan loyalists. In this case, the need to create a sense of difference functioned as one campaign exigence, whereas Reagan's popularity functioned as a constraint. Nixon faced a similar problem in assuming the presidency in 1969—how to make his Vietnam policy different from that of Lyndon Johnson's administration when, on the surface at least, Nixon promised more of the same. Of course, creating distinctions is not only a problem for presidents. Gloria Steinem's defense of the trial judge's decision to throw out Paula Jones's sexual harassment lawsuit against Clinton depended on her ability to develop grounds for distinguishing Clinton's behavior from that of other male public figures (e.g., Clarence Thomas, Bob Packwood) who earned the wrath of feminists, as depicted by her in an opinion essay in the March 22, 1998, issue of the *New York Times.*

But the need to create and maintain distinctions is more complicated than the first two examples, which focus more on issues of personality. Consider all of the *substantive* distinctions that advocates attempt to reinforce in various policy debates. Calling on abolitionists to dissolve the union, the radical Wendell Phillips, in a speech titled "The Philosophy of the Abolitionist Movement" in Boston in January 1853, struggled to "preserve the distinction between *submission* and *obedience*—between *submission* and *support.*" Black Power advocates during the late 1960s had to distinguish between voluntary "separation" and enforced "segregation." Contemporary defenders of affirmative action distinguish between "quotas" and "hiring goals." Proponents of a shift in drug policy in the direction of decriminalization argue the need to distinguish between drug "use" and drug "abuse." In his 1984 speech defending his position on the political inexpediency of antiabortion radicalism, Mario Cuomo had to distinguish between "personal morality" (which dictates an individual's personal behavior) and "technical" political questions (which are, he argued, best decided on standards other than personal morality). These are just a few examples of the way in which creating and maintaining distinctions can function as an exigence (usually a secondary one) in a complex controversy.

At other times, advocates attempt the opposite; they try to remove distinctions that might be made between groups of people or positions on policy questions. For example, defenders of the status quo frequently refuse to distinguish between moderate and radical forms of dissent, thereby discrediting the moderates by associating them with the radicals. For example, opponents of the Equal Rights Amendment (ERA) face the challenge of trying to associate ERA supporters with "radical feminists." If successful, they could (and did) discredit the ERA. Conservative politicians satisfy this need through the use of ad hominem attacks, whereby female nominees for federal office who have feminist sympathies are derided as "radical feminists," or female advocates for proportional representation (an alternative to the "winner take all" electoral process) are dismissed as "quota queens." When used effectively, this rhetorical challenge becomes an effective rhetorical weapon.

Solve a Prudential Dilemma

One sense of the concept of **prudence** involves the process of balancing or negotiating competing principles. The paradigm case of this dilemma might be the Old Testament account of Abraham being ordered by God to sacrifice his son Isaac. The tension in this case was between Abraham's personal sense of what is *right* and the external *command* from the figure of ultimate authority. Many young American men during the late 1960s faced a version of this dilemma: Should they do what their government ordered them to do (report for military service) or what their consciences told them was right (resist an unjust war). This type of personal/external tension is common, but it is not the only form that a prudential dilemma can take.

Prudential dilemmas are a recurring public exigence. Consider a controversy between birth parents and adoptive parents. Whose "rights" are most important in this case? An advocate in a legal case or one defending a proposed policy in this area will need to wrestle with this dilemma. Consider the constant need to adjudicate between conflicting rights. Where does the "right" to privacy end and the public's "right" to legislative (and juridical) intervention begin? Imagine that an individual in a crowded store sees a parent severely disciplining a child. Should the individual step in and intervene (so as to prevent "child abuse"), or should the individual grant the parent the privacy right to discipline the child as he or she sees fit? As another example, how do we balance a woman's civil rights (e.g., to inhabit an environment free of degrading images) and the right of free speech and free expression? Should pornography be banned because it degrades and offends many women, or should the rights of producers and consumers of pornography be upheld? Is it more important to be fair and equitable in how we deal with people or that we honor the terms of an explicit written contract (whose terms might not be judged as "fair" by one of the parties at a later date)? These are just a small sample of the range of prudential dilemmas that inhabit contemporary American culture. Rendering a decision or making a **judgment** normally will involve invoking a principle or norm to construct at least a temporary **value hierarchy.**

Specific prudential dilemmas tend to form around particular spheres of human activity. In politics, for example, a recurring dilemma occurs when we try to balance the impulse to innovate against the impulse to conserve traditional practices (Garver, 1987). In the law, a frequent problem is the need to balance the rights of the majority against the rights of the minority. In education, teachers continually negotiate the tension between ends (e.g., helping students to achieve autonomy or an ability to think for themselves) and means (e.g., forms of imitation, rules to follow). Prudential dilemmas sometimes are resolved by creating distinctions or by introducing new concepts that help to describe the world in a different way. An innovative concept such as "marital rape," for example, restructures how we think about gender relations and the tension between public obligations and private rights.

Provide an Authoritative Interpretation of a Key Document (a "hermeneutic problem")

Public controversies often center on the meaning of some key document (e.g., the Constitution, a treaty). Advocates need to develop a convincing interpretation of the document so as to secure their ultimate objective. Various interpretive approaches (e.g., appeals to authorial intention, appeals to accepted meanings of terms, appeals to context) function as *inventional resources* for public **argument** (Mailloux, 1989). For example, during the 19th century, advocates debated the Bible's stance on slavery and women's rights and the constitutionality of a national bank. The Bible and the U.S. Constitution remain at the center of many contemporary controversies. Does the Constitution establish a right of privacy? Does the Second Amendment prohibit restrictions on firearms? What types of speech fall under the protection of the First Amendment? Does the Bible prohibit female priests? What does the Bible teach with respect to homosexuality? In addition to the Bible and the Constitution, other recurrent sources of hermeneutic conflict include treaties (e.g., the debate over whether the Reagan administration's "Star Wars" missile defense proposal was permissible under the terms of the 1972 Anti-Ballistic Missile Treaty), legal agreements (e.g., the controversy over the question of whether Microsoft is violating an earlier agreement by integrating an Internet browser with its operating system), and written contracts (e.g., disputes between landlords and tenants, disputes between union workers and management).

This list of common exigences is not exhaustive. The range of problems confronting people that either demand or suggest discursive responses is vast. Nor are these exigences mutually exclusive. As some of the examples offered indicated, rhetorical situations sometimes are complex, presenting numerous exigences for advocates to negotiate. A specific situation, and its controlling exigence, often is embedded (or nested) in a somewhat broader situation. For example, Abraham Lincoln's immediate rhetorical situation when he faced his audience at Cooper Union in New York in 1860 was, according to Leff and Mohrmann (1974), focused on the problem of "ingratiation"—on Lincoln's need to win support from eastern Republicans to further his quest for the presidency. But Leff and Mohrmann recognized that this immediate situation was embedded in the broader struggle over the issue of slavery. So, Lincoln confronted at least two key exigences: the need to establish his **ethos** and the policy question regarding slavery. The nesting of a local situation within a more encompassing rhetorical problem is relatively common.

One of the first things that a critic often does in approaching a text is to reconstruct the situation—both the immediate situation and any broader problems in which the local situation is nested—so as to identify the relevant exigences, constraints, resources, and audiences. Situational analysis and assessment is at the root of any effort to understand the *instrumental* function of rhetorical practice. So long as rhetorical scholars are interested in exploring the instrumental capacity of discourse, the concept of the rhetorical situation will play a significant role.

Notes

1. Exigence is similar to, but not identical to, the concept of *ill* in the **stock topics of policy disputes.**

2. It might, of course, be possible to alter behavior through a nondiscursive process of positive reinforcement and negative punishment such as director Stanley Kubrick depicted in the film *A Clockwork Orange.* Bitzer's unwillingness to confront this possibility might reflect a humanistic bias that privileges persuasion over potentially dehumanizing modes of behavioral modification.

3. Bitzer (1980) would add *resources* as a co-equal part of this third constituent.

4. Compare Bitzer's (1980) account to Crable and Vibbert's (1985) discussion of the developmental nature of "issues."

5. For a concrete case study, see Buehler (1998).

6. On the general topic of constructionism, see Potter (1996).

7. Blumenberg (1987) maintained that "being compelled to act is itself not an utterly 'real' circumstance. . . . [It] is constructed" (p. 441).

8. For a study of one discursive effort to fix or stabilize the meaning of the war in Vietnam, see Dionisopoulos and Goldzwig (1992).

9. See also the discussion of *communal exigences* in the entry for **epideictic discourse.**

10. See the discussion in the entry for **deliberative discourse.**

11. See also Campbell's (1984) discussion of human mortality as the "ultimate" or "omnipotent" exigence (p. 236).

References and Additional Reading

Benoit, W. L. (1994). The genesis of rhetorical action. *Southern Communication Journal, 59,* 342-355.

Biesecker, B. A. (1989). Rethinking the rhetorical situation from within the thematic of *différance. Philosophy and Rhetoric, 22,* 110-130.

Bitzer, L. (1968). The rhetorical situation. *Philosophy and Rhetoric, 1,* 1-14.

Bitzer, L. (1980). Functional communication: A situational perspective. In E. E. White (Ed.), *Rhetoric in transition: Studies in the nature and uses of rhetoric.* University Park: Pennsylvania State University Press.

Blumenberg, H. (1987). An anthropological approach to the contemporary significance of rhetoric (R. M. Wallace, Trans.). In K. Baynes, J. Bohman, & T. McCarthy (Eds.), *After philosophy: End or transformation?* Cambridge, MA: MIT Press.

Brinton, A. (1981). Situation in the theory of rhetoric. *Philosophy and Rhetoric, 14,* 234-248.

Buehler, D. O. (1998). Permanence and change in Theodore Roosevelt's conservation jeremiad. *Western Journal of Communication, 62,* 439-458.

Campbell, J. A. (1984). A rhetorical interpretation of history. *Rhetorica, 2,* 227-266.

Consigny, S. (1974). Rhetoric and its situations. *Philosophy and Rhetoric, 7,* 175-186.

Crable, R. E., & Vibbert, S. L. (1985). Managing issues and influencing public policy. *Public Relations Review, 6,* 3-16.

Dionisopoulos, G. N., & Goldzwig, S. R. (1992). "The meaning of Vietnam": Political rhetoric as revisionist cultural history. *Quarterly Journal of Speech, 78,* 61-79.

Fisher, W. R. (1970). A motive view of communication. *Quarterly Journal of Speech, 56,* 131-139.

Garrett, M., & Xiaosui, X. (1993). The rhetorical situation revisited. *Rhetoric Society Quarterly, 23,* 30-40.

Garver, E. (1987). *Machiavelli and the history of prudence.* Madison: University of Wisconsin Press.

Goffman, E. (1967). On face-work. In E. Goffman, *Interaction ritual: Essays on face-to-face behavior.* Garden City, NY: Anchor.

Gorrell, D. (1997). The rhetorical situation again: Linked components in a Venn diagram. *Philosophy and Rhetoric, 30,* 395-412.

Hauser, G. (1986). *An introduction to rhetorical theory.* New York: Harper & Row.

Hunsaker, D. M., & Smith, C. R. (1976). The nature of issues: A constructive approach to situational rhetoric. *Western Journal of Speech Communication, 40,* 144-156.

Jamieson, K. M. H. (1973). Generic constraints and the rhetorical situation. *Philosophy and Rhetoric, 6,* 162-170.

Larson, R. L. (1970). Lloyd Bitzer's "rhetorical situation" and the classification of discourse: Problems and implications. *Philosophy and Rhetoric, 3,* 165-169.

Leff, M. C., & Mohrmann, G. P. (1974). Lincoln at Cooper Union: A rhetorical analysis of the text. *Quarterly Journal of Speech, 60,* 346-358.

Mailloux, S. (1989). *Rhetorical power.* Ithaca, NY: Cornell University Press.

Marx, K. (1967). *The eighteenth brumaire of Louis Bonaparte.* New York: International Publishers.

Miller, A. B. (1972). Rhetorical exigence. *Philosophy and Rhetoric, 5,* 111-118.

O'Leary, S. D. (1997). Apocalyptic argument and the anticipation of catastrophe: The prediction of risk and the risks of prediction. *Argumentation, 11,* 293-313.

Patton, J. H. (1979). Causation and creativity in rhetorical situations: Distinctions and implications. *Quarterly Journal of Speech, 65,* 36-55.

Potter, J. (1996). *Representing reality: Discourse, rhetoric and social construction.* London: Sage.

Smith, C. R., & Lybarger, S. (1996). Bitzer's model reconstructed. *Communication Quarterly, 44,* 197-213.

Vatz, R. E. (1973). The myth of the rhetorical situation. *Philosophy and Rhetoric, 6,* 154-161.

SOCIAL KNOWLEDGE

What is the substance or material of rhetorical practice and, in particular, of rhetorical argument? This question is rather abstract and impossible to answer with any absolute finality.[1] Nonetheless, it is important because the answer that one gives will shape the nature and scope of rhetoric and the tasks of rhetorical theory. Two common answers to the question are (a) certain techniques or strategies (including the doctrine of **topics/topoi, argument** strategies, and **style**) and (b) common opinion (**doxa**), evidence, and/or *data.* Considering these possibilities, Farrell (1976) remarked, "Whenever I participate in a *rhetorical* process, however, I am depending upon much more than information, data, evidence, even the armory of persuasive tactics which still compromise our lexicons" (p. 5). For Farrell, neither of these common answers adequately identifies the substance of rhetorical argument.

In proposing an answer to this question of substance, Farrell (1976) returned to Aristotle's seminal work on rhetoric. According to Farrell,

> Aristotle formulated a functional relationship between a fully developed art of rhetoric and a generally accepted body of knowledge pertaining to matters of public concern. . . . In Aristotle's early expansive vision, then, rhetoric was the art which employed the common knowledge of a particular audience to inform and guide reasoned judgments about matters of public interest. (p. 1)

From Aristotle, Farrell recovered common knowledge as the substance of rhetorical argument. But the process of recovery is complicated because it is not entirely clear whether we understand what Aristotle meant by common knowledge. Over time, our understanding of the concept of knowledge has shifted, and "with each alteration in our conception of knowledge . . ., the art of rhetoric . . . altered its status and function accordingly" (pp. 2-3). Farrell's recovery project, focused on the concept of **social knowledge,** is both a reconstruction/reformulation of Aristotelian theory and a contribution to the growing literature on the **epistemic** status of rhetorical practice.

What did Farrell mean by social knowledge? Let us begin by considering a hypothetical case. Imagine that an individual is walking down the street in a large urban city. Someone is sitting on the curb. The individual walking is asked to describe what he or she sees. The individual might begin by noting the person's gender, then might report the person's approximate age, and then might turn to physical appearance—size, hair, clothing, and so on. So far, the description comports with what Searle (1969) labeled as "brute facts." But what else does the individual "see" sitting on the curb? Someone who is homeless? A victim of the ongoing economic restructuring of the nation that has ruined the lives of millions of Americans? A shiftless bum? Someone who lacks willpower, self-discipline, and personal initiative? A fellow human? Another of God's creatures? In Searle's philosophical perspective, when a person perceives brutes facts *as something* (e.g., when a person perceives physical movement by individuals *as* a football play or a sequence of words *as* a threat), he or she has moved into the realm of what Searle termed *institutional facts.* The person's perception has been shaped, enabling him or her to see certain things *as* something in particular. What is it that shapes a person's perception? What allows one person to perceive an intricate play in an athletic contest, while a person from a different culture seated nearby can "see" only random movement? What enables one person to perceive a shiftless bum and another to "see" a victim of economic exploitation? Farrell's (1976) response was social knowledge. He wrote, "Social knowledge . . . enabl[es] isolated 'bits' of information to achieve meaning and significance. . . . Social knowledge gives *form* to information" (p. 12). In the abstract, social knowledge is that structure of usually implicit assumptions that shapes how a person perceives and interacts with elements of the social world.

But Farrell (1976) was interested in more than an abstract account of social knowledge. He wanted to describe the "functional characteristics" (p. 2) of social knowledge as the substance of rhetorical argument. Farrell identified five central characteristics, noting that social knowledge (a) is an attributed consensus posited in the course of rhetorical argument, (b) is audience dependent, (c) exists in a state of potentiality or incipience, (d) is generative along at least three trajectories, and (e) is normative in its implications. Each of these characteristics merits additional elaboration.

Farrell (1976) maintained that "social knowledge rests upon a peculiar kind of consensus. . . . It rests upon a consensus which is attributed to an audience rather than concretely shared" (p. 6). What does it mean to say that consensus, or agreement, is attributed to an audience in the course of rhetorical argument? It means, in its simplest sense, that an advocate must assume some point of agreement, or some common ground, before proceeding to whatever specific advocacy task might be at hand. For example, an advocate will assume that an audience possesses certain interests and values that, when applied to specific material conditions, will result in the perception of an *ill* or *exigence*. There might not be an actual consensus between audience and advocate on the existence of an ill, but the advocate begins by attributing such a consensus. In the course of a rhetorical performance, the advocate attempts to actualize the consensus.

As any advocate or performer knows quite well, every audience is different. Social knowledge always is dependent on a particular audience and the specific interests of its members (p. 9). Farrell (1976) suggested that all advocacy is rooted in a democratic faith that people "may become conscious that the suffering of others is pertinent to their own interests" or in a belief in "certain human potentialities" to perceive problems and the need for collective action (p. 8). We must assume the possibility of agreement or consensus (the first characteristic) for advocacy to take place (if we did not think it was possible, then we would have no reason to engage in advocacy). But that possibility has to be realized with real live audiences with different social knowledge assumptions. Social knowledge emerges as particular audiences are engaged.

To say that social knowledge emerges suggests that it exists in a state of potentiality or incipience. It only becomes relevant—it only comes alive—in the practice of rhetorical advocacy. We might then ask the question: How and/or where is social knowledge "stored" or "housed" when it is not in use or when it is in the state of incipience? In one sense, it is "in" all of us; we carry around elements of the dominant culture's (and various subcultures') social knowledge assumptions as part of our individual cognitive structures. Social knowledge exists more concretely in aphorisms and proverbs,[2] in the morals or lessons of common **myths** and **narratives,** and in the propositions of various **ideologies.** But social knowledge functions rhetorically only when it is applied to specific cases in the practice of advocacy. Then, "through the reasoned action of an audience, the potential state of social knowledge is actualized" (p. 9).

Social knowledge is generative in at least three senses. First, rhetorical advocacy generates social knowledge by bringing it into being; as Farrell (1976) observed, rhetorical arguments are able to "generate what they can initially only assume" (p. 11). Second, social knowledge is generative in that, when attributed and actualized in advocacy, "it also establishes social precedents for future attributions of consensus in situations which have yet to be encountered" (p. 10). Third, social knowledge is generative in that "each particular decision" made by an audience through the agency of social knowledge "gives increasing form and specificity to our relationship with others as social beings" (p. 6). The nature of any human collectivity is determined by its practices, especially its "public" practices (e.g., laws, policies, institutional procedures). Public practices in a democratic society are, for the most part, the result of rhetorical deliberation. In this way, social knowledge not only shapes the perceptions of the members of a community, it also shapes the nature of the community. As Farrell noted, "The overarching function of social knowledge is to transform the society into a community" (p. 11).

According to Farrell (1976), "The most elusive and important characteristic of social knowledge . . . [is] its affective or normative impact upon decision-making" (p. 10); put differently, social knowledge has a normative and "imperative" (p. 11) impact on audiences. Farrell noted that humans are bombarded by thousands of bits of information on a daily basis. But when we encounter social knowledge, or when a bit of information (e.g., the perception of the person sitting on the curb) is transformed by way of social knowledge, "the very apprehension and comprehension of such knowledge requires that some form of action be taken" (p. 10). For Farrell, social knowledge is not *simply* ignored because "even the attempt to ignore, to detach it from our lives . . ., is itself an action of sorts; it is the decision to do nothing" (p. 10). Social knowledge, then, demands *some* type of response from an audience because it does not merely convey information to which we may or may not pay attention; it contains a normative or value dimension that impels an audience to respond. Farrell's definition seems to suggest that someone who fails to respond to social knowledge (leaving aside, for the moment, the problem of operationalizing "failure to respond") is not really a member of the community. This problem of failing to respond reveals a critical and recurrent issue in rhetorical studies: Can advocacy proceed when individuals fail to perceive the normative characteristic of social knowledge? In Farrell's perspective, all that the advocate can do is search for some possible attributable consensus that can serve as the social knowledge ground for advocacy. But what happens when the advocate and audience come from completely incommensurable communities? Can social knowledge be the substance of advocacy in this case?[3]

Farrell's social knowledge thesis has had a significant impact on contemporary rhetorical studies. In addition to staking out one of the positions in the rhetoric as **epistemic** debate and helping to popularize the project of Aristotelian reconstruction,[4] two other aspects of the social knowledge position merit brief consideration. First, as Leff (1978) observed, Farrell's account of social knowledge not only responded to the question "What is the substance of rhetoric?" but also addressed the recurrent binary opposition of substance versus process/function. Leff's reading of Farrell's essay revealed that social knowledge is *both* substance and functional process; in other words, it is **recursive**. Leff wrote, "Rhetoric is functional, but it only functions in cases where social knowledge is engaged" (p. 89). He suggested that the social knowledge thesis is a creative "synthesis of the classical and the more expansive contemporary views of the scope of rhetoric" (p. 89). Second, Farrell's exposition of the social knowledge thesis developed, in part, by way of a contrast to what Farrell termed *technical knowledge.* Leff wrote, "Whereas technical or specialized knowledge is actualized through its perceived correspondence to the external world, social knowledge is actualized through the decision and action of an audience" (p. 4). Technical knowledge is necessary "to control, produce, or appropriate resources of the natural environment" (p. 4), whereas social knowledge is necessary "whenever members of a social system experience the need for coordinating their conduct" (p. 5). The distinction, although challenged by scholars holding a more "radical" or nonrestricted rhetoric as epistemic position (e.g., Carleton, 1978), has resonated within the field. The distinction has proven useful in helping to explain the decline in public discourse. A growing number of scholars suggest that, more and more frequently, public deliberation dependent on social knowledge is being replaced by a sphere of specialized argument drawing on technical knowledge (e.g., Goodnight, 1982). As Farrell (1978) observed,

> Many former matters of statecraft or practical wisdom seem now to be the prerogative of bureaucratized and specialized imaginations. This "technical" knowledge is grounded upon a consensus removed from public scrutiny. It is no more likely to be questioned than the latest meteorological forecast. (p. 330)

Given the growing globalization of the economy, the general technologization of life, and the ensuing "cult" of expertise, critical reflection on the forms and limits of technical knowledge and technical reasoning, which Farrell's formulation encourages, will be needed in the foreseeable future.

Notes

1. Part of the reason why the question cannot be answered with precision lies in the fact that rhetoric as practice (*rhetorica utens*) is defined in different ways.

2. See, for example, Burke's (1957) wonderful discussion of proverbs in "Literature as Equipment for Living" and Mieder's (1997) detailed discussion of their force and function.

3. Critics of the social knowledge position argue that the problem of seemingly incommensurable perspectives reveals the position's relativism. Cherwitz and Hikins (1983), for example, argued that the social knowledge perspective is only a "mitigated subjectivism" (pp. 254-255).

4. This project culminated in Farrell's (1993) *Norms of Rhetorical Culture.*

References and Additional Reading

Bitzer, L. F. (1978). Rhetoric and public knowledge. In D. M. Burks (Ed.), *Rhetoric, philosophy, and literature: An exploration.* West Lafayette, IN: Purdue University Press.

Burke, K. (1957). Literature as equipment for living. In K. Burke, *The philosophy of literary form* (rev. ed.). New York: Vintage.

Carleton, W. M. (1978). What is rhetorical knowledge? A response to Farrell—and more. *Quarterly Journal of Speech, 64,* 313-328.

Cherwitz, R. A., & Hikins, J. W. (1983). Rhetorical perspectivism. *Quarterly Journal of Speech, 69,* 249-266.

Farrell, T. B. (1976). Knowledge, consensus, and rhetorical theory. *Quarterly Journal of Speech, 62,* 1-14.

Farrell, T. B. (1978). Social knowledge II. *Quarterly Journal of Speech, 64,* 329-334.

Farrell, T. B. (1993). *Norms of rhetorical culture.* New Haven, CT: Yale University Press.

Goodnight, G. T. (1982). The personal, technical, and public spheres of argument: A speculative inquiry into the art of public deliberation. *Journal of the American Forensic Association, 18,* 214-227.

Leff, M. C. (1978). In search of Ariadne's thread: A review of the recent literature on rhetorical theory. *Central States Speech Journal, 29,* 73-91.

Mieder, W. (1997). *The politics of proverbs: From traditional wisdom to proverbial stereotypes.* Madison: University of Wisconsin Press.

Searle, J. (1969). *Speech acts: An essay in the philosophy of language.* Cambridge, UK: Cambridge University Press.

STASIS

The origins of the classical doctrine or theory of **stasis** (the Latin *status*) are commonly attributed to the 2nd-century BC Greek thinker Hermagoras. Two factors seem central to the emergence of this theory. First, the scope of rhetorical practice was gradually narrowing as the need for civic deliberation on policy questions declined, leaving the law courts as the principal space for rhetorical performance. Second, writers on the subject of rhetoric after Aristotle struggled to render comprehensible his system of **invention,** especially the idea of **topoi** or topics. Kennedy (1980) noted that Hermagoras's "theory of stasis . . . restated Aristotle's theory of topics as a system of categories adapted to the law courts, which a student of rhetoric could memorize and apply to any situation" (p. 88).

But what is stasis? The origins of the term are complex (Dieter, 1950), but its meaning in the tradition of rhetoric is relatively clear. Kennedy (1972) defined stasis as "a series of steps or questions to ask which [lead] to the heart of the matter" (p. 117). Fahnestock and Secor (1983) described stasis as "a taxonomy, a system of classifying the kinds of questions that can be at issue in a controversy" (p. 137). The traditional stases are questions organized and arranged in such a way that, when employed, they allow participants or observers to understand the essence—the central issue or dispute—in a legal case. These questions are arranged hierarchically; this pattern of arrangement recognized that it would be impossible to resolve a question lower on the hierarchy until the prior, higher level question or questions had been resolved.

Hermagoras's original treatise did not survive, but his approach to the doctrine of stasis was incorporated in Cicero's early work on rhetoric, *De Inventione.* According to Cicero, "Every subject which contains in itself a controversy to be resolved by speech and debate involves a question about a fact, or about a definition, or about the nature of an act, or about legal processes" (I, 8, 10). The first question or point of stasis concerns the existence or nonexistence of fact; the Latin question is *an sit* or "is it." A trial for murder can illustrate how this, along with the other stasis questions, locates the central issue or organizes the flow of issues. The question of whether a fact exists would focus on whether or not someone is dead. Obviously, if there is a body that has been pronounced dead, then the issue is resolved. But imagine that an individual is on trial for murder, and the prosecution has not produced the body of the supposed victim. The defendant or the defense attorney would be in a position to raise the first stasis issue. How can it be known that the person is dead? Perhaps the person is on a mysterious trip of some sort. Or, perhaps the person had reason to drop out of public view and go underground. Unless this matter is resolved favorably for the prosecution, the defense wins the question and the trial is over. The second question or point of stasis concerns the definition or classification of an act; the Latin question is *quid sit* or "what is it." Assume that the prosecution produces a body that has been pronounced dead. Now the question shifts to the manner of death. How is this fact classified? Is it known that the person did not die from natural causes? Is it known that the person did not die in an accident? Is it known that the person did not commit suicide? If the defense can establish one of these definitions of the act, then the charge of murder cannot be sustained. Assume that the prosecution has been able to establish that the manner of death was homicide; someone else was responsible for the death. The trial then shifts to the third question or point of stasis concerning the quality of the established fact or act; the Latin question is *quale sit* or "what kind is it." The defense might approach this question in one of two different ways. On the one hand, the defense might argue that this act was not murder but rather self-defense; it was not the type of act that the prosecution claims. On the other hand, the defense might object to the prosecution's characterization of the act. The prosecution might have charged the individual with murder in the first degree; this characterization of the act implies, among other things, that the defendant committed it with premeditation. The defense might argue that the act took place (the defendant murdered the person) but that it was not premeditated murder but rather an act of spontaneous rage or passion. Hence, the defendant is not guilty of murder in the first degree but rather is guilty of a lesser crime. Finally, the fourth question or point of stasis might come into play concerning the issue of procedure and/or jurisdiction. The defense might argue that proper procedures were not followed in this case. Although Cicero could not have imagined the Miranda requirements in effect in the United States today, the fourth stasis point speaks to the issue. If the prosecution is relying on the individual's confession as a major source of evidence, and if that confession was obtained improperly, then an appeal to the procedural stasis might be an avenue to an acquittal. Or, in other cases, it might not be a question of procedure but rather one of jurisdiction. Is this court properly authorized to hear and decide on this case? Is another court a more appropriate forum for this case? As Fahnestock and Secor (1983) noted, "Although stasis theory is not a formal part of legal education in the United States . . ., it operates in the procedures of the courtroom. The stases have in fact become ritualized in the formalities of the courts and plea bargaining procedures" (p. 139).

What has been the impact of stasis theory? As discussed in the next entry, one trajectory of stasis theory has contributed to the development of **stock topics in policy disputes.** The stock issues attempt to do for policy deliberation what stasis did for legal cases—identify the recurrent points or issues that organize and shape disputes. But the contemporary recuperation of stasis is not limited to the realm of stock issues. One line of contemporary inquiry, overlapping to a degree with stock issues, focuses on the value of stasis as a tool for rhetorical **invention.** This is the dominant thrust of Fahnestock and Secor's (1983) discussion. Another approach seeks to elaborate and/or adapt the stasis doctrine as a tool for criticism and analysis. Kline (1979), for example, argued that the analytic potential of stasis can be enhanced by considering "stases as resident within the structure of the communicative act itself" (p. 103). Kline found precedent for such a reformulation of stasis in the works of contemporary language philosophers, in particular the communication theory of Jürgen Habermas. According to Habermas, every act of communication presupposes four essential "validity claims": that what the speaker or writer says is true, that the speaker or writer is sincere, that the communicative act is appropriate, and that it is intelligible. Kline contended that "Cicero and Quintilian's general conception of stasis as the point around which arguments are settled matches Habermas's conception of validity claims as focal points of discourse" (p. 101). By reformulating the stasis doctrine as a form of universal validity claim, Kline extended the range of applicability; the idea of stasis no longer is limited to legal discourse and can used to analyze a range of communicative practices.

Rhetorical critics have found different ways of employing stasis theory in their critical practice. Prelli (1989) adapted stasis to the analysis of scientific discourse. In O'Leary's (1994) analysis of **apocalyptic discourse,** he suggested,

> The classical theory of forensic stases could . . . be used to illuminate the problem of evil. . . . If one imagines God on trial for the "crime" of creating a universe full of evil and suffering, the dynamics of theological and philosophical arguments about evil can be understood as the movement of argument through the conceptual levels of forensic controversy. (p. 37)

Whereas both Prelli and O'Leary employed the entire stasis system, Zarefsky (1990) illustrated how the procedural or jurisdictional issue can shed light on the dynamics of 19th-century arguments over slavery. Specifically, Zarefsky argued that Stephen Douglas's efforts to avoid addressing substantive questions regarding slavery can be understand as a type of **transcendence** through recourse to the procedural stasis. As Zarefsky remarked,

> Raising the procedural *stasis* preempts consideration of the substantive [issues] since it is idle to consider a matter until it is clear that one is entitled to do so—that one has jurisdiction over the matter. In distinguishing between congressional and territorial action, Douglas wished to redirect the issue to the classical *stasis* in place or procedure rather than focusing on the substance of the issue. (p. 137)

A dynamic similar to what Zarefsky uncovered in Douglas can be found in a number of contemporary controversies. Consider two examples. In the brief prepared by lawyers for the state of Kansas in the landmark Supreme Court case *Brown v. Board of Education,* the lawyers explicitly stated that they "do not propose to advocate the policy of segregation of any racial group within the school system." Like Douglas, the state's lawyers attempted to preempt the substantive question. They claimed that the issue of school policy regarding race was "the exclusive province of the legislature." In effect, then, the state maintained that the issue of school segregation was *political* and not *legal.* The lawyers suggested that the policy question of whether or not a school district segregated students on the basis of race should be determined in the proper forum following the appropriate practices of that forum. The proper forum for deciding this question, the state argued, was the political sphere where political practices (e.g., public deliberation, elections, legislative action) would be employed to resolve the issue. This position implied that a legal remedy imposed by the judiciary was inappropriate on forum and procedural grounds.

More recently, a coalition of international environmental and local community organizations filed a lawsuit in the United States against Texaco, alleging that the company's environmental practices in Ecuador were a violation of accepted international environmental standards (e.g., the 1972 Stockholm Declaration, the 1992 Rio Declaration). Lawyers for this coalition claimed that an obscure piece of legislation from 1789, the Alien Tort Claims Act, gives these groups the right to sue in U.S. courts. Texaco spokespeople have denied the substantive claims of these groups. But more important for the present discussion, an implicit appeal to the fourth stasis point has been a key part of their overall strategy. Texaco's lawyers have invoked the legal doctrine known as *forum non conveniens* to argue that the trial should be held in Ecuador, a location that is more "convenient" for the plaintiffs and closer to where the alleged violations occurred. Of course, Texaco's contention that a U.S. court was an inappropriate forum for the case might be based on more than its commitment to an abstract legal principle. For example, as Eyal Press explained in an article in the May 31, 1999, issue of *The Nation*, because Ecuadoran law does not recognize the concept of class action lawsuits, every plaintiff would have to file an individual suit against Texaco. The impact of these individual suits might well paralyze the local Ecuadoran judicial system. Like the *Brown* case, the Texaco example illustrates the stasis principle that the question of appropriate forum needs to be resolved before the substantive issues in a case can be addressed.

References and Additional Reading

Braet, A. (1987). The classical doctrine of *status* and the rhetorical theory of argumentation. *Philosophy and Rhetoric, 20,* 79-93.

Cicero. (1949). *De Inventione* (H. M. Hubbell, Trans.). Cambridge, MA: Harvard University Press.

Crowley, S., & Hawhee, D. (1999). *Ancient rhetorics for contemporary students* (2nd ed.). Boston: Allyn & Bacon.

Dieter, O. A. L. (1950). Stasis. *Speech Monographs, 17,* 345-369.

Fahnestock, J. R., & Secor, M. J. (1983). Grounds for argument: Stasis theory and the topoi. In D. Zarefsky (Ed.), *Argument in transition: Proceedings of the Third Summer Conference on Argumentation.* Annandale, VA: Speech Communication Association.

Hohmann, H. (1989). The dynamics of stasis: Classical rhetorical theory and modern legal argumentation. *American Journal of Jurisprudence, 34,* 171-197.

Kennedy, G. (1972). *The art of rhetoric in the Roman world.* Princeton, NJ: Princeton University Press.

Kennedy, G. (1980). *Classical rhetoric and its Christian and secular tradition from ancient to modern times.* Chapel Hill: University of North Carolina Press.

Kline, S. L. (1979). Toward a contemporary linguistic interpretation of the concept of stasis. *Journal of the American Forensic Association, 16,* 95-103.

McKeon, R. (1966). The methods of rhetoric and philosophy: Invention and judgment. In L. Wallach (Ed.), *The classical tradition: Literary and historical studies in honor of Harry Caplan.* Ithaca, NY: Cornell University Press.

Nadeau, R. (1959). Classical systems of *stases* in Greek: Hermagoras to Hermogenes. *Greek, Roman and Byzantine Studies, 2,* 51-71.

Nadeau, R. (1964). Hermogenes' *On Stases:* A translation with an introduction and notes. *Speech Monographs, 31,* 361-424.

O'Leary, S. D. (1994). *Arguing the apocalypse: A theory of millennial rhetoric.* New York: Oxford University Press.

Prelli, L. J. (1989). *A rhetoric of science: Inventing scientific discourse.* Columbia: University of South Carolina Press.

Raign, K. R. (1989). Stasis theory revisited: An inventional *techne* for empowering students. *Focuses, 2,* 19-26.

Thompson, W. (1972). *Stasis* in Aristotle's *Rhetoric. Quarterly Journal of Speech, 58,* 134-141.

Trimpi, W. (1983). *Muses of one mind: The literary analysis of experience and its continuity.* Princeton, NJ: Princeton University Press.

Zarefsky, D. (1990). *Lincoln, Douglas, and slavery: In the crucible of public debate.* Chicago: University of Chicago Press.

STOCK TOPICS/ISSUES IN POLICY DISPUTES

It is difficult to identify with precision the origins of the contemporary doctrine of **stock topics in policy disputes.** Some scholars (e.g., Reinard, 1991) suggest that the doctrine evolved out of the classical concept of **stasis,** but specifying the process of conceptual revision and innovation is difficult. Hultzén (1966) noted the conceptual similarities between the two concepts and articulated one of the earliest and clearest versions of the doctrine of stock topics. But as Hultzén acknowledged in the notes to his essay, the transition from stasis to stock topics had begun earlier in the 20th century. During the first quarter of the century, Shaw (1922) outlined four "possibilities of proof" (p. 151) in policy debate. These possibilities are that (a) change is necessary, (b) proposed policy change is beneficial, (c) proposed policy change will not introduce new or worse problems, and (d) no substitute policy is available. As Shaw recognized, these four possible proofs could organize debate as each side would argue the opposite position on each point (e.g., the affirmative would contend that change is necessary while the negative would assert that no change is necessary, the affirmative would argue that proposed change is beneficial while the negative would argue that proposed change would not produce the benefits claimed by the affirmative). Shaw did not use the label "stock topics," nor did he link his notion of the four possible proofs to the classical doctrine of stasis. But his discussion set the stage for a more careful elaboration of the central points in policy debates or controversies.

By the time Bryant and Wallace (1947) wrote around mid-century, they referred to the "traditional scheme" for "seeing the essentials of a controversy" (p. 406). Hultzén (1966) drew on both Shaw's and Bryant and Wallace's works in elaborating "a system of analysis" that can apply to "all deliberative situations" (p. 109). Other scholars defined the doctrine of stock topics as "a systematic methodology for breaking the [debate] proposition down into its vital component parts" (Ziegelmueller, Kay, & Dause, 1990, p. 39). Hultzén's essay is the reference point for most contemporary discussions of stock topics. He identified four "frames" within his analytical scheme. Subsequent writers on stock topics sometimes reduced the number of topics or issues to three or expanded the number to five; the variation is due largely to how many sub-issues or sub-topics are located within a major issue or topic. Hultzén employed a medical *metaphor* as a way of labeling each major frame.[1] His four frames, or four topics, organize the discussion that follows.

Ill

Does a problem exist? If it does not exist right now, how probable is it that the ill will develop? Is it urgent? How long will it last? How significant (in terms of qualitative *severity* and quantitative *magnitude*) is it?

These and other similar questions are at the root of policy controversies or disputes. The type of answers that are formulated and made persuasive determine the shape and direction of the controversy. If proponents of a policy proposal cannot establish the existence of an ill, then it is extremely unlikely that anything will come of their persuasive efforts.

In some cases, the ill is defined as a tangible material state of affairs. For example, the problem of air and water quality functioned as the ill that generated the environmental movement and various legislative acts to remedy the situation. In other cases, the ill is not so much a clear defect as a felt sense by many that things should be better than they are at present.[2] In this case, the ill is defined as a failure to meet goals or objectives. Consider the situation of a college football coach whose 5-year record is marginally above .500. At some institutions, this record would be viewed as a success, and the coach's contract would be extended. But at other institutions, this record could very easily be viewed as a failure; the members of the institution (administrators, faculty, alumni, and students) had considerably higher expectations than a .500 record, and consequently, this record would constitute an ill that needed to be cured (in all likelihood, by firing the coach).

Let us consider a more significant way in which these two senses of ill can shape a dispute. During the 1950s and 1960s, the ill of racial discrimination became widely recognized. As a result of extensive advocacy efforts, over time the nation eliminated the most obvious forms of racial discrimination. America's form of apartheid—racial segregation—ended. For many Americans, therefore, the problem or ill of race relations was remedied. Race relations no longer was a controversial issue. But agitation and advocacy on racial issues remains a central fact of American life today. Political leaders such as Bill Clinton have called for a national conversation on the topic of race relations. Why? In part, the continued presence of race as an issue on the public policy agenda has to do with the two alternative ways of understanding the ill sketched previously. Many white Americans believe that the ill of racial discrimination and segregation is over. They point to numerous laws and policies adopted over the past 25 years and the changes in the social and political conditions of minority groups as proof that the ill has been cured. But many Americans of color argue that the ill of race relations still exists in America. How is it possible for these two groups to disagree on the *status* of the ill?

It is possible because white America and black America appeal to different ways of conceptualizing the ill. Many Americans of color argue that the ill still exists because the goals and objectives of the civil rights movement, adopted to at least some degree by the nation at large, have not yet been realized. Significant economic, social, and political disparity persists despite the laws, programs, and policies enacted over the past 25 years. Until these disparities are remedied, and until the promises of the American dream are fulfilled, many Americans (of all races) will continue to perceive an ill or a problem with respect to race relations. In short, the contemporary issue of race relations is so perplexing because, in part, it is based on two different ways of conceptualizing or understanding the nature of the ill or problem.

Finally, we need to acknowledge how the status of programs, institutions, and policy proposals can shift over time. What one **generation** believes to be a cure might become, to a later generation, an ill or a problem. A clear example of such a shift in status can be found in contemporary discussions of poverty and welfare. Lyndon Johnson's "Great Society" programs, an extension of Franklin Roosevelt's vision of a more activist government, were directed at the ill of poverty in America. A variety of programs, now commonly lumped together under the heading of "welfare," were introduced to battle the problem. After more than 30 years of these programs in operation, Americans now are trying to determine whether or not they have been a success. Many have concluded that the programs have failed to solve the ill that they were designed to remedy, and to make matters worse, the programs have introduced unexpected negative consequences or new problems such as the "cycle of dependency." So, the problem of poverty has evolved into the problem of welfare; what was thought to be a cure, or at least a partial remedy, has been discovered to be worse than the disease. Debate now focuses on how to cure the ill of welfare dependency, and the original ill—poverty—has been pushed to the margins of public discourse.

The example of status shift in the case of welfare policy reveals an ambiguity in how the stock topics can be applied. Technically, welfare dependency (if it exists) is a negative consequence of a policy (governmental assistance programs) designed to combat a social ill (poverty). In certain cases, it appears that significant negative consequences might constitute a "new" ill or problem. But in general, it is best to avoid confusing the ill that a policy attempts to rectify and any potentially negative consequences that the policy's implementation might generate.[3] The same rule of thumb applies to policies themselves. The negative (or anti-policy) side in most policy disputes views the proposed policy as problematic, but this tendency does not transform the policy into an ill. Consider the policy dispute over physician-assisted suicide. Novice argument analysts often assume that the ill of the dispute is the act of assistance or its legalization. Opponents of physician-assisted suicide raise many questions about this policy in an effort to make the policy appear problematic. But the policy itself is not the ill. To understand the debate over physician-assisted suicide, the argument analyst needs to uncover the problem that physician-assisted suicide is trying to solve. Supporters of this policy believe that the medical establishment at present does not provide sufficient relief for the often excruciating pain associated with terminal diseases and other maladies. The ill or problem in the physician-assisted suicide debate is the existence of intolerable pain and suffering. Supporters of the policy believe that the only way of remedying this ill is to allow individuals to choose to end their own lives. Opponents of the policy have numerous argumentative options (see the entry for **case construction strategies**). Some might choose to dispute the existence of the ill by, for example, denying the severity of the pain and suffering of the terminally ill. Other opponents might grant the existence of the ill but contend that there are other remedies available or argue that physician-assisted suicide produces such extensive negative consequences that it should be rejected despite its ability to offer relief to the afflicted. But the policy of physician-assisted suicide, or any potential negative consequences, is not the ill.

Blame or Cause

Who or what is responsible for the ill? Was it done on purpose, or was it an accident? Is the ill *inherent* in the human condition or in the social structure (e.g., some political economists believe that a degree of unemployment is endemic to a free enterprise/market-driven economy, making the ill of unemployment inherent)? If it is, are there ways in which we can palliate it? If not, is it reformable or capable of remediation?

It is important to think carefully on the relationship between ill and blame because at times it can be confusing. Consider advocacy on the issue of guns in America. Some Americans believe that restrictions on access to firearms would be in the public's interest, whereas others believe that open access to firearms is both sound policy and a constitutional right. So, the ill in this dispute is the presence of guns. Although on the surface that might look to be the case, it is not an accurate application of the stock issues of ill and blame to the controversy. The ill that appears to be at the center of ongoing debate about guns is violence. Advocates in favor of restricting access to firearms point to homicide rates in America, they compare these rates to those in other nations, they point to the number of accidents and crimes of passion that occur in this country, and they conclude that America is beset by violence. Supporters of gun control argue that the blame or cause is, in large part, the wide availability of guns. Opponents of gun control largely concede the opposition's claim regarding the ill; they agree that violence is a crucial problem in America. The controversy does not center on the question of whether or not an ill exists; both sides of the dispute generally agree that it does. The two issues that drive the debate are who or what is to blame and how to solve the problem. Opponents of gun control reject the proponents' claim that guns are an important contributing factor to the problem of violence. In other words, they reject the attribution of blame made by supporters of gun control. In the well-known expression used by the opposition, "Guns don't kill people; people kill people." People, not guns, are to blame.

The sub-issue of inherency often is critical in a policy controversy. The claim of inherency usually is developed in one of two ways: *structural* inherency (the problem is caused by existing rules, procedures, practices, or structures that prevent the status quo from solving the problem) or *attitudinal* inherency (the problem is attributed to values, beliefs, or attitudes held by a significant majority of the society's members). Establishing inherency is an important way for the affirmative to offset the negative's potential reliance on the **case construction strategy** of minor repairs. When a problem is inherent, minor repairs are insufficient. But inherency often complicates the affirmative's need to establish *solvency* (discussed later). For example, if an individual claims that a problem is caused by existing attitudes, then he or she must try to establish how the proposed policy remedy will alter the problematic attitudes.

Cure

What is the proposed solution for the ill? How feasible is the cure? Does the cure promise to remove the ill completely—solve the problem—or is it merely a temporary palliative while we look for a more permanent solution?

The sub-issue of *solvency,* or whether the cure really solves the problem, is a key element in a policy controversy. Claims on behalf of the cure's solvency potential always are claims of *future fact;* at best, the advocate might be able to make a parallel case argument (what Aristotle discussed under the category of *example*) showing that the proposed cure solved a similar problem somewhere else. But the existence of a parallel case, or even a number of parallel cases, never can guarantee that the cure will solve *this* problem. Hence, solvency remains the Achilles' heel of many affirmative policy arguments.

Possible courses of action that advocates want to defend might not be able to solve or remove a problem completely. When one thinks about the complicated problems that afflict America (or any nation or community), establishing that a proposed cure will solve the problem can be an exceedingly difficult (if not impossible) task. This fact opens the proposed cure to criticism from opponents who might view it as a mere "Band-Aid" approach and not a solution to the problem. The dynamics of a specific controversy or dispute might lead to numerous replies. The opposition's attack might be recharacterized as a sham because, although they critique the proposal, they do not offer a substantive alternative. Or, the advocates for change can try to argue that although the proposal will not solve the problem completely, it is a necessary first step that will make it possible to solve the problem fully somewhere down the road. Advocates can defend the proposal as a realistic first step and attack the opposition for seemingly demanding perfection when that is impossible to achieve. Or, advocates can acknowledge that although the proposal might not be necessary in the strict sense of that term, the proposal still merits adoption because it will lessen the impact or extent of the problem while the search for a better solution continues.

The second key sub-issue under cure is *workability.* Not only must a cure offer solvency, it must do so in a way that is workable or feasible. Ronald Reagan's "Star Wars" missile defense system promised to solve the problem of nuclear conflict, at least in terms of America's vulnerability to attack, but the proposal generated considerable controversy with respect to its workability. A number of experts believed that it simply would not work—that it was not technologically feasible. Workability can arise in ways beyond technological competence. A policy for dealing with the ill of pornography might be attacked as unworkable given our current interpretation of the Constitution and Bill of Rights. Or, a policy requiring women to register for the draft might be rejected because it violates our beliefs about the appropriate duties and responsibilities of the different genders; the policy is unworkable given the current state of gender roles and expectations. The sub-issue of workability, as it is explored in an extended policy dispute, often intersects with the final stock topic of consequences.

Consequences

Assuming that the cure can in fact solve the problem, we still can argue about the additional consequences—what might be called the *side effects*—of the cure. A lobotomy might "cure" a person's severe headache, but he or she probably is reluctant to get one because of its other consequences. In his famous Essay No. 10 of the *Federalist Papers,* James Madison used an analogy between political faction (a serious ill for most of the nation's founders) and fire to demonstrate that certain cures, although they no doubt would "solve" the problem of faction, are in fact worse than the disease itself. Opponents of a policy try to discover those unpleasant side effects that might make that particular cure less desirable. Discussion of negative consequences or costs usually falls into one of two categories. The first is *material* consequences or costs. A proposed cure might solve the ill but would cost more money than we currently have available to spend on the problem, or a proposed cure to an ill such as gang violence might require more material resources than currently are available. The second category of negative consequences is *social.* Some cures might not exact material costs but still might require that a community give up important social practices, customs, and/or beliefs. For example, if a proposed cure for poverty destroys the fabric of the nuclear family, this social consequence will lead many to oppose the policy cure.

On the other hand, supporters of a policy cure try to uncover its extra benefits (what other good things will happen besides curing the ill) to make the policy more attractive. A cure for poverty can be strengthened if advocates can show that, in addition to alleviating the problem of poverty, the policy will increase individual responsibility and initiative as well as promote stable nuclear families given that these are important values in American society.

Advocates use these stock issues and subissues in strategic planning; they are extremely useful in the process of rhetorical **invention.** Critics can use them as a tool for analyzing policy disputes. How? Stock issues serve as points where competing claims meet (e.g., a significant ill exists/no significant ill exists, *x* is the cause of the problem/*x* is not the cause of the problem). Critics analyze (a) *how* advocates establish claims regarding ill, blame, cure, and consequences and (b) *how* advocates respond to or negotiate the claims made by the opposition. Close analyses or detailed "readings" of **controversies,** in some cases following the stock issues format closely and in other cases departing from them by locating particular **topics/topoi** immanent to the controversy, have emerged as an important form of critical practice in contemporary rhetorical studies.

Notes

1. Hultzén (1966) acknowledged that the metaphor is not essential but might be explainable given the long tradition of using medical metaphors to discuss rhetoric.
2. In contemporary public discourse, this sense of ill can be detected in Newman's (1993) book, *Declining Fortunes.*
3. When examining a controversy, it is useful to distinguish between the ill that a community is trying to resolve and the potential *negative consequences* of the cure (even if individual advocates might blur this distinction in their discourse). But as the discussion in the previous paragraph tried to suggest, this distinction can blur over time as negative consequences evolve into a social ill.

References and Additional Reading

Braet, A. (1987). The classical doctrine of "status" and the rhetorical theory of argumentation. *Philosophy and Rhetoric, 20,* 79-93.

Bryant, D. C., & Wallace, K. R. (1947). *Fundamentals of public speaking.* New York: Appleton-Century-Crofts.

Freeley, A. J. (1996). *Argumentation and debate: Critical thinking for reasoned decision making* (9th ed.). Belmont, CA: Wadsworth.

Hultzén, L. S. (1966). Status in deliberative analysis. In D. C. Bryant (Ed.), *The rhetorical idiom: Essays in rhetoric, oratory, language, and drama.* New York: Russell and Russell.

Katula, R., & Roth, R. (1980). A stock issues approach to writing arguments. *College Composition and Communication, 31,* 183-196.

Newman, K. (1993). *Declining fortunes: The withering of the American dream.* New York: Basic Books.

Reinard, J. C. (1991). *Foundation of argument: Effective communication for critical thinking.* Dubuque, IA: William C. Brown.

Rybacki, K. C., & Rybacki, D. J. (1991). *Advocacy and opposition: An introduction to argumentation* (2nd ed.). Englewood Cliffs, NJ: Prentice Hall.

Shaw, W. C. (1922). *The art of debate.* Boston: Allyn & Bacon.

Ziegelmueller, G., Kay, J., & Dause, C. (1990). *Argumentation: Inquiry and advocacy.* Englewood Cliffs, NJ: Prentice Hall.

STYLE

Style is one of the five traditional **canons** or subdivisions in classical rhetorical theory. It is, Hochmuth (1955) argued, "that most allusive of all aspects of the speaking act" (p. 18); it is a subject that is exceedingly difficult to conceptualize with precision and consistency (Hariman, 1995). Various approaches to style can be found in the tradition of rhetorical thought. One of the earliest, and most common, efforts to theorize style culminated in the identification of three types of style: the low or plain style, the middle style, and the grand style (Kennedy, 1980; Vickers, 1988, pp. 80-82). Over time, the realm of rhetoric was reduced to the domain of style.[1] Many contemporary thinkers resist the reduction of rhetoric to style, but at the same time, they encourage greater attention to, and reflection on, the nature and function of style (Hariman, 1995). What might it mean to take style seriously as a topic for theoretical reflection and critical analysis?

We frequently take issues of style for granted. Most of us were taught that reading involves looking *through* the form or style of the words on the page to locate the meaning of the text (Lanham, 1983). According to this traditional perspective, the meaning of a text resides in its content, and content exists apart from the text's form or style; at best, style "dresses up" the language or content of a text. It does not, and it cannot, contribute in any substantial way to its meaning or significance. This radical separation of content from style or form has been called into question during recent years.[2] Many scholars now believe that meaning, as well as persuasive force, emerges from a complex interaction of discursive elements. As Carter and Nash (1990) wrote, "Particular linguistic or stylistic choices are not innocent value-free selections from a system; they work to conceal and reveal certain realities rather than others, establishing or reinforcing ideologies in the process and refracting (as opposed to reflecting) particular points of view" (p. 24). **Argument,** structure or **arrangement,** language (*idioms,* **ideographs,** and word choice), syntax (grammatical structure and sentence patterns), and style (to name some of the more common elements) all contribute to meaning and persuasive force. The challenge posed by recent developments in rhetorical, literary, and linguistic theory is to learn how to look *at,* rather than *through,* the style or *texture* of a text so as to discover how it works and what it might be doing.

So, the first step in taking style seriously is to overcome the problematic disjunction between style and content. Style possesses cognitive, communicative, and persuasive force. But how might we study the elusive domain of style? Cooper's (1989) Burkeian-influenced discussion of "levels of structure" in public discourse (p. 194) provides a useful way of proceeding. Acknowledging that structure, like style, is difficult to codify, Cooper borrowed from Burke to establish three levels of analysis: large-scale structures, intermediate structures, and small-scale structures. The same three-part scheme can help to organize the desultory domain of style.

Large-Scale Stylistic Patterns

This analytic level focuses on identifying texts that share certain central characteristics. The characteristics linking different texts constitute a large-scale discursive style. Consider some examples. Brown (1966) identified five large-scale styles in the realm of prose discourse: *deliberative, expository, tumbling, prophetic,* and *indentured.* Each stylistic pattern tends to inhabit certain spheres of life (but large-scale styles rarely, if ever, are completely restricted to any specific sphere). For example, the indentured style inhabits the legal sphere, whereas the deliberative style is most common in politics. Each stylistic pattern has a defining texture or a set of characteristics that give it its particular shape. Brown summarized his discussion of the five styles as follows:

> The genius of deliberative writing seems to me to show itself most characteristically in a highly organic, climactic movement; that of exposition in the form of the equation and in series of parallel terms, which often exhibit some common element of form; that of prophecy in bold, loosely connected,

> terse, paradoxical aphorisms; that of tumbling prose in a crowded stress-patterning reminiscent of that of alliterative-accentual verse, though a characteristic diction in this style is almost as near its center; and that of the traditional indenture in the stretching of a single sentence to include the whole contents of the document. (p. 16)[3]

Hariman's (1995) analysis of political style proceeded in a similar manner. Political style was defined as

> (1) a set of rules for speech and conduct guiding the alignment of signs and situations, or texts and acts, or behavior and place; (2) informing practices of communication and display; (3) operating through a repertoire of rhetorical conventions depending on aesthetic reactions; and (4) determining individual identity, providing social cohesion, and distributing power. (p. 187)

Hariman's acknowledged that his sense of style is "expansive" (p. 12). But he suggested that such expansion is necessary if rhetorical scholars are to break with a tedious formalism that does nothing but "catalog elements of design independently of substantive meaning" (p. 8). Hariman not only contributed to a general reassessment of the nature of rhetorical or political style but also described, in some detail, four common styles in political discourse: the *realist,* the *courtly,* the *republican,* and the *bureaucratic.* Each style in Hariman's typology merits additional critical attention (see, e.g., Hariman, 1996; Murphy, 1994).

Not every discussion of large-scale style eventuates in a typology of styles. Some scholars emphasize the clash of styles as in Robertson's (1995) discussion of the *hortatory, laudatory,* and *admonitory* styles in the United States and Great Britain. Many scholars in and out of the discipline of rhetorical studies focus attention on a specific large-scale pattern. Bormann (1985), for example, defined style expansively as "recurring patterns of communication" or "the broad usage of a community of people" (p. 19). This definition supports his analysis of the "puritan" rhetorical style and its subsequent evolution into a style that Bormann labeled "romantic pragmatism." One particular large-scale stylistic pattern that has generated substantial attention within and outside rhetorical studies is the "paranoid style" first discussed by historian Richard Hofstadter during the mid-1960s (Hofstadter, 1965/1979). The characteristics and conventions of *paranoid* discourse have been a subject of inquiry and debate (Bass, 1992; Hutson, 1984; Sanders & Newman, 1971; Short, 1987; Singh, 1997; Smith, 1977; Wood, 1982). Another large-scale pattern to attract considerable attention, especially among rhetorical scholars, is the **feminine style** (Campbell, 1989; Jamieson, 1988, pp. 67-89). These examples of large-scale stylistic patterns are not exhaustive; they illustrate just some of the lines of inquiry pursued by rhetoricians and scholars in other fields.[4]

Intermediate Stylistic Patterns

This analytic level identifies patterns and structures that generally operate at the level of the sentence and/or paragraph. The line separating intermediate patterns from small-scale patterns is not clear; intermediate patterns such as *asyndeton* and *polysyndeton* might be recategorized as small-scale patterns, whereas some of the small-scale patterns (e.g., *anaphora*) exist over a series of phrases, clauses, sentences, or (sometimes) paragraphs (e.g., John F. Kennedy's use of "To those" to open successive paragraphs in his "Inaugural Address").

Noun Style versus Verb Style

These two stylistic patterns (Lanham, 1983; see also Wells, 1960) employ different types of verbs. The noun style features variations on the copula (connecting verb) "is," whereas the verb style features "active" verbs (but not in the sense of active voice vs. passive voice). In the noun style, verbs tend to be *nominalized* or turned into nouns and adjectives. Compare the following:

Noun style: Preparation is the key to success.
Verb style: Prepare for success.

What makes the first sentence an example of the noun style is (a) the presence of the linking verb "is" and (b) the nominalized verb ("prepare" becomes "preparation").

Lanham (1983) described the classic pattern of noun style sentences as

noun + "is" + prepositional phrase(s).

Prepositional phrases also can be found in the opening sections of a noun style sentence (e.g., in examining "In Lanham's discussion, the function of noun style sentences is clear," two prepositional phrases—"in Lanham's discussion" and "of noun style sentences"—appear before the verb "is," which departs from the classic pattern). Here is an example with a pile of prepositional phrases at the end:

The proposed policy (+) is (+) an example
of liberal plans
to destroy the family
in order
to establish
by law
without public support a
godless society.

The key active verbs in this sentence, "destroy" and "establish," have not been nominalized, but their infinitive form ("to" + verb) allows them to function as nouns. The sentence can be rewritten to, in a sense, unleash the verbs: "The liberal's policy destroys the family and establishes a godless society without public support."

The verb style describes a world of action; the noun style renders the world more static. This can create problems because the noun style frequently is used for descriptive purposes. The challenge becomes trying to describe action through static sentences (see the discussion of *ironic iconicity* in the entry for **iconicity**). The verb style tends to be more direct, whereas the noun style is more indirect and occasionally is evasive (Williams, 1990). Consider the example of the sentence criticizing an unnamed liberal policy. The verb style sentence advances a more direct claim (the "liberal's policy destroys"), whereas the noun style sentence makes the point more indirectly (in a sense, the point gets buried in the prepositional phrase structure). The verb style tends to "move" more quickly; things happen. The noun style tends to "move" at a much slower pace.

Parataxis (paratactic style) versus Hypotaxis (hypotactic style)

Parataxis is a form of "syntactic democracy" (Lanham, 1983). Elements in a sentence are merely juxtaposed, or placed next to each other, without any clear sense of their relationship. What this means is that in the paratactic style, the syntax or structure (e.g., use of complex sentences with clear patterns of subordination) of sentences does not add details such as relationships and a sense of causality. Lanham's (1983) paradigmatic example is "I came, I saw, I conquered." Lanham suggested that Hemingway's prose is a prime example of extended parataxis. An example of Hemingwayesque parataxis can be found in Barry Lopez's essay, "Apologia" (Lopez, 1990/1998). The vast majority of Lopez's sentences were simple or compound ones; there were very few complex sentences in the essay. Lopez placed clause and clause, as well as sentence and sentence, next to each other. There was a chronological structure that gave the essay a sense of order, but the readers were not given many other syntactical clues to help figure out how events related to each other or what the "meaning" of the whole essay might be. But Lanham's observations about Hemingway provide a way of deciphering Lopez's parataxis. Lanham argued that Hemingway's paratactic style in *A Farewell to Arms* disclosed a narrator unable to understand the world (understanding would be "communicated" through hypotactic structures); Hemingway's narrator was passive and simply endured an existence that could not be comprehended. Similar observations might be made about Lopez's narrator; he also seemed unable to fully understand the events and actions that he described. The paratactic style suggests that the essay was, in part, about the narrator's struggle to understand his own behavior.

Hypotactic style allows syntax and structure to supply useful information. Instead of simple juxtaposition of elements by way of simple and compound sentences, hypotactic structures rely more on complex sentences to establish relationships among elements.[5] Perelman and Olbrechts-Tyteca (1969) observed, "The hypotactic construction is the argumentative construction par excellence. . . . Hypotaxis creates frameworks [and] constitutes the adoption of a position" (p. 158). So, Lanham's paradigmatic example can be rewritten as "First I came, then I saw, and consequently I conquered." We can find more elaborate hypotactic structures in Martin Luther King, Jr.'s "Letter From Birmingham Jail" in April 1963. The diagrams in Figure S.1 use a variation of Lanham's method of charting sentences to bring out their hypotactic structure. Each sentence contains numerous subordinate or dependent clauses along with prepositional phrases to create the ranking that Lanham believed is characteristic of hypotaxis. Did King's hypotaxis have a potential rhetorical function? Consider the context of the letter. King was responding to criticism of his decision to proceed with the direct action campaign in Birmingham, Alabama. His judgment had been called into question. King's critics suggested that he did not understand the situation in Birmingham and perhaps in the South as well. King defended his judgment in the letter, and his use of numerous hypotactic structures reinforced his argument. Hypotaxis is the style of someone who understands what is going on and can reflect that understanding in complex grammatical constructions.

Periodic Style versus Running Style

The running style *looks like* the way in which a person's mind responds to the world without benefit of reflection (Lanham, 1983). If an individual could somehow hook up a transcriber to his or her brain so that it took down the person's thoughts as he or she went through the day, the result would be something like the running style. Writers (and sometimes speakers) will invite their readers (audiences) to experience the world along with them or to get inside their heads and see or experience things along with them. The most common form of the running style is what is termed *stream of consciousness* writing (e.g., James Joyce). Something very close to the running style can appear in public advocacy when advocates let the readers or audience experience the way in which they have deliberated about an issue. For example, an advocate might use a *residue* argument structure to give the readers or audience members the impression (remember that we are dealing with a *style* here) that they are overhearing the way in which the advocate thought through his or her final position on the issue. We might find this style in a politician publicly agonizing over a vote on abortion or in a prosecutor defending a decision to seek the death penalty.

The periodic style *looks like* the way in which a person's mind is *after* the individual has sorted through the complexity of his or her experience. If the transcription of a person's brain represents the running style, then a diary entry made after the day's events have been the subject of reflection can represent the periodic style. The periodic style exhibits a sense of control and direction lacking in the running style. What is known as the *periodic sentence*—usually long and containing numerous (usually balanced) parenthetical digressions, with its point made clear at the end—reflects, despite the apparent hesitations and twists and turns, a mind that has reflected on and organized the material it confronts. Martin (1958) wrote, "The periodic sentence 'shapes' its structure more formally,

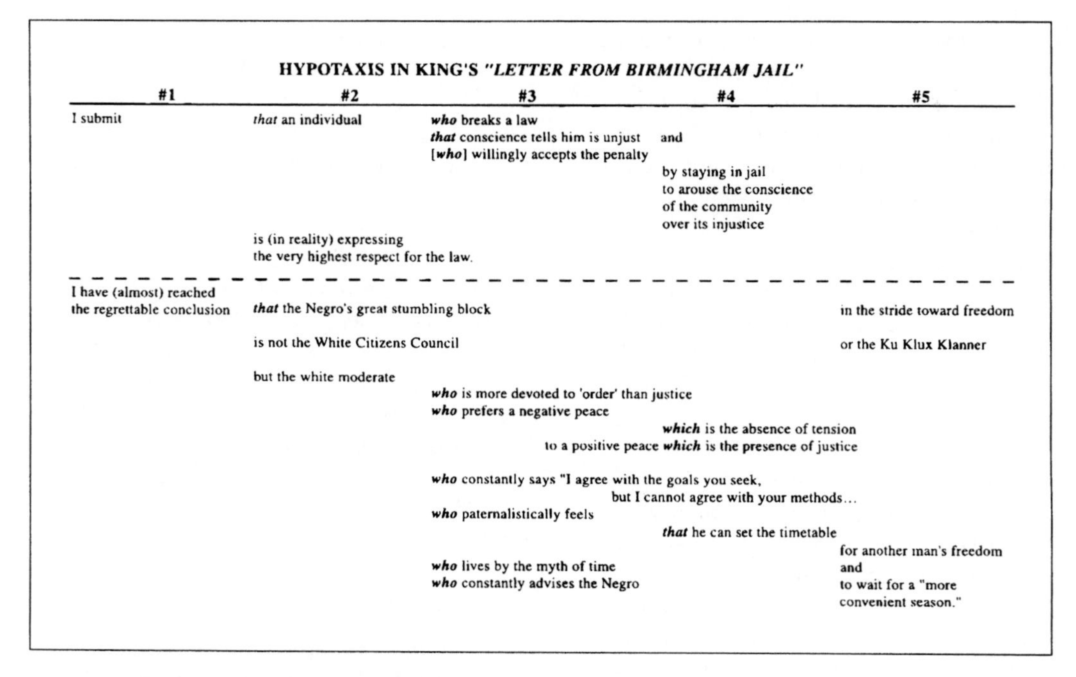

Figure S.1. Hypotaxis in King's "Letter From Birmingham Jail"

placing modifiers so that the predication of the sentence, and therefore its direction and intent, is not clear until at or near the end" (p. 114). Here is a simple example from Ralph Waldo Emerson's essay, "Self-Reliance": "To believe your own thought, to believe that what is true for you in your private heart is true for all man [sic]—that is *genius*" (Emerson, 1841/1979). Martin (1958) suggested that the periodic style is a "flexible instrument" that, in the hands of a novelist such as Henry James, can embody deep "introspection" while also being capable of supporting a "thunderous indictment" (p. 115). Martin provided the following example of each use:

Periodic introspection: "He knew with the suddenness of insight to which he had grown accustomed in his new mental state that these, the infertile flowers of a life too long spent in what had been, from whatever point of view one chose to examine it, a manner excessively solitary, were not now, and never had been the sort of tributes to lay at the feet, if so pagan and oriental a tradition of worship were not presumptuous and uncharacteristic for him to consider, of his beloved, and too long neglected, friend" (p. 114).

Periodic thunder: "This man, long the consort of criminals and enemy of the law-abiding, a petty tyrant of back alleys made powerful by the corruption of those in high places and relentless by his insatiable greed and vanity, has again demonstrated his cunning as well as the indifference of those charged with the public welfare by seizing in our time of greatest need the very resources on which we most depended for our sustenance" (p. 115).

Asyndetic Style versus Polysyndetic Style

These terms are used to describe the presence or absence of linguistic connectors (e.g., and, but, then, after). An asyndetic style features few connectors, whereas a polysyndetic style features a liberal use of connectors. Abraham Lincoln's *peroration* in the "Gettysburg Address," "that government of the people, by the people, for the people, shall not perish from the earth," and Aristotle's (1954) conclusion to the *Rhetoric,* "I have spoken. You have heard; you know the facts; now render your judgment," illustrate the asyndetic style. The following passage from the Book of Revelations in the Bible illustrates the polysyndetic style:

> *And* I stood upon the sand of the sea, *and* saw a beast rise up out of the sea, having seven heads *and* ten horns, *and* upon his horns ten crowns, *and* upon his heads the name of blasphemy. *And* the beast which I saw was like unto a leopard, *and* his feet were as the feet of a bear, *and* his mouth as the mouth of a lion: *and* the dragon gave him his power, *and* his seat, *and* great authority.

Notice the polysyndetic quality in the following passage from Jesse Jackson's "The Rainbow Coalition" speech at the 1984 Democratic National Convention:

> If we cut that military budget without cutting our defense, *and* we use that money to rebuild bridges *and* put steelworkers back to work, *and* use that money, *and* provide jobs for our citizens, *and* use that money to build schools *and* train teachers *and* educate our children, *and* build hospitals *and* train doctors *and* train nurses, the whole nation will come running to us.

Given Jackson's training as a preacher, the biblical "feel" of the passage is understandable; the repetitive use of "and" by Jackson not only reveals a religious "voice" but also underscores the process of coalition building that Jackson was attempting throughout the speech.

The asyndetic and polysyndetic styles can be combined as well. Consider this passage from Luke: "*And* as it was in the days of Noah so shall it be also in the days of the Son of man. They did eat, they drank, they married wives, they were given in marriage, until the day that Noah entered into the ark, *and* the flood came, *and* destroyed them all."

Tropes and Figures of Speech (or small-scale stylistic patterns)

Tropes and figures have been the focus of attention in rhetorical studies for more than 2,000 years. This discussion is *one* way of understanding some of the more common figures. These definitions, it must be noted, are *not* definitive.

Alliteration

Alliteration is a repetitious pattern of consonant sounds. Tongue twisters such as "Sally sells sea shells by the sea shore" use it abundantly. Daniel Webster was fond of alliteration, as in this example from his 1825 "Bunker Hill Monument Address": "They have thought that for this object no time could be more propitious than the present prosperous and peaceful period." Lanham (1983) described alliteration as a "powerful glue [that] can connect elements without logical relationship" (p. 125); alliteration pulls words together (p. 132). King used alliteration to help reinforce his famous "promissory note" metaphor: "It is obvious today that America has defaulted on this promissory note insofar as her citizens of color are concerned." Corbett (1971) suggested that the appeal of alliteration has declined but noted its continued presence as a "mnemonic device" in advertising slogans such as "better business builds bigger bankrolls" (p. 471).

Alliterative Antithesis

Alliterative antithesis is a pattern of consonant sounds that links words/ideas together while semantic content pushes them apart (making them *antithetical*), creating what Lanham (1983) described as a "paradoxical electricity" (p. 129). In King's admonishment to judge his children not "by the color of their skin but by the content of their character" in his August 1963 "I Have a Dream" speech, the alliterative "c" sound links the material while the semantic level contrasts two forms of judgment: one based on race and the other based on personal character. Malcolm X employed the same pattern in 1964 in his "The Ballot or the Bullet" speech. The repetition of both the "b" and "l" sounds links the two terms—ballot and bullet—while their semantic contrast pushes them apart.

Anadiplosis

Anadiplosis[6] is when a word at or near the end of one clause or sentence is used to begin the following clause or sentence. Anadiplosis creates the pattern A → B, B → C, C → D, D → E, suggesting a logical relationship among the terms in the expression. Here is an example: "Justice requires the rule of law. The rule of law exists through wise legislation. And wise legislation is the essence of government." Colonial spokesperson John Dickinson, in his famous *Letters From a Farmer in Pennsylvania* (Dickinson, 1768), employed the strategy:

> Let these *truths* be indelibly impressed on our minds—*that we cannot be HAPPY, without being FREE*—that we cannot be free, *without being secure in our property*—that *we* cannot be secure in our property, *if, without our consent, others may, as by right, take it away*—that *taxes imposed on us by parliament,* do thus take it away. (Letter XII)

In a speech in the Senate in 1832, Henry Clay defended his economic program (known as the "American system") with this strategy: "Now, the truth is that the [American] system *excites* and *creates* labor, and this labor creates wealth, and this new wealth communicates additional ability to consume, which acts on all the objects contributing to human comfort and enjoyment." Corbett (1971) cited the following passages as more contemporary examples. From Howard Griffin's book, *Black Like Me,* he quoted, "The laughter had to be gross or it would turn to sobs, and to sob would be to realize, and to realize would be to despair." From Herman Wouk's *The Caine Mutiny,* he quoted the following line of Captain Queeg's: "Aboard my ship, excellent performance is standard. Standard performance is sub-standard. Sub-standard performance is not permitted to exist." Malcolm X employed the pattern in his "The Ballot or the Bullet" speech when he observed, "The Dixiecrats in Washington, D.C., control the key committees that run the government. The only reason the Dixiecrats control these committees is because they have seniority. The only reason they have seniority is because they come from states where Negroes can't vote." We find the pattern again in Jackson's 1984 speech to the Democratic National Convention: "Suffering breeds character. Character breeds faith. And in the end, faith will not disappoint." Here is a slight variation that combined anadiplosis with some anaphora from Ortman's (1993) collection of popular expressions: "If you can't ignore an insult, top it; if you can't top it, laugh it off; and if you can't laugh it off, it's probably deserved" (p. 110). Anadiplosis also can be used to create a circular effect. A teenager might say something to this effect: "I want a job. But to get a job, I need a car to get to work. To get a car, I need money. And to get money, I need a job."

Anaphora

Anaphora is the repetition of a word or phrase at the beginning of successive sentences or paragraphs. Anaphora can be very useful for building to a climax, as in this example from King's "I Have a Dream" speech:

> There are those who ask the devotees of civil rights, "When will you be satisfied?" *We can never be satisfied* as long as the Negro is the victim of the unspeakable horrors of police brutality. *We can never be satisfied* as long as our bodies, heavy with fatigue of travel, cannot gain lodging in the motels of the highways and the hotels of the city. *We cannot be*

> *satisfied* as long as the Negro's basic mobility is from a smaller ghetto to a larger one. *We can never be satisfied* as long as our children are stripped of their selfhood and robbed of their dignity by signs stating "for whites only." *We cannot be satisfied* as long as the Negro in Mississippi cannot vote and a Negro in New York believes he has nothing for which to vote. No, *we are not satisfied,* and *we will not be satisfied* until justice rolls down like waters and righteousness like a mighty stream.

Corbett (1971) noted that anaphora tends to "produce a strong emotional effect" (p. 473). King's use in the passage just quoted illustrates this potential.

Anastrophe

Anastrophe[7] is the inversion of the usual or common word order. Corbett (1971) noted that "because such deviation surprises expectations, anastrophe can be an effective device for gaining attention" (p. 466). As an example, Corbett cited the caption from a Peugeot automobile ad: "One ad does not a survey make." The poet Robert Bridges employed the same inversion pattern in a line from his poem "I Love All Beauteous Things": "I too will something make." This is a rather common pattern. A sportswriter commenting on the local team might write, "One win does not a contender make." Anastrophe often is used to add emphasis. Consider a comic example. In a Dilbert cartoon strip published on March 5, 1998, the pointy-haired boss announces that he will begin using the "chaos theory of management." Dilbert's co-worker Wally replies, "And this will be different how?" Normally, we would place the interrogative adverb "how" at the beginning of the sentence (as in "How would this be different?"). By deviating from the normal word order, Wally places extra emphasis on the *question* of difference. Wally's extra emphasis suggests that the new theory will not dramatically change the boss's behavior.

Antithesis

Antithesis is a compact expression of contrast or opposition sometimes combined with alliteration and/or parallelism. Here is a simple example from an essay by the linguistic anthropologist Benjamin Whorf:

> Language is not simply a reporting device for experience
> but a defining framework for it.
> (Whorf, 1956)

Two contrasting views of language were contrasted and the parallelism underscored that contrast. The next example, from the opening of Kennedy's "Inaugural Address," is a bit more elaborate:

> We observe today
> not a victory of party
> but a celebration of freedom

The sentence continued with an elaborate antithetical parallel structure:

> symbolizing an end as well as a beginning
> signifying renewal as well as change.

This was reinforced by alliteration and *homoioteleuton* (similar ending to words). Or, consider this example from the same address:

> If a free society cannot help the many who are poor,
> it cannot save the few who are rich.

Clinton often linked himself to Kennedy; in this passage from his "First Inaugural Address" in 1992, Clinton borrowed Kennedy's flair for antithesis: "This ceremony is held in the depth of winter, but by the words we speak and the faces we show the world, we force the spring." Burke (1966) observed,

> Antithesis is an exceptionally effective rhetorical device. There is its sheerly *formal* lure, giving dramatic saliency and at least apparent clarity to any issue. One may find himself [sic] hard-put to define a policy purely in its own terms, but one can advo-

> cate it persuasively by an urgent assurance that it is decidedly *against* such-and-such other policy with which people may be disgruntled. (p. 19)

Corbett (1971) suggested that "nicely managed antithesis can produce the effect of aphoristic neatness and can win the author a reputation for wit" (p. 465).

Aporia

Aporia is an expression of incompetence, humility (both feigned and real), lack of sophistication, or ignorance of generic and/or situational expectations. It is a member of the *irony* family. Aporia often is incorporated into the beginning of a message. A speaker who notes "My talents do not match the task before me today" is employing aporia. When a person claims that he or she cannot put thoughts into words, but then does so at great length, he or she is employing aporia. Lincoln's observation in the "Gettysburg Address" that "the world will little note nor long remember what we say here" denigrated his speech and, therefore, falls into the aporia family. In the opening of Frederick Douglass's 1852 address, "What to the Slave Is the Fourth of July," he stated,

> I do not remember ever to have appeared as a speaker before any assembly more shrinkingly, nor with a greater distrust of my ability, than I do this day. A feeling has crept over me quite unfavorable to the exercise of my limited powers of speech. The task before me is one which requires much previous thought and study for its proper performance.

In a somewhat unusual move, Douglass then immediately acknowledged his strategy to seemingly destabilize the **genre** (Jasinski, 1997): "I know that apologies of this sort are generally considered flat and unmeaning. I trust, however, that mine will not be so considered."

Apostrophe

Apostrophe is a device by which a speaker begins to address an audience other than the one to which he or she is speaking. Like aporia, it is part of the irony family. In the middle section of his 1860 address at Cooper Union in New York, Lincoln purported to "say a few words" to the people of the South. In so doing, he spoke to his New York audience by using fictional southern listeners as a frame. John Hancock did something similar in his 1774 speech commemorating the Boston Massacre when he purported to address the British soldiers: "Tell me, ye bloody butchers! Ye villains high and low! Ye wretches who contrived, as well as you who executed the inhuman deed! Do you not feel the goads and strings of conscious guilt pierce through your savage bosoms?" Apostrophe is not necessarily restricted to oral composition. A newspaper ad from a tobacco company purportedly directed at young people, but appearing in the business or editorial section of the newspaper, uses young people as a frame through which to reach a different audience.

Catachresis

Catachresis is an extravagant or outrageous *metaphor.* This was Lanham's (1983) example: "Mom will have kittens when she hears this" (p. 252). This strategy most commonly is found in poetry, as when Emily Dickinson described the need to "cool one's pain" or when e. e. cummings described "the voice of your eyes is deeper than all roses" (Quinn, 1982, p. 56).

Chiasmus

The term *chiasmus* is derived from the Greek letter for X and describes an inverted repetition pattern as in A → B, B → A. Following is an example:

> When the going gets tough,
> the tough get going.

Following is a passage from Quintilian:

Write quickly and
you will never write well;
write well and
you will soon write quickly.

Chiasmus are particularly useful to reinforce the idea of reversal. The National Rifle Association, for example, seeks to "reverse" the idea that gun control laws will promote public safety with its chiasmus slogan:

If guns are outlawed
only outlaws will have guns.

Or, here is how James Madison wrote about the progress of the new American nation in 1792:

In Europe, charters of liberty have been
granted by power.
America has set the example . . . of charters of power
granted by liberty.

Chiasmus also can be found in serious philosophical discourse. Karl Marx, intent on reversing the doctrines of Hegelian philosophy, was fond of chiasmus, as in these examples:

Life is not determined by consciousness,
but consciousness by life.
Circumstances make men just as much as
men make circumstances.

Chiasmus also can develop more indirectly. Here is an example from Jesse Jackson's speech to the Democratic National Convention in 1984:

The disabled have their handicap revealed and their genius concealed
while the able-bodied have their genius revealed and their disability concealed.

In the preceding passage, a weak chiasmus (weak in the sense that the A term switches in the second line from "handicap" to "disability") helps to reinforce the antithetical parallelism of the passage.

More complex patterns involving chiasmus also are possible.[8] Here is an example of a double chiasmus that includes *polyptoton* from Lyndon Johnson's national eulogy for Kennedy in 1963:

We will demonstrate anew
that the strong can be just in the use of strength
and the just can be strong in the defense of justice.

Finally, chiasmus also can be suggested through sound reversal, as in this passage from Jackson's 1984 address:

To be strong leaders
we must be long suffering.

Climax

Climax is a discursive structure, usually relying on forms of repetition and parallelism, that builds or grows in intensity until a breaking point is reached. The passage from King's "I Have a Dream" speech quoted earlier illustrated how anaphoric repetition builds to a climax. A common variation discussed by Lanham (1983) is the antithetical climax. We can see this pattern in Winston Churchill's account of the air battle over Britain during World War II: "Never in the field of human conflict was so much owed by so many to so few." We find repetition (combined with alliteration in the *so* much and the *so* many) and parallelism at work, but the climax subverts our expectations (yet still feels "right"). As Lanham explained, " 'So much' and 'so many' lead us to expect a third repetition," but Churchill subverted this expectation through an antithesis "so few" that completed the climactic progression (p. 130).

Diacope

Diacope is the repetition of a word in a sentence with one or a small number of words in between. Roosevelt's "First Inaugural Address" contained the following example: "Let me assert my firm belief that the only thing we have to fear is fear itself." C. S. Lewis used diacope in his *Surprised by Joy* to capture the repetitiveness of human life: "Term, holidays, term, holidays, till we leave school, and then work, work, work till we die" (Lewis, 1955). Tautological expressions such as "boys will be boys" also fall into this category.

Ellipsis

Elipsis is the omission of a word or words. Corbett (1971) noted that ellipsis "can be an artful and arresting means of securing economy of expression" (p. 469). For example, consider this "sentence" from Lopez's (1990/1998) essay, "Apologia": "The signature of a tractor-trailer truck: 78,000 pounds at 65 mph." No subject and no predicate verb were provided. But the "sentence" packed a punch coming at the end of a paragraph describing the effects of the collision on a deer. When the verb is omitted, scholars refer to the figure as *zeugma*. In the same Lopez essay, we find these "sentences": "In Illinois, west of Kankakee, two raccoons as young as the ones in Oregon. In Indiana, another raccoon, a gray squirrel." Neither sentence had a verb; we are not told what has happened to either animal.

Epanaphora

Epanaphora is intensive anaphora.

Epiphora or Epistrophe

Epiphora or *epistrophe* is the repetition of a word or phrase at the end of a clause or sentence. An example is the biblical passage from Corinthians: "When I was a child, I spoke as a child; I understood as a child; I thought as a child; but when I became a man, I put away childish things." Another example is this passage from a Malcolm X speech in February 1965: "When you teach a man to hate his lips, the lips that God gave him, the shape of the nose that God gave him, the texture of the hair that God gave him, the color of the skin that God gave him, you've committed the worst crime that a race of people can commit." A form of epiphora also can be created by way of polyptoton (variations on a word). An ad for Suffolk University features the statement, "Politics is your life. Now make it your living" ("life" and "living" both are derived from the old English word *libban*). Epiphora can be combined with parallelism, as in the following expression attributed to both Lincoln and P. T. Barnum: "You can fool some of the people all of the time and all of the people some of the time, but you can't fool all of the people all of the time."

Epithet

Epithet is a characterizing phrase such as "the great communicator" or "silver-tongued devil."

Epitrope

Another member of the irony family, epitrope[9] consists of an essentially ironic expression of agreement with an opponent that is then turned to the advantage of the speaker or writer. For example, in his "Letter From Birmingham Jail," King wrote,

> I would not hesitate to say that it is unfortunate that so-called demonstrations are taking place in Birmingham at this time, but I would say in more emphatic terms that it is even more unfortunate that the white power structure of this city left the Negro community with no other alternative.

King opened the sentence by affirming a point made by the eight white ministers to which he was responding—demonstrations are unfortunate. But King's agreement, it turned out, was ironic. We see this in the second clause of the sentence when King introduced a truncated *residue* **argument** (there is "no other alternative") that "trumped" the agreement in the opening clause. King appeared to agree with his critics, but this agreement was quickly turned against the critics.

We can distinguish between what might be called weak and strong forms of the epitrope. In the weak case, an arguer will accept the *terms* that the opposition introduces into the debate (terms can mean figurative or argumentative strategies). Consider the following exchange between Charles Fried, special assistant U.S. attorney general in George Bush's administration, and Frank Susman, a lawyer representing Missouri abortion clinics, during oral arguments in the *Webster v. Reproductive Health Services* case in 1989:

> **Fried:** We are not asking the court to unravel the fabric of unenumerated and privacy rights. . . . Rather, we are asking the court to pull this one thread.
>
> **Susman:** I think [that Fried] is somewhat disingenuous when he suggests to this court that he does not seek to unravel the whole cloth of procreational rights but merely to pull a thread. It has always been my personal experience that when I pull a thread, my sleeve falls off.

In this exchange, Susman accepted the metaphorical terms employed by Fried—rights figuratively depicted as a thread and cloth—but he appropriated these terms and used them to subvert the substance of Fried's position on abortion rights. Gesturing toward a *directional* **argument,** Susman maintained that one cannot pull a thread without the sleeve falling off—one cannot alter one right without endangering the whole structure of unenumerated rights. This same strategy can be used for humorous effect. In an episode of the television show *Frasier,* Frasier gloats about his success with women to his brother Niles by remarking, "I'm catnip." Niles responds, "I feel a fur ball coming up."

In the strong case of epitrope, an arguer will appear to accept a *claim* introduced by the opposition. Here is a brief example. In defending the death penalty, Jacob Sullum agreed with his anti-death penalty opponents that one potential problematic issue was

> the inconsistent application of the death penalty. To pick just one notorious example, isn't it unjust to give Hillside strangler Angelo Buono—who kidnapped, tortured, and murdered nine women—a life sentence, while sending [convicted killer Robert Alton] Harris to death row? Yes, but the injustice is not in executing Harris; it's in failing to execute Buono.

In this passage from the June 1990 issue of *Reason* Magazine, Sullum's apparent agreement with the opposition's claim that it is unjust to execute one individual while allowing other convicted killers to live was turned against the opposition; the injustice, Sullum asserted, was in not executing both of these murderers. Here is another example. In a 1989 speech on American drug policy, former Secretary of Education William Bennett argued in support of a criminal justice approach to the problem. But Bennett realized that some people were suspicious of that policy strategy. He acknowledged,

> Whenever discussion turns to the need for more police and stronger penalties, [liberals] cry that our constitutional liberties are in jeopardy. Well, yes, they are in jeopardy, but not from drug *policy.* On this score, the guardians of our Constitution can sleep easy. Constitutional liberties are in jeopardy instead from drugs themselves, which every day scorch the earth of our common freedom.

Bennett's strategy paralleled that used by Sullum. There was an apparent agreement with the opposition's claim (that constitutional liberties were in jeopardy) that was turned into a rejection of the opposition's position (that drug policy presented a threat to constitutional liberties).

Consider a final historical example. Arguing in 1854 in defense of his proposed territorial policy that would explicitly overturn the 1820 Missouri Compromise that established a dividing line between "free" territory and territory open to slavery, Illinois Senator Stephen Douglas wanted to subvert the proposition that the 1820 compromise was a "solemn compact" that must not be altered. One way in which he did this was to grant his opponents' claim; he considered the 1820 compromise to be a solemn compact. But in typical epitropic fashion, he used this apparent agreement to undercut his opponents' position. Douglas proceeded to argue that because the North failed to abide by the terms of the compact, the compact had in fact never been ratified and, therefore, was not binding on the parties. The proposition that the 1820 compromise was a solemn compact was subverted through a strategy of initial agreement that was turned against the opposition.

Epizeuxis

Epizeuxis is an emphatic repetition of a word or phrase with nothing else in between. A parent mourning a dead child wails, "Why? Why? Why?" A relatively common form of epizeuxis is created by repeating a demonstrative pronoun, as in "This, this is what I get in return for all my hard work."

Euphemism

Euphemism is the use of a vague term or expression in place of something more disagreeable. Politicians, for example, will speak about "revenue enhancement" rather than "raising taxes." During the war in Vietnam, military leaders would refer to the destruction of villages as "pacification."

Homoioteleuton

Homoioteleuton is a series of words with similar endings such as those with the Latinate suffixes "-ion" (e.g., presentation, action, elaboration, interpretation), "-ence" (e.g., emergence), and "-ance" (e.g., resemblance, performance). These suffixes work to nominalize verbs (transform verbs into nouns) and tend to appear most regularly in what Williams (1990) referred to as the various "-eses" idioms such as "legalese" and "bureaucratese" (p. 37). Like other patterns of repetition, homoioteleuton helps to build or reinforce connections, as in this example from the English politician Lord Rosebery in an 1899 speech: "Imperialism, sane imperialism . . . is nothing but this—a larger patriotism."

Hyperbole

Hyperbole is a moment of excessive exaggeration (Fogelin, 1987). Comedian Woody Allen published "My Speech to the Graduates" in the August 10, 1979, issue of the *New York Times.* In this hypothetical commencement address, Allen employed abundant hyberbole. In discussing our dependence on science and medicine, Allen observed,

> Science is something we depend on all the time. If I develop a pain in the chest, I must take an X-ray. But what if the radiation from the X-ray causes me deeper problems? Before I know it, I'm going in for surgery. Naturally, while they're giving me oxygen, an intern decides to light up a cigarette. The next thing you know, I'm rocketing over the World Trade Center in bed clothes.

Later in the same piece, Allen discussed the state of technology: "My toaster has never once worked properly in four years. I follow the instructions and push two slices of bread down in the slots, and seconds later they rifle upwards. Once they broke the nose of a woman I loved very dearly."

Hyperbole and exaggeration are not always used for (intentionally) comic purposes. After Gloria Steinem published an essay in the March 22, 1998, issue of the *New York Times* defending Clinton and claiming that his behavior toward women such as Kathleen Willey and Paula Jones did not constitute sexual harassment because he understood that when a woman says no a man must halt his sexual advances, another columnist, Abe Rosenthal, responded with an essay on March 27, 1998, claiming that Clinton's unwanted exposure was in fact a terribly dangerous act. Building off of a story about the tragic death of his sister, Rosenthal suggested that acts such as Clinton's might actually frighten a woman to such an extent that she would take rash action that could lead to her death.

Rosenthal's equation or **articulation** of "genital exposure" and "death" appeared to be a bit of an exaggeration (statistically, at least, "genital exposure" and "death" are not frequently correlated). It might be comic to some readers, but the thrust of Rosenthal's column was to emphasize, or make present (see the entry for **presence**), the vile nature of Clinton's behavior. Noncomic hyperbole is a common feature of **conspiracy arguments** such as Lincoln's account of the "slave power" in his 1858 "House Divided" address.

Irony

An extremely complex topic, *irony* has a number of different levels or modes including situational irony, dramatic irony, and sarcasm (for an introduction, see Booth, 1974; Muecke, 1969, 1970). As Muecke (1970) noted, "The principal obstacle in the way of a simple definition of irony is the fact that irony is not a simple phenomenon" (p. 8). Rhetorical scholars generally focus on verbal irony or statements that imply something other than their literal or ostensible meanings. Consider some of these recurrent forms of verbal irony: *ironic concern* (e.g., a person responds to another's mishap by saying "Oh, you poor, poor baby" in a way that lets us know that the person really has very little concern for the injured party), *ironic compliment* (e.g., a student tells a classmate "That was a good answer" in a way that lets us know that the student did not think highly of the answer), *ironic question* (e.g., a reporter asks a politician a question during a press conference in an effort to embarrass the politician rather than to solicit information from him or her), *ironic insult* (e.g., a disparaging utterance, spoken between friends, works to reaffirm the relationship), and *ironic warning* (e.g., a husband imitating Jackie Gleason's Ralph Cramden character from *The Honeymooners* television show tells his wife, "You do that again and it's 'to the moon, Alice' "). Almost any speech act can be ironized.

Meiosis

Meiosis[10] is a statement that depicts something important in terms that lessen or belittle it. Allen's fictitious graduation speech discussed earlier alternated between hyperbole and meiosis. Discussing the crisis of alienation in society, Allen remarked, "Man [sic] has seen the ravages of war, he has known natural catastrophes, he has been to singles bars." Commenting on the benefits of democracy, Allen observed, "In a democracy at least, civil liberties are upheld. No citizen can be wantonly tortured, imprisoned, or made to sit through certain Broadway shows." The pattern in each case was the same. Allen introduced a "serious" topic, began to treat it in a dignified and elevated manner, but ended on a note of understatement.

Understatement is not only used for comic effect. Consider the case of Clinton's purported White House encounter with Willey. After she described the encounter on the television program *60 Minutes,* a number of feminists accused Clinton of sexual assault. In a March 22, 1998, essay in the *New York Times* defending the president, Steinem employed understatement in describing the encounter as "a clumsy sexual pass." Any verbal effort to make an event, an idea, or a person less significant is a form of meiosis (it can be thought of as the opposite of efforts to give something **presence**).

Metaphor

In its most general sense, *metaphor* involves talking about one thing in terms of another. It often is considered the paradigm instance of discursive **figuration.** In their important book, *Metaphors We Live By,* Lakoff and Johnson (1980) asserted that "the essence of metaphor is understanding and experiencing one kind of thing in terms of another" (p. 5). In her address "The Solitude of Self," delivered in Washington, D.C., in January 1892, Elizabeth Cady Stanton relied on metaphor to help convey her central theme of human solitude. For example, she spoke of how women "must take the voyage of life alone," inviting her audience to understand one thing, human life, in terms of something else, in this case a voyage. Images of life's "voyage," "harbor of safety," and "drift with the current" appeared throughout the address and extended the voyage metaphor. Metaphoric extension, or the development of a root metaphor, can be found in King's "check" or "promissory note" metaphor (justice for African Americans was understood in terms of "cashing a check") that structured an early portion of his "I Have a Dream" speech.

Scholars use different terms for describing the parts of a metaphor. Richards's (1936) distinction between the *tenor* (John) and *vehicle* (is a pig) is used by many contemporary rhetorical scholars. An issue of some significance, treated at length by Lakoff and Johnson (1980) and a number of other scholars, is whether metaphor is a mere vehicle of style or whether it possesses important conceptual and cognitive significance. The consensus that has emerged over the past two decades favors a conceptual and cognitive approach to metaphor. As Lakoff and Johnson argued, "Our ordinary conceptual system, in terms of which we both think and act, is fundamentally metaphorical in nature. . . . Human thought processes are largely metaphorical" (pp. 3, 6). A growing number of rhetorical scholars have begun to explore both the conceptual and strategic value of metaphor (Carpenter, 1990; Ivie, 1987; Leff, 1983; Osborn, 1967, 1977).

Metonymy

Metonymy is a form of substitution in which something that is associated with *x* is substituted for *x*. When a professional athlete explains his or her motivation by stating "I want a ring," ring functions as a metonymic substitute for championship. Lakoff and Johnson (1980) provided an example where one waitress says to another, "The ham sandwich is waiting for his check" (p. 35); an attribute of the customer—he ordered a ham sandwich—functions as a substitute. Metonymy differs from metaphor, Lakoff and Johnson argued, because there is little (if any) interaction between the two elements (e.g., ring/championship, ham sandwich/customer). Metonymy simply "allows us to use one entity to *stand for* another" (p. 36).

Neologism

Neologism refers to the creation of new words. Gustafson (1992) noted that neology, or linguistic experimentation in general, is an important part of the American spirit, discussed and endorsed over the years by Jefferson, Emerson, Thoreau, and Whitman. Plotnik (1996) identified six sources for creating new words or types of neology: (a) *creating* new words from scratch (often based on the principle of *onomatopoeia* or the relationship between sounds and words, as in the word "burp," which sounds like the activity of that name); (b) *borrowing* from another language; (c) *combining* (using prefixes and suffixes to create new words such as "*green*washing" and "travel*gate*"); (d) *shortening* (e.g., some subcultures will "dis" someone (meaning to disrespect him or her), others will have "staff devo" meetings (meaning staff development); (e) *blending* (sometimes referred to as a *portmanteau word*), which involves combining and shortening (e.g., "infomercial," "Reaganomics," Apple computer's use of the term "resolutionary" to describe its new computer monitor, the bumper sticker reading "Don't Californicate Washington," "collabopetitors" (referring to the relationship among computer technology firms such as Microsoft, Apple, and Netscape); and (f) *shifting* word meaning through new grammatical functions (e.g., the transitive verb "hurl" ["She hurled the rock at the police"] acquires an intransitive meaning ["He hurled"] or a word develops a new *euphemistic* meaning as in the case of using the word "uninstalled" instead of "fired") or through *eponymic naming* where proper names for a person or product are turned into nouns, verbs, or modifiers (e.g., the prophet Jeremiah produces the word "jeremiad," Hoover vacuum cleaners lead us to the verb "hoovered," specific products such as a Xerox photocopy and a Kleenex tissue become general verbs or nouns ["Go xerox this document," "Please hand me a kleenex"]).

Occupatio

Another member of the irony family, *occupatio*[11] is a form of *ironic denial.* A person denies that he or she is going to do something, but the act of denial ironically does the very thing that the person denies he or she is doing. A politician might say "I will not call my opponent a liar" or "I will not raise my opponent's extramarital affair as an issue in this campaign." But what is the result of both of these denials? The politician does, in fact, question the opponent's honesty and does raise the issue of the opponent's marital situation. A television commercial for halogen light bulbs enacts a form of occupatio with a humorous touch. The voice-over for the commercial engages in denial, telling the viewers that buying these bulbs will not transform their homes. But visually, this verbal denial is subverted as viewers are shown pictures of homes that have been transformed into palaces.

A more complicated version of occupatio can be found in Angelina Grimké's famous speech before a committee of the Massachusetts legislature in 1838. In the *exordium* of the speech (the only part that has been preserved), Grimké related the tale of the Persian queen Esther's attempt to win the lives of her people from the Persian king. According to Grimké, Esther had to rely on various forms of "personal influence" to accomplish her goal because other, more direct means of persuasion were unavailable to her. Grimké then noted that she had a mission similar to that of Esther; she was trying to save the lives of innocent southern slaves and, as a women in 19th-century America, was denied access to more direct means of persuasion. But Grimké insisted that she was not going to rely on the forms of "personal influence" that Esther exploited. Grimké told her legislative audience,

> I thank God that we live in an age of the world too enlightened and too moral to admit the adoption of the same means to obtain as holy an end. I feel that it would be an insult to this committee were I to attempt to win [committee members'] favor by arraying my person in gold, and silver, and costly apparel, or by inviting them to partake of the luxurious feast, or the banquet of wine. I understand the spirit of the age too well to believe that you could be moved by such sensual means—means as unworthy of you, as they would be beneath the dignity of the cause of humanity. Yes, I feel that if you are reached at all, it will not be by me but by the truths I shall endeavor to present to your understandings and your hearts. The heart of the eastern despot was reached through the lowest propensities of his animal nature, by personal influence; yours, I know, cannot be reached but through the loftier sentiments of the intellectual and moral feelings.

What was going on in this passage? On the one hand, Grimké denied that "personal influence" is an appropriate means of persuasion. What exactly did she mean by personal influence? Her examples in the speech included "personal charms" and "sensual gratification," but it seems fair to include the practice of flattery within the orbit of these rejected means of persuasion. But notice how Grimké, despite the rejection of personal influence, seemed to employ the resources of flattery. In essence, she told the legislative committee that "you're too smart, you're too intelligent, you're too noble in spirit to fall for an appeal based on personal influence." Yet, in saying this to the legislative committee, she was relying on flattery as a form of personal influence. Telling audience members that they are too smart to fall for a rhetorical "trick" is merely a different type of rhetorical tactic—occupatio.[12] Grimké denied the appropriateness of personal influence as she ironically exploited those very resources in her appeal to the committee. The presence of occupatio in the speech can be explained, as Japp (1985) suggested, by Grimké's ambivalent relationship with the Esther **persona.**[13] Although Grimké wanted to move beyond the slave/queen status that 19th-century American women shared with Esther, she nevertheless remained constrained by this status. The presence of occupatio reflects her ongoing struggle to escape the cultural constraints placed on women advocates during the 19th century.

Oxymoron

Oxymoron is a condensed paradox such as "icy hot" and (for some) "military intelligence." Sometimes, we might encounter *performative oxymoron,* as when a company that stresses "thinking outside the box" creates a list of rules to regulate individualism and idiosyncratic employee behavior. A number of rhetorical critics (e.g., Campbell, 1973; Gunderson, 1977; Jasinski, 1992) find the figure of the oxymoron to be an important, and often pervasive, feature of public discourse.

Parallelism

Consider this sentence from Lopez's (1990/1998) essay, "Apologia" (discussed earlier): "We treat the attrition of lives on the road like the attrition of lives in war: horrifying, unavoidable, justified." It offered a *simile;* one thing is "like" another. But notice how the comparison was reinforced by the structure of the sentence. We can "chart" the sentence (Lanham, 1983) to make this structure clearer:

> We treat the attrition of lives on the road
> like the attrition of lives in war:
> horrifying, unavoidable, justified.

This type of structure is referred to as parallelism.

Corbett (1971) argued that parallelism

> is one of the basic principles of grammar and rhetoric. The principle demands that equivalent things be set forth in coordinate grammatical structures. . . . When this principle is ignored, not only is the grammar of coordination violated, but the rhetoric of coherence is wrenched. Students [of rhetoric] must be made to realize that violations of parallelism are serious, not only because they impair communication but [also] because they reflect disorderly thinking. (pp. 463-464)

Parallelism can exist at the level of phrase, clause, and sentence. When the parallel elements are linked by not only their general structure but also the number of words or syllables, some scholars refer to the pattern as *isocolon.* In some cases, the parallel elements complement each other; in other cases, there can be tension. Consider some examples from Lucretia Coffin Mott's "Discourse on Woman" speech in Philadelphia in December 1849. We can "chart" the examples to highlight the parallelism. Discussing the restrictions placed on women, Mott noted the following:

> These restrictions have enervated her mind
> and paralyzed her powers.

Discussing women's abilities to assist in the process of social reform, Mott made this observation:

> They are efficient co-workers,
> their talents are called into profitable exercise,
> their labors are effective in each department of reform.

Continuing on the theme of women as reformers, Mott extended the pattern of parallelism to include *climax:*

> If she is to shrink from being such an iconoclast . . .
> if she is to fear to exercise her reason . . . lest she should be thought
> if she is to be satisfied with the narrow sphere . . . lest she should transcend .
> truly it is a mournful prospect for woman.

Paramologia

Paramologia is a concession or admission that ultimately functions to further an advocate's position. Paramologia often is referred to as "the figure of admission." A simple example might be a politician admitting, "I may be guilty of a few things. I may have stolen a few things in my youth. But unlike my opponent, I have never stolen from the poor and from those who can least afford it." Here is a more elaborate example. Discussing the condition of former slaves in the South during a speech in April 1888, Frederick Douglass remarked,

> I admit that the Negro, and especially the plantation Negro, the tiller of the soil, has made little progress from barbarism to civilization, and that he [sic] is in a deplorable condition since his emancipation. That he is worse off, in many respects, than when he was a slave, I am compelled to admit, but I contend that the fault is not his but that of his heartless accusers. He is the victim of a cunningly devised swindle, one which paralyzes his energies, suppresses his ambition, and blasts all his hopes; and though he is nominally free, he is actually a slave.

Douglass opened the passage by conceding a point often made during the post-Reconstruction era: Most southern blacks were worse off than they were under slavery. But this was only a strategic concession that Douglass introduced before going on the attack. Although he granted the "truth" of the claim, Douglass insisted that the freed slaves were not responsible for their present condition. He argued that former slave owners had constructed a system that effectively reduced the former slaves to their earlier condition. Douglass closed the passage with **dissociation** to reinforce the point: The former slave was "nominally free" (appearance) when in *reality* "he [was] actually a slave."

Paronomasia

Paronomasia is a play on words or a "homonymic pun" (Lanham, 1983, p. 124). Michelob commercials employ this figure with slogans such as "Lite up the night" (promoting "lite" beer) and "Don't be afraid of the dark" (promoting dark beer).

Polyptoton

Polyptoton is the repetition of words that stem from the same root. Mario Cuomo employed polyptoton and other strategies in this phrase from his 1984 Democratic National Convention keynote address: "ever since Franklin Roosevelt *lifted* himself from his wheelchair to *lift* this nation from its knees." Herbert Spencer also mixed polyptoton with other strategies in this passage from one of his essays: "The ultimate result of shielding men [sic] from the effects of *folly* is to fill the world with *fools*" (Spencer, 1880).

Prolepsis

Prolepsis[14] is responding to the anticipated objections of one's opponents. In some cases, the strategy is obvious as the speaker or writer formulates the words that the opposition might use. For example, in 1852, Douglass stated,

> But I fancy I hear someone of my audience say, it is just in this circumstance that you and your brother abolitionists fail to make a favorable impression on the public mind. Would you argue more and denounce less, would you persuade more and rebuke less, your cause would be much more likely to succeed. But, I submit, where all is plain, there is nothing to be argued.

Douglass first voiced the concerns of many in the North (**polyphony** or voice appropriation) and then responded. Lincoln used the same strategy, combined with apostrophe, in his 1860 address at Cooper Union in New York when he identified, and then responded to, the charges made by the South against the Republican party.[15]

Prolepsis will not always be explicitly marked as in the cases of Douglass and Lincoln. Advocates also can engage in indirect forms of anticipation. If an advocate understands the objections that have been raised against a policy proposal, then the advocate can address these objections *without explicitly marking* that fact. For example, concerns about *workability* or *solvency* could be addressed without necessarily attributing these concerns to a specific person or group. Consider the case of Henry Highland Garnet's 1843 "Address to the Slaves." In the address, Garnet urged slave resistance and solicited northern free black support for this course of action. Shortly after introducing his proposal, Garnet remarked, "If [slaveholders] then commence the work of death, they, not you, will be responsible for the consequences." In this remark, Garnet indirectly acknowledged a common objection to the policy of resistance—it will lead to violence—and then discounted the objection by maintaining that any violence that might result would be due to the actions of the slaveowners, not the resisting slaves.[16] Garnet continued the strategy of indirect anticipation shortly after that, addressing the slaves and states as follows: "Your stern energies have been beaten out upon the anvil of severe trial. Slavery has done this, to make you subservient to its own purposes; but it has done more than this, it has prepared you for any emergency." How might we read this passage? Why did Garnet insert it into the address? One of its functions might have been to counteract the feeling that slaves would not be able to resist because they lacked the resources or the personal strength to do so. Garnet transformed the slaves' oppression into a resource in responding to the objection. Yes, the slaves had been treated brutally by the slaveholders, but this severe treatment had not left them incapable of resistance; it had, ironically, prepared the slaves for any emergency including the emergencies that would arise from the path of resistance. In both of these passages, Garnet can be read as addressing typical objections to the policy of resistance without explicitly incorporating these objections into his text.[17]

Prosopopoeia

Over the centuries, some rhetoricians have conflated *personification* and *prosopopoeia,* whereas others have distinguished between these similar stylistic strategies. Those who distinguish the two usually maintain that personification occurs when some nonhuman entity (e.g., an animal, a granite monument) is given human characteristics, especially the power of speech. Prosopopoeia, on the other hand, refers to the process of giving voice to someone who is absent, especially someone who is dead.[18]

Prosopopoeia goes beyond quoting someone else's words. When it is employed well, an advocate will (if only briefly) become some other person. For example, a coach might speak to his or her players at halftime and borrow the voice of a hospitalized star player ("If Smith were here, he [or she] would say . . ."). At times, an advocate can employ a weak form of prosopopoeia by giving voice to the concerns of an absent group while not directly attempting to speak in its voice. King did this in his 1967 anti-Vietnam war speech, "A Time to Break Silence."[19] In an 1829 Fourth of July speech, William Lloyd Garrison, like King in 1967, sought to give voice to those who were voiceless. Unlike King, Garrison employed a strong sense of prosopopoeia when he constructed, following the pattern of the Declaration of Independence, a list of African American grievances:

> Speaking at first from the shores of Africa, and changing their situation with the course of events, they would say: "They (the American people), arrogantly styling themselves the champions of freedom, for a long course of years have been guilty of the most cruel and protracted tyranny. They have invaded our territories, depopulated our villages, and kindled among us the flames of an exterminating war. They have wedged us into the holds of their 'floating hells,' with suffocating compactness. . . . They have brought us to a free and Christian land and sold us in their marketplaces like cattle. . . . They have cruelly torn the wife from her husband, the mother from her daughter, and children from their parents, and sold them into perpetual exile. . . . They have confined us in loathsome cells and secret prisons. . . . They have lacerated our bodies

> with whips, and brands, and knives. . . . Nor have they deprived us merely of our liberties. They would destroy our souls."

One common form of prosopopoeia is to speak from the perspective, as well as in the voice, of someone who is a *stranger* to the culture. Alexander Hamilton used this technique in Essay No. 24 of the *Federalist Papers.* He initially set up the prosopopoeia by introducing "a stranger to our politics" who was asked to reflect on the ongoing **debate** over the proposed Constitution. Hamilton then staged the internal dialogue of this "stranger" as he tried to understand the vehement sentiments expressed in the newspapers: "He would naturally say to himself, it is impossible that all this vehement and pathetic declamation can be without some colorable pretext." But search as he might, Hamilton's "stranger" was unable to locate a valid foundation for the *fear appeals* employed by the anti-Federalists. During the 20th century, the stranger often was a visitor from another planet. For example, in a November 1972 essay in *Harper's* Magazine on the Republican National Convention held that summer, novelist Kurt Vonnegut opened his remarks by speaking in the voice of "a visitor from another planet." Many films, although not technically employing the prosopopoeia strategy, capture its spirit as they try to use an alien's perspective to comment on American culture.[20]

Speaking in the voice of the dead is another common form of prosopopoeia. Knute Rockne spoke in George Gipp's voice and told his Notre Dame football team to "win one for the Gipper." A widow might use this strategy if, when speaking to her child, she says, "If your father were alive, I know he would say . . ." Clinton employed this strategy in his November 13, 1993, speech to the convocation of the Church of God in Christ meeting in Memphis, Tennessee, when he spoke to the ministers in the voice of King. The 18th-century American minister Jonathan Edwards employed this strategy with great zest as he asked his audiences to listen to the voices of those suffering in hell. Consider this passage from his well-known sermon, "Sinners in the Hands of an Angry God," in July 1741:

> If it were so that we could come to speak with them, and could inquire of them, one by one, whether they expected, when alive, and when they used to hear about hell, ever to be subjects of that misery, we, doubtless, should hear one and another reply, "No, I never intended to come here: I had laid out matters otherwise in my mind; I thought I should contrive well for myself; I thought my scheme good; I intended to take effectual care; but it came upon me unexpectedly; I did not look for it at that time, and in that manner; it came as a thief; death outwitted me . . ., then sudden destruction came upon me."

Prosopopoeia can have different functions. One common function is to introduce anticipated objections (prolepsis). Here is a passage from Douglass's "What to the Slave Is the Fourth of July" speech that illustrates this way of employing prosopopoeia:

> But I fancy I hear someone of my audience say, "It is just in this circumstance that you and your brother abolitionists fail to make a favorable impression on the public mind. Would you argue more and denounce less, would you persuade more and rebuke less, your cause would be much more likely to succeed."

Douglass then immediately responded to this anticipated objection: "But I submit, where all is plain there is nothing to be argued."

Synecdoche

Synecdoche is a form of *substitution* in which a part is used to represent the whole, as in "all hands on deck" (where the part [hands] stands in for the whole [person or crew]); the material out of which something is made is used to refer to the finished product, as in "raise the canvas" (where the material [canvas] stands in for the finished product [sail]); or the species is used to represent the larger genus, as in "give us this day our daily bread" (where the species [bread] stands in for the larger genus [food]).[21]

Tricolon

Tricolon is a pattern of three-part parallel repetition (phrases, clauses, or sentences). Lincoln's peroration in the "Gettysburg Address"—"government of the people, by the people, for the people, shall not perish from the earth"—employed the three-part tricolon structure embodied in the short prepositional phrases. Lincoln, of course, was borrowing the strategy (and sentiment) from Daniel Webster's January 26, 1830, speech on Foote's resolution: "The people government, made for the people, made by the people, and answerable to the people." Kennedy employed the pattern when discussing the issue of religion in his 1960 "New Frontier" speech: "I am telling you now what you are entitled to know: that my decisions on every public policy will be my own—as an American, a Democrat, and a free man." Lyndon Johnson's speechwriters often made him sound Kennedyesque through the use of tricolon, as in this passage from a July 1966 speech on American policy in Southeast Asia ("charted" to bring out the three-part parallelism and the way in which alliteration and epiphora reinforce it):

We are at war against the poverty	that deprives	him,
the unemployment	that degrades	him,
and the prejudice	that defies	him.

Ortman (1993) provided the following anonymous aphorisms that illustrate tricolon ("charted" to bring out the three-part parallelism):

Tell	me and I'll forget;	Stand up to be seen;
show	me and I may remember;	speak up to be heard;
involve	me and I'll understand.	shut up to be appreciated.

Notes

1. For a discussion of this trend, see Vickers (1988). For an example, see Dubois and colleagues (1981).

2. In rhetorical studies, see, for example, Hariman (1995), Leff (1983), and Leff and Sachs (1990). For a classic statement on this issue, see Wimsatt (1941).

3. For an alternative five-part scheme, see Myers (1996). For two alternative typologies, see Gibson (1966) and Myers (1996).

4. For an example of another larger scale pattern, see Boyer's (1992) discussion of an **apocalyptic** style.

5. On the potential rhetorical implications of sentence types and other basic grammatical categories, see also Weaver (1953).

6. This also is referred to as *reduplicatio.* Intense cases sometimes are termed *gradatio.*

7. This also is referred to as *hyperbaton.*

8. In addition to the examples discussed, consider Terrill's (2000) claim regarding "chiasmus in large scale" (p. 77) in Malcolm X's February 16, 1965, address in Rochester, New York.

9. This literally means to give up or yield.

10. This also is referred to as *diminutio* or *understatement.* see Fogelin (1987).

11. This also is referred to as *occultatio* or *paralepsis.*

12. In other words, the occupatio produces *comprobatio* or the strategy of flattering the audience.

13. Interestingly, Richardson (1987) perceived a similar tension between two different voices in the public speeches of Maria W. Stewart, an African American orator who preceded Grimké to the platform by approximately 5 years.

14. This also is referred to as *praemunitio* or the strategy of anticipation.

15. Leff and Goodwin (2000) argued that Lincoln's use of prolepsis, along with prosopopoeia, functioned as a form of "dialectical argument."

16. King employed a similar strategy in his "Letter From Birmingham Jail." In King's case, his refutation was explicitly marked; he was responding to the objections of eight white ministers published in a local newspaper.

17. Sloane (1997) observed that the Renaissance scholar/humanist Erasmus's "Letter to Mountjoy" on the subject of marriage made "frequent use of prolepsis or anticipatory refutation" (p. 81). This letter, published in 1518, is another excellent illustration of the proleptic strategy.

18. Prosopopoeia is derived from the Greek *prosopon* and *poein,* which together mean "to make a face." For a discussion of the complex relationship between personification and prosopopoeia, see Paxson (1994).

19. Hillary Rodham Clinton did something similar in her 1995 speech to the U.N. Conference on Women in Bejing, China.

20. Films in this tradition include the 1950s classic *The Day the Earth Stood Still* as well as the more recent *Starman* and *E.T.* and even the television show *Mork and Mindy.*

21. See Brummett's (1981) discussion of the role of synecdoche in political discourse.

References and Additional Reading

Aristotle. (1954). *Rhetoric* (W. R. Roberts, Trans.). New York: Modern Library.

Bass, J. D. (1992). The paranoid style in foreign policy: Ronald Reagan's control of the situation in Nicaragua. In M. Weiler & W. B. Pearce (Eds.), *Reagan and public discourse in America.* Tuscaloosa: University of Alabama Press.

Booth, W. C. (1974). *A rhetoric of irony.* Chicago: University of Chicago Press.

Bormann, E. G. (1985). *The force of fantasy: Restoring the American dream.* Carbondale: Southern Illinois University Press.

Boyer, P. (1992). *When times shall be no more: Prophecy belief in modern American culture.* Cambridge, MA: Harvard University Press.

Brown, H. (1966). *Prose styles: Five primary types.* Minneapolis: University of Minnesota Press.

Brummett, B. (1981). Gastronomic references, synecdoche, and political images. *Quarterly Journal of Speech, 67,* 138-145.

Bryant, D. C. (1957). Of style. *Western Speech, 21,* 103-110.

Burke, K. (1966). *Language as symbolic action: Essays on life, literature, and method.* Berkeley: University of California Press.

Campbell, K. K. (1973). The rhetoric of women's liberation: An oxymoron. *Quarterly Journal of Speech, 59,* 74-86.

Campbell, K. K. (1989). *Man cannot speak for her: A critical study of early feminist rhetoric* (Vol. 1). New York: Greenwood.

Carpenter, R. H. (1969). The essential schemes of syntax: An analysis of rhetorical theory's recommendations for uncommon word orders. *Quarterly Journal of Speech, 55,* 161-168.

Carpenter, R. H. (1990). America's tragic metaphor: Our twentieth-century combatants as frontiersmen. *Quarterly Journal of Speech, 76,* 1-22.

Carter, R., & Nash, W. (1990). *Seeing through language: A guide to styles of English writing.* London: Basil Blackwell.

Cooper, M. (1989). *Analyzing public discourse.* Prospect Heights, IL: Waveland.

Corbett, E. P. J. (1971). *Classical rhetoric for the modern student* (2nd ed.). New York: Oxford University Press.

DeVito, J. A. (1967). Style and stylistics: An attempt at definition. *Quarterly Journal of Speech, 53,* 248-255.

Dickinson, J. (1768). *Letters from a farmer in Pennsylvania.* Boston: Mein and Fleeming.

Dubois, J., Edeline, F., Klinkenberg, J.-M., Minguet, P., Pire, F., & Trinon, H. (1981). *A general rhetoric* (P. B. Burrell & E. M. Slotkin, Trans.). Baltimore, MD: Johns Hopkins University Press.

Emerson, R. W. (1979). Self-reliance. In R. W. Emerson, *Collected works of Ralph Waldo Emerson* (2nd ed.). Cambridge, MA: Harvard University Press. (Original work published 1841)

Fogelin, R. J. (1987). Some figures of speech. In F. H. van Eemeren, R. Grootendorst, J. A. Blair, & C. A. Willard (Eds.), *Argumentation: Across the lines of discipline.* Dordrecht, Netherlands: Foris Publications.

Gibson, W. (1966). *Tough, sweet, and stuffy: An essay on modern American prose style.* Bloomington: Indiana University Press.

Gunderson, R. G. (1977). The oxymoron strain in American rhetoric. *Central States Speech Journal, 28,* 92-95.

Gustafson, T. (1992). *Representative words: Politics, literature, and the American language, 1776-1865.* Cambridge, UK: Cambridge University Press.

Hariman, R. (1995). *Political style: The artistry of power.* Chicago: University of Chicago Press.

Hariman, R. (1996). Henry Kissinger: Realism's rational actor. In F. A. Beer & R. Hariman (Eds.), *Post-realism: The rhetorical turn in international affairs.* East Lansing: Michigan State University Press.

Hochmuth, M. (1955). The criticism of rhetoric. In M. Hochmuth (Ed.), *A history and criticism of American public address* (Vol. 3). New York: Longmans, Green.

Hofstadter, R. (1979). *The paranoid style in American politics and other essays.* Chicago: University of Chicago Press. (Original work published 1965)

Hutson, J. H. (1984). The origins of "The Paranoid Style in American Politics": Public jealousy from the age of Walpole to the age of Jackson. In D. D. Hall, J. M. Murrin, & T. W. Tate (Eds.), *Saints and revolutionaries: Essays on early American history.* New York: Norton.

Ivie, R. L. (1987). Metaphor and the rhetorical invention of cold war "idealists." *Communication Monographs, 54,* 165-182.

Jamieson, K. H. (1988). *Eloquence in an electronic age: The transformation of political speechmaking.* New York: Oxford University Press.

Japp, P. (1985). Esther or Isaiah? The abolitionist-feminist rhetoric of Angelina Grimké. *Quarterly Journal of Speech, 71,* 335-348.

Jasinski, J. (1992). Antithesis and oxymoron: Ronald Reagan's figurative rhetorical structure. In M. Weiler & W. B. Pearce (Eds.), *Reagan and public discourse in America.* Tuscaloosa: University of Alabama Press.

Jasinski, J. (1997). Rearticulating history in epideictic discourse: Frederick Douglass's "The Meaning of the Fourth of July to the Negro." In T. W. Benson (Ed.), *Rhetoric and political culture in nineteenth-century America.* East Lansing: Michigan State University Press.

Kennedy, G. A. (1980). *Classical rhetoric and its Christian and secular tradition from ancient to modern times.* Chapel Hill: University of North Carolina Press.

Kozy, J., Jr. (1970). The argumentative use of rhetorical figures. *Philosophy and Rhetoric, 3,* 141-151.

Lakoff, G., & Johnson, M. (1980). *Metaphors we live by.* Chicago: University of Chicago Press.

Lanham, R. A. (1983). *Analyzing prose.* New York: Scribner.

Lanham, R. A. (1991). *A handlist of rhetorical terms* (2nd ed.). Berkeley: University of California Press.

Leff, M. (1983). Topical invention and metaphoric interaction. *Southern Speech Communication Journal, 48,* 214-229.

Leff, M., & Goodwin, J. (2000). Dialogic figures and dialectical argument in Lincoln's rhetoric. *Rhetoric and Public Affairs, 3,* 59-69.

Leff, M., & Sachs, A. (1990). Words the most like things: Iconicity and the rhetorical text. *Western Journal of Speech Communication, 54,* 252-273.

Lewis, C. S. (1955). *Surprised by joy.* New York: Harcourt Brace Jovanovich.

Lopez, B. (1998). Apologia. In B. Lopez, *About the life: Journeys on the threshold of memory.* New York: Vintage. (Original work published 1990)

Martin, H. C. (1958). *The logic and rhetoric of exposition.* New York: Rinehart.

Muecke, D. C. (1969). *The compass of irony.* London: Methuen.

Muecke, D. C. (1970). *Irony.* London: Methuen.

Murphy, J. M. (1994). Republicanism in the modern age: Adlai Stevenson in the 1952 presidential campaign. *Quarterly Journal of Speech, 80,* 313-328.

Myers, M. (1996). Style and worldviews in literature and public discourse. In M. Myers, *Changing our minds: Negotiating English and literacy.* Urbana, IL: National Council of Teachers of English.

Nichols, M. H. (1971). Rhetoric and style. In J. Strelka (Ed.), *Patterns of literary style.* University Park: Pennsylvania State University Press.

Ortman, M. (1993). *Now that makes sense.* Kirkland, WA: Wise Owl Books.

Osborn, M. (1967). Archetypal metaphor in rhetoric: The light-dark family. *Quarterly Journal of Speech, 53,* 115-126.

Osborn, M. (1976). *Orientations to rhetorical style.* Chicago: SRA.

Osborn, M. (1977). The evolution of the archetypal sea in rhetoric and poetic. *Quarterly Journal of Speech, 63,* 347-363.

Paul, A. M. (1970). Figurative language. *Philosophy and Rhetoric, 3,* 225-248.

Paxson, J. J. (1994). *The poetics of personification.* Cambridge, UK: Cambridge University Press.

Perelman, C., & Olbrechts-Tyteca, L. (1969). *The new rhetoric* (J. Wilkinson & P. Weaver, Trans.). Notre Dame, IN: University of Notre Dame Press.

Plotnik, A. (1996). *The elements of expression.* New York: Henry Holt.

Quinn, A. (1982). *Figures of speech: Sixty ways to turn a phrase.* Salt Lake City, UT: Gibbs M. Smith.

Richards, I. A. (1936). *The philosophy of rhetoric.* New York: Oxford University Press.

Richardson, M. (1987). Introduction. In M. Richardson, *Maria W. Stewart: America's first black woman political writer.* Bloomington: Indiana University Press.

Robertson, A. W. (1995). *The language of democracy: Political rhetoric in the United States and Britain, 1790-1900.* Ithaca, NY: Cornell University Press.

Rosteck, T. (1992). Synecdoche and audience in *See It Now*'s "The Case of Milo Radulovich." *Southern Speech Communication Journal, 57,* 229-240.

Sanders, K. R., & Newman, R. P. (1971). James A. Stormer and the Hofstadter hypothesis. *Central States Speech Journal, 22,* 218-227.

Short, B. (1987). Comic book apologia: The "paranoid" rhetoric of Congressman George Hanson. *Western Journal of Speech Communication, 51,* 189-203.

Singh, R. (1997). *The Farrakhan phenomenon: Race, reaction, and the paranoid style in American politics.* Washington, DC: Georgetown University Press.

Sloane, T. O. (1997). *On the contrary: The protocol of traditional rhetoric.* Washington, DC: Catholic University of America Press.

Smith, C. A. (1977). The Hofstadter hypothesis revisited: The nature of evidence in politically "paranoid" discourse. *Southern Speech Communication Journal, 42,* 274-289.

Spencer, H. (1880). *Essays: Moral, political, and aesthetic* New York: D. Appleton.

Terrill, R. E. (2000). Colonizing the borderlands: Shifting circumference in the rhetoric of Malcolm X. *Quarterly Journal of Speech, 86,* 67-85.

Vickers, B. (1988). *In defense of rhetoric.* Oxford, UK: Clarendon.

Weaver, R. (1953). Some rhetorical aspects of grammatical categories. In R. Weaver, *The ethics of rhetoric.* South Bend, IN: Regnery/Gateway.

Wells, R. (1960). Nominal and verbal style. In T. A. Sebeok (Ed.), *Style in language.* Cambridge, MA: MIT Press.

Williams, J. M. (1990). *Style: Toward grace and clarity.* Chicago: University of Chicago Press.

Wimsatt, W. K., Jr. (1941). Style as meaning. In W. K. Wimsatt, Jr., *The prose style of Samuel Johnson.* New Haven, CT: Yale University Press.

Winterowd, W. R. (1970). Style: A matter of manner. *Quarterly Journal of Speech, 66,* 161-167.

Wood, G. S. (1982). Conspiracy and the paranoid style: Causality and deceit in the eighteenth century. *William and Mary Quarterly, 39,* 401-441. (Series 3)

SUBJECT/SUBJECTIVITY

"The so-called 'I' is merely a unique combination of partially conflicting 'corporate we's.' . . . Sometimes these various corporate identities work fairly well together. At other times they conflict, with disturbing moral consequences." Burke (1984, p. 264) published these thoughts on human "identity" or the nature of human subjectivity in *Attitudes Towards History* (originally published in 1937). Students of Burke's work are accustomed to the way in which he uncannily anticipated many of the issues and trends in contemporary social and critical theory. His fairly brief comments on identity in *Attitudes* are another example of Burke's proleptic power.[1]

The nature of human **subjectivity,** or what it means to be a discrete person or human **subject,** is a central issue in much current social and critical theory with important implications for rhetorical studies. Contemporary discussions of this topic frequently begin by uncovering the purportedly basic features or the essence of the *modern individual.* Sarup (1989) began his introduction to postmodernism by remarking that the term *individual* "dates from the Renaissance and presupposes that man [sic] is a free, intellectual agent and that thinking processes are not coerced by historical or cultural circumstances" (p. 1). Similarly, McKerrow (1993) wrote,

> In the modern world, dominated by Cartesian rationality, the subject, both in its empirical, physical presence to the world and in its transcendental "I," occupies center stage. A subject, conscious of its own presence in the world and actively engaged in thought about the world, operates as the originator of action. (p. 54)

Kamberelis and Scott (1992) focused on the tradition of *liberal humanist* thought (considered to be one of the pillars of modernity) and remarked that, within that tradition, "subjectivity has been conceived as a transcendent consciousness that functions unencumbered by social and material conditions and that is the source of all knowledge and the agent of all action. Such a self is unified, coherent, autonomous, and noncontradictory" (p. 360). Finally, Calhoun (1994) noted a modern tendency to conceive of the self in "essentialist" terms stipulating that "individual persons can have singular, integral, altogether harmonious and unproblematic identities" (p. 13). Even scholars who reconstruct a more complex and complicated history of the modern subject and modern subjectivity (e.g., Cascardi, 1992; Taylor, 1989) reach many of these same conclusions. As Foucault (1972) wrote, in the modern world, the subject is sovereign (p. 12).

There is, as Soper (1986) observed, a decidedly *anthropocentric* drift to humanism and to the modern view of the human subject. That is, gradually over the past 300 or 400 years, people began to perceive that humans, both individually and collectively, were the most important thing or entity in the world. Soper continued, "Such anthropocentrism has now itself come under attack from the 'anti-humanists' on the grounds that it mythologizes the object—humankind—of which it aspires to provide a rational or scientific understanding" (p. 11). This growing "attack" not only has challenged the idea that humans are the most essential ingredient in the world but also has given rise to a serious and sustained interrogation of the concept of the individual self or subject. Increasingly over the past few decades, scholars are asking whether or not the individual self is as autonomous, purposeful, unified, coherent, and harmonious as once was thought to be the case.

The anti-humanist turn that Soper described did not develop overnight. Contemporary scholars point to an important line of thinkers—Nietzsche, Marx, Freud, Heidegger, Althusser, Lacan, Foucault, and Derrida, to name a few of the most cited ones—who have contributed to this intellectual development.

The contributions of traditions such as sociology and social psychology, traditions from which Burke derived much inspiration, often are overlooked. Calhoun (1994) observed that "a sociologist is apt to think that the new poststructuralist rhetoric of 'subject positions' and 'enactments' is an unnecessary reinvention of the familiar vocabulary of status and role" (p. 12). To gain some additional perspective on the emergence of the anti-humanist critique of the human subject, as well as to avoid some potential confusion, a brief detour into American social psychology is warranted.

A key figure in the development of sociology and social psychology in the United States was George Herbert Mead.[2] Human communication, in Mead's view, is essential to the emergence of a self. Mead (1934) wrote, "It is impossible to conceive of a self arising outside of social experience" (p. 140). He insisted, "The self is essentially a social structure, and it arises in social experience" (p. 141). What he termed "significant speech" was a crucial component in the social experience that produced the self. Mead continued,

> We carry on a whole series of different relationships to different people. We are one thing to one man [sic] and another thing to another. There are parts of the self which exist only for the self in relationship to itself. We divide ourselves up in all sorts of different selves with reference to our acquaintances. We discuss politics with one and religion with another. There are all sorts of different selves answering to all sorts of different social reactions. It is the social process itself that is responsible for the appearance of the self; it is not there as a self apart from this type of experience. (p. 142)

He concluded, "A multiple personality is in a certain sense normal" (p. 142).

In the language of contemporary social and critical theory, Mead has, to a degree, "decentered" the self. That is, by insisting that selves arise only through social interaction, Mead helped to destroy the image of an autonomous, self-sufficient individual; he argued that an individual becomes the type of person he or she is not through some act of individual will but rather through interaction with others. A person's identity as an individual depends on his or her interaction with other people. Furthermore, Mead recognized a degree of fragmentation within any individual self. Mead (1934) wrote, "There are all sorts of different selves answering to all sorts of different social reactions" (p. 142). These different selves, or social *roles* (e.g., student, roommate, sister, employee), raise questions about the degree of harmony or unity within an individual self. But as Calhoun (1994) pointed out, it is at this point that we can perceive the key difference between Mead's more rudimentary form of decentering and contemporary manifestations. Calhoun observed that "most versions of role theory tacitly posited a kind of ontological independence of the individual from his/her various roles" (p. 13). There is, in other words, a core self that is separate from the various roles that a person may inhabit or enact that embodies the essence of the person.

This seemed to be Mead's (1934) position. Recall the passage from *Mind, Self, and Society* noted earlier: "A multiple personality is *in a certain sense* normal" (emphasis added). What did Mead mean by the qualifier "in a certain sense"? Fragmentation exists, but it appears to be contained in Mead's view by a more encompassing sense of "a unified self" (p. 143). He wrote,

> The unity and structure of the complete self reflects the unity and structure of the social process as a whole. . . . The various elementary selves which constitute, or are organized into, a complete self are the various aspects of the structure of that complete self answering to the various aspects of the structure of the social process as a whole; the structure of the complete self is thus a reflection of the complete social process. (p. 144)

Mead's belief that there is some core self behind or beneath the various roles that one might assume was further reflected in his discussion, following the earlier work of James (1890), of the "I" and "me" as the basic constituent elements of the self (Mead, 1934, pp. 173-178, 192-200). In broad terms, Mead saw the "me" as an internalized expression of the attitudes of others that is continually being reconstructed as an individual moves between different spheres of activity and social roles. On the other hand, although the "I" develops through social interaction, it functions as a point of stability or as an anchor; it is the essence of an individual's uniqueness.

Contemporary accounts of the subject and human subjectivity agree with Mead's general position that the individual self is a social creature. But they differ from Mead's more rudimentary form of decentering by denying that there is any "I" or any core or essential sense of identity with, in Calhoun's (1994) terms, "ontological independence." Individuals simply are the collection of socially constructed roles, or *subject positions,* that they find themselves inhabiting. Consider how some contemporary theorists define the self/subject. Culler (1975) wrote that "subjectivity is not so much a personal core as an intersubjectivity, the track or the furrow left by texts of all kinds" (p. 140). Smith (1988) defined the subject as "the series or the conglomeration of *positions,* subject positions, provisional and not necessarily indefeasible, into which a person is called momentarily by the discourses and the world that he/she inhabits" (p. xxxv).[3] In a similar vein, Wess (1996) argued that the "subject consists of a conjuncture of conflicting motivational discourses in a single body" (pp. 22-23), and Cascardi (1992) maintained that "the subject exists at the intersection of a series of discourses or cultural spheres" (p. 2). Collection, conglomeration, conjuncture, and intersection appear over and over in contemporary discussions of human subjectivity; these terms try to describe what it means to exist as a decentered subject. Socially constructed and lacking any coherent essential core, the individual subject no longer is accorded the central status it once held. It is considered to be not the cause or originator of action but rather the effect of action (see also the essays collected in Battaglia, 1995).

An exhaustive or even modestly thorough account of the various important issues stemming from the postmodern reconceptualization of human subjectivity is well beyond the scope of this entry. But a few key issues and questions merit some additional attention. First, let us return for a moment to Mead's (1934) observation that "a multiple personality is in a certain sense normal." Many contemporary thinkers would agree with this claim provided that Mead's qualifier is deleted. Decentering the subject contributes to a conception of subjectivity as essentially contested. This sense of *contested subjectivity* is reflected in Wess's (1996) discussion of the "crisis among subject positions" (p. 195) and in Smith's (1988) account of "the contradictions and disturbances in and among subject positions" (p. xxxv). Therborn (1980) illustrated the idea of contested subjectivity in his discussion of how a labor organizer must persuade his or her audience to identify with the subject position of "worker" rather than with some other position (e.g., Catholic, citizen, father/mother). Scholars such as Wess (1996) admit the possibility of a "contingent hierarchy" (pp. 25, 146)[4] of subject positions eventuating in a type of locally stable self; the possibility of locally stable selves is a type of midpoint between the modernist or humanist idea of the completely unified self and an extreme form of decentering that sees the subject as completely fragmented and beset by internal conflicts.[5]

Scholars influenced by the French philosopher Louis Althusser's concept of **interpellation** (e.g., Charland, 1987) tend to emphasize how discourse inserts people into particular subject positions or how discourse is used to negotiate issues of contested subjectivity. Individuals (or at least *most* individuals) are depicted as passive; the discourse of others (e.g., social and political elites, the "state," religious institutions) "positions" us in specific ways. As McKerrow (1993) noted, "The subject that does exist as displaced appears passive as the result of forces not of its own making" (p. 58). In other words, individuals become "workers" or "students" as an effect of discourse practice. For example, the economic and business discourse of a nation both shapes and inserts individuals into the position of workers, and the discourse of a university both shapes and inserts individuals into the position of students (at that institution). But is it possible for an individual to use discourse to position himself or herself—to engage in a process that Greenblatt (1980) labeled "self-fashioning" and Foucault (1988) referred to as a "technology" for constituting the self? Can a person, in short, use discourse to create his or her self? This is an extremely controversial issue in the broad realm of contemporary social and critical theory. A number of scholars who reject the traditional or modern view of the autonomous individual nevertheless maintain that individual subjects exert at least some control or direction over their identities. For example, Giddens (1979) maintained that "to study the production of the text is at the same time in a definite sense to study the production of its author. . . . The 'author' helps constitute him- or herself through the text via the very process of production of that text" (pp. 43-44).[6] Giddens tried to make clear that his position was not "a return to a form of subjectivism" but rather an effort "to promote *a recovery of the subject* without lapsing into subjectivism" (p. 44). As Soper (1986) suggested, individuals are "both 'makers' and 'made' " (p. 151); put differently, individual identity or the individual self is forged through a never-ending interaction of self-fashioning (creating a sense of self through discourse) and interpellation (being positioned or inserted into subject positions by discourse).[7]

A crucial issue for Giddens and others sharing this perspective on the subject is the status accorded to the *intentions* of an author or a speaker.[8] As Scott (1980) noted, "Traditionally, rhetorical theory has taken the intention of a speaker, either actual or potential, as the starting place of analysis and the focus for synthesis" (p. 53). He wrote, "To say that intention is an unexamined assumption in the notion of persuasive discourse throughout classical literature is not too great an oversimplification" (p. 40). For some scholars, decentering the subject means a complete rejection of the idea of intentions, with the concept of intentions being linked to the discredited modernist sense of subjectivity. But the works of Giddens and others illustrate a different and narrower sense of decentering. Giddens indicated that it is possible to retain the idea of intentions, and include them as a factor in various forms of social or critical analysis, but refuse to grant them absolute priority or a privileged position. We can see this type of decentering frequently in our everyday lives. Imagine that an individual says something that hurts another person's feelings. The individual might try to diffuse the situation by denying that it was his or her intention to hurt the other person's feelings (this is common in the **genre** of the **apologia**). But is this always sufficient? It might be in some cases, but in other cases the person whose feelings were hurt might bracket the individual's intentions, decenter the individual, and insist that he or she be held accountable for the impact or result of the statement despite the purported lack of any cruel intentions. In short, we commit to the principle that all action, and the meanings that we derive from that action, is not completely controlled or determined by the person who is acting. And this principle is part of what scholars mean when they talk about decentering the subject. Or, consider a different case. Imagine that an individual does something that another person considers to be dumb, so the other person asks the individual why he or she did it. But for any of a number of different reasons, the other person doubts that the intention that is related is the "real" reason for individual's behavior. Perhaps the individual is so embarrassed by the behavior that he or she refuses to disclose the real reason for the behavior. Or, the other person might reach another conclusion. Perhaps the individual does not know what his or her real intention was. If the other person reaches this conclusion, then he or she again is demonstrating a form of decentering by removing intention from the center of the "analysis" of the situation. With intention decentered, the other person starts to explore other explanations that might account for the individual's behavior. And this decentering is at the heart of Burke's work, according to Wess (1996), who wrote that Burke's "new rhetoric decenters the rhetor in introducing a level of motivation beyond its deliberate control" (p. 189). The concept of **motive,** so central to Burke's work, is understandable only in the context of Burke's implicit decentering of intentionality.

The discussion of intention in the preceding paragraph leads to another key issue in contemporary discussions of subjectivity—the possibility of human agency. What capacity, if any, do individuals possess for novel or creative action? The anti-humanist attack on the autonomous individual is taken, by some, to also entail an attack on the possibility for human action. In some of its extreme forms, the decentered subject becomes a marionette whose actions are completely determined by those cultural forces that effectively are "pulling the strings." Some feminists have been particularly sensitive to the implications of the critique of modernist subjectivity. Harstock (1989-1990), for example, noted the irony in the (mostly male) attack on the concept of the individual subject just as women were beginning to emerge as potent subjects and active participants in public life. The recurrent danger, as the passage from Giddens (1979) noted earlier recognizes, is that as soon as one starts talking about the topic of human agency (and related issues such as choice and rhetorical **invention**), there is the possibility of lapsing back into an essentialistic subjectivism.

One of the most sustained and rigorous attempts to theorize the possibility of human agency in the context of decentered subjectivity can be found in Smith's (1988) *Discerning the Subject.* Smith contended that "all notions of the 'subject' as essentially subjected and dominated need to be questioned" (p. 154). He wrote, "The interpellation of the 'subject' into oppressed positions is not complete and monolithic; rather, interpellation also produces contradiction and negativity" (p. 152). Smith maintained that what was described earlier as contested subjectivity—the tensions that exist between the subject positions into which individuals are inserted—is an inevitable part of the process of interpellation. And these tensions serve, in Smith's view, as the conditions for human agency; human action emerges as part of a complex (and, to a certain degree, unconscious) response to the experience of "contradiction and negativity." As individuals experience the tensions between, say, the subject position of workers in a petrochemical plant and the position of residents in the community where the plant is located, the possibility of action or agency is generated (in terms of this example, the result is what sometimes is called the "environmental justice" movement). A question worth considering might be to what degree Smith's approach to the question of human agency is a radical reformulation of the psychological doctrine of *cognitive dissonance.*

Another question to consider regarding Smith's position is the degree to which it limits action to resistance—to efforts at thwarting domination and oppression—and neglects to consider the need for affirmative forms of action. McKerrow (1993), for example, noted the problem of raising resistance "to heroic status" (p. 63). Smith denied that his position valorizes resistance in this way. He wrote, "To exploit the negativity which, I've claimed, constitutes the links of the 'subject's' colligations is not to privilege the action of resistant or rebellious will" (p. 157). Notice, however, that Smith's point was to not privilege the resistant *will* (as a type of mental capacity or faculty). As such, the overall thrust of his project remained constant—to uncover the "conditions of *oppositional* practice" (p. 158, emphasis added). The question for rhetorical scholars is how Smith's account of agency (or other possible accounts) helps to reveal the possibilities for affirmative advocacy (e.g., a vision of the "common good") as well as the possibilities for discursive resistance to oppressive realities.

The issue raised at the end of the preceding paragraph leads to the final topic to be considered. Simply put, what is the significance of the reconceptualized individual—the subject—for rhetorical studies? This question, like the general topic of subjectivity, merits extensive discussion beyond the scope of this entry. But we can focus on three specific issues where the concept of the subject has had an impact on the field: (a) critical practice, (b) rhetorical **invention,** and (c) the traditional concept of **ethos.**

Recent work by Gaonkar (1993, 1997)[9] has brought the issue of the subject to the center of discussion in the realm of rhetorical criticism. One of Gaonkar's (1997) central claims was that critical practice in rhetorical studies tends to be shaped by an "ideology of human agency" (p. 336) that, in attributing all textual details to the work of "authorial cunning" (p. 352), inadvertently defers the text and disables critical practice. Gaonkar maintained that "to insist on individual consciousness and its contents as the originary site of public discourse . . . is surely to cripple the critical enterprise before it gets off the ground" (p. 337). According to Gaonkar, robust critical practice in rhetorical studies needs to decenter or displace the authorial subject so as to "engage the public text as a cultural artifact" (p. 352). Gaonkar's position is generally understood as representing the postmodern movement in scholarship. But hints of his position can be found in earlier rhetorical scholarship. Scott (1976), for example, maintained that rhetorical scholarship "will be much too limited by taking a speaker-oriented rhetoric only. . . . If there is a new social rhetoric, it must be rooted firmly in an enlarged notion of rhetorical roles" (p. 260). Gaonkar's position may be both a radicalization of ideas that have been circulating in the field for 20 years and an effort to incorporate recent insights in postmodern social theory.

As the preceding discussion has suggested, there is some ambiguity as to what decentering the authorial subject means in critical practice. Campbell (1997) argued that when decentering involves the complete elimination of the subject, it is "nonsense" (p. 121) but allows for other forms of bracketing authors and/or speakers in ways that, as Gaonkar argued, foster critical practice. Campbell seemed to endorse the position of Soper described earlier: Individuals are both "makers and made" or beings that create and get created. But then Campbell suggested that the *real* function of rhetorical criticism is to study individuals as "makers" or "points of origin" rather than as bodies inserted into subject positions (p. 123). One ongoing challenge for rhetorical critics is to determine ways of integrating these rival, but linked, perspectives on the subject in critical practice.

Alterations in how we think about the individual person or subject also have an impact on how the process of discursive invention can be conceptualized. The postmodern challenge calls into question a *romantic* model of invention that explains the act of discursive creation as the result of individual "genius" or inspiration. Invention, like the subject, has to be understood as a *social* process (LeFevre, 1987). Some strands in contemporary critical thought provide alternatives to the model of romantic genius. Such alternatives include a Bakhtinian view of the author as "orchestrator" or organizer of social languages and voices[10] and the concept of the rhetor as **bricoleur** proposed by scholars affiliated with the **critical rhetoric** movement.[11] The images of orchestrator and bricoleur both emphasize how authors, speakers, and advocates all exist in a world saturated by texts, images, arguments, narratives, and tropes and figures of speech. In such a world, the individual does not always, or even usually, create something "new"; instead, the aspiring speaker, writer, or advocate works with the discursive materials at hand, taking bits of material from various sources and configuring them into a rhetorical utterance.

Finally, how does the reconceptualization of the subject fit with the traditional concept of **ethos** or character? To a certain extent, the postmodern view of subjectivity challenges the relevance of the concept of character. That is, if character is understood as something that is stable and unchanging, or something that is essential to an individual's identity, then the postmodern approach would encourage a skeptical response that challenges the underlying ideas of stability or essence. Postmodern theorists argue that there is no essence, only the shifting configurations or conjunctures of subject positions that we inhabit from moment to moment. But just as there appears to be an important interaction, or **dialectic,** between the sense of individual as maker and the sense of individual as something that is made, there might be a way of conceptualizing the relationship between ethos or character and subjectivity dialectically, thereby overcoming an either/or binary opposition. The postmodern concepts of the subject and subject positions are fundamentally *spatial* and *synchronic.* A common image, the individual as a "point of intersection" (Gaonkar, 1993), captures the spatial aspect of postmodern thinking. The individual exists in a space carved out from a series of different positions. At any particular moment, the individual exists in a space that is carved out for him or her and that the individual also helps to carve out for himself or herself. These spaces are synchronic to the degree that they have no connection with one another over time. The space/position that a person inhabits today has no clear relationship to the spaces/positions that the person inhabited yesterday or those that he or she will inhabit tomorrow. But it is equally possible to alter our perspective and think about the individual in *temporal* and *diachronic* terms. The individual not only exists in a particular space or position but also exists *over time;* the individual lives through blocks of time organized in different ways (e.g., episodes in a relationship, terms of office, prison sentences). And the existence in time is diachronic to the degree that there is some relationship between events that happen at different points in time. The concepts of ethos and character speak to our sense of ourselves as temporal creatures who experience diachronic connections between events.[12] In short, an individual not only exists *in* a subject position but also exists *as* a flow or movement between such positions. Just as there is conflict in the form of contested subjectivity at specific points in time (e.g., between the demands of being a "good soldier" and those of being an "ethical person" during a war), there also can be temporal conflict within a subject position (e.g., as an individual's understanding of what being a "good soldier" means is put into dispute and changes) and between subject positions (e.g., when an individual who acts as a "ruthless businessman" one day is pushed into the position of "concerned parent" the next day). Critical scholarship might profitably be directed at uncovering the ways in which subjectivity is constructed and contested in space (synchronically) and over time (diachronically). Subjectivity and ethos need not, then, be understood as antagonistic concepts; each emphasizes a different dimension of what it means to be human.

Notes

1. For extended discussions of Burke's thinking on the nature of subjectivity, see Biesecker (1997), Jameson (1978), and Wess (1996).

2. For Mead's influence on the development of rhetorical studies and speech communication scholarship, see Arnold and Frandsen (1983).

3. On the discursive character of subject positions, see Laclau and Mouffe (1985).

4. See also Biesecker's (1992) discussion of the "provisional stabilization" of the subject.

5. On this issue, see Laclau and Mouffe's (1985) distinction between the "*dispersion* of subject positions" and "an effective *separation* among them" (p. 116). See also Miller's (1993) account of the tensions between the positions of "citizen" and "consumer" in contemporary society. In critical scholarship, two studies of Deborah Sampson Gannett's 1802 lecture tour in the United States indirectly address the issue of contested subjectivity. As Campbell (1995) noted, in Gannett's public performance, "Woman and warrior [are] at war . . ., embodying and enacting two conflicting selves and speaking in two competing voices" (p. 490). See also Gustafson's (2000) discussion of Gannett (pp. 246-257).

6. On this issue, see also Kamberelis and Scott's (1992) discussion of the "coarticulation of texts and subjectivities."

7. On this interaction, see also Montrose's (1989) discussion of the duality inherent in the process of *subjectification* and Butler's (1997) account of the "paradoxical" process of *subjection*.

8. For a recent overview on this topic, see Lyons (1995).

9. See also Biesecker (1992) and McKerrow (1993).

10. See Kamberelis and Scott (1992) and the entries for **heteroglossia** and **polyphony**.

11. See Charland (1991) and the entry for **bricolage**.

12. Carr (1986), MacIntyre (1981), and Schectman (1996) discussed the way in which **narratives** organize an individual's temporal experience, encouraging us to think, in MacIntyre's (1981) terms, "of a human life as a narrative unity" (p. 211).

References and Additional Reading

Arnold, C. C., & Frandsen, K. D. (1983). Conceptions of rhetoric and communication. In C. C. Arnold & J. W. Bowers (Eds.), *Handbook of rhetorical and communication theory.* Boston: Allyn & Bacon.

Battaglia, D. (Ed.). (1995). *Rhetorics of self-making.* Berkeley: University of California Press.

Biesecker, B. (1992). Coming to terms with recent attempts to write women into the history of rhetoric. *Philosophy and Rhetoric, 25,* 140-161.

Biesecker, B. A. (1997). *Addressing postmodernity: Kenneth Burke, rhetoric, and a theory of social change.* Tuscaloosa: University of Alabama Press.

Burke, K. (1984). *Attitudes toward history* (3rd ed.). Berkeley: University of California Press.

Butler, J. (1997). *The psychic life of power: Theories in subjection.* Stanford, CA: Stanford University Press.

Cadava, E., Connor, P., & Nancy, J. L. (Eds.). (1991). *Who comes after the subject?* New York: Routledge.

Calhoun, C. (1994). Social theory and the politics of identity. In C. Calhoun (Ed.), *Social theory and the politics of identity.* Cambridge, UK: Blackwell.

Campbell, J. A. (1997). Strategic reading: Rhetoric, intention, and interpretation. In A. G. Gross & W. M. Keith (Eds.), *Rhetorical hermeneutics: Invention and interpretation in the age of science.* Albany: State University of New York Press.

Campbell, K. K. (1995). Gender and genre: Loci of invention and contradiction in the earliest speeches by U.S. women. *Quarterly Journal of Speech, 81,* 479-495.

Carr, D. (1986). *Time, narrative, and history.* Bloomington: Indiana University Press.

Cascardi, A. J. (1992). *The subject of modernity.* Cambridge, UK: Cambridge University Press.

Charland, M. (1987). Constitutive rhetoric: The case of the peuple Québécois. *Quarterly Journal of Speech, 73,* 133-150.

Charland, M. (1991). Finding a horizon and telos: The challenge to critical rhetoric. *Quarterly Journal of Speech, 77,* 71-74.

Culler, J. (1975). *Structuralist poetics: Structuralism, linguistics, and the study of literature.* Ithaca, NY: Cornell University Press.

Farrell, F. B. (1994). *Subjectivity, realism, and postmodernism: The recovery of the world.* Cambridge, UK: Cambridge University Press.

Foucault, M. (1972). *The archaeology of knowledge* (A. M. Sheridan Smith, Trans.). New York: Pantheon.

Foucault, M. (1988). Technologies of the self. In L. H. Martin, H. Gutman, & P. H. Hutton (Eds.), *Technologies of the self: A seminar with Michel Foucault.* Amherst: University of Massachusetts Press.

Gaonkar, D. P. (1993). The idea of rhetoric in the rhetoric of science. *Southern Communication Journal, 58,* 258-295.

Gaonkar, D. P. (1997). Close readings of the third kind: Reply to my critics. In A. G. Gross & W. M. Keith (Eds.), *Rhetorical hermeneutics: Invention and interpretation in the age of science.* Albany: State University of New York Press.

Gergen, K. J. (1991). *The saturated self: Dilemmas of identity in contemporary life.* New York: Basic Books.

Giddens, A. (1979). *Central problems in social theory: Action, structure, and contradiction in social analysis.* Berkeley: University of California Press.

Giddens, A. (1991). *Modernity and self-identity: Self and society in the late modern age.* Stanford, CA: Stanford University Press.

Greenblatt, S. (1980). *Renaissance self-fashioning.* Chicago: University of Chicago Press.

Gustafson, S. M. (2000). *Eloquence is power: Oratory and performance in early America.* Chapel Hill: University of North Carolina Press.

Hall, S. (1996). Introduction: Who needs "identity"? In S. Hall & P. du Gay (Eds.), *Questions of cultural identity.* London: Sage.

Harstock, N. (1989-1990). Postmodernism and political change: Issues for feminist theory. *Cultural Critique,* No. 14, pp. 15-33.

James, W. (1890). *The principles of psychology.* New York: Henry Holt.

Jameson, F. R. (1978). The symbolic inference: Or, Kenneth Burke and ideological analysis. *Critical Inquiry, 4,* 507-523.

Kamberelis, G., & Scott, K. D. (1992). Other people's voices: The coarticulation of texts and subjectivities. *Linguistics and Education, 4,* 359-403.

Laclau, E., & Mouffe, C. (1985). *Hegemony and socialist strategy: Towards a radical democratic politics.* London: Verso.

Langsdorf, L. (1997). Refusing individuality: How human beings are made into subjects. *Communication Theory, 7,* 321-342.

LeFevre, K. B. (1987). *Invention as a social act.* Carbondale: Southern Illinois University Press.

Lyons, W. (1995). *Approaches to intentionality.* Oxford, UK: Clarendon.

MacIntyre, A. (1981). *After virtue: A study in moral theory.* Notre Dame, IN: University of Notre Dame Press.

McKerrow, R. E. (1993). Critical rhetoric and the possibility of the subject. In I. Angus & L. Langsdorf (Eds.), *The critical turn: Rhetoric and philosophy in postmodern discourse.* Carbondale: Southern Illinois University Press.

Mead, G. H. (1934). *Mind, self, and society.* Chicago: University of Chicago Press.

Miller, T. (1993). *The well-tempered self: Citizenship, culture, and the postmodern subject.* Baltimore, MD: Johns Hopkins University Press.

Montrose, L. (1989). Professing the Renaissance: The poetics and politics of culture. In H. A. Veeser (Ed.), *The new historicism.* New York: Routledge.

Ransom, J. S. (1997). *Foucault's discipline: The politics of subjectivity.* Durham, NC: Duke University Press.

Sarup, M. (1989). *An introductory guide to poststructuralism and postmodernism.* Athens: University of Georgia Press.

Schectman, M. (1996). *The constitution of selves.* Ithaca, NY: Cornell University Press.

Schrag, C. O. (1986). *Communicative praxis and the space of subjectivity.* Bloomington: Indiana University Press.

Scott, R. L. (1976). On viewing rhetoric as epistemic: Ten years later. *Central States Speech Journal, 27,* 258-266.

Scott, R. L. (1980). Intentionality in the rhetorical process. In E. E. White (Ed.), *Rhetoric in transition: Studies in the nature and uses of rhetoric.* University Park: Pennsylvania State University Press.

Smith, P. (1988). *Discerning the subject.* Minneapolis: University of Minnesota Press.

Soper, K. (1986). *Humanism and anti-humanism.* London: Hutchinson.

Steele, M. (1997). *Theorizing textual subjects: Agency and oppression.* Cambridge, UK: Cambridge University Press.

Taylor, C. (1989). *Sources of the self: The making of the modern identity.* Cambridge, MA: Harvard University Press.

Therborn, G. (1980). *The ideology of power and the power of ideology.* London: Verso.

Wess, R. (1996). *Kenneth Burke: Rhetoric, subjectivity, postmodernism.* Cambridge, UK: Cambridge University Press.

T

TEXT

The questions "What is a text?" and "What is the nature of a rhetorical text?" admit different levels of complexity. A simple answer to the first question would be that a **text** is a discrete communicative act or a specific message. A poem, a letter to a friend (or, more commonly today, an e-mail message), an essay in a magazine, a newspaper editorial, a book (anything from a recipe book to a philosophical treatise on the nature of human knowledge)—all of these are specific discrete messages or texts. A simple answer to the second question ("What is the nature of a rhetorical text?") is commonly framed in one of two ways. First, a simple definition of a rhetorical text is that it is a speech or an oratorical performance (typically, one that has been transcribed or recorded in some manner and re-embodied in print). Abraham Lincoln's "Gettysburg Address," Elizabeth Cady Stanton's "The Solitude of Self" speech, and Malcolm X's "The Ballot or the Bullet" speech all are speech or rhetorical texts. A second common way of identifying the nature of a rhetorical text is to focus on function. Functionally, rhetorical texts are defined as those messages that manifest a relatively clear persuasive intention and/or objective. A television commercial by a political candidate soliciting votes, a newspaper ad on the dangers of gun control from the National Rifle Association, a pamphlet on the virtues of reproductive choice distributed by Planned Parenthood, a newspaper opinion editorial from the president of a local teachers union asking voters to defeat a property tax cap referendum, a sermon by a local minister on the evils of abortion, and a speech by a community organizer at a rally trying to generate support for a homeless shelter all manifest a rather clear persuasive function and satisfy the second common way of identifying a rhetorical text.

But as one might expect, these questions can lead to a host of complicated conceptual issues. Although the simple answers just outlined are sufficient for certain limited purposes (e.g., the answers probably are a satisfactory way of identifying the materials to be studied in an undergraduate course in American public address or contemporary public advocacy), they do not provide an adequate conceptual grounding for careful and rigorous critical inquiry in rhetorical studies. Despite the potential difficulties involved, further reflection on these basic questions is warranted.

This process of reflection on the questions "What is a text?" and "What is the nature of a rhetorical text?" can be organized through a third question that tries to identify the fundamental conceptual issues at stake on the topic of the text: "What is the *ontic* or *ontological* status of a rhetorical text?" Put as simply as possible, the terms *ontic* and *ontological* in this question try to identify the essential qualities or characteristics of something (ontology generally is understood as the study of human existence or human *being*). For example, to pose the question "What is the ontic or ontological status of a rhetorical text?" is to ask the question: "What is the essence—what are the essential properties or characteristics—of a text and, more specifically, of a rhetorical text?"[1]

One way of approaching this question is to trace the various conceptualizations of text and rhetorical text that have been developed by scholars in the contemporary tradition of rhetorical studies. During the formative period of contemporary rhetorical studies in the first quarter of the 20th century, two strategies for circumscribing the nature of the rhetorical text were clearly evident. In key essays by Hudson (1923) and Wichelns (1925/1962), the essence of the rhetorical text was (a) clarified by way of an *antithetical* comparison to the poetic or literary text and (b) associated with its purportedly unique function (cf. Gaonkar, 1990). For Hudson, Wichelns, and many of the modern founders of rhetorical studies, there existed a clear opposition between poetry (aesthetic discourse in general) and rhetoric. In the emerging language of literary **new criticism,** the aesthetic text (e.g., the poem, the novel, the short story) was thought to possess the following essential attributes or characteristics. It was autotelic (an end in itself and lacking in didactic purpose), autonomous or self-sufficient (a structured, unified, and self-contained whole rather than an assemblage of parts), coherent (with all elements contributing toward realizing its end, an idea that was commonly embodied in an organic *metaphor* that compared the poem or literary work with a living thing whose parts worked together in harmony), and stable (with its value not depending on the historical situation given that the aesthetic text was thought to transcend its situation). The rhetorical text lacked these characteristics. In a famous passage, Wichelns (1925/1962) wrote, "For poetry always is free to fulfill its own law [i.e., it is autotelic], but the writer of rhetorical discourse is, in a sense, perpetually in bondage to the occasion and the audience; and in that fact we find the line of cleavage between rhetoric and poetry" (p. 212). But Wichelns' strategy of definition by negation said very little about the essential features or nature of the rhetorical text. What Wichelns did was define the nature of the rhetorical text by its function (persuasion) and by its end. And the end of rhetoric, Wichelns insisted, was *effect.* But in effect, the two-part strategy of Wichelns and the other founders of the field led to a deferral of the central question as to the ontic status of the rhetorical text. Wichelns told us what the rhetorical text is not (it is not poetic) and what it does (it produces persuasive effects), but he sidestepped the problem of the status or nature of the rhetorical text.

As Gaonkar (1989) and others have noted, the deferral of the text would remain a central feature of rhetorical criticism for more than 50 years. Although an engagement with the text, and the question of its ontic status, was deferred, critics nevertheless employed a range of metaphors that contributed (if only indirectly) to the gradual specification of its basic features.[2] Most of these metaphors, such as text as a *window,* as a *mirror,* as a *move in a game,* and as an *engine for change,* extend and/or refine Wichelns's (1925/1962) discussion of function and effect. But functional metaphors still have *entailments* that contribute to the ongoing prefiguration of the text in rhetorical studies. For example, the functional characterization of a rhetorical text as a window into a culture prefigures the text as **transparent,** as in the following hypothetical critical statement: "Malcolm X's 'The Ballot or the Bullet' can provide a lens for viewing the phenomenon of black nationalism during the mid-1960s." The text is characterized not as something that we must *look at* but rather as something we *look through.* As Gaonkar (1990) observed, the tradition in rhetorical criticism that extends from Wrage to Baskerville "prefigured the oratorical text as a *passive receptacle,* something so *transparent* that it inspired little or no methodological self-reflexiveness" (p. 298, emphasis added; see also Gaonkar, 1997). In short, attention to the common text metaphors present in rhetorical criticism reveals an object lacking in ontic substance or significance. The common conceptualization of the rhetorical text implicit in much critical practice maintains that it is insubstantial, transparent, ephemeral, and devoid of distinctiveness.

Given this recurrent (if only implicit) characterization of the rhetorical text, it is not surprising that critical innovations during the 1960s and 1970s depended on analytic methods and conceptual formulations that further marginalized the text (Leff & Sachs, 1990). But the movement in rhetorical criticism known as **close reading** or close textual analysis has dramatically challenged the once dominant conceptualization and, in so doing, has brought the question of the ontic status of the rhetorical text to the forefront of contemporary rhetorical studies. One key feature of the close reading approach is its destabilization of the rigid rhetoric-poetic dichotomy set in place by Hudson and Wichelns. Close reading restores a range of *aesthetic* qualities such as "texture," "structure," "density," "unity," and "integrity" to the rhetorical text. Leff (1986) insisted that the rhetorical text, especially in the traditional form of a public speech or oration, is an "artistic construction" (p. 381). Another important element in Leff's (1987) argument for close reading was his negotiation of the traditional "product" versus "process" tension. Many (or perhaps most) rhetorical scholars treat rhetorical products—individual texts—as "an occasion for studying a process" (p. 3), and this tendency leads scholarship away from the nuances and ontology of the text. Leff responded by reconceptualizing the text as a dynamic process. He wrote, "The substance of rhetoric . . . does not arise from processes attached to the logical, ethical, or psychological coordinates of discourse; instead, it arises from the way such processes congeal within a particular rhetorical artifact" (p. 4). A rhetorical text, especially one shaped or informed by an internal principle of **decorum,** is a site of interaction or the location of a dynamic process of "mediation," "balance," and "negotiation" among advocate, audience, purpose, concrete circumstances, and linguistic and symbolic resources (pp. 6-7). At a minimum, then, close reading responds to the question "What is the ontic status of the rhetorical text" with an affirmation of its aesthetic features and complex interactive character; the rhetorical text is a discrete (cf. Brummett, 1994), dense, yet dynamic configuration of linguistic, stylistic, figurative, narrative, and argumentative elements.

Beyond emphasizing the aesthetic and structural complexity of the rhetorical text, close reading features a key metaphor that further clarifies the ontic status, or the essential nature, of the rhetorical text. Often overlooked in discussions of the close reading approach is its central metaphor for specifying the nature of the text: The rhetorical text is a *field of action* (Gaonkar, 1989; Leff, 1986; Leff & Sachs, 1990; Rosteck & Leff, 1989). The spatial component of the metaphor—text as *field*—is fairly common; literary new criticism has given a prominent place to the spatially derived architectural metaphor "structure" in its effort to uncover the ontology of the text (Ransom, 1941). Leff (1986) argued that the spatial metaphor of field leads to an effort "to conceive [the] boundaries that delimit the field" and establish "the conceptual space" of any particular text (pp. 386-387). But this sense of field incorporates one of the entailments of the literary metaphor of structure; for Leff, the field of the rhetorical text is not a smooth surface but rather a multilevel space with both surface and *depth.* He maintained, "Recent studies of the tropes, metaphor in particular, clearly indicate that such [textual] boundaries normally consist in images or clusters of images that subsist below the surface action of the discourse" (pp. 386-387).

But the metaphor of field provides an incomplete account of the nature of the rhetorical text. As Leff (1986) remarked, "After all, to do nothing more than reduce the discourse to its conceptual bases is to convert a field of action into a set of static entities" (p. 387). The second term in the metaphor—text as a field of action—is essential in that it tries to capture the dynamic character of the rhetorical text. As Leff argued, the rhetorical text is not a static entity. Specific elements within its field interact; they support, subvert, extend, qualify, and/or conflict with other elements as the text unfolds, sentence by sentence, paragraph by paragraph, over time. The emphasis on action, then, balances the spatial aspects of field with a sense of the way in which action occurs over time.

Leff's readings of key texts in the history of oratory tended to emphasize a specific form of action within the text's conceptual field. He identified what he termed the "intrinsic" dimension (the formal or artistic impulse that enters the text's field) and the "extrinsic" dimension (the referential or representational impulse) of textual production that intersect in the end product.[3] Leff (1986) noted,

> To rely exclusively either upon a formal/intrinsic or a representational/extrinsic criterion is to distort the rhetorical integrity of the discourse. Though critical analysis can separate these dimensions, the fact is that they occur simultaneously and work cooperatively within the fabric of the discourse. (pp. 381-382)

The rhetorical text is, in short, the intersection between aesthetic form and representational content. The interaction between these dimensions, Leff suggested, is the primal or generative action that takes place within a text's field.

We might qualify Leff's account of the ontic status or nature of the rhetorical text in two ways. First, Leff concentrated on the harmony between form and content or the aesthetic and the representational; as he noted just quoted, their interaction is cooperative. This cooperative relationship was further developed in Leff's discussion of **iconicity** (Leff & Sachs, 1990). But we might note that where there is cooperation there also is antagonism and conflict lurking in the shadows.[4] Attention to this "dark side," so to speak, leads to the possibility that at least some texts exist as a field of disruption and not cooperative action. Lanham (1983), for example, described the irony of a text whose representational content is a description of the dynamic quality of social existence (the sociological idea of dramatism) that is undercut or disrupted by an aesthetic form that is lifeless and static. This brief example suggests that rhetorical scholars need to remain open to the possibility of textual deconstruction and **polysemy** or the idea that a text's field of action is marked by conceptual ruptures and semantic instability (Sarup, 1989).

Second, Leff's (1986) conception of textual "unity" stemmed from his belief that authorial intention or "purpose" serves a coordinating function, organizing the play of intrinsic and extrinsic impulses manifest in the text (p. 382). But what if, as adherents to various strands of *postmodern* critical theory argue, there is no autonomous self with an unambiguous and coherent purpose (see the entry for **subject**)? Does the phenomenon of the "decentered subject" call Leff's model of the text as a field of action into question? Not necessarily. Leff (1997) acknowledged the "need to modify the received notion that rhetors are purely strategic agents employing neutral instruments to adjust people to ideas and ideas to people" (p. 133). What contemporary thinking on the issues of self and subjectivity does is to expand the range of forces that may be active within a text's field of action. If postmodern critical theorists are correct and there is no essential self standing behind and completely determining the action within the text's field, then it becomes possible to view the text as a field within which various "subject positions" interact and struggle with each other. In the process of producing texts, authors also produce contingent, *locally stable* selves (Giddens, 1979; Kamberelis & Scott, 1992). There are, it would appear, a variety of forces and structures—linguistic, psychoanalytical, religious, metaphysical, sociological, ideological, and so on—that constitute the text's conditions of possibility or the materials that allow the text to come into existence and that the text, in turn, brings to life. Expanding on Leff's metaphor allows rhetorical scholars to conceptualize the interaction of these forces and structures as the essence of textual action. As Culler (1982) remarked, the play of "languages and structures, rather than authorial self or consciousness, become[s] the major source of [critical] explanation" (p. 21; cf. Gaonkar, 1997).

While the close reading movement in rhetorical criticism has been engaged in the project of recovering and reconceptualizing the text, the other dominant strand of contemporary rhetorical thought—**critical rhetoric**—has been attempting to problematize the concept of the text (e.g., McGee, 1990; Solomon, 1993). Indebted to the work of Becker (1971) within the field, and to the works of Barthes (1981), Derrida (1979), Foucault (1972), and other theorists and critics, more recent scholarship by McGee (1990) and McKerrow (1989) offers an alternative conceptualization of the rhetorical text as *fragment.* Becker's (1971) description of the fragmentary nature of the text is based on an account "of what man [sic] as receiver is exposed to rather than what man as source creates" (p. 31). Becker argued that people rarely are exposed to "whole" texts in our media-dominated culture; rather, people are bombarded by countless "fragments or bits of information on an immense number of topics" (p. 33). He suggested that the task for rhetorical scholarship no longer is the analysis of single messages or texts; rather, the urgent challenge is to study the way in which the bits or fragments interact and are organized by individual audiences. Foucault's (1972) account of the text emerged from an effort to rethink the standard forms of "unity" that undergird fields of knowledge such as history. Whereas Leff appeared confident that the "boundaries" or "borders" of a text can be identified, Foucault's writing expressed strong doubts. He wrote, "The frontiers of a book are never clear-cut; beyond the title, the first lines, and the last full stop, beyond its internal configuration and its autonomous form, it is caught up in a system of references to other books, other texts, other sentences; it is a node within a network" (p. 23). Both Becker and Foucault, in different ways, dissolved the discrete autonomous text; its status was reduced to that of a fragment or "node" within some larger, encompassing, linguistic and/or discursive universe.[5]

The shift to the notion of text as fragment advanced by the growing critical rhetoric tradition displaces the discrete text from the position of prominence it has enjoyed within the close reading movement. The locus of attention is directed toward discursive fragments (e.g., a sentence, a metaphor, an **ideograph,** a narrative anecdote, a particular pattern of argument) and their relationship to each other (the phenomenon of **intertextuality**) and/or their interrelationships within some broader "diffuse text" (Brummett, 1994) or **discursive formation.** The formation (e.g., an academic discipline such as psychology, a social **movement** such as pro-life, a political **ideology** such as neo-liberalism, a sphere of practice such as the law, a "language game" such as international diplomacy), and not any particular text that might fall within its (often flexible) borders, is the object in need of critical analysis. Critical attention and analytic energy is directed toward reconstructing the "logic" or dynamics—the "rules" (Foucault, 1972) or protocols—of the formation or the *intertextual* field.

This brief history of the text in contemporary rhetorical scholarship has revealed a line of continuity as well as a process of substitution. The line of continuity can be seen in the tendency for the field to employ dichotomies or *disjunctions* in its efforts to locate the essence of the text. The process of substitution emerges as an internal disjunction (field of action vs. fragment) and replaces an external one (rhetorical text vs. poetic or literary text). But is there any way of bridging the oppositions and synthesizing the competing accounts so as to develop a single, all-encompassing conceptualization of the rhetorical text? To answer this question, we need to return to, and reassess, the question that organized this quest for the ontic status of the rhetorical text. Although that question is useful, it also has the potential to distort our understanding of the relevant issues. The question "What is the ontic status of the rhetorical text?" is framed in the singular, suggesting that that status is monodimensional. But what if the text exists in different modalities, with none reflecting *the* single and unified ontic status of the text? Both Leff (1997) and McGee (1990) appeared to grant this possibility. McGee did so by suggesting that any discrete units of discourse "are simultaneously structures of fragments, finished texts, and fragments themselves to be accounted for in subsequent discourse" (p. 279). That is, the ontic status of the text is not singular but rather multiple; a text exists (a) as a **bricolage** of arguments, images, narratives, and so on; (b) as a unified (as well as, in some cases, an internally divided) field of action; and (c) as an element within a larger discursive system. Leff (1997) made a similar point when he described the text as "an assimilative social product" that "is at once a point of local closure, an event in the ongoing development of a genre of utterance, and a productive moment in the unending process of interpreting and re-interpreting the social world" (p. 134).

What research directives might be gleaned from these observations? Two seem to stand out. First, critical research can, and should, continue along all various fronts. Rhetorical critics can trace the ancestry of the materials, the "structure of fragments," from which a text is composed (e.g., Slagell, 1991); they can probe the unities and/or ruptures within the "finished" text's field of action (e.g., Leff, 1988), or they can assemble discursive fragments to reconstruct the logic of a discursive formation or system (e.g., Sloop, 1996). Second, rather than trying to synthesize these different modalities into a unified account or theory of the text, critics can engage in diachronic studies that trace the "career" of a text—how it emerges out of the various resources or materials available to the author or speaker, how it achieves a degree of unity or manifests a degree of rupture as it enters a **rhetorical situation** and the stream of history, and how it then circulates within a society (how it is used, and possibly abused, in subsequent discourse or how it functions as a resource that is used in fashioning "new" texts) or how it affirms or contests the logic or rules of the discursive formation of which it is a part (Solomon, 1993). These directives do not exhaust the possibilities of how the concept of text might be deployed in critical practice, but they do recognize both the relative autonomy of and interaction between the various modalities—the different modes of existence—of this seminal concept in rhetorical studies.

Notes

1. For an example of how this question is treated in literary studies, see Ransom (1941) and Wellek and Warren (1956, chap. 12). For different approaches to the "ontology of rhetoric" and the rhetorical text, see Leff (1987) and Valesio (1980).

2. On the importance of locating and analyzing these *metaphorical prefigurations* of the text, see Aune (1989) and Baskerville (1977).

3. In Leff and Sachs (1990), these moments were rendered as the more traditional concepts of "form" and "content."

4. This is exemplified, for example, in Burke's (1950) observation about the relationship between **identification** and division and, even more to the point, in Weaver's (1953) discussion of "congruence" and "friction" in form-content relationships (pp. 116-117).

5. The dissolution of the text is a recurrent theme in much contemporary literary theory. See, for example, Fish (1980) and Frow (1990).

References and Additional Reading

Aune, J. A. (1989). Public address and rhetorical theory. In M. C. Leff & F. J. Kauffeld (Eds.), *Texts in context: Critical dialogues on significant episodes in American political rhetoric.* Davis, CA: Hermagoras Press.

Barthes, R. (1981). Theory of the text. In R. Young (Ed.), *Untying the text: A post-structuralist reader.* London: Routledge and Kegan Paul.

Baskerville, B. (1977). Must we all be "rhetorical critics"? *Quarterly Journal of Speech, 63,* 107-116.

Becker, S. L. (1971). Rhetorical studies for the contemporary world. In L. F. Bitzer & E. Black (Eds.), *The prospect of rhetoric.* Englewood Cliffs, NJ: Prentice Hall.

Brummett, B. (1994). *Rhetoric in popular culture.* New York: St. Martin's.

Burke, K. (1950). *The rhetoric of motives.* New York: Prentice Hall.

Culler, J. (1982). *On deconstruction: Theory and criticism after structuralism.* Ithaca, NY: Cornell University Press.

Derrida, J. (1979). Living on: Border lines. In G. Hartman (Ed.), *Deconstruction and criticism.* New York: Seabury Press.

Fish, S. (1980). *Is there a text in this class? The authority of interpretive communities.* Cambridge, MA: Harvard University Press.

Foucault, M. (1972). *The archaeology of knowledge* (A. M. Sheridan Smith, Trans.). New York: Pantheon.

Frow, J. (1990). Intertextuality and ontology. In M. Worton & J. Still (Eds.), *Intertextuality: Theories and practices.* Manchester, UK: Manchester University Press.

Gaonkar, D. P. (1989). The oratorical text: The enigma of arrival. In M. C. Leff & F. J. Kauffeld (Eds.), *Texts in context: Critical dialogues on significant episodes in American political rhetoric.* Davis, CA: Hermagoras Press.

Gaonkar, D. P. (1990). Object and method in rhetorical criticism: From Wichelns to Leff and McGee. *Western Journal of Speech Communication, 54,* 290-316.

Gaonkar, D. P. (1997). Close readings of the third kind: Reply to my critics. In W. Keith & A. Gross (Eds.), *Rhetorical hermeneutics.* Albany: State University of New York Press.

Giddens, A. (1979). *Central problems in social theory: Action, structure, and contradiction in social analysis.* Berkeley: University of California Press.

Hudson, H. H. (1923). The field of rhetoric. *Quarterly Journal of Speech Education, 9,* 167-180.

Kamberelis, G., & Scott, K. (1992). Other people's voices: The co-articulation of texts and subjectivities. *Linguistics and Education, 4,* 359-403.

Lanham, R. A. (1983). *Analyzing prose.* New York: Scribner.

Leff, M. (1986). Textual criticism: The legacy of G. P. Mohrmann. *Quarterly Journal of Speech, 72,* 377-389.

Leff, M. (1987). The habitation of rhetoric. In J. W. Wenzel (Ed.), *Argument and critical practices: Proceedings of the Fifth SCA/AFA Conference on Argumentation.* Annandale, VA: Speech Communication Association.

Leff, M. (1988). Dimensions of temporality in Lincoln's second inaugural. *Communication Reports, 1,* 26-31.

Leff, M. C. (1997). Lincoln among the nineteenth-century orators. In T. W. Benson (Ed.), *Rhetoric and political culture in nineteenth-century America.* East Lansing: Michigan State University Press.

Leff, M., & Sachs, A. (1990). Words the most like things: Iconicity and the rhetorical text. *Western Journal of Speech Communication, 54,* 252-273.

McGee, M. C. (1990). Text, context, and the fragmentation of contemporary culture. *Western Journal of Speech Communication, 54,* 274-289.

McKerrow, R. E. (1989). Critical rhetoric: Theory and praxis. *Communication Monographs, 56,* 91-111.

Ransom, J. C. (1941). *The new criticism.* Norfolk, CT: New Directions.

Rosteck, T., & Leff, M. (1989). Piety, propriety, and perspective: An interpretation and application of key terms in Kenneth Burke's *Permanence and Change. Western Journal of Speech Communication, 53,* 327-341.

Sarup, M. (1989). *An introductory guide to post-structuralism and postmodernism.* Athens: University of Georgia Press.

Slagell, A. R. (1991). Anatomy of a masterpiece: A close textual analysis of Abraham Lincoln's second inaugural address. *Communication Studies, 42,* 155-171.

Sloop, J. M. (1996). *The cultural prison: Discourse, prisoners, and punishment.* Tuscaloosa: University of Alabama Press.

Solomon, M. (1993). The things we study: Texts and their interactions. *Communication Monographs, 60,* 62-68.

Valesio, P. (1980). *Novantiqua: Rhetorics as a contemporary theory.* Bloomington: Indiana University Press.

Weaver, R. (1953). Some rhetorical aspects of grammatical categories. In R. Weaver, *The ethics of rhetoric.* South Bend, IN: Regnery/Gateway.

Wellek, R., & Warren, A. (1956). *Theory of literature* (3rd ed.). New York: Harcourt Brace.

Wichelns, H. A. (1962). The literary criticism of oratory. In A. M. Drummond (Ed.), *Studies in rhetoric and public speaking in honor of James Albert Winans.* New York: Russell and Russell. (Original work published 1925)

TONE

The British theorist and critic I. A. Richards played a key role in popularizing the concept of **tone** in literary and rhetorical studies. In his book *Practical Criticism,* originally published in 1929, Richards (1962) noted that a writer or speaker ordinarily has "*an attitude to his* [sic] *listener.* . . . The tone of his utterance reflects his awareness of this relation, his sense of how he stands towards those he is addressing" (p. 175). For Richards, then, tone refers primarily to a speaker's or writer's attitude toward his or her audience—the relationship that the speaker or writer believes exists between them or that is *inscribed* or enacted in an utterance or text (see also Booth's [1970] discussion of various forms of *rhetorical stance*). For example, a text might manifest a *familiar tone* (assumes that some degree of cordial relations exists between the author or advocate and the audience), a *formal tone* (assumes that the relationship between the author and the reader is governed by institutional or cultural rules that prescribe how they should interact), a *condescending tone* (assumes that the author or advocate occupies a superior position with respect to the audience), a *critical tone* (assumes that the author is in a position to evaluate some aspect of the reader's behavior), an *ingratiating tone* (assumes that no substantive relationship currently exists between the speaker and the audience and reflects the speaker's desire to establish such a relationship with the audience), a *hesitant* or *reticent tone* (assumes that a relationship exists between the author and the reader but reflects the author's inability to determine whether introducing a certain topic would violate the terms of that relationship), or a *supplicating* or *obsequious tone* (assumes that the audience occupies a position superior to that of the advocate and possesses something that the advocate wants or needs). This list of examples is far from exhaustive.

A somewhat more expansive conceptualization of tone can be detected in the scholarly literature. Voloshinov (1987) suggested that tone or *intonation* is "oriented *in two directions:* with respect to the listener as ally or witness and with respect to the object of the utterance as the third living participant whom the intonation scolds or caresses, denigrates or magnifies" (pp. 104-105). Put differently, Voloshinov broadened tone to include a speaker's or writer's attitude *toward his or her subject* as well as the audience. This expanded sense of tone also can be found in Booth and Gregory's (1987) discussion of the topic. They wrote,

> "Tone" is a musical metaphor for writers' relationships with readers that result from writers making two decisions: (1) how they will express or imply their *feelings* about their subject and (2) how they will place themselves socially, intellectually, or morally with regard to their implied readers—as their superiors, looking down; as their inferiors, looking up; or as their equals, addressing them eye-to-eye. (p. 288)

An author or advocate might adopt a *playful tone* toward a subject (demonstrating that the author or advocate does not take the subject too seriously), a *serious tone* (demonstrating that the author or advocate believes that the subject merits careful reflection), a *neutral* or *dispassionate tone* (demonstrating a lack of emotional involvement with the subject), or a *sarcastic tone* (demonstrating a negative attitude toward the subject). Summarizing the more expansive sense of tone, Abrams (1993) wrote, "The way we speak reveals, by subtle clues, our conception of, and attitude to[ward], the things we are talking about, our personal relation to our auditor, as well as our assumptions about the social level, intelligence, and sensitivity of that auditor" (p. 156).

Perhaps the best way of exploring the expanded sense of tone is to look at two texts dealing with the same general topic. Consider the following texts: first, an essay by Carrie R. Leana, professor in the School of Business at the University of Pittsburgh, from the April 14, 1996, issue of *Chicago Tribune Magazine* titled "Why Downsizing Won't Work" and, second, the book *Downsize This!* (Moore, 1996), written by Michael Moore, creator of the television program *TV Nation* and the documentary films *Roger and Me* and *The Big One.* As the titles of the texts indicate, they treated the subject of corporate downsizing. Both texts reached the same conclusion: Downsizing is a bad policy. And they both recommended that steps be taken to regulate corporate behavior. But the tone of each text was different. Let us look at each text a little more closely.

Whereas Leana concluded that the corporate sector's rush to embrace "restructuring" (a common corporate term for downsizing that Leana employed throughout her essay) is misguided, her writing treats the topic dispassionately or objectively. She assumed that her readers expected serious argument and analysis, and that is what she provided. She reasoned with her readers. For example, Leana wrote early in the essay,

> But if you look inside American firms, as I and other researchers have done, you find a disturbing paradox. The very qualities that many executives say their firms need in order to compete—flexibility, teamwork, innovation, etc.—are in fact being destroyed by the organizational culture they're creating. Advocates of this new culture of "permanent restructuring" and "contingent workers" see great savings but don't count the costs. And here I am not talking about the well-documented human costs, such as employee dislocation and financial distress. Real damage is being done to the ability of our firms to compete and succeed over the long run.

This passage summarizes the basic thrust of Leana's argument. Let us compare it to a passage that encapsulates Moore's position:

> And downsizing is one of those things that is hurting us. I'm not talking about legitimate layoffs, when a company is losing money and simply doesn't have the cash reserves to pay its workers. I'm talking about companies like GM [General Motors], AT&T, and GE [General Electric], which fire people at a time when the company is making record profits in the billions of dollars. Executives who do this are not scorned, picketed, or arrested—they are hailed as heroes! They make the covers of *Fortune* and *Forbes*. They lecture at the Harvard Business School about their success. They throw big campaign fund-raisers and sit next to the president of the United States. They are the masters of the universe simply because they make huge profits regardless of the consequences to our society. Are we insane or what? Why do we allow this to happen? It is *wrong* to make money off people's labor and then fire them after you've made it. It is *immoral* for a CEO [chief executive officer] to make millions of dollars when he [sic] has just destroyed the livelihood[s] of 40,000 families. And it's just plain *nuts* to allow American companies to move factories overseas at the expense of our own people. (pp. 255-256)

How does Moore's depiction compare to that of Leana? For one thing, Moore expressed an emotional reaction toward his subject. He was angry; Leana was analytic. Moore described the situation as "immoral" and "wrong"; Leana noted a "disturbing paradox." Moore was outraged, and he assumed that his audience shared (or should share) that sentiment; Leana assumed that her readers shared her disposition toward objective inquiry. Moore created an audience of potential comrades-in-arms, exhorting them to storm the gates of corporate power; Leana created an audience of concerned but reasonable civic leaders. Moore sympathized with the plight of the downsized worker; Leana related to the pressures facing the current generation of corporate managers. And these attitudes were conveyed to the readers primarily through word choice as well as through syntax, **style** (e.g., *anaphora*), typographical choices (e.g., use of italics for emphasis), and punctuation (e.g., exclamation points), all resources for enacting tone (see also the entry for **accent**).

This brief analysis only scratches the surface of these two texts. Numerous factors shape the texts and give them their uniqueness; tone is only one element. But tone is one of the defining features of Leana's and Moore's texts. Tone saturates human discourse; every text conveys attitudes and makes evaluations about its readers and subjects.[1] As Burke (1950) observed, tonality provides the "proper slant," or the perspective, that an advocate takes toward the audience and subject, and this slant—sometimes subtle and other times obvious—often can be more important than explicit argument in the process of persuasion or **identification** (p. 98). Tone can be an elusive object of study, but its centrality to the process of advocacy and influence appears beyond doubt.

Note

1. On the evaluative dimension of tonality and intonation, see Booth (1983, p. 74) and Morson and Emerson's (1990) discussion of Bakhtin (p. 134).

References and Additional Reading

Abrams, M. H. (1993). *A glossary of literary terms* (6th ed.). Fort Worth, TX: Harcourt Brace.

Booth, W. C. (1970). *Now don't try to reason with me: Essays and ironies for a credulous age.* Chicago: University of Chicago Press.

Booth, W. C. (1983). *The rhetoric of fiction* (2nd ed.). Chicago: University of Chicago Press.

Booth, W. C., & Gregory, M. W. (1987). *The Harper and Row rhetoric: Writing as thinking, thinking as writing.* New York: Harper & Row.

Burke, K. (1950). *A rhetoric of motives.* New York: Prentice Hall.

Gibson, W. (1966). *Tough, sweet, and stuffy: An essay on modern American prose styles.* Bloomington: Indiana University Press.

Moore, M. (1996). *Downsize this!* New York: Crown.

Morson, G. S., & Emerson, C. (1990). *Mikhail Bakhtin: Creation of a prosaics.* Stanford, CA: Stanford University Press.

Richards, I. A. (1962). *Practical criticism: A study of literary judgment.* New York: Harcourt Brace.

Voloshinov, V. N. (1987). Discourse in life and discourse in poetry (concerning sociological poetics). In I. R. Titunik & N. R. Bruss (Eds.), *Freudianism: A critical sketch* (I. R. Titunik, Trans.). Bloomington: Indiana University Press.

TOPICS/TOPOI

According to Leff (1983a), "The term 'topic' is notoriously ambiguous, and even in its technical uses, its meaning ranges from recurrent themes appearing in a certain kind of discourse to abstract patterns of inference" (p. 220; see also Leff, 1983b). Virtually all commentators on classical rhetoric agree that the concept of **topics**[1] occupied a central place in theories of rhetoric and **invention.** But although ancient writers on rhetoric agreed on the centrality of topics, Leff noted that they disagreed on the substance of the concept. The questions "What is a topic?" and "How does it function in the process of rhetorical invention?" received widely divergent answers.

Prior to Aristotle, a topic was considered primarily as a recurrent *theme* or *image* that appeared in discourse and could be used by speakers and writers to help generate discourse. Discussing **topoi** during the Homeric period of ancient Greece, D'Angelo (1984) wrote, "We already know what some of the material was like: stock epithets, figures of speech, exempla, proverbs, sententiae, quotations, praises or censures of people and things, and brief treatises on virtues and vices" (p. 54; see also Lanham, 1991, pp. 169-170; Ong, 1967). Such commonplace themes and images often were gathered into collections; orators acquainted with these topoi could then draw on them in a variety of situations.

Commonplace topics provided orators with a stock of familiar material to which audiences often responded positively. Whereas other senses of topoi would be introduced by subsequent rhetorical theorists, this sense of topoi also would persist. Leff (1996) noted their presence as *loci communes* in the Latin treatises of Cicero and (especially) Quintilian. Other scholars have traced this line of thought to the formulas found in "commonplace books" during the Medieval and Renaissance periods and beyond. Commonplace books, perhaps the most famous being Erasmus's *De Copia,* were designed to enhance a speaker's or writer's resourcefulness or ability to respond to almost any situation.[2] Leff wrote that the loci communes of Latin rhetorics were "finished products that integrate logical argument, emotional appeal, and style into a single structure" (p. 448). Walter Mondale's use of the television commercial line "Where's the beef?" to attack rival presidential aspirant Gary Hart during the 1984 Democratic primaries illustrates one way in which a commonplace expression can combine argument, emotion, and style. As the quotation from Leff (1983a) at the beginning of the entry noted, scholars continue to use the term *topoi* to refer to recurring elements of discursive practice (Hahn & Gustainis, 1987; Ivie, 1980; McCloskey, 1985; Nothstine, 1988; O'Leary, 1994; Prelli, 1989; Wiethoff, 1981).

The concept of topoi underwent significant revision in Aristotle's (1954) *Rhetoric* and in his work on **dialectical** argumentation (*The Topics* [Aristotle, 1960]). A considerable body of commentary on Aristotle's approach to topoi has emerged (Brake, 1965; Conley, 1978; Grimaldi, 1958; Leff, 1983b; Leff & Hewes, 1981; Ochs, 1969; Owen, 1968; Stump, 1978). Scholars agree that, at least in the realm of rhetoric, Aristotle identified two types of topics: the *universal* (*koinoi topoi*) and the *special* (*eide topoi*).[3] The key questions then become "What links the universal and special topoi?" (or what is it that they have in common that makes them part of a larger genus?) and "What differentiates the universal and special topoi?" (or what makes them separate species of a larger genus?). Building off of, while still disagreeing with, earlier commentators (especially Grimaldi), Leff (1983a, 1983b) answered these two questions as follows. In response to the first question, Leff (1983b) argued that both forms of Aristotelian topoi function as a "process of inference" (p. 26) or are used heuristically to assist in the "discovery of inferential connectives" (p. 29). They all are elements in the process of human reasoning; they work to support and/or subvert *concrete* propositional *claims* (e.g., we should go to war against Country X, we should raise taxes on cigarettes by $1.00 a pack).[4] Aristotelian topoi fulfill their function, or relate to claims, in different ways. This leads to the second question. Leff (1983a) wrote that universal topics provide "an abstract category of inference," whereas the special topics are "an inventory of propositions expressing abstract beliefs and values generally accepted by the public" (pp. 220-221). We need to probe Leff's suggested distinction further to understand the different, yet similar, functions of the Aristotelian topoi.

Aristotelian universal topics "take the form of a word or short phrase expressing a highly abstract pattern of relationship relevant to any subject of argument whatsoever" (Leff, 1983b, p. 26). Leff (1983b) continued, "the [universal] topic 'from degree' includes, among other things, the principle that if something has happened where it is less likely, it will happen where it is more likely" (p. 26). The principle, derived from the universal topic, can then be inserted into an argument such as the following: State University (probably) will win the meet because its players performed well in today's events in which they are not very strong and should perform as well or better tomorrow in the events that are their strong suit. Lanham (1991) noted that Aristotle's list of 28 universal topics "is often shortened to basic types: genus and species, nature, authority, consequences, time and place, word, etc." (p. 152). The Aristotelian universal topics identify common *lines of argument* (e.g., analogy, cause) or modes of **exposition** and thematic development (e.g., comparison, contrast, definition)[5] that can be employed on a wide variety of topics.

The special topics, on the other hand, are "propositions that express . . . generally accepted beliefs and values" (Leff, 1983b, p. 26) or draw on a community's stock of **social knowledge** (p. 25) and **ideographs.** Burke (1966) made a similar observation when he wrote, "By 'topics,' Aristotle obviously has in mind something quite close to what contemporary sociologists would call 'values' " (p. 302). For example, Leff (1983a) identified the special topic "What is rare is a greater good than what is more plentiful" (p. 221).[6] This topic is more limited in scope than the more abstract universal topoi. It is relevant, Aristotle believed, in the realm of **deliberation,** where an evaluative choice is to be made among various courses of action.[7] An environmentalist might rely on this special topic in choosing to support a course of action (a policy) that protects the habitat of an endangered species (what is rare) rather than an alternative course of action (which might promise material benefits for a large number of people).

Leff insisted that the essence of Aristotelian topoi, both universal and special, is their role in the production of argumentative inferences. Topoi, on Leff's reading, are similar to Toulmin's concept of a *warrant* (see also Bird, 1962); both function to "link . . . the data from which an argument begins and the conclusion with which it ends" (Leff, 1983a, p. 220). This specific function of Aristotelian topics can be grasped more clearly when, to employ a common expository topoi, it is *contrasted* with the discussion of topoi in Latin rhetorical theory. Leff (1983b) wrote,

> Latin rhetorical theorists . . . depart from the Aristotelian concept of topics as inferential strategies. Instead, they base the topics of argument on a conception of the generic subject of rhetorical discourse. (p. 26) . . . The focus of the [topical] system shifts from the discovery of inferential connectives to the discovery of materials for argument. (p. 29)

This third sense of topoi requires careful explication.

Latin rhetorical theorists such as Cicero (1949) in *De Inventione* and Quintilian accepted, but downplayed, Aristotle's doctrine of **genres** that located three distinct "subjects" of rhetorical discourse. Cicero apparently believed that there was a general or "generic subject" on which all rhetorical practice focused. Leff (1983b) explained Cicero's approach to the problem of rhetoric's subject in these terms:

> When rhetorical is considered at the broadest, most general level, its subject matter consists of persons and acts. But since an argument must proceed from what is better known or more readily believed to that which is doubtful, the very subjects of the argument . . . cannot themselves furnish the resources of argument. Consequently, the argument must proceed from the attributes of persons and acts in order to resolve doubt about the particular person and act in question. (p. 27)

Cicero's topical scheme attempted to provide would-be advocates with a *systematic method* for analyzing *any* issue or controversy. The 11 attributes of the person and the four main divisions of the attributes of the act[8] identify all of the key issues that might arise in a dispute or controversy. By using the topoi as an analytic or *heuristic* device that is applied to concrete specific cases, advocates can unearth all that might be said with respect to those cases. Unlike the general themes and images collected under the rubric of commonplaces, Latin topoi function as a systematic method for rhetorical **invention.** But unlike the Aristotelian approach that emphasized, in Leff's reading, the discovery of argumentative warrants, the Latin topical method helped advocates to discover discursive material that "then must be integrated into a larger argumentative structure" (Leff, 1983b, p. 29).

The Latin attempt to generate an exhaustive heuristic for rhetorical invention had a substantial impact on 20th-century rhetorical thinking. Corbett (1986) commented, "When one closely examines the heuristic systems that have been developed in this century, one notes the affinity that many of them have with the classical system of topics" (p. 55).[9] Numerous authors have either called for or proposed a new topical system or scheme. Few (if any) of these contemporary schemes make the claim to comprehensiveness found in many Latin rhetorical treatises. Some of the more recent topical systems that have been proposed include Larson's (1968) method of systematic questioning, Steele and Redding's (1962) inventory of American cultural values (which they indicated might function as argumentative premises), and Wilson and Arnold's (1983) 16-point scheme of common attributes and relationships. These and other heuristic topoi, Corbett (1971) wrote, might be thought of

> as "suggesters," as "prompters," as "initiators," as a "checklist" of ideas on some subject. Being general heads or categories, the topics "prime the pump," as it were; by suggesting general strategies of development, they help to overcome inertia. . . . The term "checklist" suggests that one goes through the list of topics, one by one, asking oneself whether this particular topic will turn up any material for the development of our subject. (pp. 108-109)

The value of topical schemes to the task of rhetorical invention has been challenged. As Corbett (1986) observed, a number of theorists argue that "the topics are unduly complicated, stifle creativity, and produce dull, trivial discourse" (p. 51). Nevertheless, topical theory retains an important place in many introductions to rhetorical thinking (e.g., Hauser, 1991; McCroskey, 1997). There also has been a shift in function as topical theory has been incorporated into rhetorical criticism (e.g., McCloskey, 1985; Prelli, 1989). Whether as a storehouse of clichés and aphorisms, a procedure for uncovering warrants, a method for discovering things to say about a specific topic, or a concept with interpretive value, topics or commonplaces remain of interest to rhetorical scholars.

Notes

1. Other roughly synonymous terms include *commonplace* and *locus* (and the plural *loci* and *loci communes*).

2. See Kennedy (1980) and Sloane (1997, pp. 56-79).

3. For an exception, see Kinneavy (1971).

4. Rhetorical claims (often defined as *hypotheses* in ancient rhetorical manuals) are concrete. Dialectical claims (often referred to as *theses*) are abstract; they are not embedded in a particular context. The claims "war is good" and "taxes are bad" are abstract dialectical claims.

5. D'Angelo (1984) noted how abstract analytic topoi "become displaced as inventional strategies [only to] reappear in nineteenth-century British and American textbooks as methods of developing paragraphs" (p. 66).

6. This example also illustrates Perelman and Olbrechts-Tyteca's (1969) locus of quality (pp. 90-91). On the argumentative function of this and other loci, see the discussion in the entry for **argument.**

7. Deliberative topics do not appear bound to the realm of deliberation in an absolute sense. Leff (1983a) used his example of a deliberative special topic ("That is good on which much labor or money has been spent") to support a rather nondeliberative claim ("Helen must have been good").

8. The four divisions of attributes of the act consist of (a) topics coherent with the act (e.g., motive), (b) topics involved in the performance or execution of the act (e.g., time, place, resources), (c) topics that represent adjuncts of the act (essentially ways of comparing the act to other acts), and (d) topics relating to the consequence(s) of the act (e.g., the response to the act). See Leff (1983b, pp. 27-28).

9. Corbett's (1986) observation might be qualified by noting, as the earlier discussion indicated, that there was not a single classical theory of topics. Historically, the Aristotelian and Latin approaches to topoi were collapsed, giving the impression of conceptual unity. Scholarship such as Leff's (1983b) has called attention to the differences in classical topical thought.

References and Additional Reading

Aristotle. (1954). *Rhetoric* (W. R. Roberts, Trans.). New York: Modern Library.

Aristotle. (1960). *The topics* (E. S. Forster, Trans.). Cambridge, MA: Harvard University Press.

Bailey, D. (1964). A plea for a modern set of *topoi. College English, 26,* 111-117.

Bilsky, M., Hazlett, M., Streeter, R. E., & Weaver, R. M. (1953). Looking for an argument. *College English, 14,* 210-216.

Bird, O. (1961). The re-discovery of the topics: Professor Toulmin's inference-warrants. *Mind, 70,* 534-539.

Bird, O. (1962). The tradition of the logical topics: Aristotle to Ockham. *Journal of the History of Ideas, 23,* 307-323.

Brake, R. J. (1965). A reconsideration of Aristotle's concept of topics. *Central States Speech Journal, 16,* 106-112.

Burke, K. (1966). *Language as symbolic action: Essays on life, literature, and method.* Berkeley: University of California Press.

Cicero. (1949). *De inventione* (H. M. Hubbell, Trans.). Cambridge, MA: Harvard University Press.

Conley, T. M. (1978). "Logical hylomorphism" and Aristotle's *koinoi topoi. Central States Speech Journal, 29,* 92-97.

Corbett, E. P. J. (1971). *Classical rhetoric for the modern student* (2nd ed.). New York: Oxford University Press.

Corbett, E. P. J. (1986). The *topoi* revisited. In J. D. Moss (Ed.), *Rhetoric and praxis: The contribution of classical rhetoric to practical reasoning.* Washington, DC: Catholic University of America Press.

Crowley, S., & Hawhee, D. (1999). *Ancient rhetorics for contemporary students* (2nd ed.). Boston: Allyn & Bacon.

D'Angelo, F. J. (1975). *A conceptual theory of rhetoric.* Cambridge, UK: Winthrop.

D'Angelo, F. J. (1984). The evolution of the analytic *topoi:* A speculative inquiry. In R. J. Connors, L. S. Ede, & A. A. Lunsford (Eds.), *Essays on classical rhetoric and modern discourse.* Carbondale: Southern Illinois University Press.

Dick, R. C. (1964). *Topoi:* An approach to inventing arguments. *Speech Teacher, 13,* 313-319.

Grimaldi, W. M. A. (1958). The Aristotelian *topics. Traditio, 14,* 1-16.

Hahn, D. F., & Gustainis, J. J. (1987). Defensive tactics in presidential rhetoric: Contemporary *topoi.* In T. Windt & B. Ingold (Eds.), *Essays in presidential rhetoric* (2nd ed.). Dubuque, IA: Kendall/Hunt.

Hauser, G. A. (1991). *Introduction to rhetorical theory.* Prospect Heights, IL: Waveland.

Ivie, R. L. (1980). Images of savagery in American justifications for war. *Communication Monographs, 47,* 279-294.

Jost, W. (1991). Teaching the topics: Character, rhetoric, and liberal education. *Rhetoric Society Quarterly, 21,* 1-16.

Kennedy, G. A. (1980). *Classical rhetoric and its Christian and secular tradition from ancient to modern times.* Chapel Hill: University of North Carolina Press.

Kinneavy, J. L. (1971). *A theory of discourse.* Englewood Cliffs, NJ: Prentice Hall.

Lanham, R. A. (1991). *A handlist of rhetorical terms* (2nd ed.). Berkeley: University of California Press.

Larson, R. L. (1968). Discovering through questioning: A plan for teaching rhetorical invention. *College English, 30,* 126-134.

Leff, M. (1983a). Topical invention and metaphorical interaction. *Southern Speech Communication Journal, 48,* 214-229.

Leff, M. C. (1983b). The topics of argumentative invention in Latin rhetorical theory from Cicero to Boethius. *Rhetorica, 1,* 23-44.

Leff, M. (1996). Commonplaces and argumentation in Cicero and Quintilian. *Argumentation, 10,* 445-452.

Leff, M. C., & Hewes, D. E. (1981). Topical invention and group communication: Towards a sociology of inference. In G. Ziegelmueller & J. Rhodes (Eds.), *Dimensions of argument: Proceedings of the Second Summer Conference on Argument.* Annandale, VA: Speech Communication Association.

McCloskey, D. N. (1985). *The rhetoric of economics.* Madison: University of Wisconsin Press.

McCroskey, J. C. (1997). *An introduction to rhetorical communication* (7th ed.). Boston: Allyn & Bacon.

McKeon, R. (1973). Creativity and the commonplace. *Philosophy and Rhetoric, 6,* 199-210.

Nelson, W. F. (1969). Topoi: Evidence of human conceptual behavior. *Philosophy and Rhetoric, 2,* 1-11.

Nothstine, W. L. (1988). "Topics" as ontological metaphor in contemporary rhetorical theory and criticism. *Quarterly Journal of Speech, 74,* 151-163.

Ochs, D. J. (1969). Aristotle's concept of formal topics. *Speech Monographs, 36,* 419-425.

Ochs, D. J. (1982). Cicero's *Topica:* A process view of invention. In R. E. McKerrow (Ed.), *Explorations in rhetoric: Studies in honor of Douglas Ehninger.* Glenview, IL: Scott, Foresman.

O'Leary, S. D. (1994). *Arguing the apocalypse: A theory of millennial rhetoric.* New York: Oxford University Press.

Ong, W. L. (1967). *The presence of the word.* New Haven, CT: Yale University Press.

Owen, G. E. L. (Ed.). (1968). *Aristotle on dialectic: The topics.* Oxford, UK: Oxford University Press.

Perelman, C., & Olbrechts-Tyteca, L. (1969). *The new rhetoric: A treatise on argumentation* (J. Wilkinson & P. Weaver, Trans.). Notre Dame, IN: University of Notre Dame Press.

Prelli, L. J. (1989). *A rhetoric of science: Inventing scientific discourse.* Columbia: University of South Carolina Press.

Sloane, T. O. (1997). *On the contrary: The protocol of traditional rhetoric.* Washington, DC: Catholic University of America Press.

Steele, E. D., & Redding, W. C. (1962). The American value system: Premises for persuasion. *Western Speech, 26,* 83-91.

Stump, E. (1978). Dialectic and Aristotle's *Topics.* In E. Stump, *Boethius's DE TOPICIS DIFFERENTIIS* (E. Stump, Trans.). Ithaca, NY: Cornell University Press.

Wallace, K. R. (1972). *Topoi* and the problem of invention. *Quarterly Journal of Speech, 58,* 387-395.

Wiethoff, W. E. (1981). *Topoi* of religious controversy in the American Catholic debate over vernacular reform. *Western Journal of Speech Communication, 45,* 172-181.

Wilson, J. F., & Arnold, C. C. (1983). *Public speaking as a liberal art* (5th ed.). Boston: Allyn & Bacon.

TOUCHSTONE

Like a number of concepts found in the sciences and the humanities, the concept of a **touchstone** emerged *metaphorically.* The earliest use of the term was to refer to a piece of stone that could be used to test the purity of gold and silver. In his famous essay, "The Study of Poetry" (Arnold, 1880/1973), the English literary critic Matthew Arnold used the term to refer to poetic passages that could function in the realm of poetic evaluation in a manner analogous to the evaluation of gold and silver. According to Arnold,

> Indeed there can be no more useful help for discovering what poetry belongs to the class of the truly excellent, and can therefore do us the most good, than to have always in one's mind lines and expressions of the great masters and to apply them as a touchstone to other poetry. (p. 168)

Arnold believed that evaluations of poetic quality by way of the touchstone method would be objective; the evaluation would be based not on the critic's personal standards but rather on a comparison of the poem to the great masterpieces of the past that had survived the (metaphorical) "test" of time. The idea that evaluation based on the touchstone method could be objective assumes that there is universal agreement on what works constitute the category of touchstones. This assumption has been rigorously challenged in contemporary literary and rhetorical criticism (see the entry for **canon**).

The idea of rhetorical touchstones was popularized by Edwin Black in his influential book, *Rhetorical Criticism* (Black, 1965/1978), originally published in 1965. Black maintained that rhetorical critics can justify their "appraisals of specific discourses by recourse to generally accepted touchstones of rhetorical excellence—Demosthenes, Cicero, [and] Edmund Burke, for example—and show the relative merit of a discourse by comparing it to these touchstones" (p. 67). Such a procedure was necessary, Black argued, if the critic was to evaluate a discourse based on *rhetorical* criteria—"*good* in a rhetorical sense" (p. 66)—and avoid falling into the trap of evaluating discourse based on its effects. In suggesting the touchstone system, Black was careful to warn critics away from possible misapplications and to direct critics in the proper use of the method. He wrote,

> Obviously, no critic could reasonably demand of a contemporary rhetor that he [sic] speak in exactly the same way as, say, Edmund Burke. Touchstones are not models for copying. Rather, the touchstone system would demand that the contemporary rhetor treat his subject as well as Burke treated his before the contemporary would be awarded the highest accolade. (p. 67)

In the final analysis, the touchstone approach to criticism does not provide the critic with

> explicit, mechanically applicable standards; [it] provide[s] him [sic] with that vague quality, *taste,* without which no set of explicit standards can be judiciously applied. The touchstone system, then, is extremely useful to the training of the critic, to the sharpening of his perceptions and the elevation of his expectations. (pp. 67-68)[1]

Elements of the touchstone system are present in Leff's version of the critical strategy of **close reading.** For Leff, the aim of close reading is a grounded reconstruction of the principles of artistic rhetorical practice. Leff (1986) argued that exemplars or touchstones possess the capacity for "generating theoretical understanding of rhetorical action" (p. 382).[2] As Gaonkar (1990) observed, Leff's appropriation of the idea of touchstones of excellence as the concrete ground for uncovering the theoretical principles of rhetorical action taps into a mode of thinking that predates Arnold's method for poetic evaluation. Leff's version of the touchstone system resembles the mode of oratorical instruction outlined in Cicero's *De Oratore.* Gaonkar averred,

> There is a striking similarity between Antonius' [a character in Cicero's dialogue] program for oratorical education and Leff's

> program for rhetorical criticism. In Leff's scheme, masterpieces are the paradigmatic models, recognized as such by the interpretive community, that contain within them the secrets of eloquence. . . . His rationale for privileging the touchstone system is more theoretical than pedagogical. For Leff, rhetorical criticism, like psychoanalysis, is an interpretive discipline that seeks to understand an incomplete and elusive art through its concrete manifestations. When properly interpreted, the oratorical masterpiece discloses better than any other type of rhetorical text the actual functioning of the art. (p. 312)

In short, Leff redirected the thrust of the touchstone system. The traditional view from Arnold to Black saw the touchstone as part of the process of critical evaluation, whereas Leff understood the touchstone as a means for reconstructing the principles of rhetorical action.

But developing theory by way of touchstones also poses a dilemma for rhetorical scholars. Farrell (1993) outlined the terms of the dilemma in the following question: "If rhetoric is such a practical art, why is it that only exceptional cases of eloquent oratory are invoked as evidence of its craft?" (pp. 276-277). Put directly, this is the dilemma: Can a *practical* and *public* art be defined and explicated through touchstones produced almost exclusively by social elites? Some scholars, such as Ono and Sloop (1995), have eschewed touchstones rather decidedly in favor of an emphasis on **vernacular** discourse. The debate between scholars favoring a touchstone approach to criticism and theory building and those defending the study of vernacular discourse is a key issue in contemporary rhetorical studies.

Notes

1. For a variation on Black's (1965/1978) argument for touchstone criticism, see Rosenfield's (1968) discussion of the "analog modality" in critical practice.

2. Leff's (1986) point here extended Rosenfield's (1968) observation that the "analog modality . . . provides a point of departure which enables the critic to derive new categories and precepts from his [sic] investigation" (p. 68).

References and Additional Reading

Arnold, M. (1973). The study of poetry. In R. H. Super (Ed.), *The complete prose works of Matthew Arnold: English literature and Irish politics* (Vol. 9). Ann Arbor: University of Michigan Press. (Original work published 1880)

Black, E. (1978). *Rhetorical criticism: A study in method.* Madison: University of Wisconsin Press. (Original work published 1965)

Farrell, T. B. (1993). *Norms of rhetorical culture.* New Haven, CT: Yale University Press.

Gaonkar, D. P. (1990). Object and method in rhetorical criticism: From Wichelns to Leff and McGee. *Western Journal of Speech Communication, 54,* 290-316.

Leff, M. (1986). Textual criticism: The legacy of G. P. Mohrmann. *Quarterly Journal of Speech, 72,* 377-389.

Ono, K. A., & Sloop, J. M. (1995). The critique of vernacular discourse. *Communication Monographs, 62,* 19-46.

Rosenfield, L. W. (1968). The anatomy of critical discourse. *Speech Monographs, 35,* 50-69.

TRADITION

The English term **tradition** derives from two Latin words: the verb *tradere* (meaning to transmit as well as to give for safekeeping) and the noun *traditio* (referring to the process of transmission) (Gross, 1992). Beginning with the Enlightenment, the idea of tradition—of things handed down or transmitted from one generation to the next—was widely reviled as the *antithesis* of reason. But the status of tradition was on the upsurge during the latter portion of the 20th century, and this reevaluation has some significance for rhetorical studies.

One of the first tasks facing scholars interested in the topic of tradition is definitional: What exactly is meant by the concept of tradition? In his classic study, Shils (1981) wrote,

> Tradition means many things. In its barest, most elementary sense, it means simply a *traditum;* it is anything which is transmitted or handed down from the past to the present. . . . Tradition—that which is handed down—includes material objects, beliefs about all sorts of things, images of persons and events, practices and institutions. It includes buildings, monuments, landscapes, sculptures, paintings, books, tools, [and] machines. (p. 12)

Similarly, Gross (1992) remarked,

> The term "tradition" refers to a set of practices, a constellation of beliefs, or a mode of thinking that exists in the present but was inherited from the past. . . . A tradition, then, can be a set of observances, a collection of doctrines or teachings, a particular type of behavior, a way of thinking about the world or oneself, a way of regarding others or interpreting reality. (p. 8; see also Pocock, 1971)[1]

Efforts to define tradition must distinguish it from other related concepts. Shils (1981), for example, considered tradition in relation to the idea of *fashion* or **style.** He wrote, "A fashion existing within a short time period might be the practice or belief of a single generation, let us say those between fifteen and twenty years of age" (p. 15). But these fashionable beliefs or practices are not transmitted to the next generation or age cohort. Shils suggested that "brevity of duration is the mark of a fashion" (p. 16). If we are going to distinguish between traditions and fashions based on their respective durations, then what is the minimum duration that a belief or practice must meet to qualify as a tradition? Shils responded to this question by observing that "how long?"

> is an academic question, difficult to answer in a wholly satisfactory way but also not necessary to answer except to say that, at [a] minimum, two transmissions over three generations are required for a pattern of belief or action to be considered a tradition. (p. 15)

Gross (1992) generally endorsed Shils's two-transmission/three-generation definitional criterion (p. 10). He also raised the question of the relationship between tradition and *custom.* Gross wrote,

> A custom is an established social usage that has been built up through repetition over a long period of time. It may originate to satisfy some immediate need, but in the course of being repeated from one generation to another it gradually comes to be accepted simply because it is convenient or because it has been in operation for so long that no one questions its rationale. (p. 12)

Customs and traditions both involve transmission between generations, so on what grounds might they be distinguished? Gross explained the difference in this way:

> Though the lines between the two are easily blurred, there are some notable differences. Customs are social practices which, when considered from the point of view of society as a whole, are judged to be much less important than traditions. Because customs involve mostly superficial modes of behavior, they are not as heavily invested with value as traditions are. . . . Customs are often adhered to out of expediency or inertia. Moral censure is rarely incurred if one deviates from them, whereas traditions carry some amount of moral authority. (p. 12)

Gross's account of the differences between custom and tradition introduced another important aspect of tradition—its "moral authority" or, in Shils's terms, its "normative element" (p. 23). Shils continued,

> Tradition is thus far more than the statistically frequent recurrence over a succession of generations of similar beliefs, practices, institutions, and works. The recurrence is a consequence of the normative conse-

> quences—sometimes the normative intention—of presentation and of the acceptance of the tradition as normative. It is this normative transmission which links the generations of the dead with the generation of the living in the constitution of a society. (p. 24)

Traditions, in short, frequently are prescriptive; they structure or guide beliefs and behaviors. As will be discussed a little more fully in what follows, the normativity of tradition has important rhetorical implications.

The concept of tradition has relevance for rhetorical studies in at least two broad ways. First, rhetorical theory (or *rhetorica docens*) constitutes a significant tradition of thought. Its classical roots have been transmitted to succeeding generations for roughly two millennia, making it one of the most durable of intellectual traditions. Its normative or prescriptive character has been noted by countless scholars. And like many traditions, it is the subject of periodic reflection and reevaluation that can then lead to alterations of the tradition.[2] But the rhetorical tradition is different from many intellectual traditions in that its central concept—the idea of *rhetoric*—admits multiple definitions. The rhetorical tradition, as it has developed for more than two millennia, consists of multiple perspectives and voices.

The concept of tradition also has significance for rhetoric as a discursive practice (or *rhetorica utens*). The practical significance of tradition emerges in at least three ways. First, tradition can function as a *practical strategy.* Given its normative component, it should not be surprising that advocates try to harness this potential as a strategic resource. Advocates can appeal to the value of tradition (Perelman & Olbrechts-Tyteca, 1969), or they can employ tradition as an *authoritative* argumentative *warrant.* Tradition frequently is invoked as a strategy for *affirming* the status quo or the existing social order. Some scholars maintain that appeals to tradition or traditional values and beliefs are problematic; therefore, some logic and argument textbooks consider this strategy to be a **fallacy.**[3] To determine whether appeals to tradition are fallacious, it probably will be necessary to engage the complex question of whether or not traditions—what have been passed down to us from preceding generations—are reasonable or rational.[4]

Second, traditions have practical significance because they often function as a *situational constraint.* In a well-known passage from his essay, *The Eighteenth Brumaire of Louis Bonaparte,* Marx (1967) claimed that "the tradition of all the dead generations weighs like a nightmare on the brain of the living." Shils (1981) noted the tendency to conceptualize tradition *metaphorically* as a weight or a drag (p. 201). He continued, "Tradition hems an individual in; it sets the condition of his [sic] actions; it determines his resources. . . . It is very difficult for the individual to change what has been given" (p. 197). Any advocate who urges alteration of the status quo faces the constraint of tradition. One way in which advocates negotiate the constraint of tradition is by engaging in a rereading or reconceptualization of the tradition (Pocock, 1971). Advocates search for lost or neglected aspects of the tradition that might be used to open up new possibilities in the present. In 1852, black abolitionist Frederick Douglass reread the traditional beliefs concerning the American Revolution so as to uncover or recover resources that could be used in the struggle against slavery (Jasinski, 1997b). While acknowledging that tradition can function as a constraint, scholars also have begun to explore the way in which tradition might function as a resource for promoting social change (e.g., Calhoun, 1983).

Third, in addition to tradition being viewed as a strategy and as a potential constraint and/or resource, tradition is understood to be a *medium* of human existence or an inescapable part of human reality. This expansive approach to tradition has been developed in certain quarters of continental philosophy, especially the works of the German philosopher Hans-Georg Gadamer (e.g.,

Gadamer, 1982).[5] Summarizing some of the general aspects of the Gadamerian view of tradition, MacIntyre (1988) wrote, "There is no standing ground, no place for enquiry, no way to engage in the practices of advancing, evaluating, accepting, and rejecting reasoned argument apart from that which is provided by some particular tradition or other" (p. 350). In short, tradition is ubiquitous; it saturates our shared human reality. All thinking, all advocacy, and all critical reflection depend on tradition; these practices are impossible without it.

Gadamer's account of tradition is a type of rehabilitation; he rescued tradition from the scrap heap to which Enlightenment philosophers had consigned it. A revitalized sense of tradition has begun to play an important role in contemporary rhetorical studies. Bineham (1995) explored in some detail tradition's role as a medium of human existence. When so understood, tradition becomes the absolute foundation of rhetorical **invention**; all discursive production emerges from an advocate's engagement with tradition. Other scholars (Darsey, 1997; Jasinski, 1997a; Murphy, 1997) point to ways in which an expansive sense of tradition might function in rhetorical criticism. These studies position concepts such as rhetorical tradition and performative tradition at the center of critical scholarship, illustrating yet another way in which tradition is relevant to rhetorical studies.

Notes

1. Gross (1992) questioned whether material objects should be designated as part of a tradition. Material objects, he suggested, should be considered "conduits of traditional attitudes or patterns of conduct, but they are not themselves traditions" (p. 8).

2. On the tendency for traditions to evolve based on intensive reflection and scrutiny, see Gross (1992, pp. 77-91) and Shils (1981, pp. 213-261). For examples of this process in contemporary rhetorical studies, see Kastely (1997) and Poulakos (1993).

3. See, for example, Damer (1995) and Inch and Warnick (1998). See also the discussion of the *ad verecundiam* fallacy.

4. For an introduction to this complicated issue, see MacIntyre (1988, pp. 349-369).

5. For commentaries on Gadamer, see also Bineham (1995), Risser (1997), and Warnke (1987).

References and Additional Reading

Allan, G. (1986). *The importance of the past: A meditation on the authority of tradition.* Albany: State University of New York Press.

Bineham, J. L. (1995). The hermeneutic medium. *Philosophy and Rhetoric, 28,* 1-16.

Bruns, G. L. (1991). What is tradition? *New Literary History, 22,* 1-21.

Calhoun, C. J. (1983). The radicalism of tradition: Community strength or venerable disguise and borrowed language? *American Journal of Sociology, 88,* 886-914.

Damer, T. E. (1995). *Attacking faulty reasoning: A practical guide to fallacy-free arguments* (3rd ed.). Belmont, CA: Wadsworth.

Darsey, J. (1997). *The prophetic tradition and radical rhetoric in America.* New York: New York University Press.

Eliot, T. S. (1920). Tradition and individual talent. In T. S. Eliot, *The sacred wood: Essays on poetry and criticism.* London: Methuen.

Gadamer, H. G. (1982). *Truth and method* (G. Barden & J. Cumming, Trans.). New York: Crossroad.

Gross, D. (1992). *The past in ruins: Tradition and the critique of modernity.* Amherst: University of Massachusetts Press.

Hobsbawm, E., & Ranger, T. (Eds.). (1983). *The invention of tradition.* Cambridge, UK: Cambridge University Press.

Inch, E. S., & Warnick, B. (1998). *Critical thinking and communication: The use of reason in argument* (3rd ed.). Boston: Allyn & Bacon.

Jasinski, J. (1997a). Instrumentalism, contextualism, and interpretation in rhetorical criticism. In A. G. Gross & W. M. Keith (Eds.), *Rhetorical hermeneutics.* Albany: State University of New York Press.

Jasinski, J. (1997b). Rearticulating history in epideictic discourse: Frederick Douglass's "The Meaning of the Fourth of July to the Negro." In T. W. Benson (Ed.), *Rhetoric and political culture in nineteenth-century America.* East Lansing: Michigan State University Press.

Kastely, J. L. (1997). *Rethinking the rhetorical tradition: From Plato to postmodernism.* New Haven, CT: Yale University Press.

MacIntyre, A. (1988). *Whose justice? Which rationality?* Notre Dame, IN: University of Notre Dame Press.

Marx, K. (1967). *The eighteenth brumaire of Louis Bonaparte.* New York: International Publishers.

Murphy, J. M. (1997). Inventing authority: Bill Clinton, Martin Luther King, Jr., and the orchestration of rhetorical traditions. *Quarterly Journal of Speech, 83,* 71-89.

Perelman, C., & Olbrechts-Tyteca, L. (1969). *The new rhetoric: A treatise on argument* (J. Wilkinson & P. Weaver, Trans.). Notre Dame, IN: University of Notre Dame Press.

Pocock, J. G. A. (1971). Time, institutions, and action: An essay on traditions and their understanding. In J. G. A. Pocock, *Politics, language, and time.* New York: Atheneum.

Poulakos, T. (Ed.). (1993). *Rethinking the history of rhetoric: Multidisciplinary essays on the rhetorical tradition.* Boulder, CO: Westview.

Risser, J. (1997). *Hermeneutics and the voice of the other: Re-reading Gadamer's philosophical hermeneutics.* Albany: State University of New York Press.

Shils, E. A. (1981). *Tradition.* Chicago: University of Chicago Press.

Warnke, G. (1987). *Gadamer: Hermeneutics, tradition, and reason.* Stanford, CA: Stanford University Press.

TRANSCENDENCE

Discussing the concept of **transcendence** in *Attitudes Toward History,* Burke (1984) remarked,

> We are trying to bring up an issue rather than to persuade anyone that we can make it crystal-clear. The point to be stressed is that the process of transcendence, basic to thought, is revealed most simply in didactic-moralistic literature. There must be many ways by which "transcendence" takes place. (p. 86)

As Burke acknowledged in the preceding passage, the concept of transcendence is elusive and difficult to pin down. But because it appears with regularity in "didactic" or persuasive discourse, it probably should remain of interest to rhetorical scholars.

Other scholars echo Burke's observation on the centrality of transcendence to human life. Evens (1990) described transcendence as a basic "modality of human existence" that is "fundamental to social life" (p. 1). Evens added that transcendence "describes a kind of being, both protean and indistinct, by which society everywhere develops and proceeds" (p. 3). Generalizing from the observations of Burke and Evens, we can tentatively conclude that transcendence is central to human existence but is also hard to grasp. How *have* scholars tried to define the basic nature of transcendence?

Burke's (1984) classic definition is as follows: "When approached from a certain point of view, A and B are 'opposites.' We mean by 'transcendence' the adoption of another point of view from which they cease to be opposites." Burke noted that this is "the nearest approach we can make to the process by verbal means" (p. 336). Consider a few hypothetical examples that illustrate Burke's definition. Two factions emerge within a religious order, with each opposed to the ideas of the other. If the two factions continue on their antagonistic course, the continued existence of the religious order is in jeopardy. How might an advocate intervene in this *rhetorical* **situation**? Employing the strategy of transcendence, an advocate might encourage both factions to focus on doing God's will on this earth. The advocate might try to overcome or transcend the factional strife by getting both groups to turn their attention away from each other (at least what they do not like about each other) and to focus instead on their shared calling to serve God. Consider a second case. The marketing and production departments at a large manufacturing operation are at odds. Each blames the other for the company's inability to increase its market share. If the tension between these two departments persists, then the company will have little chance of attaining economic growth. How might someone in senior management try to resolve this *exigence*? If the senior manager elects the strategy of transcendence (rather than, say, **scapegoating**), then he or she might call a company-wide meeting to announce that the competition is developing a new product that will pose an even greater threat to the company's market share. "Our only hope," the manager might implore, "is to pull together to defeat the competition." In this case, the manager would be trying to transcend the interdepartmental squabbling by directing attention away from the company and instead focusing on a common "enemy." Consider a final example. Two political parties are at odds, with each believing that the ideas supported by the other party threaten the health of the nation. Given this situation, how might a political advocate build support for a particular policy proposal? The advocate might try to transcend the interparty disputes by focusing attention on how the policy actually is in the "national interest" (as Burke [1984] noted, "Professional partisans like to advocate their measures as *transcending* factional antithesis" [p. 78]). Use of the abstract *ultimate term* (Burke, 1950) or the **ideograph** "national interest" might encourage the members of both parties to stand together and support what is in everyone's best interest.[1]

The pattern in each case is basically the same. The substance of the appeal might be different in each of the examples—in one case the advocate appeals to God, in another case the advocate creates an **enemy,** and in the final case the advocate introduces an abstract *principle*—but they all function in a similar manner. None of the appeals deals with the substance of what separates A and B; in each case, the transcendence strategy refocuses the attention of the disputants onto something of value they share (God or the national interest) or something they share through opposition (a competing company). In each case, the individuals and groups that constitute the A and B are given a new point of view—a new *perspective*—that allows them to overcome their differences.

Wess (1996) pointed out that Burke's sense of transcendence is fundamentally "rhetorical" (p. 87). What was Wess getting at when he described Burke's position in this way? Wess's point appeared to be this: Unlike some schools of philosophy (sometimes referred to as *transcendental* philosophy) that seek out some final or absolute (foundational) point of view that will organize and order the world, Burke's sense of transcendence is decidedly *nonfoundational.* According to Wess, Burke understood transcendence "as always relative to historically engendered tensions. A perspective that is transcendent in one situation is not necessarily transcendent in others" (p. 87). Burke discussed transcendence not in an effort to transcend differences and establish an absolute foundation but rather in the hope of calling attention to a pervasive aspect of human life and the discursive practices that sustain it.

But Burke might not have been entirely consistent in his account of transcendence. In a later essay on Emerson, Burke (1966) described transcendence as "the building of a *terministic bridge,* whereby one realm is *transcended* by being viewed *in terms of* a realm 'beyond' it" (p. 187). Some scholars read this discussion of transcendence as describing a process of change or *transformation* (p. 189; see also Burke, 1969). That is, transcendence occurs when A *becomes* B rather than when something else intervenes to overcome an opposition *between* A and B. Duncan (1962), for example, understood transcendence as a form of "symbolic transformation" (p. 157).[2] Duncan drew attention to Burke's discussion of "upward" and "downward" transcendence. Upward transcendence occurs when an act is reconceptualized or transformed; what was at first a selfish act of acquisition is, by way of upward transcendence, transformed into an act that protects the health of the larger economic system.[3] Downward transcendence occurs when something usually viewed as noble is reduced to its most elemental constituent parts. This form of transcendence appears to be at work in a BBC documentary series titled "The Human Body." The writer and narrator for the documentary, Sir Robert Winston, noted that "the cells in our bodies are made up of atoms which have existed since the start of the universe. They are constantly being exchanged and recycled. So today what makes up our bodies [was] once parts of plants, animals, trees—indeed, other humans." A critic of the documentary series, Steven Chalke, implicitly drew our attention to the downward transcendence embedded in the series when he protested "this reduction of humanity to nothing but a race of gene machines."

Another way of conceptualizing the concept of transcendence is to see it as an essentially spiritual movement from incompleteness or fragmentation to a state of wholeness or completion. For example, Rushing (1985) described the "modern need for transcendence" as a desire for "transcendent wholeness" (p. 188). The desire to overcome "the contemporary sense of fragmentation" is reflected in a variety of media texts, such as the film *E.T.*, that offer their audiences "visions of transcendence" (pp. 189, 199). Daughton (1996) uncovered a similar, albeit more gender-inflected, movement in the radical transformation of Bill Murray's character in the film *Groundhog Day* from selfish sexist pig to sensitive and caring human.

Extant scholarship does not provide one definitive definition of the concept of transcendence. But the scholarship does describe a range of practices that merit continued attention and reflection. As Evens (1990) noted, "Transcendence may connote the mystical and the occult, the visionary and divine. But whatever its particular connotation . . ., it is fundamental to social life" (p. 1).

Notes

1. Appeals to ultimate terms and ideographs are forms of "bridging devices." Burke (1984) defined a *bridging device* as a "symbolic structure whereby one 'transcends' a conflict in one way or another" (p. 224). Carlson (1994) illustrated some of the critical potential of the concept in her study of Lucretia Coffin Mott's important 1849 oration, "Discourse on Woman." In her analysis, Carlson argued that "Mott's artistry arises in rhetorical bridging of accepted differences between man and woman by subsuming them to the transcendent ideal of 'inner light' [a key concept in Quaker theology]. . . . Mott uses the 'inner light' as a 'bridging device' to transcend the differences between the sexes dictated by society" (p. 87). See also Carlson (1999).

2. See also Bertelsen (1993) and Brummett (1981, 1982). Hearit (1997) combined both senses of transcendence in an exploration of their **apologia** functions.

3. This is a variation on Brummett's (1981) reading of Ronald Reagan's transcendence strategy in the 1980 presidential election.

References and Additional Reading

Bertelsen, D. A. (1993). Kenneth Burke's conception of reality: The process of transformation and its implications for rhetorical criticism. In J. W. Chesebro (Ed.), *Extensions of the Burkeian system.* Tuscaloosa: University of Alabama Press.

Brummett, B. (1981). Burkean scapegoating, mortification, and transcendence in presidential campaign rhetoric. *Central States Speech Journal, 32,* 254-264.

Brummett, B. (1982). Burkean transcendence and ultimate terms in rhetoric by and about James Watt. *Central States Speech Journal, 33,* 547-556.

Burke, K. (1950). *A rhetoric of motives.* New York: Prentice Hall.

Burke, K. (1966). *Language as symbolic action: Essays on life, literature, and method.* Berkeley: University of California Press.

Burke, K. (1969). *A grammar of motives.* Berkeley: University of California Press.

Burke, K. (1984). *Attitudes toward history.* Berkeley: University of California Press.

Burkholder, T. R. (1989). Kansas populism, woman suffrage, and the agrarian myth: A case study in the limits of mythic transcendence. *Communication Studies, 40,* 292-307.

Carlson, A. C. (1994). Defining womanhood: Lucretia Coffin Mott and the transformation of femininity. *Western Journal of Communication, 58,* 85-97.

Carlson, A. C. (1999). "You know it when you see it": The rhetorical hierarchy of race and gender in *Rhinelander v. Rhinelander. Quarterly Journal of Speech, 85,* 111-128.

Chandler, R. C., Hobbs, J. D., King, A. S., & Walts, C. (2000). Scapegoating, transcendence, mortification, and forgiveness: Compensatory arguments of blame after Littleton. In T. A. Hollihan (Ed.), *Argument at century's end: Reflecting on the past and envisioning the future.* Annandale, VA: National Communication Association.

Daughton, S. M. (1993). Metaphoric transcendence: Images of the holy war in Franklin Roosevelt's first inaugural. *Quarterly Journal of Speech, 79,* 427-446.

Daughton, S. M. (1996). The spiritual power of repetitive form: Steps toward transcendence in *Groundhog Day. Critical Studies in Mass Communication, 13,* 138-154.

Duncan, H. D. (1962). *Communication and social order.* London: Oxford University Press.

Evens, T. M. S. (1990). Introduction. In T. M. S. Evens & J. L. Peacock (Eds.), *Comparative social research,*

Suppl. 1: *Transcendence in society: Case studies.* Greenwich, CT: JAI.

Hearit, K. M. (1997). On the use of transcendence as an apologia strategy: The case of Johnson Controls and its fetal protection policy. *Public Relations Review, 23,* 217-231.

Parson, D. W. (1993). "If you want me to be your president": H. Ross Perot's strategies of rhetorical transcendence. In R. E. McKerrow (Ed.), *Argument and the postmodern challenge: Proceedings of the Eighth SCA/AFA Conference on Argumentation.* Annandale, VA: Speech Communication Association.

Rasmussen, K. (1994). Transcendence in Leonard Bernstein's *Kaddish Symphony. Quarterly Journal of Speech, 80,* 150-173.

Rushing, J. H. (1985). *E.T.* as rhetorical transcendence. *Quarterly Journal of Speech, 71,* 188-203.

Wess, R. (1996). *Kenneth Burke: Rhetoric, subjectivity, postmodernism.* Cambridge, UK: Cambridge University Press.

TRANSPARENCY THESIS

In his essay on the legacy of G. P. Mohrmann, Leff (1986) identified a persistent tendency among rhetorical critics. Leff wrote that even as critical scholarship "drifted away from its original moorings, the *transparency of the text* persisted as a general assumption" (p. 384). Focusing on the "persistent and crucial" relationship "between time and rhetoric" (p. 383), Leff argued that the durability of specific rhetorical events or performances commonly has been conceptualized as "entirely diachronic, something charted across the arc of historic change" (p. 384). Consequently, what Leff referred to as the internal timing of the text—the "order and relation of elements within its own pattern of utterance" (p. 385)—typically has been deferred. Leff suggested that this deferral illustrates an unarticulated logic inscribed in most rhetorical criticism—the logic of the transparent text.[1] A text's or performance's internal timing has been neglected because critics have assumed that rhetorical artifacts—speeches, orations, essays, and so on—lack "artistic density" (p. 385), that they pose no interpretive problems, or that they do not require careful attention to the internal dynamics of their construction. In short, as the underlying metaphor of transparency suggests, critics have tended to *look through* the text rather than fix their analytic gaze on it. It is worth observing that the idea of the transparent text is not unique to the field of rhetorical studies; it has deep roots in American thinking about political discourse (Aune, 1996) and rhetorical style (Lanham, 1983).

Gaonkar's (1990) **metacritical** essay referred to Leff's observation as the transparency thesis (see also Gaonkar, 1997). Gaonkar (1990) argued that Leff negotiated the text's purported transparency, and the related issue of textual resistance to **close reading,** through a strategy of reversal. Transparency is not a textual characteristic to be denied but rather one to be appreciated and analyzed more deeply. For Leff, it becomes "the hallmark of rhetorical artistry" (p. 313). Gaonkar identified the following critical passage from Leff's essay:

> Unlike poetry and other "purer" forms of verbal art, the oration does not call attention to its own status as an art form. Oratory succeeds best when it appears to blend into the context of ordinary experience. It is a genre of discourse that effaces its own construction. (p. 381)[2]

Gaonkar added that the "seeming reducibility" of the rhetorical text to either its referential or ideological dimensions "is precisely the work of rhetorical art. The cunning of the oratorical text consists in creating an illusion of [unmediated or objective] referentiality and ideological plausibility" (p. 313). Through Leff's reversal strategy, "the oratorical text loses its transparency" (p. 313), but (somewhat paradoxically) the text gains a new or reconfigured form of transparency—an artistic appearance of transparency that reveals the text to be "dense and opaque" (p. 313) and, hence, in need of careful disciplined reading. In short, for Leff, transparency is an artistic achievement and not a natural or inevitable effect of linguistic **representation.**

But Gaonkar argued that Leff's reversal of the rhetorical text's transparency was based on a "misreading" of the transparency thesis. For Gaonkar, this misreading becomes clear when the question of transparency is connected to the issue of textual resistance. He asserted that Leff's diagnosis of the problems in current rhetorical criticism "is preoccupied with *the resistance to the text* rather than with *the resistance of the text.* But there is a key difference" (p. 310). The difference has to do with the source of resistance. Gaonkar argued that Leff located resistance outside of the text—in "the methodological monism of the old guard or the excessive theoreticism of revisionists"—but that Leff did not "seriously engage" the possibility that resistance emanates from within the text. Leff's negotiation of the transparency thesis "misreads the resistance of the text as having no resistance whatsoever" (p. 310). For Leff, the appearance of transparency does not repel or inhibit careful reading; it makes it necessary. But Gaonkar observed that "this move deflects our attention from a more radical notion of resistance" that can be found, for example, in McGee's (1990) claim that all texts are simply "fragments" that are continually assembled, disassembled, and reassembled. Gaonkar maintained that a form of radical resistance residing in the **text** would require significant modifications in the critical program that follows from Leff's negotiation of the transparency thesis.

Gaonkar (1997) outlined the basic elements of an alternative critical program that he labeled "close reading of the third kind" (p. 350). He began his outline by displacing the idea of the "transparent" text and replacing it with a sense of the "translucent" text (pp. 350-351). Gaonkar explained,

> The difference between the transparent and the translucent is notable. The latter implies partial transparency. According to the dictionary, *translucent* refers both to what is shining or glowing (hence, *luminous*) and what is readily perceptible (hence, *lucid*). The crossing of the luminous and the lucid creates an effect of "admitting and diffusing light so that objects beyond cannot be clearly distinguished." The surface of the public text is translucent in precisely this sense. It is readily perceptible and distracting. Its electric surface is easy and tempting to consume, but its glare deflects a close reading. (p. 351)

With the concept of the translucent text, Gaonkar identified a more radical form of textual resistance; it is this translucent quality of the text that is the source of its resistance or what makes reading such a deceptively simple, and thus rather complicated, process.

Neither of the two dominant reading strategies in contemporary rhetorical criticism—what Gaonkar (1997) labeled the instrumental and the contextual (p. 351)—is adequate for grasping the translucent text. Gaonkar adumbrated an alternative by way of a mundane yet striking *metaphor:*

> The surface of the public text . . . [is] like that of a clear pond. . . . Just as the pond becomes unsettled and muddied in unseasonable weather, the text is unsettled under a certain kind of reading. In CRTK [close reading of the third kind], unsettling the text is like stirring a pond with a stick. . . . To extend the metaphor, the critic stirs the seemingly translucent pond/text until it becomes muddy; then, she [sic] reads the sedimented particles that have surfaced from the base, identifying their character and formation and their gradual return to the base. (pp. 350-351)

The metaphor certainly is suggestive but devoid of concrete critical or interpretive directives. In a more prosaic moment, Gaonkar asserted the need to "engage the public text as a cultural artifact rather than as a manifestation of a rhetor's strategic consciousness . . . [or] to map the articulatory practices of a cultural conjuncture and not that of an authorial cunning" (p. 352). The one clear directive that Gaonkar offered is a version of the **postmodern** "decentering" of the **subject.**

Finally, Jasinski (1997), following Bineham (1995), extended the transparency thesis into the conceptual domains of **context** and **tradition.** Responding to a perceived problem in how context has been conceptualized in critical practice, Jasinski (1997) argued that the orchestration of *performative traditions* in rhetorical practice requires the attention of critics. But he acknowledged that such a shift raises the problem of transparency:

> The turn to close reading over the last decade or so has done much to recover the artfulness of the seemingly innocent text. But the problem of transparency has a second level or dimension that requires attention. While the techniques of rhetorical art receive increased emphasis in close textual analysis, the material of art still remains rather transparent. (p. 214)

Tradition, along with **doxa** or **social knowledge,** is one of the primary materials of rhetorical art. But as Bineham (1995) noted, although tradition might be an "encompassing" medium of human life, it frequently is "unnoticed" and "transparent" (p. 5). Quoting the hermeneutic philosopher Richard Palmer, Bineham wrote, "Tradition is 'not over against us but something in which we stand and through which we exist; for the most part, it is so transparent a medium that it is invisible to us—as invisible as water to a fish' " (p. 8). Part of the contemporary critic's challenge, Jasinski suggested, is to not only negotiate the transparency of rhetorical art as manifest in specific texts but also engage the transparency of performative traditions as a way of thickening critical practice.

Notes

1. On the transparency of rhetorical effect, see also Blumenberg (1987).

2. In this passage, Leff (1986) was extending one of Aristotle's insights on **style.** Aristotle (1954) wrote in the *Rhetoric,* "We can now see that a writer must disguise his [sic] art and give the impression of speaking naturally and not artificially" (1404b17-1404b19).

References and Additional Reading

Aristotle. (1954). *Rhetoric* (W. R. Roberts, Trans.). New York: Modern Library.

Aune, J. A. (1996, September). *Eloquence, transparency, and the emergence of the populist style: A reading of* The Key of Liberty. Paper presented at the Fifth Biennial Public Address Conference, Urbana, IL.

Bineham, J. L. (1995). The hermeneutic medium. *Philosophy and Rhetoric, 28,* 1-16.

Blumenberg, H. (1987). An anthropological approach to the contemporary significance of rhetoric (R. M. Wallace, Trans.). In K. Baynes, J. Bohman, & T. McCarthy (Eds.), *After philosophy: End or transformation?* Cambridge, MA: MIT Press.

Gaonkar, D. P. (1990). Object and method in rhetorical criticism: From Wichelns to Leff and McGee. *Western Journal of Speech Communication, 54,* 290-316.

Gaonkar, D. P. (1997). Close readings of the third kind: Reply to my critics. In W. Keith & A. Gross (Eds.), *Rhetorical hermeneutics.* Albany: State University of New York Press.

Jasinski, J. (1997). Instrumentalism, contextualism, and interpretation in rhetorical criticism. In W. Keith & A. Gross (Eds.), *Rhetorical hermeneutics.* Albany: State University of New York Press.

Lanham, R. A. (1983). *Analyzing prose.* New York: Scribner.

Leff, M. (1986). Textual criticism: The legacy of G. P. Mohrmann. *Quarterly Journal of Speech, 72,* 377-389.

McGee, M. C. (1990). Text, context, and the fragmentation of contemporary culture. *Western Journal of Speech Communication, 54,* 274-289.

VALUES AND VALUE HIERARCHY

Philosopher William Frankena observed,

> Philosophers from the time of Plato had discussed a variety of questions under such headings as the good, the end, the right, obligation, virtue, moral judgment, aesthetic judgment, the beautiful, truth, and validity. In the nineteenth century, the conception was born—or reborn, because it is essentially to be found in Plato—that all these questions belong to the same family, since they are all concerned with value or what ought to be, not with fact or what is, was, or will be. (Frankena, 1967, p. 229)

Frankena suggested that the concept of value is multifaceted: "In its widest use, 'value' is a generic noun for all kinds of critical or pro and con predicates, as opposed to descriptive ones, and is contrasted with existence or fact." In a somewhat narrower sense, value often is used

> to refer to what is valued, judged to have value, thought to be good, or desired. The expressions "his values," "her value system," and "American values" refer to what a man, a woman, and Americans value or think to be good. Such phrases are also used to refer to what people think is right or obligatory. (pp. 229-230)

The term *values,* then, often is a shorthand way of saying "things we believe to be good." Because values frequently are communal in nature and connected to action (as in the act of *evaluation*), we might think of values as shared dispositions of what is desirable and undesirable.[1]

Values and value hierarchies have been the focus of considerable scholarly attention for a number of years. For example, values can be categorized in various ways. Following Rokeach (1973), many scholars distinguish between *instrumental* and *terminal* values. Instrumental values consist of positive or negative evaluations of courses of conduct or behavior (e.g., lying is bad/telling the truth is good). Terminal values identify desirable conditions or states of existence (e.g., the Aristotelian notion that happiness is the *telos* or end of human existence). Some scholars (e.g., Walhout, 1978) also distinguish between *social* or political values (e.g., liberty, freedom) and those that, although shared within a society, operate in a more *personal* realm (e.g., health, friendship). Finally, some scholars differentiate between *abstract* and *concrete* values. Perelman and Olbrechts-Tyteca (1969) wrote that a concrete value is "one attaching to a living being, a specific group, or a particular object, considered as a unique entity"

(p. 77). Family is a very concrete value in the world depicted in the three *Godfather* films. Abstract values such as truth and justice **transcend** particular circumstances (p. 77). Because of their generality, abstract values "seem to provide criteria for one wishing to change the established order" (p. 79). Like most efforts at categorization, the distinctions between instrumental and terminal values, between social and personal values, and between concrete and abstract values are not absolute. Gray areas between these categories no doubt exist.

According to Perelman and Olbrechts-Tyteca (1969), "Values enter into every argument. . . . In the fields of law, politics, and philosophy, values intervene as a basis for argument at all stages of the developments" (p. 75). Although they were not the first scholars to notice the relationship between values and **argument,** Perelman and Olbrechts-Tyteca helped to stimulate theoretical reflection on the role of values in rhetorical practice. Values enter into the process and/or practice of argument in numerous ways. It is quite common in contemporary argumentation theory to speak of *value claims.* But Sillars and Ganer (1982) warned scholars not to reduce the function of values in argument to one of simply specifying a type of claim (pp. 188-189). They wrote that "in argumentation, values are strategically significant" (p. 191). But what exactly are some of the ways in which values enter into argumentative or rhetorical practice?

First, as noted by Sillars and Ganer (1982), among others (e.g., van Eemeren, Grootendorst, & Henkemans, 1996), values often function, in Toulmin's vocabulary, as an argument *warrant* or as *backing* for a warrant. Sillars and Ganer (1982) wrote,

> Any argument involves reasoning, and any reasoning can be driven back to a value orientation. That value orientation will most frequently and importantly serve as warrants for claims or when the warrant is a belief, values will back it. . . . In argumentation . . ., values form warrants for arguments. (pp. 195-196, 198)

For example, the value of "family security" frequently appears near the tops of surveys of public values. This value has the potential to warrant a variety of **deliberative** *policy claims.* Consider the following reconstructions of *classification* arguments in support of policy claims:

Example 1

Major premise (value warrant): Social policies that promote family security are good.

Minor premise (data): The provisions of the proposed crime bill will enhance family security.[2]

Conclusion (claim): The proposed crime bill is good (and because it is good, we should support it).

Example 2

Major premise (value warrant): Courses of action that protect family security are good.

Minor premise (data): Saving 10% of take-home pay for future emergencies will enhance family security.

Conclusion (claim): Saving 10% of take-home pay is good (and because it is good, we should do it).

Using values as warrants usually entails the application of values to specific objects or, in other words, engaging in the process of *evaluation.* The dynamics of this process were treated in detail by Inch and Warnick (1998).[3] They suggested that the argumentative process of evaluation reveals certain standard or *stock issues* that parallel the more widely known **stock topics of policy discourse.** They identified five value stock issues: *definition, field, criteria, application,* and *hierarchies* (pp. 252-256). Evaluative argument begins by identifying an object to be appraised. Inch and Warnick wrote, "A value object is an idea, practice, event, policy, or state of affairs that is to be judged by means of an evaluation" (p. 252). The first possible issue or point of dispute is **definition.** How will the object be circumscribed? Consider a simple example.

An individual who recently moved into a new town gets into a discussion with a co-worker about which of the local news shows is best. One of the first things that needs to happen in this discussion, if only implicitly, is reaching an agreement over what "local" and "newscast" will mean. They need to decide what gets included and what gets excluded so that an evaluation can proceed. The second issue, according to Inch and Warnick, is the **argument field** "or perspective within which the value object will be evaluated" (p. 253). It will be virtually impossible for the individual and co-worker to reach a consensus if they are proceeding from different fields. If the co-worker is using economics as a field, arguing that the newscast that makes the most money is best, then he or she will have difficulty in persuading the new individual if that person is using the assumptions of a different field such as journalism. Even when arguers agree on a field, they still can disagree on the specific *field-dependent criteria* that should be used in the evaluative process. Various criteria can be derived from the field of journalism to evaluate local newscasts. The individual might assert that the amount of attention devoted to local politics is the principal criterion that should be used, whereas the co-worker might counter by claiming that community service features is the appropriate standard. Finally, the specific criteria or standards must be applied to the value object. The individual and the co-worker might agree that attention to local politics is the most appropriate criterion, but they still might disagree about the *application* process. The co-worker might try to argue that the local NBC affiliate devotes the most attention to local politics, whereas the new individual might assert that the local independent station devotes more attention. Because disputes over application usually involve *factual claims,* advocates frequently will appeal to empirical evidence to resolve them.

Inch and Warnick's (1998) fifth value stock issue, *value hierarchies,* leads into a distinct aspect of value argument. Values enter into argument not only as warrants or as part of the process of evaluation; at times, value conflicts are at the center of a controversy, and such conflicts are resolved through the construction of value hierarchies. Value hierarchies simply place one value (or value object) in a position of superiority relative to another value (or value object).[4] Inch and Warnick wrote that there are "many value hierarchies that are recognized and accepted in American society." They pointed to our tendency to value the "objective" over the "subjective" or the "ends" over the "means" (p. 204). In some cases, advocates draw on value hierarchies in constructing persuasive appeals. For example, a local real estate developer might try to win support for a new shopping mall by suggesting that the economic needs of the community are more important than the extremist environmental concerns raised by outsiders. Numerous hierarchies are at work—economic needs over environmental needs, local residents over outsiders, and reasonable over extreme.

But how are value hierarchies constructed or overturned? Perelman and Olbrechts-Tyteca (1969) offered some insight into this issue. They wrote, "When a speaker wants to establish values or hierarchies . . ., he [sic] may . . . resort to premises of a very general nature which we shall term *loci*" or commonplaces (p. 83).[5] These general "premises" are grouped into six clusters: quantity, quality, order, existent, essence, and the person (pp. 85-95).[6] We can illustrate how the loci work by considering the question: Which is more valuable, justice or courage? At first glance, this seems to be a hopelessly abstract and difficult question. Thinkers influenced by Plato or the Platonic tradition probably would argue that the question could not be answered unless we understood the nature of each value. Without adequate knowledge of justice and courage, the question could not be answered. A rhetorician familiar with the loci would reply that this is nonsense and that we can build an argument in support of a hierarchy by asking one additional question: Which gets used more often, justice or courage? If we reply that the value of justice should operate in the world everyday whereas the value of courage is important only in certain situations, then we can assert that justice is more valuable because we use it more often. This argument is built on the locus of quantity and the specific (major) *premise:* What gets used more often is more valuable than what is used less often.[7] The same locus and premise could help to mediate a conflict between different value objects. If someone asks, "Who is more valuable, a pitcher such as Greg Maddux or Randy Johnson or an outfielder such as Sammy Sosa or Ken Griffey, Jr.?," then one can reply, "Sosa and Griffey play every day (unless they get injured), whereas Maddux and Johnson pitch only every fourth or fifth game, so Sosa or Griffey is more valuable because he plays more often."

The loci also can work to *subvert* existing hierarchies or evaluations. Perelman and Olbrechts-Tyteca (1969) observed that the "*loci* of quality occur in argumentation when the strength of numbers is challenged. . . . They are used by reformers or those in revolt against commonly held opinions" (p. 89). Appeals to particular qualitative loci such as the *unique,* the *precarious,* and the *irreparable* become ways of undercutting arguments grounded in a quantitative hierarchy (Cox, 1982). The locus of order also illustrates this subversive potential. A music critic can draw on premises relating to order in arguing that early REM or U2 recordings are better than their later recordings. The premise would be something to the effect of "What comes earlier is more authentic or purer than what comes later." But a different premise of order, something like "What comes later is more refined or polished than what comes earlier," could be used to argue the opposite position.

Rhetorical scholars have explored the role of values in public discourse intermittently over the past few decades (Sillars, 1995; Steele, 1958; Steele & Redding, 1962; Walker & Sillars, 1990; Wenzel, 1977). Sillars (1995) made a strong case for what he described as "a value-centered theory of argumentation." The central task of such a theory is to study "how the participants in argumentation use values." He claimed that value analysis "brings us closer to what actually happens in argumentation" (p. 2). Sillars' work is a concrete manifestation of the place of value inquiry in contemporary rhetorical studies.

Notes

1. For classic definitions, see Rescher (1969) and Rokeach (1973). For a useful summary, see Inch and Warnick (1998, pp. 247-249).

2. The data or minor premise might, of course, need to be supported further.

3. Inch and Warnick's (1998) discussion extended Taylor (1961) and Warnick (1981).

4. Discussing the inevitability of hierarchical ordering when values are at stake, Gunn (1987) wrote, "By values . . ., I do not mean anything as restrictive as ideals or norms, conscious or otherwise. Rather, I refer to the categories of significance, of assessed meaning, by which we arrange experience—any experience, all experience—hierarchically. We do so, apparently, because we have to. Life continually confronts us with choices, options between which we must decide. We decide only on the basis of preference, which requires valuation and produces ranking" (p. 127).

5. See also the discussion in the entry for **topics/topoi.**

6. See also Cox (1980, 1982), Depoe (1991), and Inch and Warnick (1998, pp. 250-251).

7. It is possible, of course, to employ a qualitative locus and argue that courage is more important because, without courage, it would not be possible for a community to maintain its independence and, without independence, a community would not need justice.

References and Additional Reading

Cox, J. R. (1980). "Loci communes" and Thoreau's arguments for wilderness in "Walking" (1851). *Southern Speech Communication Journal, 46,* 1-16.

Cox, J. R. (1982). The die is cast: Topical and ontological dimensions of the *locus* of the irreparable. *Quarterly Journal of Speech, 68,* 227-239.

Depoe, S. P. (1991). Space and the 1960 presidential campaign: Kennedy, Nixon, and "public time." *Western Journal of Speech Communication, 55,* 215-233.

Frankena, W. K. (1967). Value and valuation. In P. Edwards (Ed.), *The encyclopedia of philosophy* (Vol. 8). New York: Macmillan.

Gunn, G. (1987). *The culture of criticism and the criticism of culture.* New York: Oxford University Press.

Inch, E. S., & Warnick, B. (1998). *Critical thinking and communication: The use of reason in argument* (3rd ed.). Boston: Allyn & Bacon.

Perelman, C., & Olbrechts-Tyteca, L. (1969). *The new rhetoric: A treatise on argumentation* (J. Wilkinson & P. Weaver, Trans.). Notre Dame, IN: University of Notre Dame Press.

Rescher, N. (1969). *Introduction to value theory.* Englewood Cliffs, NJ: Prentice Hall.

Rokeach, M. (1973). *The nature of human values.* New York: Free Press.

Sillars, M. O. (1995). Values: Providing standards for audience-centered argumentation. In S. Jackson (Ed.), *Argumentation and values: Proceedings of the Ninth SCA/AFA Conference on Argumentation.* Annandale, VA: Speech Communication Association.

Sillars, M. O., & Ganer, P. (1982). Values and beliefs: A systematic basis for argumentation. In J. R. Cox & C. A. Willard (Eds.), *Advances in argumentation theory and research.* Carbondale: Southern Illinois University Press.

Steele, E. (1958). Social values in public address. *Western Speech, 22,* 38-42.

Steele, E., & Redding, W. C. (1962). The American value system: Premises for persuasion. *Western Speech, 26,* 83-91.

Taylor, P. W. (1961). *Normative discourse.* Englewood Cliffs, NJ: Prentice Hall.

van Eemeren, F. H., Grootendorst, R., & Henkemans, F. S. (1996). *Fundamentals of argumentation theory: A handbook of historical backgrounds and contemporary developments.* Mahwah, NJ: Lawrence Erlbaum.

Walhout, D. (1978). *The good and the realm of values.* Notre Dame, IN: University of Notre Dame Press.

Walker, G. B., & Sillars, M. O. (1990). Where is argument? Perelman's theory of values. In R. Trapp & J. Schuetz (Eds.), *Perspectives on argumentation.* Prospect Heights, IL: Waveland.

Warnick, B. (1981). Arguing value propositions. *Journal of the American Forensic Association, 18,* 109-118.

Wenzel, J. W. (1977). Toward a rationale for value-centered argument. *Journal of the American Forensic Association, 13,* 150-158.

VERNACULAR

The English term **vernacular** is derived from the Latin *vernaculus* (meaning native) and *verna* (referring to a slave born in a master's house). These two elements of the term's etymology—something native to a region and something subservient to something else—are part of its contemporary sense. Vernacular refers to a linguistic dialect or *idiom* that is (a) indigenous or native to a region or class (vernacular as the language of the working class or the language of the urban inner city) and (b) usually considered substandard in comparison to literary or cultured speech. More generally, the term *vernacular* is used to refer to the everyday, the quotidian, or the common in contrast to the important, the significant, or the special.

Scholarly interest in everyday life and vernacular discourse has been on the rise for a number of decades (e.g., Baker, 1984). Consider the specific case of the discipline and practice of history. For a long time, the history of a nation (or a smaller social unit) was related through a narrative that recounted the deeds and actions of its social elite (e.g., military leaders, prominent politicians and public figures, business tycoons). The lives and language of common people were of little interest. As the discipline of history evolved throughout the 20th century, specific subbranches emerged. Among those subbranches was what is called "social history," whose focus tends to be on the quotidian and the vernacular. Bodnar's (1992) study of commemoration practices and public **memory** is an example of this trend. For Bodnar, public memory emerges through the often antagonistic interaction, or "intersection" (p. 13), of a society's "official culture"[1] and its various forms of "vernacular culture." According to Bodnar, vernacular culture

> represents an array of specialized interests that are grounded in parts of the whole. They are diverse and changing and can be reformulated from time to time. . . . Defenders of such cultures are numerous and intent on protecting values and restating views of reality [see the entry for **definitions of the situation**] derived from firsthand experience in small-scale communities rather than the "imagined" communities of a large nation. . . . Normally, vernacular expressions convey what social reality feels like

> rather than what it should be like. Its very existence threatens the sacred and timeless nature of official expressions. (p. 14)

Previous modes of historical inquiry privileged what Bodnar termed the "official culture" and largely ignored the vernacular. For Bodnar, it is impossible to understand a society's public memory without devoting significant attention to its vernacular culture.

In contemporary rhetorical studies, the most significant statement on the necessity of studying vernacular discourse can be found in Ono and Sloop's (1995) essay, "The Critique of Vernacular Discourse."[2] Ono and Sloop began by recounting what has become a familiar story of how, for the most part, rhetorical critics have been preoccupied with the discourse of the powerful and the (seemingly) socially significant. "Great speakers and speeches," almost always white men, have been the object of rhetorical study.[3] Like social historians of previous decades, as well as a number of feminist scholars (see the entry for **gynocritics/gynocriticism**), Ono and Sloop contended that the field of rhetoric is "missing out on, and writing 'out of history,' important texts that gird and influence local cultures" (p. 19). These texts, or vernacular discourses, must be brought to the center of disciplinary attention.

The qualifier of "for the most part" in the preceding paragraph is important. Ono and Sloop (1995) recognized that the discipline of rhetorical studies already has begun to attend to vernacular voices and practices. Largely as a reaction to the social and cultural ferment of the 1960s and early 1970s, rhetorical critics turned to the practices of those without social and political power (both in the past as well as in the present) and made those practices the object of critical reflection. Although Ono and Sloop applauded this trend, they maintained that it is only a partial or preliminary encounter with the reality of the vernacular. For the most part, current studies are of the "recuperative" or "descriptive" variety that can help to bring vernacular voices to new audiences and chart basic discursive processes. But what is needed, Ono and Sloop argued, is "a critical framework within which to discuss vernacular discourse" (p. 21). Too often, efforts at studying vernacular discourse are thwarted by critical tools and methods derived from the study of elite or canonical texts. Ono and Sloop maintained that such tools and methods are incapable of grasping the nuances and dynamics of vernacular practices.[4] By engaging the vernacular critically and conceptually, "new tools and new critical capacities will be shaped" (p. 40).

Ono and Sloop (1995) offered a "prolegomenon" (p. 40) or starting point for a critical theory of vernacular discourse. They maintained that vernacular discourse is speech that "emanates from" (p. 39) and "resonates within local communities" (p. 20) demarcated along the lines of race, ethnicity, gender, sexual orientation, class, or geographical location. The discursive practices of lesbian feminists, African American "black nationalists," ethnic working class enclaves, immigrant communities, and rural farmers fall within this definition of the vernacular. Drawing on extant scholarship in literary and cultural studies, Ono and Sloop highlighted two central characteristics of vernacular discourse that can help to orient the critic trying to approach this form of practice. The first characteristic is *cultural syncretism,* which refers to the complex **dialectic** of *affirmation and subversion* that shapes most vernacular practices. Vernacular discourse "functions syncretically, to affirm and protest" (p. 24); vernacular practices affirm aspects of the dominant cultural system and affirm alternatives to it (*residual* as well as *emergent*) while simultaneously protesting or subverting other aspects of the dominant or **hegemonic** culture. Put differently, vernacular discourse is a constant rhetorical *double gesture* of affirmation and subversion. The second characteristic of vernacular discourse is its common mode of construction. Vernacular discourse emerges through a "process of pastiche" (p. 23) in which "cultural fragments" are continually assembled and reassembled. Considered from a Bakhtinian perspective, vernacular discourse is constructed through a process of appropriating and incorporating other languages (**heteroglossia**) and other voices (**polyphony**) into a "new" textual practice.

While affirming the importance of vernacular practices, Ono and Sloop (1995) were careful to guard against "idealized versions of vernacular discourse" (p. 25). They acknowledged that there is a tendency to at times valorize the vernacular, treating it as inherently positive and worthy of approbation. In contrast to the valorization temptation, Ono and Sloop insisted that "vernacular discourse does not, by definition, enable constituents of vernacular cultures to articulate liberatory political identities and subject positions" (p. 25). As they illustrated in their case study of the construction of women in the Japanese American periodical *Pacific Citizen*, vernacular discourse can affirm aspects of the dominant culture (in terms of gender relations) while protesting other aspects (discrimination against Japanese Americans). A similar warning against the valorization of vernacular practices can be found in the work of social historians Stuart and Elizabeth Ewen. The key danger that Ewen and Ewen (1982) perceived was "the commercial appropriation of the vernacular . . ., the ability [of the corporate sector] to translate the vernacular into a viable commercial form" (p. 31). They argued that vernacular practices of specific subcultures (their styles of dress, language practices, forms of music, etc.) frequently are co-opted and made to serve the interests of the dominant culture.

As Ono and Sloop (1995) noted, their essay did not articulate a finished research agenda; rather, they were attempting to reorient, to at least some degree, the focus of critical scholarship in rhetorical studies. Did their essay imply that elite or canonical discourse should *not* be studied? Not necessarily.[5] The deconstruction and/or emulation of "documents of power" (p. 19), in both criticism and pedagogy, has a secure place in rhetorical studies. What Ono and Sloop's essay did is help rhetorical scholars see how the analysis of vernacular discourse can enhance our understanding of the relationship between discursive and textual practice and various cultural forms and processes (e.g., **ideology, power, tradition, ritual**) and refine our understanding of the dynamic, always changing possibilities of language and linguistic practice.

Notes

1. The official culture "originates in the concerns of cultural leaders or authorities at all levels of society" (Bodnar, 1992, p. 13).

2. See also Sloop and Ono (1997). In addition, see Becker's (1970) earlier call to study "mundane sorts of communication encounters" (p. 26) and Hauser's (1998, 1999) outline of a "vernacular rhetoric model of public opinion."

3. For part of the rationale, see the entries for **canon** and **touchstone.**

4. A similar argument often is advanced in the context of feminist critical scholarship.

5. Compare Ono and Sloop's (1995) position to the one articulated by Biesecker (1992, p. 158).

References and Additional Reading

Baker, H. A., Jr. (1984). *Blues, ideology, and Afro-American literature: A vernacular theory.* Chicago: University of Chicago Press.

Becker, S. (1970). Rhetorical studies for the contemporary world. In L. F. Bitzer & E. Black (Eds.), *The prospect of rhetoric.* Englewood Cliffs, NJ: Prentice Hall.

Biesecker, B. (1992). Coming to terms with recent attempts to write women into the history of rhetoric. *Philosophy and Rhetoric, 25,* 140-161.

Bodnar, J. (1992). *Remaking America: Public memory, commemoration, and patriotism in the twentieth century.* Princeton, NJ: Princeton University Press.

Ewen, S., & Ewen, E. (1982). *Channels of desire: Mass images and the shaping of American consciousness.* New York: McGraw-Hill.

Goldzwig, S. R., & Sullivan, P. A. (1997, November). *Interrogating theoretical and critical praxis: Self-reflexivity, local communities, and cultures.* Paper presented at the meeting of the National Communication Association, Chicago.

Hauser, G. A. (1998). Vernacular dialogue and the rhetoricality of public opinion. *Communication Monographs, 65,* 83-107.

Hauser, G. A. (1999). *Vernacular voices: The rhetoric of publics and public spheres.* Charleston: University of South Carolina Press.

Labov, W. (1972). *Language in the inner city: Studies in the black English vernacular.* Philadelphia: University of Pennsylvania Press.

McLaughlin, T. (1996). *Street smarts and critical theory: Listening to the vernacular.* Madison: University of Wisconsin Press.

Ono, K. A., & Sloop, J. M. (1995). The critique of vernacular discourse. *Communication Monographs, 62,* 19-46.

Sloop, J. M., & Ono, K. A. (1997). Out-law discourse: The critical politics of material judgment. *Philosophy and Rhetoric, 30,* 50-69.

Name Index

Subject Index

About the Author

James Jasinski (Ph.D., Northwestern University, 1986) is Associate Professor in the Department of Communication and Theatre Arts at the University of Puget Sound, where he teaches courses in rhetorical criticism, rhetorical theory, and the critical analysis of public discourse. He previously taught at Southern Illinois University–Carbondale and the University of Illinois, Urbana-Champaign. His scholarly work in rhetorical studies has focused on various texts and episodes in American antebellum political culture and has appeared in the *Quarterly Journal of Speech, Rhetoric Society Quarterly,* and numerous collections of essays. His essay, "The Feminization of Liberty, Domesticated Virtue, and the Reconstitution of Power and Authority in Early American Political Discourse," received the Distinguished Scholarship Award from the Public Address division of the National Communication Association in 1993. Some of his more recent metacritical work has examined key concepts (e.g., context, method and its relationship to theory) in contemporary rhetorical critical criticism. He has served on the editorial boards of the *Quarterly Journal of Speech, Western Journal of Communication,* and *Communication Studies.*

CPSIA information can be obtained at www.ICGtesting.com
Printed in the USA
LVOW072043161112

307204LV00003BA/2/P